Contemporary Communication Systems

M F Mesiya

Rensselaer Polytechnic Institute

Connect
Learn
Succeed™

The McGraw-Hill Companies

Mc Graw Hill — Connect Learn Succeed™

CONTEMPORARY COMMUNICATION SYSTEMS
International Edition 2013

Exclusive rights by McGraw-Hill Education (Asia), for manufacture and export. This book cannot be re-exported from the country to which it is sold by McGraw-Hill. This International Edition is not to be sold or purchased in North America and contains content that is different from its North American version.

Published by McGraw-Hill, a business unit of The McGraw-Hill Companies, Inc., 1221 Avenue of the Americas, New York, NY 10020. Copyright © 2013 by The McGraw-Hill Companies, Inc. All rights reserved. No part of this publication may be reproduced or distributed in any form or by any means, or stored in a database or retrieval system, without the prior written consent of The McGraw-Hill Companies, Inc., including, but not limited to, in any network or other electronic storage or transmission, or broadcast for distance learning.
Some ancillaries, including electronic and print components, may not be available to customers outside the United States.

10 09 08 07 06 05 04 03 02 01
20 15 14 13 12
CTP SLP

All credits appearing on page or at the end of the book are considered to be an extension of the copyright page.

When ordering this title, use ISBN 978-007-108661-5 or MHID 007-108661-7

Printed in Singapore

www.mhhe.com

In loving memory of my parents
Aisha and Kassem Mesiya

To

Sieglinde for her tremendous patience and support

Yasmin and Misha for inspiring me to pursue
the opportunities the future offers

Brief Contents

Table of Contents

CHAPTER   3
Simulation of Communication Systems Using MATLAB/Simulink   104

CHAPTER   4
Amplitude Modulation   141

CHAPTER 5

Angle Modulation   206

CHAPTER 6

Probability and Random Processes   278

CHAPTER   9

Digital Baseband Modulation   489

CHAPTER   10

Detection of Baseband Signals in Noise   532

CHAPTER   11

Digital Information Transmission Using Carrier Modulation   *592*

CHAPTER   12

Digital Signal Transmission Through Time Dispersive Channels   *679*

CHAPTER   13

Digital Multiplexing and Synchronization   *741*

CHAPTER   14
Information Theory and Compression Techniques   *787*

CHAPTER   15
Channel Coding Techniques   *854*

APPENDIX   A

Mathematical Tables   927

APPENDIX   B

Abbreviations   932

APPENDIX   C

List of Symbols   934

Preface

Communication systems transfer information between different points in space or time. *Contemporary Communication Systems* provides a comprehensive introduction to analog and digital communication systems that form the infrastructure of today's optical fiber, wireless, and satellite communication networks. The book not only provides a logical and easy-to-understand presentation of the fundamental principles but also engages students in the issues relevant to system and product implementation. As such, the book covers several topics that get scant coverage in other textbooks but are very relevant in implementing modern analog and digital communication systems.

The book is designed for introductory courses in communication systems and in digital communications at the upper-level undergraduate, and first-year graduate programs in electrical and computer engineering. It provides detailed coverage of the background required to study communication systems in two chapters, one on signals and systems with emphasis on the frequency-domain analysis, and the other on the probability theory and random processes. Analog communications systems are covered in Chapters 4, 5, and 7. These chapters include not only the traditional material but some new topics that are relevant to the design of today's wireless communication receivers and optical networks employing cascade of optical amplifiers. Digital transmission is the enabling technology for global Internet, optical fiber, and new generations of wireless networks. Chapters 8 to 15 cover various aspects of digital communications systems.

Organization

Chapter 1 provides an introduction to communication systems, the history of their development, and major trends driving their evolution.

Chapter 2 is a review of signals and systems with an emphasis on the frequency domain analysis of signal transmission through LTI systems.

Chapter 3 introduces the capabilities of Simulink® for modeling and the simulation of analog and digital communication systems.

Chapter 4 is devoted to various amplitude modulation schemes. We also discuss multiplexing techniques and key operations implemented in communication transmitters and receivers. The chapter concludes with a discussion of various receiver architectures implemented in modern communication systems.

Chapter 5 covers angle modulation systems (FM and PM). This is followed by a detailed treatment of analog phase-locked loops and analog NTSC TV system.

Chapter 6 reviews the basic concepts of probability theory and random processes that are relevant to the modeling and analysis of information signals and ubiquitous noise in communication systems. Transmission of random signals and noise through LTI systems are then analyzed in both time and frequency domains.

Chapter 7 addresses the effect of noise in the demodulation of amplitude- and angle-modulated signals. We compare the performance of analog communication systems and study the effects of transmission losses and noise on the design of analog transmission systems with repeaters.

Chapter 8 considers the conversion of analog signals into digital format. We study sampling theorem and quantization techniques followed by waveform coding methods such as PCM, DPCM, and DM. The chapter concludes with a discussion of sigma-delta converters and bandpass sampling.

Chapter 9 presents baseband modulation schemes for transmission of digital data. Key requirements and characteristics of various line coding schemes are explained. We also study the design of pulse shapes to improve the spectral efficiency of digital baseband transmission systems.

In Chapter 10 we consider the detection of transmission symbols being conveyed in the digitally modulated signals in the presence of additive white Gaussian noise (AWGN). We introduce the representation of signal waveforms and AWGN as vectors in finite-dimensional vector spaces and use these concepts to develop optimum detector structures and analyze their performance.

Chapter 11 considers the transmission of digital data by modulating a carrier. We consider binary and quadrature modulation schemes and analyze their performance using vector space concepts. Frequency shift keying and minimum shift keying are also treated.

Noncoherent and differentially coherent schemes are then discussed. The chapter concludes with spectral analysis and a comparison of various digital carrier modulation schemes.

Chapter 12 treats the transmission of digitally modulated signals through channels that introduce inter-symbol interference (ISI) in addition to AWGN. We consider signal design and equalization schemes for the mitigation of ISI and noise.

Chapter 13 addresses two major topics in digital communications: digital multiplexing and synchronization. Multiplexing is used to combine multiple user signals for the efficient sharing of a high-speed communication channel. This is followed by the coverage of carrier, symbol timing, and frame sync recovery circuits that are used to properly recover and demultiplex the constituent signals at the receiver.

Chapter 14 is an introduction to information theory where we explain fundamental limits on communication of information. After introducing the concepts of information content of a source and capacity of a communication channel, we study Shannon's theorems on source coding and channel capacity. The chapter concludes with a detailed treatment of text, image, and video compression schemes.

Chapter 15 is devoted to channel coding for reliable transmission of information over noisy communication channels. We consider both linear block codes and convolutional codes and their performance using hard- and soft-decision decoding strategies. Coding for bandlimited channels and capacity-achieving turbo codes are also treated.

Pedagogical Features

The pedagogical features of the book include the following:

- Chapter introductions that preview the material covered in that chapter and its relevance in practice.
- Numerous examples, including MATLAB® exercises, to reinforce the key concepts and mathematical results.
- End-of-chapter problems with varying degrees of difficulty. MATLAB exercises are provided with extensive help to assist students in programming problem solutions.
- Simulink is used as a key pedagogical tool to help students understand theoretical results and develop familiarity with key elements in the design of communication systems. The author believes that Simulink can be used as a *virtual laboratory* to conduct experiments in the classroom setting to
  - Display signal waveforms and spectra at various points in communication systems.
  - Analyze the performance of systems and compare them with theoretical results.
  - Study the design approaches and possible trade-offs.
- Each chapter concludes with final remarks that reiterate the key concepts and comment on important developments.
- Each chapter includes a list of references that point to further reading materials.
- Extensive resources for instructors and students on the book's website are provided.
- The development of communication systems has a rich and interesting history. A special effort has been made in the text to chronicle the milestone events in the field with historical boxes sprinkled throughout the book.
- Most chapters include interviews with modern pioneers and renowned contributors in the field of communications that should inspire and motivate students.

Course Options

The book can be used to offer a variety of courses in communication systems. By a selective choice of chapters and sections therein, the instructor can provide the desired concentration for the course or adjust the content for the background of the students. An important consideration in this context is whether or not the students have already taken a course in probability and random processes at a senior level. We offer the following options for consideration, although many variants are possible.

- A one-semester course in analog and digital communication systems: Selected review of sections from Chapters 2 and 6, Chapters 3 through 5, Chapter 7: Sections 7.1 to 7.5, Chapter 8: Sections 8.1 to 8.4, Chapter 9: Sections 9.1 to 9.2, Chapter 10: Sections 10.1 to 10.2, Chapter 11: Sections 11.1 to 11.2, and selections from Chapters 14 through 15 if time permits.
- A one-semester course in digital communications: Selected review of sections from Chapters 2 and 6, Chapter 3, and Chapters 8 through 15.
- A two-semester course sequence in analog and digital communication systems:
  - Chapters 2 through 8 for the first course
  - Chapters 9 through 15 for the second course

Online Resources

A website to accompany this text can be found at www.mhhe.com/mesiya. The site contains an instructor's solutions manual, lecture PowerPoints, MATLAB m-files, Simulink models for all experiments, additional problems, and an image library. Instructors can also obtain access to COSMOS—a Complete Online Solutions Manual Organization System, which instructors can use to create exams and assignments, create custom content, and edit supplied problems and solutions.

Electronic Textbook Option

This text is offered through CourseSmart for both instructors and students. CourseSmart is an online resource where students can purchase the complete text online at almost half the cost of a traditional text. Purchasing the eTextbook allows students to take advantage of CourseSmart's web tools for learning, which include full text search, notes and highlighting, and email tools for sharing notes between classmates. To learn more about CourseSmart options, contact your sales representative or visit www.CourseSmart.com.

McGraw-Hill Create™

Craft your teaching resources to match the way you teach. With McGraw-Hill Create™, you can rearrange chapters, combine material from other content sources, and quickly upload content you have written, such as your course syllabus or teaching notes. Find the content you need in McGraw-Hill Create by searching through thousands of leading McGraw-Hill textbooks. Arrange your book to fit your teaching style. McGraw-Hill Create even allows you to personalize your book's appearance by selecting the cover and adding your name, school, and course information.

Acknowledgments

The writing of a new textbook takes the input and recommendations of many people. The author is indebted to the following individuals, who reviewed chapters of the manuscript in various stages.

Vijay Bhargava	University of British Columbia
Deva Borah	New Mexico State University
Lakshmi S. Chennupati	California State University–Sacramento
Tolga M. Duman	Arizona State University
Satyabrata Jit	Banaras Hindu University
James Kang	California State Polytechnic University–Pomona
Hyuck M. Kwon	Wichita State University
Tongtong Li	Michigan State University
Timothy Pratt	Virginia Polytechnic Institute
P. R. Sahu	IIT Guwahati
Masoud Salehi	Northeastern University
Gary J. Saulnier	Rensselaer Polytechnic Institute
Jitendra K. Tugnait	Auburn University

Among the many reviewers, the author would like to especially acknowledge the contribution of Dr. Deva Borah, for his careful and thorough review of the entire manuscript for accuracy and many suggestions. The author is grateful to Raghu Srinivasan, Global Publisher, at McGraw-Hill for his continued enthusiasm and support for the project. Many thanks are due to Lora Neyens who worked with me on various aspects of this project with enthusiasm over the last four years. In addition, the author expresses his appreciation to Michael Hackett, Peter Massar, and Darlene Schueller for their help and encouragement during their association with the project. Jane Mohr managed this project through the production phase and she deserves thanks for her helpful support and flexibility in dealing with uncertainties. The author gratefully acknowledges tremendous effort of Erika Jordan and her team at Laserwords in getting this book ready for production. The author wishes to thank Naomi Fernandes and Dr. Houman Zarrinkoub at Mathworks, Inc. for their helpful support and encouragement. Finally, the author expresses his sincere appreciation to Yasmin Sarah Mesiya for reviewing the historical content in the book.

Notational Conventions

1. Random variables are denoted in a bold font $x, y, \ldots$ and the values assumed by them will be displayed by the corresponding lowercase letters $x, y, \ldots$

2. The symbol $x[n]$ is used to denote the entire sequence (i.e., discrete-time signal) as well as the nth sample or number in the sequence. The intended meaning will be obvious from the context. We occasionally use curly brackets $\{\}$ to enclose sequences.

3. Finite-dimensional vectors are denoted by lowercase letters with an underscore. For example, $\underline{x}$ denotes a vector. The ith element of the vector $\underline{x}$ is denoted by x_i.

4. Matrices are denoted by uppercase letters with an underscore. For example, $\underline{A}$ denotes a matrix. The (i, j)-th element of the matrix $\underline{A}$ is denoted by A_{ij}.

5. The length or norm of a vector $\underline{x}$ is denoted by $\|\underline{x}\|$. The Euclidean distance between the vectors $\underline{x}$ and $\underline{y}$ is denoted by $\|\underline{x} - \underline{y}\|$.

6. The inner product between the vectors $\underline{x}$ and $\underline{y}$ is denoted by $(\underline{x} \bullet \underline{y})$.

7. The use of an asterisk as superscript denotes complex conjugate. For example, y^* is complex conjugate of y.

8. The symbol $|\,|$ represents the magnitude of the complex number or the function contained within.

9. The symbol $\angle$ denotes the phase of the complex number or function.

10. The symbol $\xleftrightarrow{\;\Im\;}$ represents a Fourier transform pair. For example, $x(t) \xleftrightarrow{\;\Im\;} X(f)$, where a lowercase letter denotes the time function and a corresponding uppercase letter denotes its Fourier transform.

11. The symbol $\otimes$ denotes convolution of two continuous-time functions or sequences.

12. The symbol $\oplus$ denotes modulo-2 addition. In Chapter 15, all arithmetic involving binary sequences is modulo-2 whether or not specifically indicated by $\oplus$ or ordinary $+$ sign.

13. The use of a hat over an unknown parameter or variable indicates the estimate of the unknown parameter or variable. For example, $\hat{a}$ denotes an estimate of the unknown parameter a.

14. The use of a tilde over a function indicates the complex envelope of a bandpass signal. For example, $\tilde{x}(t)$ denotes the complex envelope of the bandpass signal $x(t)$.

15. The symbol $E\{\ \}$ denotes the expected value of a random variable or process inside the brackets.

16. The symbol $Var(\ )$ denotes the variance of a random variable inside the parentheses.

17. The symbol $Cov(\ )$ denotes the covariance of the two random variables inside the parentheses.

CHAPTER 1

Introduction

Communication is the transfer of information. It is the most natural and social of human needs as evidenced by the ubiquitous presence and use of cell phones for voice communication and text messaging. In our twenty-first-century society, the exchange of information between humans and machines has become as important as that between humans. Communication systems convey or transmit information. In this book, we will be mainly concerned with electrical communication systems where information from a source to a destination is conveyed in the form of an electromagnetic signal. Electrical communication systems enable interaction *at a distance* almost *instantaneously*. For example, we can download a Web page with a click of the mouse from anywhere on the globe. This illustrates the important role that communication systems play in our modern information age.

Most signals we encounter in the real world are **analog** in nature. That is, they are continuous functions of time and assume a continuum of values in a given amplitude range. Examples include speech, music, images, and video signals. **Digital** signals, on the other hand, can change values at discrete instants of time, assuming one of a finite number of amplitude levels. For example, binary digital signals can assume one of two values, say, $\{0, A\}$. Figure 1.1 compares analog and digital signals.

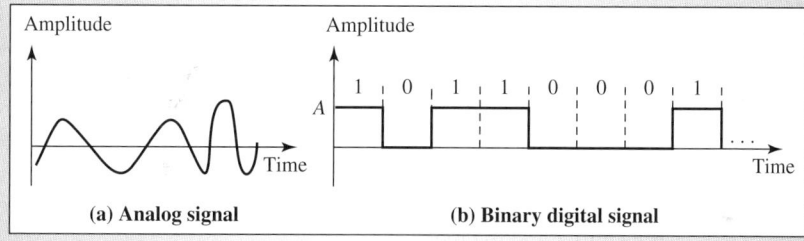

Figure 1.1 Analog and digital signals.

The chapter is organized into the following sections:

1.1 ELEMENTS OF A COMMUNICATION SYSTEM.
This section considers the functional components of a communication system for the transfer of information between two points.

1.2 COMMUNICATION CHANNELS.
We review various transmission media (or communication channels) that make the physical transfer of information in the form of waveforms possible.

1.3 ANALOG AND DIGITAL COMMUNICATION SYSTEMS.
In this section we first consider analog communication systems, where the message being transferred is an analog signal. Next we explain digital communication systems, where the information being transmitted is a sequence of symbols that assume values in an alphabet of finite size. The section concludes with a discussion of the significant advantages offered by digital transmission systems.

1.4 HISTORY OF COMMUNICATIONS.
We review major events in the history of electrical communications, which spans almost two centuries. The major innovations that form the building blocks of all communication systems are discussed.

1.5 KEY THEMES AND DRIVERS.
The major themes and drivers fueling the dramatic growth of the communications industry are reviewed in this section.

The chapter concludes with final remarks and a selected list of references.

1.1   ELEMENTS OF A COMMUNICATION SYSTEM

An electrical communication system transmits information from a source to a destination in the form of an electromagnetic signal. A typical communication system is represented by the block diagram of Figure 1.2. An information source generates a message, which may be either an analog signal or a sequence of symbols or characters from a finite alphabet. Speech, music, images, and video are examples of analog signals. If the message signal does not originate as an electrical signal, it is converted to an electrical form by an input transducer. Examples of input transducers include microphones, still cameras, and TV cameras. Text, Web, and MP3 audio files are examples of digital messages. Regardless of the application, a communication system consists of three functional components to convey the message to an end user at a remote destination:

- **Transmitter.** The transmitter converts the message into a form that is suitable for transmission over a physical medium or channel. The output of the transmitter is an electromagnetic signal that can be either sent over a cable or launched into free space. Obviously, the transmitter output signal contains the necessary information being conveyed in the original message.
- **Transmission medium or channel.** The communication channel is the transmission medium that conveys the energy of an electromagnetic signal from the transmitter to a receiver. Examples include twisted wire pair, coaxial or optical fiber cable, radio or satellite link. One common characteristic of all transmission media is that the signal undergoes degradation from transmitter to receiver. This degradation often results from noise and other interference, but it also occurs because of the attenuation and distortion produced by the channel.
- **Receiver.** The function of the receiver is to recover the original message from the received signal. This is feasible only if the signal is not degraded beyond a certain limit. The limit is determined by the signal processing performed jointly by the transmitter and the receiver.

1.2   COMMUNICATION CHANNELS

For information transfer to occur, we must have a communication channel that conveys the energy of a signal from the transmitter to the receiver. There are two basic types of communication channels:

1. **Wired media.** The signal energy is contained and guided within a solid medium. Examples include copper twisted wire pairs, coaxial cable, and optical fibers.
2. **Wireless media.** The signal energy propagates in the form of unguided electromagnetic waves. Radio and infrared light are examples.

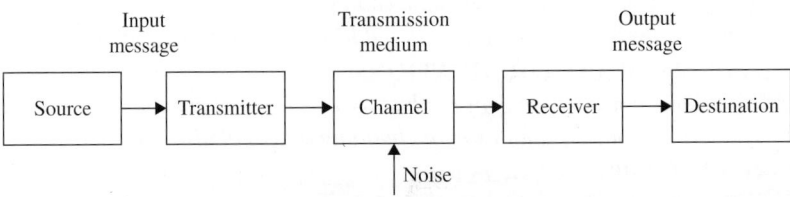

Figure 1.2 A typical communication system.

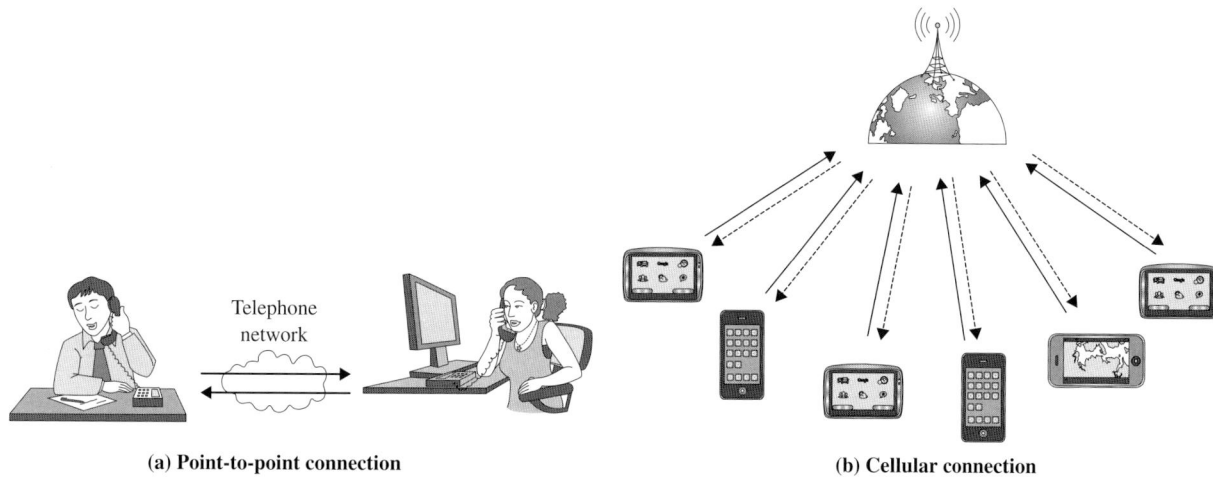

(a) **Point-to-point connection**   (b) **Cellular connection**

Figure 1.3 Wired and wireless transmission media.

Wired and wireless media differ in a fundamental way. Basically, wired media provide **point-to-point** connectivity. That is, users communicate via a point-to-point physical link or channel. Wireless media generally operate in a **broadcast** mode. That is, the medium is *shared* within a certain geographical coverage area, and users communicate via the shared communication channel. Thus, there is a possibility of interference as users try to access the medium simultaneously. This is illustrated in Figure 1.3.

Twisted wire pair (**TWP**) is ubiquitous in the subscriber loop plant of **telephone companies (telcos),** where it was originally installed to provide voice communication in the form of **plain old telephone service** (**POTS**). Today, TWPs are used to offer a rich set of voice and data services to residential customers utilizing **Integrated Services Digital Network (ISDN)** and **Asymmetric Digital Subscriber Line (ADSL)** technologies. For business customers, telcos provide voice and high-speed data services over existing TWP network using various **Digital Subscriber Line (DSL)** systems. TWP is also the medium of choice for **Local Area Network (LAN)** wiring infrastructure in the enterprise environment. A twisted pair wire consists of two wires that are twisted together to reduce their susceptibility to interference. The close proximity of the wires means that any interference will be picked up by both, and so the differences between the wires should be largely unaffected by the interference. Twisting also helps to reduce (but not eliminate) the crosstalk interference that occurs when multiple pairs are placed within one cable. Because multiple pairs are bundled together within one telephone cable, the amount of crosstalk is still significant, especially at higher frequencies. TWPs of different wire sizes are specified in **American Wire Gauge (AWG)** standard. The lower the AWG number of the TWP, the bigger the wire diameter and the lower the attenuation. Telcos usually deploy 22 (0.0254 inch), 24 (0.0201 inch), and 26 (0.0159 inch) AWG cables. For inside premises wiring, several **categories** (**Cat**) of twisted pair cabling systems (includes cables, junctions, and connectors) have been standardized by **ANSI/EIA (American National Standards Institute/Electronic Industries Association).** Cat cabling systems, according to EIA 568 standard, differ in terms of the data rates that they can sustain effectively. For example, Cat 5 cabling system is designed to

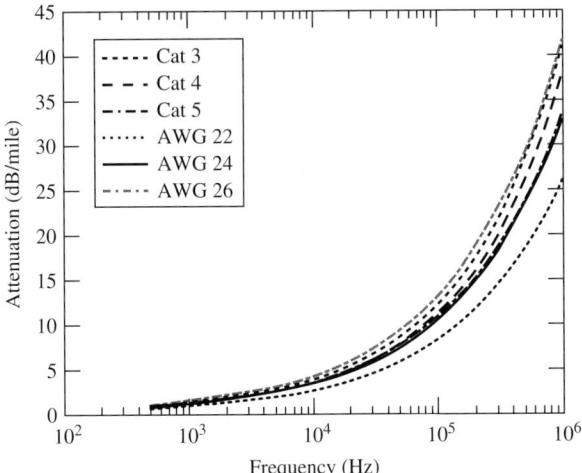

Figure 1.4 Attenuation characteristics of twisted wire pairs.

support 10/100 Mb/s Ethernet networks. Figure 1.4 displays the attenuation characteristics of popular TWP cables.

1.2.1   Coaxial Cable

Coaxial cables are used in cable television (CATV) systems to distribute TV signals. In coaxial cable, a solid center conductor is located coaxially within a cylindrical outer conductor. Cables with a solid copper or aluminum outer conductor are used for **trunk** and **feeder** applications, while a braided design is used for **drop** cable application. The two conductors are separated by a foam dielectric, and the outer conductor is covered with a plastic sheath as shown in Figure 1.5. The coaxial arrangement of the two conductors provides much better immunity to interference and crosstalk than twisted wire pair does. Coaxial cables with copper-clad solid aluminum center conductor and seamless aluminum tube outer conductor are used for CATV trunk and feeder applications. 500-F (outer conductor diameter 0.5 inch) and 625-F (outer conductor diameter 0.625 inch) in Figure 1.6 are examples of these cable designs. For distribution and inside premises applications, lower cost coaxial cables with braided outer conductor are used. RG-59 and RG-6 in Figure 1.6 are the most widely used of such cable types.

Figure 1.6 displays the attenuation characteristics of some coaxial cables. A comparison of Figures 1.4 and 1.6 indicates that coaxial cables have a much higher frequency range (bandwidth) of operation than TWPs, several hundred megahertz versus a few megahertz.

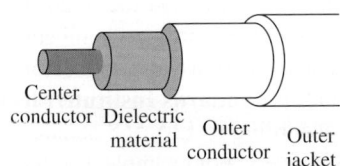

Figure 1.5 Coaxial cables.

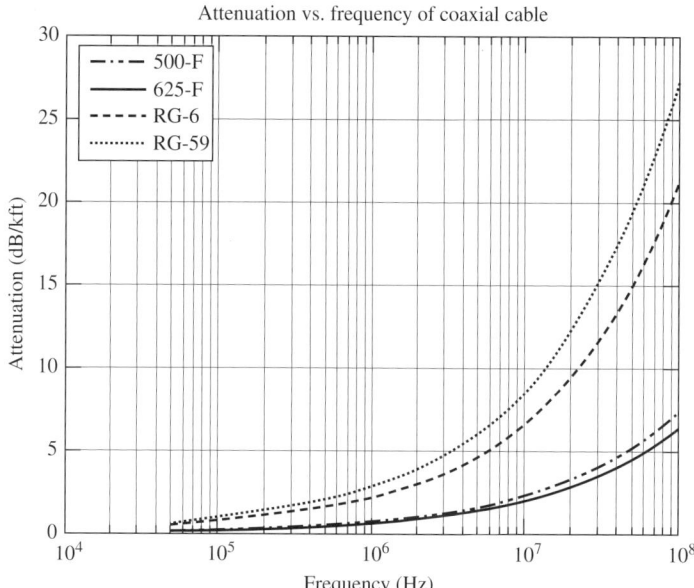

Figure 1.6 Attenuation characteristics of coaxial cables.

1.2.2 Optical Fibers

Optical fiber is a cylindrical waveguide and consists of a glass **core** of refractive index n_1 as shown in Figure 1.7. The core is surrounded by a glass **cladding,** which has refractive index n_2 that is less than n_1. A third layer—**buffer coating**—is applied over the cladding to protect a very fragile core-cladding structure.

Consider the propagation of light within an optical fiber as shown in Figure 1.8. The ratio of the indices of refraction of the core and cladding determines a critical angle ϕ_c. When a light wave ("ray") from the core approaches the core-cladding interface at greater than or equal to the critical incidence angle, ϕ_c, then the wave is completely reflected back into the core and none escapes into the cladding. This is called **total internal reflection.** The wave then crosses to the other side of the core, and because the fiber is more or less straight, the wave will meet the cladding on the other side at an angle that again causes total internal reflection to occur. The wave is then reflected back

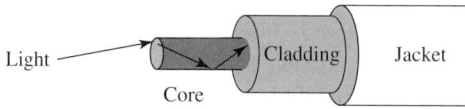

Figure 1.7 Structure of optical fiber.

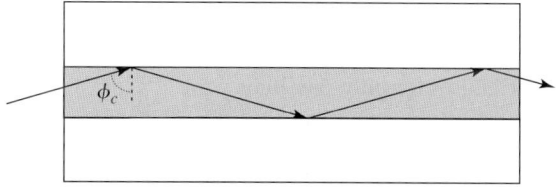

Figure 1.8 Propagation of light in optical fibers.

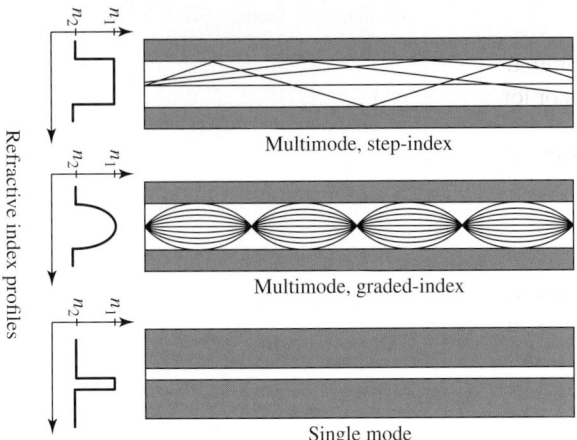

Figure 1.9 Propagation in different types of optical fiber.

across the core again and the same thing happens. In this way the light wave zigzags its way along the fiber. This means that the light wave will be transmitted to the end of the fiber via a series of total internal reflections at the interface of the silica core and the slightly lower refractive index silica cladding.

There are three types of optical fiber as shown in Figure 1.9.

- Step-index multimode
- Graded-index multimode
- Single mode

Step-index multimode fiber has a refractive index profile that undergoes a step change from high to low at the cladding boundary. It is characterized by a relatively large core diameter (50−200 μm) and numerical aperture. **Numerical aperture (NA)** describes the ability of an optical fiber to capture light from an optical source that, in turn, can propagate inside the fiber as a result of total internal reflection. The cladding diameter of a typical multimode fiber is 125 to 400 μm. The term **multimode** refers to the fact that multiple optical light waves propagate through the fiber. Higher NA implies that more light waves are coupled into the fiber resulting in higher coupled power but at the cost of more pulse spreading. Therefore, the choice of NA in the range 0.2–0.3 is a design compromise depending on the application need. Step-index multimode fiber may be used in LAN or campus network applications that require moderate bandwidth over relatively short distances.

Graded-index multimode fiber offers a compromise between the large core diameter and NA of step-index multimode fiber and the higher bandwidth of single-mode fiber. The core diameter is typically 50 μm with a 125 μm cladding. We observe from Figure 1.9 that the core's refractive index decreases away from the center toward the cladding in a parabolic fashion. Hence the light waves striking the core-cladding boundary at higher angles of incidence travel faster. This tends to compensate for the longer paths taken by higher incidence-angle waves versus the shorter paths taken by those waves striking at lower angles of incidence, thus decreasing the amount of pulse spreading and increasing the bandwidth of the fiber.

Single-mode fiber allows for only one light wave ("axial" ray) to travel within the fiber. To achieve this mode of operation, the core diameter is typically restricted to between 8 and 10 μm with a 125 μm cladding. Unlike multimode fibers, there is only single light wave propagating through the fiber, so there is no similar pulse spreading. The bandwidth of a single-mode fiber is limited, however, because the light coupled from an optical source contains energy at different wavelengths in the single light wave. Different wavelengths travel at different speeds through the fiber, thus leading to pulse spreading depending on the spectral content of the source. Because of very high bandwidth and low signal loss offered by single-mode fibers, they are used in applications where multi-gigabit data rates or long spans are required as in telecommunication networks.

Advantages of Optical Fibers

Optical fibers have many advantages over metallic-based transmission media. These advantages include:

- **Low transmission loss.** Attenuation for single-mode fibers in the 1.55 μm wavelength region is around 0.25 dB/km as shown in Figure 1.10. Unlike TWP and coaxial cables, this performance is independent of the frequency of the electrical signal being transmitted through the fiber. For comparison, RG-6 coaxial cable has an attenuation of 22.6 dB/km at 100 MHz.
- **Enormous potential bandwidth.** The region from 1.25 μm to 1.625 μm offers the potential for bandwidth as high as 50 THz.
- **Small size and weight.** Optical fiber strands are the size of human hair. Optical fiber cables are lighter and more compact than metallic media types.
- **Low cost.** A few cents per foot. A cost comparison on the basis of information-carrying capacity is even more favorable.
- **Electrical isolation.** Dielectric medium. No ground loops. Ideally suited for electrically hostile environments.
- **Immunity to interference and crosstalk.** No **electromagnetic interference (EMI)** ingress or egress during transmission due to the dielectric nature of the medium.
- **Signal security.** Signal energy cannot be tapped from fiber in a noninvasive manner.

We will demonstrate in Chapter 2 that for all wired transmission media the attenuation exhibits a linear dependence on distance d. That is,

$$\text{Attenuation for wired media} = \alpha d \text{ dB} \qquad (1.1)$$

where α is attenuation in dB/km if the distance is specified in kilometers. α is frequency dependent for most transmission media except single-mode optical fibers. That is, attenuation is higher for higher frequencies. Because higher frequency components of the signal are attenuated more while propagating through the communication channel, the output of the channel is a distorted version of the input signal.

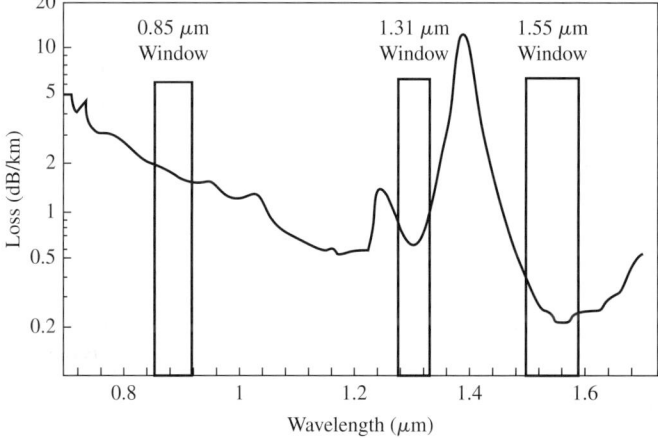

Figure 1.10 Attenuation characteristics of optical fibers.

1.2.3 Radio Channels

The **radio frequency (RF)** spectrum extends from 3 kHz to 300 GHz. For radio transmission through space, the transmitter output signal is converted to an electromagnetic (EM) wave by an appropriate transmitting antenna for propagation through space. The RF spectrum is allocated on a worldwide basis by the International Telecommunication Union (ITU) to various classes of service. Within the United States and its possessions, the RF spectrum is further allocated between nongovernment and government users. The Federal Communications Commission (FCC), acting under the authority of Congress, is responsible for the allocation and assignment of frequencies to nongovernment users. The National Telecommunications and Information Administration (NTIA) is responsible for the allocation and assignment of frequencies to departments and agencies of the U.S. government.

Table 1.1 summarizes the frequency bands in the RF spectrum. Figure 1.11 displays the allocation of the frequency spectrum to various communication applications. Digital cellular communication systems operate in two frequency bands: 800/900 MHz and 1800/1900 MHz. Wireless LANs (Wi-Fi) use the 2.4 and 5 GHz frequency bands. Satellite communication systems operate in the 4/6, 11/14, and 20/30 GHz bands, where the first number indicates the downlink (from satellite) frequency and the second number the uplink (to satellite) frequency.

For wireless media, the attenuation of the transmitted signal is proportional to d^n where n is called the **path loss exponent.**[1] The attenuation for wireless media in dB is given by

$$\text{Attenuation for wireless media (``Path loss'')} = \alpha n \log_{10} d \text{ dB} \qquad (1.2)$$

Table 1.1 RF Spectrum Allocation

Frequency Band	Frequency Range
Very Low Frequency (VLF)	3–30 kHz
Radio navigation	
Fixed maritime mobile communications	
Submarine communications	
Low Frequency (LF)	30–300 kHz
Fixed maritime mobile communications	
Radio navigation	
Medium Frequency (MF)	300–3000 kHz
AM radio broadcasting	530–1700 kHz
Traveler's information service	
High Frequency (HF)	3–30 MHz
Shortwave radio broadcasting	5.95–26.1 MHz
Very High Frequency (VHF)	30–300 MHz
TV channels 2–6	54–88 MHz
FM radio broadcast	88–108 MHz
TV channels 7–13	174–216 MHz
Ultra High Frequency (VHF)	300–3000 MHz
TV channels 14–83	420–890 MHz
Cellular telephony	824–894 MHz
Industrial, scientific, and medical (ISM): Wi-Fi	902–928 MHz
Global positioning system (GPS)	1227.6, 1575.4 MHz
Cellular telephony: Personal communications services (PCS)	1850–1990 MHz
ISM: Wi-Fi	2400–2483.5 MHz
Superhigh (Microwave) Frequencies (SHF)	3–30 GHz
G band: Geostationary satellite communications	4–6 GHz
J band: Geostationary satellite communications	10.7–14.5 GHz
Ka band: Satellite communications	26.5–40 GHz

[1] J. Andersen, T. Rappaport, and S. Yoshida, "Propagation Measurements and Models for Wireless Communication Channels," *IEEE Communications Magazine* 33, no. 1 (1995): 42–49.

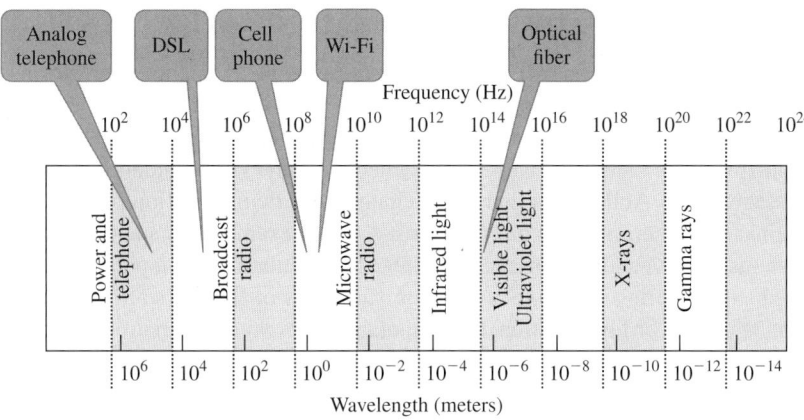

Figure 1.11 Allocation of the frequency spectrum.

Equation (1.2) implies that attenuation in wireless media increases logarithmically with distance d. Thus, signals in wireless channels attenuate much more slowly with distance than in wired systems. Attenuation for radio systems increases with rainfall. Radio systems are also subject to other channel impairments. These include shadowing, multipath fading, and interference from other users. Shadow fading models variations in the signal attenuation as various physical obstructions are encountered in the transmitter-receiver path. Multipath fading refers to the degradation of the received waveform resulting from two or more copies of the transmitted signal arriving via different paths. If the arriving signals are 180° out of phase, total annihilation of the signal occurs at the receiver. Figure 1.12 displays measured values of path loss as a function of distance for five cities in Germany.[2] We observe that the model (1.2) with the path loss exponent value between 2 and 4 provides a good fit with the measured data.

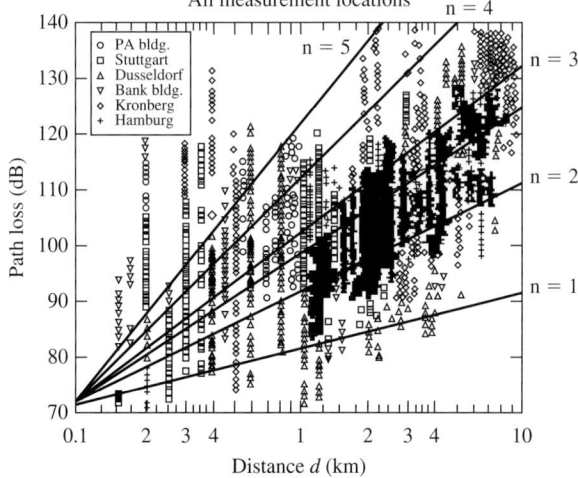

Figure 1.12 Scatter plot of path loss.

Andersen, J., T. Rappaport, & S. Yoshida, "Propagation Measurements and Models for Wireless Communication Channels," IEEE Communications Magazine, vol. 33, no. 1, January 1995, ©1995 IEEE.

[2] Andersen, Rappaport, and Yoshida, "Propagation Measurements and Models for Wireless Communication Channels," 42–49.

1.3   ANALOG AND DIGITAL COMMUNICATION SYSTEMS

Analog communication systems convert analog message signals into waveforms suitable for transmission over a communication channel. The conversion process is called **modulation.** Usually, modulation involves varying the amplitude, phase, or frequency of a high-frequency sinusoidal waveform (called a **carrier**) in accordance with the analog message signal. At the other end of the channel, the **demodulation** process recovers the original analog message signal. The most familiar examples of analog communication systems are AM and FM broadcasting. In AM modulation, the input message signal is embedded in the instantaneous amplitude variations of the carrier waveform. Similarly, in the case of FM modulation, the instantaneous frequency variations of the carrier embed the information signal. The block diagram of an analog communication system is displayed in Figure 1.13. In addition to modulation, the transmitter performs certain other essential functions (labeled "Transmitter output processing") such as filtering the modulated signal, frequency translation, and output signal amplification. At the other end of the system, the receiver also performs additional functions (labeled "Receiver input processing") prior to demodulation of the original message signal. These include low-noise amplification, frequency slot selection ("tuning"), and filtering.

The performance objective in the design of analog communication systems is an exact reproduction of the original analog message at the receiver output. In practice, however, perfect reproduction in the presence of noise and channel impairments cannot be achieved. So some degree of distortion is acceptable, depending on the application.

1.3.1   Digital Communication Systems

In a digital communication system, the message is a sequence of symbols from a finite alphabet. An example is a text file that consists of characters from the English or Chinese alphabet. If the source is analog, such as a voice signal from a microphone, the output of a sensor, or a video waveform, the output is converted into a sequence of binary digits by sampling and an analog-to-digital (A/D) conversion process. The block diagram of a typical digital communication system is shown in Figure 1.14. Most sources possess redundancy, which manifests itself as a correlation between successive source output symbols. That is, the probabilities of their occurrence are not equal. For example, in the English language the probability of occurrence of the letter *E* is 10.73%, while the letter *B* occurs with a probability of 1.18%. The function of a **source coding** or **compression** scheme is to remove the redundancy and obtain an efficient binary representation of the source output for transmission through the system. Transmission of digital information through a communication channel always results in some errors at the receiver due to noise and other channel impairments. The acceptable level of error rate depends on the application. For example, certain financial transactions require virtually error-free

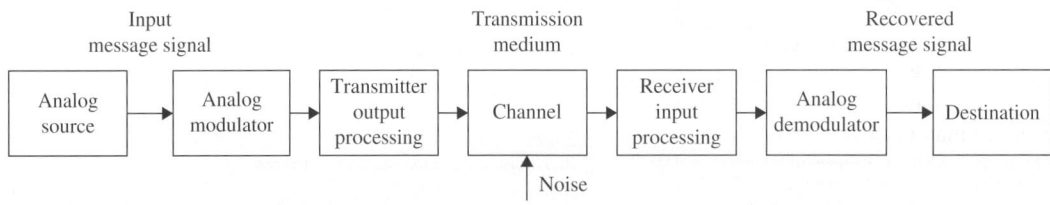

Figure 1.13 Block diagram of an analog communication system.

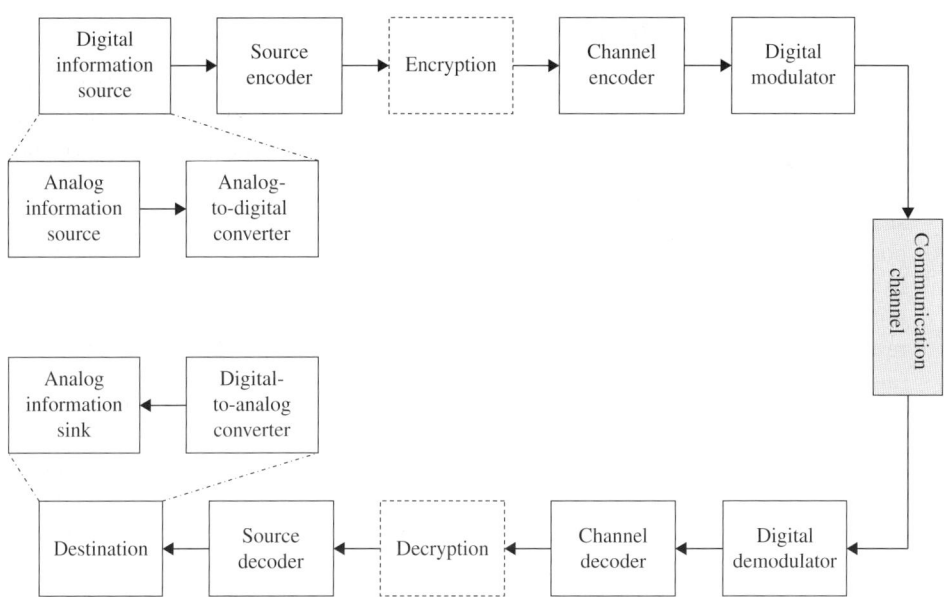

Figure 1.14 Block diagram of a typical digital communication system.

transmission, whereas audio/video applications are error-tolerant. The purpose of channel coding is to improve the error performance that is delivered to the application when the inherent error rate of a digital communication system is unacceptable. The **channel encoder** introduces in a controlled manner some redundancy in the source encoder output binary sequence, which can be used at the receiver to overcome the effects of noise and interference encountered in the transmission of the signal through the channel. The output of the channel encoder is a succession of codewords or coded sequences. It is passed to the **digital modulator,** which serves as the interface to the communication channel. The digital modulator maps a block of channel encoder output bits into a continuous-time waveform suitable for transmission through the channel.

At the receiving end of a digital communication system, the **digital demodulator** processes the channel-distorted and noisy received waveform and generates an estimate of the channel encoder output sequence. For example, in the case of binary transmission, the demodulator detects the signal in the received waveform and decides whether a binary 0 or 1 was transmitted during a bit interval. The **channel decoder** takes advantage of the redundancy contained in the received data and attempts error detection and correction to reconstruct the source encoder binary output sequence. The **source decoder** accepts the bit sequence (possibly corrupted) from the channel decoder and converts it into a more-or-less faithful replica of the original source output symbol sequence. The uncompressed data can now be converted into analog format by a digital-to-analog (D/A) conversion process. Due to channel decoding errors and possible distortion introduced by the source encoder and, perhaps, the source decoder (including D/A converter), the signal at the output is an *approximation* to the original source output. Encryption is optionally used to assure the security of message transmission, that is, only the intended receiver can understand the message and only the authorized sender can transmit it. A decryption stage may decipher the data using the proper decryption key.

Modern communication networks today are increasingly based on digital communications. This trend has largely been driven by the advantages of digital versus analog transmission and the semiconductor revolution.

1.3.2   Why Digital Transmission?

The advantages of digital transmission over analog transmission become apparent when transmitting over a long distance. For example, consider a coaxial **cable television (CATV)** system that distributes TV signals in a neighborhood. As the system length increases, the output of the coaxial cable is increasingly attenuated, and the original shape of the signal is distorted. The distortion occurs because different frequency components of the signal are attenuated differently in the cable, as illustrated in Figure 1.6. In addition, interference from extraneous sources, such as radiation from radio transmitters, car ignitions, and power lines, as well as noise inherent in electronic systems, results in the addition of random noise to the transmitted signal. Therefore, amplifiers (also called **analog repeaters**) are placed approximately every 2000 feet to compensate for the attenuation and distortion of the signal, as shown in Figure 1.15. The amplifier boosts the signal level and attempts to equalize the high-frequency roll-off produced by the cable. It then launches this reconditioned signal into the next cable segment. Unfortunately, the input noise is also amplified in this process. Each succeeding amplifier adds the noise and amplifies the noise contributions of the previous amplifiers. Therefore, the signal quality continues to degrade due to the accumulation of noise. This, in turn, severely limits the length of the system (i.e., number of amplifiers in the cascade) in practical systems.

The most important advantage of a digital transmission system is the ability to reconstruct the transmitted digital signal almost perfectly even after it has been impaired by the transmission medium (attenuation + distortion) and noise. The process of reconstruction is performed by **regenerative repeaters** which are spaced along the transmission path. Consider a digital transmission system where binary information consisting of a string of 0's and 1's is conveyed by a sequence of positive and negative pulses. As the length of the transmission link (e.g., a TWP segment) increases, the pulses are increasingly distorted as shown in Figure 1.16. In addition, noise is added as in the analog transmission case.

The job of a regenerative repeater, however, is simple; it does not need to completely recover the original shape of the transmitted signal as in the case of an analog transmission system. In the example displayed in Figure 1.17, it needs to determine only the presence or absence of a pulse in each bit interval. The regenerative repeater also uses a preamp and equalizer to compensate for the attenuation and signal distortion introduced

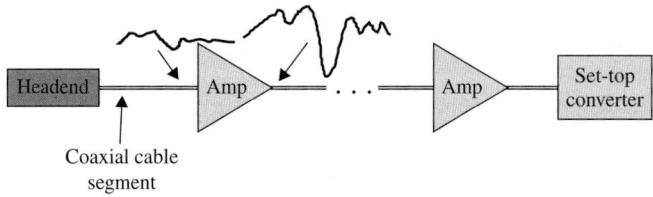

Figure 1.15 Analog CATV system.

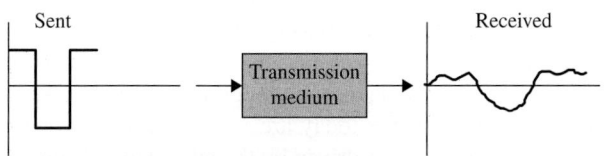

Figure 1.16 Distortion and attenuation of digital signal.

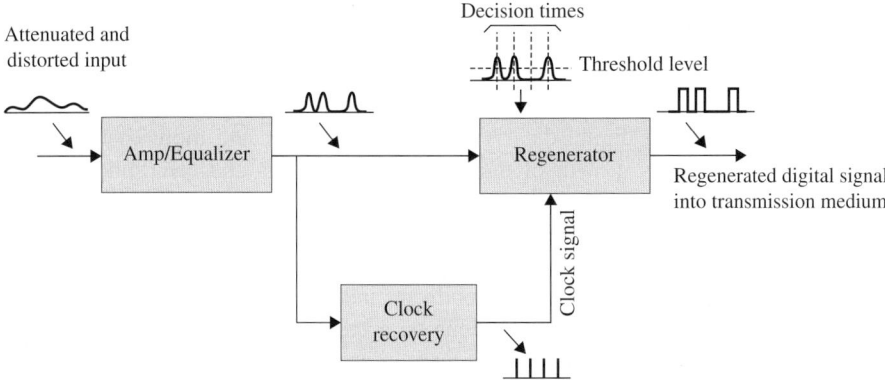

Figure 1.17 Digital regenerative repeater.

by the channel. A timing recovery circuit generates the clock signal that is used by the regenerator to sample the preamp/equalizer output (reshaped pulse + noise) at the midpoint of each pulse period. The **regenerator** will produce a *clean* pulse whenever the magnitude of the sample is above the threshold value. An error occurs when the noise and interference are large enough that the received signal sample value crosses the threshold at the sampling point when no pulse is transmitted. In a properly designed system, the original symbol can be recovered error free virtually every time, and there is *no* accumulation of noise and interference. Consequently, the binary digital signal can be **regenerated** virtually error-free over a large number of repeaters and hence over arbitrarily long distances. The impact on signal quality in multiple regenerative repeaters is similar to the digital recording of music in MP3 format, where the signal is stored as a file of binary information. The file can be copied any number of times, and the quality of the sound is unaffected by the number of times the file is copied.

We can conclude from the preceding discussion that digital transmission has superior performance over analog transmission. Regenerative repeaters eliminate the accumulation of noise that occurs in analog systems and provide performance that is nearly independent of distance. Other advantages of digital transmission systems include:

- **One network for all services.** Digital transmission systems can carry all types of information, whether inherently analog or digital, in one network. Analog signals such as speech, audio, and video, once converted into bits, can be treated like any other form of the digital data. They can be combined with e-mails, text files, and other data for transmission over the same digital transmission system. Thus, communication networks with digital transmission infrastructure can handle all types of traditional as well as new and emerging services.
- **Lower transmitted power.** Digital transmission systems require several orders of magnitude less received power than analog systems for the same user experience or performance (voice or picture quality). In analog communication systems, noise accompanying the signal shows up as distortion at the receiver output. This requires higher received signal level (relative to noise) so that the signal impairment is not objectionable to the user. In the digital case, the signal can be restored perfectly by regeneration as long as the received power level is sufficient to determine whether the transmitted bit is a 0 or 1. The superior sensitivity of the receiver plays a pivotal role in improving the coverage area of cells in cellular systems. In addition, lower transmitted power translates into smaller battery size and less frequent recharging intervals. This is of crucial importance for battery-operated devices such as cell and smart phones.

- **Enhanced capabilities.** Digital transmission enables easier implementation of multiplexing, error control coding, and compression techniques. These capabilities have made feasible the availability of multimedia services and applications on a global scale.
- **Security.** Encrypting digital data is easier, more secure, and more cost effective. With the tremendous growth of mobile communications and electronic financial transactions, protection of information has become very important.
- **Benefits of Moore's law.** The silicon chips inside the digital transmission equipment follow Moore's law, which states that the number of transistors on a chip will double about every two years. Semiconductor industry has kept that pace for more than 40 years, providing more functions on a chip at significantly lower cost per function. Such an exponential improvement in performance of the digital chips can be exploited to cost-effectively integrate sophisticated error control, compression, equalization, and encryption capabilities.

1.4   HISTORY OF COMMUNICATIONS

It is an interesting fact of history that electronic communication began as a digital communication system with the demonstration in 1938 of the first prototype telegraph equipment by Samuel Morse. Morse was granted a United States patent for his invention in 1840. This was followed by the first commercial wire-line telegraph system demonstration between Baltimore and Washington, D.C. in 1844 by him. Morse invented the efficient code that converts text messages into sequences of dots and dashes, as illustrated in Table 1.2. Each dot or dash was communicated by transmitting a short or long pulse of electrical current over a copper wire. Morse also conceived the idea of using short code words to represent more frequently occurring letters such as *e* and *i* and long code words to represent less frequently occurring letters. The concept of variable-length coding is widely used today in compression schemes such as the **Joint Photographic Experts Group (JPEG)** standard. Morse's telegraph system was obviously a binary digital transmission system and a precursor of the modern digital communication systems.

During the second half of the nineteenth century, wire-line telegraphy experienced tremendous growth as increasing numbers of telegraph lines spanned much of Europe, North America, and the Middle East. The expansion of telegraphy across the Atlantic Ocean posed many fundamental challenges. The major difficulty with submarine telegraphy was the attenuation and spreading of pulses propagating through enormous spans of cable across the ocean. Lord Kelvin was the first to analyze this as an engineering

Table 1.2 International Morse Code

	Morse Code		Morse Code		Morse Code		Morse Code
A	. —	J	. — —	S	. . .	2	. . — — —
B	— . . .	K	— . —	T	—	3	. . . — —
C	— . —	L	. — . .	U	. . —	4	. . . . —
D	— . .	M	— —	V	. . . —	5	. . . . .
E	.	N	— .	W	. — —	6	— . . . .
F	. . — .	O	— —	X	— . . —	7	— — . . .
G	— — .	P	. — —	Y	— . — —	8	— — — . .
H	. . . .	Q	— — .	Z	— — . .	9	— — — — .
I	. .	R	. — .	1	. — — —	0	— — — — —

problem in the modern sense. He applied Fourier analysis to study the transmission of electrical pulses through a long submarine cable. By separating the signal (telegraphic pulses) from the system (cable), he was able to develop optimized cable designs and to improve signaling equipment for shaping and detecting the pulses. This was a revolutionary idea, and it signifies the point at which communications engineering was placed on a firm scientific foundation.

Telephone

Telephony was invented in 1875 by Alexander Graham Bell while he was investigating the use of sinusoidal signals for conveying several telegraph signals down the same wire line. During his work, he realized that if a telegraph line could convey several tones, it could also transmit human speech. Bell filed his U.S. patent application in 1876 and he developed the first telephone that could transmit the entire voice signal. That same year he gave the first public demonstration of a two-way long-distance telephone conversation (16 miles) using a borrowed telegraph circuit. The telephone quickly caught on for local service, and by 1880 the Bell Company leased nearly 100,000 instruments. Simple telephone service became a commodity, and it was augmented by many other uses for the telephone, such as the 1887 simultaneous telephone and telegraph service on the same line, and leased line service in 1881. Long-distance telephone transmission, like submarine telegraphy, suffered from attenuation and dispersion. Intelligible speech could be transmitted over a copper wire pair for no more than 100 miles. Successful long-distance telephony required two major engineering advances: inductive loading to counteract line capacitance and signal amplification.

The need for signal amplification led to the beginning of the electronics age with its profound consequences for our civilization. It began with Edison who in 1883 discovered that current flows in a vacuum through the space between two electrodes. It was John Fleming who devised the term *diode* for such a two-element vacuum tube and who observed that an AC current would flow only in one direction. The invention of the vacuum tube was a revolutionary idea. It could be called the beginning of electronics as it laid the foundations for many further inventions. In 1906 Lee De Forest placed a third electrode between the cathode and anode, inventing the triode, which became the fundamental building block of both amplifiers and oscillators. The invention made it possible to introduce signal amplification in telephone communication systems and, thus, to allow for telephone signal transmission over great distances. As a result, transcontinental telephone transmission became operational in 1915. By now the analog telephone had replaced the telegraph as the chosen instrument of human communication. With the advent of amplifiers, limitations imposed by electronic noise were discovered, resulting in the development of noise theory by Nyquist in 1928.

Radio and TV Broadcasting

The invention of the vacuum tube also paved the way for the development of radio communication systems. Broadcasting began in 1906 when Fessenden successfully transmitted a Christmas Eve broadcast to ships at sea from Massachusetts. It was Edwin Armstrong's work on the design of stable oscillator circuits, using a vacuum tube triode and the invention of the superheterodyne receiver, which led to the feasibility of commercial radio broadcasting. The first scheduled radio broadcast was initiated in 1920 by KDKA, Pittsburg, followed by the British Broadcasting Corporation (BBC) in 1922. These radio broadcasts used amplitude modulation (AM). With AM, the noise generated by the radio electronics produced static in the audio output. Another invention by

Pioneers in the Field

Library of Congress Prints and
Photographs Division
[LC-DIG-cwpbh-00852]

Samuel Morse co-inventor of the telegraph, was born in Charlestown, Massachusetts, on April 27, 1791. Though he majored in art at Yale University, Morse also studied chemistry, natural philosophy, and electricity. After his graduation in 1810, he studied painting at the Royal Academy in London and would later become a well-known portrait artist. In 1829, Morse returned to Europe as an artist. On his voyage back to the United States in 1832, he joined a group of passengers discussing the growing field of electricity. A fellow traveler pointed out that electricity could propagate almost instantly through any length of wire. Morse immediately saw the possibility of the telegraph and soon sketched the concept of equipment. His idea was to use an electromagnet, operated at a distance by making and breaking the current in a battery-powered circuit, to move a pencil, which would make marks on a moving strip of paper. As a result of his limited technical background, it took Morse four years after his original concept to complete his first crude telegraph equipment prototype. With this prototype model, Morse was able to record signals, but only to a distance of about 40 feet. To increase the range of his device, Morse sought the aid of two partners: Leonard Gale, a professor of science at New York University, and Alfred Vail, who offered both his mechanical skills and the use of his family's company, New Jersey Iron Works, to help construct better telegraph models. By the following year, the team developed an improved system that used Morse code to represent the letters of the English alphabet and numerical digits by sequences of dots and dashes. Although the code bears the name of Morse, it was jointly developed by Morse and Vail. In 1838, at an exhibition of his telegraph in New York, Morse and Vail transmitted 10 words per minute, using the Morse code that would become standard throughout the world.

After much lobbying, Morse convinced Congress in 1842 to appropriate $30,000 to construct an experimental telegraph line from Baltimore to Washington, D.C. On May 24, 1844, the line was officially opened as Morse coded the message from the Supreme Court chamber in Washington, D.C. to the Pratt Street railroad station in Baltimore. In Baltimore, Vail received the message, which translated as, "What hath God wrought?" This biblical quote had been chosen by the daughter of the patents commissioner.

By 1846, private companies, using Morse's patent, had built telegraph lines from Washington to Boston and Buffalo, and were pushing even further. The telegraph spread across the United States faster than the railroads had, whose routes the wires often followed. By 1854, there were 23,000 miles of telegraph wire in operation. Western Union was founded in 1851, and in 1866, the first successful trans-Atlantic cable link was established. It is a surprising fact in the historical context that a portrait painter with little formal scientific or technical education established the first electrical communications system in the United States. Throughout his life, Morse remained telegraphy's greatest promoter, driving its rapid development and adoption across the globe.

Armstrong in the 1930s, frequency modulation (FM), provided improved noise immunity and superior audio quality. However, commercial FM broadcasting didn't begin in the United States until 1961.

The first all-electronic television system was demonstrated by Philo Farnsworth in 1928, and then independently by Vladimir Zworkin in 1929. Commercial television broadcasting began in London in 1936 by the BBC. The Federal Communications Commission (FCC) authorized television broadcasting in the United States in 1941 using the NTSC black-and-white television standard.

Digital Communications

Digital communication began with the invention of pulse-code modulation (PCM) by Alec Reeves in 1937. His work relied on the earlier work of Carson in 1920 and Hartley and Nyquist in 1924 demonstrating that a band-limited analog waveform can be exactly represented by samples taken at a rate at least twice the maximum frequency present in the waveform. The MTRC16 digital microwave radio relay system delivered in 1945 to the U.S. Army during World War II for encrypted messaging was probably the first deployment of PCM. The economic feasibility of digital communications needed one more invention—the transistor in 1948 at Bell Labs by Shockley, Brattain, and Barden. This provided the base for the next giant step. The integrated circuit was invented in 1958

Pioneers in the Field

Alexander Graham Bell was born on March 3, 1847, in Edinburgh, Scotland, into a family with a passion for communication. His father, Alexander Melville Bell, was a professor of elocution and developed a technique called *visible speech—* a set of symbols that represented speech sounds. The elder Bell used the technique to teach the hearing impaired to speak. Young Bell followed in the footsteps of his father, and by the time he was twenty, he was teaching visible speech in London. In 1870, he immigrated with his parents to Canada. The next year, Bell moved to Boston to lecture on visible speech and to teach the hearing impaired. In 1872, he became a professor of elocution at Boston University.

Since Samuel Morse completed his first telegraph line in 1844, the telegraph network spread not only over the continent, but across the Atlantic Ocean as well. Motivated by the potential of financial reward from the Western Union Telegraph Company, Bell started working on a "harmonic telegraph" that would transmit multiple messages by using musical tones of several frequencies. Bell's harmonic telegraph attracted financial support from Gardiner Hubbard and Thomas Saunders, both parents of his students, and enabled him to employ Thomas Watson as his assistant. While working on the harmonic telegraph, Bell realized that to transmit speech on a telegraph circuit, he needed a transmitter capable of producing an undulating current (that is, an analog signal) in response to vibration of the membrane by the voice and a receiver that would reproduce the audio variations.

On February 14, 1876, Bell filed his patent application covering "the method of, and apparatus for, transmitting vocal or other sounds telegraphically . . . by causing electrical undulations, similar in form to the vibrations of the air accompanying the said vocal or other sound." The patent included both a variable-resistance "liquid" transmitter and an electromagnetic device for both transmission and reception. Another application for a telephone was filed by Elisha Gray only a few hours after Bell's application was filed. Because Bell had filed an application while Gray had only submitted the intent to file an application, Bell's application was granted and Gray's rejected. On March 7, 1876, Bell was issued patent number 174,465 for his invention of the telephone. Three days after the patent was issued, Bell succeeded in getting his telephone to work, using a liquid transmitter similar to Gray's design. Vibration of the membrane by the voice caused a wire to vibrate in the liquid (battery acid), varying the electrical resistance in the circuit. Bell made history when he spoke the famous words, "Mr. Watson, come here. I want to see you!" into the liquid transmitter. Difficulties with the liquid transmitter caused Bell to revert to the electromagnetic design which he was soon able to perform satisfactorily.

Seizing upon the opportunity to promote his new invention, Alexander Graham Bell introduced the telephone to the world at the Centennial Exhibition in Philadelphia in 1876. Brazilian Emperor Dom Pedro exclaimed, "My God, it talks," as Bell performed passages from *Hamlet* over the line from the main building 100 yards away. The success of Bell's telephone was now the talk of the international scientific community. In 1878, Rutherford B. Hayes was the first U.S. president to have a telephone installed in the White House. The Bell Telephone Company (which would eventually become AT&T) was created in 1877, and by 1886, more than 150,000 people in the United States owned telephones.

---

by Jack Kilby at Texas Instruments. The first fully operational time-division multiplexed PCM system for voice communications was implemented in the United States by 1962. This first interoffice digital transmission system, called T1 carrier, time-multiplexed 24-telephone channels sampled 8000 times per second with 8-bit resolution/sample for a total of 1.5 million bits per second (bps). After the development of T1 carrier, a complete family of digital transmission systems was eventually developed, including the 4000-channel DR18 digital radio system in 1969 and the 4000-channel T4 coaxial cable system in 1975.

At the time of the invention of the transistor in 1948, Claude Shannon also worked at Bell Labs and published his landmark paper, "A Mathematical Theory of Communication."[3] Shannon's paper and the invention of the transistor laid the foundation of the Digital Age. Shannon's paper not only proposed the architecture for the design of digital communication systems, as shown in Figure 1.14, but also defined the fundamental limits of information transmission. Shannon showed that every

---

[3] C. Shannon, "A Mathematical Theory of Communication," *Bell Syst. Tech. J.* 27 (1948): 379–423.

communications channel has a maximum rate for reliable data transmission, which he called the channel capacity, measured in bits per second. He demonstrated that data can be transmitted at speeds up to the channel capacity, virtually error free, and with surprisingly low transmitting power by using certain coding schemes—an astonishing result that surprised engineers at the time. Before Shannon's work, engineers thought that to reduce transmission error rate it was necessary to reduce the data rate. So since 1948, communication engineers and theorists have been busy devising coding techniques to achieve good reliability at rates not too far from channel capacity, aiming to fulfill Shannon's prophecy. Shannon's ideas of data compression and channel coding involved complex processing and algorithms, and were it not for the powerful silicon chips (Moore's law) and software, they would have remained for the most part a curiosity. Today **turbo** and **low-density parity check (LDPC)** codes achieve performance that is within a fraction of a decibel of Shannon's prediction.

Optical Fiber Communications

Barely a decade after the invention of the transistor came another major invention in 1959—the laser. This suggested the possibility of transmitting information using light pulses at a very high data rate, but a suitable transmission medium did not yet exist. A breakthrough occurred in 1966 when K. C. Kao and G. A. Hockham proposed optical fiber and predicted that a loss of 20 dB/km should be attainable, a remarkable prediction given that the fibers of the time had losses on the order of 1000 dB/km. By 1968, researchers had prepared bulk silica samples with losses as low as 5 dB/km. In 1970, R. Maurer, P. Schultz, and D. Keck of Corning Glass Works reported the development of a fiber with a loss of 20 dB/km. That same year I. Hayashi and others at Bell Labs demonstrated successful transmission at this attenuation figure using a semiconductor laser. Although actual installation in the field would not occur until the mid-1970s, these and other researchers had demonstrated the feasibility of using semiconductor lasers and optical fibers for communications. During the late 1980s and early 1990s, the capacity of optical fiber transmission systems continued to double every year, reaching a practical limit of 40 Gb/s. Then in 1989 came the innovation of Erbium-Doped Fiber Amplifier (EDFA) that brought about a revolutionary improvement in optical fiber communications. The revolutionary impact of these optical amplifiers is derived from their ability to boost information signals carried by many different wavelengths or "colors" of light. This capability is significant, as the transmission capacity of optical fiber transmission systems can be increased to terabit range by using dense-wavelength-division multiplexing (DWDM), in which many different wavelengths of light are sent down the same fiber, each carrying different information. Today, DWDM optical fiber transmission systems with 1 terabit/second are commercially available.

1.4.1   Wireless Communications

Wireless communications has its origins in James Maxwell's unified theory of electromagnetism, published in 1864, which predicted the existence of electromagnetic wave propagation. However, it took almost a quarter century for Maxwell's theory to be confirmed by the young German physicist Heinrich Hertz, who demonstrated the generation and detection of electromagnetic radiation in the laboratory. During the early 1890s, scientists in several countries experimented with electromagnetic waves. In Russia, Vladimir Popov built some of the earliest radio detectors, while the young Irish-Italian Guglielmo Marconi investigated radio communication systems. It was Marconi who transmitted detectable radio signals across the Atlantic in 1900 and then demonstrated wireless telegraphy the following year. Until the rise of broadcasting after 1920, the major application of radio and specifically wireless telegraphy was for maritime communications.

Mobile Communications

Mobile communications have undergone spectacular development in the last 40 years that continues at a fast pace. In 1947 Reudink and Young of Bell Labs proposed the cellular mobile radio concept, in which frequencies could be reused in nonadjacent cells by mobile radios of limited power. The first trial of the Advanced Mobile Telephone Service (AMPS) utilizing the cellular concept was held in 1978 in the Chicago suburbs. The first-generation (1G) analog AMPS carried frequency-modulated voice signals in the 30 kHz frequency slot. The second-generation (2G) systems using new digital technologies were introduced in the 1990s, particularly time-division multiple access (TDMA) and spread spectrum code-division multiple access (CDMA). TDMA was realized in the IS-136 standard used in the United States and Japan and in the GSM system deployed in Europe and more recently around the world. The first- and second-generation mobile network systems were optimized to carry voice traffic, although low-speed data applications became quite popular. The third-generation (3G) network, first launched in Japan in 2001 by NTT DoCoMo using WCDMA technology, offers faster access to the Internet and other data services, with typical downstream speeds ranging from 400 kilobytes per second (kbps) up to several megabits per second (Mbps) for the user. In October 2010, ITU set standards for 4G networks capable of delivering peak download speeds of 100 Mbps to support high speed mobile broadband applications.

Table 1.3 summarizes major events in the long and interesting history of communication.

1.5   KEY THEMES AND DRIVERS

The key developments in the communications landscape during the second half of the nineteenth century and the first few decades of the twentieth century were driven mostly by the development of devices and communication circuits. In the twentieth century, innovations in the communication field increasingly began to emerge from the mathematical analysis of communication systems and the study of various performance trade-offs. The most influential work in this context was Shannon's paper,[4] which laid the foundation of digital communications and established the field of information theory. Shannon's work presented concepts, architecture, and fundamental limits on the performance of digital communication systems that can be achieved using complex processing. It required two additional revolutions to realize Shannon's prophecy:

- Semiconductor revolution in the form of Moore's law that enabled the development of powerful silicon chips.
- Software revolution beginning with the development of stored-program computer concept by Von Nuemann. Complex coding and compression algorithms are implemented in software to run on these silicon chips.

This marriage of communication and computers has produced a paradigm shift in the design of digital communication systems and networks. It is the ideas and algorithms rather than the devices and circuits that drive innovations in the twenty-first-century communications industry. It is fair to say that several multibillion-dollar industries, such as wireless, consumer electronics, and broadband, would not exist without the

---

[4] Shannon, "A Mathematical Theory of Communication," 379–423.

Table 1.3 Important Milestones in History of Communications

Year	Event
1820	Oersted shows electric currents create magnetic fields
1830–1840	Henry discovers induction; Faraday and others show changing magnetic fields produce electric fields
1838	Samuel Morse demonstrates telegraph
1844	First commercial telegraph link from Baltimore to Washington
1864	James C. Maxwell predicts electromagnetic radiation
1866	Transatlantic telegraph
1876	Alexander Graham Bell files patent application for the invention of telephone
1878	Alexander Graham Bell installs first telephone exchange in New Haven, Connecticut
1887	Hertz experimentally verifies Maxwell theory
1895	Radio, or "wireless," born when Guglielmo Marconi experiments with wireless telegraphy
1901	First transatlantic radio message by Marconi, United Kingdom to Canada
1904–1906	Fleming announces diode tube; DeForest announces triode
1906	AM radio broadcasting
1918	Edwin Armstrong devises superheterodyne receiver
1920	First modern radio broadcast by KDKA, Pittsburgh, Pennsylvania
1924–1928	Mechanical TV system demonstrations by John Baird, London
1928	Gaussian thermal noise papers of Johnson and Nyquist
	First all-electronic television system demonstrated by Philo Farnsworth, and also independently by Vladimir Zworkin in 1929
1933	Edwin Armstrong invents FM
1936	Commercial TV broadcasting by British Broadcasting Corporation, London
1937	Alec Reeves patents pulse-code modulation (PCM) in England
1943	D. O. North introduces matched filter for radar detection application
1947	Kotelnikov in Russia introduces signal space concepts to develop theory of optimal reception of digital signals in the presence of noise
1948	Brattain, Bardeen, and Shockley demonstrate transistor in the United States; Claude Shannon publishes *A Mathematical Theory of Communication*
1949	Shannon publishes sampling theorem in the context of communication; Kotelnikov arrived at similar results in 1933 independently
1950–1955	Beginnings of computer software; beginnings of microwave long-haul transmission
1956	First transatlantic telephone cable
1959	Jack Kilby patents integrated circuit
1960s	Error-correcting codes begin rapid development
1960	Theodore Maiman introduces the first working laser in the United States
1962	AT&T introduces T1 digital carrier system, the transmission of voice in digital format
	First communication satellite, Telstar I, launched
1967	Viterbi proposes algorithm for efficient decoding of convolutional codes
1970	Low-loss optical fibers demonstrated
1971	Microprocessor invented
1975	Robert Metcalfe and others file a patent for Ethernet at Xerox PARC
1976	Apple I home computer invented
1979	First commercial citywide cellular network is launched in Japan by NTT
1981	IBM launches its personal computer (PC)
1983	FT3C (90 Mb/s) digital optical fiber system linking Washington D.C. to New York installed
1983	16-bit DSP chips commercially available
1985–1990	Cellular mobile telephones become widespread in Europe
1987	EDFA optical amplifier invented, a key enabling technology for wavelength-division multiplexing (WDM) systems
1988	Flash memory commercially available (key technology for PDAs, laptop computers, MP3 players, digital cameras, and cellular phones)
1991	Second-generation (digital) cellular system, GSM, begins operation in Europe
1993	Turbo coding invented by C. Berrou and others, approaches Shannon limit
1996	Demonstration of Tbit/sec rate transmission on single-mode fibers using WDM
Late-1990s	Internet proliferates
2001	First commercial launch of third-generation (3G) cellular network in Japan by NTT DoCoMo using WCDMA technology

scientific underpinnings provided by Shannon's ideas and the revolutionary improvements in semiconductor and software technologies. Other significant trends in the communication landscape include:

- **Transition from electrons to photons.** Transmission of information by photons instead of electrons has made bandwidth abundant and cheap. Digital transmission over optical fibers has resulted in nearly limitless capacity in the long-haul telecommunication networks. This evolution will continue, and the photonic information pipe to the home is becoming a reality.
- **Discrete-time processing.** Because of the tremendous improvements in analog-to-digital conversion technologies, there is an increasing trend to push the signal processing complexity from the analog into the digital domain. The resultant cost and performance benefits are then increasingly driven by Moore's law. The smart phone is an example.
- **Mobility.** Mobile communication has become the preferred way of communication, information gathering, and entertainment as evidenced by the increasing dominance of smart phones in our society. It is driven by the people's need to be connected whenever and wherever they are.

FINAL REMARKS

Shannon's paper and Shockley's invention of the transistor (and its progeny, large-scale integrated circuits) have been referred to by Andrew Viterbi[5] as the "double big bang," which led to the creation of the modern communications industry. We anticipate dramatic growth in wireless and broadband communications systems as the prophecies of Shannon and Moore continue to be fulfilled.

---

[5] Lecture at MIT.

FURTHER READINGS

Readings [2, 4] were consulted in preparing the historical review of communications in this chapter. Reading [3] contains many interesting articles on the history of communications. Netravali [6] is a good survey of the impact of the semiconductor revolution on computing and communications.

1. Andersen, J., T. Rappaport, and S. Yoshida. "Propagation Measurements and Models for Wireless Communication Channels." *IEEE Communications Magazine* 33, no. 1 (1995): 42–49.

2. Joel, A. R. "Telecommunications and the IEEE Communications Society." *IEEE Communications Magazine,* 50th Anniversary Commemorative Issue (May 2002): 6–14, 162–164 6*ff.*

3. "100 Years of Communication Progress." *IEEE Communications Magazine* 22, no. 5 (1984).

4. Anderson, J., and R. Johannesson. *Understanding Information Transmission.* Hoboken, NJ: IEEE Press, Wiley-Interscience, 2005.

5. Shannon, C. "A Mathematical Theory of Communication." *Bell Syst. Tech. J.* 27, (1948): 379–423.

6. Netravali, A. "The Impact of Solid-State Electronics on Computing and Communications." *Bell Labs Tech. J.* 2, no. 4 (Autumn 1997): 126–154.

An Interview with John Mayo

Courtesy of John Mayo

Why did you choose a career in the communications field?

Electronics was the blooming technology of my youth, so it was natural for my entire family to get involved with communications. I never considered any other career.

Tell us about a few memorable moments of your lifelong career at Bell Labs.

Most memorable was when we were able to devise a command code that returned the Telstar satellite to service after it encountered serious radiation damage and did not respond to normal commands. Many memorable moments came from hard work and long hours spent with coworkers. I was fortunate to be able to ride the crest of the digital revolution, so the success of digital carrier on wire pairs and fiber-optic cable, of large-scale digital switching, and automation of network operations were especially rewarding.

In your opinion, what are the major innovations that have contributed to the information age we live in? What has been the impact of the semiconductor revolution? Optical fiber revolution? Marriage of computers and communications?

The transistor is the invention that changed the world. Next in importance are the innovations of materials, scientists, and engineers that produced silicon so pure millions of transistors can be put in a tiny chip and glass so pure it transmits light hundreds of miles. The semiconductor revolution drove the cost, size, and power consumption of an electronic circuit to near zero by putting millions of interconnecting "wires" on the surface of the silicon chip. That opened the door to the digital revolution with its focus on microcomputers and software. Optical fibers favor digital over analog transmission and have the enormous bandwidth required to interconnect the world as well as local neighborhoods. The resulting marriage of computers and communications enabled the personal computer, cell phones, and the Internet to change our way of life. The world today would be a very different place if the transistor invention had not enabled Japan to prosper by supplying the world with low-cost electronics during the Cold War, enabled the USA to create Silicon Valley, and later made it clear to the Russians that their form of communism was not compatible with the Internet and other elements of the digital revolution.

1948 was the year of "double big bang": the invention of transistor and publication of Shannon's seminal papers.

With the disappearance of Bell system research model, are we doing enough fundamental research to drive the next round of major innovations?

The Bell Labs research model exists not only at Bell Labs, but now at many places around the world, especially in Silicon Valley and in research-focused companies and countries. Key to the Bell Labs model is that world class does not come from managing people. It comes from managing ideas. It starts with hiring the very best people from around the world and helping them reach their full potential. Ideas are gathered from the group and from around the world with the goal of solving serious problems for which there are no good solutions. The transistor was not an abstract invention. It was Bell Labs' answer to the developing crisis in telecommunications as an enormous number of vacuum tubes were being introduced into the telephone network and they were too unreliable, too power hungry, and too large to provide the quality of service that would be required in a rapidly growing public network.

Tell us about the development of the T1 carrier system. What were the major technical challenges faced by the development team? In retrospect, how do you view the impact of this milestone event toward the realization of an all digital network?

The T1 carrier was a major milestone in telecommunications for it brought high-speed digital technology to the large cables of wire pairs that were the backbone of the telephone network. It simplified the network of wires and cables and also opened the door for digital switching, integrated services, and the oncoming digital revolution. Our challenges for T1 were cross-talk between wire pairs in the same cable, extraction of a timing wave from a random group of pulses, timing jitter in a long string of repeaters, and the high cost of digital circuitry compared to analog equivalents.

You made major contributions toward the development of circuit-switched network. While at Bell Labs, did you anticipate such a phenomenal growth of packet-switched network technologies and TCP/IP applications? Internet?

Anticipation is a time-frame concept. As a young engineer I would have said wiring up a million circuits on a tiny chip is a pipe dream, and sending light through a hundred miles of glass is crazy. One's views change as reality develops. We talked about packet switching in the T1 days, but the technology and the marketplace were not ready for it. Analog packet switching was reduced to practice in TASI, a system for increasing capacity on the transatlantic cables, and packet multiplexing (called time-compression) was considered for putting many Picturephone signals on a wideband channel. Exponential growth of the digital revolution made it clear long ago that wireless networks, packet switching, and the Internet are key components that will grow exponentially also.

Who inspired you professionally?

Vannevar Bush was a great inspiration. I doubt there will ever be another technologist quite like him. All the people of Bell Labs were inspiring and helpful. Julius Molnar had this great gift of managing ideas and encouraging people to their full potential.

Do you have any advice for the new generation of students and researchers entering the communications field?

Time will reveal many new concepts in communications, and they will come to those who work hard to find better solutions to today's worsening problems. What you have learned is like a newly planted field. You must continue to develop new knowledge throughout your entire career, or else "weeds" will overtake your knowledge base and prevent a bountiful harvest.

John S. Mayo was born February 26, 1930, in Greenville, North Carolina. He received his B.S., M.S., and Ph.D. degrees in Electrical Engineering from North Carolina State in 1952, 1953, and 1955, respectively. Dr. Mayo began his career with Bell Labs in 1955, working on the design of the first transistorized digital computer, a military development project named Tradic. Later, he worked on another early experimental programmable computer named Leprechaun. He also contributed to the Telstar communications satellite program. He led the development of the T1 carrier system and the #4ESS long-distance digital switching system. At Bell Labs, Dr. Mayo has been director of the Ocean Systems Laboratory, executive director of the Ocean Systems division, executive director of the Toll Electronic Switching division and vice president of Electronics Technology. He became the seventh president of Bell Labs in 1991 and continued in this position until his retirement in 1995. During forty years service at the Labs, he played a key role in transitioning telecommunications from a people-intensive analog telephone network to a computer-intensive digital multiservice network. This was achieved through his leadership in guiding the fundamental research and development of systems that underlie today's global all-digital communications network. Dr. Mayo has been awarded many honors in recognition of his outstanding contributions, including the National Medal of Technology from President George H. W. Bush.

Review of Signals and Linear Systems

Communication systems transfer information using signals. **Signals** are functions of time that convey information from the transmitter to the receiver at the other end of the transmission medium. In electrical communication systems, signals take the form of electromagnetic waves that can be transmitted over wired or wireless media. Examples of wired media include twisted wire pair, coaxial cable, and optical fiber in which the signal energy is contained and guided within the medium. In wireless media, on the other hand, the signal energy propagates in the form of unguided electromagnetic waves. Radio, microwave, and infrared are examples of wireless media.

A **system** is an interconnection of devices and subsystems chosen to perform a desired function on signals. In this chapter, we review representative signal types and system models frequently encountered in modern communication systems. We next consider frequency domain representation of signals and linear, time-invariant systems. Many practical communication subsystems and channels can be closely modeled by this important subclass of systems. Thus it is useful to understand the effect of linear, time-invariant systems on transmission of signals.

The chapter is organized into the following sections:

2.1   BASIC SIGNAL CONCEPTS.
We consider various signal classifications useful in the study of communication systems. We then describe basic signals encountered in modeling of such systems.

2.2   BASIC SYSTEM CONCEPTS.
This section introduces **linear time-invariant (LTI)** *systems and their characterization in time-domain. The concepts of causality and stability are also introduced.*

2.3   FREQUENCY DOMAIN REPRESENTATION.
The frequency domain representation of signals is introduced in this section. We discuss additional insight offered by the frequency domain analysis and its use in the design of communication systems.

2.4   FOURIER SERIES.
This section describes Fourier series representation, which is applicable to periodic signals.

2.5   FOURIER TRANSFORM.
The concept of Fourier transform and its many useful properties are discussed in this section. We conclude by considering Fourier transforms of periodic signals.

2.6   TIME-BANDWIDTH PRODUCT.
The inverse relationship between time- and frequency-domain descriptions of a signal is considered in this section.

2.7   TRANSMISSION OF SIGNALS THROUGH LTI SYSTEMS.
The concept of the frequency response of a linear, time-invariant system is introduced. The requirements for distortionless transmission of signals over such systems are then studied using frequency domain analysis techniques.

2.8   LTI SYSTEMS AS FREQUENCY SELECTIVE FILTERS.
We introduce filtering as a key application of an LTI system. The most commonly realized filter characteristics are then described, and issues related to practical realization are discussed.

2.9   POWER SPECTRAL DENSITY.
The section studies the **power spectral density (PSD)** *as a useful measure for describing the power content of a signal as a function of the frequency.*

2.10   FREQUENCY RESPONSE CHARACTERISTICS OF TRANSMISSION MEDIA.
The characteristics of popular transmission media in terms of their frequency response performance are discussed in this section.

2.11   FOURIER TRANSFORMS FOR DISCRETE-TIME SIGNALS.

We introduce two alternative Fourier transform representations for discrete-time signals that lead to efficient computational algorithms.

The chapter concludes with final remarks and a selected list of readings.

2.1   BASIC SIGNAL CONCEPTS

A signal $x(t)$ is called a **continuous-time (CT) signal** if it is defined for every instant of time t in the range $-\infty$ to ∞. On the other hand, a **discrete-time (DT) signal** is defined for discrete instants of time, and hence it is a sequence of numbers, called **samples.** It is denoted by $\{x[n], n =$ integer in the range $-\infty$ to $\infty\}$. In this book, we will use the notation $x[n]$ to denote the entire sequence as well as the nth sample or number in the sequence. The intended meaning will be obvious from the context. It is important to recognize that the sequence $x[n]$ is defined only for integer values of n. Figure 2.1(a) and (b) display examples of CT and DT signals.

Analog and Digital Signals

A continuous-time signal that assumes a continuum of amplitude values between given maximum and minimum is called an **analog signal.** Most signals we encounter in the real world are analog in nature. Examples include speech, music, image, and video signals. **Digital signals,** on the other hand, can change values at discrete instants of time, assuming one of a finite number of amplitude levels. Figure 2.1(c) shows examples of binary and quaternary digital signals.

So far we have considered real signals for which the amplitude of the signal takes its values from the set of real numbers, that is, $x(t) \in \mathbb{R}, -\infty < t < \infty$. A **complex signal,** on the other hand, takes its values from the set of complex numbers, that is, $x(t) \in \mathbb{C}$, $-\infty < t < \infty$. Complex signals are used to model signals that convey information in both amplitude and phase.

Deterministic and Random Signals

A **deterministic signal** $x(t)$ is completely specified for each value of time t—that is, its amplitude is known either graphically or analytically for all values of t. An example is a simple sinusoidal waveform $\sin(4\pi t)$, which is displayed in Figure 2.2. On the

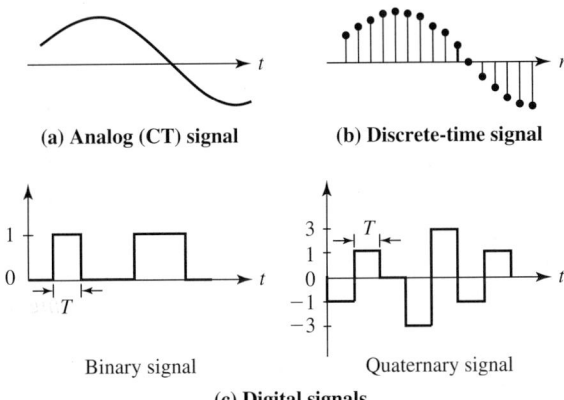

Figure 2.1 Examples of signals.

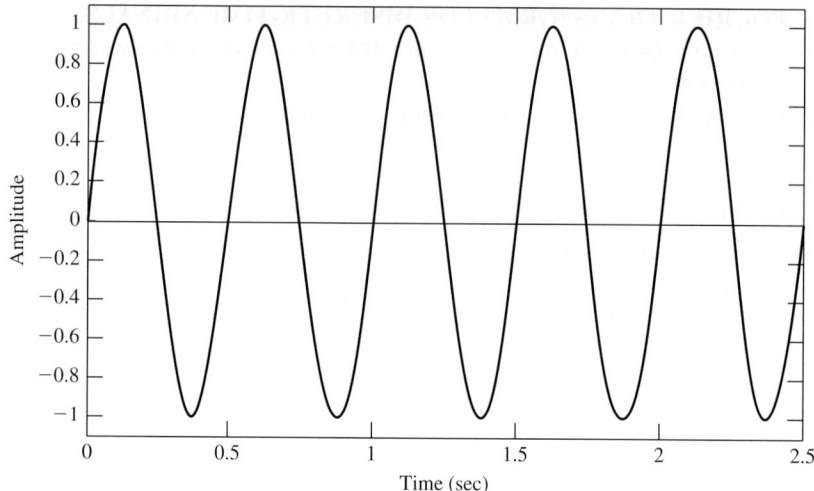

Figure 2.2 Example of a deterministic signal: sine wave.

other hand, a **random signal** is not precisely known for each value of *t*—it can only be specified in terms of probabilities. This is a very important class of signals that includes noise signals and all information-carrying signals, such as speech and data signals. The variations of these signals are extremely complex, and we have only partial specifications available. Figure 2.3 shows an example of a random signal.

Periodic and Aperiodic Signals

A CT signal $x_p(t)$ is **periodic** with period T if and only if

$$x_p(t) = x_p(t + kT), \quad -\infty < t < \infty \quad T > 0 \tag{2.1}$$

where k is any integer. From equation (2.1) it is obvious that $x_p(t)$ repeats its values at integer multiples of its period T. The minimum value of the period $T > 0$ that satisfies (2.1) is called the **fundamental period** of the signal and is denoted as T_o. A signal not

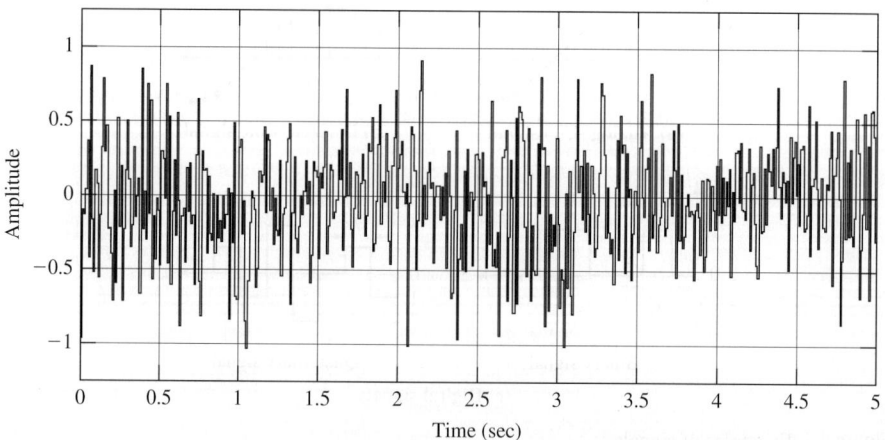

Figure 2.3 Example of a random signal.

satisfying the periodicity condition (2.1) is called an **aperiodic signal.** The sinusoidal waveform displayed in Figure 2.2 is an example of a continuous-time periodic signal with fundamental period $T_o = 0.5$ sec.

A discrete-time signal (sequence) $x_p[n]$ satisfying

$$x_p[n] = x_p[n + kN], \ N > 0 \tag{2.2}$$

is called a **periodic sequence** with period N where k is any integer. The smallest value of the period N that satisfies (2.2) is called the fundamental period N_o of the sequence. Figure 2.4 shows an example of a discrete-time periodic signal.

A sequence not satisfying the periodicity condition (2.2) is called an **aperiodic sequence.**

2.1.1 Some Useful Basic Signals

In the study of communication systems, certain signal types occur recurrently. These signals are defined next.

The Sinusoidal Signal

The most common real-valued signal is the sinusoidal waveform

$$x(t) = A \cos(2\pi f_o t + \phi) \tag{2.3}$$

where A, f_o, and ϕ are its amplitude, frequency, and phase, respectively. A sinusoidal signal $x(t) = 5\sin(4\pi t + \pi/4)$ is shown in Figure 2.5. Sinusoidal signals are important

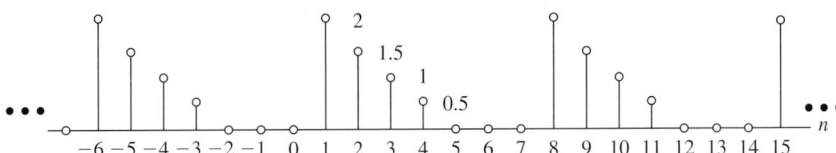

Figure 2.4 Discrete-time periodic signal with fundamental period $N_o = 7$.

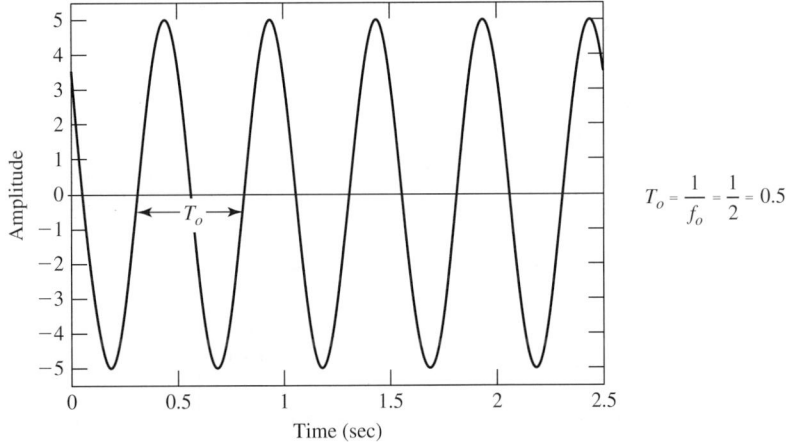

$$T_o = \frac{1}{f_o} = \frac{1}{2} = 0.5$$

Figure 2.5 Sinusoidal signal where $A = 5, f_o = 2$, and $\phi = \pi/4$.

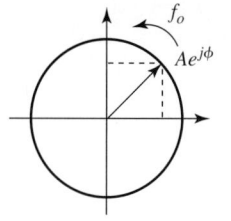

Figure 2.6 Interpretation of a complex exponential signal as a rotating phasor.

because they can be used to synthesize many waveforms. An arbitrary signal defined over a finite interval can be expressed as a sum of sinusoidal signals with different frequencies, amplitudes, and phases. Pure musical notes are essentially sinusoidal signals at different frequencies.

The Complex Exponential Signal

The complex exponential signal is defined by

$$x(t) \triangleq Ae^{j(2\pi f_o t + \phi)} \tag{2.4}$$

where A, f_o, and ϕ are again amplitude, frequency, and phase, respectively. $Ae^{j\phi}$ is known as the signal's complex amplitude or **phasor.** A complex exponential signal can be interpreted as a rotating phasor as illustrated in Figure 2.6. The frequency f_o of the complex exponential signal corresponds to the number of times the phasor rotates per second. Its horizontal and vertical projections at any time correspond to the real and imaginary parts of $x(t)$, respectively. It should be noted that the sinusoidal signal in equation (2.3) is a real part of the complex exponential signal.

The Unit Step Signal

This signal is defined as

$$u(t) \triangleq \begin{cases} 1, & t \geq 0 \\ 0, & \text{otherwise} \end{cases} \tag{2.5}$$

The corresponding signal in the discrete-time domain is called a **unit step sequence.** It is defined as

$$u[n] \triangleq \begin{cases} 1, & n \geq 0 \\ 0, & \text{otherwise} \end{cases} \tag{2.6}$$

Figure 2.7 displays the unit step signal $u(t)$ and its discrete-time version $u[n]$.

A signal $x(t)$ is called **causal** if $x(t) = 0$ for all $t < 0$. Otherwise, the signal is called **noncausal.** For a noncausal signal $x(t)$, we can generate a causal version of it by multiplying it with $u(t)$. That is,

$$x(t)u(t) = \begin{cases} x(t), & t \geq 0 \\ 0, & \text{otherwise} \end{cases} \tag{2.7}$$

Example 2.1

The sinusoidal signal $x(t) = A\cos(2\pi f_c t + \phi)$ is a noncausal signal. However, $A\cos(2\pi f_c t + \phi)u(t)$ is a causal signal.

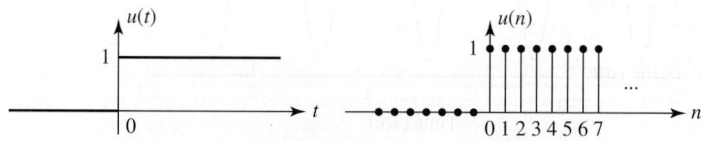

Figure 2.7 Continuous- and discrete-time versions of the unit step signal.

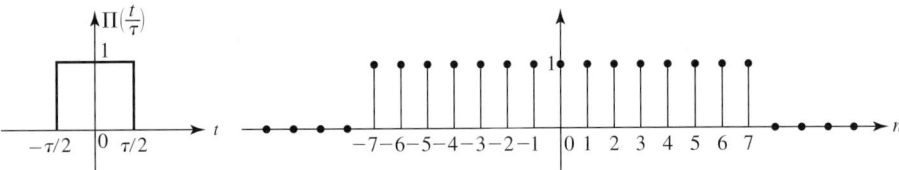

Figure 2.8 Rectangular pulse and corresponding discrete-time sequence.

The Rectangular Pulse

The rectangular pulse $\Pi\left(\dfrac{t}{\tau}\right)$ is a pulse of unit amplitude and width τ centered at $t = 0$.

$$\Pi\left(\frac{t}{\tau}\right) \triangleq \begin{cases} 1, & -\tau/2 \leq t \leq \tau/2 \\ 0, & \text{otherwise} \end{cases} \qquad (2.8)$$

Figure 2.8 displays the rectangular pulse $\Pi\left(\dfrac{t}{\tau}\right)$ and a discrete-time version of it.

The triangular pulse $\Lambda\left(\dfrac{t}{\tau}\right)$ is defined by

$$\Lambda\left(\frac{t}{\tau}\right) \triangleq \begin{cases} 1 + \dfrac{2t}{\tau}, & -\tau/2 \leq t \leq 0 \\ 1 - \dfrac{2t}{\tau}, & 0 \leq t \leq +\tau/2 \\ 0, & \text{otherwise} \end{cases} \qquad (2.9)$$

Figure 2.9 displays the triangular pulse $\Lambda\left(\dfrac{t}{\tau}\right)$.

The Impulse Signal

The impulse signal $\delta(t)$ is defined by the equations

$$\int_{-\infty}^{\infty} \delta(t)dt = 1 \qquad (2.10)$$

and

$$\delta(t) = 0, \ t \neq 0$$

Thus the impulse signal $\delta(t)$ is zero everywhere except at the origin, and it has unit area or **weight.** Note that the impulse signal is defined by its properties rather than its values. We depict the impulse signal as a vertical arrow as illustrated in Figure 2.10(a) where the number beside the arrow indicates its weight. In mathematics, $\delta(t)$ is referred to as Dirac delta function or functional. The impulse signal can be viewed as a narrow pulse with large amplitude and having a unit area. In the limit, as the width of the pulse approaches zero, its amplitude increases such that the area of the pulse remains unity. Figure 2.10(b) shows the impulse signal as a limit of the narrowing rectangular pulse.

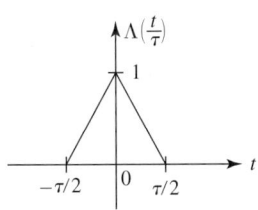

Figure 2.9 Triangular pulse.

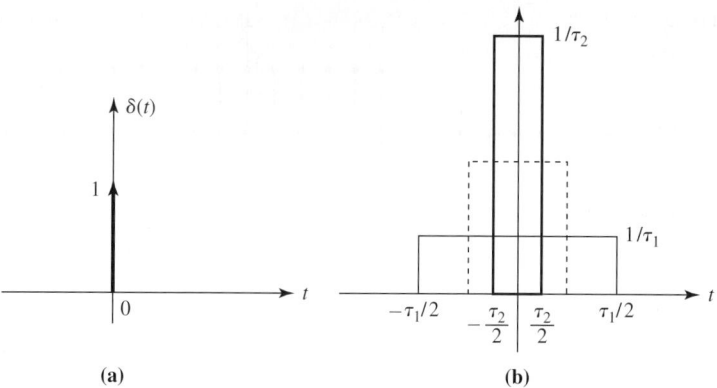

Figure 2.10 (a) Impulse signal; (b) approximating the impulse signal with narrowing rectangular pulses.

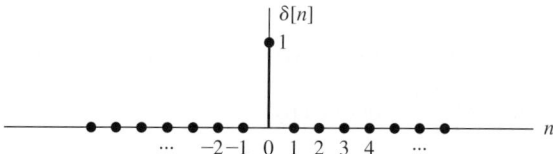

Figure 2.11 Unit impulse sequence.

The impulse signal is a mathematical representation for excitation or action that is highly localized in time.

In discrete-time domain, a **unit impulse** or **sample sequence** is defined by

$$\delta[n] \triangleq \begin{cases} 1, & n = 0 \\ 0, & \text{otherwise} \end{cases} \tag{2.11}$$

Figure 2.11 illustrates a unit impulse sequence.

The following properties of the impulse signal can be derived from its definition:

1. $x(t)\delta(t - t_o) = x(t_o)\delta(t - t_o)$ \hfill (2.12)

Equation (2.12) follows from the fact that $\delta(t - t_o) = 0$ everywhere except at $t = t_o$.

2. $\delta(\alpha t) = \dfrac{1}{|\alpha|}\delta(t)$ \hfill (2.13)

3. $\displaystyle\int_{-\infty}^{\infty} x(t)\delta(t - t_o)dt = x(t_o)$ \hfill (2.14)

Equation (2.14) is obtained by substituting (2.12) into the integral as follows:

$$\int_{-\infty}^{\infty} x(t)\delta(t - t_o)dt = \int_{-\infty}^{\infty} x(t_o)\delta(t - t_o)dt = x(t_o)\int_{-\infty}^{\infty} \delta(t - t_o)dt = x(t_o)$$

This is called the **sampling** or **sifting** property of the impulse signal.

4. $x(t) \otimes \delta(t) = \displaystyle\int_{-\infty}^{\infty} x(\tau)\delta(t - \tau)d\tau = x(t)$ \hfill (2.15)

Equation (2.15) is obtained by using the property $\delta(t) = \delta(-t)$ and a change of variables as follows:

$$x(t) \otimes \delta(t) = \int_{-\infty}^{\infty} x(\tau)\delta(\tau - t)d\tau = x(t)\int_{-\infty}^{\infty} \delta(\tau - t)d\tau = x(t)$$

Similarly,

$$x(t) \otimes \delta(t - t_o) = \int_{-\infty}^{\infty} x(\tau)\delta(t - t_o - \tau)d\tau = \int_{-\infty}^{\infty} x(\tau)\delta[\tau - (t - t_o)]d\tau = x(t - t_o)$$

$$(2.16)$$

Thus, the convolution of an arbitrary signal with the impulse signal yields the signal itself. Further, the convolution of an arbitrary signal with a shifted impulse signal yields the signal shifted by the same amount.

Example 2.2

Evaluate the following expressions.

a. $\sin(3500\pi t)\delta(t)$

b. $\cos(\pi t)\delta(4t - 1)$

c. $\int_{-\infty}^{\infty} [t^2 - \cos(\pi t)]\delta(t - 2)dt$

d. $\int_{-\infty}^{\infty} [e^{-t} + \cos(10\pi t)]\delta(2t - 4)dt$

Solution

a. Applying Property 1 of the impulse signal yields

$$\sin(3500\pi t)\delta(t) = \sin(0)\delta(t) = 0 \times \delta(t) = 0$$

b. Using Property 2, we obtain

$$\cos(\pi t)\delta(4t - 1) = \frac{1}{4}\cos(\pi t)\delta\left(t - \frac{1}{4}\right)$$

Now applying Property 1 yields

$$\cos(\pi t)\delta(4t - 1) = \frac{1}{4}\cos\left(\frac{\pi}{4}\right)\delta\left(t - \frac{1}{4}\right) = \frac{1}{4\sqrt{2}}\delta\left(t - \frac{1}{4}\right)$$

c. Using Property 3, we can write

$$\int_{-\infty}^{\infty} [t^2 - \cos(\pi t)]\delta(t - 2)dt = [t^2 - \cos(\pi t)]\big|_{t=2} = 4 - 1 = 3$$

d. Applying Property 2 yields

$$\int_{-\infty}^{\infty} [e^{-t} + \cos(10\pi t)]\delta(2t - 4)dt = \int_{-\infty}^{\infty} [e^{-t} + \cos(10\pi t)]\delta[2(t - 2)]dt$$

$$= \frac{1}{2}\int_{-\infty}^{\infty} [e^{-t} + \cos(10\pi t)]\delta(t - 2)dt$$

Now using Property 3, we obtain

$$\int_{-\infty}^{\infty} [e^{-t} + \cos(10\pi t)]\delta(2t - 4)dt = \frac{e^{-t} + \cos(10\pi t)}{2}\bigg|_{t=2} = \frac{1}{2}[e^{-2} + 1] = \frac{1.135}{2} = 0.567$$

Sinc Signal

The sinc signal is defined as

$$\text{sinc}(t) \triangleq \frac{\sin(\pi t)}{\pi t} \tag{2.17}$$

The waveform of the sinc signal is displayed in Figure 2.12. We observe from Figure 2.12 that the sinc signal undergoes zero crossings at $t = \pm 1, \pm 2, \pm 3, \ldots$ The sinc signal assumes a maximum value of 1 at $t = 0$ (obtained as a limit using L'Hopital's rule).

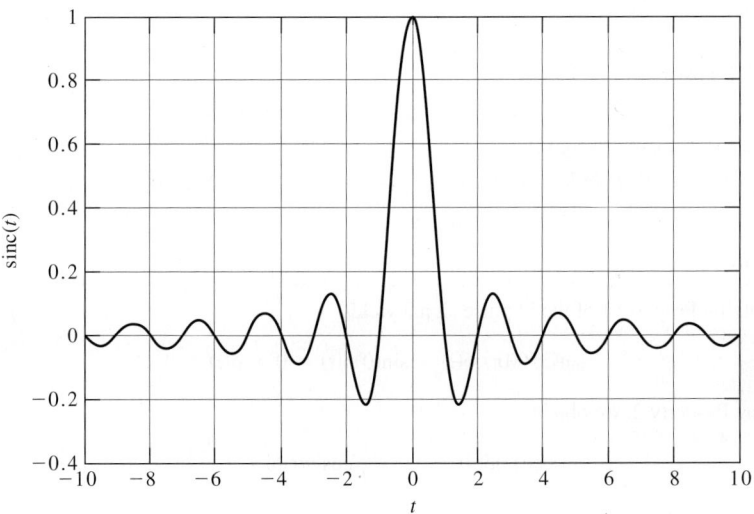

Figure 2.12 The sinc signal.

Sign or Signum Signal

The sign signal sgn(t) is defined as

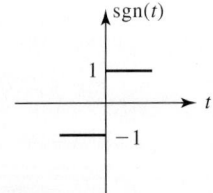

Figure 2.13 The sign or signum signal.

$$\text{sgn}(t) \triangleq \begin{cases} 1, & t > 0 \\ -1, & t < 0 \\ 0, & \text{otherwise} \end{cases} \tag{2.18}$$

Note that sgn(t) denotes the sign of the independent variable t. Figure 2.13 depicts the sign signal.

2.1.2   Energy and Power Signals

Energy and power are useful parameters of a signal. The **normalized energy** of a signal $x(t)$ is defined as the energy dissipated by a voltage $x(t)$ applied across a 1-ohm resistor (or a current $x(t)$ passing though a 1-ohm resistor).

$$E_x \triangleq \lim_{T \to \infty} \int_{-T/2}^{T/2} |x(t)|^2 dt = \int_{-\infty}^{\infty} |x(t)|^2 dt \qquad (2.19)$$

The energy of a signal is meaningful only if the limit in (2.19) exists (that is, finite). Such signals are called **energy signals.**

Example 2.3

Find the energy of a rectangular pulse $x(t) = A\Pi(t/T_b)$.

$$x(t) = \begin{cases} A, & |t| \leq T_b/2 \\ 0, & \text{otherwise} \end{cases}$$

Solution

Using (2.19), the energy is given by

$$E_x = \int_{-\infty}^{\infty} |x(t)|^2 dt = \int_{-T_b/2}^{T_b/2} A^2 dt = A^2 T_b$$

Example 2.4

Find the energy of the carrier pulse $x(t) = A\Pi(t/T_b)\cos(2\pi f_o t)$.

$$x(t) = \begin{cases} A\cos(2\pi f_o t), & |t| \leq T_b/2 \\ 0, & \text{otherwise} \end{cases}$$

Solution

Substituting into (2.19) yields

$$E_x = \int_{-\infty}^{\infty} |x(t)|^2 dt = A^2 \int_{-T_b/2}^{T_b/2} \cos^2(2\pi f_o t) dt = \frac{A^2}{2} \int_{-T_b/2}^{T_b/2} [1 + \cos(4\pi f_o t)] dt = \frac{A^2 T_b}{2}$$

where we have used the trigonometric identity $2\cos^2(\theta) = 1 + \cos(2\theta)$. The integral of the second term is zero because $f_o \gg 1/T_b$ has been assumed. The energy content of the signal becomes infinite in the limit as $T_b \to \infty$.

Example 2.5

Find the energy of the sinusoidal waveform $x(t) = A\cos(2\pi f_o t)$.

Solution

$$E_x = \lim_{T \to \infty} \int_{-T/2}^{T/2} |x(t)|^2 dt = A^2 \lim_{T \to \infty} \int_{-T/2}^{T/2} \cos^2(2\pi f_o t) dt = \lim_{T \to \infty} \frac{A^2 T}{2} \to \infty$$

Therefore, this signal is not an energy signal. In such cases, the concept of power of a signal is meaningful.

The normalized power of a signal $x(t)$ is the power dissipated by a voltage $x(t)$ applied across a 1-ohm resistor (or a current $x(t)$ passing though a 1-ohm resistor). The **normalized average power** of a signal $x(t)$ is defined as

$$P_x \triangleq \lim_{T \to \infty} \frac{1}{T} \int_{-T/2}^{T/2} |x(t)|^2 dt \tag{2.20}$$

The normalized average power of a signal is meaningful only if the limit in (2.20) exists (that is, finite). Such signals are called **power** signals. For a periodic signal $x_p(t)$ with fundamental period T_o, (2.20) simplifies to

$$P_x = \frac{1}{T_o} \int_{-T_o/2}^{T_o/2} |x_p(t)|^2 dt \tag{2.21}$$

A signal cannot be both power- and energy-type, because $P_x = 0$ for energy signals and $E_x = \infty$ for power signals. A signal may be neither energy-type nor power-type.

Example 2.6

Calculate the power of sinusoidal signal $x_p(t) = A\cos(2\pi f_o t + \phi)$.

Solution

Substituting $A\cos(2\pi f_o t + \phi)$ into (2.21) yields

$$P_x = \frac{A^2}{T_o} \int_{-T_o/2}^{T_o/2} \cos^2(2\pi f_o t + \phi) dt$$

$$= \frac{A^2}{2T_o} \left[\int_{-T_o/2}^{T_o/2} dt + \int_{-T_o/2}^{T_o/2} \cos(4\pi f_o t + 2\phi) dt \right] = \frac{A^2}{2} + 0 = \frac{A^2}{2}$$

The second integral is zero because it evaluates the integrand $\cos(4\pi f_o t + 2\phi)$ over two complete periods.

2.1.3 Logarithmic Power Calculations

In communication systems, it is often convenient to work with power levels and component losses (gains) in logarithmic units. Engineers prefer to express power levels as dB above or below 1 milliWatt (mW) and call it **dBm.** The power level in dBm is defined as

$$\text{Power level in dBm} = 10\log_{10}\frac{P}{1\text{mW}} \tag{2.22}$$

where P is power level in mW. Thus, 1 mW is 0 dBm and 100 mW equals 20 dBm. To convert from dBm to mW, the following formula can be used:

$$\text{Power level in mW} = 10^{(\text{dBm}/10)} \tag{2.23}$$

The power level at any point in a transmission link can now be calculated by adding the algebraic sum of gains (in dB) up to that point to the input level in dBm. The following example illustrates the advantage of using logarithmic units.

Example 2.7

A semiconductor laser couples 5 mW into an optical fiber link. The optical signal travels through a group of components (e.g., cable, connectors, splitters) with gains specified in Figure 2.14. Compute the power input to the optical receiver.

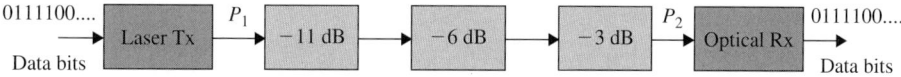

Figure 2.14 Optical fiber link.

Solution

Power coupled into the optical fiber by the laser transmitter (Tx) $P_1 = 5$ mW

Input optical power P_1 in dBm $= 10\log_{10}\dfrac{5\text{ mW}}{1\text{ mW}} = 7$ dBm

Total accumulated gain in the optical fiber link $= -11 - 6 - 3 = -20$ dB
Output optical power P_2 in dBm $= P_1$ (dBm) + Gain (dB)
$$= 7 - 20 = -13 \text{ dBm}$$
Power input to the optical receiver $= -13$ dBm
Power input to the optical receiver in micro Watts $= 10^{(-13/10)} = 50$

2.1.4 Some Basic Operations on Signals

We consider four basic operations on signals in time-domain. These include time reversal, time shifting, time scaling, and amplitude scaling.

Time Reversal

In time reversal we create a new signal $x_1(t)$ by flipping the original signal $x(t)$ around vertical axis.

$$x_1(t) = x(-t) \tag{2.24}$$

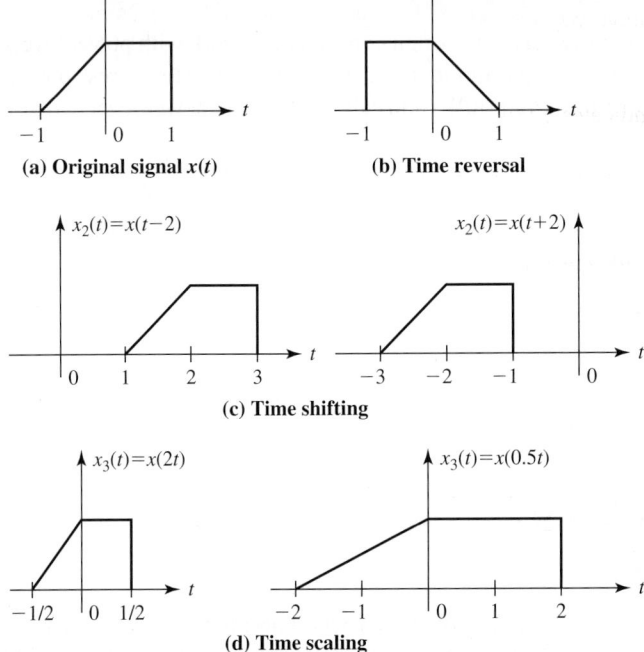

Figure 2.15 Transformations of signals in time-domain.

Figure 2.15(b) illustrates time reversal operation. Note that the resultant signal $x_1(t)$ is mirror image of the original signal $x(t)$.

Time Shifting

Given a CT signal $x(t)$, a time-shifted version of this signal is

$$x_2(t) = x(t - t_o), \quad t_o = \text{constant} \tag{2.25}$$

If t_o is positive, the time-shifted signal is delayed in time. The resultant signal $x_2(t)$ is shifted by t_o to the right of the original signal. On the other hand, if t_o is negative, the time-shifted signal is advanced in time. The resultant signal $x_2(t)$ is shifted by t_o to the left of the original signal. Figure 2.15(c) illustrates time-shifting operation.

Time Scaling

Given a CT signal $x(t)$, a time-scaled version of this signal is

$$x_3(t) = x(\alpha t), \quad \alpha = \text{constant} \tag{2.26}$$

Time scaling results in either an expanded or compressed version of the original signal $x(t)$. If $\alpha > 1$, the resultant signal $x_3(t)$ is compressed or contracted in time. On the other hand, the signal $x_3(t)$ is expanded in time for $\alpha < 1$. Figure 2.15(d) illustrates time scaling operation.

Amplitude Scaling

Given a CT signal $x(t)$, an amplitude-scaled version of this signal is

$$x_4(t) = Ax(t) + B, \quad A, B = \text{constants} \tag{2.27}$$

If $A > 1$, it indicates amplification of the original signal $x(t)$. The nonzero value of B shifts the DC level of the resultant signal $x_4(t)$.

   In general, a combination of the above operations may be involved in generating the new signal.

Example 2.8

Plot the following signals.

a. $x_1(t) = \Pi\left(\dfrac{t}{100}\right) + \Pi\left(\dfrac{t}{50}\right)$

b. $x_2(t) = 2\Pi\left(\dfrac{t}{12}\right) + 2\Pi\left(\dfrac{t}{6}\right) + 2\Lambda\left(\dfrac{t}{6}\right)$

c. $x_3(t) = \Lambda\left(\dfrac{t}{2} - 1\right) + \Lambda\left(\dfrac{t}{2} + 1\right)$

Solution

The waveforms are illustrated in Figure 2.16.

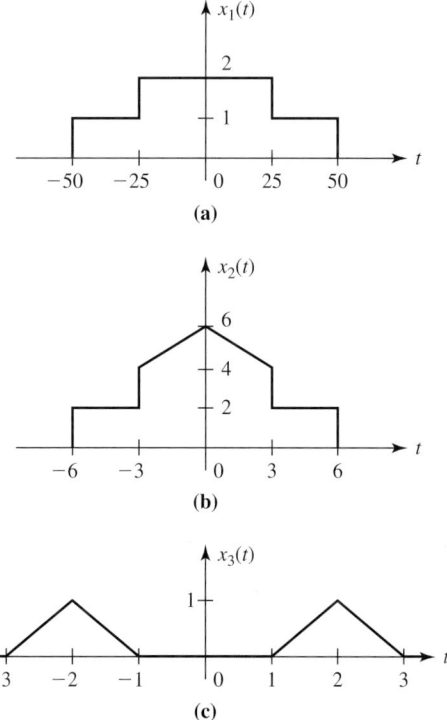

Figure 2.16 Example 2.8 signal waveforms.

2.2 BASIC SYSTEM CONCEPTS

A continuous-time system operates on a continuous-time input signal $x(t)$, according to some well-defined rule or **transformation** $\mathcal{T}$, to produce a continuous-time output signal $y(t)$ as a result of it. We will use the following notation to denote the action of a system:

$$\text{Continuous-time (CT) system:} \quad x(t) \xrightarrow{\mathcal{T}} y(t) \tag{2.28}$$

Note that the output $y(t)$ for any value of t may depend on $x(t)$ for all values of t. Similarly, a discrete-time system accepts an input sequence $x[n]$ to produce an output sequence $y[n]$

$$\text{Discrete-time (DT) system:} \quad x[n] \xrightarrow{\mathcal{T}} y[n] \tag{2.29}$$

As in the case of continuous-time systems, the output $y[n]$ for any value of n may depend on $x[n]$ for all values of n. Figure 2.17 shows a block diagram representation of the CT and DT systems.

In the context of communication systems, the system entity may represent the effect of transmission media or signal processing operations on signals. An example is the attenuation and distortion of the output signal produced by the twisted copper wire pair. Another example modeled by a system entity is the filtering action produced by an interconnection of circuit elements (ICs, resistors, capacitors, etc.) on the received signal with the intent to remove out-of-band noise.

Example 2.9

The square law device is a simple example of a continuous-time system. It is defined by the input-output relation

$$y(t) = x^2(t)$$

which states that the output signal value at time t is equal to the square of the input signal value at that same time.

Example 2.10

Another simple example is the ideal delay system defined by

$$y(t) = x(t - t_o)$$

where t_o is the time delay introduced by the system.

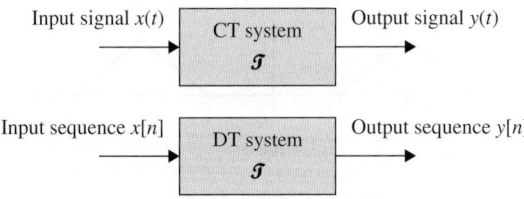

Figure 2.17 Block diagram of a system.

Example 2.11

The **accumulator**

$$y[n] = \sum_{l=-\infty}^{n} x[\ell] = \sum_{l=-\infty}^{n-1} x[\ell] + x[n] = y[n-1] + x[n]$$

is a discrete-time system. The output at time instant n is the sum of the current input sample $x[n]$ and the previous output $y[n-1]$. $y[n-1]$, in turn, is the sum of all previous input sample values from $-\infty$ to $n-1$. The system cumulatively adds, that is, it accumulates all input sample values.

In all the aforementioned cases, the input–output relation defining the system lends itself to simple mathematical definition. The rule for obtaining the output from the input can alternatively be defined by a graph or a table (e.g., in a read-only memory [ROM]).

2.2.1 Classification of Systems

There are various ways to classify systems based on the input–output relation of the system.

Linear Systems

The most widely used system model, and the one that we frequently use in this text, is a **linear** system for which the **superposition principle** always holds. More precisely, a system $x(t) \xrightarrow{\mathcal{T}} y(t)$ is linear, if $x_1(t)$ results in the output $y_1(t)$ and $x_2(t)$ results in the output $y_2(t)$, then the response due to the input is

$$x(t) = \alpha x_1(t) + \beta x_2(t) \tag{2.30}$$

is given by

$$y(t) = \alpha y_1(t) + \beta y_2(t) \tag{2.31}$$

The superposition property must hold for any arbitrary constants α and β, and for all possible inputs $x_1(t)$ and $x_2(t)$. This property makes it feasible to compute the response to a complex signal that can be decomposed as a weighted combination of some fundamental signals, such as unit impulse or complex exponential signals. In this case, the desired output is given by a similarly weighted combination of outputs to the constituent fundamental signals. A system that does not satisfy the superposition property is called a **nonlinear** system.

Similarly, a DT system $x[n] \xrightarrow{\mathcal{T}} y[n]$ is linear if and only if

$$x_1[n] \xrightarrow{\mathcal{T}} y_1[n]$$

$$x_2[n] \xrightarrow{\mathcal{T}} y_2[n]$$

then

$$\alpha x_1[n] + \beta x_2[n] \xrightarrow{\mathcal{T}} \alpha y_1[n] + \beta y_2[n] \tag{2.32}$$

for any arbitrary constants α and β.

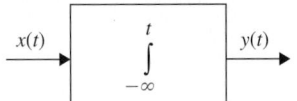

Figure 2.18 Integrator.

Example 2.12

The integrator in Figure 2.18 is a linear system. The output of the integrator is related to its input by

$$y(t) = \int_{-\infty}^{t} x(\tau)d\tau$$

To show this, let $x(t) = \alpha x_1(t) + \beta x_2(t)$ be the system input. The corresponding output is

$$y(t) = \int_{-\infty}^{t} x(\tau)d\tau = \int_{-\infty}^{t} [\alpha x_1(\tau) + \beta x_2(\tau)]d\tau$$

$$= \alpha \int_{-\infty}^{t} x_1(\tau)d\tau + \beta \int_{-\infty}^{t} x_2(\tau)d\tau$$

$$= \alpha y_1(t) + \beta y_2(t)$$

Thus, the integrator is a linear system.

Example 2.13

The square law device $y(t) = x^2(t)$ is a nonlinear system. To see this, let $x(t) = \alpha x_1(t) + \beta x_2(t)$ be the system input. The corresponding output is

$$y(t) = x^2(t) = [\alpha x_1(t) + \beta x_2(t)]^2$$

$$= \alpha^2[x_1(t)]^2 + 2\alpha\beta x_1(t)x_2(t) + \beta^2[x_2(t)]^2$$

$$\neq \alpha y_1(t) + \beta y_2(t)$$

where $y_1(t) = [x_1(t)]^2$ and $y_2(t) = [x_2(t)]^2$. Therefore the system is nonlinear.

Example 2.14

The accumulator $y[n] = \sum_{l=-\infty}^{n} x[\ell]$ is a linear system. Let

$$y_1[n] = \sum_{l=-\infty}^{n} x_1[\ell], \ y_2[n] = \sum_{l=-\infty}^{n} x_2[\ell]$$

For an input $x[n] = \alpha x_1[n] + \beta x_2[n]$, the output is

$$y[n] = \sum_{l=-\infty}^{n} (\alpha x_1[\ell] + \beta x_2[\ell])$$

$$= \alpha \sum_{l=-\infty}^{n} x_1[\ell] + \beta \sum_{l=-\infty}^{n} x_2[\ell]$$

$$= \alpha y_1[n] + \beta y_2[n]$$

Hence, the system is linear.

Memoryless Systems

A memoryless system is one whose current value of the output depends only on the current value of the input; that is, the current value of the output does not depend on either past values or future values of the input. The integrator $y(t) = \int_{-\infty}^{t} x(\tau)d\tau$ in Example 2.12 is an example of a system with memory. The integrator's current output depends on the history of its input. The square law device $y(t) = x^2(t)$ in Example 2.13 is an example of a memoryless system. Its current output depends on its current input value only.

Time-Invariant Systems

A system $x(t) \xrightarrow{\mathcal{J}} y(t)$ is said to be **time-invariant** if the delayed input $x_1(t) = x(t - t_o)$ results in the delayed output. That is,

$$y_1(t) = y(t - t_o) \tag{2.33}$$

for all t_o.

Similarly, a DT system $x[n] \xrightarrow{\mathcal{J}} y[n]$ is said to be **shift-invariant** if the delayed input sequence $x_1[n] = x[n - n_o]$ results in the delayed output sequence. That is,

$$y_1[n] = y[n - n_o] \tag{2.34}$$

for all n_o.

For a system to be time- (shift-) invariant, this relationship between the input and output must hold for any arbitrary input signal (sequence) and the corresponding output signal (sequence). Time (shift) invariance ensures that the same input signal always generates the same output signal, regardless of the time when the input signal is applied to the system. Of course the output signal is a delayed replica corresponding to the delay in the input signal.

Example 2.15

The integrator is a time-invariant system.

To show this, let $x_1(t) = x(t - t_o)$ be the system input. The corresponding output is

$$y_1(t) = \int_{-\infty}^{t} x_1(\tau)d\tau = \int_{-\infty}^{t} x(\tau - t_o)d\tau = \int_{-\infty}^{t-t_o} x(v)dv = y(t - t_o)$$

Therefore, the integrator is time-invariant.

Example 2.16

The amplitude modulator (Figure 2.19) defined by $y(t) = x(t)\cos(2\pi f_c t)$ is a time-varying system.

To show this, let $x_1(t) = x(t - t_o)$ be the system input. The corresponding output is

$$y_1(t) = x_1(t)\cos(2\pi f_c t) = x(t - t_o)\cos(2\pi f_c t) \neq y(t - t_o)$$

Therefore the amplitude modulator is not time-invariant.

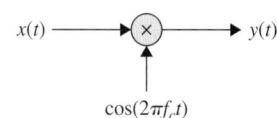

Figure 2.19 Amplitude modulator.

Example 2.17

The M-point moving average system $y[n] = \dfrac{1}{M}\displaystyle\sum_{k=0}^{M-1} x[n - k]$ is shift-invariant. To prove it, let $x_1[n] = x[n - n_o]$. Then

$$y_1[n] = \frac{1}{M}\sum_{k=0}^{M-1} x[n - n_o - k]$$

Also,

$$y[n - n_o] = \frac{1}{M}\sum_{k=0}^{M-1} x[n - n_o - k]$$

Because $y_1[n] = y[n - n_o] = \dfrac{1}{M}\displaystyle\sum_{k=0}^{M-1} x[n - n_o - k]$, the DT system is shift-invariant.

A system satisfying both the linearity and the time-invariance properties is called a **linear time-invariant (LTI)** system. LTI systems are mathematically easy to analyze, and consequently, easy to design.

2.2.2 Characterization of LTI Systems

We will next derive a very important result that the impulse response completely determines the behavior of an LTI system. For this purpose, we will start with an approximation of an arbitrary CT signal $x(t)$ by a sum of shifted, scaled pulses as shown in Figure 2.20(a). That is,

$$\hat{x}(t) = \sum_{k=-\infty}^{\infty} x(k\Delta)\delta_\Delta(t - k\Delta)\Delta \tag{2.35}$$

where $\delta_\Delta(t)$ is unit area pulse in Figure 2.20(b). In the limit as $\Delta \to 0$, the summation approaches the integral (2.15).

$$\hat{x}(t) \xrightarrow{\Delta \to 0} \int_{-\infty}^{\infty} x(\tau)\delta(t - \tau)d\tau \tag{2.36}$$

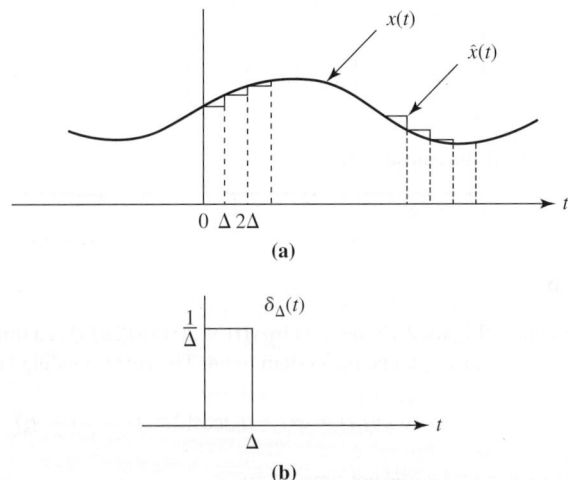

(a)

(b)

Figure 2.20 Staircase approximation to a CT signal.

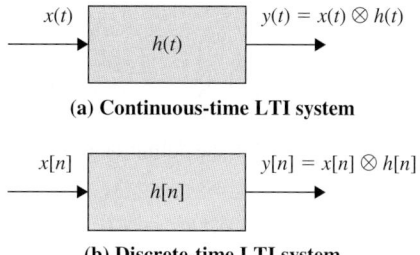

(a) Continuous-time LTI system

(b) Discrete-time LTI system

Figure 2.21 Characterization of LTI system.

Let $h_\Delta(t)$ be the response of the system to the pulse $\delta_\Delta(t)$. That is,

$$\delta_\Delta(t) \xrightarrow{\ \mathcal{J}\ } h_\Delta(t) \tag{2.37}$$

Then, using linearity and time-invariance properties, we obtain

$$\hat{x}(t) = \sum_{k=-\infty}^{\infty} x(k\Delta)\delta_\Delta(t - k\Delta)\Delta \xrightarrow{\ \mathcal{J}\ } \hat{y}(t) = \sum_{k=-\infty}^{\infty} x(k\Delta)h_\Delta(t - k\Delta)\Delta \tag{2.38}$$

In the limit as $\Delta \to 0$, $\delta_\Delta(t) \xrightarrow{\Delta \to 0} \delta(t)$ and $h_\Delta(t) \xrightarrow{\Delta \to 0} h(t)$. Therefore, we can write

$$y(t) = \lim_{\Delta \to 0} \hat{y}(t) = \int_{-\infty}^{\infty} x(\tau)h(t - \tau)d\tau = x(t) \otimes h(t) \tag{2.39}$$

where

$$\delta(t) \xrightarrow{\ \mathcal{J}\ } h(t) \tag{2.40}$$

$h(t)$ is called the **impulse response** of the LTI system. Equation (2.39) states that the response of the system to an arbitrary input $x(t)$ is the convolution of $x(t)$ with the system impulse response $h(t)$. Similarly, it can be shown that for a DT system, the output sequence $y[n]$ is the convolution sum of input sequence $x[n]$ with the system impulse response $h[n]$. Summarizing

$$\text{CT system: } y(t) = x(t) \otimes h(t) = \int_{-\infty}^{\infty} x(\tau)h(t - \tau)d\tau = \int_{-\infty}^{\infty} h(\tau)x(t - \tau)d\tau \tag{2.41}$$

$$\text{DT system: } y[n] = x[n] \otimes h[n] = \sum_{k=-\infty}^{\infty} x[k]h[n - k] = \sum_{k=-\infty}^{\infty} x[n - k]h[k] \tag{2.42}$$

Figure 2.21 displays these relationships for LTI systems. As a consequence of (2.41) and (2.42), an LTI system is **completely characterized** by its impulse response. If the system is nonlinear or time-variant, its impulse response describes only part of the system's characteristics.

Example 2.18

The impulse response of an integrator is a unit step function. To show this, let $x(t) = \delta(t)$ be the system input. The corresponding output is

$$h(t) = \int_{-\infty}^{t} \delta(\tau)d\tau$$

Now

$$\int_{-\infty}^{t} \delta(\tau)d\tau = \begin{cases} 1, & t \geq 0 \\ 0, & t < 0 \end{cases} \tag{2.43}$$

But the right-hand side of (2.43) is identical to the definition of the unit step signal in (2.5). So

$$h(t) = \int_{-\infty}^{t} \delta(\tau)d\tau = u(t) \tag{2.44}$$

Equation (2.44) states that impulse response function of the integrator is a unit step function.

Example 2.19

The output of a **unit delay** system is $x(t-1)$ to an input $x(t)$. Using the property (2.16) of the impulse signal, we can write

$$x(t) \otimes \delta(t-1) = x(t-1)$$

Therefore, the impulse response of a unit delay system is $h(t) = \delta(t-1)$.

Example 2.20

The impulse response of the accumulator $y[n] = \sum_{l=-\infty}^{n} x[\ell]$ is obtained by setting $x[n] = \delta[n]$ resulting in $h[n] = \sum_{l=-\infty}^{n} \delta[\ell]$.

Now

$$\sum_{l=-\infty}^{n} \delta[\ell] = \begin{cases} 1, & n \geq 0 \\ 0, & \text{otherwise} \end{cases}$$

is a unit step sequence $u[n]$. Thus, impulse response of the accumulator is unit step sequence.

Causal Systems

A system is said to be **causal** if its current output depends only on its current and past inputs. If the output depends on future inputs, the system is said to be **noncausal** or **anticipatory.** In a CT causal system, for every choice of t_o, the output signal value $y(t_o)$ depends only on the input signal values $x(t)$ for $t \leq t_o$ and does not depend on input signal values for $t > t_o$. A causal system does not anticipate the future. No physical system has such a capability. Thus every physical system is causal, and causality is a necessary condition for a system to be realizable in the real world.

For an LTI system, it is possible to derive a very simple condition for causality in terms of its impulse response $h(t)$. A CT LTI system is causal iff its impulse response satisfies the following condition:

$$h(t) = 0, \ t < 0 \tag{2.45}$$

The equivalent condition for a DT system is that its impulse response $h[n]$ satisfies the following condition for causality.

$$h[n] = 0, \; n < 0 \tag{2.46}$$

Example 2.21

The integrator is a causal system because its impulse response is a unit step function and thus satisfies the property (2.45).

Example 2.22

The impulse response of a unit delay system is given by $h(t) = \delta(t - 1)$. It is causal because it satisfies the property (2.45).

Stable Systems

A system is **stable** if for every bounded input, the output is bounded. This implies that, if the input $|x(t)| \leq B$ for all values of t, then the output of the system $|y(t)| \leq C$ for all values of t, where B and C are finite constants. This type of stability is referred to as **bounded input, bounded output (BIBO)** stability.

For an LTI system, it is possible to derive a very simple condition for stability in terms of its impulse response. A CT LTI system is stable if its impulse response $h(t)$ is absolutely integrable, that is,

$$\int_{-\infty}^{\infty} |h(t)| dt < \infty \tag{2.47}$$

The equivalent condition for a DT system is that its impulse response $h[n]$ is absolutely summable for BIBO stability.

$$\sum_{n=-\infty}^{\infty} |h(n)| < \infty \tag{2.48}$$

One important consequence of (2.48) is that a DT system whose impulse response is of finite length ("FIR system"), the stability condition is always satisfied as long as $|h[n]| < \infty$.

Example 2.23

The integrator system is unstable. The impulse response of the integrator is $h(t) = u(t)$, so applying the criterion (2.47) leads to

$$\int_{-\infty}^{\infty} |h(t)| dt = \int_{-\infty}^{\infty} |u(t)| dt = \int_{0}^{\infty} dt \to \infty$$

Therefore, the integrator is an unstable system.

2.3   FREQUENCY DOMAIN REPRESENTATION

Although electrical signals used in communication systems are commonly viewed as functions of time, it is very useful to think of them in terms of their frequency content. Certain characteristics of signals are easier to analyze and measure in the frequency domain. In addition, the frequency domain analysis of many important operations on signals leads to unique and valuable insights toward understanding their effects. That is why the frequency domain representation and analysis of signals and systems is an integral part of design tools for communication systems.

Figure 2.22(a) shows the time domain representation of a 10 Hz sine wave embedded in noise. It is difficult to identify a simple 10 Hz waveform in the presence of wideband ("white") noise by simply looking at it on an oscilloscope. However, if we look at the same signal and noise in the frequency domain using a spectrum analyzer, it is very easy to identify the 10 Hz tone. We observe from Figure 2.22(b) that the noise is spread out over all frequencies and forms the floor of the spectrum analyzer display. In more complex situations, the composite signal may consist of hundreds of channels or carriers. An example is a CATV system where a few hundred channels or signals are present. Analyzing such a complex signal in the time domain is not very useful. The frequency domain analysis, however, provides valuable insight into the effects of system impairments and noise.

In this chapter, we will consider two useful frequency domain representations of continuous-time signals:

1. Fourier series (FS)
2. Fourier transform (FT)

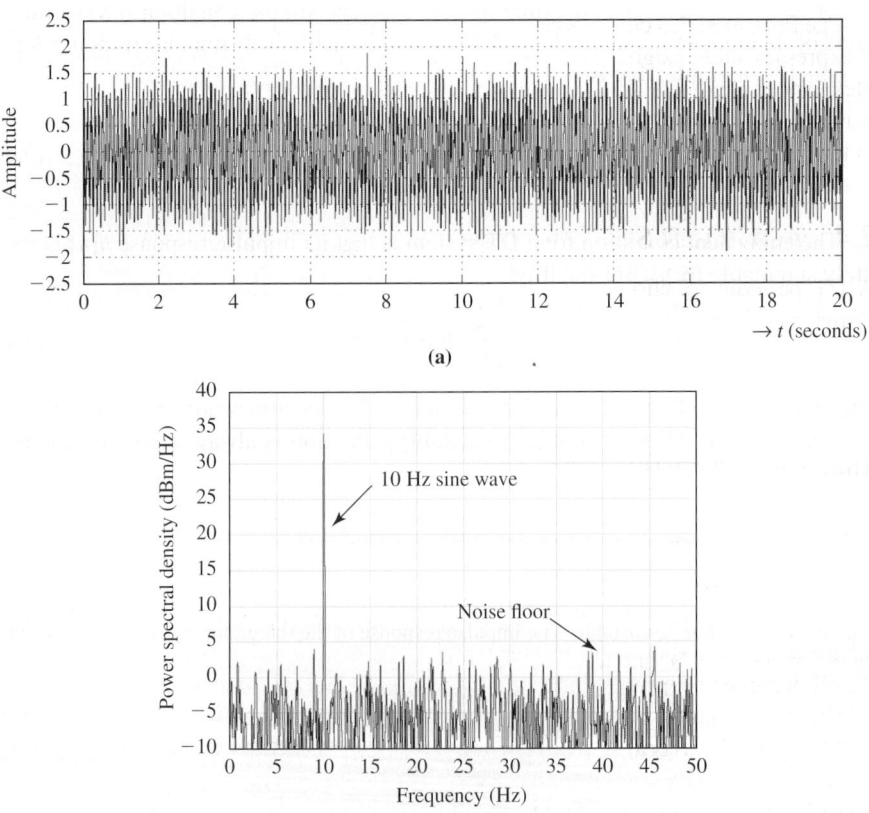

(a)

(b)

Figure 2.22 (a) Time and (b) frequency domain representation of a sine wave embedded in noise.

Pioneers in the Field

Jean Baptiste Joseph Fourier was born in Auxerre, France in 1768. He was orphaned at age eight and grew up with his aunt and uncle in the same town. On the recommendation of the Bishop of Auxerre, Fourier was offered a place at the nearby École Royale Militaire. He demonstrated such proficiency in mathematics in his early years that he later became a teacher there. When the École Normale was founded in 1794 in Paris, Fourier was among its first students, and, in 1795, he began teaching there. That same year, Fourier joined the faculty at the brand new École Polytechnique and became a colleague of Gaspard Monge and other mathematicians.

Fourier accompanied Napoléon Bonaparte on his Egyptian expedition in 1798. He was appointed governor of Lower Egypt and secretary of the Institut d'Égypte. While there, he organized ammunition workshops to support the French army during the war with the English. He also contributed several mathematical papers to the Egyptian Institute (also called the Cairo Institute), which Napoléon founded in Cairo, with a view of weakening English influence in the East. After the French defeat in 1801,

Fourier returned to France and became prefect of Isère. It was here that he carried out his investigation of propagation of heat in the solid bodies. These experiments led to the development of the Fourier series and Fourier integral. Fourier claimed that an arbitrary function defined in a finite interval can be expressed as a sum of sinusoids. He submitted his initial work on heat transfer to the Institut de France in 1807. The judges, including the great French mathematicians Laplace, Lagrange, Monge, and LaCroix admitted the originality and significance of Fourier's work, but criticized its lack of mathematical rigor. Fourier believed the criticism was unjustified but was unable to defend his claim because the tools required for operations with infinite series were not available at the time. Although three of the four judges were in favor of publication, the paper was rejected for publication because of the forceful opposition by Lagrange. Fourier was elected to the Académie des Sciences in 1817 and became its secretary in 1822. Fifteen years after he presented the results, the Académie des Sciences published his prize-winning essay *Théorie analytique de la chaleur* in 1822. The book is now considered a classic.

The Fourier series can be used to represent periodic signals in the frequency domain. It expresses such a signal as a **superposition** of an infinite ($\approx$ large) number of complex exponential waveforms. The Fourier transform, however, is applicable to aperiodic waveforms in a strict mathematical sense. Both provide a simpler description of signals in terms of magnitudes and phases of the constituent frequency components.

2.4 FOURIER SERIES

A CT periodic function $x_p(t)$ with period T_o can be represented by an **exponential Fourier series (FS)**

$$x_p(t) = \sum_{n=-\infty}^{\infty} C_n e^{j2\pi n f_o t} \tag{2.49}$$

The series coefficients C_n are related to $x_p(t)$ by

$$C_n = \frac{1}{T_o} \int_{T_o} x_p(t) e^{-j2\pi n f_o t} dt \tag{2.50}$$

where $f_o = 1/T_o$ is called the **fundamental frequency** of the periodic signal $x_p(t)$. From (2.49), it can be observed that the Fourier series expands a periodic function as an infinite sum of complex phasor signals $C_n e^{j2\pi n f_o t}$. The term C_0 corresponding to $n = 0$ in (2.49) equals the **average** or **DC** component of the signal, and is given by

$$C_0 = \frac{1}{T_o} \int_{T_o} x_p(t) dt \tag{2.51}$$

The phasor signal $C_1 e^{j2\pi f_o t}$ represents the fundamental frequency (f_o) component in the periodic signal $x_p(t)$. The terms in summation (2.49) for $n \geq 2$ consist of phasor signals at **harmonic frequencies** $f = nf_o$, $n = 0, 1, 2, 3, \ldots$ in the FS expansion of the signal $x_p(t)$. They are called its **frequency** or **spectral components**. Each phasor term in (2.49) can be written as

$$C_n e^{j2\pi nf_o t} = |C_n| e^{j(2\pi nf_o t + \angle C_n)} \qquad (2.52)$$

Magnitude of the frequency   Phase of the frequency
component at $f = nf_o$ component at $f = nf_o$

Plots of $|C_n|$ and $\angle C_n$ as function of frequency are called the **magnitude** and the **phase** spectrum of the signal, respectively. Because the magnitude and phase spectra of periodic signals contain spectral components at discrete frequencies $f = nf_o$, $n = 0, 1, 2, 3, \ldots$, these are called **line spectra.** For $x_p(t)$ real function of time, we have

$$C_{-n} = \frac{1}{T_o} \int_{T_0} x_p(t) e^{j2\pi nf_o t} dt = \left(\frac{1}{T_o} \int_{T_o} x_p(t) e^{-j2\pi nf_o t} dt \right)^* = C_n^* \qquad (2.53)$$

From (2.53) it follows that for a real signal, the magnitude spectrum is an even function, and the phase spectrum is an odd function of frequency.

2.4.1   Trigonometric Fourier Series

We next derive a second form of the Fourier series for real signals. For this purpose, we write (2.49) as

$$x_p(t) = C_o + \sum_{n=1}^{\infty} C_{-n} e^{-j2\pi nf_o t} + \sum_{n=1}^{\infty} C_n e^{j2\pi nf_o t} = C_o + \sum_{n=1}^{\infty} C_n^* e^{-j2\pi nf_o t} + \sum_{n=1}^{\infty} C_n e^{j2\pi nf_o t}$$

$$= C_0 + \sum_{n=1}^{\infty} |C_n| [e^{-j(2\pi nf_o t + \angle C_n)} + e^{j(2\pi nf_o t + \angle C_n)}]$$

$$= C_0 + 2 \sum_{n=1}^{\infty} |C_n| \cos(2\pi nf_o t + \angle C_n) \qquad (2.54)$$

Equation (2.54) is called the **trigonometric Fourier series.** We can write an alternative form of (2.54) by expanding the cosine function as follows:

$$x_p(t) = A_0 + \sum_{n=1}^{\infty} A_n \cos(2\pi nf_o t) + \sum_{n=1}^{\infty} B_n \sin(2\pi nf_o t) \qquad (2.55)$$

where

$$A_n = 2|C_n| \cos(\angle C_n) = C_n + C_n^* = \frac{2}{T_o} \int_{T_o} x_p(t) \cos(2\pi nf_o t) dt \qquad (2.56)$$

$$B_n = -2|C_n| \sin(\angle C_n) = -(C_n - C_n^*)/j = \frac{2}{T_o} \int_{T_o} x_p(t) \sin(2\pi nf_o t) dt \qquad (2.57)$$

The coefficients of the exponential and trigonometric forms of the Fourier series are related by

$$C_o = A_o; \quad 2C_n = A_n - jB_n \tag{2.58}$$

We can conclude from (2.56) and (2.57) that if

1. $x_p(t)$ is an even function of time, its Fourier series expansion will contain only cosine terms, i.e., $B_n = 0, n = 1, 2, \ldots$
2. $x_p(t)$ is an odd function of time, its Fourier series expansion will contain only sine terms, i.e., $A_n = 0, n = 1, 2, \ldots$

Example 2.24

Determine the Fourier series expansion of a periodic pulse train $g_{T_o}(t) = \sum\limits_{n=-\infty}^{\infty} \Pi\left[\dfrac{(t - nT_o)}{\tau}\right]$ of rectangular pulses shown in Figure 2.23.

Solution

Each pulse in Figure 2.23 has unity amplitude and duration τ. The Fourier coefficients are given by

$$C_n = \frac{1}{T_o} \int_{T_o} g_{T_o}(t) e^{-j2\pi n f_o t} \, dt = \frac{1}{T_o} \int_{-\tau/2}^{\tau/2} e^{-j2\pi n f_o t} \, dt$$

$$= -\frac{1}{j2\pi n f_o T_o} \left[e^{-j\pi n f_o \tau} - e^{j\pi n f_o \tau} \right]$$

$$= \frac{\tau}{T_o} \frac{\sin(\pi n f_o \tau)}{\pi n f_o \tau} = \frac{\tau}{T_o} \text{sinc}(n f_o \tau) \tag{2.59}$$

The magnitude spectrum, given by $|C_n| = \dfrac{\tau}{T_o} |\text{sinc}(n f_o \tau)|$, is shown in Figure 2.24 for the case $\dfrac{\tau}{T_o} = 0.25$. Because the sinc function is always real, the phase spectrum in Figure 2.24 assumes values $0°$ or $180°$, depending on the sign of the $\text{sinc}(n f_o \tau)$ function. Note the following points about the magnitude spectrum of the periodic pulse train:

a. The value of the DC coefficient is τ/T_o.
b. The frequency spacing between adjacent spectral components is $f_o = 1/T_o$ Hz.
c. The zero crossings of the envelope occur at integral multiples of $4f_o = 1/\tau$ Hz.

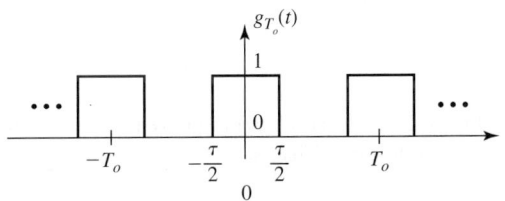

Figure 2.23 Rectangular pulse train.

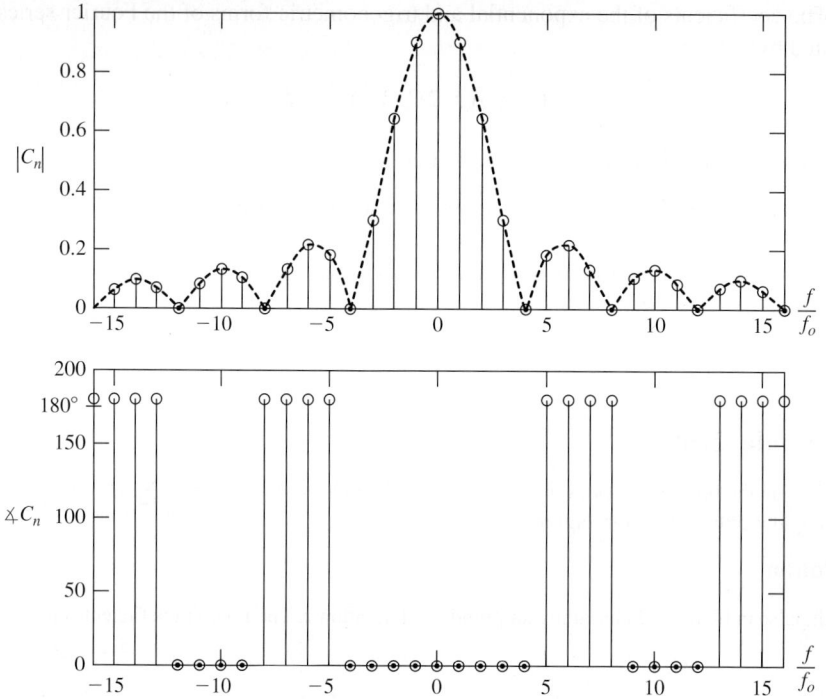

Figure 2.24 Magnitude and phase spectra of a rectangular pulse train.

Example 2.25

Suppose that a binary information source sends a repetition of pattern 01111110 at a rate of 8 Kbps. A binary 1 is transmitted by sending a rectangular pulse of 1 V with a width of 0.125 ms, and a 0 is transmitted by sending a pulse of -1 V. Find the Fourier series expansion of the periodic waveform $x_p(t)$ shown in Figure 2.25.

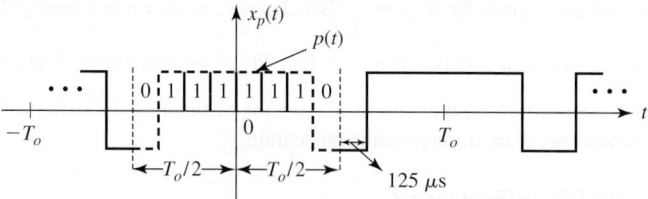

Figure 2.25 Periodic waveform $x_p(t)$ corresponding to repeated pattern 01111110.

Solution

The periodic waveform $x_p(t)$ in Figure 2.25 can be expressed as

$$x_p(t) = \sum_{k=-\infty}^{\infty} p(t - kT_o)$$

where $p(t)$ is defined in Figure 2.25. Because $x_p(t)$ is an even function of time, its Fourier series expansion will contain only cosine terms. That is,

$$x_p(t) = A_0 + \sum_{n=1}^{\infty} A_n\cos(2\pi nf_o t)$$

where

$$f_0 = \frac{1}{T_o} = 1000 \text{ Hz}$$

$$A_0 = \frac{1}{T_o} \int_{T_o} x_p(t)dt = \frac{1}{T_o} \int_0^{T_o} p(t) \, dt = \frac{1}{T_o}\left[\frac{6T_o}{8} - \frac{2T_o}{8}\right] = 0.5$$

$$A_n = \frac{2}{T_o} \int_{T_o} x_p(t)\cos(2\pi n f_o t) \, dt = \frac{4}{T_o} \int_0^{T_o/2} p(t)\cos(2\pi n f_o t) \, dt$$

$$= \frac{4}{T_o}\left\{ \int_0^{3T_o/8} \cos(2\pi n f_o t)dt - \int_{3T_o/8}^{T_o/2} \cos(2\pi n f_o t)dt \right\} = \frac{4}{\pi n} \sin(3\pi n/4)$$

The FS representation for $x_p(t)$ can now be written as

$$x_p(t) = A_0 + \frac{4}{\pi}\sum_{n=1}^{\infty} \frac{\sin(3\pi n/4)}{n} \cos(2\pi n f_o t)$$

$$= 0.5 + \frac{4}{\pi} \sin\left(\frac{3\pi}{4}\right)\cos(2\pi \times 1000t) + \frac{4}{2\pi} \sin\left(\frac{3\pi}{2}\right)\cos(2\pi \times 2000t)$$

$$+ \frac{4}{3\pi} \sin\left(\frac{9\pi}{4}\right)\cos(2\pi \times 3000t) + \frac{1}{\pi} \sin(3\pi)\cos(2\pi \times 4000t) - \ldots$$

Figure 2.26 displays the plot of Fourier coefficients A_n as a function of frequency.

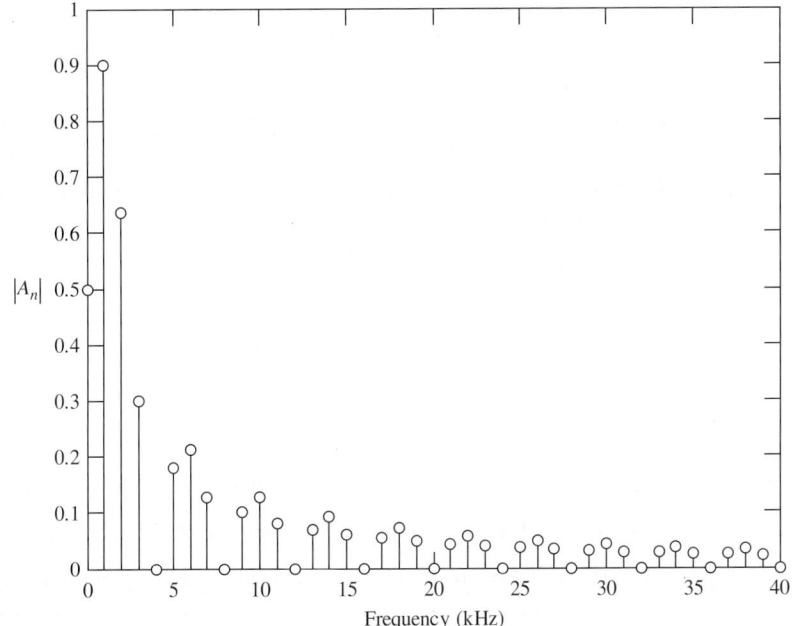

Figure 2.26 One-sided magnitude spectrum for $x_p(t)$.

2.4.2 Parseval's Theorem

The normalized average power P_x of a periodic signal is given from (2.21) as

$$P_x = \frac{1}{T_o} \int_{T_o} |x_p(t)|^2 dt = \frac{1}{T_o} \int_{T_o} x_p(t) x_p^*(t) dt \qquad (2.21)$$

Substituting the FS expansion for $x_p^*(t)$ from (2.49) into (2.21), we get

$$P_x = \frac{1}{T_o} \int_{T_o} x_p(t) \left[\sum_{n=-\infty}^{\infty} C_n^* e^{-j2\pi n f_o t} \right] dt$$

$$= \sum_{n=-\infty}^{\infty} \left[\frac{1}{T_o} \int_{T_o} x_p(t) e^{-j2\pi n f_o t} dt \right] C_n^*$$

$$= \sum_{n=-\infty}^{\infty} C_n C_n^* = \sum_{n=-\infty}^{\infty} \underbrace{|C_n|^2}_{\substack{\text{Average power in} \\ \text{the frequency} \\ \text{component at } f = nf_o}} \qquad (2.60)$$

The normalized average power of a periodic signal is the sum of the average power of its frequency components.

Bandwidth of a Signal

The **bandwidth** of a signal is a measure of the range of significant frequency components present in the signal. The term significant here implies inclusion of those frequencies that represent the signal with acceptable distortion. The latter is determined by the relevance in a given application. If the significant energy of the signal lies in the range of positive frequencies $f_1 < f < f_2$, the bandwidth would be $f_2 - f_1$. There are many definitions of bandwidth, depending on how frequencies f_1 and f_2 are defined. If f_1 and f_2 are chosen so that the spectrum of the signal is zero outside the frequency band $f_1 < f < f_2$, the quantity $f_2 - f_1$ is called the **absolute bandwidth.**

Example 2.26

Determine the absolute bandwidth of a periodic pulse train of rectangular pulses shown in Example 2.24.

   The magnitude spectrum of a periodic pulse train of rectangular pulses, shown in Figure 2.23, is given by $|C_n| = \dfrac{\tau}{T_o} |\text{sinc}(n f_o \tau)|$. The values of the sinc function become smaller and smaller as $n \to \infty$, yet they remain nonzero. Therefore, the absolute bandwidth of this signal is infinite.

In another popular definition of bandwidth, the frequencies f_1 and f_2 are chosen so that 99% of the power resides in the frequency band $f_1 < f < f_2$. In this case the quantity $f_2 - f_1$ is called the **99% power bandwidth.**

Example 2.27

Determine the 99% power bandwidth of the periodic pulse train of rectangular pulses shown in Example 2.24. Assume $T_o = 1\ \mu\text{sec}$ and $\tau/T_o = 0.5$.

Solution

From Example 2.24, the FS expansion of the periodic pulse train $x_p(t)$ can be expressed as

$$x_p(t) = \sum_{n=-\infty}^{\infty} C_n e^{j2\pi n f_o t}$$

where

$$C_n = \frac{\tau}{T_o} \text{sinc}(n f_o \tau)$$

Now

$$f_o = \frac{1}{T_o} = 1\ \text{MHz}$$

$$C_0 = \frac{\tau}{T_o} = 0.5$$

$$C_n = \frac{\tau}{T_o} \text{sinc}(n f_o \tau) = 0.5\ \text{sinc}(n/2)$$

Using Parseval's theorem, we can write

$$P_x = \sum_{n=-\infty}^{\infty} |C_n|^2 = C_0^2 + 2 \sum_{n=1}^{\infty} |C_n|^2$$

$$= 0.25 + 0.5 \sum_{n=1}^{\infty} |\text{sinc}(n/2)|^2$$

Table 2.1 displays Fourier coefficients and the accumulated power up to and including frequency $f = n f_o$. As the table shows, we need to include 21 Fourier coefficients to get 99% power in the signal. Because each spectral component is separated by 1 MHz, the 99% power bandwidth of the periodic pulse train is approximately 21 MHz.

Table 2.1 Power in the Fourier Components of the Rectangular Pulse Train

n	C_n	Accumulated Power (Up to and Including Frequency $f = n f_o$)
0	0.25	0.25
1	0.6366	0.4526
3	−0.212	0.4752
5	0.1273	0.4833
7	−0.091	0.4874
9	0.0707	0.4899
11	−0.058	0.4916
13	0.0490	0.4928
15	−0.0424	0.4937
17	0.0374	0.4944
19	−0.0335	0.4949
21	0.0303	0.4954

We observe that the normalized average power in the periodic pulse train is 0.5 W as shown below:

$$P_x = \frac{1}{T_o} \int_{-T_o/2}^{T_o/2} |g_{T_o}(t)|^2\, dt = \frac{1}{T_o} \int_{-T_o/2}^{T_o/2} \Pi^2\left(\frac{t}{\tau}\right) dt = \frac{1}{T_o} \int_{-\tau/2}^{\tau/2} dt = \frac{\tau}{T_o} = 0.5$$

2.4.3 Convergence of Fourier Series

It is interesting to consider the sequence of signals that we obtain as we incorporate finite number of terms into the Fourier series of a signal. The partial sum representing the FS approximation to $x_p(t)$ can be expressed as

$$S_N(t) = \sum_{n=-N}^{N} C_n e^{j2\pi n f_o t} \tag{2.61}$$

It is quite reasonable to expect that as more and more terms are included in the partial sum (2.61), the approximation should get better and better, yielding zero approximation error as $n \to \infty$. The fundamental result on the convergence of Fourier series, due to Dirichlet, states that the approximation error

$$\varepsilon_N = \max_{t \in [0, T_o]} |x_p(t) - S_N(t)| \tag{2.62}$$

decreases to zero as $n \to \infty$ for all values of t where the function is continuous. However, if the function is discontinuous at a point t_o, the partial sum $S_N(t)$ at $t = t_o$ converges to the value $\dfrac{x_p(t_o^+) + x_p(t_o^-)}{2}$. Thus the maximum error is always half the size of the jump in the waveform at the discontinuity point. However, on each side of the discontinuity, $S_N(t)$ has oscillatory **overshoot** with peak value of about 9% of the size of the discontinuity as shown in Figure 2.27. This behavior is independent of value of N except that the period of oscillation changes to $T_o/2N$. This is also known as **Gibbs phenomenon** in the theory of Fourier series.

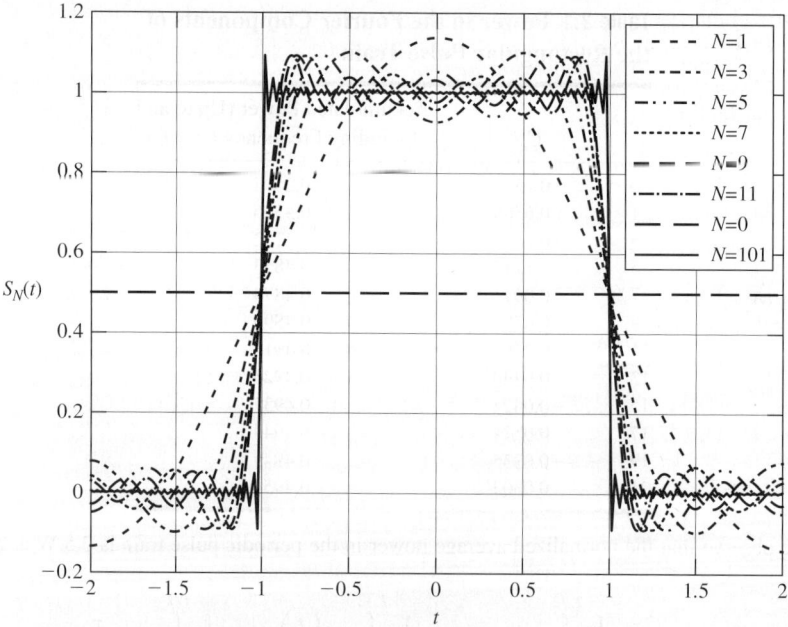

Figure 2.27 FS approximations to a rectangular pulse train.

2.5 FOURIER TRANSFORM

The Fourier coefficients of the rectangular pulse train are spaced at a discrete set of frequencies $nf_o = n/T_o$. The component frequencies are separated by $1/T_o$ Hz. Note that as the period T_o gets larger, the frequency separation gets smaller. Obviously, as the period approaches infinity, the frequency separation tends to zero. Thus a nonperiodic function, which can be viewed as a periodic function with infinite period, contains all frequencies in its Fourier expansion rather than just a discrete set. The Fourier expansion of a nonperiodic function is defined in terms of an integral rather than the infinite sum in (2.49). That is,

$$x(t) = \int_{-\infty}^{\infty} X(f) e^{j2\pi ft} \, df \tag{2.63}$$

where $X(f) = \Im\{x(t)\}$ is the **Fourier transform (FT)** of the signal $x(t)$. It is defined by the following formula

$$X(f) = \int_{-\infty}^{\infty} x(t) e^{-j2\pi ft} \, dt \tag{2.64}$$

We will use the following notation to denote the FT and its inverse operation:

FT operation

$$x(t) \xrightarrow{\Im} X(f) \colon X(f) = \Im\{x(t)\} = \int_{-\infty}^{\infty} x(t) e^{-j2\pi ft} \, dt$$

Inverse FT operation

$$X(f) \xrightarrow{\Im^{-1}} x(t) \colon x(t) = \Im^{-1}\{X(f)\} = \int_{-\infty}^{\infty} X(f) e^{j2\pi ft} \, df$$

Most frequently, the notation $\xleftrightarrow{\Im}$ will be used to denote either the FT operation or its inverse. The meaning will be obvious from the context. Equations (2.63) and (2.64) form the Fourier transform pair.

We observe from (2.64) that $X(f)$ is defined over all frequencies f and plays the same role for nonperiodic signals as Fourier coefficients C_n do for periodic signals. $X(f)$ is called the **frequency spectrum** of the nonperiodic signal $x(t)$. It is a continuous spectrum as opposed to the line spectrum produced by coefficients C_n for a periodic signal. In general, $X(f)$ is a complex function of the real variable f and can be written as

$$X(f) = |X(f)| e^{j\angle X(f)} \tag{2.65}$$

where $|X(f)|$ and $\angle X(f)$ are, respectively, called the **magnitude** and the **phase spectrum** of the signal $x(t)$.

$$\text{For real } x(t), \ X(-f) = \int_{-\infty}^{\infty} x(t) e^{j2\pi ft} dt = X^*(f) \tag{2.66}$$

Comparing magnitude and phase responses of both sides of (2.66) yields

$$|X(-f)| = |X(f)| \tag{2.67}$$

$$\angle X(-f) = -\angle X(f) \tag{2.68}$$

Thus $|X(f)|$ and $\angle X(f)$ are even and odd functions of f, respectively.

2.5.1   Fourier Transforms of Some Common Signals

Rectangular Pulse

$$x(t) = A\Pi(t/\tau)$$

$$X(f) = A\int_{-\infty}^{\infty} e^{-j2\pi ft}dt = A\int_{-\tau/2}^{\tau/2} e^{-j2\pi ft}dt = A\frac{e^{-j\pi f\tau} - e^{j\pi f\tau}}{-j2\pi f} = A\frac{\sin(\pi f\tau)}{\pi f}$$

$$= A\tau\,\mathrm{sinc}(f\tau) \qquad (2.69)$$

The magnitude and phase spectra of the rectangular pulse are plotted in Figure 2.28. It is interesting to note that the width of the mainlobe increases as the pulse width τ narrows.

Unit Impulse Signal

$$x(t) = \delta(t)$$

$$X(f) = \int_{-\infty}^{\infty} \delta(t)e^{-j2\pi ft}\,dt = \int_{-\infty}^{\infty} \delta(t)dt = 1 \qquad (2.70)$$

Equation (2.70) states that the unit impulse signal contains all frequencies with equal magnitudes as shown in Figure 2.29.

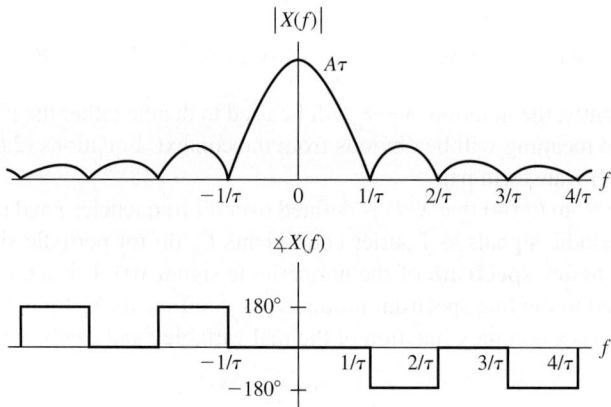

Figure 2.28 Magnitude and phase spectra of the rectangular pulse.

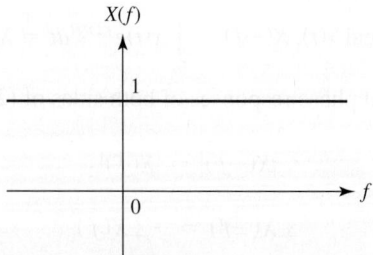

Figure 2.29 Fourier transform of the unit impulse signal.

Complex Exponential Signal

The Fourier transform of the complex exponential signal $e^{j2\pi f_c t}$ is $\delta(f - f_c)$. This can be verified by substituting $\delta(f - f_c)$ in the inverse Fourier transform formula as follows:

$$\int_{-\infty}^{\infty} \delta(f - f_c) e^{j2\pi ft} \, df = \int_{-\infty}^{\infty} \delta(f - f_c) e^{j2\pi f_c t} \, df = e^{j2\pi f_c t} \tag{2.71}$$

Figure 2.30 displays the result. It is intuitively satisfying in that it affirms that the spectrum of a complex sinusoid $e^{j2\pi f_c t}$ contains energy at only single frequency f_c.

Substituting $f_c = 0$ into (2.71), we obtain the FT of a DC signal as

$$1 \xleftrightarrow{\Im} \delta(f).$$

Signum Signal

The signum signal $\mathrm{sgn}(t)$ in (2.18) can be expressed as

$$\mathrm{sgn}(t) = \begin{cases} 1, & t \geq 0 \\ -1, & t \leq 0 \end{cases} = \lim_{\alpha \to 0} \begin{cases} e^{-\alpha t}, & t \geq 0 \\ -e^{\alpha t}, & t \leq 0 \end{cases} \tag{2.72}$$

The FT of $\mathrm{sgn}(t)$ can now be written as

$$\begin{aligned}
\Im\{\mathrm{sgn}(t)\} &= \lim_{\alpha \to 0} \left[-\int_{-\infty}^{0} e^{\alpha t} e^{-j2\pi ft} \, dt + \int_{0}^{\infty} e^{-\alpha t} e^{-j2\pi ft} \, dt \right] \\
&= \lim_{\alpha \to 0} \left[-\int_{-\infty}^{0} e^{(\alpha - j2\pi f)t} \, dt + \int_{0}^{\infty} e^{-(\alpha + j2\pi f)t} \, dt \right] \\
&= \lim_{\alpha \to 0} \frac{-4j\pi f}{\alpha^2 + 4\pi^2 f^2} = \frac{1}{j\pi f}
\end{aligned} \tag{2.73}$$

Unit Step Signal

The unit step function $u(t)$ can be expressed as

$$u(t) = \frac{1}{2} + \frac{1}{2} \mathrm{sgn}(t) \tag{2.74}$$

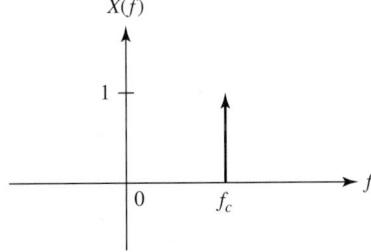

Figure 2.30 Fourier transform of a complex exponential signal.

Taking the FT of both sides of (2.74) yields

$$U(f) = \frac{1}{2}\delta(f) + \frac{1}{j2\pi f} \tag{2.75}$$

Table 2.2 tabulates Fourier transforms of frequently used signal types.

2.5.2 Properties of Fourier Transform

There are a number of important properties of the Fourier transform that are useful in the analysis and design of communication systems.

Linearity

$$\alpha x(t) + \beta y(t) \overset{\Im}{\longleftrightarrow} \alpha X(f) + \beta Y(f) \tag{2.76}$$

where α and β are arbitrary real or complex constants.

Table 2.2 Basic Fourier Transform Pairs

Time Function $x(t)$	Fourier Transform $X(f)$
DC signal A	$A\delta(f)$
Rectangular pulse $\Pi(t/\tau)$	$\tau\,\text{sinc}(f\tau)$
Triangular pulse $\Lambda(t/\tau)$	$\dfrac{\tau}{2}\,\text{sinc}^2\!\left(\dfrac{f\tau}{2}\right)$
Decaying exponential $e^{-\alpha t}u(t)$	$\dfrac{1}{\alpha + j2\pi f}$
$e^{-\alpha\lvert t\rvert}$	$\dfrac{2\alpha}{\alpha^2 + (2\pi f)^2}$
Unit impulse $\delta(t)$	1
$\delta(t - t_o)$	$e^{-j2\pi f t_o}$
Sinc pulse $\text{sinc}(2Wt)$	$\dfrac{1}{2W}\Pi(f/2W)$
Complex sinusoid $e^{j2\pi f_c t}$	$\delta(f - f_c)$
Sinusoid $\sin(2\pi f_c t)$	$\dfrac{1}{2j}[\delta(f - f_c) - \delta(f + f_c)]$
Sinusoid $\cos(2\pi f_c t)$	$\dfrac{1}{2}[\delta(f - f_c) + \delta(f + f_c)]$
Gaussian pulse $e^{-\pi t^2}$	$e^{-\pi f^2}$
$\text{sgn}(t)$	$\dfrac{1}{j\pi f}$
Unit step $u(t)$	$\dfrac{1}{2}\delta(f) + \dfrac{1}{j2\pi f}$
$\dfrac{1}{\pi t}$	$-j\,\text{sgn}(f)$
$\delta'(t)$	$j2\pi f$

To prove this property, let us take the FT of the left-hand side to obtain

$$\alpha x(t) + \beta y(t) \overset{\Im}{\longleftrightarrow} \int\limits_{-\infty}^{\infty} [\alpha x(t) + \beta y(t)]e^{-j2\pi ft}dt = \alpha \int\limits_{-\infty}^{\infty} x(t)e^{-j2\pi ft}dt + \beta \int\limits_{-\infty}^{\infty} y(t)e^{-j2\pi ft}dt$$

$$= \alpha X(f) + \beta Y(f)$$

Time Shifting

$$x(t - t_o) \overset{\Im}{\longleftrightarrow} X(f)e^{-j2\pi ft_o} \tag{2.77}$$

This can be proved by using the inverse Fourier transform formula as follows:

$$x(t - t_o) = \int\limits_{-\infty}^{\infty} X(f)e^{j2\pi f(t-t_o)}df = \int\limits_{-\infty}^{\infty} [X(f)e^{-j2\pi ft_o}]e^{j2\pi ft}df = \Im^{-1}\{X(f)e^{-j2\pi ft_o}\}$$

The Fourier transform of a signal $x(t)$ represents the magnitude and phase of all the frequency components in it. Now, if $x(t)$ is shifted in time by t_o seconds, it is equivalent to shifting all the component sinusoids by the same amount. This does not change their magnitudes, so the magnitude of $X(f)$ remains unchanged with a time shift. However, the phase of each constituent sinusoid does change with a time shift, and the higher the frequency of the sinusoid, the larger the phase change.

Frequency Translation

$$x(t)e^{j2\pi f_c t} \overset{\Im}{\longleftrightarrow} X(f - f_c) \tag{2.78}$$

Taking the Fourier transform of the left-hand side yields

$$\int\limits_{-\infty}^{\infty} x(t)e^{j2\pi f_c t}e^{-j2\pi ft}dt = \int\limits_{-\infty}^{\infty} x(t)e^{-j2\pi(f-f_c)t}dt = X(f - f_c)$$

This property states that multiplication of a signal $x(t)$ by $e^{j2\pi f_c t}$ translates its frequency spectrum $X(f)$ by the amount f_c (to the right on a graph). Communication systems often use frequency translation to assign frequency slots within a shared frequency spectrum to individual users on a demand basis—as in cellular telephone networks, for example.

Convolution

$$x(t) \otimes y(t) \overset{\Im}{\longleftrightarrow} X(f)Y(f) \tag{2.79}$$

To prove this property, recall that $x(t) \otimes y(t) = \int\limits_{-\infty}^{\infty} x(\tau)y(t - \tau)d\tau$. If we take the Fourier transform of the right-hand side and exchange the order of integration, we get

$$\int\limits_{-\infty}^{\infty} \left[\int\limits_{-\infty}^{\infty} x(\tau)y(t - \tau)d\tau\right] e^{-j2\pi ft}dt = \int\limits_{-\infty}^{\infty} d\tau x(\tau) \left[\int\limits_{-\infty}^{\infty} y(t - \tau)e^{-j2\pi ft}dt\right]$$

$$= \int\limits_{-\infty}^{\infty} x(\tau)Y(f)e^{-j2\pi f\tau}d\tau$$

where we have used the time-shifting property of the Fourier transform on $y(t - \tau)$. Now taking $Y(f)$ outside the integral yields

$$\int_{-\infty}^{\infty} x(\tau)y(t - \tau)d\tau \;\overset{\Im}{\longleftrightarrow}\; Y(f)\int_{-\infty}^{\infty} x(\tau)e^{-j2\pi f\tau}d\tau = Y(f)X(f)$$

Equation (2.79) states that the convolution operation in the time domain is *equivalent* to multiplication in the frequency domain. This is a very useful result.

Time/Frequency Scaling

$$x(at) \;\overset{\Im}{\longleftrightarrow}\; \frac{1}{|a|}X\!\left(\frac{f}{a}\right) \tag{2.80}$$

To prove this property, we first assume $a > 0$. Using the change of variable $u = at$, we have

$$x(at) \;\overset{\Im}{\longleftrightarrow}\; \int_{-\infty}^{\infty} x(at)e^{-j2\pi ft}dt = \frac{1}{a}\int_{-\infty}^{\infty} x(u)e^{-j2\pi(f/a)u}\,du = \frac{1}{a}X\!\left(\frac{f}{a}\right)$$

Now with $a < 0$, substituting $u = -|a|t$ yields

$$x(at) \;\overset{\Im}{\longleftrightarrow}\; \int_{-\infty}^{\infty} x(-|a|t)e^{-j2\pi ft}dt = \frac{1}{|a|}\int_{-\infty}^{\infty} x(u)e^{j2\pi(f/|a|)u}\,du = \frac{1}{|a|}X\!\left(-\frac{f}{|a|}\right) = \frac{1}{|a|}X\!\left(\frac{f}{a}\right)$$

The function $x(at)$, for $a > 0$, is a time-compressed (by a factor a) version of $x(t)$. On the other hand, a function $X(f/a)$ represents a function $X(f)$ expanded by the same factor a. The scaling property therefore states that compressing a signal in the time domain will stretch its Fourier transform. Similarly, stretching a time signal will compress its Fourier transform. The result is intuitively satisfying because compression in time by the factor a means that the function is varying rapidly in time by the same amount. Consequently, the extent of its frequency spectrum will be increased by the factor a. The converse can also be justified by a similar argument.

Duality

$$\text{If } x(t) \;\overset{\Im}{\longleftrightarrow}\; X(f), \text{ then } X(t) \;\overset{\Im}{\longleftrightarrow}\; x(-f) \tag{2.81}$$

To prove this property, we begin with

$$x(t) = \int_{-\infty}^{\infty} X(f)e^{j2\pi ft}df$$

Making a change of variable $f = -v$ yields

$$x(t) = \int_{-\infty}^{\infty} X(-v)e^{-j2\pi vt}dv$$

If we set $t = -f$, we get

$$x(-f) = \int\limits_{-\infty}^{\infty} X(-v)e^{j2\pi fv}dv$$

Finally, substituting t for $-v$, we get

$$x(-f) = \int\limits_{-\infty}^{\infty} X(t)e^{-j2\pi ft}dt = \Im\{X(t)\}$$

Example 2.28

Calculate the Fourier transform of the sinc pulse $2W\mathrm{sinc}(t2W)$.

Solution

From Table 2.2, the Fourier transform of a rectangular pulse is a sinc function in the frequency domain.

$$\Pi(t/\tau) \overset{\Im}{\longleftrightarrow} \tau \,\mathrm{sinc}(f\tau)$$

Using the duality property, we obtain

$$2W\mathrm{sinc}(t2W) \overset{\Im}{\longleftrightarrow} \Pi(f/2W)$$

Thus the Fourier transform of a sinc pulse is a rectangular function in frequency.

Differentiation Property

$$\frac{d}{dt}x(t) \overset{\Im}{\longleftrightarrow} j2\pi f X(f) \tag{2.82}$$

To prove this, we have

$$\frac{d}{dt}x(t) = \frac{d}{dt}\int\limits_{-\infty}^{\infty} X(f)e^{j2\pi ft}df = \int\limits_{-\infty}^{\infty} X(f)\left(\frac{d}{dt}e^{j2\pi ft}\right)df = \int\limits_{-\infty}^{\infty} [j2\pi f X(f)]e^{j2\pi ft}df \tag{2.83}$$

From (2.83) we conclude that

$$\Im^{-1}\{j2\pi f X(f)\} = \frac{d}{dt}x(t)$$

or

$$\Im\left\{\frac{d}{dt}x(t)\right\} = j2\pi f X(f)$$

Equation (2.82) states that the differentiation in the time domain is equivalent to multiplication by $j2\pi f$ in the frequency domain. With repeated application of the differentiation property, we obtain the following relation

$$\Im\left\{\frac{d^n}{dt^n}x(t)\right\} = (j2\pi f)^n X(f) \tag{2.84}$$

Differentiation in Frequency Domain

$$tx(t) \overset{\Im}{\longleftrightarrow} \frac{j}{2\pi}\frac{d}{df}X(f) \tag{2.85}$$

The proof follows the same basic steps as involved in proving the differentiation theorem.

Integration Property

$$\int_{-\infty}^{t} x(\tau)d\tau \overset{\Im}{\longleftrightarrow} \frac{X(f)}{j2\pi f} + \frac{1}{2}X(0)\delta(f) \tag{2.86}$$

To prove this, we first note that

$$\int_{-\infty}^{t} x(\tau)d\tau = x(t) \otimes u(t)$$

Using the convolution property of the FT, we can write

$$\Im\left\{\int_{-\infty}^{t} x(\tau)d\tau\right\} = X(f)U(f) \tag{2.87}$$

Substituting (2.75) into (2.87) yields

$$\Im\left\{\int_{-\infty}^{t} x(\tau)d\tau\right\} = X(f)\left\{\frac{1}{j2\pi f} + \frac{1}{2}\delta(f)\right\} = \frac{X(f)}{j2\pi f} + \frac{1}{2}X(0)\delta(f)$$

Parseval's Relation

$$\int_{-\infty}^{\infty} x(t)y^*(t)dt = \int_{-\infty}^{\infty} X(f)Y^*(f)df \tag{2.88}$$

To prove this, we substitute

$$y^*(t) = \int_{-\infty}^{\infty} Y^*(f)e^{-j2\pi ft}df$$

into the left-hand side of (2.88) and exchanging the order of integration yields

$$\int\limits_{-\infty}^{\infty} x(t)y^*(t)dt = \int\limits_{-\infty}^{\infty} x(t)\left[\int\limits_{-\infty}^{\infty} Y^*(f)e^{-j2\pi ft}df\right]dt$$

$$= \int\limits_{-\infty}^{\infty} Y^*(f)\left[\int\limits_{-\infty}^{\infty} x(t)e^{-j2\pi ft}dt\right]df = \int\limits_{-\infty}^{\infty} Y^*(f)X(f)df$$

If we let $y(t) = x(t)$ in Parseval's formula, we get the well-known relationship for the energy of a signal in time and frequency domains.

$$E_x = \int\limits_{-\infty}^{\infty} |x(t)|^2 dt = \int\limits_{-\infty}^{\infty} |X(f)|^2 df \qquad (2.89)$$

Equation (2.89) states that the energy of a signal is given by the area under the $|X(f)|^2$ curve. $|X(f)|^2$ is called the **energy density spectrum** of $x(t)$. Note that the quantity $|X(f_o)|^2 \, \Delta f$ represents the energy contained in a spectral band of Δf Hz centered at frequency f_o. Thus $|X(f)|^2$ may be interpreted as the energy per Hz of bandwidth contained in spectral components of $x(t)$ centered at frequency f. It is specified in units of Joules/Hz.

Table 2.3 summarizes important properties of the Fourier transform. The following example illustrates how the properties in Table 2.3 may be used to calculate the FT of other signals not listed in Table 2.2.

Table 2.3 Fourier Transform Properties

Property	Time Function $x(t)$ $y(t)$	Fourier Transform $X(f)$ $Y(f)$
Linearity	$\alpha x(t) + \beta y(t)$	$\alpha X(f) + \beta Y(f)$
Time-shifting	$x(t - t_o)$	$X(f)e^{-j2\pi ft_o}$
Frequency translation	$x(t)e^{j2\pi f_c t}$	$X(f - f_c)$
Convolution	$x(t) \otimes y(t)$	$X(f)Y(f)$
Multiplication	$x(t)y(t)$	$X(f) \otimes Y(f)$
Time/Frequency scaling	$x(at)$	$\dfrac{1}{|a|}X\left(\dfrac{f}{a}\right)$
Duality	$X(t)$	$x(-f)$
Differentiation in time	$\dfrac{d}{dt}x(t)$	$j2\pi f X(f)$
Differentiation in frequency	$tx(t)$	$\dfrac{j}{2\pi}\dfrac{d}{df}X(f)$
Integration	$\displaystyle\int\limits_{-\infty}^{t} x(\tau)d\tau$	$\dfrac{X(f)}{j2\pi f} + \dfrac{1}{2}X(0)\delta(f)$
Parseval's relation	$\displaystyle\int\limits_{-\infty}^{\infty} x(t)y^*(t)dt = \int\limits_{-\infty}^{\infty} X(f)Y^*(f)df$	

Example 2.29

Calculate the FT of the signals in Figure 2.31(a) and (b).

Solution

a. $x_1(t) = -\Pi\left[\dfrac{2(t + \tau/4)}{\tau}\right] + \Pi\left[\dfrac{(t - \tau/2)}{\tau}\right]$

Now

$$\Pi\left(\frac{2t}{\tau}\right) \overset{\Im}{\longleftrightarrow} \frac{\tau}{2}\,\text{sinc}\left(\frac{f\tau}{2}\right)$$

Applying the time-shifting property of the FT yields

$$\Pi\left[\frac{2(t + \tau/4)}{\tau}\right] \overset{\Im}{\longleftrightarrow} \frac{\tau}{2}\,\text{sinc}\left(\frac{f\tau}{2}\right)e^{j\pi f\tau/2}$$

and

$$\Pi\left[\frac{(t - \tau/2)}{\tau}\right] \overset{\Im}{\longleftrightarrow} \tau\,\text{sinc}(f\tau)e^{-j\pi f\tau}$$

Adding

$$X_1(f) = -\frac{\tau}{2}\,\text{sinc}\left(\frac{f\tau}{2}\right)e^{j\pi f\tau/2} + \tau\,\text{sinc}(f\tau)e^{-j\pi f\tau}$$

b. As shown in Figure 2.31(c), differentiating $x_2(t)$ yields

$$\frac{dx_2(t)}{dt} = \Pi(t + 1/2) - \delta(t - 1)$$

Taking the FT of both sides and using the differentiation property, we obtain

$$j2\pi f X_2(f) = \Im\{\Pi(t + 1/2) - \delta(t - 1)\}$$

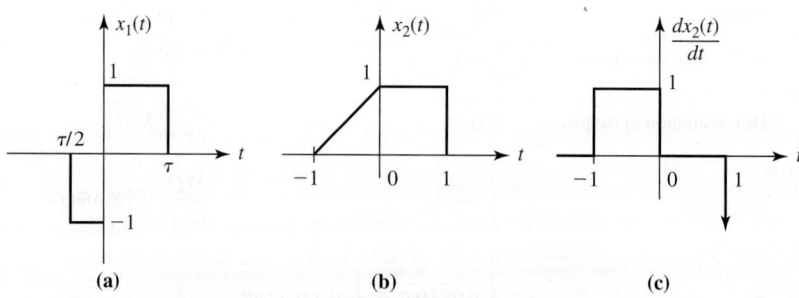

Figure 2.31 Waveforms: Example 2.29.

Now $\Pi(t) \overset{\Im}{\longleftrightarrow} \text{sinc}(f)$. Applying the time-shifting property of the FT, we can write

$$\Pi(t + 1/2) \overset{\Im}{\longleftrightarrow} \text{sinc}(f)e^{j\pi f}$$

Also $\delta(t) \overset{\Im}{\longleftrightarrow} 1$. Again, using the time-shifting property of the FT, we get

$$\delta(t - 1) \overset{\Im}{\longleftrightarrow} e^{-j2\pi f}$$

Adding

$$j2\pi f X_2(f) = \text{sinc}(f)e^{j\pi f} - e^{-j2\pi f}$$

or

$$X_2(f) = \frac{1}{j2\pi f}[\text{sinc}(f)e^{j\pi f} - e^{-j2\pi f}]$$

2.5.3 Fourier Transforms of Periodic Signals

The Fourier transform is strictly defined for finite energy signals. However, the Fourier transform of a real sinusoidal signal exists, as is evident from Table 2.2. Thus it is possible to formally determine the Fourier transform of a periodic signal by taking the Fourier transform of its complex Fourier series term by term. The FS expansion for a periodic function $x_p(t)$ can be written from (2.49) as

$$x_p(t) = \sum_{n=-\infty}^{\infty} C_n e^{j2\pi nf_o t}$$

Taking the Fourier transform of both sides, we have

$$X_p(f) = \Im\left\{ \sum_{n=-\infty}^{\infty} C_n e^{j2\pi nf_o t} \right\} = \sum_{n=-\infty}^{\infty} C_n \Im\{e^{j2\pi nf_o t}\} = \sum_{n=-\infty}^{\infty} C_n \delta(f - nf_o) \quad (2.90)$$

Equation (2.90) states that the FT of a periodic signal consists of impulses located at harmonic frequencies of the signal. The weight of the impulse located at $f = nf_o$ in the FT $X_p(f)$, denoted by $X_p(nf_o)$, is equal to the corresponding coefficient in the exponential FS expansion of $x_p(t)$. That is,

$$X_p(nf_o) = C_n \quad (2.91)$$

Example 2.30

Calculate the Fourier transform of a cosine wave $A\cos(2\pi f_c t + \phi)$.

Solution

$$x(t) = A\cos(2\pi f_c t + \phi) = \frac{A}{2}e^{j(2\pi f_c t + \phi)} + \frac{A}{2}e^{-j(2\pi f_c t + \phi)}$$

Taking the FT of both sides and using Table 2.2, we obtain

$$X(f) = \frac{A}{2}e^{j\phi}\delta(f - f_c) + \frac{A}{2}e^{-j\phi}\delta(f + f_c) \tag{2.92}$$

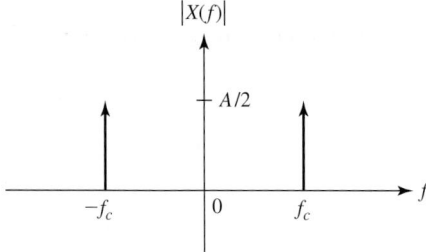

Figure 2.32 Fourier transform of $A\cos(2\pi f_c t + \phi)$.

Figure 2.32 displays the magnitude of the Fourier transform of $A\cos(2\pi f_c t + \phi)$. Similarly, it can be shown that

$$A\sin(2\pi f_c t + \phi) \overset{\Im}{\longleftrightarrow} \frac{A}{2j}e^{j\phi}\delta(f - f_c) - \frac{A}{2j}e^{-j\phi}\delta(f + f_c) \tag{2.93}$$

Example 2.31

Determine the FT of the periodic impulse train displayed in Figure 2.33.

Solution

The periodic impulse train with period T_o is given by

$$\delta_p(t) = \sum_{n=-\infty}^{\infty} \delta(t - nT_o) \tag{2.94}$$

The FS expansion for this signal can be expressed as

$$\delta_p(t) = \sum_{n=-\infty}^{\infty} C_n e^{j2\pi n f_o t} \tag{2.95}$$

where

$$f_o = \frac{1}{T_o}$$

$$C_n = \frac{1}{T_o}\int_{T_o}\delta_p(t)e^{-j2\pi n f_o t}dt = \frac{1}{T_o}\int_{-T_o/2}^{T_o/2}\delta(t)e^{-j2\pi n f_o t}dt = \frac{1}{T_o} = f_o \tag{2.96}$$

Substituting into (2.95) yields

$$\delta_p(t) = f_o \sum_{n=-\infty}^{\infty} e^{j2\pi n f_o t} \tag{2.97}$$

Taking the Fourier transform of both sides of (2.97), we obtain

$$\Delta_p(f) = \Im\{\delta_p(t)\} = f_o \sum_{n=-\infty}^{\infty} \delta(f - n f_o) \tag{2.98}$$

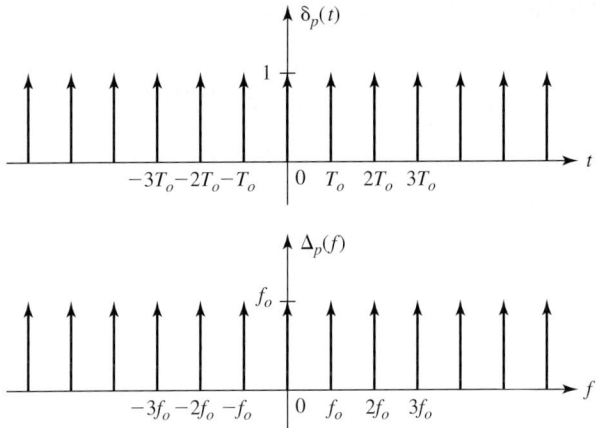

Figure 2.33 Periodic impulse train and its Fourier transform.

Equation (2.98) states that the Fourier transform $\Delta_p(f)$ of a periodic impulse train with period T_o is also a periodic impulse train but with period $f_o = \dfrac{1}{T_o}$. The weight of each impulse in $\Delta_p(f)$ is f_o as displayed in Figure 2.33.

Poisson Sum Formula

Consider the signal $y(t)$ obtained by convolving an energy signal $x(t)$ with the periodic impulse train in (2.94).

$$y(t) = \delta_p(t) \otimes x(t) = x(t) \otimes \sum_{n=-\infty}^{\infty} \delta(t - nT_o) = \sum_{n=-\infty}^{\infty} x(t - nT_o) \qquad (2.99)$$

It is obvious from (2.99) that $y(t)$ is a periodic and is referred to as a **periodic extension** of $x(t)$. Now using the convolution property of Fourier transform and (2.98), we obtain

$$\sum_{n=-\infty}^{\infty} x(t - nT_o) = x(t) \otimes \sum_{n=-\infty}^{\infty} \delta(t - nT_o) \overset{\Im}{\longleftrightarrow} X(f)\Delta_p(f)$$

$$= X(f)f_o \sum_{n=-\infty}^{\infty} \delta(f - nf_o) = f_o \sum_{n=-\infty}^{\infty} X(nf_o)\delta(f - nf_o)$$

That is,

$$\sum_{n=-\infty}^{\infty} x(t - nT_o) \overset{\Im}{\longleftrightarrow} f_o \sum_{n=-\infty}^{\infty} X(nf_o)\delta(f - nf_o) \qquad (2.100)$$

Now taking the inverse Fourier transform of the right-hand side of (2.100) yields

$$\Im^{-1}\left\{ f_o \sum_{n=-\infty}^{\infty} X(nf_o)\delta(f - nf_o) \right\} = f_o \sum_{n=-\infty}^{\infty} X(nf_o)e^{j2\pi nf_o t} \qquad (2.101)$$

Combining (2.100) and (2.101) yields the Poisson sum formula

$$\sum_{n=-\infty}^{\infty} x(t - nT_o) = \frac{1}{T_o} \sum_{n=-\infty}^{\infty} X(nf_o)e^{j2\pi nf_o t} \qquad (2.102)$$

Equation (2.102) states that the sample values $X(nf_o)$ of the Fourier transform of $x(t)$ are the FS coefficients of the periodic signal $T_o \sum_{n=-\infty}^{\infty} x(t - nT_o)$. As a special case, setting $t = 0$ in (2.102), we obtain

$$\sum_{n=-\infty}^{\infty} x(nT_o) = \frac{1}{T_o} \sum_{n=-\infty}^{\infty} X(nf_o) \qquad (2.103)$$

2.6   TIME-BANDWIDTH PRODUCT

Recall the scaling property of the Fourier transform, which states that the compression in the time domain is equivalent to the expansion in the frequency domain, and vice versa. Thus, the frequency- and time-domain behaviors of a signal are **inversely** related. This important relationship is captured in the statement that the time-bandwidth product of a signal is constant.

$$\text{Time Duration} \times \text{Frequency Bandwidth} = k \qquad (2.104)$$

where k is some constant determined by the precise definitions of **duration** in the time domain and **bandwidth** in the frequency domain. For example,

1. The unit impulse signal, which has zero duration, has a Fourier transform with infinite extent.
2. The sinc signal, which has infinite time duration, has a Fourier transform with finite bandwidth.

Thus, a signal cannot be both duration-limited and bandwidth-limited. We provide the proof of (2.104) by choosing the pulse duration definition as the width Δt of a rectangle whose height matches its peak value (say $x(0)$ for convenience), and whose area is the same as that under the pulse $x(t)$. This is illustrated in Figure 2.34.

$$\Delta t = \frac{\int_{-\infty}^{\infty} x(t)dt}{x(0)} \qquad (2.105)$$

We define the bandwidth Δf in a similar manner as

$$\Delta f = \frac{\int_{-\infty}^{\infty} X(f)df}{X(0)} \qquad (2.106)$$

The product of these two is

$$\Delta f \Delta t = \frac{\int_{-\infty}^{\infty} X(f)df}{X(0)} \frac{\int_{-\infty}^{\infty} x(t)dt}{x(0)} \qquad (2.107)$$

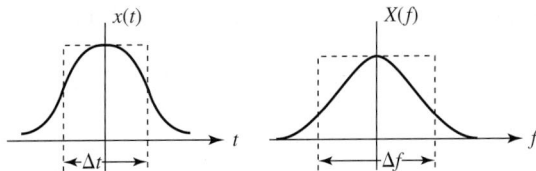

Figure 2.34 Definition of pulse width and bandwidth.

Now from the definition of Fourier transform pair, we have

$$X(0) = \int_{-\infty}^{\infty} x(t)e^{-j2\pi ft}dt\Big|_{f=0} = \int_{-\infty}^{\infty} x(t)dt \qquad (2.108)$$

$$x(0) = \int_{-\infty}^{\infty} X(f)e^{j2\pi ft}df\Big|_{t=0} = \int_{-\infty}^{\infty} X(f)df \qquad (2.109)$$

Substituting into (2.107) yields

$$\Delta f \Delta t = 1 \qquad (2.110)$$

(2.110) states that the product of the pulse duration and its bandwidth is unity. If we instead use **root-mean-square (RMS)** definitions for signal duration and bandwidth, it can be shown that

$$\Delta f_{rms}\Delta t_{rms} \geq \frac{1}{4\pi} \qquad (2.111)$$

where

$$\Delta t_{rms} = \frac{\displaystyle\int_{-\infty}^{\infty} t^2|x(t)|^2 dt}{\displaystyle\int_{-\infty}^{\infty} |x(t)|^2 dt} \qquad (2.112)$$

$$\Delta f_{rms} = \frac{\displaystyle\int_{-\infty}^{\infty} f^2|X(f)|^2 df}{\displaystyle\int_{-\infty}^{\infty} {}^2|X(f)|^2 df} \qquad (2.113)$$

For a Gaussian pulse $e^{-\pi t^2}$, (2.111) is satisfied with the equality sign. Again, the time duration and bandwidth of a signal have an inverse relationship. This leads to the general conclusion that the time duration of a signal and its bandwidth cannot both be made arbitrarily small. The relationship (2.111) is also known as the **uncertainty principle** in quantum physics, where Δf_{rms} and Δt_{rms} are interpreted as resolutions in frequency and time, respectively. Frequency resolution means the ability to clearly identify signal components that are concentrated at particular frequencies, and time resolution implies the precision to clearly identify signal events that manifest during a short time interval. The uncertainty principle sets a fundamental limit on resolution in both time and frequency.

2.7 TRANSMISSION OF SIGNALS THROUGH LTI SYSTEMS

An LTI system is completely characterized in the time domain by its impulse response function $h(t)$. Recall that the input–output relationship in the time domain of an LTI system with impulse response function $h(t)$ is given by the convolution integral of (2.41) and is of the form

$$y(t) = x(t) \otimes h(t) = \int_{-\infty}^{\infty} x(\tau)h(t - \tau)d\tau \tag{2.41}$$

where $y(t)$ and $x(t)$ are, respectively, the output and the input signals. We now consider the response of an LTI system to complex exponential signal $e^{j2\pi f_c t}$. From (2.41), the output is given by

$$y(t) = \int_{-\infty}^{\infty} e^{j2\pi f_c \tau} h(t - \tau)d\tau = \int_{-\infty}^{\infty} e^{j2\pi f_c(t-u)} h(u)du = e^{j2\pi f_c t} \underbrace{\int_{-\infty}^{\infty} e^{-j2\pi f_c u} h(u)du}_{H(f_c)}$$

$$= e^{j2\pi f_c t} H(f_c) \tag{2.114}$$

where

$$H(f) \xleftrightarrow{\ \Im\ } h(t)$$

Note that $H(f)$ is FT of the impulse response function $h(t)$ and provides frequency domain description of the system. It is called **frequency response function** of the LTI system. (2.114) states that for a complex exponential input of frequency f_c, the output $y(t)$ is also a complex exponential signal of the *same* frequency but *scaled* by the complex weight $H(f_c)$. We can write (2.114) as

$$y(t) = |H(f_c)|e^{j[2\pi f_c t + \angle H(f_c)]} \tag{2.115}$$

It is obvious from (2.115) that the value of $H(f)$ at f_c determines the magnitude and phase shifts introduced by the system in passing the input complex exponential signal from input to output. Equation (2.115) implies that the response of the system to a real sinusoidal input signal $x(t) = \cos(2\pi f_c t)$ of frequency f_c is given by

$$y(t) = |H(f_c)|\cos[2\pi f_c t + \angle H(f_c)] \tag{2.116}$$

Similarly, the response of the system to sinusoidal input signal $x(t) = \sin(2\pi f_c t)$ is

$$y(t) = |H(f_c)|\sin[2\pi f_c t + \angle H(f_c)] \tag{2.117}$$

For a periodic input signal $x_p(t)$ represented by its Fourier series (2.49), the output of an LTI system can be obtained by applying (2.114) to each discrete frequency component as follows:

$$y_p(t) = \sum_{n=-\infty}^{\infty} C_n H(nf_o)e^{j2\pi nf_o t} \tag{2.118}$$

Equation (2.118) states that the output of an LTI system to a periodic input is *also* periodic and FS coefficients of the output signal are given by $C_n H(nf_o)$.

Example 2.32

The frequency response $H(f)$ of an LTI system is given by

$$H(f) = \frac{2}{1 + j0.0025\pi f}$$

Determine the output $y(t)$ for an input $x(t) = \sin(800\pi t) + 2\sin(2000\pi t + \pi/4)$.

Solution

The response of the system to input sinusoidal signal $\sin(800\pi t)$ is given by

$$H(400) = 0.184 - j0.578$$

This can be represented in the magnitude-phase form as

$$|H(400)| = 0.6066$$

$$\angle H(400) = -72.34°$$

The output of the system for an input $\sin(800\pi t)$ can now be expressed using (2.117) as $0.6066\sin(800\pi t - 72.34°)$.

The response of the system to input sinusoidal signal $2\sin(2000\pi t + \pi/4)$ is

$$H(1000) = 0.032 - j0.2506$$

This can be represented in the magnitude-phase form as

$$|H(1000)| = 0.2526$$

$$\angle |H(1000)| = -82.75°$$

The output of the system for an input $2\sin(2000\pi t + \pi/4)$ can now be expressed using (2.117) as $0.5052\sin(2000\pi t - 82.75° + \pi/4)$.

Therefore, the combined output is

$$y(t) = 0.6066\sin(800\pi t - 72.34°) + 0.5052\sin(2000\pi t - 82.75° + \pi/4)$$

For any arbitrary input, the frequency domain response of an LTI system can be obtained by applying the FT to both sides of (2.41) and using the convolution property (2.79).

$$Y(f) = X(f)H(f) \tag{2.119}$$

Equation (2.119) states that the output of the system in the frequency domain is given by multiplying the Fourier transform of the input by the system frequency response $H(f)$. $H(f)$, in general, is a complex function of f and can be expressed in the magnitude-phase form as

$$H(f) = |H(f)|e^{j\angle H(f)} \tag{2.120}$$

where $|H(f)|$ and $\angle H(f)$ are, respectively, called the **magnitude** and the **phase responses** of the system.

Design specifications for the LTI system, in many applications, are given in terms of the magnitude and phase responses. If $h(t)$ is a real function of time, then it follows from (2.67) and (2.68) that $|H(f)|$ is an even function of f

$$|H(f)| = |H(-f)| \tag{2.121}$$

and the phase function $\angle H(f)$ is an odd function of f

$$\angle H(f) = -\angle H(-f) \tag{2.122}$$

In the frequency domain, the magnitude and the phase of the system input and output are related by

$$|Y(f)| = |X(f)||H(f)| \tag{2.123}$$

$$\angle Y(f) = \angle X(f) + \angle H(f) \tag{2.124}$$

The magnitude and the phase effects represented by (2.123) and (2.124) can be either *intentional* or *undesirable*. In the latter case, these effects of an LTI system on a signal are referred to as magnitude and phase distortions, respectively.

Example 2.33

Determine the magnitude and phase response of the RC low-pass filter shown in Figure 2.35.

Solution

The transfer function of the RC low-pass filter is obtained from Figure 2.35 as

$$H(f) = \frac{Y(f)}{X(f)} = \frac{1/j2\pi fC}{R + 1/j2\pi fC} = \frac{1}{1 + j2\pi fRC} = \frac{1}{1 + j(f/f_{3\text{dB}})} \tag{2.125}$$

where

$$f_{3\text{dB}} = \frac{1}{2\pi RC} \tag{2.126}$$

The magnitude and phase responses of the RC low-pass filter can now be expressed as

$$|H(f)| = \frac{1}{\sqrt{1 + (f/f_{3\text{dB}})^2}} \tag{2.127}$$

$$\angle H(f) = -\tan^{-1}(f/f_{3\text{dB}}) \tag{2.128}$$

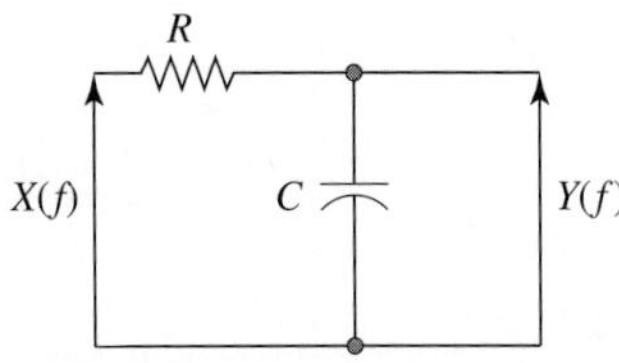

Figure 2.35 RC low-pass filter.

$f_{3\text{dB}}$ is called the **3-dB cutoff frequency** or **3-dB bandwidth** of the low-pass filter because its magnitude-squared response drops by 3 dB (i.e., one-half the power) at $f = f_{3\text{dB}}$ as shown below:

$$10\log_{10}|H(f_{3\text{dB}})|^2 = 20\log_{10}\frac{1}{\sqrt{2}} = -3 \text{ dB} \tag{2.129}$$

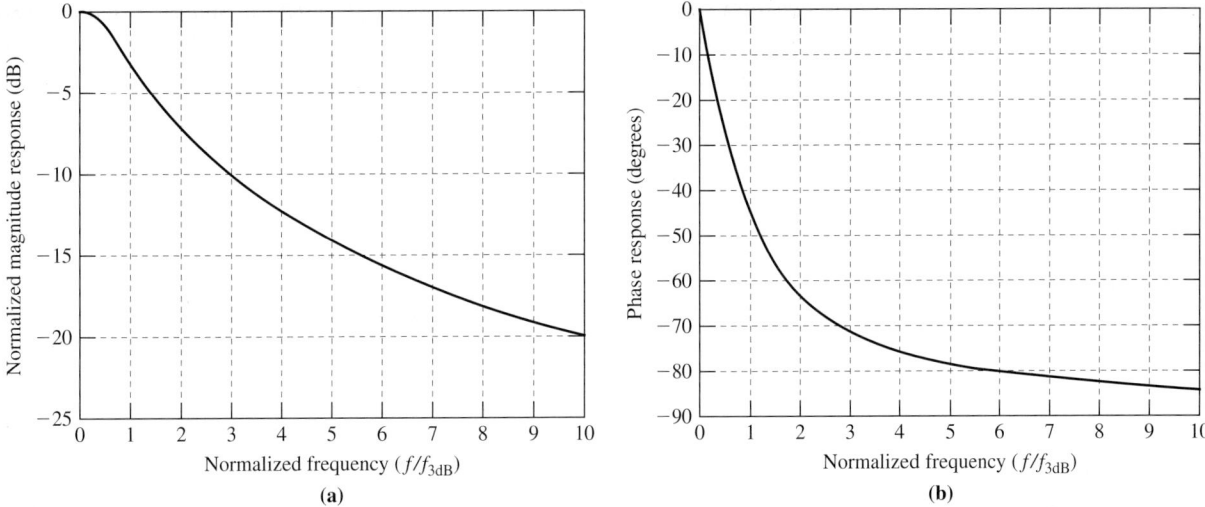

Figure 2.36 (a) Magnitude and (b) phase responses of the RC low-pass filter.

Equation (2.129) states that the input signal frequency component at $f = f_{3dB}$ is attenuated by 3 dB compared with that at $f = 0$ in the filter output waveform. Figure 2.36 shows the magnitude and phase responses of the low-pass filter with 3-dB bandwidth equal to 1 Hz.

Taking inverse FT of both sides of (2.125), the impulse response of the RC low-pass filter is given by

$$h(t) = 2\pi f_{3dB} e^{-2\pi f_{3dB} t} u(t) = \frac{1}{RC} e^{-t/RC} u(t) \tag{2.130}$$

2.7.1 Distortionless Transmission

In general, both the magnitude and phase of spectral components of the input signal will be altered as the signal passes through an LTI system as indicated by (2.123) and (2.124). This amounts to **distortion** in signal transmission. An LTI system is termed **distortionless** if it introduces the same attenuation to all spectral components and offers linear phase response over the frequency band of interest, that is,

$$H_{ideal}(f) = \begin{cases} H_o e^{-j2\pi f t_o}, & f_1 \leq f \leq f_2 \\ 0, & \text{otherwise} \end{cases} \tag{2.131}$$

Substituting (2.131) into (2.119) yields

$$Y(f) = X(f)H_{ideal}(f) = H_o X(f) e^{-j2\pi f t_o} \tag{2.132}$$

Taking inverse FT of both sides of (2.132), the output of a distortionless LTI system due to an arbitrary input signal $x(t)$ is given by

$$y(t) = H_o x(t - t_o) \tag{2.133}$$

Consequently, the output of a distortionless LTI system is simply a delayed and scaled replica of the input.

Group Delay

The **group delay** of an LTI system is defined as

$$\tau_g(f) \triangleq -\frac{1}{2\pi} \frac{d\angle H(f)}{df} \tag{2.134}$$

The phase response of a distortionless LTI system from (2.131) is a linear function of frequency as given by

$$\angle H_{ideal}(f) = -2\pi f t_o, \quad f_1 \leq f \leq f_2 \tag{2.135}$$

where t_o is a constant. For a linear phase LTI system, we obtain

$$\tau_g(f) = -\frac{1}{2\pi} \frac{d(-2\pi f t_o)}{df} = t_o = \text{constant} \tag{2.136}$$

Equation (2.136) states that for a linear phase LTI system, the group delay is constant. We interpret the group delay $\tau_g(f)$ as the time delay that a spectral component at frequency f undergoes as it passes through the LTI system. In this case of a linear phase LTI system, all frequency components of the input signal undergo the same time delay.

Phase Delay

The **phase delay** of an LTI system is defined as

$$\tau_p(f) \triangleq -\frac{1}{2\pi f} \angle H(f) \tag{2.137}$$

For a linear phase LTI system, the phase delay is given by

$$\tau_p(f) = -\frac{1}{2\pi f}(-2\pi f t_o) = t_o = \text{constant} \tag{2.138}$$

2.8   LTI SYSTEMS AS FREQUENCY SELECTIVE FILTERS

One key application of LTI systems is to design **filters** that separate the desired information-bearing signal from unwanted interference and noise. By definition, filters pass certain frequency components in the input signal (sequence) with minimum distortion and block all other frequency components.

2.8.1   Ideal Filters

An ideal filter designed to pass signal components of certain frequencies without any distortion should have a magnitude response that is flat over these frequencies and should totally block signal components at all other frequencies. The range of frequencies

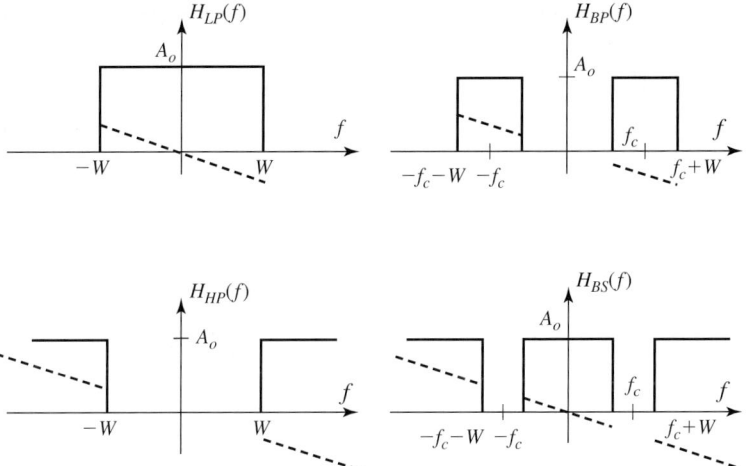

Figure 2.37 Magnitude and phase responses of ideal filters.

where the magnitude response takes the constant value and where the phase response is a linear function of frequency is called the **passband.** The range of frequencies where the frequency response is zero is called the **stopband** of the filter. Figure 2.37 displays the frequency response characteristics of ideal filters.

Ideal Low-Pass Filter

The magnitude response of an ideal **low-pass (LP)** filter is defined as

$$|H_{LP}(f)| = \begin{cases} A_o, & -W \leq f \leq W \\ 0, & \text{otherwise} \end{cases} \tag{2.139}$$

The range of frequencies $0 \leq f \leq W$ is the passband of the filter. The range of frequencies $f > W$ is the stopband of the filter.

The frequency response of an ideal LP filter can now be expressed as

$$H_{LP}(f) = A_o \Pi(f/2W)e^{-j2\pi f t_o} \tag{2.140}$$

Taking the inverse Fourier transform yields the impulse response $h_{LP}(t)$ of the ideal LP filter as

$$h_{LP}(t) = 2WA_o \operatorname{sinc}[2W(t - t_o)] \tag{2.141}$$

Figure 2.38 displays the impulse response of an ideal LP filter.

Ideal High-Pass Filter

The magnitude response of an ideal **high-pass (HP)** filter is defined as

$$|H_{HP}(f)| = \begin{cases} 0, & -W \leq f \leq W \\ A_o, & \text{otherwise} \end{cases} \tag{2.142}$$

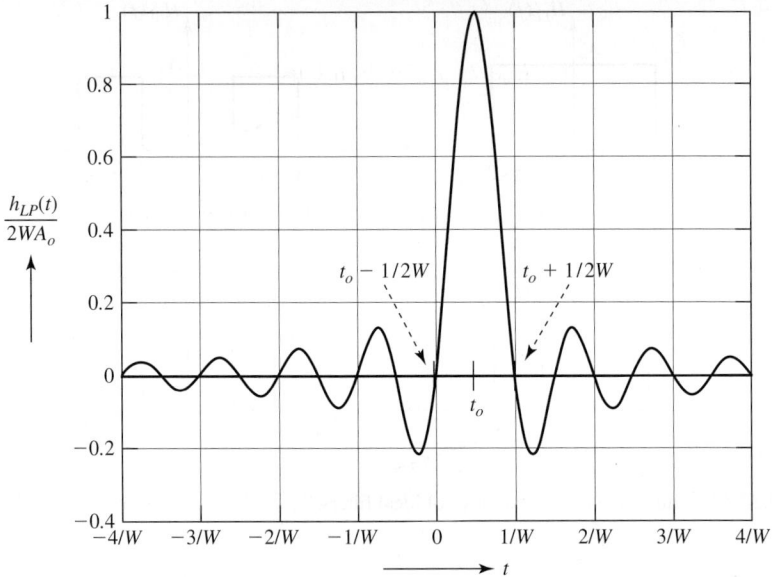

Figure 2.38 Impulse response of an ideal LP filter.

The range of frequencies $f \leq W$ is the stopband of the filter. The range of frequencies $f > W$ is the passband of the filter. The frequency response of an ideal HP filter can now be written as

$$H_{HP}(f) = A_o[1 - \Pi(f/2W)]e^{-j2\pi ft_o} \tag{2.143}$$

Taking the inverse Fourier transform yields the impulse response $h_{HP}(t)$ of the ideal HP filter as

$$h_{HP}(t) = A_o\{\delta(t - t_o) - 2W\,\mathrm{sinc}[2W(t - t_o)]\} \tag{2.144}$$

Ideal Bandpass Filter

The magnitude response of an ideal **bandpass (BP)** filter is defined as

$$|H_{BP}(f)| = \begin{cases} A_o, & f_c - W \leq |f| \leq f_c + W \\ 0, & \text{otherwise} \end{cases} \tag{2.145}$$

The range of frequencies $f_c - W \leq |f| \leq f_c + W$ is the passband of the filter. The range of frequencies $|f| > f_c + W$ and $|f| < f_c - W$ are the stopband regions of the filter. The frequency response of an ideal BP filter can now be written as

$$H_{BP}(f) = H_o(f - f_c) + H_o(f + f_c) \tag{2.146}$$

where

$$H_o(f) = A_o\Pi(f/2W)e^{-j2\pi ft_o} \tag{2.147}$$

is an LP filter with impulse response

$$h_o(t) = 2WA_o\,\mathrm{sinc}[2W(t - t_o)] \tag{2.148}$$

Because

$$H_o(f - f_c) \overset{\Im}{\longleftrightarrow} h_o(t)e^{j2\pi f_c t} \tag{2.149}$$

$$H_o(f + f_c) \overset{\Im}{\longleftrightarrow} h_o(t)e^{-j2\pi f_c t} \tag{2.150}$$

we can now write the impulse response $h_{BP}(t)$ of the bandpass filter as

$$h_{BP}(t) = 4WA_o \operatorname{sinc}[2W(t - t_o)] \left[\frac{e^{j2\pi f_c t} + e^{-j2\pi f_c t}}{2} \right]$$

$$= 4WA_o \operatorname{sinc}[2W(t - t_o)] \cos(2\pi f_c t) \tag{2.151}$$

Thus, the impulse response of the bandpass filter is an oscillatory function. For the important case $f_c \gg 2W$, $h_{BP}(t)$ can be viewed as the slowly varying signal $4WA_o \operatorname{sinc}(2Wt)$ shifted by t_o seconds and modulating the high-frequency sinusoidal signal $\cos(2\pi f_c t)$. Figure 2.39 displays the impulse response of the ideal bandpass filter.

Ideal Bandstop Filter

The magnitude response of an ideal **bandstop (BS)** filter is defined as

$$|H_{BS}(f)| = \begin{cases} A_o, & \text{otherwise} \\ 0, & f_c - W \leq |f| \leq f_c + W \end{cases} \tag{2.152}$$

The range of frequencies $f_c - W \leq |f| \leq f_c + W$ is the stopband of the filter. The range of frequencies $|f| > f_c + W$ and $|f| < f_c - W$ is the passband region of the filter.

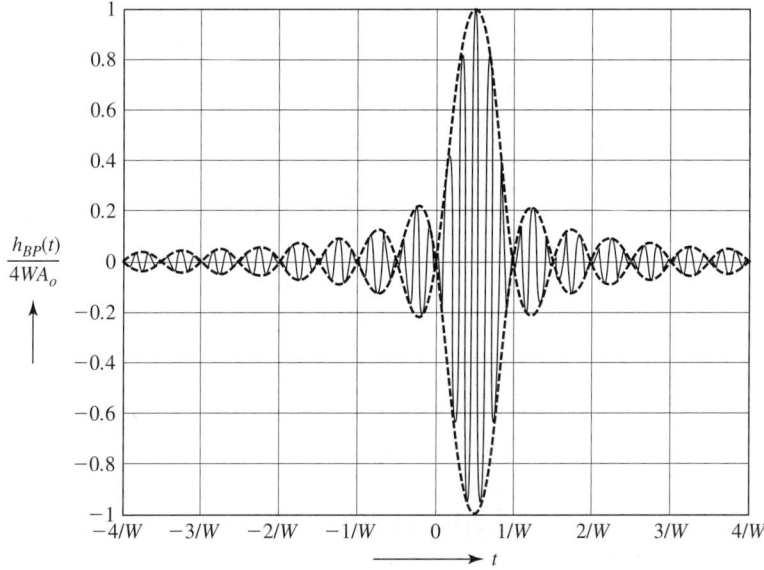

Figure 2.39 Impulse response of an ideal BP filter.

2.8.2   Realizable Approximations to Ideal Filters

In practice, it is impossible to realize a filter with the ideal **brick wall** characteristic of Figure 2.37 because the corresponding impulse response is not causal and extends from $-\infty$ to ∞. In order to develop realizable filter transfer functions, the ideal frequency response specifications of Figure 2.37 are relaxed by including a transition band between the passband and the stopband to permit the magnitude response to decay more gradually from its maximum value in the passband to the zero value in the stopband as shown in Figure 2.40. Moreover, the magnitude response is allowed to vary by a small amount both in the passband and stopband.

The magnitude response specifications for a realizable approximation $|H_a(f)|$ to the ideal brick wall characteristic consists of acceptable tolerances as shown in Figure 2.40. In the **passband** defined by $0 \leq f \leq f_p$, we require

$$1 - \delta_p \leq |H_a(f)| \leq 1 + \delta_p \tag{2.153}$$

that is, the magnitude approximates unity within an error of $\pm\delta_p$. In the **stopband,** defined by $f_s \leq |f| \leq \infty$, we require

$$|H_a(f)| \leq \delta_s \tag{2.154}$$

implying that the magnitude approximates zero within an error of δ_s. The frequencies f_p and f_s are, respectively, called the **passband edge frequency** and the **stopband edge frequency.** The limits of the tolerances in the passband and stopband, δ_p and δ_s, are called the **peak ripple values.** The peak passband ripple in dB is

$$R_p = -20\log(1 - \delta_p) \tag{2.155}$$

The minimum stopband attenuation in dB is given by

$$R_s = -20\log(\delta_s) \tag{2.156}$$

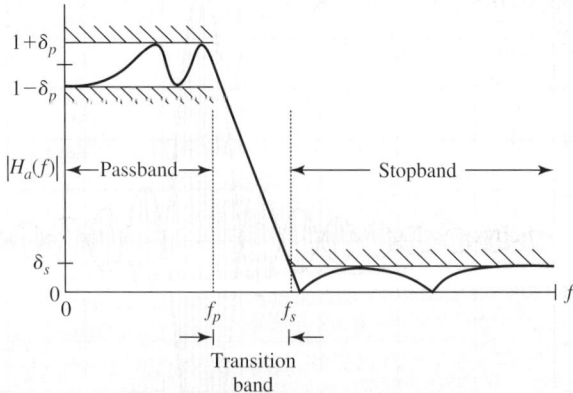

Figure 2.40 Typical magnitude specification of an LP filter.

Now we consider three design approaches to achieve the specifications described in Figure 2.40. These include

1. Butterworth approximation
2. Chebyshev approximation
3. Elliptic approximation

All these methods realize $|H_a(f)|^2$ by an expression of the form

$$|H_a(f)|^2 = \frac{1}{1 + \varepsilon^2 C^2(f)} \tag{2.157}$$

where $C(f)$ is called the **characteristic function,** which is unique to the design approach selected.

Butterworth Approximation

The frequency response of the Butterworth filter is maximally flat (i.e., it has no ripples) in the passband and rolls off toward zero in the stopband. For Butterworth filters,

$$C(f) = (f/f_c)^N \tag{2.158}$$

$$\varepsilon = 1$$

The magnitude-squared response of the Butterworth filter is given by

$$|H_a(f)|^2 = \frac{1}{1 + (f/f_c)^{2N}} \tag{2.159}$$

where f_c is the 3-dB cutoff frequency. Note that as the filter order $N \rightarrow \infty$, $|H_a(f)|$ approaches the ideal brick wall characteristic. That is, the passband and the stopband magnitude responses approach the ideal characteristic with a corresponding decrease in the transition band. Butterworth filters have a monotonically decreasing magnitude response with f.

Chebyshev Approximation

Chebyshev filters minimize the peak error between the approximation and the ideal brick wall characteristic over the specified frequency range of the filter. In fact, the magnitude error is equiripple in the passband. For Chebyshev filters,

$$C(f) = T_N(f/f_p) \tag{2.160}$$

where $T_N(x)$ is a Chebyshev polynomial of order N given by the recursion relation

$$T_n(x) = 2xT_{n-1}(x) - T_{n-2}(x), n \geq 2 \tag{2.161}$$

and

$$T_1(x) = x, \quad T_0(x) = 0 \tag{2.162}$$

The parameter ε specifies peak ripple in the passband. For a Chebyshev filter of fixed order N, there is a trade-off between the ripple and passband width. If one wants a small ripple, then the passband must be narrow. If both a small ripple and a wide passband are required, then a sufficiently large filter order N must be chosen. For a given filter order N, a Chebyshev design provides a sharper transition roll-off than the Butterworth filter. Like the Butterworth, the Chebyshev filter stopband roll-off is monotonic.

Elliptic Approximation

The magnitude-squared response of the Elliptic or Cauer filter of order N is given by

$$|H_a(f)|^2 = \frac{1}{1 + \varepsilon^2 R_N^2(f/f_p)} \tag{2.163}$$

where $R_N(x)$ is an elliptic polynomial of order N and ε determines passband ripple. Although an Elliptic filter achieves faster roll-off than either Butterworth or Chebyshev varieties, it introduces ripple in both the passband and the stopband. Also, the Elliptic filter roll-off is not monotonic, eventually reaching an attenuation limit, called the stopband floor.

Figure 2.41 displays the magnitude response of a sixth-order Elliptic filter designed to achieve 2-dB ripple in the passband ($f_p = 2$ kHz) and a 50-dB stopband floor ($f_s = 2.5$ kHz). For comparison, the magnitude responses of the same-order Butterworth and Chebyshev designs are plotted as well. The Elliptic filter has a predictably sharper roll-off characteristic than the other two approximations. However, the faster roll-off in the transition band is accompanied with a nonlinear phase response characteristic as well.

2.8.3　Analog Filter Design Using MATLAB

The **Signal Processing Toolbox** in MATLAB includes a large number of built-in functions to develop analog filter transfer functions for meeting given frequency response specifications. The design procedure consists of two steps:

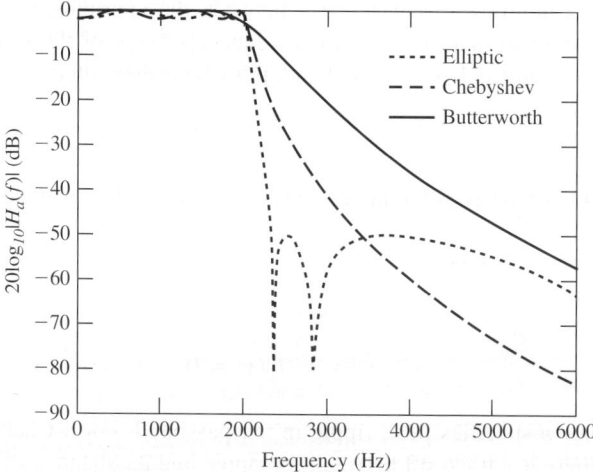

Figure 2.41 Comparison of the frequency responses of three types of analog LP filters.

1. Estimate the order of the filter $H_a(s)$ using any one of the magnitude approximation techniques, that is, Butterworth, Chebyshev, and Elliptic approximations. Specifically, the following M-file functions are available:

```
[N,Wn]  =  buttord(Wp,Ws,Rp,Rs,'s')
[N,Wn]  =  cheb1ord(Wp,Ws,Rp,Rs,'s')
[N,Wn]  =  ellipord(Wp,Ws,Rp,Rs,'s')
```

where Wp and Ws, respectively, are passband and stopband edge frequencies in radians/sec with Wp < Ws for a LP filter. The other two parameters, Rp and Rs, are the passband ripple and the minimum stopband attenuation in dB, respectively. The outputs of these functions are the filter order N and the frequency scaling factor Wn. To meet the specified response specifications, Wn is a 3-dB angular cutoff frequency in the case of Butterworth design, whereas it is an angular passband edge frequency for Chebyshev and Elliptic filters.

2. Design the LP analog filter $H_a(s)$ using any of the following M-files corresponding to the approximation approach selected:

```
[b,a]  =  butter(N,Wn,'s')
[b,a]  =  cheby1(N,Rp,Wn,'s')
[b,a]  =  ellip(N,Rp,Rs,Wn,'s')
```

The output data files of these functions are the length $N + 1$ column vectors b and a providing, respectively, the numerator and denominator coefficients in descending powers of s. The form of the transfer function obtained is given by

$$H_a(s) = \frac{B(s)}{A(s)} = \frac{b(1)s^N + b(2)s^{N-1} + \ldots + b(N)s + b(N+1)}{a(1)s^N + a(2)s^{N-1} + \ldots + a(N)s + a(N+1)} \quad (2.164)$$

After these coefficients have been calculated, the frequency response can be computed using the M-file function freqs(b,a,w), where w is a specified set of angular frequencies (radians/sec). The function freqs(b,a,w) generates a complex vector of frequency response samples $H_a(\omega)$ from which magnitude or phase response samples of the filter can be readily computed.

Example 2.34

Design and plot the gain response of an analog Elliptic LP filter with the following specifications:

- Passband frequency $f_p = 800$ Hz
- Stopband frequency $f_s = 1000$ Hz
- Maximum passband ripple $R_p = 1$ dB
- Minimum stopband ripple $R_s = 40$ dB

Solution

To determine the order of the Elliptic filter meeting the specifications, we use the command [N,Wn] = ellipord(Wp,Ws,Rp,Rs,'s') with Wp = $2\pi(800)$, Ws = $2\pi(1000)$, Rp = 1, Rs = 40. The outputs generated are N = 5 and Wn = $2\pi(800)$. Next we design the filter using the command [b,a] = ellip(N,Rp,Rs,Wn,'s'). Figure 2.42 displays the sample MATLAB code for this example. The magnitude response of the desired filter of order N = 5 is shown in Figure 2.43.

```
% Program to Design Elliptic Low-pass Filter
%
% Read in passband edge frequency,stopband edge frequency
% passband ripple in dB and minimum stopband
% attenuation in dB
Fp = input('Fp =Passband edge frequency in Hz = ');
Fs = input('Fs =Stopband edge frequency in Hz = ');
Rp = input('Passband ripple in dB = ');
Rs = input('Minimum stopband attenuation in dB = ');
Wp=2*pi*Fp
Ws=2*pi*Fs
%Determine the order of Elliptic filter
[N,Wn] = ellipord(Wp,Ws,Rp,Rs,'s')
%Determine the coefficients of the transfer function
[num,den] = ellip(N,Rp,Rs,Wn,'s');
% Compute and plot the frequency response
omega = [0: 20: 6*Fp*pi];
h = freqs(num,den,omega);
plot (omega/(2*pi),20*log10(abs(h)));
grid on;
title('Magnitude Response of Elliptic LP Filter');
axis([0 3*Fp -80 5])
xlabel('Frequency, Hz');
ylabel('Magnitude Response(dB)');
```

Figure 2.42 MATLAB m-file to design LP Elliptic filter.

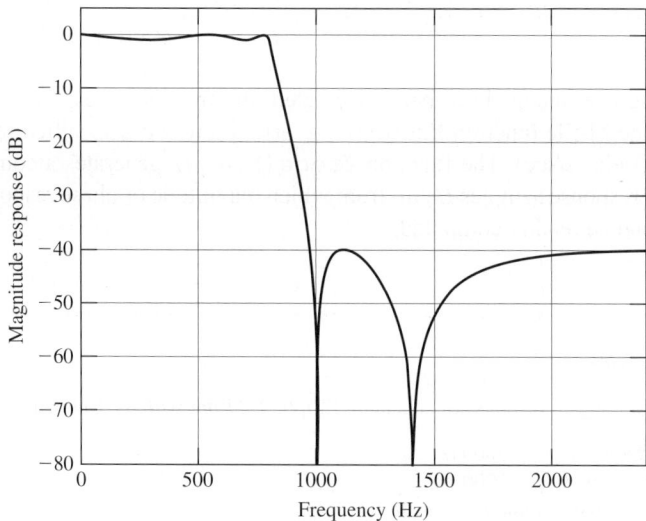

Figure 2.43 Magnitude response of the LP Elliptic filter.

For designing HP, BP, and BS digital filters, the order of the three types of filters can be estimated using the same MATLAB functions as before but with the following differences: For HP filters, Wp > Ws. For BP and BS digital filters, Wp and Ws are vectors of length 2 specifying the transition bandedges. For example, Wp = [wp1 wp2] with wp1<w<wp2. wp1 and wp2 are, respectively, the lower and upper passband edge frequencies. As before, the parameters Rp and Rs are the passband ripple and the minimum stopband attenuation in dB, respectively. The outputs of these functions are the filter order N

and the frequency scaling factor `Wn`. `Wn` is a vector of length 2 for bandpass and bandstop filters. `N` and `Wn` are used as input to the following MATLAB functions for filter design:

```
[b,a] = butter(N,Wn,'filtertype','s')
[b,a] = cheby1(N,Rp,Wn,'filtertype','s')
[b,a] = ellip(N,Rp,Rs,Wn,'filtertype','s')
```

For example, the command

```
[b,a] = butter(N,Wn,'s')
```

is used to design a BP Butterworth filter of order 2N with Wn being a two-element vector. By default, if Wn is a two-element vector, a BP or BS filter is assumed.

For designing high-pass (HP) digital filters, the string `'filtertype'` is `'high'` in all of the preceding commands with Wn being a scalar. For example, the command

```
[b,a] = cheby1(N,Rp,Wn,'high','s')
```

is used to design a HP Chebyshev filter of order N.

Similarly, the string "filtertype" is `'stop'` in all of the preceding commands for designing BS digital filters. For example, the command

```
[b,a] = ellip(N,Rp,Rs,Wn,'stop','s')
```

is used to design a BS Elliptic filter of order 2N with `Wn` being a two-element vector.

Example 2.35

Design and plot the gain response of an Elliptic BP filter with the following specifications:

- Passband edge frequencies $[f_{p1}, f_{p2}] = [4000, 7000]$ Hz
- Stopband edge frequencies $[f_{s1}, f_{s2}] = [3000, 8000]$ Hz
- Maximum passband ripple $R_p = 1$ dB
- Minimum stopband ripple $R_s = 40$ dB

```
% Program to Design Elliptic Bandpass Filter
%
% Read in passband edge frequency,stopband edge frequency
% passband ripple in dB and minimum stopband
% attenuation in dB
Fp = input('Fp =Passband edge frequencies in Hz = ');
Fs = input('Fs =Stopband edge frequencies in Hz = ');
Rp = input('Passband ripple in dB = ');
Rs = input('Minimum stopband attenuation in dB = ');
Wp=2*pi*Fp
Ws=2*pi*Fs
%Determine the order of Elliptic filter
[N,Wn] = ellipord(Wp,Ws,Rp,Rs,'s')
%Determine the coefficients of the transfer function
[num,den] = ellip(N,Rp,Rs,Wn,'s');
% Compute and plot the frequency response
omega = [0: 200: 4*Fp(2)*pi];
h = freqs(num,den,omega);
plot (omega/(2*pi),20*log10(abs(h)));
grid on;
title('Magnitude Response of Elliptic Bandpass Filter');
axis([0 2*Fp(2) -80 5]);
xlabel('Frequency, Hz');
ylabel('Magnitude Response(dB)');
```

Figure 2.44 MATLAB m-file to design BP Elliptic filter.

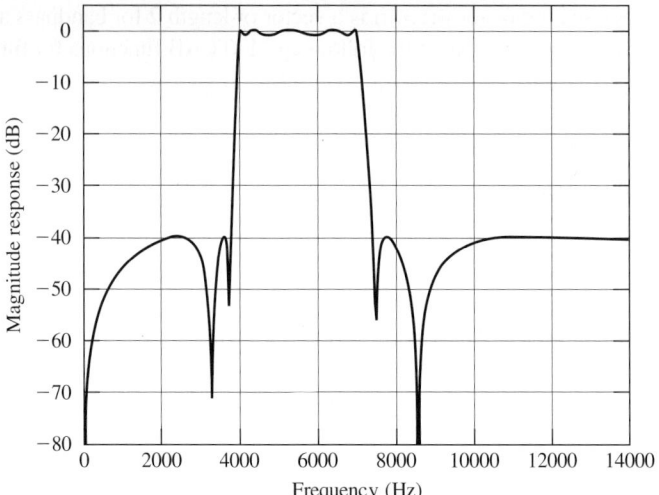

Figure 2.45 Magnitude response of the BP Elliptic filter.

To determine the order of the Elliptic filter meeting the specifications, we use the command $[\mathtt{N},\mathtt{Wn}]$ $= \mathtt{ellipord}(\mathtt{Wp},\mathtt{Ws},\mathtt{Rp},\mathtt{Rs},\mathtt{'s'})$ with $\mathtt{Wp} = 2\pi[4000, 7000]$, $\mathtt{Ws} = 2\pi[3000, 8000]$, $\mathtt{Rp} = 1$, $\mathtt{Rs} = 40$. Next we design the filter using the command $[\mathtt{b},\mathtt{a}] = \mathtt{ellip}(\mathtt{N},\mathtt{Rp},\mathtt{Rs},\mathtt{Wn},\mathtt{'s'})$. Figure 2.44 displays the sample MATLAB code for this example. The magnitude response of the desired filter of order $\mathtt{N} = 10$ is shown in Figure 2.45.

2.9   POWER SPECTRAL DENSITY

In the design of communication systems, we are interested in power distribution of a power signal in the frequency domain. Recall from Section 2.1 that the normalized average power of a signal $x(t)$ was defined in (2.20) as

$$P_x = \lim_{T \to \infty} \frac{1}{T} \int_{-T/2}^{T/2} |x(t)|^2 dt \qquad (2.20)$$

Note that the average power defined here is a **time-average mean-square value** to distinguish it from statistical mean-square value to be discussed in Chapter 6. The problem in dealing with power signals in the frequency domain is that their Fourier transform may not exist as they have infinite energy. To overcome this problem, we define a new function $x_T(t)$ by truncating $x(t)$ outside the interval $|t| > T/2$.

$$x_T(t) = \begin{cases} x(t), & -T/2 \le t \le T/2 \\ 0, & \text{otherwise} \end{cases} \qquad (2.165)$$

$x_T(t)$ has finite energy as long as T is finite. We can now write an expression for the energy of $x_T(t)$ by using Parseval's relation (2.89) as follows:

$$E_{x_T} = \int_{-\infty}^{\infty} |x_T(t)|^2 dt = \int_{-\infty}^{\infty} |X_T(f)|^2 df \qquad (2.166)$$

where

$$x_T(t) \xleftrightarrow{\mathfrak{F}} X_T(f)$$

Because

$$\int_{-\infty}^{\infty} |x_T(t)|^2 dt = \int_{-T/2}^{T/2} |x(t)|^2 dt \qquad (2.167)$$

we can write

$$\frac{1}{T} \int_{-T/2}^{T/2} |x(t)|^2 dt = \int_{-\infty}^{\infty} \frac{|X_T(f)|^2}{T} df \qquad (2.168)$$

The normalized average power can now be expressed by substituting (2.168) into (2.20) as

$$P_x = \lim_{T \to \infty} \int_{-\infty}^{\infty} \frac{|X_T(f)|^2}{T} df \qquad (2.169)$$

Because $x(t)$ is a power signal, the integral on the right-hand side of (2.169) exists in the limit as $T \to \infty$. Therefore, we can change the order of integration and limit yielding

$$P_x = \lim_{T \to \infty} \int_{-\infty}^{\infty} \frac{|X_T(f)|^2}{T} df = \int_{-\infty}^{\infty} \lim_{T \to \infty} \frac{|X_T(f)|^2}{T} df \qquad (2.170)$$

The **power spectral density (PSD)** $\mathcal{G}_x(f)$ of power signal $x(t)$ is defined as

$$\mathcal{G}_x(f) \triangleq \lim_{T \to \infty} \frac{|X_T(f)|^2}{T} \qquad (2.171)$$

This allows us to express the normalized average power as

$$P_x = \int_{-\infty}^{\infty} \mathcal{G}_x(f) df \qquad (2.172)$$

From (2.172), it is obvious $\mathcal{G}_x(f_o)\Delta f$ represents the power contained in a spectral band of Δf Hz centered at frequency f_o. Thus $\mathcal{G}_x(f)$ may be interpreted as the power contained in spectral components of $x(t)$ centered at frequency f per Hz of bandwidth. It is specified in units of W/Hz.

Power Spectral Density of a Periodic Signal

For a periodic signal $x_p(t)$, the normalized average power is given from (2.60) as

$$P_x = \sum_{n=-\infty}^{\infty} |C_n|^2$$

Because $|C_n|^2$ is power contained in the spectral component at $f = nf_o$, the PSD $\mathcal{G}_x(f)$ of a periodic signal can be expressed as

$$\mathcal{G}_x(f) = \sum_{n=-\infty}^{\infty} |C_n|^2 \delta(f - nf_o) \qquad (2.173)$$

Substituting (2.91) into (2.173) yields

$$\mathcal{G}_x(f) = \sum_{n=-\infty}^{\infty} |X_p(nf_o)|^2 \delta(f - nf_o) \tag{2.174}$$

2.9.1 Time-Average Autocorrelation Function

The **time-average autocorrelation function** of a power signal $x(t)$ is defined as

$$\mathcal{R}_x(\tau) = \lim_{T \to \infty} \frac{1}{T} \int_{-T/2}^{T/2} x(t)x(t - \tau)dt \tag{2.175}$$

The normalized average power P_x of $x(t)$ is related to $\mathcal{R}_x(\tau)$ by

$$P_x = \lim_{T \to \infty} \frac{1}{T} \int_{-T/2}^{T/2} |x(t)|^2 dt = \mathcal{R}_x(0) \tag{2.176}$$

It can be shown that the PSD of a power signal $x(t)$ is the Fourier transform of its time-average autocorrelation function.

$$\mathcal{G}_x(f) \overset{\mathfrak{I}}{\longleftrightarrow} \mathcal{R}_x(\tau) \tag{2.177}$$

Example 2.36

Determine the time-average autocorrelation function and PSD of the sinusoidal signal $x(t) = A\cos(2\pi f_o t + \phi)$

Solution

The time-average autocorrelation function is obtained using the definition (2.175) as

$$\mathcal{R}_x(\tau) = \lim_{T \to \infty} \frac{1}{T} \int_{-T/2}^{T/2} x(t)x(t - \tau)dt$$

$$= \lim_{T \to \infty} \frac{1}{T} \int_{-T/2}^{T/2} A^2 \cos(2\pi f_o t + \phi)\cos[2\pi f_o(t - \tau) + \phi]dt$$

$$= \frac{A^2}{2}\cos(2\pi f_o\tau) + \lim_{T \to \infty} \frac{1}{T} \int_{-T/2}^{T/2} \cos[4\pi f_o t - 2\pi f_o\tau + 2\phi]dt$$

The second integral is zero yielding

$$\mathcal{R}_x(\tau) = \frac{A^2}{2}\cos(2\pi f_o\tau) \tag{2.178}$$

Because the PSD of a power signal $x(t)$ is the Fourier transform of its time-average autocorrelation function, we obtain using Table 2.2

$$\mathcal{G}_x(f) = \Im\{\mathcal{R}_x(\tau)\} = \Im\left\{\frac{A^2}{2}\cos(2\pi f_o\tau)\right\} = \frac{A^2}{4}[\delta(f - f_o) + \delta(f + f_o)]$$

The normalized average power may be obtained by using (2.172) as

$$P_x = \int_{-\infty}^{\infty}\mathcal{G}_x(f)df = \int_{-\infty}^{\infty}\frac{A^2}{4}[\delta(f - f_o) + \delta(f + f_o)]df = \frac{A^2}{2}$$

2.9.2   Relationship Between Input and Output Power Spectral Densities

For a linear system with transfer function $H(f)$, the output $y(t)$ of the system in response to the input signal $x(t)$ is given in the frequency domain from (2.119) as

$$Y(f) = X(f)H(f) \tag{2.119}$$

The PSD of a power signal $y(t)$ can be written using (2.169) as

$$\mathcal{G}_y(f) = \lim_{T\to\infty}\frac{|Y_T(f)|^2}{T} \tag{2.179}$$

The relationship in the frequency domain between the truncated versions of $y(t)$ and $x(t)$ is obtained using (2.119) as

$$Y_T(f) = X_T(f)H(f) \tag{2.180}$$

Substituting (2.180) into (2.179) yields

$$\mathcal{G}_y(f) = \lim_{T\to\infty}\frac{|X_T(f)H(f)|^2}{T} = |H(f)|^2\lim_{T\to\infty}\frac{|X_T(f)|^2}{T} = |H(f)|^2\mathcal{G}_x(f) \tag{2.181}$$

Equation (2.181) states that the output signal PSD in an LTI system depends on the magnitude of $H(f)$ and is given by $|H(f)|^2$ times the input PSD.

Example 2.37

The periodic pulse train in Example 2.24 is input to a fourth order Butterworth LPF with 3-dB cutoff frequency $f_c = 4$ MHz. Assume $T_o = 1$ μsec and $\tau/T_o = 0.25$. Plot the output PSD.

Solution

The PSD $\mathcal{G}_x(f)$ of periodic pulse train is given by substituting (2.59) into (2.173).

$$\mathcal{G}_x(f) = \left(\frac{\tau}{T_o}\right)^2\sum_{n=-\infty}^{\infty}\left|\text{sinc}\left(\frac{n\tau}{T_o}\right)\right|^2\delta(f - nf_o) = \frac{1}{16}\sum_{n=-\infty}^{\infty}|\text{sinc}(n/4)|^2\delta(f - nf_o) \tag{2.182}$$

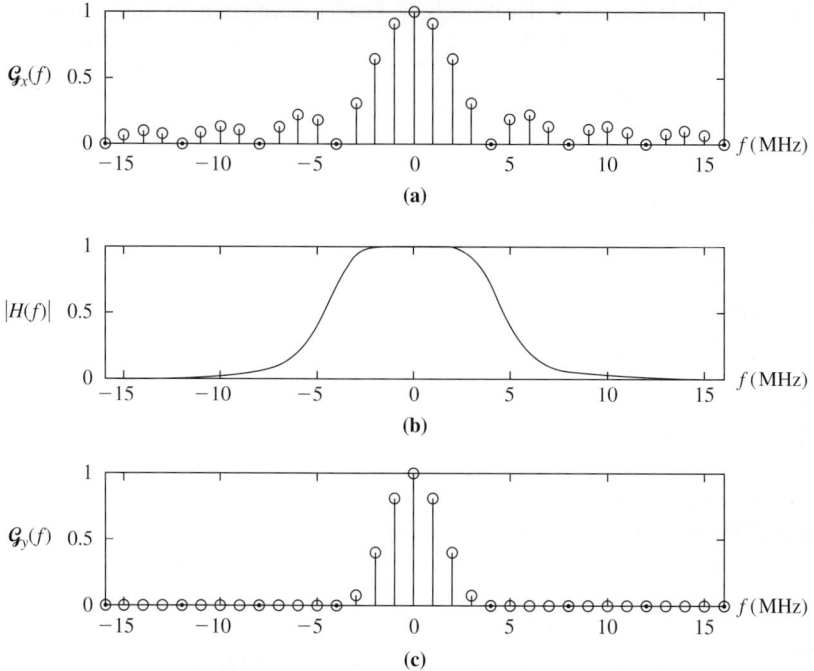

Figure 2.46 Input and output spectral densities.

Substituting (2.182) and (2.181) yields the output PSD $\mathcal{G}_y(f)$ as

$$\mathcal{G}_y(f) = |H(f)|^2 \mathcal{G}_x(f) = \frac{1}{16}|H(f)|^2 \sum_{n=-\infty}^{\infty} |\text{sinc}(n/4)|^2 \delta(f - nf_o)$$

$$= \frac{1}{16} \sum_{n=-\infty}^{\infty} |H(nf_o)|^2 |\text{sinc}(n/4)|^2 \delta(f - nf_o) \qquad (2.183)$$

Figure 2.46(a) displays the PSD $\mathcal{G}_x(f)$ of the periodic pulse train. The magnitude response of the fourth order Butterworth LPF with 3-dB cutoff frequency $f_c = 4$ MHz is illustrated in Figure 2.46(b). The output PSD $\mathcal{G}_y(f)$ calculated using (2.183) is shown in Figure 2.46(c).

2.10 FREQUENCY RESPONSE CHARACTERISTICS OF TRANSMISSION MEDIA

We consider transmission of signals through widely used wired media such as TWP and coaxial cables.

2.10.1 Twisted Wire Pairs

To obtain frequency domain characterization of twisted wire pairs (TWPs) and coaxial cables, we use transmission line theory concepts. The distributed circuit model of the transmission line consists of a cascade of many transmission line segments of the type shown in Figure 2.47. Each transmission line segment is characterized by an equivalent circuit with lumped-circuit elements R, L, C, and G where

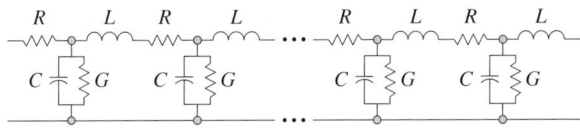

Figure 2.47 Transmission line model of a TWP.

- R = Series resistance per meter
- L = Series inductance per meter
- C = Shunt capacitance per meter
- G = Shunt conductance per meter

The line is **lossless** if $R = G = 0$. R depends on frequency and has the form $R(f) \approx c_o \sqrt{2\pi f}$ at high frequencies because of the **skin effect.** This refers to the tendency of high frequencies in a signal to travel near the surface of a conductor in a layer some tens of microns thick.

If voltage $x_i(t)$ is applied at the input to the transmission line at time $t = 0$, the voltage along the line declines exponentially with distance. At time t its value is given by

$$x(z, t) = x_i(t)e^{-\gamma z} \qquad (2.184)$$

where z is the distance in meters. γ is called the **propagation constant** of the TWP. It determines the variation of voltage along the line. As a special case, if the input is a complex sinusoidal signal $x_i(t) = Ae^{j2\pi ft}$ of frequency f Hz, the voltage along the line at distance z is

$$x(z, t) = Ae^{j2\pi ft}e^{-\gamma z} \quad \text{at time } t \qquad (2.185)$$

The propagation constant is a complex function of frequency and is given in terms the lumped-circuit model element values as

$$\gamma(f) = \alpha(f) + j\beta(f) = \sqrt{(R + j2\pi fL)(G + j2\pi fC)} \qquad (2.186)$$

where α = attenuation coefficient (= 0 for lossless line), and β = phase shift coefficient = $2\pi/\lambda$ (radians/meter). Substituting (2.186) into (2.185) yields

$$x(z, t) = Ae^{-[\alpha(f)+j\beta(f)]z}e^{j2\pi ft} = Ae^{-\alpha(f)z}e^{j[2\pi ft-\beta(f)z]} \qquad (2.187)$$

Equation (2.187) states that the entering phasor signal's magnitude decays along the line as $e^{-\alpha(f)z}$. Further, a phase shift of $-\beta(f)z$ radians is introduced in the input phasor signal. Another important parameter of the transmission line is its **characteristic impedance,** Z_o. It is defined as the input impedance of an infinite line or that of a finite line terminated with a load impedance, $Z_L = Z_o$. It is given in terms the lumped-circuit model element values as

$$Z_o = \sqrt{\frac{R + j2\pi fL}{G + j2\pi fC}} \qquad (2.188)$$

For a transmission line terminated with its characteristic impedance, the transfer function $H_{TWP}(f, \ell)$ is given by

$$H_{TWP}(f, \ell) = e^{-\gamma(f)\ell} \qquad (2.189)$$

where ℓ is line length. The **attenuation** or **insertion loss** is defined as the reduction or loss in signal power as it is transferred across the transmission medium. It is determined by the magnitude of its transfer function, which is given by

$$|H_{TWP}(f, \ell)| = e^{-\alpha(f)\ell} \tag{2.190}$$

where $\alpha(f)$ = real part of the propagation constant in (2.186). The attenuation of a TWP is usually expressed in dB as

$$\text{Insertion Loss} = -20\log_{10}|H_{TWP}(f, \ell)| = -20\log_{10}e^{-\alpha(f)\ell} = 8.686\alpha(f)\ell \text{ dB} \tag{2.191}$$

The parameter $\alpha(f)$ has the form

$$\alpha(f) = c_1\sqrt{f} + c_2 f \tag{2.192}$$

where f is in Hz. For $f \geq 300$ kHz, $\alpha(f) \approx c_1\sqrt{f}$ Substituting in (2.191) allows us to write the following simplified expression for the attenuation of a TWP:

$$\text{Insertion Loss} = 8.686c_1\sqrt{f}\ell \text{ dB}, \ f \geq 300 \text{ kHz} \tag{2.193}$$

where f and ℓ are specified in Hz and miles, respectively. Attenuation of the TWP increases both with the length and the frequency of operation. The increase in attenuation is linear with length and is proportional to $\sqrt{f}$ at high frequencies because of the skin effect. The parameters c_1 and c_2 for popular TWP cables are listed in Table 2.4.

Figure 2.48 shows insertion losses that are produced using the parameters from Table 2.4 for a length of 1 mile. The attenuation for a TWP, measured in dB/mile, can range from a few dB/mile at 1 kHz to 15 to 30 dB/mile at 500 kHz, depending on the AWG of the wire. Because the insertion loss of a TWP increases linearly with distance, the bandwidth decreases correspondingly with the length of TWP drop.

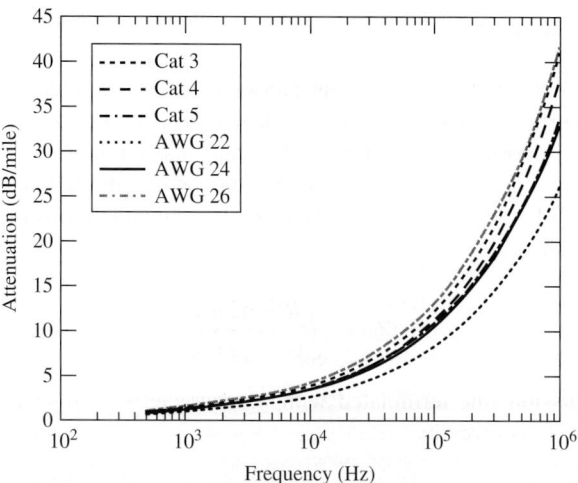

Figure 2.48 Attenuation characteristics of TWP.

Table 2.4 c_1 and c_2 **Parameters for Popular TWP Cables**

Type	c_1	c_2
Cat 3	4.31×10^{-3}	4.26×10^{-7}
Cat 4	3.89×10^{-3}	4.82×10^{-7}
Cat 5	3.83×10^{-3}	2.41×10^{-8}
AWG 26	4.8×10^{-3}	-1.71×10^{-8}
AWG 24	3.8×10^{-3}	-0.54×10^{-8}
AWG 22	3.0×10^{-3}	0.035×10^{-8}

Example 2.38

The element values in the lumped-circuit model of 24-AWG TWP are given as

$C = 0.05 \ \mu\text{F/km}$
$L = 0.673 \ \text{mH/km}$
$R = 180 \ \text{ohms/km}$
$G = 0$

In telephone network, subscriber loops are limited to 18,000 feet ($\sim$ 5.45 km). Determine the output of 6-km TWP for an input sinusoidal signal $x(t) = 5\cos(6800\pi t)$.

Solution

Substituting these element values in (2.186) yields

$$\gamma(f)|_{f=3.4 \text{ kHz}} = \sqrt{(180 + j6.8\pi \times 0.673)(0 + j6.8\pi \times 0.05 \times 10^{-3})}$$

$$= 0.2979 + j0.3227 = 0.4392 \angle 47.3°$$

Therefore, α at 3.4 kHz = 0.2979 km^{-1}. The attenuation at f = 3.4 kHz is obtained by substituting α into (2.191) as $8.686 \times 0.2979 \approx 2.6$ dB/km.

The transfer function value for 6-km TWP loop at 3.4 kHz is given from (2.189) as

$$H_{TWP}(f)|_{f=3.4 \text{ kHz}} = e^{-6 \times \gamma(f)|_{f=3.4 \times 10^3}} = e^{-(0.2979 + j0.3227) \times 6}$$

$$= -0.0598 - j0.1563 = 0.1674 \angle -110.9°$$

Substituting into (2.116), the output of 6-km TWP loop for a sinusoidal input $x(t) = 5\cos(6800\pi t)$ can be written as

$$y(t) = |H_{TWP}(f)|_{f=3.4 \text{ kHz}} \times 5\cos[6800\pi t + \angle H_{TWP}(f)|_{f=3.4 \text{ kHz}}]$$

$$= 5 \times 0.1674\cos(6800\pi t - 110.9°) = 0.837\cos(6800\pi t - 110.9°)$$

Example 2.39

If the maximum run length using Category (Cat) 5 TWP from the desktop to the nearest wiring closet is restricted to 100 feet, what is the expected power level at the closet assuming the desktop network interface launches 250 mW at 100 MHz?

Solution

The attenuation of a Cat 5 TWP is given by

Insertion Loss $= 8.686 \times 3.83 \times 10^{-3} \times \sqrt{10^8}$ dB/mile $= 8.686 \times 38.3 = 332.67$ dB/mile

Therefore, loss for $\ell = 100$ foot drop of Cat 5 TWP cable $= 332.67 \times 100/5000 = 6.65$ dB.

Power launched by the desktop $= 250$ m$W = 10\log_{10}(250) = 24$ dBm

Power level at the wiring closet $=$ Power launched by the desktop $-$ loss $= 24 - 6.65 = 17.35$ dBm $= 10^{17.35/10} = 54$ mW

2.10.2   Coaxial Cable

The insertion loss of coaxial cables can be modeled by the following:

$$\text{Insertion Loss} = 20\log_{10}|H_{coax}(f, \ell)| = (k_1\sqrt{f} + k_2 f)\ell \ \ \text{dB} \qquad (2.194)$$

where

$f =$ frequency in MHz

$\ell =$ cable length in kft

For high frequencies, $k_1\sqrt{f}$ term in (2.194) dominates. This allows us to write the following simplified expression for the attenuation of a coaxial cable:

$$\text{Insertion Loss} = k_1\sqrt{f}\,\ell \ \text{dB}, f \geq 300 \ \text{kHz} \qquad (2.195)$$

where f and ℓ are specified in MHz and kft, respectively. Attenuation of the coaxial cable also increases both with frequency and the cable length. The increase in attenuation is linear with length and proportional to $\sqrt{f}$ at high frequencies because of the skin effect. The parameters k_1 and k_2 characterize the coaxial cable type; k_1 basically indicates the amount of conductor loss while k_2 indicates the amount of dielectric loss.

Table 2.5 k_1 and k_2 Parameters for Popular Coaxial Cables

	500-F	625-F	RG-6	RG-59
k_1	0.69	0.6058	2.1144	2.7155
k_2	3.7×10^{-3}	1.6×10^{-3}	2.1×10^{-3}	1.5×10^{-3}

The parameters for different types of cables are listed in Table 2.5.

RG-59 and RG-6 cables are used in the distribution segment of a CATV network for subscriber drops. 500-F and 625-F are examples of cables that originate from a fiber distribution node to form the trunk and feeder portion of the CATV network. Figure 2.49 displays the attenuation characteristics of both cable types. By comparing the results in Figure 2.49 with those in Figure 2.48, it can be seen that coaxial cables can provide much larger frequency range of operation (up to 1 GHz) than twisted wire pair (a few MHz). Today's **cable television (CATV)** systems use a frequency range of 1 GHz.

2.11   FOURIER TRANSFORMS FOR DISCRETE-TIME SIGNALS

For discrete-time signals $x[n]$, two alternative frequency domain representations are extremely useful.

- Discrete-time Fourier transform (DTFT)
- Discrete Fourier transform (DFT)

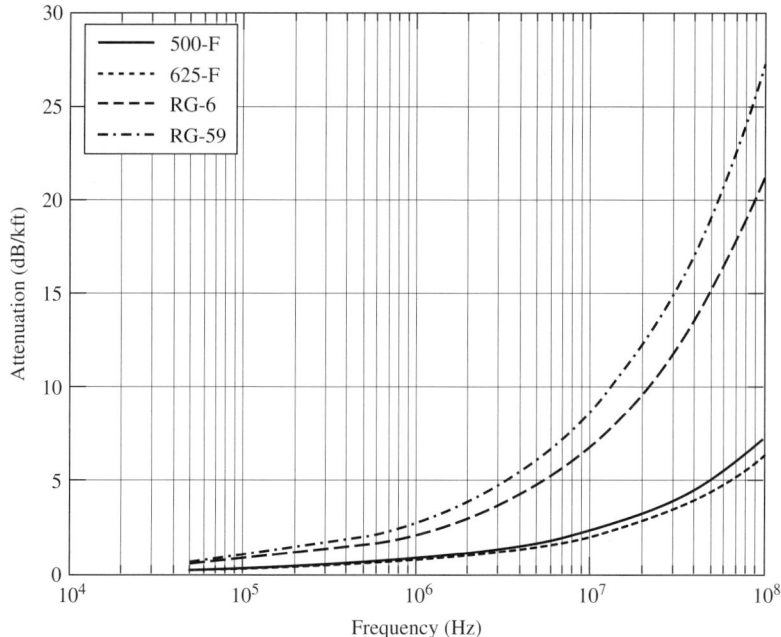

Figure 2.49 Attenuation characteristics of coaxial cables.

The DTFT $X(e^{j\hat{\omega}})$ of a sequence $x[n]$, obtained by sampling an analog signal $x(t)$ at the rate $f_s = 1/T_s$ samples/sec, is defined by

$$X(e^{j\hat{\omega}}) = \sum_{n=-\infty}^{\infty} x[n]e^{-j\hat{\omega}n} \tag{2.196}$$

where $\hat{\omega}$ is normalized angular frequency $\hat{\omega} = 2\pi f T_s$ in radians/sample. $X(e^{j\hat{\omega}})$ is, in general, a complex and *continuous* function of the real variable $\hat{\omega}$ and can be written as

$$X(e^{j\hat{\omega}}) = |X(e^{j\hat{\omega}})|e^{j \measuredangle X(e^{j\hat{\omega}})} \tag{2.197}$$

where both magnitude $|X(e^{j\hat{\omega}})|$ and phase $\measuredangle X(e^{j\hat{\omega}})$ are real functions of $\hat{\omega}$. The DTFT $X(e^{j\hat{\omega}})$ of a sequence $x[n]$ is a periodic function of $\hat{\omega}$ with period 2π.

$$X\left[e^{j(\hat{\omega}+2\pi k)}\right] = \sum_{n=-\infty}^{\infty} x[n]e^{-j(\hat{\omega}+2\pi k)n} = \sum_{n=-\infty}^{\infty} x[n]e^{-j\hat{\omega}n} = X(e^{j\hat{\omega}}) \tag{2.198}$$

Figure 2.50 displays the relationship between the FT of a continuous signal $x(t)$ and its sampled version $x[n]$. The values of $\hat{\omega} = \pm\pi$ correspond to half the sampling rate, that is, $f_s/2$.

In the case of a finite-length sequence $x[n]$, $0 \le n \le N - 1$, there is a simpler frequency domain representation in terms of its DFT. The DFT $X[k]$ of a sequence $x[n]$ is defined by

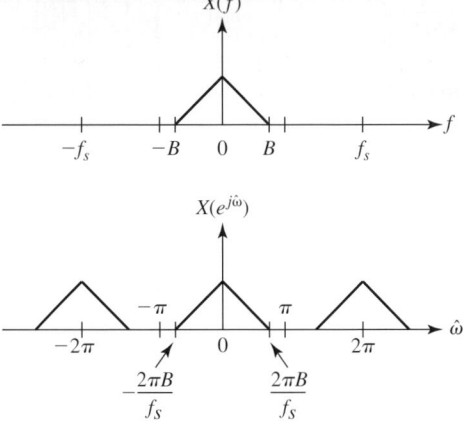

Figure 2.50 Relationship between FT and DTFT of a sampled signal.

$$X[k] = \sum_{n=0}^{N-1} x[n] e^{-j2\pi kn/N}, \quad k = 0, 1, \ldots, N-1 \tag{2.199}$$

Note that DFT is applicable *only* to a finite-length sequence. The length of the DFT sequence $X[k]$ is also N. $X[k]$ is, therefore, referred to as **N-point** DFT of $x[n]$. Because

$$X[k] = X(e^{j\hat{\omega}})|_{\hat{\omega} = 2\pi k/N}, \tag{2.200}$$

the DFT $X[k]$ can be viewed as *uniformly spaced* samples of the corresponding DTFT $X(e^{j\hat{\omega}})$ over $[0, 2\pi]$ at frequencies $\hat{\omega}_k = \dfrac{2\pi k}{N}, k = 0, 1, \ldots, N-1$. It is easy to prove that $X[k]$ is periodic with period N.

$$X[k] = X[k + mN], \quad m \text{ any integer}$$

Because there are N frequency samples in the interval f_s (corresponding to $[0, 2\pi]$ on $\hat{\omega}$ axis), the frequency resolution of DFT is given by

$$\Delta f = \frac{f_s}{N} = \frac{1}{NT_s} = \frac{1}{T} \tag{2.201}$$

where T is the total duration of the signal. Equation (2.201) states that the frequency resolution of DFT is determined by the signal record length. To obtain the original sequence $x[n]$ from the DFT sequence, we use the **inverse DFT (IDFT)** defined by

$$x[n] = \frac{1}{N} \sum_{k=0}^{N-1} X[k] e^{+j2\pi kn/N}, \quad n = 0, 1, \ldots, N-1 \tag{2.202}$$

Equations (2.199) and (2.202) form a DFT pair.

The **Fast Fourier transform (FFT)** is an extremely efficient algorithm for computing DFT. The FFT requires that the sequence length N is an integer power of 2. This is usually accomplished by appending zeros on either side of discrete-time sequence $x[n]$.

Zero-padding increases the number of points in the DFT thereby improving the DFT's approximation of the DTFT $X(e^{j\hat\omega})$. In MATLAB, the m-file `fft(x)` is used for computing the *N*-point FFT of a length-*N* sequence $x[n]$. The m-file `ifft(X)` computes the inverse FFT of length-*N* DFT sequence $X[k]$.

Example 2.40

Consider a rectangular pulse of unit amplitude and duration $T = 1$ sec.

a. Sample the pulse at 20 Hz and append zeros on either side to generate a discrete-time sequence $x[n]$ of length 512.
b. Obtain the DFT X[k] of $x[n]$ by using m-file `fft(x)`. Plot `fftshift(X)`.

Solution

The m-file in Figure 2.51(b) computes the FFT as a rectangular pulse of unit amplitude and duration $T = 1$ sec. The sampling rate is chosen so that 20 samples are obtained within the pulse interval to account for the wide bandwidth of the pulse due to its sharp edges. Figure 2.54(a) displays the sampled sequence $x[n]$ and magnitude of the 512-point FFT.

```
% Example_2.41.m
% Matlab script to illustrate the FFT of a rectangular pulse
%

clear all;

% Time axis: Sampling period is 50 milliseconds
delt=1/20
t = -12.5:delt:12.5;
fs=1/delt

% A rectangular pulse of duration 1 second

x = rectpuls (t,1);
subplot (2,1,1);
stem(t,x)
axis([-5 5 0 1.1])
title ('x[n]')
xlabel('Time')

% Fast Fourier Transform of x[n]

X = fft(x,512);

% Compute the magnitude of FFT and center it

XX = abs(fftshift(X(1:512)));
f = fs*(-256:255)/512;
subplot (2,1,2);
stem(f,XX)
axis([-0.5*fs 0.5*fs 0 25])
title('DFT X[k]')
xlabel('Frequency (Hz)')
```

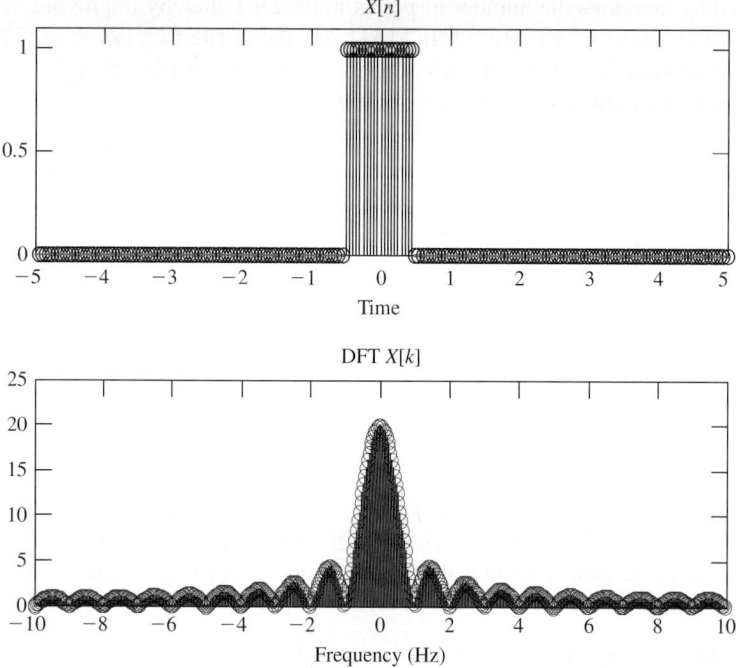

Figure 2.51 (a) Sampled sequence $x[n]$ and magnitude of the 512-point FFT; (b) m-file for computing the FFT of a rectangular pulse.

FINAL REMARKS

In this chapter we reviewed fundamental concepts about signals and their processing by linear systems. Although signals are usually described as functions of time, the frequency domain description was introduced to analyze the signals and linear systems. The Fourier transform serves as a fundamental tool in this context for relating the time-domain and frequency-domain descriptions.

An inverse relationship exists between the time-domain and frequency-domain parameters that characterize signals and systems. An important consequence of this inverse relationship is that the duration–bandwidth product of a signal is constant. Thus, a signal cannot arbitrarily be both duration and bandwidth limited.

The response of linear time-invariant systems to input signals was considered in both time- and frequency-domains. The output signal in general is a distorted version of the input as a result of nonideal magnitude and phase response characteristics of the system. An important signal processing operation in communication systems is that of linear filtering. We studied various ideal filter types and investigated realizable designs using MATLAB.

The transmission characteristics of different transmission media were then studied in the frequency domain. Signal transmission and distortion properties of wired media such as twisted wire pair and coaxial cable were reviewed.

FURTHER READINGS

Signals and systems are covered in the undergraduate texts on the subject [1–4]. References [5] and [6] review the material from the perspective of its relevance in the study of communication systems.

1. Kamen, E., and B. Heck. *Fundamentals of Signals and Systems,* 3rd ed. Upper Saddle River, NJ: Prentice Hall, 2006.

2. McClellan J., R. Schafer, and M. Yoder. *Signal Processing First.* Upper Saddle River, NJ: Prentice Hall, 2003.

3. Lathi, B. *Linear Systems and Signals,* 2nd ed. New York: Oxford University Press, 2004.

4. Oppenheim, A., A. Willsky, and S. Nawab. *Signals and Systems,* 2nd ed. Upper Saddle River, NJ: Prentice Hall, 1996.

5. Ziemer, R., and W. Tranter. *Principles of Communications: Systems, Modulation, and Noise,* 5th ed. New York: John Wiley, 2001.

6. Carlson, B., P. Crilly, and J. Rutledge. *Communication Systems,* 4th ed. New York: McGraw-Hill, 2002.

7. Mitra, S. *Digital Signal Processing: A Computer-Based Approach,* 3rd ed. New York: McGraw-Hill, 2006.

8. MATLAB + Signal Processing Toolbox, Student Version Release 14, available at www.mathworks.com/student.

PROBLEMS

2.1. Consider the signals displayed in Figure P2.1. Show that each of these signals can be expressed as the sum of rectangular $\Pi(t)$ or triangular $\Lambda(t)$ pulses.

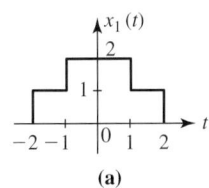

(a)

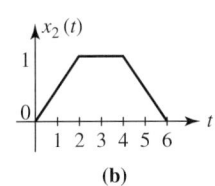

(b)

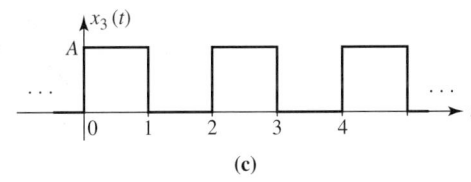

(c)

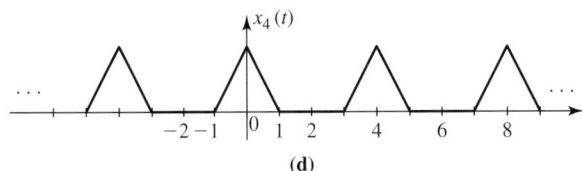

(d)

Figure P2.1

2.2. For the signal $x_2(t)$ in Figure P2.1(b) plot the following signals:

a. $x_2(t - 3)$

b. $x_2(-t)$

c. $x_2(2t)$

d. $x_2(3 - 2t)$

2.3. Plot the following signals:

a. $x_1(t) = 2\Pi(t/2)\cos(6\pi t)$

b. $x_2(t) = 2\left[\dfrac{1}{2} + \dfrac{1}{2}\,\mathrm{sgn}(t)\right]$

c. $x_3(t) = x_2(-t + 2)$

d. $x_4(t) = \mathrm{sinc}(2t)\Pi(t/2)$

2.4. Determine whether the following signals are periodic. For periodic signals, determine the fundamental period.

a. $x_1(t) = \sin(\pi t) + 5\cos(4\pi t/5)$

b. $x_2(t) = e^{j3t} + e^{j9t} + \cos(12t)$

c. $x_3(t) = \sin(2\pi t) + \cos(10t)$

d. $x_4(t) = \cos\left(2\pi t - \dfrac{\pi}{4}\right) + \sin(5\pi t)$

2.5. Classify the following signals as odd or even or neither.

a. $x_1(t) = -4t$

b. $x_2(t) = e^{-|t|}$

c. $x_3(t) = 5\cos(3t)$

d. $x_4(t) = \sin\left(3t - \dfrac{\pi}{2}\right)$

e. $x_5(t) = u(t)$

f. $x_6(t) = \sin(2t) + \cos(2t)$

2.6. Determine whether the following signals are energy or power, or neither and calculate the corresponding energy or power in the signal.

a. $x_1(t) = u(t)$

b. $x_2(t) = 4\cos(2\pi t) + 3\cos(4\pi t)$

c. $x_3(t) = \dfrac{1}{t}$

d. $x_4(t) = e^{-\alpha t}u(t)$

e. $x_5(t) = \Pi(t/3) + \Pi(t)$

f. $x_6(t) = 5e^{(-2t + j10\pi t)}u(t)$

g. $x_7(t) = \displaystyle\sum_{n=-\infty}^{\infty} \Lambda[(t - 4n)/2]$

2.7. Evaluate the following expressions by using the properties of the delta function:

a. $x_1(t) = \delta(4t)\sin(2t)$

b. $x_2(t) = \delta(t)\cos\left(30\pi t + \dfrac{\pi}{4}\right)$

c. $x_3(t) = \delta(t)\text{sinc}(t + 1)$

d. $x_4(t) = \delta(t - 2)e^{-t}\sin(2.5\pi t)$

e. $x_5(t) = \displaystyle\int_{-\infty}^{\infty} \delta(2t)\text{sinc}(t)dt$

f. $x_6(t) = \displaystyle\int_{-\infty}^{\infty} \delta(t - 3)\cos(t)dt$

g. $x_7(t) = \displaystyle\int_{-\infty}^{\infty} \delta(2 - t)\dfrac{1}{1 - t^3}dt$

h. $x_8(t) = \displaystyle\int_{-\infty}^{\infty} \delta(3t - 4)e^{-3t}dt$

i. $x_9(t) = \delta'(t) \otimes \Pi(t)$

2.8. For each of the following continuous-time systems, determine whether or not the system is (1) linear, (2) time-invariant, (3) memoryless, and (4) causal.

a. $y(t) = x(t - 1)$

b. $y(t) = 3x(t) - 2$

c. $y(t) = |x(t)|$

d. $y(t) = [\cos(2t)]x(t)$

e. $y(t) = e^{x(t)}$

f. $y(t) = tx(t)$

g. $y(t) = \displaystyle\int_{-\infty}^{t} e^{-3(t-\tau)}x(\tau - 1)d\tau$

2.9. Calculate the output $y(t)$ of the LTI system for the following cases:

a. $x(t) = e^{-2t}u(t)$ and $h(t) = u(t - 2) - u(t - 4)$

b. $x(t) = e^{-t}u(t)$ and $h(t) = e^{-2t}u(t)$

c. $x(t) = u(-t)$ and $h(t) = \delta(t) - 3e^{-2t}u(t)$

d. $x(t) = \delta(t - 2) + 3e^{3t}u(-t)$ and $h(t) = u(t) - u(t - 1)$

2.10. The impulse response of a continuous-time LTI system is displayed in Figure P2.2(b). Assuming the input $x(t)$ to the system is waveform illustrated in Figure P2.2(a), determine the system output waveform $y(t)$ and sketch it.

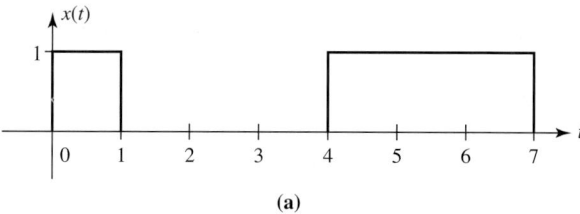

(a)

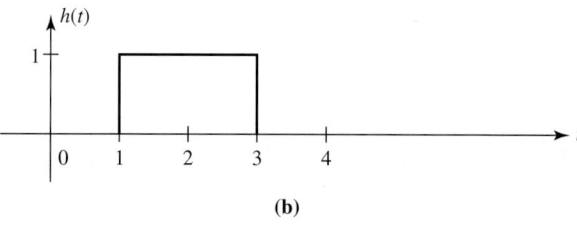

(b)

Figure P2.2

2.11. An LTI system has the impulse response

$$h(t) = e^{-0.5(t - 2)}u(t - 2).$$

a. Is the system causal?

b. Is the system stable?

c. Repeat parts (a) and (b) for $h(t) = e^{-0.5(t + 2)}u(t + 2)$.

2.12. a. Write down the exponential Fourier series coefficients of the signal

$$x(t) = 5\sin(40\pi t) + 7\cos(80\pi t - \pi/2) - \cos(160\pi t + \pi/4).$$

b. Is $x(t)$ periodic? If so, what is its period?

2.13. A signal has the two-sided spectrum shown in Figure P2.3.

a. Write the equation for $x(t)$.

b. Is the signal periodic? If so, what is its period?

c. Does the signal have energy at DC?

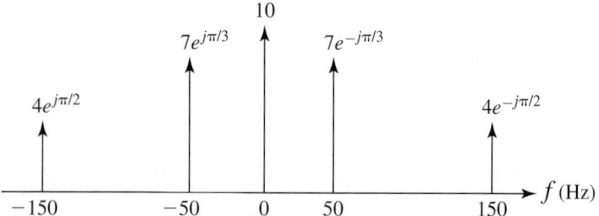

Figure P2.3

2.14. Write down the complex exponential Fourier series for each of the periodic signals shown in Figure P2.4. Plot the magnitude and phase spectra.

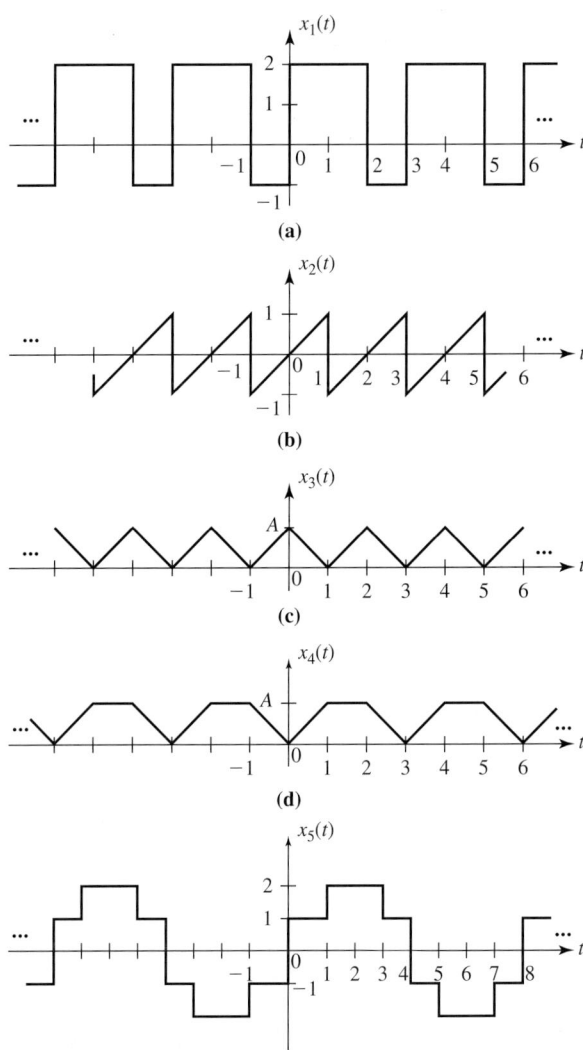

(a)

(b)

(c)

(d)

(e)

Figure P2.4

2.15. For the rectangular pulse train in Figure 2.24, compute the Fourier coefficients of the new periodic signal $y(t)$ given by

a. $y(t) = x(t - 0.5T_o)$

b. $y(t) = x(t)e^{j2\pi t/T_o}$

c. $y(t) = x(\alpha t)$

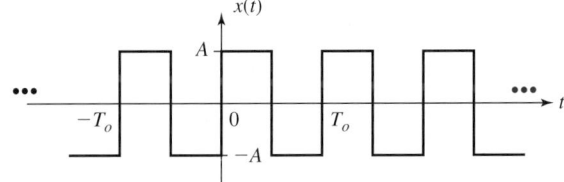

Figure P2.5

2.16. Draw the one-sided magnitude power spectrum for the square wave in Figure P2.5 with duty cycle 50%.

a. Calculate the normalized average power.

b. Determine the 99% power bandwidth of the pulse train.

2.17. Determine the Fourier transforms of the signals shown in Figure P2.6.

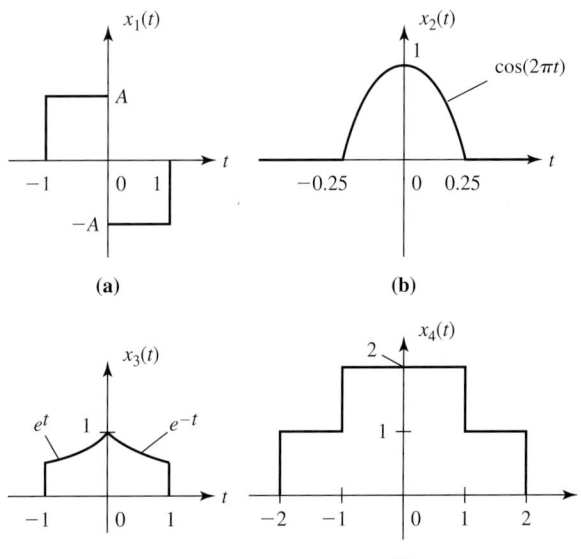

(a)   **(b)**

(c)   **(d)**

Figure P2.6

2.18. Use properties of the Fourier transform to compute the Fourier transform of following signals.

a. $\text{sinc}^2(Wt)$

b. $\Pi(t/T)\cos(2\pi f_c t)$

c. $(e^{-t}\cos 10\pi t)u(t)$

d. $te^{-t}u(t)$

e. $e^{-\pi t^2}$

f. $4\text{sinc}^2(t)\cos(100\pi t)$

2.19. Find the following convolutions:

a. $\text{sinc}(Wt) \otimes \text{sinc}(2Wt)$

b. $\text{sinc}^2(Wt) \otimes \text{sinc}(2Wt)$

2.20. The FT of a signal $x(t)$ is described by

$$X(f) = \frac{1}{5 + j2\pi f}$$

Determine the FT $V(f)$ of the following signals:

a. $v(t) = x(5t - 1)$ What is the impulse response $h(t)$?

b. $v(t) = x(t)\cos(100\pi t)$

c. $v(t) = x(t)e^{j10t}$

d. $v(t) = \dfrac{dx(t)}{dt}$

e. $v(t) = x(t) \otimes u(t)$

2.21. Consider the delay element $y(t) = x(t - 3)$.

    a. What is the impulse response $h(t)$?

    b. What is the magnitude and phase response function of the system?

2.22. The periodic input $x(t)$ to an LTI system is displayed in Figure P2.7. The frequency response function of the system is given by

$$H(f) = \frac{2}{2 + j2\pi f}$$

    a. Write the complex exponential FS of input $x(t)$.

    b. Plot the magnitude and phase response functions for $H(f)$.

    c. Compute the complex exponential FS of the output $y(t)$.

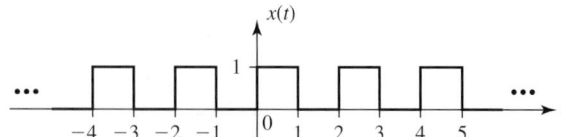

Figure P2.7

2.23. The frequency response of an ideal LP filter is given by

$$H(f) = \begin{cases} 5e^{-j0.0025\pi f}, & |f| < 1000 \text{ Hz} \\ 0, & |f| > 1000 \text{ Hz} \end{cases}$$

Determine the output signal in each of the following cases:

    a. $x(t) = 5\sin(400\pi t) + 2\cos(1200\pi t - \pi/2)$
$- \cos(2200\pi t + \pi/4)$

    b. $x(t) = 2\sin(400\pi t) + \dfrac{\sin(2200\pi t)}{\pi t}$

    c. $x(t) = \cos(400\pi t) + \dfrac{\sin(1000\pi t)}{\pi t}$

    d $x(t) = 5\cos(800\pi t) + 2\delta(t)$

2.24. The frequency response of an ideal HP filter is given by

$$H(f) = \begin{cases} 4, & |f| > 20 \text{ Hz,} \\ 0, & |f| < 20 \text{ Hz} \end{cases}$$

Determine the output signal $y(t)$ for the input

    a. $x(t) = 5 + 2\cos(50\pi t - \pi/2) - \cos(75\pi t + \pi/4)$

    b. $x(t) = \cos(20\pi t - 3\pi/4) + 3\cos(100\pi t + \pi/4)$

2.25. The frequency response of an ideal BP filter is given by

$$H(f) = \begin{cases} 2e^{-j0.0005\pi f}, & 900 < |f| < 1000 \text{ Hz,} \\ 0, & \text{otherwise} \end{cases}$$

Determine the output signal $y(t)$ for the input

    a. $x(t) = 2\cos(1850\pi t - \pi/2) - \cos(1900\pi t + \pi/4)$

    b. $x(t) = \text{sinc}(60t)\cos(1900\pi t)$

    c. $x(t) = \text{sinc}^2(30t)\cos(1900\pi t)$

2.26. The signal $2e^{-2t}u(t)$ is input to an ideal LP filter with passband edge frequency equal to 5 Hz. Find the energy density spectrum of the output of the filter. Calculate the energy of the input signal and the output signal.

2.27. Calculate and sketch the power spectral density of the following signals:

    a. $x(t) = 2\cos(1000\pi t - \pi/2) - \cos(1850\pi t + \pi/4)$

    b. $x(t) = [1 + \sin(200\pi t)]\cos(2000\pi t)$

    c. $x(t) = \cos^2(200\pi t)\sin(1800\pi t)$

Calculate the normalized average power of the signal in each case.

MATLAB PROBLEMS

2.28. Consider the square wave $x(t)$ with $T_o = 1$ in Figure P2.5. It is applied to a filter with frequency response

$$H(f) = \frac{1}{1 + j0.2\pi f}$$

    a. Verify using Symbolic MATLAB that FS coefficients of $x(t)$ are given by

$$C_n = \begin{cases} -j\dfrac{2A}{\pi n}, & n \text{ odd} \\ 0, & n \text{ even} \end{cases}$$

    b. Use MATLAB `stem` command to plot the magnitude spectrum $|C_n|$, $0 \le |n| \le 10$.

    c. Calculate and plot the filter output magnitude spectrum $|D_n|$, $0 \le |n| \le 10$.

Plot the FS approximation of the filter output for $n = 10$.

    d. Repeat parts (b) and (c) for $T_o = 0.1$. Comment on the differences in the filter output waveform.

2.29. Consider the periodic signal

$x(t) = 1.5\sin(400\pi t) + 0.75\cos(800\pi t) + 2\sin(1200\pi t)$.

    a. Generate a discrete-time sequence $x[n]$ of length 2048 by sampling the signal at 2.4 kHz. Plot $x[n]$.

    b. Obtain the DFT X[k] of $x[n]$ by using function `fft(x)`. Plot `fftshift(X)`.

2.30. Consider the signal $x(t)$ described by

$$x(t) = \begin{cases} t + 4, & -4 \le t \le -1 \\ 1, & -1 < t \le 1 \\ t - 4, & 1 < t \le 4 \\ 0, & \text{otherwise} \end{cases}$$

a. Sample the pulse at 16 Hz and append zeros on either side to generate a discrete-time sequence $x[n]$ of length 256.

b. Obtain the DFT $X[k]$ of $x[n]$ by using function `fft(x)`. Plot `fftshift(X)`.

2.31. A rectangular pulse of unit amplitude and duration $T = 50$ msec is applied to an Elliptic filter with following specifications:

Passband frequency $f_p = B$ Hz

Stopband frequency $f_s = 1.25B$ Hz

Maximum passband ripple $R_p = 1$ dB

Minimum stopband ripple $R_s = 40$ dB

a. Generate a discrete-time sequence $x[n]$ of length 1024 by sampling the signal at 1 kHz over the interval $[-512,512]$ msec This has the effect of appending zeros prior to the beginning and at the end of the pulse.

b. Design an Elliptic filter $BT = 0.5$ as illustrated in Example 2.34. Now use function `filter(num,den,x)` to calculate the output $y[n]$ of the filter. Calculate the 10–90% rise-time t_r of the output pulse.

c. Repeat (b) for $BT = 1, 2, 5, 10$. Derive an approximate relationship between B and t_r.

2.32. Consider the square wave $x(t)$ depicted in Figure P2.5. Assume $T_o = 20$ msec and sampling rate = 3.2 kHz.

a. Generate the 2,048-point sequence `x[n]` of 50% duty cycle square wave using m-file `square`

b. Obtain the DFT $X[k]$ of `x[n]` after appending zeros on both sides. Plot using `stem` command the output of `fftshift(X)`. What is the frequency resolution achieved by FFT here?

c. Compute the FS coefficients of the square wave and plot them using `stem` command. Compare with plot obtained in (b) and comment.

2.33. Consider the triangular wave $x(t)$ in Figure P2.8. Assume $T_o = 50$ msec.

a. Calculate and plot sketch the power spectral density of $x(t)$ using MATLAB.

b. The signal is passed through an ideal LP filter with frequency response $H(f) = \Pi(f/B)$, where the filter bandwidth B is chosen so that $BT_o = 5$. Plot the power spectral density of the output.

c. Repeat (b) for the Elliptic filter designed in Problem 2.31 with $BT_o = 5$.

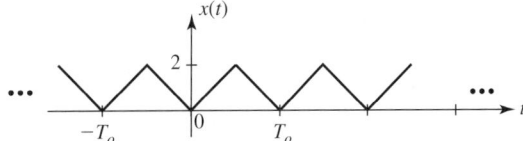

Figure P2.8

An Interview with Herwig Kogelnik

Why did you choose a career in the optical communication field?
You know that many of the early laser pioneers thought of optical communications as a primary laser application and anticipated many communications concepts. I was doing research at Oxford University in plasma physics applied to energy production via nuclear fusion. I was just finishing up and writing my PhD thesis in 1960, just after the first laser had been demonstrated by Maiman. There was a visitor from the United States. He was Rudi Kompfner from Bell Labs, and already in 1960 he went around the world looking for people he was interested in, persuaded them to change fields, come to Bell Labs, and switch into the new field of lasers and optical communications. That's indeed what he did with me also. I still remember his key words that convinced me.

He talked about lasers and reminded me of their extremely high carrier frequency compared to microwave sources. Usually you get 5–10% of this as signal bandwidth, so with lasers you get an enormous bandwidth to transmit information. He said "think of all this bandwidth." I still remember it clearly, and it is still an important guideline today. And in many ways, this was the key line that persuaded me to quit the field of plasma physics, go to America, and join Bell Labs and their laser and optical communications effort.

In your opinion what are the major innovations that have contributed to the information age we live in? What has been the impact of semiconductor revolution? Optical fiber revolution?
Clearly, transistors and integrated circuits are a highly important part of the revolution in information technology during the past three decades. There has been fine progress in the speed of electronics, but its growth rate is only a factor of 10 every 10 years. On the other hand, computing power is growing × 100 every 10 years, making our

(continued)

computers obsolete very quickly. Computers achieve their growth in processing speed by using parallel processing in addition to faster ICs. Now, there is Amdahl's law that says that networking speed has to match computing power: 1 MIPS networked computing power requires 1 Mbps I/O bandwidth. So optical fiber transmission capacity has to grow $\times$ 100 every 10 years to keep up. In recent years it has done this by using wavelength division multiplexing. It is hard to find such revolutionary growth rates in other modern technologies, but there is yet another one in information technology. This is the information storage density in magnetic storage.

Tell us about the invention of the distributed-feedback (DFB) laser which is widely used in optical fiber communications. What were the challenges in developing this single-mode laser design necessary to exploit the huge bandwidth offered by single-mode fibers?

Up to then feedback in lasers was provided by mirrors, not easily integrated. Integrated optics had just been proposed. So Chuck Shank and I were wondering whether we could make a compact laser, integrable on a photonic integrated circuit (PIC), and possibly make it to work in a single frequency. I had early contact with periodic structures during my PhD thesis in Vienna. So we came up with the idea of using a periodic structure for feedback and add gain to make an oscillator. Chuck was working on dye lasers. So, as a first test of the DFB principle, we thought of using a film of dichromated gelatin as in holography into which we dissolved a dye to provide the gain. This was pumped optically, and we were glad to see that DFB laser work. Of course we wanted the same principle applied to the semiconductor lasers envisaged for optical communications, and we patented several ideas right away. But to translate that idea to semiconductor lasers was difficult at first. The first room-temperature continuously operating double heterostructure lasers had just barely been demonstrated at the time. They required very delicate chemistry for their preparation. So it took time and effort by researchers worldwide to develop a practical DFB junction laser.

Multi-wavelength optical systems that can achieve 1 Tbps capacity are now widely available. What is the status of key component technologies, such as wide-range tunable lasers, cost-effective WDM devices, etc.? To build optical fiber rings, we need wavelength division multiplex add/drop devices which are remotely configurable. Are these devices commercially available for deployment in carrier networks?

Advances in optical fiber transmission are due to innovations such as wavelength-division-multiplexing and advanced modulation formats. The most recent innovation is coherent detection which can handle advanced modulation formats, correct linear impairments, and provide ideal optical filtering for high spectral efficiencies. The associated system

complexity must be handled with ever higher levels of integration in PICs. Several of these PICs are already deployed in commercial systems. Examples are tunable optical dispersion compensator modules, tunable laser PICs, and the integrated coherent receivers of the recent transmission systems using 100 Gbps channels. The research community has already demonstrated highly sophisticated PICs, such as a monolithic four-channel dual polarization dual quadrature coherent receiver and the InP 16 QAM modulator PIC. However it will take time for the more sophisticated technologies to mature until they are ready for commercial introduction.

Although optical fiber provides almost infinite bandwidth, service providers continue to invest in extending the life of TWP plant (using technologies like DSL) instead of fiber infrastructure for the last mile. Do we need some major innovation in this area to make fiber a more attractive option?

Fiber-to-the-home (FTTH) technology, which provides the broadband communications infrastructure for the last mile, is a complex issue and the answers throughout the world depend strongly on local cost regulations and policies. Recent OECD statistics show that the U.S. is not among the top 10 countries with the most broadband subscribers where there are up to 35 subscribers per 100 inhabitants. While there is still quite a bit of DSL deployed, FTTH deployment is already larger than DSL deployment in advanced countries such as South Korea and Japan. As demand for bandwidth continues to increase worldwide, FTTH is regarded as a future-proof installation. Of course, reduction of costs will make it an even more attractive option. And it appears that fiber is already getting cheaper than copper. In the U.S., FTTH service is now available to about 18 million homes with about 6 million subscribing to the service. About 60% of this is provided by Verizon. Google has announced recently that it is planning to provide fiber-optic connections for up to 500,000 users with a capacity of 1 Gbps per user. They are starting with a small 1 Gbps pilot project at Stanford.

What are the new frontiers of innovation in optical fiber communications? High-spectral efficiency coherent communications?

In the past three decades, the capacity of long-haul optical fiber transmission has increased by a factor of 100 every 10 years. The latest advances have used wavelength division multiplexing and erbium doped fiber amplifiers. Recent research demonstrations have achieved capacities of up to 70 Tbps per fiber. This is approaching the Shannon capacity limits of a fiber, as modified for impairments due to fiber nonlinearities. New approaches are needed to continue this trend in the future. Among these are advanced modulation formats and the use of coherent detection allowing higher spectral efficiencies, as you mention. In addition, researchers are exploring amplifiers with larger bandwidth as well as the use of multimode and multicore fibers to increase the degrees of freedom available for higher capacity transmission via modal multiplexing.

Who inspired you professionally the most?
This was clearly Rudi Kompfner, the man who had recruited and hired me to Bell Labs. Rudi was a director in the Bell Labs Research area at the time, and he was the primary champion of optical communications at Bell Labs. He was building up a strong and broad research effort in all the relevant enabling technologies, and this was more than 20 years before fiber communications was a success in the market. I learned from him another line: "You have to have a hundred new ideas before you have a really good one." He practiced that one diligently, and asked us to help him throw out the bad ideas among the many he created.

Do you have any advice for the new generation of students and researchers entering the optical fiber communications field?
Well, in information technology we live in a time of tremendous innovation and constant change. Learn to use and enjoy that change, even though it may appear painful at first. Think of the line "Change is inevitable, suffering is optional." Switching fields can bring a tremendous benefit, namely cross-fertilization by transporting the ideas and experiences of one field to the other.

Herwig Kogelnik was born in Graz, Austria, in 1932. He received the Dipl. Ing. and Doctor of Technology Degrees, both from the Technische Hochschule Wien, Vienna, Austria, in 1955 and 1958, respectively, and the Ph.D. Degree from Oxford University, Oxford, England, in 1960.

He joined Bell Labs (currently Alcatel-Lucent), Holmdel, New Jersey, in 1961, where he has been concerned with research in optics, electronics, and communications, including work on lasers, holography, optical guided-wave devices, and integrated optics. He is presently Adjunct Photonics Research Vice President.

Dr. Kogelnik is a Fellow of the IEEE and the OSA. He was elected to the National Academy of Engineering in 1978 and to the National Academy of Sciences in 1994. He is the recipient of the 1984 Frederic Ives Medal of OSA, the 1989 David Sarnoff Award, and the 1991 Quantum Electronics Award from the IEEE. He was elected Honorary Fellow of St. Peter's College at Oxford University in 1992. He is the recipient of the 2001 IEEE Medal of Honor and received the 2001 Marconi International Fellowship. In 2006 he was named Honorary Member of OSA, was awarded the Okawa Prize from the Okawa Foundation for Information and Telecommunications, and received the 2006 National Medal of Technology.

CHAPTER 3

Simulation of Communication Systems Using MATLAB/Simulink

Simulink is a software package for modeling, simulation, and analysis of dynamic systems. For modeling, Simulink provides a **graphical user interface (GUI)** for building models as block diagrams, using click-and-drag mouse operations. Simulink includes a comprehensive library of blocks for modeling sources, sinks, and various signal processing components. The custom blocks for a given application can be constructed by combining existing blocks or creating new blocks using MATLAB m-files or C code. Additional libraries of blocks (called "blocksets") are available that specifically facilitate simulation and analysis of wired/wireless communication systems as well as various signal processing and control applications. The simulation models used in this text would require the capability of *the Student Version of MATLAB and Simulink* which includes MATLAB and Simulink as well as various toolboxes and *Signal Processing Blockset*.

Simulation of a dynamic system is a two-step process in Simulink. First, a block diagram of the system is created, using the Simulink model editor, that graphically depicts a time-dependent model of the dynamic system. The user then commands the Simulink software to simulate the system represented by the model from a specified start time to a specified stop time. In this chapter, we will focus on capabilities and features of the Simulink that students can quickly learn to simulate analog and digital communication systems. This, in turn, should enable them to study signal waveforms and spectra at different stages in the system. Also, it would be quite beneficial for them to make simulated measurements of key system performance metrics and compare them with theoretical results.

The chapter is organized into the following sections:

3.1   GETTING STARTED IN SIMULINK.
This section describes how to create a simple model using Simulink software, and how to simulate that model. The basic techniques used to create and simulate this simple model are the same as those for more complex models. We conclude with a brief discussion of solvers provided in Simulink.

3.2   MODELING IN SIMULINK.
In this section, we review important features of standard blocks available in Simulink for modeling a system. Next we build hierarchical models and build custom blocks to facilitate modeling of complex systems.

3.3   SIMULATION OF SIGNAL AND NOISE SOURCES.
We discuss models to generate deterministic and random signal waveforms required in simulation of analog and digital communication systems. The section concludes with a study of noise models to simulate the effect of additive white Gaussian noise channel.

3.4   MODELING OF COMMUNICATION SYSTEMS.
*We consider Simulink models for communication subsystems described in either time or one of the various transform domains. In this context, we study digital filter design capabilities in MATLAB and **Signal Processing (SP)** blockset.*

3.5   DISPLAYING SIGNALS IN FREQUENCY DOMAIN.
This section introduces Spectrum Scope block from SP blockset to provide display of signal spectra and effect of various operations in frequency domain.

3.6   USING SIMULINK WITH MATLAB.
This section explains how to import and export data between a Simulink model and MATLAB workspace. This facilitates the modeling of systems as well as the setup of simulation runs and further analysis of resultant data.

The chapter concludes with final remarks and a selected list of references.

3.1   GETTING STARTED IN SIMULINK

Simulink is started from the MATLAB in two ways:

- On the MATLAB toolbar, click the Simulink icon.
- Enter simulink at the prompt >> in the MATLAB command window.

```
>> simulink
```

The Simulink Library Browser opens. The libraries of standard blocks appear as a tree-structured folder in the left pane as illustrated in Figure 3.1. The contents of the library selected in the left pane appear in the Library tab to the right of the pane. A library can be opened by either selecting it in the left pane or double-clicking it in the Library tab. One builds models by copying blocks from a library into a model window.

Opening a Model

One can open existing Simulink models or create new models from the Simulink Library Browser. To create a new model:

- Select **File > New > Model** in the Simulink Library Browser.

  The software opens an empty model window. It is displayed in Figure 3.2.

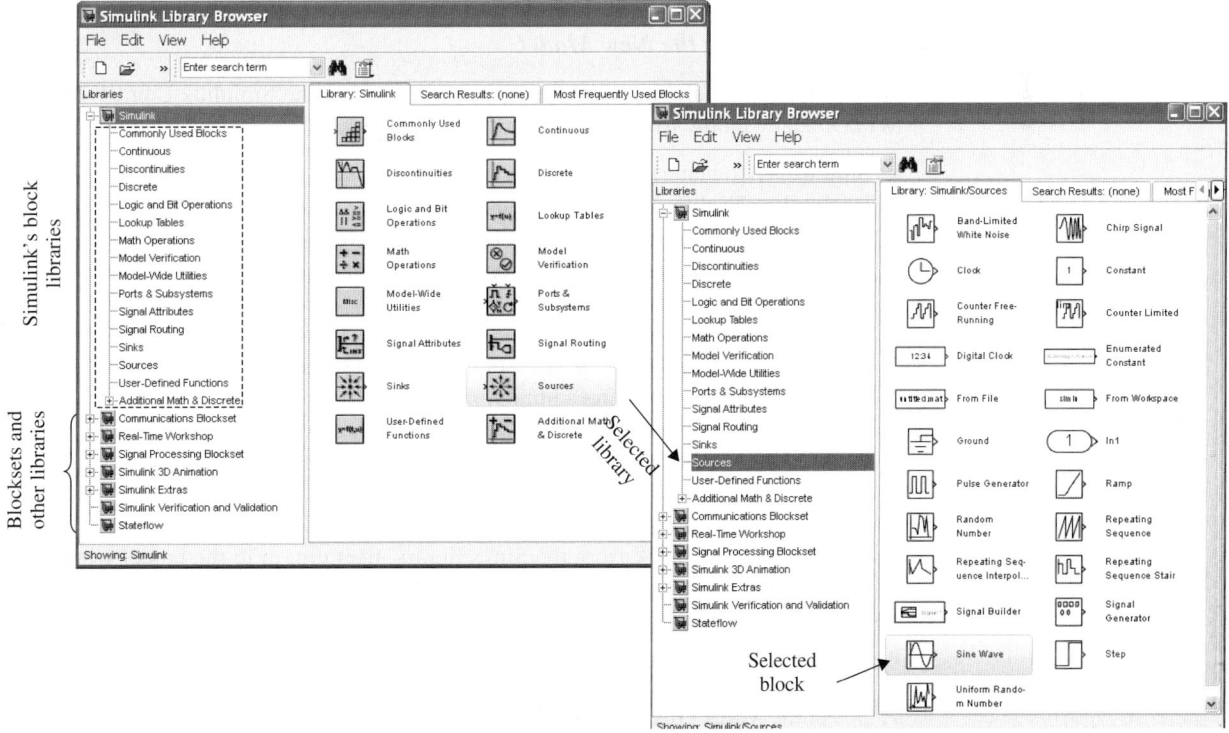

Figure 3.1 Simulink Library Browser.

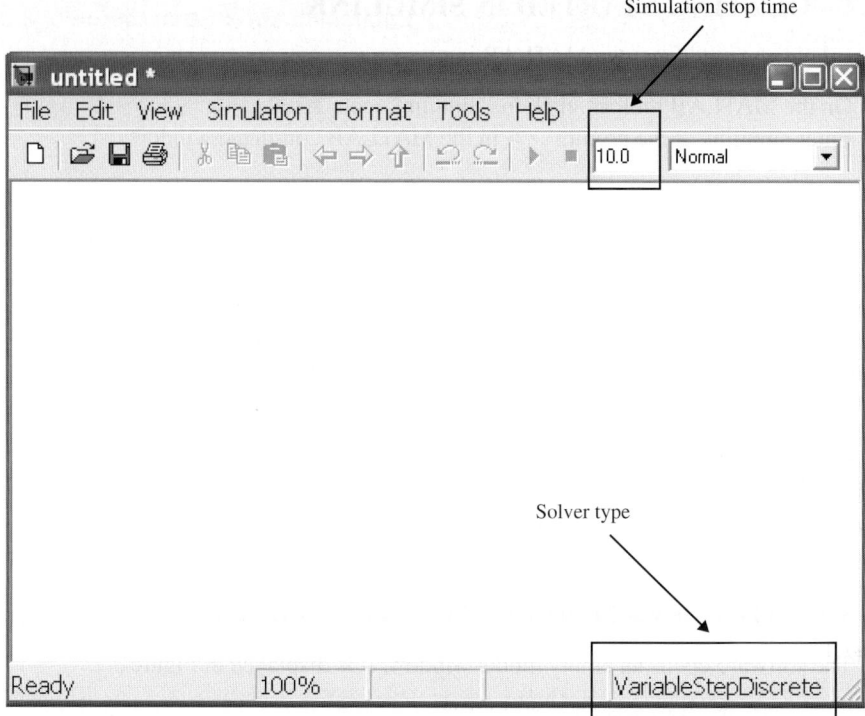

Figure 3.2 Empty model window.

Adding Blocks to the New Model

To construct a model, one should first copy blocks from the Simulink Library Browser to the model window. To create the simple model in this example, we need four blocks:

- **Sine wave.** To generate an input signal for the model.
- **Derivative.** To differentiate the input signal.
- **Sign.** To generate a square wave from the sine wave.
- **Scope.** To display the signals (like oscilloscope) in the model.

To add blocks to your model:

1. Select the **Sources** library in the Simulink Library Browser. The Simulink Library Browser displays the Sources library.
2. Select the Sine Wave block in the Simulink Library Browser, then drag it to the model window. A copy of the Sine Wave block appears in the model window as shown in Figure 3.3.
3. Select the **Sinks** library in the Simulink Library Browser.
4. Select the Scope block from the Sinks library, then drag it to the model window. A Scope block appears in the model window.
5. Select the **Continuous** library in the Simulink Library Browser.
6. Select the Derivative block from the Continuous library, then drag it to the model window. A Derivative block appears in the model window.
7. Select the **Math Operations** library in the Simulink Library Browser.
8. Select the Sign block from the Math Operations library, then drag it to the model window. A Sign block appears in the model window.

Figure 3.4 displays all the blocks in the model window.

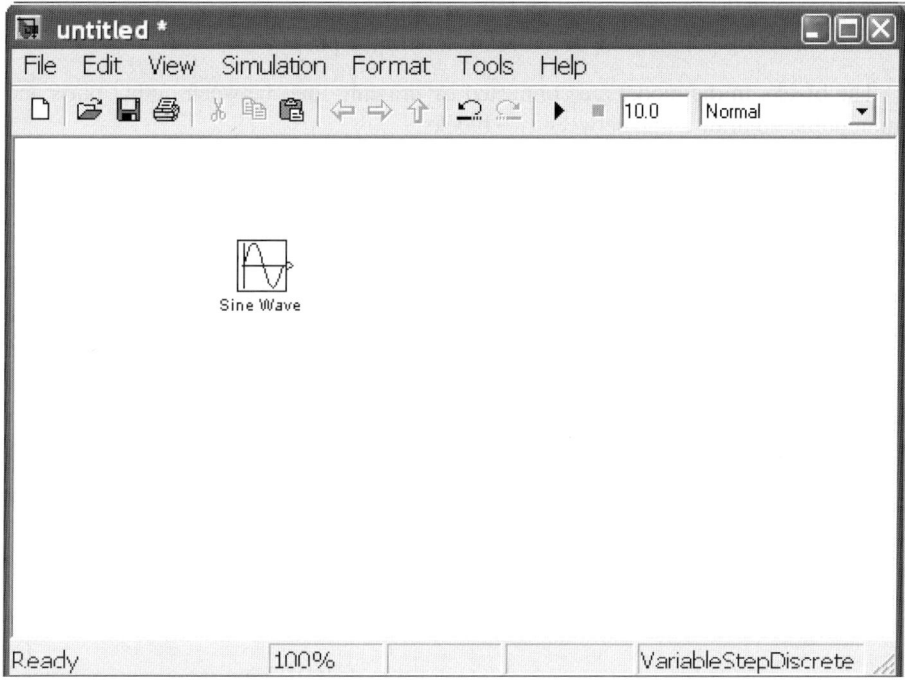

Figure 3.3 Sine Wave block added to model window.

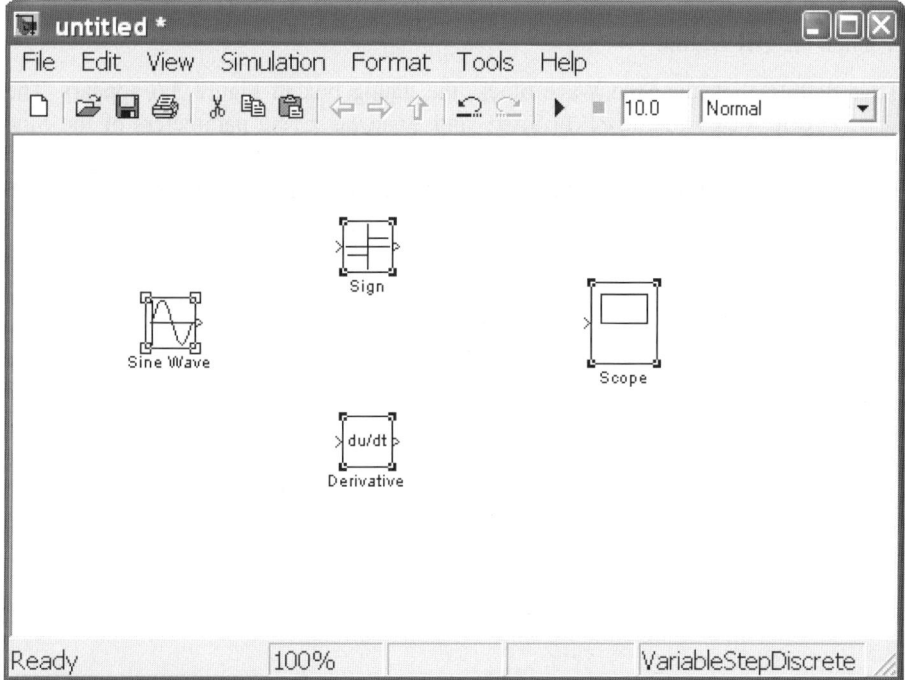

Figure 3.4 All blocks added to the model window.

Connecting Blocks in the Model Window

After blocks are added to the model window, we need to connect them to represent the signal connections within the model. Notice that each block has angle brackets on one or both sides. These angle brackets represent input and output ports.

- The > symbol pointing into a block is an **input port.**
- The > symbol pointing out of a block is an **output port.**

The blocks in the model are connected by drawing lines between output ports and input ports. To draw a line between two blocks:

1. Position the mouse pointer over the output port of the Sine Wave block. Note that the pointer turns into crosshairs (+) while over the port.
2. Click and drag a line from the output port to the input port of the Sign block. Note that the line is dashed while you hold the mouse button down, and that the pointer turns into double crosshairs as it approaches the input port of the Sign block.
3. Release the mouse button over the input port. If the connection is successful, a solid line appears connecting the blocks with the arrow indicating the direction of signal flow. Otherwise, the line is red and dashed.
4. To weld a connection to an existing line ("branch line"), position the mouse pointer on the line between the Sine Wave and the Sign block. Press and hold the Ctrl key, then drag a line to the Derivative block's input port. The software draws a line between the starting point and the input port of the Derivative block.

Figure 3.5 illustrates these operations.

Defining the Block Parameters

Next we specify the parameters of each block using the following steps:

1. Double-click the block. This brings up the block Parameters dialog box.
2. Replace each relevant field with a proper value or selection.
3. Click the **OK** button.

If we double-click the Sine Wave block, the dialog box in Figure 3.6 appears. The `Amplitude`, `Frequency`, `Phase`, and `Sample time` parameters of the Sine

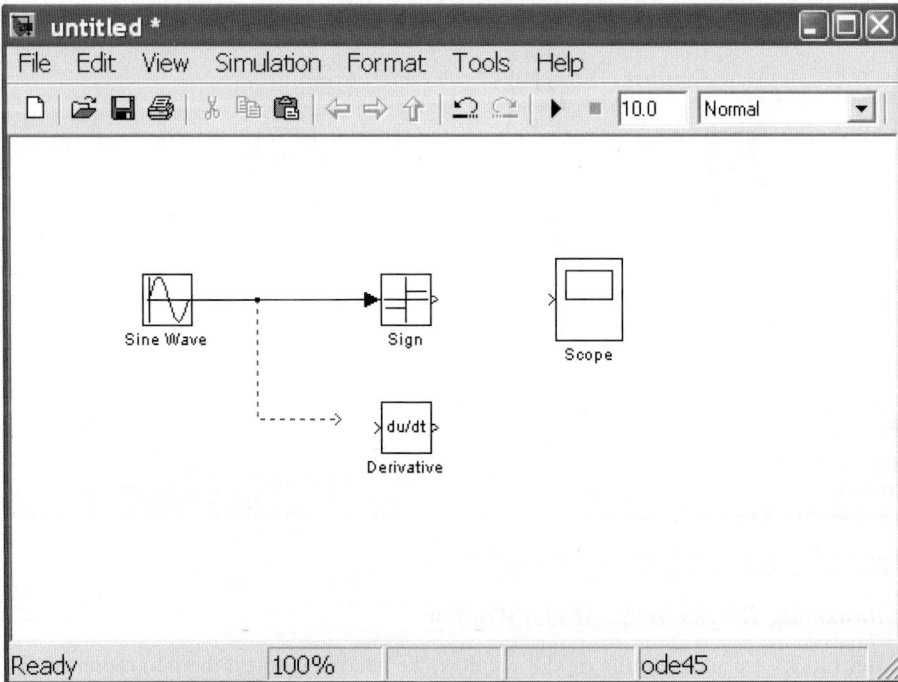

Figure 3.5 Connecting blocks: lines and branch lines.

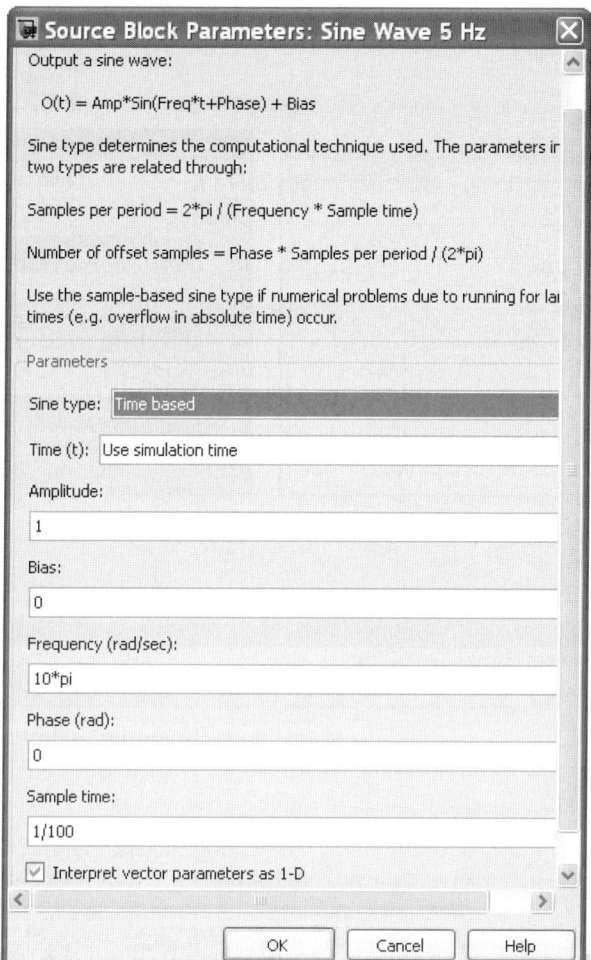

Figure 3.6 Parameters dialog box of the Sine Wave block.

Wave source are selected and then saved by clicking the **OK** button. Other blocks can keep their default parameter values.

The Scope block provides temporal display of multiple input waveforms. To select the number of input waveforms to be displayed, double-click the Scope block. The Scope display appears as shown in Figure 3.7(a). Click the ⊟ icon in the Scope's toolbar and a new window labeled "Scope parameters" will pop up as displayed in Figure 3.7(b). Change the value in the field for `Number of axes` to 3 from 1. Click the **OK** and **Apply** buttons. The Scope display changes to Figure 3.7(c). Close the Scope display. Note that the Scope in the model window now has three input ports to accept three signal waveforms. Finish making the block connections. The model is now complete: It should look similar to Figure 3.8.

Saving the Model

After the model is completed, it can be saved as follows:

1. Select **File > Save As** in the model window.
2. Specify the location to which you want to save the model.
3. Enter `Example_3_1` in the **File name** field.
4. Click **Save.**

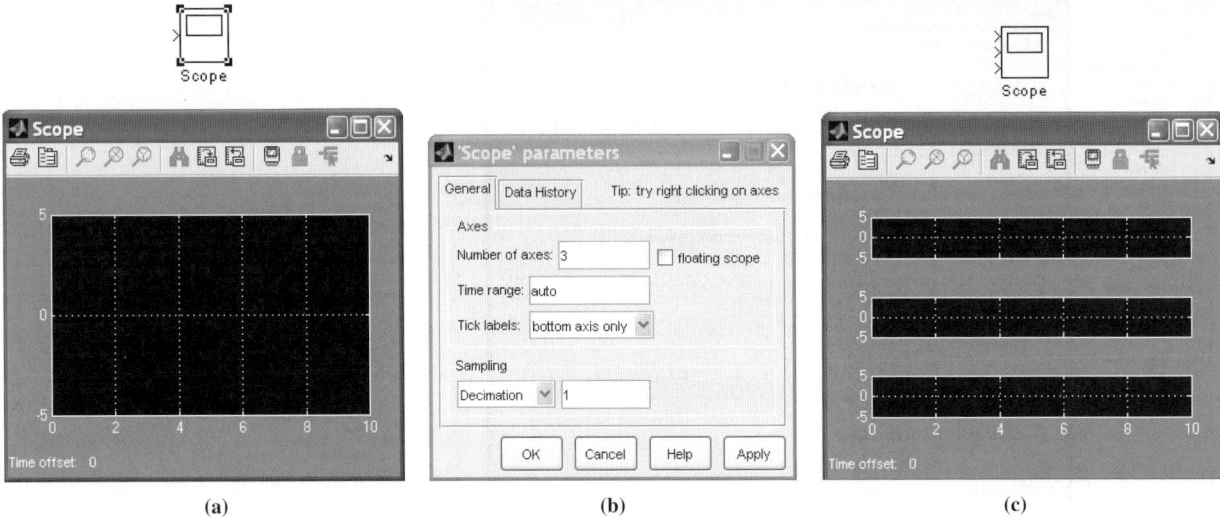

Figure 3.7 Selecting Scope's parameters.

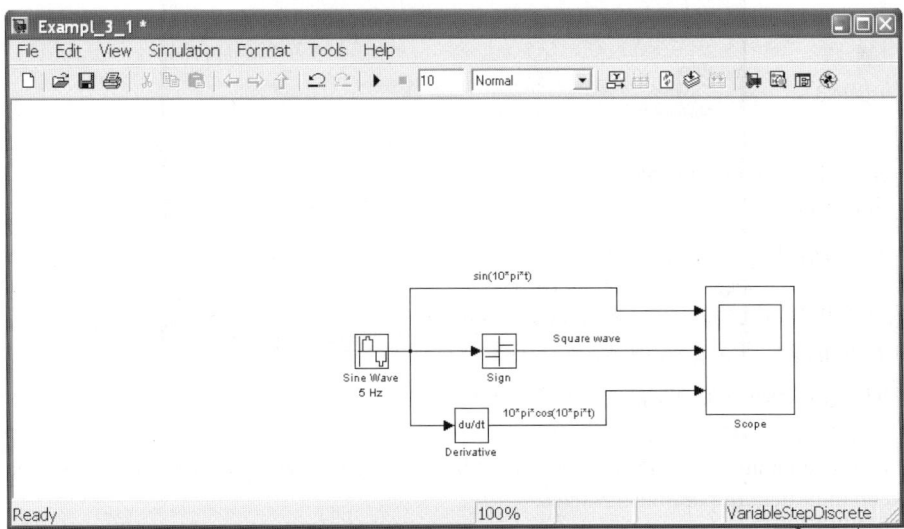

Figure 3.8 Completed Simulink model.

Note the name change in the model window from `untitled` to the saved file name.

Setting Simulation Options

Before running the simulation of the sample model, we can set simulation options such as the start and stop time, and the type of solver that Simulink software uses to solve the model at each time step. These options can be specified using the Configuration Parameters dialog box. To specify simulation options for the sample model:

1. Select **Simulation > Configuration Parameters** in the model window. The software displays the Configuration Parameters dialog box shown in Figure 3.9.
2. Enter `10` in the Stop time field.
3. Select Solver options as shown.
4. Click **OK.**

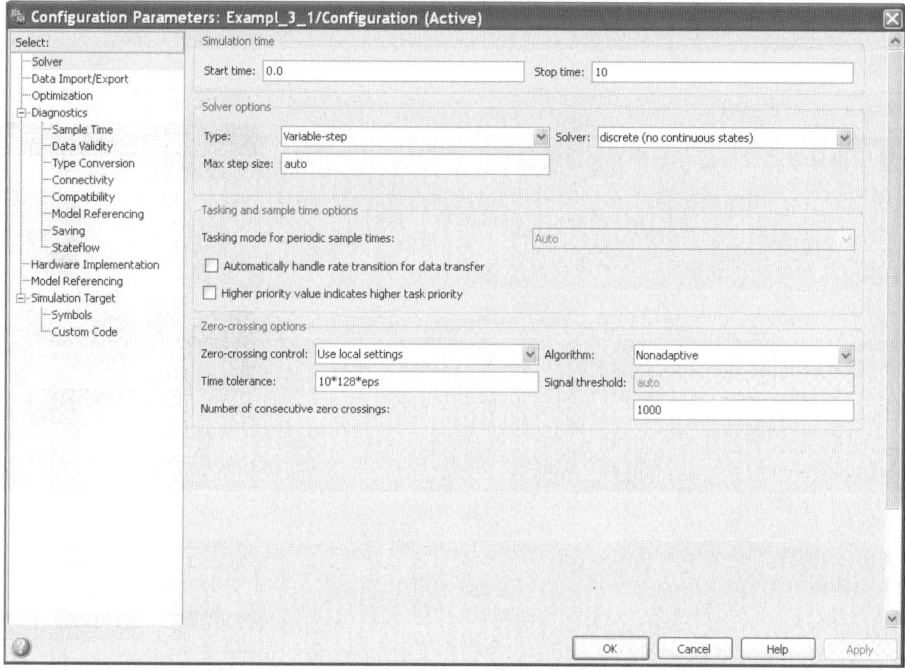

Figure 3.9 Configuration Parameters dialog box.

Simulink applies the changes to the parameters and closes the Configuration Parameters dialog box.

Run the Simulation

To run the simulation:

1. Select **Simulation > Start** in the model window.

The software runs the model, stopping when it reaches the stop time specified in the Configuration Parameters dialog box.

On computers running the Microsoft Windows operating system, click the **Start simulation** button ▶ and **Stop simulation** button ■ in the model window toolbar to start and stop a simulation.

2. Double-click the Scope block in the model window. The Scope window displays the simulation results in Figure 3.10.

3.1.1 Solvers

A Simulink model, in essence, is a piece of software code that defines a set of difference or differential equations describing component blocks of the system being simulated. Running a simulation of the model entails solving this set of difference or differential equations numerically using one of the **solvers** provided in the Simulink software. This involves computing model's inputs, outputs, and states at time intervals from the simulation start time to the simulation end time. No one method for solving a model is suitable for all models. Simulink therefore provides an assortment of solvers, each geared to solving a specific type of model. The Simulink library of solvers is divided into two major types in the **fixed-step** and **variable-step.** Both fixed-step

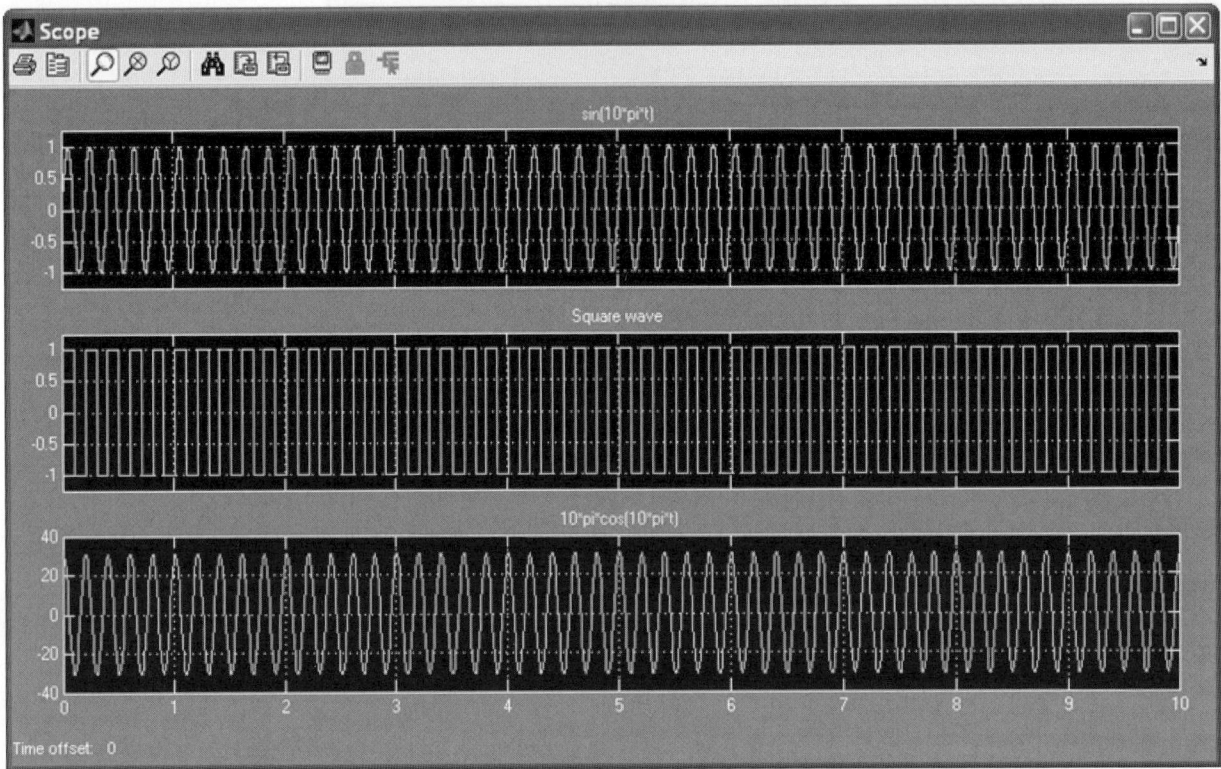

Figure 3.10 Simulation results from the sample model.

and variable-step solvers compute the next simulation time as the sum of the current simulation time and a quantity known as the **step size.** With a fixed-step solver, the step size remains constant throughout the simulation. In contrast, with a variable-step solver, the step size can vary from step to step, depending on the model dynamics. It is generally best to use the variable-step solvers as they continuously adapt the step size to maximize efficiency, while meeting specified error tolerances. Simulink also provides the choice of **continuous-** versus **discrete-time** solvers. Discrete solvers exist primarily to solve purely discrete models. Unless otherwise specified, we will use discrete type, variable-step solvers to run simulations.

3.2   MODELING IN SIMULINK

Simulink has the ability to simulate discrete-time (sampled data) systems, including systems whose components operate at different sampling rates (**multirate systems**) and systems that mix discrete and continuous components (**hybrid systems**). A Simulink block diagram is a pictorial model of a dynamic system that is being simulated. It represents the instantaneous behavior of a dynamic system. Determining a system's behavior over time thus entails repeatedly solving the model at intervals, called time steps, from the start of the time span to the end of the time span. The process of solving a model at successive time steps is referred to as **simulating** the system that the model represents. The block diagram consists of a set of symbols, called **blocks,** interconnected by lines. Blocks embody functionality to generate, process, output, and display signals in a Simulink model. The blocks are interconnected by **lines** which transfer signals from

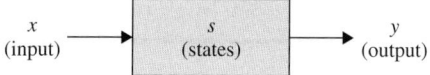

Figure 3.11 Representing a block.

one block's output to another block's input. As illustrated in Figure 3.11, each block represents an elementary dynamic system that comprises one or more of the following: a set of inputs, a set of states, and a set of outputs.

A block's output is a function of time and the block's inputs and states (if any). Blocks with states represent subsystems with memory because the current output of the system is function of the current input as well as the current state of the system. An example is **Integrator** block that has a state (memory). The Integrator block outputs the integral of the input signal from the start of the simulation to the current time. The integral at the current time step depends on the history of the Integrator block's input. The integral therefore is a state of the Integrator block and is, in fact, its only state. Another example of a block with states is the Simulink **Memory** block. A Memory block stores the values of its inputs at the current simulation time and outputs them at a later time. The states of a Memory block are the previous values of its inputs. The Simulink **Gain** block is an example of a stateless block. It has no memory because the current output is current input signal multiplied by the gain. Other examples of stateless blocks include the **Sum** and **Product** blocks. The output of these blocks is purely a function of the current values of their inputs (the sum in one case, the product in the other). Thus, these blocks have no states.

Table 3.1 summarizes a description of these libraries. Key properties of many standard blocks are user selected via the block's Parameters dialog box as discussed in Section 3.1. For example, the gain value of the Simulink Gain block is a parameter that can be set to different values to represent different gain blocks at different locations in the model. The block parameterization thus allows each standard block to represent a family of blocks, thereby greatly increasing the modeling power of the standard Simulink libraries.

Continuous versus Discrete Blocks

The library of built-in blocks in Simulink includes continuous blocks and discrete blocks. Continuous blocks respond continuously to continuously changing input. Discrete blocks, by contrast, respond to changes in input only at integer multiples of a fixed interval called the block's **sample time.** Discrete blocks hold their output constant between successive sample time hits. Examples of continuous blocks include the Constant block and the blocks in the Continuous blocks library. Examples of discrete blocks include the Discrete Pulse Generator block and the blocks in the Discrete blocks library. Many Simulink blocks, for example, the Gain block, can be either continuous or discrete, depending on whether they are driven by continuous or discrete blocks. Each discrete block includes a `Sample time` parameter that is user selected. The sample time is specified as a vector `[Ts, To]` where `Ts` is the time interval or period between consecutive sample times and `To` is an initial offset to the sample time. (If `To` $= 0$, the sample time is specified as scalar `Ts`. The sample time can be an **inherited** type by specifying it symbolically as `[-1,0]` or -1. In this case, the block inherits the sample time from the block connected to its input. Exceptions include blocks in the Continuous library and blocks that do not have inputs (e.g., blocks from the Sources library). Figure 3.12 displays Parameters dialog boxes of continuous- and discrete-time Integrator blocks. Note that the discrete-time Integrator block requires specification of sample time.

Table 3.1 Simulink Standard Block Libraries

Block Library	Description
Commonly used blocks	Contains a group of the most commonly used blocks, such as the **Constant, In1, Out1, Scope,** and **Sum** blocks. Each of the blocks in this library is also included in other libraries.
Continuous	Contains blocks that model continuous-time linear functions, such as the **Derivative** and **Integrator** blocks.
Discontinuous	Contains blocks with outputs that are discontinuous functions of their inputs, such as the **Saturation** block.
Discrete	Contains blocks that represent discrete-time functions, such as the **Unit Delay** block.
Logic and bit operations	Contains blocks that perform logic or bit operations, such as the **Logical Operator** and **Relational Operator** blocks.
LookUp tables	Contains blocks that use lookup tables to determine their outputs from their inputs, such as the **Cosine** and **Sine** blocks.
Math operations	Contains blocks that perform mathematical and logical functions, such as the **Gain, Product,** and **Sum** blocks.
Ports and subsystems	Contains blocks that allow the user to create subsystems, such as the **In1, Out1,** and **Subsystem** blocks.
Signal attributes	Contains blocks that modify the attributes of signals, such as the **Data Type Conversion** block.
Signal routing	Contains blocks that route signals from one point in a block diagram to another, such as the **Mux** and **Switch** blocks.
Sinks	Contains blocks that display or export output, such as the **Out1** and **Scope** blocks.
Sources	Contains blocks that generate or import system inputs, such as the **Constant, In1,** and **Sine Wave** blocks.
User-defined functions	Contains blocks that allow the user to define custom functions, such as the **Embedded MATLAB Function** block.

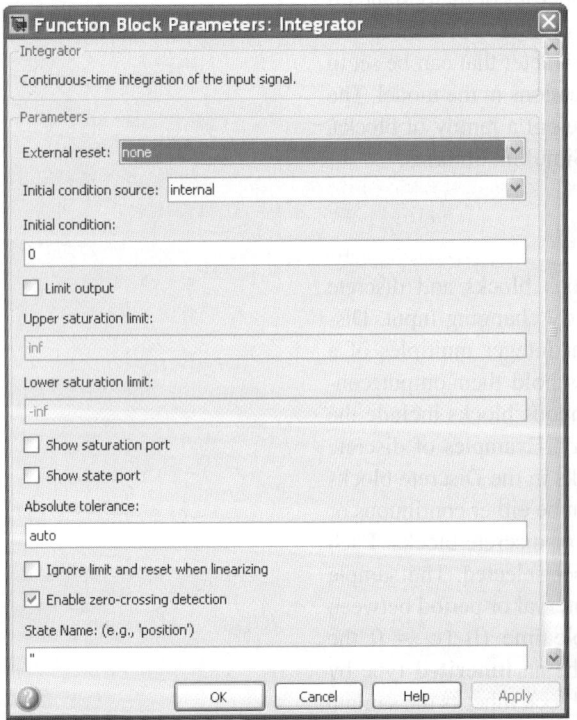
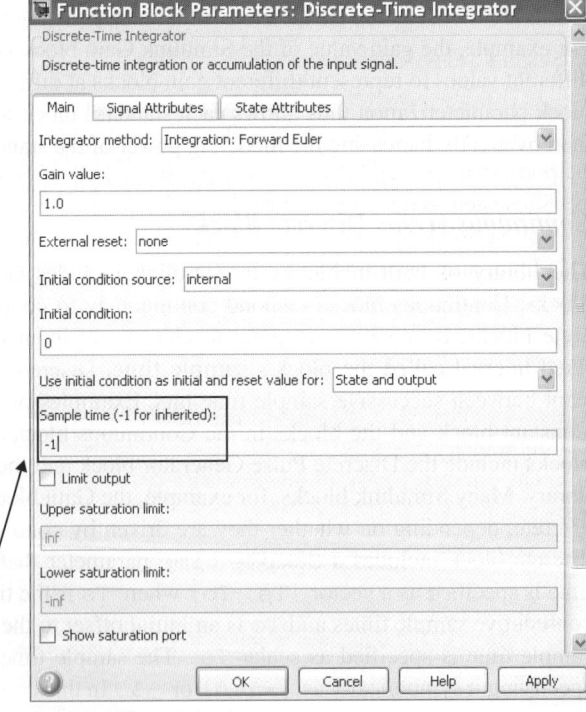

A discrete block requires specification of sample time

Figure 3.12 Parameters dialog boxes of continuous- and discrete-time integrators.

3.2.1 Subsystems

As models grow larger and more complex, they can easily become difficult to understand, maintain, and display. Simulink allows us to model a complex system as a set of interconnected subsystems each of which is represented by a block diagram. A subsystem is a set of blocks that have been replaced by a single block called a **Subsystem** block. As models increase in size and complexity, they can be simplified by grouping blocks into subsystems. Using subsystems has these advantages:

- It helps reduce the number of blocks displayed in the model window.
- It allows to us to keep functionally related blocks together.
- It enables us to establish a hierarchical block diagram, where a Subsystem block is on one layer and the blocks that make up the subsystem are on another.

To create a subsystem from a collection of blocks:

1. Enclose the blocks and connecting lines that are included in the subsystem within a bounding box.
   a. Define the starting corner of a bounding box by positioning the pointer at one corner of the box, then pressing and holding down the mouse button. Notice the shape of the cursor.
   b. Drag the pointer to the opposite corner of the box. A dotted rectangle encloses the selected blocks and lines.
   c. Release the mouse button. All blocks and lines at least partially enclosed by the bounding box are selected.

Figure 3.13(a) displays the selected blocks in the system model being considered here.

2. Select **Create Subsystem** from the **Edit** menu.

A new Subsystem block replaces the selected blocks. Figure 3.13(b) shows the model after selecting the Create Subsystem command (and resizing the Subsystem block so the port labels are readable). To display the hidden contents of subsystem, double-click the Subsystem block. This opens the new block diagram window displaying the contents of the subsystem as illustrated in Figure 3.13(c). Notice that the Simulink software adds Input and Output blocks to represent input from and output to blocks outside the subsystem.

Masking a Subsystem

A mask is a custom user interface for a subsystem that hides the subsystem's contents, making it appear to the user as a custom block with its own icon and Parameters dialog box. The Simulink Mask Editor enables us to create a mask for any subsystem. Masking allows us to:

- Replace the parameter dialogs of a subsystem's contents with a single parameter dialog with its own block description, parameter prompts, and help text.
- Replace a subsystem's standard icon with a custom icon that depicts its purpose.
- Prevent unintended modification of subsystems by hiding their contents behind a mask.
- Create a custom block with its own block diagram that defines the block's behavior in a masked subsystem and then placing the masked subsystem in a library.

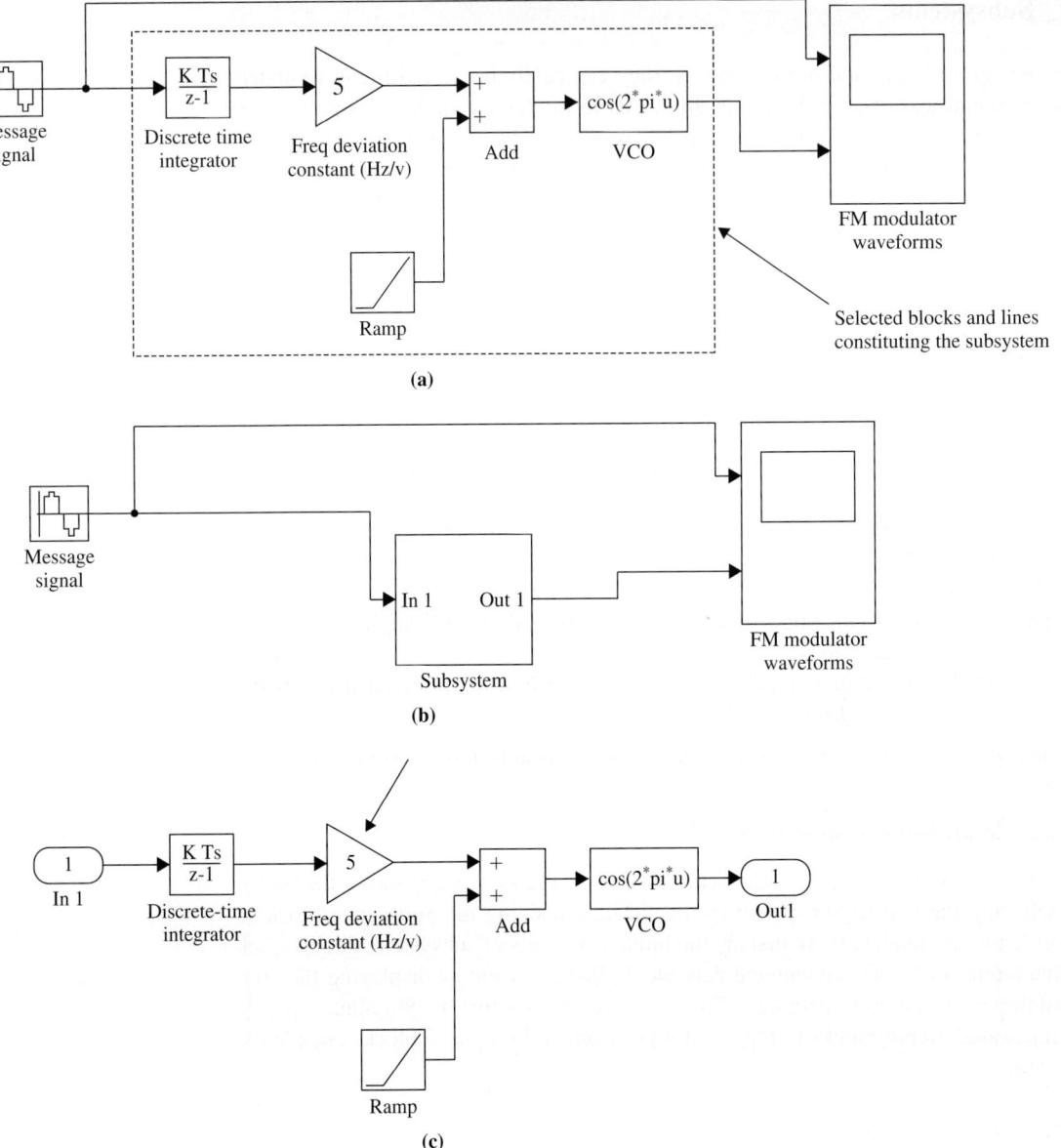

Figure 3.13 Creating subsystems.

Creating a Subsystem Mask

To mask a subsystem:

1. Select a subsystem.
2. Select **Edit → Mask.** This brings up the Mask Editor.

The Mask Editor contains four panes:

- **Icon.** For specifying the icon.
- **Parameters.** For defining the parameters dialog.
- **Initialization.** For entering initialization commands.
- **Documentation.** For entering block documentation and help.

After a subsystem is masked, the mask can be modified by selecting **Edit → Edit Mask.**

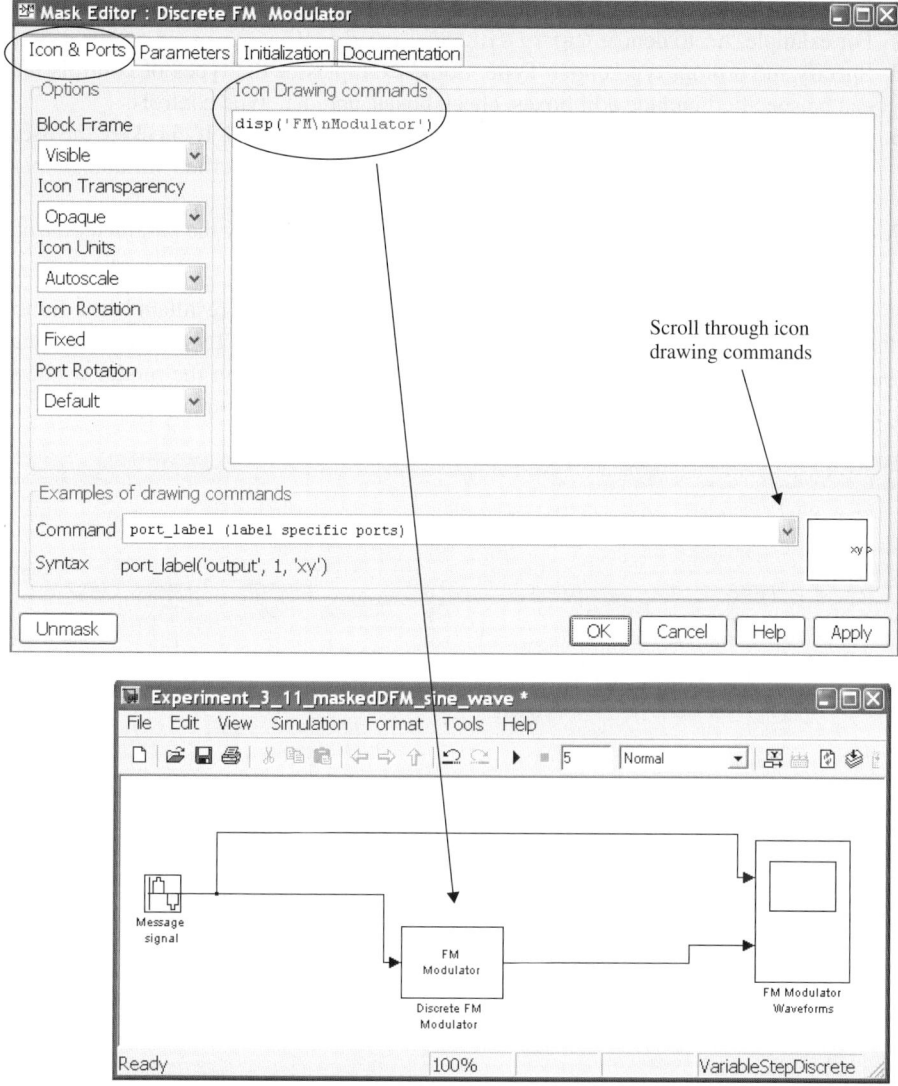

Figure 3.14 Specifying a masked subsystem icon.

As an example, we consider masking the subsystem created in Figure 3.13. Click the Subsystem block in Figure 3.13(b) to select it. Choose **Edit → Mask** to open the Mask Editor.

To create a block icon:

1. Select the **Icon & Ports** pane of the Mask Editor.
2. Scroll through **Icon Drawing commands** and type the selected command in the window of the Icon pane.

As an example we type the command `display ('FM\nModulator')` in the window to specify the icon for the subsystem block in Figure 3.13(b). Click **Apply** and **OK** to save. Figure 3.14 displays the result.

To build a custom subsystem interface, it is desirable to define parameters that the users can easily specify and tune via a dialog. To define block parameters:

1. Select the **Parameters** pane of the Mask Editor.

2. Click the ⇥ icon to add a new prompt.

3. Enter the prompt string under **Prompt.** For example, `Carrier Amplitude(V)`.

4. Under **Variable,** enter the name of the variable assigned to the entry in step 3 above. For example, `Ac` to denote `Carrier Amplitude(V)`.

5. Specify the prompt type under **Type.** Some examples of the types of controls that can be specified include edit boxes, check boxes, and data type controls.

6. Under **Evaluate,** check the box if you want the entry evaluated. If checked, the user-entered expression is evaluated before it is assigned to the specified variable. Otherwise, the entry is treated as a string.

7. Under **Tunable,** check the box if you want to be able to modify the parameter during run time.

Repeat steps 2 to 7 above to define additional parameters. The resultant Mask Editor display is shown in Figure 3.15(a). Click **Apply** and **OK** to save. To see the Parameters dialog box created here, double-click the FM Modulator block in the model window. Figure 3.15(b) displays the result with values selected for the parameters.

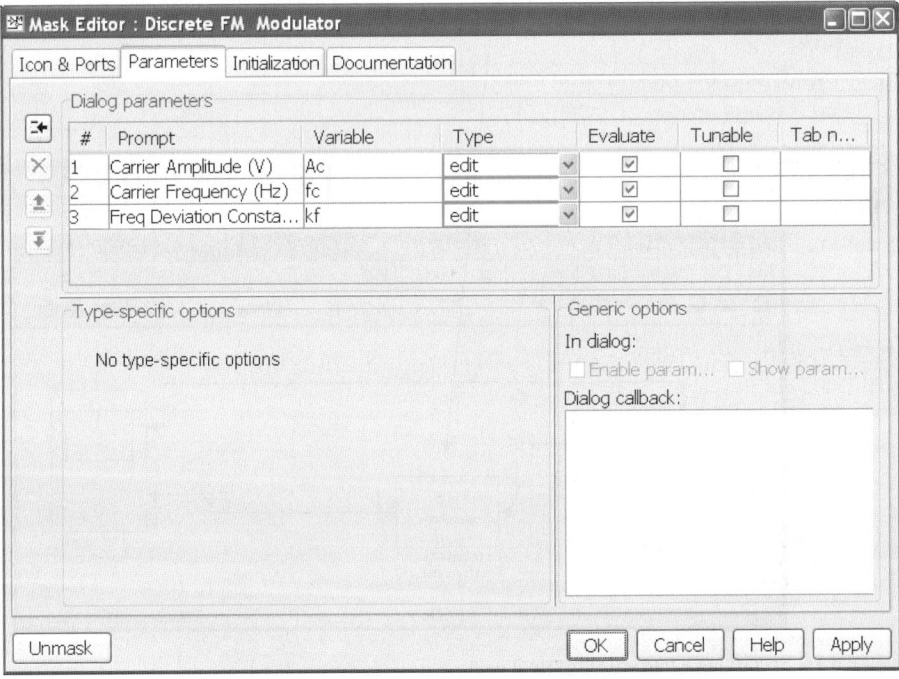

(a)

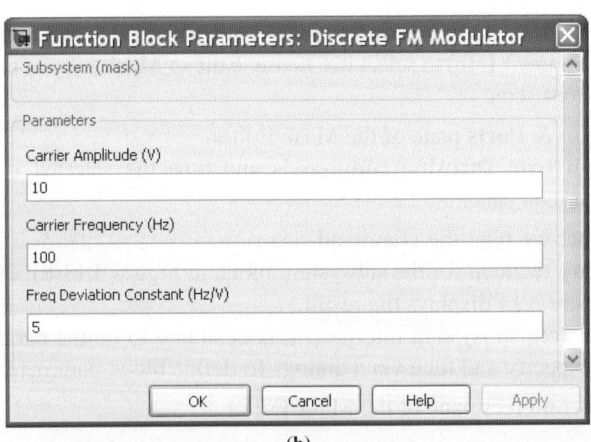

(b)

Figure 3.15 Defining masked subsystem block parameters.

3.3 SIMULATION OF SIGNAL AND NOISE SOURCES

Simulink supports a large variety of deterministic and random signal sources for the simulation of analog and digital communication systems. The source models are provided in Simulink's Sources library and SP blockset's **Signal Processing Sources** library as illustrated in Figures 3.1 and 3.16, respectively. The models for Gaussian noise, which is representative of the noise introduced by many important communication channels, are also provided by these libraries. For more complex channel models, the user needs to use the blocks provided in Communications blockset, which is not included in the Student Version of MATLAB and Simulink.

3.3.1 Deterministic Signals

We observe from Figure 3.1 that Simulink Source library provides blocks for generating sinusoidal, square, triangular, sawtooth, and other periodic waveforms. Blocks also exist that produce nonperiodic signals, such as step and ramp waveforms. We next discuss a generation of sinusoidal waveforms and clock signals.

Sinusoidal Waveforms

The simplest way to generate a sinusoidal waveform is to use the Sine Wave block from the Simulink Sources library as illustrated in Figure 3.1. It generates a sine wave of

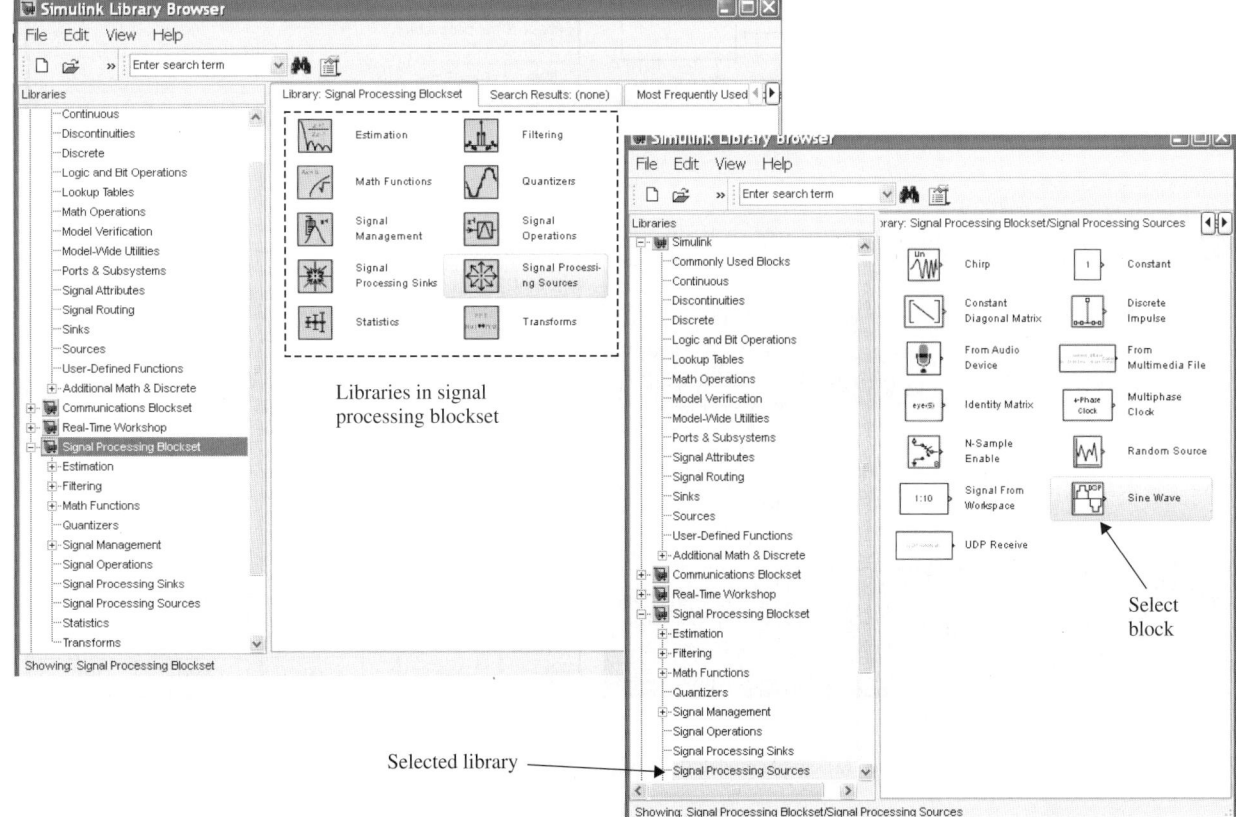

Figure 3.16 Signal and noise sources in SP blockset.

specified amplitude, frequency, and phase. To generate a cosine wave, the phase parameter is specified as $\pi/2$. The parameters dialog for a Sine Wave block is illustrated in Figure 3.6. The block can operate in time-based or sample-based mode. Time-based mode has two submodes: **continuous** or **discrete.** The value of the `Sample time` parameter determines whether the block operates in continuous submode or discrete submode:

- 0 (the default) causes the block to operate in continuous submode.
- > 0 causes the block to operate in discrete submode.

In discrete submode, a `Sample time` parameter value greater than zero causes the block to behave as if it were driving a **Zero-order hold (ZOH)** block whose sample time is set to that value. The sample-based method of computing the block's output does not depend on the result of the previous time step to compute the result at the current time step. It therefore avoids round-off error accumulation.

Another way to generate a sine wave in the Simulink is to use the Sine Wave block from the Signal Processing Sources library in the SP blockset. This block generates a multichannel sinusoidal signal, with independent amplitude, frequency, and phase in each output channel. Figure 3.17 displays the sample model to generate and display the signal consisting of three different sinusoidal waveforms. The parameters of waveforms are selected via the dialog box as shown in Figure 3.17(c).

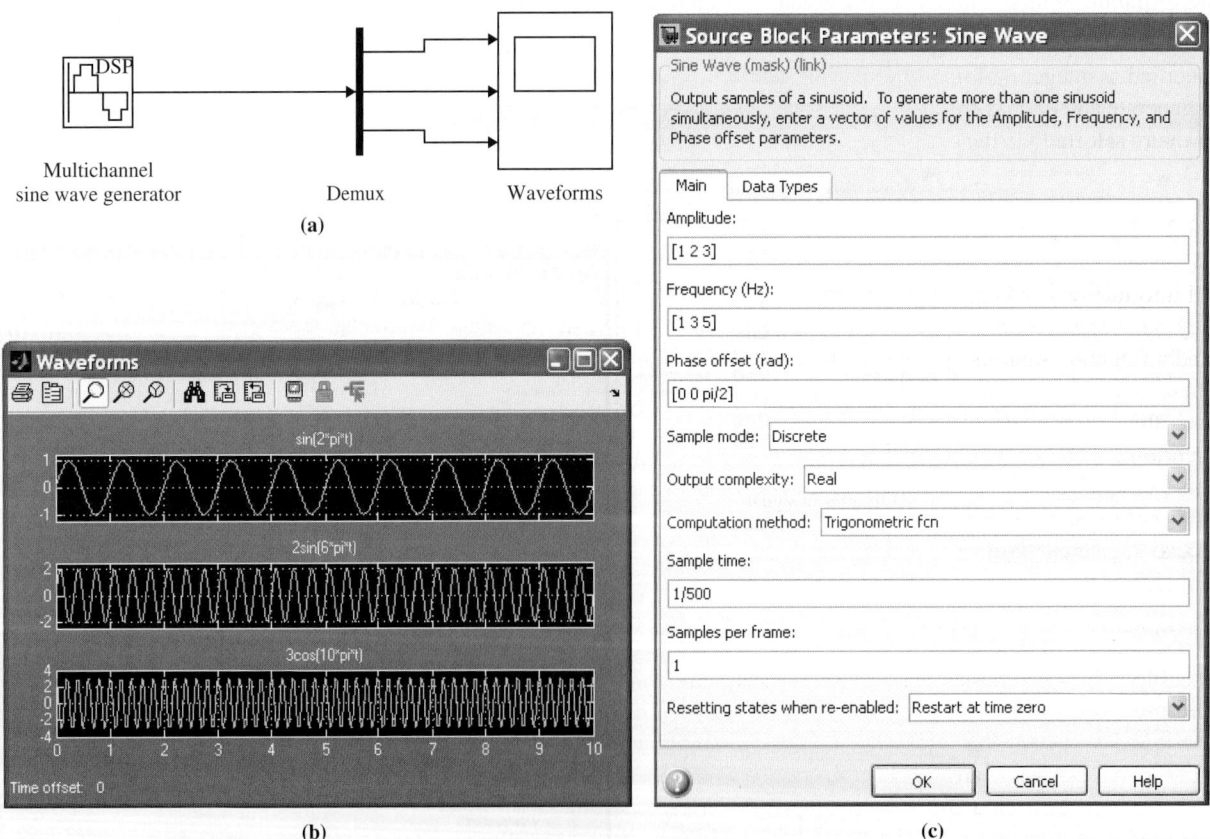

Figure 3.17 Sine Wave block in SP blockset: (a) sample model; (b) waveform; (c) parameters dialog box.

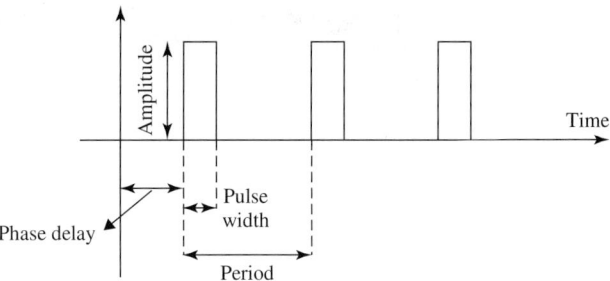

Figure 3.18 Parameters of the Pulse Generator block.

Clock Signal

In a digital communication system, a clock signal is required to regenerate the transmitted signal at the receiver. It is very convenient to use the **Pulse Generator** block in Simulink's Sources library to create the appropriate clock signal. It generates a periodic pulse train as illustrated in Figure 3.18. The shape of the waveform is determined by `Amplitude`, `Pulse Width`, `Period`, and `Phase Delay` parameters.

The `Pulse type` parameter is used to specify whether the block's output is time-based or sample-based. If `time-based` is selected as the block's pulse type, the pulse's phase delay and period must be specified in units of seconds. On the other hand, if `sample-based` is specified, the block's sample time in seconds must be specified using the `Sample time` parameter. The block's phase delay and period must then be specified as integer multiples of the sample time. Figure 3.19 displays the sample model to generate and display the clock signal of duty cycle 20%. The parameters of the waveform are selected via the dialog box as illustrated in Figure 3.19(c).

3.3.2 Random Signals

All information-carrying signals, whether analog or digital, are random in the sense that they cannot be predicted or exactly described prior to their actual occurrence. To simulate random signals, Simulink and SP blockset provide blocks to generate random waveforms. These are, in fact, **pseudo-random** waveforms because although they appear to be random, they repeat after a very long period. Each of these Simulink blocks implements a **pseudo-random number (PRN)** generator followed by a ZOH. The ZOH holds the random number for the period specified by the `Sample time` parameter.

Simulink and SP blockset provide Uniform Random Number and Random Source blocks to generate uniformly distributed pseudo-random numbers.

Uniform Random Number Block

This block in the Simulink Sources library generates a sequence of uniformly distributed pseudo-random numbers over a specified amplitude range with a specified seed. The `minimum` and `maximum` limits of the amplitude range as well as the `Sample time` parameter value are set by using the Parameters dialog box. The random number generation starts from a `seed` value, which is any user-specified nonnegative integer. The seed is reset each time a simulation starts. If the same seed is used repeatedly, the same sequence of random numbers is generated.

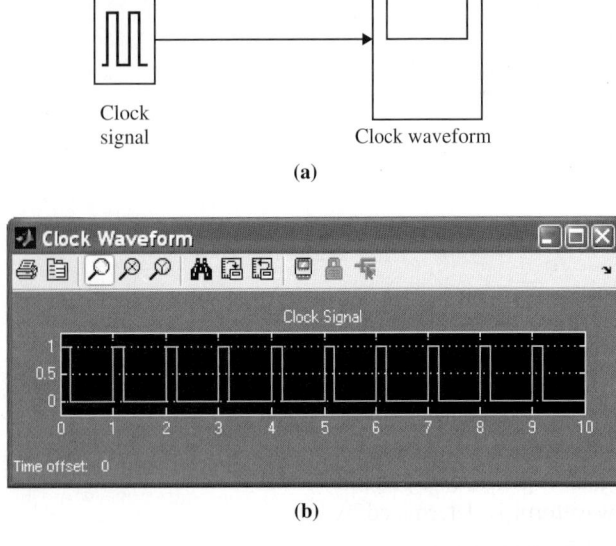

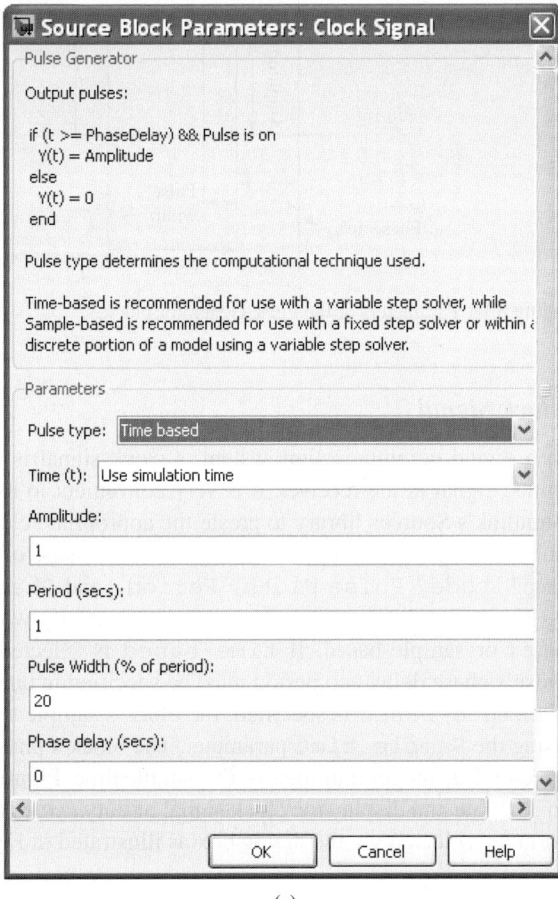

Figure 3.19 Pulse Generator block: (a) sample model; (b) waveform; (c) parameters dialog box.

Random Source Block

This block in the Signal Processing Sources library from the SP blockset provides another option to generate a sequence of uniformly distributed pseudo-random numbers. For this purpose, the Source type parameter is set to Uniform in the Parameters dialog box. The minimum and maximum limits of the amplitude range as well as the Sample time parameter value (in the Discrete mode) are set as previously noted. The Repeatability parameter determines whether or not the block outputs the same sequence each time the simulation is run. The choices are Not repeatable, Repeatable, or Specify seed. In the Repeatable and Specify seed settings mode, the block outputs the same sequence every time the simulation is run.

Example 3.1

For comparison, display the sequences of uniformly distributed random numbers generated by the Uniform Random Number block and the Random Source block. Use a Sample time parameter of 1/10 and amplitude range of $[-1, 1]$.

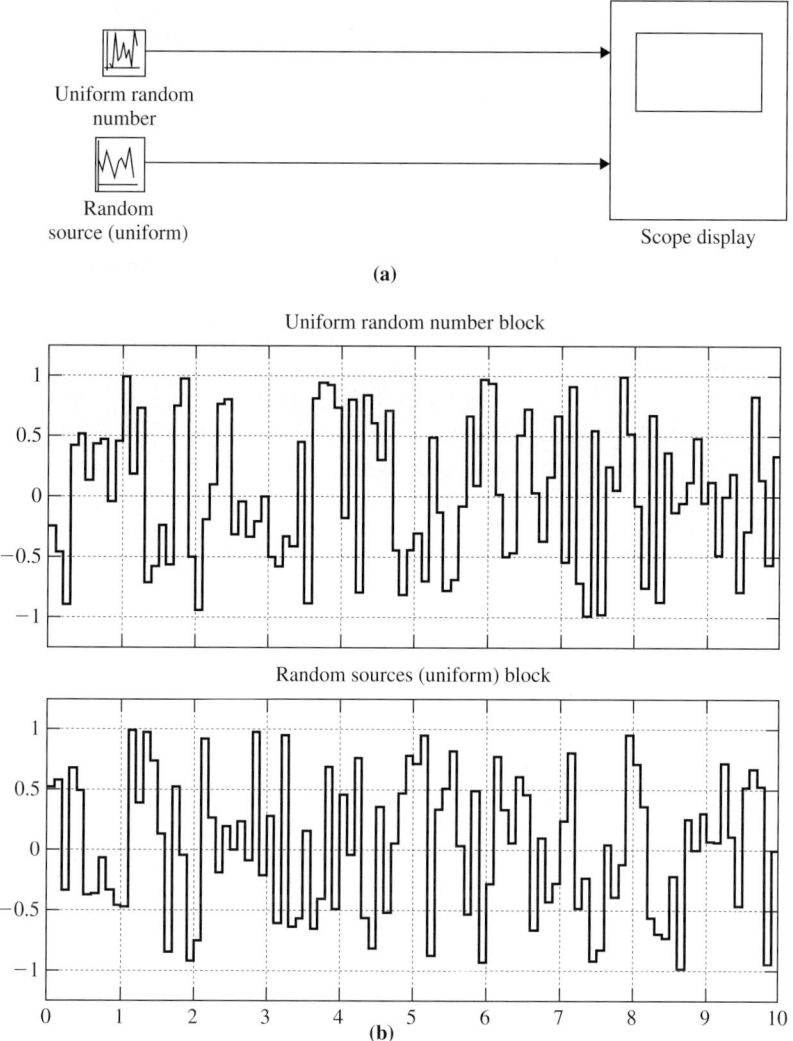

Figure 3.20 Uniformly distributed random sequences: (a) model; (b) Scope display.

Solution

The Simulink model for this example is shown in Figure 3.20(a). The same seed value was used for initializing both blocks. Figure 3.20(b) displays the random sequences generated by the two blocks. It appears that two different algorithms are used to generate these uniformly distributed PRN sequences.

Next we illustrate the application of uniformly distributed random sequences to generate binary and quaternary polar digital signals.

Example 3.2

Develop Simulink models for generating pseudo-random binary and quaternary polar digital signals. Use a `Sample time` parameter of 1/10.

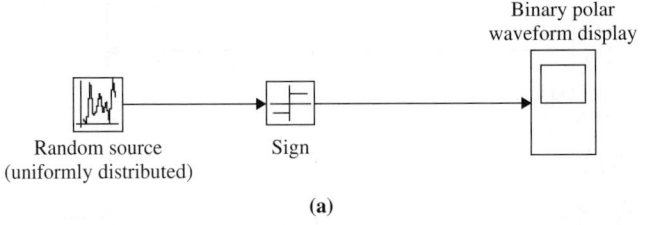

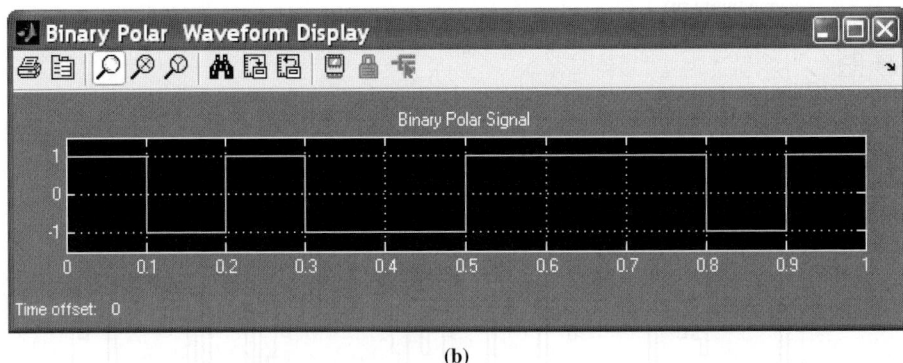

Figure 3.21 Binary polar signal source: (a) model; (b) waveform.

Solution

The model for generating binary polar digital signals consists of a Random Source block followed by the Sign block from Simulink's Math Operations library. This is illustrated in Figure 3.21(a). The Random Source block generates pulse waveforms assuming amplitude values in the interval $[-1, 1]$ with equal probability. The Sign block output is 1 when the input amplitude is greater than zero. Similarly, the output is -1 when the input amplitude is less than zero. Thus, output of the Sign block is a binary digital signal assuming values ± 1 with probability 0.5. Note that bit duration of the output digital signal equals the Sample time parameter set in the Random Source block. Figure 3.21(b) displays the binary polar signal.

The model for generating quaternary polar digital signals consists of a Random Source block followed by the MATLAB Fcn block from Simulink's **User Defined Functions** library. This is illustrated in Figure 3.22(a). The Random Source block generates pulse waveforms assuming amplitude values in the interval $[-1, 1]$ with equal probability. The MATLAB Fcn implements following mapping to generate pulse levels in the set $\{-3, -1, 1, 3\}$ from uniformly distributed random numbers:

$$u \rightarrow 2*fix(M*u) - M_1$$

where $M_1 = M - 1$ and $M = 4$ for quaternary signaling. u is a uniformly distributed random number generated by the Random Source block. Note that the symbol or pulse duration of the output quaternary waveform equals the Sample time parameter set in the Random Source block. Figure 3.22(b) displays the quaternary polar signal.

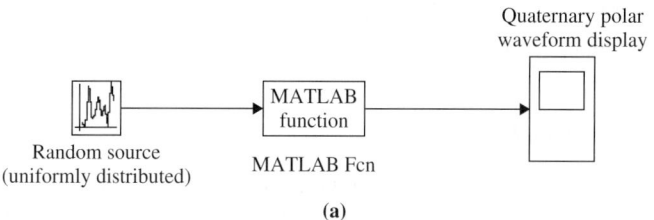

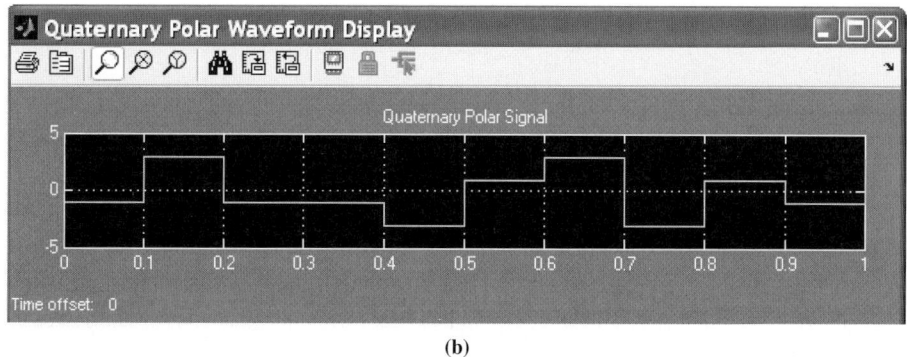

(b)

Figure 3.22 Quaternary polar signal source: (a) model; (b) waveform.

3.3.3 Modeling of AWGN Channel

Noise and interference degrade the information-bearing signal as it passes through the communication system from information source to the destination. Accurate modeling of these systems requires algorithms for generating sampled versions of random wave-forms (noise, interference, etc.). In this context, we will limit consideration to channels where the signal degradation effects can be modeled by an additive white Gaussian noise (WGN) process. We will show in Section 6.15.3 that samples of WGN are statistically independent Gaussian random variables with zero mean and variance σ^2 given by (6.344). That is,

$$\sigma^2 = \frac{N_o}{2T_s} \tag{3.1}$$

where $N_o/2$ is two-sided power spectral density of the noise and T_s is sampling interval. We will see in Section 6.11.2 that the autocorrelation function of continuous-time WGN is an impulse, that is, its correlation time $t_c = 0$. In Simulink software, the effect of white noise can be simulated by using a random sequence with a correlation time that is much smaller than the shortest time constant of the system. Simulink documentation suggests that for good results the correlation time is selected according to the following rule:

$$t_c = \frac{1}{100} \frac{2\pi}{\omega_{max}} \tag{3.2}$$

where ω_{max} is the bandwidth of the system in rad/sec.

Simulink and SP blockset provide Random Number, Bandlimited White Noise, and Random Source blocks to generate samples of Gaussian noise.

Random Number Block

This block in the Simulink Sources library generates Gaussian noise samples with `mean` and `variance` specified using the Parameters dialog box. The time interval between the samples is selected via the `Sample time` parameter.

Bandlimited White Noise Block

This block in the Simulink Sources library generates WGN samples with two-sided `noise power` spectral density ($N_o/2$) and `Sample time` specified using the Parameters dialog box. It is suitable for use in continuous or hybrid systems. The primary difference between this block and the Random Number block is that the Bandlimited White Noise block produces output at a specific sample rate. The sample time is the correlation time of the noise according to equation (3.2).

Random Source Block

This block in the Signal Processing Sources library from the SP blockset provides another option to generate WGN samples. For this purpose, the `Source` type parameter is set to `Gaussian` in the Parameters dialog box. If the `Method` parameter is selected `Ziggurat`, the block computes the output Gaussian random values using the Ziggurat method, which is the same method used by the MATLAB `randn` function. The `Repeatability` parameter is set as discussed previously for generating uniformly distributed random numbers.

Example 3.3

Generate and display the sequences of Gaussian distributed random numbers generated by using the following blocks

1. Random Number block
2. Bandlimited White Noise block
3. Random Source block
4. AWGN Channel block from the Communications blockset

Use `variance` and `Sample time` parameter values of 0.15 and 1/100, respectively. All blocks should be initialized with the same seed for comparison purposes.

Solution

The Simulink model for the example is shown in Figure 3.23(a). The Gaussian noise samples generated by different blocks are illustrated in Figure 3.23(b). For comparison, we are also displaying output of the AWGN Channel block from the Communications blockset. It is designed to add WGN to a real or complex input signal. We observe that algorithms used in Random Number and Bandlimited White Noise blocks are identical as evident from the waveforms shown in Figure 3.23(b). On the other hand, Random Source (Gaussian) and AWGN Channel blocks use the Ziggurat method to produce identical noise samples.

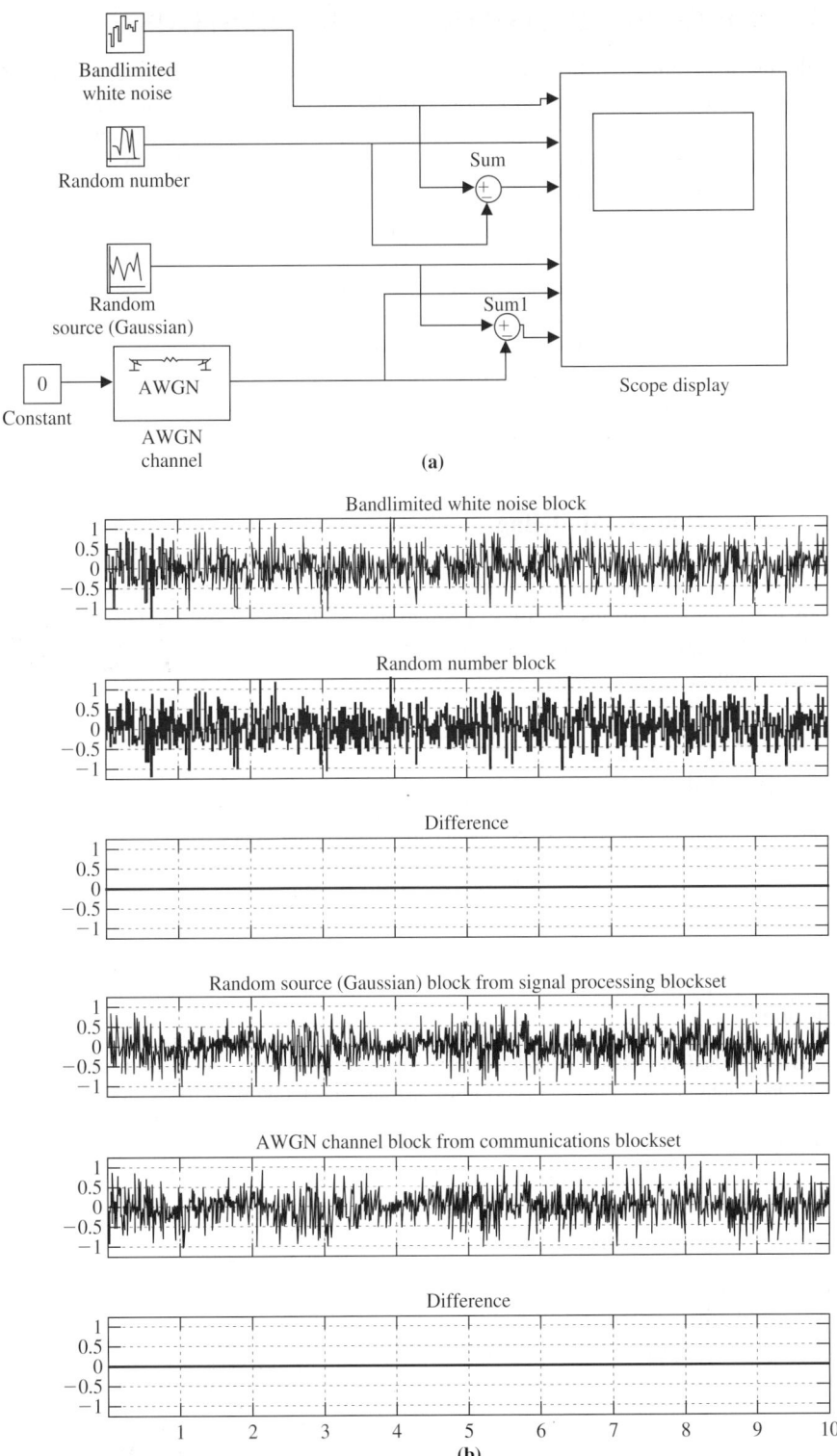

Figure 3.23 Gaussian distributed random sequences: (a) model; (b) Scope display.

3.4   MODELING OF COMMUNICATION SYSTEMS

Modeling of a communication system involves subsystems that are best represented by block diagram models in either time or one of the transform (that is s, ω, or z) domains. Most nonlinear signal processing functions are represented in time domain either by a mathematical relationship or in a tabular or graphic form. LTI signal processing functions, on the other hand, can be represented either by a linear difference equation model or more conveniently in frequency or z domains. For example, a digital filter is specified by a template in the frequency domain, whereas it is represented by its z-domain transfer or system function in a Simulink model. Further, some other signal processing functions required in a communication system are better stated in the textual language of the MATLAB software than in the graphical language of Simulink. For this purpose, `MATLAB Fcn` and `Embedded MATLAB Function` blocks from the Simulink's **User-Defined Functions** library can be used. Simulink provides multi-domain modeling environment for end-to-end simulation of communication systems.

3.4.1   Time-Domain Modeling

It is very straightforward to model a discrete-time subsystem by using blocks from **Discrete** and Math Operations libraries of Simulink. Each block from the Discrete library is assumed to have a sampler at the input and a ZOH at the output. We illustrate this by a few examples.

Example 3.4

Develop a Simulink model for DSB-SC modulator whose output is described by

$$x(t) = s(t)c(t) = \cos(2\pi f_m t)A_c\cos(2\pi f_c t) \tag{3.3}$$

Assume $f_m = 1$ Hz, $f_c = 10$ Hz, $A = 10$. Display message, carrier, and modulator output waveforms.

Solution

The DSB-SC AM modulator is modeled by the cascade of Product and Gain blocks from the Math Operations library. Figure 3.24(a) illustrates the generation of DSB-SC AM signal. The

Figure 3.24 Modeling DSB-SC AM modulator.

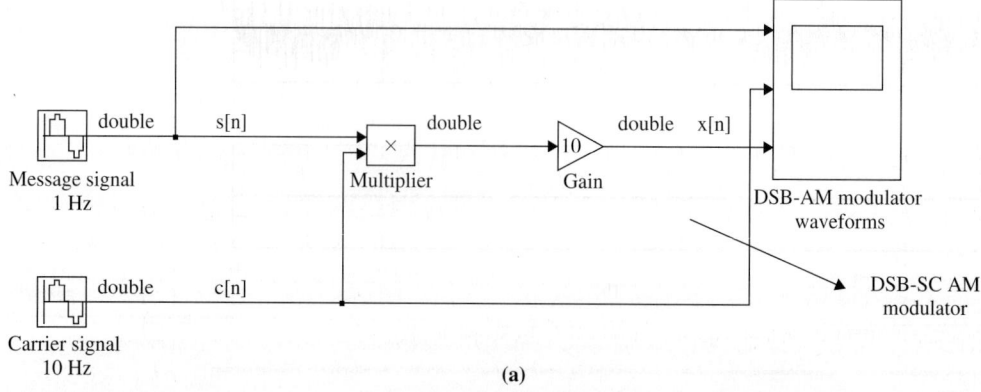

(a)

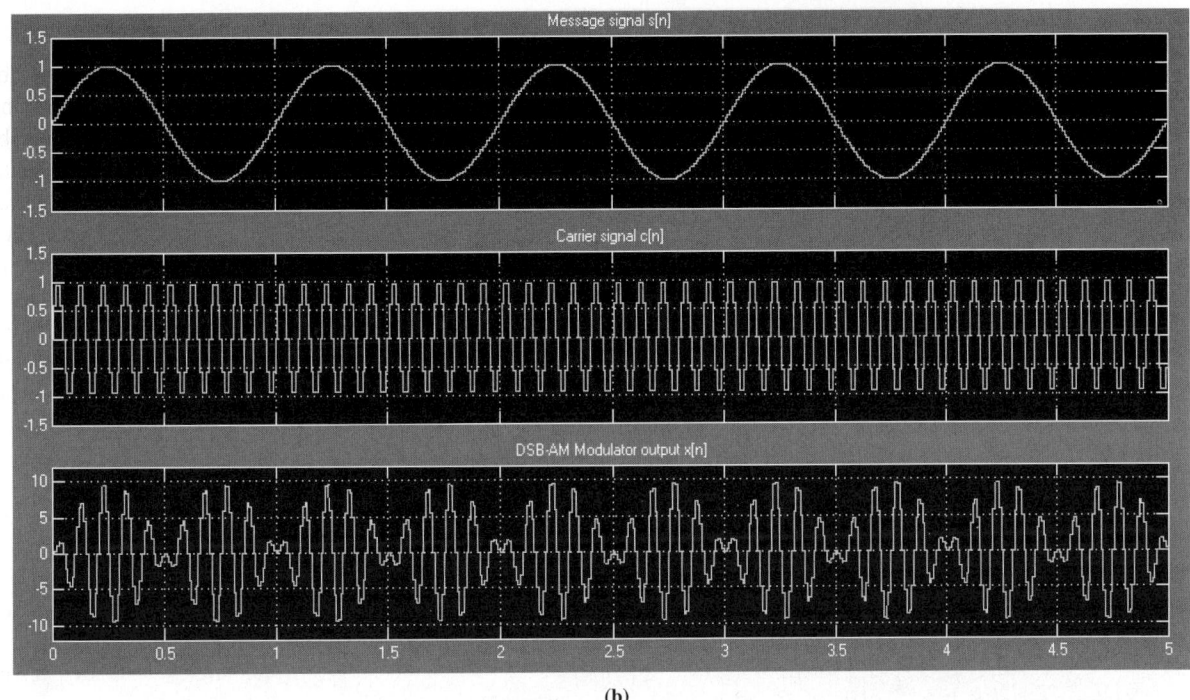

(b)

message and carrier waveforms are generated by the Sine Wave block from the Sources library. The `Sample time` parameter value of 1/100 is selected. Various modulator waveforms are displayed in Figure 3.24(b).

Example 3.5

Develop a Simulink model for an FM modulator whose output is described by

$$x_{FM}(t) = A_c \cos\left[2\pi f_c t + 2\pi k_f \int_{-\infty}^{t} s(\alpha)d\alpha\right] \quad (3.4)$$

Assume $k_f = 5$ Hz/V, $f_c = 10$ Hz, and modulating waveform $s(t) = \cos(2\pi t)$. Display the message and modulator output waveforms.

Solution

The message signal is processed by the cascade of Discrete-Time Integrator block (from the Simulink Discrete library) and Gain block (from Math Operations library) to generate the $k_f \int_{-\infty}^{t} s(\alpha)d\alpha$ term in (3.4). A Ramp block from Simulink Sources library is used to produce the $f_c t$ term in (3.4). The combined signal $f_c t + k_f \int_{-\infty}^{t} s(\alpha)d\alpha$ is applied to an **Fcn** block

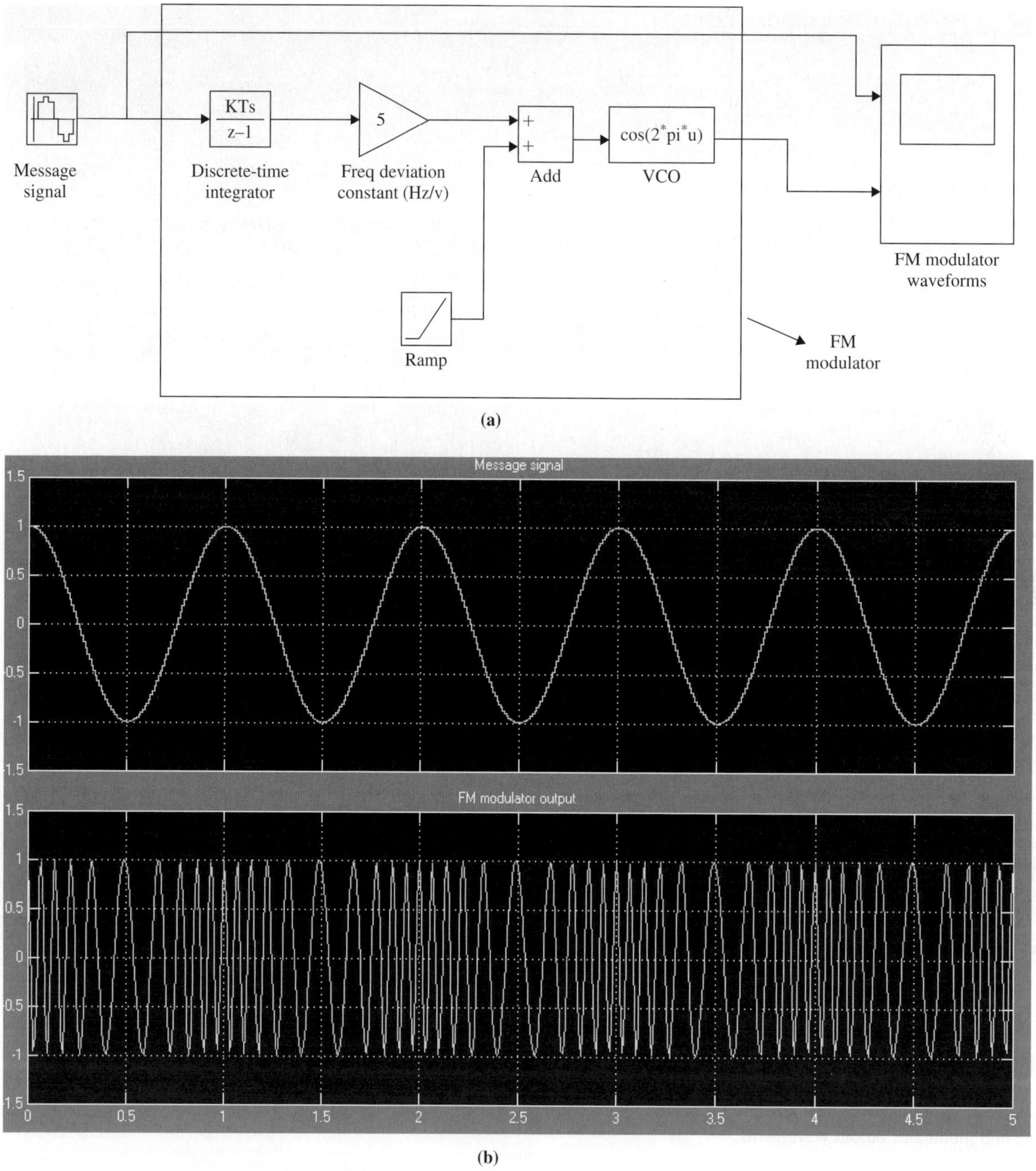

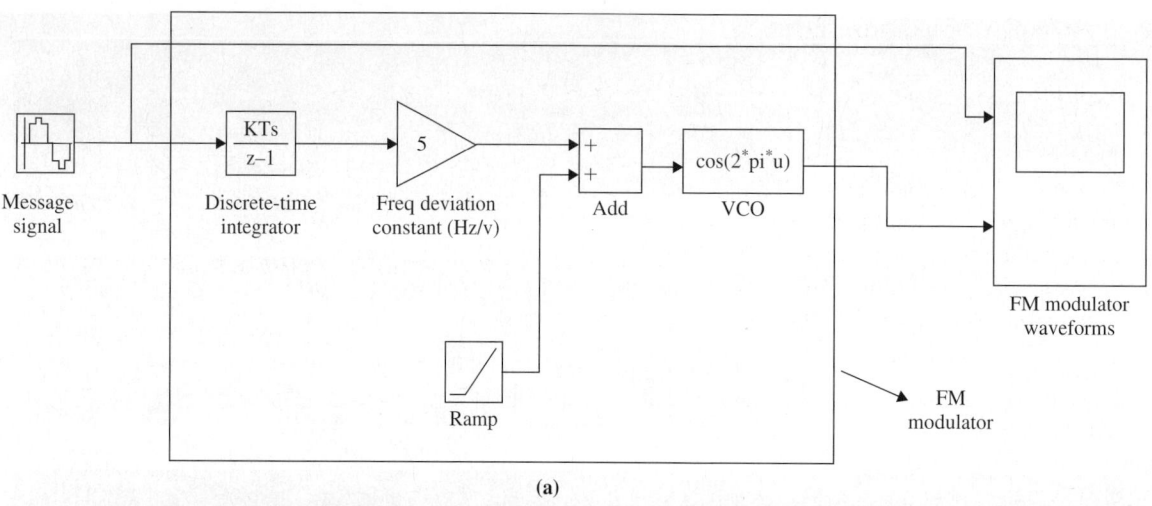

(a)

(b)

Figure 3.25 Modeling FM modulator.

from the User-Defined Functions library to produce the FM signal in (3.4). The resultant model of an FM modulator is illustrated in Figure 3.25(a). The Sample time parameter value of 1/100 is selected. The message and FM signal waveforms are displayed in Figure 3.25(b).

3.4.2   Transform-Domain Description

The goal of filtering is to perform frequency-dependent alteration of a signal. In communication systems, filters are used to shape signal spectra and remove out of band noise. The requirements of filters are obviously described in frequency-domain. However, the design of filters is usually accomplished in either *s*-domain (analog filters) or *z*-domain (digital filters). As we discussed in Section 2.8.2, the specifications for filter design include edge frequencies, passband ripple, and stopband attenuation. Various methods are supported in the MATLAB and Simulink environments to design both analog and digital filters. We will mainly use the following options:

- **Filtering** library in the SP blockset. As illustrated in Figure 3.26, if the **Filter Designs** option is selected, it offers a menu of classic filter designs (LP, HP, BP, BS) as well as other selections. The desired filter is simply dragged into the model window like any other block. The filter design parameters then need to be selected via the dialog box.

  All digital filter design functions in MATLAB and Simulink use a frequency scaling that is somewhat nonstandard. When entering the normalized passband and stopband edge frequencies $\hat{\omega}_p$ and $\hat{\omega}_s$ (radians/sample), the values must be divided by π.

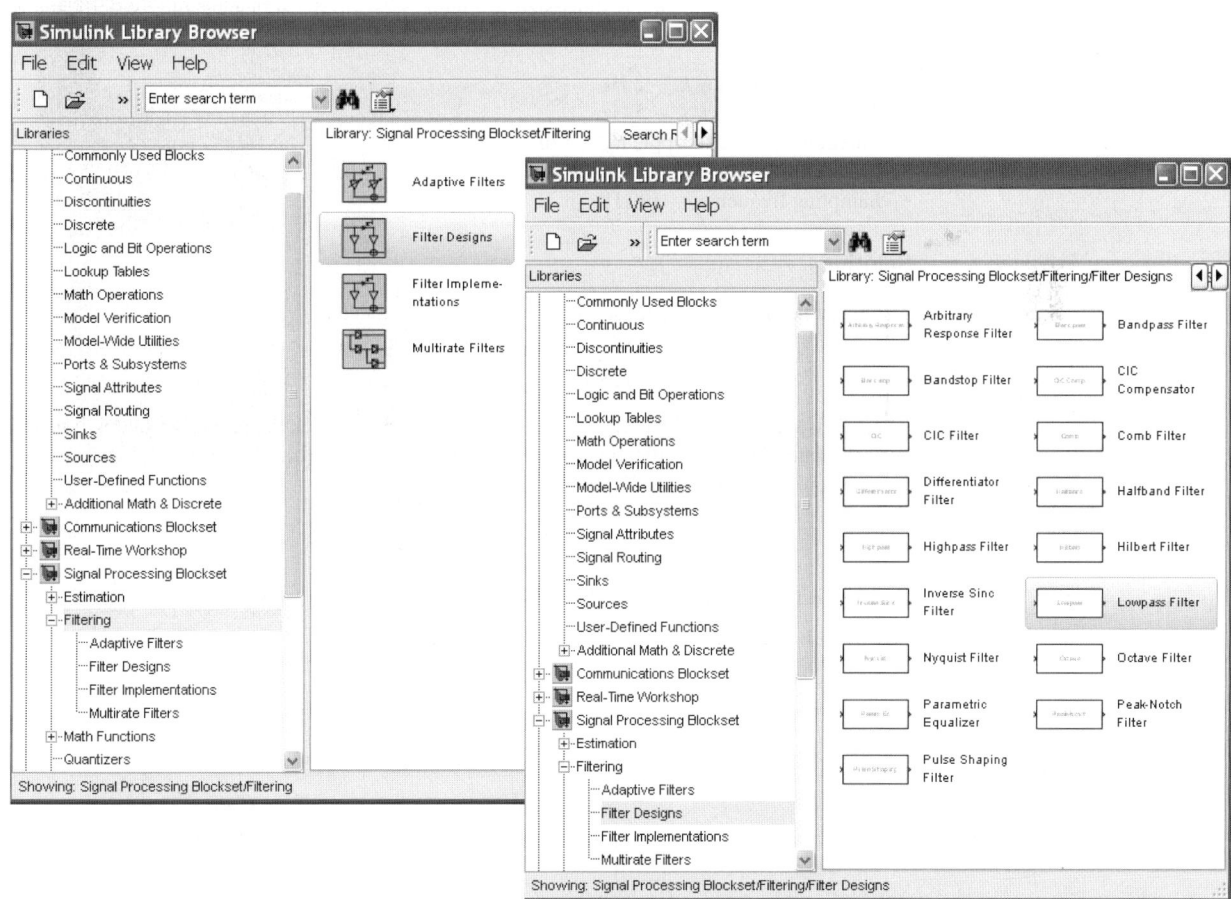

Figure 3.26 Digital filter design options in SP blockset.

Thus, an edge frequency specified as $\hat{\omega} = 0.22\pi$ would be entered as 0.22 in MAT-LAB. Therefore, if the specifications call for a passband edge frequency of 1000 Hz when the sampling frequency is 5000 Hz, we must enter 0.4 in MATLAB, because the normalized edge frequency in radians is $\hat{\omega}_p = 2\pi f_p T_s = 2\pi(1000/5000) = 2\pi(0.2) = 0.4\pi$.

- **Discrete Filter** and **Discrete Transfer Fcn** blocks from Simulink's Discrete library. Both blocks require that coefficients of the transfer function's numerator and denominator polynomials be provided via the dialog box. These blocks are equivalent except differing in the definition of the coefficients for the function's numerator and denominator polynomials. The `Discrete Filter` block requires the vectors of coefficients of polynomials in ascending powers of z^{-1}, whereas the `Discrete Transfer Fcn` block requires the vectors of coefficients of polynomials in descending powers of z. In both cases, the filter coefficients may be computed using MATLAB in a companion m-file.

Example 3.6

Consider the design of an LP digital filter using an SP blockset to limit out-of-band Gaussian noise in the Simulink model as illustrated in Figure 3.27(a). The following filter specifications are selected:

- Passband frequency $f_p = 2$ Hz
- Stopband frequency $f_s = 5$ Hz
- Maximum passband ripple $R_p = 1$ dB
- Minimum stopband ripple $R_s = 60$ dB
- Sampling frequency $= 100$ Hz

Solution

The normalized angular frequencies $\hat{\omega}_p$ and $\hat{\omega}_s$ are calculated as

$$\hat{\omega}_p = 2\pi f_p T_s = 2\pi(2/100) = 2\pi(0.02) = 0.04\pi$$
$$\hat{\omega}_s = 2\pi f_s T_s = 2\pi(5/100) = 2\pi(0.05) = 0.1\pi$$

where T_s is the sampling interval. To design the LP filter, we click the parameter dialog box and enter the filter design specifications as illustrated in Figure 3.27(b). The designed filter's magnitude response is displayed in Figure 3.27(c).

Figure 3.27 LP filter design using SP blockset in Example 3.6.

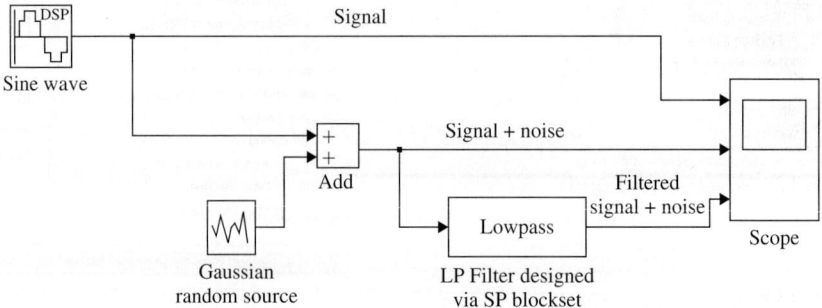

(a)

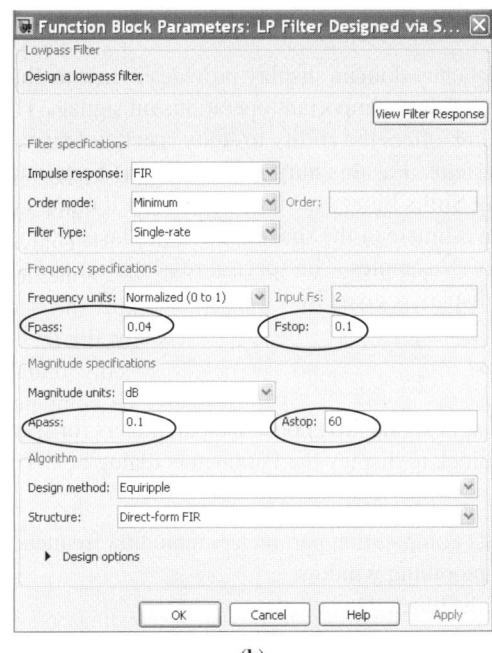

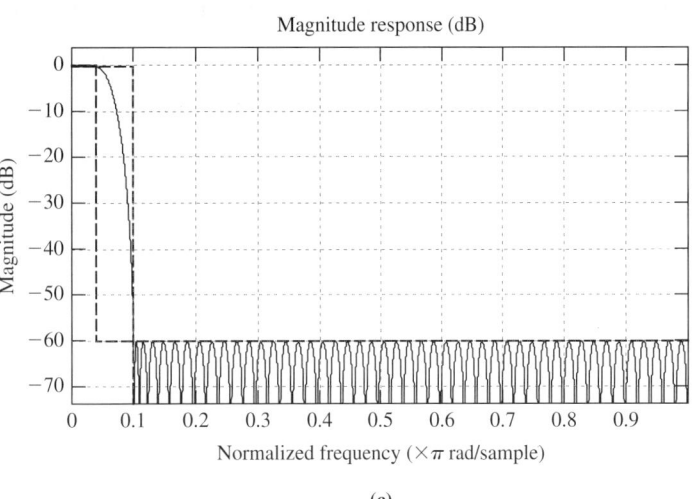

(b)

(c)

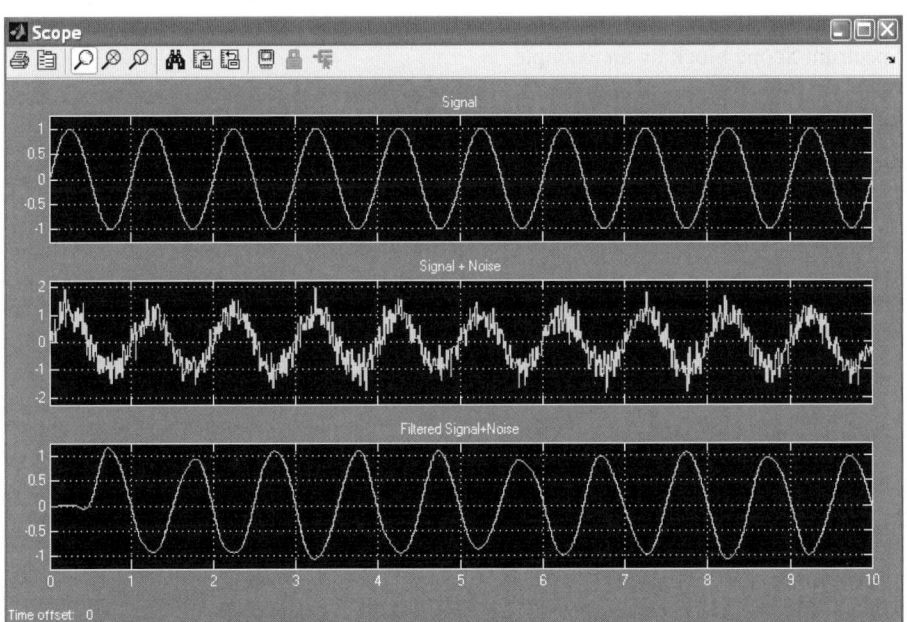

Figure 3.28 Waveforms in Example 3.6.

We observe from Figure 3.28 that the LP filter does a very good job of removing the noise from the signal. There is a slight waveform distortion in the filtering process.

3.5   DISPLAYING SIGNALS IN FREQUENCY DOMAIN

As we discussed in Section 2.3, the frequency domain display provides a unique ability to analyze and understand the effects of many important operations on signals. The spectral density display facility in Simulink offers the ability to study spectra of signals in analog and digital communication systems. For this purpose, we use the **Spectrum Scope** block from the **Signal Processing Sinks** library of the SP blockset. It computes the periodogram of the input signal as an estimate of the spectral density. The periodogram is obtained by computing the FFT of 2^N samples. The spectral resolution Δf of the resulting power spectral density (PSD) display is given by

$$\Delta f = \frac{f_s}{2^N} \tag{3.5}$$

where f_s is a sampling frequency of the input signal. To choose the parameters for spectral display, click the **Spectrum Scope** block to display the Parameters dialog box. The dialog box contains four panes:

- **Scope properties.** For specifying PSD computation parameters including frequency range, length of FFT, and choice of smoothing window.
- **Display properties.** For setting how the block displays data.
- **Axis properties.** For entering the sample time and setting the PSD display limits.
- **Line properties.** For defining parameters to distinguish two or more channels of data on the scope.

Figure 3.29 displays the scope properties pane. Note that we have selected sample-based input for PSD computation. The selection of PSD display parameters is accomplished using axis properties pane shown in Figure 3.30. We illustrate the use of the Spectrum Scope block by an example.

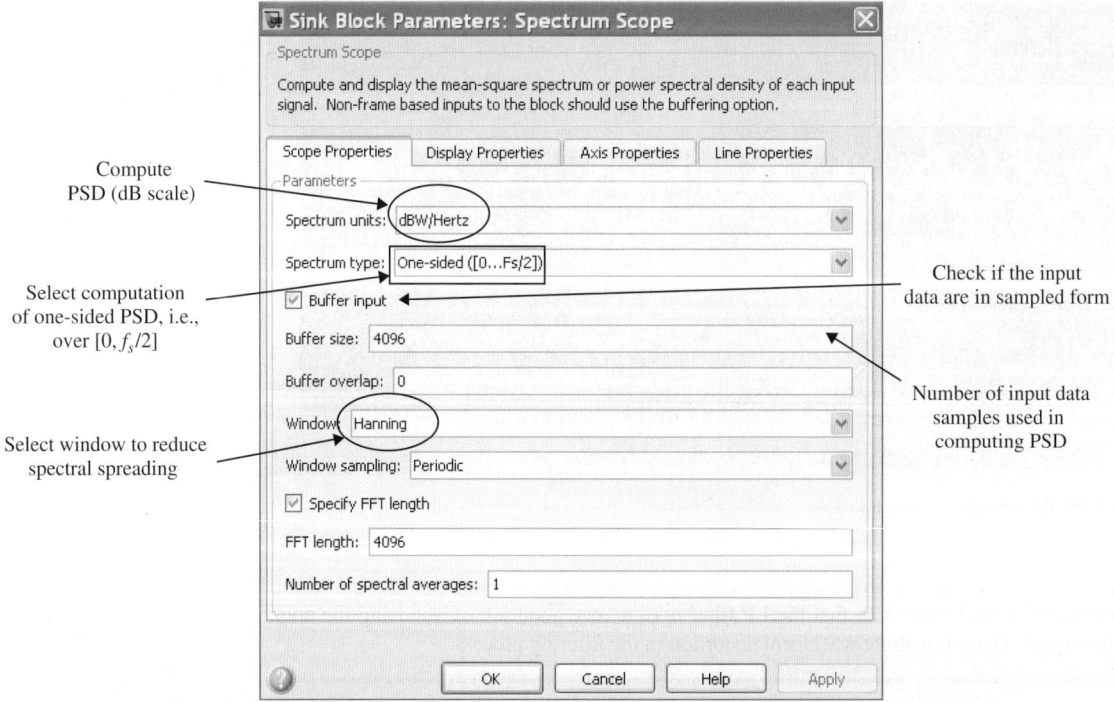

Figure 3.29 Scope properties pane of the Spectrum Scope block.

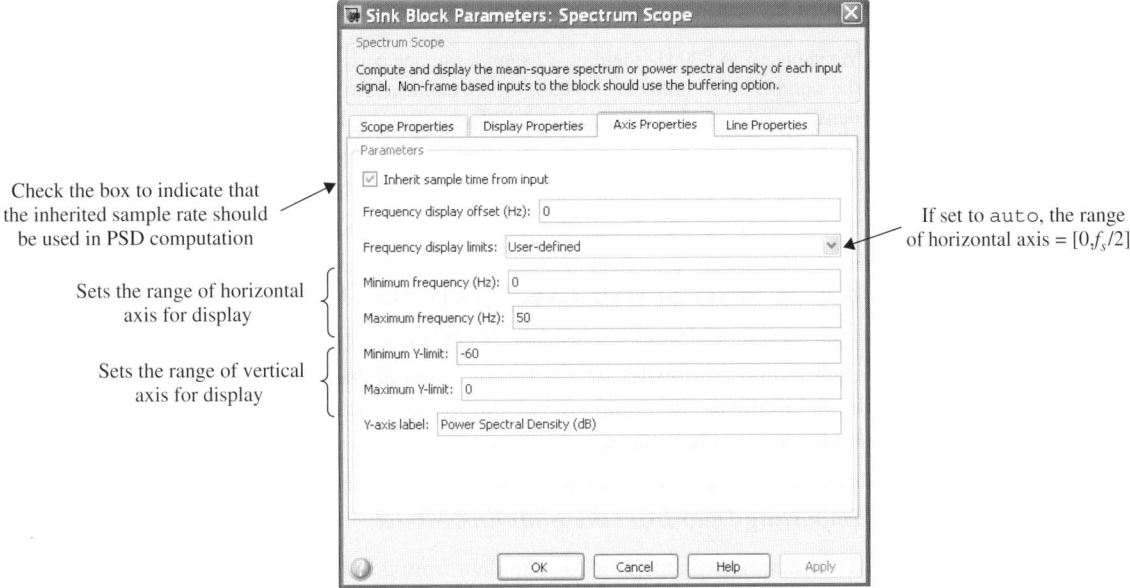

Figure 3.30 Axis properties pane of the Spectrum Scope block.

Example 3.7

Consider the Simulink model for spectral display in Figure 3.31(a) using the FM modulator model from Example 3.5. Display the spectral density of modulated signal assuming the following parameters: $f_m = 1$ Hz, $f_c = 25$ Hz, $A = 1.0$ V, $k_f = 5$ Hz/V.

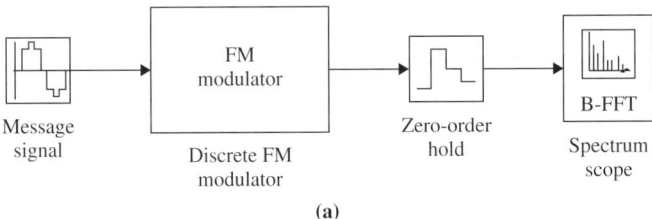

(a)

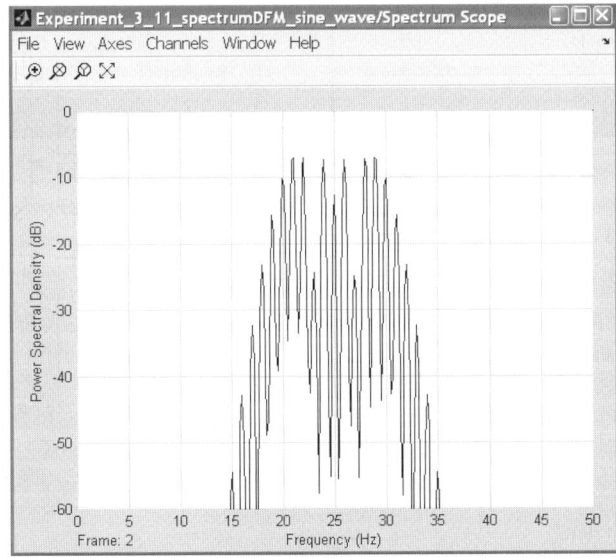

Figure 3.31 Spectrum of FM signal.

(b)

Solution

We choose $f_s = 800$ Hz yielding 32 samples in one period of 25-Hz carrier waveform. If we select the number of samples $2^N = 4096$, the frequency resolution Δf of the resulting power spectral density (PSD) display from equation (3.5) is ~ 0.2 Hz. The setting of Spectrum scope parameters is displayed in Figures 3.29 and 3.30. The spectrum of the FM signal is shown in Figure 3.31(b).

3.6   USING SIMULINK WITH MATLAB

This section describes how to use MATLAB to extend the capabilities of Simulink. We discuss how to transfer data between a model and the MATLAB workspace. We also explain how to run simulations from the command line or an m-file, and how to run multiple simulations.

Importing Data from the Simulink Model

This section explains how to send data from a Simulink model to the MATLAB workspace so the results of simulations can be analyzed further. For example, a Monte Carlo simulation of a communication system in Simulink produces the necessary data that can be further processed by a MATLAB m-file to generate SNR or BER performance curves of the system. For this purpose, a **Signal to Workspace** block from the Signal Processing Sinks library of the SP blockset can be used to send data to the MATLAB workspace as a vector. As an example, the model in Figure 3.32 simulates bit error rate calculation in a binary digital communication system. To transfer simulated error rate data to an m-file, we have inserted a Signal to Workspace block by dragging it into the model window and connecting it as shown in the figure. Next we configure the Signal to Workspace block using the following steps:

1. Double-click the block to display its dialog box.
2. Type `error_rate` in the `Variable name` field.

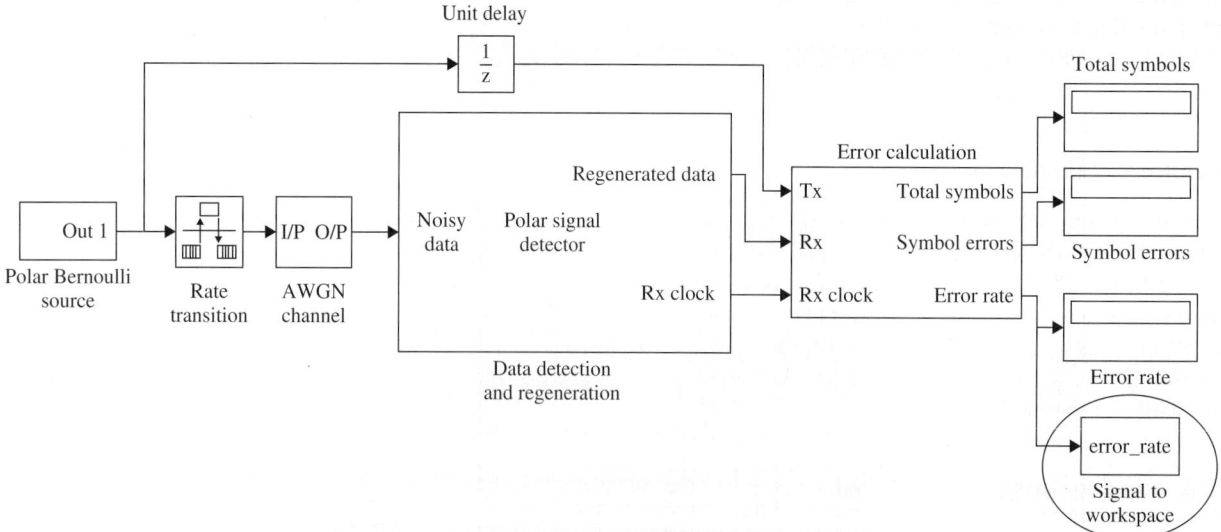

Figure 3.32   Model of a binary digital communication system.

3. Type 1 in the `Limit data points to last` field. This limits the output vector to the values at the final time step of the simulation.

4. Click **OK**.

When the simulation is run, the model sends the output of the **Error Calculation** block to the workspace as a scalar, called `error_rate`. The value of this scalar is the same as that shown by the **Error Rate Display** block. After running a simulation, one can view the output of the Signal to Workspace block by typing the following commands at the MATLAB prompt:

```
format short e
error_rate
```

The scalar output is the following:

```
error_rate =
2.0002e-004
```

3.6.1 Running Simulations from MATLAB

This section describes how to run simulations from the command line using the `sim` command. This is especially useful for running multiple simulations on a model.

Running a Single Simulation

As an example, consider the model in Figure 3.32 saved as `Example_3_12.mdl`. To run the model from the command line, enter

```
sim('Example_3_12')
```

in the MATLAB Command window. This runs the model in the background without opening the model window. While the simulation is running, the MATLAB prompt is unavailable and one cannot enter another MATLAB command. After the simulation stops, the prompt reappears. We can then view the results of the simulation by typing `Example_3_12` to open the model. It is not necessary to open the model window when running a simulation from the command line. Usually we want to send the results of the simulation to the MATLAB workspace, for example, if we are running multiple simulations on a single model.

Running Multiple Simulations

We can run multiple simulations, with different parameters, from the command line using a MATLAB script in the command window or an m-file. This section describes how to run the `Example_3_12` model with varying amounts of channel noise. This can be accomplished by running multiple simulations, each with a different SNR/bit (E_b/N_o) parameter. The m-file in Figure 3.33 runs the simulations in a loop and stores the results in a vector called `BER_Vec`. When the simulation ends, the results of the simulation are printed as follows:

```
BER_Vec =
0.0294 0.0094 0.0020 0.0002 0 0 0
```

The results of the simulation can also be plotted as illustrated in Figure 3.34. Bit error-rate results were obtained with 10,000 bits. This allows us to simulate error rates

```
%
% Set-up to run multiple simulations of Example_3_12 model
%
clc
BER_Vec=[];      % Initialize BER vector
Bit_rate=1       % Bit rate of binary digital communication system
T=1/Bit_rate;    % Bit interval
Tsim=10000       % Number of simulations to calculate BER
Ts=T/32          % sampling interval
Fs=1/Ts          % sample rate
%
% Loop parameters
%
EbNovec=[3 5 7 9 11 13 15];% Vector of Eb/No values
%
% Run multiple simulations
%
for n=1:length(EbNovec);
EbNo=EbNovec(n);
zz=10^(0.1*EbNo);
sigma2=Fs/(2*zz)
sim('Experiment_3_12');% Run simulation of Experiment_3_12_model
BER_Vec(n)=error_rate  % Output of the Error calculation block
end;
%
% Plot the results of multiple simulations:Ber vs Eb/No
%
semilogy(EbNovec,BER_Vec,'--*');
xlabel('Eb/No(db)');ylabel('BER');
axis([3 15 1e-6 1e-1])
title('BER Performance of Antipodal Signaling');
```

Various block and simulation parameters for the model set

Variance of WGN source in the model for different Eb/No values set here

Error rate calculation data from the model received via To workspace block

Figure 3.33 m-file for running multiple simulations of `Example_3_12` model.

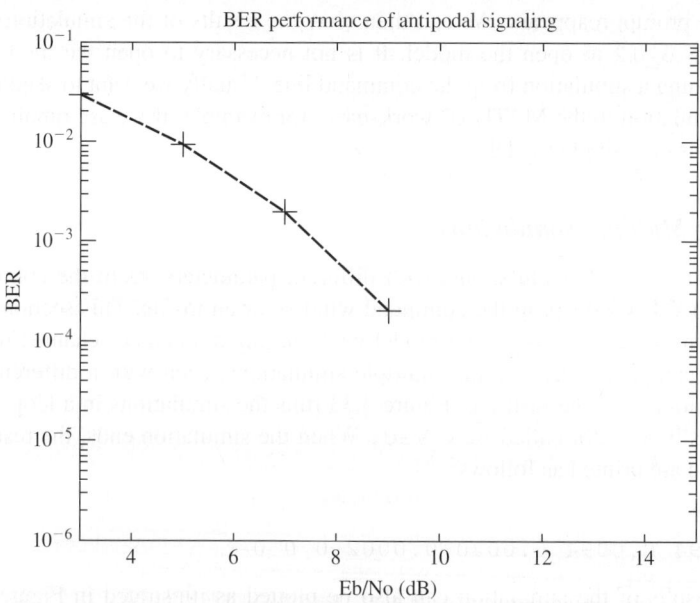

Figure 3.34 BER performance of system in Figure 3.32.

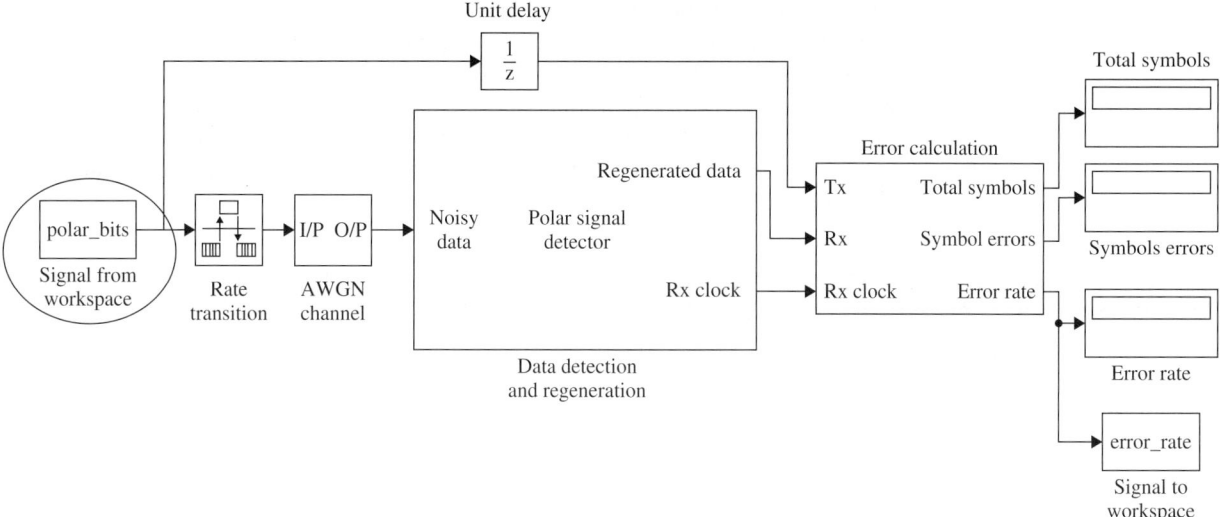

Figure 3.35 Importing a signal from the workspace.

of 10^{-3} or higher. To simulate error rates of 10^{-5}, the number of transmitted bits should be at least 500,000 to see any errors. Otherwise 0 errors will be displayed in BER_Vec for higher values of SNR/bit.

Importing Data to the Simulink Model

We can import data into a model directly from the MATLAB workspace using the **Signal from Workspace** block, in the Signal Processing Sources library. This enables us to run simulations on data that is created in the workspace or import from outside MATLAB. To import a signal that is created in the workspace, Signal from Workspace block is used as a source. An example is the model shown in Figure 3.35. This model is the same as the one shown in Figure 3.32 except that the Polar Bernoulli Source block has been replaced with a Signal from Workspace block. To build this model, follow these steps:

1. Replace the Polar Bernoulli Source block with a Signal from Workspace block from the Signal Processing Sources library.
2. In the Signal from Workspace block's dialog, change the Signal parameter to polar_Bits (or another variable name).

Before using the model, we need to define the vector polar_Bits in the MATLAB workspace. For example, the following code segment can be added to the m-file in Figure 3.33. This defines data as a random polar binary vector of length Tsim.

```
% Signal to Workspace data generation
%
bn= rand(1,Tsim);
polar_bits=sign(bn-0.5)
```

FINAL REMARKS

This chapter introduces Simulink and MATLAB as a *virtual laboratory* to develop understanding of the important concepts in the design and analysis of communication systems. By using their laptops, students can conduct experiments to model all types of communication systems in a classroom environment. They can study signal waveforms and spectra at various points in the communication system using soft scopes and spectrum analyzers. The performance of systems can be measured and compared with theory results studied in the class. Because of the flexibility of this platform, it can serve as a convenient tool to study various design trade-offs (e.g., equipment complexity, bandwidth, and power) as well.

FURTHER READINGS

The MathWorks publications [1, 2] provide extensive information on Simulink. Each Simulink block also has help screens that are accessible via the Parameters dialog box. The help screen provides useful and detailed information required in model building effort. Reference [4] provides a good tutorial introduction to the subject.

1. "Simulink 7 User's Guide," Revised for Simulink 7.5 (Release 2010a), *The MathWorks,* March 2010.

2. "Simulink 7 Getting Started Guide," Revised for Simulink 7.3 (Release 2009a), *The MathWorks,* March 2009.

3. "Communications Blockset Getting Started Guide," Version 4.2 (Release 2009a), *The MathWorks,* March 2009.

4. Dabney, J., and F. T. Harman. *Mastering Simulink.* Upper Saddle River, NJ: Prentice Hall, 2004.

Amplitude Modulation

Modulation is the process by which a message or information-bearing signal is transformed into another signal to facilitate transmission over a communication channel (e.g., radio, satellite, twisted wire pair [TWP]). Modulation involves the use of an auxiliary waveform, usually sinusoidal, called a **carrier.** A **modulated carrier** is generated by varying some characteristic (e.g., amplitude, frequency, or phase) of the carrier in accordance with the message signal. Modulation is performed to accomplish one or more of these objectives: frequency translation, channelization, practical equipment design, or noise performance improvement.

Frequency Translation

The frequency content of an information-bearing signal usually extends from direct current (DC) to some maximum frequency. The need for frequency translation arises because a communication channel usually offers optimal transmission performance (e.g., least attenuation) in a frequency range different from that of the information signal. This is taken into consideration by the governmental organizations, like the FCC in the United States, which regulates the allocation of available spectrum to **service providers,** such as AT&T and Verizon. Modulation allows the energy of the information signal to be *transferred* to a specific frequency band that is determined by the frequency of the carrier. As an example, the frequency band 869 to 894 MHz is allocated to cellular systems for downstream transmission. Human speech contains significant energy in the low frequency range (up to 4 kHz). The speech signal can be translated to a frequency slot within the allocated frequency band for transmission using one of the modulation techniques.

Channelization

Channelization refers to partitioning the bandwidth of a wideband channel into many smaller bandwidth subchannels or frequency slots to accommodate simultaneous transmission of multiple information signals. This allows efficient and cost-effective utilization of available bandwidth resources. For example, in Cable TV (CATV) systems, the frequency band 54 MHz–1 GHz is used for downstream transmission of a variety of signals, including analog TV channels, digital TV programming, high-speed Internet, and cable telephony signals. This is achieved by dividing the frequency band into 6-MHz frequency slots. A program channel from a network (e.g., CBS or NBC or ABC) may now be transmitted using one of these frequency slots (e.g., channel 2 in the 54–60 MHz slot).

Practical Equipment Design

For radio channels, the signal is converted to an electromagnetic (EM) wave for transmission by an appropriate antenna. The size of antenna for the transmission and reception of EM waves is determined by the wavelength λ_c of the carrier, where $\lambda_c = c/f_c$, c = speed of EM waves in free space (3×10^8 m/s), and f_c = frequency of the carrier. Antennas are typically $\lambda_c/4$ in size. The higher the transmitted signal frequency, the smaller the antenna size required. For example, in cellular telephony, the use of a 900 (1800) MHz carrier requires an antenna of about 8 (4) cm. Without carrier modulation to high frequencies, transmission of low frequency signals, such as speech, through free space would require unmanageably large antenna sizes.

Noise Performance Improvement

Modulation can be used to minimize the effects of noise and interference. The increased immunity is obtained by trading the extra bandwidth for the modulated signal. For example, the improved audio quality of FM radio reception is achieved at the cost of a 200-kHz channel bandwidth versus 10 kHz for AM.

In this chapter we begin the study of the transmission of analog signals by carrier modulation. First we consider the modulation of an analog signal by impressing it on the amplitude of the carrier signal. In Chapter 5, we discuss the modulated carrier, which is generated by changing the frequency or the phase of the carrier according to the amplitude of the message signal. Demodulation methods for these modulation schemes to recover the original message signal are also considered. Chapter 7 treats the performance of analog transmission systems in the presence of noise.

There are several different ways of amplitude modulating the carrier signal by message signal. These include

- Double-sideband, suppressed-carrier (DSB-SC) amplitude modulation (AM)
- Conventional AM
- Single-sideband AM (SSB-AM)
- Vestigial-sideband AM (VSB-AM)

Each modulation scheme results in different spectral characteristics for the transmitted signal.

The chapter is organized into the following sections:

4.1 LOW-PASS AND BANDPASS SIGNALS.

    This section introduces the concepts of LP and BP signals.

4.2 DOUBLE-SIDEBAND SUPPRESSED-CARRIER AM.

    The simplest of the amplitude modulation schemes is considered here. We study the spectral characteristics of the modulated waveform and then analyze the demodulation process to recover the message signal.

4.3 CONVENTIONAL AMPLITUDE MODULATION.

    We explain this very popular amplitude modulation system, its spectral characteristics, and its power efficiency. This type of AM lends itself to a very simple demodulating technique using an envelope detector.

4.4 ALTERNATIVE REPRESENTATIONS FOR BP SIGNALS AND SYSTEMS.

    The complex envelope representation for BP signals and systems is introduced to facilitate a simplified analysis of many carrier modulated systems.

4.5 SINGLE-SIDEBAND AM.

    This section introduces a bandwidth-efficient AM system where only one of the sidebands is transmitted. The two approaches for generating SSB-AM are described and issues related to practical realization are discussed.

4.6 VESTIGIAL-SIDEBAND AM.

    We explain the VSB-AM modulation scheme in this section. The characteristics of the VSB filtering to achieve bandwidth efficiency without introducing signal distortion are considered.

4.7 QUADRATURE MULTIPLEXING.

    We discuss the transmission of two message signals in the same frequency slot by using quadrature carriers.

4.8 MULTIPLEXING.

    In this section we consider frequency-division-multiplexing as a means of efficiently sharing the bandwidth resources of a communication channel or medium for simultaneous transmission of multiple lower-bandwidth user signals.

4.9 FREQUENCY TRANSLATION AND SELECTION.

    We explain these key operations implemented in communication transmitters and receivers. The section concludes with a discussion of down-conversion mixer-design approaches for image rejection.

4.10 COMMUNICATION RECEIVERS.

    This section considers key performance objectives for a communication receiver and various design approaches to achieve them. After explaining the superheterodyne receiver, we explore zero- and low-IF receiver options because of their attractiveness for realization as an integrated design using complementary metal oxide semiconductor (CMOS) technology.

APPENDIX 4A

    Discusses the Hilbert transform and its properties.

This chapter concludes with final remarks and a selected list of references.

Pioneers in the Field

Reginald Fessenden, a prolific inventor, was born October 6, 1866, in Knowlton, Quebec, Canada. From early on, he was a very gifted student. At age eleven he attended Trinity College School in Port Hope, Ontario, and at age fourteen, the Bishop's College in Lennoxville, Quebec, granted him a mathematics mastership. Fessenden left Bishop's College when he was eighteen, just short of completing his degree. During the next two years, he worked at the Whitney Institute in Bermuda, where he served as the sole teacher and principal, and met his future wife, Helen Trott.

Like many aspiring inventors of his time, Fessenden wanted to work for Thomas Edison. To this end, he moved to New York City, and through his perseverance, landed a job with Edison's company. He became interested in wireless technology after hearing about Guglielmo Marconi's work. Fessenden recognized that the spark technology used by Marconi was inefficient because the resultant spectral splatter wasted both power and bandwidth. He envisioned a simpler, cleaner technology that involved continuous wave transmission, and his idea was to develop a high-speed alternator that produced electrical currents at tens of kilohertz, that is, a radio frequency (RF) signal. Then, he could *amplitude modulate* the RF carrier wave by inserting a carbon microphone between the high-speed alternator and the antenna.

Fessenden contracted with General Electric to help design and produce a series of high-frequency alternator-transmitters. On December 21, 1906, Fessenden used the new alternator-transmitter to make a demonstration of wireless speech transmission at Brant Rock, Massachusetts. Three days later, he made the world's first radio broadcast from Brant Rock. The transmission included a speech by Fessenden, selected Christmas music, and his rendition of Handel's Largo on the violin. That first broadcast was heard by radio operators onboard U.S. Navy and United Fruit Company ships at various distances over the South and North Atlantic, and as far away as the West Indies. It was a pleasant surprise for those lonely sailors at sea to hear Christmas music followed by a perfectly clear speech.

Another major advance made by Fessenden was the development of the *heterodyne* principle, whereby two signals are multiplied to generate a signal at a third frequency. He undertook experiments with this in 1901; however, given the state of wireless technology, they were well ahead of their time and not used for over 10 years afterward (requiring the availability of stable continuous wave signal sources which were not practicable until the vacuum tube was invented). Although Reginald Fessenden held over 250 patents, he never really received the recognition that he deserved. Nonetheless, he did receive the Scientific American Gold medal in 1929.

4.1   LOW-PASS AND BANDPASS SIGNALS

An LP signal $s(t)$ has its spectral energy clustered around the DC or zero frequency. All practical LP signals will have a frequency above which their spectral components may be considered negligible, as shown in Figure 4.1. This frequency, denoted by B, is called the **bandwidth** of the LP signal.

A BP signal $x(t)$ has spectral components concentrated in the vicinity of a frequency f_c, which is usually much higher than the bandwidth of the signal. Figure 4.2 displays the spectrum of the BP signal.

An arbitrary BP signal $x(t)$ can be expressed as

$$x(t) = A(t)\cos\left[2\pi f_c t + \psi(t)\right] \qquad (4.1)$$

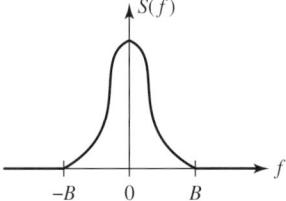

Figure 4.1 Spectrum of an LP signal.

where $A(t) \geq 0$ is the time-varying **amplitude** or **envelope** of the modulated signal and $\psi(t)$ is the time-varying phase. The carrier frequency f_c is assumed to be sufficiently large compared with the amplitude and phase variations of $x(t)$ so that its spectrum does not contain energy at low frequencies, including the DC. Equation (4.1) is called the **amplitude-phase representation** of the BP signal. In Section 4.4, we will study alternative representations of BP signals and systems that will lead to simplified analysis in many cases.

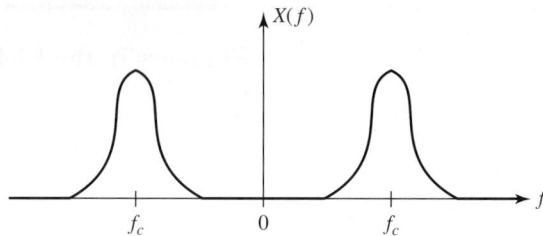

Figure 4.2 Spectrum of a BP signal.

4.2   DOUBLE-SIDEBAND SUPPRESSED-CARRIER AM

A double-sideband suppressed-carrier (DSB-SC) AM signal is obtained by multiplying the message signal $s(t)$ with the carrier signal $c(t) = A_c\cos(2\pi f_c t)$ as shown in Figure 4.3. Thus, we have the amplitude-modulated signal

$$x_{DSB}(t) = s(t)c(t) = A_c s(t)\cos(2\pi f_c t) \tag{4.2}$$

Figure 4.4 displays an assumed message signal and corresponding DSB-SC AM waveforms. Note that the modulated waveform retains the key characteristics of the message signal. Therefore, it can be used to recover the message signal at the receiver by appropriate signal processing.

4.2.1   Spectrum of the DSB-SC AM Signal

The spectrum of the modulated signal can be obtained by taking the Fourier transform (FT) of $x_{DSB}(t)$ and using the convolution property (2.79). This yields

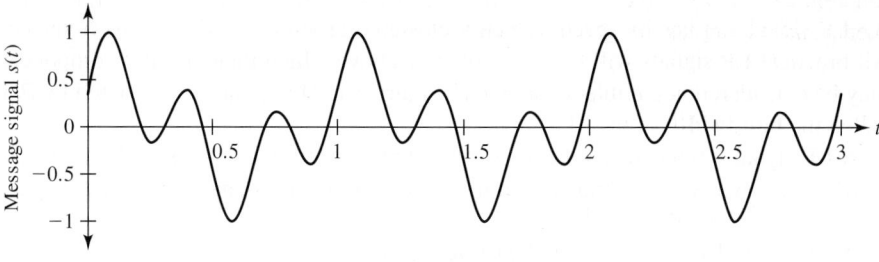

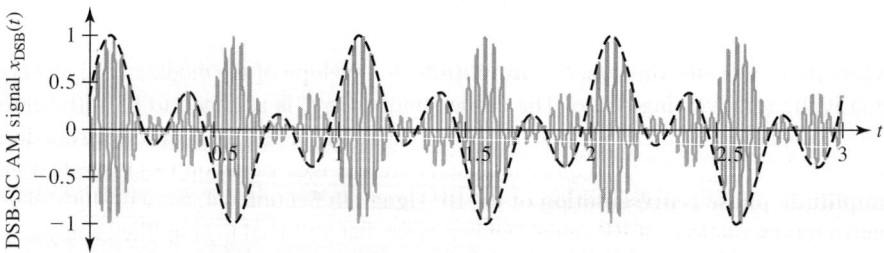

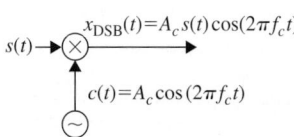

Figure 4.3 DSB-SC amplitude modulation.

Figure 4.4 DSB-SC modulation waveforms.

$$X_{DSB}(f) = S(f) \otimes C(f) = \frac{A_c}{2}S(f) \otimes \left[\delta(f - f_c) + \delta(f + f_c)\right]$$

$$= \frac{A_c}{2}\left[S(f - f_c) + S(f + f_c)\right] \tag{4.3}$$

Figure 4.5 displays the magnitude spectra for $S(f)$ and $X_{DSB}(f)$. The message spectrum $S(f)$ is chosen for the purpose of illustration only and it does not correspond to $s(t)$ in Figure 4.4. We observe that the modulation has translated the magnitude spectrum of the message signal $s(t)$ by the frequency $\pm f_c$. Further, the amplitude-modulated signal occupies a bandwidth of $2B$, whereas the bandwidth of the message signal $s(t)$ is B. Therefore, the bandwidth required to transmit the modulated signal $x_{DSB}(t)$ is given by

$$B_T = 2B \tag{4.4}$$

The spectrum of the modulated signal $x_{DSB}(t)$ in the frequency band $|f| > f_c$ is called the **upper sideband** of $X_{DSB}(f)$ and the spectrum in the frequency band $|f| < f_c$ is called the **lower sideband** of $X_{DSB}(f)$. Note that either one of the sidebands of $X_{DSB}(f)$ contains all of the information content that is in $S(f)$. For example, the frequency content of the upper sideband for $f > f_c$ corresponds to the frequency components of $S(f)$ for $f > 0$, and the frequency content for $f < -f_c$ corresponds to the frequency content of $S(f)$ for $f < 0$. Similarly, the lower sideband of $X_{DSB}(f)$ also contains all the spectral components of the message signal $S(f)$. Because $X_{DSB}(f)$ contains both the upper and the lower sidebands, it is called a **double-sideband** AM **signal.**

The other characteristic of the modulated signal $x_{DSB}(t)$ is that it does not contain energy at the carrier frequency f_c. For this reason, $x_{DSB}(t)$ is called a **suppressed-carrier signal.** Because all the transmitted power resides in the sidebands, the resultant power efficiency makes the DSB-SC modulation scheme attractive. However for coherent demodulation, a locally generated carrier, that is frequency- and phase-locked with the carrier used for modulation at the transmitter, is required. The generation of such a coherent carrier, when the received signal has no spectral component at the carrier frequency, adds complexity to the receiver design.

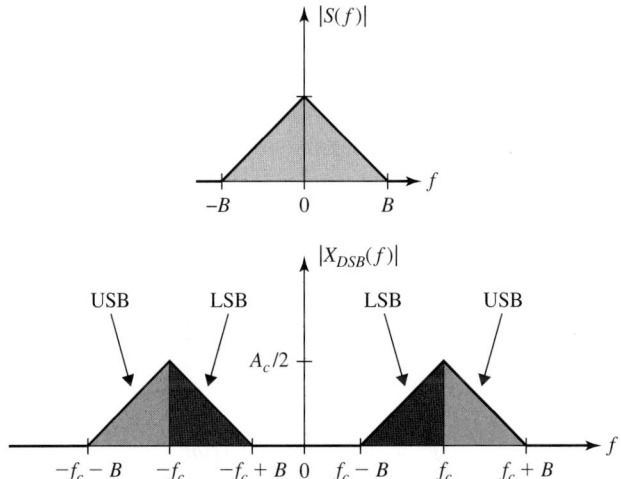

Figure 4.5 Spectra of the message and DSB-SC AM signals.

Example 4.1

Let the modulating signal be a single tone $s(t) = A_m\cos(2\pi f_m t)$. Determine the spectrum of corresponding DSB-SC AM signal $x(t)$ and plot it.

Solution

The DSB-SC AM signal $x_{DSB}(t)$ is given from (4.2) as

$$x_{DSB}(t) = s(t)c(t) = A_c A_m\cos(2\pi f_c t)\cos(2\pi f_m t)$$

$$= \frac{A_c A_m}{2}\left\{\cos\left[2\pi(f_c + f_m)t\right] + \cos\left[2\pi(f_c - f_m)t\right]\right\}$$

Taking the Fourier transform of both sides, we obtain

$$X_{DSB}(f) = \frac{A_c A_m}{4}\left\{\begin{array}{l}\delta\left[f - (f_c + f_m)\right] + \delta\left[f + (f_c + f_m)\right]\\ +\delta\left[f - (f_c - f_m)\right] + \delta\left[f + (f_c - f_m)\right]\end{array}\right\}$$

Figure 4.6 displays the spectrum of a DSB-SC AM signal for the special case of a sinusoidal message signal. Note the spectrum consists of impulses at $f_c \pm f_m$, and $-f_c \pm f_m$. There is no spectral energy at the carrier frequency, as expected.

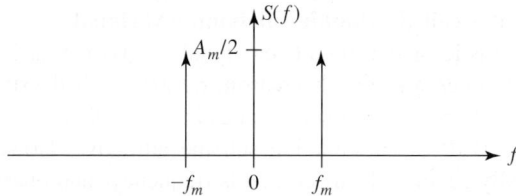

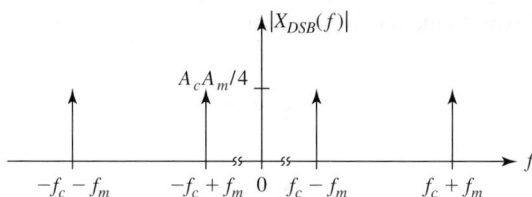

Figure 4.6 Spectrum of a DSB-SC signal with single-tone modulating signal.

Power Content of DSB-SC AM Signal

The normalized average power of a DSB-SC AM signal can be obtained by using (2.20) as

$$P_x = \lim_{T\to\infty}\frac{1}{T}\int_{-T/2}^{T/2} x_{DSB}^2(t)dt \tag{2.20}$$

Substituting (4.2) into (2.20) yields

$$P_x = \lim_{T \to \infty} \frac{A_c^2}{T} \int\limits_{-T/2}^{T/2} s^2(t) \cos^2(2\pi f_c t) dt$$

$$= \frac{A_c^2}{2} \lim_{T \to \infty} \frac{1}{T} \int\limits_{-T/2}^{T/2} s^2(t) \left[1 + \cos(4\pi f_c t) \right] dt \qquad (4.5)$$

The second integral in (4.5) is zero because it evaluates the integrand $s^2(t)\cos(4\pi f_c t)$, where $s(t)$ is slowly varying versus the high-frequency carrier term $\cos(4\pi f_c t)$. Therefore, we can simplify (4.5) into the following form:

$$P_x = \frac{A_c^2}{2} P_s \qquad (4.6)$$

where P_s represents the normalized average power in the baseband message waveform $s(t)$. $\dfrac{A_c^2}{2}$ is the normalized average power of the unmodulated carrier signal.

Often, the power of amplitude modulated signals is specified in terms of the normalized **peak envelope power (PEP).** It is defined as the average power supplied by the modulator to a 1 ohm load during one carrier frequency cycle at the crest of the modulation envelope. It is equivalent to the average power supplied to a 1 ohm load by a sinusoidal waveform with amplitude equal to the peak of the modulated waveform. For DSB-SC AM signals, the PEP is given by

$$PEP_{DSB} = \text{Power supplied by a sinusoidal waveform with amplitude } A_c \left[\max_t s(t) \right]$$

$$= \frac{A_c^2 \left[\max\limits_t s(t) \right]^2}{2} \qquad (4.7)$$

where $\max\limits_t s(t)$ is peak amplitude of the message signal $s(t)$.

For the sinusoidal modulating signal considered in Example 4.1, the normalized average power of the DSB-SC AM signal is $P_x = \dfrac{A_c^2 A_m^2}{4}$. The PEP supplied by the DSB-SC AM waveform is given by $PEP_{DSB} = \dfrac{A_m^2 A_c^2}{2}$. Thus, $PEP_{DSB} = 2P_x$. For a message signal consisting of human voice, the PEP is about three to four times the average power.

4.2.2   Demodulation of DSB-SC AM Signals

For the purpose of analysis in this section, we neglect channel noise and assume that the received signal at the demodulator is an attenuated version of the transmitted signal.

$$r(t) = \alpha x_{DSB}(t), \ \alpha < 1 \qquad (4.8)$$

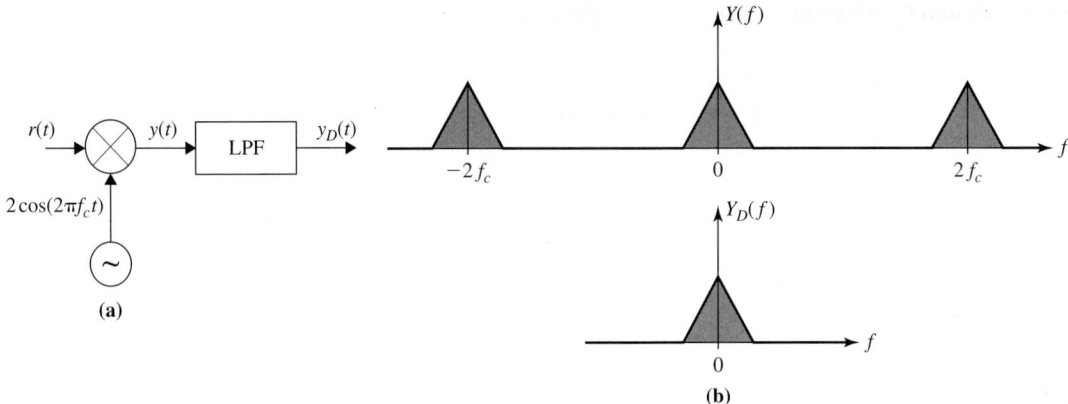

Figure 4.7 (a) Coherent demodulation of DSB-SC AM signal; (b) spectra of signals in DSB-SC demodulation process.

where α represents the attenuation produced by the channel. We assume $\alpha = 1$ without any loss of generality. We now demonstrate that the message waveform $s(t)$ can be recovered by first multiplying the received waveform $r(t)$ with a locally generated carrier and then LP filtering the product signal as illustrated in Figure 4.7(a). If the locally generated carrier is frequency- and phase-locked to the carrier used for modulation at the transmitter, the demodulation scheme is called **coherent.** Under this condition, the multiplier output is given by

$$y(t) = r(t) \times 2\cos(2\pi f_c t) = x_{DSB}(t) \times 2\cos(2\pi f_c t)$$

$$= A_c s(t)\cos(2\pi f_c t) \times 2\cos(2\pi f_c t)$$

$$= A_c s(t) + \underbrace{A_c s(t)\cos(4\pi f_c t)}_{\substack{\text{Double carrier frequency term.} \\ \text{Filtered out.}}} \tag{4.9}$$

The demodulation process in the frequency domain is illustrated in Figure 4.7(b). The multiplier output $y(t)$ after LP filtering and appropriate amplification yields

$$y_D(t) = s(t) \tag{4.10}$$

Next let us assume a frequency and phase error in the locally generated carrier at the demodulator. In this case, the multiplier output is given by

$$y(t) = r(t) \times 2\cos\left[2\pi(f_c + \Delta f)t + \phi\right] = A_c s(t)\cos(2\pi f_c t) \times 2\cos\left[2\pi(f_c + \Delta f)t + \phi\right]$$

$$= A_c s(t)\cos(\Delta ft + \phi) + \underbrace{A_c s(t)\cos\left[2\pi(2f_c + \Delta f)t + \phi\right]}_{\substack{\text{Double carrier frequency term.} \\ \text{Filtered out.}}} \tag{4.11}$$

The demodulated output $y_D(t)$ is

$$y_D(t) = s(t)\cos(\Delta ft + \phi) \tag{4.12}$$

The coherent detection case corresponds to $\Delta f = 0$ and $\phi = 0$. For $\Delta f = 0$, the demodulator output is given by

$$y_D(t) = s(t)\cos\phi \qquad (4.13)$$

We note from (4.13) that the desired signal $s(t)$ in the demodulated output is attenuated by the factor $\cos(\phi)$ that depends on the phase error ϕ between the locally generated carrier and the carrier used for modulation at the transmitter. For example, if $\phi = 45°$, the amplitude of the desired signal is reduced by $\sqrt{2}$ and the signal power is reduced by a factor of two. If $\phi = 90°$, the desired signal is totally annihilated. This justifies the need for coherent demodulation of the received DSB-SC signal to recover the message signal $s(t)$.

To implement a coherent demodulation scheme, a coherent carrier needs to be generated locally. This is difficult because there is no spectral component at the carrier frequency in the received DSB-SC signal. One method of generating a coherent carrier utilizes some form of nonlinear processing, such as a square-law device as shown in Figure 4.8. The output of the square-law device is given by

$$r^2(t) = A_c^2 s^2(t)\cos^2(2\pi f_c t)$$

$$= \frac{1}{2}A_c^2 s^2(t) + \frac{1}{2}A_c^2 s^2(t)\cos(4\pi f_c t) \qquad (4.14)$$

It is reasonable to assume that $s(t)$ is a power signal implying, by definition, that $s^2(t)$ has a nonzero DC average. That is, $s^2(t)$ has a nonzero spectral component at DC. By invoking the frequency translation property (2.78) of the Fourier transform, we can state that $s^2(t)\cos(4\pi f_c t)$ has a spectral component at $2f_c$ that can be extracted using a narrowband BP filter. The coherent carrier required for demodulation is now obtained using a frequency scaler (divider).

Another method of providing coherent carrier is to add a relatively small amplitude pilot tone at the carrier frequency. This produces a DSB signal, but it is no longer a suppressed carrier signal. A narrowband BP filter at the receiver extracts the pilot tone that is used to recover the desired signal. In Chapter 13 we will discuss the **Costas loop,** which is a popular method of carrier recovery when the received signal does not have a spectral component at the carrier frequency.

Figure 4.8 DSB-SC carrier recovery using a square law device.

Experiment 4.1   *DSB-SC AM Modulation and Demodulation*

In this experiment, we model a DSB-SC AM system using Simulink and MATLAB. Figure 4.9(a) illustrates the Simulink model for the system. The models of modulator and demodulator depict the block diagrams in Figures 4.3 and 4.7(a), respectively. The message signal is 1-Hz sine wave and the carrier frequency is selected as 20 Hz. The `Sample time` parameter value of 1/1000 is used. The parameters of simulation including message signal frequency, carrier frequency, and sampling rate are set up by a companion MATLAB m-file. The m-file also computes the transfer function of the BP and LP filters in the DSB-AM coherent demodulator. Figures 4.9(b) and 4.9(c) display modulator and demodulator waveforms. The spectra of various waveforms are shown in Figures 4.9(d).

Figure 4.9 (a) Simulink model of DSB-SC AM system; (b) modulator waveforms; (c) demodulator waveforms; (d) spectra of waveforms.

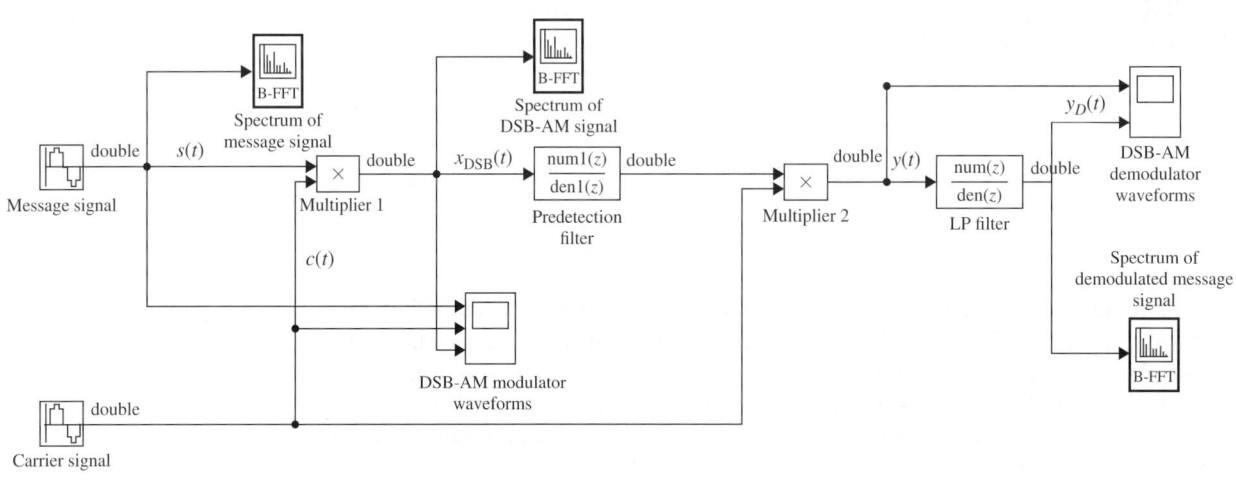

(a)

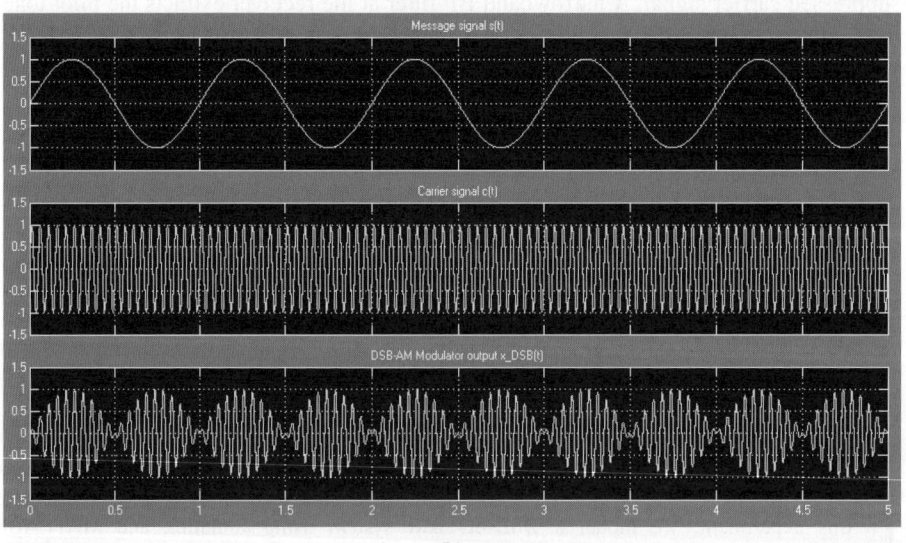

(b)

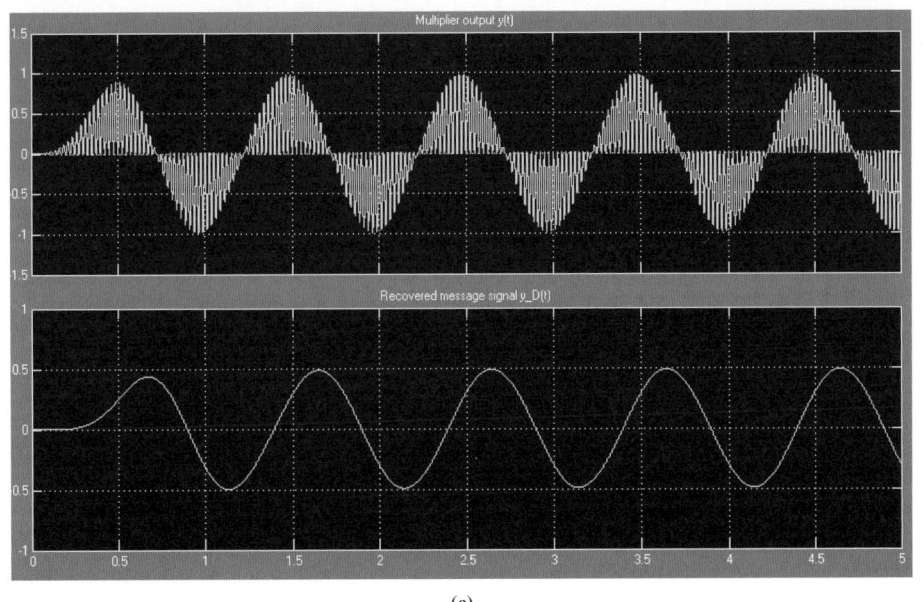

(c)

Spectrum of message signal

Spectrum of DSB-AM signal

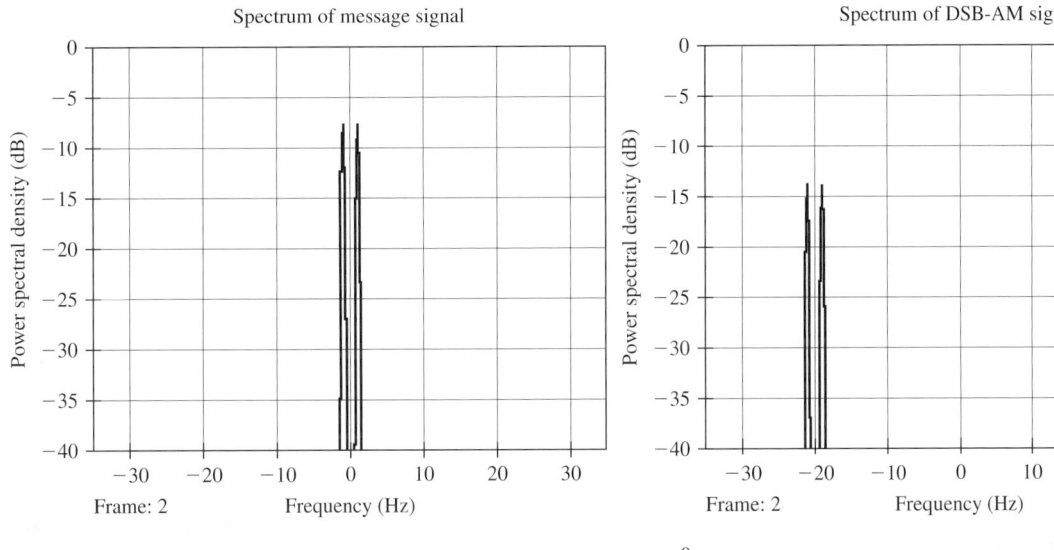

Spectrum of demodulated
message signal

(d)

4.3   CONVENTIONAL AMPLITUDE MODULATION

In the conventional amplitude modulation scheme, a portion of the sinusoidal carrier is added to the DSB-SC AM signal, which greatly simplifies the demodulation process. The transmitted signal is given by

$$x_{AM}(t) = A_c\cos(2\pi f_c t) + s(t)\cos(2\pi f_c t)$$

$$= \big[A_c + s(t)\big]\cos(2\pi f_c t) \tag{4.15}$$

Equation (4.15) can be written in a more convenient form as

$$x_{AM}(t) = A_c\big[1 + m_a s_n(t)\big]\cos(2\pi f_c t) \tag{4.16}$$

where $s_n(t)$ is a normalized version of $s(t)$ defined by

$$s_n(t) \triangleq \frac{s(t)}{\left|\min_t s(t)\right|}, \quad \left|\min_t s(t)\right| \neq 0 \tag{4.17}$$

We note from (4.17) that the normalized signal $s_n(t) \geq -1$. The parameter m_a determines the extent to which the carrier has been amplitude-modulated. It is called the **modulation index** and is defined as

$$m_a \triangleq \frac{\left|\min_t s(t)\right|}{A_c} \tag{4.18}$$

Let $A_{\max}$ and $A_{\min}$ be maximum and minimum values of the envelope $A_c[1 + m_a s_n(t)]$, respectively. Because the minimum value of $s_n(t)$ is -1,

$$A_{\min} = A_c(1 - m_a) \tag{4.19}$$

Also,

$$A_{\max} = A_c\{\max_t[1 + m_a s_n(t)]\} \tag{4.20}$$

If the message signal is symmetrical in the sense that $\left|\max_t s_n(t)\right| = \left|\min_t s_n(t)\right|$, it follows from (4.20) that $A_{\max} = A_c(1 + m_a)$. In this case, we can express the modulation index as

$$m_a = \frac{A_{\max} - A_c}{A_c} = \frac{A_c - A_{\min}}{A_c} = \frac{A_{\max} - A_{\min}}{2A_c} = \frac{A_{\max} - A_{\min}}{A_{\max} + A_{\min}} \tag{4.21}$$

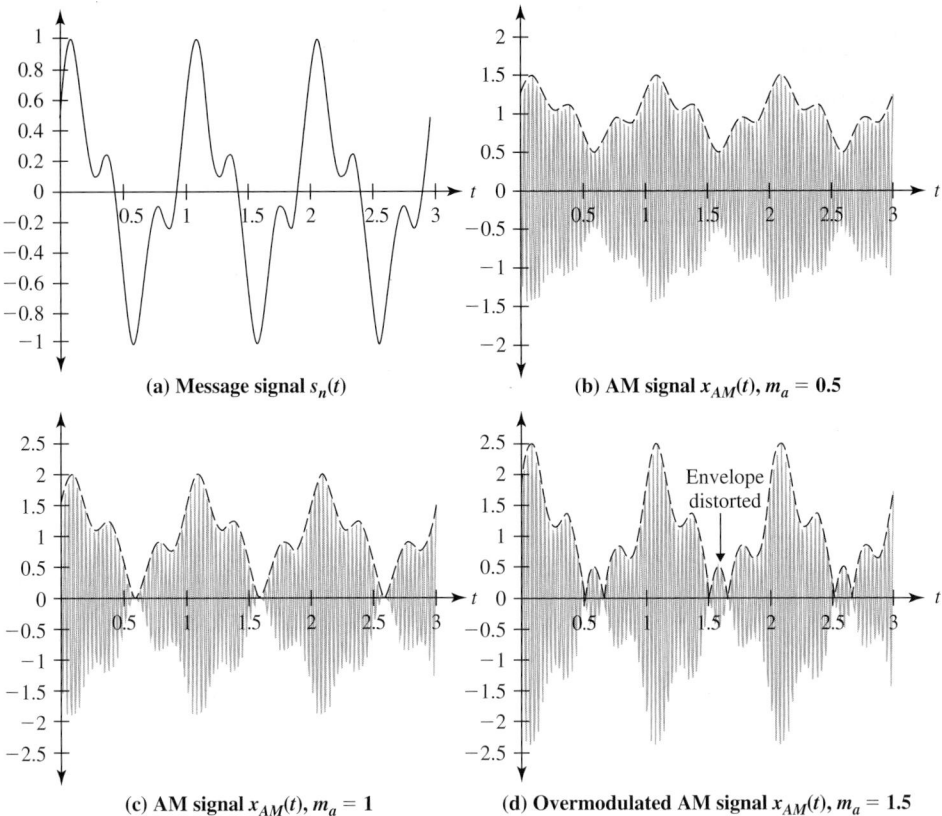

(a) Message signal $s_n(t)$

(b) AM signal $x_{AM}(t)$, $m_a = 0.5$

(c) AM signal $x_{AM}(t)$, $m_a = 1$

(d) Overmodulated AM signal $x_{AM}(t)$, $m_a = 1.5$

Figure 4.10 Conventional AM signal.

With 100% modulation (i.e., $m_a = 1$), the envelope varies between $A_{\min} = 0$ and $A_{\max} = 2A_c$.

Figure 4.10 displays a message signal $s_n(t)$ and the corresponding AM waveforms for three different values of m_a. We observe from the figure that the envelope of $x_{AM}(t)$ retains the shape of the message signal if $A_{\min}$ stays positive. From (4.19), $A_{\min}$ is always positive if

$$1 - m_a \geq 0 \tag{4.22}$$

or

$$m_a \leq 1$$

Equation (4.22) states that if the value modulation index m_a is less than 1, the envelope of the modulated signal $x_{AM}(t)$ is always positive, and hence retains the shape of the message signal. Therefore, the message signal $s_n(t)$ can be easily recovered from $x_{AM}(t)$ by using a simple envelope detector. Envelope detection of the overmodulated ($m_a > 1$) signal results in recovery of a distorted message signal as illustrated by Figure 4.10(d).

Example 4.2

A conventional AM waveform $x_{AM}(t)$ is shown in Figure 4.11. Calculate the modulation index.

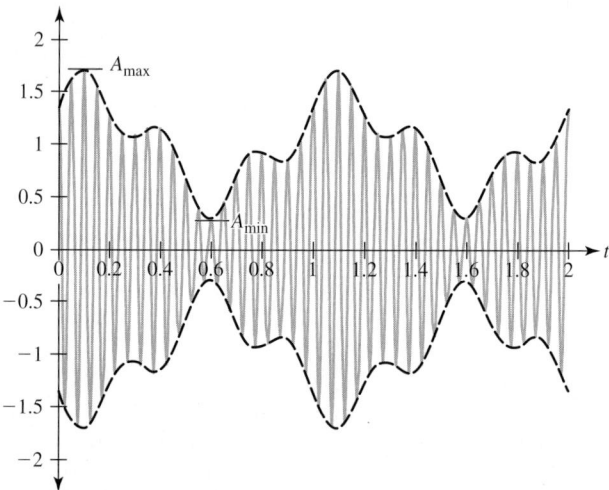

Figure 4.11 AM waveform in Example 4.2.

Solution

We note from the figure that

$$A_{\max} = 1.707$$

$$A_{\min} = 0.293$$

$$m_a = \frac{A_{\max} - A_{\min}}{A_{\max} + A_{\min}} = \frac{1.707 - 0.293}{1.707 + 0.293} = \frac{1.414}{2} = 0.707$$

4.3.1   Spectrum of the Conventional AM Signal

The spectrum of the AM signal $x_{AM}(t)$ in (4.15) is given by

$$X_{AM}(f) = \Im\big\{A_c\big[1 + m_a s_n(t)\big]\cos(2\pi f_c t)\big\}$$

$$= \Im\{A_c\cos(2\pi f_c t)\} + \Im\{A_c m_a s_n(t)\cos(2\pi f_c t)\}$$

$$= \frac{A_c}{2}\big[\delta(f - f_c) + \delta(f + f_c)\big] + \frac{A_c m_a}{2}\big[S_n(f - f_c) + S_n(f + f_c)\big] \qquad (4.23)$$

Figure 4.12 displays the spectrum $X_{AM}(f)$ of the conventional AM signal for the sample message spectrum $S(f)$. We observe the presence of impulses at $\pm f_c$ indicating that a carrier component is present in the modulated signal $x_{AM}(t)$. The message signal information is conveyed in the sidebands of the AM signal spectrum. It is obvious from the figure that the spectrum of a conventional AM signal occupies twice the bandwidth of the message signal.

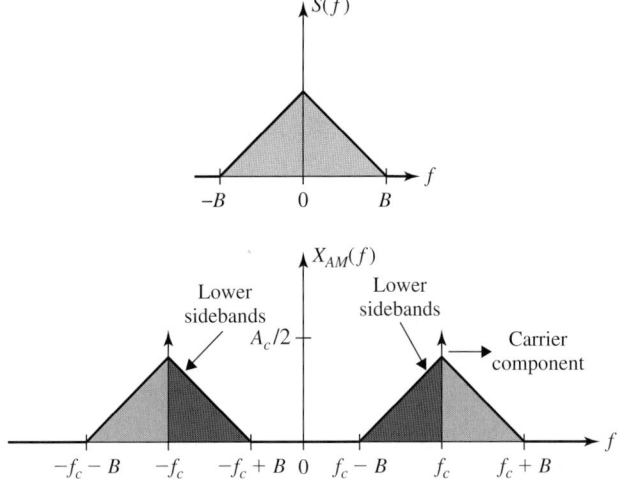

Figure 4.12 Spectrum of the conventional AM signal.

Example 4.3

A single tone message signal

$$s(t) = A_m\cos(2\pi f_m t) \tag{4.24}$$

modulates the carrier waveform $c(t) = A_c\cos(2\pi f_c t)$. Determine and plot the spectrum of the resultant conventional AM signal $x_{AM}(t)$.

Solution

The normalized message signal is

$$s_n(t) = \cos(2\pi f_m t) \tag{4.25}$$

The corresponding conventional AM signal is obtained by applying (4.16) and (4.18) as

$$x_{AM}(t) = A_c\big[1 + m_a\cos(2\pi f_m t)\big]\cos(2\pi f_c t)$$

$$= A_c\cos(2\pi f_c t) + \frac{m_a A_c}{2}\Big\{\cos\big[2\pi(f_c + f_m)t\big] + \cos 2\pi(f_c - f_m)t\big]\Big\} \tag{4.26}$$

where

$$m_a = \frac{A_m}{A_c} \tag{4.27}$$

Taking the Fourier transform of both sides, we get

$$X_{AM}(f) = \frac{A_c}{2}\big[\delta(f - f_c) + \delta(f + f_c)\big]$$

$$+ \frac{m_a A_c}{4}\left\{\begin{array}{l}\delta[f - (f_c + f_m)] + \delta[f + (f_c + f_m)] \\ +\delta[f - (f_c - f_m)] + \delta[f + (f_c - f_m)]\end{array}\right\} \tag{4.28}$$

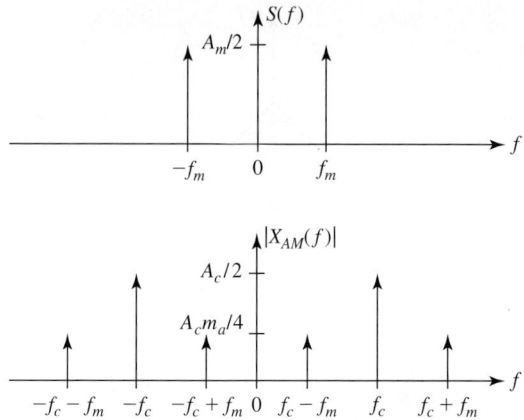

Figure 4.13 Spectrum of a conventional AM signal with single-tone modulating signal.

Figure 4.13 displays the spectrum of a conventional AM signal for the special case of a sinusoidal message signal. The spectrum consists of impulses at $f_c \pm f_m$, and $-f_c \pm f_m$ as in the case of DSB-SC AM. Note, however, the presence of spectral lines at $\pm f_c$, indicating spectral energy at the carrier frequency.

Power Content of Conventional AM Signal

The normalized average power of a conventional AM signal is obtained by using (2.20) as

$$P_x = \lim_{T \to \infty} \frac{1}{T} \int_{-T/2}^{T/2} x_{AM}^2(t)dt$$

$$= \lim_{T \to \infty} \frac{A_c^2}{T} \int_{-T/2}^{T/2} [1 + m_a s_n(t)]^2 \cos^2(2\pi f_c t)dt$$

$$= \frac{A_c^2}{2} \lim_{T \to \infty} \frac{1}{T} \int_{-T/2}^{T/2} [1 + m_a s_n(t)]^2 [1 + \cos(4\pi f_c t)]dt \qquad (4.29)$$

The integration of terms containing $\cos(4\pi f_c t)$ on the right-hand side of (4.29) yields zero. Therefore,

$$P_x = \frac{A_c^2}{2} \lim_{T \to \infty} \frac{1}{T} \int_{-T/2}^{T/2} [1 + m_a s_n(t)]^2 dt \qquad (4.30)$$

Assuming that the time average of the message signal $s_n(t)$ is zero, (4.30) can be expressed as

$$P_x = \frac{A_c^2}{2} + \frac{A_c^2 m_a^2}{2} P_{s_n} \qquad (4.31)$$

where P_{s_n} represents power in the normalized modulating signal $s_n(t)$. The first term in (4.31) represents power in the carrier component. It is wasted power because it does not carry any information. The signal power, contained in the sidebands, is given by the second term and is usually much smaller than the carrier power. The **power** or **modulation efficiency** of the conventional AM scheme is given by

$$\eta = \frac{\text{Signal power}}{\text{Total Power}} = \frac{(m_a A_c)^2 P_{s_n}/2}{A_c^2/2 + (m_a A_c)^2 P_{s_n}/2} = \frac{m_a^2 P_{s_n}}{1 + m_a^2 P_{s_n}} \le 0.5 \qquad (4.32)$$

Thus maximum power efficiency of 50% is achieved when a square-wave modulating signal ($P_{s_n} = 1$) is used and $m_a = 1$. For the sinusoidal message signal in Example 4.3, assuming 100% modulation ($m_a = 1$), the power efficiency is given by

$$\eta = \frac{m_a^2 P_{s_n}}{1 + m_a^2 P_{s_n}} = \frac{0.5}{1 + 0.5} = 0.333 \text{ or } 33.3\% \qquad (4.33)$$

Because the normalized peak envelope power is the average power supplied by the modulator to a 1 ohm load during one carrier frequency cycle at the crest of the modulation envelope, it is obtained for a conventional AM signal by using (4.20) as

$PEP_{AM} =$ Power supplied by a sinusoidal waveform with peak amplitude $A_{\max}$

$$= \frac{A_{\max}^2}{2} = \frac{A_c^2}{2}\left(\max_t[1 + m_a s_n(t)]\right)^2 \qquad (4.34)$$

For a sinusoidal modulating signal considered in Example 4.3, the normalized average power of the conventional AM signal from (4.31) is $P_x = \frac{A_c^2(1 + 0.5 m_a^2)}{2}$. The PEP supplied by the conventional AM waveform is given by $PEP_{AM} = \frac{A_c^2(1 + m_a)^2}{2}$. For $m_a = 0.875$,

$$\frac{PEP_{AM}}{P_x} = \frac{(1 + 0.875)^2}{1 + 0.5 \times 0.875^2} = 2.54$$

Example 4.4

A conventional AM waveform $x_{AM}(t)$ is shown in Figure 4.14. Calculate (a) the modulation index and (b) the power efficiency.

Solution

We note from the figure that

$$A_{\max} = 1.5$$
$$A_{\min} = 0.5$$

a. $m_a = \dfrac{A_{\max} - A_{\min}}{A_{\max} + A_{\min}} = \dfrac{1.5 - 0.5}{1.5 + 0.5} = \dfrac{1}{2} = 0.5$

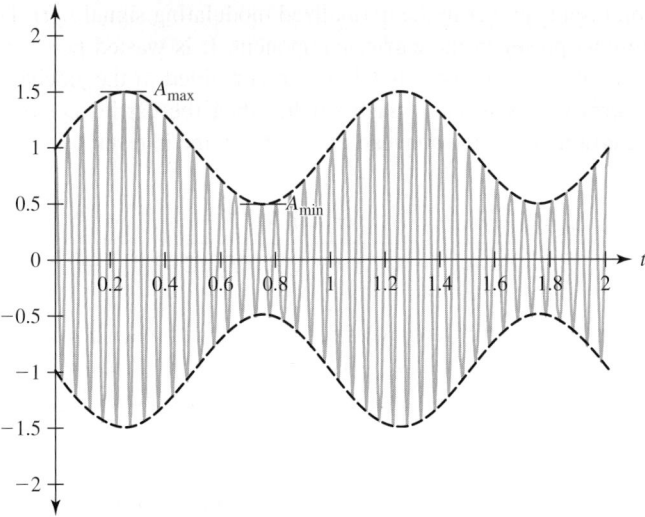

Figure 4.14 AM waveform for Example 4.4.

b. From the figure, the normalized message signal is $\sin(2\pi t)$. Therefore,

$$P_{s_n} = \frac{1}{T}\int\limits_{-T/2}^{T/2} \sin^2(2\pi t)\,dt = \frac{1}{2T}\int\limits_{-T/2}^{T/2}\left[1 - \cos(2\pi t)\right]dt = \frac{1}{2}$$

Substituting into (4.32) yields

$$\eta = \frac{(0.5)^2 \times 0.5}{1 + (0.5)^2 \times 0.5} = \frac{0.125}{1 + 0.125} = 11.11\%$$

Example 4.5

A conventional AM signal is given by

$$x_{AM}(t) = \left[15 + 2\cos(80\pi t) + 5\sin(120\pi t)\right]\cos(4000\pi t)$$

a. Plot the spectrum of $x_{AM}(t)$.
b. Determine the power in carrier and sideband spectral components.
c. Calculate the modulation index and the power efficiency.

Solution

a. Using trigonometric identities, $x_{AM}(t)$ can be expanded as

$$x_{AM}(t) = 15\cos(4000\pi t) + \cos(4080\pi t) + \cos(3920\pi t) - 2.5\sin(3880\pi t) + 2.5\sin(4120\pi t)$$

Taking the FT of both sides, we obtain

$$X_{AM}(f) = 7.5\left[\delta(f - 2000) + \delta(f + 2000)\right] + 0.5\left[\delta(f - 2040) + \delta(f + 2040)\right]$$

$$+ 0.5\big[\delta(f - 1960) + \delta(f + 1960)\big] - \frac{1.25}{j}\big[\delta(f - 1940) - \delta(f + 1940)\big]$$

$$+ \frac{1.25}{j}\big[\delta(f - 2060) - \delta(f + 2060)\big]$$

Figure 4.15 (a) displays the spectrum $X_{AM}(f)$.

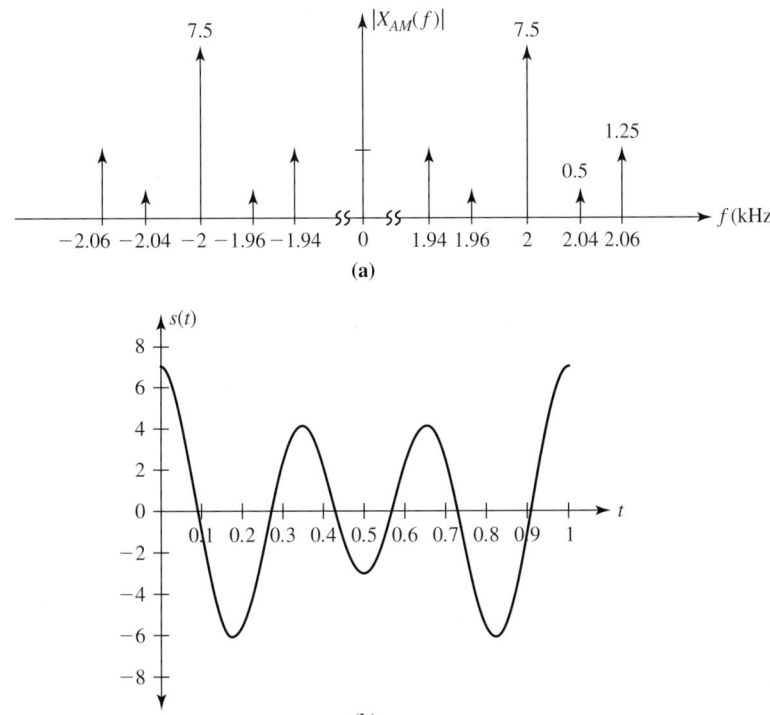

(a)

(b)

Figure 4.15 (a) AM waveform; (b) modulating signal for Example 4.5.

b. Power in the carrier component of the modulated signal $= \dfrac{(15)^2}{2} = 112.5$ W

Power in the sideband components (signal) of the modulated signal $=$

$$\frac{(1)^2}{2} + \frac{(1)^2}{2} + \frac{(2.5)^2}{2} + \frac{(2.5)^2}{2} = 0.5 + 0.5 + 6.25 = 7.25 \text{ W}$$

c. The message signal $s(t) = 2\cos(80\pi t) + 5\sin(120\pi t)$ is displayed in Figure 4.15(b). The minimum value of $s(t) = -6.1178$. The modulation index is given from (4.18) as

$$m_a = \frac{\left|\min_t s(t)\right|}{A_c} = \frac{6.1178}{15} = 0.408$$

The normalized message signal is

$$s_n(t) = 0.327\cos(80\pi t) + 0.817\sin(120\pi t)$$

The power in P_{s_n} in the normalized message signal is $\dfrac{(0.327)^2}{2} + \dfrac{(0.817)^2}{2} = 0.387$. Therefore,

$$\eta = \frac{(0.408)^2 \times 0.387}{1 + (0.408)^2 \times 0.387} = \frac{0.166 \times 0.387}{1 + 0.166 \times 0.387} = 6.05\%$$

4.3.2   Demodulation of Conventional AM Signal

Like DSB-SC, a conventional AM signal can be demodulated by means of a coherent demodulator which requires a locally generated carrier that is synchronized with the carrier used for modulation at the transmitter. Because the envelope of the modulated signal retains the shape of the message signal for $m_a \leq 1$, the demodulation of AM signal can alternatively be accomplished by using a simple envelope detector. An envelope detector can be constructed using a diode rectifier followed by a first-order RC filter as shown in Figure 4.16(a). The diode is forward-biased on the positive half-cycle of the input signal and the capacitor charges up rapidly to the full value of the input signal. When the input signal falls below this value, the diode becomes reverse-biased and the capacitor C discharges slowly through the load resistor R_L. The discharging continues until the next positive half-cycle. The diode conducts again when the input signal voltage exceeds the voltage across the capacitor. This process is repeated as shown in Figure 4.16(b). It is important to choose time constant $R_L C$ appropriately so that the capacitor output voltage follows the envelope of the AM waveform. Initially, we will assume that the diode is ideal with zero-forward resistance and infinite resistance in the reverse-biased state. The discharging time constant $R_L C$ must be large enough so that the capacitor discharges slowly through load resistor R_L between successive positive peaks of the carrier waveform. However, it must be small enough so the envelope detector can track the maximum rate of change of the message signal. That is,

$$\frac{1}{f_c} << R_L C << \frac{1}{B} \tag{4.35}$$

where B is bandwidth of the message signal $s(t)$. As a rule of thumb, the time constant $R_L C$ is chosen to be approximately 5 to 10% of $1/B$. Under ideal conditions, the charging time constant is zero. However, if we assume that the detector circuit is fed by a source with series resistance R_s and that the diode has nonzero forward resistance R_f, the charging time constant is $(R_f + R_s)C$. The charging time constant must be small compared to $1/f_c$ so that the capacitor charges rapidly to the carrier peak and thereby follows the message signal envelope.

$$(R_f + R_s)C << \frac{1}{f_c} \tag{4.36}$$

As displayed in Figure 4.16(b), the envelope detector output follows the carrier envelope, except that it has superimposed on it a sawtooth waveform at the carrier frequency. Because the carrier frequency is assumed to be much higher than the maximum frequency in the modulating signal, the sawtooth distortion of the demodulated envelope is easily removed by an LP filter. The DC component in $y_D(t)$ can be blocked out by a series or coupling capacitor in the following gain stage. Figure 4.16(c) displays the conventional AM demodulator using an envelope detector.

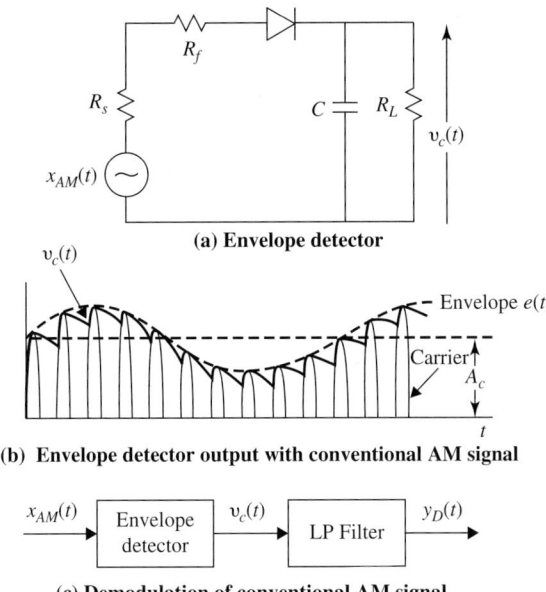

(a) Envelope detector

(b) Envelope detector output with conventional AM signal

(c) Demodulation of conventional AM signal

Figure 4.16 Demodulation of conventional AM signal using envelope detection.

The reason for the wide popularity of conventional AM is the simplicity of the demodulator circuit that can be used in a receiver. This was the overwhelming consideration in the choice of conventional AM as the transmission technology for AM radio broadcasting in spite of its poor power transmission efficiency. There are billions of radio receivers worldwide but only a relatively small number of broadcast transmitters. This justifies the sacrifice in power efficiency for AM transmitters as a favorable trade-off for a simple and inexpensive implementation of the demodulation process at the receivers.

Example 4.6

Consider the envelope detection of the single-tone modulated conventional AM signal in Example 4.3. Show that if the detector output is to follow the envelope at all times, the time constant $R_L C$ satisfies

$$R_L C \leq \frac{1}{2\pi f_m} \frac{\sqrt{1 - m_a^2}}{m_a} \tag{4.37}$$

Solution

The envelope of a single-tone modulated conventional AM signal in (4.26) is given by

$$e(t) = A_c \left[1 + m_a \cos(2\pi f_m t) \right], \ 0 < m_a < 1 \tag{4.38}$$

Figure 4.17 displays the envelope of $x(t)$ and the voltage $v_c(t)$ across the capacitor C in Figure 4.16. The time interval between two successive carrier peaks is $1/f_c$. The capacitor discharges from the carrier peak value $V_o = A_c[1 + m_a \cos(2\pi f_m t_o)]$, where t_o is some arbitrary instant where the carrier peak occurs. The voltage across the capacitor is given by

$$v_c(t) = V_o e^{-(t - t_o)/R_L C}, \ t_o \leq t < t_o + \frac{1}{f_c} \tag{4.39}$$

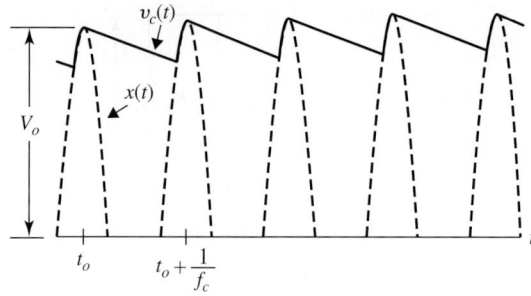

Figure 4.17 Capacitor output voltage in an envelope detector.

Because $R_L C \gg 1/f_c$ is by design, the capacitor voltage $v_c(t)$, therefore, discharges for a short time interval (compared with time constant $R_L C$) between successive cycles. Using the approximation $e^{-x} \approx 1 - x$, $x \ll 1$, we can write

$$v_c(t) \cong V_o \left[1 - \frac{t - t_o}{R_L C} \right], \quad t_o \leq t < t_o + \frac{1}{f_c} \tag{4.40}$$

In order that the capacitor output voltage follows the envelope of the AM waveform, it is required that

$$v_c(t) \leq e(t)|_{t = t_o + \frac{1}{f_c}}$$

That is,

$$\left[1 + m_a \cos(2\pi f_m t_o) \right] \left[1 - \frac{1}{R_L C f_c} \right] \leq 1 + m_a \cos\left[2\pi f_m \left(t_o + \frac{1}{f_c} \right) \right] \tag{4.41}$$

Now

$$\cos\left[2\pi f_m \left(t_o + \frac{1}{f_c} \right) \right] = \cos(2\pi f_m t_o) \cos\left(\frac{2\pi f_m}{f_c} \right) - \sin(2\pi f_m t_o) \sin\left(\frac{2\pi f_m}{f_c} \right) \tag{4.42}$$

For $f_m \ll f_c$, we can approximate (4.42) as

$$\cos\left[2\pi f_m \left(t_o + \frac{1}{f_c} \right) \right] = \cos(2\pi f_m t_o) - \sin(2\pi f_m t_o) \left(\frac{2\pi f_m}{f_c} \right) \tag{4.43}$$

Substituting (4.43) into (4.41) yields

$$\left[1 + m_a \cos(2\pi f_m t_o) \right] \left[1 - \frac{1}{R_L C f_c} \right] \leq 1 + m_a \cos(2\pi f_m t_o) - m_a \sin(2\pi f_m t_o) \left(\frac{2\pi f_m}{f_c} \right)$$

Hence,

$$\left[1 + m_a \cos(2\pi f_m t_o) \right] \left(\frac{1}{R_L C f_c} \right) \geq m_a \sin(2\pi f_m t_o) \left(\frac{2\pi f_m}{f_c} \right)$$

or

$$m_a \left[2\pi f_m \sin(2\pi f_m t_o) - \frac{1}{R_L C} \cos(2\pi f_m t_o) \right] \leq \frac{1}{R_L C} \tag{4.44}$$

Multiplying and dividing the left-hand side of (4.44) by $\sqrt{(2\pi f_m)^2 + \left(\dfrac{1}{R_L C}\right)^2}$, we obtain

$$m_a \sqrt{(2\pi f_m)^2 + \left(\frac{1}{R_L C}\right)^2}$$

$$\times \left[\frac{2\pi f_m}{\sqrt{(2\pi f_m)^2 + \left(\dfrac{1}{R_L C}\right)^2}} \sin(2\pi f_m t_o) - \frac{1/R_L C}{\sqrt{(2\pi f_m)^2 + \left(\dfrac{1}{R_L C}\right)^2}} \cos(2\pi f_m t_o) \right] \le \frac{1}{R_L C} \quad (4.45)$$

We can write (4.45) as

$$m_a \sqrt{(2\pi f_m)^2 + \left(\frac{1}{R_L C}\right)^2} \sin(2\pi f_m t_o - \theta) \le \frac{1}{R_L C} \quad (4.46)$$

where

$$\theta = \tan^{-1} \frac{1}{2\pi f_m R_L C}$$

Because the condition (4.46) must be satisfied for every t_o, we must have

$$m_a \sqrt{(2\pi f_m)^2 + \left(\frac{1}{R_L C}\right)^2} \le \frac{1}{R_L C} \quad (4.47)$$

That is,

$$m_a^2 \left[(2\pi f_m)^2 + \left(\frac{1}{R_L C}\right)^2 \right] \le \left(\frac{1}{R_L C}\right)^2$$

or

$$m_a^2 (2\pi f_m)^2 \le \left(\frac{1}{R_L C}\right)^2 (1 - m_a^2)$$

or

$$(R_L C)^2 \le \frac{(1 - m_a^2)}{m_a^2 (2\pi f_m)^2}$$

This yields an upper bound on $R_L C$ for a sinusoidal message signal as

$$R_L C \le \frac{1}{2\pi f_m} \frac{\sqrt{1 - m_a^2}}{m_a}$$

Figure 4.18 displays the results of envelope detection of the AM signal $x_{AM}(t) = [1 + m_a \sin(2\pi t)] \sin(100\pi t)$ over the time period $0 \le t \le 1$ for various values of $R_L C$. For Figure 4.18(a), $R_L C = 0.1$ was used. The value is a little bit too small.

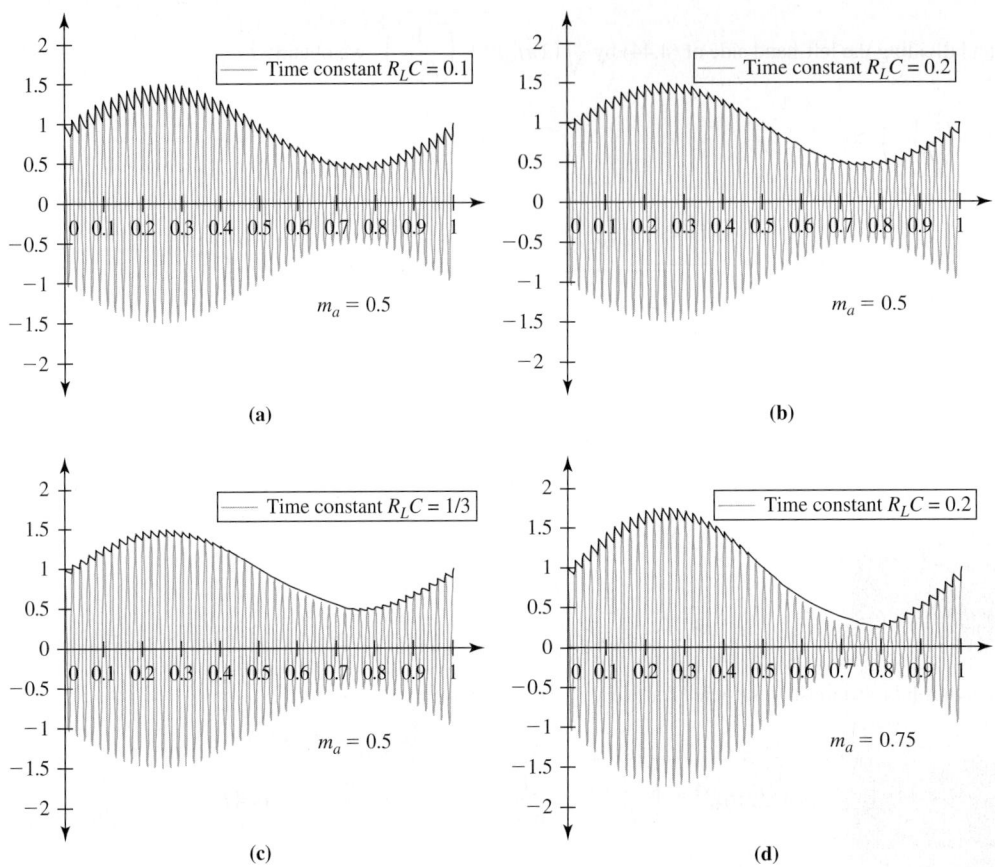

Figure 4.18 Envelope detection for various values of time constant R_LC.

For Figure 4.18(b), $R_LC = 0.2$ was selected. The value is just about right. $R_LC = 1/3$ was chosen for Figure 4.18(c). This value is a bit too large; the envelope detector output floats above the true envelope resulting in distortion of the recovered message signal. It is obvious from (4.44) that the choice of time constant R_LC depends on the modulation index m_a. Smaller values of R_LC are required as m_a gets larger. For example, the choice of $R_LC = 0.2$ was right for $m_a = 0.5$. However, this value is too large for $m_a = 0.75$ as illustrated by the envelope distortion in Figure 4.18(d).

Experiment 4.2   *Conventional AM Modulation and Demodulation*

In this experiment, we model a conventional AM system using Simulink and MATLAB. Figure 4.19(a) illustrates the Simulink model for the system. The carrier frequency is 20 Hz and the message signal is a 1.5-Hz sine wave. The Sample time parameter value of 1/1000 is used. The choice of modulation index is made by setting the gain value in the Gain block. For this experiment, $m_a = 0.5$ has been selected. The parameters of simulation including message signal frequency, carrier frequency, modulation depth, and sampling rate are set up by a companion MATLAB m-file. The m-file also computes transfer functions of the BP and LP filters in the AM demodulator using an envelope detector. Figure 4.19(b) and (c) displays modulator and demodulator waveforms. The spectra of waveforms are shown in Figure 4.19(d).

Figure 4.19 (a) Simulink model of conventional AM system; (b) conventional AM modulator waveforms; (c) conventional AM demodulator waveforms; (d) spectra of waveforms in conventional AM.

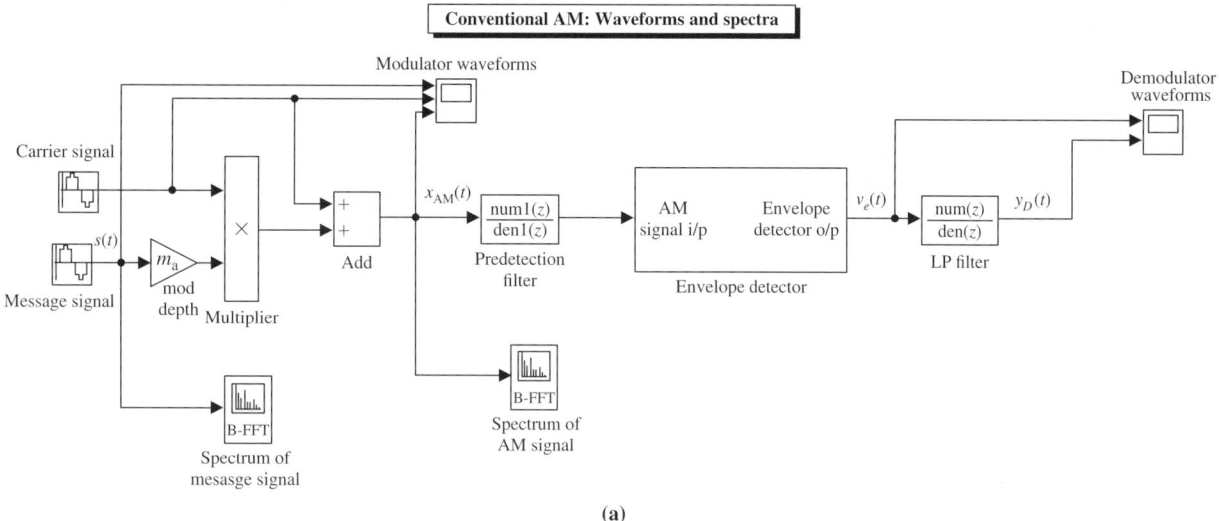

(a)

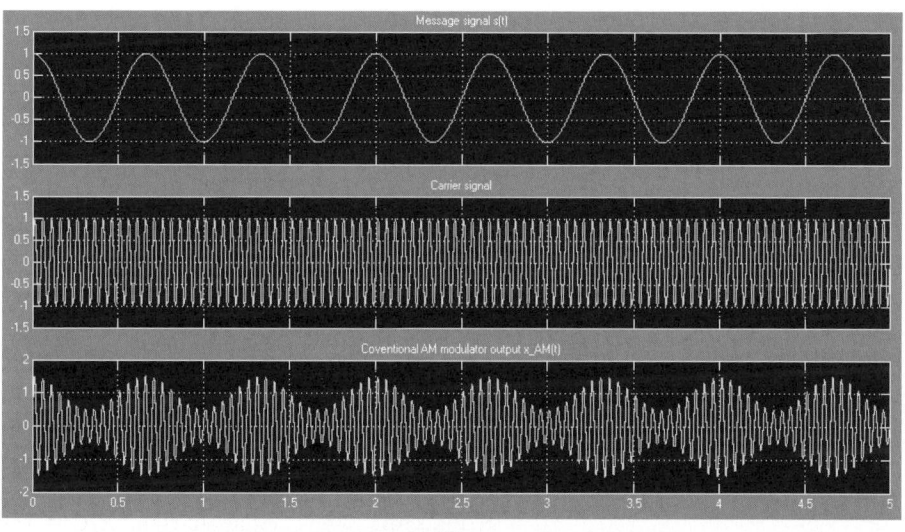

(b)

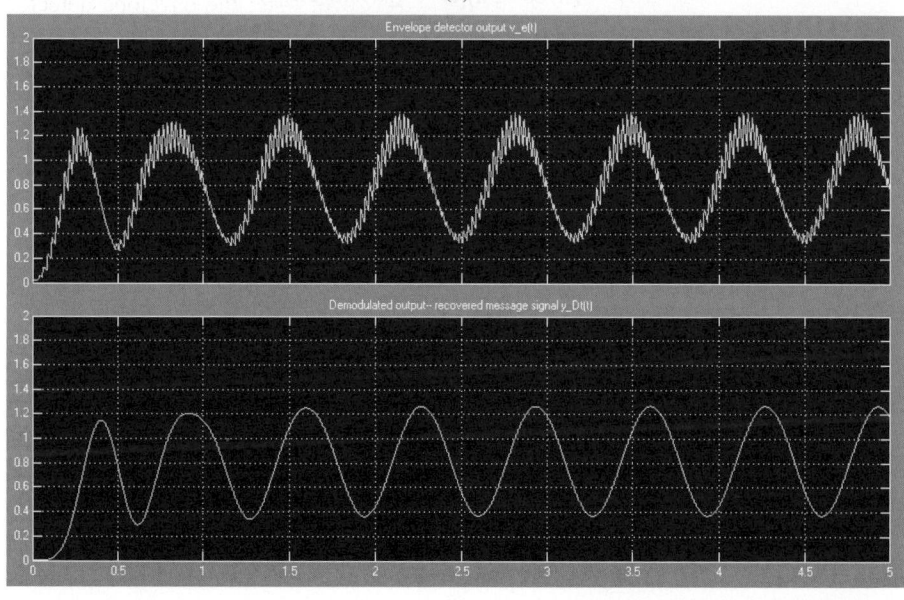

(c)

(*continued*)

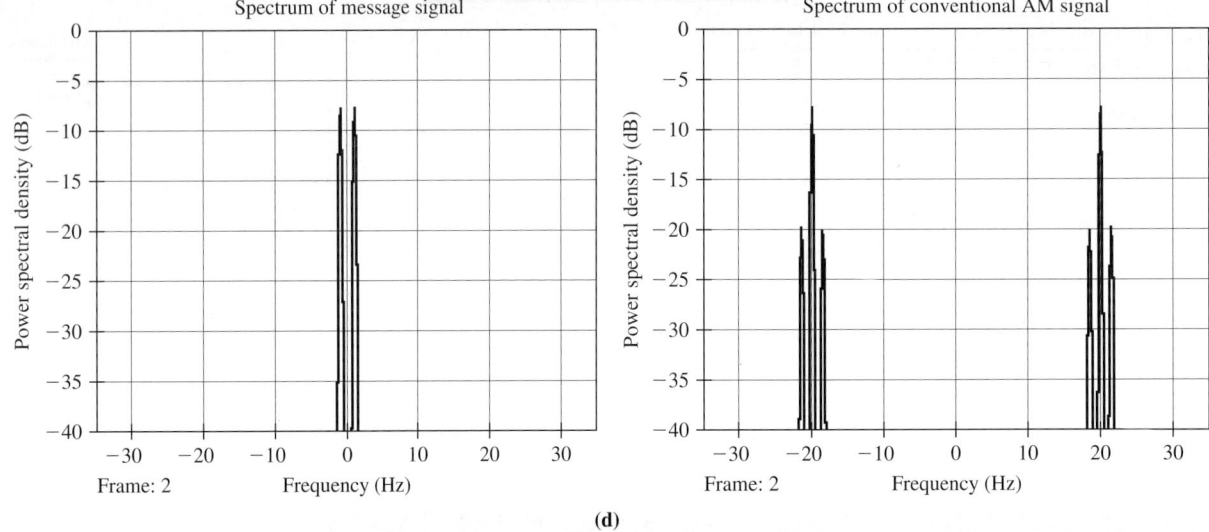

(d)

4.4 ALTERNATIVE REPRESENTATIONS FOR BP SIGNALS AND SYSTEMS

The amplitude-phase representation of a BP signal is given from (4.1) as

$$x(t) = A(t)\cos\left[2\pi f_c t + \psi(t)\right] \tag{4.1}$$

Equation (4.1) can be equivalently expressed, using the trigonometric identity $\cos(u + v) = \cos(u)\cos(v) - \sin(u)\sin(v)$, in the **quadrature** form as

$$x(t) = I(t)\cos(2\pi f_c t) - Q(t)\sin(2\pi f_c t) \tag{4.48}$$

The LP signals $I(t)$ and $Q(t)$, called the **in-phase** and **quadrature components** of $x(t)$, are related to $A(t)$ and $\psi(t)$ by

$$I(t) = A(t)\cos\psi(t) \tag{4.49}$$

$$Q(t) = A(t)\sin\psi(t) \tag{4.50}$$

Further,

$$A(t) = \sqrt{I^2(t) + Q^2(t)} \tag{4.51}$$

$$\psi(t) = \tan^{-1}\left(\frac{Q(t)}{I(t)}\right) \tag{4.52}$$

It is convenient to seek an equivalent LP representation for the BP waveform $x(t)$ in terms of its in-phase (I) and quadrature (Q) components. This can be done by defining an equivalent complex signal called the **complex envelope** $\tilde{x}(t)$ as

$$\tilde{x}(t) \triangleq I(t) + jQ(t) \tag{4.53}$$

Substituting (4.49) and (4.50) into (4.53), we obtain

$$\tilde{x}(t) = A(t)e^{j\psi(t)} \tag{4.54}$$

The real BP signal $x(t)$ in (4.1) can now be written in terms of its complex envelope as

$$x(t) = \operatorname{Re}\left\{\tilde{x}(t)e^{j2\pi f_c t}\right\} \tag{4.55}$$

Because the complex envelope representation eliminates explicit consideration of the carrier frequency f_c, it has been found to be very convenient in analyzing BP signals and systems.

Another complex representation for the BP signal $x(t)$ is the **analytic signal**

$$x^+(t) = \tilde{x}(t)e^{j2\pi f_c t} \tag{4.56}$$

Substituting (4.53) into (4.56) yields

$$
\begin{aligned}
x^+(t) &= \left[I(t) + jQ(t)\right]\left[\cos(2\pi f_c t) + j\sin(2\pi f_c t)\right] \\
&= \left[I(t)\cos(2\pi f_c t) - Q(t)\sin(2\pi f_c t)\right] + j\left[I(t)\sin(2\pi f_c t) + Q(t)\cos(2\pi f_c t)\right] \quad (4.57)
\end{aligned}
$$

Comparing the real part of (4.57) with (4.48), it is obvious that the original BP signal $x(t)$ equals the real part of the analytic signal $x^+(t)$.

$$x(t) = \operatorname{Re}\left\{x^+(t)\right\} \tag{4.58}$$

It is easy to show using the properties (4A.13) and (4A.14) of the Hilbert transform that the imaginary part of (4.57) is the Hilbert transform of the BP signal $x(t)$. Thus, the imaginary part of the analytic signal $x^+(t)$ is the Hilbert transform of the real BP signal $x(t)$.

$$\hat{x}(t) = \operatorname{Im}\left\{x^+(t)\right\} \tag{4.59}$$

Combining (4.58) and (4.59) yields

$$x^+(t) = x(t) + j\hat{x}(t) \tag{4.60}$$

Finally, the in-phase component $I(t)$ and the quadrature component $Q(t)$ can be expressed using the signal $x(t)$ and its Hilbert transform $\hat{x}(t)$ as

$$
\begin{aligned}
I(t) &= \operatorname{Re}\left\{\tilde{x}(t)\right\} = \operatorname{Re}\left\{x^+(t)e^{-j2\pi f_c t}\right\} \\
&= \operatorname{Re}\left\{\left[x(t) + j\hat{x}(t)\right]e^{-j2\pi f_c t}\right\} \\
&= x(t)\cos(2\pi f_c t) + \hat{x}(t)\sin(2\pi f_c t) \tag{4.61}
\end{aligned}
$$

Similarly, it can be shown that

$$Q(t) = \hat{x}(t)\cos(2\pi f_c t) - x(t)\sin(2\pi f_c t) \qquad (4.62)$$

Thus, four equivalent forms for representing a real BP signal $x(t)$ with carrier frequency f_c are:

- Amplitude and phase $A(t)$, $\psi(t)$
- Quadrature components $I(t)$, $Q(t)$
- Complex envelope $\tilde{x}(t)$
- Analytic $x^+(t)$

Example 4.7

A BP signal is given by

$$x(t) = \text{sinc}(10^3 t)\cos(2\pi \times 10^6 t) + 3\,\text{sinc}(10^3 t)\sin(2\pi \times 10^6 t).$$

Write the various representations of the BP signal.

Solution

The carrier frequency is 1 MHz. The in-phase and quadrature components are

$$I(t) = \text{sinc}(10^3 t)$$

$$Q(t) = -3\,\text{sinc}(10^3 t)$$

The complex envelope is

$$\tilde{x}(t) = \text{sinc}(10^3 t) - j3\,\text{sinc}(10^3 t)$$

The amplitude and phase of the complex envelope signal are

$$A(t) = |\tilde{x}(t)| = \text{sinc}(10^3 t)\sqrt{1 + 9} = \sqrt{10}\,\text{sinc}(10^3 t)$$

$$\psi(t) = \tan^{-1}\left(-\frac{3}{1}\right) = -71.6°$$

The analytic signal is given by

$$x^+(t) = (1 - j3)\text{sinc}(10^3 t)e^{j2\pi 10^6 t}$$

4.4.1   Frequency Spectrum of Complex Envelope and Analytic Representations

It is instructive to look at the characteristics of various BP signal representations in the frequency domain. Taking the Fourier transform of both sides of (4.60) and using the property (4A.7) of the Hilbert transform yields

$$X^+(f) = X(f)\big[1 + \text{sgn}(f)\big] = \begin{cases} 2X(f), & f > 0 \\ 0, & f < 0 \end{cases} \tag{4.63}$$

where

$$X^+(f) \xleftrightarrow{\ \Im\ } x^+(t)$$

Equation (4.63) states that $X^+(f)$ represents the positive frequency portion of $X(f)$ and is identically zero for negative frequencies. Let us define the complex conjugate of analytic signal $x^+(t)$ as

$$x^-(t) \triangleq \big[x^+(t)\big]^* = x(t) - j\hat{x}(t) \tag{4.64}$$

Taking the Fourier transform of both sides,

$$X^-(f) = X(f)\big[1 - \text{sgn}(f)\big] = \begin{cases} 0, & f > 0 \\ 2X(f), & f < 0 \end{cases} \tag{4.65}$$

where

$$X^-(f) \xleftrightarrow{\ \Im\ } x^-(t)$$

Thus $X^-(f)$ represents the negative frequency portion of $X(f)$ and is identically zero for positive frequencies.

We note from (4.56) that the spectrum of the analytic signal $x^+(t)$ is simply the Fourier transform of its complex envelope translated in frequency by f_c.

$$X^+(f) = \tilde{X}(f - f_c) \tag{4.66}$$

where

$$\tilde{X}(f) \xleftrightarrow{\ \Im\ } \tilde{x}(t)$$

On the other hand, the spectrum of the complex envelope of a signal $x(t)$ is the Fourier transform of its analytic signal translated in frequency by $-f_c$.

$$\tilde{X}(f) = X^+(f + f_c) \tag{4.67}$$

Figure 4.20 illustrates frequency spectra of $x(t)$ and its equivalent representations $\tilde{x}(t)$, $x^+(t)$, and $x^-(t)$. We conclude by expressing the spectrum of a BP waveform $x(t)$ in terms of the spectrum of its complex envelope. To accomplish this, we write $x(t)$ from (4.55) in the form

$$x(t) = \text{Re}\big\{\tilde{x}(t)e^{j2\pi f_c t}\big\}$$

$$= \frac{1}{2}\big\{\tilde{x}(t)e^{j2\pi f_c t} + \tilde{x}^*(t)e^{-j2\pi f_c t}\big\} \tag{4.68}$$

Taking the Fourier transform of both sides of (4.68) yields

$$X(f) = \frac{1}{2}\big[\tilde{X}(f - f_c) + \tilde{X}^*(-f - f_c)\big] \tag{4.69}$$

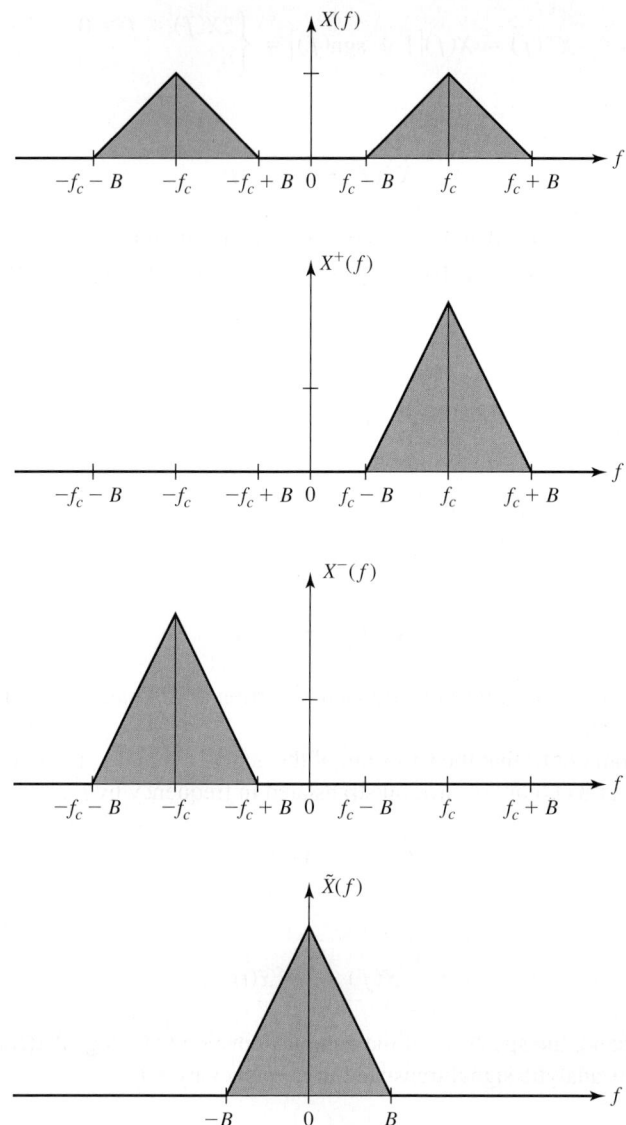

Figure 4.20 Spectra of a BP signal, its complex envelope, and analytic representations.

4.4.2   Complex Envelope Representation of BP Systems

Consider a BP system with impulse response $h(t)$, which is represented in terms of its complex envelope $\widetilde{h}(t)$ as

$$h(t) = 2\text{Re}\{\widetilde{h}(t)e^{j2\pi f_c t}\} \tag{4.70}$$

Note the scaling factor 2 has been added in (4.70) to obtain the convolution integral relationship with complex envelopes similar in form to (2.24). Using (4.69), the frequency response of a BP filter can be written in terms of the FT of its complex envelope as

$$H(f) = \left[\widetilde{H}(f - f_c) + \widetilde{H}^*(-f - f_c)\right] \tag{4.71}$$

Using (2.41), the output of an LTI system with impulse response $h(t)$ to an input signal $x(t)$ is given by

$$y(t) = x(t) \otimes h(t) = \int_{-\infty}^{\infty} h(\tau)x(t - \tau)d\tau \tag{4.72}$$

In the frequency domain, (4.72) is equivalent to

$$Y(f) = X(f)H(f) \tag{4.73}$$

Substituting (4.69) and (4.71) into (4.73), we obtain

$$Y(f) = \frac{1}{2}\left[\begin{matrix} \widetilde{H}(f - f_c)\widetilde{X}(f - f_c) + \widetilde{H}^*(-f - f_c)\widetilde{X}(f - f_c) \\ + \widetilde{H}(f - f_c)\widetilde{X}^*(-f - f_c) + \widetilde{H}^*(-f - f_c)\widetilde{X}^*(-f - f_c) \end{matrix}\right] \tag{4.74}$$

$\widetilde{H}^*(-f - f_c)\widetilde{X}(f - f_c)$ is zero because $\widetilde{X}(f - f_c)$ is nonzero for $f > 0$, whereas $\widetilde{H}^*(-f - f_c)$ is nonzero for $f < 0$. The same argument applies for $\widetilde{H}(f - f_c)\widetilde{X}^*(-f - f_c)$ and is also zero. Therefore,

$$Y(f) = \frac{1}{2}\left[\widetilde{H}(f - f_c)\widetilde{X}(f - f_c) + \widetilde{H}^*(-f - f_c)\widetilde{X}^*(-f - f_c)\right] \tag{4.75}$$

By comparing (4.75) and (4.69), we deduce that

$$\widetilde{Y}(f - f_c) = \widetilde{H}(f - f_c)\widetilde{X}(f - f_c) \tag{4.76}$$

where $\widetilde{Y}(f) \xleftrightarrow{\Im} \widetilde{y}(t)$. (4.76) implies that

$$\widetilde{Y}(f) = \widetilde{H}(f)\widetilde{X}(f) \tag{4.77}$$

Equation (4.77) can be written in the time domain as

$$\widetilde{y}(t) = \widetilde{x}(t) \otimes \widetilde{h}(t) = \int_{-\infty}^{\infty} \widetilde{h}(\tau)\widetilde{x}(t - \tau)d\tau \tag{4.78}$$

This is a very significant result as it greatly simplifies the analysis of BP systems. Equation (4.78) states that the response of a BP system can be calculated by using the complex envelopes of the input and the system impulse response function, $\widetilde{x}(t)$ and $\widetilde{h}(t)$, respectively. Once $\widetilde{y}(t)$ is known, the output BP waveform $y(t)$ can be calculated using (4.55).

$$y(t) = \text{Re}\left\{\widetilde{y}(t)e^{j2\pi f_c t}\right\} \tag{4.79}$$

Analysis of transmission problems involving BP signals and systems is usually messy because of the presence of sinusoidal factors $\cos(2\pi f_c t)$. By using the concept of complex envelope, we have managed to convert the BP analysis problem into an equivalent LP one as $\widetilde{x}(t)$, $\widetilde{y}(t)$, and $\widetilde{h}(t)$ are LP functions.

Example 4.8

The impulse response of a BP filter is given by

$$h(t) = 2e^{-\alpha t}\cos(2\pi f_c t)u(t)$$

Determine the response of the system to a carrier burst $x(t) = \Pi\left[(t - \tau/2)/\tau\right]\cos(2\pi f_c t)$.

Solution

The complex envelopes of the input and the system impulse response function, $\widetilde{x}(t)$ and $\widetilde{h}(t)$, are given by

$$\widetilde{x}(t) = \Pi\left[(t - \tau/2)/\tau\right]$$

$$\widetilde{h}(t) = e^{-\alpha t}u(t)$$

The complex envelope of the output is given from (4.78) as

$$\widetilde{y}(t) = \widetilde{x}(t) \otimes \widetilde{h}(t) = \int_{-\infty}^{\infty} \widetilde{h}(v)\widetilde{x}(t - v)dv = \int_{-\infty}^{\infty} e^{-\alpha v}u(v)\Pi\left[(t - v - \tau/2)/\tau\right]dv$$

$$= \int_{0}^{\infty} e^{-\alpha v}\Pi\left[(t - v - \tau/2)/\tau\right]dv$$

For $0 \leq t \leq \tau$, we have

$$\int_{0}^{\infty} e^{-\alpha v}\Pi\left[(t - v - \tau/2)/\tau\right]dv = \int_{0}^{t} e^{-\alpha v}dv = \frac{1 - e^{-\alpha t}}{\alpha}$$

For $t > \tau$, we obtain

$$\int_{0}^{\infty} e^{-\alpha v}\Pi\left[(t - v - \tau/2)/\tau\right]dv = \int_{t}^{t+\tau} e^{-\alpha v}dv = \frac{\left[1 - e^{-\alpha\tau}\right]e^{-\alpha t}}{\alpha}$$

Therefore, the complex envelope of the output is

$$\widetilde{y}(t) = \begin{cases} \dfrac{1 - e^{-\alpha t}}{\alpha}, & 0 \leq t \leq \tau \\ \dfrac{\left[1 - e^{-\alpha\tau}\right]}{\alpha}e^{-\alpha t}, & t > \tau \end{cases}$$

The BP output is now obtained from (4.79) as

$$y(t) = \begin{cases} \dfrac{\left[1 - e^{-\alpha t}\right]\cos(2\pi f_c t)}{\alpha}, & 0 \leq t \leq \tau \\ \dfrac{\left[1 - e^{-\alpha\tau}\right]e^{-\alpha t}\cos(2\pi f_c t)}{\alpha}, & t > \tau \end{cases}$$

4.5 SINGLE-SIDEBAND AM

In our study of DSB-SC scheme, we observed that either sideband in the modulated signal contains the necessary information to recover the message signal. Elimination of one of the sidebands prior to transmission results in a **single-sideband AM (SSB-AM)** signal, which reduces the required transmission bandwidth W_T from $2B$ to B Hz, where B is the bandwidth of the message signal. One obvious method of generating a SSB-AM signal is to generate a DSB-SC AM signal and then employ a BP filter to select one of the sidebands as shown in Figure 4.21. This is called the **filtering method,** and it provides a very cost-effective solution for generating a SSB-AM signal when the message signal does not have spectral content in the vicinity of zero frequency. Low-cost crystal filters can be used to achieve the necessary sideband suppression in such applications.

Another method of generating a SSB-AM signal based on the concept of the analytic signal (Section 4.4) is illustrated in Figure 4.22. It is called the **phasing method** and requires the use of an ideal phase shifter to perform the Hilbert transforming operation. From Figure 4.22, the output of the phase-shift modulator is obtained as

$$x_{USB}(t) = \frac{A_c}{2}\{s(t)\cos(2\pi f_c t) - \hat{s}(t)\sin(2\pi f_c t)\} \tag{4.80}$$

where $\hat{s}(t)$ is the Hilbert transform of $s(t)$. We now investigate the spectral characteristics of $x_{USB}(t)$ in (4.80) to prove that it represents the upper sideband SSB-AM signal.

To prove this, we write (4.80) in terms of analytic signal $s^+(t)$ as

$$x_{USB}(t) = \frac{A_c}{2}\operatorname{Re}\{s^+(t)e^{j2\pi f_c t}\} \tag{4.81}$$

Equation (4.81) can be expressed as

$$x_{USB}(t) = \frac{A_c}{4}\{s^+(t)e^{j2\pi f_c t} + s^{+*}(t)e^{-j2\pi f_c t}\} \tag{4.82}$$

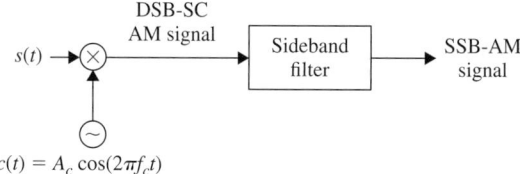

Figure 4.21 Filtering method of generating a SSB-AM signal.

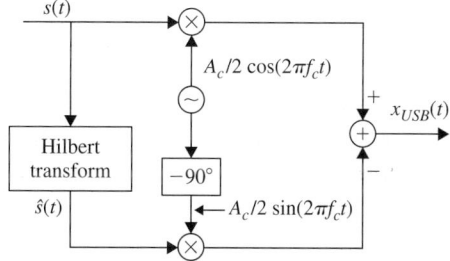

Figure 4.22 Generation of an upper-sideband SSB-AM signal using the phasing method.

Substituting (4.64) into (4.82), we obtain

$$x_{USB}(t) = \frac{A_c}{4}\{s^+(t)e^{j2\pi f_c t} + s^-(t)e^{-j2\pi f_c t}\} \tag{4.83}$$

We know from (4.63) that $S^+(f)$ contains only the positive frequency components of $S(f)$. Similarly, $S^-(f)$ contains only the negative frequency components of $S(f)$ as indicated in (4.65). Taking FT of both sides of (4.83), the spectrum of $x_{USB}(t)$ can be expressed as

$$X_{USB}(f) = \frac{A_c}{2}\left\{\frac{S^+(f - f_c)}{2} + \frac{S^-(f + f_c)}{2}\right\} \tag{4.84}$$

$\dfrac{S^+(f - f_c)}{2}$ represents the positive frequency portion of $S(f)$ shifted in frequency by the carrier frequency f_c. On the other hand, $\dfrac{S^-(f + f_c)}{2}$ represents the negative frequency portion of $S(f)$ shifted in frequency by the amount $-f_c$. Thus, (4.84) is spectrum of an upper sideband SSB-AM signal with modulating signal spectrum $S(f)$. Figure 4.23 displays the spectra of various signals involved in the generation of upper sideband SSB-AM signal $x_{USB}(t)$.

Similarly, if we use the plus sign in (4.80), that is,

$$x_{LSB}(t) = \frac{A_c}{2}\{s(t)\cos(2\pi f_c t) + \hat{s}(t)\sin(2\pi f_c t)\} \tag{4.85}$$

the lower sideband SSB-AM signal is obtained.

Power Content of SSB-AM Signal

The normalized average power of a SSB-AM signal is obtained by using (2.20) as

$$P_x = \lim_{T \to \infty} \frac{1}{T} \int_{-T/2}^{T/2} x_{SSB}^2(t)dt$$

$$= \lim_{T \to \infty} \frac{A_c^2}{4T} \int_{-T/2}^{T/2}\left[s^2(t)\cos^2(2\pi f_c t) + \hat{s}^2(t)\sin^2(2\pi f_c t) \pm s(t)\hat{s}(t)\underbrace{2\cos(2\pi f_c t)\sin(2\pi f_c t)}_{\sin(4\pi f_c t)} \right]dt$$

$$= \frac{A_c^2}{8}(P_s + P_{\hat{s}} + 0) = \frac{A_c^2}{8}(P_s + P_{\hat{s}}) \tag{4.86}$$

where P_s and $P_{\hat{s}}$, respectively, represent power in $s(t)$ and $\hat{s}(t)$. Because $s(t)$ and $\hat{s}(t)$ are slowly varying relative to $\sin(4\pi f_c t)$ in the last integral, its value is equal to zero. Using (4A.11), the normalized average power of a SSB-AM signal is obtained as

$$P_x = \frac{A_c^2 P_s}{4} \tag{4.87}$$

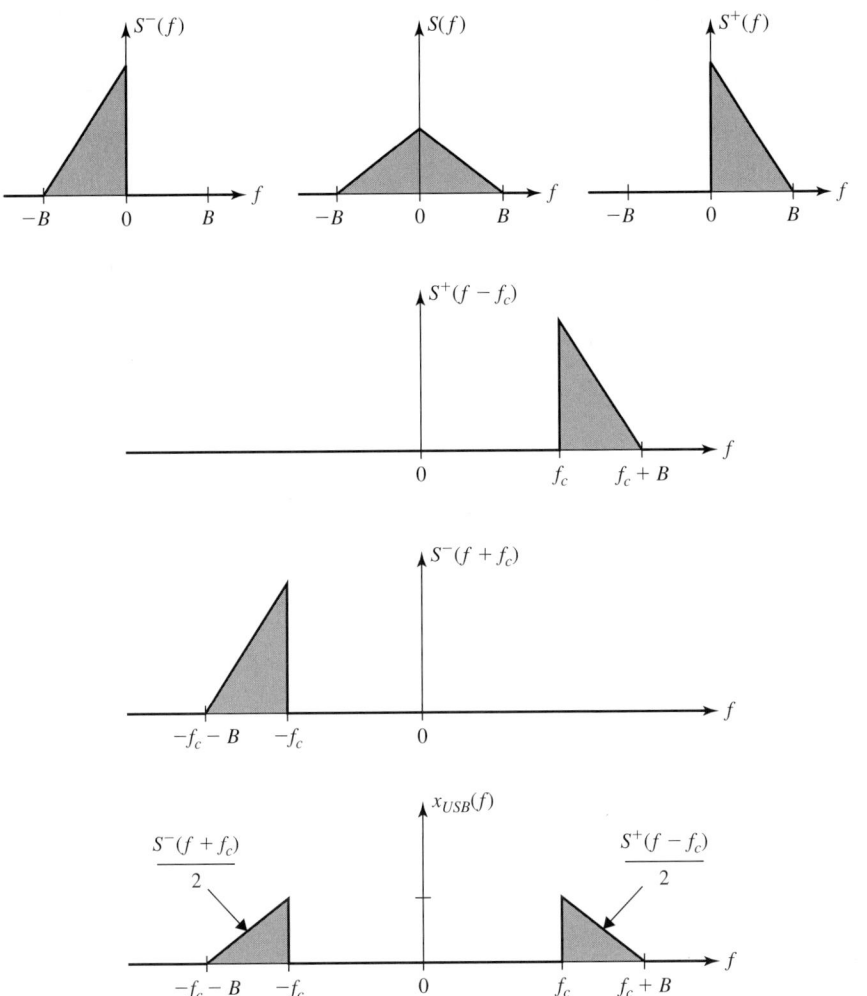

Figure 4.23 Phasing method of generating a SSB-AM signal in frequency domain.

To calculate the peak envelope power of a SSB-AM signal, we express SSB-AM signals in (4.80) and (4.85) in the amplitude-phase format as

$$x_{SSB}(t) = \frac{A_c}{2}\sqrt{s^2(t) + \hat{s}^2(t)}\,\cos\!\left[2\pi f_c t \pm \tan^{-1}\!\left(\hat{s}(t)/s(t)\right)\right] \qquad (4.88)$$

We observe that the amplitude and phase in (4.88) are slowly varying relative to the carrier $\cos(2\pi f_c t)$. The normalized peak envelope power of the SSB-AM signal, PEP_{SSB}, is given by

$$PEP_{SSB} = \text{Power supplied by a sinusoidal waveform with amplitude}$$
$$\frac{A_c}{2}\left[\max_t \sqrt{s^2(t) + \hat{s}^2(t)}\right]$$
$$= \frac{A_c^2 \max_t\left[s^2(t) + \hat{s}^2(t)\right]}{8} \qquad (4.89)$$

For a sinusoidal modulating signal $s(t) = \cos(2\pi f_m t)$, the normalized average power of the SSB-AM signal from (4.86) is $P_x = \dfrac{A_c^2}{8}$. The PEP supplied by the SSB-AM waveform from (4.89) is given by $PEP_{SSB} = \dfrac{A_c^2}{8}$.

Example 4.9

The signal $s(t) = \cos(2\pi t) + 3\cos(6\pi t)$ modulates the carrier $A_c \cos(20\pi t)$.

1. Write an expression for the USB-AM signal in time-domain.
2. Sketch the spectrum of the USB-AM signal.

Solution

a. $\hat{s}(t)$ is obtained by using (4A.2) as

$$\hat{s}(t) = \sin(2\pi t) + 3\sin(6\pi t)$$

We can write $x_{USB}(t)$ from (4.80) as

$$x_{USB}(t) = \frac{A_c}{2}\big[s(t)\cos(2\pi f_c t) - \hat{s}(t)\sin(2\pi f_c t)\big]$$

$$= \frac{A_c}{2}\big\{\big[\cos(2\pi t) + 3\cos(6\pi t)\big]\cos(20\pi t) - \big[\sin(2\pi t) + 3\sin(6\pi t)\big]\sin(20\pi t)\big\}$$

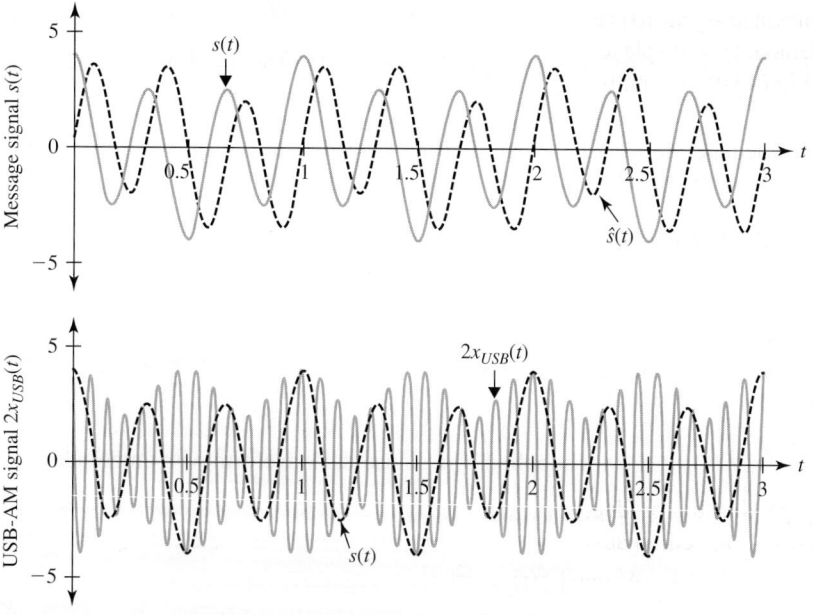

Figure 4.24   (a) USB modulation in time-domain ($A_c = 1$).

Rearranging the terms, we obtain

$$x_{USB}(t) = \frac{A_c}{2}\left\{\begin{array}{l}[\cos(2\pi t)\cos(20\pi t) - \sin(2\pi t)\sin(20\pi t)]\\ + 3[\cos(6\pi t)\cos(20\pi t) - \sin(6\pi t)\sin(20\pi t)]\end{array}\right\}$$

$$= \frac{A_c}{2}\left\{\cos(22\pi t) + 3\cos(26\pi t)\right\}$$

Figure 4.24(a) displays message and modulation waveforms.

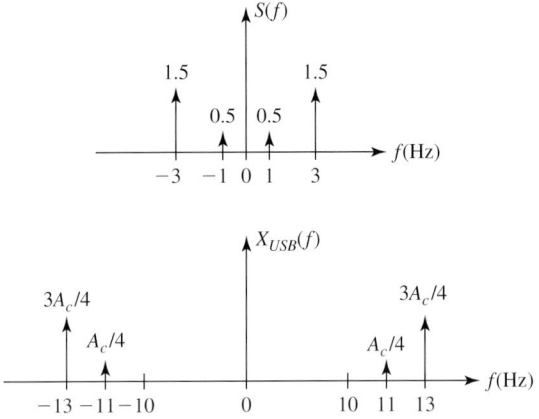

Figure 4.24 (b) USB modulation in frequency-domain.

b. The spectrum of the USB-AM signal is shown in Figure 4.24(b).

4.5.1 Demodulation of SSB-AM Signals

The message signal $s(t)$ can be recovered from either SSB-AM signal by using a coherent demodulator displayed in Figure 4.7(a) for DSB-SC AM signals. For a USB-AM signal in (4.80), the multiplier output is given by

$$y(t) = x_{USB}(t) \times 2\cos(2\pi f_c t + \phi) = \frac{A_c}{2}\left\{s(t)\cos(2\pi f_c t) - \hat{s}(t)\sin(2\pi f_c t)\right\} \times 2\cos(2\pi f_c t + \phi)$$

$$= \frac{A_c}{2}\left\{2s(t)\cos(2\pi f_c t)\cos(2\pi f_c t + \phi) - 2\hat{s}(t)\sin(2\pi f_c t)\cos(2\pi f_c t + \phi)\right\}$$

$$= \frac{A_c}{2}\left\{s(t)\left[\underbrace{\cos(4\pi f_c t + \phi)}_{\text{Filtered out by filter}} + \cos(\phi)\right] - \hat{s}(t)\left[\underbrace{\sin(4\pi f_c t + \phi)}_{\text{Filtered out by filter}} - \sin(\phi)\right]\right\}$$

$$(4.90)$$

By passing the product signal in (4.90) through a LP filter, the double-frequency components are eliminated leaving us with

$$y_D(t) = \frac{A_c}{2}\left\{s(t)\cos(\phi) + \hat{s}(t)\sin(\phi)\right\} \qquad (4.91)$$

For coherent demodulation, $\phi = 0$. A nonzero phase offset ϕ not only reduces the amplitude of the desired signal $s(t)$ by $\cos(\phi)$, but it also results in an undesirable sideband signal due to the presence of $\hat{s}(t)$ in $y_D(t)$. The latter component was not present in the demodulation of a DSB-SC signal. However, it is a factor that contributes to the distortion of the demodulated signal. Instead of generating a coherent carrier at the receiver for demodulation, a pilot tone at the carrier frequency can be transmitted along with the SSB signal for this purpose. This, of course, implies that a portion of the transmitted power needs to be allocated for the pilot tone.

Envelope Demodulation of SSB-AM Signals

Another technique for demodulation of an SSB signal involves carrier reinsertion prior to demodulation. We next show that envelope detection can be used to recover the message waveform for a sufficiently large reinserted carrier signal. The resultant signal for the LSB waveform in (4.85) is given by

$$x_c(t) = \frac{A_c}{2}\left[s(t)\cos(2\pi f_c t) + \hat{s}(t)\sin(2\pi f_c t)\right] + k\cos(2\pi f_c t)$$

$$= \left[\frac{A_c s(t)}{2} + k\right]\cos(2\pi f_c t) + \frac{A_c \hat{s}(t)}{2}\sin(2\pi f_c t) \tag{4.92}$$

where k is amplitude of the added carrier. Equation (4.92) can be expressed in the amplitude-phase form as

$$x_c(t) = e(t)\cos\left[2\pi f_c t + \psi(t)\right] \tag{4.93}$$

where

$$e(t) = \sqrt{\left(\frac{A_c s(t)}{2} + k\right)^2 + \left(\frac{A_c \hat{s}(t)}{2}\right)^2} = \sqrt{\left(\frac{A_c s(t)}{2}\right)^2 + kA_c s(t) + k^2 + \left(\frac{A_c \hat{s}(t)}{2}\right)^2}$$

$$\tag{4.94}$$

and

$$\psi(t) = -\tan^{-1}\frac{\hat{s}(t)}{s(t) + \dfrac{2k}{A_c}} \tag{4.95}$$

If the reinserted carrier amplitude k is large such that $k \gg A_c s(t)$ and $k \gg A_c \hat{s}(t)$, the envelope detector output $e(t)$ can be approximated as

$$e(t) \approx k\sqrt{1 + \frac{A_c}{k}s(t)} \tag{4.96}$$

For $|x| \ll 1$, $\approx \sqrt{1 + x} \approx 1 + \dfrac{x}{2}$. Using this approximation, we can express (4.96) as

$$e(t) \approx k\left[1 + \frac{A_c}{2k}s(t) \right] = k + \frac{A_c}{2}s(t) \qquad (4.97)$$

$k + \dfrac{A_c}{2}s(t)$ is always positive because $k >> A_c s(t)$. Therefore, the resultant SSB-AM signal can be recovered using an envelope detector without distortion. The reinsertion of a large carrier signal, however, reduces the power efficiency of SSB-AM.

The spectral efficiency of SSB AM made this modulation method very attractive for use in voice communications over analog cable and microwave systems in the predigital communications era. In this application, a pilot tone is transmitted for synchronous demodulation and shared among several channels.

Experiment 4.3 *SSB-AM Modulation and Demodulation*

In this experiment, we model an SSB-AM system using Simulink and MATLAB. Figure 4.25(a) illustrates the Simulink model for the system. The message signal $s(t) = \cos\left(2\pi t + \dfrac{\pi}{4} \right) + 3\sin(6\pi t)$ is used. The carrier frequency of 25 Hz is selected for this example. The `Sample time` parameter value of 1/1000 is used. The parameters of simulation including carrier frequency and sampling rate are set up by a companion MATLAB m-file. The m-file also computes transfer functions of the BP and LP filters in the USB-AM receiver using coherent demodulation. Figures 4.25(b) and (c) display modulator and demodulator waveforms. The spectra of various waveforms are shown in Figures 4.25(d).

Figure 4.25 (a) Simulink model of SSB-AM system; (b) modulator waveforms; (c) demodulator waveforms; (d) spectra of waveforms.

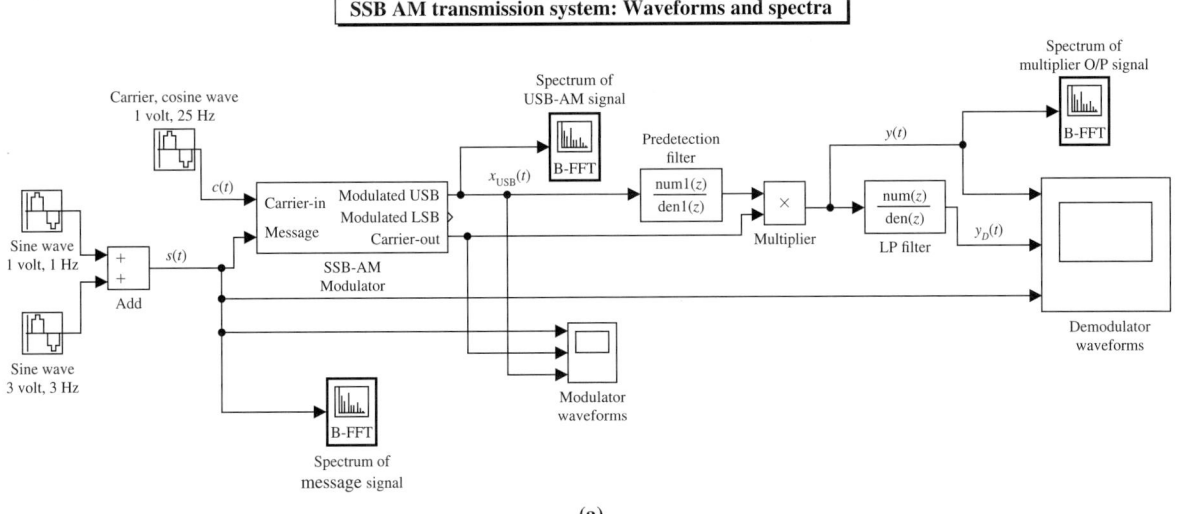

(a)

(*continued*)

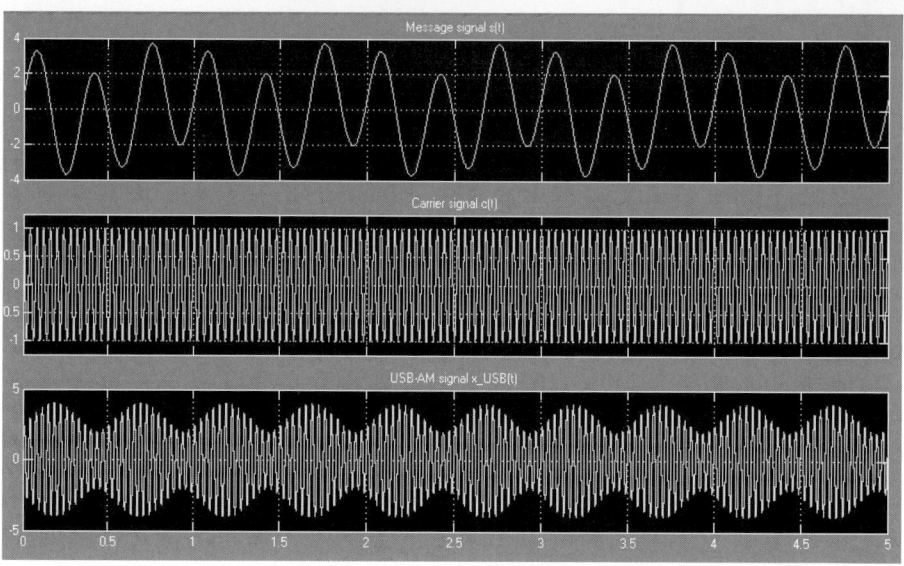

(b)

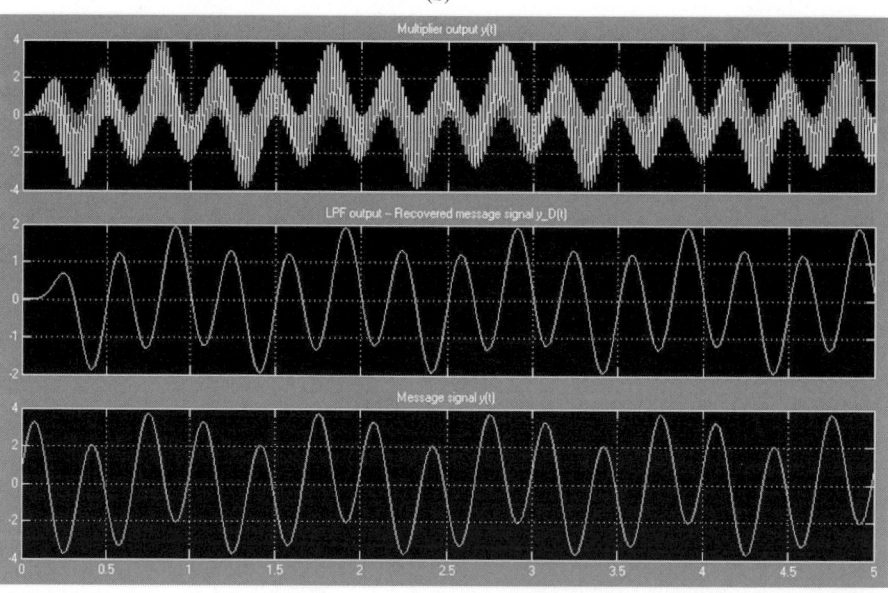

(c)

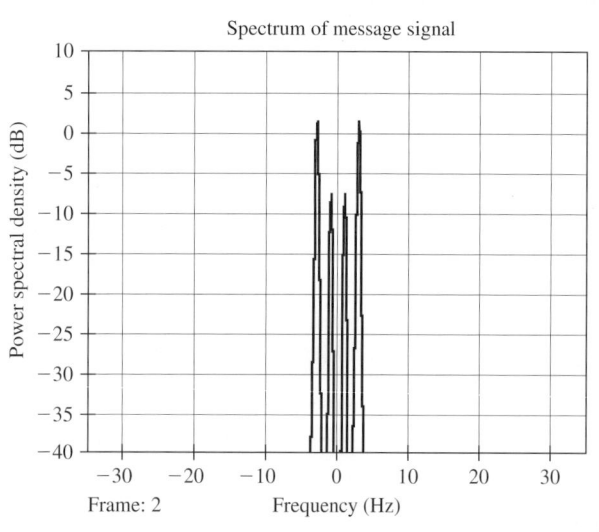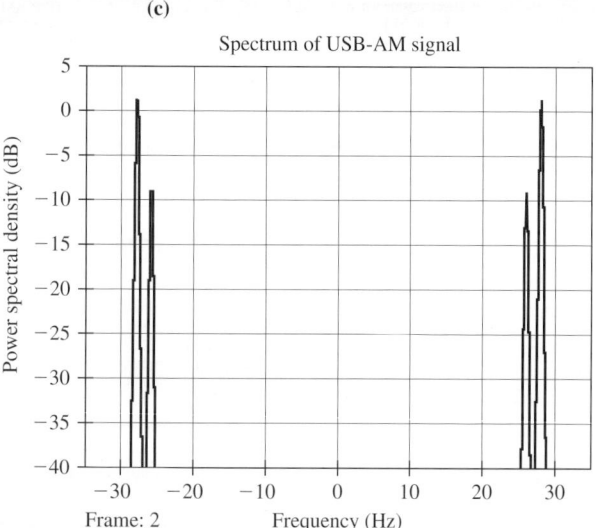

(d)

4.6 VESTIGIAL-SIDEBAND AM

Vestigial-sideband (VSB) AM systems offer an efficient way of conserving bandwidth for the transmission of baseband signals such as television and data that possess frequency content down to zero frequency. For such signals, the SSB scheme is not feasible because it requires filters with an extremely sharp cutoff frequency response characteristic in order to reject the second sideband. Such filter characteristics are very difficult to implement in practice. VSB-AM achieves a useful compromise by allowing a portion ("vestige") of the unwanted sideband to appear at the output of the modulator. This implies that VSB-AM requires slightly higher bandwidth than SSB-AM. However, it allows the designer to relax the stringent requirements on the frequency response of the sideband filter.

A VSB-AM signal is generated by partially suppressing one of the sidebands of a DSB-SC signal by a sideband-shaping filter as shown in Figure 4.26. The VSB-AM signal $x_{VSB}(t)$ can be expressed as

$$x_{VSB}(t) = x_{DSB}(t) \otimes h(t) = \left[A_c s(t)\cos(2\pi f_c t)\right] \otimes h(t) \tag{4.98}$$

where $h(t)$ is the impulse response of the VSB filter. Taking the Fourier transform of both sides in (4.98), we obtain

$$X_{VSB}(f) = \frac{A_c}{2}\left[S(f - f_c) + S(f + f_c)\right]H(f) \tag{4.99}$$

where $H(f)$ is the frequency response of the VSB filter.

The VSB-AM signal $x_{VSB}(t)$ is coherently demodulated by multiplying it with the carrier $2\cos(2\pi f_c t)$ and LP filtering the output to remove the double frequency terms as shown in Figure 4.7(a). The output of the multiplier is

$$y(t) = x_{VSB}(t) \times 2\cos(2\pi f_c t) \tag{4.100}$$

In the frequency domain, the output signal can be expressed as

$$Y(f) = \left[X_{VSB}(f - f_c) + X_{VSB}(f + f_c)\right] \tag{4.101}$$

Now substituting $X_{VSB}(f)$ from (4.99) into (4.101) yields

$$Y(f) = \frac{A_c}{2}\left[S(f - 2f_c) + S(f)\right]H(f - f_c) + \frac{A_c}{2}\left[S(f) + S(f + 2f_c)\right]H(f + f_c) \tag{4.102}$$

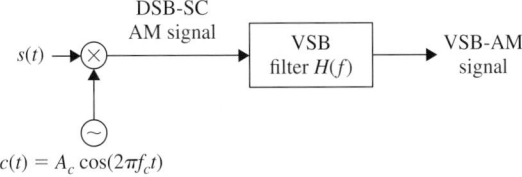

Figure 4.26 Filtering method of generating a VSB-AM signal.

Equation (4.102) can be rearranged as follows:

$$Y(f) = \frac{A_c}{2}\left\{\begin{array}{l} S(f)[H(f - f_c) + H(f + f_c)] \\ + [S(f - 2f_c)H(f - f_c) + S(f + 2f_c)H(f + f_c)] \end{array}\right\} \quad (4.103)$$

The LP filter in the demodulator removes the message signal terms in (4.103) translated to frequencies $f = \pm 2f_c$. Hence, the signal spectrum at the output of the ideal LP filter is given by

$$Y_D(f) = \frac{A_c}{2}\left\{S(f)\left[H(f - f_c) + H(f + f_c)\right]\right\} \quad (4.104)$$

The demodulated message signal in (4.104) can be recovered without any distortion if the VSB filter $H(f)$ satisfies the property

$$H(f - f_c) + H(f + f_c) = C, \quad |f| \leq B \quad (4.105)$$

where C is a real constant that can be taken as unity without loss of generality. Equation (4.105) is called **vestigial symmetry condition.** Figure 4.27(a) displays a frequency response of a VSB filter that truncates the lower sideband of the DSB-SC signal. We observe that the VSB filter roll off characteristic exhibits *odd* symmetry in the transition width of $2f_v$ around the carrier frequency f_c.

$$|H(f_c + f_1)| + |H(f_c - f_1)| = 1, \quad f_1 \leq f_v$$

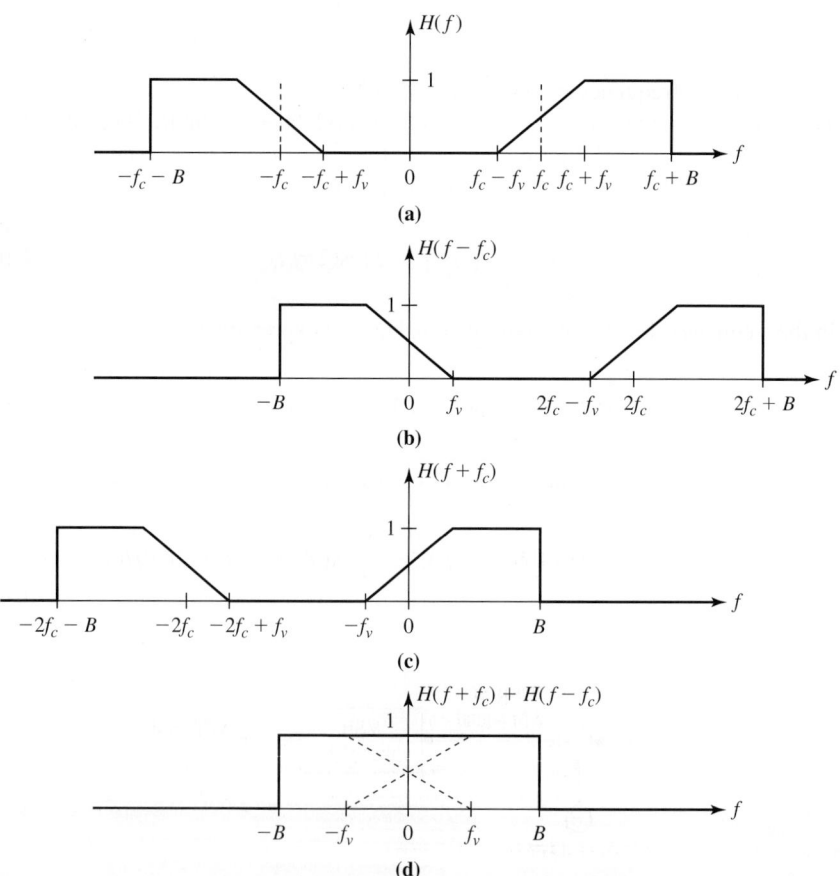

Figure 4.27 VSB filter frequency response characteristic.

where f_v is the width of the vestigial sideband. Note that the filter totally attenuates the lower sideband spectral energy beyond f_v Hz away from the carrier frequency. Figures 4.27(b), (c), and (d) illustrate how the filter in Figure 4.27(a) satisfies the required condition (4.105).

As in the case of SSB-AM signals, a carrier component can be added to the VSB signal. This variant of VSB, called **VSB + C,** can now be demodulated using an envelope detector. It is the approach used in TV broadcasting because it makes the VSB demodulator in the TV receiver much simpler.

Example 4.10

Let the message signal be sum of two sinusoidal signals $s(t) = A_1\cos(2\pi f_1 t) + A_2\cos(2\pi f_2 t)$. The resultant carrier-modulated DSB-SC signal is passed through a VSB filter with characteristic illustrated in Figure 4.28(a). Show that the coherent demodulator can successfully recover the original message signal.

Solution

The DSB-SC AM signal is given by

$$
\begin{aligned}
x_{DSB}(t) &= \left[A_1\cos(2\pi f_1 t) + A_2\cos(2\pi f_2 t)\right]\cos(2\pi f_c t) \\
&= \frac{A_1}{2}\left\{\cos\left[2\pi(f_c + f_1)t\right] + \cos\left[2\pi(f_c - f_1)t\right]\right\} \\
&\quad + \frac{A_2}{2}\left\{\cos\left[2\pi(f_c + f_2)t\right] + \cos\left[2\pi(f_c - f_2)t\right]\right\}
\end{aligned} \qquad (4.106)
$$

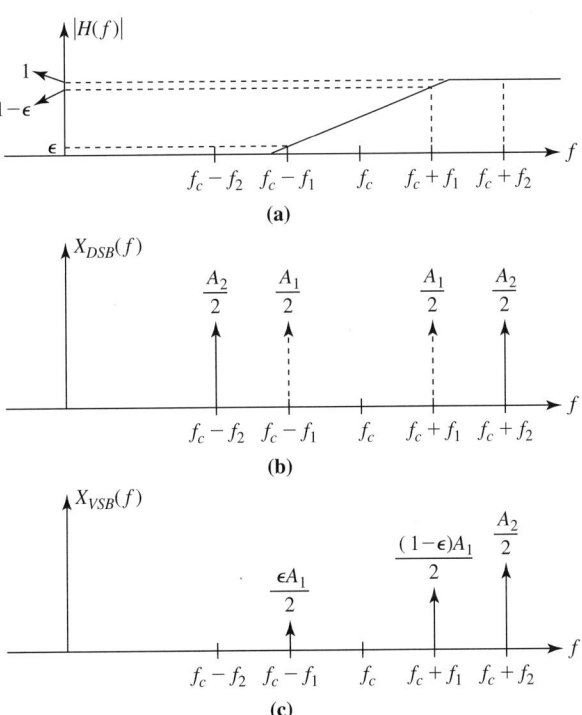

Figure 4.28 VSB filtering example: (a) VSB filter characteristic; (b) DSB signal spectrum; (c) VSB signal spectrum.

The one-sided spectrum of the signal in (4.106) is shown in Figure 4.28(b). The VSB-AM signal is generated by using the VSB filter whose frequency response is shown in Figure 4.28(a). The VSB filter exhibits odd symmetry around the carrier frequency f_c as required. The values of the VSB filter magnitude response at frequencies $f_c - f_1, f_c + f_1$, and $f_c + f_2$ are, respectively, $\varepsilon, 1 - \varepsilon$, and 1. The output of the VSB filter to the input (4.106) is obtained by using (2.116) as

$$x_{VSB}(t) = \frac{A_1(1 - \varepsilon)}{2}\cos\left[2\pi(f_c + f_1)t\right] + \frac{A_1\varepsilon}{2}\cos\left[2\pi(f_c - f_1)t\right] + \frac{A_2}{2}\cos\left[2\pi(f_c + f_2)t\right] \quad (4.107)$$

The message signal is recovered using coherent demodulation. Multiplying $x_{VSB}(t)$ by $2\cos(2\pi f_c t)$ and LP filtering the output to reject double frequency terms, we obtain

$$y(t) = x_{VSB}(t) \times 2\cos(2\pi f_c t)$$

$$= \frac{A_1(1 - \varepsilon)}{2}\cos(2\pi f_1 t) + \frac{A_1\varepsilon}{2}\cos(2\pi f_1 t) + \frac{A_2}{2}\cos(2\pi f_2 t)$$

$$= \frac{A_1}{2}\cos(2\pi f_1 t) + \frac{A_2}{2}\cos(2\pi f_2 t)$$

This is the desired message signal $s(t)$.

Example 4.11

The bandwidth of the baseband video signal is 4.2 MHz. If DSB-AM were used, it would require 8.4 MHz of spectrum allocation for transmission of the video component of the TV signal. TV broadcasting, therefore, uses the VSB-AM transmission format to reduce the required channel bandwidth to 6 MHz for both the video and audio signals. The audio signal is transmitted using

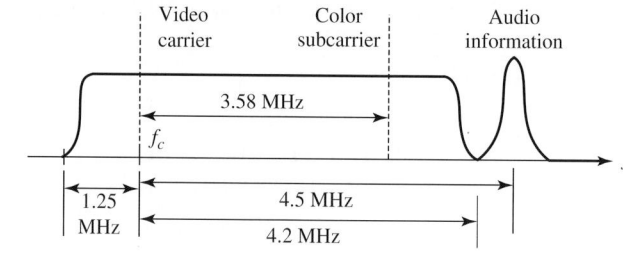

(a) Spectrum of the transmitted TV signal

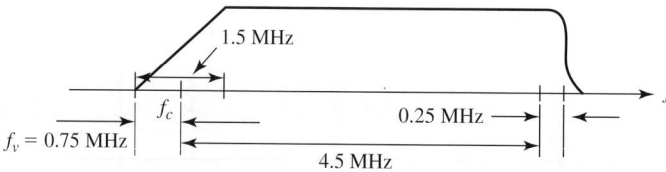

(b) Magnitude response of the VSB filter in the TV receiver

Figure 4.29 VSB filtering in broadcast TV transmission.

the frequency modulation technique on a carrier located at 4.5 MHz above the picture carrier f_c. The precise shaping of the vestigial sideband is not carried out at the transmitter, but at the receiver, where signal levels are low. The spectrum of the transmitted TV signal is shown in Figure 4.29(a). The transmitter filter bandlimits the upper sideband of the video signal to about 4.2 MHz so that it does not interfere with the sound carrier. The lower sideband of the video signal is transmitted without attenuation up to 0.75 MHz and is entirely attenuated at 1.25 MHz. Figure 4.29(b) shows the amplitude response of the receiver VSB filter with $f_v = 0.75$ MHz. As the filter characteristic satisfies the condition (4.104), the video modulation signal can be recovered without distortion at the receiver.

4.7   QUADRATURE MULTIPLEXING

The transmission bandwidth required for the DSB-SC signal is twice that of the baseband message signal. **Quadrature multiplexing** is a technique whereby two carriers in quadrature are used to transmit two DSB-SC signals over the same frequency slot as shown in Figure 4.30. Let the message signal $s_1(t)$ modulate **in-phase carrier** $\cos(2\pi f_c t)$ to produce the DSB signal $s_1(t)\cos(2\pi f_c t)$. The modulated signal occupies a frequency bandwidth of $2B$ Hz centered around f_c. Similarly, let the message signal $s_2(t)$ modulate **quadrature carrier** $\sin(2\pi f_c t)$ to produce the DSB signal $s_2(t)\sin(2\pi f_c t)$. Note that this modulated signal will also have its power located within the same frequency band as the DSB signal $s_1(t)\cos(2\pi f_c t)$. The composite signal

$$x_{QAM}(t) = s_1(t)\cos(2\pi f_c t) + s_2(t)\sin(2\pi f_c t) \tag{4.108}$$

is a **quadrature-carrier multiplexed signal.** It is also referred to as a **quadrature amplitude modulated (QAM) signal.**

Because the baseband message signals $s_1(t)$ and $s_2(t)$ modulate quadrature carriers $\cos(2\pi f_c t)$ and $\sin(2\pi f_c t)$, respectively, they can be recovered from the composite signal $x_{QAM}(t)$ by coherent demodulation as shown in Figure 4.30. By multiplying $x_{QAM}(t)$ with $2\cos(2\pi f_c t)$ and then LP filtering the resulting signal, we recover the message signal $s_1(t)$ as follows:

$$x_{QAM}(t) \times 2\cos(2\pi f_c t) = \left[s_1(t)\cos(2\pi f_c t) + s_2(t)\sin(2\pi f_c t)\right] \times 2\cos(2\pi f_c t)$$

$$= 2s_1(t)\cos^2(2\pi f_c t) + 2s_2(t)\sin(2\pi f_c t)\cos(2\pi f_c t)$$

$$= s_1(t)\left[1 + \cos(4\pi f_c t)\right] + s_2(t)\sin(4\pi f_c t)$$

$$= s_1(t) + \text{double frequency } (2f_c) \text{ terms} \tag{4.109}$$

Similarly, the message signal $s_2(t)$ is recovered by multiplying $x_{QAM}(t)$ with $2\sin(2\pi f_c t)$ and then LP filtering the output. Thus two baseband signals, each of bandwidth B Hz, can be transmitted simultaneously without any distortion over the same frequency channel of bandwidth $2B$ Hz by using quadrature carriers. Quadrature-carrier multiplexing, therefore, achieves the bandwidth efficiency of SSB-AM.

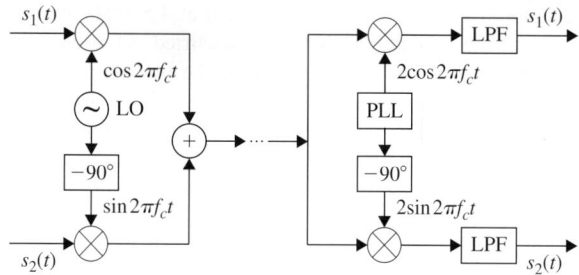

Figure 4.30 Quadrature multiplexing.

4.8   MULTIPLEXING

In many applications, it is desirable to transmit multiple user signals simultaneously over a single communication link. **Multiplexing** is the process of combining multiple user signals into a composite signal such that individual signals can be separated at the receiving end without any distortion. There are three common methods for signal multiplexing:

- Frequency division multiplexing (FDM)
- Time division multiplexing (TDM)
- Code division multiplexing (CDM)

Time and code division multiplexing schemes are used to combine digital signals. Frequency division multiplexing may be used for combining carrier-modulated analog or digital signals and is considered here.

4.8.1   Frequency Division Multiplexing

In FDM, the total system bandwidth is divided into nonoverlapping frequency slots, called **channels.** Each user is assigned a unique channel to prevent interference during simultaneous signal transmissions. Multiplexing is desirable when the bandwidth of individual connections is much smaller than the total bandwidth of the communication system. For example, commercial AM broadcasting is assigned the frequency band 535 to 1605 kHz for the transmission of voice and music programming. The standard AM radio signal occupies 10 kHz, so multiplexing is used to simultaneously carry multiple radio signals over the AM band.

The block diagram of an FDM scheme is shown in Figure 4.31. N user signals are modulated on N different subcarriers $f_1, f_2, \ldots, f_N$ at the transmitter. The outputs of N modulators are then combined to generate the frequency division multiplexed signal. Note in Figure 4.32 that each modulated user signal is assigned a different frequency slot as determined by the corresponding subcarrier frequency. It is assumed that the appropriate BP filtering in each modulator's output stage ensures that the spectral energy of each modulated signal is contained in the assigned frequency slot to minimize any adjacent channel interference. At the receiver, the N outputs from the signal splitter are applied to a bank of BP filters centered at different subcarrier frequencies $f_1, f_2, \ldots, f_N$. The bandwidth of each BP filter is wide enough to pass the desired signal without significant distortion while sufficiently attenuating adjacent carriers. The output of each BP filter is demodulated to recover the original user signal. The bandwidth allocated to each frequency slot is slightly larger than the bandwidth needed by the modulated signal. This extra frequency band, called a **guardband,** allows systems to use less expensive (less steep roll-off) BP filters.

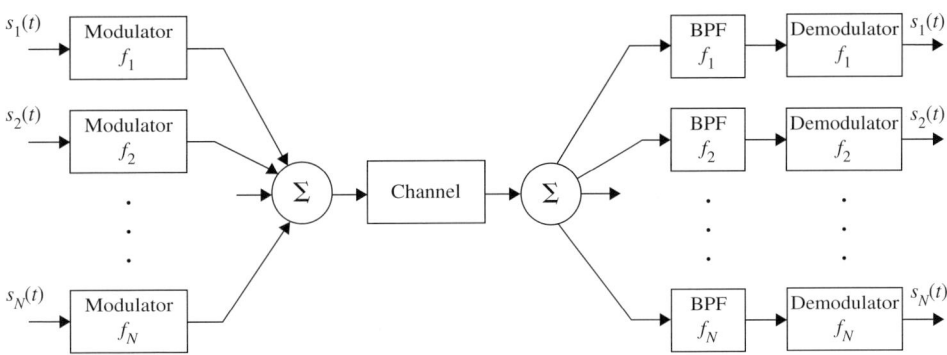

Figure 4.31 Frequency division multiplexing.

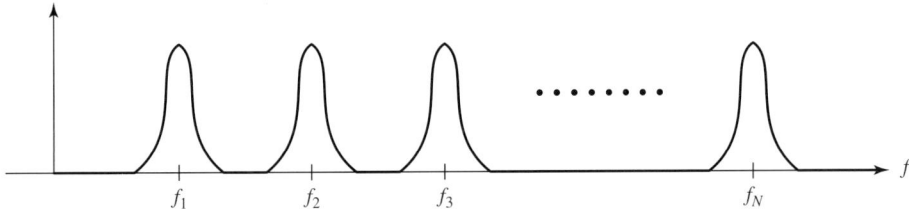

Figure 4.32 Spectrum of the frequency division multiplexed signal.

Example 4.12

FDM was introduced in the telephone network in the 1930s. Because the filter technology needed to separate the signals was not as advanced, multiplexing took place in several stages, called a **hierarchy.** Each voice channel using SSB-AM modulation requires 3.4 kHz, but the channels are assigned 4 kHz of bandwidth to provide a guardband between them. The basic multiplexing building block is a **group** that combines 12 voice channels that occupies a frequency band from 60 to 108 kHz. Five groups are then combined into a **supergroup** of 60 channels that occupies a frequency band from 312 to 552 kHz. Note that for the purposes of multiplexing, each group is treated as an individual signal. Ten supergroups can then be combined to form a **mastergroup** of 600 channels that occupies a frequency band from 564 to 3084 kHz. Finally, six mastergroups interspersed with four supergroups make up a **jumbogroup** of 3840 channels that occupies a frequency band from 564 to 17,548 kHz. Note that the mastergroup and jumbogroup have guardbands added to the bandwidth. Figure 4.33 illustrates the FDM hierarchy used in the analog telephone network. Table 4.1 summarizes the details of the North American and ITU FDM standard used in the analog telephone network.

Table 4.1 North American FDM Standard for Telephony

Multiplex Level	Number of Voice Circuits	Frequency Band (kHz)	BW (kHz)
Voice channel	1	0–4	4
Group	12	60–108	48
Supergroup	60	312–552	240
Mastergroup	600	564–3084	2520
Supergroup	3600	564–17,548	16,984

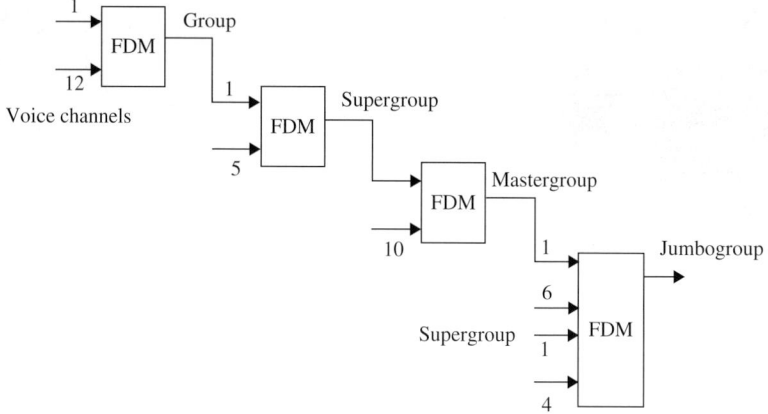

Figure 4.33 North American FDM hierarchy.

Example 4.13

There are more than 11,000 CATV systems in the United States. They provide a high capacity, nearly ubiquitous, broadband two-way information infrastructure serving both the business and residential communities. Modern CATV systems deploy a hybrid fiber coax (HFC) architecture in which fiber trunks provide transmission to and from fiber nodes. Each fiber node serves small neighborhoods of a few hundred homes (about 500) as shown in Figure 4.34. From there on, the connections are over coaxial cable. The coaxial cable portion of the CATV network is used as a bidirectional transmission path for simultaneous transmission of information in both directions. This is achieved by segregating the high- and low-frequency bands of the coax for downstream (forward path) and upstream (reverse path) transmissions, respectively.

In the downstream direction, the band from 54 to 552 MHz is used for the distribution of analog TV signals. This frequency band is divided into 6 MHz frequency slots (channels) and carries the analog TV signal in VSB-AM format. Up to 78 analog TV channels are carried using the FDM with channel 2 and 78 subcarriers at 55.25 and 547.25 MHz, respectively. The band from 552 to 1,002 MHz is used to carry digital video as well as downstream data (high-speed Internet) and telephony signals. The digital signals are carried in 6-MHz frequency slots again using the FDM technique.

The upstream frequency band from 5 to 42 MHz, which was originally intended for Impulse Pay-per-View (IPPV) signaling, is now used for upstream data and telephony communications.

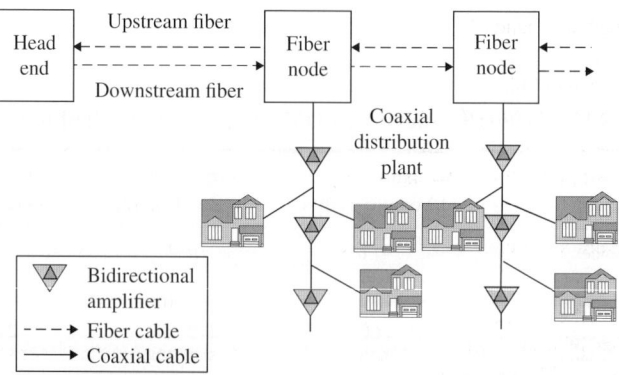

Figure 4.34 Topology of a HFC CATV system.

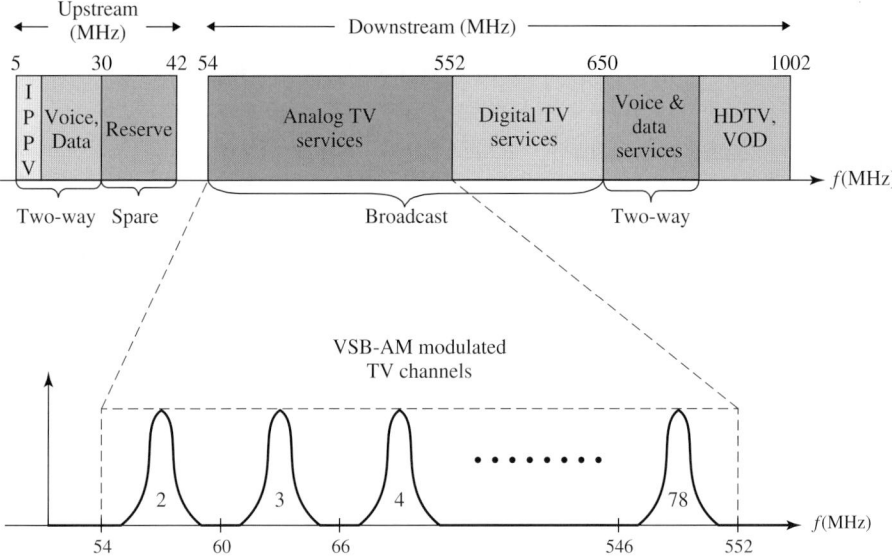

Figure 4.35 Spectrum allocation in modern CATV systems.

This band is divided into different width frequency slots (0.2, 0.4, 0.8, 1.6, and 3.2 MHz) to accommodate different information rates. Again, various reverse path signals are carried using different subcarriers in the FDM format. The frequency plan used by a modern CATV system is shown in Figure 4.35. The reverse path is subject to much worse interference and noise than the downstream path and therefore requires different digital carrier modulation schemes (Chapter 11) than the forward path.

Note that the frequency plan of Figure 4.35 exploits the FDM for transporting a large number of RF subcarriers, each modulated with analog or digital information. This ability to transport multiple subcarriers carrying different kinds of information allows us to build a single network to offer a wide variety of services.

Example 4.14

AMPS is the analog mobile phone system standard developed by Bell Laboratories and officially introduced in 1984. Bandwidth for wireless systems is a scarce resource. Cellular service providers procure available frequency spectrum in auctions conducted by governmental agencies (e.g., the FCC in the United States), spending billions of dollars. Multiplexing enables them to share the assigned frequency band among the maximum number of simultaneous users and for a variety of services, such as voice, data, and music/video clip downloads. AMPS uses a 25-MHz frequency band in each uplink (e.g., 824–849 MHz in the United States), and a 25-MHz band in each downlink (e.g., 869–894 MHz in the United States). AMPS allocates 30-kHz channel spacing for each forward and reverse channel. Because a 10-kHz guardband is allocated at each edge of the 25-MHz frequency band, the total number of channels supported by an AMPS system is given by

$$\text{Number of channels} = \frac{25 \times 10^6 - 2 \times 10 \times 10^3}{30 \times 10^3} = 832 \text{ channels}$$

The standard specifies that 21 of the available channels are reserved for control signaling. Therefore, the number of user channels is $832 - 21 = 811$. Figure 4.36 displays the FDM access scheme used in the AMPS system.

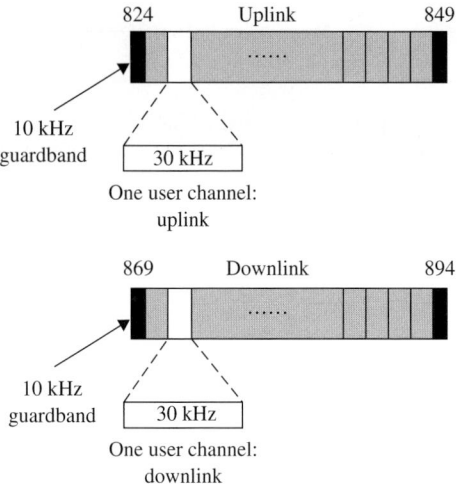

Figure 4.36 AMPS FDM access scheme.

4.9   FREQUENCY TRANSLATION AND SELECTION

In many applications, we want to translate a BP signal to a different center frequency. Frequency translation is usually a necessary step in the design of communication transmitters and receivers. In a receiver, this is usually from a higher **radio frequency (RF)** to a lower **intermediate frequency (IF).** In a transmitter, it's the inverse. The process of frequency translation is performed by a multiplier (called **mixer**) that multiplies the input BP signal by a fixed amplitude sinusoidal output from a **local oscillator (LO).** In a **down-conversion mixer,** the input port is driven by the RF signal, and the output is at a lower IF. In an **up-conversion mixer,** the input is the IF signal and the output is the RF signal. Figure 4.37 illustrates down- and up-conversion mixers.

4.9.1   Down-Conversion Mixer

Suppose that the mixer RF input and LO signals are given by

$$x_{RF}(t) = A(t)\cos\left[2\pi f_c t + \psi(t)\right] \tag{4.110}$$

$$v_{LO}(t) = V_o \cos(2\pi f_{LO} t) \tag{4.111}$$

where f_{LO} is the output frequency of the local oscillator. The mixer output $y(t)$ consists of sum and difference frequency terms

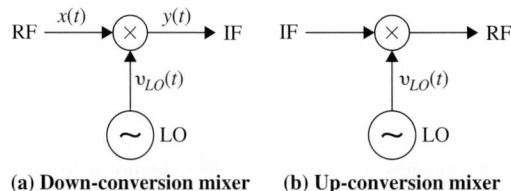

(a) Down-conversion mixer   **(b) Up-conversion mixer**

Figure 4.37 Down- and up-conversion mixers.

$$y(t) = x_{RF}(t) \times v_{LO}(t) = \frac{A(t)V_o}{2}\Big\{\cos[2\pi f_{IF}t + \psi(t)] + \cos[2\pi(f_c + f_{LO})t + \psi(t)]\Big\}$$

$$(4.112)$$

Equation (4.112) states that the down-conversion mixer translates the input signal at frequency f_c to the intermediate frequency (f_{IF}) given by

$$f_{IF} = f_c - f_{LO} \qquad (4.113)$$

The undesired (sum frequency) term in (4.112) is removed by filtering. Note that the LO frequency can be below the RF or carrier frequency

$$f_{LO} = f_c - f_{IF} \quad \textbf{(low-side injection)} \qquad (4.114)$$

or above the RF or carrier frequency

$$f_{LO} = f_c + f_{IF} \quad \textbf{(high-side injection)} \qquad (4.115)$$

Further, for a given choice of f_{IF}, the input frequency $f_c + 2f_{IF}$ is also converted to the same IF frequency for the high-side injection. Similarly, for the low-side injection, the input frequency $f_c - 2f_{IF}$ is also converted to the same IF frequency. These frequencies that are separated from the desired frequencies by $2f_{IF}$ are called **image frequencies.** Figure 4.38 displays location of image frequencies in low- and high-side injection schemes. This is a potential problem because the noise and interference at the image frequency can corrupt the desired signal at the receiver. Therefore, image-reject filtering must precede any down-conversion operation to an intermediate frequency to avoid the interference to the desired signal as shown in Figure 4.39.

The most common method of image suppression is to place an image-reject filter immediately before the mixer. This filter must have low loss in the signal band and large attenuation in the image band as shown in Figure 4.40.

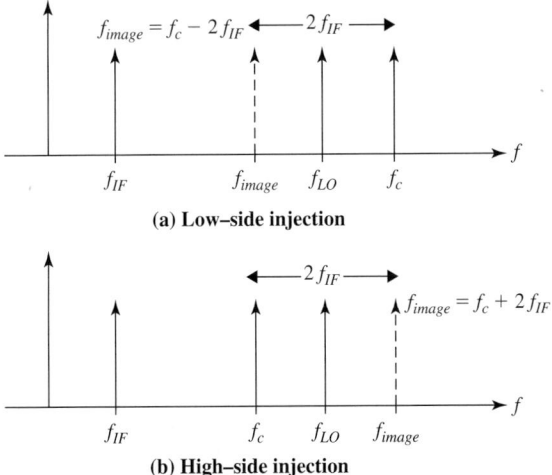

Figure 4.38 Image frequencies.

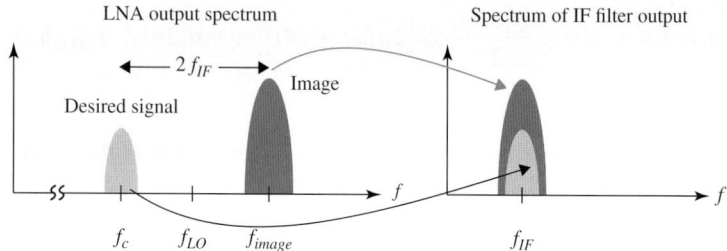

Figure 4.39 Masking of the desired signal by an interferer at the image frequency: high-side injection.

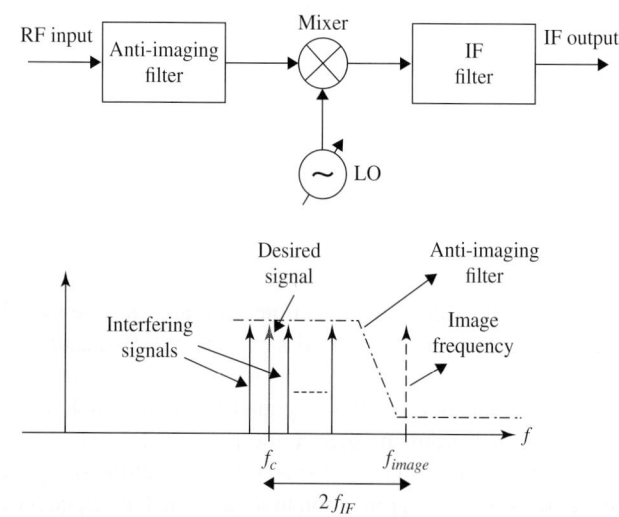

Figure 4.40 Image-reject filtering: high-side injection.

4.9.2 Image-Reject Mixers

An alternative approach to image-reject filtering is the use of a cancellation scheme to perform image suppression. The key idea in an image-reject mixer is to process the signal and the image differently, allowing the cancellation of the image by its negated replica. An image-reject mixer design originating from a SSB modulator introduced by Hartley in 1928 is illustrated in Figure 4.41.[1]

Suppose that the RF input signal is given by

$$x(t) = A_c \cos(2\pi f_c t) + A_{image} \cos(2\pi f_{image} t) \qquad (4.116)$$

where the first term in (4.116) represents the desired channel and the second term the image. The input is applied to two down-conversion mixers fed by quadrature LO inputs, that is, $\cos(2\pi f_{LO} t)$ and $\sin(2\pi f_{LO} t)$. Assuming low-side injection, the following relationship is obvious from Figure 4.38.

$$f_{IF} = f_c - f_{LO} = f_{LO} - f_{image} \qquad (4.117)$$

[1] R. Hartley, *Single-Sideband Modulation System,* United States Patent No. 1666, 206, 1928.

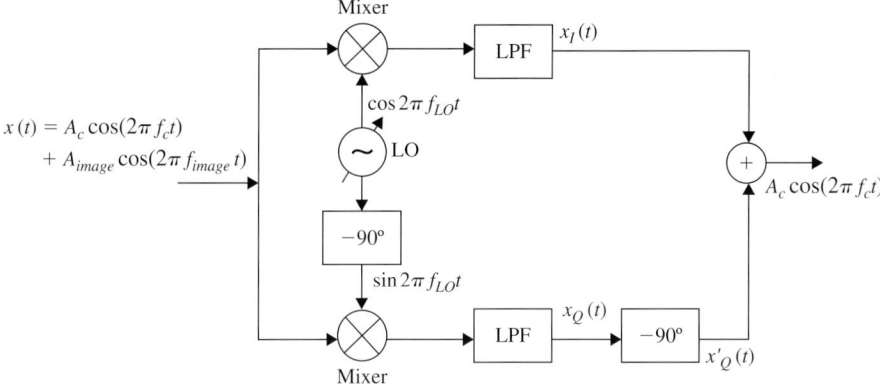

Figure 4.41 Image-reject mixer.

Two IF outputs, $x_I(t)$ and $x_Q(t)$, are obtained by LP filtering the output of each mixer. As explained in Section 4.9.1, this is done to reject the double (carrier) frequency terms in each mixer's output.

$$x_I(t) = \frac{A_c}{2}\cos\left[2\pi(f_c - f_{LO})t\right] + \frac{A_{image}}{2}\cos\left[2\pi(f_{image} - f_{LO})t\right] \qquad (4.118)$$

$$x_Q(t) = -\frac{A_c}{2}\sin\left[2\pi(f_c - f_{LO})t\right] + \frac{A_{image}}{2}\sin\left[2\pi(f_{LO} - f_{image})t\right] \qquad (4.119)$$

The quadrature path IF output, $x_Q(t)$, is now phase shifted by 90° yielding

$$x_Q'(t) = -\frac{A_c}{2}\sin\left[2\pi(f_c - f_{LO})t - \frac{\pi}{2}\right] - \frac{A_{image}}{2}\sin\left[2\pi(f_{image} - f_{LO})t + \frac{\pi}{2}\right]$$

$$= +\frac{A_c}{2}\cos\left[2\pi(f_c - f_{LO})t\right] - \frac{A_{image}}{2}\cos\left[2\pi(f_{image} - f_{LO})t\right] \qquad (4.120)$$

Upon the addition of $x_I(t)$ and $x_Q'(t)$, the desired signal adds coherently yielding $A_c\cos(2\pi f_I t)$, while the image signal cancels. Thus the RF signal $x(t)$ is down-converted to IF with total suppression of the image signal. The drawback of Hartley's design is that the image rejection is highly dependent on the accuracy of the phase shift and the gain matching in the upper and lower branches of Figure 4.41. Image rejection in excess of 60 dB requires a phase accuracy of less than 0.5°, which is difficult to realize in a monolithic implementation.

4.10 COMMUNICATION RECEIVERS

The purpose of a communication receiver is to extract the desired signal in the presence of noise and interfering signals that coexist with that signal. The key functions of a communication receiver include:

- **Reception/amplification.** Low-noise amplification in the front end for improved sensitivity. **Sensitivity** is a measure of a receiver's ability to receive weak signals in the presence of noise with an acceptable signal-to-noise ratio. Several stages of amplification are provided as necessary to make up for the attenuation in the transmission path and to deliver the signal to the demodulation stage in the acceptable range.

- **Channel or signal selection.** Tuning of the desired signal (frequency slot) from the received signal that may contain other signals in addition to noise, essentially distinguishing it from adjacent channels. This is called *selectivity*. **Selectivity** is the measure of the ability of a receiver to select a particular frequency or a particular band of frequencies and reject all other unwanted frequencies.
- **Demodulation.** Recovering the original baseband message signal.

The receivers used in communication systems can be classified into three main types[2]:

- Superheterodyne receivers
- Direct-conversion receivers
- Low IF receivers

4.10.1 Superheterodyne Receivers

The superheterodyne receiver was invented in 1918 by Edwin H. Armstrong and is still the most universally used. The key idea in a superheterodyne receiver is to down-convert the incoming RF signal at the antenna to some fixed lower IF (f_{IF}). The desired signal selection is then accomplished at IF using a highly selective IF BP filter to remove unwanted adjacent channels. The block diagram of a superheterodyne receiver is shown in Figure 4.42.

The front end of the receiver consists of an RF filter followed by the **low noise amplifier (LNA).** The input to the receiver is an FDM signal containing all the channels specified by some sort of national or international standard, such as cellular, CATV, broadcast AM or FM. The RF filter performs a first-order attenuation of out-of-band signals. After the RF filter, the entire FDM signal is amplified by the LNA, which is optimized to contribute a minimal amount of noise. The image-reject BP filter at the LNA output performs additional filtering to attenuate undesirable spectral energy (other signals as well as LNA output noise) at the image frequency. The resulting signal is then translated to an out-of-band IF by a down-conversion mixer. We recall that if the desired signal is centered at f_c, then image-band signals centered at $f_c - 2f_{IF}$ (for low-side injection) must be filtered out prior to mixing. Otherwise, they can corrupt the desired signal by down-converting to the same intermediate frequency, f_{IF}. Typical receiver requirements for image rejection range from 40 to 90 dB. The choice of low- or high-side injection is dictated by the spectral occupancy of in-band signals as well as technology/cost considerations. In the case of CATV, the lower band edge of the downstream (forward) signal spectrum starts at 54 MHz (channel 2), so high-side injection is used. Cellular/wireless transceivers, however, use low-side injection as transmission signals occupy 25 MHz band around a center frequency of either 1 or 2 GHz. For the rest of the discussion, we will assume low-side injection.

Tuning of the receiver is accomplished by varying the frequency of the local oscillator. The latter is usually implemented as a PLL frequency synthesizer that feeds the correct frequency ($f_c - f_{IF}$) to the mixer to recover the desired channel centered at frequency f_c. Thus the frequency translation of the desired carrier is always to the *same* IF frequency f_{IF}. This is an important feature of a superheterodyne receiver that the desired channel always appears at the same IF frequency independent of the carrier frequency. This implies that the IF filter does not need to be tunable. It is, however, a highly

[2] B. Razavi, *RF Microelectronics* (Upper Saddle River, NJ: Prentice Hall, 1998), Chapter 5.

selective (i.e., sharp roll-off) transfer function designed to perform the desired channel selection by the suppression of adjacent channel signals. Consequently, in many systems, an IF filter is implemented using **surface acoustic wave (SAW)** or similar technology capable of achieving high filter quality (Q) factors. The desired channel at the IF is next amplified utilizing a **variable gain amplifier (VGA)** and is then demodulated to baseband for further signal processing. Figure 4.43 displays frequency spectra at various stages in the receiver.

The choice of intermediate frequency f_{IF} is a trade-off between the receiver's sensitivity and selectivity. The sensitivity of a superheterodyne receiver is largely determined by the image-reject filtering, whereas its selectivity is typically concentrated in the IF filter. As shown in Figure 4.40, the image-reject filter must attenuate signals in the image band located only $2f_{IF}$ away from the desired signal. The two requirements imposed upon an image-reject filter, (1) a well-controlled response in the signal passband and (2) a steep attenuation in the image band, can be met simultaneously if $2f_{IF}$ is sufficiently large. However, a large value of f_{IF} creates technological challenges in implementing highly selective IF filter designs. As a rule of thumb, IF frequency is chosen to be on the order of 10% of the RF carrier frequency f_c. Therefore, when the carrier of the incoming RF signal is situated between 1 and 2 GHz, an IF between 100 and 200 MHz is a typical choice.

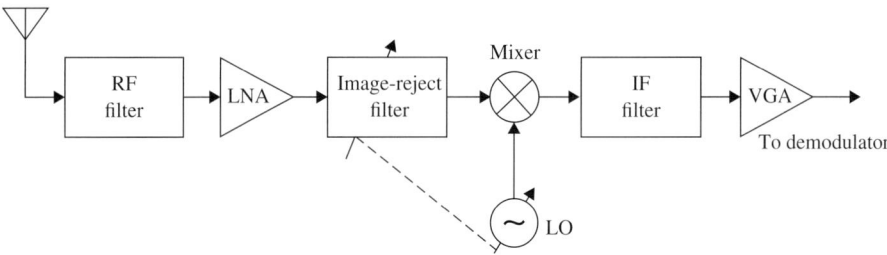

Figure 4.42 Superheterodyne receiver architecture.

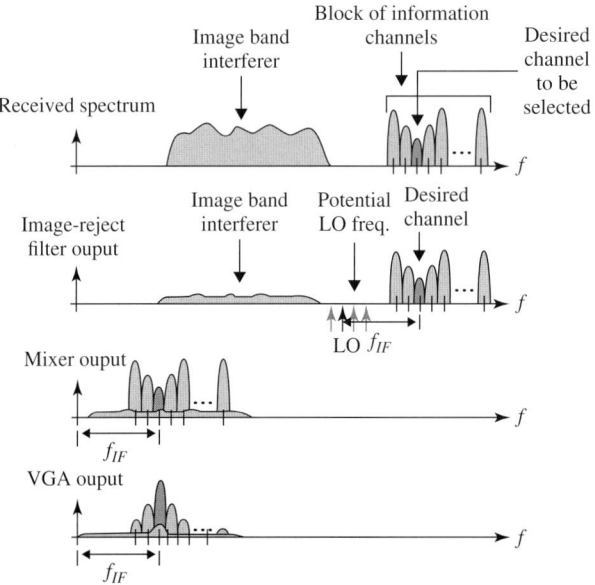

Figure 4.43 Spectra at various stages in a superheterodyne receiver.

Example 4.15

AM radio broadcasting utilizes a frequency band of 535 to 1605 kHz. The carrier frequency allocations range from 540 to 1600 kHz with 10 kHz spacing. The baseband message signal $s(t)$ is limited to a bandwidth of 5 kHz. The radio receiver for AM broadcasting uses 455 kHz IF.

a. Determine the LO tuning range for high-side injection.
b. Determine the LO tuning range for low-side injection.

Solution

a. Using (4.115) for high-side injection, we have

$$f_{LO} = f_c + f_{IF} = f_c + 455$$

When $f_c = 540$ kHz, $f_{LO} = 540 + 455 = 995$ kHz. Similarly, when $f_c = 1600$ kHz, $f_{LO} = 1600 + 455 = 2055$ kHz. Therefore, the tuning range of the LO is 995 to 2055 kHz.

b. Using (4.114) for low-side injection, we have

$$f_{LO} = f_c - f_{IF} = f_c - 455$$

When $f_c = 540$ kHz, $f_{LO} = 540 - 455 = 85$ kHz. Similarly, when $f_c = 1600$ kHz, $f_{LO} = 1600 - 455 = 1145$ kHz. Therefore, the tuning range of the LO is 85 to 1145 kHz.

The LO tuning range for low-side injection is $1145/85 \approx 14$ versus $2055/995 \approx 2$ for high-side injection. It is easier and more cost-effective to design an LO with a frequency range of 2 rather than 14. Therefore, an AM superheterodyne receiver uses high-side injection.

4.10.2   Direct-Conversion Receivers

Direct-conversion receivers were considered as early as 1924, while one of the first radios to be built using direct conversion appeared in 1947. In the simplest form, the direct-conversion receiver can be considered a superheterodyne receiver where the IF is 0 Hz. The received FDM signal, with a center frequency of many GHz in many applications, is translated directly to baseband in one conversion, hence the name **direct conversion** or the other commonly used name, **zero-IF (ZIF).** This approach removes the IF stage from the receiver and eliminates the need for image rejection. Energy from undesired channels is removed with on-chip low-pass filtering at baseband. Figure 4.44 displays the spectra of waveforms at different stages of a direct-conversion receiver.

The direct-conversion receiver has several advantages over the superheterodyne design.[3] First, the problem of image is circumvented because the IF is zero. Second, the LNA need not drive a 50-ohm load because no discrete image-reject filter is required. Third, the IF SAW filter and subsequent stages are replaced with LP filters and baseband amplifiers that are amenable to monolithic integration. Direct translation of the spectrum to zero frequency, however, entails a number of issues that do not exist or are not as serious in a superheterodyne receiver. The most important problem is feedthrough coupling between the LO and the inputs of RF filter, mixer, and LNA as shown in Figure 4.45. This effect, called **LO leakage,** arises from capacitive and substrate coupling and, if the LO signal is provided externally, bond wire coupling. The leakage signal appearing at the inputs of the RF filter, the LNA, and the mixer is now

[3] Razavi, *RF Microelectronics,* Chapter 5.

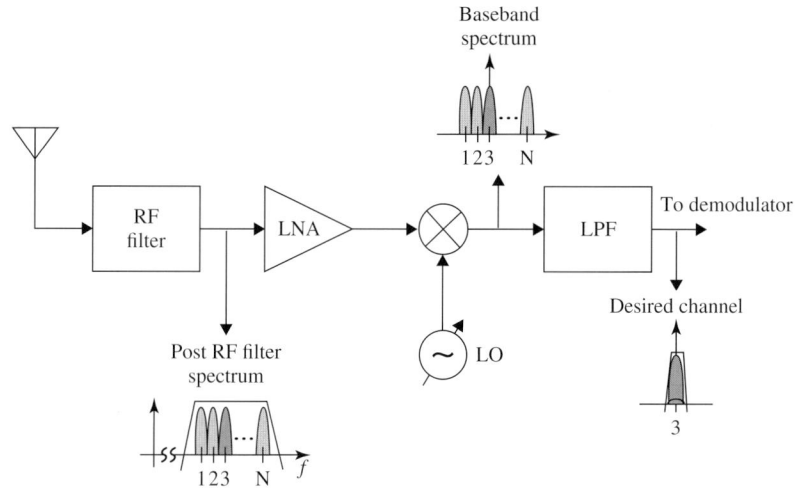

Figure 4.44 Direct-conversion receiver architecture.

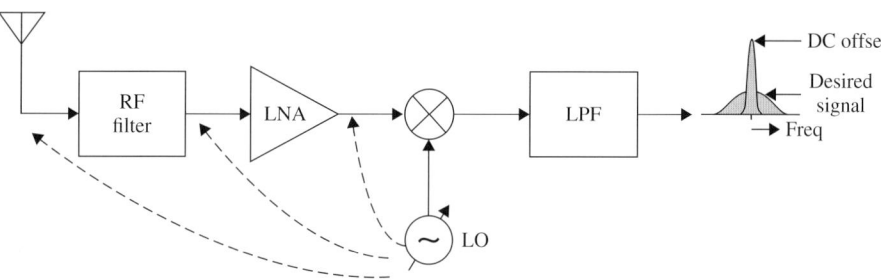

Figure 4.45 LO leakage paths in direct-conversion receivers.

mixed with the LO signal, thus producing time-varying DC components (**DC offsets**) in the desired signal spectrum at the mixer output. This phenomenon is called **self-mixing.** Other mechanisms that create DC interference include second-order intermodulation and accumulated offset created by the baseband blocks.

Certain carrier modulation schemes (covered in Chapter 11) popular in digital cellular systems (e.g., GSM) have spectral energy at DC. Hence, DC coupling is generally considered mandatory. However, any DC offset adds directly to the information signal, resulting in distortion. This problem could be reduced by allowing DC-blocking capacitors to be used. With maximum cutoff frequencies around 50 Hz, impractical capacitor sizes are called for. This makes DC blocking unsuited for IC implementations. As a result, direct-conversion receivers for GSM cellular radio need offset-canceling algorithms to cope with the DC-offset problem.

4.10.3 Low-IF Receiver Architectures

An obvious alternative to address the DC-offset problems introduced in a zero-IF receiver is to down-convert the carrier to a very low IF, rather than directly to baseband. The **low-IF receiver,** shown in Figure 4.46, leverages the performance advantages of the superheterodyne receiver with the economic and integration advantages of the direct

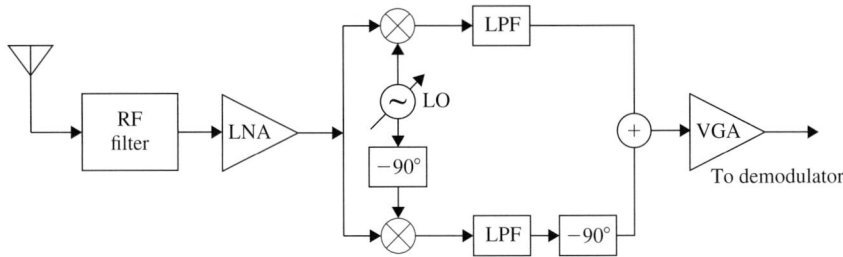

Figure 4.46 Low-IF receiver architecture.

conversion approach. This is accomplished by band selecting and down-converting the desired RF signal to a low IF—one or two channel bandwidths away from DC. Similar to a direct-conversion receiver, the low-IF architecture requires the use of only one discrete filter, the RF filter. The advantages of a low-IF receiver compared to a zero-IF receiver are clear. There is absolutely no DC-offset problem simply because the desired signal is not situated around DC. Similar to the zero-IF receiver, the low-IF receiver is able to eliminate the off-chip IF SAW filter. As in the case of the superhetero-dyne receiver, the low-IF receiver needs to attenuate signals in the image band located only $2f_{IF}$ away from the desired signal. Because of the low-IF design, it is prohibi-tively difficult to use BP filtering to meet the required image suppression specification. Instead, an image-reject mixer (Section 4.8.2) is typically employed to down-convert the RF signal to IF.

Low-IF receivers implemented in RF CMOS ICs are developing a strong presence in the marketplace. For applications such as wireless LAN (WLAN) and Bluetooth, they are dominant, and in areas such as GSM cellular transceivers and GPS receivers, they are making inroads. The Alcatel Bluetooth transceiver design uses an IF of 1 MHz, while Broadcom and Ericsson implementations use an IF of 2 MHz.[4]

FINAL REMARKS

In this chapter, we began our study of various analog modulation schemes where the message signal is embedded in the carrier by varying one of its characteristic param-eters in one-to-one correspondence. Modulation is performed to achieve efficient transmission and to enable frequency division multiplexing for spectrum sharing. This chapter was devoted to amplitude modulation where the information is embedded in the amplitude of the carrier. Table 4.2 compares the performance of various amplitude modulation schemes.

It is important to note that although FDM was studied here in the context of analog transmission systems, it is widely applicable in modern digital communication systems as well. For example, in the **second generation (2G)** digital cellular systems (e.g., GSM), the 25-MHz band for each direction is divided into 124 channels, 200-kHz wide, using FDM. Each channel supports digital transmission at 270.833 kbps. Similarly, the superheterodyne receiver architecture, developed here in the context of analog commu-nication systems, is also relevant in modern digital communication systems. Not only is it used in every radio and TV set, and every CATV set-top unit, but it also forms the front end in digital 2G cellular handsets.

---

[4] A. Abidi, "RF CMOS Comes of Age," *IEEE Journal of Solid-State Circuits* 39, no. 4 (2004): 549–561.

Table 4.2 Comparison of Amplitude Modulation Schemes

Type of Modulation	Transmission Bandwidth	Power Efficiency	Equipment Complexity	Comment
DSB-SC	$2B$	100%	Medium	Coherent demodulator only
Conventional AM	$2B$	$< 50\%$	Low	Envelope detector can be used
SSB	B	100%	High	Coherent demodulator only; complex sideband filtering required at modulator
SSB + C	B	Depends upon the magnitude of the carrier	Medium	Envelope detector can be used; complex sideband filtering required at modulator
VSB	$B + f_v, f_v/B \approx 0.2 - 0.3$	100%	Medium	Coherent demodulator required
VSB + C	$B + f_v, f_v/B \approx 0.2 - 0.3$	Depends upon the magnitude of the carrier	Low	Envelope detector can be used

FURTHER READINGS

AM modulation schemes are covered in the undergraduate communication systems texts [1–5]. The concepts of superheterodyne and other receiver architectures originally developed in the context of analog communications are flourishing today in digital cellular and WLAN communications. There is great excitement in this field with the developments of new transceiver architectures made possible by Moore's law and progress in RF CMOS ICs. References [8] and [9] provide a survey of these rapidly developing fields.

1. Ziemer, R., and W. Tranter. *Principles of Communications: Systems, Modulation, and Noise,* 5th ed. New York: John Wiley, 2001.

2. Carlson, B., P. Crilly, and J. Rutledge. *Communication Systems,* 4th ed. New York: McGraw-Hill, 2002.

3. Proakis, J., and M. Salehi. *Fundamentals of Communication Systems,* 1st ed. Upper Saddle River, NJ: Prentice Hall, 2005.

4. Couch, L. *Digital and Analog Communication Systems,* 6th ed. Upper Saddle River, NJ: Prentice Hall, 2001.

5. Haykin, S. *Communication Systems,* 4th ed. New York: John Wiley, 2000.

6. Orchard, H., and G. Temes. "Design Technique for Vestigial-Sideband Filters." *IEEE Transactions on Communications* COM-22, no. 7 (1974): 956–964.

7. Hartley, R. *Single-Sideband Modulation System.* United States Patent No. 1666, 206, 1928.

8. Razavi, B. *RF Microelectronics.* Upper Saddle River, NJ: Prentice Hall, 1998

9. Abidi, A. "RF CMOS Comes of Age." *IEEE Journal of Solid-State Circuits* 39, no. 4 (2004): 549–561.

PROBLEMS

4.1. The message signal $s_1(t) = \sin(100\pi t)$ modulates the carrier $c(t) = \cos(3600\pi t)$ to generate the DSB-SC AM signal.

a. Sketch the spectrum of the message signal.

b. Determine and sketch the spectrum of the resulting DSB-SC AM signal. Identify the upper and lower sidebands in the spectrum.

c. Repeat (a) and (b) for $s_2(t) = \cos(600\pi t)\sin(1800\pi t)$.

4.2. The message signal $s(t) = 2\cos(6\pi t) + 0.5\sin(10\pi t)$ modulates the carrier signal $c(t) = A_c\cos(100\pi t)$ using DSB-SC AM scheme.

a. Write an expression for the modulated signal $x(t)$.

b. Determine and sketch the spectrum of the modulated signal $x(t)$.

c. Calculate the average power contained in the modulated signal $x(t)$.

4.3. A message signal $s(t) = 2\cos(6\pi t) + 5\sin(10\pi t)$ modulates the carrier signal $c(t) = 100\cos(1000\pi t)$ using convention AM scheme. The modulator operates with a modulation index of 0.7.

a. Write an expression for the modulated signal $x(t)$.

b. Determine and sketch the spectrum of the modulated signal $x(t)$.

c. Compare the power contained in the sidebands to the total power in the modulated signal. What is the power efficiency in this AM scheme?

d. Calculate the PEP supplied by the AM transmitter.

4.4. The output of an AM modulator is given by

$$x(t) = A_c\cos(2000\pi t) + 50\cos(2100\pi t) + 50\cos(1900\pi t)$$

The carrier power is 5 kW.

a. Determine the modulation index m_a.

b. Write an expression for the normalized modulating signal.

c. Calculate the power efficiency.

d. Calculate the PEP supplied by the AM transmitter and compare it with the normalized average power and the carrier power.

4.5. The envelope detector shown in Figure 4.16(a) is used to demodulate the message signal $s(t)$ from the conventional AM signal $x(t) = A_c[1 + s(t)]\cos(2\pi f_c t)$ where $s(t)$ is a square wave taking on the values 1 and -1 and having a period $T_o \gg 1/f_c$. Sketch the demodulated signal if $R_L C = T_o/40$ and $T_o/4$.

4.6. Consider the demodulation of conventional AM signals using a square law detector with transfer characteristic $y(t) = k_1 x_{AM}(t) + k_2 x_{AM}^2(t)$, where k_1 and k_2 are constants with $k_2 \gg k_1$.

a. Calculate the detector output $y(t)$.

b. Calculate the output $y_D(t)$ of the LP filter. Note that it contains the desired signal as well as the distortion term. Show that if $A_c \gg s(t)$, the distortion can be neglected.

4.7. The spectrum of signal $x(t)$ is illustrated in Figure P4.1. Derive an expression for the spectrum of the signal

$$y(t) = x(t)\cos(2\pi f_c t) + \hat{x}(t)\sin(2\pi f_c t)$$

Assume $B \ll f_c$. Sketch the spectrum $Y(f)$.

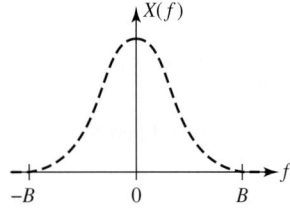

Figure P4.1

4.8. Find the Hilbert transform of the following time signals:

a. $x(t) = \text{sinc}(t)$

b. $x_2(t) = \dfrac{\sin(4\pi t)}{t}\cos(300\pi t)$

c. $x_3(t) = \cos(300\pi t) + 3\sin(600\pi t)$

4.9. If $x(t)$ and $y(t)$ are signals with nonoverlapping spectra, where $x(t)$ is LP and $y(t)$ is BP signal, prove that

$$\mathcal{H}\{x(t)y(t)\} = x(t)\hat{y}(t)$$

4.10. Consider the signal $x(t) = \left[2W\text{sinc}(2Wt) + W\text{sinc}^2(Wt)\right]\cos(2\pi f_c t)$.

a. Determine and sketch the spectrum of analytic signal $x^+(t)$.

b. Determine and sketch the spectrum of the complex envelope $\tilde{x}(t)$.

c. Write an expression for the complex envelope $\tilde{x}(t)$.

4.11. An LSB-AM signal is generated by modulating a 1-kHz carrier by the message signal $s(t) = 2\cos(6\pi t) + 0.5\sin(10\pi t)$. The carrier power is 5 kW.

a. Determine the signal $\hat{s}(t)$.

b. Write an expression for the LSB-AM signal.

c. Determine and sketch the amplitude spectrum of the LSB-AM signal.

d. Compare the PEP and the normalized average power of the LSB-AM signal.

4.12. Suppose the message signal $s(t) = \text{sinc}(2t)$ modulates the carrier signal $c(t) = 10\cos(50\pi t)$ to generate the USB-AM signal.

a. Plot the spectrum of the resultant USB-AM signal and compare it with that of corresponding DSB-SC signal.

b. From the plot of the Fourier transform of the USB signal, show that the USB signal is given by

$$x_{USB}(t) = 5\cos(51\pi t)\text{sinc}(t)$$

c. Now show that $5[s(t)\cos(50\pi t) - \hat{s}(t)\sin(50\pi t)]$ equals $x_{USB}(t)$ of part (b).

4.13. Consider the LSB-AM signal

$$x(t) = \frac{A_c}{2}\left[s(t)\cos(2\pi f_c t) + \hat{s}(t)\sin(2\pi f_c t)\right]. \text{ Assume that}$$

the LO at the demodulator generates a carrier with a fixed phase offset ϕ. That is, the receiver multiplies $x(t)$ with $\cos(2\pi f_c t + \phi)$ and LP filters the output to produce the demodulated signal $y_D(t)$.

a. Find $y_D(t)$ in terms of $s(t)$ and $\hat{s}(t)$. Comment on the distortion in the demodulated signal introduced by the phase offset.

b. Show that the output spectrum $Y_D(f)$ is given by

$$Y_D(f) = \begin{cases} \dfrac{A_c}{2}S(f)e^{j\phi}, & f \geq 0 \\[2mm] \dfrac{A_c}{2}S(f)e^{-j\phi}, & f < 0 \end{cases}$$

4.14. The main technical difficulty in the phasing method of generating SSB-AM signal (Figure 4.22) is implementing the Hilbert transformer over a wide range of frequencies. An alternative method of generating an SSB-AM signal proposed by Weaver is shown in Figure P4.2. Although it is a more complex design, it avoids the use of wide-band phase shifter. The message signal $s(t)$ is band-limited to B Hz. Assume ideal LP filters with cutoff frequency $B/2$. Prove that $x(t)$ is a USB-AM signal.

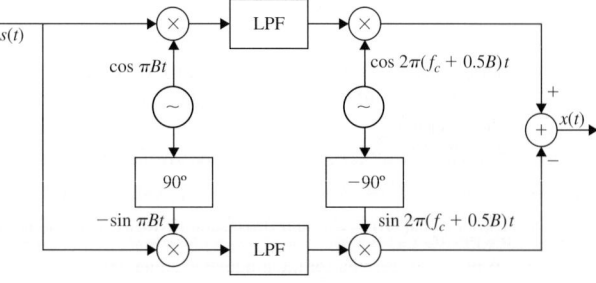

Figure P4.2

4.15. One disadvantage of coherent demodulation of SSB-AM signals is the interference caused by the presence of residual frequency components from the removed sideband. By using a quadrature demodulation scheme shown in Figure P4.3, it is possible to demodulate either the upper or lower sideband and cancel the other sideband. Prove that by choosing the sign of 90° phase shifter, either the upper or lower sideband component is demodulated while suppressing the other.

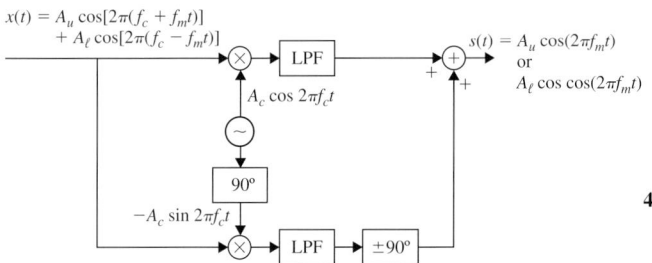

Figure P4.3

4.16. Consider the phasing method illustrated in Figure 4.22 to generate a USB-AM signal. The modulating signal is a single tone of frequency f_m. The 90° phase-shift network introduces a constant phase offset of ϕ_o between the in-phase and quadrature carriers.

 a. Calculate the output of the USB-AM modulator.

 b. Calculate the residual power in the lower sideband as a percentage of the power in the desired sideband.

 c. Evaluate the magnitude of undesired sideband rejection for phase offset $\phi_o = 1.5\,°$.

4.17. A VSB-AM signal is generated from an input $s(t)$ by first generating a conventional AM signal ($m_a = 0.875$) with a carrier frequency $f_c = 45.75$ MHz and then passing this signal through a filter whose frequency response is given by

$$|H(f)| = \begin{cases} \dfrac{f - f_c + f_v}{2f_v}, & f_c - f_v \le |f| < f_c + f_v \\ 1, & f_c + f_v \le |f| < f_c + 4.2 \text{ MHz} \\ 0, & \text{otherwise} \end{cases}$$

where $f_v = 0.75$ MHz.

 a. Determine an expression for the resulting VSB signal if $s_1(t) = \cos(30\pi \times 10^3)$.

 b. Determine the spectrum of the VSB signal.

 c. Calculate the ratio of the PEP to the average power.

 d. Repeat (a) through (c) for $s_2(t) = \cos(\pi \times 10^6)$ and $s_3(t) = \cos(4\pi \times 10^6)$.

4.18. A superheterodyne receiver is designed to cover the RF frequency range of 45 to 860 MHz, with channel spacings of 8 MHz and an IF of 40 MHz. Assume high-side injection.

 a. If the receiver down-converts the RF signals to an IF of 40 MHz, calculate the range of frequencies for the LO.

 b. Calculate the range of image frequencies.

 Note that band of image frequencies and the signal band overlap. This is undesirable. So we consider up-conversion to a higher IF of 1.2 GHz.

 c. Calculate the range of frequencies for the LO.

 d. Determine the range of image frequencies.

 e. Is there any overlap between image and signal bands?

 f. Because it is difficult to realize highly selective filtering at high IF, *a dual-conversion* superheterodyne design is a desirable choice for a wide bandwidth receiver spanning several octaves. Draw the block diagram of *a dual-conversion* superheterodyne receiver and specify the reasons for your choice of first and second IF frequencies.

MATLAB PROBLEMS

4.19. The message signal $s(t)$ is given by

$$s(t) = \begin{cases} \text{sinc}^2(10t), & t \le 2 \\ 0, & \text{otherwise} \end{cases}$$

The message signal modulates a carrier $c(t) = \cos(200\pi t)$ to generate a DSB-AM signal $x(t)$.

 a. Sample the message signal $s(t)$ at 100 Hz to generate a 256-point message sequence s[n]. Plot it.

 b. Sample the DSB-AM signal $x(t)$ at 1000 Hz to generate a 2048-point sequence x[n]. Plot it.

 c. Obtain the DFT S[k] of s[n]. Plot the magnitude spectrum of the message signal (that is, fftshift(S)) using the function stem.

 d. Plot the magnitude spectrum of the DSB-AM signal x[n].

4.20. The message signal

$$s(t) = \begin{cases} 2\cos(20\pi t) + \sin(4\pi t), & t \le 2 \\ 0, & \text{otherwise} \end{cases}$$

modulates a carrier $c(t) = \cos(200\pi t)$ to generate a conventional-AM signal. Assume modulation index $m_a = 0.5$.

 a. Sample the message signal $s(t)$ at 100 Hz to generate a 256-point message sequence s[n]. Plot it.

 b. Sample the conventional-AM signal $x(t)$ at 1000 Hz to generate a 2048-point sequence x[n]. Plot it.

 c. Obtain the DFT S[k] of s[n]. Plot the magnitude spectrum of the message signal.

 d. Plot the magnitude spectrum of the conventional-AM signal x[n].

4.21. The message signal

$$s(t) = \begin{cases} 2\sin(2\pi t), & 0 \le t < 1 \\ 0, & 1 \le t < 1.3 \\ 4\cos(2.5\pi t + \pi/4), & 1.3 \le t \le 2.1 \\ 0, & \text{otherwise} \end{cases}$$

modulates a carrier $c(t) = \cos(50\pi t)$ to generate a USB-AM signal.

a. Sample the message signal $s(t)$ at 250 Hz to generate a 1024-point message sequence s[n]. Plot it.

b. Use the MATLAB function `hilbert(s)` to obtain the Hilbert transform of the message sequence s[n]. Note that this function returns the analytic signal sequence $s^+[n] = s[n] + j\,\hat{s}[n]$. The real part of $s^+[n]$ is the original sequence s[n], while the imaginary part contains the Hilbert transform ŝ[n]. Plot ŝ[n].

c. Plot the magnitude spectra of s[n] and s^+[n] using DFT.

d. Generate and plot 1024-point USB-AM sequence x[n] = s[n]c[n] − ŝ[n] ĉ[n], where c[n] is discrete-time sequence corresponding to the carrier signal $c(t)$.

e. Obtain the DFT X[k] of x[n]. Plot the magnitude spectrum of the USB-AM signal.

4.22. The DSB-AM signal x[n] in Problem 4.19 is demodulated by the coherent demodulation scheme displayed in Figure 4.7(a). The LP filter is fourth order Butterworth filter with cutoff frequency of 50 Hz.

a. For the carrier phase offset values of 0°, 30°, 60°, and 90° between the modulator and demodulator, compute the demodulated output sequences y_D[n] using MATLAB function `filter`.

b. Make a composite plot of the demodulated output sequences generated in (a). Comment on the results.

4.23. The conventional-AM signal x[n] in Problem 4.20 is demodulated by the envelope detector followed by a LPF displayed in Figure 4.16(c). The LP filter is fourth order Butterworth filter with cutoff frequency of 50 Hz. The envelope detector characterized by time-constant R_LC can be simulated in MATLAB by the following code segment:

```
vcout(1) = x(1)
for i = 2:length(x)
if x(i) > vcout(i-1)
  vcout(i) =x(i);
else
  vcout(i) = vcout(i-1)*exp(-Ts/RC);
end
end
```

where vcout is the envelope detector output sequence and Ts is the sampling interval used in generating the conventional-AM signal x[n].

a. Plot the envelope detector output sequence to display how it tracks the carrier envelope for R_LC values 0.1 to 0.5. Assume modulation index $m_a = 0.8$.

b. Calculate the demodulated output sequence and plot it along with the original message sequence for each case in (a). Comment on the results.

4.24. The USB-AM signal x[n] in Problem 4.21 is demodulated by the coherent demodulation scheme displayed in Figure 4.7(a). The LP filter is fourth order Butterworth filter with cutoff frequency of 12.5 Hz.

a. For the carrier phase offset values of 0°, 30°, 60°, and 90° between the modulator and demodulator, compute the demodulated output sequences y_D[n] using MATLAB function `filter`.

b. Make a composite plot of the demodulated output sequences generated in (a). Comment on the results.

4.25. The message signal

$$s(t) = \begin{cases} 2\cos(20\pi t) + \sin(4\pi t), & t \le 2.048 \\ 0, & \text{otherwise} \end{cases}$$

modulates a carrier $c(t) = \cos(200\pi t)$ to generate a DSB-AM signal. The DSB-AM signal is passed through the VSB filter response illustrated in Figure P4.4.

a. Generate a VSB-AM signal $x_{VSB}(t)$.

b. Reinsert the carrier signal $k\cos(200\pi t)$.

c. Sample the composite signal $x_{VSB}(t) + k\cos(200\pi t)$ at 1000 Hz to generate a 2048-point sequence.

d. Design an envelope detector and appropriate LP filter to recover the original message signal. Plot it.

e. Start with value of $k = 0.85$ and repeat (c) and (d) for higher values to demonstrate the viability of an envelope detection scheme.

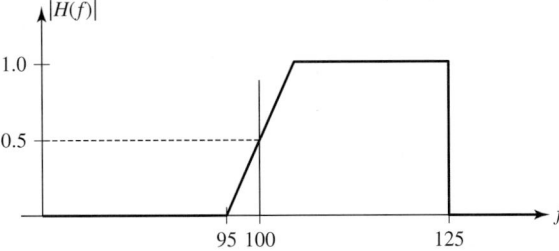

Figure P4.4

Appendix 4A

Hilbert Transform

The **Hilbert transform** of the signal $x(t)$ is defined as the signal whose frequency components are all phase shifted by $-\pi/2$ radians. The resulting signal is denoted

$$\hat{x}(t) = \mathcal{H}\{x(t)\} \tag{4A.1}$$

Therefore, $\hat{x}(t)$ has exactly the same frequency components as are present in $x(t)$ without any amplitude change. However, a 90° phase delay is incurred by each component in the process of transformation.

Example 4A.1

$$x_1(t) = A\cos(2\pi f_c t + \phi) \overset{\mathcal{H}}{\longleftrightarrow} A\cos\left(2\pi f_c t + \phi - \frac{\pi}{2}\right) = A\sin(2\pi f_c t + \phi) \tag{4A.2}$$

$$x_2(t) = A\sin(2\pi f_c t + \phi) \overset{\mathcal{H}}{\longleftrightarrow} A\sin\left(2\pi f_c t + \phi - \frac{\pi}{2}\right) = -A\cos(2\pi f_c t + \phi) \tag{4A.3}$$

The two results obtained in Example 4A.1 can be combined to show that

$$Ae^{j(2\pi f_c t + \phi)} \overset{\mathcal{H}}{\longleftrightarrow} Ae^{j(2\pi f_c t + \phi - \frac{\pi}{2})} \tag{4A.4}$$

For an arbitrary signal, $\hat{x}(t)$ is obtained by passing $x(t)$ through a filter with transfer function

$$H(f) = -j\,\mathrm{sgn}(f) \tag{4A.5}$$

Equation (4A.5) describes the effect of the Hilbert transform in the frequency domain. For positive frequencies, the spectrum of the input signal, $X(f)$, is multiplied by $-j$. This corresponds to a phase shift of $-\pi/2$ radians as shown in Figure 4A.1. The input spectrum $X(f)$ is multiplied by j for negative frequencies corresponding to a phase shift of $\pi/2$ radians.

From (4A.5), it is possible to write the following expression for the amplitude and phase response of $H(f)$:

$$|H(f)| = 1$$

$$\angle H(f) = -\frac{\pi}{2}\,\mathrm{sgn}(f) \tag{4A.6}$$

The Fourier transform of $\hat{x}(t)$ is given by

$$\Im\{\hat{x}(t)\} = X(f)H(f) = -j\,\mathrm{sgn}(f)X(f) = \begin{cases} -jX(f), & f > 0 \\ 0, & f = 0 \\ jX(f), & f < 0 \end{cases} \tag{4A.7}$$

The impulse response of $H(f)$ from Table 2.2 is

$$h(t) = \frac{1}{\pi t} \tag{4A.8}$$

Using the convolution theorem of Fourier transform (2.58), it is easy to conclude from (4A.7) that the Hilbert transform is a convolution operation in the time domain.

$$\hat{x}(t) = x(t) \otimes h(t) = x(t) \otimes \frac{1}{\pi t} = \frac{1}{\pi} \int_{-\infty}^{\infty} \frac{x(\tau)}{t - \tau} d\tau \qquad (4A.9)$$

4A.1   Properties of Hilbert Transform

1. Sign Reversal.

$$\hat{\hat{x}}(t) = -x(t) \qquad (4A.10)$$

Because Hilbert transform corresponds to a phase shift of $-\pi/2$ radians, we note that the Hilbert transform of $\hat{x}(t)$ corresponds to the transfer function $(-j\mathrm{sgn}(f))^2 = -1$, or a phase shift of $-\pi$ radians.

2. Energy. The energy (power) in a signal $x(t)$ and its Hilbert transform $\hat{x}(t)$ are equal.

$$|\Im\{\hat{x}(t)\}|^2 = |-j\mathrm{sgn}(f)X(f)|^2 = |-j\mathrm{sgn}(f)|^2|X(f)|^2 = |X(f)|^2 \qquad (4A.11)$$

Because the energy spectral densities for $x(t)$ and its Hilbert transform of $\hat{x}(t)$ are equal, their energies are also equal.

3. Orthogonality. A signal $x(t)$ and its Hilbert transform $\hat{x}(t)$ are orthogonal.

Using Parseval's theorem of the Fourier transform, we get

$$\int_{-\infty}^{\infty} x(t)\hat{x}^*(t)dt = \int_{-\infty}^{\infty} X(f)\hat{X}^*(f)df$$

$$= \int_{-\infty}^{\infty} X(f)\big[-j\mathrm{sgn}(f)X(f)\big]^*df = -j\int_{-\infty}^{0} |X(f)|^2df + j\int_{-\infty}^{0} |X(f)|^2df = 0$$

If $x(t)$ and $y(t)$ are signals with nonoverlapping spectra, where $x(t)$ is low-pass and $y(t)$ is high-pass, then

$$x(t)y(t) \xrightarrow{\;\mathscr{H}\;} x(t)\hat{y}(t) \qquad (4A.12)$$

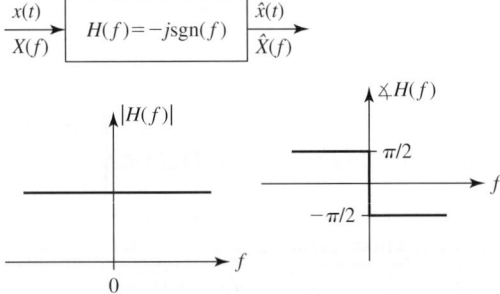

Figure 4A.1 Hilbert transform in the frequency domain.

Example 4A.2

Calculate Hilbert transforms of carrier-modulated waveforms

a. $x_1(t) = s(t)\cos(2\pi f_c t + \phi)$
b. $x_2(t) = s(t)\sin(2\pi f_c t + \phi)$.

Solution

Using (4A.12), we can write

$$x_1(t) = s(t)\cos(2\pi f_c t + \phi) \xleftrightarrow{\mathcal{H}} s(t)\sin(2\pi f_c t + \phi) \qquad (4A.13)$$

$$x_2(t) = s(t)\sin(2\pi f_c t + \phi) \xleftrightarrow{\mathcal{H}} -s(t)\cos(2\pi f_c t + \phi) \qquad (4A.14)$$

CHAPTER 5

Angle Modulation

This chapter will consider two other forms of analog modulation—**frequency modulation (FM)** and **phase modulation (PM)**—both of which are commonly known as **angle modulation.** Both FM and PM find extensive use in communication systems. The use of FM in radio broadcasting is obviously the most well-known application. FM is also employed for the transmission of the sound signal in the analog TV standard, for private land-mobile radio systems, and for cordless telephone systems, just to name a few common applications. PM by itself and in combination with AM is used extensively in modern data-communications systems. Angle modulation has a very important advantage over AM in its ability to provide increased immunity to noise. This improvement is achieved at the expense of an increase in transmission bandwidth. That is, channel bandwidth may be exchanged for improved noise performance in angle modulation systems. Such a trade-off is *not* possible with AM.

The chapter is organized into the following sections:

5.1   FM AND PM SIGNALS.
    This section introduces basic concepts of phase- and frequency-modulated signals.

5.2   SPECTRUM OF ANGLE-MODULATED SIGNALS.
    The spectrum of an angle-modulated carrier with sinusoidal message signal is considered in this section. The results are then used to develop a measure of bandwidth for arbitrary modulation signals.

5.3   NARROWBAND FM.
    We explain narrowband angle modulation and compare its spectral characteristics with DSB-AM.

5.4   DEMODULATION OF ANGLE-MODULATED SIGNALS.
    Various techniques for demodulation of angle-modulated signals are considered in this section. After analyzing the ideal frequency discriminator, practical discriminator implementations are described.

5.5   PHASE-LOCKED LOOP.
    Analog phase-locked loops (PLLs) are introduced in this section. We consider the linear model of PLLs to study their behavior in the locked state. After describing the characteristics of first- and second-order loops, we study the acquisition process in PLLs.

5.6   PLL AS FM DEMODULATOR.
    An important application of PLLs for the demodulation of FM signals is considered in this section

5.7   FM BROADCASTING.
    In this section we describe FM radio broadcasting, including stereo FM.

5.8   ANALOG TELEVISION.
    This section studies the principles of black-and-white and color analog television systems. After explaining the concepts of scanning, synchronization, and video resolution, we proceed to a discussion of compatible color TV signal formats. We next describe how chrominance and audio information are multiplexed in broadcast TV signals.

The chapter concludes with final remarks and a selected list of references.

5.1   FM AND PM SIGNALS

In angle modulation, the information-bearing signal is embedded in the instantaneous phase or frequency of the carrier. The amplitude of the carrier does not contain any information and is held constant. Instead the instantaneous phase or frequency of the carrier is varied linearly with the message signal $s(t)$. An **angle-modulated** signal can be expressed as

$$x(t) = A_c \cos[2\pi f_c t + \theta(t)] \tag{5.1}$$

The **instantaneous phase** of $x(t)$ is defined as

$$\phi_i(t) \triangleq 2\pi f_c t + \theta(t) \tag{5.2}$$

where $\theta(t)$ is called the **excess phase** of the angle-modulated signal. We can write (5.1) in terms of (5.2) as

$$x(t) = A_c \cos \phi_i(t) \tag{5.3}$$

The **instantaneous frequency** of $x(t)$ is defined as

$$f_i(t) \triangleq \frac{1}{2\pi} \frac{d\phi_i}{dt} \tag{5.4}$$

Integrating both sides of (5.4) yields

$$\phi_i(t) = 2\pi \int_{-\infty}^{t} f_i(\alpha) d\alpha \tag{5.5}$$

Equations (5.4) and (5.5) describe how the instantaneous phase and frequency of an angle-modulated waveform $x(t)$ are related.

There are two kinds of angle modulation:

- Phase modulation (PM)
- Frequency modulation (FM)

Phase Modulation

In PM, excess phase of the carrier is varied linearly with the message signal $s(t)$. That is,

$$\theta(t) = k_p s(t) \tag{5.6}$$

where k_p is called the **phase sensitivity** of the phase modulator, expressed in radians/volt. We can write (5.6) as

$$\theta(t) = k_p s(t) = k_p \max|s(t)| \frac{s(t)}{\max|s(t)|} = \Delta\phi_{\max} s_n(t) \tag{5.7}$$

where

$$s_n(t) = \frac{s(t)}{\max|s(t)|} = \text{normalized message signal } s(t) \tag{5.8}$$

and

$$\Delta\phi_{\max} \triangleq \max|\theta(t)| = k_p \max|s(t)| \tag{5.9}$$

$\Delta\phi_{\max}$, called the **maximum phase deviation,** represents maximum instantaneous phase change of the PM signal produced by the modulating signal. Substituting (5.7) into (5.2) yields the instantaneous phase of the PM signal as

$$\phi_i(t) = 2\pi f_c t + \Delta\phi_{\max} s_n(t) \tag{5.10}$$

Substituting (5.10) into (5.3), we can write the following expression for a PM signal

$$x_{PM}(t) = A_c \cos\left[2\pi f_c t + \Delta\phi_{max} s_n(t)\right] \qquad (5.11)$$

The instantaneous frequency of a PM signal is obtained by application of (5.4) to (5.10). That is,

$$f_i(t) = \frac{1}{2\pi} \frac{d\phi_i(t)}{dt} = f_c + \frac{\Delta\phi_{max}}{2\pi} \dot{s}_n(t) \qquad (5.12)$$

Frequency Modulation

In FM, the instantaneous frequency of the carrier is varied linearly with the message signal $s(t)$. That is,

$$f_i(t) = f_c + k_f s(t) \qquad (5.13)$$

where k_f is called the **frequency sensitivity** of the FM modulator, expressed in Hz/volt. Substituting (5.8) into (5.13), we obtain

$$f_i(t) = f_c + k_f \max|s(t)| s_n(t) \qquad (5.14)$$

We observe from (5.14) that the maximum instantaneous frequency change from the carrier frequency produced by the modulating signal is given by

$$\Delta f_{max} \triangleq \max|f_i(t) - f_c| = k_f \max|s(t)| \qquad (5.15)$$

Δf_{max} is called the **maximum frequency deviation** of the FM signal. Substituting (5.15) into (5.14), the instantaneous frequency of the FM signal can be expressed as

$$f_i(t) = f_c + \Delta f_{max} s_n(t) \qquad (5.16)$$

The instantaneous phase of the FM signal is obtained by substituting (5.16) into (5.5). That is,

$$\phi_i(t) = 2\pi \int_{-\infty}^{t} f_i(\alpha)d\alpha = 2\pi \int_{-\infty}^{t} \left[f_c + \Delta f_{max} s_n(\alpha)\right]d\alpha = 2\pi f_c t + 2\pi\Delta f_{max} \int_{-\infty}^{t} s_n(\alpha)d\alpha \quad (5.17)$$

We can now write the following expression for an FM signal by combining (5.17) and (5.3).

$$x_{FM}(t) = A_c \cos\left[2\pi f_c t + 2\pi\Delta f_{max} \int_{-\infty}^{t} s_n(\alpha)d\alpha\right] \qquad (5.18)$$

Note that the second term in (5.18) represents excess phase of the FM signal. That is,

$$\theta(t) = 2\pi\Delta f_{max} \int_{-\infty}^{t} s_n(\alpha)d\alpha \qquad (5.19)$$

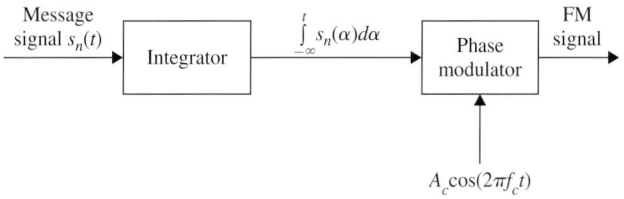

(a) Generating an FM signal using a phase modulator

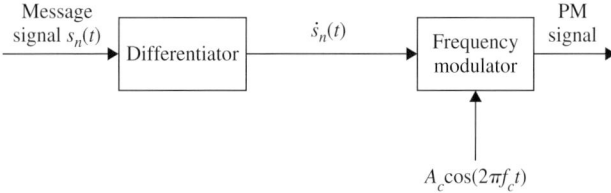

(b) Generating a PM signal using a frequency modulator

Figure 5.1 Relationship between phase and frequency modulation.

The special relationship between PM and FM is apparent from (5.11) and (5.18). An FM waveform corresponding to the message signal $s_n(t)$ is also a PM waveform corresponding to the signal $\int_{-\infty}^{t} s_n(\alpha)d\alpha$. Similarly, a PM waveform corresponding to message signal $s_n(t)$ is also an FM waveform corresponding to signal $\dot{s}_n(t)$. Therefore, it is not possible to identify by inspection whether an angle-modulated signal is an FM or PM waveform because it can be interpreted as either. Figure 5.1 illustrates the relationship between PM and FM.

Table 5.1 summarizes key definitions and relationships for PM and FM signals.

Table 5.1 Definitions and Relationships for PM and FM Signals

	PM	FM
Key parameters	k_p = phase sensitivity (rad/V) $\Delta\phi_{max}$ = max phase deviation (rad)	k_f = frequency sensitivity (Hz/V) Δf_{max} = max frequency deviation (Hz)
Excess phase $\theta(t)$	$\Delta\phi_{max}s_n(t)$	$2\pi\Delta f_{max}\int_{-\infty}^{t} s_n(\alpha)d\alpha$
Instantaneous phase $\phi_i(t)$	$2\pi f_c t + \Delta\phi_{max}s_n(t)$	$2\pi f_c t + 2\pi\Delta f_{max}\int_{-\infty}^{t} s_n(\alpha)d\alpha$
Instantaneous frequency $f_i(t)$	$f_c + \dfrac{\Delta\phi_{max}}{2\pi}\dot{s}_n(t)$	$f_c + \Delta f_{max}s_n(t)$
Modulated signal	$A_c\cos[2\pi f_c t + \Delta\phi_{max}s_n(t)]$	$A_c\cos\left[2\pi f_c t + 2\pi\Delta f_{max}\int_{-\infty}^{t} s_n(\alpha)d\alpha\right]$

Example 5.1

Display FM and PM waveforms for the square-wave modulating signal shown in Figure 5.2(a). The frequency and phase modulator sensitivities k_f and k_p are 5 Hz/V and $\pi/2$ rad/V, respectively. The carrier frequency f_c is 10 Hz.

Solution

Because $\Delta f_{\max} = 5$ Hz, the instantaneous frequency for the FM signal is obtained from (5.16) as

$$f_i(t) = f_c + \Delta f_{\max} s_n(t) = f_c + k_f s_n(t) = 10 + 5 s_n(t)$$

As the amplitude of $s_n(t)$ changes from 1 to -1 and vice versa, the instantaneous frequency switches between 15 and 5 Hz. The FM signal can be written from (5.18) as

$$x_{FM}(t) = \begin{cases} \cos(30\pi t), & s_n(t) = 1 \\ \cos(10\pi t), & s_n(t) = -1 \end{cases}$$

The PM signal can be expressed from (5.11) as

$$x_{PM}(t) = A_c \cos\left[2\pi f_c t + \Delta\phi_{\max} s_n(t)\right]$$

$$= A_c \cos\left[2\pi f_c t + k_p s_n(t)\right] = A_c \cos\left[2\pi f_c t + \frac{\pi}{2} s_n(t)\right]$$

Therefore,

$$x_{PM}(t) = \begin{cases} A_c \cos(2\pi f_c t + \pi/2) = -A_c \sin(2\pi f_c t), & s_n(t) = 1 \\ A_c \cos(2\pi f_c t - \pi/2) = A_c \sin(2\pi f_c t), & s_n(t) = -1 \end{cases}$$

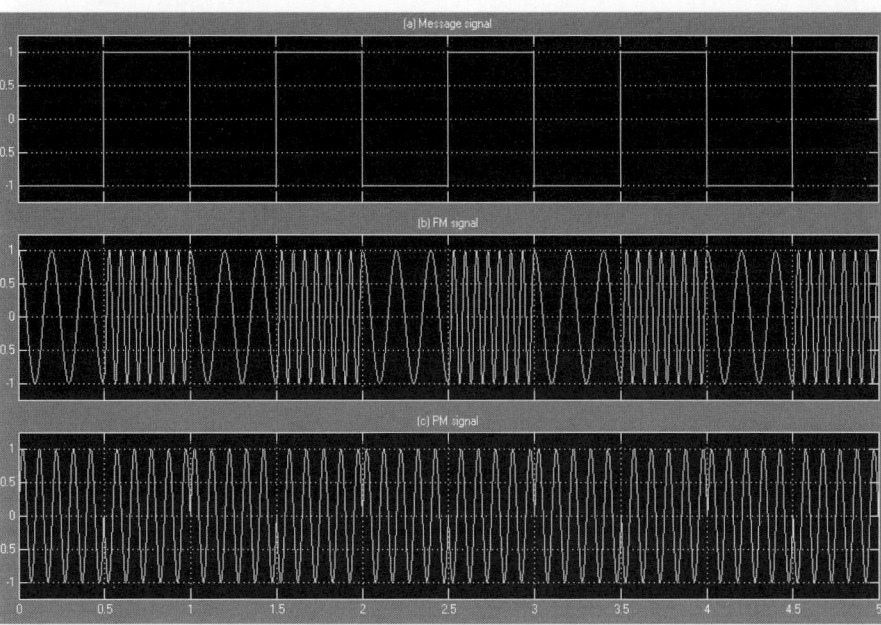

Figure 5.2 FM and PM waveforms for square-wave modulating signal.

Figure 5.2 displays the FM and PM waveforms for the square-wave modulating signal. Note that the PM signal has phase discontinuities of π radians where $s_n(t)$ switches from 1 to -1 and vice versa.

5.1.1 FM and PM Signals with Sinusoidal Modulating Signal

For the sinusoidal modulating waveform

$$s(t) = A_m \cos(2\pi f_m t) \tag{5.20}$$

the normalized signal is given by

$$s_n(t) = \cos(2\pi f_m t) \tag{5.21}$$

FM Signal

The instantaneous frequency for the resulting FM signal is obtained from (5.16) as

$$f_i(t) = f_c + \Delta f_{\max} \cos(2\pi f_m t) \tag{5.22}$$

For the waveform in (5.20), the maximum frequency deviation $\Delta f_{\max}$ is given from (5.15) as

$$\Delta f_{\max} = k_f A_m \tag{5.23}$$

We observe from (5.23) that $\Delta f_{\max}$ is proportional to the peak amplitude of the sinusoidal modulating signal and does not depend on its frequency. The instantaneous phase of the FM waveform is obtained by substituting (5.21) into (5.17) as

$$\phi_i(t) = 2\pi f_c t + 2\pi \Delta f_{\max} \int_{-\infty}^{t} \cos(2\pi f_m t) dt = 2\pi f_c t + \frac{\Delta f_{\max}}{f_m} \sin(2\pi f_m t)$$

$$= 2\pi f_c t + \beta \sin(2\pi f_m t) \tag{5.24}$$

The ratio

$$\beta = \frac{\Delta f_{\max}}{f_m} \tag{5.25}$$

is called the **modulation index** of the FM signal. The resultant FM signal is, therefore, given by substituting (5.24) into (5.3) as

$$x_{FM}(t) = A_c \cos\left[2\pi f_c t + \beta \sin(2\pi f_m t)\right] \tag{5.26}$$

From (5.26), it can be observed that for the sinusoidal modulating waveform, β also represents the maximum value of the phase deviation for the FM signal.

PM Signal

For the modulating signal in (5.20), the maximum phase deviation $\Delta \phi_{\max}$ can be obtained from (5.9) as

$$\Delta \phi_{\max} = k_p A_m \tag{5.27}$$

We observe from (5.27) that $\Delta\phi_{max}$ is proportional to the peak amplitude of the sinusoidal waveform. Substituting (5.27) into (5.10) yields

$$\phi_i(t) = 2\pi f_c t + k_p A_m \cos(2\pi f_m t) \qquad (5.28)$$

The resultant PM signal is, therefore, given from (5.3) as

$$x_{PM}(t) = A_c \cos\left[2\pi f_c t + \underbrace{k_p A_m \cos(2\pi f_m t)}_{\Delta\phi_{max}}\right] \qquad (5.29)$$

The expression for the PM signal in (5.29) is identical to (5.26) except for the substitution of $\Delta\phi_{max}\cos(2\pi f_m t)$ in lieu of $\beta\sin(2\pi f_m t)$. For analysis purposes, we will henceforth use

$$x(t) = A_c \cos\left[2\pi f_c t + \beta\sin(2\pi f_m t)\right] \qquad (5.30)$$

to represent both FM and PM signals resulting from sinusoidal modulation. The results will be applicable for phase modulation with $\beta = \Delta\phi_{max}$ and $\pi/2$ phase offset added to $\sin(2\pi f_m t)$.

Example 5.2

Consider FM and PM signals generated by modulating a 10-Hz carrier by the sinusoidal waveform $\cos(2\pi t)$. Assume that FM and PM modulators have frequency and phase sensitivities k_f and k_p of 5 Hz/V and 2π rad/V, respectively.

a. Write expressions for FM and PM signals. Plot them.
b. Derive expressions for the instantaneous frequency for both FM and PM signals.

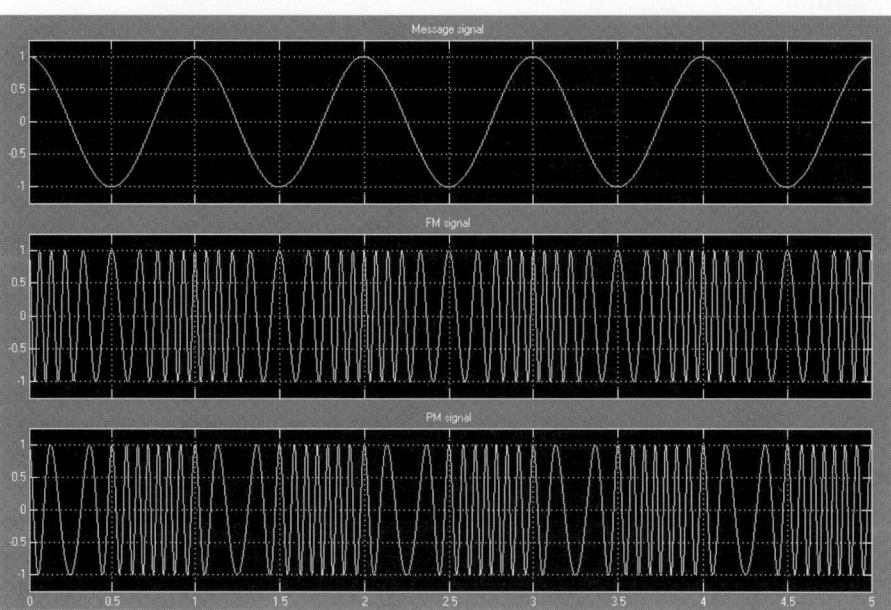

Figure 5.3 FM and PM waveforms with 1-Hz sine wave modulating signal.

Solution

In the present case,

$$\Delta f_{\max} = k_f = 5 \text{ yielding } \beta = 5$$

$$\Delta \phi_{\max} = k_p = 2\pi$$

Substituting into (5.26) and (5.29), we obtain

$$x_{FM}(t) = A_c \cos\left[20\pi t + 5\sin(2\pi t)\right]$$

$$x_{PM}(t) = A_c \cos\left[20\pi t + 2\pi \cos(2\pi t)\right]$$

Figure 5.3 displays FM and PM waveforms.

For the FM signal, the instantaneous frequency is given from (5.22) as

$$f_i(t) = f_c + \Delta f_{\max} \cos(2\pi f_m t) = 10 + 5\cos(2\pi t)$$

The instantaneous frequency varies sinusoidally between upper and lower limits of 15 and 5 Hz, respectively.

For the PM signal, the instantaneous frequency is given from (5.12) as

$$f_i(t) = f_c + \frac{\Delta \phi_{\max}}{2\pi} \dot{s}_n(t) = 10 - 2\pi \sin(2\pi t)$$

The instantaneous frequency of the PM signal varies sinusoidally between upper and lower limits of $10 + 2\pi$ and $10 - 2\pi$ Hz, respectively.

Example 5.3

An angle-modulated signal is described by

$$x(t) = 2\cos\left[2\pi(100 \times 10^6)t + \underbrace{5\sin(10 \times 10^3 \times \pi t)}_{\theta(t)}\right] \tag{5.31}$$

Determine

a. Frequency modulation index β
b. Maximum frequency deviation $\Delta f_{\max}$
c. Maximum phase deviation $\Delta \phi_{\max}$
d. The normalized message signal

Solution

a. Comparing (5.31) with (5.26), it is obvious that the FM modulation index $\beta = 5$.
b. The modulating signal frequency f_m is 5×10^3. Therefore, the frequency deviation $\Delta f_{\max}$ is given by using (5.25) as

$$\Delta f_{\max} = \beta f_m = 5 \times 5 \times 10^3 = 2.5 \times 10^4 \text{ Hz}$$

c. The maximum phase deviation $\Delta \phi_{\max}$ is the maximum value of the excess phase $\theta(t) = 5\sin(10 \times 10^3 \times \pi t)$, which equals 5 radians.

d. Considering the angle-modulated signal (5.31) as a PM signal, the normalized message signal is given by

$$s_n(t) = \sin(10 \times 10^3 \times \pi t)$$

Now let the angle-modulated signal (5.31) be an FM signal. From (5.31) and (5.19), the excess phase is given by

$$\theta(t) = 2\pi\Delta f_{max} \int\limits_{-\infty}^{t} s_n(t) dt = 5\sin(10 \times 10^3 \times \pi t)$$

Taking the derivative of both sides yields

$$2\pi\Delta f_{max} s_n(t) = 50 \times 10^3 \times \pi\cos(10 \times 10^3 \times \pi t)$$

or

$$s_n(t) = \frac{50 \times 10^3 \times \pi}{2.5 \times 10^4 \times 2\pi} \cos(10 \times 10^3 \times \pi t) = \cos(10 \times 10^3 \times \pi t)$$

Therefore, the normalized message signal is $s_n(t) = \cos(10 \times 10^3 \times \pi t)$.

5.1.2 Power in Angle-Modulated Signal

The normalized power content of an angle-modulated signal is obtained by substituting (5.1) into (2.16) as

$$P_x = \lim_{T \to \infty} \frac{A_c^2}{T} \int\limits_{-T/2}^{T/2} \cos^2\left[2\pi f_c t + \theta(t)\right] dt$$

$$= \frac{A_c^2}{2} \lim_{T \to \infty} \frac{1}{T} \int\limits_{-T/2}^{T/2} \left\{1 + \cos\left[4\pi f_c t + 2\theta(t)\right]\right\} dt$$

$$= \frac{A_c^2}{2} \lim_{T \to \infty} \frac{1}{T} \left(\int\limits_{-T/2}^{T/2} dt + \int\limits_{-T/2}^{T/2} \cos\left[4\pi f_c t + 2\theta(t)\right] dt \right) \tag{5.32}$$

The second integral on the right side of (5.32) is negligible due to the fact that $\theta(t)$ varies slowly relative to f_c.

$$P_x = \frac{A_c^2}{2} \tag{5.33}$$

Equation (5.33) states that the average power of an angle-modulated signal is constant independent of the message signal. This is not a surprising result because an angle-modulated signal has constant amplitude.

5.2 SPECTRUM OF ANGLE-MODULATED SIGNALS

The derivation of the spectral characteristics of an angle-modulated signal is usually a complex problem. However, if the modulating signal is a sinusoidal waveform, it is easy to obtain the spectrum of the resultant FM signal. Although we are treating here a very simple message waveform, the results provide significant insight into the spectral properties of angle-modulated signals in general. The FM signal resulting from a sinusoidal modulating signal is given from (5.30) as

$$x_{FM}(t) = A_c \cos[2\pi f_c t + \beta \sin(2\pi f_m t)]$$

This signal can be expressed as

$$x_{FM}(t) = A_c \text{Re}\left\{ e^{j[2\pi f_c t + \beta \sin(2\pi f_m t)]} \right\} = A_c \text{Re}\left\{ e^{j2\pi f_c t} e^{j\beta \sin(2\pi f_m t)} \right\} \tag{5.34}$$

The function $e^{j\beta \sin(2\pi f_m t)}$ is periodic with period $1/f_m$, and therefore it can be expanded in a complex Fourier series:

$$e^{j\beta \sin(2\pi f_m t)} = \sum_{n=-\infty}^{\infty} C_n e^{j2\pi n f_m t} \tag{5.35}$$

where

$$C_n = f_m \int_0^{1/f_m} e^{j\beta \sin(2\pi f_m t)} e^{-j2\pi n f_m t} dt = \frac{1}{2\pi} \int_0^{2\pi} e^{j(\beta \sin z - nz)} dz \tag{5.36}$$

The integral on the right-hand side of (5.36) is the well-known Bessel function of order n and is denoted by $J_n(\beta)$. The integral does not have a closed-form solution, but it is well tabulated. Therefore, we can write the Fourier series expansion for $e^{j\beta \sin 2\pi f_m t}$ as

$$e^{j\beta \sin(2\pi f_m t)} = \sum_{n=-\infty}^{\infty} J_n(\beta) e^{j2\pi n f_m t} \tag{5.37}$$

Substituting (5.37) into (5.34) yields

$$x_{FM}(t) = \text{Re}\left\{ A_c \sum_{n=-\infty}^{\infty} J_n(\beta) e^{jn2\pi f_m t} e^{j2\pi f_c t} \right\}$$

$$= A_c \sum_{n=-\infty}^{\infty} J_n(\beta) \cos[2\pi(f_c + n f_m)t] \tag{5.38}$$

Equation (5.38) shows that the FM signal not only contains the carrier frequency term ($n = 0$) but also components ($n \neq 0$) at multiples of the signal frequency on both sides of the carrier. These components at $f_c \pm n f_m$, $n = 1, 2, \ldots$ are called **sidebands** of the FM signal. The amplitudes of the spectral components in the Fourier expansion (5.38) are given by the Bessel functions, $J_n(\beta)$. Figure 5.4 displays Bessel functions of various orders.

Some interesting properties of the Bessel function are

1. $J_n(\beta) = J_{-n}(\beta), \quad n$ even
    $J_n(\beta) = -J_{-n}(\beta), \quad n$ odd $\tag{5.39}$

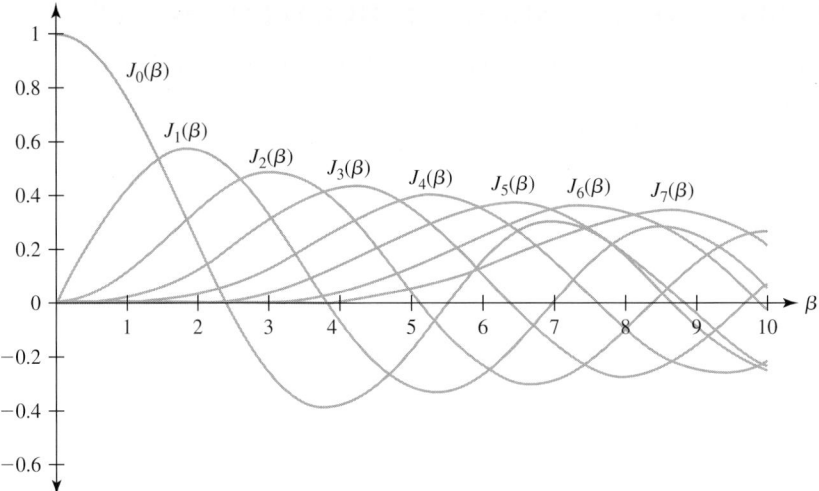

Figure 5.4 Plots of Bessel functions of various orders.

2. $\displaystyle\sum_{n=-\infty}^{\infty} J_n^2(\beta) = 1$ for any value of β $\hspace{3cm}$ (5.40)

We note from Figure 5.4 that, for $\beta = 0$, $J_0(0) = 1$, while all other J_n's are zero. Thus, as expected when there is no modulation, only the carrier, of normalized amplitude unity, is present, while all sidebands have zero amplitude. As β slowly approaches unity, $J_1(\beta)$ acquires a magnitude that is significant in comparison with unity, while all higher-order J_n's are negligible in comparison. Accordingly, for $\beta \ll 1$, the FM signal is composed of the carrier and a single pair of sidebands with frequencies $f_c \pm f_m$. Further, as β continues to increase, $J_2, J_3, \ldots$ begin to acquire significant magnitude, giving rise to sideband pairs at frequencies $f_c \pm 2f_m, f_c \pm 3f_m, \ldots$. Although the modulating signal in (5.30) is a single tone of frequency f_m, the spectrum of FM signal $x_{FM}(t)$ contains an infinite number of sinusoidal components at frequencies $f_c + nf_m$, $n = 0, \pm 1, \pm 2, \ldots$ as displayed in Figure 5.5.

5.2.1 Bandwidth of a Sinusoidally Modulated FM Signal

Because a sinusoidally modulated FM signal contains an infinite number of sinusoidal components separated in frequency by the modulating frequency f_m, the bandwidth of the modulated signal, in a strict sense, is *infinite*. For fixed β and sufficiently large n, the amplitudes of sinusoidal components, $J_n(\beta)$, decrease asymptotically as

$$J_n(\beta) \approx \frac{\beta^n}{2^n n!} \hspace{3cm} (5.41)$$

Because the values of $J_n(\beta)$ become negligible for sufficiently large n, the bandwidth of the angle-modulated signal is determined by the finite number of sidebands in the sum (5.38) that contain *significant* power. The term *significant* implies that no serious distortion of the signal results by neglecting the sidebands outside this bandwidth. Because each term in the sum (5.38) is a sine wave, the power contained in

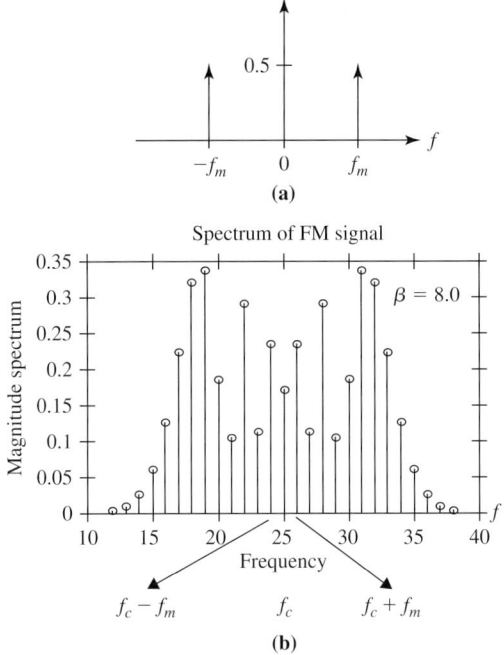

Figure 5.5 Spectra of (a) Sinusoidal modulating signal and (b) FM signal for $f_m = 1$ Hz and $\beta = 8$.

the carrier and M sideband components is given by $\dfrac{A_c^2}{2} \displaystyle\sum_{n=-M}^{M} J_n^2(\beta)$. The **in-band power ratio** $P_{IB}(M)$ is defined as the ratio of the power contained in the carrier and M sideband components to the total power in the modulated signal. It is given by

$$P_{IB}(M) = \frac{\dfrac{A_c^2}{2} \displaystyle\sum_{n=-M}^{M} J_n^2(\beta)}{\dfrac{A_c^2}{2}} = \sum_{n=-M}^{M} J_n^2(\beta)$$

$$= J_0^2(\beta) + 2\sum_{n=1}^{M} J_n^2(\beta) \tag{5.42}$$

The value of M corresponding to $P_{IB}(M) \geq 0.98$ contains at least 98% of the signal power. The **98% power bandwidth** of the FM signal is, therefore, defined as

$$B_T = 2Mf_m \tag{5.43}$$

where M is the number of significant sidebands so that $P_{IB}(M) \geq 0.98$. An estimate of M may be obtained by examining Table 5.2, where $J_n(\beta)$ is tabulated for various values of n and β. In each column of Table 5.2, a line has been drawn after the entries that accounts for at least 98% of the power. We observe that for $\beta \geq 0.5$, the horizontal lines in Table 5.2 occur for values of n equal to the integer part of $\beta + 1$. Thus, for sinusoidal modulation, the 98% power bandwidth of the resultant FM signal includes $M = \beta + 1$ significant sideband components. Substituting into (5.43) yields

$$B_T = 2(\beta + 1)f_m \tag{5.44}$$

Table 5.2 Values of the Bessel Functions $J_n(\beta)$

n	$\beta = 0.1$	$\beta = 0.2$	$\beta = 0.5$	$\beta = 1$	$\beta = 2$	$\beta = 5$	$\beta = 8$	$\beta = 10$	n
0	0.998	0.990	0.938	0.765	0.224	−0.178	0.172	−0.246	0
1	0.050	0.100	0.242	0.440	0.577	−0.328	0.235	0.043	1
2	0.001	0.005	0.031	0.115	0.353	0.047	−0.113	0.255	2
3				0.020	0.129	0.365	−0.291	0.058	3
4				0.002	0.034	0.391	−0.105	−0.220	4
5					0.007	0.261	0.186	−0.234	5
6					0.001	0.131	0.338	−0.014	6
7						0.053	0.321	0.217	7
8						0.018	0.223	0.318	8
9						0.006	0.126	0.292	9
10						0.001	0.061	0.207	10
11							0.026	0.123	11
12							0.010	0.063	12
13							0.003	0.029	13
14							0.001	0.012	14
15								0.004	15
16								0.001	16

For example, consider the case $\beta = 2$. From Table 5.2, $M = 3$. Substituting in (5.42) yields

$$P_{IB}(3) = J_0^2(2) + 2\sum_{n=1}^{3} J_n^2(2) = (0.2239)^2 + 2[(0.5767)^2 + (0.3528)^2 + (0.1289)^2] \approx 0.99$$

Using (5.25), we may write (5.44) in the alternative form

$$B_T = 2(\Delta f_{\max} + f_m) \tag{5.45}$$

That is, the bandwidth of the FM signal is twice the sum of the maximum frequency deviation $\Delta f_{\max}$ and the modulating frequency f_m.

The magnitude spectra for a sinusoidally modulated FM signal are displayed in Figure 5.6(a) for values of $\beta = 0.2$, 1, 5, and 10. The sinusoidal modulating signal has constant frequency f_m in Figure 5.6(a), so the modulation index β is proportional to its amplitude. Figure 5.6(b) displays the FM spectra for $\beta = 5$, 10, 50, and 100 subject to the condition that $\Delta f_{\max}$ is held constant by keeping the amplitude of the sinusoidal modulating signal fixed. Consequently, f_m is decreased to increase β. We observe that as β is increased while keeping $\Delta f_{\max}$ fixed, an increasing number of spectral components crowd into the fixed frequency interval $[-\Delta f_{\max}, \Delta f_{\max}]$ centered at f_c. Further, unlike AM schemes, the amplitude of the spectral component at the carrier frequency is not constant and varies as $J_o(\beta)$. Because the power of an angle-modulated signal is a constant (independent of the modulation index β), the power in the sidebands may appear only at the expense of the power in the carrier.

For PM signals, we can similarly show that the **98% power bandwidth** for a sinusoidal modulating signal is given by

$$B_T = 2(\Delta\phi_{\max} + 1)f_m \tag{5.46}$$

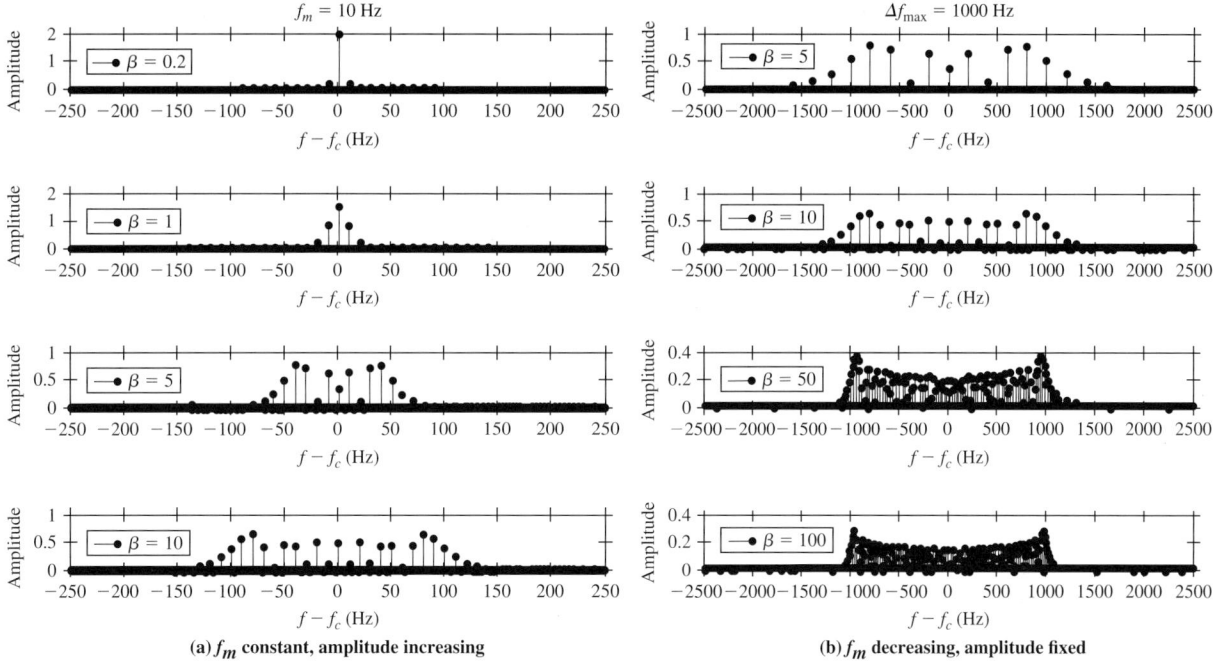

Figure 5.6 Magnitude spectra for FM with sinusoidal modulation for different values of β.

In summary, for a sinusoidal modulating signal, the bandwidth of an angle-modulated signal is given by

$$B_T = \begin{cases} 2(\Delta f_{\max} + f_m), & \text{FM} \\ 2(\Delta\phi_{\max} + 1)f_m, & \text{PM} \end{cases} \tag{5.47}$$

where $\Delta f_{\max}$ and $\Delta\phi_{\max}$ are, respectively, defined by (5.23) and (5.27).

5.2.2 Bandwidth of an FM Signal Modulated by Arbitrary Message Signal

For an arbitrary message signal $s(t)$ having the bandwidth B, it is possible to generalize (5.45) to obtain an approximate expression for the bandwidth of the resultant FM signal. In this context, we define the **deviation ratio**

$$D = \frac{\text{Maximum frequency deviation}}{\text{Bandwidth of the message signal}} = \frac{\Delta f_{\max}}{B} \tag{5.48}$$

where $\Delta f_{\max}$, defined in (5.15), is the peak frequency deviation produced by an arbitrary message signal $s(t)$. The deviation ratio D plays the same role in determining the FM signal bandwidth for an arbitrary modulating signal as the modulation index β plays for the sinusoidal message signal. Substituting D for β and replacing f_m with B in (5.44), we can write

$$B_T = 2(D + 1)B = 2(\Delta f_{\max} + B) \tag{5.49}$$

This rule for the bandwidth of FM signals is called **Carson's rule.** Similarly, the bandwidth of a PM signal is obtained by replacing f_m with B in (5.46) as

$$B_T = 2(\Delta\phi_{\max} + 1)B \tag{5.50}$$

where $\Delta\phi_{max}$, defined in (5.9), is the peak phase deviation produced by an arbitrary message signal $s(t)$. To summarize, the bandwidth of an angle-modulated signal produced by an arbitrary modulating signal of bandwidth B is given by

$$B_T = \begin{cases} 2(\Delta f_{max} + B), & \text{FM} \\ 2(\Delta\phi_{max} + 1)B, & \text{PM} \end{cases} \tag{5.51}$$

where Δf_{max} and $\Delta\phi_{max}$ are, respectively, defined by (5.15) and (5.9).

For **wideband FM (WBFM)** signals characterized by high deviation ratios ($D \gg 1$), the transmission bandwidth from (5.49) can be approximated as

$$B_T = 2(D + 1)B \approx 2DB = 2\Delta f_{max} \tag{5.52}$$

Thus the transmission bandwidth for a WBFM signal equals twice the peak frequency deviation and is independent of the modulating signal bandwidth. This is evident in Figure 5.6(b) for the case $\beta = 100$.

Example 5.4

The FM signal is described by

$$x_{FM}(t) = 100\cos\Big[2\pi(100 \times 10^6)t + \underbrace{5\sin(10^4 \times \pi t) + 3\sin(2 \times 10^4 \times \pi t)}_{\theta(t)}\Big] \tag{5.53}$$

Determine

a. Maximum frequency deviation Δf_{max}
b. Maximum phase deviation $\Delta\phi_{max}$
c. Deviation ratio D
d. Bandwidth of the modulated signal
e. Power of the modulated signal

Solution

a. The instantaneous phase of the FM signal is

$$\phi_i(t) = 2\pi(100 \times 10^6)t + 5\sin(10^4 \times \pi t) + 3\sin(2 \times 10^4 \times \pi t)$$

The instantaneous frequency of the signal is obtained by using (5.4) as

$$f_i(t) = \frac{1}{2\pi}\frac{d\phi_i(t)}{dt} = 100 \times 10^6 + 2.5 \times 10^4\cos(10^4 \times \pi t) + 3 \times 10^4\cos(10^4 \times 2\pi t)\Big] \tag{5.54}$$

The maximum frequency deviation Δf_{max} from the carrier frequency occurs when both cosine terms in (5.54) add in phase.

$$\Delta f_{max} = 5.5 \times 10^4$$

b. The maximum phase deviation $\Delta\phi_{max}$ is the maximum value of the angle

$$\theta(t) = 5\sin(10^4 \times \pi t) + 3\sin(2 \times 10^4 \times \pi t), \text{ which equals 8 radians.}$$

c. The bandwidth of the modulating signal frequency B is 10 kHz. Therefore, the deviation ratio D is obtained from (5.48) as

$$D = \frac{\Delta f_{\max}}{B} = \frac{5.5 \times 10^4}{10^4} = 5.5$$

d. The bandwidth of the modulated signal is given from (5.49) as

$$B_T = 2(D + 1)B = 2(5.5 + 1)10^4 = 130 \text{ kHz}$$

e. The power of the angle-modulated signal is given by using (5.33) as

$$P_x = \frac{A_c^2}{2} = \frac{100^2}{2} = 5 \text{ kW}$$

Example 5.5

Commercial FM radio broadcasting utilizes the frequency band 88 to 108 MHz for the transmission of voice and music signals. The bandwidth of the information signal is set at 15 kHz, and the peak frequency deviation is specified at 75 kHz. Calculate the bandwidth of the FM signal.

Solution

Substituting $B = 15$ kHz, $\Delta f_{\max} = 75$ kHz into (5.48) yields

$$D = 75/15 = 5.$$

The bandwidth of the FM signal using (5.49) is calculated as

$$B_T = 2(\Delta f_{\max} + B) = 2(D + 1)B = 2(5 + 1) \times 15 = 180 \text{ kHz}.$$

The carrier frequencies in the FM-broadcasting scheme are, therefore, separated by 200 kHz. Each station is identified by the center frequency within its channel (e.g., 91.5 MHz, 103.7 MHz). The 20-MHz allocated frequency spectrum can provide radio listeners with their choice of up to 100 different radio stations.

5.3   NARROWBAND FM

By using the trigonometric identity $\cos(u + v) = \cos(u)\cos(v) - \sin(u)\sin(v)$, the single-tone, angle-modulated signal in (5.30) can be expressed as

$$x_{FM}(t) = A_c \cos\left[2\pi f_c t + \beta \sin(2\pi f_m t)\right]$$

$$= A_c \left[\cos(2\pi f_c t)\cos(\beta \sin 2\pi f_m t) - \sin(2\pi f_c t)\sin(\beta \sin 2\pi f_m t)\right] \tag{5.55}$$

For a narrowband FM (NBFM) system, $\beta \ll 1$. In this case, (5.55) can be approximated as follows by using $\cos(u) \approx 1$ and $\sin(u) \approx u$ for $|u| \ll 1$.

$$x_{FM}(t) \approx A_c \left[\cos(2\pi f_c t) - \beta \sin(2\pi f_m t)\sin(2\pi f_c t)\right]$$

$$= A_c \cos(2\pi f_c t) + \frac{A_c \beta}{2}\cos\left[2\pi(f_c + f_m)t\right] - \frac{A_c \beta}{2}\cos\left[2\pi(f_c - f_m)t\right] \tag{5.56}$$

Pioneers in the Field

National Oceanic and
Atmospheric Administration/
Department of Commerce

Edwin Howard Armstrong, inventor of FM radio, was born on December 18, 1890, in New York City. He was interested in radio from an early age and built a makeshift antenna on his family's front lawn to study radio reception. After he finished high school, Armstrong entered Columbia University's school of engineering, where he pursued his wireless studies further. During his third year at Columbia in 1913, Armstrong discovered his first major invention: the regenerative (positive feedback) amplifier, using the triode vacuum tube recently discovered by Lee De Forest. Armstrong's single-circuit design provided such high gain that it became a key component in building the continuous-wave radio transmitters and relatively inexpensive high-sensitivity receivers. Soon after his graduation, Armstrong was sent to Paris to serve in the U.S. Army Signal Corps as a captain during World War I. There, he designed his second major invention, the superheterodyne receiver, while working on a project to improve the army's ability to intercept shortwave enemy communications. He developed the idea to use a tunable oscillator followed by a fixed narrow filter in order to obtain more selective and sensitive radio receivers. The superheterodyne receiver is still part of virtually every tuner in today's radios, TVs, and cellular handsets. In 1920, Westinghouse bought Armstrong's patent for the superheterodyne receiver and started up the nation's first radio station, KDKA, in Pittsburgh.

Armstrong is most well-known for his invention of a wide-deviation FM system, which he developed while trying to solve an AM radio static problem. Armstrong's discovery was at odds with John Renshaw Carson's ("Carson's rule") claim that FM did not offer any particular advantage. While Carson was focused only on narrowband FM, Armstrong was successful in demonstrating significant advantages of wide-deviation FM versus AM radio. In 1940, Armstrong received a permit for the first FM station, which he established in Alpine, New Jersey. RCA fought Armstrong's claim to patent FM radio, while lobbying against the standardization of FM radio by the FCC to protect their existing AM business. In 1946, the FCC's decision to use Armstrong's FM system as the standard for National Television Systems Committee (NTSC) television sound afforded him another opportunity to obtain royalty payments. However, RCA refused to pay royalties and encouraged other TV set makers and broadcasters to follow suit. After years of unsuccessfully battling the giant corporations profiting from his patents, Armstrong committed suicide in 1954. Armstrong's widow continued to fight his legal battles and won millions of dollars in damages over the next several years. By the late 1960s, FM was established as the superior radio system and has since then even been used in cellular and earth-to-space communication.

In 1917, Armstrong became the first recipient of IEEE's Medal of Honor. For his wartime work on radio, the French government gave him the Legion of Honor in 1919. He was awarded the 1941 Franklin Medal and the AIEE's Edison Medal in 1942. Armstrong was inducted into the National Inventors Hall of Fame in 1980 and was commemorated on a U.S. postage stamp in 1983.

The expression (5.56) for an NBFM signal resembles that of a conventional AM signal in (4.26).

$$x_{AM}(t) = A_c\cos(2\pi f_c t) + \frac{A_c m_a}{2}\cos\left[2\pi(f_c + f_m)t\right] + \frac{A_c m_a}{2}\cos\left[2\pi(f_c - f_m)t\right] \quad (4.26)$$

Comparing (5.56) and (4.26), we see that the main difference between the angle-modulated and AM cases is the phase reversal of the lower sideband. The magnitude spectrum of the NBFM signal is shown in Figure 5.7(a). As in the case of the conventional AM signal, the spectrum of the NBFM signal occupies twice the bandwidth of the message signal, that is, $2f_m$.

It is interesting to compare the NBFM and conventional AM signals using the phasor diagrams shown in Figures 5.7(b) and (c). We assume that the coordinate system in both figures rotate counterclockwise at frequency f_c. Referring to Figure 5.7(b), the phasor for the carrier term in (5.56) is, therefore, stationary and oriented in the horizontal direction. The phasor for the sideband $\dfrac{A_c\beta}{2}\cos\left[2\pi(f_c + f_m)t\right]$

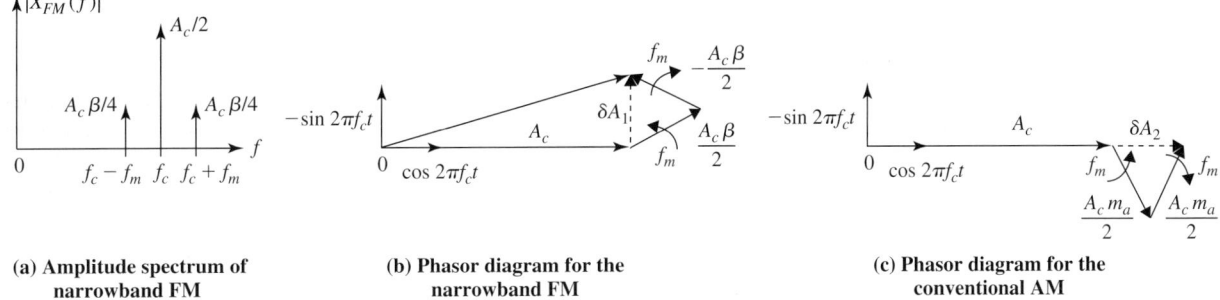

(a) Amplitude spectrum of
narrowband FM

(b) Phasor diagram for the
narrowband FM

(c) Phasor diagram for the
conventional AM

Figure 5.7 Comparison of NBFM and conventional AM.

rotates in a counterclockwise direction at frequency f_m, while the sideband $-\dfrac{A_c\beta}{2}\cos\left[2\pi(f_c - f_m)t\right]$ phasor rotates in a clockwise direction at frequency f_m. The phasor δA_1 is perpendicular to the carrier phasor and has the magnitude $\beta\sin 2\pi f_m t$. Thus the maximum amplitude variation in the narrowband angle-modulated signal is limited to $\beta \ll 1$. Figure 5.7(c) displays the components in (4.24) for a conventional AM signal as phasors. The phasor δA_2 is always parallel to the carrier phasor and has the magnitude $m_a A_c \cos 2\pi f_m t$. Hence, the carrier phasor varies in amplitude between $A_c(1 - m_a)$ and $A_c(1 + m_a)$. Thus, the conventional AM scheme has significantly more amplitude variation than NBFM. The angle-modulation schemes should not exhibit any amplitude variations by design. The small variation in the amplitude of the resultant phasor, shown in Figure 5.7(b), is caused because higher sidebands are neglected in the approximation (5.56).

5.4   DEMODULATION OF ANGLE-MODULATED SIGNALS

An FM demodulator recovers the message signal from the received FM waveform that is generally corrupted by noise. This requires a circuit that produces an output that is linearly proportional to the instantaneous frequency of the input FM signal. FM demodulators can be classified into the following three broad categories based on their principle of operation:

- **Frequency discrimination.** An FM signal is converted into AM signal by a differentiator and then an envelope detector is used to recover the message signal from the converted waveform. This is a noncoherent demodulation method.
- **Phase-shift discrimination.** An FM signal is converted into a PM signal and then a phase detector is used to recover the message signal. In practice, it is implemented using a **quadrature detector.** This is also a noncoherent demodulation method.
- **Phase-locked loop (PLL) detector.** A PLL detector uses a voltage-controlled oscillator (VCO) and feedback to extract the message signal. This is a coherent demodulation scheme and will be discussed in Section 5.6.

In modern FM systems, if a noncoherent FM demodulator is required, then the quadrature detector is used. Examples include low- and medium-quality FM receivers and audio FM demodulators in TV sets. PLL chips are now widely used as FM demodulators for their superior performance and declining costs.

5.4.1   Bandpass Limiter

Although amplitude of an FM carrier is constant, the signal entering the FM discriminator may have amplitude variations due to addition of the channel noise. All FM discriminators are, therefore, preceded by a **BP limiter** to ensure that the discriminator input signal is constant in amplitude. A BP limiter consists of a **hard limiter** followed by a BP filter as shown in Figure 5.8(a). The transfer characteristic of a hard limiter, shown in Figure 5.8(b), is described by

$$x_L[r] = \begin{cases} 1, & r > 0 \\ -1, & r < 0 \end{cases} \tag{5.57}$$

The hard limiter thus clips the input signal and converts it to a square waveform. If input to the hard limiter is an angle-modulated signal

$$r(t) = A(t)\cos\left[2\pi f_c t + \theta(t)\right] = A(t)\cos\phi_i(t) \tag{5.58}$$

the output is given by

$$x_L[\phi_i] = \begin{cases} 1, & \cos\phi_i > 0 \\ -1, & \cos\phi_i < 0 \end{cases} \tag{5.59}$$

$x_L[\phi_i]$ is a periodic square waveform with period 2π. Thus it can be expressed by a Fourier series:

$$x_L[\phi_i] = \frac{4}{\pi}\left[\cos(\phi_i) - \frac{1}{3}\cos(3\phi_i) + \frac{1}{5}\cos(5\phi_i) - \ \dots \right] \tag{5.60}$$

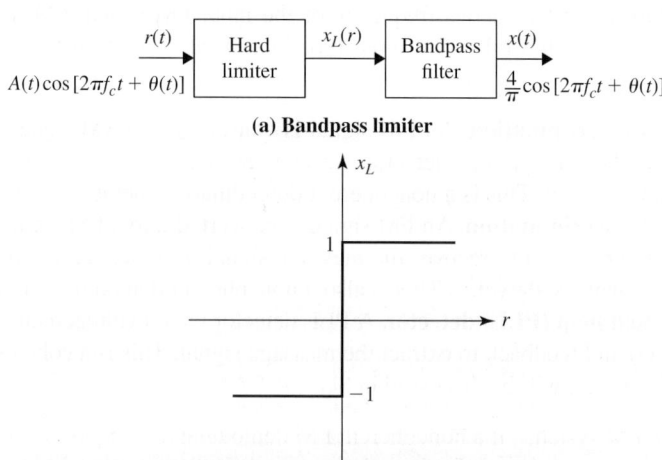

(a) Bandpass limiter

(b) Transfer characteristic of the hard limiter

Figure 5.8 Bandpass limiter.

Note that (5.60) contains only cosine terms because $x_L[\phi_i]$ is an even function of ϕ_i. Substituting $\phi_i(t) = 2\pi f_c t + \theta(t)$, (5.60) can be expressed as

$$x_L[\phi_i] = \frac{4}{\pi}\left\{\cos[2\pi f_c t + \theta(t)] - \frac{1}{3}\cos[6\pi f_c t + 3\theta(t)] + \frac{1}{5}\cos[10\pi f_c t + 5\theta(t)] - \ldots\right\}$$

$$(5.61)$$

Equation (5.61) states that the output of the hard limiter contains not only the original FM signal but also its odd harmonics. The BP filter following the limiter suppresses all harmonics, and its output is the desired angle-modulated signal with constant amplitude

$$x(t) = \frac{4}{\pi}\cos[2\pi f_c t + \theta(t)]$$

$$(5.62)$$

5.4.2 Frequency Discriminator

Recall from Chapter 2 that a differentiator has linear frequency-to-amplitude transfer function

$$H_{diff}(f) = K_{FD}j2\pi f$$

$$(5.63)$$

where K_{FD} is frequency discriminator gain constant, expressed in V/Hz. In the time domain, this corresponds to

$$K_{FD}j2\pi f \xrightarrow{\;\Im^{-1}\;} K_{FD}\frac{d}{dt}$$

$$(5.64)$$

Therefore, if the input FM signal is given by $x_{FM}(t) = A_c\cos[2\pi f_c t + \theta(t)]$, the output of the differentiator circuit is given by

$$v(t) = K_{FD}\frac{dx_{FM}(t)}{dt} = K_{FD}\frac{d\cos[2\pi f_c t + \theta(t)]}{dt}$$

$$= -K_{FD}\left[2\pi f_c + \frac{d\theta(t)}{dt}\right]\sin[2\pi f_c t + \theta(t)]$$

$$(5.65)$$

In practice, $2\pi f_c >> \dfrac{d\theta(t)}{dt}$. Therefore, $2\pi f_c + \dfrac{d\theta(t)}{dt}$ is always positive. Hence, the output of the envelope detector is given by

$$y(t) = K_{FD}\left[2\pi f_c + \frac{d\theta(t)}{dt}\right]$$

$$(5.66)$$

From Table 5.1, the excess phase $\theta(t) = 2\pi\Delta f_{max}\displaystyle\int_{-\infty}^{t} s_n(t)dt$ is for an FM signal. Substituting into (5.66) yields

$$y(t) = K_{FD}2\pi[f_c + \Delta f_{max}s_n(t)]$$

$$(5.67)$$

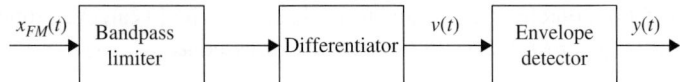

Figure 5.9 Frequency discriminator.

The DC term $K_{FD}2\pi f_c$ in (5.67) is blocked by the AC-coupled circuitry. Combining (5.66) and (5.67), the discriminator output can be expressed as

$$y_D(t) = K_{FD}\frac{d\theta(t)}{dt} = K_{FD}2\pi\Delta f_{\max}s_n(t) \qquad (5.68)$$

We observe from (5.68) that the discriminator output is proportional to the message signal $s_n(t)$. Figure 5.9 illustrates the frequency discriminator with a differentiator.

The discriminator in Figure 5.9 can also be used to demodulate PM signals. Because the excess phase $\theta(t)$ is proportional to $s_n(t)$ for a PM signal, $y_D(t)$ given by (5.68) is proportional to $\dot{s}_n(t)$. The message signal can therefore be recovered by integrating the frequency discriminator output. Thus, a PM demodulator can be realized as a frequency discriminator followed by an integrator. The PM demodulator output can now be written as

$$y_D(t) = K_{PD}\theta(t) = K_{PD}\Delta\phi_{\max}s_n(t) \qquad (5.69)$$

where K_{PD} is PM demodulator gain constant, expressed in V/radian.

Experiment 5.1 *Simulink Model of an FM System with Frequency Discriminator*

In this experiment, we use the Simulink to model FM modulator and demodulator. The parameters of simulation including carrier and message signal frequencies, FM modulator sensitivity, and LP filter are set up by a companion MATLAB m-file. The carrier frequency is 25 Hz and the message signal is 1-Hz sine wave. The FM modulator sensitivity k_f is set at 10 Hz/volt. The Simulink model is illustrated in Figure 5.10. We use the Simulink model for the FM modulator

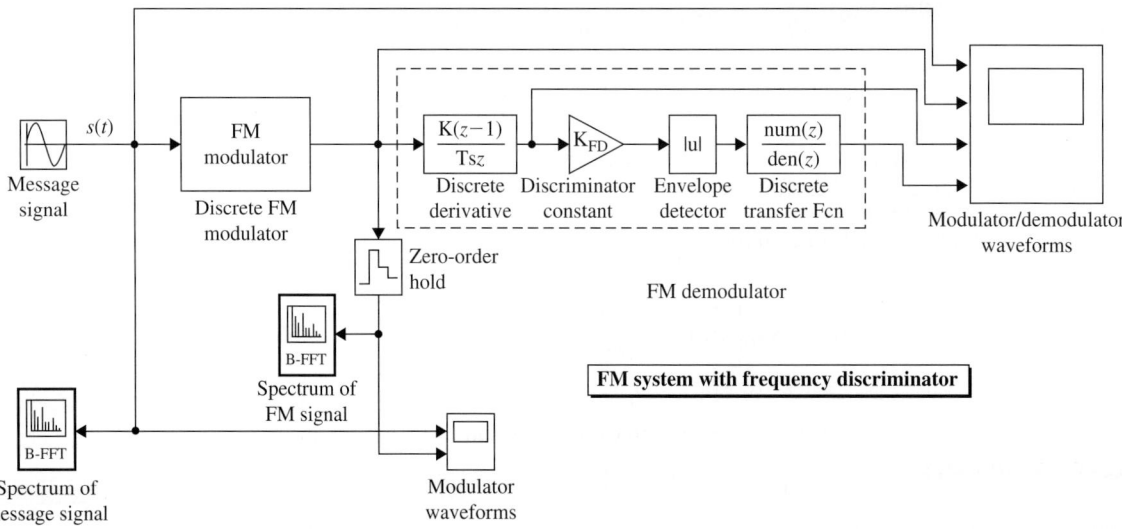

Figure 5.10 Simulink model of FM system.

Figure 5.11 Modulator/demodulator waveforms.

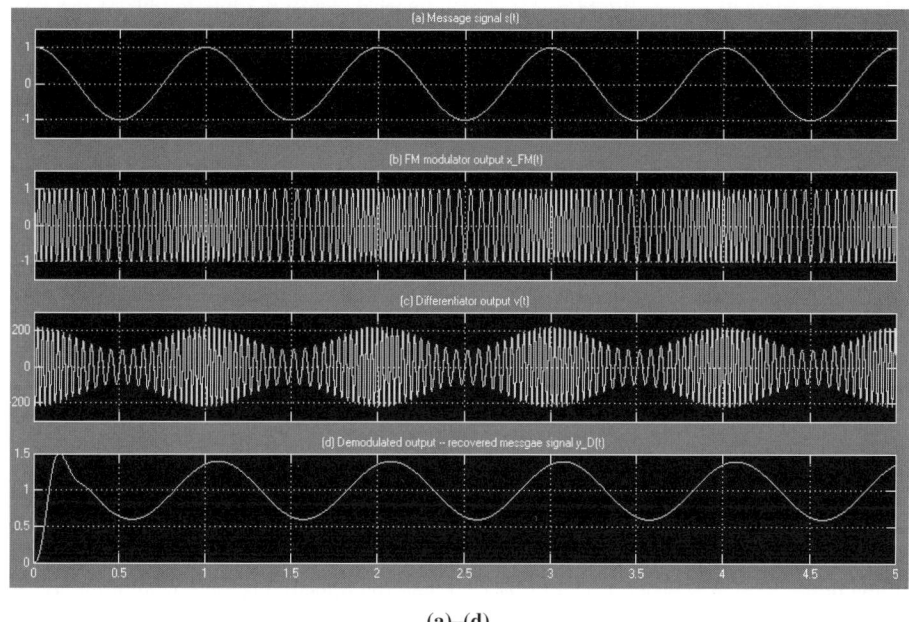

(a)–(d)

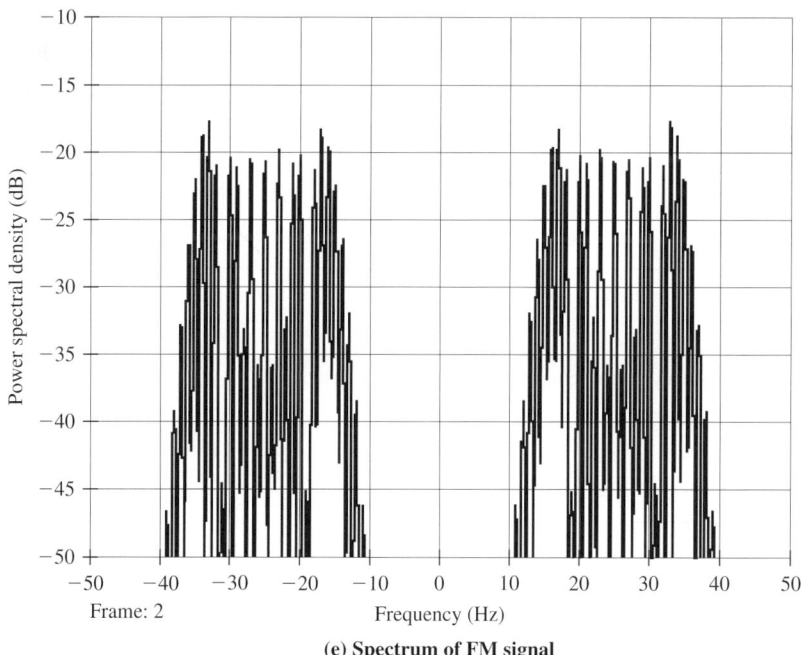

(e) Spectrum of FM signal

developed in Section 3.2.1 here. The FM demodulator model utilizes the frequency discriminator defined in (5.63). The output of the differentiator is shown in Figure 5.11(c). Note that its envelope displays the message signal that is embedded in the instantaneous frequency of the FM signal. The envelope detection circuitry following the discriminator recovers the message signal as illustrated in Figure 5.11(d). The spectrum of the FM signal is displayed in Figure 5.11(e).

In practice, the differentiator in (5.63) is approximated by a **slope detector** that has a linear frequency-to-amplitude transfer characteristic over the bandwidth of the FM signal. The frequency response function of a slope detector can be expressed as

$$|H_{\text{slope\_det}}(f)| = \begin{cases} 2\pi K_{FD}\left|f - \left(f_c - \dfrac{B_T}{2}\right)\right|, & f_c - \dfrac{B_T}{2} \leq f \leq f_c + \dfrac{B_T}{2} \\[3mm] 2\pi K_{FD}\left|f + \left(f_c - \dfrac{B_T}{2}\right)\right|, & -f_c - \dfrac{B_T}{2} \leq f \leq -f_c + \dfrac{B_T}{2} \\[3mm] 0, & \text{otherwise} \end{cases} \tag{5.70}$$

where B_T is Carson's bandwidth. The magnitude response in (5.70) is displayed in Figure 5.12.

The slope detector can be realized using a tuned circuit as shown in Figure 5.13(a). The magnitude of the frequency response function is linear over the narrow band shown in Figure 5.13(b).

To solve this problem, a **balanced slope detector** is used with two tuned circuits as shown in Figure 5.14(a). The upper and lower tuned circuits are tuned to frequencies f_1 and f_2, respectively, that are above and below the carrier frequency f_c. Figure 5.14(b) displays the magnitude responses of these two tuned circuits. The FM-AM transfer characteristic of the upper branch is proportional to $|H_1(f)|$, and the transfer characteristic of the lower branch is proportional to $|H_2(f)|$. The overall FM-AM transfer characteristic $H(f)$ of the balanced slope detector is thus proportional to $|H_1(f)| - |H_2(f)|$. It is linear over a wider frequency range than would be possible with a single tuned circuit. Further, the DC terms from both branches cancel each other to make $H(f_c) = 0$. The linearity of the useful portion of the overall S-shaped FM-AM transfer characteristic is determined by the separation

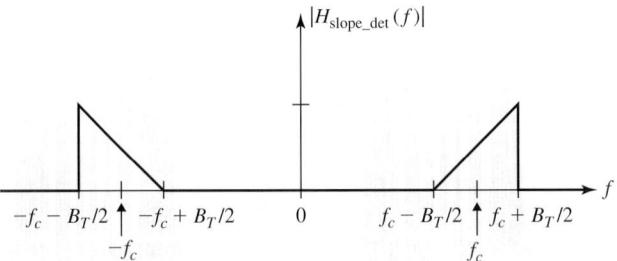

Figure 5.12 Frequency response characteristic of a slope detector.

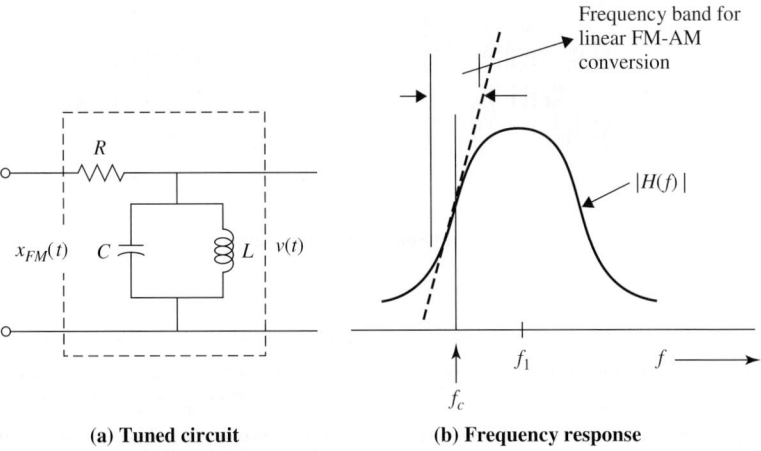

(a) **Tuned circuit**   (b) **Frequency response**

Figure 5.13 Implementation of a slope detector using a tuned circuit.

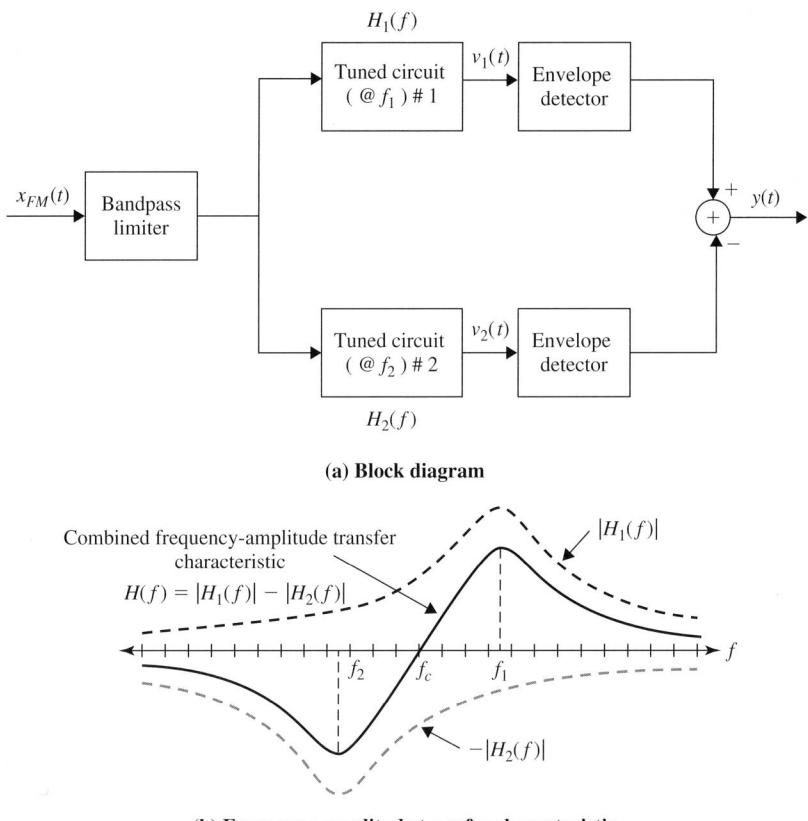

(a) Block diagram

(b) Frequency-amplitude transfer characteristic

Figure 5.14 Frequency discriminator: balanced slope detector.

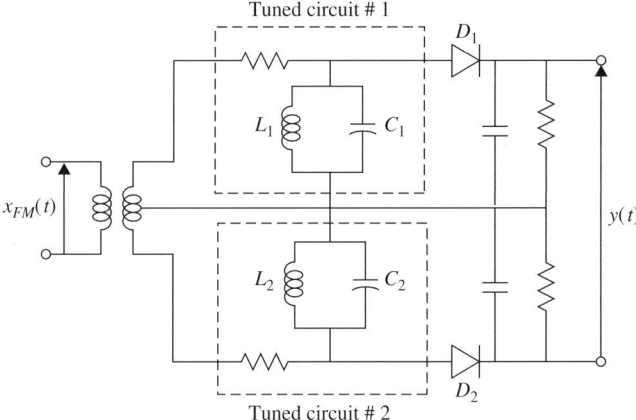

Figure 5.15 Implementation of a balanced slope detector.

of the resonant frequencies f_1 and f_2. For the best performance, the resonant frequency f_1 is chosen approximately $3 \times \Delta f_{max}$ above the carrier frequency f_c. Similarly, the second resonant frequency f_2 is chosen approximately $3 \times \Delta f_{max}$ below the carrier frequency f_c.

Figure 5.15 shows the realization of a balanced slope detector where a center-tapped transformer feeds the two tuned circuits 180° out of phase. If the frequency of the input signal is in the vicinity of f_1, it will produce maximum output across diode D_1, and negligible output across D_2. When the frequency of the input signal is in the vicinity of

f_2, it will produce negligible output across diode D_1, and maximum output across D_2. When the frequency of the input signal is f_c, the output voltages for both diodes would be equal, and hence, the net output will be zero. Thus the output $y(t)$ will increase as the frequency of the input signal increases from f_c to f_1, and it becomes more negative as the frequency of the input signal decreases from f_c to f_2.

Experiment 5.2   *FM Demodulation with Balanced Slope Detector*

In this experiment, we use a balanced slope detector to perform FM-AM conversion. The Simulink models of the system and the slope detector are illustrated in Figure 5.16(a) and (b), respectively. The parameters of simulation including carrier and message signal frequencies, FM modulator sensitivity, and characteristics of two tuned filters are set up by a companion MATLAB m-file. The carrier frequency is chosen as 101 MHz and the message signal is 1-Hz sine wave. The FM modulator sensitivity k_f is set at 5 Hz/volt. The resonant frequencies f_1 and f_2 of the upper and lower tuned circuit are selected as 115 and 85 MHz, respectively. The transfer characteristic of the balanced slope detector is shown in Figure 5.16(c). The FM modulator and

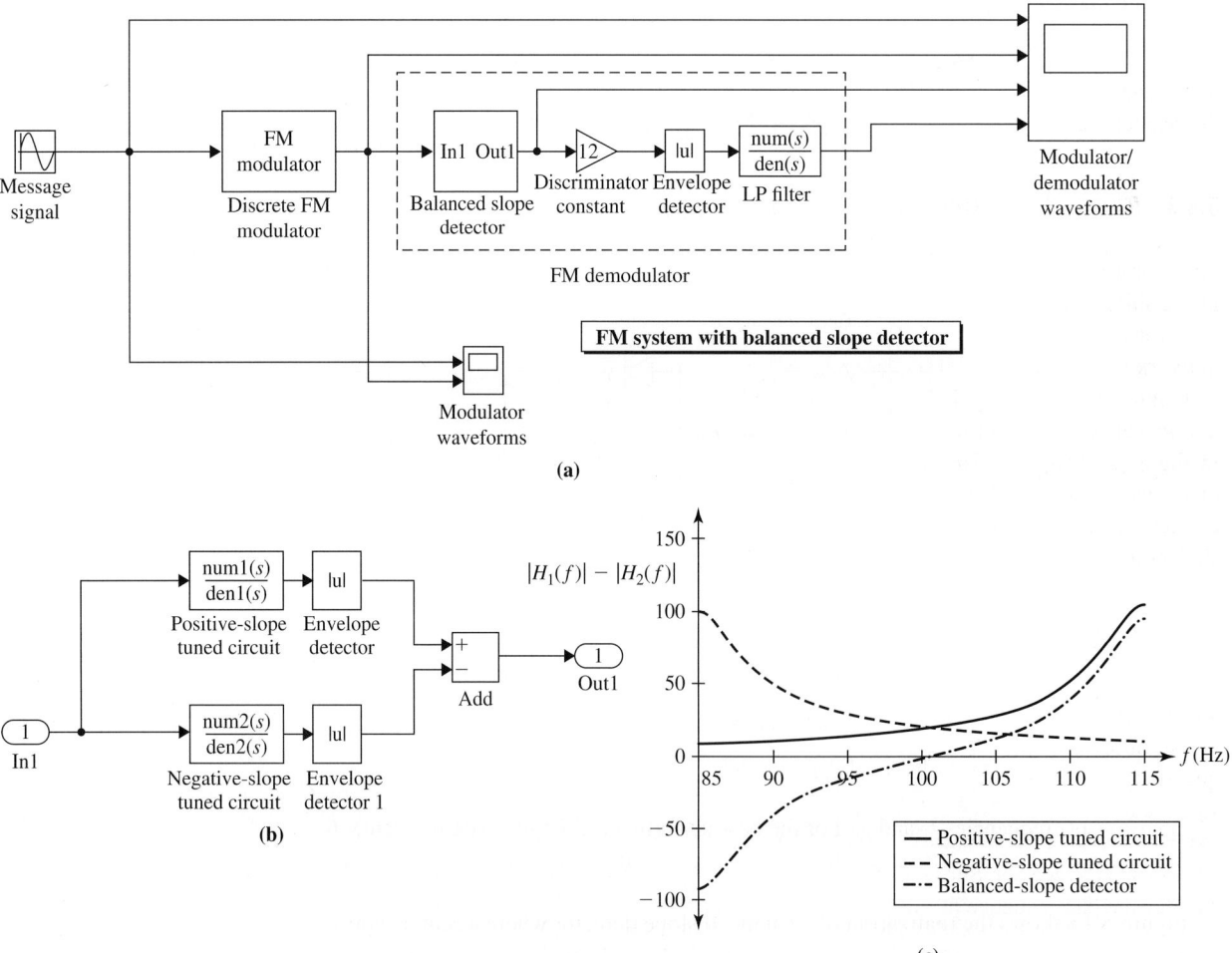

Figure 5.16 Simulink model of an FM system with balanced-slope detector.

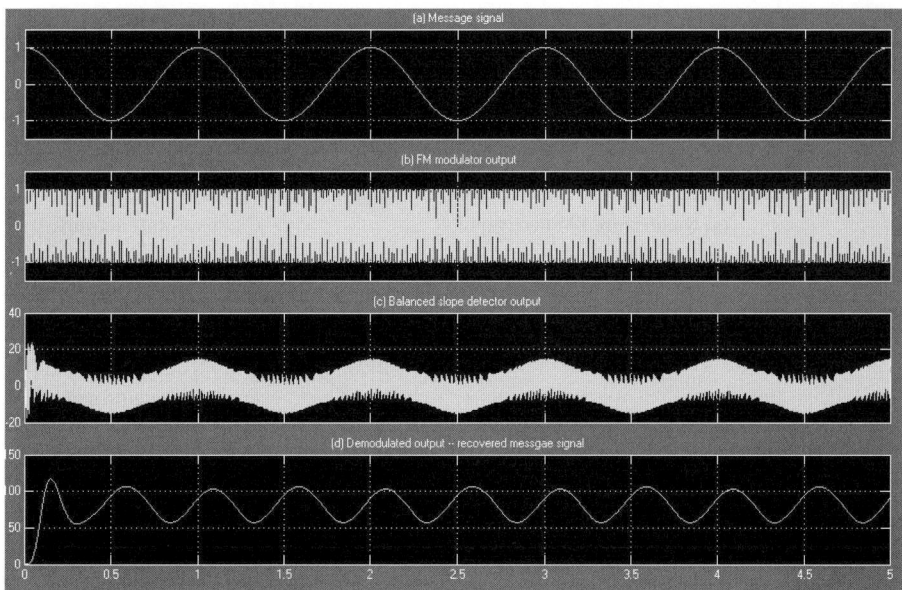

Figure 5.17　FM modulator/demodulator waveforms.

demodulator waveforms are illustrated in Figure 5.17. Note that there is no apparent distortion in the demodulated signal.

5.4.3　Phase-shift Discriminator: Quadrature Detector

A quadrature detector converts instantaneous frequency deviation in an FM signal to phase shift and then detects the change of phase. The block diagram of a quadrature FM detector is displayed in Figure 5.18(a). The FM carrier is passed through a phase-shift network that preserves the FM while introducing a phase shift that is proportional to the instantaneous frequency deviation of the FM signal. The phase-shift network consists of a large capacitor (C_s) in series with a parallel tuned circuit (R_p, L_p, and C_p) as illustrated in Figure 5.18(b). The large capacitor provides a 90° phase shift, and the tuned circuit provides an additional phase shift that is linearly proportional to the instantaneous frequency deviation (from f_c) of the FM signal. The transfer characteristic of the phase-shift network is described by

$$\Delta\psi = -\frac{\pi}{2} + K_1\big[f_i(t) - f_c\big] \tag{5.71}$$

where K_1 denotes the slope of the phase-shift circuit about f_c.

We observe from (5.71) that the phase shift produced by the circuit at the carrier frequency f_c equals $-90\,^\circ$. Figure 5.19 displays the phase response of a phase-shift circuit suitable for use in an FM radio receiver. Note that the phase shift is linearly proportional to the instantaneous frequency deviation in the vicinity of the IF frequency $f_{IF} = 10.7$ MHz used in such a receiver. Substituting (5.16) into (5.71), we can write the following expression for the phase change produced by the phase-shift network:

$$\Delta\psi = -\frac{\pi}{2} + K_1\Delta f_{\max}s_n(t) \tag{5.72}$$

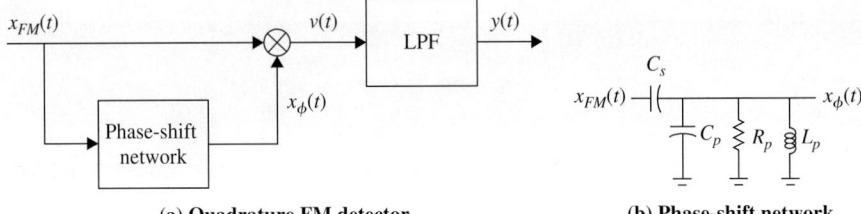

(a) Quadrature FM detector   **(b) Phase-shift network**

Figure 5.18 FM demodulator: quadrature detector.

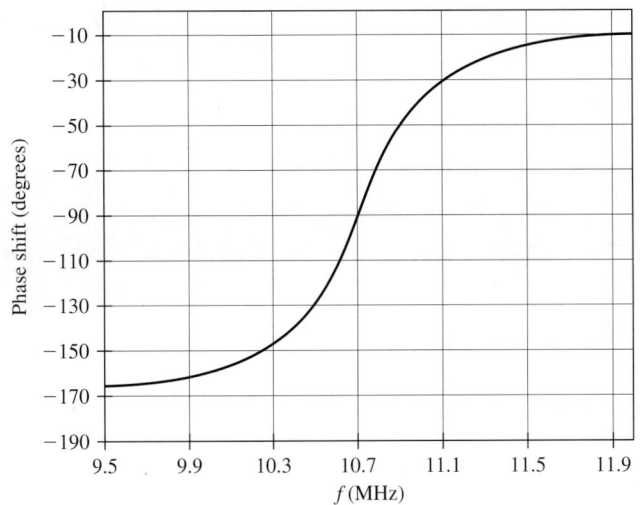

Figure 5.19 Phase response of a typical phase-shift circuit used in FM radio.

Therefore, the output of the phase-shift network to an input

$$x_{FM}(t) = A_c\cos\left[2\pi f_c t + 2\pi\Delta f_{max}\int_{-\infty}^{t} s_n(\alpha)d\alpha\right] \tag{5.18}$$

is given by

$$x_\phi(t) = K_2 A_c\cos\left[2\pi f_c t + 2\pi\Delta f_{max}\int_{-\infty}^{t} s_n(\alpha)d\alpha + K_1\Delta f_{max}s_n(t) - \frac{\pi}{2}\right] \tag{5.73}$$

where K_2 is a phase-shift network constant. Note that $x_{FM}(t)$ carries only FM while $x_\phi(t)$ carries both FM and PM.

We use the cascade of a mixer and LP filter as the phase detector. Its output is given by

$$v(t) = K_m x_{FM}(t)x_\phi(t)$$

$$= K_m K_2 A_c^2\cos\left[2\pi f_c t + 2\pi\Delta f_{max}\int_{-\infty}^{t} s_n(\alpha)d\alpha\right]\cos\left[2\pi f_c t + 2\pi\Delta f_{max}\int_{-\infty}^{t} s_n(\alpha)d\alpha + K_1\Delta f_{max}s_n(t) - \frac{\pi}{2}\right]$$

$$= K_m K_2 A_c^2\cos\left[2\pi f_c t + 2\pi\Delta f_{max}\int_{-\infty}^{t} s_n(\alpha)d\alpha\right]\sin\left[2\pi f_c t + 2\pi\Delta f_{max}\int_{-\infty}^{t} s_n(\alpha)d\alpha + K_1\Delta f_{max}s_n(t)\right]$$

$$= \frac{K_m K_2 A_c^2}{2} \left\{ \sin\left[K_1 \Delta f_{\max} s_n(t)\right] + \text{double frequency term} \right\} \tag{5.74}$$

where K_m is the mixer gain constant. The LP filter suppresses the double-frequency term, yielding

$$y(t) = \frac{K_m K_2 A_c^2}{2} \sin\left[K_1 \Delta f_{\max} s_n(t)\right] \tag{5.75}$$

Assuming K_1 to be sufficiently small, the output becomes

$$y(t) \approx \frac{K_m K_2 A_c^2}{2} K_1 \Delta f_{\max} s_n(t) \tag{5.76}$$

Thus the quadrature detector recovers the original message signal.

5.5 PHASE-LOCKED LOOP

Phase-locked loop (PLL) is one of the most versatile circuit blocks used in both communication and instrumentation systems. PLLs are widely used in cell phones, televisions, radios, pagers, computers, and storage devices. An incomplete list of specific tasks performed by PLLs includes clock generation, frequency synthesis, carrier recovery, clock recovery, and frequency and phase demodulation.

Basically, a PLL is a negative feedback control system in which an oscillator-generated signal is phase and frequency locked to the input reference signal. It is possible to have a phase offset between input reference and oscillator output, but when locked, the frequencies must exactly track. Thus, under the **phase-locked condition,** a PLL satisfies the following properties:

$$\omega_{out} = \omega_{in} \tag{5.77}$$

and

$$\theta_{out}(t) = \theta_{in}(t) + \text{constant} \tag{5.78}$$

where

ω_{in} = Frequency of the input reference signal (rad/s)
ω_{out} = Frequency of the oscillator output (rad/s)
θ_{in} = Excess phase of the input reference signal
θ_{out} = Excess phase of the oscillator output

The block diagram of a PLL is shown in Figure 5.20. It consists of three components:

- **Phase detector (PD).** Produces an error signal proportional to the difference between the phase of the input reference signal and the phase of a locally generated VCO signal.

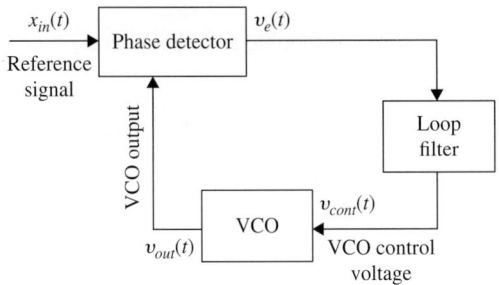

Figure 5.20 Phase-locked loop components.

- **Loop filter.** Filters the error signal to produce the control signal that forms the VCO input.
- **Voltage-controlled oscillator (VCO).** Produces an output signal whose frequency is proportional to the control signal applied to it.

The operation of the PLL is as follows: The phase detector compares the phase of the input reference signal $x_{in}(t)$ against the phase of the VCO output $v_{out}(t)$ and produces an error signal $v_e(t)$. This error signal is then filtered in order to remove noise and other unwanted frequency components. The frequency of the VCO is varied according to the value of the control voltage $v_{cont}(t)$ until the phase lock is achieved. Once the PLL has acquired the lock, the VCO will track the input reference signal frequency over some range, provided that the input frequency changes slowly. The PLL output can be taken from either $v_{cont}(t)$, the filtered (baseband) VCO control voltage, or the output of the VCO, depending on the application. The baseband output tracks the phase variation at the input. The VCO output can be used as a local oscillator waveform or to generate a clock signal for a digital system.

There are many types of PLLs, depending on the implementation technologies for loop components as shown in Table 5.3.

Only the APLL is discussed in this section.

5.5.1 Analog Phase-Locked Loop

The phase detector in an APLL consists of an analog mixer followed by an LP filter to remove the double-frequency terms. Figure 5.21(a) illustrates the block diagram of an APLL. Let the PLL input reference signal be given by

$$x_{in}(t) = A\sin\left[\omega_c t + \theta_{in}(t)\right] \qquad (5.79)$$

Table 5.3 Classification of PLL Types

PLL Type	Phase Detector	Loop Filter	Controlled Oscillator
Analog PLL (APLL)	Analog mixer	RC passive or active	Voltage
Digital PLL (DPLL)	Digital detector	RC passive or active	Voltage
All digital PLL (ADPLL)	Digital detector	Digital filter	Digitally controlled

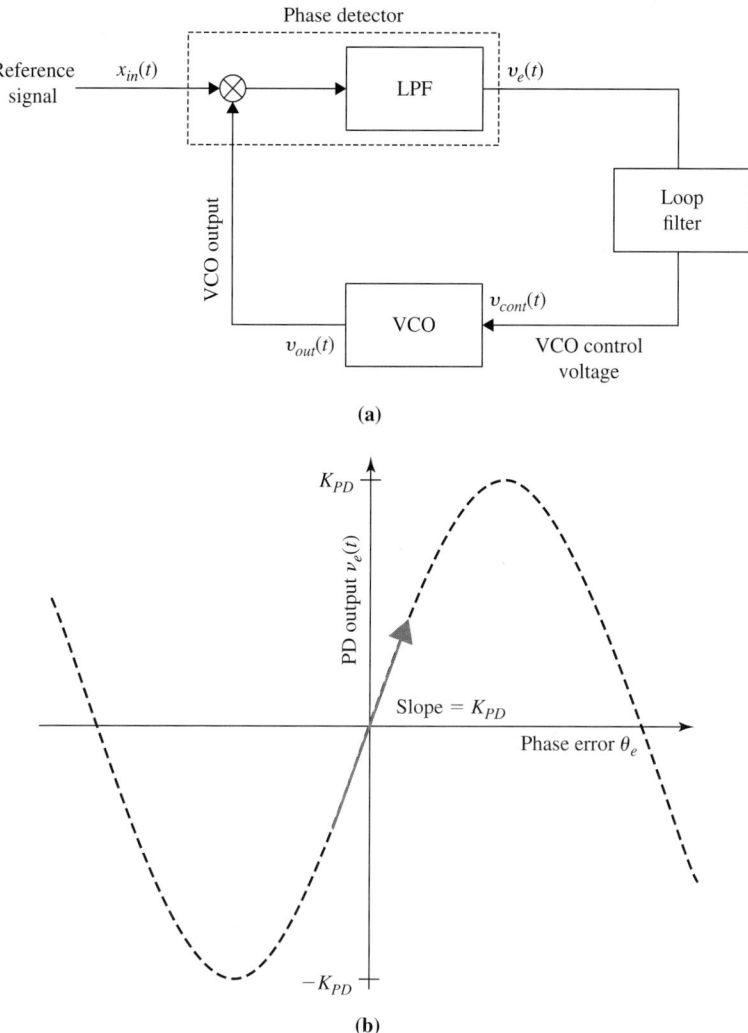

Figure 5.21 (a) Analog phase-locked loop; (b) mixer-low-pass filter (LPF) phase detector characteristic.

The VCO output in the locked state can be expressed as

$$v_{out}(t) = B\cos\left[\omega_c t + \theta_{out}(t)\right] \tag{5.80}$$

The analog mixer in the PD multiplies the input reference signal $x_{in}(t)$ by the VCO output $v_{out}(t)$, producing both the difference- and sum-frequency terms. The LP filter eliminates the sum-frequency component yielding

$$v_e(t) = \frac{1}{2}ABK_m\sin\left[\theta_{in}(t) - \theta_{out}(t)\right] \tag{5.81}$$

where K_m is mixer constant. We observe that the PD output in (5.81) is periodic and a nonlinear function of the difference between the input and VCO excess phases $\theta_e = \theta_{in} - \theta_{out}$. Figure 5.21(b) displays the PD output as a function of the phase error θ_e.

It is convenient to express the PD output as

$$v_e(t) = K_{PD}\sin\left[\theta_e(t)\right]$$

(5.82)

where

$$K_{PD} \triangleq \left.\frac{dv_e}{d\theta_e}\right|_{\theta_e=0} = \left.\frac{1}{2}ABK_m\cos(\theta_e)\right|_{\theta_e=0} = \frac{1}{2}ABK_m$$

(5.83)

is referred to as the **PD gain constant.** It represents slope of the PD transfer characteristic at $\theta_e = 0$ as illustrated in Figure 5.21(b). The units of K_{PD} are in volts/radian. We observe from (5.79) and (5.80) that under phase-lock condition, a $90°$ built-in phase offset exists between the input reference and VCO output, that is, they lock in **quadrature.** In other words, if the phase difference is $90°$, the phase error is considered to be zero.

VCO

The VCO oscillates at an instantaneous frequency that is linearly proportional to the control voltage $v_{cont}(t)$. That is,

$$\omega_{out}(t) = \omega_o + K_{VCO}v_{cont}(t)$$

(5.84)

where ω_o is a **free-running frequency** when the control voltage $v_{cont}(t)$ is zero. K_{VCO} is the VCO gain constant in radians/sec-volt. Substituting (5.84) into (5.5) yields the instantaneous phase of the VCO output

$$\phi_{out}(t) = \omega_o t + K_{VCO}\int_{-\infty}^{t} v_{cont}(\alpha)d\alpha$$

(5.85)

The excess phase of the VCO output is given by the second term in (5.85) as

$$\theta_{out}(t) = K_{VCO}\int_{-\infty}^{t} v_{cont}(\alpha)d\alpha$$

(5.86)

It is obvious from (5.84) that to obtain an arbitrary output frequency (within the VCO tuning range), a finite v_{cont} is required. Suppose an output frequency ω_1 is needed. From Figure 5.22(a), we see that a control voltage v_1 will be necessary to produce this output frequency.

$$v_1 = \frac{\omega_1 - \omega_o}{K_{VCO}}$$

(5.87)

The phase detector can produce v_1 only by maintaining a phase error or offset θ_1 at its input as displayed in Figure 5.22(b).

$$\theta_1 = \frac{v_1}{K_{PD}} = \frac{\omega_1 - \omega_o}{K_{PD}K_{VCO}}$$

(5.88)

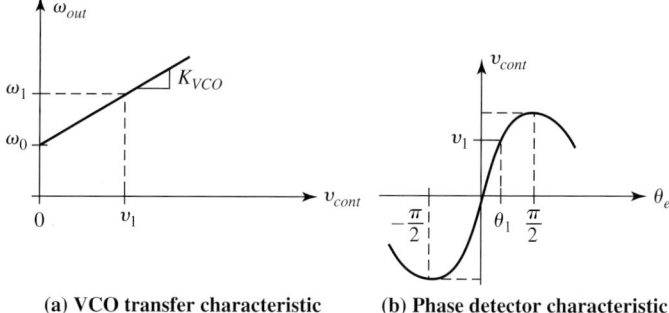

(a) VCO transfer characteristic   **(b) Phase detector characteristic**

Figure 5.22 VCO and phase detector transfer characteristics.

In order to minimize the required phase offset, the PLL loop gain, $K_{PD}K_{VCO}$, should be maximized.

Loop Filter

The primary function of the loop filter is to determine loop dynamics, that is, how does the loop respond to various internal and external disturbances, such as changes in the input signal frequency or phase, additive and VCO phase noise, and so on. Some important considerations in the selection of loop filter include the range over which the loop can achieve lock as well as how fast the loop achieves lock and the output noise variance. Depending on the application, this may require the use of one of the filter types displayed in Figure 5.23.

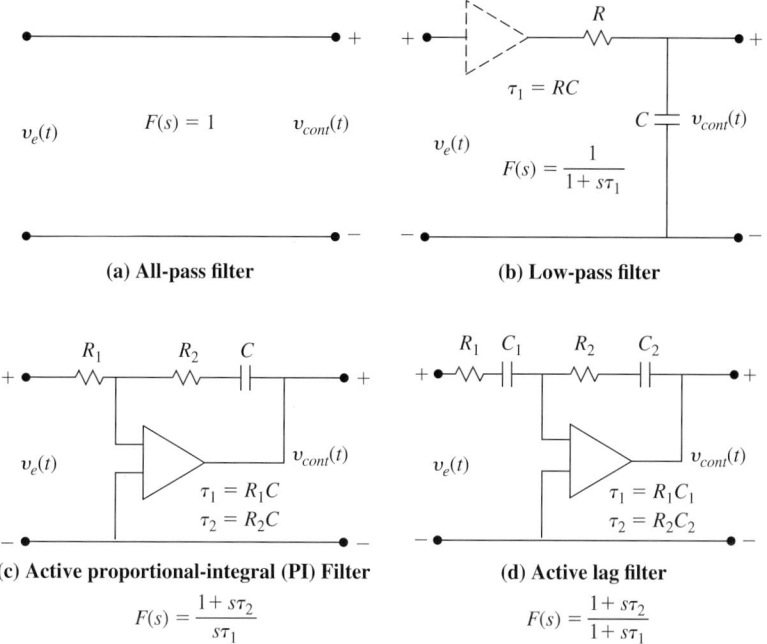

(a) All-pass filter

$$F(s) = 1$$

(b) Low-pass filter

$$\tau_1 = RC$$

$$F(s) = \frac{1}{1 + s\tau_1}$$

(c) Active proportional-integral (PI) Filter

$$\tau_1 = R_1C$$
$$\tau_2 = R_2C$$

$$F(s) = \frac{1 + s\tau_2}{s\tau_1}$$

(d) Active lag filter

$$\tau_1 = R_1C_1$$
$$\tau_2 = R_2C_2$$

$$F(s) = \frac{1 + s\tau_2}{1 + s\tau_1}$$

Figure 5.23 Loop filters.

5.5.2 APLL Linear Model

When the phase error θ_e is small, $\sin\theta_e \approx \theta_e$, the phase-detector output is obtained from (5.82) as

$$v_e(t) \approx K_{PD}\theta_e(t) \tag{5.89}$$

Equation (5.89) represents the linearized model of the phase detector. We can use (5.89) to obtain a linearized model of the PLL as illustrated in Figure 5.24(a) where excess phases of the reference input and the VCO output are used instead of the signals themselves. Now we can analyze the PLL using linear system techniques. If we take Laplace transform of all signals and systems in Figure 5.24(a), we obtain the equivalent *s*-domain model for the PLL, which is displayed in Figure 5.24(b).

From the Figure 5.24(b), the open-loop transfer function of the PLL is obtained as

$$G(s) = \frac{K_{PD}F(s)K_{VCO}}{s} = \frac{KF(s)}{s} \tag{5.90}$$

where

$$K = K_{VCO}K_{PD} \tag{5.91}$$

is called the **loop gain** of the PLL and has the dimension of (1/sec). The loop gain K is a critical PLL design parameter, and it may be necessary in many cases to insert an actual

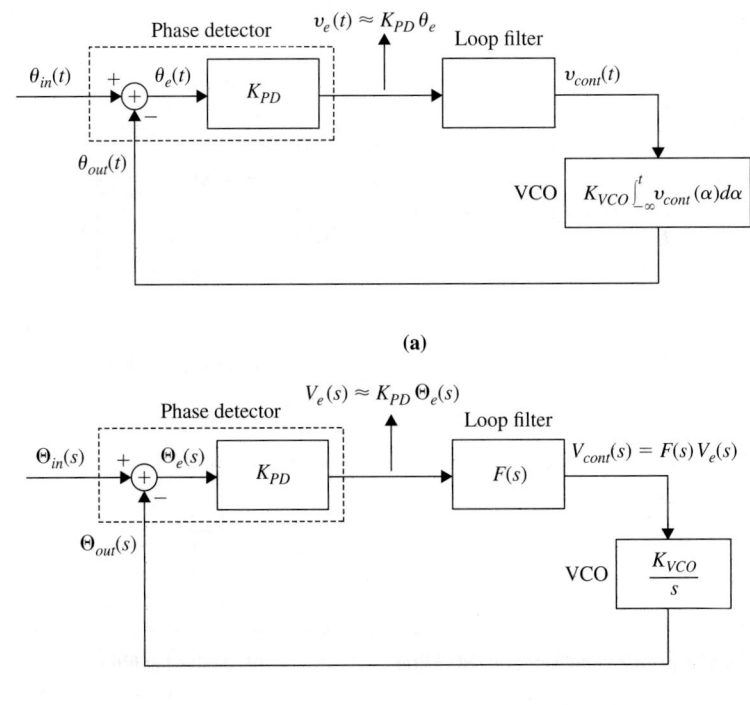

(a)

(b)

Figure 5.24 Linearized model of APLL: (a) time-domain; (b) *s*-domain.

gain block in the loop to implement it. The closed-loop transfer function of the PLL can now be written using (5.90) as

$$H(s) = \frac{\Theta_{out}(s)}{\Theta_{in}(s)} = \frac{G(s)}{1 + G(s)} = \frac{KF(s)}{s + KF(s)} \qquad (5.92)$$

A loop filter with m poles produces a PLL with closed-loop transfer function having $m + 1$ poles. Such a PLL is called $(\boldsymbol{m + 1})$-**order** PLL. Another important function characterizing the performance of a PLL is the **phase error transfer function** relating the phase error to the input phase. It is given by

$$H_e(s) = \frac{\Theta_e(s)}{\Theta_{in}(s)} = \frac{\Theta_{in}(s) - \Theta_{out}(s)}{\Theta_{in}(s)} = 1 - H(s) \qquad (5.93)$$

Substituting (5.92) into (5.93), the phase error function can be expressed as

$$H_e(s) = \frac{s}{s + KF(s)} \qquad (5.94)$$

We can now write the following relationship between the phase error and the input excess phase by using (5.93) and (5.94).

$$\Theta_e(s) = \Theta_{in}(s)H_e(s) = \Theta_{in}(s)\frac{s}{s + KF(s)} \qquad (5.95)$$

It is interesting to consider the steady-state behavior of the PLL—in particular, the steady-state error remaining in the loop at the PD output. It is the value of $\theta_e(t)$ after all transients have died out (i.e., after the PLL reaches the steady-state condition). Substituting (5.95) in the final value theorem of the Laplace transform, the steady-state phase error $\theta_e(\infty)$ is given by

$$\theta_e(\infty) = \lim_{s \to 0} s\Theta_e(s) = \lim_{s \to 0} s\Theta_{in}(s)\frac{s}{s + KF(s)} = \lim_{s \to 0}\frac{s^2\Theta_{in}(s)}{s + KF(s)} \qquad (5.96)$$

Equation (5.96) can be used to calculate the steady-state error for a given input excess phase $\Theta_{in}(s)$. Ideally, the PLL phase error should approach zero without significant delay. The choice of the loop filter plays an important role in realizing this performance.

5.5.3 First-Order PLL

A loop filter with no poles, that is $F(s) = 1$, produces a first-order PLL. Substituting into (5.92), the closed-loop transfer function of the first-order PLL is obtained as

$$H(s) = \frac{K}{s + K} \qquad (5.97)$$

Equation (5.97) states that the loop is stable when the loop gain $K > 0$. The 3-dB bandwidth of the loop is K. The shortcoming of the first-order PLL is that the loop gain K is the only parameter available for adjustment.

The phase-error transfer function is given from (5.94) as

$$H_e(s) = \frac{s}{s + K} \tag{5.98}$$

Assuming that the loop is initially locked, we next consider the transient response of the first-order PLL to some important step changes.

Phase Step

For an input signal with a phase step, the excess phase is given by

$$\theta_{in}(t) = (\Delta\theta)u(t) \tag{5.99}$$

where $\Delta\theta$ is the magnitude of the phase step. Its Laplace transform is given by

$$\Theta_{in}(s) = \frac{\Delta\theta}{s} \tag{5.100}$$

Substituting (5.100) into (5.96), the steady-state phase error for the first-order PLL is obtained as

$$\theta_e(\infty) = \lim_{s \to 0} \frac{s\Delta\theta}{s + K} = 0 \tag{5.101}$$

It follows from (5.101) there is zero steady-state phase error for a phase step applied to the first-order PLL input.

Frequency Step

For an input signal with a frequency step, the instantaneous frequency is given by

$$\omega_{in}(t) = \omega_c + (\Delta\omega)u(t) \tag{5.102}$$

where $\Delta\omega$ is the magnitude of the frequency step. Integrating the second term in (5.102) yields the excess phase

$$\theta_{in}(t) = (\Delta\omega)t \tag{5.103}$$

Note that for a frequency step, the excess phase is a ramp function. Its Laplace transform is given by

$$\Theta_{in}(s) = \frac{\Delta\omega}{s^2} \tag{5.104}$$

Substituting (5.104) into (5.96), the steady-state phase error for a frequency step is given by

$$\theta_e(\infty) = \lim_{s \to 0} \frac{\Delta\omega}{s + K} = \frac{\Delta\omega}{K} \tag{5.105}$$

Equation (5.105) shows that for a first-order PLL, there is a steady-state phase error for a frequency step applied to the reference input. However, the error can be made small by making the loop gain K large. If a large loop gain is needed to ensure good tracking, the 3-dB bandwidth will also be large. If good tracking and a narrow bandwidth (for noise suppression) are desired, a first-order loop cannot be used.

Example 5.6

Consider a first-order PLL with parameters $K_{VCO} = 2\pi \times 10^8$ rad/sec-volt, and $K_{PD} = 0.8$ V/radians, and the VCO free-running frequency $f_o = 500$ MHz. Sketch the control voltage $v_e(t)$ at the output of the phase detector if the input frequency jumps from 500 to 550 MHz.

Solution

The phase error for a first-order PLL in s-domain is obtained from (5.95) as

$$\Theta_e(s) = \frac{s}{s + K}\Theta_{in}(s) \tag{5.106}$$

For a frequency step, the excess phase in s-domain is given from (5.104) by

$$\Theta_{in}(s) = \frac{\Delta\omega}{s^2} \tag{}$$

Substituting into (5.106), we obtain

$$\Theta_e(s) = \frac{\Delta\omega}{s(s + K)} \tag{5.107}$$

From Figure 5.24(b), we can write the following s-domain relationship between the phase error $\theta_e(t)$ and the resultant control voltage $v_e(t)$:

$$V_e(s) = K_{PD}\Theta_e(s) \tag{5.108}$$

Substituting (5.107) into (5.108) yields

$$V_e(s) = \frac{K_{PD}\Delta\omega}{s(s + K)} \tag{5.109}$$

The control voltage $v_e(t)$ can now be obtained by taking the inverse Laplace transform of (5.109). That is,

$$v_e(t) = \mathcal{L}^{-1}\{V_e(s)\} = \frac{K_{PD}\Delta\omega}{K}(1 - e^{-Kt}) \tag{5.110}$$

Now

$$K = 200\pi \times 10^6 \times 0.8 = 160\pi \times 10^6 \text{ sec}^{-1}, \Delta\omega = 2\pi \times 50 \times 10^6$$

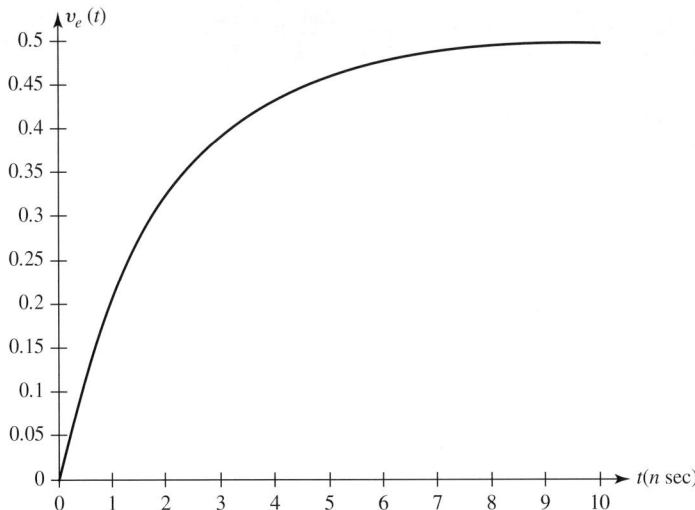

Figure 5.25 VCO control voltage for a first-order PLL.

Substituting these values, we obtain

$$v_e(t) = \frac{0.8\pi \times 10^8}{160\pi \times 10^6}\left(1 - e^{-160\pi \times 10^6 t}\right) = 0.5\left(1 - e^{-502.65 \times 10^6 t}\right)$$

A plot of the VCO control voltage $v_e(t)$ is illustrated in Figure 5.25.

Experiment 5.3 *First-Order PLL*

In this experiment, we study the dynamic response of a first-order analog PLL to a frequency step using Simulink and MATLAB. Figure 5.26 displays the Simulink model of the first-order APLL. The parameters of simulation including reference sinusoidal signal frequency, frequency step magnitude, and VCO gain constant are set up by a companion MATLAB m-file. The input reference signal is a 1-kHz sinusoidal waveform before the frequency step is applied. The phase detector is implemented by the cascade of a mixer and a sixth order Butterworth low-pass filter (LPF)

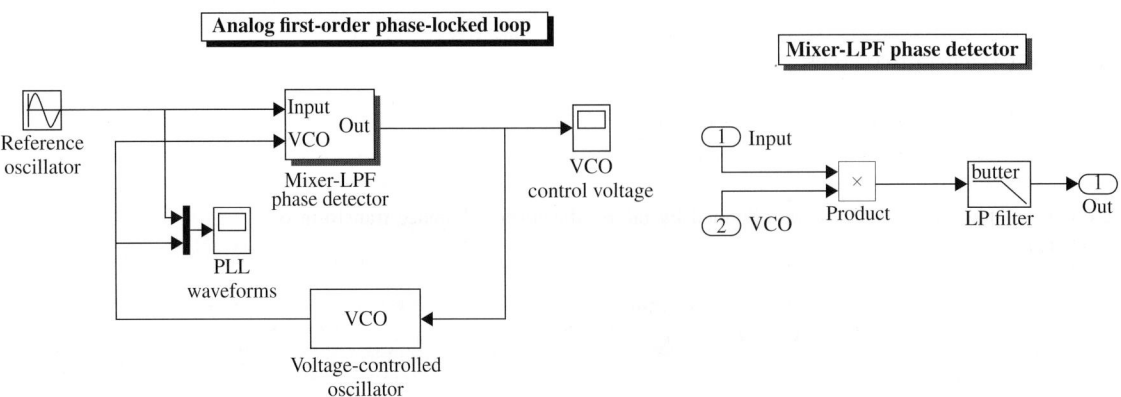

Figure 5.26 Simulink model for a first-order PLL.

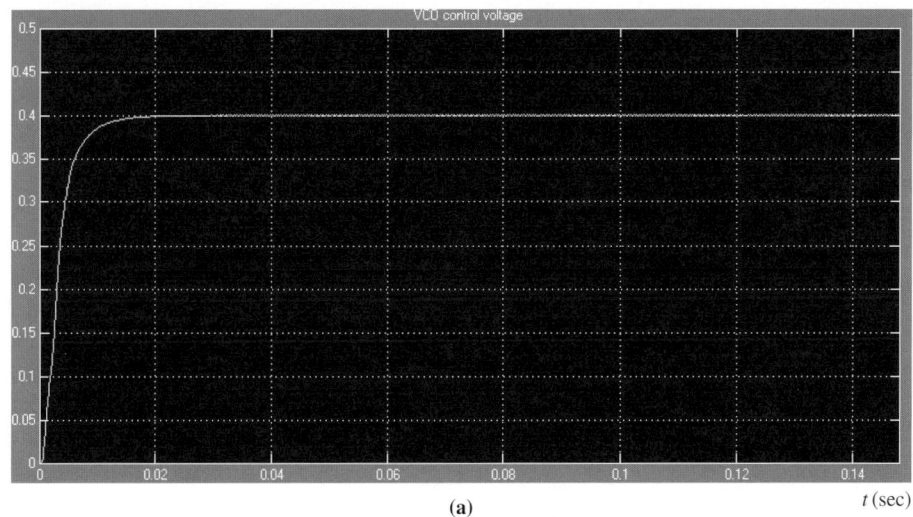

(a) t (sec)

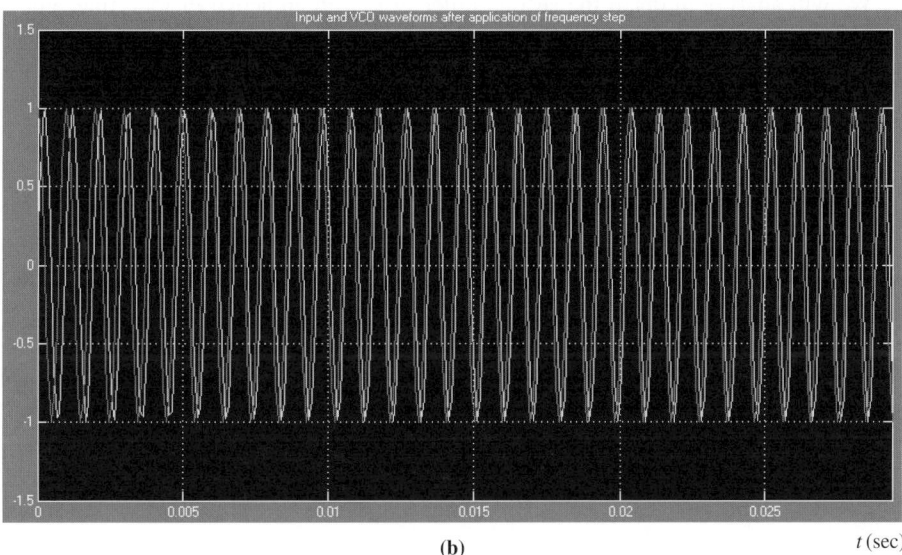

(b) t (sec)

Figure 5.27 (a) VCO control voltage; (b) input and VCO waveforms after the application of a frequency step.

with 500-Hz 3-dB cutoff frequency. The VCO gain constant K_{VCO} is chosen as 100 Hz/V. When the input frequency is increased by a frequency step $\Delta\omega = 80\pi$ radians/sec, it causes the phase difference to grow with time because a frequency step is a phase ramp. As a result, the zero crossings of the input reference signal increasingly lead those of the VCO output, as shown in Figure 5.27(b). As the phase difference increases, it creates a higher control voltage at the output of the phase detector, thereby increasing the VCO frequency ω_{out}. As ω_{out} increases, the phase error reduces. The settling time of the PLL is approximately 0.02 second. Beyond this point, the phase error is reduced to zero and the VCO control voltage is settled around 0.4 volt as displayed in Figure 5.27(a).

5.5.4 Second-Order PLL

The use of a loop filter with a single pole produces a second-order PLL. We will consider following three filter types illustrated in Figures 5.23(b) through (d):

1. LP filter:

$$F(s) = \frac{1}{1 + s\tau_1} \tag{5.111}$$

2. Active PI filter:

$$F(s) = \frac{1 + s\tau_2}{s\tau_1} \tag{5.112}$$

3. Active lag filter:

$$F(s) = \frac{1 + s\tau_2}{1 + s\tau_1} \tag{5.113}$$

We will analyze in detail the second-order PLL with an active PI loop filter given by (5.112). The results for the other filter types are summarized in Table 5.4. The open-loop transfer function $G(s)$ for the loop with an active PI filter is obtained by substituting (5.112) into (5.90) as

$$G(s) = \frac{K(1 + s\tau_2)}{s^2\tau_1} \tag{5.114}$$

Substituting (5.112) into (5.92), the closed-loop transfer function $H(s)$ is given by

$$H(s) = \frac{K(1 + s\tau_2)}{s^2\tau_1 + K(1 + s\tau_2)} = \frac{\dfrac{K}{\tau_1}(1 + s\tau_2)}{s^2 + \dfrac{K}{\tau_1}(1 + s\tau_2)} = \frac{\dfrac{K}{\tau_1}\tau_2 s + \dfrac{K}{\tau_1}}{s^2 + \dfrac{K}{\tau_1}\tau_2 s + \dfrac{K}{\tau_1}} \tag{5.115}$$

Because it is customary to characterize the performance of a linear second-order PLL in terms of the **natural frequency** ω_n and **damping factor** ζ, we write (5.115) in the standard form

$$H(s) = \frac{2s\zeta\omega_n + \omega_n^2}{s^2 + 2s\zeta\omega_n + \omega_n^2} \tag{5.116}$$

where

$$\omega_n = \sqrt{\frac{K}{\tau_1}} \tag{5.117}$$

$$\zeta = \frac{\tau_2}{2}\sqrt{\frac{K}{\tau_1}} \tag{5.118}$$

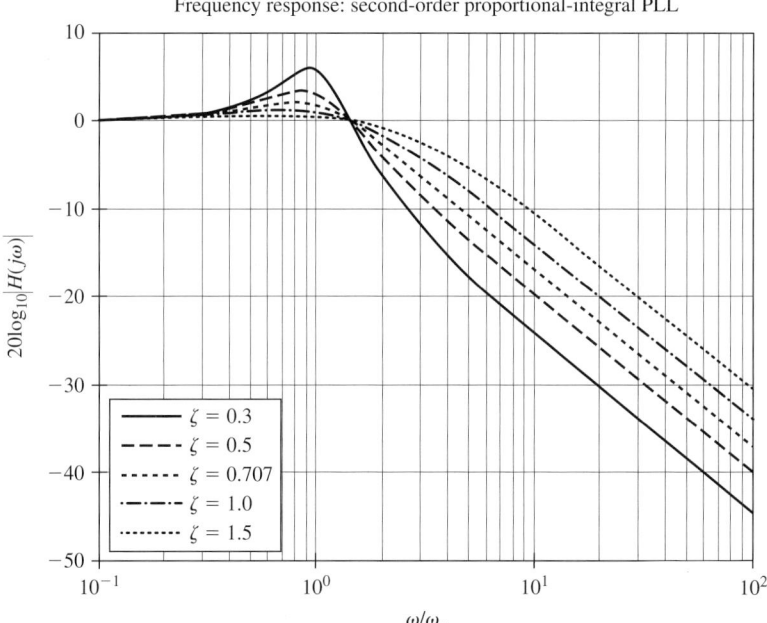

Figure 5.28 Closed-loop frequency response of the second-order active PI loop.

The phase error transfer function $H_e(s)$ can now be obtained by substituting (5.116) into (5.93) as

$$H_e(s) = 1 - \frac{2s\zeta\omega_n + \omega_n^2}{s^2 + 2s\zeta\omega_n + \omega_n^2} = \frac{s^2}{s^2 + 2s\zeta\omega_n + \omega_n^2} \qquad (5.119)$$

The closed-loop frequency response of the second-order active PI loop is displayed in Figure 5.28. We observe that the PLL has a low-pass filter characteristic with flat response up to ω_n (albeit with some peaking depending on the value of damping factor ζ). This implies that the PLL can track phase and frequency variations of the reference input signal up to frequency ω_n. The damping factor ζ has significant influence in determining the transient behavior of the PLL. For $\zeta = 1$, the PLL is critically damped. For $\zeta < 1$, the transient response becomes oscillatory, with overshoot becoming larger as ζ is made smaller. The choice of $\zeta = 0.707$, which represents a second-order Butterworth filter, provides a good compromise between the flatness and the settling behavior for the loop.

PLL Bandwidth

The bandwidth of a PLL is another important parameter that characterizes its performance along with ω_n and ζ. The frequency response of the second-order active PI loop is obtained from (5.116) by substituting $s = j\omega$ as

$$H(j\omega) = \frac{2j\zeta\omega_n\omega + \omega_n^2}{(\omega_n^2 - \omega^2) + 2j\zeta\omega_n\omega} \qquad (5.120)$$

At $\omega = \omega_{3dB}$, $|H(j\omega_{3dB})|^2 = \dfrac{1}{2}$. This implies

$$\frac{\omega_n^4 + 4\zeta^2\omega_n^2\omega_{3dB}^2}{(\omega_n^2 - \omega_{3dB}^2)^2 + 4\zeta^2\omega_n^2\omega_{3dB}^2} = \frac{1}{2}$$

Solving for ω_{3dB}, we have

$$\omega_{3dB} = \omega_n\left[1 + 2\zeta^2 + \sqrt{(1 + 2\zeta^2)^2 + 1}\,\right]^{1/2} \tag{5.121}$$

For a damping factor ζ of 0.707, $\omega_{3dB} = 2.06\omega_n$, which is about twice the natural frequency. Another parameter useful in characterizing the PLL performance in the presence of noise is its noise-equivalent bandwidth B_N. For a PLL, it is defined as

$$B_N = \int_0^\infty |H(f)|^2 df \tag{5.122}$$

Substituting (5.120) into (5.122), we obtain

$$B_N = \int_0^\infty \frac{\omega_n^4 + (4\pi\zeta\omega_n)^2 f^2}{(\omega_n^2 - \omega^2)^2 + 4\zeta^2\omega_n^2\omega^2} df = \int_0^\infty \frac{\omega_n^4 + (4\pi\zeta\omega_n)^2 f^2}{(2\pi f)^4 - 8\pi^2\omega_n^2 f^2 + 16\zeta^2\pi^2\omega_n^2 f^2 + \omega_n^4} df$$

$$= \int_0^\infty \frac{\omega_n^4}{(2\pi f)^4 + 8\pi^2\omega_n^2 f^2(2\zeta^2 - 1) + \omega_n^4} df + \int_0^\infty \frac{(4\pi\zeta\omega_n)^2 f^2}{(2\pi f)^4 + 8\pi^2\omega_n^2 f^2(2\zeta^2 - 1) + \omega_n^4} df \tag{5.123}$$

Both integrals on the right-hand side of (5.123) have closed-form solutions. Substituting yields

$$B_N = \frac{\omega_n}{8\zeta} + \frac{\omega_n\zeta}{2}$$

Table 5.4 summarizes transfer functions and key performance parameters of the four loops considered here.

Transient Response

Assuming that the loop is initially locked, we next consider the transient response of the second-order PLL by considering some important reference input signals. For the second-order active PI loop, the phase error in the s-domain is given by substituting (5.119) into (5.95) as

$$\Theta_e(s) = \{\Theta_{in}(s)H_e(s)\} = \Theta_{in}(s)\frac{s^2}{s^2 + 2s\zeta\omega_n + \omega_n^2} \tag{5.124}$$

Table 5.4 Transfer Functions and Loop Parameters for First- and Second-Order PLLs

Loop Type	Loop Filter $F(s)$	Open-Loop Transfer Function $G(s)$	Natural Frequency ω_n (rad/sec)	Damping Factor ζ	Closed-Loop Transfer Function $H(s)$	Phase Error Transfer Function $H_e(s) = 1 - H(s)$	Noise Equivalent Bandwidth B_N(Hz)
First-order	1	$\dfrac{K}{s}$	K	—	$\dfrac{K}{s+K}$	$\dfrac{s}{s+K}$	$\dfrac{K}{4}$
Second-order lag (two-pole)	$\dfrac{1}{1+s\tau_1}$	$\dfrac{K}{s(1+s\tau_1)}$	$\sqrt{\dfrac{K}{\tau_1}}$	$\dfrac{1}{2\sqrt{K\tau_1}}$	$\dfrac{\omega_n^2}{s^2+2s\zeta\omega_n+\omega_n^2}$	$\dfrac{s^2+2s\zeta\omega_n}{s^2+2s\zeta\omega_n+\omega_n^2}$	$\dfrac{K}{4}$ or $\dfrac{\omega_n}{8\zeta}$
Second-order active PI	$\dfrac{1+s\tau_2}{s\tau_1}$	$\dfrac{K(1+s\tau_2)}{s^2\tau_1}$	$\sqrt{\dfrac{K}{\tau_1}}$	$\dfrac{\tau_2}{2}\sqrt{\dfrac{K}{\tau_1}}$	$\dfrac{2s\zeta\omega_n+\omega_n^2}{s^2+2s\zeta\omega_n+\omega_n^2}$	$\dfrac{s^2}{s^2+2s\zeta\omega_n+\omega_n^2}$	$\dfrac{\omega_n}{8\zeta}+\dfrac{\omega_n\zeta}{2}$
Second-order active lead-lag	$\dfrac{1+s\tau_2}{1+s\tau_1}$	$\dfrac{K(1+s\tau_2)}{s(1+s\tau_1)}$	$\sqrt{\dfrac{K}{\tau_1}}$	$\dfrac{1}{2}\sqrt{\dfrac{K}{\tau_1}}\left(\tau_2+\dfrac{1}{K}\right)$	$\dfrac{s\omega_n\left(2\zeta-\dfrac{\omega_n}{K}\right)+\omega_n^2}{s^2+2s\zeta\omega_n+\omega_n^2}$	$\dfrac{s^2+(\omega_n^2/K)s}{s^2+2s\zeta\omega_n+\omega_n^2}$	$\dfrac{\omega_n}{8\zeta}+\dfrac{\omega_n}{8K^2}\zeta(2\zeta K-\omega_n)^2$

K = Loop gain

Phase Step

For an input reference signal with phase step $\theta_{in}(t) = (\Delta\theta)u(t)$, the steady-state phase error is obtained by substituting (5.100) into (5.96) as

$$\theta_e(\infty) = \lim_{s \to 0} \frac{s\Delta\theta}{s + K_{VCO}K_{PD}F(s)} = \frac{0}{0 + K_{VCO}K_{PD}F(0)} = 0 \qquad (5.125)$$

Thus, the second-order PLL will track out the phase error for a phase step applied to the reference input. Next we investigate how long it will take to achieve the phase lock. The answer to this question is important in many applications and thus helps us determine the key loop parameters. To answer this question, we obtain the phase error for an active PI loop due to a phase step by substituting (5.100) into (5.124) as

$$\Theta_e(s) = \frac{\Delta\theta}{s} \frac{s^2}{s^2 + 2s\zeta\omega_n + \omega_n^2} = \frac{\Delta\theta s}{s^2 + 2s\zeta\omega_n + \omega_n^2} \qquad (5.126)$$

Next we obtain the phase error expression in the time domain by taking the inverse Laplace transform of (5.126) as

$$\theta_e(t) = \mathcal{L}^{-1}\{\Theta_e(s)\} = \mathcal{L}^{-1}\left\{\frac{\Delta\theta s}{s^2 + 2s\zeta\omega_n + \omega_n^2}\right\}$$

$$= \begin{cases} \Delta\theta\left(\cos(\sqrt{1 - \zeta^2}\omega_n t) - \dfrac{\zeta}{\sqrt{1 - \zeta^2}} \sin(\sqrt{1 - \zeta^2}\omega_n t)\right)e^{-\zeta\omega_n t}, & \zeta < 1 \\ \Delta\theta(1 - \omega_n t)e^{-\zeta\omega_n t}, & \zeta = 1 \end{cases}$$

$$(5.127)$$

The normalized phase error, $\dfrac{\theta_e(t)}{\Delta\theta}$, has been plotted in Figure 5.29 for various values of damping factor ζ. The initial phase error equals $\Delta\theta$ and the phase error approaches zero as $t \to \infty$ as stated in (5.125). The phase error decays with a time constant $(\zeta\omega_n)^{-1}$. The time to reach steady-state is related inversely to ω_n. Thus, increasing the natural frequency ω_n decreases the settling time. But a large value for the natural frequency also increases the bandwidth of the loop and thus lets in more noise.

Frequency Step

For a reference input signal with frequency step $\Delta\omega$, the steady-state phase error is given by substituting (5.104) into (5.96) as

$$\theta_e(\infty) = \lim_{s \to 0} s\Theta_e(s) = \lim_{s \to 0} \frac{2\pi\Delta f}{s + KF(s)} = \frac{2\pi\Delta f}{KF(0)} \qquad (5.128)$$

The steady-state phase error for a second-order PLL due to a frequency step does not go to zero as in the case of phase step input, except for an active PI loop. It can be made acceptably small by making the loop gain K as large as possible. Table 5.5 summarizes steady-state phase errors achievable for various loop filters. We observe from the table that to track the frequency offset with zero phase error, an active PI loop filter is required.

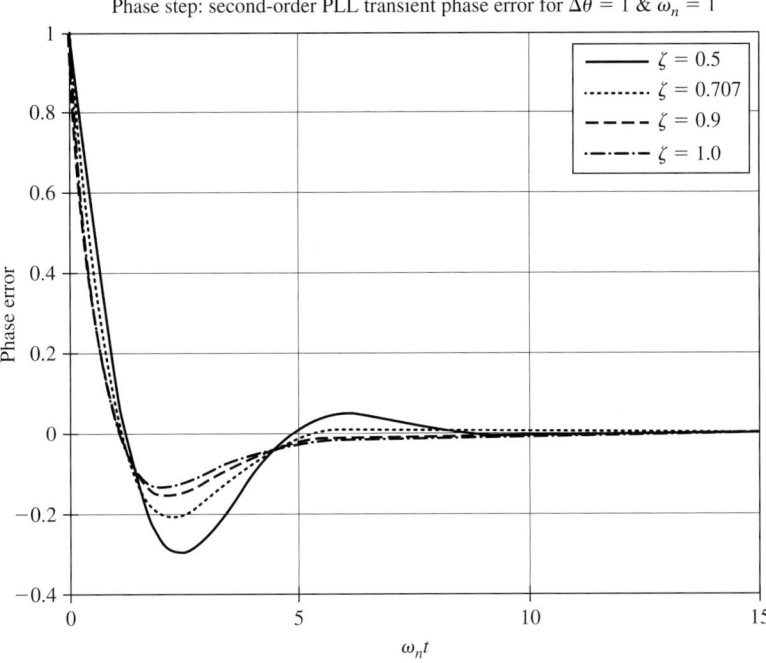

Figure 5.29 Second-order active PI PLL: transient phase error for a phase step.

To study the behavior of the phase error in the time domain, we substitute (5.104) into (5.124) to obtain

$$\Theta_e(s) = \frac{\Delta\omega}{s^2} \frac{s^2}{s^2 + 2s\zeta\omega_n + \omega_n^2} = \frac{\Delta\omega}{s^2 + 2s\zeta\omega_n + \omega_n^2} \qquad (5.129)$$

Taking the inverse Laplace transform of (5.129) yields

$$\theta_e(t) = \mathcal{L}^{-1}\{\Theta_e(s)\} = \mathcal{L}^{-1}\left\{\frac{\Delta\omega}{s^2 + 2s\zeta\omega_n + \omega_n^2}\right\}$$

Table 5.5 Steady-State Phase Errors for Various Loop Filters

Loop Type	Loop Filter $F(s)$	$F(0)$	Steady-State Phase Error Due to Phase Step $\Delta\theta$	Steady-State Phase Error Due to Frequency Step $\Delta\omega$
First-order	1	1	0	$\dfrac{\Delta\omega}{K}$
Second-order lag (two-pole)	$\dfrac{1}{1 + s\tau_1}$	1	0	$\dfrac{\Delta\omega}{K}$
Second-order active PI	$\dfrac{1 + s\tau_2}{s\tau_1}$	∞	0	0
Second-order active lead-lag	$\dfrac{1 + s\tau_2}{1 + s\tau_1}$	1	0	$\dfrac{\Delta\omega}{K}$

$$
= \begin{cases} \dfrac{\Delta\omega}{\omega_n}\left(\dfrac{1}{\sqrt{1-\zeta^2}}\sin(\sqrt{1-\zeta^2}\,\omega_n t)\right)e^{-\zeta\omega_n t}, & \zeta < 1 \\[3mm] \dfrac{\Delta\omega}{\omega_n}(\omega_n t)e^{-\zeta\omega_n t}, & \zeta = 1 \end{cases} \tag{5.130}
$$

The initial phase error equals zero. The phase error is sinusoidal with frequency $\sqrt{1-\zeta^2}\,\omega_n$ that decays with a time constant $(\zeta\omega_n)^{-1}$. The phase error, $\dfrac{\theta_e(t)}{\Delta\omega}$, has been plotted in Figure 5.30 for various values of damping factor ζ. As in the case of phase step, the settling time to achieve acceptable error specification is related inversely to ω_n, that is, increasing the natural frequency ω_n decreases the settling time.

The frequency error $\Delta\omega_e$ corresponding to the phase error $\theta_e(t)$ is given by

$$
\Delta\omega_e = \frac{\theta_e(t)}{t} \tag{5.131}
$$

Substituting (5.130) into (5.131) yields

$$
\Delta\omega_e = \frac{\Delta\omega}{\omega_n t}\left(\frac{1}{\sqrt{1-\zeta^2}}\sin(\sqrt{1-\zeta^2}\,\omega_n t)\right)e^{-\zeta\omega_n t}
$$

$$
= \Delta\omega(\mathrm{sinc}(2\sqrt{1-\zeta^2}\,f_n t))e^{-\zeta\omega_n t}, \quad \zeta \le 1 \tag{5.132}
$$

Figure 5.31 displays the normalized frequency error, $\dfrac{\Delta\omega_e}{\Delta\omega}$, for various values of damping factor ζ.

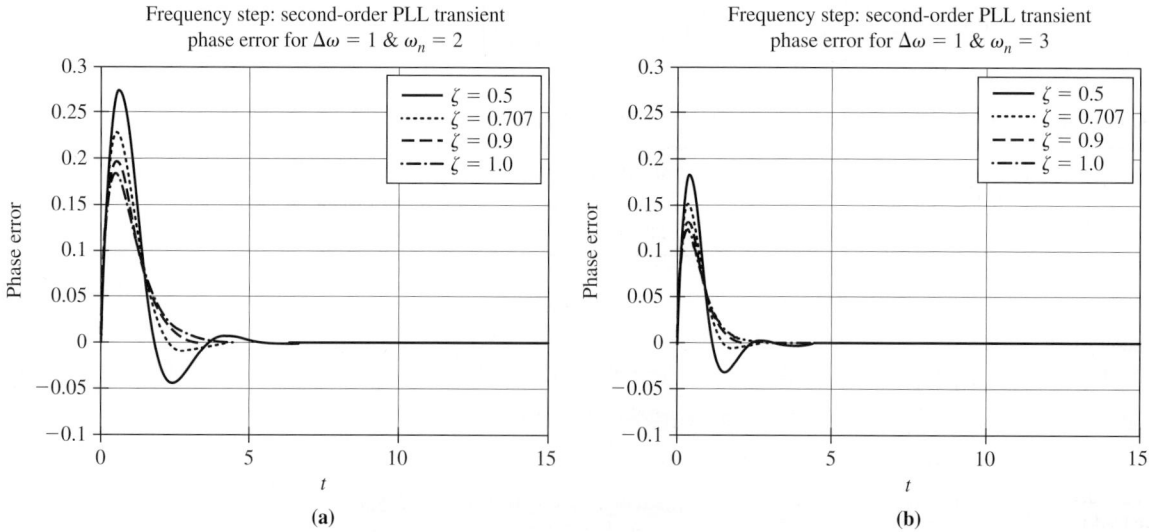

Figure 5.30 Second-order active PI PLL: transient phase error for frequency step: (a) $\omega_n = 2$; (b) $\omega_n = 3$.

Example 5.7

In the GSM TDMA cellular system, there are 124 channels (eight users per channel) of 200-kHz width in the RF band. The frequency bands used by the cell phone in the GSM-900 system are: Transmit (880–915 MHz) and Receive (925–960 MHz). Suppose the mobile is instructed by the base station to change the channel frequency from 910 MHz to 910.2 MHz. Assuming a 3-dB loop bandwidth of 20 kHz, how long does the PLL output frequency take to settle within 100 Hz of its final value?

Solution

$\Delta\omega = 2\pi \times 200$ kHz, $\Delta\omega_e = 2\pi \times 100$ Hz. Substituting these values into (5.132), we have

$$\frac{100}{200 \times 10^3} = (\text{sinc}(2\sqrt{1 - \zeta^2} f_n t))e^{-\zeta\omega_n t} \tag{5.133}$$

The maximum value of the sinc function is unity. If we use this value in (5.133), it gives a slightly optimistic value for the settling time.

$$e^{-\zeta\omega_n\tau} = \frac{100}{200 \times 10^3} = 0.0005 \Rightarrow \zeta\omega_n t = 7.6 \tag{5.134}$$

Assuming $\zeta = 0.707$, (5.121) yields $\omega_n = \dfrac{2\pi \times 20 \times 10^3}{2.06}$ kHz. Substituting into (5.134), we obtain

$$t = \frac{7.6}{\zeta\omega_n} = \frac{7.6}{0.707 \times 2\pi \times 10^4} = 0.171 \text{ ms}$$

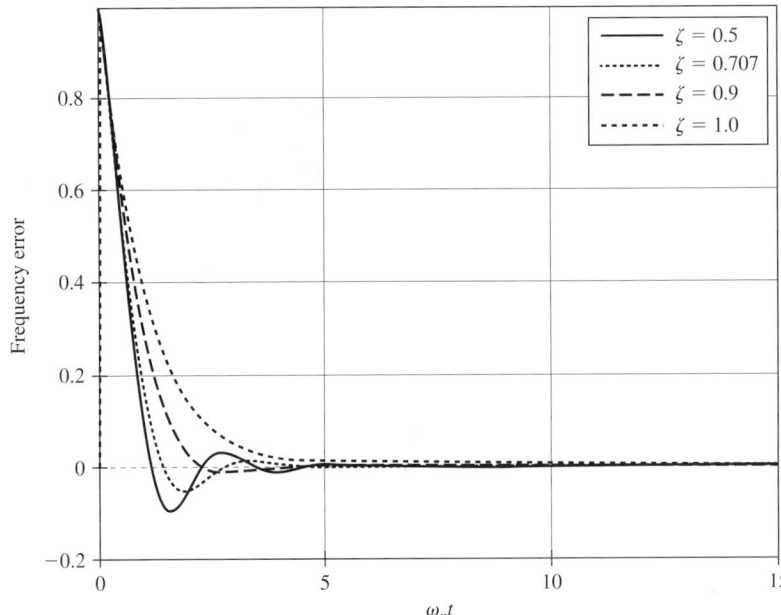

Frequency step: second-order PLL transient frequency error for $\Delta\omega = 1$ & $\omega_n = 1$

Figure 5.31 Second-order active PI PLL: transient frequency error for a frequency step.

Experiment 5.4 *Second-Order PLL*

In this experiment, we study the dynamic response of a second-order analog PLL to a frequency step using Simulink and MATLAB. Figure 5.32 displays the Simulink model of the second-order APLL. The parameters of simulation including reference sinusoidal signal frequency, frequency step, and VCO gain constant are set up by a companion MATLAB m-file. The input reference signal is a 1-kHz sinusoidal waveform before the frequency step is applied. The phase detector is implemented by the cascade of a mixer and a sixth-order Butterworth LPF with 500-Hz 3-dB cutoff frequency. The VCO gain constant K_{VCO} is chosen as 100 Hz/V. The simulation uses an active lead-lag loop filter. Figure 5.33 displays the VCO control voltage waveforms for two different frequency steps. The settling time for frequency step $\Delta\omega = 300\pi$ is approximately 120 ms compared with 20 ms for $\Delta\omega = 150\pi$. It is easy to verify from Figure 5.34 that beyond $t = 120$ ms VCO and input waveforms are locked in quadrature.

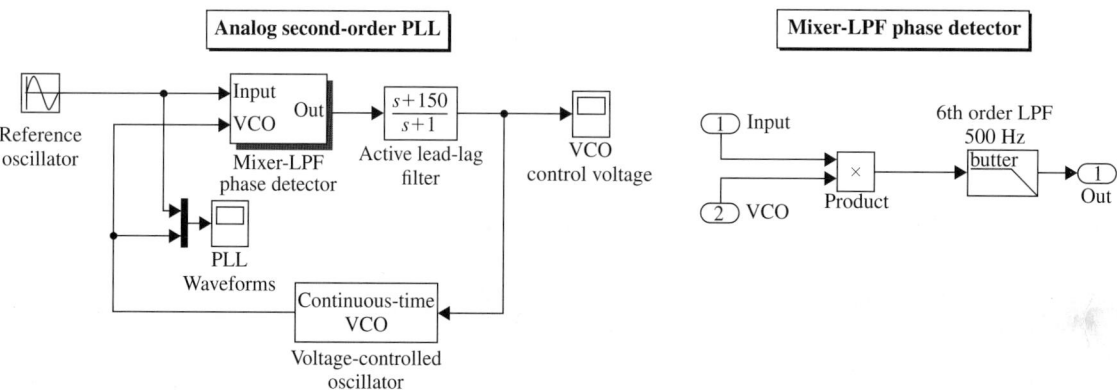

Figure 5.32 Simulink model of the second-order PLL.

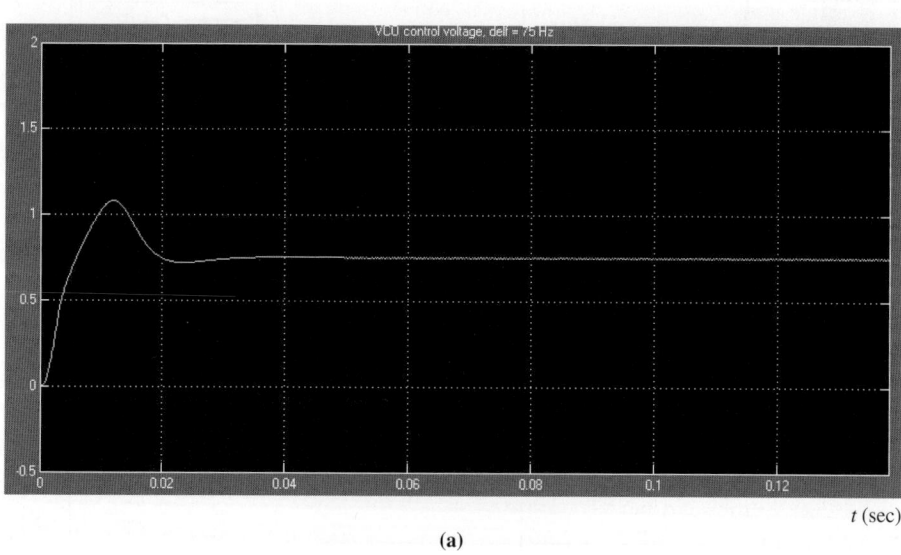

(a)

Figure 5.33 VCO control voltage: (a) $\Delta\omega = 150\pi$

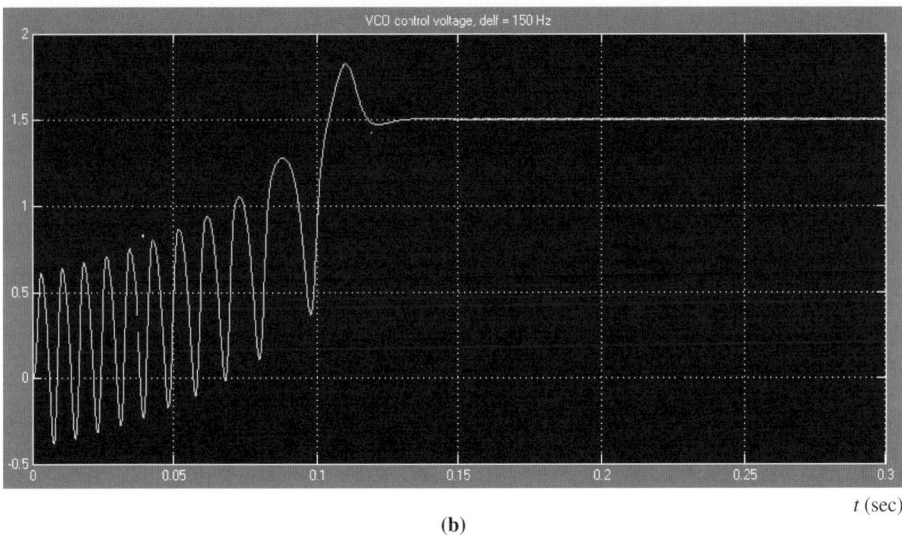

(b)

Figure 5.33 VCO control voltage: (b) $\Delta\omega = 300\pi$ radians/sec step.

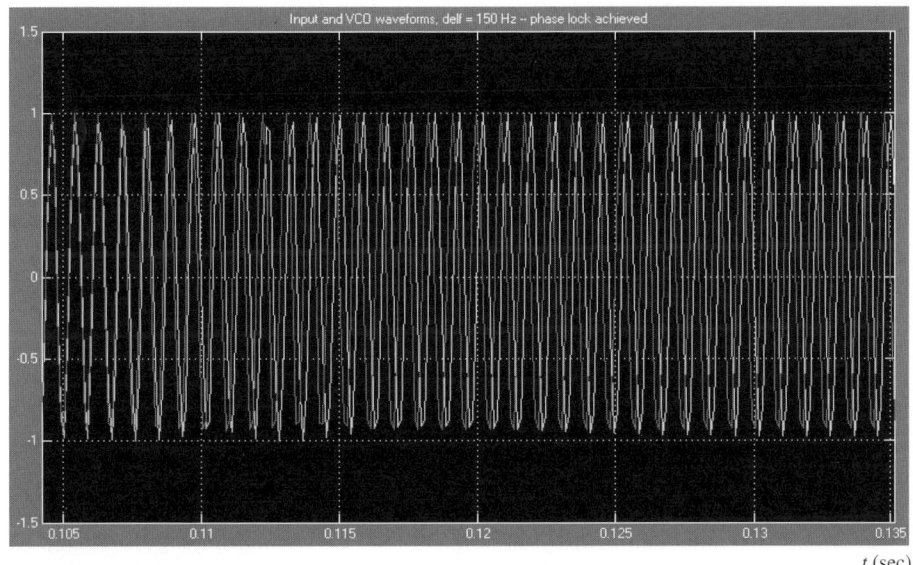

Figure 5.34 Input and VCO waveforms after the application of $\Delta\omega = 300\pi$ step.

5.5.5   Acquisition Process: APLL in the Unlocked State

If the PLL is initially unlocked, the phase error, θ_e, can take on arbitrarily large values and as a result, the linear model is no longer valid. If the input frequency is inside the **pull-in** (or **capture**) **range** ($\Delta\omega_P$) of the PLL, the VCO frequency and phase adjust to the input frequency and phase to achieve the phase lock. The process of acquiring phase lock from the unlocked state is called the **acquisition process.** This is a highly

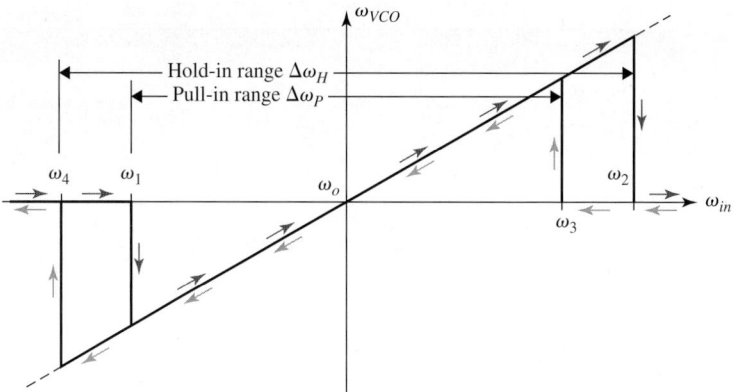

Figure 5.35 PLL acquisition process.

nonlinear process, and it is very hard to analyze. If the input frequency is outside the pull-in range, the PLL will not acquire lock, and the VCO reverts to its free-running frequency. Figure 5.35 displays the VCO output frequency as a function of the input frequency. As the input frequency is increased from the unlocked state, the PLL acquires lock at some frequency ω_1. The frequency $\omega_1 = \omega_o - \Delta\omega_P/2$ is the lower limit of the pull-in range. As the input frequency continues to increase, the PLL goes out of lock at some higher frequency ω_2. The frequency $\omega_2 = \omega_o + \Delta\omega_H/2$ is the upper limit of the **hold-in** or **tracking range** ($\Delta\omega_H$). If the input frequency is higher than ω_2 and the frequency is decreased, at some frequency ω_3, the PLL acquires lock. The frequency $\omega_3 = \omega_o + \Delta\omega_P/2$ represents the upper end of the pull-in range. As the input frequency is decreased, at some frequency ω_4, the PLL goes out of lock. The frequency $\omega_4 = \omega_o - \Delta\omega_H/2$ is the lower end of the hold-in range. The key operating frequency ranges of the PLL are described below.

The hold-in range ($\Delta\omega_H$) is the input frequency range over which a PLL remains locked once it acquires the phase lock. This can be limited either by the phase detector or by the VCO frequency range. If limited by the phase detector, $-\pi/2 < \theta_e < \pi/2$ is the active range where lock can be maintained for the phase detector type shown in Figure 5.20. The phase detector characteristic slope reverses outside this range. Thus the frequency would change in the opposite direction from that required to maintain the locked condition. We can see from Figure 5.20(b) that the PD output varies over the range $2K_{PD}$. We can obtain the hold-in range of the PLL by multiplying the change in PD output by $K_{VCO}F(0)$. That is,

$$\Delta\omega_H = 2K_{VCO}K_{PD}F(0) = 2KF(0) \qquad (5.135)$$

The DC gain of the loop filter is used in (5.134) because the input frequency is changed slowly to determine the hold-in range. As an example, the hold-in range for a first-order PLL is given by $\Delta\omega_H = 2K_{VCO}K_{PD}$. The hold-in range for the second-order PLL with active PI loop filter is infinite because of its infinite gain at DC. In practice, however, the actual hold-in range is limited by the frequency range of the VCO.

The pull-in (or capture) range ($\Delta\omega_P$) is the maximum initial frequency difference $|\omega_{in} - \omega_o|$ between the input and VCO free-running frequencies for which the PLL eventually achieves the phase-locked condition. The pull-in range is determined by the loop filter characteristics, and it never exceeds the hold-in range.

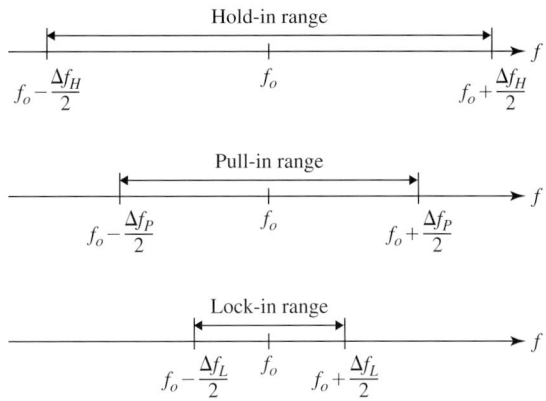

Figure 5.36 Frequency ranges of the PLL.

The **lock-in range** ($\Delta\omega_L$) is the frequency range within which a PLL locks within one single-beat note between the reference input and the VCO output frequencies. Normally, the operating frequency range of a PLL is restricted to the lock-in range.

Figure 5.36 displays the key operating frequency ranges of the PLL.

5.6   PLL AS FM DEMODULATOR

The PLL input signal is FM carrier

$$x_{FM}(t) = A_c \cos\left[\omega_c t + \theta_{in}(t)\right] \tag{5.1}$$

From (5.19), the excess phase $\theta_{in}(t)$ is related to the message signal $s(t)$ by

$$\theta_{in}(t) = 2\pi\Delta f \int\limits_{-\infty}^{t} s_n(\alpha)d\alpha = 2\pi k_f \int\limits_{-\infty}^{t} s(\alpha)d\alpha$$

Taking the Fourier transform on both sides, the excess phase of the FM signal in the frequency domain is given by

$$\Theta_{in}(j\omega) = \frac{2\pi k_f}{j\omega} S(j\omega) \tag{5.136}$$

where

$$\theta_{in}(t) \xleftrightarrow{\Im} \Theta_{in}(j\omega)$$

$$s(t) \xleftrightarrow{\Im} S(j\omega)$$

$S(j\omega)$ is the Fourier transform of the baseband message signal $s(t)$ that is to be detected. To simplify our analysis, we assume that the VCO free-running frequency equals the carrier frequency of the input FM waveform (that is, $\omega_o = \omega_c$), and that the linearized model of the PLL is valid. The relationship between the VCO control voltage and its output in the frequency domain is given from (5.86) as

$$\Theta_{out}(j\omega) = \frac{K_{VCO}}{j\omega} V_{cont}(j\omega)$$

or

$$V_{cont}(j\omega) = \frac{j\omega}{K_{VCO}}\Theta_{out}(j\omega) \tag{5.137}$$

Substituting (5.92) into (5.137) yields

$$V_{cont}(j\omega) = \frac{j\omega}{K_{VCO}}H(j\omega)\Theta_{in}(j\omega) \tag{5.138}$$

where $H(j\omega)$ is the closed-loop transfer function of the PLL in the frequency domain. Combining (5.136) and (5.138) yields

$$V_{cont}(j\omega) = \frac{2\pi k_f}{K_{VCO}}H(j\omega)S(j\omega) \tag{5.139}$$

Substituting (5.97) and (5.91) into (5.139), we obtain

$$V_{cont}(j\omega) = \frac{2\pi k_f}{K_{VCO}}\frac{K_{VCO}K_{PD}F(j\omega)}{j\omega + K_{VCO}K_{PD}F(j\omega)}S(j\omega) \tag{5.140}$$

We can get better insight into the behavior of the PLL by considering a first-order loop. That is, $F(j\omega) = 1$. This yields

$$V_{cont}(j\omega) = 2\pi k_f\frac{K_{PD}}{j\omega + K_{VCO}K_{PD}}S(j\omega) \tag{5.141}$$

If 3-dB bandwidth of the loop $\omega_{3dB} = K_{VCO}K_{PD} \gg 2\pi B$, then

$$V_{cont}(j\omega) \approx \frac{2\pi k_f}{K_{VCO}}S(j\omega), \quad |\omega| \le 2\pi B \tag{5.142}$$

Equation (5.142) states that the PLL demodulates the FM signal if the loop 3-dB bandwidth $\omega_{3dB} \gg 2\pi B$, where B is bandwidth of the message signal $s(t)$ in Hz. In time-domain, the control voltage of the VCO is given by

$$v_{cont}(t) = \frac{2\pi k_f}{K_{VCO}}s(t) \tag{5.143}$$

Note that $v_{cont}(t)$ is proportional to the message signal $s(t)$. Thus the PLL acts as an FM demodulator, and the detected output is given by $v_{cont}(t)$. This configuration is called a "modulation tracking loop."

Experiment 5.5   *PLL as FM Demodulator*

In this experiment, we study the operation of a PLL for demodulation of FM signal using Simulink and MATLAB. Figure 5.26 displays the Simulink model of the system. The parameters of simulation including message signal frequency, FM sensitivity, VCO and LP filter characteristics are set up by a companion MATLAB m-file. The message signal is chosen as a 1-Hz sinusoidal waveform. The carrier frequency of the FM modulator and free-running frequency of the PLL VCO are assumed to be 100 Hz. Because FM sensitivity $k_f = 10$ Hz/V for FM modulator, the bandwidth of the modulated signal is 22 Hz. The loop filter is selected as second-order

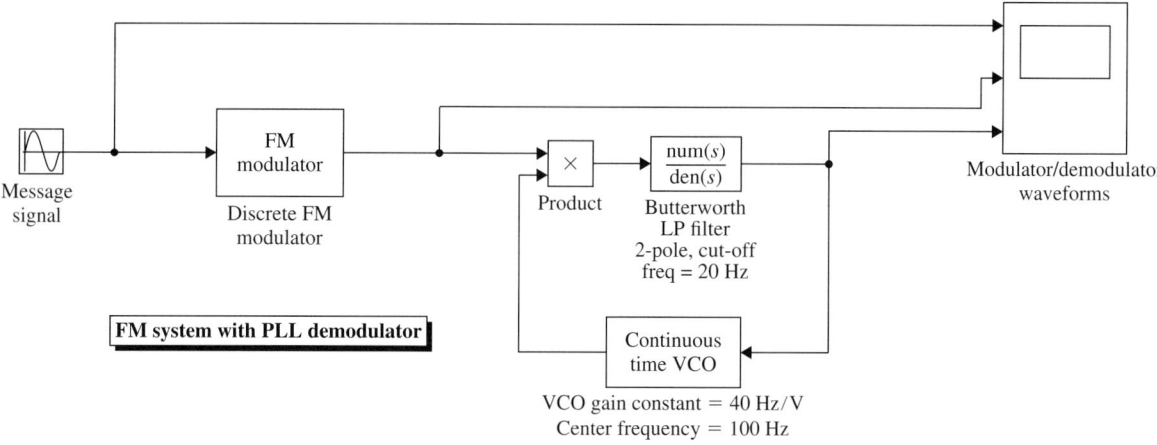

Figure 5.37 Simulink model of the PLL FM demodulator.

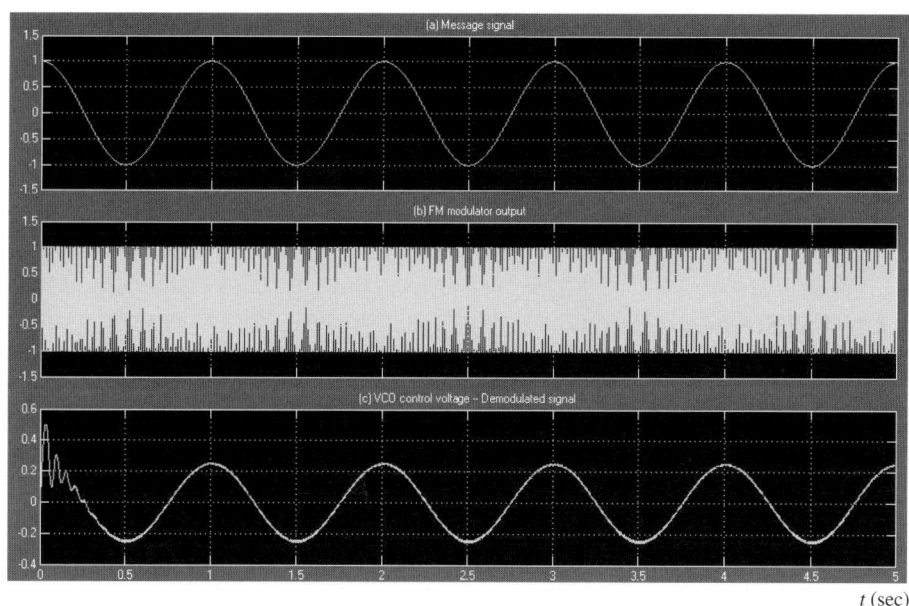

t (sec)

Figure 5.38 PLL FM demodulator original and recovered message waveforms.

Butterworth LPF with 3-dB cutoff frequency equal to 20 Hz. The VCO gain constant K_{VCO} is chosen as 40 Hz/V. Figure 5.37 displays a Simulink model of the FM system with a PLL demodulator. The original and recovered message waveforms are shown in Figure 5.38.

Example 5.8

Consider the demodulation of FM signal $x_{FM}(t) = \cos[1000\pi t + 50\sin(20\pi t))]$. Assuming a first-order PLL with $K_{PD} = 0.5$, $K_{VCO} = 1000\pi$, determine the demodulated PLL output.

Solution

Assuming that the modulating signal peak amplitude is unity, $k_f = \Delta f$. In the present case, $\beta = 50$ and $f_m = 10$. Therefore, $k_f = \Delta_f = \beta f_m = 500$ and $s(t) = \cos(20\pi t)$. Using (5.141), we have

$$\left.\frac{V_{cont}(\omega)}{S(\omega)}\right|_{\omega=20\pi} = 2\pi k_f \left.\frac{K_{PD}}{j\omega + K_{VCO}K_{PD}}\right|_{\omega=20\pi} = \frac{500\pi}{j20\pi + 500\pi} = 1\angle -2.3°$$

Therefore, the demodulated PLL output is

$$v_{cont}(t) \approx \cos(20\pi t - 2.3°)$$

5.7 FM BROADCASTING

Commercial FM radio broadcasting uses the frequency band 88 to 108 MHz for the transmission of voice and music signals. The maximum frequency (bandwidth) of the information signal is set at 15 kHz and the peak frequency deviation is fixed at 75 kHz. The 88 to 108 MHz frequency band is divided into 200-kHz channels using FDM as discussed in Example 5.5. The stations are identified by the center frequencies within their channels (e.g., 90.5 MHz, 101.1 MHz). The bandwidth of each channel is sufficient to ensure high-quality FM broadcast of music.

The FM radio broadcast receiver is very similar to the superheterodyne receiver described in Section 4.10. The only differences are in the range of frequencies of the image-reject filter and the local oscillator. An IF of 10.7 MHz is used. The FM demodulator includes a BP limiter and discriminator stages. The output is then passed to the audio amplifier stage which also incorporates a deemphasis function. The preemphasis and deemphasis functions for FM are discussed in Section 7.4. The **automatic frequency control (AFC)** circuit ensures that the LO frequency is stable in spite of changes in temperature and aging. The block diagram of such a receiver is shown in Figure 5.39.

5.7.1 FM Stereo

FM stereo broadcasting was introduced during the early 1960s. The selected scheme was designed to be compatible with the monaural FM radios that were in existence at the time. FM stereo is a method of sending two independent audio signals simultaneously within the same FM channel. Essentially, the system performs the frequency-division multiplexing of two signals into a complex baseband signal that modulates the FM carrier. Figure 5.40 shows a block diagram of an FM stereo transmitter. At the

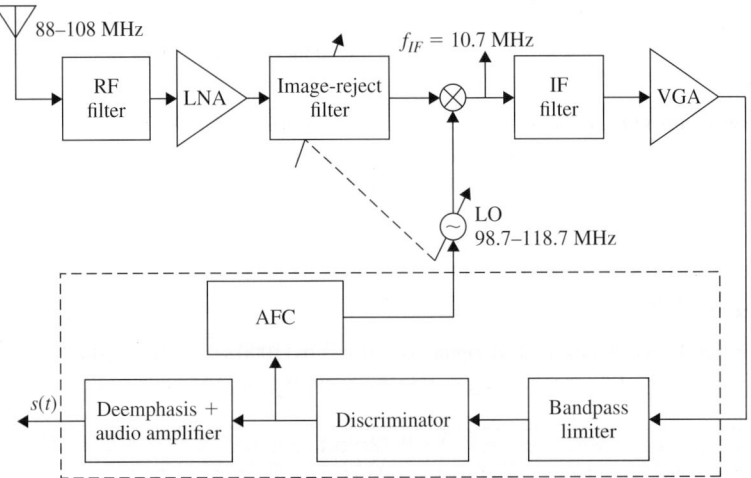

Figure 5.39 FM receiver.

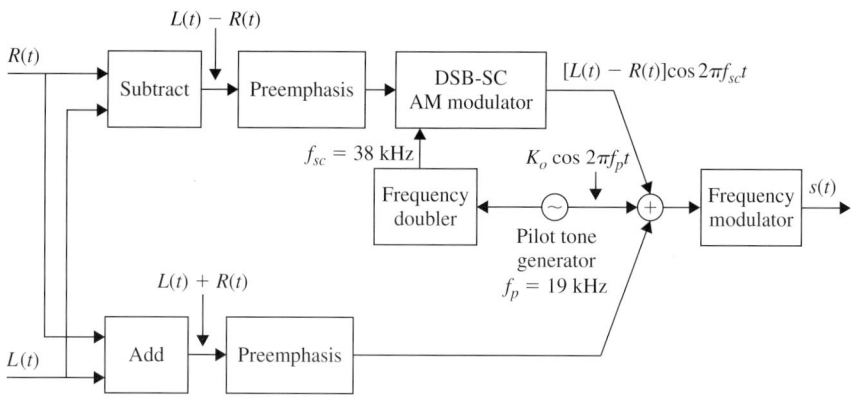

Figure 5.40 FM stereo transmitter.

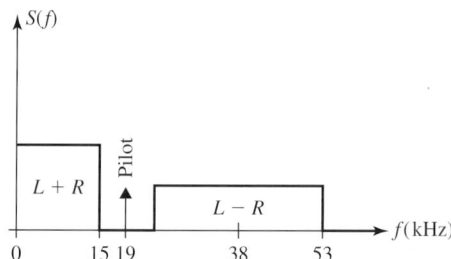

Figure 5.41 FM stereo baseband frequency spectrum.

recording studio, left-hand audio signal $L(t)$ and right-hand signal $R(t)$ are added and subtracted to generate the sum $L + R$ and the difference signal $L - R$. The sum and difference signals are each preemphasized and bandlimited to 15 kHz by the filters. The sum signal is left unchanged while the difference signal is DSB-SC modulated using a 38-kHz subcarrier that is generated from a 19-kHz pilot tone. The pilot tone is transmitted along with $L + R$ and $L - R$ signals for the purpose of demodulating the DSB-SC AM signal at the receiver. The composite stereo signal

$$s(t) = \left[L(t) + R(t)\right] + \left[L(t) - R(t)\right]\cos 2\pi f_{sc}t + K_o\cos 2\pi f_P t \qquad (5.144)$$

is used to frequency modulate a carrier. The constant K_o determines the level of the pilot carrier relative to other components of the composite signal (5.144). Figure 5.41 shows the spectrum of the composite baseband stereo signal.

At the FM stereo receiver, the composite baseband stereo signal is recovered by the FM demodulator as shown in Figure 5.42. The three component signals are separated by two BPFs and one LPF. The $L + R$ signal, which occupies the 0 to 15 kHz range, is obtained by passing the LPF output through the deemphasis stage. The 19-kHz pilot tone is separated by a narrow BPF centered at 19 kHz. This signal undergoes a frequency doubling to 38 kHz and is then applied to a coherent demodulator. The DSB-SC modulated $L - R$ signal is recovered by another BPF centered at 38 kHz, and it is also applied to the coherent demodulator. The coherent demodulator output after deemphasis consists of the $L - R$ signal. At this point the $L + R$ and $L - R$ signals are applied to adder circuits (sometimes referred to as a matrix) that yield the separate left and right signals. The signals are then fed to identical audio amplifiers.

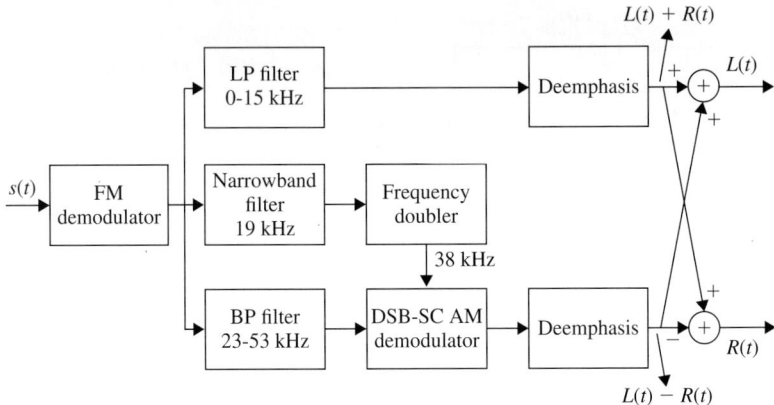

Figure 5.42 FM stereo receiver.

5.8   ANALOG TELEVISION

Television and related display technologies in laptops, cell phones, PDAs, and video iPods play a very influential role in our daily lives. Television permits the reproduction and storage of two-dimensional fixed or moving images by converting them into electrical signals. Once a visual image is converted to an electrical signal, it can be transmitted using electronic communication systems across the globe, making **vision at a distance** possible. The format of television signals varies from country to country. In the United States, Canada, and Japan, the **National Television Systems Committee (NTSC)** format is used. In Europe, the **Phase Alternating Line (PAL)** format is common. PAL, developed after NTSC, is an improvement over NTSC. The **Sequential Coleur avec Memoire** (SECAM) standard is used in France and the former Soviet Union. None of these formats are compatible with each other. Although they all utilize the same basic scanning system and represent color with a type of phase modulation, they differ in specific scanning frequencies, number of scan lines, and color modulation techniques, among others.

5.8.1   Black-and-White Image

The black-and-white image can be thought of as being formed by a large number of picture elements, called **pixels,** arranged in rows and columns as shown in Figure 5.43(a). The light intensity of each pixel is a function of spatial coordinates x and y. Because the electrical signal is a one-dimensional function of time, a technique is needed to encode the light intensity of each pixel $I(x,y)$ into electrical signal $s(t)$. This is accomplished by **raster scanning,** as shown in Figure 5.43(b). We start from the upper left-hand corner of the image and scan the first horizontal line. This produces an electrical signal corresponding to the light intensity of each pixel in the line. The scanning beam is then moved to the beginning of the next horizontal line by a fast retrace as shown by the dashed lines. The second row of pixels is scanned next. The process of scanning and retrace continues this way until the last horizontal line is scanned. One complete set of lines makes a **frame** of the image.

Synchronization Signals

Synchronization (sync) signals are added by the TV camera to allow reconstruction of the image at the receiver/monitor. A **horizontal synchronizing pulse** is inserted at the end of each row of pixels (or horizontal line) scanned to indicate the beginning of the

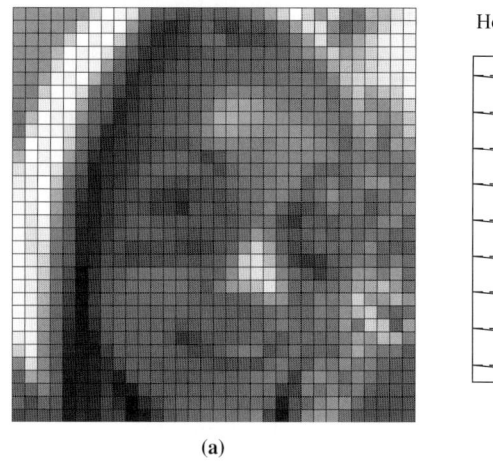 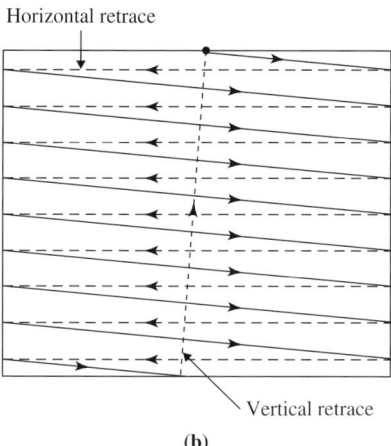

(a)   **(b)**

Figure 5.43   (a) Pixels; (b) raster scanning.

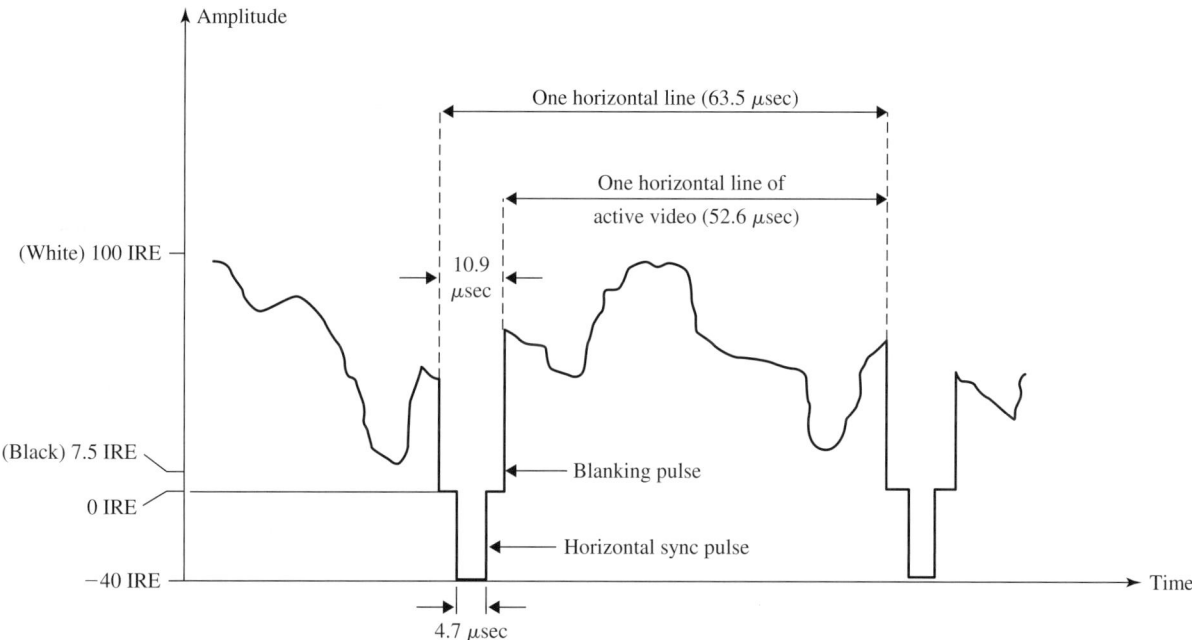

Figure 5.44   Black-and-white video composite waveform.

next line to the video receiver. During the retrace from right to left as indicated by the dashed lines, a **horizontal blanking pulse** (at the black level) is transmitted to blank the display. A **vertical blanking pulse** is added at the end of each frame scan to retrace to the top of the screen and start displaying the next frame.

The composite video waveform, called the **luminance signal,** obtained by scanning a black-and-white visual image is displayed in Figure 5.44. It consists of two parts: the active video and sync. The **active video** is the analog waveform portion whose amplitude represents the light intensity of pixels in each horizontal line scan. The sync portion of the luminance signal consists of a periodic sequence of synchronizing and blanking pulses to allow the reconstruction of the image at the receiver/monitor. Note that the

Table 5.6 Video Amplitude Levels

Level	IRE Units/Amplitude
White	100/714 mV
Black	7.5/53.55 mV
Blanking	0/0 V
Sync tip	−40/−286 mV

sync portion doesn't interfere with the active video because it's below the black level and can't be seen. Any signal below the black level is said to be **blanked.** The black and blanking levels are the same in every format except NTSC composite. The composite TV waveform is 1 V peak-to-peak. The various amplitude levels in a TV waveform are specified in terms of an **Institute of Radio Engineers (IRE)** scale. According to the IRE scale, 140 IRE units = 1V peak-to-peak. The amplitudes of various levels in both IRE units and volts are specified in Table 5.6.

5.8.2   Black-and-White Television

The human eye retains an image for a fraction of a second after it views the image. This property (called **persistence of vision**) is essential to all visual display technologies, including television and motion pictures. If a sequence of images is displayed in quick succession showing progressively different stages of the motion, the persistence of vision integrates these still frames to provide the illusion of motion. A minimum frame rate of around 40 frames/second is required so that the human eye does not perceive flicker. The NTSC system uses 525 lines/frame and displays 30 frames/second. PAL and SECAM systems use 625 lines/frame and a display rate of 25 frames/second. At these rates some flicker is still noticeable, but instead of increasing the frame rate, a technique called **interlacing** is used. A frame is divided into two **fields** that consist of the odd and even lines, respectively. Odd and even fields are displayed in alternation, resulting in a display rate of 60 fields/second. The odd and even fields draw lines in nonoverlapping portions of the picture as shown in Figure 5.45. Interlacing relies on human persistence of vision to give the appearance of 60 frames/second, because the odd and even fields display lines in nonoverlapping portions of the image.

Video Resolution

Visual resolution is a measure of the smallest detail that can be seen in an image. It is defined as the number of alternating (i.e., black and white) lines that can be discerned in the full screen. The **vertical resolution** defines the capability of the system to resolve horizontal lines. It is expressed as the number of distinct horizontal lines, alternately black and white, which can be satisfactorily resolved on a television screen as illustrated by the checkerboard pattern in Figure 5.46. Ideally, the vertical resolution would be equal to the number of scanning lines per frame. This would happen if the scanning lines were centered on the picture details. However, the scanning lines cannot be assumed to occupy a fixed position relative to vertical detail at all times. From subjective data, obtained with progressive (noninterlaced) scanning, it has been found that the vertical resolution is equal to 70% (the **Kell factor**) of the number of raster lines.

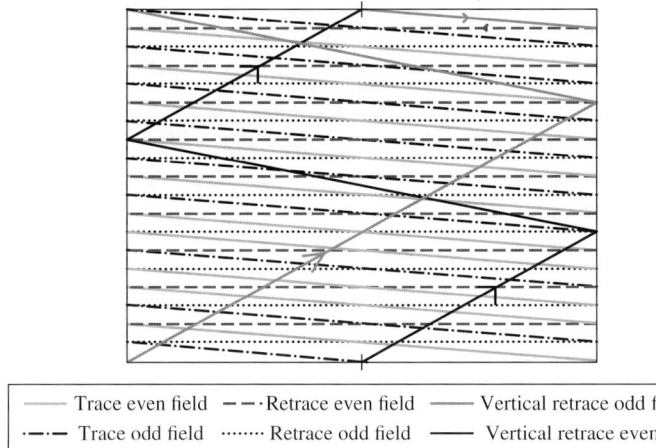

Figure 5.45 Interlaced scanning.

Vertical resolution is further reduced because of the loss of lines during vertical retrace between fields. The resulting number of pixels that can be resolved in the vertical direction is given by

$$N_v = 0.7(N - N_{vb}) \qquad (5.145)$$

where

N_v = Effective vertical resolution
N = Total number of raster (scanning) lines
N_{vb} = Number of raster lines lost during vertical retrace

In the NTSC standard, there is a total of 525 horizontal lines per frame, of which about 20 lines are blanked per field during vertical retrace. The effective vertical resolution achieved in the NTSC video is, therefore, given by

$$N_v = 0.7(525 - 2 \times 20) = 0.7 \times 485 \approx 339 \text{ lines} \qquad (5.146)$$

Note that the vertical resolution is independent of the system bandwidth.

The **horizontal resolution** defines the capability of the system to resolve vertical lines. It is expressed as the number of distinct vertical lines, alternately black and white, which can be satisfactorily resolved on a full screen. Subjective tests indicate that satisfactory results are obtained if horizontal resolution is made approximately equal to vertical resolution. The desired horizontal resolution, N_h, is given by

$$N_h = AN_v \qquad (5.147)$$

A is called the **aspect ratio** of the picture and is defined as

$$A = \frac{\text{image width}}{\text{image height}} \qquad (5.148)$$

In the NTSC system, an aspect ratio of 4:3 is used. This results in horizontal resolution of $339 \times 4/3 \approx 452$ lines.

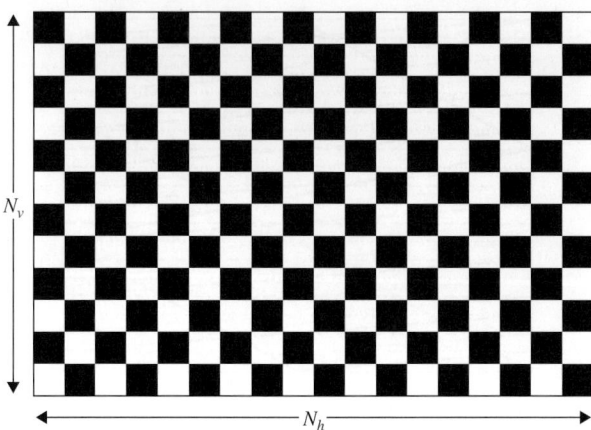

Figure 5.46 Horizontal and vertical resolution.

Bandwidth Requirements

For a TV system to display full horizontal resolution, it should be able to reproduce the checkerboard test pattern consisting of N_h alternate black-and-white pixels during the active horizontal scan. Such a pattern would be produced by a sine wave signal of frequency f_{max} that would undergo $N_h/2$ cycles during the time interval $t_h - t_{hb}$. That is,

$$\frac{N_h}{2} = f_{max}(t_h - t_{hb}) \tag{5.149}$$

where

t_h = Total horizontal scanning line duration
t_{hb} = Horizontal blanking interval

The maximum frequency, f_{max}, resulting from the scanning process is, therefore, given by

$$f_{max} = \frac{N_h}{2(t_h - t_{hb})} \tag{5.150}$$

In the NTSC standard, $N_h = 452$, $t_h = 63.5$ μsec, and $t_{hb} = 10.9$ μsec. Substituting into (5.150), we get

$$f_{max} = \frac{452}{2(63.5 - 10.9) \times 10^{-6}} \approx 4.29 \text{ MHz} \tag{5.151}$$

Thus, the maximum transmitted baseband video frequency is ~4.3 MHz using the NTSC standard. The significant point to note here is that channel bandwidth determines the horizontal resolution. If the bandwidth is restricted for any reason, the horizontal detail in the image will be degraded.

Spectrum of Video Signal

The scanning process determines the basic distribution of energy in the resulting electrical signal. Line scanning of the image concentrates the energy in the harmonics of the line frequency f_h. In addition, the 60-Hz field scan rate gives rise to spectral lines spaced at multiples of 60 Hz on each side of the line frequency harmonic. Figure 5.47 displays the spectrum of a still image. Note that the periodic scanning of an image yields a spectrum with energy clustered around the harmonics of f_h with large gaps between clusters. The amplitude and phase of various spectral components will vary depending on the details of the image being scanned. In the case of motion video, the spectrum retains the concentration of energy at harmonics of the line frequency as in the case of still images. The effect of motion is to transform spectral line clusters around harmonics of f_h into clumps as a result of spectral spreading. But gaps still exist between these energy concentrations at harmonics of f_h. This characteristic of the video signal spectrum is used to advantage for multiplexing additional information in a color TV signal.

The bandwidth allocated for video signals by the FCC for commercial TV broadcasting is set at 4.2 MHz. The audio signal bandwidth is limited to 10 kHz. It is frequency modulated with a frequency deviation $\Delta f = 25$ kHz, resulting in a bandwidth of 70 kHz. The FM audio signal is frequency division multiplexed with the video signal using a 4.5-MHz subcarrier. The resulting multiplexed signal has a bandwidth of 4.535 MHz. The transmission bandwidth allowed by the FCC for broadcast TV signals is 6 MHz. As discussed in Example 4.5, commercial TV broadcasting uses the VSB-AM transmission format to limit the transmission bandwidth to 5.785 MHz, leaving approximately 250-kHz guardband between the channels. The spectrum of a black-and-white TV signal after VSB-AM is shown in Figure 5.48.

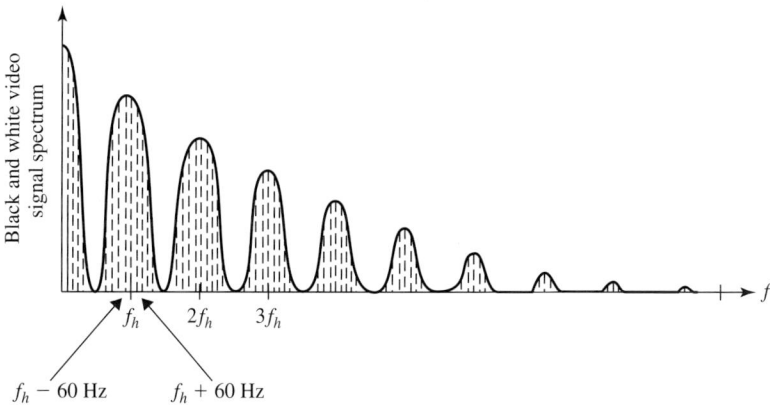

Figure 5.47 Spectrum of black-and-white video signal.

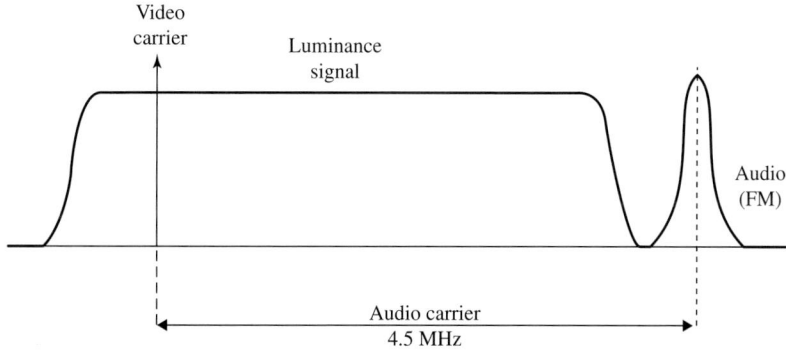

Figure 5.48 Spectrum of VSB-AM black-and-white TV signal.

Black-and-White TV Transmitters and Receivers

The block diagram of a black-and-white TV transmitter is displayed in Figure 5.49. The details of the corresponding receiver are shown in Figure 5.50. It is a single-conversion, superheterodyne design with an IF frequency band of 41 to 47 MHz. The portion of the TV receiver that performs the translation of the selected channel to the IF band is called a **tuner.** The IF filter is usually a **surface acoustic wave (SAW)** type, which also provides the VSB filter shaping (Section 4.6) prior to VSB-AM demodulation. The output of the IF stage is envelope detected to produce the multiplexed baseband signal.

The audio portion of the signal centered at 4.5 MHz is filtered by an audio subcarrier filter and amplifier. The output is next passed to an FM demodulator. The baseband audio output is then amplified by an audio amplifier stage whose output drives the TV speaker(s). The video portion of the multiplexed baseband signal is amplified by a

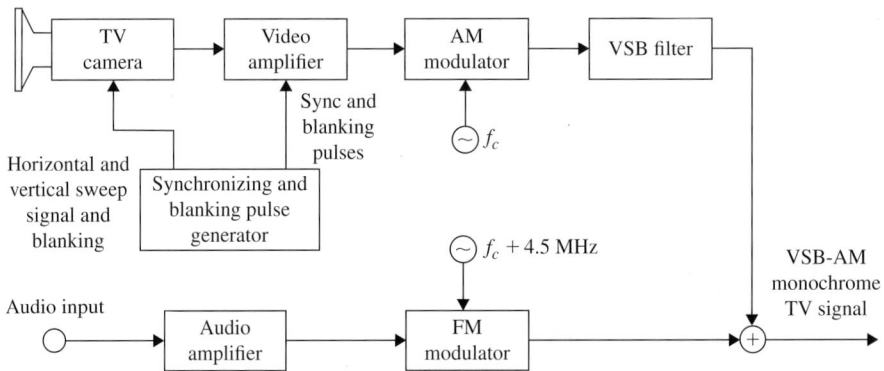

Figure 5.49 Black-and-white TV transmitter.

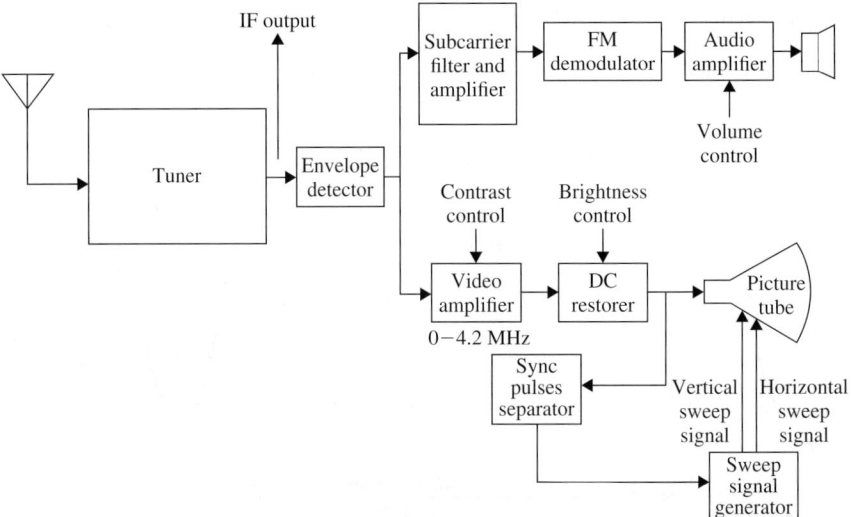

Figure 5.50 Black-and-white TV receiver.

DC-coupled video amplifier. Its output is passed to DC restoration circuitry that clamps the blanking pulses and sets the correct DC level. The DC-restored video signal is then fed to the picture tube. The synchronization signals contained in the received video signal are separated and applied to the TV display circuitry for proper line and field synchronization of the images.

5.8.3 Color Television

All colors can be synthesized by combining in appropriate proportions three primary colors: **red, green,** and **blue (*R, G,* & *B*).** Thus, a color image or video signal can be transmitted by sending three **component signals**—$s_R(t)$, $s_G(t)$, $s_B(t)$—one for each primary color. The NTSC was mandated by the FCC in the early 1950s to develop a color TV system that would be backward compatible with the existing black-and-white TV system so as not to render obsolete thousands of black-and-white television sets overnight. The challenge for the NTSC was to combine both luminance and chrominance information into one broadcast signal that could then be transmitted within the bandwidth allocated to a monochrome TV channel. To create a compatible transmission format, the three component signals are linearly combined so that one of the signals yields the equivalent luminance or black-and-white signal. The remaining two signals, called the **chrominance signals,** contain additional information that can be used by the color TV set to reconstruct $s_R(t)$, $s_G(t)$, and $s_B(t)$. The three signals used in the NTSC system can be expressed in terms of the RGB components as

$$Y: s_Y(t) = 0.3s_R(t) + 0.59s_G(t) + 0.11s_B(t)$$

$$I: s_I(t) = 0.6s_R(t) - 0.28s_G(t) - 0.32s_B(t)$$

$$Q: s_Q(t) = 0.21s_R(t) - 0.52s_G(t) + 0.31s_B(t) \tag{5.152}$$

Y is the luminance signal that produces a black-and-white image in a conventional monochrome TV receiver. I and Q signals are obtained by rotating (that is, phase-shifting) $33°$ counterclockwise from the difference signals $(R - Y)$ and $(B - Y)$, respectively. Equations (5.152) are called the ***YIQ*** representation of NTSC color TV signals. Because these are linearly independent equations, the inverse of matrix

$$M = \begin{bmatrix} 0.30 & 0.59 & 0.11 \\ 0.60 & -0.28 & -0.32 \\ 0.21 & -0.52 & 0.31 \end{bmatrix} \tag{5.153}$$

exists. Thus primary color signals $s_R(t)$, $s_G(t)$, and $s_B(t)$ can be obtained from $s_Y(t)$, $s_I(t)$, and $s_Q(t)$ at the receiver by inverse transformation. Figure 5.51 displays *RGB* and *YIQ* component signals produced in a horizontal scan line of a color bar test pattern.

As each horizontal line is scanned, the **color subcarrier vector** $I - jQ$ moves around in the $I - Q$ plane. The amplitude of this vector

$$A_{sc} = \sqrt{I^2 + Q^2} \tag{5.154}$$

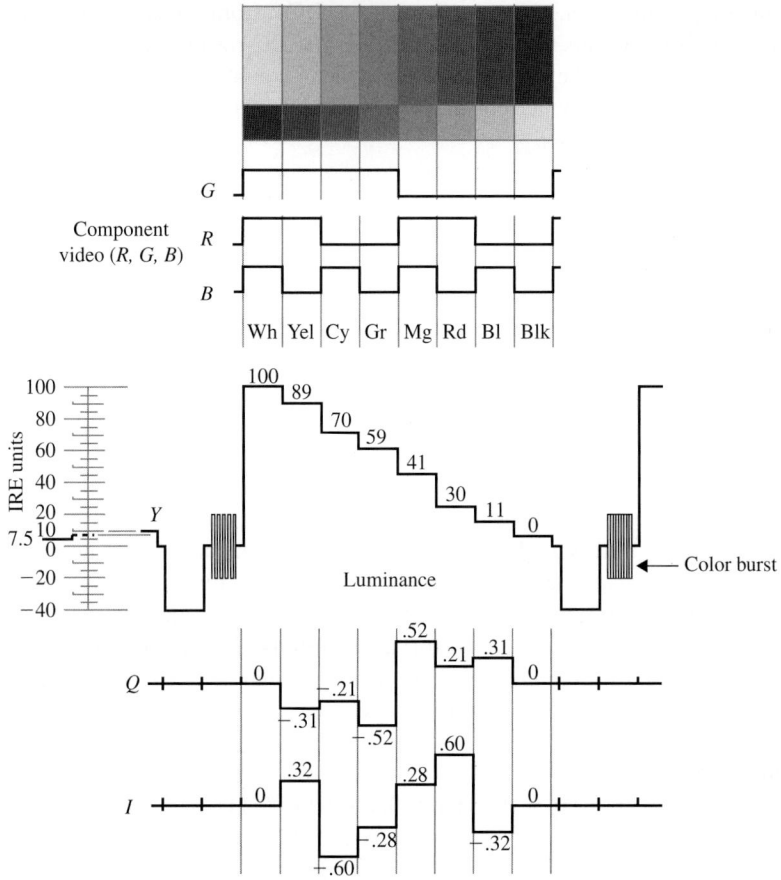

Figure 5.51 Color bar test pattern: *RGB* and *YIQ* component signals.

represents the amount of color or **saturation,** and its phase

$$\phi_{sc} = \tan^{-1}\left(-\frac{Q}{I}\right) \tag{5.155}$$

represents the tint or **hue** of the color information. Hue specifies the color, such as red, yellow, green, blue, or any other color in between. Saturation specifies the intensity or purity of color. For example, a deep red has 100% saturation, but pink is a blend of red and white and thus will have less saturation. The faithful reproduction of color information requires that the phase ϕ_{sc} of the color subcarrier vector relative to the phase of the color subcarrier (at the transmitter) is accurately decoded at the receiver. To ensure this, an eight-cycle burst of the subcarrier waveform, called the **color burst,** is included on the back porch of the blanking pulses at the transmitter for synchronizing the locally generated color subcarrier at the receiver. The color subcarrier vector $I - jQ$ can be viewed using a **vectorscope** instrument, which is widely used to make critical video quality measurements in the industry. Figure 5.52 shows the vectorscope display where $B - Y$ and $R - Y$ signals lie along the x and y axes, respectively. The I vector is offset $33°$ from the $R - Y$ axis. The phase of the color burst is chosen as $90°$ with respect to the $R - Y$ axis. If the chrominance signal is completely orange-cyan, then it will lie directly

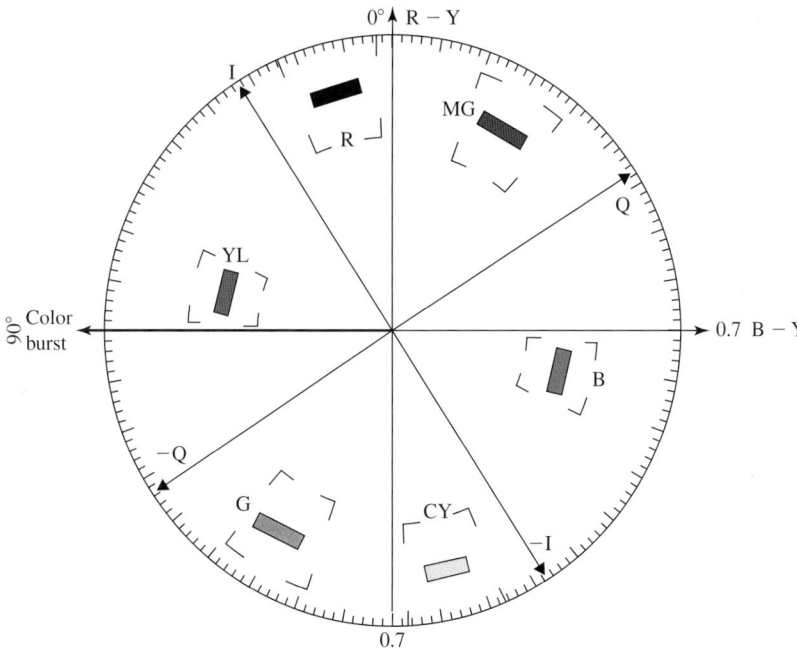

Figure 5.52 Vectorscope representation of color vectors.

on the I vector. It will lie directly along the Q vector if it is completely green-purple. If the chrominance signal is completely yellow-green, then it will lie directly on the color burst vector.

Example 5.9

Determine the color subcarrier vectors for red, green, and blue colors.

Solution

For saturated red, $R = 1$, $G = 0$, $B = 0$. Substituting these values in (5.152) yields $I = 0.6$, $Q = 0.21$. Now using (5.154) and (5.155), we can compute the amplitude and phase of the color subcarrier vector corresponding to red color as follows:

$$A_{sc} = \sqrt{I^2 + Q^2} = \sqrt{0.36 + 0.0441} = 0.636$$

$$\phi_{sc} = \tan^{-1}\left(-\frac{Q}{I}\right) = \tan^{-1}\left(-\frac{0.21}{0.6}\right) = -19.3°$$

Thus the saturated red color vector equals $0.636 \angle -19.3°$. It makes an angle of $-19.3°$ with the I axis. With respect to the $R - Y$ axis, it is offset by $-19.3° + 33° = 13.7°$. It makes an angle of $13.7° - 90° = -76.3°$ with the color burst axis.

By using similar calculations, it can be shown that the saturated green color vector equals $0.59 \angle 118°$. It makes an angle of $118°$ with the I axis. With respect to the $R - Y$ axis, it is offset by $118° + 33° = 151°$. It makes an angle of $151° - 90° = 61°$ with the color burst axis.

The saturated blue color vector equals $0.45 \angle 224°$. It makes an angle of $224°$ with the I axis. With respect to the $R - Y$ axis, it is offset by $224° + 33° = 257°$. It makes an angle of $257° - 90° = 167°$ with the color burst axis.

Color TV Transmission Format

The luminance signal $s_Y(t)$ is allocated 4.2 MHz bandwidth and transmitted in VSB-AM format as in black-and-white TV transmission. During the development effort leading to the NTSC color television system standard, it was observed that the human visual system has much less sensitivity to spatial variation of chrominance information than of luminance information—that is, it can perceive luminance in higher resolution than the chrominance. Color TV systems make use of this difference in sensitivity by transmitting the chrominance signals at a lower bandwidth without any perceptible impairment in the quality of the reconstructed picture. According to NTSC standards, $s_I(t)$ and $s_Q(t)$ signals are band-limited to 1.6 and 0.6 MHz, respectively, prior to transmission. These signals are quadrature-carrier multiplexed (see Section 4.7) on a **color subcarrier** at frequency $f_{sc} = f_c + 3.579545$ MHz, which is chosen (discussed later) so that the resultant color subcarrier signal will not interfere with the luminance signal.

Figure 5.53 illustrates the multiplexing of luminance, chrominance, and audio components to form the composite baseband color TV signal. The chrominance signal $s_I(t)$ is DSB-SC modulated using the in-phase carrier to generate the modulated signal $s_I(t)\cos(2\pi f_{sc}t)$. Because the modulated signal spectrum extends to about 5.18 MHz, a VSB filter follows the modulator to suppress upper sideband spectral components above 4.2 MHz. The chrominance signal $s_Q(t)$ is DSB-SC modulated using the quadrature carrier to generate $s_Q(t)\sin(2\pi f_{sc}t)$. The baseband composite color TV signal, therefore, is given by

$$s(t) = \underbrace{s_Y(t)}_{\substack{\text{Baseband} \\ \text{luminance} \\ \text{signal}}} + \underbrace{s_Q(t)\sin(2\pi f_{sc}t)}_{\substack{\text{DSB-SC} \\ \text{modulated } s_Q(t)}} + \underbrace{s_I(t)\cos(2\pi f_{sc}t) + \hat{s}_I(t)\sin(2\pi f_{sc}t)}_{\text{VSB modulated } s_I(t)} \qquad (5.156)$$

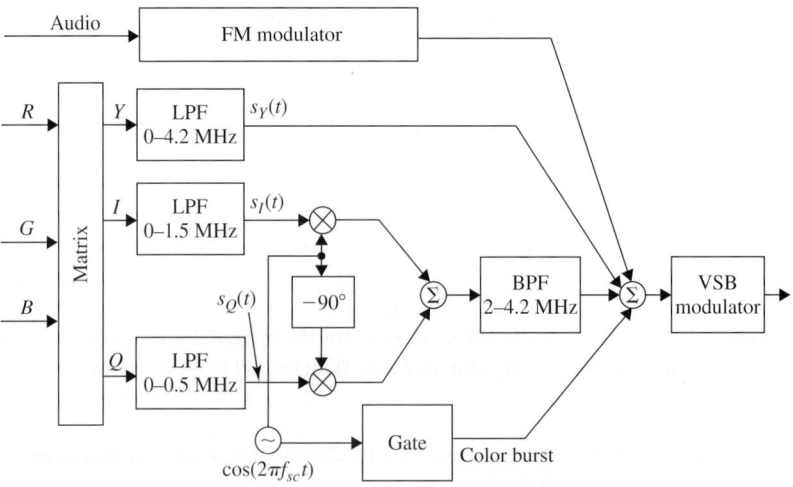

Figure 5.53 Generation of color TV signal.

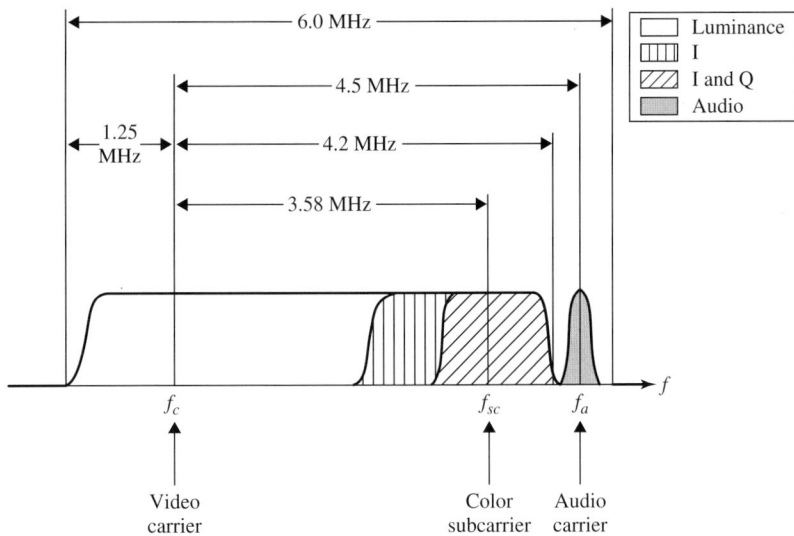

Figure 5.54 Spectrum of composite color TV signal.

Horizontal and vertical synchronizing pulses are next added to $s(t)$. The resultant color TV signal is now VSB modulated and frequency translated to the desired TV channel frequency slot for transmission. The spectrum of the composite color TV signal is displayed in Figure 5.54.

At the color TV receiver, the baseband composite color TV signal $s(t)$ is recovered by the envelope detector. As illustrated in Figure 5.55, the luminance signal is recovered by passing the composite video signal through a comb filter to remove the chrominance components. The chrominance signals are then coherently demodulated by using the color subcarrier synchronized with the transmitted color burst. The demodulated luminance and chrominance signals are linearly combined to produce the original RGB signals.

$$s_R(t) = s_Y(t) - 0.96s_I(t) + 0.62s_Q(t)$$

$$s_G(t) = s_Y(t) - 0.28s_I(t) - 0.64s_Q(t)$$

$$s_B(t) = s_Y(t) - 1.10s_I(t) + 1.70s_Q(t) \tag{5.157}$$

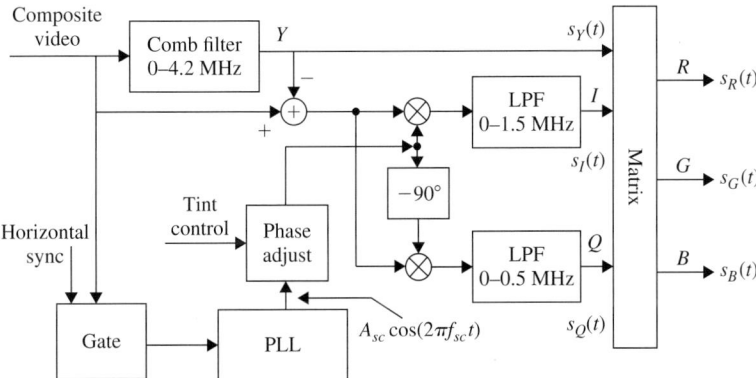

Figure 5.55 Demultiplexing of video component signals at the receiver.

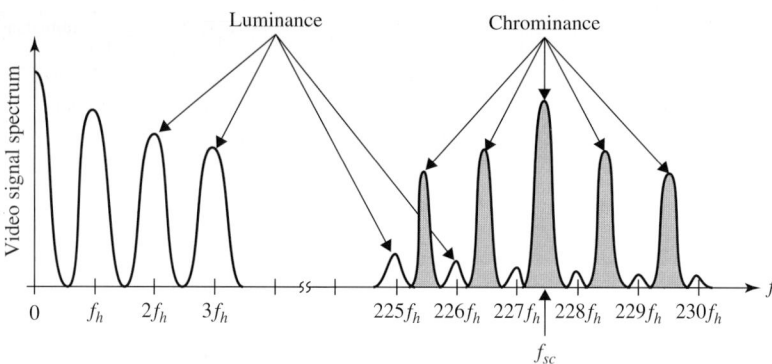

Figure 5.56 Multiplexing of luminance and chrominance signals.

Choice of Color Subcarrier Frequency

The frequency of the color subcarrier is chosen to lie exactly between the 227th and 228th harmonic of the horizontal line frequency f_h.

$$f_{sc} = \frac{455}{2}f_h = 227.5 \times 15.75 \times 10^3 = 3.583125 \text{ MHz} \qquad (5.158)$$

The effect of this is to interleave the components of the chrominance signal spectrum between the luminance signal spectral components as illustrated in Figure 5.56. The chrominance signal sidebands on either side of the color subcarrier frequency vary in amplitude and phase in accordance with the hue and saturation information being transmitted. When a color signal is applied to a monochrome picture tube, the viewer does not see the sinusoidal variations produced by the color subcarrier and its sidebands. This is because all of these sideband components are exactly an odd multiple of one-half the line frequency, and they reverse in phase from line to line and from field to field. Because of the persistence of vision, these variations are averaged out over time and space, making them essentially invisible to the viewer. In practice, f_{sc} is chosen as 3.579545 MHz, which is slightly smaller than $227.5f_h$ to avoid a visible beat frequency with the audio carrier, which lies at 4.5 MHz. Because $f_h = f_{sc}/227.5$, it is slightly modified to the value 15.7326 kHz, and the field frequency is actually 59.94 rather than 60. The beat frequency now occurs at $4.5 - 3.579545 = 920.455 \text{ kHz} = (107/2)f_h$, which is an invisible frequency.

5.8.4   Multichannel Television Sound

The original NTSC TV signal standard included a monophonic audio signal (equivalent to $L + R$ signal in stereo FM). In 1984 the FCC adopted the **Broadcast Television Systems Committee (BTSC) system** to provide multiple audio channels within the NTSC TV signal. The system, better known as **Multichannel Television Sound (MTS),** maintains compatibility with existing nonstereo TV receivers while providing high-quality stereo sound and **Secondary Audio Program (SAP).** MTS incorporates an advanced noise reduction system developed by the dbx Corporation. The stereo and SAP subcarriers were chosen to be multiples of the NTSC video horizontal line frequency f_h (15.734 kHz). These subcarriers are phase locked to the horizontal sync in the video signal to minimize the visibility of any impairments in the picture. The spectrum of the

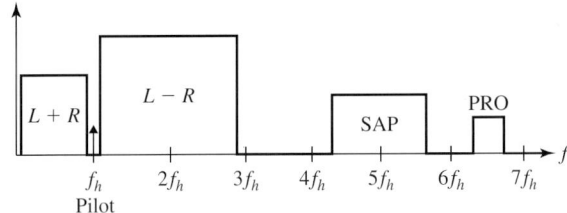

Figure 5.57 Spectral format of an MTS signal.

composite baseband multiplex signal is shown in Figure 5.57. A description of various components of the MTS composite signal follows:

- **Mono channel.** The mono channel carries the $L + R$ signal, which is identical to the monaural signal used in the original NTSC audio format to maintain compatibility with existing monaural-only receivers.
- **Stereo subchannel.** The stereo subchannel carries the difference $L - R$ signal to recover left and right audio at the receiver. This channel is similar to the stereo $L - R$ subchannel used in FM stereo. In the MTS system, however, the $L - R$ signal is processed through a noise reduction system. The encoded $L - R$ signal then modulates a subcarrier of 31.468 kHz ($2f_h$) to produce a DSB-SC signal. The $L - R$ sidebands occupy an approximately 30 kHz bandwidth centered at 31.468 kHz.
- **Pilot.** A pilot tone at the NTSC video horizontal line frequency f_h (15.734 kHz) is added to recover the $L - R$ audio channel at $2f_h$, and the SAP and PRO channels located at $5f_h$ and $6.5f_h$. The pilot is needed for the coherent demodulation of the $L - R$ signal, which is transmitted without a subcarrier in the DSB-SC format. As in the case of stereo FM, the receiver generates a reference subcarrier at 31.468 kHz from the pilot tone using a PLL. The pilot tone is also used by the receiver to detect the presence of a stereo audio signal.
- **Secondary audio program (SAP).** This channel allows other audio, such as a second language, to be broadcast along with the stereo signal. The SAP audio is sent through a dbx noise reduction system identical to that of the stereo $L - R$ subchannel. The SAP signal frequency modulates its 78.671 kHz ($5f_h$) subcarrier. The modulating audio has a frequency range of 50 Hz to 10 kHz.
- **Professional (PRO) channel.** This channel is included to transfer telemetry, such as information from remote television crews, back to the production studios. It is not used to transmit broadcast information.

FINAL REMARKS

This chapter introduced angle modulation schemes by which the message signal is embedded in the carrier by varying its phase or frequency in one-to-one correspondence. The bandwidth of angle-modulated signals, in a strict sense, is infinite. Fortunately, most of the signal energy is contained in the finite bandwidth, which can be estimated using Carson's rule. In Chapter 7 we will show that angle modulation systems offer improved noise performance when compared to AM systems by trading the increased transmission bandwidth.

PLLs were introduced in the context of their application in the demodulation of FM signals. However, the concepts will also be useful in the study of carrier and clock recovery circuits. Black-and-white and color analog TV systems were also introduced; here analog modulation and multiplexing schemes have been successfully applied in the development of this major technology innovation.

FURTHER READINGS

Angle modulation schemes are covered in the undergraduate communication systems texts [1–5]. References [6] and [7] provide in-depth coverage of PLLs. Grob [8] is a good reference on TV systems.

1. Ziemer, R., and W. Tranter. *Principles of Communications: Systems, Modulation, and Noise,* 5th ed. New York: John Wiley, 2001.

2. Carlson, B., P. Crilly, and J. Rutledge. *Communication Systems,* 4th ed. New York: McGraw-Hill, 2002.

3. Proakis, J., and M. Salehi. *Fundamentals of Communication Systems.* Upper Saddle River, NJ: Prentice Hall, 2005.

4. Couch, L. *Digital and Analog Communication Systems,* 7th ed. Upper Saddle River, NJ: Prentice Hall, 2006.

5. Haykin, S. *Communication Systems,* 4th ed. New York: John Wiley, 2000.

6. Gardner, F. *Phaselock Techniques,* 2nd ed. New York: John Wiley, 1979.

7. Best, R. *Phase-Locked Loops: Design, Simulation, and Applications,* 5th ed. New York: McGraw-Hill, 2003.

8. Grob, B., and C. E. Herndon. *Basic Television and Video Systems,* 6th ed. New York: McGraw Hill, 1999.

9. Pritchard, D. "U.S. Color Television Fundamentals." *IEEE Trans. Consum. Electron* CE-23 (1977): 467–478.

PROBLEMS

5.1. A message signal $s(t)$ is shown in Figure P5.1. Sketch the FM and PM waveforms if the carrier frequency is 50 Hz, $k_f = 30$ and $k_p = 10\pi$.

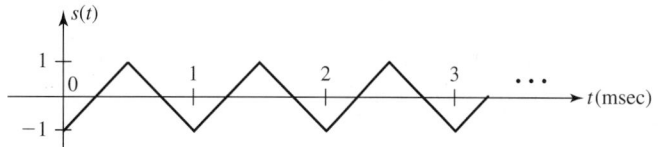

Figure P5.1

5.2. An angle-modulated signal is described by

$$x(t) = 100\cos\left[2\pi \times 10^5 t + 0.01\cos(4\pi \times 10^3 t)\right]$$

a. Write an expression for the instantaneous frequency of $x(t)$.

b. If $x(t)$ is an FM signal, what is the message signal $s_n(t)$?

c. If $x(t)$ is a PM signal, what is the message signal $s_n(t)$?

5.3. An angle-modulated signal is given by

$$x(t) = 10\cos\left[2\pi \times 10^6 t + 2\sin(4\pi \times 10^3 t)\right]$$

a. Determine the peak phase deviation.

b. Determine the peak frequency deviation.

c. Calculate the average power in the modulated signal $x(t)$.

d. Is this a frequency- or phase-modulated signal?

5.4. Consider an FM signal generated by modulating a 10-MHz carrier by a 1-kHz sinusoidal waveform such that peak frequency deviation is 2.5 kHz.

a. Determine the bandwidth of the modulated signal.

b. If the modulating signal amplitude is doubled, determine the bandwidth of the modulated signal.

c. Determine the bandwidth of the modulated signal if the modulating signal frequency is doubled.

d. Determine the bandwidth of the modulated signal if both the amplitude and frequency of the modulating signal are doubled.

5.5. Let the modulating signal be

$$s(t) = 10\cos(2\pi \times 300t) + 25\cos(2\pi \times 600t)$$

a. Write an expression for the FM waveform $x_{FM}(t)$ when $A_c = 100, f_c = 5$ MHz, and $k_f = 200$ Hz/V.

b. Determine maximum frequency deviation Δf_{max}, maximum phase deviation $\Delta \phi_{max}$, and deviation ratio D of the modulated signal.

c. Determine the bandwidth of the modulated signal.

5.6. Consider a PM signal generated by modulating a 10-MHz carrier with a 1-kHz sinusoidal waveform with peak phase deviation of 1 radian.

a. Write an expression for the PM signal and determine its Carson bandwidth.

b. Plot the spectral density of the PM signal.

c. Determine the normalized average power in the PM signal.

d. Calculate the percentage of the total power at the carrier frequency.

e. Repeat parts (a) and (d) if the amplitude of the modulating signal is doubled.

5.7. A single-tone modulated FM signal is given by

$$x_{FM}(t) = 10\cos\left[2\pi \times 10^6 t + 4\sin(4\pi \times 10^3 t)\right]$$

a. Plot the spectral density of the FM signal.

b. Determine Carson's bandwidth of the FM signal.

c. Determine the normalized average power of the FM signal.

d. Calculate the percentage of the total power at the carrier frequency. How does the magnitude of power contained in the carrier frequency component changes if the amplitude of the modulating signal is doubled?

5.8. The message signal $s(t)$ modulates a carrier at 1 MHz to produce an angle-modulated signal. $s(t)$ is periodic waveform with period T_o as shown in Figure P5.2. Assume $A_m = 1$ and $T_o = 1$ sec.

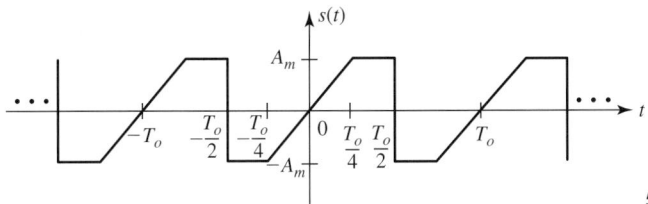

Figure P5.2

a. Determine the 97% bandwidth of the message signal.

b. Calculate the bandwidth of the resultant FM signal with $k_f = 100$ Hz/V.

c. Calculate the bandwidth of the resultant PM signal with $k_P = \pi/2$.

d. Calculate the bandwidth of the resultant FM signal with $k_f = 1000$ Hz/V.

e. How do the answers to parts (a) through (c) change for the case where $A_m = 2$ and $T_o = 1$ msec.

f. How do the answers to parts (a) through (c) change for the case where $A_m = 1$ and $T_o = 0.5$ msec.

5.9. A 1-MHz carrier is frequency-modulated by a single tone of frequency 2 kHz, resulting in the peak frequency deviation of 10 kHz.

a. What is the bandwidth occupied by the modulated signal? Plot the spectrum of the FM signal (only sidebands in the Carson's bandwidth).

b. If the amplitude of the modulating sinusoidal signal is increased by a factor of 3 and its frequency is decreased to 1 kHz, how is the bandwidth of the modulated signal modified? Plot the spectrum of the FM signal.

c. Repeat part (b) with the frequency of the modulating sinusoidal signal increased to 3 kHz.

5.10. Consider the parallel RLC tuned circuit in Figure P5.3 used as a slope detector.

a. Show that the transfer function of the tuned circuit is given by

$$H(j\omega) = \frac{V(j\omega)}{X(j\omega)} = \frac{j\omega\omega_o Q}{\omega_o^2 - \omega^2 + j\omega\omega_o Q}$$

where

$$\omega_o = \frac{1}{\sqrt{LC}}, \omega_{3dB} = \frac{1}{RC}$$

$$Q = \frac{\omega_o}{\omega_{3dB}} = R\sqrt{\frac{C}{L}}$$

b. Determine appropriate values for R, L, and C for $\omega_o = 2\pi \times 10^6$ and $Q = 20$.

c. Plot the magnitude frequency response of the parallel RLC tuned circuit from 940 kHz to 1 MHz. Select the discriminator center frequency, discriminator constant K_{FD}, and permissible peak frequency deviation for the input signal.

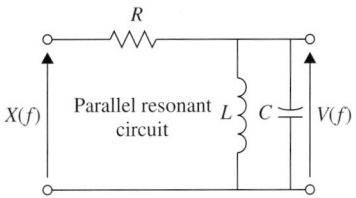

Figure P5.3

5.11. Delay-line FM discriminator. Consider the FM signal

$$x_{FM}(t) = A_c\cos\left[2\pi f_c t + \theta(t)\right]$$

where $\theta(t) = 2\pi\Delta f_{\max}\int_{-\infty}^{t} s_n(t)dt$. We use the FM demodulation scheme illustrated in Figure P5.4. The input FM signal is passed through a delay line that produces a delay of $\pi/2$ radians at the carrier frequency f_c. That is, $2\pi f_c t_d = \pi/2$. The output of the delay line is subtracted from the incoming FM signal, and the resulting difference signal is envelope detected. Let

$$y(t) = x_{FM}(t) - x_{FM}(t - t_d)$$

Assume $|\theta(t) - \theta(t - t_d)| \ll 1$.

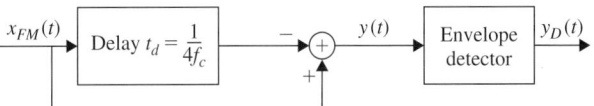

Figure P5.4

a. Show that the envelope of $y(t)$ is given by

$$v(t) = 2A_c\sin\left[\frac{\pi}{4} + \frac{\theta(t) - \theta(t - t_d)}{2}\right]$$

b. Show that the envelope detector output can be expressed as

$$y_D(t) = \frac{1}{\sqrt{2}}\left[1 + \frac{1}{2}\frac{d\theta}{dt}t_d\right] = \frac{1}{\sqrt{2}}\left[1 + \pi\Delta f_{\max}t_d s_n(t)\right]$$

c. Calculate the output $y_D(t)$ for a single-tone modulated FM signal

$$x_{FM}(t) = A_c\cos[2\pi f_c t + \beta\sin 2\pi f_m t]$$

Assume $f_c \gg f_m$ so that $f_m t_d \ll 1$.

5.12. A superheterodyne FM receiver operates in the frequency range of 88 to 108 MHz. Assuming that an IF of 10.7 MHz is selected, determine the range of variation of the local oscillator frequency f_{LO}. Does the range of image frequencies fall outside of the 88 to 108 MHz band?

5.13. A first-order PLL has phase detector characteristic shown in Figure P5.5. Assume that the phase detector output voltage swing is ± 1.5 V. Determine

a. Phase detector gain constant.

b. Capture range of the PLL.

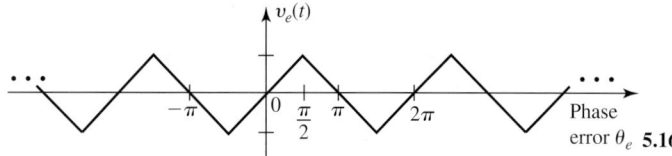

Figure P5.5

5.14. A first-order PLL is operating in phase lock when a frequency step $\Delta\omega$ is applied. Assume that the loop gain $K = 500\pi$. Assume $K_{PD} = 0.8$ V/radians.

    a. Determine the steady-state phase error, in degrees, for $\Delta\omega = 100\pi, 200\pi$, and 800π.

    b. Plot the control voltage in each case. What is the steady-state control voltage after the initial transients have died?

    c. What is the 3-dB bandwidth of the loop in each case? Comment on the trade-off between the noise performance of the first-order PLL versus its steady-state phase error in part (a).

5.15. Consider two-pole, second-order PLL with loop filter

$$F(s) = \frac{1}{1 + s\tau_1}$$

    a. Derive closed-loop transfer function of the PLL in the standard form.

    b. Determine and compare the 3-dB bandwidth and noise equivalent bandwidth B_N of the PLL.

5.16. A frequency step of $\Delta\omega$ is applied to the second-order PLL with loop active PI loop filter analyzed in Section 5.5.4.

    a. Derive an expression for the control voltage applied to the VCO. What is the steady-state control voltage after the initial transients have died?

    b. Calculate the peak phase error for the step frequency change $\Delta\omega$.

5.17. Consider the second-order PLL with loop active PI loop filter. A single tone modulated FM signal with peak deviation Δf_{max} is applied to the PLL, where Δf_{max} peak frequency deviation.

    a. Calculate the magnitude of the phase error.

    b. For fixed Δf_{max}, calculate the value of modulating signal frequency f_m for which the peak phase deviation occurs. What is the corresponding value of the peak phase deviation?

    c. Calculate the parameters of PLL (K, τ_1, τ_2) for a FM signal with $\Delta f_{max} = 75$ kHz and $f_m = 15$ kHz. The PLL uses the phase detector with characteristic in Figure P5.5. Assume $\zeta = 0.707$, and $\tau_1 = \tau_2$.

MATLAB PROBLEMS

5.18. Consider the FM signal produced by modulating a 100-Hz carrier signal with a 5-Hz sinusoidal modulating waveform. Assume $\Delta f_{max} = 25$ Hz.

    a. Generate 4,000-point modulating signal sequence s[n] with a sampling rate of 4096 Hz. Plot it.

    b. Generate 4,000-point FM signal sequence x[n]. Use MATLAB function cumsum(x) to integrate. Plot x[n].

    c. Obtain the DFT X[k] of x[n]. Using the function stem, plot the magnitude spectrum of the FM signal (that is, fftshift(X)).

    d. Repeat for $\Delta f_{max} = 15$ and 35 Hz. Estimate 98% bandwidth of the FM signal in each case.

5.19. The FM signal x[n] in Problem 5.18 is demodulated by the frequency discriminator in Figure 5.9 followed by a LPF.

    a. Design the FIR differentiator by using the Remez algorithm. Use the following code segment

```
fm_det = firpm(60,[0 1],[0 1],
'differentiator');
```

    Plot the magnitude and phase response of the differentiator by using the MATLAB function freqz.

    b. Calculate the differentiator output by using the following code segment

```
y = filter(fm_det,1,x);
```

    c. Envelope detection can be accomplished by using the following code segment:

```
y_env = abs(y);
```

    d. Remove the DC content from the envelope detector output. Design the 60th-order LP fir1 filter with passband edge frequency of 5 Hz. Calculate the demodulated output yD[n] using the MATLAB command filter. The following code segment may be used.

```
y1 = y_env - mean(y_env);
num = fir1(60,fm*Ts);
yD = filter(num,1,y1);
```

    e. Plot the demodulated output sequence yD[n] and compare it with transmitted message sequence s[n]. Comment on the results.

5.20. Consider the PM signal produced by modulating a 100 Hz carrier signal with a 5-Hz sinusoidal modulating waveform. Assume $\Delta\phi_{max} = \pi$.

    a. Generate 4,000-point modulating signal sequence s[n] with a sampling rate of 4096 Hz. Plot it.

    b. Generate 4,000-point PM signal sequence x[n]. Plot x[n].

    c. Obtain the DFT X[k] of x[n]. Using the function stem, plot the magnitude spectrum of the PM signal (that is, fftshift(X)).

    d. Repeat for modulating waveform $s(t) = \cos(6\pi t) + \cos(10\pi t)$. Estimate 98% bandwidth of the PM signal in each case.

5.21. The FM signal x[n] in Problem 5.18 is demodulated by the delay discriminator illustrated in Figure P5.4 followed by an LPF.

    a. Calculate the differentiator output $y[n] = x[n] - x[n - \Delta]$, where $\Delta = \dfrac{1}{4f_c}$.

    b. Envelope detection can be accomplished by using the following code segment:

```
y_env = abs(y);
```

    c. Remove the DC content from the envelope detector output. Design the 100th-order LP `fir1` filter with passband edge frequency of 5 Hz. Calculate the demodulated output yD[n] using the MATLAB command `filter`.

    d. Plot the demodulated output sequence yD[n] and compare it with that obtained in Problem 5.11(c) as well as the original message sequence s[n]. Comment on the results.

CHAPTER 6

Probability and Random Processes

In our study of signals so far, we have dealt with deterministic signals. These signals can be specified either analytically or graphically or in a tabular form at all instants of time. Information signals (speech, music, text, video) or the ever-present noise in communication systems cannot be predicted or exactly described prior to their actual occurrence. This seems reasonable, for if the signals could be predicted they would convey no information upon their occurrence. This chapter provides an overview of probability theory and random processes to familiarize us with the tools required for mathematical modeling of random signals and noise.

Probability theory deals with the study of random experiments, which under repeated trials yield unpredictable outcomes that exhibit certain underlying regularities or patterns. As a consequence, characterization of these phenomena in terms of probabilities and statistical averages is possible. In the case of random processes, the outcomes of random experiments are functions of time, or waveforms. The complete statistical description of the random process is difficult to obtain from the empirical data. Fortunately, analyses of random signal transmission through linear systems require knowledge of only the second-order statistics or the equivalent frequency domain description of random processes.

The chapter is organized into the following sections:

6.1   PROBABILITY CONCEPTS.
This section provides a brief review of probability theory that will prove useful in developing mathematical models of random signals and noise.

6.2   RANDOM VARIABLES.
The concept of a random variable, which assigns numbers to outcomes of a random experiment, is introduced. Next we discuss discrete random variables and characterize them in terms of probability mass functions.

6.3   CONTINUOUS RANDOM VARIABLES.
This section considers continuous random variables and their characterization in terms of cumulative distribution and probability density functions. We then study some common continuous random variables.

6.4   FUNCTIONS OF A RANDOM VARIABLE.
We discuss here the probability density function of the random variable that results from the mapping or transformation of another random variable.

6.5   STATISTICS OF RANDOM VARIABLES.
The partial description of random variables in terms of certain statistical averages, such as mean and variance, is considered in this section.

6.6   PAIRS OF RANDOM VARIABLES.
This section considers the joint and marginal distributions of a pair of random variables that result from a random experiment. Next we study the statistical averages of the functions of two random variables.

6.7   CONDITIONAL DISTRIBUTIONS.
In this section we discuss the conditional probability distributions of a random variable given the knowledge of the other random variable in the pair. This leads to the important concept of independent random variables.

6.8   JOINTLY GAUSSIAN RANDOM VARIABLES.
Here we study some properties of jointly Gaussian random variables, and we conclude the section with a discussion of the Rayleigh probability density function and the central limit theorem.

6.9   RANDOM PROCESSES: INTRODUCTION.
In this section we consider fundamental concepts of random processes and their description in terms of various order probability density functions. The mean and autocorrelation function of a random process are

introduced as key statistics to characterize the time-domain behavior of the process. Wide-sense stationary and ergodic processes, which form two very important classes of random processes, are then discussed.

6.10 POWER SPECTRUM OF A RANDOM PROCESS.

We consider the frequency-domain description of a random process in terms of its power spectral density function. Next we derive the output spectral density of a random process after transmission through a linear time-invariant system.

6.11 SOME IMPORTANT RANDOM PROCESSES.

We review some random processes that are frequently used to model random phenomena in communication systems.

6.12 NARROWBAND NOISE.

This section considers the characterization of narrowband noise that frequently occurs in carrier-modulated communication systems. Next we introduce the Ricean probability density function to model the statistics of sine waves embedded in narrowband Gaussian noise.

6.13 NOISE SOURCES IN COMMUNICATION SYSTEMS.

We discuss various physical processes that give rise to generation of noise in electronic systems and review suitable models to characterize them.

6.14 CHARACTERIZATION OF SYSTEM NOISE.

This section considers the noise performance of a system in terms of two important parameters: noise figure and effective noise temperature. We develop expressions for the system's total output noise power from a knowledge of these parameters for component subsystems.

6.15 MATLAB SIMULATION OF RANDOM PROCESSES.

We conclude this chapter with a discussion of techniques for simulation of random processes.

6.1 PROBABILITY CONCEPTS

The fundamental concept in the probability theory is the notion of a **random experiment,** which is any experiment the outcome of which cannot be predicted with certainty. A simple example is a coin tossing experiment. We know that heads and tails are possible outcomes, although the outcome (heads or tails?) of a particular experiment (toss) is uncertain. Let us define the following concepts associated with a random experiment:

- **Outcome** (ξ). The result of a random experiment.
- **Sample space** (Ω). The set of all possible outcomes of a random experiment.
- **Event** (A). Any collection of outcomes, in other words, a subset of Ω.

The empty subset ϕ is called the **null** or **impossible event,** and the whole set Ω is called the **whole** or **sure event.**

6.1.1 Relative Frequency

Although outcomes of a random experiment are unpredictable, a certain statistical regularity can be observed about them. Take, for example, the coin tossing experiment. In a large number of tries, the outcome is heads approximately 50% of the time and tails the other 50% of the time. Thus we can say that each outcome in this experiment occurs with a relative frequency of approximately 1/2. The relative frequency of an event A is defined as

$$f(A) = \frac{n_A}{n} \tag{6.1}$$

where n_A is the number of occurrences of A and n is the total number of trials. Although the fraction n_A/n may vary considerably for small values of n, it approaches a limit as $n \to \infty$. Using the relative frequency concept, the probability $P(A)$ of an event A is defined as

$$P(A) = \lim_{n \to \infty} \frac{n_A}{n} \tag{6.2}$$

This is reasonable because the probability of an event is intuitively understood to mean the likelihood of occurrence of an event.

6.1.2 Probability Axioms

The relative frequency definition of probability has great intuitive appeal. However, it requires that an experiment be performed a very large ("infinite") number of times. In the axiomatic approach, we do not begin with how to compute the probability of an event. Instead, the probability is defined as a function that assigns a real number, denoted by $P(A)$, to every event A in the sample space Ω such that:

1. $P(A) \geq 0$ $\tag{6.3}$
2. The whole event Ω will occur each time we perform the random experiment.

$$P(\Omega) = 1 \tag{6.4}$$

3. If the events $A_1, A_2, \ldots$ are **mutually exclusive** or **disjoint** (i.e., they cannot occur at the same time), the probability of their union is the sum of their probabilities.

$$P(A_1 \cup A_2 \cup \ldots) = P(A_1) + P(A_2) + \ldots \tag{6.5}$$

Equations (6.3) to (6.5) are called the **axioms** of probability. If the event A contains k outcomes $\xi_1, \xi_2, \ldots, \xi_k$, the probability $P(A)$ is given by

$$P(A) = \sum_{i=1}^{k} P(\xi_i) \tag{6.6}$$

Equation (6.6) follows by the application of (6.5) to mutually exclusive events $\{\xi_i\}$—each containing a single outcome from the set $A = \{\xi_1, \xi_2, \ldots, \xi_k\}$.

By using the preceding axioms, we can derive the following important properties of the probability function:

4. The probability of the null event is zero.

$$P(\phi) = 0 \tag{6.7}$$

5. $P(\overline{A}) = 1 - P(A)$, where $\overline{A}$ denotes the complement of A. $\tag{6.8}$
6. $P(A) \leq P(B)$ if $A \subseteq B$ $\tag{6.9}$
7. In the case of two events A and B that are not mutually exclusive, we have

$$P(A \cup B) = P(A) + P(B) - P(A \cap B) \tag{6.10}$$

Unless otherwise necessary for clarification, we shall use the notation $P(AB)$ to denote the probability of the joint event $P(A \cap B)$.

Pioneers in the Field

Andrey Nikolaevich Kolmogorov was born on April 25, 1903, in Tambov, Russia. His unwed mother died in childbirth, and he was raised by her sister in Tunoshna, near Yaroslavl, at the estate of his grandfather, a wealthy nobleman. He always felt the deepest affection for her. His father, an agriculturist by trade, was exiled from Saint Petersburg for participation in the revolutionary movement. He later disappeared and was presumed to have been killed in the Russian Civil War.

In 1920, Kolmogorov began to study at Moscow State University. While still an undergraduate, Kolmogorov obtained several important results in set theory as well as in the theory of Fourier series. In 1925, Kolmogorov graduated from Moscow State University. His pioneering work, *Analytical Methods of Probability Theory,* was published (in German) in 1931. That same year he also became a professor at Moscow University. In 1933, Kolmogorov published the book *Foundations of the Theory of Probability,* laying the modern axiomatic foundations of probability theory and establishing his reputation as the world's leading living expert in this field. In 1935, Kolmogorov became the first chairman of probability theory at Moscow State University. In 1939, he was elected a full member of the USSR Academy of Sciences. In a 1938 paper, Kolmogorov established the basic theorems for smoothing and predicting stationary stochastic processes. This paper would have major military applications during the Cold War to come. In his study of stochastic processes, especially Markov processes, Kolmogorov and the British mathematician Sydney Chapman independently developed the pivotal set of equations in the field, the Chapman-Kolmogorov equations.

Kolmogorov pursued a vigorous teaching career throughout his life, not only at the university level, but also with younger children, as he was actively involved in developing a pedagogy for gifted children in literature and music, as well as in mathematics. Kolmogorov is considered the foremost contemporary Soviet mathematician and one of the greatest mathematicians of the twentieth century.

Example 6.1

Suppose a six-sided fair dice is rolled, and let the number of dots on the top face denote the outcome. Calculate the probabilities of the following events:

a. Each outcome
b. Roll yields an odd number
c. Roll yields a number less than 4

Solution

Let i denote the outcome of each roll, that is, the number of dots on the top face. Because the dice is assumed to be fair, it implies that each outcome is equally likely. Therefore,

a. $P(i) = 1/6, i = 1, 2, \ldots, 6$
b. The event in this case is defined as $A = \{1, 3, 5\}$. Using (6.5), we can write

$$P(A) = P\{i = 1 \text{ or } 3 \text{ or } 6\} = 1/6 + 1/6 + 1/6 = 1/2$$

c. The event in this case is defined as $A = \{1, 2, 3\}$. Using (6.5), we can write

$$P(A) = P\{i = 1 \text{ or } 2 \text{ or } 3\} = 1/6 + 1/6 + 1/6 = 3/6 = 1/2$$

6.1.3 Union Bound

If the events $A_1, A_2, \ldots$ are not mutually exclusive, the probability of their union is upper-bounded by the sum of the probabilities of the constituent events. That is,

$$P(A_1 \cup A_2 \cup \ldots) \leq P(A_1) + P(A_2) + \ldots \qquad (6.11)$$

6.1.4 Conditional Probability

The probability $P(A)$ of the occurrence of an event A is commonly called its a priori probability because it reflects our knowledge of A before a certain random experiment is performed. For example, we can say that the a priori probability of observing, say 3, in a roll of a die is 1/6. In many practical situations, we are interested in the probability of the event A after we know that the outcome of a random experiment belongs to the event set B. That is, we are interested in the a posteriori probability of A knowing that B has already occurred. It is reasonable to assume that the knowledge of B provides additional information about the occurrence of A. This is captured in a new measure called the **conditional probability** $P(A|B)$ of the event A given the occurrence of the event B. It is defined as

$$P(A|B) = \frac{P(AB)}{P(B)}, \quad P(B) > 0 \tag{6.12}$$

Conditioning by event B has the effect of restricting the universe of outcomes for the event A to the subset B of Ω.

Example 6.2

Suppose a six-sided fair die is rolled. Let $A = \{\text{even number}\}$ and $B = \{\text{less than or equal to 3}\}$. Calculate $P(B)$, $P(AB)$, and $P(A|B)$.

Solution

The sample space for the experiment is

$$\Omega = \{1, 2, 3, 4, 5, 6\}$$
$$\searrow B$$

$$P(B) = P\{i = 1 \text{ or } 2 \text{ or } 3\} = 1/6 + 1/6 + 1/6 = 1/2$$

Because $A = \{2, 4, 6\}$, $AB = \{2\}$. Therefore, $P(AB) = P\{i = 2\} = 1/6$

Given the knowledge of B, $P(A|B)$ is simply the probability that the outcome is an even number (i.e., 2) in the subset $B = \{1, 2, 3\}$. Therefore, $P(A|B) = 1/3$. Note that a priori probability $P(A) = 0.5$. $P(A|B)$ can also be calculated using (6.12) as follows:

$$P(A|B) = \frac{P(AB)}{P(B)} = 1/3$$

The preceding definition (6.12) of the conditional probability satisfies all probability axioms discussed earlier. We shall sketch here the proof of axiom 3. That is, if $A_1, A_2, \ldots$ are pairwise disjoint and their union is A, then

$$P(A|B) = \sum_i P(A_i|B) \tag{6.13}$$

Using the set theory, it can be shown that

$$AB = A \cap B = (A_1 \cup A_2 \cup \ldots) \cap B = (A_1 \cap B) \cup (A_2 \cap B) \cup \ldots \tag{6.14}$$

Substituting (6.14) into (6.12) yields

$$P(A|B) = \frac{P(AB)}{P(B)} = \frac{P\{(A_1 \cap B) \cup (A_2 \cap B) \cup \dots\}}{P(B)}$$

$$= \sum_i \frac{P(A_i \cap B)}{P(B)} = \sum_i P(A_i|B) \qquad (6.15)$$

Law of Total Probability

The law of total probability allows us to calculate the probability of an event that can occur in different ways. If an event occurs when either of the subevents B_1 or $B_2 \dots$ or B_k occurs, then the probability of event A is given by

$$P(A) = \sum_{i=1}^{k} P(B_i)P(A|B_i) \qquad (6.16)$$

where $B_1 \cup B_2 \cup \dots \cup B_k = \Omega$. Thus if we know the a priori probabilities $P(B_i)$ and conditional probabilities $P(A|B_i)$ describing different ways event A can occur, the probability of event A can then be computed using (6.16). The proof is obvious from Figure 6.1. Now

$$A = \bigcup_{i=1}^{k} (AB_i) \qquad (6.17)$$

because AB_i are disjoint events.

The probability of the event A can be expressed by applying (6.5) as

$$P(A) = P\left(\bigcup_{i=1}^{k}(AB_i)\right) = \sum_{i=1}^{k} P(AB_i) = \sum_{i=1}^{k} P(B_i)P(A|B_i) \qquad (6.18)$$

For the special case when event A can occur in two different ways, the probability of the occurrence of event A is given by

$$P(A) = P(B_1)P(A|B_1) + P(B_2)P(A|B_2) \qquad (6.19)$$

$P(A|B_1)$ = Probability of event A given that B_1 occurs
$P(A|B_2)$ = Probability of event A given that B_2 occurs

where $B_1 \cup B_2 = \Omega$

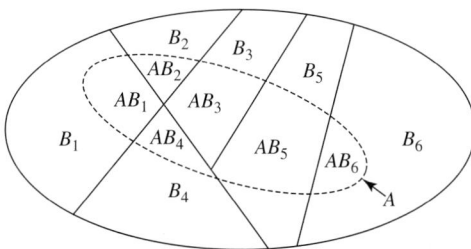

Figure 6.1 Venn diagram.

Example 6.3

A binary digital communication system transmits information by sending bits 1 and 0. Suppose the noise in the system causes, on the average, 1 out of 10,000 bits to be in error when binary 1 is transmitted and 2 out of every 10,000 bits to be in error when binary 0 is transmitted. Find the probability of bit error for the system. Assume bits 1 and 0 are transmitted with equal probability.

Solution

Let us define the following events:

B_1 = {Binary 1 transmitted}
B_2 = {Binary 0 transmitted}
e = {error in received bit}

Using this notation, we can write the following expression for the probability of bit error from (6.19):

$$P(e) = P(B_1)P[e\,|\,B_1] + P(B_2)P[e\,|\,B_2] \tag{6.20}$$

Now

$$P(B_1) = P(B_2) = 0.5$$

$$P[e\,|\,B_1] = \frac{1}{10,000} = 10^{-4}$$

$$P[e\,|\,B_2] = \frac{2}{10,000} = 2 \times 10^{-4}$$

Substituting into (6.20) yields

$$P(e) = 0.5 \times 10^{-4} + 0.5 \times 2 \times 10^{-4} = 1.5 \times 10^{-4}$$

The system noise causes, on average, 1.5 out of 10,000 bits to be in error.

Baye's Rule

Suppose $B_1, B_2, \ldots, B_k$ is a collection of events that we cannot observe directly, but we would like to make some inference about them by observing an event A. The a priori probabilities $P(B_i)$ are known to us before making the observation. Now if we have knowledge of conditional probabilities $P(A\,|\,B_i)$ after we observe A, the a posteriori probabilities $P(B_i\,|\,A)$ can be computed by applying (6.12) and (6.16) as

$$P(B_i\,|\,A) = \frac{P(A\cap B_i)}{P(A)} = \frac{P(A\,|\,B_i)P(B_i)}{\sum\limits_{i=1}^{k} P(A\,|\,B_i)P(B_i)} \tag{6.21}$$

Baye's rule is frequently stated in the following form

$$P(B\,|\,A) = \frac{P(A\,|\,B)P(B)}{P(A)} \tag{6.22}$$

Example 6.4

For the binary digital communication system in Example 6.3, suppose that during a test we find that the received bit is in error. What is the probability that the bit in error was a binary 1?

Solution

We are interested in finding the conditional probability $P[B_1|e]$. Using Baye's rule,

$$P[B_1|e] = \frac{P[e|B_1]P(B_1)}{P(e)}$$

$$= \frac{10^{-4} \times 0.5}{1.5 \times 10^{-4}} = \frac{1}{3}$$

Note that a priori probability $P(B_1) = 0.5$. However, the receipt of a bit in error provides us more information. Because $P[B_1|e] = \frac{1}{3} < 0.5$, it is more likely at this point that binary 0 must have been transmitted. This is because the conditional probability of bit error for binary 0 is twice as much as that for a binary 1.

Independent Events

A and B are said to be **independent events** if

$$P(AB) = P(A)P(B) \tag{6.23}$$

The reader should not confuse independent events with mutually exclusive events. Mutually exclusive events have no outcome in common, that is, $AB = \phi$ implying that $P(AB) = 0$. Independent events in most cases are not disjoint. Substituting (6.23) into the definition of conditional probability (6.12), we get

$$P(A|B) = \frac{P(AB)}{P(B)} = \frac{P(A)P(B)}{P(B)} = P(A) \tag{6.24}$$

The conditional probability $P(A|B)$ describes our knowledge of the event A given the information that the outcome of the random experiment is included in the event B. On the other hand $P(A|B) = P(A)$ implies that the occurrence of B does not provide any more information about the event A. It makes no difference to the likelihood of occurrence of the event A whether or not B has occurred. It is in this probabilistic sense that the events are independent. The concept of independence can be extended to k events defined on Ω. The events $A_1, A_2, \ldots, A_k$ are independent if for $m = 2, \ldots, k$,

$$P(A_{i_1} A_{i_2}, \ldots, A_{i_m}) = P(A_{i_1})P(A_{i_2}), \ldots, P(A_{i_m}) \tag{6.25}$$

where $1 \leq i_1 < i_2 < \ldots < i_m \leq k$. For $k = 3$, as an example, A_1, A_2, A_3 are independent if

$$P(A_1 A_2) = P(A_1)P(A_2) \quad P(A_1 A_3) = P(A_1)P(A_3)$$

$$P(A_2 A_3) = P(A_2)P(A_3) \quad P(A_1 A_2 A_3) = P(A_1)P(A_2)P(A_3) \tag{6.26}$$

It is obvious from (6.26) that pairwise independence alone *does not* imply independence.

Example 6.5

Consider the random experiment consisting of two consecutive tosses of a fair coin. Let A = head on first toss, B = head on second toss, and C = outcomes of the two tosses are different. Calculate $P(AB)$, $P(AC)$, and $P(BC)$.

Solution

From Figure 6.2, there are four equally likely outcomes of the random experiment each with probability = 1/4. Because $A = \{HH, HT\}$, $P(A) = 1/2$. Similarly, $P(B) = P(C) = 1/2$.

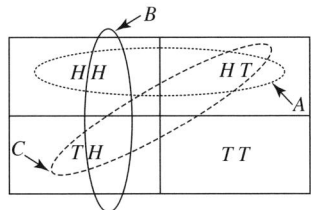

Figure 6.2 Sample space of Example 6.5.

Now $P(AB) = P(HH) = 1/4$. Therefore, $P(AB) = P(A)P(B)$, implying that events A and B are independent. Also,

$P(AC) = P(HT) = 1/4 = P(A)P(C)$, implying that events A and C are independent.
$P(BC) = P(TH) = 1/4 = P(B)P(C)$, implying that events B and C are independent.

Therefore A, B, and C are pairwise independent. Now $P(AB|C) = P(\phi) = 0$. But $P(AB) = 1/4$. Thus, $P(AB|C) \neq P(AB)$, implying that A, B, and C are not independent.

6.2   RANDOM VARIABLES

In many applications, measurements and observations are conveniently described by numbers. These numbers vary each time these measurements and observations are repeated. For example,

- Number of call requests arriving/sec at telephone company central office switch.
- Number of photons arriving at the photo detector during a bit interval.
- Number of integrated circuits (ICs) passing the final test from each wafer.

The real numbers in each of these examples represent possible outcomes of an underlying random experiment.

A **random variable** is defined as a rule that assigns a real number to each possible outcome of a random experiment. Thus, random variable is a function that maps every outcome ξ in sample space Ω to a unique real number x as illustrated in Figure 6.3.

We will denote random variables in a bold font $x, y, \ldots$ and the values assumed by them will be displayed by the lowercase letters $x, y, \ldots$. Random variables may be discrete, continuous, or mixed, depending on the range of values they can assume.

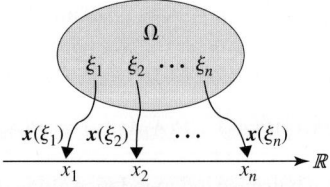

Figure 6.3 Conceptual model of a random variable.

6.2.1 Discrete Random Variables

A **discrete** random variable x can take on a **countable** number of values $x_1, x_2, x_3, \ldots$ with probabilities $P\{x = x_i\}$, $i = 0, 1, 2, \ldots$ Examples of discrete random variables include

1. Number of packet arrivals at a network router in a fixed interval
2. Number of calls serviced by a telephone company central office switch at any time
3. Number of defective chips from a semiconductor wafer
4. Number of photons arriving at the photodetector during a bit interval in an optical receiver

The set $S_x = \{x_1, x_2, x_3, \ldots\}$ of values assumed by the discrete random variable x is called its **range.**

A **probability mass function (PMF)** $p_x(x)$ completely characterizes a discrete random variable. It is defined as

$$p_x(x_i) = P\{x = x_i\} \tag{6.27}$$

$P\{x = x_i\}$ is calculated by adding the probabilities of all outcomes ξ in Ω such that $x(\xi) = x_i$. That is,

$$p_x(x_i) = P\{x(\xi) = x_i | \xi \in \Omega\} \tag{6.28}$$

Because $p_x(x_i)$ is a probability, it is a number satisfying

$$0 \le p_x(x_i) \le 1 \tag{6.29}$$

$$\sum_i p_x(x_i) = \sum_i P\{x(\xi) = x_i | \xi \in \Omega\} = 1 \tag{6.30}$$

Equation (6.30) is obvious as it represents the sum of probabilities of all possible outcomes ξ in the sample space Ω of the random experiment.

Example 6.6

Suppose a six-sided fair dice is rolled twice. Let $F = \{\text{outcome of first roll}\}$ and $S = \{\text{outcome of second roll}\}$. Let $x = \max(F, S)$. Calculate the PMF of x.

Solution

The sample space of random variable x is displayed in Figure 6.4. The random variable $x = \max(F, S)$ assumes values $\{1, 2, 3, 4, 5, 6\}$. From Figure 6.4, we can define the following mapping between values of random variable and corresponding outcomes:

$$x(\xi) = \begin{cases} 1, \ \xi = \{(1, 1)\} \\ 2, \ \xi = \{(1, 2), (2, 2), (2, 1)\} \\ 3, \ \xi = \{(1, 3), (2, 3), (3, 3), (3, 1), (3, 2)\} \\ 4, \ \xi = \{(1, 4), (2, 4), (3, 4), (4, 4), (4, 3), (4, 2), (4, 1)\} \\ 5, \ \xi = \{(1, 5), (2, 5), (3, 5), (4, 5), (5, 5), (5, 1), (5, 2), (5, 3), (5, 4)\} \\ 6, \ \xi = \{(1, 6), (2, 6), (3, 6), (4, 6), (5, 6), (6, 6), (6, 1), (6, 2), (6, 3), (6, 4), (6, 5)\} \end{cases}$$

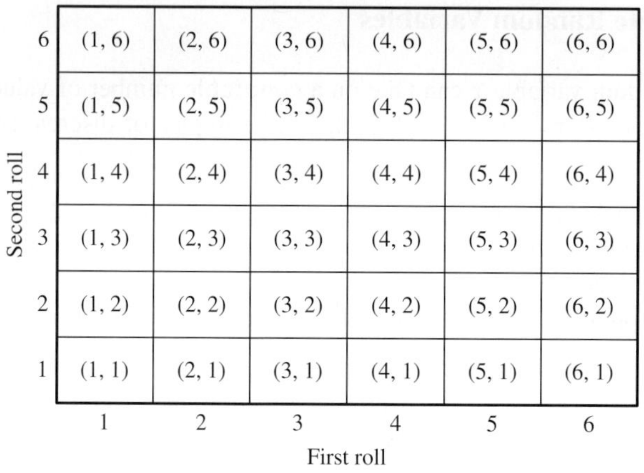

Figure 6.4 Sample space of Example 6.6.

We can now write the PMF of x as follows:

$$p_x(1) = P\{x = 1\} = 1/36$$
$$p_x(2) = P\{x = 2\} = 3/36 = 1/12$$
$$p_x(3) = P\{x = 3\} = 5/36$$
$$p_x(4) = P\{x = 4\} = 7/36$$
$$p_x(5) = P\{x = 5\} = 9/36 = 1/4$$
$$p_x(6) = P\{x = 6\} = 11/36$$

The **cumulative distribution function (CDF)** of a discrete random variable x is defined as

$$F_x(x) = P\{x \le x\} = \sum_{i:x_i \le x} p_x(x_i) \tag{6.31}$$

For any real number x, the CDF measures the probability that the random variable x is no larger than x. The CDF of a discrete random variable is a stair-step function with jump discontinuities at $x = x_i$ where the magnitude of the jump equals $P\{x = x_i\} = p_x(x_i)$. For adjacent points $x_{i-1} < x_i$,

$$p_x(x_i) = F_x(x_i) - F_x(x_{i-1}) \tag{6.32}$$

Figure 6.5 displays the CDF and PMF of a discrete random variable. We will study the properties of CDF in Section 6.3.

6.2.2 Some Common Discrete Random Variables

Here we introduce four important discrete random variables:

- Uniform
- Bernoulli
- Binomial
- Poisson

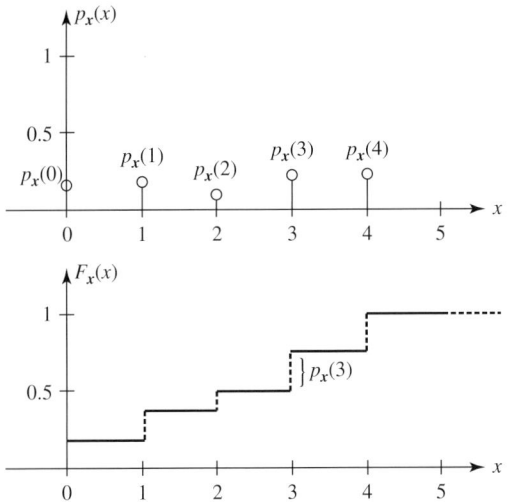

Figure 6.5 PMF and CDF of a discrete random variable.

Uniform Random Variable

When an experiment results in a finite number of "equally likely" or "totally random" outcomes, we model it with uniform random variables. x is a uniformly distributed random variable assuming values from the set $\{0, 1, 2, \ldots, M-1\}$ if

$$P\{x = k\} = \frac{1}{M}, \qquad k = 0, 1, 2, \ldots, M-1 \tag{6.33}$$

Its PMF can be written from (6.33) as

$$p_x(x) = \begin{cases} 1/M, & k = 0, 1, 2, \ldots, M-1 \\ 0, & \text{otherwise} \end{cases} \tag{6.34}$$

Bernoulli Random Variable

Bernoulli random variables are binary valued. A binary random variable x assumes values, say 0 and 1, with probabilities

$$P\{x = 1\} = p$$
$$P\{x = 0\} = 1 - p \tag{6.35}$$

Its PMF can be written from (6.35) as

$$p_x(x) = \begin{cases} p, & x = 1 \\ 1 - p, & x = 0 \end{cases} \tag{6.36}$$

where $0 < p < 1$. Bernoulli random variables are used to model random experiments whose outcomes are binary, for example, whether a bit is received in error, or whether a packet is dropped by a congested router.

Binomial Random Variable

Binomial random variables model the number of successes in a sequence of n independent trials of a random experiment, each of which yields success with probability p. x is a binomial random variable if its PMF is of the form

$$p_x(k) = P\{x = k\} = P\{k \text{ success in } n \text{ trials}\}$$

$$= \binom{n}{k} p^k (1 - p)^{n-k}, \; k = 0, 1, 2, \ldots, n \tag{6.37}$$

where $0 < p < 1$ and $n \geq 1$.

Example 6.7

a. If a fair coin is tossed 10 times, what is the probability of observing 3 heads (and 7 tails)?
b. Using an unfair coin such that the probability of a head $p = 0.35$ and the probability of a tail $(1 - p) = 0.65$, what is the probability of observing 5 heads in 10 tosses?

Solution

$$p_x(k) = P\{k \text{ successes in } n \text{ trials}\} = \binom{n}{k} p^k (1 - p)^{n-k}$$

where p = probability of success (observing a head)

a. $P\{3 \text{ heads in } 10 \text{ trials}\} = \binom{10}{3}(0.5)^3(0.5)^7 = 0.117$

b. $P\{5 \text{ heads in } 10 \text{ trials}\} = \binom{10}{5}(0.35)^5(0.65)^5 = 0.154$

Poisson Random Variable

The Poisson random variable x models the number of events (k) occurring in any interval $(t_o, t_o + \tau)$ if the occurrence of these events, at an average rate λ, is independent of t_o and depends only on the length of interval τ. It is common in the literature to refer to the occurrence of a Poisson event as an arrival. x is a Poisson random variable if its PMF is of the form

$$p_x(k) = P(x = k) = P\{k \text{ arrivals in a time interval } \tau\}$$

$$= e^{-\lambda\tau}\frac{(\lambda\tau)^k}{k!}, \; k = 0, 1, 2, \ldots, \infty \tag{6.38}$$

where λ = average arrival rate

Example 6.8

The number of call requests to a telco central office over a 1-second interval is a Poisson random variable x with an average arrival rate of $\lambda = 0.5$ call requests per second.

a. Calculate the probability that there are no requests in an interval of 0.3 seconds.
b. What is the probability that there are no more than three requests in an interval of 2 seconds?

Solution

a. Because $\lambda = 0.5$ and $\tau = 0.3$, the PMF of x can be written as

$$p_x(k) = e^{-0.15}\frac{(0.15)^k}{k!}, \quad k = 0, 1, 2, \ldots, \infty$$

The probability of the event that there are zero call arrivals in a 0.3-second interval is

$$p_x(0) = e^{-0.15} = 0.861$$

b. Because $\lambda = 0.5$ and $\tau = 2$, the PMF of x can be written as

$$p_x(k) = e^{-1}\frac{(1)^k}{k!} = \frac{e^{-1}}{k!}, \quad k = 0, 1, 2, \ldots, \infty$$

The probability of the event that there are no more than 3 arrivals in a 2-second interval is

$$P\{\text{no more than 3 arrivals}\} = P\{0 \text{ or } 1 \text{ or } 2 \text{ or } 3 \text{ arrivals}\}$$

$$= p_x(k = 0) + p_x(k = 1) + p_x(k = 2) + p_x(k = 3)$$

$$= \frac{e^{-1}}{0!} + \frac{e^{-1}}{1!} + \frac{e^{-1}}{2!} + \frac{e^{-1}}{3!} = 0.981$$

6.3 CONTINUOUS RANDOM VARIABLES

A **continuous random variable** x takes values in a continuous set of numbers. The range S_x of x may consist of the whole real line $\mathbb{R}$ or an interval thereof. Continuous random variables model many real-life phenomena that include file download time on the Internet, voltage across a resistor, and the phase of a carrier signal produced by a radio transmitter. One characteristic that distinguishes a continuous random variable from a discrete one is that the probability of an individual outcome is zero. That is, $P\{x = x\} = 0$, where x is any number in the range of x. Therefore, we cannot use the probability mass function $p_x(x)$ for a continuous random variable. However, we can use the cumulative distribution function as an appropriate probability measure in this case.

The **cumulative distribution function (CDF)** of a continuous random variable x is defined as

$$F_x(x) = P\{x \le x\} \tag{6.39}$$

Note that $F_x(x)$ measures the probability of the event $A = \{\xi \in \Omega : x(\xi) \le x\}$. While the concept of the CDF applies to any random variable, there is one key difference between CDFs of continuous and discrete random variables. Whereas the CDF of a discrete random variable is a staircase function, it is a continuous function for the continuous random variable. For any random variable x,

1. $0 \le F_x(x) \le 1$ (6.40)

2. $\lim_{x \to -\infty} F_x(x) = 0$ and $\lim_{x \to \infty} F_x(x) = 1$ (6.41)

3. $P\{a < x \le b\} = F_x(b) - F_x(a)$ (6.42)

4. $F_x(x)$ is nondecreasing

From (6.42), the probability that x is in the interval Δx_1 to the right of x_1 is

$$P\{x_1 < x \leq x_1 + \Delta x_1\} = F_x(x_1 + \Delta x_1) - F_x(x_1)$$

$$= \frac{F_x(x_1 + \Delta x_1) - F_x(x_1)}{\Delta x_1} \Delta x_1 \qquad (6.43)$$

In the limit as $\Delta x_1 \to 0$

$$P\{x_1 < x \leq x_1 + \Delta x_1\} = \left. \frac{dF_x(x)}{dx} \right|_{x=x_1} \Delta x_1 \qquad (6.44)$$

We conclude from (6.44) that the derivative of CDF evaluated at x_1 is an indicator of probability of observing the random variable x *near* x_1.

The **probability density function (PDF)**, $f_x(x)$, of a continuous random variable x is derivative of its CDF. That is,

$$f_x(x) = \frac{dF_x(x)}{dx} \qquad (6.45)$$

We observe from (6.44) and (6.45) that $f_x(x_1)$ indicates the probability that x is in the close vicinity of x_1. Like CDF, the PDF also provides a complete description of the random variable x.

The important properties of $f_x(x)$ include

a. $f_x(x) \geq 0$ for all x (6.46)

b. $F_x(a) = \displaystyle\int_{-\infty}^{a} f_x(x)dx$ (6.47)

c. $\displaystyle\int_{a}^{b} f_x(x)dx = P\{a < x \leq b\}$ (6.48)

d. $\displaystyle\int_{-\infty}^{\infty} f_x(x)dx = 1$ (6.49)

The proofs of these statements follow.

a. Because $F_x(x)$ is nondecreasing,

$$f_x(x) = \frac{dF_x(x)}{dx} = \lim_{\Delta x \to 0} \frac{F_x(x + \Delta x) - F_x(x)}{\Delta x} \geq 0$$

b. The second result follows from the definition of $F_x(x)$.

c. $\displaystyle\int_{a}^{b} f_x(x)dx = \int_{-\infty}^{b} f_x(x)dx - \int_{-\infty}^{a} f_x(x)dx = F_x(b) - F_x(a) = P\{a < x \leq b\}$

d. $\displaystyle\int_{-\infty}^{\infty} f_x(x)dx = F_x(\infty) - F_x(-\infty) = 1 - 0 = 1$

As a special case of (6.48), the probability of observing x in the interval $(x, x + \Delta x)$, as $\Delta x \to 0$, is given by

$$P\{x \leq x \leq x + \Delta x\} = f_x(x)\Delta x \qquad (6.50)$$

Example 6.9

The PDF of a random variable is given by

$$f_x(x) = \begin{cases} Ce^{-x}, & x \geq 0 \\ 0, & \text{otherwise} \end{cases} \qquad (6.51)$$

Find

a. The constant C
b. The CDF $F_x(x)$
c. $P\{0 < x \leq 5\}$
d. $P\{-3 < x \leq 3\}$

Solution

a. Substituting (6.51) into (6.49) yields

$$1 = \int_0^\infty Ce^{-x}dx = C\frac{e^{-x}}{-1}\bigg|_0^\infty = -C(0 - 1) = C \Rightarrow C = 1$$

b. For $x > 0$,

$$F_x(x) = \int_0^x e^{-t}dt = \frac{e^{-t}}{-1}\bigg|_0^x = 1 - e^{-x}$$

Therefore,

$$F_x(x) = \begin{cases} 1 - e^{-x}, & x \geq 0 \\ 0, & x < 0 \end{cases}$$

c. $P\{0 < x \leq 5\} = F_x(5) - F_x(0) = 1 - e^{-5} \approx 0.993$
d. $P\{-3 < x \leq 3\} = F_x(3) - F_x(-3) = 1 - e^{-3} \approx 0.950$

6.3.1 Some Common Continuous Random Variables

We now introduce three important continuous random variables:

- Uniform
- Gaussian
- Exponential

Uniform Random Variable

x is a uniform continuous random variable if its PDF is given by

$$f_x(x) = \begin{cases} \dfrac{1}{b - a}, & a \leq x \leq b \\ 0, & \text{otherwise} \end{cases} \qquad (6.52)$$

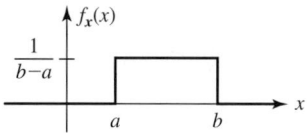

Figure 6.6 PDF of the uniform random variable $\mathcal{U}[a, b]$.

The uniform random variable, denoted by $\mathcal{U}[a, b]$, is a good model when each outcome of a random experiment is equally likely, and constrained to lie in the interval $[b, a]$, $b > a$. Figure 6.6 displays the PDF of a uniformly distributed random variable.

Example 6.10

In the digital carrier modulation schemes to be studied in Chapter 11, the phase offset between the transmitter and the receiver is modeled by a random variable θ that is uniformly distributed between $[-\pi, \pi]$. Find

a. $P\{\theta \leq 0\}$
b. $P\{\theta \leq \pi/4\}$

Solution

Because θ is uniformly distributed between $[-\pi, \pi]$, its PDF is given 0 factorial by

$$f_\theta(\theta) = \begin{cases} \dfrac{1}{2\pi}, & -\pi \leq \theta \leq \pi \\ 0, & \text{otherwise} \end{cases}$$

a. $P\{\theta \leq 0\} = \displaystyle\int_{-\infty}^{0} f_\theta(\theta)d\theta = \int_{-\pi}^{0} \frac{1}{2\pi}d\theta = \frac{\pi}{2\pi} = \frac{1}{2}$

b. $P\{\theta \leq \pi/4\} = \displaystyle\int_{-\infty}^{\pi/4} f_\theta(\theta)d\theta = \int_{-\pi}^{\pi/4} \frac{1}{2\pi}d\theta = \frac{\dfrac{\pi}{4} + \pi}{2\pi} = \frac{5}{8}$

Gaussian or Normal Random Variable

x is a normal or Gaussian random variable if its PDF is given by

$$f_x(x) = \frac{1}{\sqrt{2\pi\sigma_x^2}}e^{-(x-m_x)^2/2\sigma_x^2} \tag{6.53}$$

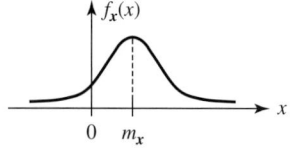

Figure 6.7 Gaussian or normal random variable PDF.

Figure 6.7 displays the bell-shaped PDF curve, symmetric around the parameter m_x—called the **mean** of the Gaussian random variable. m_x can assume any finite value. The parameter σ_x is called the **standard deviation** and can assume any finite positive value. The square of the standard deviation, σ_x^2, is called the **variance.** A Gaussian random variable with mean m_x and variance σ_x^2 is denoted by $\mathcal{N}(m_x, \sigma_x^2)$. The random variable $\mathcal{N}(0, 1)$ is usually called **standard normal.**

The CDF $F_x(x)$ of the $\mathcal{N}(m_x, \sigma_x^2)$ Gaussian random variable x is obtained by substituting (6.53) into (6.47) as

$$F_x(x) = P\{x \leq x\} = \int_{-\infty}^{x} \frac{1}{\sqrt{2\pi\sigma_x^2}}e^{-(t-m_x)^2/2\sigma_x^2}dt \tag{6.54}$$

There is no closed-form solution for the integral on the right-hand side of (6.54). However, it can be written in terms of the Q-function where

$$Q(a) = P\{x > a\} = \frac{1}{\sqrt{2\pi}} \int_a^\infty e^{-y^2/2} dy \qquad (6.55)$$

The Q-function represents the area under the tail of a standard normal random variable and is widely tabulated. Some interesting properties of the Q-function are

$$Q(0) = \frac{1}{2} \qquad (6.56)$$

$$Q(-\infty) = 1 \qquad (6.57)$$

$$Q(-x) = \frac{1}{\sqrt{2\pi}} \int_{-x}^\infty e^{-y^2/2} dy = \frac{1}{\sqrt{2\pi}} \int_{-\infty}^\infty e^{-y^2/2} dy - \frac{1}{\sqrt{2\pi}} \int_x^\infty e^{-y^2/2} dy = 1 - Q(x) \quad (6.58)$$

Table 6.1 displays the values of this function for various values of x. By making the change of variable $z = \dfrac{m_x - t}{\sigma_x}$, the CDF in (6.54) can be expressed in terms of Q-function as

$$F_x(x) = \int_{-\infty}^{\frac{x-m_x}{\sigma_x}} \frac{1}{\sqrt{2\pi}} e^{-z^2/2} dz = 1 - \int_{\frac{x-m_x}{\sigma_x}}^\infty \frac{1}{\sqrt{2\pi}} e^{-z^2/2} dz$$

$$= 1 - Q\left(\frac{x - m_x}{\sigma_x}\right) = Q\left(\frac{m_x - x}{\sigma_x}\right) \qquad (6.59)$$

Using (6.59), we can write

$$P\{x > x\} = 1 - F_x(x) = 1 - Q\left(\frac{m_x - x}{\sigma_x}\right) = Q\left(\frac{x - m_x}{\sigma_x}\right) \qquad (6.60)$$

The Gaussian random variable is the most frequently used random variable in the analysis and modeling of communication systems. Thermal noise, which is ubiquitously present in communication systems, has a Gaussian PDF.

Example 6.11

A Gaussian random variable x has the probability density function

$$f_x(x) = \frac{1}{\sqrt{30\pi}} \exp[-(x - 12)^2/30]$$

Express the following probabilities in terms of the Q-function:

a. $P(x \le 11)$
b. $P(10 < x \le 12)$
c. $P(11 < x \le 13)$
d. $P(9 < x \le 12)$

Solution

a. $P(x \leq 11) = Q\left(\dfrac{12 - 11}{\sqrt{15}}\right) = Q\left(1/\sqrt{15}\right)$

b. $P(10 < x \leq 12) = P\{x \leq 12\} - P\{x \leq 10\} = Q(0) - Q\left(2/\sqrt{15}\right)$

c. $P(11 < x \leq 13) = Q\left(-1/\sqrt{15}\right) - Q\left(1/\sqrt{15}\right) = 1 - 2Q\left(1/\sqrt{15}\right)$

d. $P(9 < x \leq 12) = Q(0) - Q\left(3/\sqrt{15}\right) = 0.5 - Q\left(3/\sqrt{15}\right)$

Table 6.1 Values of Q-function

x	$Q(x)$	x	$Q(x)$	x	$Q(x)$	x	$Q(x)$
0.00	0.5	2.30	0.010724	4.55	2.6823×10^{-6}	6.80	5.231×10^{-12}
0.05	0.48006	2.35	0.0093867	4.60	2.1125×10^{-6}	6.85	3.6925×10^{-12}
0.10	0.46017	2.40	0.0081975	4.65	1.6597×10^{-6}	6.90	2.6001×10^{-12}
0.15	0.44038	2.45	0.0071428	4.70	1.3008×10^{-6}	6.95	1.8264×10^{-12}
0.20	0.42074	2.50	0.0062097	4.75	1.0171×10^{-6}	7.00	1.2798×10^{-12}
0.25	0.40129	2.55	0.0053861	4.80	7.9333×10^{-7}	7.05	8.9459×10^{-13}
0.30	0.38209	2.60	0.0046612	4.85	6.1731×10^{-7}	7.10	6.2378×10^{-13}
0.35	0.36317	2.65	0.0040246	4.90	4.7918×10^{-7}	7.15	4.3389×10^{-13}
0.40	0.34458	2.70	0.003467	4.95	3.7107×10^{-7}	7.20	3.0106×10^{-13}
0.45	0.32636	2.75	0.0029798	5.00	2.8665×10^{-7}	7.25	2.0839×10^{-13}
0.50	0.30854	2.80	0.0025551	5.05	2.2091×10^{-7}	7.30	1.4388×10^{-13}
0.55	0.29116	2.85	0.002186	5.10	$1.e983 \times 10^{-7}$	7.35	9.9103×10^{-14}
0.60	0.27425	2.90	0.0018658	5.15	1.3024×10^{-7}	7.40	6.8092×10^{-14}
0.65	0.25785	2.95	0.0015889	5.20	9.9644×10^{-8}	7.45	4.667×10^{-14}
0.70	0.24196	3.00	0.0013499	5.25	7.605×10^{-8}	7.50	3.1909×10^{-14}
0.75	0.22663	3.05	0.0011442	5.30	5.7901×10^{-8}	7.55	2.1763×10^{-14}
0.80	0.21186	3.10	0.0009676	5.35	4.3977×10^{-8}	7.60	1.4807×10^{-14}
0.85	0.19766	3.15	0.00081635	5.40	3.332×10^{-8}	7.65	1.0049×10^{-14}
0.90	0.18406	3.20	0.00068714	5.45	2.5185×10^{-8}	7.70	6.8033×10^{-15}
0.95	0.17106	3.25	0.00057703	5.50	1.899×10^{-8}	7.75	4.5946×10^{-15}
1.00	0.15866	3.30	0.00048342	5.55	1.4283×10^{-8}	7.80	3.0954×10^{-15}
1.05	0.14686	3.35	0.00040406	5.60	1.0718×10^{-8}	7.85	2.0802×10^{-15}
1.10	0.13567	3.40	0.00033693	5.65	8.0224×10^{-9}	7.90	1.3945×10^{-15}
1.15	0.12507	3.45	0.00028029	5.70	5.9904×10^{-3}	7.95	9.3256×10^{-16}
1.20	0.11507	3.50	0.00023263	5.75	4.4622×10^{-9}	8.00	6.221×10^{-16}
1.25	0.10565	3.55	0.00019262	5.80	3.3157×10^{-9}	8.05	4.1397×10^{-16}
1.30	0.0968	3.60	0.00015911	5.85	2.4579×10^{-9}	8.10	2.748×10^{-16}
1.35	0.088508	3.65	0.00013112	5.90	1.8175×10^{-9}	8.15	1.8196×10^{-16}
1.40	0.080757	3.70	0.0001078	5.95	1.3407×10^{-9}	8.20	1.2019×10^{-16}
1.45	0.073529	3.75	8.8417×10^{-5}	6.00	9.8659×10^{-10}	8.25	7.9197×10^{-17}
1.50	0.066807	3.80	7.2348×10^{-5}	6.05	7.2423×10^{-10}	8.30	5.2056×10^{-17}
1.55	0.060571	3.85	5.9059×10^{-5}	6.10	5.3034×10^{-10}	8.35	3.4131×10^{-17}
1.60	0.054799	3.90	4.8096×10^{-5}	6.15	3.8741×10^{-10}	8.40	2.2324×10^{-17}
1.65	0.049471	3.95	3.9076×10^{-5}	6.20	2.8232×10^{-10}	8.45	1.4565×10^{-17}
1.70	0.044565	4.00	3.1671×10^{-5}	6.25	2.0523×10^{-10}	8.50	9.4795×10^{-18}
1.75	0.040059	4.05	2.5609×10^{-5}	6.30	1.4882×10^{-10}	8.55	6.1544×10^{-18}
1.80	0.03593	4.10	2.0658×10^{-5}	6.35	1.0766×10^{-10}	8.60	3.9858×10^{-18}
1.85	0.032157	4.15	1.6624×10^{-5}	6.40	7.7688×10^{-11}	8.65	2.575×10^{-18}
1.90	0.028717	4.20	1.3346×10^{-5}	6.45	5.5925×10^{-11}	8.70	1.6594×10^{-18}
1.95	0.025588	4.25	1.0689×10^{-5}	6.50	4.016×10^{-11}	8.75	1.0668×10^{-18}
2.00	0.02275	4.30	8.5399×10^{-6}	6.55	2.8769×10^{-11}	8.80	6.8408×10^{-19}
2.05	0.020182	4.35	6.8069×10^{-6}	6.60	2.0558×10^{-11}	8.85	4.376×10^{-19}
2.10	0.017864	4.40	5.4125×10^{-6}	6.65	1.4655×10^{-11}	8.90	2.7923×10^{-19}
2.15	0.015778	4.45	4.2935×10^{-6}	6.70	1.0421×10^{-11}	8.95	1.7774×10^{-19}
2.20	0.013903	4.50	3.3977×10^{-6}	6.75	7.3923×10^{-12}	9.00	1.1286×10^{-19}
2.25	0.012224						

Exponential Random Variable

x is an exponential random variable if its PDF is given by

$$f_x(x) = \begin{cases} \lambda e^{-\lambda x}, & x \geq 0 \\ 0, & \text{otherwise} \end{cases} \qquad (6.61)$$

where $\lambda > 0$.

The exponential random variable is frequently used to model lifetimes (e.g., duration of a phone call) or waiting times (e.g., until some event happens). Figure 6.8 displays the PDF of an exponential random variable. As λ increases, the height increases and the width decreases. It is easy to show that the PDF integrates to one.

$$\int_0^\infty \lambda e^{-\lambda x} dx = -e^{-\lambda x}\Big|_0^\infty = -0 + 1 = 1$$

For $x \geq 0$,

$$F_x(x) = P\{x \leq x\} = \int_0^x \lambda e^{-\lambda t} dt = \int_0^x \lambda e^{-\lambda x} dx = -e^{-\lambda t}\Big|_0^x = 1 - e^{-\lambda x}$$

Therefore, the CDF of an exponential random variable can be written as

$$F_x(x) = \begin{cases} 1 - e^{-\lambda x}, & x \geq 0 \\ 0, & x < 0 \end{cases} \qquad (6.62)$$

From (6.62), we can write for $x \geq 0$

$$P\{x > x\} = 1 - P\{x \leq x\} = 1 - F_x(x) = e^{-\lambda x} \qquad (6.63)$$

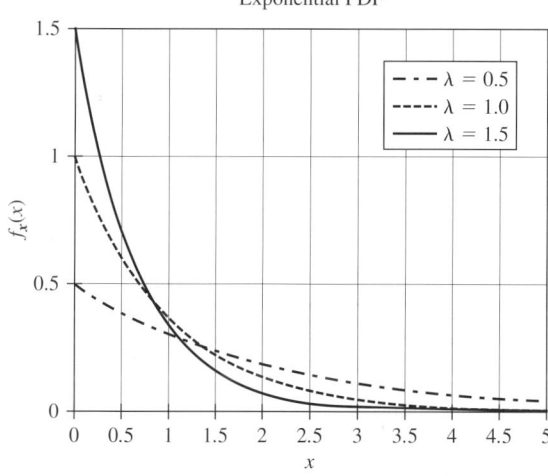
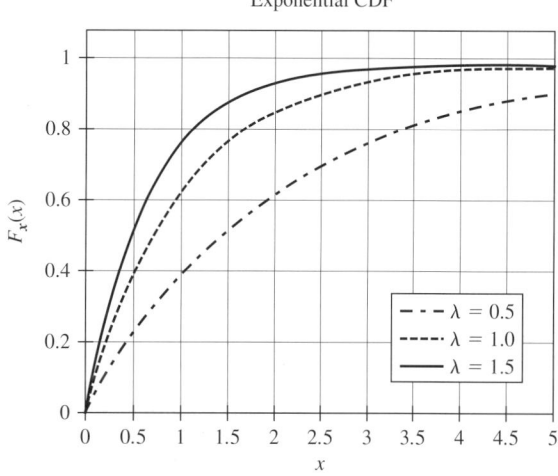

Figure 6.8 PDF and CDF of the exponential random variable.

Example 6.12

The holding time of a telephone call is modeled as an exponential random variable x with PDF

$$f_x(x) = \begin{cases} 0.25e^{-0.25x}, & x \geq 0 \\ 0, & \text{otherwise} \end{cases}$$

a. What is the probability that a telephone call lasts more than 5 minutes?
b. Calculate the probability that a telephone conversation lasts between 1 and 3 minutes.

Solution

a. Using (6.63), we have

$$P\{x > 5\} = e^{-0.25 \times 5} = 0.286$$

b. $P\{1 \leq x \leq 3\} = F_x(3) - F_x(1) = 1 - e^{-0.25 \times 3} - 1 + e^{-0.25} = 0.306$

6.3.2 PDFs for Discrete and Mixed Random Variables

Strictly speaking, a discrete random variable does not have a PDF. However, we can define a PDF for a discrete random variable by use of the delta function. The PDF of a discrete random variable has the form

$$f_x(x) = \sum_i p_x(x_i)\delta(x - x_i) \tag{6.64}$$

where $x_i \in S_x$. Figure 6.9 illustrates the PDF $f_x(x)$ of the discrete random variable x whose PMF and CDF are shown in Figure 6.5. Note that the weight of the impulse at $x = x_i$ equals the probability $P\{x = x_i\}$.

The CDF of a continuous random variable is continuous everywhere, while it is a staircase function (that is, consists of only jumps) for a discrete random variable. For a **mixed random variable,** the CDF is continuous, in general, except for a countable number of jumps as displayed in Figure 6.10(a). The PDF of a mixed random variable

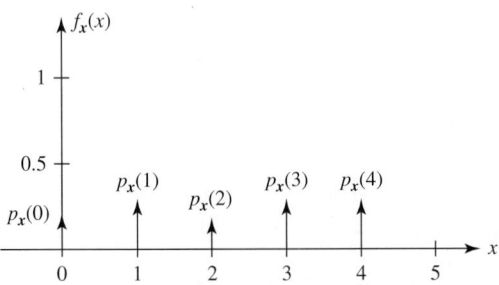

Figure 6.9 PDF of a discrete random variable.

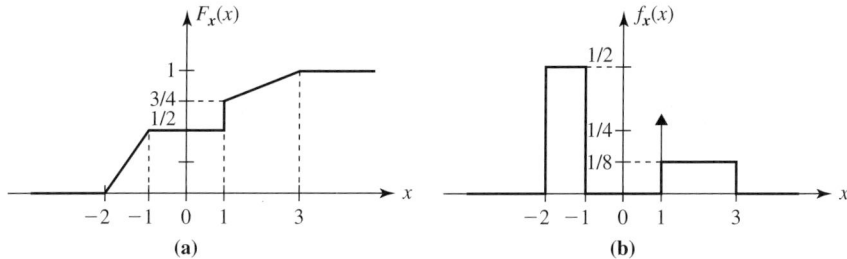

Figure 6.10 CDF and PDF for a mixed random variable.

contains impulses as well as nonzero, finite-valued continuous part(s). The PDF of a mixed random variable is of the form

$$f_x(x) = \sum_i p_x(x_i)\delta(x - x_i) + f_x^c(x) \qquad (6.65)$$

where $f_x^c(x)$ is the continuous portion without any impulses. Figure 6.10(b) illustrates the PDF corresponding to the CDF in Figure 6.10(a) for a mixed random variable x. The impulse occurs because the derivative of a step function is a delta function. The weight of the delta function equals the magnitude of the jump.

6.4 FUNCTIONS OF A RANDOM VARIABLE

We are frequently interested in statistics of a random signal after passage through a system. Let x be a random variable whose PDF is known and suppose that $g(.)$ denotes the transfer characteristic of a linear or nonlinear system. We want to determine the PDF $f_y(y)$ of the new random variable y related to x by

$$y = g(x) \qquad (6.66)$$

6.4.1 Case I: $g(x)$ Monotonically Increasing or Decreasing

This implies that $g(x)$ maps each x in the range of random variable x to only one value of y. For a monotonically increasing function $g(x)$, the interval $(x, x + \Delta x)$ is mapped into a unique interval $(y, y + \Delta y)$ as shown in Figure 6.11. Therefore, the probability of observing y in the interval $(y, y + \Delta y)$ is the same as the probability of observing x in the interval $(x, x + \Delta x)$.

$$P\{x \le x \le x + \Delta x\} = P\{y \le y \le y + \Delta y\} \qquad (6.67)$$

Using (6.50), we can express (6.67) as

$$f_x(x)\Delta x = f_y(y)\Delta y \qquad (6.68)$$

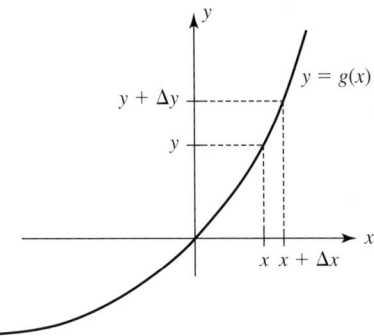

Figure 6.11 Monotonically increasing function of a random variable.

Similarly, for a monotonic decreasing function $g(x)$, the probability that x lies in the interval $(x, x + \Delta x)$ is the same as the probability that y lies in the interval $(y, y - \Delta y)$. That is,

$$f_x(x)\Delta x = -f_y(y)\Delta y \tag{6.69}$$

Combining (6.68) and (6.69), we get

$$f_y(y) = \frac{f_x(x)}{|dy/dx|} = \frac{f_x(x)}{|g'(x)|} \tag{6.70}$$

Because $f_y(y)$ is a function of y, the right-hand side of (6.70) is expressed in terms of y by substituting $x = g^{-1}(y)$. For a monotonically increasing or decreasing function, such an inverse exists, yielding

$$f_y(y) = \left.\frac{f_x(x)}{|g'(x)|}\right|_{x=g^{-1}(y)} \tag{6.71}$$

Example 6.13

Consider the linear transfer characteristic

$$y = g(x) = ax + b$$

If the input random variable x is $\mathcal{N}(0, 1)$, determine the PDF of y.

Solution

The PDF of y is given from (6.71) by

$$f_y(y) = \left.\frac{f_x(x)}{|g'(x)|}\right|_{x=g^{-1}(y)}$$

Substituting $g'(x) = a$ and $x = (y - b)/a$ yields

$$f_y(y) = \left.\frac{f_x(x)}{a}\right|_{x=(y-b)/a} = \frac{1}{a}f_x\left(\frac{y-b}{a}\right)$$

Now the PDF of x is

$$f_x(x) = \frac{1}{\sqrt{2\pi}}e^{-x^2/2}$$

Substituting into (6.71), the output PDF is given by

$$f_y(y) = \left.\frac{1}{a}\frac{1}{\sqrt{2\pi}}e^{-x^2/2}\right|_{x=(y-b)/a} = \frac{1}{\sqrt{2\pi a^2}}e^{-(y-b)^2/2a^2}$$

6.4.2   Case II: Arbitrary $g(x)$

In this case $g(x)$ consists of piecewise monotonic segments over the range of random variable x. Figure 6.12 shows $g(x)$ with three piecewise monotonic segments. As a result the intervals $(x_1, x_1 + \Delta x_1)$, $(x_2, x_2 + \Delta x_2)$, and $(x_3, x_3 + \Delta x_3)$ are mapped by $g(x)$ into the same interval $(y, y + \Delta y)$. The probability that y lies in the interval $(y, y + \Delta y)$ is, therefore, equal to the probability that x lies in any one of the three disjoint intervals $(x_1, x_1 + \Delta x_1)$, $(x_2 - \Delta x_2, x_2)$, and $(x_3, x_3 + \Delta x_3)$. Hence we have

$$f_y(y)|\Delta y| = f_x(x_1)|\Delta x_1| + f_x(x_2)|\Delta x_2| + f_x(x_3)|\Delta x_3| \tag{6.72}$$

Equation (6.72) can be expressed in a format similar to (6.71) as

$$f_y(y) = \left.\frac{f_x(x_1)}{|g'(x_1)|}\right|_{x_1=g^{-1}(y)} + \left.\frac{f_x(x_2)}{|g'(x_2)|}\right|_{x_2=g^{-1}(y)} + \left.\frac{f_x(x_3)}{|g'(x_3)|}\right|_{x_3=g^{-1}(y)} \tag{6.73}$$

where x_1, x_2, and x_3 are roots of the equation $g(x) = y$.

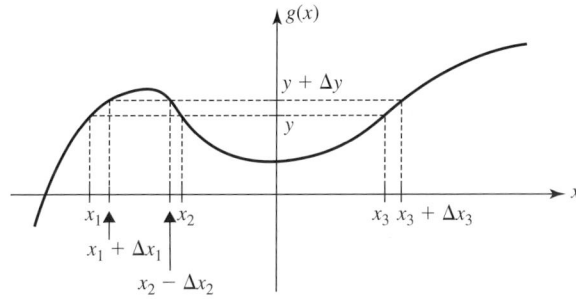

Figure 6.12 Nonmonotonic function of a random variable.

Example 6.14

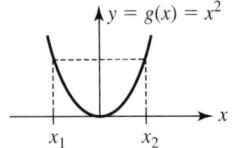

Figure 6.13 Square-law device transfer characteristic.

Consider the square-law device shown in Figure 6.13. Its transfer characteristic is given by $g(x) = x^2$. Determine the PDF of $y = g(x)$. If the input random variable x is exponential, determine the PDF of y.

Solution

The PDF of y is given from (6.73) as

$$f_y(y) = \frac{f_x(x_1)}{|g'(x_1)|}\bigg|_{x_1 = g^{-1}(y)} + \frac{f_x(x_2)}{|g'(x_2)|}\bigg|_{x_2 = g^{-1}(y)}$$

In this case $g'(x) = 2x$. From Figure 6.13, the two roots of $x^2 = y$ are

$$x_1 = \sqrt{y} \text{ and } x_2 = -\sqrt{y}$$

Substituting into the expression for $f_y(y)$, we get

$$f_y(y) = \frac{f_x(x_1)}{|2x_1|}\bigg|_{x_1 = \sqrt{y}} + \frac{f_x(x_2)}{|2x_2|}\bigg|_{x_2 = -\sqrt{y}} = \frac{1}{\sqrt{y}}\left[f_x\left(\sqrt{y}\right) + f_x\left(-\sqrt{y}\right)\right]$$

The PDF of y is therefore given by

$$f_y(y) = \begin{cases} \dfrac{1}{\sqrt{y}}\left[f_x\left(\sqrt{y}\right) + f_x\left(-\sqrt{y}\right)\right], & y > 0 \\ 0, & \text{otherwise} \end{cases}$$

Now if the PDF of x is

$$f_x(x) = \begin{cases} \lambda e^{-\lambda x}, & x \geq 0 \\ & \lambda > 0, \\ 0, & \text{otherwise} \end{cases}$$

$f_y(y)$ is given by

$$f_y(y) = \begin{cases} \dfrac{1}{\sqrt{y}}\lambda e^{-\lambda\sqrt{y}}, & y > 0 \\ 0, & \text{otherwise} \end{cases}$$

6.5   STATISTICS OF RANDOM VARIABLES

Although a random variable x is completely characterized by its PDF $f_x(x)$, we are often interested in a partial description of its behavior in terms of certain averages. In this context, we introduce two such parameters—mean and variance—that are universally used to represent the important properties of a random variable.

The **mean** or the **expected** value of a continuous random variable x is defined as

$$m_x = \bar{x} = E\{x\} = \int_{-\infty}^{\infty} x f_x(x) dx \qquad (6.74)$$

If x is a discrete random variable, the expected value is given by

$$m_x = \bar{x} = E\{x\} = \sum_i x_i p_x(x_i) = \sum_i x_i P\{x = x_i\} \qquad (6.75)$$

The mean or the expected value of a random variable represents the average value of the random variable in a very large number of trials.

Example 6.15

x is a uniformly distributed random variable $\mathcal{U}[a, b]$. Calculate its mean.

Solution

The PDF of x is given by

$$f_x(x) = \begin{cases} \dfrac{1}{b - a}, & a \leq x \leq b, \\ 0, & \text{otherwise.} \end{cases}$$

Therefore,

$$m_x = \int_a^b \frac{x}{b - a} dx = \frac{1}{b - a} \frac{x^2}{2} \Big|_a^b = \frac{b^2 - a^2}{2(b - a)} = \frac{a + b}{2}$$

Note that the mean of a random variable uniformly distributed in $[a, b]$ is the midpoint of its range.

The **mean** or the **expected value** of the function $y = g(x)$ of a continuous random variable x is given by

$$m_y = \bar{y} = \int_{-\infty}^{\infty} y f_y(y) dy \qquad (6.76)$$

where $f_y(y)$ can be determined from $f_x(x)$ by using the relationship (6.71) or (6.73). However, it is more convenient to find the mean of the function $g(x)$ directly by using

$$\overline{g(x)} = E\{g(x)\} = \int_{-\infty}^{\infty} g(x) f_x(x) dx \qquad (6.77)$$

Equation (6.77) is a useful result because it allows us to calculate the expected value of certain functions of the random variable x that may provide additional useful information about it.

The variance $Var(x)$ of a random variable x is defined as

$$Var(x) = \sigma_x^2 = E\{(x - m_x)^2\} = \int_{-\infty}^{\infty} (x - m_x)^2 f_x(x) dx \qquad (6.78)$$

Because the integrand in (6.78) is nonnegative, $\sigma_x^2 \geq 0$. The variance of a random variable x describes the spread of its PDF around the expected value m_x. For small values of σ_x^2, the most likely values of x are concentrated in a relatively narrow range around its mean value. On the other hand, the most likely values of x are spread over a wider range for a larger value of variance. Expanding (6.78) and using the linearity of the integrals, we get

$$
\begin{aligned}
Var(x) &= \int_{-\infty}^{\infty} (x^2 - 2xm_x + m_x^2) f_x(x) dx \\
&= \int_{-\infty}^{\infty} x^2 f_x(x) dx - 2m_x \int_{-\infty}^{\infty} x f_x(x) dx + m_x^2 \\
&= E\{x^2\} - m_x^2 = \overline{x^2} - \overline{x}^2 \qquad (6.79)
\end{aligned}
$$

where $\overline{x^2} = E\{x^2\}$ is called the **mean-square value** of the random variable x. For a random variable x with zero mean,

$$Var(x) = E\{x^2\} \qquad (6.80)$$

The **standard deviation** of a random variable x is defined as

$$\sigma_x = \sqrt{Var(x)} \qquad (6.81)$$

6.5.1 Moments and Characteristic Functions

For the special case of $g(x) = x^n$, the **nth moment** of a real-valued random variable x is obtained from (6.77) as

$$E\{x^n\} = \int_{-\infty}^{\infty} x^n f_x(x) dx \qquad (6.82)$$

The first moment of x is its mean $m_x = E\{x\}$ and the second moment is its mean-square value $E\{x^2\}$. The **nth central moment** of a real-valued random variable x is defined as

$$E\{(x - m_x)^n\} = \int_{-\infty}^{\infty} (x - m_x)^n f_x(x) dx \qquad (6.83)$$

Hence the variance $Var(x)$ is the second central moment of x.

Example 6.16

Find the mean and variance of exponential random variable x with PDF

$$f_x(x) = \begin{cases} \lambda e^{-\lambda x}, & x \geq 0 \\ 0, & \text{otherwise} \end{cases}$$

where $\lambda > 0$.

Solution

We will calculate the nth moment of x.

$$E\{x^n\} = \lambda \int_0^\infty x^n e^{-\lambda x} dx$$

Using integration by parts, we obtain

$$\lambda \int_0^\infty x^n e^{-\lambda x} dx = \lambda \left[-\frac{1}{\lambda} x^n e^{-\lambda x} \Big|_0^\infty + \frac{n}{\lambda} \int_0^\infty x^{n-1} e^{-\lambda x} dx \right] \tag{6.84}$$

The first term on the right-hand side of (6.84), $x^n e^{-\lambda x}$, equals zero for both limits. Therefore, we can write

$$E\{x^n\} = \left[n \int_0^\infty x^{n-1} e^{-\lambda x} dx \right] = \frac{n}{\lambda} E\{x^{n-1}\}$$

For $n = 1$, we have $E\{x\} = \bar{x} = \frac{1}{\lambda} E\{x^0\} = \frac{1}{\lambda}$

For $n = 2$, we have $E\{x^2\} = \overline{x^2} = \frac{2}{\lambda} E\{x\} = \frac{2}{\lambda} \frac{1}{\lambda} = \frac{2}{\lambda^2}$

$$Var(x) = \overline{x^2} - \bar{x}^2 = \frac{2}{\lambda^2} - \frac{1}{\lambda^2} = \frac{1}{\lambda^2}$$

The **characteristic function** of a random variable x is defined as

$$\Phi_x(j\omega) = E\{e^{j\omega x}\} = \int_{-\infty}^\infty e^{j\omega x} f_x(x) dx \tag{6.85}$$

We observe from (6.85) that the characteristic function is a Fourier transform of the PDF except for a sign change in the exponent (that is, $e^{j\omega x}$ versus $e^{-j\omega x}$). Obviously the PDF $f_x(x)$ can be obtained by computing the inverse Fourier transform of $\Phi_x(j\omega)$. That is,

$$f_x(x) = \int_{-\infty}^\infty \Phi_x(j\omega) e^{-j\omega x} d\omega \tag{6.86}$$

We can easily show from (6.85) that

$$|\Phi_x(j\omega)| = |\int_{-\infty}^{\infty} e^{j\omega x}f_x(x)dx| \leq \int_{-\infty}^{\infty} \underbrace{|e^{j\omega x}|}_{=1}f_x(x)dx = \Phi_x(0) = 1 \tag{6.87}$$

Differentiating both sides of (6.85) yields

$$\frac{d\Phi_x(j\omega)}{d\omega} = \frac{d}{d\omega}\left[\int_{-\infty}^{\infty} f_x(x)e^{j\omega x}dx\right] = j\int_{-\infty}^{\infty} xf_x(x)e^{j\omega x}dx \tag{6.88}$$

We recognize from (6.88) that the derivative of $\Phi_x(j\omega)$ evaluated at $\omega = 0$ is the first moment of the random variable x. That is,

$$\frac{d\Phi_x(j\omega)}{d\omega}\bigg|_{\omega=0} = j\int_{-\infty}^{\infty} xf_x(x)dx = jE\{x\} \tag{6.89}$$

Similarly, the nth moment of the random variable x is obtained by taking the nth derivative of $\Phi_x(j\omega)$ at $\omega = 0$.

$$E\{x^n\} = (-j)^n\frac{d^n\Phi_x(j\omega)}{d\omega^n}\bigg|_{\omega=0} \tag{6.90}$$

Typically it is easier to calculate the moments of x by finding the characteristic function and differentiating it rather than by integrating $x^nf_x(x)$.

Example 6.17

Calculate the characteristic function of Gaussian random variable $x \sim \mathcal{N}(m_x, \sigma_x^2)$.

Solution

The FT of a Gaussian pulse from Table 2.2 is

$$e^{-\pi x^2} \overset{\mathfrak{I}}{\longleftrightarrow} e^{-\pi f^2} \tag{6.91}$$

For a Gaussian random variable $x \sim \mathcal{N}(m_x, \sigma_x^2)$, the FT of the PDF is obtained by applying the scaling and time-shifting properties to the FT of the Gaussian pulse in (6.91).

$$\frac{1}{\sqrt{2\pi\sigma_x^2}}e^{-(x-m_x)^2/2\sigma_x^2} \overset{\mathfrak{I}}{\longleftrightarrow} \left[e^{-\omega^2\sigma_x^2/2}\right]e^{j\omega m_x} = e^{j\omega m_x - \frac{1}{2}\omega^2\sigma_x^2} \tag{6.92}$$

The characteristic function of the Gaussian random variable $x \sim \mathcal{N}(m_x, \sigma_x^2)$ can, therefore, be written as

$$\Phi_x(j\omega) = e^{j\omega m_x - \frac{1}{2}\omega^2\sigma_x^2} \tag{6.93}$$

The nth order moments of the Gaussian random variable is obtained by substituting (6.93) into (6.90) as

$$E\{x^n\} = (-j)^n \left. \frac{d^n \left(e^{j\omega m_x - \frac{1}{2}\omega^2 \sigma_x^2}\right)}{d\omega^n} \right|_{\omega=0} \tag{6.94}$$

Equation (6.94) states a significant result that the higher-order moments of the Gaussian random variable are uniquely determined by its second-order statistical averages (that is, mean and variance).

6.6 PAIRS OF RANDOM VARIABLES

In this section, we consider random experiments where the outcomes are described by a pair of random variables x and y. That is, the vector function $(x(\xi), y(\xi))$ assigns a pair of real numbers to each outcome $\xi \in \Omega$ of the random experiment. In many situations, we are interested in studying the *joint* behavior of random variables x and y. An example is the cumulative GPA (x) and SAT score (y) of a graduating high school senior in Connecticut. Other examples include:

- Signal x emitted by a radio transmitter and the corresponding signal y that eventually arrives at the receiver
- Strength y of the signal received at a base station and the distance x of the cell phone from the base station

The **joint cumulative distribution function** of two random variables x and y is defined as

$$F_{xy}(x, y) = P\{x \le x, y \le y\} \tag{6.95}$$

We observe that $F_{xy}(x, y)$ measures the probability of the event $A = \{\xi \in \Omega : x(\xi) \le x, y(\xi) \le y\}$. The range of (x, y) is the whole real plane $\mathbb{R}^2$ or a subset thereof. For any pair of random variables x and y,

1. $0 \le F_{xy}(x, y) \le 1$ (6.96)
2. $F_{xy}(\infty, \infty) = 1$ (6.97)
3. $F_{xy}(x, -\infty) = F_{xy}(-\infty, y) = 0$ (6.98)
4. $F_{xy}(x, y)$ is nondecreasing

For discrete random variables x and y, the **joint probability mass function (PMF)** is defined as

$$p_{xy}(x_i, y_j) = P\{x = x_i, y = y_j\} \tag{6.99}$$

Thus for any pair of real numbers, the PMF is the probability of observing these numbers.

The **joint probability density function** $f_{xy}(x, y)$ of two random variables x and y is defined as

$$f_{xy}(x, y) = \frac{\partial^2 F_{xy}(x, y)}{\partial x \, \partial y} \tag{6.100}$$

From the definition (6.100), it follows that

$$F_{xy}(x, y) = \int_{-\infty}^{x} \int_{-\infty}^{y} f_{xy}(u, v)dudv \tag{6.101}$$

The important properties of $f_{xy}(x, y)$ include:

1. $f_{xy}(x, y) \geq 0$ for all (x, y) \hfill (6.102)

2. $\int_{-\infty}^{+\infty} \int_{-\infty}^{+\infty} f_{xy}(x, y)dxdy = F_{xy}(\infty, \infty) = 1$ \hfill (6.103)

3. For a rectangle $\{a < \pmb{x} \leq b, c < \pmb{y} \leq d\}$ in x–y plane,

$$P\{a < \pmb{x} \leq b, c < \pmb{y} \leq d\} = \int_{a}^{b} \int_{c}^{d} f_{xy}(x, y)dxdy \tag{6.104}$$

As a special case of (6.104), the probability of finding random variable pair $(\pmb{x}, \pmb{y})$ in the infinitesimal rectangle is given by

$$P\{x < \pmb{x} \leq x + \Delta x, y < \pmb{y} \leq y + \Delta y\} = \int_{x}^{x+\Delta x} \int_{y}^{y+\Delta y} f_{xy}(u, v)dudv \approx f_{xy}(x, y)\Delta x\Delta y \tag{6.105}$$

Equation (6.105) states that the probability of finding random variable pair $(\pmb{x}, \pmb{y})$ in the vicinity of point (x, y) is product of the PDF value $f_{xy}(x, y)$ and the area of the infinitesimal rectangle.

Example 6.18

The joint CDF of random variables $\pmb{x}$ and $\pmb{y}$ is given by

$$F_{xy}(x, y) = \begin{cases} A(1 - e^{-x} - e^{-y} + e^{-(x+y)}), & x \geq 0, \ y \geq 0 \\ 0, & \text{otherwise} \end{cases}$$

a. Calculate A.
b. Calculate the PDF $f_{xy}(x, y)$.
c. What is the probability $P\{\pmb{x} \leq 1, \pmb{y} \leq 3\}$?

Solution

a. $F_{xy}(\infty, \infty) = A(1 - 0 - 0 + 0) = 1 \Rightarrow A = 1$

b. For $x, y \geq 0, f_{xy}(x, y) = \dfrac{\partial^2 F_{xy}(x, y)}{\partial x\, \partial y} = e^{-x}e^{-y} = e^{-(x+y)}$

$$f_{xy}(x, y) = \begin{cases} e^{-(x+y)}, & x \geq 0, \ y \geq 0 \\ 0, & \text{otherwise} \end{cases}$$

c. $P\{\pmb{x} \leq 1, \pmb{y} \leq 3\} = F_{xy}(1, 3) = 1 - e^{-1} - e^{-3} + e^{-4} \approx 0.6$

6.6.1 Marginal Distributions

Although a random experiment may produce two random variables x and y, we may be interested in the statistics of each individual random variable in certain cases. The **marginal CDFs** of random variables x and y with the joint CDF $F_{xy}(x, y)$ are obtained by setting the other variable to ∞. That is,

$$F_x(x) = F_{xy}(x, \infty) \tag{6.106}$$

$$F_y(y) = F_{xy}(\infty, y) \tag{6.107}$$

To prove (6.106), we observe that the set $\{x \leq x\}$ in $\mathbb{R}^2$ can be expressed as

$$\{x \leq x\} = \{x \leq x\} \cap \{y \leq \infty\}$$

so that

$$F_x(x) = P\{x \leq x\} = P\{x \leq x, y \leq \infty\} = F_{xy}(x, \infty)$$

The **marginal PDFs** of random variables x and y with the joint PDF $f_{xy}(x, y)$ are obtained by integrating out the other variable as shown below:

$$f_x(x) = \int_{-\infty}^{\infty} f_{xy}(x, y)dy \tag{6.108}$$

$$f_y(y) = \int_{-\infty}^{\infty} f_{xy}(x, y)dx \tag{6.109}$$

In general, the joint CDF and PDF cannot be obtained from marginal CDFs and PDFs, respectively.

To prove (6.108), we make use of (6.106) and (6.101) to obtain

$$F_x(x) = F_{xy}(x, \infty) = \int_{-\infty}^{x} \int_{-\infty}^{+\infty} f_{xy}(u, y)du\,dy \tag{6.110}$$

Now taking derivative of the right-hand side of (6.110) with respect to x yields (6.108). We observe that $f_x(x_1)\Delta x_1 = P\{x_1 < x \leq x_1 + \Delta x_1, y \leq \infty\}$ is the probability that the random variable x lies in the infinitesimal strip shown in Figure 6.14.

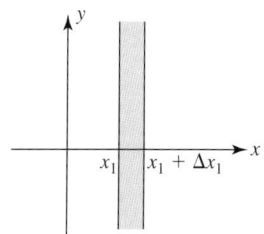

Figure 6.14 Interpretation of marginal PDF

Example 6.19

For the joint CDF of random variables x and y in Example 6.18, determine

a. Marginal CDFs $F_x(x)$ and $F_y(y)$
b. Marginal PDFs $f_x(x)$ and $f_y(y)$

Solution

a. $F_x(x) = F_{xy}(x, \infty) = 1 - e^{-x} - 0 + 0 = 1 - e^{-x}, \quad x \geq 0$

$$F_x(x) = \begin{cases} 1 - e^{-x}, & x \geq 0 \\ 0, & \text{otherwise} \end{cases}$$

$$F_y(y) = F_{xy}(\infty, y) = 1 - 0 - e^{-y} + 0 = 1 - e^{-y}, \ y \ge 0$$

$$F_y(y) = \begin{cases} 1 - e^{-y}, & y \ge 0 \\ 0, & \text{otherwise} \end{cases}$$

b. $\displaystyle f_x(x) = \int_{-\infty}^{+\infty} f_{xy}(x, y) dy = \int_0^{+\infty} e^{-(x+y)} dy = e^{-x} \int_0^{+\infty} e^{-y} dy = e^{-x} \left[-e^{-y} \Big|_0^{\infty} \right] = e^{-x}$

$$f_x(x) = \begin{cases} e^{-x}, & x \ge 0 \\ 0, & \text{otherwise} \end{cases}$$

Similarly, we can show that

$$f_y(y) = \begin{cases} e^{-y}, & y \ge 0 \\ 0, & \text{otherwise} \end{cases}$$

6.6.2   Function of Two Random Variables: Expected Values

Often in the study of communication systems, we are interested in the statistical characterization of a certain function of two random variables x and y. For example, the receiver input signal (z) usually consists of the desired signal (x) embedded in noise (y). That is,

$$z = x + y \tag{6.111}$$

Example 6.20

Let $z = x + y$, where x and y are jointly distributed random variables with the joint PDF $f_{xy}(x, y)$. Find the CDF and PDF of z.

Solution

The CDF of z is given by

$$F_z(z) = P(z \le z) = P(x + y \le z) = \int_{-\infty}^{\infty} dy \left[\int_{-\infty}^{z-y} f_{xy}(x, y) dx \right] \tag{6.112}$$

By differentiating the right-hand side of (6.112), we can write the PDF of z as

$$f_z(z) = \frac{\partial F_z(z)}{\partial z} = \int_{-\infty}^{\infty} f_{xy}(z - y, y) dy \tag{6.113}$$

Although the CDF and PDF of z provide a complete description of $z = g(x, y)$, we may be satisfied with the knowledge of certain statistics of z in many cases. The expected value of a function $z = g(x, y)$ of two random variables x and y is given by

$$E\{z\} = E\{g(x, y)\} = \int_{-\infty}^{\infty} \int_{-\infty}^{\infty} g(x, y) f_{xy}(x, y) dx dy \tag{6.114}$$

Let $g(x, y) = x + y$. Substituting into (6.114) yields

$$E\{x + y\} = \int_{-\infty}^{\infty}\int_{-\infty}^{\infty}(x + y)f_{xy}(x, y)dxdy = \int_{-\infty}^{\infty}\int_{-\infty}^{\infty}xf_{xy}(x, y)dxdy + \int_{-\infty}^{\infty}\int_{-\infty}^{\infty}yf_{xy}(x, y)dxdy$$

$$= \int_{-\infty}^{\infty}xf_x(x)dx + \int_{-\infty}^{\infty}yf_y(y)dy = E\{x\} + E\{y\} \qquad (6.115)$$

Equation (6.115) states that the expected value of a sum of two random variables x and y equals the sum of the expected values. The important point to note is that the calculation of $E\{x\}$ and $E\{y\}$ requires the knowledge of marginal PDFs $f_x(x)$ and $f_y(y)$, respectively. We do not need the joint PDF $f_{xy}(x, y)$ which simplifies the problem. At this point we can state a more general result that the expectation is a **linear operator.** That is,

$$E\left\{\sum_{i=1}^{n}\alpha_i x_i\right\} = \sum_{i=1}^{n}\alpha_i E\{x_i\} \qquad (6.116)$$

The variance of the sum of two random variables x and y is

$$Var(x + y) = E\{[x + y - (m_x + m_y)]^2\} = E\{[(x - m_x) + (y - m_y)]^2\}$$

$$= E\{(x - m_x)^2\} + 2E\{(x - m_x)(y - m_y)\} + E\{(y - m_y)^2\}$$

$$= Var(x) + Var(y) + 2E\{(x - m_x)(y - m_y)\} \qquad (6.117)$$

Note that unlike the expectation, the variance is not a linear operator. Further, we require the knowledge of the joint PDF $f_{xy}(x, y)$ for the calculation of variance.

The **covariance** $Cov(x, y)$ of two random variables x and y is defined as

$$Cov(x, y) = E\{(x - m_x)(y - m_y)\} \qquad (6.118)$$

Substituting (6.118) into (6.117), we obtain the following relationship

$$Var(x + y) = Var(x) + Var(y) + 2Cov(x, y) \qquad (6.119)$$

The **cross-correlation** of two random variables x and y is defined as

$$R_{xy} = E\{xy\} \qquad (6.120)$$

It is a very simple exercise to prove that

$$Cov(x, y) = E\{xy\} - E\{x\}E\{y\} = R_{xy} - m_x m_y \qquad (6.121)$$

x and y are called **uncorrelated random variables** if $Cov(x, y) = 0$. That is,

$$E\{xy\} = E\{x\}E\{y\} \qquad (6.122)$$

The **correlation coefficient** ρ_{xy} of two random variables x and y is defined as

$$\rho_{xy} = \frac{Cov(x, y)}{\sigma_x \sigma_y} \tag{6.123}$$

It is left as an exercise to prove that $-1 \leq \rho_{xy} \leq 1$ (see Problem 6.14). The correlation coefficient provides a measure of similarity between random variables x and y. $\rho_{xy} = 0$ implies that the random variables x and y are uncorrelated. A positive value of correlation coefficient ($\rho_{xy} \geq 0$) suggests that x and y move in the same direction. That is, if x is high relative to its mean, y also tends to be high and vice versa. A negative value of correlation coefficient ($\rho_{xy} < 0$) suggests that x and y move in the opposite direction.

Joint Moments and Characteristic Functions

The joint moments of two random variables x and y summarize information about their joint behavior. The **kmth joint moment** of x and y is defined as

$$E[x^k y^m] = \int_{-\infty}^{\infty} \int_{-\infty}^{\infty} x^k y^m f_{xy}(x, y)\,dxdy \tag{6.124}$$

The **joint characteristic function** of two random variables x and y is defined as

$$\Phi_{xy}(ju, jv) = E\{e^{j(xu+yv)}\} = \int_{-\infty}^{\infty} \int_{-\infty}^{\infty} e^{j(xu+yv)} f_{xy}(x, y)\,dxdy \tag{6.125}$$

Equation (6.125) states that the joint characteristic function of two random variables x and y is a two-dimensional Fourier transform of their joint PDF $f_{xy}(x, y)$, except for a sign change in the exponent (that is, $e^{j(xu + yv)}$ versus $e^{-j(xu + yv)}$). The joint PDF $f_{xy}(x, y)$ can be obtained from $\Phi_{xy}(ju, jv)$ by its inverse two-dimensional Fourier transform.

$$f_{xy}(x, y) = \int_{-\infty}^{\infty} \int_{-\infty}^{\infty} \Phi_{xy}(ju, jv) e^{-j(xu+yv)}\,dudv \tag{6.126}$$

Note that

$$|\Phi_{xy}(ju, jv)| \leq \Phi_{xy}(0, 0) = 1 \tag{6.127}$$

The marginal characteristic functions $\Phi_x(ju)$ and $\Phi_y(jv)$ can be obtained from the joint characteristic function by setting other variables to zero.

$$\Phi_x(ju) = \Phi_{xy}(ju, 0)$$

$$\Phi_y(jv) = \Phi_{xy}(0, jv) \tag{6.128}$$

It is easy to show that the joint moments can be obtained by taking an appropriate set of derivatives.

$$E\{x^n y^m\} = (-j)^{n+m} \left. \frac{\partial^{n+m} \Phi_{xy}(u, v)}{\partial^n u \partial^m v} \right|_{u=0,\, v=0} \tag{6.129}$$

6.7 CONDITIONAL DISTRIBUTIONS

Recall from Section 6.1 that the conditional probability $P(A|B)$ provides a modified probability model for the event A based on the knowledge that outcome of the random experiment is in set B. For a random variable x with the probability distribution function $F_x(x)$, the **conditional** CDF of x given the occurrence of event B is defined as

$$F_x(x|B) = P\{x(\xi) \le x|B\} = \frac{P\{(x(\xi) \le x) \cap B\}}{P(B)} \tag{6.130}$$

Obviously, the random variable x and the event B are defined on the same sample space Ω. $F_x(x|B)$ satisfies all the properties of a CDF discussed in Section 6.3. For example,

$$F_x(\infty|B) = \frac{P\{(x(\xi) \le \infty) \cap B\}}{P(B)} = \frac{P(B)}{P(B)} = 1 \tag{6.131}$$

The conditional PDF $f_x(x|B)$ is the derivative of the conditional CDF $F_x(x|B)$.

$$f_x(x|B) = \frac{dF_x(x|B)}{dx} \tag{6.132}$$

Given the PDF $f_x(x|B)$, the conditional CDF $F_x(x|B)$ can be obtained using

$$F_x(x|B) = \int_{-\infty}^{x} f_x(u|B)du \tag{6.133}$$

Using (6.42) and (6.133), we can write

$$P(x_1 < x(\xi) \le x_2|B) = F_x(x_2|B) - F_x(x_1|B) = \int_{x_1}^{x_2} f_x(x|B)dx \tag{6.134}$$

Next we consider conditioning by the special event $B = \{y < y \le y + \Delta y\}$. The conditional CDF of random variable x given $y < y \le y + \Delta y$, is given from (6.103) as

$$F_x(x|y < y \le y + \Delta y) = P\{x(\xi) \le x|y < y \le y + \Delta y\}$$

$$= \frac{P\{(x(\xi) \le x) \cap y < y(\xi) \le y + \Delta y\}}{P(y < y(\xi) \le y + \Delta y)}$$

$$= \frac{\displaystyle\int_{-\infty}^{x} \int_{y}^{y+\Delta y} f_{xy}(x, y)dxdy}{\displaystyle\int_{y}^{y+\Delta y} f_y(y)dy} \tag{6.135}$$

In the limit as $\Delta y \to 0$, (6.135) represents the conditional CDF of random variable x given $\{y = y\}$. That is,

$$F_x(x|y = y) = \frac{\Delta y \int_{-\infty}^{x} f_{xy}(x, y)dx}{\Delta y f_y(y)} = \frac{\int_{-\infty}^{x} f_{xy}(x, y)dx}{f_y(y)} \qquad (6.136)$$

The derivative of $F_x(x|y = y)$ with respect to x is the conditional PDF $f_x(x|y)$.

$$f_x(x|y) = f_x(x|y = y) = \frac{f_{xy}(x, y)}{f_y(y)}, \quad f_y(y) > 0 \qquad (6.137)$$

Note that for each y, the conditional PDF $f_x(x|y = y)$ provides a new probabilistic description of the random variable x. Similarly, we can obtain the conditional PDF of random variable y given $\{x = x\}$

$$f_y(y|x) = f_y(y|x = x) = \frac{f_{xy}(x, y)}{f_x(x)}, \quad f_x(x) > 0 \qquad (6.138)$$

Bayes's Rule for Random Variables

From (6.138) and (6.137), we can write the joint PDF of random variables x and y in terms of their conditional PDFs as follows:

$$f_{xy}(x, y) = f_y(y|x = x)f_x(x) \qquad (6.139)$$

$$f_{xy}(x, y) = f_x(x|y = y)f_y(y) \qquad (6.140)$$

Substituting (6.139) into (6.137) yields

$$f_x(x|y = y) = \frac{f_y(y|x = x)f_x(x)}{f_y(y)}, \quad f_y(y) > 0 \qquad (6.141)$$

Similarly, substituting (6.140) into (6.138), we obtain

$$f_y(y|x = x) = \frac{f_x(x|y = y)f_y(y)}{f_x(x)}, \quad f_x(x) > 0 \qquad (6.142)$$

Equations (6.141) and (6.142) represent Bayes's rule for continuous random variables.

In certain instances, we may have to deal with discrete and continuous random variables jointly. If x is a discrete random variable and y is a continuous random variable, then the probability of the event $\{x = x \text{ and } y < y \le y + \Delta y\}$ is given by

$$P\{x = x \text{ and } y < y \le y + \Delta y\} = P\{x = x|y < y \le y + \Delta y\}P\{y < y \le y + \Delta y\}$$

$$= P\{x = x|y < y \le y + \Delta y\}f_y(y)\Delta y \qquad (6.143)$$

Alternatively, we can express $P\{x = x \text{ and } y < y \leq y + \Delta y\}$ as

$$P\{x = x \text{ and } y < y \leq y + \Delta y\} = P\{y < y \leq y + \Delta y \mid x = x\}P\{x = x\}$$

$$= P\{x = x\}f_y(y \mid x = x)\Delta y \qquad (6.144)$$

Comparing right-hand sides of (6.143) and (6.144), we obtain

$$P\{x = x \mid y < y \leq y + \Delta y\}f_y(y) = P\{x = x\}f_y(y \mid x = x) \qquad (6.145)$$

Now

$$\lim_{\Delta y \to 0} P\{x = x \mid y < y \leq y + \Delta y\} = P\{x = x \mid y = y\}$$

Substituting into (6.145) yields a mixed form of Bayes's rule

$$P\{x = x \mid y = y\} = \frac{P\{x = x\}f_y(y \mid x = x)}{f_y(y)} \qquad (6.146)$$

Example 6.21

The joint PDF of two random variables is

$$f_{xy}(x, y) = \begin{cases} C(1 + xy), & 0 \leq x \leq 6, \ 0 \leq y \leq 5 \\ 0, & \text{otherwise} \end{cases}$$

Find the following:

a. The constant C
b. $F_{xy}(0.1, 1.5)$
c. $f_{xy}(x, 3)$
d. $f_x(x \mid y)$

Solution

a. $\displaystyle \int_{-\infty}^{\infty}\int_{-\infty}^{\infty} f_{xy}(x, y)dxdy = \int_{0}^{6}\int_{0}^{5} C(1 + xy)dxdy = 1 \Rightarrow C = 1/255$

b. $\displaystyle F_{xy}(0.1, 1.5) = \int_{0}^{0.1}\int_{0}^{1.5} f_{xy}(x, y)dxdy = \frac{1}{255}\int_{0}^{0.1}\int_{0}^{1.5}(1 + xy)dxdy = 6.1 \times 10^{-4}$

c. $f_{xy}(x, 3) = \begin{cases} \dfrac{1}{255}(1 + 3x), & 0 \leq x \leq 6 \\ 0, & \text{otherwise} \end{cases}$

d. $f_x(x \mid y) = \dfrac{f_{xy}(x, y)}{f_y(y)}$

Now

$$f_y(y) = \int_{0}^{6} f_{xy}(x, y)dx = \frac{1}{255}\int_{0}^{6}(1 + xy)dx = \frac{1}{255}\left(x + y\frac{x^2}{2}\right)\Big|_{0}^{6}$$

$$= \frac{1}{255}(6 + 18y) = \frac{6}{255}(1 + 3y)$$

Therefore,

$$f_x(x|y) = \frac{1 + xy}{6(1 + 3y)}, \quad 0 \le x \le 6, \; 0 \le y \le 5$$

6.7.1 Conditional Expected Values

The conditional PDFs can be used to obtain the conditional averages. The **conditional expected value** of $g(x, y)$ given $y = y$ is defined as

$$E\{g(x, y)|y = y\} = \int_{-\infty}^{\infty} g(x, y)f_x(x|y)dx \tag{6.147}$$

The conditional expected value of x given $y = y$ is a special case of (6.147).

$$m_{x|y} = E\{x|y = y\} = \int_{-\infty}^{\infty} xf_x(x|y)dx \tag{6.148}$$

The conditional variance of x given $y = y$ is obtained by using (6.78), (6.147), and (6.148) as

$$Var(x|y = y) = E\{(x - m_{x|y})^2|y = y\} = \int_{-\infty}^{+\infty} (x - m_{x|y})^2 f_x(x|y)dx$$

$$= E\{x^2|y = y\} - m_{x|y}^2 \tag{6.149}$$

6.7.2 Independent Random Variables

Two random variables x and y are said to be **statistically independent** if

$$F_{xy}(x, y) = P\{x \le x, y \le y\} = P\{x \le x\}P\{y \le y\}$$

$$= F_x(x)F_y(y) \tag{6.150}$$

The condition for statistical independence in (6.150) can alternatively be expressed as

$$f_{xy}(x, y) = f_x(x)f_y(y) \tag{6.151}$$

Substituting (6.151) into (6.137) we obtain

$$f_x(x|y) = \frac{f_{xy}(x, y)}{f_y(y)} = \frac{f_x(x)f_y(y)}{f_y(y)} = f_x(x) \tag{6.152}$$

That is, if x and y are statistically independent, the PDF of x after knowledge of the event $\{y = y\}$ is the same as its PDF before the knowledge of the event.

Example 6.22

The joint PDF of random variables x and y is given by

$$f_{xy}(x, y) = \begin{cases} 6xy^2, & 0 \leq y \leq 1, \ 0 \leq x \leq 1, \\ 0, & \text{otherwise} \end{cases}$$

Show that random variables x and y are statistically independent.

Solution

$$f_x(x) = \int\limits_{-\infty}^{\infty} f_{xy}(x, y)dy = 6x \int\limits_{0}^{1} y^2 dy$$

$$= 2x, \quad 0 \leq x \leq 1$$

Similarly,

$$f_y(y) = \int\limits_{-\infty}^{\infty} f_{xy}(x, y)dx = 6y^2 \int\limits_{0}^{1} x dx$$

$$= 3y^2, \quad 0 \leq y \leq 1$$

That is,

$$f_{xy}(x, y) = f_x(x)f_y(y)$$

Hence x and y are independent random variables.

Example 6.23

Let $z = x + y$, where x and y are independent random variables with the joint PDF $f_{xy}(x, y)$. Find the PDF of z.

Solution

The PDF of z from (6.113) is

$$f_z(z) = \int\limits_{-\infty}^{\infty} f_{xy}(z - y, y)dy \tag{6.113}$$

We can write (6.113) using (6.151) as

$$f_z(z) = \int\limits_{-\infty}^{\infty} f_x(z - y)f_y(y)dy = f_x(z) \otimes f_y(z) \tag{6.153}$$

Equation (6.153) states that the PDF of the sum of two independent random variables is convolution of their marginal PDFs.

For independent random variables *x* and *y,* the following statements about the expected values are stated without proof:

1. $E\{g(x)h(y)\} = E\{g(x)\}E\{h(y)\}$ (6.154)
2. $Cov(x, y) = \rho_{xy} = 0$ (6.155)
3. $Var(x + y) = Var(x) + Var(y)$ (6.156)
4. $E\{x|y = y\} = E\{x\}$ (6.157)
5. $E\{y|x = x\} = E\{y\}$ (6.158)

It follows from (6.155) that statistical independence implies uncorrelatedness. The reverse is not always true.

     x and *y* are said to be **orthogonal** if

$$R_{xy} = E\{xy\} = 0 \qquad (6.159)$$

From (6.159) and (6.121), it follows that if either *x* or *y* has zero mean, then orthogonality implies uncorrelatedness and vice versa.

6.8   JOINTLY GAUSSIAN RANDOM VARIABLES

The joint PDF of two Gaussian random variables $x \sim \mathcal{N}(m_x, \sigma_x^2)$ and $y \sim \mathcal{N}(m_y, \sigma_y^2)$ is given by

$$f_{xy}(x, y) = \frac{1}{2\pi\sigma_x\sigma_y\sqrt{1 - \rho_{xy}^2}} \, e^{\frac{-1}{2(1-\rho_{xy}^2)}\left(\frac{(x-m_x)^2}{\sigma_x^2} - \frac{2\rho_{xy}(x-m_x)(y-m_y)}{\sigma_x\sigma_y} + \frac{(y-m_y)^2}{\sigma_y^2}\right)} \qquad (6.160)$$

where $|\rho_{xy}| < 1$. Equation (6.160) is also called the **bivariate Gaussian density.** Figure 6.15(a) illustrates $f_{xy}(x, y)$ for $\rho_{xy} = 0$. Equi-level contours of $f_{xy}(x, y)$ are displayed in Figure 6.15(b).

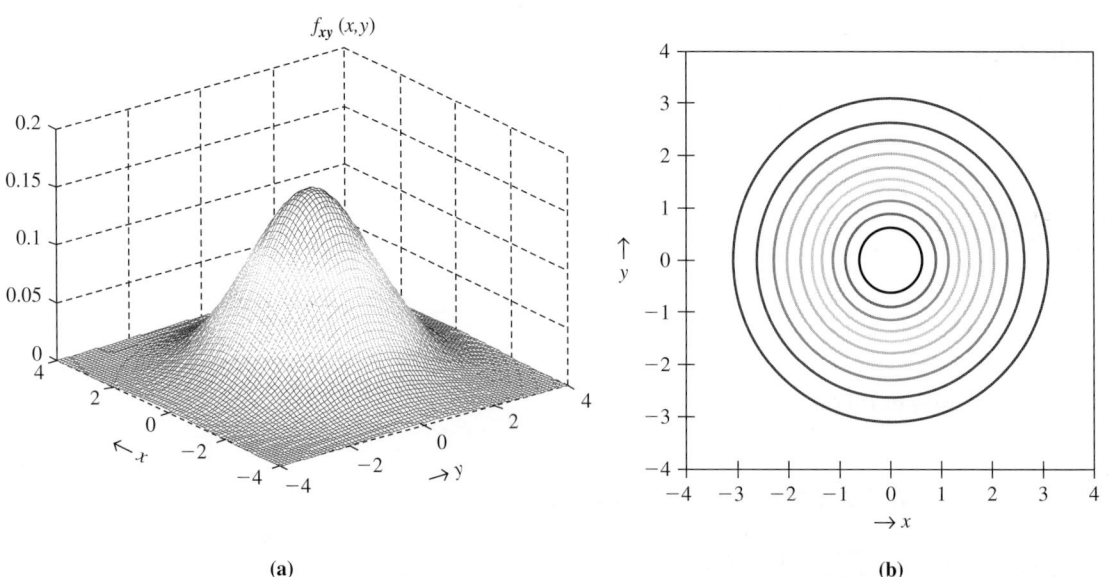

(a)   **(b)**

Figure 6.15   (a) Bivariate Gaussian density $f_{xy}(x, y)$ for $\rho_{xy} = 0$; (b) equi-level contours.

The marginal PDFs for x or y can be obtained from (6.160) by integrating over y or x as

$$f_x(x) = \frac{1}{\sqrt{2\pi\sigma_x^2}} e^{-(x-m_x)^2/2\sigma_x^2} \tag{6.161}$$

$$f_y(y) = \frac{1}{\sqrt{2\pi\sigma_y^2}} e^{-(y-m_y)^2/2\sigma_y^2} \tag{6.162}$$

For uncorrelated Gaussian random variables, $\rho_{xy} = 0$. Substituting into (6.160) yields the following simplified expression for the joint PDF

$$f_{xy}(x, y)|_{\rho_{xy}=0} = \frac{1}{\sqrt{2\pi\sigma_x^2}} e^{-(x-m_x)^2/2\sigma_x^2} \frac{1}{\sqrt{2\pi\sigma_y^2}} e^{-(y-m_y)^2/2\sigma_y^2} \tag{6.163}$$

Equation (6.163) states that uncorrelated Gaussian random variables ($\rho_{xy} = 0$) are also statistically independent. This statement is not valid for all random variable types. Further, it is not always possible to obtain the joint PDF by knowing the marginal PDFs unless the random variables are statistically independent. The only exception is Gaussian random variables where the condition of statistical independence is relaxed to uncorrelatedness.

The joint characteristic function of Gaussian random variables x and y is obtained by taking the two-dimensional FT of (6.160) as

$$\Phi_{xy}(ju, jv) = E\{e^{j(xu+yv)}\} = e^{j(m_xu+m_yv)-\frac{1}{2}(\sigma_x^2u^2+2\rho_{xy}\sigma_x\sigma_y\,uv+\sigma_y^2v^2)} \tag{6.164}$$

Letting $v = 0$ in (6.164), we get the marginal characteristic function of x as

$$\Phi_x(ju) = \Phi_{xy}(ju, 0) = e^{jm_xu-\frac{1}{2}\sigma_x^2u^2} \tag{6.165}$$

Example 6.24

Consider two random variables $x \sim \mathcal{N}(m_x, \sigma_x^2)$ and $y \sim \mathcal{N}(m_y, \sigma_y^2)$. Let $z = ax + by$. Determine the PDF $f_z(z)$.

Solution

We make use of characteristic function to solve this problem. The characteristic function of random variable z is given by

$$\Phi_z(u) = E\{e^{jzu}\} = E\{e^{j(aux+buy)}\} = \Phi_{xy}(au, bu)$$

From (6.164) with u and v replaced by au and bu respectively, we obtain

$$\Phi_z(u) = e^{j(am_x+bm_y)u-\frac{1}{2}(a^2\sigma_x^2+2\rho ab\sigma_x\sigma_y+b^2\sigma_y^2)u^2} = e^{jm_zu-\frac{1}{2}\sigma_z^2u^2} \tag{6.166}$$

where

$$m_z = am_x + bm_y \tag{6.167}$$

$$\sigma_z^2 = a^2\sigma_x^2 + 2\rho ab\sigma_x\sigma_y + b^2\sigma_y^2 \tag{6.168}$$

Notice that (6.166) has the same form as (6.93), and hence we conclude that $z = ax + by$ is also Gaussian with mean and variance in (6.167)–(6.168). That is, *any linear combination of jointly Gaussian random variables generates a Gaussian random variable.*

We can extend the above discussion to **Gaussian random vector** $\underline{x} = [x_1, x_2, \ldots, x_n]^T$ of n jointly Gaussian random variables $x_i \sim \mathcal{N}(m_i, \sigma_i^2)$. The joint PDF of $\underline{x}$ is given by

$$f_{\underline{x}}(\underline{x}) = \frac{1}{(2\pi)^{n/2}|\underline{C}|^{1/2}} e^{(-\frac{1}{2}(\underline{x}-\underline{m})^T \underline{C}^{-1}(\underline{x}-\underline{m}))} \tag{6.169}$$

where

$$\underline{m} = \begin{bmatrix} m_1 \\ m_2 \\ \vdots \\ m_n \end{bmatrix} = \begin{bmatrix} E\{x_1\} \\ E\{x_2\} \\ \vdots \\ E\{x_n\} \end{bmatrix} \tag{6.170}$$

and $\underline{C}$ is the covariance matrix defined by

$$\underline{C} = \begin{bmatrix} Var(x_1) & Cov(x_1 x_2) & \ldots & Cov(x_1 x_n) \\ Cov(x_2 x_1) & Var(x_2) & \ldots & Cov(x_2 x_n) \\ \vdots & \vdots & & \vdots \\ \vdots & \vdots & & \vdots \\ Cov(x_n x_1) & Cov(x_n x_2) & \ldots & Var(x_n) \end{bmatrix} \tag{6.171}$$

For n uncorrelated Gaussian random variables $x_i \sim \mathcal{N}(m_i, \sigma_i^2)$, $\underline{C}$ becomes a diagonal matrix and the joint PDF in (6.169) simplifies to

$$f_{\underline{x}}(\underline{x}) = \prod_{i=1}^{n} f_{x_i}(x_i) = \prod_{i=1}^{n} \frac{1}{\sqrt{2\pi\sigma_i^2}} e^{-(x_i - m_i)^2/2\sigma_i^2} \tag{6.172}$$

For n zero mean, and independent Gaussian random variables $\mathcal{N}(0, \sigma^2)$, (6.172) can be expressed as

$$f_{\underline{x}}(\underline{x}) = \prod_{i=1}^{n} \frac{1}{\sqrt{2\pi\sigma^2}} e^{-x_i^2/2\sigma^2} = \frac{1}{(2\pi\sigma^2)^{n/2}} e^{-\frac{1}{2\sigma^2}\sum_{i=1}^{n} x_i^2} \tag{6.173}$$

Example 6.25

Consider two jointly Gaussian random variables x and y with means 1 and 2, respectively, and covariance matrix

$$\underline{C} = \begin{pmatrix} 4 & 0 \\ 0 & 4 \end{pmatrix}$$

a. Write the joint PDF $f_{xy}(x, y)$ of x and y.
b. Try to factor the joint PDF into marginal PDFs. Are the random variables x and y statistically independent?
c. Compute the probability $x > 3$ and $y > 3$.
d. Compute the probability $x > 1$ and $y < 2$.

Solution

a. $f_{\underline{x}}(\underline{x}) = \dfrac{1}{(2\pi)^{n/2}|\underline{C}|^{1/2}} e^{(-\frac{1}{2}(\underline{x}-\underline{m})^T \underline{C}^{-1}(\underline{x}-\underline{m}))}$

$$|\underline{C}|^{1/2} = 4$$

$$\underline{C}^{-1} = \frac{1}{16}\begin{pmatrix} 4 & 0 \\ 0 & 4 \end{pmatrix} = \begin{pmatrix} 1/4 & 0 \\ 0 & 1/4 \end{pmatrix}$$

$$f_{xy}(x, y) = \frac{1}{8\pi} e^{-\frac{1}{2}(x-1 \quad y-2)\begin{pmatrix} 1/4 & 0 \\ 0 & 1/4 \end{pmatrix}\begin{pmatrix} x-1 \\ y-2 \end{pmatrix}}$$

$$= \frac{1}{8\pi} e^{-\left[\frac{(x-1)^2}{8} + \frac{(y-2)^2}{8}\right]}$$

b. $f_{xy}(x, y) = \dfrac{1}{\sqrt{8\pi}} e^{-\frac{(x-1)^2}{8}} \dfrac{1}{\sqrt{8\pi}} e^{-\frac{(y-2)^2}{8}}$

Thus we see that $x \sim \mathcal{N}(1, 4)$ and $y \sim \mathcal{N}(2, 4)$ are statistically independent.

c. $P\{x > 3 \text{ and } y > 3\} = P\{x > 3\}P\{y > 3\} = Q\left(\dfrac{3-1}{2}\right)Q\left(\dfrac{3-2}{2}\right) = 0.1586 \times 0.5 = 0.0793$

d. $P\{x > 1 \text{ and } y < 2\} = P\{x > 1\}P\{y < 2\} = Q\left(\dfrac{1-1}{4}\right)Q\left(\dfrac{2-2}{4}\right) = 0.25$

6.8.1 Two Functions of Two Random Variables

Consider two monotonic functions $g(x, y)$ and $h(x, y)$ of the random variables x and y with joint PDF $f_{xy}(x, y)$

$$v = g(x, y)$$

$$w = h(x, y) \tag{6.174}$$

Using arguments that led to the derivation of (6.67), we obtain

$$P\{v \le v \le v + \Delta v, w \le w \le w + \Delta w\} = P\{x \le x \le x + \Delta x, y \le y \le y + \Delta y\}$$

Now applying (6.105) yields

$$f_{vw}(v, w)\Delta v \Delta w = f_{xy}(x, y)\Delta x \Delta y$$

Therefore, the PDF $f_{vw}(v, w)$ is related to $f_{xy}(x, y)$ by

$$f_{vw}(v, w) = \frac{\Delta x \Delta y}{\Delta v \Delta w} f_{xy}(x, y) \tag{6.175}$$

where $\Delta v \Delta w$ is the infinitesimal area in the vw plane corresponding to the infinitesimal area $\Delta x \Delta y$ in the xy plane. The ratio of these areas is given by the **Jacobian** defined as

$$J(v, w) = \frac{\Delta x \Delta y}{\Delta v \Delta w} = \det \begin{vmatrix} \dfrac{\partial x}{\partial v} & \dfrac{\partial x}{\partial w} \\[2mm] \dfrac{\partial y}{\partial v} & \dfrac{\partial y}{\partial w} \end{vmatrix}_{x = g^{-1}(v, w),\, y = h^{-1}(v, w)} \tag{6.176}$$

where $\det|A|$ denotes the determinant of the matrix A. Substituting (6.176) into (6.175), the PDF $f_{vw}(v, w)$ is given by

$$f_{vw}(v, w) = f_{xy}(x, y) J(x, y)\big|_{x = g^{-1}(v, w),\, y = h^{-1}(v, w)} \tag{6.177}$$

The inverses $g^{-1}(v, w)$ and $h^{-1}(v, w)$ exist because the mappings in (6.174) are one-to-one. We will now use these results to introduce the Rayleigh PDF in Example 6.26.

Example 6.26

Assume that the random variables x and y are $\mathcal{N}(0, \sigma^2)$ and statistically independent. Let r and ϕ be the polar coordinate representation of x and y

$$r = g(x, y) = \sqrt{x^2 + y^2} \tag{6.178}$$

$$\phi = h(x, y) = \tan^{-1}\frac{y}{x} \tag{6.179}$$

Determine the PDFs of r and ϕ.

Solution

The joint PDF of independent Gaussian random variables x and y is obtained from (6.163) as

$$f_{xy}(x, y) = \frac{1}{2\pi\sigma^2} e^{-(x^2 + y^2)/2\sigma^2} \tag{6.180}$$

The inverse transformations are obtained by solving for x and y from (6.178) and (6.179) as

$$x = r\cos\phi = g^{-1}(r, \phi), \quad 0 \le r < \infty,\ -\pi \le \phi \le \pi \tag{6.181}$$

$$y = r\sin\phi = h^{-1}(r, \phi) \tag{6.182}$$

The Jacobian $J(r, \phi)$ is given by

$$J(r, \phi) = \det \begin{pmatrix} \dfrac{\partial x}{\partial r} & \dfrac{\partial x}{\partial \phi} \\[2mm] \dfrac{\partial y}{\partial r} & \dfrac{\partial y}{\partial \phi} \end{pmatrix}_{x = g^{-1}(r, \phi),\, y = h^{-1}(r, \phi)}$$

$$= \det \begin{pmatrix} \cos\phi & -r\sin\phi \\ \sin\phi & r\cos\phi \end{pmatrix} = r \qquad (6.183)$$

The joint PDF $f_{r\phi}(r, \phi)$ is obtained by substituting (6.180) through (6.183) into (6.177) as

$$f_{r\phi}(r, \phi) = \frac{r}{2\pi\sigma^2}e^{-r^2/2\sigma^2}, \quad 0 \le r < \infty, -\pi \le \phi \le \pi \qquad (6.184)$$

The PDF in (6.184) is independent of the angle ϕ, which implies that random variables r and ϕ are statitiscally independent. We integrate out ϕ in (6.184) to obtain the marginal PDF $f_r(r)$ as

$$f_r(r) = \frac{r}{\sigma^2}e^{-r^2/2\sigma^2}, \quad 0 \le r < \infty \qquad (6.185)$$

Equation (6.185) is referred to as the **Rayleigh's PDF.** It is displayed in Figure 6.16. If we now integrate (6.184) over r, it can be shown that ϕ is uniformly distributed over $[-\pi, \pi]$.

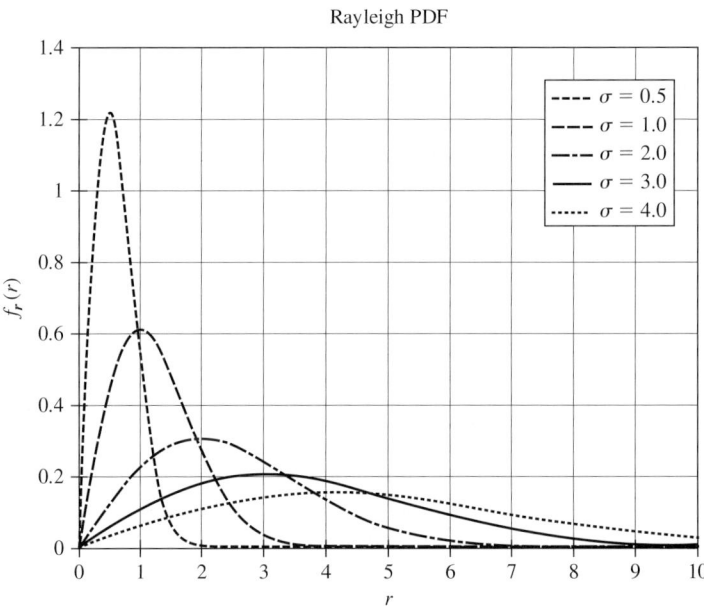

Figure 6.16 Rayleigh PDF.

6.8.2   Central Limit Theorem

Let $x_1, x_2, \ldots$ be **independent and identically distributed (iid)** random variables with finite mean m and variance σ^2. Let z_n be a sequence of random variables with zero mean and unity variance, defined by

$$z_n = \frac{\displaystyle\sum_{i=1}^{n}x_i - nm}{\sigma\sqrt{n}} \qquad (6.186)$$

Then

$$\lim_{n \to \infty} P\{z_n \leq z\} = \int_{-\infty}^{z} \frac{1}{\sqrt{2\pi}} e^{-u^2/2} du \qquad (6.187)$$

That is, the CDF of z_n converges to a Gaussian CDF $\mathcal{N}(0, 1)$ as n approaches ∞, independent of the distribution of random variables x_i. This result is known as the **central limit theorem.** In a nutshell, the central limit theorem states that the sum of almost any set of independent random variables rapidly converges to the Gaussian distribution. This explains why the Gaussian distribution arises so commonly in practice to reflect the additive effect of a large number of random occurrences.

6.9   RANDOM PROCESSES: INTRODUCTION

Random variables assign one or more numbers to each outcome ξ of a random experiment. In the case of random process $x(t)$, every such outcome is assigned a waveform $x(t, \xi)$. $x(t, \xi)$ is called the **sample function,** and the **ensemble** of all such sample functions or realizations over time represents the random process $x(t)$. Figure 6.17 displays the correspondence between the sample space of a random experiment and the ensemble of sample functions of a random process. Note that various sample functions themselves are deterministic. There is no randomness associated with the sample function waveform. The randomness is associated with the occurrence of a particular outcome, which in turn determines the sample function observed.

Figure 6.18 displays sample functions of three commonly encountered random processes in communications. The Gaussian random process models thermal noise in electronic systems. The amplitude of noise sample at any instant is a Gaussian random variable. The Poisson process is a counting process for the number of events that have occurred up to a particular time. Examples that are well-modeled as Poisson processes include the radioactive decay of atoms, telephone calls arriving at a central office switch, and the number of hits to a Web site. Figure 6.18(c) illustrates the binary random process where the sample functions correspond to sequence of random data bits conveying the message information. These random binary sequences may represent text, speech, image, or video information signals.

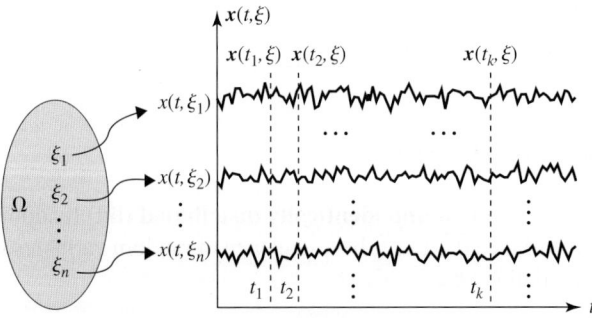

Figure 6.17 Conceptual representation of a random process.

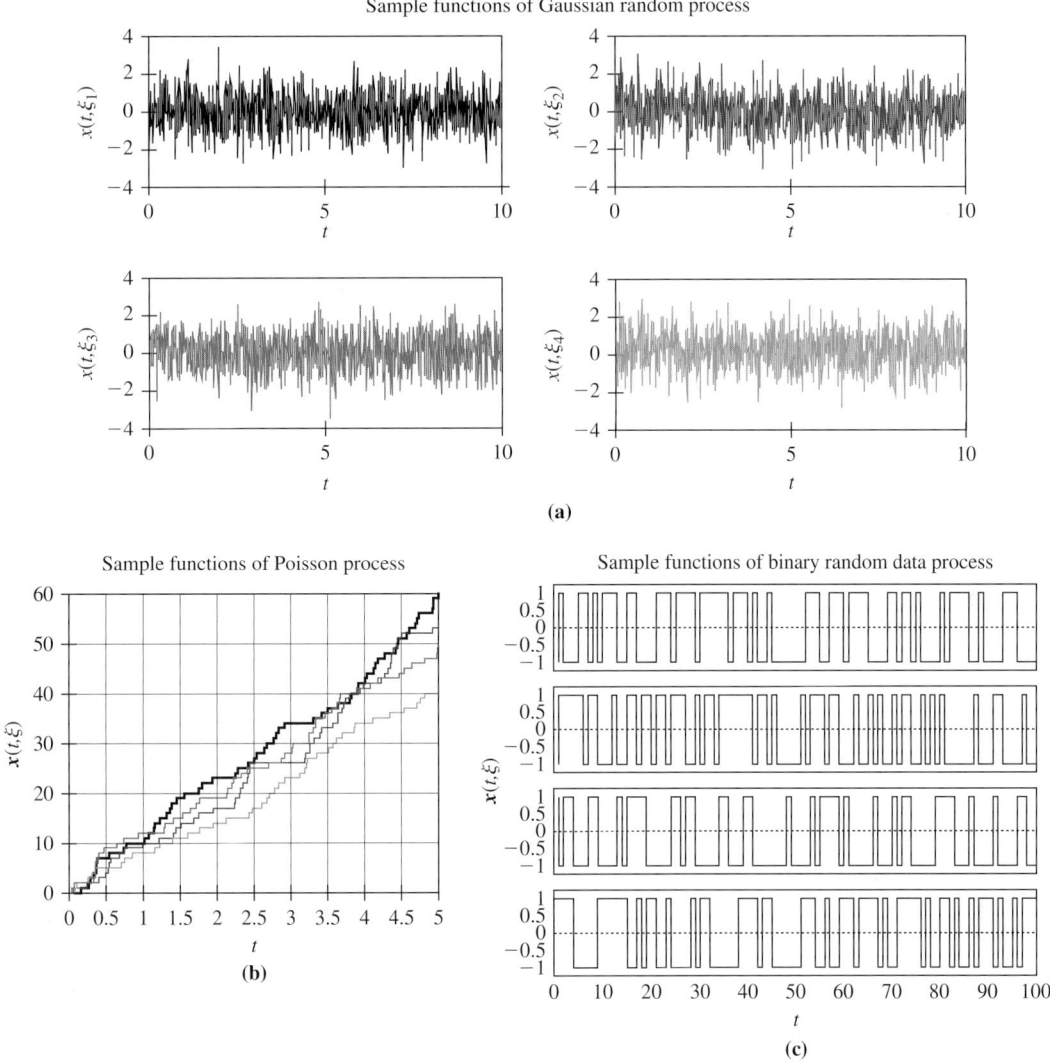

Figure 6.18 Sample functions of commonly encountered random processes.

Example 6.27

Consider the random process

$$x(t, \xi) = A(\xi)\sin(2\pi f_0 t + \theta), \quad -\infty < t < \infty \tag{6.188}$$

where the amplitude $A(\xi)$ is a uniformly distributed random variable in the interval $[-1, 1]$. The sample functions of this random process are sinusoidal waveforms that assume amplitudes in the range $[-1, 1]$ with equal likelihood. The amplitude $A(\xi)$ corresponds to a particular outcome ξ of a random experiment. Figure 6.19(a) displays the realizations of this random process for the case $\theta = 0$.

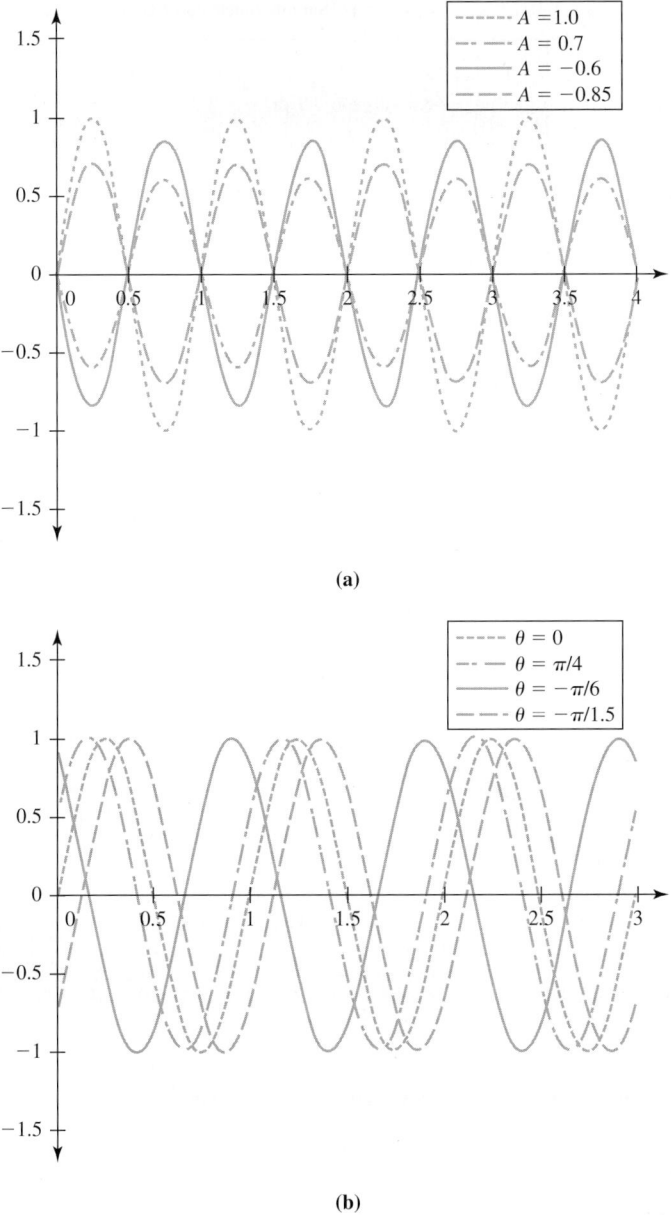

Figure 6.19 Sample functions of random process in Example 6.27

Next we consider the random process

$$x(t, \xi) = A\sin[2\pi f_0 t + \boldsymbol{\theta}(\xi)], \quad -\infty < t < \infty \tag{6.189}$$

where the random phase $\boldsymbol{\theta}(\xi)$ is a uniformly distributed random variable in the range $[-\pi, \pi]$. The sample functions of this random process are sinusoidal waveforms that incur random phase shifts in the range $[-\pi, \pi]$ with equal likelihood. The phase shift $\boldsymbol{\theta}(\xi)$ corresponds to a particular outcome ξ of a random experiment. Figure 6.19(b) displays the realizations of this random process for the case $A = 1$.

6.9.1 Characterization of a Random Process

A random process is described by its ensemble of sample functions (waveforms) and the probability distribution function over the ensemble. Consider the random process $x(t)$ in Figure 6.17 at a fixed time t_1. Each time we perform the random experiment, a number $x(t_1, \xi)$ is observed at $t = t_1$ depending upon the particular outcome ξ and the corresponding realization $x(t, \xi)$. The amplitudes of sample functions at instant t_1, therefore, represent the random variable $x(t_1, \xi)$. We will use the notation x_1 to represent the random variable $x(t_1, \xi)$ at instant t_1. Thus, random variables $x_1, x_2, \ldots, x_n$ represent amplitudes of sample functions at $t = t_1, t_2, \ldots, t_n$. A random process can, therefore, be viewed as a collection of an infinite number of random variables. Consequently, it is completely described by the nth order joint PDF $f_x(x_1, x_2, \ldots, x_n, t_1, t_2, \ldots, t_n)$ for all n and for any choice of $t_1, t_2, \ldots, t_n$. In many cases, this description would be extremely difficult to generate. Because we are mainly concerned with the transmission of random signals through linear systems, we will not need the knowledge of the nth order PDF. For our purpose, the knowledge of the first- and second-order PDFs would suffice to estimate certain averages (mean and mean-square values) and frequency content (power spectrum) of the process $x(t)$. We will use the notation $x(t)$ to represent the random process as well as the random variable $x(t, \xi)$ at instant t.

The first-order distribution function of the random variable $x(t)$ is defined as

$$F_x(x, t) = P\{x(t) \leq x\} \tag{6.190}$$

Notice that $F_x(x, t)$ depends on t, because for a different t, we obtain a different random variable. Further, the PDF of random variable $x(t)$ is

$$f_x(x, t) = \frac{dF_x(x, t)}{dx} \tag{6.191}$$

The first-order PDF describes the amplitude distributions of the sample functions at a single instant of time t. The knowledge of first-order PDF $f_x(x, t)$ allows us to determine the expected value and the mean-square value of the random process. The expected value of the random process $x(t)$ is defined as

$$m_x(t) = \overline{x(t)} = E\{x(t)\} = \int\limits_{-\infty}^{+\infty} x f_x(x, t) dx \tag{6.192}$$

In general, $m_x(t)$ is a function of time. Similarly, the mean-square value of the random process $x(t)$ is given by

$$\overline{x^2(t)} = E\{x^2(t)\} = \int\limits_{-\infty}^{+\infty} x^2 f_x(x, t) dx \tag{6.193}$$

Example 6.28

Find the first-order PDF $f_x(x, t)$ for the random process

$$x(t) = A\cos(\omega_0 t + \theta)$$

where θ is a uniformly distributed random variable over the range $[0, 2\pi]$.

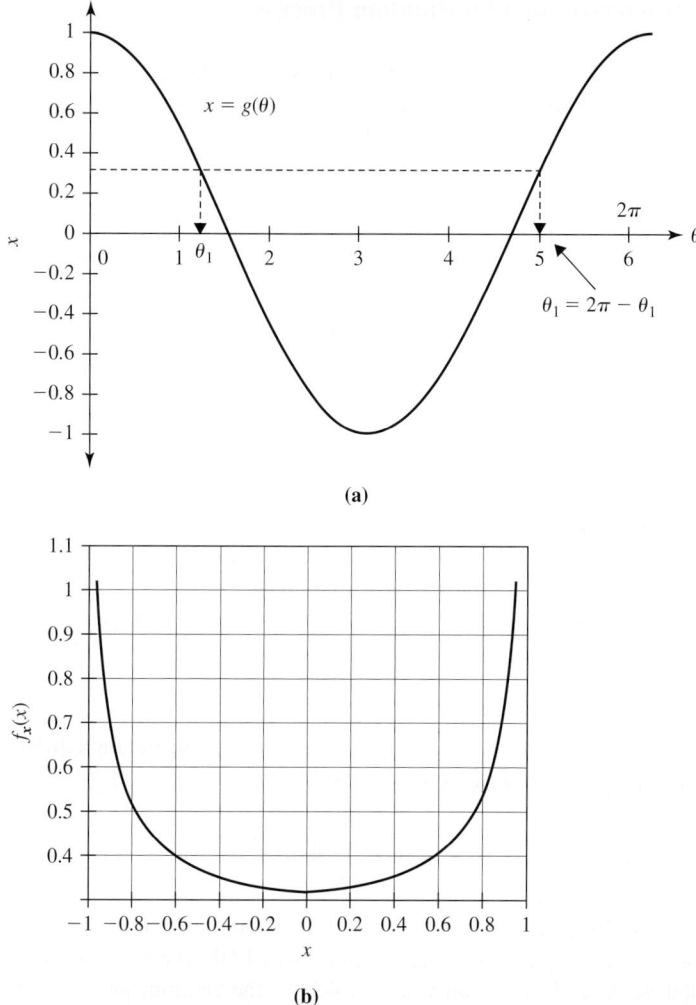

Figure 6.20 Sinusoidal waveform with random phase: (a) mapping $x = g(\theta)$; (b) first-order PDF of **x**.

Solution

At a specific time instant t, the values of random process $\mathbf{x}(t)$ define a random variable, say, $x = A\cos(\omega_0 t + \boldsymbol{\theta})$. Now the random variable $\mathbf{x}$ is a function of another random variable $\boldsymbol{\theta}$. That is,

$$x = g(\boldsymbol{\theta}) = A\cos(\omega_0 t + \boldsymbol{\theta})$$

Note from Figure 6.20(a) that $\mathbf{x}$ is a double-valued function of $\boldsymbol{\theta}$. That is, for each value of x, there are two values of θ: θ_1 and $\theta_2 = 2\pi - \theta_1$. Using (6.73), we can write

$$f_x(x) = \left.\frac{f_\theta(\theta_1)}{|g'(\theta_1)|}\right|_{\theta_1 = g^{-1}(x)} + \left.\frac{f_x(\theta_2)}{|g'(\theta_2)|}\right|_{\theta_2 = g^{-1}(x)} \tag{6.194}$$

Now

$$g'(\theta)|_{\theta=\theta_1=g^{-1}(x)} = \frac{d}{d\theta}A\cos(2\pi f_0 t + \theta)|_{\theta=\theta_1} = -A\sin(2\pi f_0 t + \theta_1)$$

$$= -A\sin[\cos^{-1}(x/A)] = -\sqrt{A^2 - x^2} \qquad (6.195)$$

Substituting (6.195) into (6.194) yields

$$f_x(x) = \frac{1}{2\pi\sqrt{A^2 - x^2}} + \frac{1}{2\pi\sqrt{A^2 - x^2}} = \frac{1}{\pi\sqrt{A^2 - x^2}}$$

The range of random variable x is $[-A, A]$. Therefore, the first-order PDF of x can be written as

$$f_x(x) = \begin{cases} \dfrac{1}{\pi\sqrt{A^2 - x^2}}, & -A < x < A \\ 0, & \text{otherwise} \end{cases} \qquad (6.196)$$

Figure 6.20(b) displays $f_x(x)$.

The first-order PDF is inadequate to describe the spectral characteristics of the random process. The latter depends on how rapidly the random signal amplitude changes as a function of time. The second-order CDF provides a complete statistical description of the behavior of random signal amplitudes $x(t_1)$ and $x(t_2)$ at time instants t_1 and t_2, respectively. The second-order CDF of the random process $x(t)$ is defined as

$$F_x(x_1, x_2, t_1, t_2) = P\{x(t_1) \le x_1, x(t_2) \le x_2\} \qquad (6.197)$$

The second-order PDF of the process $x(t)$ is

$$f_x(x_1, x_2, t_1, t_2) = \frac{\partial^2 F_x(x_1, x_2, t_1, t_2)}{\partial x_1 \partial x_2} \qquad (6.198)$$

A partial second-order description of the random process is given by the statistical average of the product of the random variables $x(t_1)$ and $x(t_2)$. This is called the **auto-correlation function** of the random process $x(t)$. It is defined as

$$R_x(t_1, t_2) = E\{x(t_1)x(t_2)\} \qquad (6.199)$$

It is a measure of correlation between sample function values of the random process $x(t)$ at time instants t_1 and t_2.

In many situations we are interested in the joint behavior of more than one random process at a time. A common example involves analyzing the interaction between random process $x(t)$ that is input to a system and another process $y(t)$ that is the output of a system. The **cross-correlation function** $R_{xy}(t_1, t_2)$ provides a measure of correlation between sample function amplitudes of processes $x(t)$ and $y(t)$ at time instants t_1 and t_2, respectively. It is defined as

$$R_{xy}(t_1, t_2) = E\{x(t_1)y(t_2)\} \qquad (6.200)$$

Example 6.29

Find the autocorrelation function of the random process

$$x(t) = A\cos(\omega_0 t + \theta)$$

where θ is a uniformly distributed random variable with range $[0, 2\pi]$.

Solution

$$R_x(t, t + \tau) = E\{x(t)x(t + \tau)\} = E\{A^2\cos(\omega_0 t + \theta)\cos[\omega_0(t + \tau) + \theta]\}$$

$$= \frac{A^2}{2}E\{\cos(\omega_0\tau) + \cos(2\omega_0 t + \omega_0\tau + 2\theta)\}$$

$$= \frac{A^2}{2}\Big[\cos(\omega_0\tau) + E\{\cos(2\omega_0 t + \omega_0\tau + 2\theta)\}\Big]$$

Now

$$E\{\cos[2\omega_0 t + \omega_0\tau + 2\theta]\} = \int_{-\infty}^{\infty} f_\theta(\theta)\cos[2\omega_0 t + \omega_0\tau + 2\theta]d\theta$$

$$= \frac{1}{2\pi}\int_{0}^{2\pi} \cos[2\omega_0 t + \omega_0\tau + 2\theta]d\theta = 0$$

$$R_x(t, t + \tau) = \frac{A^2}{2}\cos(\omega_0\tau)$$

6.9.2 Stationary Random Processes

A process whose statistical properties do not change with time is called a **stationary random process.** If a random process $x(t)$ is stationary, then its first-order PDF does not depend on t. That is,

$$f_x(x, t) = f_x(x) \tag{6.201}$$

A random process $x(t)$ satisfying (6.201) is called a **first-order (strict-sense) stationary process.** It is obvious that in this case the mean and mean-square values of $x(t)$ are time invariant. That is,

$$m_x(t) = \overline{x(t)} = E\{x(t)\} = \int_{-\infty}^{\infty} xf_x(x)dx = \text{constant} \tag{6.202}$$

$$\overline{x^2(t)} = E\{x^2(t)\} = \int_{-\infty}^{\infty} x^2f_x(x)dx = \text{constant} \tag{6.203}$$

Similarly, a random process $x(t)$ is called a **second-order (strict-sense) stationary process** if

$$f_x(x_1, x_2, t_1, t_2) = f_x(x_1, x_2, t_1 - t_2) \tag{6.204}$$

That is, the second-order PDF of a stationary process is independent of the time origin and depends only on the time difference $t_1 - t_2 = \tau$. As a consequence of (6.204), the autocorrelation function is given by

$$R_x(t_1, t_2) = E\{x(t_1)x(t_2)\} = \int\limits_{-\infty}^{\infty} \int\limits_{-\infty}^{\infty} x_1 x_2 \, f_x(x_1, x_2, t_1 - t_2) dx_1 dx_2$$

$$= R_x(t_1 - t_2) = R_x(\tau) \qquad (6.205)$$

Equation (6.205) states that the autocorrelation function of a second-order stationary process depends only on the time difference τ. Equations (6.202) and (6.205) are consequences of the random process being first- and second-order strict sense stationary. Because the conditions for the first- and second-order stationarity are usually difficult to verify in practice, we define the concept of wide-sense stationarity that represents a less stringent requirement.

6.9.3   Wide-Sense Stationary Random Processes

A random process $x(t)$ is said to be **wide-sense stationary (WSS)** if

$$m_x(t) = \overline{x(t)} = E\{x(t)\} = \text{constant} \qquad (6.206)$$

$$R_x(t, t + \tau) = R_x(\tau) \qquad (6.207)$$

Thus, in order for a random process to be WSS, we only require that its mean is a constant and that the autocorrelation function depends only on the time difference. We observe that the random signal in Example 6.29 is a WSS process. Because (6.206) and (6.207) follow from (6.201) and (6.204), it follows that a strict-sense stationary random process is always wide-sense stationary. However, the converse is not true in general, except for the Gaussian random process. That is, if a Gaussian random process is wide-sense stationary, it is stationary in the strict sense as well. This is because the nth-order joint PDF of a Gaussian random process, as indicated in (6.169), depends only on the first- and second-order statistics that form the basis of the wide-sense stationarity definition.

The random processes $x(t)$ and $y(t)$ are said to be **jointly stationary in wide-sense** if (a) $x(t)$ is WSS; (b) $y(t)$ is WSS; and (c) their cross-correlation is invariant under the shift of time origin. That is,

$$R_{xy}(t, t + \tau) = R_{xy}(\tau) \qquad (6.208)$$

6.9.4   Ergodic Random Processes

The computation of statistical averages (e.g., mean and autocorrelation function) of a random process requires an ensemble of sample functions (data records) that may not always be feasible. In many real-life applications, it would be very convenient to calculate the averages from a single data record. This is possible in certain random processes called **ergodic processes.** Because it is possible to calculate only time averages from a single sample function, it follows that in an ergodic process the time averages are *identical* to the ensemble averages. The ergodic assumption implies that any sample function of the process takes all possible values in time with the same relative frequency that an ensemble will take at any given instant.

Because time averages by definition are independent of time variable, it follows that an ergodic process is always stationary. The reverse, of course, is not always true. A stationary process may not necessarily be an ergodic process. Thus, ergodic processes form a subcategory of stationary processes, as illustrated in Figure 6.21. It is difficult to establish whether a random process is ergodic or not, because we must verify equivalence between time and ensemble averages of all orders. However, in many applications, stationary processes are ergodic with respect to first- and second-order averages. That is,

$$\overline{x(t)} = E\{x(t)\} = \lim_{T \to \infty} \frac{1}{T} \int_{-T/2}^{T/2} x(t)dt = \langle x(t) \rangle \tag{6.209}$$

$$R_x(\tau) = E\{x(t)x(t + \tau)\} = \lim_{T \to \infty} \frac{1}{T} \int_{-T/2}^{T/2} x(t)x^*(t - \tau)dt = \mathcal{R}_x(\tau) \tag{6.210}$$

where $\langle x(t) \rangle$ and $\mathcal{R}_x(\tau)$ are time-average mean and autocorrelation function (Section 2.9.1) of $x(t)$.

6.9.5   Properties of the Autocorrelation Function

For a WSS random process $x(t)$, the autocorrelation function has the following important properties:

1. $R_x(0) = E\{x^2(t)\} = \overline{x^2(t)} \geq 0$ $\tag{6.211}$

Thus $R_x(0)$ represents the total power of the random signal $x(t)$.

2. $R_x(\tau) = R_x(-\tau)$ $\tag{6.212}$

3. $\lim_{|\tau| \to \infty} R_x(\tau) = \lim_{|\tau| \to \infty} E\{x(t)x(t + \tau)\} = E\{x(t)\}E\{x(t + \tau)\} = \overline{x(t)}^2$ $\tag{6.213}$

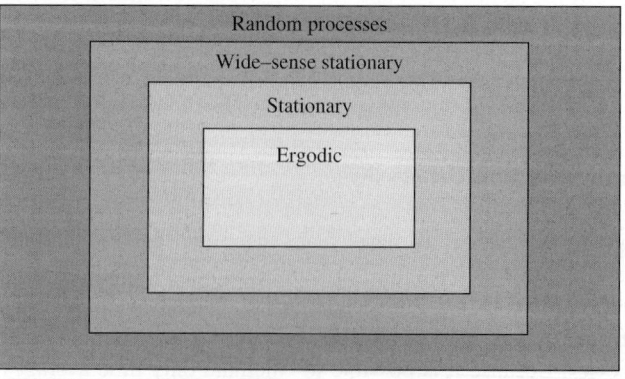

Figure 6.21 Classification of random processes.

For $|\tau|$ large, $R_x(\tau)$ represents the average or DC power of the random signal.

4. $|R_x(\tau)| \le |R_x(0)|$ for all τ $\hspace{4cm}$ (6.214)

6.9.6 Uncorrelated, Orthogonal, and Independent Random Processes

The random processes $x(t)$ and $y(t)$ are said to be **uncorrelated** if their cross-correlation function is equal to the product of their statistical means for arbitrary choice of t and τ; that is,

$$R_{xy}(t, t + \tau) = E\{x(t)y(t + \tau)\} = E\{x(t)\}E\{y(t + \tau)\} \hspace{1cm} (6.215)$$

If $x(t)$ and $y(t)$ are also WSS,

$$R_{xy}(\tau) = E\{x(t)y(t + \tau)\} = E\{x(t)\}E\{y(t)\} \hspace{1cm} (6.216)$$

It follows from (6.180) that the cross-covariance function of uncorrelated processes is zero for arbitrary choice of t and τ.

$$Cov(x(t), y(t + \tau)) = E\{x(t)y(t + \tau)\} - E\{x(t)\}E\{y(t + \tau)\} = 0 \hspace{0.5cm} (6.217)$$

Random processes $x(t)$ and $y(t)$ are said to be **orthogonal** if their cross-correlation function is zero for arbitrary choice of t and τ; that is,

$$R_{xy}(\tau) = 0 \hspace{4cm} (6.218)$$

Note that if either of the processes $x(t)$ and $y(t)$ has a zero mean, uncorrelatedness implies orthogonality and vice versa.

$x(t)$ and $y(t)$ are said to be **independent random processes** if the set of random variables $x(t_1), x(t_2), \ldots, x(t_n)$ is statistically independent of the set of random variables $y(t_1'), y(t_2'), \ldots, y(t_n')$ for any choice of $t_1, t_2, \ldots, t_n$ and $t_1', t_2', \ldots, t_n'$. Independence implies that the joint PDF of the random variables is the product of the PDFs of the individual variables.

6.10 POWER SPECTRUM OF A RANDOM PROCESS

As discussed in Section 2.10, the power spectral density of a deterministic power signal $x(t)$ is defined as

$$\mathcal{G}_x(f) \equiv \lim_{T \to \infty} \frac{|X_T(f)|^2}{T} \hspace{3cm} (2.171)$$

where $X_T(f)$ is the FT of the truncated time function $x_T(t)$ defined in (2.165). We can apply (2.171) to each sample function, $x(t, \xi_i)$, of the random process $x(t)$. This yields the power spectral density function associated with $x(t, \xi_i)$ as

$$\mathcal{G}_x(f, \xi_i) = \lim_{T \to \infty} \frac{|X_T(f, \xi_i)|^2}{T} \hspace{3cm} (6.219)$$

Pioneers in the Field

Courtesy MIT Museum

Norbert Wiener was born on November 26, 1894, in Columbia, Missouri. Wiener, a child prodigy, graduated in mathematics from Tufts University in 1909 at the age of fourteen. He spent a year at Harvard as a graduate student in zoology but left after discovering his ineptitude with laboratory work. At his father's suggestion, he began to study philosophy and completed his Ph.D. at Harvard in 1913 with a dissertation on mathematical logic. On a grant from Harvard, Wiener went first to England to study mathematical logic at the University of Cambridge under Bertrand Russell, and then to the University of Göttingen in Germany to study with David Hilbert. He also began a serious study of general mathematics, in which he was strongly influenced by Russell (who had advised him in this direction), by the English pure mathematician Godfrey Hardy, and to a lesser extent by Hilbert.

During the 1920s, Wiener's highly innovative work on stochastic processes and, in particular, on the theory of Brownian motion and on generalized harmonic analysis, made significant contributions to the field of mathematical analysis. During the Second World War, Wiener worked on gunfire control, namely, the problem of pointing a gun to fire at a moving target. His findings led to *Extrapolation, Interpolation, and Smoothing of Stationary Time Series* in 1949, which first appeared as a classified report and established Wiener as a codiscoverer, along with the Russian mathematician Andrey Kolmogorov, of the theory on the prediction of stationary time series. It introduced certain statistical methods into control and communications engineering ("Wiener filtering") and exerted great influence in these areas. This work also led him to formulate the concept of cybernetics, a formalization of the notion of feedback, with many implications for engineering, systems control, computer science, biology, philosophy, and the organization of society.

Wiener had an extraordinarily wide range of interests and contributed to many areas in addition to those mentioned above. In 1963, Wiener was awarded the National Medal of Science; he was presented with the medal a few weeks before his death the following year.

where $X_T(f, \xi_i)$ is the FT of the truncated sample function $x_T(t, \xi_i)$. Using (6.219), we can generate an ensemble of power spectral density functions—one for each sample function of $x(t)$. Therefore, a meaningful definition for the power spectral density of a random process would be the ensemble average of the power spectral density spectra of all the sample functions. That is,

$$G_x(f) \triangleq \lim_{T \to \infty} \frac{E\{|X_T(f)|^2\}}{T} \tag{6.220}$$

6.10.1 Wiener-Khinchin Theorem

For a wide-sense stationary random process $x(t)$, the power spectral density $G_x(f)$ defined by (6.220) is the Fourier transform of the autocorrelation function $R_x(\tau)$. That is,

$$G_x(f) = \Im[R_x(\tau)] = \int_{-\infty}^{\infty} R_x(\tau)e^{-j2\pi f\tau}d\tau \tag{6.221}$$

Conversely,

$$R_x(\tau) = \Im^{-1}[G_x(f)] = \int_{-\infty}^{\infty} G_x(f)e^{j2\pi f\tau}df \tag{6.222}$$

The proof of the Wiener-Khinchin theorem can be found in reference.[1] Combining (6.211) with (6.222) yields

$$\overline{x^2(t)} = R_x(0) = \int_{-\infty}^{\infty} G_x(f)df \qquad (6.223)$$

We conclude from (6.223) that the area under $G_x(f)$ represents the total power of the random process $x(t)$; hence $G_x(f)$ truly represents the power spectral density.

Example 6.30

The spectral density of a random signal $x(t)$ is shown in Figure 6.22.
    Determine the following:

a. The autocorrelation function
b. The total power
c. The DC power

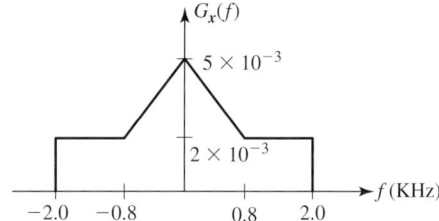

Figure 6.22 Spectral density of $x(t)$ in Example 6.30.

Solution

a. From Figure 6.22, the spectral density of $x(t)$ can be expressed as

$$G_x(f) = 2 \times 10^{-3} \, \Pi\left(\frac{f}{4 \times 10^3}\right) + 3 \times 10^{-3} \, \Lambda\left(\frac{f}{1.6 \times 10^3}\right)$$

Using Table 2.2, we can write

$$\Pi\left(\frac{f}{4 \times 10^3}\right) \xleftrightarrow{\Im} 4 \times 10^3 \times \text{sinc}(4 \times 10^3 \tau)$$

$$\Lambda\left(\frac{f}{1.6 \times 10^3}\right) \xleftrightarrow{\Im} 0.8 \times 10^3 \times \text{sinc}^2(0.8 \times 10^3 \times \tau)$$

$$R_x(\tau) = 8 \times \text{sinc}(4 \times 10^3 \tau) + 2.4 \times \text{sinc}^2(0.8 \times 10^3 \times \tau)$$

b. Total Power $= R_x(\tau)|_{\tau=0} = 8 + 2.4 = 10.4$ Watts
c. DC Power $= \lim_{\tau \to \infty} R_x(\tau)| = \overline{x(t)}^2 = 0$

---

[1] A. Leon-Garcia, *Probability and Random Processes for Electrical Engineering,* 3rd ed, (Upper Saddle River, NJ: Prentice Hall, 2008).

6.10.2   Transmission of Random Signals Through Linear Time-Invariant Systems

The output of a **linear time-invariant (LTI)** system with impulse response function $h(t)$ to the wide-sense stationary random signal $x(t)$ is given by applying (2.41) as

$$y(t) = x(t) \otimes h(t) = \int_{-\infty}^{+\infty} x(t - u)h(u)du \tag{6.224}$$

Now applying (2.181) to each sample function $x(t, \xi_i)$ yields the power spectral density of $y(t, \xi_i)$ as

$$\mathcal{G}_y(f, \xi_i) = |H(f)|^2 \mathcal{G}_x(f, \xi_i) = |H(f)|^2 \lim_{T \to \infty} \frac{|X_T(f, \xi_i)|^2}{T} \tag{6.225}$$

The power spectral density $G_y(f)$ of the output random process $y(t)$ is the ensemble average $\mathcal{G}_y(f, \xi)$ over all ξ. That is,

$$G_y(f) = E\{\mathcal{G}_y(f, \xi)\} \tag{6.226}$$

Substituting (6.225) into (6.226), we obtain

$$G_y(f) = E\left\{|H(f)|^2 \lim_{T \to \infty} \frac{|X_T(f, \xi)|^2}{T}\right\}$$

$$= |H(f)|^2 \lim_{T \to \infty} \frac{E\{|X_T(f, \xi)|^2\}}{T} = |H(f)|^2 E\{\mathcal{G}_x(f, \xi)\} \tag{6.227}$$

Substituting (6.220) into (6.227) yields

$$G_y(f) = |H(f)|^2 G_x(f) \tag{6.228}$$

The relationship (6.228) between input and output power spectral densities for random processes is *identical* to that for deterministic signals in (2.181) with appropriate definitions for spectral densities. Figure 6.23 displays these relationships for deterministic and random signals. Equation (6.228) applies to all wide-sense stationary random processes.

Taking the inverse FT of both sides of (6.228), the autocorrelation function of the output random signal $y(t)$ is obtained as

$$R_y(\tau) = \mathfrak{I}^{-1}[G_y(f)] = \mathfrak{I}^{-1}[H(f)H^*(f)G_x(f)] \tag{6.229}$$

The application of the convolution theorem (2.79) of the FT to (6.229) yields

$$R_y(\tau) = h(\tau) \otimes h(-\tau) \otimes R_x(\tau) \tag{6.230}$$

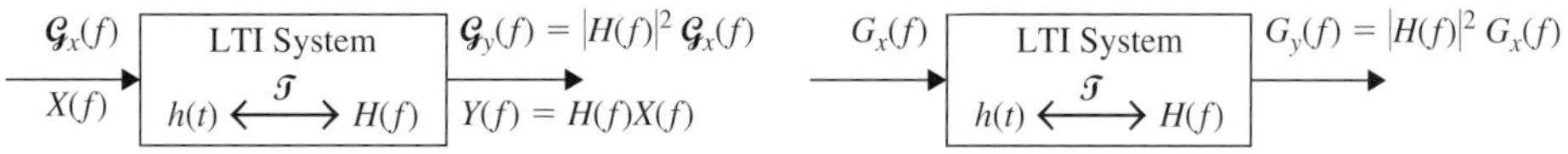

(a) Deterministic signals **(b) Random signals**

Figure 6.23 Power spectral densities of deterministic and random signals.

Let

$$R_{xy}(\tau) = E\{\boldsymbol{x}(t)\boldsymbol{y}(t+\tau)\} \tag{6.231}$$

denote the cross-correlation function between the system input and output random processes $\boldsymbol{x}(t)$ and $\boldsymbol{y}(t)$. Substituting (6.224) into (6.231) yields

$$R_{xy}(\tau) = E\left\{\boldsymbol{x}(t)\int_{-\infty}^{\infty}\boldsymbol{x}(t+\tau-u)h(u)du\right\} \tag{6.232}$$

Interchanging the order of expectation and integration, we have

$$R_{xy}(\tau) = \int_{-\infty}^{\infty}E\{\boldsymbol{x}(t)\boldsymbol{x}(t+\tau-u)\}h(u)du = \int_{-\infty}^{\infty}R_x(\tau-u)h(u)du = h(\tau)\otimes R_x(\tau) \tag{6.233}$$

Taking the Fourier transform of both sides, we get

$$G_{xy}(f) = H(f)G_x(f) \tag{6.234}$$

The mean of output random process $\boldsymbol{y}(t)$ is obtained from (6.224) as

$$m_y(t) = \overline{\boldsymbol{y}(t)} = E\{\boldsymbol{y}(t)\} = E\left\{\int_{-\infty}^{\infty}\boldsymbol{x}(t-u)h(u)du\right\} \tag{6.235}$$

Exchanging the order of integration and expectation, we have

$$m_y(t) = \int_{-\infty}^{\infty}E\{\boldsymbol{x}(t-u)\}h(u)du = m_x\int_{\infty}^{\infty}h(u)du \tag{6.236}$$

Because $\boldsymbol{x}(t)$ is wide-sense stationary, m_y is independent of t from (6.236). We can rewrite (6.236) as

$$m_y = m_x H(0) \tag{6.237}$$

The expected value of the output process depends only on the LTI system response at DC (i.e., $H(f)$ at $f = 0$). Because the mean of $\boldsymbol{y}(t)$ does not vary with the choice of t, and its autocorrelation function depends on the time difference τ only, the response of an LTI system to a wide-sense stationary random process is also wide-sense stationary. Further, it follows from (6.233) that $\boldsymbol{x}(t)$and $\boldsymbol{y}(t)$ are jointly wide-sense stationary.

6.11   SOME IMPORTANT RANDOM PROCESSES

In this section, we review some important random processes that are frequently encountered in the study of communication systems.

6.11.1   Gaussian Random Process

A random process is said to be a Gaussian process if the random variables $x(t_1)$, $x(t_2), \ldots, x(t_n)$ are jointly Gaussian for any n and for any choice of $t_1, t_2, \ldots, t_n$. Many processes that arise from natural phenomena are approximated well by Gaussian processes, using central limit theorem arguments. Examples include thermal noise in resistors and diffusion noise in semiconductors. Gaussian processes are also relatively easy to handle analytically. That is why they are so important in communication systems. Some important properties of Gaussian processes follow.

1. A Gaussian process $x(t)$ is completely specified by the set of means

$$m_i = E\{x(t_i)\} \tag{6.238}$$

and the set of autocorrelation functions

$$R_x(t_i, t_j) = E\{x(t_i)x(t_j)\} \tag{6.239}$$

As discussed in Section 6.9.1, a random process is completely described by its nth order joint PDF $f_x(x_1, x_2, \ldots, x_n, t_1, t_2, \ldots, t_n)$. For a Gaussian random process, $f_x(x_1, x_2, \ldots, x_n, t_1, t_2, \ldots, t_n)$ is the multivariate PDF (6.169) of n jointly Gaussian random variables that is completely determined by the set of means and autocorrelation functions.

2. For a Gaussian random process $x(t)$, if $x(t_1), x(t_2), \ldots, x(t_n)$ for any set of distinct time instants $t_1, t_2, \ldots, t_n$ are uncorrelated, then they are statistically independent.

In Section 6.8, we proved the above property for a pair of uncorrelated Gaussian random variables and extended in (6.172) to n such random variables.

3. If $x(t)$ is a wide-sense stationary Gaussian process, then $x(t)$ is a strictly stationary Gaussian process.

This property follows from Property (a) and the definition of WSS random process in (6.206) and (6.207).

4. For an LTI system with Gaussian input process $x(t)$, the output process $y(t)$ is also Gaussian. Moreover, $x(t)$ and $y(t)$ are jointly Gaussian processes.

The output at $t = t_i$ of an LTI system with impulse response function $h(t)$ to the Gaussian random signal $x(t)$ can be expressed using (6.224) as

$$y(t_i) = \int_{-\infty}^{+\infty} x(u)h(t_i - u)du$$

$$= \lim_{\Delta u \to 0} \sum_{n=-\infty}^{\infty} x(n\Delta u)h(t_i - n\Delta u)\Delta u \tag{6.240}$$

Equation (6.240) states that the random variable $y(t_i)$ is a linear combination of n jointly Gaussian random variables, and is, therefore, Gaussian as discussed in Example 6.24. Further, any set of $y(t_i)$ for any choice of $t_1, t_2, \ldots, t_n$ are jointly Gaussian (see Problem 6.19). Therefore, the output process $y(t)$ is also Gaussian.

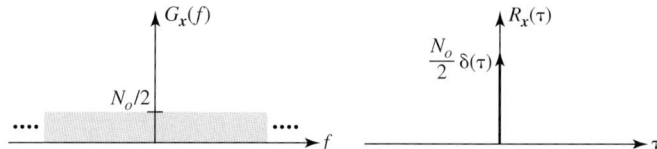

Figure 6.24 Power spectral density and autocorrelation function of WGN.

6.11.2   White Gaussian Noise

The term **white noise** is used to describe a wide-sense stationary random process whose power spectral density is flat over the entire frequency band $(-\infty, \infty)$ as shown in Figure 6.24. The constant spectral density, by convention, is denoted by $N_o/2$.

$$G_x(f) = \frac{N_o}{2} \tag{6.241}$$

Taking the inverse FT yields

$$R_x(\tau) = \frac{N_o}{2}\delta(\tau) \tag{6.242}$$

White noise represents the ultimate in randomness because (6.242) implies instantaneous decorrelation. That is, any two samples of WGN are uncorrelated no matter how closely spaced they are. White noise processes that are also Gaussian are called **white Gaussian noise (WGN).** It follows from (6.242) and the previously described property (b) of Gaussian process that WGN samples $x(t_1), x(t_2), \ldots, x(t_n)$ for any set of distinct time instants $t_1, t_2, \ldots, t_n$ are statistically independent.

WGN is an idealization of the noise observed in electronic components. This noise is caused by the chaotic motion of electrons in these components, and is commonly referred to as **thermal noise.** Because the random motion of a large number of electrons contributes to this noise, we can apply the central limit theorem to conclude that this noise is a Gaussian random process. Experiments conducted by Johnson (and verified analytically by Nyquist) in the 1920s showed that the power spectral density of thermal noise was constant for frequencies as high as 1000 GHz. Although WGN is a useful mathematical abstraction, it does not conform to any random signal or noise observed in real life. Because

$$\int_{-\infty}^{\infty} \frac{N_o}{2}df = \infty \tag{6.243}$$

WGN has infinite average power, which is physically impossible.

Example 6.31

White noise with two-sided spectral density $N_o/2$ passes through an ideal LP filter with bandwidth W Hz. Sketch and label the output noise spectral density and determine the output noise power.

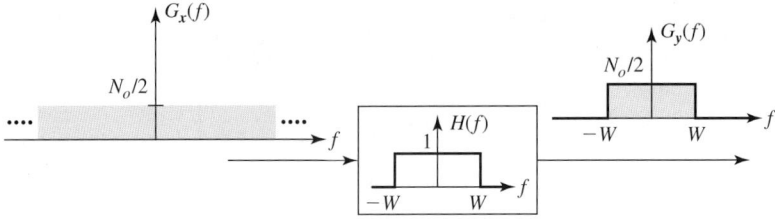

Figure 6.25 Ideal LP filter output noise spectral density.

Solution

The output spectral density is obtained by substituting (6.241) into (6.228) as

$$G_y(f) = |H(f)|^2 \, G_x(f) = \begin{cases} \dfrac{N_o}{2}, & |f| \leq W \\ 0, & \text{otherwise} \end{cases} \tag{6.244}$$

The autocorrelation function of band-limited WGN is the inverse FT of (6.244).

$$R_y(\tau) = N_o W \operatorname{sinc}(2W\tau) \tag{6.245}$$

Figure 6.25 displays the output noise spectral density. The output noise power $\overline{y^2(t)}$ is given from (6.245) as

$$\overline{y^2(t)} = R_y(0) = N_o W$$

Alternatively, it can be calculated by substituting (6.244) into (6.223) as

$$\overline{y^2(t)} = \int_{-\infty}^{\infty} G_y(f) df = \frac{N_o}{2} \int_{-W}^{W} df = N_o W \tag{6.246}$$

6.11.3   Filtered White Gaussian Noise

If WGN is passed through a nonideal filter with transfer function $H(f)$, the output noise spectral density is given by substituting (6.241) into (6.228) as

$$G_y(f) = \frac{N_o}{2} |H(f)|^2 \tag{6.247}$$

The mean-square output noise power is given by substituting (6.247) into (6.223) as

$$\overline{y^2(t)} = \int_{-\infty}^{\infty} G_y(f) df = \frac{N_o}{2} \int_{-\infty}^{\infty} |H(f)|^2 \, df$$

$$= N_o \int_{0}^{\infty} |H(f)|^2 \, df \tag{6.248}$$

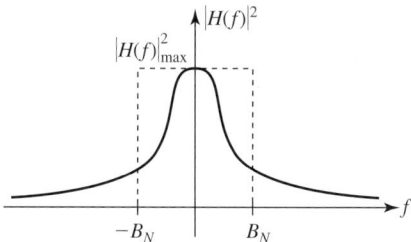

Figure 6.26 Definition of noise-equivalent bandwidth.

Noise-Equivalent Bandwidth

If the filter was ideal with bandwidth B_N and gain $|H(f)|_{\max}$ equal to the maximum gain of the nonideal filter $H(f)$ as shown in Figure 6.26, the mean-square output noise power is given by

$$\overline{y^2(t)} = \frac{N_o}{2} \times 2B_N \times |H(f)|_{\max}^2 = N_o B_N |H(f)|_{\max}^2 \tag{6.249}$$

We would now like to determine the equivalent bandwidth B_N that passes the same amount of noise power as the nonideal filter $H(f)$. Comparing (6.248) and (6.249), we obtain

$$N_o B_N |H(f)|_{\max}^2 = N_o \int_0^\infty |H(f)|^2 df$$

Solving for B_N yields

$$B_N = \frac{\displaystyle\int_0^\infty |H(f)|^2 df}{|H(f)|_{\max}^2} \tag{6.250}$$

B_N is called the **noise-equivalent bandwidth** of the nonideal filter $H(f)$.

Example 6.32

Consider the low-pass RC filter from Example 2.33. The transfer function is given by

$$H(f) = \frac{1}{1 + j(f/f_{3dB})} \tag{2.125}$$

where $f_{3dB} = \frac{1}{2\pi RC}$. Calculate the noise-equivalent bandwidth of the filter.

Solution

$$\int_0^\infty |H(f)|^2 df = \int_0^\infty \left|\frac{1}{1 + jf/f_{3dB}}\right|^2 df = \int_0^\infty \frac{1}{1 + (f/f_{3dB})^2} df \tag{6.251}$$

Making a change of variable $x = f/f_{\text{3dB}}$ in (6.251) and solving the resultant integral yields

$$\int_0^\infty |H(f)|^2 df = f_{\text{3dB}} \int_0^\infty \frac{1}{1 + x^2} dx = f_{\text{3dB}} \frac{\pi}{2} \tag{6.252}$$

Substituting $|H(f)|^2_{\max} = 1$ and (6.252) into (6.250), we have

$$B_N = \frac{\displaystyle\int_0^\infty |H(f)|^2 df}{|H(f)|^2_{\max}} = \frac{\pi f_{\text{3dB}}}{2} = \frac{\pi}{4\pi RC} = \frac{1}{4RC} \tag{6.253}$$

6.12   NARROWBAND NOISE

In many analog and digital communication systems, narrowband, WSS noise is an appropriate noise model. The power spectral density of a narrowband random process is nonzero only in a narrow frequency band which is very small compared to the center frequency f_c as illustrated in Figure 6.27.

It is convenient to represent the narrowband random process $x(t)$ in terms of quadrature components as

$$x(t) = x_c(t)\cos(2\pi f_c t) - x_s(t)\sin(2\pi f_c t) \tag{6.254}$$

or alternatively in amplitude-phase form as

$$x(t) = r(t)\cos\left[2\pi f_c t + \phi(t)\right] \tag{6.255}$$

The noise envelope $r(t)$ and phase $\phi(t)$ processes are related to quadrature noise components of $x(t)$ by

$$r(t) = \sqrt{x_c^2(t) + x_s^2(t)} \tag{6.256}$$

$$\phi(t) = \tan^{-1}\left(\frac{x_s(t)}{x_c(t)}\right) \tag{6.257}$$

We will prove that $x_c(t)$ and $x_s(t)$ are LP random processes, that is, slowly varying with respect to $\cos(2\pi f_c t)$.

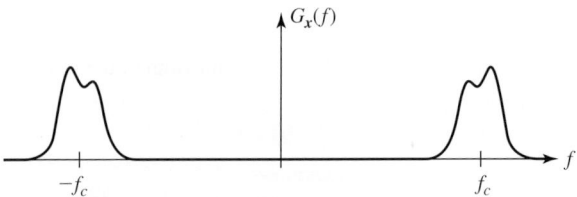

Figure 6.27 Example of a narrowband random process spectral density.

As in the case of deterministic BP signals, the quadrature components $x_c(t)$ and $x_s(t)$ can be expressed in terms of $x(t)$ and $\hat{x}(t)$ using equations similar to (4.61) and (4.62) as

$$x_c(t) = x(t)\cos(2\pi f_c t) + \hat{x}(t)\sin(2\pi f_c t) \tag{6.258}$$

$$x_s(t) = \hat{x}(t)\cos(2\pi f_c t) - x(t)\sin(2\pi f_c t) \tag{6.259}$$

where $\hat{x}(t)$ is Hilbert transform of the random process $x(t)$. The autocorrelation function of $x_c(t)$ is given by

$$
\begin{aligned}
R_{x_c}(\tau) &= E\{x_c(t)x_c(t + \tau)\} \\
&= E\{[x(t)\cos(2\pi f_c t) + \hat{x}(t)\sin(2\pi f_c t)][x(t + \tau)\cos(2\pi f_c(t + \tau)) + \hat{x}(t + \tau)\sin(2\pi f_c(t + \tau))]\} \\
&= E\{x(t)x(t + \tau)\cos(2\pi f_c t)\cos(2\pi f_c(t + \tau))\} + E\{x(t)\hat{x}(t + \tau)\cos(2\pi f_c t)\sin(2\pi f_c(t + \tau))\} \\
&\quad + E\{\hat{x}(t)x(t + \tau)\sin(2\pi f_c t)\cos(2\pi f_c(t + \tau))\} + E\{\hat{x}(t)\hat{x}(t + \tau)\sin(2\pi f_c t)\sin(2\pi f_c(t + \tau))\}
\end{aligned} \tag{6.260}
$$

Because the Hilbert transform represents an LTI system, hence $x(t)$ and $\hat{x}(t)$ are jointly WSS as discussed in Section 6.11.1. This allows us to express (6.260) as

$$
\begin{aligned}
R_{x_c}(\tau) &= R_x(\tau)\cos(2\pi f_c t)\cos(2\pi f_c(t + \tau)) + R_{x\hat{x}}(\tau)\cos(2\pi f_c t)\sin(2\pi f_c(t + \tau)) \\
&\quad + R_{\hat{x}x}(\tau)\sin(2\pi f_c t)\cos(2\pi f_c(t + \tau)) + R_{\hat{x}}(\tau)\sin(2\pi f_c t)\sin(2\pi f_c(t + \tau))
\end{aligned} \tag{6.261}
$$

where $R_x(\tau)$ and $R_{\hat{x}}(\tau)$ are autocorrelation functions of $x(t)$ and $\hat{x}(t)$, respectively.

Using (6.233) and (4A.9), we obtain the following relationship for the crosscorrelation function $R_{x\hat{x}}(\tau)$

$$R_{x\hat{x}}(\tau) = E\{x(t)\hat{x}(t + \tau)\} = h(\tau) \otimes R_x(\tau) = \mathcal{H}\{R_x(\tau)\} = \hat{R}_x(\tau) \tag{6.262}$$

where the impulse response function $h(\tau)$, given by (4A.8), represents Hilbert transform filtering operation. Similarly, it can be shown that

$$R_{\hat{x}x}(\tau) = -\hat{R}_x(\tau) \tag{6.263}$$

$$R_{\hat{x}}(\tau) = R_x(\tau) \tag{6.264}$$

Substituting (6.262) through (6.264) into (6.261), we obtain

$$
\begin{aligned}
R_{x_c}(\tau) &= R_x(\tau)\{\cos(2\pi f_c t)\cos(2\pi f_c(t + \tau)) + \sin(2\pi f_c t)\sin(2\pi f_c(t + \tau))\} \\
&\quad + \hat{R}_x(\tau)\{\cos(2\pi f_c t)\sin(2\pi f_c(t + \tau)) - \sin(2\pi f_c t)\cos(2\pi f_c(t + \tau))\} \\
&= R_x(\tau)\cos(2\pi f_c \tau) + \hat{R}_x(\tau)\sin(2\pi f_c \tau)
\end{aligned} \tag{6.265}
$$

We can show by following a similar procedure that

$$R_{x_s}(\tau) = R_{x_c}(\tau) = R_x(\tau)\cos(2\pi f_c \tau) + \hat{R}_x(\tau)\sin(2\pi f_c \tau) \tag{6.266}$$

Taking FT of both sides of (6.266) and noting that $\hat{R}_x(\tau) \overset{\Im}{\longleftrightarrow} -j\text{sgn}(f)G_x(f)$, the spectral density for $x_c(t)$ and $x_s(t)$ is obtained as

$$G_{x_c}(f) = G_{x_s}(f) = \frac{1}{2}\left[G_x(f+f_c) + G_x(f-f_c)\right]$$

$$-\frac{1}{2}\left[\text{sgn}(f-f_c)G_x(f-f_c) - \text{sgn}(f+f_c)G_x(f+f_c)\right] \quad (6.267)$$

(6.267) simplifies to yield the following expression for the spectral density of $x_c(t)$ and $x_s(t)$:

$$G_{x_c}(f) = G_{x_s}(f) = \begin{cases} G_x(f+f_c) + G_x(f-f_c), & |f| \le f_c \\ 0, & \text{otherwise} \end{cases} \quad (6.268)$$

Figure 6.28 illustrates the relationship between spectra of narrowband process $x(t)$ and its quadrature components. It is evident from Figure 6.28(d) that both $x_c(t)$ and $x_s(t)$ are LP random processes. We further observe from Figure 6.28(a) and (d) that areas under the spectral density functions $G_x(f)$, $G_{x_c}(f)$, and $G_{x_s}(f)$ are equal. Therefore, we can state that

$$\overline{x^2(t)} = \overline{x_c^2(t)} = \overline{x_s^2(t)} \quad (6.269)$$

The **cross-spectral density** of $x_c(t)$ and $x_s(t)$ is given by (Problem 6.32)

$$G_{x_c x_s}(f) = \begin{cases} j\left[G_x(f+f_c) - G_x(f-f_c)\right], & |f| \le f_c \\ 0, & \text{otherwise} \end{cases} \quad (6.270)$$

It should be noted that for the quadrature representation in (6.254), it is not necessary that f_c be the center frequency of the narrowband random process spectrum. We can obtain a quadrature representation for another carrier frequency f_c' that is not the center frequency of the spectrum. As such, the quadrature representation (6.254) is not unique. An infinite number of choices exist for the carrier frequency, and each choice leads to a distinct quadrature representation for the narrowband random process. This is illustrated in Example 6.33. If the spectral density $G_x(f)$ of the narrowband noise process $x(t)$ is *symmetrical* about the carrier frequency f_c, the cross-spectral density $G_{x_c x_s}(f) = 0$. Under this condition, $R_{x_c x_s}(\tau) = 0$, implying that $x_c(t)$ and $x_s(t)$ are uncorrelated. Further, if $x(t)$ is Gaussian, $x_c(t)$ and $x_s(t)$ are independent processes.

6.12.1 Narrowband White Gaussian Noise

Consider the noise $n(t)$ obtained by passing white Gaussian noise with spectral density $N_o/2$ through an ideal BP filter of bandwidth $2B$ centered at frequency f_c. It is assumed that $f_c \gg B$. Figure 6.29(a) displays the spectral density $G_n(f)$. $n(t)$ can be expressed in terms of its quadrature components $n_c(t)$ and $n_s(t)$ as

$$n(t) = n_c(t)\cos(2\pi f_c t) - n_s(t)\sin(2\pi f_c t) \quad (6.271)$$

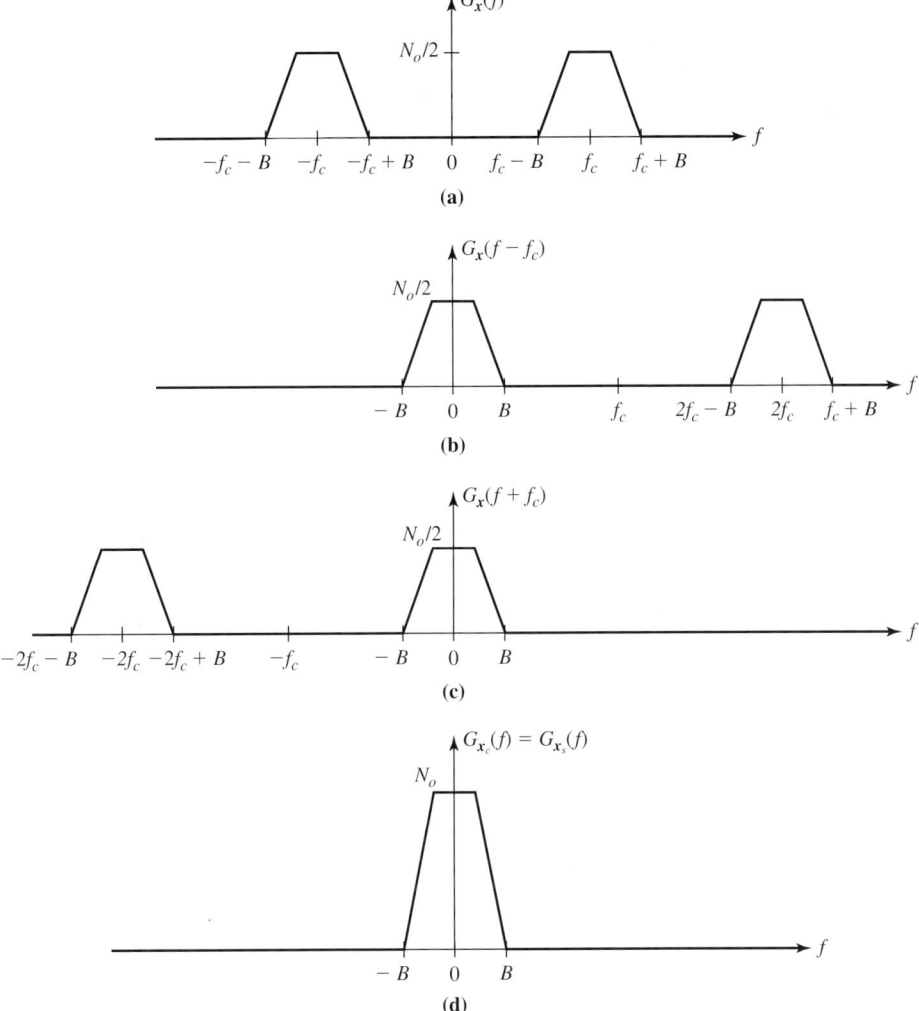

Figure 6.28 Spectral densities of quadrature noise components.

The spectral densities of $n_c(t)$ and $n_s(t)$ can be obtained from (6.268) as

$$G_{n_c}(f) = G_{n_s}(f) = \begin{cases} N_o, & |f| \le B \\ 0, & \text{otherwise} \end{cases} \tag{6.272}$$

Figure 6.29(b) displays spectral densities of $n_c(t)$ and $n_s(t)$. By application of (6.223), we obtain

$$\overline{n^2(t)} = 2 \int_{f_c - B}^{f_c + B} \frac{N_o}{2} df = 2N_o B \tag{6.273}$$

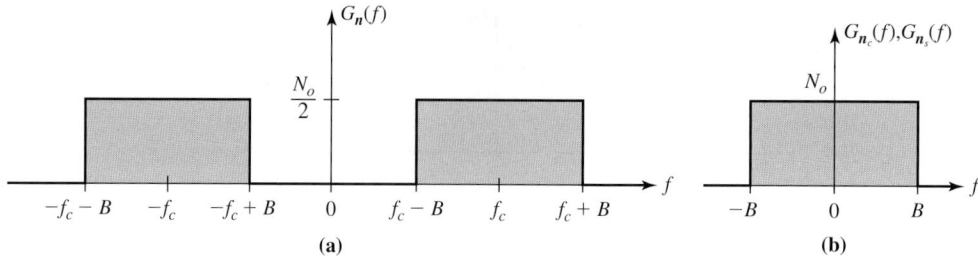

Figure 6.29 Spectral densities of narrowband WGN quadrature components.

$$\overline{n_c^2(t)} = \overline{n_s^2(t)} = \int_{-B}^{B} N_o df = 2N_o B \tag{6.274}$$

Therefore, $\overline{n^2(t)} = \overline{n_c^2(t)} = \overline{n_s^2(t)} = 2N_o B = \sigma^2$. Because $n_c(t)$ and $n_s(t)$ are $\mathcal{N}(0, \sigma^2)$ and statistically independent, their joint PDF is given by

$$f_{n_c n_s}(x, y) = \frac{1}{2\pi\sigma^2} e^{-(x^2 + y^2)/2\sigma^2} \tag{6.275}$$

As discussed in Example 6.26, the joint PDF of amplitude r and phase ϕ of the narrowband WGN can be obtained from (6.275) as

$$f_{r\phi}(r, \phi) = \frac{r}{2\pi\sigma^2} e^{-r^2/2\sigma^2}, \quad 0 \le r < \infty, \quad -\pi \le \phi \le \pi \tag{6.276}$$

where $\sigma^2 = 2N_o B$.

Example 6.33

Consider the narrowband WGN $n(t)$ with zero mean and spectral density $N_o/2$ over frequency band 5 to 9 Hz as shown in Figure 6.30(a).

a. If $f_c = 7$, calculate $G_{n_c}(f)$, $G_{n_s}(f)$, $G_{n_c n_s}(f)$, and $R_{n_c n_s}(\tau)$ for $n(t)$.
b. How will the results change if $f_c = 6$ Hz?

Solution

a. For $f_c = 7$, $G_n(f - 7) + G_n(f + 7) = N_o$ for $|f| \le 2$. Therefore, we can write the spectral density of $n_c(t)$ and $n_s(t)$ using (6.268) or (6.272) as

$$G_{n_c}(f) = G_{n_s}(f) = \begin{cases} N_o, & |f| \le 2 \\ 0, & \text{otherwise} \end{cases}$$

It is displayed in Figure 6.30(b). Because $G_n(f - 7) = G_n(f + 7)$ for $|f| < 2$,

$$G_{n_c n_s}(f) = j[G_n(f + 7) - G_n(f - 7)] = 0 \text{ for all } f \Rightarrow R_{n_c n_s}(\tau) = 0$$

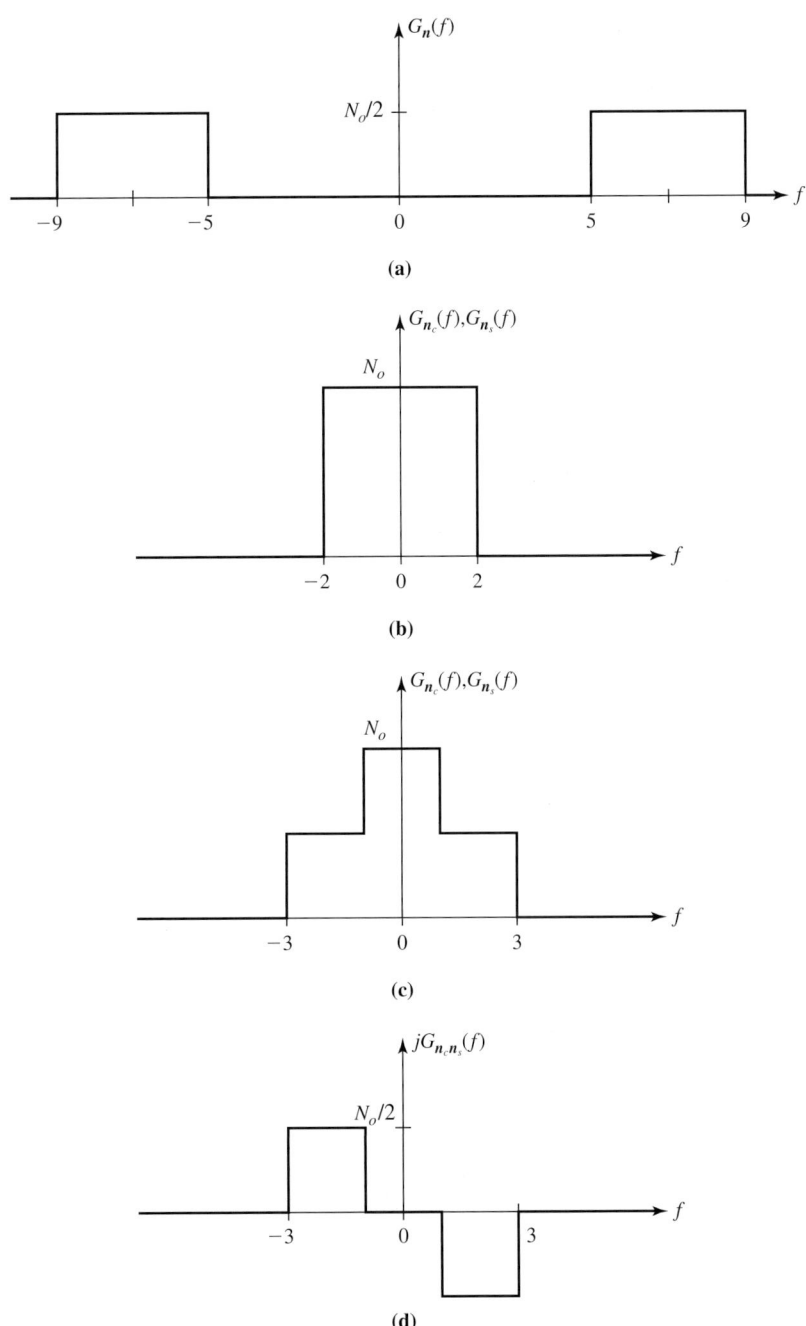

Figure 6.30 Spectral densities for Example 6.33.

b. With $f_c = 6$ Hz, the spectral density of $n_c(t)$ and $n_s(t)$ using (6.268) can be expressed as

$$G_{n_c}(f) = G_{n_s}(f) = \begin{cases} N_o/2, & 1 < |f| \leq 3 \\ N_o, & |f| \leq 1 \\ 0, & \text{otherwise} \end{cases}$$

The cross-spectral density is given from (6.270) by

$$G_{n_c n_s}(f) = \begin{cases} jN_o/2, & -3 < f < -1 \\ -jN_o/2, & 1 < f < 3 \\ 0, & \text{otherwise} \end{cases}$$

Figures 6.30(c) and 6.30(d) illustrate these spectra. The cross-correlation function $R_{n_c n_s}(\tau)$ is obtained by taking the inverse FT of $G_{n_c n_s}(f)$. That is,

$$R_{n_c n_s}(\tau) = \Im^{-1}\left\{ -j\frac{N_o}{2}\left(\Pi\left[\frac{f-1}{2}\right] - \Pi\left[\frac{f+1}{2}\right] \right) \right\}$$

$$= -j\frac{N_o}{2}2\text{sinc}(2\tau)[e^{j2\pi\tau} - e^{-j2\pi\tau}]$$

$$= 2N_o\text{sinc}(2\tau)\sin(2\pi\tau)$$

6.12.2   Envelope of Sine Wave in Narrowband Noise

In many communication system models, a sinusoidal waveform is received in the presence of additive narrowband white Gaussian noise. The received signal can be expressed as

$$z(t) = A\cos(2\pi f_c t + \theta) + n(t) \tag{6.277}$$

where $n(t)$ is zero-mean narrowband Gaussian noise with power spectral density $G_n(f) = N_o/2$ centered at f_c. Expanding the narrowband noise $n(t)$ into quadrature components around the carrier frequency, we can write (6.277) as

$$z(t) = [A + n_c(t)]\cos(2\pi f_c t + \theta) - n_s(t)\sin(2\pi f_c t + \theta)$$

$$= r(t)\cos[2\pi f_c t + \phi(t) + \theta] \tag{6.278}$$

where the envelope $r(t)$ and phase $\phi(t)$ processes are given by

$$r(t) = \sqrt{[A + n_c(t)]^2 + n_s^2(t)} \tag{6.279}$$

$$\phi(t) = \tan^{-1}\frac{n_s(t)}{A + n_c(t)} \tag{6.280}$$

$n_c(t)$ and $n_s(t)$ are statistically independent Gaussian random variables with mean zero and variance $\sigma^2 = 2N_o B$. Hence the joint PDF of random variables $x = A + n_c(t)$ and $y = n_s(t)$ is given by

$$f_{xy}(x, y) = \frac{1}{2\pi\sigma^2}e^{-[(x-A)^2 + y^2]/2\sigma^2} \tag{6.281}$$

Equation (6.281) can be written in terms of random variables r and phase $\boldsymbol{\phi}$ as

$$f_{r\phi}(r, \phi) = \frac{r}{2\pi\sigma^2}e^{-(r^2 + A^2 - 2rA\cos\phi)/2\sigma^2}, \quad 0 \le r < \infty, -\pi \le \phi \le \pi \quad (6.282)$$

The PDF of r is obtained by integrating out ϕ.

$$f_r(r) = \int_{-\infty}^{\infty} f_{r\phi}(r, \phi)d\phi = \frac{r}{\sigma^2}e^{-(r^2 + A^2)/2\sigma^2}\frac{1}{2\pi}\int_{-\pi}^{\pi} e^{rA\cos\phi/\sigma^2}d\phi \quad (6.283)$$

The integral in brackets on the right-hand side of (6.283) is the modified Bessel function of the first kind and order zero defined as

$$I_0(x) = \frac{1}{2\pi}\int_{-\pi}^{\pi} e^{x\cos\phi}d\phi = \frac{1}{2\pi}\int_{0}^{2\pi} e^{x\cos\phi}d\phi \quad (6.284)$$

Like the Q-function, the modified Bessel function does not have a closed-form solution, but is widely tabulated. In MATLAB, it can be evaluated using the `besseli` function. Substituting (6.284) in (6.283), the PDF of the envelope of a sinusoidal waveform embedded in narrowband Gaussian noise can be expressed as

$$f_r(r) = \frac{r}{\sigma^2}e^{-(r^2 + A^2)/2\sigma^2}I_0\left(\frac{rA}{\sigma^2}\right), \quad r \ge 0, A \ge 0 \quad (6.285)$$

This is known as the **Rician PDF.** Rician PDF is usually described in terms of the Rician K factor, which is defined as

$$K = \frac{A^2}{2\sigma^2} \quad (6.286)$$

Figure 6.31 displays Rician PDF for various values of parameter K. It is easy to see from (6.285) and Figure 6.31 that the Rician PDF converges to the Rayleigh PDF as K goes to zero (corresponding to $A \to 0$). The Rician random variable, on the other hand, converges to $\mathcal{N}(A, \sigma^2)$ as $K \to \infty$.

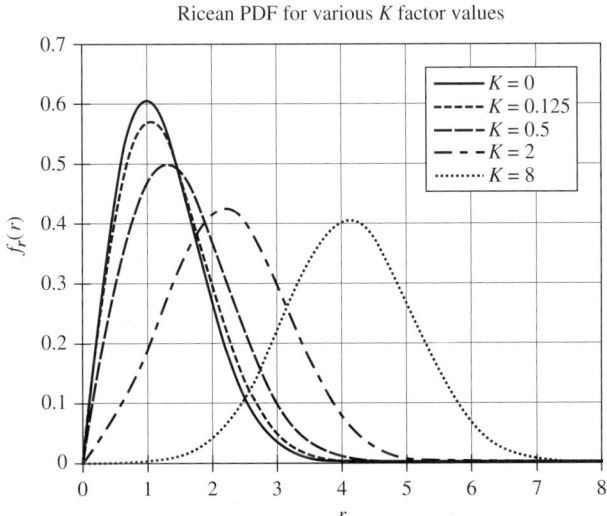

Figure 6.31 Rician PDF.

6.13 NOISE SOURCES IN COMMUNICATION SYSTEMS

Noise is always present in all electronic systems. In communication systems, its effect is usually dominant at the receiver because the signal is the weakest on arrival here after attenuation by the transmission channel or medium. The necessary amplification and filtering of the input signal as it passes through various stages of the receiver is accomplished by using circuits consisting of active devices (diodes, transistors, etc.) and resistors. These devices add noise in processing the signal, which is generated by various physical phenomena:

- **Thermal noise.** Produced by random motion of electrons in the conductors (e.g., resistors)
- **Shot noise.** Manifests as random fluctuations of the current flow in electronic devices (diodes, transistors) because the electric current at any instant consists of a stream of random numbers of carriers (e.g., those crossing the depletion region in a P-N junction)

Besides thermal and shot noise, all active devices as well as some passive components (e.g., carbon resistors) exhibit a low-frequency noise known as **flicker noise.** The spectral density of flicker noise varies inversely as a function of frequency f (i.e., $\propto 1/f$). The amplitude distribution of flicker noise is often non-Gaussian. Another type of low-frequency noise found in some integrated circuits and discrete transistors is called **burst noise.** Its spectral density rolls off inversely as a function of f^2 (i.e., $\propto 1/f^2$).

Noise may also be added to the signal by the sources external to the communication system. Examples include atmospheric disturbances, extraterrestrial radiation, and man-made sources, such as ignition noise. The effects of many external noise sources can be minimized or eliminated by proper engineering design, such as shielding. We confine our discussion here to internal noise generation mechanisms within devices that determine the ultimate performance of a communication system.

6.13.1 Thermal Noise

At temperatures above absolute zero ($0°K$), electrons move randomly in any conductor. Random thermal motion of electrons in a resistor manifests as a fluctuating voltage across its terminals. This fluctuating voltage is called **thermal noise.** It is also referred to as **Johnson** or **Nyquist noise** after the two engineers at Bell Labs who first studied it experimentally and theoretically. Because the random motion of a large number of electrons contributes to this noise, we can apply the central limit theorem to conclude that this noise is a Gaussian random process.

The mean-square noise voltage appearing at the terminals of a resistor R at temperature $T°K$ is given by

$$\overline{v_T^2} = 4kTRB \text{ Volt}^2 \tag{6.287}$$

where

k = Boltzmann's constant = 1.38×10^{-23} W/Hz/$°K$
B = Measurement or receiver bandwidth (Hz)

Thus a noisy resistor can be represented as a noiseless resistor in series with a voltage source with RMS voltage $\sqrt{\overline{v_T^2}}$ as displayed in Figure 6.32(a). Using Norton's

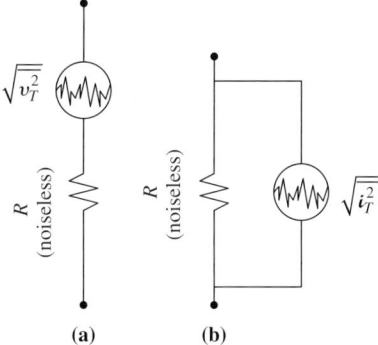

Figure 6.32 Model of a noisy resistor: (a) Thevenin and (b) Norton equivalent circuits.

theorem, we can alternatively represent a resistor by a noiseless resistor and a parallel current source with RMS output current $\sqrt{\overline{i_T^2}}$ as shown in Figure 6.32(b).

$$\overline{i_T^2} = \frac{4kT}{R}B\,\text{Amp}^2 \tag{6.288}$$

It has been experimentally found that the power spectrum of thermal noise is flat over frequencies as high as 10^4 GHz. Because electronic communication systems operate well below this frequency range, thermal noise is modeled as white Gaussian noise.

Example 6.34

Calculate the RMS noise voltage appearing at the output terminals of a 20-kΩ resistor at room temperature in a 1-MHz bandwidth.

Solution

Assuming room temperature equals 23°C, we have $T = 23 + 273 = 296$°K. Substituting into (6.287) yields

$$\overline{v_T^2} = 4kTRB = 4 \times 1.38 \times 10^{-23} \times 296 \times 20 \times 10^3 \times 10^6 = 29.6 \times 10^{-12} \text{ Volt}^2$$

This corresponds to an RMS thermal noise voltage $\sqrt{\overline{v_T^2}} = 5.44 \, \mu\text{V}$ across a 20-kΩ resistor

If we put two resistors R_1 and R_2 in series, then the mean-square noise voltage is given by

$$\overline{v_T^2} = 4kT(R_1 + R_2)B = \overline{v_{T1}^2} + \overline{v_{T2}^2} \tag{6.289}$$

That is, thermal noise adds on the power basis. Similarly, for two resistors R_1 and R_2 in parallel, we can add the mean-square currents as follows:

$$\overline{i_T^2} = 4kT(G_1 + G_2)B = \overline{i_{T1}^2} + \overline{i_{T2}^2}\,\text{Amp}^2 \tag{6.290}$$

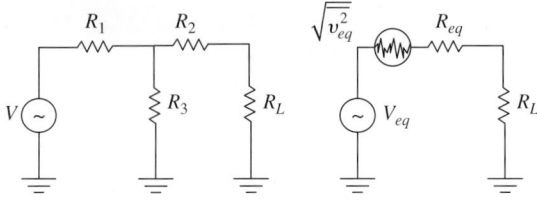

Figure 6.33 (a) Resistive circuit; (b) equivalent Thevenin circuit.

For an arbitrary circuit consisting of resistors, inductors, and capacitors, we can determine the equivalent noise source representing the contributions of all resistors by developing a Thevenin equivalent circuit. As an example, consider the resistive circuit shown in Figure 6.33(a).

$$\text{Thevenin equivalent voltage } V_{eq} = \frac{VR_3}{R_1 + R_3} \qquad (6.291)$$

$$\text{Thevenin equivalent resistance } R_{eq} = R_2 + \frac{R_1 R_3}{R_1 + R_3} = \frac{R_1 R_2 + R_2 R_3 + R_1 R_3}{R_1 + R_3} \qquad (6.292)$$

The equivalent noise source representing contributions of all resistors as seen from the output terminals is given by

$$\overline{v_{eq}^2} = 4kTR_{eq}B = 4kT\left(\frac{R_1 R_2 + R_2 R_3 + R_1 R_3}{R_1 + R_3}\right)B \qquad (6.293)$$

Figure 6.33(b) displays the Thevenin equivalent circuit.

6.13.2 Available Power

The **available power** of a source is defined as the maximum power that can be transferred from the source to a load. Consider the voltage source (v_s) with internal resistance R_s connected to a load resistor R_L as illustrated in Figure 6.34. The maximum power transfer theorem states that the maximum power is transferred to the load when its resistance $R_L = R_s$. Under this matched load condition, the voltage across the load resistor R_L equals $v_s/2$ and the power transferred is given by

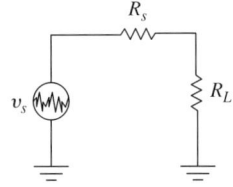

Figure 6.34 Available thermal noise.

$$P_{\text{max}} = \frac{(v_s/2)^2}{R_s} \qquad (6.294)$$

Because the source internal resistance is R_s, the resultant noise can be represented by a voltage source with RMS voltage $v_s = \sqrt{\overline{v_T^2}} = \sqrt{4kTR_sB}$ volts. Therefore, the maximum noise power transferred from this source is given by

$$N_{in} = \frac{\overline{v_T^2}}{4R_s} = \frac{4kTR_sB}{4R_s} = kTB \qquad (6.295)$$

Equation (6.295) states that the available source noise power at temperature T is kTB Watts. It is surprising to note that this value is independent of the value of the source internal resistance R_s. Therefore, the **two-sided power spectral density (PSD)** of noise due to source internal resistance is obtained from (6.295) as

$$G_n(f) = \frac{kT}{2} \text{ W/Hz} \qquad (6.296)$$

It is referred to as the two-sided PSD because the noise spectrum extends over both negative and positive frequencies. It is customary to represent the quantity kT by N_o. Using this notation, the PSD of internally generated source noise is expressed as

$$G_n(f) = \frac{N_o}{2} \qquad (6.297)$$

At the **standard temperature** $T_o = 290°$Kelvin, $N_o = kT_o = 1.38 \times 10^{-23} \times 290 = 4 \times 10^{-21}$ W/Hz. We can now write the available source noise power at temperature T by substituting (6.297) into (6.295) as

$$N_{in} = N_o B \qquad (6.298)$$

We can characterize noise sources other than resistors in terms of an **effective noise temperature** T_s. It is defined as the temperature, usually expressed in $°K$, of a hypothetical resistor that would produce the same amount of available noise power N_{source} as the noisy source in bandwidth B. That is,

$$T_s = \frac{N_{source}}{kB} \qquad (6.299)$$

For example, the effective noise temperature for an antenna represents the unwanted noise produced by itself and that picked up from the surrounding environment.

6.13.3 Shot Noise

Shot noise in electronic devices represents fluctuations in the electrical current produced by random events involving carrier emission and/or recombination. Shot noise was first studied by Schottky in 1918. The physical mechanism leading to fluctuations in the current flow varies from device to device. In semiconductor P-N junctions, the fluctuations are caused by the random diffusion of holes and electrons across the depletion region as well as random recombination of carriers outside this region. In semiconductor photodiodes, the fluctuations arise from the statistical nature of photon arrivals at the photodetector. Hence, the number of photon-generated hole-electron pairs at any particular instant is a random variable. In addition, the number of electrons producing photocurrent will vary because of their random recombinations and absorptions. The shot noise resulting from these fluctuations is thus dependent upon the magnitude of average current flow in these devices. The one-sided spectral density of shot noise, therefore, is proportional to the magnitude of the DC or average current (I_{DC}) as described by

$$G_{shot}(f) = 2qI_{DC} \text{ W/Hz} \qquad (6.300)$$

where q = electron charge = 1.6×10^{-19} Coulombs. Note that the spectral density $G_{shot}(f)$ is a constant function of frequency. That is, shot noise is a white noise process. It is also characterized as a zero mean and Gaussian. The Gaussian behavior is justified by the central limit theorem argument, because the shot noise current is composed of contributions from a large number of carriers diffusing across the P-N junction, for example, in a random and statistically independent fashion. The mean-square shot noise current in a bandwidth of B_N Hz is given by

$$\overline{i_{shot}^2(t)} = 2qI_{DC}B_N \tag{6.301}$$

where B_N = noise equivalent bandwidth of the receiver or measuring instrument.

6.14   CHARACTERIZATION OF SYSTEM NOISE

In a communication system, the input signal travels through a cascade of many different subsystems, each of which degrades the output signal-to-noise ratio (SNR) by adding noise to the signal. Examples of subsystems include amplifier, filter, and mixer stages in a communication receiver. Because every subsystem has finite passband, we model it as a two-port network with frequency response $H(f)$ as displayed in Figure 6.35(a). The signal power available to the load is given by

$$P_{out} = \mathscr{G}P_{in} \tag{6.302}$$

where

P_{in} = Available signal power at the two-port input
P_{out} = Available signal power at the two-port output
$\mathscr{G}$ = Power gain of the system

The available source noise power at the two-port input is given from (6.299) as

$$N_{in} = kT_sB_N \tag{6.303}$$

where B_N = noise equivalent bandwidth of the two-port network given by (6.250). If the two-port network is noiseless, the noise delivered to the output is given by

$$N_{out} = \mathscr{G}kT_sB_N \tag{6.304}$$

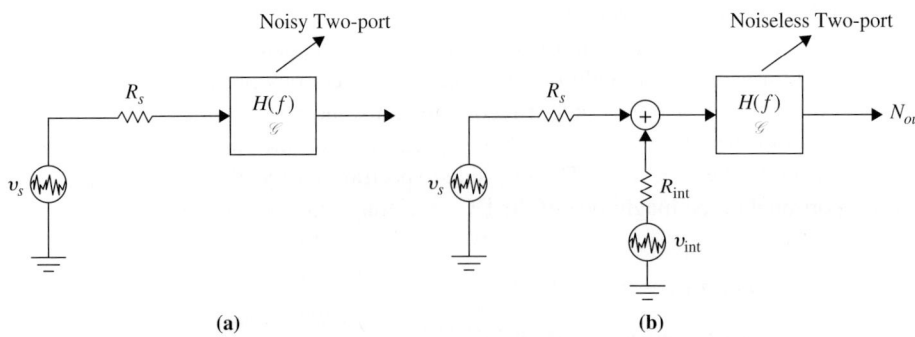

Figure 6.35 Two-port model for calculating total available noise power.

The electronic two-port network adds noise that is generated from many sources, including thermal noise and shot noise. It is modeled in Figure 6.35(b) by an *equivalent input resistive noise source* v_{int} with available noise power N_{int} connected to a noise-free two-port that will result in the same output noise power as that delivered by the noisy two-port network to the matched load. The total noise power N_{out} delivered to the matched load is obtained by combining source noise N_{in} and two-port internal noise N_{int} and then multiplying the result by the available gain $\mathscr{G}$. That is,

$$N_{out} = \mathscr{G}(N_{in} + N_{int}) = \mathscr{G}(kT_sB_N + N_{int}) \tag{6.305}$$

6.14.1 Noise Factor and Noise Figure

Noise factor (F) is used as the standard figure of merit to characterize the noise added by the system (or subsystem). According to **Institute of Electrical and Electronic Engineers (IEEE)** definition, noise factor is the ratio of the SNR at the system input $(SNR)_i$ to the SNR at the system output $(SNR)_{out}$ at a source temperature equal to T_o. That is,

$$F = \left.\frac{(SNR)_i}{(SNR)_{out}}\right|_{T_s = T_o} \tag{6.306}$$

where

$$(SNR)_i = \frac{\text{Available signal power at the system input}}{\text{Available noise power at the input}} = \left.\frac{P_{in}}{N_{in}}\right|_{T_s = T_o} \tag{6.307}$$

and

$$(SNR)_{out} = \frac{\text{Available signal power at the system output}}{\text{Available noise power at the system output}} = \left.\frac{P_{out}}{N_{out}}\right|_{T_s = T_o} \tag{6.308}$$

It can be seen from (6.306) that the noise factor determines how much SNR degradation the input signal experiences as it passes through the system. An ideal or noiseless system does not add noise to the input signal, so the output SNR is the same as that at the input and the noise factor $F = 1$. Substituting (6.302), (6.307), and (6.308) into (6.306), we get

$$F = \frac{P_{in}/N_{in}}{P_{out}/N_{out}} = \frac{N_{out}}{N_{in}(P_{out}/P_{in})} = \left.\frac{N_{out}}{N_{in}\mathscr{G}}\right|_{T_s = T_o} \tag{6.309}$$

In terms of the two-port noise factor F, the total noise power delivered to the matched load by the system is given by substituting (6.303) into (6.309) as

$$N_{out} = F\mathscr{G}N_{in} = F\mathscr{G}kT_oB_N \tag{6.310}$$

The logarithm of the noise factor expressed in dB, called the **noise figure,** is popularly used to describe the noise performance of a two-port subsystem. It is defined as

$$NF = 10\log_{10}F \,\text{dB} \tag{6.311}$$

A noise figure $NF = 3$ dB implies $F = 2$. Substituting into (6.310) and comparing with (6.305), it follows that in this case the two-port subsystem adds as much noise as the available source noise power at the input. Thus the output SNR of the system is degraded by 3 dB, that is, it is one-half that at the input.

6.14.2 Effective Input Noise Temperature of a Subsystem

Noise temperature is an alternative method for specifying the noise generated in electronic networks. This method is most commonly used in space or satellite applications where source temperatures deviate from 290°K. Noise temperature characterization does not require a specific source temperature, as is the case for the noise figure. We will now characterize the noise contributed by a subsystem in terms of an effective input noise temperature T_e. It is defined as the temperature, usually expressed in °K, required of a hypothetical resistor, placed at the input of the noiseless subsystem, in order to produce the same available noise power as that produced by the noisy subsystem. That is,

$$T_e = \frac{N_{\text{int}}}{kB_N} \tag{6.312}$$

where N_{int} is available noise power at the input of the subsystem. We emphasize that, unlike the case of a resistor, T_e does not represent the actual operating temperature of the subsystem. By making the noise temperature of the input source equal to T_o, the total noise power delivered to the matched output load can now be written by substituting (6.303) and (6.312) into (6.305) as

$$N_{out} = \mathscr{G}(N_{in} + N_{\text{int}}) = \mathscr{G}k(T_o + T_e)B_N \tag{6.313}$$

The total effective input noise temperature T_{sys} of the system, consisting of the source and the two-port, referenced to input is given by

$$T_{sys} = \frac{N_{out}}{\mathscr{G}kB_N} = \frac{\mathscr{G}(kT_o + kT_e)B_N}{\mathscr{G}kB_N} = T_o + T_e \tag{6.314}$$

We now determine the relationship between the effective input noise temperature and the noise figure of the two-port system. Substituting (6.313) and (6.303) into (6.309), we obtain

$$F = \frac{N_{out}}{N_{in}\mathscr{G}} = \frac{\mathscr{G}k(T_o + T_e)B_N}{kT_oB_N\mathscr{G}} = 1 + \frac{T_e}{T_o} \tag{6.315}$$

That is,

$$T_e = (F - 1)T_o \tag{6.316}$$

Substituting $T_o = 290$°K, (6.316) becomes

$$T_e = 290(F - 1) \tag{6.317}$$

6.14.3   Noise Figure of a Cascade of Subsystems

Consider a communication system consisting of a cascade of subsystems as shown in Figure 6.36. Initially, we shall calculate noise at the output of the first two stages. From (6.313), the available noise at the output of the first subsystem is $\mathscr{G}_1 k(T_o + T_{e_1})B_N$. It is amplified by the second stage yielding $\mathscr{G}_1\mathscr{G}_2 k(T_o + T_{e_1})B_N$. The internal noise from the second system is given by $\mathscr{G}_2 k T_{e_2} B_N$. Thus the total available noise power at the output of a two-stage cascade is given by

$$N_{out} = \mathscr{G}_1\mathscr{G}_2 k(T_o + T_{e_1})B_N + \mathscr{G}_2 k T_{e_2} B_N = \mathscr{G}_1\mathscr{G}_2 k\left(T_o + T_{e_1} + \frac{T_{e_2}}{\mathscr{G}_1}\right)B_N \quad (6.318)$$

Because the available gain for the cascade is $\mathscr{G}_1\mathscr{G}_2$, the effective temperature of a two-stage cascade is obtained by comparing (6.318) with (6.313) as

$$T_e = T_{e_1} + \frac{T_{e_2}}{\mathscr{G}_1} \quad (6.319)$$

Substituting (6.319) into (6.318) yields the available noise power at the output of a two-stage cascade as

$$N_{out} = \mathscr{G}_1\mathscr{G}_2 k(T_o + T_e)B_N \quad (6.320)$$

The overall noise figure of the cascade is obtained by using (6.315) and (6.319) as

$$F_T = 1 + \frac{T_e}{T_o} = 1 + \frac{1}{T_o}\left(T_{e_1} + \frac{T_{e_2}}{\mathscr{G}_1}\right) = 1 + \frac{T_{e_1}}{T_o} + \frac{1}{\mathscr{G}_1}\frac{T_{e_2}}{T_o} = F_1 + \frac{(F_2 - 1)}{\mathscr{G}_1} \quad (6.321)$$

The total available noise power in (6.320) at the output of two-stage cascade can be expressed in terms of the overall noise figure F_T as

$$N_{out} = \mathscr{G}_1\mathscr{G}_2 k T_o F_T B_N \quad (6.322)$$

Equation (6.321) can be generalized for a system consisting of n subsystems in cascade. The overall noise factor F_T of such a system is given by

$$F_T = F_1 + \frac{(F_2 - 1)}{\mathscr{G}_1} + \frac{(F_3 - 1)}{\mathscr{G}_1\mathscr{G}_1} + \ldots + \frac{(F_n - 1)}{\mathscr{G}_1\mathscr{G}_2, \ldots, \mathscr{G}_{n-1}} \quad (6.323)$$

This is known as the **Friis formula.** It can be observed from (6.323) that the gain in front of a noisy two-port lessens its noise contribution to the overall noise performance of the cascade. As a consequence, the noise contribution of each successive stage in a cascade is smaller and smaller. The overall noise figure of the system is dominated by the noise figure of the first stage. Thus, every communication system employs a

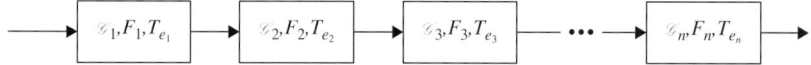

Figure 6.36   Cascade of subsystems forming a system.

low-noise amplifier (LNA) with high gain and low noise figure as the first stage to set the overall noise performance of the system. The total available noise power at the output of an *n*-stage cascade is obtained by extending (6.322) as

$$N_{out} = \mathcal{G}_1 \mathcal{G}_2, \ldots, \mathcal{G}_n F_T k T_o B_N \qquad (6.324)$$

Example 6.35

Consider the receiver cascade shown in Figure 6.37. The LNA has $G_1 = 20$ dB and $NF_1 = 2$ dB. The mixer has a conversion gain of $G_2 = 10$ dB and $NF_2 = 10$ dB. The VGA has a gain of $G_3 = 50$ dB and $NF_3 = 15$ dB. Calculate the overall noise figure of the receiver.

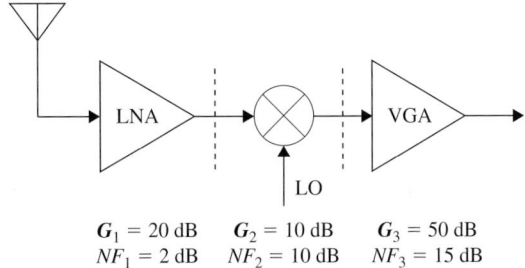

| $G_1 = 20$ dB | $G_2 = 10$ dB | $G_3 = 50$ dB |
| $NF_1 = 2$ dB | $NF_2 = 10$ dB | $NF_3 = 15$ dB |

Figure 6.37 RF receiver cascade.

Solution

The noise factor of the cascade is given from (6.323) as

$$F_T = F_1 + \frac{(F_2 - 1)}{\mathcal{G}_1} + \frac{(F_3 - 1)}{\mathcal{G}_1 \mathcal{G}_2} \qquad (6.325)$$

The noise factor and gain of each stage are tabulated below.

Stage	F	$\mathcal{G}$
1	1.585	100
2	10	10
3	31.6	10^5

Substituting into (6.325), we obtain

$$F_T = 1.585 + \frac{(10 - 1)}{100} + \frac{(31.6 - 1)}{100 \times 10} = 1.585 + 0.09 + 0.0315 = 1.7065$$

$$NF_T = 2.32 \text{ dB}$$

The effective noise temperature of the cascade can be obtained by extending (6.319) for a system consisting of *n* subsystems in cascade. It is given by

$$T_e = T_{e_1} + \frac{T_{e_2}}{\mathcal{G}_1} + \frac{T_{e_3}}{\mathcal{G}_1 \mathcal{G}_2} + \ldots + \frac{T_{e_n}}{\mathcal{G}_1 \mathcal{G}_2, \ldots, \mathcal{G}_{n-1}} \qquad (6.326)$$

The total effective noise temperature T_{sys} of the system, consisting of the source and the cascade, referenced to input is given from (6.314) as

$$T_{sys} = T_o + T_e \tag{6.327}$$

where the effective noise temperature T_e is given by (6.326). The total available noise power at the output of an n-stage cascade is obtained by extending (6.320) as

$$N_{out} = \mathscr{G}_1 \mathscr{G}_2, \ldots, \mathscr{G}_n k T_{sys} B_N = \mathscr{G}_1 \mathscr{G}_2, \ldots, \mathscr{G}_n k (T_o + T_e) B_N \tag{6.328}$$

It is obvious that (6.324) and (6.328) provide identical results.

6.14.4 Noise Factor of a Lossy Two-Port Network

An example of a lossy two-port network is a *passive* attenuator. Transmission lines and cables between subsystems have losses, and they can be considered attenuators. The power gain $\mathscr{G}$ of an attenuator is less than 1, which is equivalent to the loss $\mathscr{L} = 1/\mathscr{G}$. In dB form, let $L = 10\log_{10}\mathscr{L}$ and $G = 10\log_{10}\mathscr{G}$. Then, $L = -G$ dB for an attenuator. For example, an $\mathscr{L} = 3$ dB attenuator implies that $G = -3$ dB and $\mathscr{G} = 1/2$. An attenuator not only attenuates the signal but also adds extra noise. Assuming that the attenuator temperature is T_A, the available noise power at the attenuator output consists of two terms:

- $\mathscr{G} N_o B_N = \mathscr{G} k T_o B_N =$ source thermal noise transferred by the attenuator to the load
- $(1 - \mathscr{G}) k T_A B_N =$ attenuator-generated thermal noise transferred to the load

The available noise power at the output of the attenuator is obtained by adding these two contributions as

$$N_{out} = \mathscr{G} k T_o B_N + (1 - \mathscr{G}) k T_A B_N \tag{6.329}$$

Substituting (6.329) and (6.303) into (6.309), the noise factor of an attenuator is given by

$$F = \frac{N_{out}}{N_{in}\mathscr{G}} = \frac{\mathscr{G} k T_o B_N + (1 - \mathscr{G}) k T_A B_N}{\mathscr{G} k T_o B_N} = 1 + \frac{(1 - \mathscr{G}) k T_A B_N}{\mathscr{G} k T_o B_N}$$

$$= 1 + \left(\frac{1}{\mathscr{G}} - 1\right)\frac{T_A}{T_o} = 1 + (\mathscr{L} - 1)\frac{T_A}{T_o} \tag{6.330}$$

By comparing (6.330) with (6.315), the effective noise temperature of an attenuator can be expressed as

$$T_e = (\mathscr{L} - 1)T_A = (\mathscr{L} - 1)T_o \tag{6.331}$$

where we have assumed in (6.331) that the source, load, and lossy two-port network are in thermal equilibrium with each other (that is, $T_A = T_o$). Comparing (6.331) with (6.316), the noise factor of an attenuator is *equal* to its attenuation, that is,

$$F_{attenuator} = \mathscr{L} \tag{6.332}$$

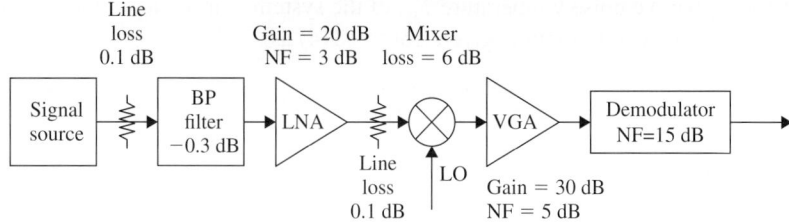

Figure 6.38 RF receiver cascade.

Because $\mathscr{G}$ represents the attenuation (i.e., loss) of any passive device, $\mathscr{G}$ would equal the insertion loss for a switch, filter, or coupler. Likewise, it would equal the conversion loss of a mixer. Thus, we can now specify the noise figure and effective noise temperature of every two-port device or subsystem.

Example 6.36

Consider the block diagram of a receiver shown in Figure 6.38. Find the overall noise figure of the receiver cascade.

Solution

The following table summarizes gains and noise factor values required to calculate the overall noise figure.

	Trans. Line	BP Filter	LNA	Trans. Line	Mixer	VGA	Demodulator
Gain G (dB)	−0.1	−0.3	20	−0.5	−6	30	
$\mathscr{G}$	0.977	0.933	100	0.891	0.25	1000	
Accumulated gain	0.977	0.912	91.2	81.2	20.3	20,300	
$\mathscr{G}_1\mathscr{G}_2,\ldots,\mathscr{G}_{n-1}$							
NF(dB)	0.1	0.3	3	0.1	6	5	15
F	1.0233	1.071	2	1.122	4	3.162	31.62

The overall noise figure of the receiver is now obtained by substituting appropriate values from the table into (6.323) as

$$F_T = 1.0233 + \frac{(1.071 - 1)}{0.977} + \frac{(2 - 1)}{0.912} + \frac{(1.122 - 1)}{91.2} + \frac{(4 - 1)}{81.2} + \frac{(3.162 - 1)}{20.3} + \frac{(31.62 - 1)}{20,300}$$

$$= 1.0233 + 0.072 + 1.096 + 0.00133 + 0.037 + 0.1065 + 0.0015 = 2.3376 = 3.69 \text{ dB}$$

6.15   MATLAB SIMULATION OF RANDOM PROCESSES

The basic building block to simulate random variables in MATLAB is the random number generator. In the context of simulation, random processes can be viewed as a sequence of random variables. MATLAB contains random number generators as part of the library of built-in functions. We start our discussion with the generation of uniformly distributed random variable $\mathcal{U}[0, 1]$ as it can be transformed to another random variable with the desired PDF. The command `rand` generates random numbers which are uniformly distributed on the interval [0, 1]. For example,

```
x[n] = rand(128,1);
```

generates a length-128 column vector of $\mathcal{U}[0, 1]$ numbers. To generate values of a uniformly distributed random variable $\mathcal{U}[a, b]$ from $\mathcal{U}[0, 1]$ numbers, we can use the following statement:

```
x[n] = a + (b - a).*rand(128,1);
```

6.15.1 Generating Arbitrary PDF Random Variables

In this section we consider the problem of generating a random variable x with given CDF $F_x(x)$. Let u be a $\mathcal{U}[0, 1]$ random variable. We will now show that the random variable

$$x = F^{-1}(u) \tag{6.333}$$

has CDF $F_x(x)$. By definition

$$P\{x \le x\} = P\{F_x^{-1}(u) \le x\} = P\{u \le F_x(x)\} \tag{6.334}$$

For a $\mathcal{U}[0, 1]$ random variable and $0 \le u \le 1$, it can be easily shown that $P\{u \le u\} = u$. Substituting into (3.333) yields

$$P\{x \le x\} = F_x(x)$$

This is the desired result. Thus, to generate a random variable x with CDF $F_x(x)$, we use the following procedure:

- Generate $u \sim \mathcal{U}[0, 1]$ random variable.
- Let $x = F^{-1}(u)$.

Example 6.37

Derive the mapping $F^{-1}(u)$ to generate exponential random variable with CDF $F_x(x) = (1 - e^{-3x})u(x)$

Solution

To invert $F_x(x)$, we set $u = F_x(x) = (1 - e^{-3x})u(x)$. Solving for x, we obtain the mapping

$$x = -\frac{1}{3}\log_e(1 - u)$$

Because the random variable $1 - u$ is also $\mathcal{U}[0, 1]$, we can replace $1 - u$ with u. Thus we may write the solution for x as

$$x = -\frac{1}{3}\log_e(u)$$

The limitation of this method is that the CDF $F_x(x)$ of the desired random variable is available in the closed form. This is not always the case. An example is Gaussian random variable. In this case other techniques can be used as illustrated in Problem 6.36. The MATLAB command `randn` generates samples of a Gaussian distributed random variable with mean 0 and variance 1. For example,

```
x[n] = randn(128,1);
```

generates a length-128 column vector of $\mathcal{N}(0, 1)$ numbers. To obtain a mean other than zero, just add or subtract a constant from the generated vector. To obtain a variance other than one, multiply the generated vector by the standard deviation (square root of the variance). For example, to generate a length-128 row vector of Gaussian distributed numbers with mean 2 and variance 5, we can use the following statement:

```
x[n] = sqrt(5).*randn(128,1) + 2;
```

6.15.2 Autocorrelation Function and Spectral Density

Let $x_1, x_2, \ldots$ be a sequence of iid random variables. The autocorrelation function of the random sequence $x_1, x_2, \ldots$ is defined as

$$R_x(i, j) = E\{x_i x_j\} \tag{6.335}$$

For a WSS random sequence, (6.335) can be expressed as

$$R_x[m] = E\{x_i x_{i+m}\} \tag{6.336}$$

The spectral density of random sequence $x_1, x_2, \ldots$ is given by the DTFT of its autocorrelation function (6.336). That is,

$$G_x(e^{j\hat{\omega}}) = \sum_{m=-\infty}^{\infty} R_x[m] e^{-j\hat{\omega}m} \tag{6.337}$$

$G_x(e^{j\hat{\omega}})$ is a measure of the power contained in the random sequence $x_1, x_2, \ldots$ as a function of frequency.

An extremely important case is the case of uncorrelated sequences. Let $x_1, x_2, \ldots$ be random sequence with autocorrelation function

$$R_x[m] = \sigma^2 \delta[m] \tag{6.338}$$

Because $R_x[m]$ is zero for $m \neq 0$, this sequence is completely uncorrelated. That is, each element of the sequence is uncorrelated from all other elements of the random sequence $x_1, x_2, \ldots$ For a Gaussian random sequence, this implies that each element of the sequence is statistically independent from all other elements of the sequence. The power spectral density of the sequence is the DTFT of (6.338).

$$G_x(e^{j\hat{\omega}}) = \sigma^2 \tag{6.339}$$

6.15.3 Samples of White Gaussian Noise

As discussed in Section 6.11.2, white Gaussian noise (WGN) has infinite bandwidth. Therefore, WGN needs to be band-limited by an anti-aliasing LP filter. The purpose of the LP filter is to limit the spectrum of WGN sampled at the rate f_s Hz to the frequency band $\left[-\dfrac{f_s}{2}, \dfrac{f_s}{2} \right]$ to prevent aliasing. The transfer function of the ideal LP filter is

$$H(f) = \begin{cases} 1, & |f| \le \dfrac{f_s}{2} \\ 0, & |f| > \dfrac{f_s}{2} \end{cases} \tag{6.340}$$

Let $n(t)$ be the band-limited output of the LP filter to WGN input $n_w(t)$ as illustrated in Figure 6.39. The spectral density and autocorrelation function of $n(t)$ are given from (6.244) and (6.245) as

$$G_n(f) = |H(f)|^2 G_{n_w}(f) = \begin{cases} \dfrac{N_o}{2}, & |f| \le \dfrac{f_s}{2} \\ 0, & \text{otherwise} \end{cases} \tag{6.341}$$

$$R_n(\tau) = \frac{N_o f_s}{2} \operatorname{sinc}(f_s \tau) \tag{6.342}$$

When $n_w(t)$ is sampled, the samples $n_w(kT_s)$, $k = 1, 2, \ldots$ are jointly Gaussian random variables. Because $n(t)$ is also Gaussian, the random sequence $n_1, n_2, \ldots$ is jointly Gaussian with zero-mean and autocorrelation function

$$\begin{aligned} R_n[m] &= E\{n(kT_s)n[(k + m)T_s]\} \\ &= R_n(mT_s) = N_o \frac{f_s}{2} \operatorname{sinc}(mf_s T_s) \\ &= \frac{N_o f_s}{2} \operatorname{sinc}(m) = \frac{N_o f_s}{2} \delta[m] \end{aligned} \tag{6.343}$$

Thus, samples of zero-mean WGN are uncorrelated random variables with zero mean and variance

$$\sigma^2 = \frac{N_o f_s}{2} = \frac{N_o}{2T_s} \tag{6.344}$$

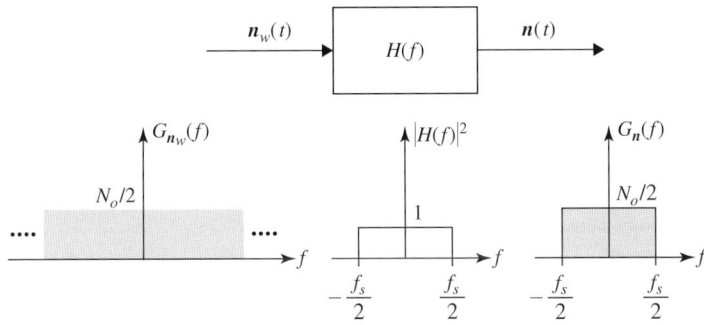

Figure 6.39 Processing of WGN prior to sampling.

FINAL REMARKS

In this chapter, we developed models for random message signals and the noise encountered in communication systems using the tools of probability theory. Although a random process is completely described by the joint PDF of all orders, a partial description in terms of the mean and autocorrelation function is adequate in many applications. Wide-sense stationary and ergodic processes were introduced as models of random phenomena frequently encountered in electronic systems. Like deterministic signals, wide-sense stationary processes lend to frequency domain representation in terms of power spectral density. This leads to the significant result for linear, time-invariant systems that the power spectra of the input and output random signals are related through the frequency response function of the system. Gaussian random processes and white noise were introduced to model physical noise processes frequently encountered in communication systems.

FURTHER READINGS

A number of undergraduate communication systems texts [1–5] deal with topics in probability and stochastic processes. Papoulis [6] is a classic reference in the field. The books by Yates [7], Gubner [8], and Leon-Garcia [9] provide excellent coverage of the subject matter at an advanced undergraduate level and are written with electrical and computer engineering students in mind.

1. Ziemer, R., and W. Tranter. *Principles of Communications: Systems, Modulation, and Noise,* 5th ed. New York: John Wiley, 2001.

2. Carlson, B., P. Crilly, and J. Rutledge. *Communication Systems,* 4th ed. New York: McGraw-Hill, 2002.

3. Proakis, J., and M. Salehi. *Fundamentals of Communication Systems.* Upper Saddle River, NJ: Prentice Hall, 2005.

4. Couch, L. *Digital and Analog Communication Systems,* 7th ed. Upper Saddle River, NJ: Prentice Hall, 2006.

5. Haykin, S. *Communication Systems,* 4th ed. New York: John Wiley, 2000.

6. Papoulis, A., and S. Pillai. *Probability, Random Variables and Stochastic Processes,* 4th ed. New York: McGraw-Hill, 2001.

7. Yates, R., and D. Goodman. *Probability and Stochastic Processes,* 2nd ed. New York: John Wiley, 2005.

8. Gubner, R. *Probability and Random Processes for Electrical and Computer Engineers.* New York: Cambridge, 2006.

9. Leon-Garcia, A. *Probability and Random Processes for Electrical Engineering,* 3rd ed. Upper Saddle River, NJ: Prentice Hall, 2008.

PROBLEMS

6.1. An unfair coin is tossed 3 times. Assume that the probability of a head $p = 0.35$ and the probability of a tail $1 - p = 0.65$.

    a. What is the sample space?

    b. Calculate $P\{HHT\}$ and $P\{1 \text{ tail}\}$.

    c. Determine $P\{\text{1st toss is not head}|1 \text{ head}\}$.

6.2. Three tetrahedral dice are rolled. Let A be the event that at least one 4 appears and B be the event that no two dice show the same value.

    a. Find $P(A)$, $P(B)$, and $P(AB)$.

    b. Are A and B statistically independent? Prove your answer.

6.3. Internet traffic from Los Angeles is routed to New York via Chicago with probability 0.8. In case of congestion, the traffic is routed via Denver with conditional probability of packet being dropped 0.3. Assuming that the conditional probability of packet being dropped via Chicago route is 0.2, determine

    a. The probability that a packet is dropped.

    b. The conditional probability that a packet is routed via Chicago given that it is not dropped.

6.4. The PMF of random variable x is given by

$$p_x(x_i) = \begin{cases} K/x_i, & x_i = 3, 6, 9, 12 \\ 0, & \text{otherwise} \end{cases}$$

    a. What is the value of K?

    b. Find $P\{x > 6\}$.

    c. Find $P\{6 \leq x \leq 12\}$.

6.5. The CDF of the random variable x is given by

$$F_x(x) = \begin{cases} 0, & x < -\dfrac{3}{2} \\ (3 + 2x)/6, & -\dfrac{3}{2} \leq x \leq \dfrac{3}{2} \\ 1, & x > \dfrac{3}{2} \end{cases}$$

    a. Plot the CDF and PDF.

    b. Find $P\{x \leq -1.5\}$.

c. Find $P\{-1 < x \le 1\}$.

d. Find $P\{x \le 2\}$.

e. Find $P\{x > 3\}$.

6.6. The PDF of the random variable x is given by $f_x(x) = K\Lambda[(x-2)/2]$.

a. What is the value of K?

b. Plot the PDF.

c. Determine and plot the CDF.

d. Calculate $P\{x \le 2\}$.

e. Find $P\{-1 \le |x - 2| \le 1\}$.

f. Find $P\{x > 2\}$.

6.7. The PDF of random variable x is given by

$$f_x(x) = 0.5e^{-\alpha|x|}, \quad -\infty < x < \infty$$

a. Determine α so that $f_x(x)$ is a PDF.

b. Determine the CDF of x.

c. Find $P\{-1 \le x \le 1\}$.

d. Calculate $E(x)$ and $Var(x)$.

6.8. The CDF of random variable x is shown in Figure P6.1.

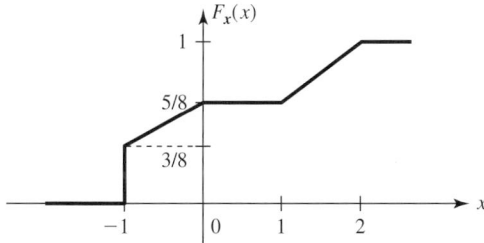

Figure P6.1

a. Sketch the PDF of x.

b. Let $y = 2x - 1$. Compute the values of $P\{-2 < y \le 1\}$.

c. Find the value of $E\{x|x > 0\}$.

6.9. The random variable x is passed through a soft limiter with transfer characteristic $y = g(x)$, shown in Figure P6.2.

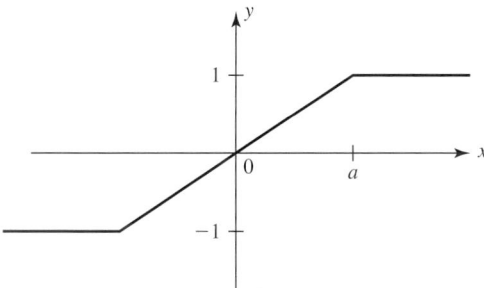

Figure P6.2

a. Find an expression for the mean and variance of the output random variable y for an arbitrary continuous random variable x.

b. If x is a Gaussian random variable, determine the PDF of the output random variable y.

c. Determine the mean and variance of the output random variable y if x is a $\mathcal{N}(0, \sigma_x^2)$.

6.10. Let $y = |x|$ be the output of a full-wave rectifier.

a. Determine the CDF of the output random variable y for an arbitrary continuous random variable x.

b. Find the PDF of y for a Gaussian random variable x.

6.11. x is a Gaussian random variable with mean $m_x = 2$ and variance $\sigma_x^2 = 16$.

a. Calculate $P\{x \le 2\}, P\{x \ge 3\}, P\{6 < x \le 10\}, P\{|x - 2| \le 4\}$ and $P\{|x| > 16\}$.

b. $P\{x > \alpha\} = 10^{-3}$, find α.

c. $P\{x \le \alpha\} = 0.995$, find α.

d. Find $P\{|x - m_x| > 6\sigma_x\}$.

6.12. x and y have joint PDF

$$f_{x,y}(x, y) = K(x^2 + y^2), \quad -1 \le x \le 1; -1 \le y \le 1$$

a. Find the value of K.

b. Determine the joint CDF $F_{x,y}(x, y)$.

c. Calculate the marginal PDFs of x and y.

6.13. x and y have joint PDF

$$f_{x,y}(x, y) = xye^{-(x+y)}, \quad x \ge 0; y \ge 0$$

a. Determine $f_x(x)$ and $f_y(y)$.

b. Are x and y statistically independent?

c. Find $f_y(y|x)$ and $f_x(x|y)$.

d. Find $E(y|x = x)$ and $E(x|y = y)$.

e. Find $E(x)$ and $E(y)$.

6.14. Show that the correlation coefficient ρ_{xy} between random variable x and y satisfies

$$-1 \le \rho_{xy} \le 1$$

6.15. Random variables x and y have joint PDF

$$f_{x,y}(x, y) = C(x + y), \quad 0 \le x \le 2; 0 \le y \le 1$$

a. Calculate C.

b. Determine $E(x)$ and $E(y)$.

c. Find $Var(x)$ and $Var(y)$.

d. Calculate $Cov(x, y)$ and ρ_{xy}.

e. What is $E(x + y)$ and $Var(x + y)$?

6.16. x and y are two $\mathcal{N}(0, 1)$ random variables. Determine the PDF of $z = x + y$ if

a. x and y are statistically independent.

b. The correlation coefficient $\rho_{xy} = -1/2$.

6.17. Let $y = e^{-ax}$.

a. Find the CDF and PDF of y if x is a uniformly distributed random variable in [0, 1]. Assume $a > 0$.

b. Find the CDF and PDF of y if x is a Gaussian random variable. For the case $a = -1$, y is called **lognormal** random variable.

6.18. The PDF of Rayleigh distributed random variable x is given by

$$f_x(x) = \frac{x}{\sigma^2} e^{-x^2/2\sigma^2}, \quad 0 \leq x < \infty$$

a. Show that $E(x) = \sigma \sqrt{\dfrac{\pi}{2}}$, $E(x^2) = 2\sigma^2$ and

$$Var(x) = \left(2 - \frac{\pi}{2}\right)\sigma^2$$

b. Find the CDF $P\{x \leq x\}$. Plot it.

c. Find $P\{x \leq 0.1 \times x_{RMS}\}$, where x_{RMS} is the **root-mean-square (RMS)** value of the random variable x.

6.19. Consider linear transformation $\underline{z} = \underline{A}\underline{x} + \underline{b}$ of a vector $\underline{x} = [x_1, x_2, \ldots, x_n]^T$ of continuous random variables. Assume that the $n \times n$ matrix $\underline{A}$ has rank n.

a. Show that the PDF of $\underline{y}$ is given by

$$f_{\underline{y}}(\underline{y}) = \frac{1}{|A|} f_{\underline{x}}\left(\underline{A}^{-1}(\underline{y} - \underline{b})\right)$$

b. If $\underline{x} = [x_1, x_2, \ldots, x_n]^T$ is a Gaussian random vector with expected value $\underline{m}_x$ and covariance matrix $\underline{C}_x$, the vector $\underline{y}$ is also Gaussian with expected value $\underline{m}_y = \underline{A}\underline{m}_x + \underline{b}$ and covariance matrix $\underline{C}_y = \underline{A}\underline{C}_x \underline{A}^T$.

6.20. Let $y = x_1 + x_2 + \ldots + x_n$ be the sum of n independent random variables.

a. Calculate the characteristic function $\Phi_y(j\omega)$.

b. If $x_1, x_2, \ldots, x_n$ are independent Gaussian random variable. Show that y is a Gaussian random variable.

6.21. A random signal is defined as $x(t) = At + B$ where A is a zero-mean Gaussian random variable.

a. Find the first-order PDF of $x(t)$.

b. Find the mean and correlation functions, $m_x(t)$ and $R_x(t_1, t_2)$.

6.22 Let $x(t)$ be a zero-mean Gaussian random process with autocorrelation function $R_x(t_1, t_2) = 2e^{-|t_2 - t_1|}$. Determine the joint PDF of $x(t)$ and $x(t + \tau)$.

6.23. Let $y(t) = x(t)\cos(2\pi f_c t + \boldsymbol{\theta})$ where $x(t)$ is another random process and $\boldsymbol{\theta}$ is a statistically independent random variable uniformly distributed in the interval $[0, 2\pi]$.

a. Find the autocorrelation function $R_y(t, t + \tau)$. Is $y(t)$ WSS?

b. Show that the spectral density of $y(t)$ is related to that of $x(t)$ by

$$G_y(f) = \frac{1}{4}[G_x(f - f_c) + G_x(f + f_c)]$$

6.24. Let $x(t) = A\cos(2\pi f_c t) + B\sin(2\pi f_c t)$ be a random process where A and B are statistically independent $\mathcal{N}(0, \sigma^2)$ random variables.

a. Find the first-order PDF of $x(t)$.

b. Find the mean and correlation functions, $m_x(t)$ and $R_x(t, t + \tau)$.

c. Is $x(t)$ stationary?

6.25. Consider the random processes

$$x(t) = A\cos(2\pi f_c t + \boldsymbol{\theta})$$

and

$$y(t) = B\sin(2\pi f_c t + \boldsymbol{\theta})$$

where $\boldsymbol{\theta}$ is a uniformly distributed random variable in the range $[-\pi, \pi]$.

a. Are $x(t)$ and $y(t)$ each WSS?

b. Find the cross-correlation function $R_{xy}(t, t + \tau)$.

c. Are the random processes jointly WSS?

d. Are the random processes uncorrelated?

6.26. The input to an LTI system with the transfer function

$$H(f) = \begin{cases} 10e^{-j2\pi f t_o}, & 0 \leq f \leq 4 \times 10^3 \\ 0, & \text{otherwise} \end{cases}$$

is a WSS process $x(t)$ with power spectral density $G_x(f) = 10^{-8}\Pi\left(\dfrac{f}{5 \times 10^5}\right)$. Let $y(t)$ denote the output of the system.

a. Find the output spectra density $G_y(f)$.

b. Determine the output autocorrelation function $R_y(\tau)$.

c. Find $E\{y^2(t)\}$.

6.27. Let $x(t)$ be a white Gaussian noise process with power spectral density $G_x(f) = N_o/2$. It is input to a first-order Butterworth filter with 3-dB cutoff frequency f_{3dB}. The transfer function is given by

$$H(f) = \frac{1}{1 + j(f/f_{3dB})}$$

a. Find the output spectra density $G_y(f)$ and autocorrelation function $R_y(\tau)$.

b. Determine the average output power.

c. Find the first-order PDF of $y(t)$.

d. Calculate the cross-spectral density $G_{xy}(f)$.

6.28. $x(t)$ is a WSS random signal with power spectral density $G_x(f)$. The signal passes through the system shown in Figure P6.3.

a. Is $y(t)$ WSS?

b. Find the output spectra density $G_y(f)$.

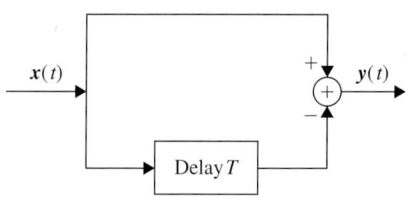

Figure P6.3

a. Find the power spectral density $G_x(f)$.

b. Find the value of $E\{x^2(t)\}$.

c. Find the RMS and 3-dB bandwidth of the process.

6.31. Suppose that narrowband noise $x(t)$ is bandlimited to $2B$ about the carrier frequency f_c. Show that the cross-spectral density of quadrature components $x_c(t)$ and $x_s(t)$ is given by

$$G_{x_c x_s}(f) = \begin{cases} j[G_x(f + f_c) - G_x(f - f_c)], & |f| \leq f_c \\ 0, & \text{otherwise} \end{cases}$$

6.29. Let $x(t)$ be WGN process with power spectral density $N_o/2$. It is applied to an ideal LP filter of bandwidth B and transfer function

$$H(f) = \Pi\left(\frac{f}{2B}\right)$$

a. Find the output autocorrelation function $R_y(\tau)$.

b. What is the maximum rate at which the filter output $y(t)$ can be sampled so that the resulting samples are independent?

6.30. The autocorrelation function of a stationary process $x(t)$ is given by

$$R_x(\tau) = e^{-\pi\tau^2}$$

6.32. Consider the block diagram of a receiver shown in Figure P6.4. Find the overall noise figure of the receiver.

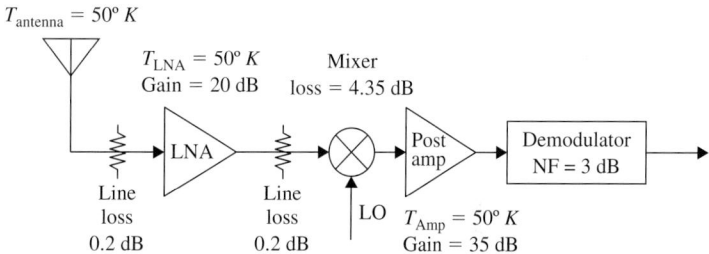

Figure P6.4

MATLAB PROBLEMS

6.33. An exponential random variable x is defined by the PDF

$$f_x(x) = 1.5e^{-1.5x}u(x).$$

a. Use the MATLAB function `rand(1,N)` to generate a sequence of iid $\mathcal{U}[0, 1]$ random variables `u[n]`. Use `N = 100`.

b. Using the inverse transform method, describe an algorithm for generating x from a uniformly distributed random variable. Generate length-N sequence `x[n]`.

c. Obtain the histogram of `x[n]` using the MATLAB function `hist` (Hint: use `H = hist(x,20)`). Use `stem` to plot the normalized (that is, scaled for unit area) histogram `H[k]` and compare it with the theoretical PDF.

d. Repeat (a) through (c) for `N = 1000`.

6.34. Central Limit Theorem Validation. Use the MATLAB function `rand(1,N)` to generate a sequence `u[n]` of iid $\mathcal{U}[0, 1]$ random variables. Use `N = 1000000`.

a. Generate a new sequence `z[k]` of length 2000 where each element `z[k]` consists of the average of 50 consecutive elements of `u[n]`. That is, `z[k] = 0.02*sum(u[k:k + 49])`.

b. Obtain the histogram of `z[k]` using the MATLAB `H = hist(z,40)`. Use `stem` to plot the normalized (that is, scaled for unit area) histogram `H[k]` and compare it with $\mathcal{N}(0, 1)$ PDF.

6.35. We use the Box-Muller algorithm to generate a pair of independent Gaussian random variables using Rayleigh random

variable. The marginal CDF $F_r(r)$ of a Rayleigh random variable r is

$$F_r(r) = \begin{cases} 0, & r < 0 \\ 1 - e^{-r^2/2\sigma^2}, & r \geq 0 \end{cases}$$

From Example 6.25, r is related to a pair of $\mathcal{N}(0, \sigma^2)$ random variables x and y by

$$x = r\cos\phi$$
$$y = r\sin\phi$$

where ϕ is uniformly distributed over $[-\pi, \pi]$. Because the CDF is monotonic, it is invertible. That is,

$$F_r(r) = 1 - e^{-r^2/2\sigma^2} = U_1$$

or

$$r = \sqrt{2\sigma^2 \log_e\left(\frac{1}{1 - U_1}\right)}$$

where U_1 is $\mathcal{U}[0, 1]$. Because $1 - U_1$ is also $\mathcal{U}[0, 1]$, we can replace $1 - U_1$ by U_1 to obtain

$$r = \sqrt{2\sigma^2 \log_e\left(\frac{1}{U_1}\right)} = \sqrt{-2\sigma^2 \log_e U_1}$$

Thus, a pair of independent Gaussian random variables x and y can be generated from a pair of $\mathcal{U}[0, 1]$ random variables U_1 and U_2 by using the algorithm

$$x = \sqrt{-2\sigma^2 \log_e U_1} \cos(2\pi U_2)$$

$$y = \sqrt{-2\sigma^2 \log_e U_1} \sin(2\pi U_2)$$

a. Use MATLAB function `rand(1,N)` to generate a pair of length-N $\mathcal{U}[0, 1]$ random sequences u_1 and u_2.

b. Generate `x[n]` and `y[n]` random sequences. Plot the normalized histograms of for `x[n]` and `y[n]` and compare with $\mathcal{N}(0, 1)$ PDF.

c. Generate a scatter plot of the ordered pair of samples (`x[n]`, `y[n]`). Use the command `plot(x, y, '.')` to plot points without connecting them with lines. Comment.

6.36. Use MATLAB function `randn(1,N)` to generate 0.3 second sequence `x[n]` of $\mathcal{N}(0, 1)$ random variables with sampling frequency of 10 kHz.

a. Calculate the spectral density of `x[n]` using the MATLAB function `periodogram`. Plot it.

b. Filter the sequence `x[n]` with length-4 moving average filter described by the following difference equation:

$$y[n] = \frac{1}{4}\{x[n] + x[n-1] + x[n-2] + x[n-3]\}$$

c. Calculate the spectral density of `y[n]` using the MATLAB function `periodogram`. Plot it.

An Interview with Gerard Foschini

Courtesy of Gerard Faschini

Why did you choose a career in the communication field?

At the time I received my NJIT BSEE, I sought a job which would enable me to pursue graduate study and an opportunity to eventually do research. I was completely open as to what that might entail. Bell Labs offered me a job in their Communication Development Training program, which included half pursuit of an NYU MEE degree and part-time work in a Military Switching area writing software specifications. Once I got my MEE, I wanted more background in fundamentals, so I left for a PhD in Math at Stevens. As I neared completion of my degree I returned to a Bell Labs to a position doing research on crosstalk among coupled wire pairs. I found the job challenging and interesting and steeped in random processes and information theory which I enjoyed learning on the job. I was finding a home in the field of communications. The more I learned, the better I could address new applications. That work on crosstalk left me especially well prepared for research decades later working out the fundamentals of wireless communications. The wireless context was different, but coupled communication paths were at the heart of it except the coupling was often extremely strong as opposed to extremely weak: The equations, at a high level, were the same.

Tell us about the concepts of spectral and spatial processing. How are they being exploited to increase the capacity of today's and future generations of wireless systems?

Shannon's work and its flourishing generalizations are growing in their impact. Communications systems are evolving on all fronts to achieve better spectral efficiency expressed in bits per second per Hertz. Spatial modes, bandwidth, and power need to be used very wisely. A top-down information theoretic view is a key to guiding designs toward that end. Fiber optic communication will likely provide much of the infrastructure for wireless communication, especially for cellular base stations. Interestingly, Shannon theory is starting to influence the advancement of fiber optic communication in much the same way. Today this includes paying close attention to exploiting multiple spatial modes of a fiber to substantially improve spectral efficiency.

In 2002, Bell Laboratories' patent on BLAST based on your work was named by MIT's *Technology Review* magazine as one of five "patents to watch." Tell us about the BLAST architecture.

Say there are n antennas in each of the transmit and receive antenna arrays. The n-dimensional received signal vector, $r(t)$, is expressed in terms of the n-dimensional transmit vector signal $s(t)$ and a random n by n matrix H and random n-dimensional received noise vector, $v(t)$, via the equation $r(t) = Hs(t) + v(t)$. Beside the uncertainty in the received signal due to added noise, the matrix, H, is also random and the transmitter does not know which H will occur. To be efficient with frequency usage, the n components of $s(t)$ were constrained to all be in the same frequency band: like n radio stations all communicating in the same band at the same time. The problem is to make sense of the receive signal under these circumstances. Back in 1948 Shannon showed *what* bit rates could ultimately be achieved under simpler circumstances when n = 1. Over the 60^+ years since, researchers have learned *how* to get extremely close to what Shannon showed was theoretically possible. The key was the continual discovery of ever better ways of coding and decoding the signal. A communication architecture to deal with all of the uncertainty of the n-dimensional channel while leveraging this 1-dimensional coding technology was called for.

Think of a virtual blank slate onto which a vector of electromagnetic waves are to be written (i.e., radiated). The slate is a discretization of space-time. The vertical dimension is space quantized by an enumeration of the antennae elements in the transmit array and the horizontal dimension of time enumerates successive time durations each of which span many transmitted symbols. The architectural question to be: How do you write on this slate and correspondingly read off the slate in a way that is most capacity efficient while leveraging the great advances of spatially 1-dimensional codes that was achieved. Remarkably, a generalization of Shannon's original mathematical analysis provides something of a blueprint on *how* to write on and read off of this slate. The solution involves writing along successive space-time diagonals. Thereby, each transmitted bit's presence is spread over *both* space and time and that is important because the transmitter does not know where or when bad impairments will occur. The linear, 1-dimensional, progression of space-time holders of encoded symbols as needed for 1-dimensional codes. As each 1-dimensional diagonal is read and subtracted away by the receiver, a layer of what would otherwise have been interference is stripped away from the signals written on the diagonals that remain. I referred to the 1-dimensional diagonals as LAyers of SpaceTime. A colleague added the B for Bell Labs to get BLAST and the name stuck. A statistically interpreted generalization of Shannon's formulation expresses what the bit rate limits are and one learns that they are approachable with 1-dimensional coders and decoders as was desired. For highly random H matrices, for fixed bandwidth and power, capacity increases linearly with n. One also learns, that as n and power grow, the penalty for the signals self interference amounts to an effective reduction of the launched power by $e = 2.718. \ldots$ This is a small, inside the log penalty for a linear outside the log capacity growth with n.

What are the new frontiers of innovation in wireless communications?

I think that the practical management of interference is in its infancy. The quest is for vast numbers of users elaborated over many square kilometers, to be exquisitely, jointly controlled. They are controlled to keep them out of each other's way even though they share the same communication resource. Just how exquisitely that can be done is a big question. The maturation of the roles of "dirty paper" coding, network coding, interference alignment, the role of relays and cognitive radio are to be determined. Besides cellular networks, peer-to-peer networks are also important to investigate. Breakthroughs in the temperature at which superconductivity is exhibited could be game changers.

Who most inspired you professionally?

Regarding accomplishment of those who led the way, I was inspired by Claude Shannon and Norbert Weiner. My Stevens Professor Larry Wallen, taught, by example, how to artfully lecture on a vast range of important fundamental analytical ideas without reliance on any notes. To again and again witness first-hand that that could be done, opened my eyes as the huge amount of information that one person could hold, contribute to, and crystal clearly articulate. His example influenced the way I try to work. Reading Professor Feller's books on probability theory, I marveled at seeing how superbly theoretical ideas could be expressed on paper. For decades I've worked on the site where Arno Penzias and Bob Wilson discovered the Big Bang. I can't imagine a more inspiring wireless discovery than that. Generally, over the years, when my own work required that I learn certain information on a topic, there was usually someone nearby who excelled in that realm who could inform me. At the same time I often found them inspiring me by virtue of the quality of their own particular achievements: Mike Gans (electromagnetics), Larry Shepp (probability), Ben Logan (harmonic analysis), Steve Rice (analysis generally), Paul Burke (queueing theory), and Giovanni Vannucci (a polymath) are some of many examples. Jack Salz exhibited superb taste in choosing problems and launching attacks on them while generously inspiring those of us who worked with him to join the attack. We'd be puzzling over some communications equations and he'd say "I tell you, this dog is barking." Once I got over my initial reaction, I came to respect his style and soon found myself saying the same thing. In short, there has been and there is now great inspirational talent all around me at Bell Labs. This includes many talented students who have worked with me. Of course, I was also inspired by countless achievements of outside researchers, besides the other interviewees, Gottfried Ungerboeck (coding), Dominique Godard (blind equalization), Tom Cover (information theory), Robert Price (decision feedback theory), and Dave Forney (MLSD theory) just to name a few. I am also inspired when I see a brilliant, elegant, simple to explain discovery enjoy enormous traction. Sivash Alamoiti's code is a fine example.

Do you have any advice for new generation of students and researchers entering the communications field?

You are now going to be at the center of an ever intensifying, roiling field of information flows and demands for you to deal with them all. Your fate may rest on how you manage, select, and adapt. Don't worry about possessing enough smarts or knowledge. If you are blessed with a genuine sense of wonder, passion, and drive to pursue your quests, that may be enough. Look to biological examples to continually transform systems theory. Keep your eye on quantum communications/computation and superconductivity advances as they may have enormous impact. Finally, don't look to old timers like me to tell you what you should do. Instead, follow Polonius' advice: "This above all: to thine own self be true."

Gerard J. Foschini received the B.S.E.E. degree from NJIT, the M.E.E. degree from NYU, and the Ph.D. degree in mathematics from Stevens Institute of Technology. He has been at Bell Laboratories for over four decades, where he is currently a Distinguished Inventor in the Wireless Research Laboratory at Crawford Hill, NJ. He has done extensive research on point-to-point communication systems as well as on networks. Dr. Foschini is best known for his seminal contributions to the science and technology of multiple-antenna wireless communications—a critical technology in today's advanced mobile broadband networking. His multiple antenna concepts make it possible to increase data transmission rates by orders of magnitude without increased power at the transmitter and without costly expanding of bandwidth. His research discoveries are core components of many of today's current and emerging wireless communications standards, including the Multiple Input Multiple Output (MIMO) architecture in IEEE WiFi (802.11n) and WiMAX (802.16e) for wireless data communication, as well as 4G cellular standards including 3GPP and 3GPP2. Dr. Foschini has published more than 100 papers and holds 15 patents. Dr. Foschini is a Fellow of IEEE and Bell Labs. He is the recipient of the 2000 Bell Labs Inventor's Award, and the 2002 Thomas Alva Edison Patent Award. He has also won the 2006 IEEE Eric E. Sumner Award, and the 2008 Alexander Graham Bell Medal. He has been elected to the National Academy of Engineering.

CHAPTER 7

Noise Performance of Analog Communication Systems

We studied several aspects of analog communication systems in Chapters 4 and 5, including the spectral characteristics of modulated signals, their bandwidth requirements, and implementation considerations for modulators and demodulators. Noise is present in all electronic systems and affects the quality of the desired signal recovered at the receiver. In this chapter, we will analyze the effect of noise on the performance of various analog communication systems.

Two parameters are frequently used to characterize the noise performance of various analog modulation schemes.

- **Carrier-to-noise power ratio** (**CNR**). It is defined as the ratio of carrier power to the noise power in a specified bandwidth, measured frequently using a spectrum analyzer. CNR measurement is performed on BP (that is, carrier modulated) waveforms. CNR is thus a predetection measurement ideally suited for characterizing impairments introduced by the transmission channel or a standalone device such as an amplifier.
- **Signal-to-noise power ratio** (**SNR**). It is defined as the ratio of signal power to noise power made at baseband before modulation or after detection or demodulation. SNR includes noise in the original signal—say, noise in the video from a TV studio camera—as well as noise contributions from the modulator/transmitter, transmission system, and demodulator/receiver. It is ideal for characterizing end-to-end performance, that is, the overall signal quality.

Accordingly, we will characterize the noise introduced by the channel or the receiver front-end in terms of appropriate CNR definition. On the other hand, we will use baseband SNR as a metric for characterizing end-to-end signal quality. The SNR measurement is performed by special test equipment designed for validating end-to-end system performance.

This chapter starts with performance analysis of AM modulation schemes in the presence of noise. Then, the effect of noise on angle-modulation systems is considered. As shown in Chapter 5, the bandwidth requirements for angle-modulation systems are considerably higher than those for AM schemes. We will find that these systems, and especially FM, can provide a high degree of noise immunity. The improved noise performance is obtained at the expense of increased transmission bandwidth. The chapter concludes by considering analog link design issues when repeaters are added to meet the system span requirements.

The chapter is organized into the following sections:

7.1 NOISE PERFORMANCE OF BASEBAND SYSTEMS.
This section studies the effect of noise in analog baseband systems.

7.2 EFFECT OF NOISE ON THE PERFORMANCE OF AM SYSTEMS.
The performance of various AM modulation schemes in the presence of noise is analyzed. DSB- and SSB-SC systems require coherent detection. For conventional AM, the performance of the system with both coherent and envelope detectors is considered.

7.3 NOISE PERFORMANCE OF ANGLE-MODULATION SYSTEMS.
In this section, the noise performance of PM and FM systems is studied. We establish that these systems offer improved SNR performance at the expense of increased transmission bandwidth. The section concludes with a review of threshold effect in FM systems.

7.4 PREEMPHASIS AND DEEMPHASIS.
The effect of pre- and deemphasis filtering in further improving the output SNR in an FM transmission system is demonstrated in this section.

7.5 COMPARISON OF ANALOG MODULATION SYSTEMS.
In this section we compare the performance of analog communication systems on the basis of bandwidth requirements, SNR achievable at the output, and equipment complexity considerations.

7.6   LINK DESIGN.

In this section, we study the effects of transmission losses and noise on the design of analog transmission systems. The effect of noise accumulation in analog repeaters on the link design is considered.

The chapter concludes with final remarks and a selected list of references.

7.1   NOISE PERFORMANCE OF BASEBAND SYSTEMS

In a baseband system, the message signal is transmitted without any carrier modulation as illustrated in Figure 7.1(a). We assume that the message signal $s(t)$ is a stationary, zero mean, low-pass random process whose spectral density is bandlimited to B Hz. Because the channel is assumed to be distortionless, it follows from Section 2.7.1 that the output signal is an attenuated and delayed version of the message signal.

$$s_o(t) = \alpha s(t - t_d), \quad \alpha < 1 \tag{7.1}$$

where α and t_d, respectively, represent the attenuation and delay introduced by the channel. We shall neglect the channel delay in further analysis without any loss of generality. The signal is received at the receiver front end in the presence of **additive white Gaussian noise** (**AWGN**) $n_i(t)$ with zero mean and two-sided power spectral density $G_{n_i}(f) = N_o/2$ W/Hz. We assume that $s(t)$ and $n_i(t)$ are statistically independent. The receiver in the baseband system consists of an ideal LP filter $H_R(f)$ with bandwidth B Hz to eliminate out-of-band noise energy while allowing the signal to pass through without any distortion. The signal at the LP filter input is given by

$$r(t) = s_o(t) + n_i(t) = \alpha s(t) + n_i(t) \tag{7.2}$$

From Figure 7.1, the output of the LP filter is

$$r_1(t) = \alpha s(t) + n_o(t) \tag{7.3}$$

The receiver output signal power is given by

$$P_R = E\{\alpha^2 s^2(t)\} = \alpha^2 \overline{s^2} \tag{7.4}$$

The power spectral density of the noise at the LP filter output is given from (6.247) as

$$G_{n_o}(f) = G_{n_i}(f)|H_R(f)|^2 = \frac{N_o}{2}|H_R(f)|^2 \tag{7.5}$$

This allows us to calculate total noise power at the receiver output as

$$P_{n_o} = \int_{-\infty}^{\infty} G_{n_o}(f)df = \int_{-\infty}^{\infty} \frac{N_o}{2}|H_R(f)|^2 df = \int_{-B}^{B} \frac{N_o}{2}df = N_o B \tag{7.6}$$

Equation (7.6) represents the **inband noise power,** that is, the noise power contained in the message signal bandwidth.

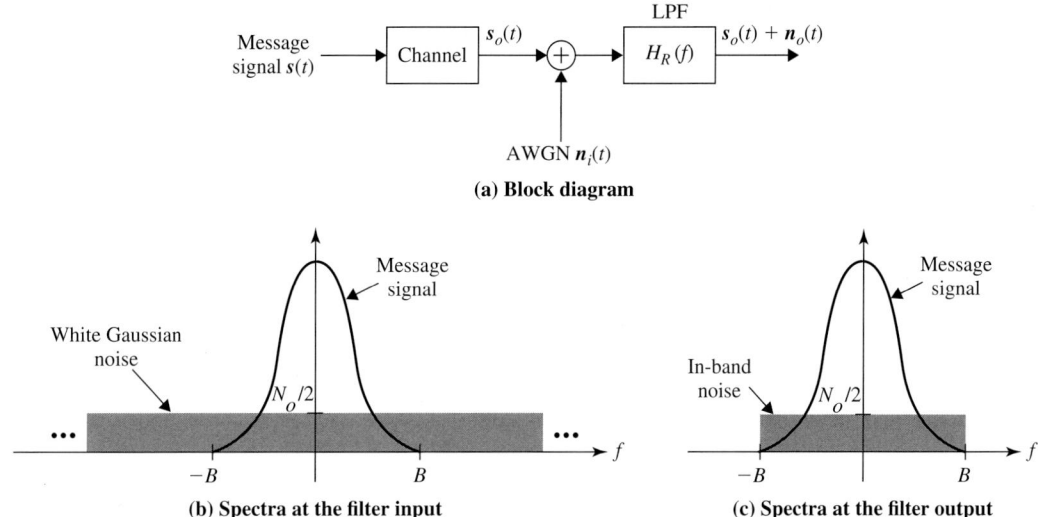

(a) Block diagram

(b) Spectra at the filter input   (c) Spectra at the filter output

Figure 7.1 Baseband system.

The SNR at the receiver output is given by

$$SNR_{BB} = \frac{P_R}{P_{n_o}} = \frac{P_R}{N_O B} = \frac{\alpha^2 \overline{s^2}}{N_O B} \tag{7.7}$$

Equation (7.7) describes the SNR achieved with a simple baseband system in which all out-of-band noise is removed by filtering. Baseband analog fiber-optic links are popular in video surveillance applications.

7.2 EFFECT OF NOISE ON THE PERFORMANCE OF AM SYSTEMS

In this section we study the performance of AM systems in the presence of noise. The quadrature model of narrowband noise developed in Section 6.12 will be useful in analyzing the noise performance of various AM and angle-modulation systems. The assumptions made in Section 7.1 regarding the statistical properties of the message signal are applicable throughout this chapter. Figure 7.2 displays the block diagram of an AM communications system. The BP channel is assumed to be distortionless over the transmission bandwidth B_T (Chapter 4). The channel output signal, therefore, is an attenuated and delayed version of the transmitter output. It

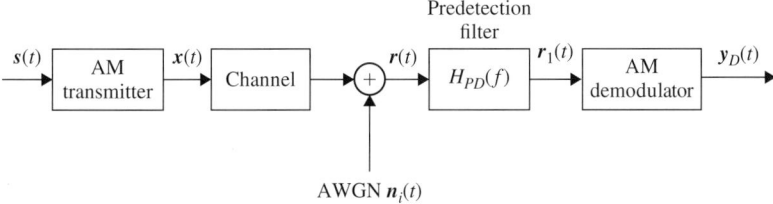

Figure 7.2 AM communication system model.

is received in the presence of AWGN $n_i(t)$ with zero mean and two-sided power spectral density $G_{n_i}(f) = N_o/2$ W/Hz. We assume that $x(t)$ and $n_i(t)$ are statistically independent. The receiver front end consists of a BP **predetection filter,** which is typically the intermediate-frequency (IF) filter in a superheterodyne receiver. The predetection filter with a bandwidth B_T passes the modulated signal without distortion while removing the out-of-band noise. The demodulator recovers the original message signal by using either a coherent or an envelope detection method, depending on the AM scheme.

7.2.1   Noise Performance of DSB-SC

In a DSB-SC AM system, the receiver consists of a coherent demodulator preceded by a predetection filter as displayed in Figure 7.3. The DSB-SC transmitter output signal is given from (4.2) as

$$x_{DSB}(t) = A_c s(t) \cos(2\pi f_c t + \phi) \tag{7.8}$$

where the message signal $s(t)$ is a stationary, zero mean, LP random process whose spectral density is bandlimited to B Hz. ϕ represents our uncertainty about the phase of the carrier waveform. The channel output signal is an attenuated version of the transmitted signal which is received in the presence of AWGN.

The input to the predetection filter can, therefore, be expressed as

$$r(t) = \alpha x_{DSB}(t) + n_i(t) = \alpha A_c s(t) \cos(2\pi f_c t + \phi) + n_i(t) \tag{7.9}$$

To calculate the signal power at the predetection filter input, we assume that ϕ is $\mathcal{U}[-\pi, \pi]$ random variable and is statistically independent of the message signal $s(t)$. Therefore,

$$P_R = E\{\alpha^2 x_{DSB}^2(t)\} = E\{\alpha^2 A_c^2 s^2(t) \cos^2(2\pi f_c t + \phi)\}$$

$$= E\{\alpha^2 A_c^2 s^2(t)\} \underbrace{E\{\cos^2(2\pi f_c t + \phi)\}}_{1/2}$$

$$= \frac{1}{2}\alpha^2 A_c^2 \overline{s^2} \tag{7.10}$$

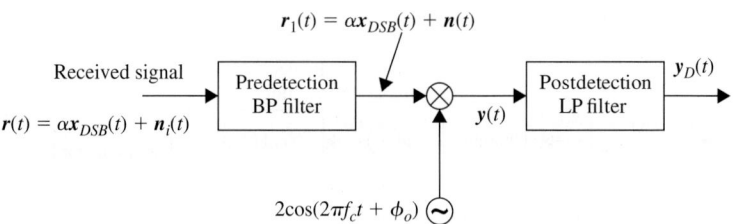

Figure 7.3 DSB-SC demodulator.

where $\overline{s^2} = E\{s^2(t)\}$ is the average power in the message signal $s(t)$. Because $n_i(t)$ has power spectral density $G_{n_i}(f) = N_o/2$ W/Hz, the noise power, measured in the bandwidth of the baseband message signal, is

$$P_{n_i} = N_o B \qquad (7.11)$$

The receiver input CNR, defined as the ratio of carrier power to the noise power in the message signal bandwidth, is given by

$$CNR_{IN} = \frac{\text{Carrier power at the receiver input}}{\text{Input noise power in the message signal bandwidth}} = \frac{P_R}{P_{n_i}} \qquad (7.12)$$

Substituting (7.10) and (7.11) into (7.12), we obtain

$$CNR_{IN} = \frac{P_R}{N_o B} = \frac{\alpha^2 A_c^2 \overline{s^2}}{2 N_o B} \qquad (7.13)$$

We assume that the predetection filter is an ideal BP filter with bandwidth equal to $B_T = 2B$. Therefore, the DSB-SC signal is passed by the predetection filter without any distortion. We write the predetection filter output as

$$r_1(t) = \alpha A_c s(t) \cos(2\pi f_c t + \phi) + n(t) \qquad (7.14)$$

The noise $n(t)$ at the predetection filter output is narrowband white Gaussian. Figure 7.4(a) illustrates noise spectrum at the predetection filter output. As discussed in Section 6.12.1, the narrowband noise $n(t)$ at the predetection filter output can be expanded into its quadrature components. This allows us to write (7.14) as

$$r_1(t) = \alpha A_c s(t) \cos(2\pi f_c t + \phi) + n_c(t) \cos(2\pi f_c t + \phi) - n_s(t) \sin(2\pi f_c t + \phi) \quad (7.15)$$

where $n_c(t)$ and $n_s(t)$ are LP Gaussian noise processes with mean zero and variance $2 N_o B$ as discussed in Section 6.12.1.

The received signal is demodulated by first multiplying the predetection filter output $r_1(t)$ with locally generated coherent carrier $2\cos(2\pi f_c t + \phi)$. The message signal $s(t)$

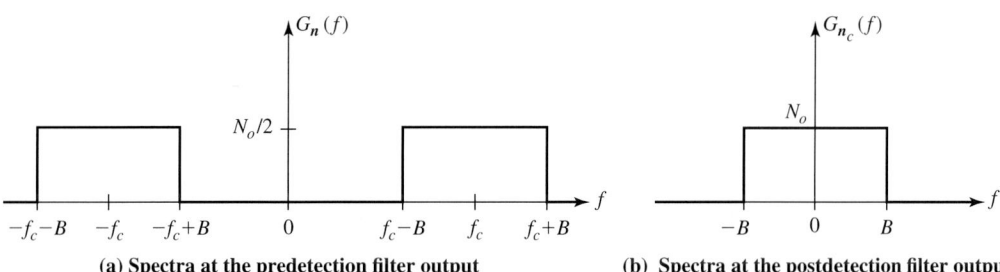

(a) Spectra at the predetection filter output   **(b) Spectra at the postdetection filter output**

Figure 7.4 Noise spectra in DSB-SC demodulation.

is then recovered from the product signal by passing it through an LP filter as illustrated in Figure 7.3. The multiplier output is given by

$$
\begin{aligned}
y(t) &= r_1(t) \times 2\cos(2\pi f_c t + \phi) \\
&= \{\alpha A_c s(t)\cos(2\pi f_c t + \phi) + n_c(t)\cos(2\pi f_c t + \phi) - n_s(t)\sin(2\pi f_c t + \phi)\} \\
&\quad \times 2\cos(2\pi f_c t + \phi) \\
&= \alpha A_c s(t) + \alpha A_c s(t)\cos(4\pi f_c t + 2\phi) + n_c(t) + n_c(t)\cos(4\pi f_c t + 2\phi) \\
&\quad - n_s(t)\sin(4\pi f_c t + 2\phi)
\end{aligned}
\tag{7.16}
$$

The postdetection LP filter of bandwidth B removes the double frequency terms and passes only the LP components. Hence, the demodulated output is given by

$$
y_D(t) = \alpha A_c s(t) + n_c(t)
\tag{7.17}
$$

The postdetection signal power is given by

$$
P_D = (\alpha A_c)^2 \overline{s^2}
\tag{7.18}
$$

The noise power at the postdetection filter output equals $P_{n_c} = 2N_o B$, as shown on Figure 7.4(b). Therefore, the output (postdetection) SNR is given by

$$
SNR_{DSB} = \frac{P_D}{P_{n_c}} = \frac{(\alpha A_c)^2 \overline{s^2}}{2N_o B} = \frac{P_R}{N_o B}
\tag{7.19}
$$

Comparing (7.19) with (7.13), we conclude that

$$
SNR_{DSB} = CNR_{IN}
\tag{7.20}
$$

Thus the output SNR of a DSB-SC AM system is equal to the receiver input CNR. The ratio of the modulation scheme's output SNR to the receiver's predetection CNR is a useful figure of merit. From (7.20), the figure of merit of a DSB-SC AM system is obtained as

$$
\frac{SNR_{DSB}}{CNR_{IN}} = 1
\tag{7.21}
$$

Experiment 7.1　*Noise Performance of a DSB-SC AM System*

In this experiment, we expand the Simulink model of a DSB-SC AM system developed in Experiment 4.1 to measure its noise performance and compare it with the theory. The carrier frequency is 20Hz and the message signal is 1-Hz sine wave. In this experiment, we compute the postdetection SNR as a function of input CNR. The Simulink model is illustrated in Figure 7.5. The computation of postdetection SNR is performed by processing the DSB-SC modulator output along two paths as follows:

1. Along the **signal path,** no noise is added. The postdetected waveform samples (**postclean**) are passed to the MATLAB workspace to calculate the demodulated signal power.

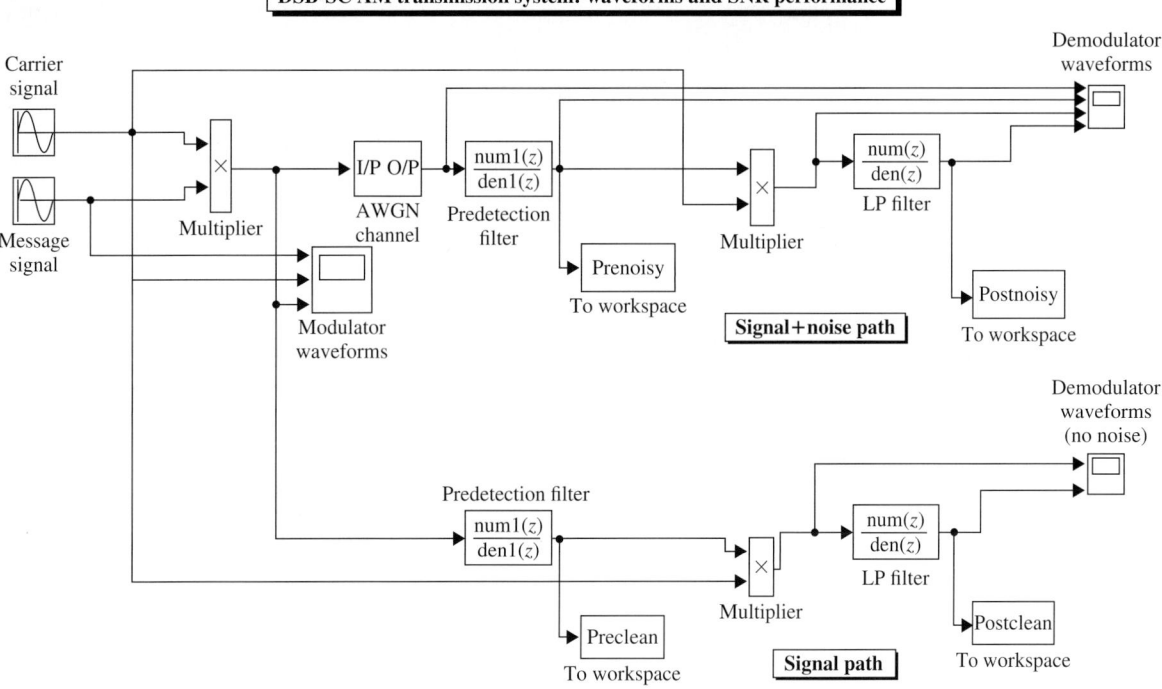

Figure 7.5 Simulink model for computing the SNR performance of a DSB-SC AM system.

2. Along the **signal + noise path,** AWGN noise is added to the DSB-SC modulator output by using the **Band-Limited White Noise (BLWN)** block from the Simulink Library. We need to set spectral density $(N_o/2)$ parameter of this block to establish a specific value of CNR_{IN} for simulation. From (7.13), the one-sided spectral density N_o for a given CNR_{IN} value is given by

$$N_o = \frac{A_c^2 \overline{s^2}}{2CNR_{IN}B} \tag{7.22}$$

For carrier amplitude $A_c = 1$ and sinusoidal modulating signal of frequency $f_m\left(\overline{s^2} = 0.5\right)$, (7.22) simplifies to

$$N_o = \frac{0.5}{2CNR_{IN}f_m} \tag{7.23}$$

The postdetected signal plus noise waveform samples (**postnoisy**) are passed to the MATLAB workspace to calculate the noise power at the LP filter output by subtracting the demodulated signal the power from the demodulated signal + noise power.

The parameters of the simulation are set up by a companion MATLAB m-file. The m-file also computes the postdetection SNR by using the signal and noise powers calculated above. Figure 7.6(a) displays demodulator waveforms. The postdetection SNR performance comparison between simulation results and the theory is illustrated in Figure 7.6(b). We can see from Figure 7.6(b) that there is close agreement between the theory and simulation results.

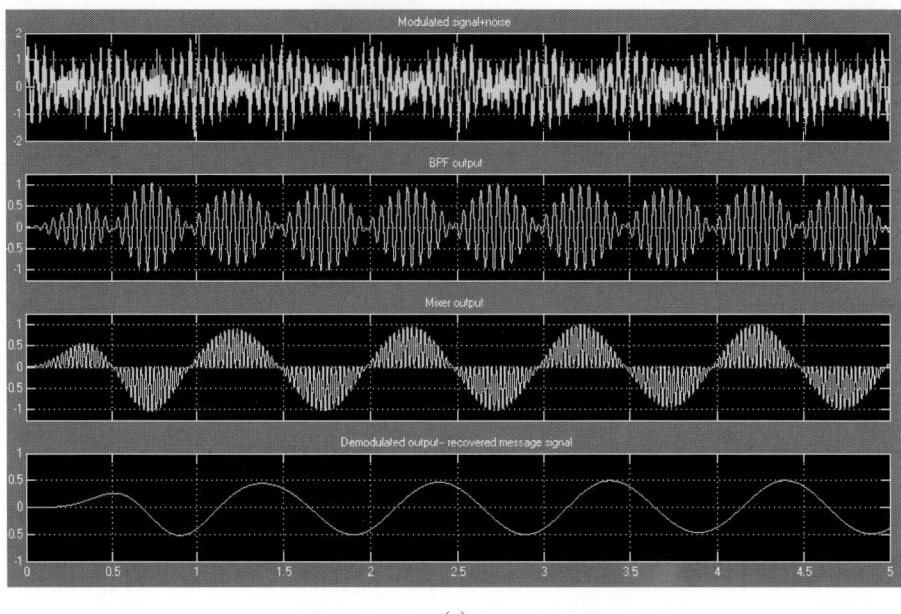

(a)

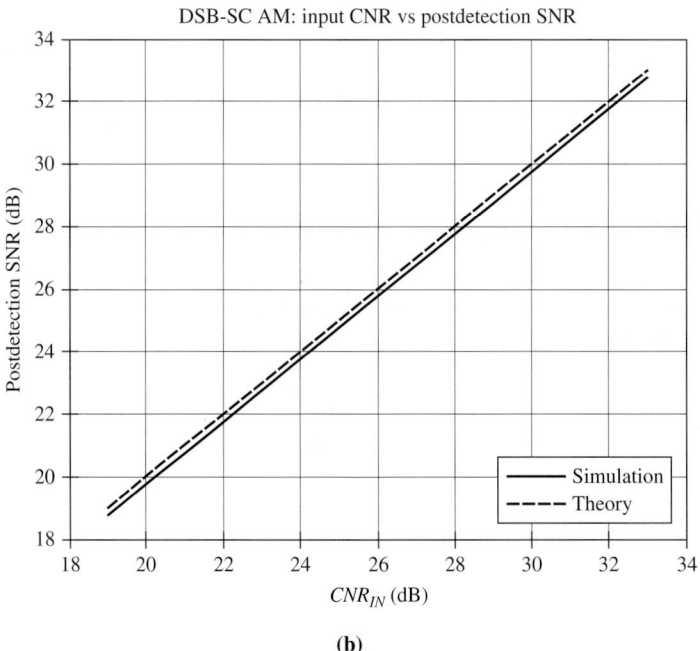

(b)

Figure 7.6 (a) Demodulator waveforms; (b) comparison of the simulated and theoretical SNR performance of a DSB-SC AM system.

7.2.2 Noise Performance of SSB-AM

The transmitted signal in the SSB-AM system using upper-sideband is given from (4.80) as

$$x_{USB}(t) = \frac{A_c}{2}\big[s(t)\cos(2\pi f_c t + \phi) - \hat{s}(t)\sin(2\pi f_c t + \phi)\big] \qquad (7.24)$$

where $\hat{s}(t)$ denotes the Hilbert transform of the random message signal $s(t)$ and ϕ represents our uncertainty about the phase of the carrier waveform. The channel output signal is an attenuated version of the transmitted signal which is received in the presence of AWGN. The predetection filter input can be written as

$$r(t) = \alpha x_{USB}(t) + n_i(t)$$

$$= \frac{\alpha A_c}{2}\big[s(t)\cos(2\pi f_c t + \phi) - \hat{s}(t)\sin(2\pi f_c t + \phi)\big] + n_i(t) \qquad (7.25)$$

The signal power at the predetection filter input is given by

$$P_R = E\big\{\alpha^2 x_{USB}^2(t)\big\} = \frac{\alpha^2 A_c^2}{4} E\big\{[s(t)\cos(2\pi f_c t + \phi) - \hat{s}(t)\sin(2\pi f_c t + \phi)]^2\big\}$$

$$= \frac{\alpha^2 A_c^2}{4}\left[\begin{array}{l} E\big\{s^2(t)\cos^2(2\pi f_c t + \phi)\big\} - 2E\big\{s(t)\hat{s}(t)\cos(2\pi f_c t + \phi)\sin(2\pi f_c t + \phi)\big\} \\ + E\big\{\hat{s}^2(t)\sin^2(2\pi f_c t + \phi)\big\} \end{array}\right]$$

$$\qquad (7.26)$$

Assuming that ϕ is $\mathcal{U}[-\pi, \pi]$ random variable and is statistically independent of the message signal $s(t)$, (7.26) can be simplified to

$$P_R = \frac{\alpha^2 A_c^2}{8}\big[E\big\{s^2(t)\big\} + E\big\{\hat{s}^2(t)\big\}\big] \qquad (7.27)$$

It was also shown in Chapter 4, Appendix 4A, that a function and its Hilbert transform have equal power. Applying this to (7.27) yields

$$P_R = \frac{\alpha^2 A_c^2 \overline{s^2}}{4} \qquad (7.28)$$

where $\overline{s^2} = E\big\{s^2(t)\big\}$ is the average power in the message signal $s(t)$. The receiver input noise power P_{n_i}, measured in the bandwidth of the baseband message signal, equals $N_o B$. Substituting (7.11) and (7.28) into (7.12), the receiver input CNR is given by

$$CNR_{IN} = \frac{P_R}{P_{n_i}} = \frac{P_R}{N_o B} = \frac{\alpha^2 A_c^2 \overline{s^2}}{4 N_o B} \qquad (7.29)$$

The predetection BP filter in the SSB-AM receiver passes the upper (or lower) sideband signal without any distortion while rejecting the out-of-band noise. As such, its minimum bandwidth is B Hz. The center frequency of the predetection filter is $f_c \pm B/2$, where the sign depends on the choice of sideband. The predetection filter output is given by

$$r_1(t) = \alpha x_{USB}(t) + n(t) = \frac{\alpha A_c}{2}\big[s(t)\cos(2\pi f_c t + \phi) - \hat{s}(t)\sin(2\pi f_c t + \phi)\big] + n(t)$$

$$\qquad (7.30)$$

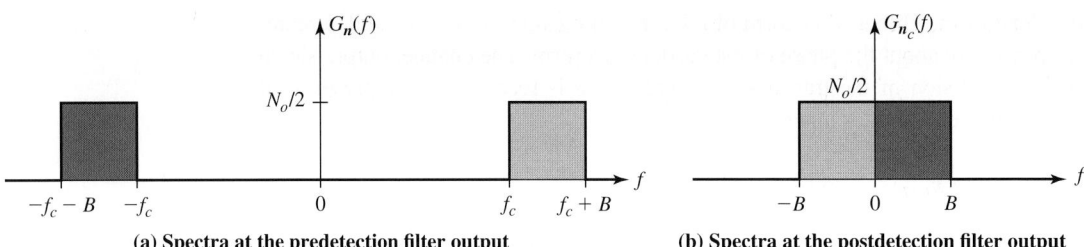

(a) Spectra at the predetection filter output   (b) Spectra at the postdetection filter output

Figure 7.7 Noise spectra in SSB demodulation.

Figure 7.7 illustrates noise spectra at the predetection and postdetection filter outputs. Expanding the narrowband noise $n(t)$ in quadrature components around the carrier frequency, the predetection filter output can be written as

$$r_1(t) = \frac{\alpha A_c}{2}\left[s(t)\cos(2\pi f_c t + \phi) - \hat{s}(t)\sin(2\pi f_c t + \phi)\right]$$

$$+ n_c(t)\cos(2\pi f_c t + \phi) - n_s(t)\sin(2\pi f_c t + \phi)$$

$$= \left[\frac{\alpha A_c}{2}s(t) + n_c(t)\right]\cos(2\pi f_c t + \phi) - \left[\frac{\alpha A_c}{2}\hat{s}(t) + n_s(t)\right]\sin(2\pi f_c t + \phi) \quad (7.31)$$

where $n_c(t)$ and $n_s(t)$ are LP Gaussian noise processes with mean zero and variance $N_o B$.

The received signal is demodulated by first multiplying the predetection filter output $r_1(t)$ with a locally generated coherent reference $2\cos(2\pi f_c t + \phi)$. The message signal $s(t)$ is then recovered from the product signal by passing it through an LP filter of bandwidth B. As in the case of DSB-SC, the demodulated output, in response to the input described by (7.31), consists of the baseband message signal and the in-phase noise component. That is,

$$y_D(t) = \frac{\alpha A_c}{2}s(t) + n_c(t) \quad (7.32)$$

From (7.32), the postdetection signal power is given by

$$P_D = \left(\frac{\alpha A_c}{2}\right)^2 \overline{s^2} \quad (7.33)$$

The noise power at the postdetection filter output equals $P_{n_c} = N_o B$ as shown in Figure 7.7(b). Therefore, the output SNR is given by

$$SNR_{SSB} = \frac{P_D}{P_{n_c}} = \frac{\alpha^2 A_c^2 \overline{s^2}}{4 N_o B} = \frac{P_R}{N_o B} \quad (7.34)$$

Comparing (7.34) with (7.29), we conclude that

$$SNR_{SSB} = CNR_{IN} \quad (7.35)$$

The figure of merit of the SSB-AM system can be expressed from (7.35) as

$$\frac{SNR_{SSB}}{CNR_{IN}} = 1 \quad (7.36)$$

Thus the output SNR of an SSB-AM system scheme is equal to the CNR at the receiver input. We further observe that the coherent demodulation of both DSB and SSB signals results in identical SNR performance.

Experiment 7.2 *Noise Performance of an SSB-AM System*

In this experiment, we expand the Simulink model of an SSB-AM system developed in Experiment 4.3 to measure its noise performance and compare it with the theory. The carrier frequency is 20Hz and the message signal is 1-Hz sine wave. In this experiment, we compute the postdetection SNR of the SSB-AM system as a function of its input CNR. The Simulink model is illustrated in Figure 7.8. The computation of postdetection SNR is performed by processing the SSB-AM modulator output along two paths as discussed in the context of Experiment 7.1. Along the **signal + noise path,** AWGN noise is added to the USB-AM modulator output by using the **BLWN** block from the Simulink Library. We need to

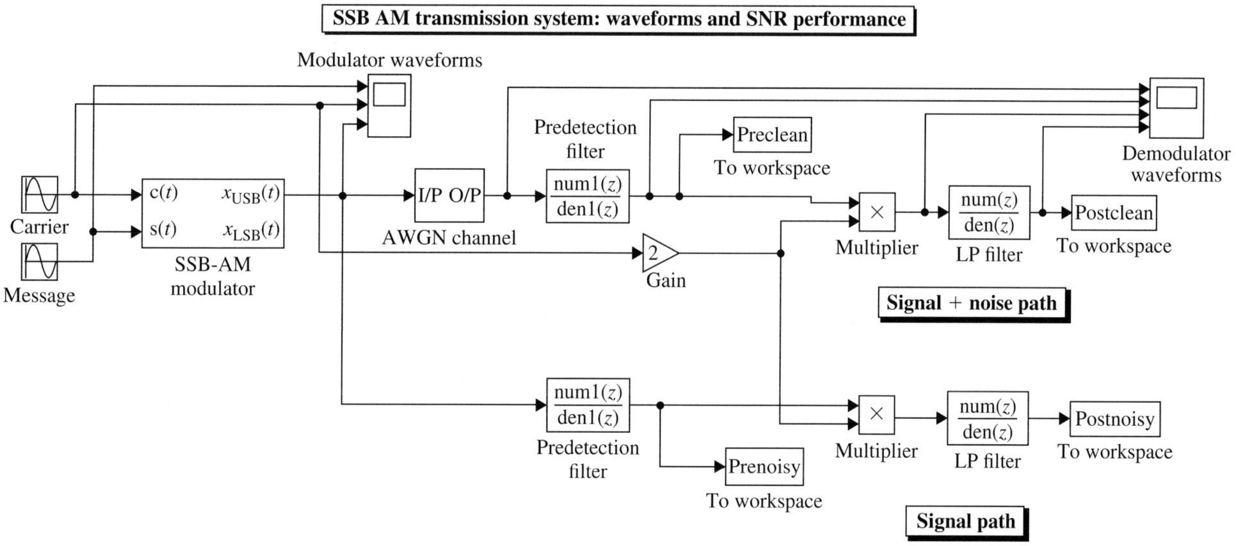

Figure 7.8 Simulink model for computing the SNR performance of an SSB-AM system.

set spectral density ($N_o/2$) parameter of this block to establish a specific value of CNR_{IN} for simulation. From (7.29), the one-sided spectral density N_o for a given CNR_{IN} value is given by

$$N_o = \frac{\alpha^2 A_c^2 \overline{s^2}}{4 CNR_{IN} B} \tag{7.37}$$

For carrier amplitude $\alpha A_c = 1$ and sinusoidal modulating signal of frequency $f_m \left(\overline{s^2} = 0.5 \right)$, (7.37) simplifies to

$$N_o = \frac{0.5}{4 CNR_{IN} f_m} \tag{7.38}$$

The parameters of the simulation are set up by a companion MATLAB m-file. The m-file also calculates the postdetection SNR by computing signal and noise powers as discussed in Experiment 7.1. Figure 7.9(a) displays demodulator waveforms. The postdetection SNR performance comparison

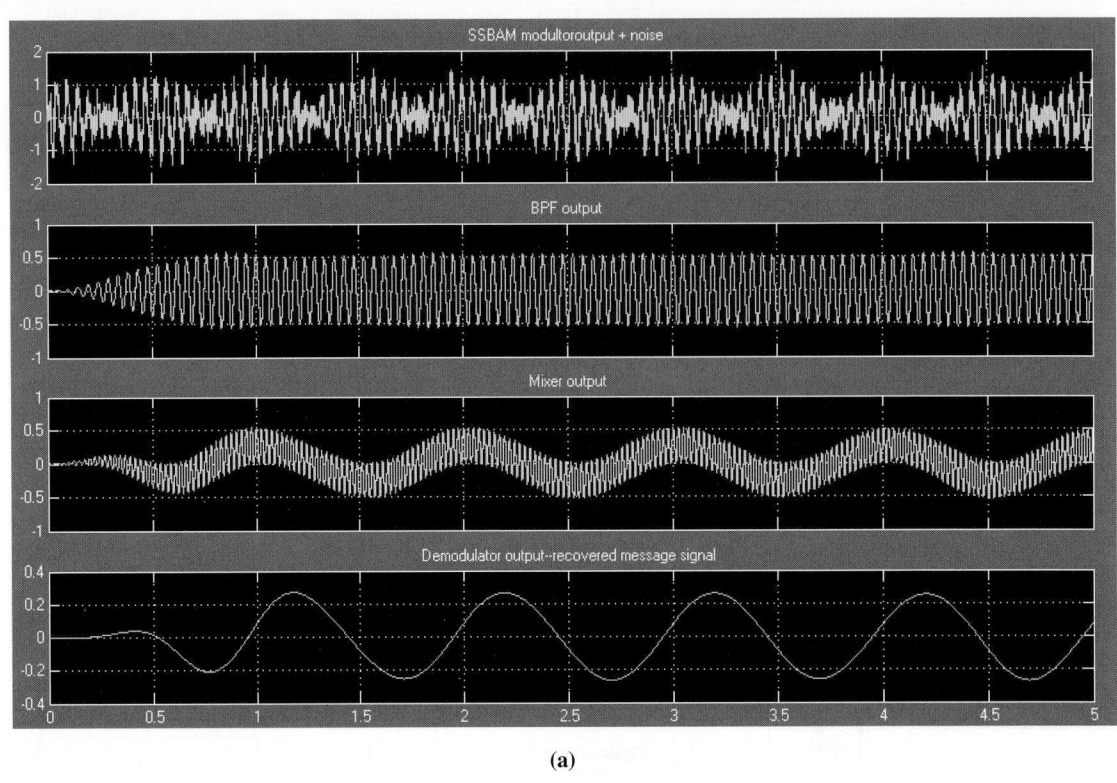

(a)

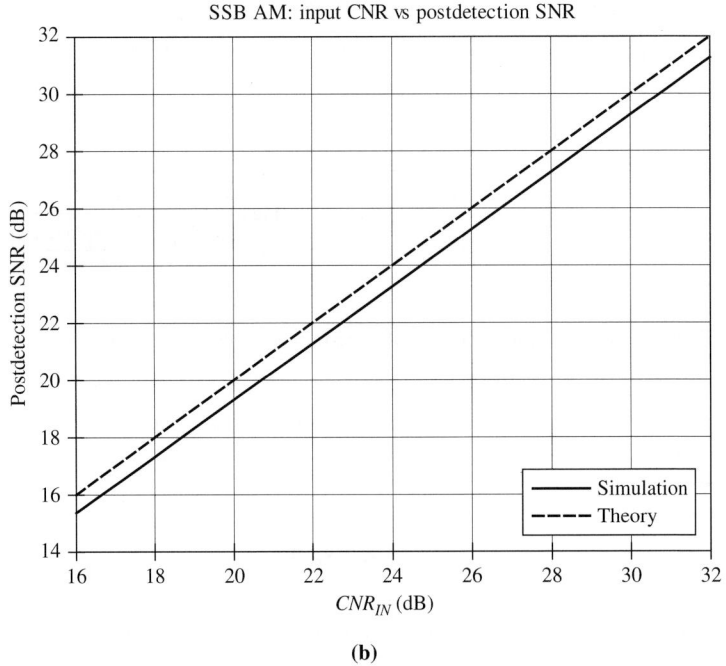

(b)

Figure 7.9 (a) Demodulator waveforms; (b) Comparison of the simulated and theoretical SNR performance of an SSB-AM system.

between simulation results and the theory is illustrated in Figure 7.9(b). It can be observed from Figure 7.9(b) that there is close agreement between the theory and simulation results.

7.2.3 Noise Performance of Conventional AM

In the conventional amplitude modulation scheme, the transmitted signal from (4.16) is given by

$$x_{AM}(t) = A_c\big[1 + m_a s_n(t)\big]\cos(2\pi f_c t + \phi) \qquad (7.39)$$

where $s_n(t)$ is normalized so that $|s_n(t)| \leq 1$ and m_a is the modulation index. The input to the predetection filter is an attenuated version of the transmitted signal in (7.39) that is received in the preference of AWGN $n_i(t)$. That is,

$$r(t) = \alpha x_{AM}(t) + n_i(t) = \alpha A_c\big[1 + m_a s_n(t)\big]\cos(2\pi f_c t + \phi) + n_i(t) \quad (7.40)$$

Again, to compute the signal power at the predetection filter input, we assume that ϕ is $\mathcal{U}[-\pi, \pi]$ random variable and is statistically independent of the message signal $s_n(t)$. Therefore

$$
\begin{aligned}
P_R &= E\big\{\alpha^2 x_{AM}^2(t)\big\} = E\big\{\alpha^2 A_c^2\big[1 + m_a s_n(t)\big]^2 \cos^2(2\pi f_c t + \phi)\big\} \\
&= E\big\{\alpha^2 A_c^2\big[1 + m_a s_n(t)\big]^2\big\} \underbrace{E\big\{\cos^2(2\pi f_c t + \phi)\big\}}_{1/2} \\
&= \frac{\alpha^2 A_c^2}{2}\big(1 + m_a^2 \overline{s_n^2}\big)
\end{aligned}
\qquad (7.41)
$$

The receiver input noise power P_{n_i}, measured in the bandwidth of the baseband message signal, equals $N_o B$. Substituting (7.41) and (7.11) into (7.12), the receiver input CNR is given by

$$CNR_{IN} = \frac{P_R}{P_{n_i}} = \frac{P_R}{N_o B} = \frac{\alpha^2 A_c^2\big(1 + m_a^2 \overline{s_n^2}\big)}{2N_o B} \qquad (7.42)$$

The predetection filter output is given by

$$r_1(t) = \alpha x_{AM}(t) + n(t) = \alpha A_c\big[1 + m_a s_n(t)\big]\cos(2\pi f_c t + \phi) + n(t) \quad (7.43)$$

Expanding the narrowband noise $n(t)$ into quadrature components around the carrier frequency, (7.43) can be expressed as

$$
\begin{aligned}
r_1(t) &= \alpha A_c\big[1 + m_a s_n(t)\big]\cos(2\pi f_c t + \phi) \\
&\quad + n_c(t)\cos(2\pi f_c t + \phi) - n_s(t)\sin(2\pi f_c t + \phi)
\end{aligned}
\qquad (7.44)
$$

Coherent Detection

It is easily shown by using a development parallel to that for DSB-SC systems that the demodulated output, in response to input described by (7.43), consists of the baseband message signal and the in-phase noise component. That is,

$$y_D(t) = \alpha A_c\big[1 + m_a s_n(t)\big] + n_c(t) \qquad (7.45)$$

The DC term in (7.45) is not considered part of the signal because it contains no information. Because AM demodulators are generally AC-coupled, the DC term is blocked out, yielding the following demodulated output:

$$y_D(t) = \alpha A_c m_a s_n(t) + n_c(t) \tag{7.46}$$

In this case, the demodulated signal power is given by

$$P_D = \alpha^2 A_c^2 m_a^2 \overline{s_n^2} \tag{7.47}$$

The noise power at the postdetection filter output equals $2N_o B$ as in the case of DSB-SC AM. Thus, the output SNR is given by

$$SNR_{AM} = \frac{P_D}{P_{n_c}} = \frac{\alpha^2 A_c^2 m_a^2 \overline{s_n^2}}{2N_o B} \tag{7.48}$$

We can express (7.48) as

$$SNR_{AM} = \frac{\alpha^2 A_c^2 m_a^2 \overline{s_n^2}}{2P_R}\left(\frac{P_R}{N_o B}\right) = \frac{\alpha^2 A_c^2 m_a^2 \overline{s_n^2}}{2P_R} CNR_{IN} \tag{7.49}$$

Substituting (7.41) and (4.32) into (7.49) yields

$$SNR_{AM} = \frac{\alpha^2 A_c^2 m_a^2 \overline{s_n^2}}{\alpha^2 A_c^2\left(1 + m_a^2 \overline{s_n^2}\right)} CNR_{IN} = \frac{m_a^2 \overline{s_n^2}}{\left(1 + m_a^2 \overline{s_n^2}\right)} CNR_{IN} = \eta CNR_{IN} \tag{7.50}$$

where η is the power efficiency of the conventional AM modulation scheme defined by (4.32). The figure of merit for the conventional AM scheme from (7.50) is

$$\frac{SNR_{AM}}{CNR_{IN}} = \eta \tag{7.51}$$

Because $\eta \leq 0.5$, (7.51) implies that, for a given value of average received power level, the output SNR in an AM system is at least 3 dB poorer than that for DSB and SSB systems using coherent demodulation. The maximum value of the SNR advantage is achieved when the power efficiency is at its maximum. The maximum value of $\eta = 50\%$ is achieved when $m_a = 100\%$ and $s(t)$ is a square wave of amplitude ± 1 volt. Typically, η is much less than 50%.

Envelope Detection

We recall from Section 4.3 that if the modulation index m_a of the conventional AM signal is restricted to less than 100%, an envelope detector can be used as an inexpensive demodulator. The envelope detector accepts the received signal and provides an output that follows the envelope of the noisy AM waveform. Because the envelope detector does not use the phase information, we can express its input from (7.44) by setting $\phi \equiv 0$ as

$$r_1(t) = \alpha A_c\left[1 + m_a s_n(t)\right]\cos(2\pi f_c t) + n_c(t)\cos(2\pi f_c t) - n_s(t)\sin(2\pi f_c t) \tag{7.52}$$

Figure 7.10 shows the phasor diagram representation of $r_1(t)$ where the first term of (7.52) is represented by a phasor of amplitude $\alpha A_c\left[1 + m_a s_n(t)\right] + n_c(t)$, while the second term is represented by a phasor perpendicular to the first and of magnitude $n_s(t)$. The envelope of $r_1(t)$ is given by

$$|r_1(t)| = \sqrt{\left(\alpha A_c\left[1 + m_a s_n(t)\right] + n_c(t)\right)^2 + n_s^2(t)} \qquad (7.53)$$

Equation (7.53) will be evaluated for two cases. First, we consider the case in which the signal component is much larger than the noise. From Figure 7.10 and (7.53), we observe that if $P\left\{|\alpha A_c\left[1 + m_a s_n(t)\right] + n_c(t)| \gg |n_s(t)|\right\} \approx 1$, then

$$|r_1(t)| \cong \alpha A_c\left[1 + m_a s_n(t)\right] + n_c(t) \qquad (7.54)$$

with a very high probability. The detected signal at the output of the LP filter after removing the DC component is given by

$$y_D(t) = \alpha A_c m_a s_n(t) + n_c(t) \qquad (7.55)$$

We observe by comparing (7.55) with (7.46) that the output of the envelope detector is identical to the output of the coherent demodulator under the assumption of high input CNR (CNR_{IN}) at the receiver. *Thus, the noise performance of coherent and envelope detectors is the same under high-CNR conditions.*

In order to analyze the low-CNR case, we use an amplitude-phase representation (6.255) of the narrowband noise $n(t)$ at the predetection filter output. That is,

$$n(t) = n_c(t)\cos(2\pi f_c t) - n_s(t)\sin(2\pi f_c t)$$
$$= e_n(t)\cos\left[2\pi f_c t + \phi_n(t)\right] \qquad (7.56)$$

where the noise envelope $e_n(t)$ and phase $\phi_n(t)$ processes are related to quadrature noise components of $n(t)$ by

$$e_n(t) = \sqrt{n_c^2(t) + n_s^2(t)} \qquad (7.57)$$

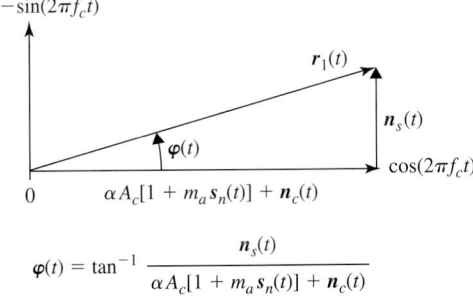

Figure 7.10 Phasor diagram of conventional AM: High-CNR case.

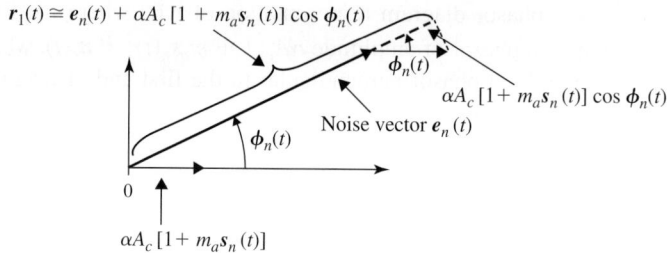

Figure 7.11 Phasor diagram of conventional AM: Low-CNR case.

$$\boldsymbol{\phi}_n(t) = \tan^{-1}\frac{\boldsymbol{n}_s(t)}{\boldsymbol{n}_c(t)} \tag{7.58}$$

Recall from Section 6.12.1 that if $\boldsymbol{n}(t)$ is Gaussian, the instantaneous amplitude $\boldsymbol{e}_n(t)$ and phase $\boldsymbol{\phi}_n(t)$ are, respectively, Rayleigh- and uniformly distributed random variables. Under low-input CNR conditions, the amplitude $\alpha A_c\big[1 + m_a s_n(t)\big]$ is much smaller when compared with $\boldsymbol{e}_n(t)$. From the phasor diagram in Figure 7.11, it is easy to write the following approximate expression for $\boldsymbol{r}_1(t)$:

$$\boldsymbol{r}_1(t) \cong \boldsymbol{e}_n(t) + A_c\big[1 + m_a s_n(t)\big]\cos\boldsymbol{\phi}_n(t) \tag{7.59}$$

It is significant to observe from (7.59) that under low-input CNR conditions, the signal term is multiplied by a random noise term $\cos\boldsymbol{\phi}_n(t)$. Thus, we have both additive and multiplicative noise at the demodulator output. Because $\boldsymbol{\phi}_n(t)$ is randomly varying in the range $-\pi$ to π, it is therefore not possible to recover the signal component. As the input CNR decreases from a high value, a **threshold** is reached. The term *threshold* signifies that for input CNR values above the threshold CNR, the output (demodulated) SNR is linearly related to the input (predetection) CNR. However for CNR values below threshold, the output SNR decreases more rapidly than the input CNR.

In summary, on strong signals, both coherent and envelope demodulators work equally well in conventional AM systems. On weak signals, coherent demodulation yields the best results because it does not exhibit the threshold condition. Most applications demand a high-output SNR specification (40 dB or higher), requiring an envelope demodulator to operate significantly above threshold.

Example 7.1

Compare the average transmitter power and channel bandwidth requirements of DSB, SSB, and conventional AM schemes for transmitting an audio signal with a bandwidth of 10 kHz with the system output SNR = 45 dB. Assume that the channel introduces an attenuation of 50 dB and that the one-sided noise power spectral density at the receiver input $N_o = 10^{-12}$ W/Hz. Assume $m_a^2\overline{s_n^2} = 0.36$ for conventional AM.

Solution

From Chapter 4, the bandwidth requirements are easily obtained as

Modulation	B_T
DSB-SC	20 kHz
SSB	10 kHz
Conventional AM	20 kHz

For DSB-SC and SSB-AM schemes,

$$SNR_{DSB} = \frac{P_R}{N_o B}$$

Substituting

$$10^{4.5} = \frac{P_R}{10^{-12} \times 10^4} \Rightarrow P_R = 10^{-3.5} = -5 \text{ dBm}$$

Because the channel produces an attenuation of 50 dB, the transmitter power P_T in the case of DSB-SC and SSB-AM schemes is given by

$$P_T = -5 + 50 = 45 \text{ dBm} = 31.62 \text{ Watts}$$

For the conventional AM scheme, we have the following relationship from (7.50).

$$SNR_{AM} = \eta CNR_{IN} = \eta \frac{P_R}{N_o B}$$

where

$$\eta = \frac{m_a^2 \overline{s_n^2}}{\left(1 + m_a^2 \overline{s_n^2}\right)} = \frac{0.36}{1 + 0.36} = 0.265$$

$$10^{4.5} = 0.265 \frac{P_R}{10^{-12} \times 10^4} \Rightarrow P_R = \frac{10^{-3.5}}{0.265} = 0.767 \text{ dBm}$$

Transmitter power P_T in the conventional AM case is given by

$$P_T = 0.767 + 50 = 50.767 \text{ dBm} = 119.316 \text{ Watts}$$

Example 7.2

The value of input CNR at the onset of threshold, $(CNR_{IN})_{th}$, in a conventional AM system with envelope detection is defined as that value of CNR_{IN} for which $e_n > A_c$ with probability 0.01. Calculate the $(CNR_{IN})_{th}$ for a single-tone modulating signal assuming modulation index $m_a = 1$.

Solution

Because the instantaneous amplitude e_n is a Rayleigh distributed random variable, we can write

$$P\{e_n \geq A_c\} = \int_{A_c}^{\infty} \frac{e_n}{\sigma_e^2} e^{-e_n^2/2\sigma_e^2} de_n = e^{-A_c^2/2\sigma_e^2}$$

where $\sigma_e^2 = 2N_o B$ is variance of e_n. At the onset of threshold, we have from the definition

$$e^{-A_c^2/4N_o B} = 0.01 \Rightarrow \frac{A_c^2}{4N_o B} = 4.605 \qquad (7.60)$$

For a single-tone modulation with $m_a = 1$, $m_a^2 \overline{s_n^2} = 0.5$. Substituting (7.60) into (7.42) yields,

$$(CNR_{IN})_{th} = \frac{A_c^2(1 + 0.5)}{2N_oB} = 2 \times 4.605 \times 1.5 = 13.8 = 12.4 \text{ dB} \qquad (7.61)$$

Now let us consider the CNR at the envelope detector input (that is, at the predetection filter output). It is defined as

$$CNR_{PD} = \frac{\text{Power in the carrier signal}}{\text{Noise power at the predetection filter output}} = \frac{P_R}{2N_oB} \qquad (7.62)$$

Comparing (7.13) and (7.62), we conclude that

$$CNR_{PD} = \frac{CNR_{IN}}{2}$$

or in dB form

$$CNR_{PD} = CNR_{IN} - 3 \text{ dB}$$

We can write the threshold condition (7.60) in terms of CNR_{PD} as

$$(CNR_{PD})_{th} = 12.4 - 3 = 9.4 \text{ dB} \qquad (7.63)$$

Equation (7.63) states that the threshold in a conventional AM system occurs when CNR_{PD} is on the order of 10 dB or less.

Experiment 7.3   *Noise Performance of a Conventional AM System*

In this experiment, we expand the Simulink model of a conventional AM system developed in Experiment 4.2 to measure its noise performance and compare it with the theory. The carrier frequency is 20Hz and the message signal is 1-Hz sine wave. In this experiment, we compute the postdetection SNR as a function of input CNR.

The modulation index m_a is set to 0.5 for the simulation. The computation of predetection CNR and postdetection SNR is performed by processing the conventional AM modulator output along two paths as discussed in the context of Experiment 7.1.

The Simulink model is illustrated in Figure 7.12. The computation of postdetection SNR is performed by processing the AM modulator output along two paths as discussed in the context of Experiment 7.1. Along the **signal + noise path,** AWGN noise is added to the conventional AM modulator output by using the **BLWN** block from the Simulink Library. We need to set spectral density ($N_o/2$) parameter of this block to establish a specific value of CNR_{IN} for simulation. From (7.42), the one-sided spectral density N_o for a given CNR_{IN} value is given by

$$N_o = \frac{\alpha^2 A_c^2 \left(1 + m_a^2 \overline{s_n^2}\right)}{2CNR_{IN}B} \qquad (7.64)$$

For carrier amplitude $\alpha A_c = 1$ and sinusoidal modulating signal of frequency $f_m \left(\overline{s_n^2} = 0.5\right)$, (7.64) simplifies to

$$N_o = \frac{\left(1 + m_a^2 0.5\right)}{4CNR_{IN}f_m} \qquad (7.65)$$

The parameters of the simulation are set up by a companion MATLAB m-file. The m-file also computes the postdetection SNR by calculating signal and noise powers as discussed in Experiment 7.1. Figure 7.13(a) displays demodulator waveforms. The postdetection SNR performance comparison between simulation results and the theory is illustrated in Figure 7.13(b). As can be observed from Figure 7.13(b), there is close agreement between the theory and simulation results.

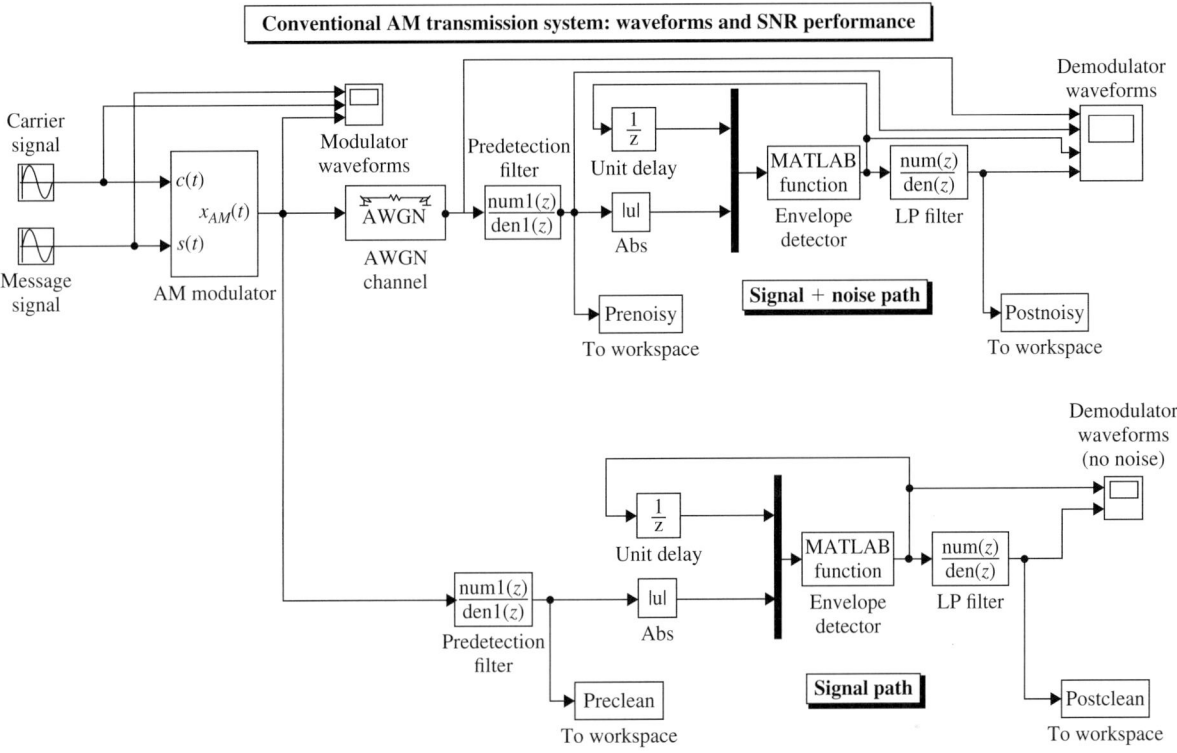

Figure 7.12 Simulink model for computing the SNR performance of a conventional AM system.

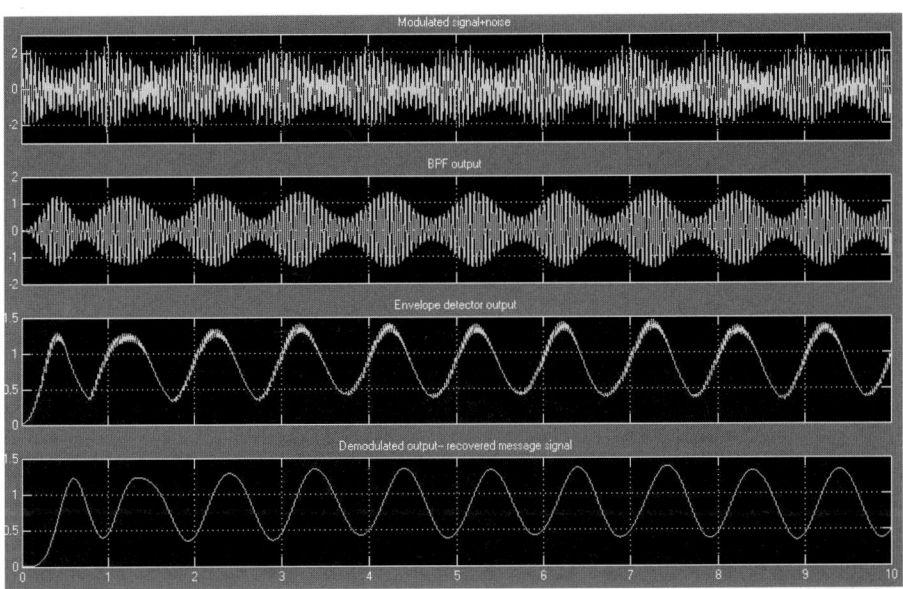

Figure 7.13 (a) Demodulator waveforms

(continued)

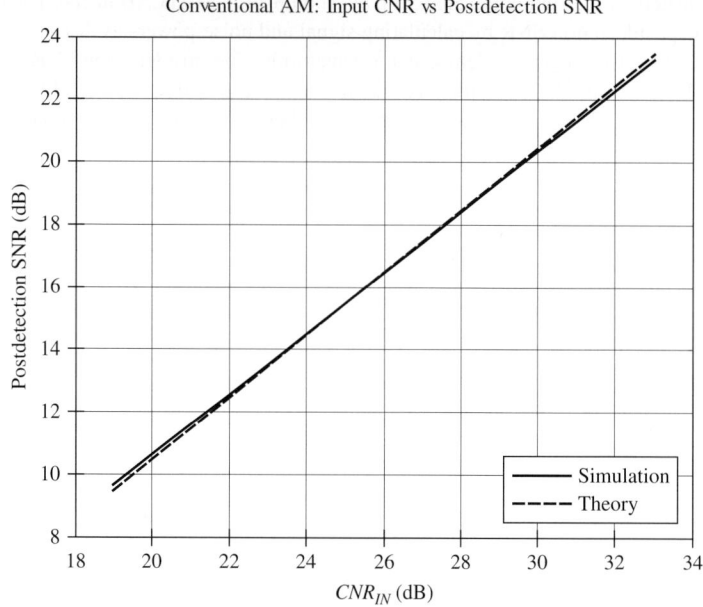

Conventional AM: Input CNR vs Postdetection SNR

Figure 7.13 (b) Comparison of the simulated and theoretical SNR performance of a conventional AM system.

7.3   NOISE PERFORMANCE OF ANGLE-MODULATION SYSTEMS

In this section, we study the performance of angle-modulated systems in the presence of noise. There are significant differences between amplitude- and angle-modulated systems when noise effects are considered. We will show how, in an FM system, an improvement in output SNR can be achieved by trading the additional bandwidth.

The block diagram of a receiver for an arbitrary angle-modulated signal is displayed in Figure 7.14. Using Carson's rule (Section 5.2.2), the predetection filter bandwidth is $B_T \approx 2(D+1)B$ Hz, where B is the bandwidth of the message signal and D is the deviation ratio. The signal input to the predetection filter is an angle-modulated waveform

$$x(t) = \alpha A_c \cos\left[2\pi f_c t + \boldsymbol{\theta}(t)\right] \tag{7.66}$$

where the excess phase $\boldsymbol{\theta}(t)$ is given by

$$\text{PM:}\ \ \boldsymbol{\theta}(t) = \Delta\phi_{\max} s_n(t) \tag{7.67}$$

$$\text{FM:}\ \ \boldsymbol{\theta}(t) = 2\pi\Delta f_{\max} \int_{-\infty}^{t} s_n(\alpha)\,d\alpha \tag{7.68}$$

where $\Delta\phi_{\max}$ is the maximum phase deviation of the PM modulator, and $\Delta f_{\max}$ is the maximum frequency deviation of the FM modulator as discussed in Section 5.1. We note that (7.66) through (7.68) are similar to their counterparts in Table 5.1 except that the normalized message signal $s_n(t)$ and, therefore, phase $\boldsymbol{\theta}(t)$ are random processes. The signal is embedded in the AWGN $\boldsymbol{n}_i(t)$ of zero mean and double-sided power spectral density

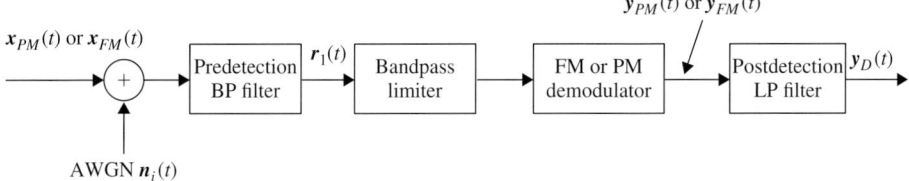

Figure 7.14 Receiver for angle-modulated systems.

$G_{n_i}(f) = N_o/2$. The receiver input CNR, defined as the ratio of carrier power to the noise power in the message signal bandwidth, is given by

$$CNR_{IN} = \frac{\text{Power in the angle-modulated signal at the receiver input}}{\text{Input noise power in the message signal bandwidth}} = \frac{P_R}{N_o B} = \frac{\alpha^2 A_c^2}{2 N_o B}$$

$$(7.69)$$

The predetection filter output can be written using amplitude-phase representation of the narrowband noise $n(t)$ as

$$r_1(t) = \alpha A_c \cos\left[2\pi f_c t + \theta(t)\right] + n(t)$$

$$= \alpha A_c \cos\left[2\pi f_c t + \theta(t)\right] + e_n(t)\cos\left[2\pi f_c t + \phi_n(t)\right] \qquad (7.70)$$

7.3.1 High-CNR Operation

Figure 7.15 illustrates the phasor representation of $r_1(t)$ under high-CNR conditions ($CNR_{IN} \gg 1$). Because $P\{\alpha A_c \gg e_n(t)\} \approx 1$, the predetection filter output, as evident from the figure, can be approximated as

$$r_1(t) \cong \left\{\alpha A_c + e_n(t)\cos\left[\phi_n(t) - \theta(t)\right]\right\}\cos\left[2\pi f_c t + \psi(t)\right] \qquad (7.71)$$

where

$$\psi(t) = \theta(t) + \phi_e(t) \qquad (7.72)$$

$$\phi_e(t) = \tan^{-1}\frac{e_n(t)\sin\left[\phi_n(t) - \theta(t)\right]}{\alpha A_c + e_n(t)\cos\left[\phi_n(t) - \theta(t)\right]} \cong \frac{e_n(t)\sin\left[\phi_n(t) - \theta(t)\right]}{\alpha A_c} \qquad (7.73)$$

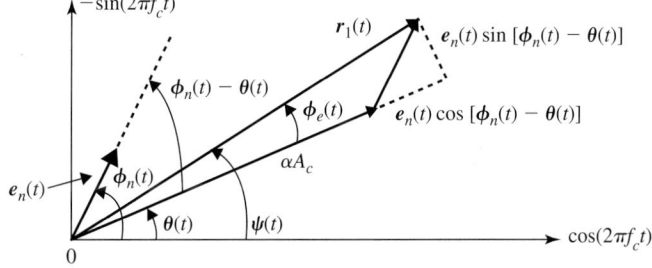

Figure 7.15 Phasor diagram for angle-modulated signal: High-CNR case.

The amplitude of $r_1(t)$ in (7.71) is irrelevant because the BP limiter removes such information prior to detection. Equation (7.72) states that, under high-SNR conditions, the phase of the predetection filter output is the sum of two terms. The first term $\theta(t)$ is the phase of the transmitted signal and is related to the message signal (7.67) or its integral (7.68). The second term represents the effect of noise—undesirable phase modulation $\phi_e(t)$. As a result, the phasor $r_1(t)$ randomly fluctuates near the signal phasor αA_c. These random phase fluctuations are translated by the demodulator into the noise in the detected signal. We observe from (7.73) that the magnitude of random phase modulation term $\phi_e(t)$ is inversely related to the signal amplitude αA_c. The higher the signal level, the lower the noise level. This noise suppression effect under high-SNR conditions is a unique characteristic of angle-modulation systems.

Substituting (7.72) into (5.68) and (5.69), the demodulator output can be expressed as

$$\text{PM:} \quad y_{PM}(t) = K_{PD}\psi(t) = K_{PD}\big[\theta(t) + \phi_e(t)\big] = K_{PD}\Delta\phi_{\max}s_n(t) + n_{PM}(t) \quad (7.74)$$

$$\text{FM:} \quad y_{FM}(t) = \frac{K_{FD}}{2\pi}\frac{d\psi(t)}{dt} = \frac{K_{FD}}{2\pi}\frac{d\big[\theta(t) + \phi_e(t)\big]}{dt}$$
$$= \frac{K_{FD}}{2\pi}\frac{d\theta(t)}{dt} + n_{FM}(t) = K_{FD}\Delta f_{\max}s_n(t) + n_{FM}(t) \quad (7.75)$$

Substituting (7.73) into (7.74) and (7.75), the noise components at the demodulator output are given by

$$n_{PM}(t) = K_{PD}\phi_e(t) = K_{PD}\frac{e_n(t)\sin\big[\phi_n(t) - \theta(t)\big]}{\alpha A_c} \quad (7.76)$$

$$n_{FM}(t) = \frac{K_{FD}}{2\pi}\frac{d\phi_e(t)}{dt} = \frac{K_{FD}}{2\pi}\frac{d}{dt}\left\{\frac{e_n(t)\sin\big[\phi_n(t) - \theta(t)\big]}{\alpha A_c}\right\} \quad (7.77)$$

PM Output SNR

The output signal power from the PM demodulator is obtained from (7.74) as

$$P_{out} = E\big\{K_{PD}^2\theta^2(t)\big\} = E\big\{K_{PD}^2(\Delta\phi_{\max})^2 s_n^2(t)\big\} = (K_{PD}\Delta\phi_{\max})^2 \overline{s_n^2} \quad (7.78)$$

To compute the power spectral density of the noise present at the demodulator output, we will set $\theta(t)$ equal to zero, so that $n_{PM}(t)$ is a function of noise alone and contains no signal component. This assumption greatly simplifies our analysis without affecting the accuracy of our results.[1] Substituting $\theta(t) \equiv 0$ into (7.76) yields

$$n_{PM}(t) = \frac{K_{PD}e_n(t)\sin\big[\phi_n(t)\big]}{\alpha A_c} = \frac{K_{PD}n_s(t)}{\alpha A_c} \quad (7.79)$$

---

[1] J. Downing, *Modulation Systems and Noise* (Upper Saddle River, NJ: Prentice Hall, 1964), 96–98.

where $n_s(t)$ is the quadrature component of the narrowband noise $n(t)$ at the demodulator input. Thus the spectral density of the noise at the demodulator output is given by

$$G_{n_{PM}}(f) = \left(\frac{K_{PD}}{\alpha A_c}\right)^2 G_{n_s}(f) \tag{7.80}$$

Because $G_{n_s}(f)$ equals N_o for $|f| \le B_T/2$, the spectral density of the noise at the demodulator output is

$$G_{n_{PM}}(f) = \begin{cases} \left(\dfrac{K_{PD}}{\alpha A_c}\right)^2 N_o, & |f| \le B_T/2 \\ 0, & \text{otherwise} \end{cases} \tag{7.81}$$

Note that the PM output noise spectrum is flat as a function of frequency (similar to AM) as displayed in Figure 7.16. Because the predetection filter bandwidth B_T is greater than twice the signal bandwidth B, the output SNR can be improved by following the demodulator with an LP filter of bandwidth B. The filter has no effect on the signal but reduces the noise output power to

$$P_{n_{PM}} = \int_{-B}^{B} G_{n_{PM}}(f)\,df = \int_{-B}^{B} \left(\frac{K_{PD}}{\alpha A_c}\right)^2 N_o\,df = \left(\frac{K_{PD}}{\alpha A_c}\right)^2 2N_o B \tag{7.82}$$

Using (7.78) and (7.82), the SNR at the PM demodulator output is obtained as

$$\begin{aligned} SNR_{PM} &= \frac{\text{Signal power at the demodulator output}}{\text{Noise power at the demodulator output}} = \frac{P_{out}}{P_{n_{PM}}} \\ &= \frac{(K_{PD}\Delta\phi_{max})^2 \overline{s_n^2}}{(K_{PD}/\alpha A_c)^2 \, 2N_o B} = (\Delta\phi_{max})^2 \overline{s_n^2} \frac{(\alpha A_c)^2}{2N_o B} \\ &= (\Delta\phi_{max})^2 \overline{s_n^2} CNR_{IN} \end{aligned} \tag{7.83}$$

where CNR_{IN} is given by (7.69). The figure of merit of a PM system is given by

$$\frac{SNR_{PM}}{CNR_{IN}} = (\Delta\phi_{max})^2 \overline{s_n^2} \tag{7.84}$$

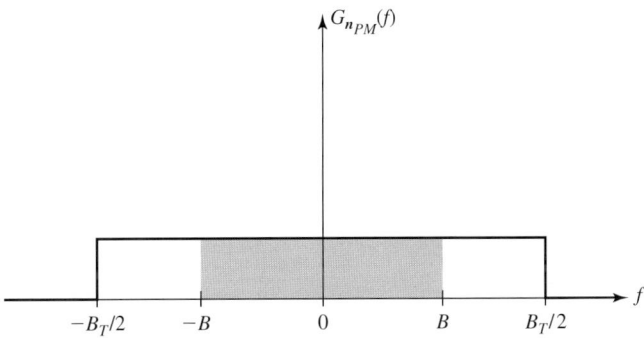

Figure 7.16 Spectrum of PM postdetection noise.

FM Output SNR

The signal power at the frequency discriminator output is obtained from (7.75) as

$$P_{out} = E\left\{ \left(\frac{K_{FD}}{2\pi} \frac{d\boldsymbol{\theta}(t)}{dt} \right)^2 \right\} = (K_{FD}\Delta f_{\max})^2 E\{s_n^2(t)\} = (K_{FD}\Delta f_{\max})^2 \overline{s_n^2} \quad (7.85)$$

To compute the power spectral density of the noise present at the discriminator output, we will set $\boldsymbol{\theta}(t)$ equal to zero, so that $\boldsymbol{n}_{FM}(t)$ is a function of noise alone and contains no signal component. This assumption greatly simplifies our analysis without affecting the accuracy of our results.[2] Substituting $\boldsymbol{\theta}(t) \equiv 0$ into (7.77) yields

$$\boldsymbol{n}_{FM}(t) = \frac{K_{FD}}{2\pi} \frac{d}{dt} \left\{ \frac{\boldsymbol{e}_n(t)\sin[\boldsymbol{\phi}_n(t)]}{\alpha A_c} \right\} = \frac{K_{FD}}{2\pi\alpha A_c} \frac{d\boldsymbol{n}_s}{dt} \quad (7.86)$$

where $\boldsymbol{n}_s(t)$ is the quadrature component of the narrowband noise $\boldsymbol{n}(t)$ at the discriminator input. The power spectral density of the noise at the discriminator output is given by

$$G_{\boldsymbol{n}_{FM}}(f) = \left(\frac{K_{FD}}{2\pi\alpha A_c} \right)^2 (2\pi f)^2 G_{\boldsymbol{n}_s}(f) = \left(\frac{K_{FD}}{\alpha A_c} \right)^2 f^2 G_{\boldsymbol{n}_s}(f) \quad (7.87)$$

Because $G_{\boldsymbol{n}_s}(f)$ equals N_0 for $|f| \geq B_T/2$, the spectral density of the noise at the discriminator output is

$$G_{\boldsymbol{n}_{FM}}(f) = \begin{cases} \left(\dfrac{K_{FD}}{\alpha A_c} \right)^2 f^2 N_o, & |f| \leq B_T/2 \\ 0, & \text{otherwise} \end{cases} \quad (7.88)$$

This spectrum of noise at the discriminator output is illustrated in Figure 7.17. It shows that the noise power spectral density has a parabolic shape, that is, it increases as f^2. This implies that the higher frequency components in the signal are subjected to higher noise levels than the lower frequency components. Because the predetection filter bandwidth B_T is greater than twice the signal bandwidth B, the output SNR can be

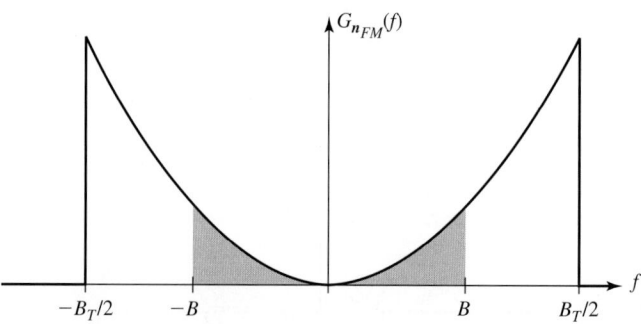

Figure 7.17 Spectrum of FM postdetection noise.

[2] Downing, *Modulation Systems and Noise*, 96–98.

improved by following the discriminator with an LP filter of bandwidth B. The filter has no effect on the signal but reduces the noise output power to

$$P_{n_{FM}} = \int_{-B}^{B} G_{n_{FM}}(f)df = \int_{-B}^{B} \left(\frac{K_{FD}}{\alpha A_c}\right)^2 f^2 N_o df$$

$$= \frac{2}{3}\left(\frac{K_{FD}}{\alpha A_c}\right)^2 N_o B^3 \tag{7.89}$$

Using (7.85) and (7.89), the SNR at the FM discriminator output is given by

$$SNR_{FM} = \frac{\text{Signal power at the discriminator output}}{\text{Noise power at the discriminator output}} = \frac{P_{out}}{P_{n_{FM}}}$$

$$= \frac{3(K_{FD}\Delta f_{max})^2 \overline{s_n^2}}{2(K_{FD}/\alpha A_c)^2 N_o B^3} = 3\left(\frac{\Delta f_{max}}{B}\right)^2 \overline{s_n^2} \frac{(\alpha A_c)^2}{2N_o B}$$

$$= 3D^2\overline{s_n^2}\frac{P_R}{N_o B} \tag{7.90}$$

Substituting (7.69) into (7.90), we obtain

$$SNR_{FM} = 3D^2\overline{s_n^2}CNR_{IN} \tag{7.91}$$

Equation (7.91) states that the output SNR in an FM system can be increased without bound by increasing the deviation ratio D. Doubling of the deviation ratio improves the FM output SNR by 6 dB. However, the transmission bandwidth requirement also increases, according to Carson's rule (5.49), as D is increased. There is a limiting value of D after which the noise power becomes unfavorably large (due to increased bandwidth) and the threshold effect occurs. The trade-off involving output SNR improvement in exchange for additional transmission bandwidth is valid as long as the input CNR_{IN} exceeds a certain **threshold** value. Above this threshold, the figure of merit of an FM system is given by

$$\frac{SNR_{FM}}{CNR_{IN}} = 3D^2\overline{s_n^2} \tag{7.92}$$

Example 7.3

Let $s_n(t) = \cos(2\pi f_m t + \varphi)$ be the message signal where φ is a $\mathcal{U}[-\pi, \pi]$ random variable. Assuming a peak frequency deviation Δf_{max}, calculate output SNR.

Solution

For a single-tone modulating signal with uniformly distributed random phase, it is easy to show that

$$E\{s_n(t)\} = \overline{s_n} = 0$$

$$E\{s_n^2(t)\} = \overline{s_n^2} = \frac{1}{2} \tag{7.93}$$

Substituting (7.93) and $D = \dfrac{\Delta f_{max}}{B} = \dfrac{\Delta f_{max}}{f_m} = \beta$ into (7.91), we get

$$SNR_{FM} = \frac{3}{2}\beta^2 CNR_{IN} \qquad (7.94)$$

Example 7.4

Calculate the SNR improvement offered by FM over DSB-SC AM for the same value of input CNR CNR_{IN}.

Solution

The output SNR in a DSB-SC AM system is given from (7.20) as

$$SNR_{DSB} = CNR_{IN}$$

The output SNR in an FM system is obtained from (7.91) as

$$SNR_{FM} = 3D^2\overline{s_n^2}CNR_{IN}$$

Therefore,

$$\frac{SNR_{FM}}{SNR_{DSB}} = 3D^2\overline{s_n^2} \qquad (7.95)$$

Equation (7.95) can be interpreted as the SNR improvement offered by an FM system over a DSB-AM system. The FM SNR improvement over a DSB-AM system can be expressed in dB form as

$$\text{FM SNR Improvement} = 10\log_{10}(D^2\overline{s_n^2}) + 4.77 \,(\text{dB}) \qquad (7.96)$$

The actual FM SNR improvement achieved in a practical system, including the effect of preemphasis and noise weighting, is significantly better as discussed in Section 7.4.

Example 7.5

Calculate the average transmitter power and channel bandwidth requirements of PM and FM schemes for transmitting an audio signal with a bandwidth of 15 kHz with the system output SNR = 60 dB. The channel introduces an attenuation of 50 dB and that the one-sided noise power spectral density at the receiver input $N_o = 10^{-12}$ W/Hz. We assume that the normalized audio signal has mean $\overline{s_n} = 0$ and variance $\overline{s_n^2} = 0.5$. Further assume that

a. Maximum phase deviation $\Delta\phi_{max} = 2.5$ for the PM modulator
b. Deviation constant $D = 5$ for the FM modulator

Compare the performance achievable in a conventional AM system with modulation index $m_a = 0.85$.

Solution

a. For PM with $\Delta\phi_{max} = 2.5$, the transmission bandwidth is computed using (5.50) as

$$B_T = 2(\Delta\phi_{max} + 1)B = 2(2.5 + 1)15 = 105 \text{ kHz}$$

From (7.83), we have

$$SNR_{PM} = (\Delta\phi_{max})^2 \overline{s_n^2} CNR_{IN}$$

Substituting $CNR_{IN} = \dfrac{P_R}{N_o B}$, we obtain

$$10^6 = SNR_{PM} = (\Delta\phi_{max})^2 \overline{s_n^2} \frac{P_R}{N_o B} = (2.5)^2 \times 0.5 \times \frac{P_R}{10^{-12} \times 1.5 \times 10^4}$$

or

$$P_R = \frac{10^6 \times 10^{-12} \times 1.5 \times 10^4}{(2.5)^2 \times 0.5} = 4.8 \text{ mW} = 6.81 \text{ dBm}$$

Because the channel produces an attenuation of 50 dB, the transmitter power P_T is given by

$$P_T = 6.81 + 50 = 56.81 \text{ dBm} = 479.7 \text{ W}$$

b. For FM with a frequency deviation constant $D = 5$, the transmission bandwidth is computed using (5.49) as

$$B_T = 2(D + 1)B = 2(5 + 1)15 = 180 \text{ kHz}$$

From (7.91), we have

$$SNR_{FM} = 3D^2 \overline{s_n^2} CNR_{IN}$$

Substituting

$$10^6 = SNR_{FM} = 3D^2 \overline{s_n^2} \frac{P_R}{N_o B} = 3(5)^2 \times 0.5 \times \frac{P_R}{10^{-12} \times 1.5 \times 10^4}$$

or

$$P_R = \frac{10^6 \times 10^{-12} \times 1.5 \times 10^4}{3(5)^2 \times 0.5} = 0.4 \text{ mW} = -4 \text{ dBm}$$

Because the channel produces an attenuation of 50 dB, the transmitter power P_T is given by

$$P_T = -4 + 50 = 46 = 39.81 \text{ W}$$

For the conventional AM scheme, the transmitted bandwidth is

$$B_T = 2B = 2 \times 15 = 30 \text{ kHz}$$

From (7.50), we have

$$SNR_{AM} = \eta CNR_{IN} = \eta \frac{P_R}{N_o B}$$

where

$$\eta = \frac{m_a^2 \overline{s_n^2}}{(1 + m_a^2 \overline{s_n^2})} = \frac{0.5(0.85)^2}{1 + 0.5(0.85)^2} = 0.265$$

$$10^6 = 0.265 \frac{P_R}{10^{-12} \times 1.5 \times 10^4} \Rightarrow P_R = \frac{0.015}{0.265} = 56.52 \text{ mW} = 17.52 \text{ dBm}$$

The transmitter power P_T in the conventional AM case is given by

$$P_T = 17.52 + 50 = 67.52 \text{ dBm} = 5.65 \text{ kW}$$

7.3.2   FM System Operation: Low-CNR Case

To analyze threshold effect, it is convenient to define CNR at the discriminator input (that is, predetection filter output).

$$CNR_{PD} = \frac{\text{Power in the FM signal at the predetection filter output}}{\text{Noise power in the predetection filter bandwidth } B_T}$$

$$= \frac{P_R}{N_o B_T} = \frac{(\alpha A_c)^2}{2N_o B_T} \tag{7.97}$$

Because the transmission bandwidth $B_T = 2B(1 + D)$ according to Carson's rule (5.49), we obtain the following relationship between CNR_{PD} and CNR_{IN}:

$$CNR_{PD} = \frac{P_R}{N_o B_T} = \frac{P_R}{N_o 2B(1 + D)} = \frac{CNR_{IN}}{2(1 + D)} \tag{7.98}$$

If the CNR at the discriminator input is low ($CNR_{PD} \ll 1$), it implies that the carrier amplitude is much smaller than the noise amplitude most of the time, that is, $P\{\alpha A_c \ll e_n(t)\} \approx 1$. This situation is illustrated by the phasor diagram representation of (7.70) in Figure 7.18. From the phasor diagram, it can be observed that

$$e_n(t)\sin\left[\phi_n(t) - \psi(t)\right] \cong \alpha A_c \sin\left[\phi_n(t) - \theta(t)\right] \tag{7.99}$$

For $\phi_n(t) - \psi(t)$ small, $\sin\left[\phi_n(t) - \psi(t)\right] \approx \phi_n(t) - \psi(t)$. Substituting into (7.99) yields

$$e_n(t)\left[\phi_n(t) - \psi(t)\right] \cong \alpha A_c \sin\left[\phi_n(t) - \theta(t)\right]$$

or

$$\psi(t) = \phi_n(t) - \frac{\alpha A_c}{e_n(t)} \sin\left[\phi_n(t) - \theta(t)\right] \tag{7.100}$$

Pioneers in the Field

Stephen O. Rice was born November 29, 1907, in Shedds, Oregon. He received his BS degree in electrical engineering from Oregon State University, Corvallis, in 1929 and carried out graduate work at California Institute of Technology and at Columbia University. In 1961 he received the honorary degree of Doctor of Science from Oregon State University. Following the graduate study, he joined Bell Labs as a Member of Technical Staff. From 1930 until 1968, Rice served as a consultant at Bell Labs on transmission engineering and carried out research in communication theory. From 1968 until his retirement in 1972, he served as Head of the Communications Analysis Research Department where he was concerned with various aspects of communication theory, particularly those areas involving random phenomena and noise.

Rice was one of the giants in the development of communication theory. His career was marked by extraordinary technical contributions to the scientific basis of telecommunications. His more than 60 papers included major contributions in the fields of noise theory, frequency modulation, nonlinear systems, and communication theory. His paper on *Mathematical Analysis of Random Noise,* published in 1944 and 1945, is widely considered to be a classic in its field. This paper, consisting of three parts, is outstanding in its clarity and detailed mathematical analysis of random noise and its properties. In Part III of this paper, Rice derived the probability density function (PDF) of a sine wave in narrowband Gaussian noise, which is now known as Rician PDF. The paper had immense scientific and engineering influence not only on electrical communications, but also on other fields of engineering where random processes are important. His other famous contribution is a 1963 paper *Noise in FM Receivers* with its ingenious original definition and analysis of "clicks." The paper solved the long mystery of the sudden deterioration of FM below a certain threshold of carrier-to-noise ratio and gave the most profound treatment of that modulation method.

Dr. Rice was a member of the National Academy of Engineering and a Fellow of the IEEE. He was the recipient of the Mervin J. Kelly Award (1965) and Alexander Graham Bell Medal (1983) awarded by the IEEE.

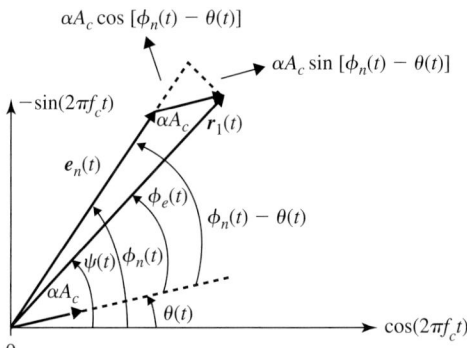

Figure 7.18 Phasor diagram for FM signal: Low-CNR case.

Note that unlike (7.72), the phase of the predetection filter output $\psi(t)$ in (7.100) does not contain a distinct signal term that can be easily separated from the noise. Actually, the signal term $\theta(t)$ in (7.100) is multiplied by the noise term. Thus under low-CNR conditions, the FM discriminator exhibits a threshold effect similar to that of the AM envelope detector.

Threshold Effect

The FM output SNR expression (7.91) was derived assuming large CNR values at the discriminator input. In such cases, $P\{\alpha A_c >> e_n(t)\} \approx 1$ and the signal and noise components are additive at the demodulator output. Referring back to Figure 7.15, we observe that the tip of the resultant vector $r_1(t)$ moves about in the vicinity of the carrier phasor αA_c due to the random fluctuations of the additive noise. As the noise at the input to the discriminator is increased, a point is reached when spikes or impulses start to appear in the discriminator output. The initial appearance of these spikes indicates the onset of the threshold effect, and the corresponding value of the CNR is called the **threshold CNR.** Under this condition, the signal and noise components are so intermingled that they are not distinguishable as indicated in (7.100), and the signal is said to have been **captured** and mutilated by the noise beyond the point of recovery.

When the carrier power and noise power at the discriminator input are comparable in magnitude ($CNR_{PD} \approx 1$), the corresponding phasors, αA_c and $e_n(t)$, are approximately of the same length. As the noise is increased further, the magnitude of the phasor $e_n(t)$ may exceed that of the carrier phasor; also the trajectory of the end point of the resultant vector $r_1(t)$ follows phase variations of the noise and may even encircle the origin. Figure 7.19 illustrates the example when the trajectory of $r_1(t)$ encircles the origin. We observe that as the variations in $\phi_n(t)$ and $e_n(t)$ follow the trajectory from t_1 to t_2, the end point of $r_1(t)$ encircles the origin in the interval $[t_1, t_2]$. The variation of the phase angle $\psi(t)$ at or near the time of occurrence of this event is shown in Figure 7.20. The angle $\psi(t)$ changes by 2π radians during the interval $[t_1, t_2]$. The output of the discriminator,

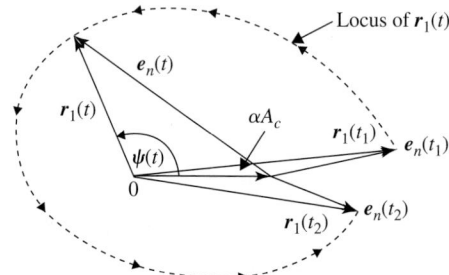

Figure 7.19 FM threshold: phasor diagram.

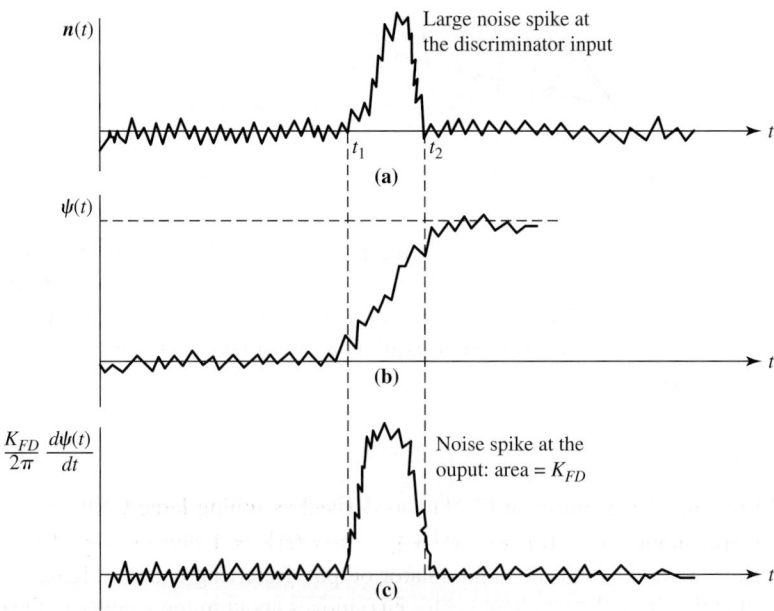

Figure 7.20 FM threshold: instantaneous noise and frequency.

which is $\dfrac{K_{FD}}{2\pi}\dfrac{d\psi(t)}{dt}$, changes by K_{FD} during the same interval, and the change appears as a spike in the output. The duration of the output noise spikes will be of the order $2/B_T$ and their frequency is dependent on the value of input CNR. The spikes can be heard as crackling or clicking sounds. As the input CNR continues to decrease beyond the threshold value, these spikes become more and more frequent and mask the signal. The noise spikes can be seen by observing the discriminator output using an oscilloscope.

The onset of threshold occurs when $CNR_{PD} \approx 10$ dB as discussed in Example 7.2. Using (7.98), an equivalent condition for the onset of threshold in an FM system is derived as

$$(CNR_{IN})_{th} = (CNR_{PD})_{th}2(D+1) \approx 20(D+1) \qquad (7.101)$$

The threshold effect was first analyzed by Rice and Stumpers.[3] An excellent tutorial presentation has been given by Taub and Schilling.[4] Their work generalizes (7.91) to describe the behavior of output SNR near the threshold. For the case of sinusoidal modulation, the generalized expression for FM output SNR is given by

$$SNR_{FM} = \dfrac{\dfrac{3}{2}\beta^2 CNR_{IN}}{1 + \dfrac{12\beta}{\pi}CNR_{IN}e^{-\frac{CNR_{IN}}{2(1+\beta)}}} \qquad (7.102)$$

It is easy to verify that (7.102) reduces to (7.94) for operation above threshold. Figure 7.21 illustrates the output SNR as a function of CNR_{IN} for various values of modulation index β. As is evident from the figure, the performance of FM systems deteriorates rapidly

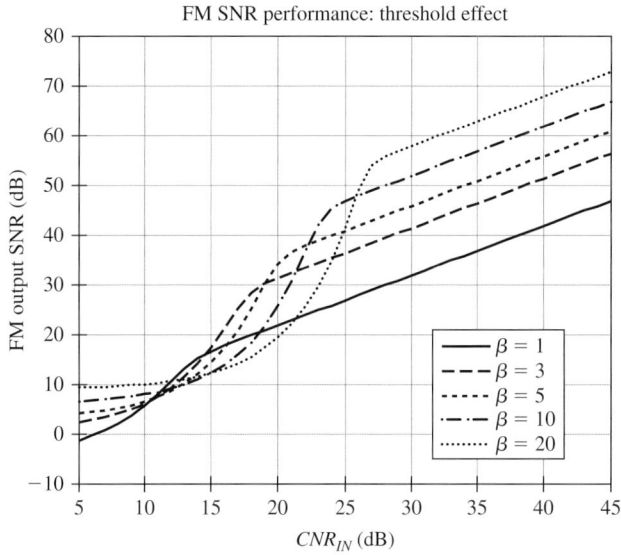

Figure 7.21 FM output SNR as a function of CNR_{IN}.

[3] S. Rice, "Statistical Properties of a Sine-Wave Plus Random Noise," *Bell System Technical Journal* 27, no. 1 (1948): 109–157; F. Stumpers, "Theory of Frequency-Modulation Noise," *Proceedings of IRE* 36, no. 9 (1948): 1081–1092.

[4] H. Taub and D. Schilling, *Principles of Communication Systems,* 2nd ed. (New York: McGraw-Hill, 1986).

as CNR_{IN} falls below the threshold value. The threshold CNR_{IN} values, as indicated by (7.101) and displayed in Figure 7.21, depend on the choice of modulation index β. Larger values of β require larger values of CNR_{IN} to operate above the threshold. This places a practical limit on the extent to which β can be increased to improve the FM SNR before the available CNR_{IN} falls below the threshold value. As a matter of fact, a favorable trade-off of bandwidth expansion for improved SNR cannot be achieved, and the system performance degrades as β is increased if the transmitter power is not appropriately increased.

Substituting (7.101) into (7.91) yields the value of output SNR at threshold

$$(SNR_{FM})_{th} = 30D^2(D + 1) \tag{7.103}$$

Equation (7.103) provides the maximum value of deviation ratio D that can be used for a given SNR_{FM} specification. This, in turn, determines the minimum value of CNR_{IN} (or equivalently, transmitter power) as required by (7.91). Another constraint on the choice of D, of course, results from the application of Carson's rule (5.49) that specifies the required transmission (channel) bandwidth.

Example 7.6

Suppose we want to design an FM system to meet $SNR_{FM} = 50$ dB specification. The channel bandwidth available is 48 MHz, and the video message signal bandwidth $B = 4$ MHz. Determine the minimum values of

a. CNR_{IN}
b. CNR_{PD}
c. Received carrier power, assuming one-sided noise power spectral density $N_o = 10^{-12}$ W/Hz

Solution

First we calculate the maximum value of D using Carson's rule (5.49).

$$48 = B_T = 2(D + 1)B = 2(D + 1)4$$

$$D + 1 = 6 \Rightarrow D = 5$$

Next we determine the maximum value of D using the threshold condition (7.103).

$$(SNR_{FM})_{th} = 10^5 = 30D^2(D + 1)$$

Solving by trial and error or using MATLAB yields $D \approx 15$. Because the value of D given by the bandwidth constraint is less than the one given by the threshold constraint, we choose the lesser of the two, that is, $D = 5$.

a. Using (7.91) and assuming $\overline{s^2} = 0.5$ for the video signal, the required CNR_{IN} is

$$CNR_{IN} = \frac{2 \times 10^5}{3 \times 5^2} = 2.667 \times 10^3 = 34.26 \text{ dB}$$

b. The corresponding CNR_{PD} is given from (7.98) as

$$CNR_{PD} = \frac{CNR_{IN}}{2(1 + D)} = \frac{2.667 \times 10^3}{2(1 + 5)} = 222.22 = 23.47 \text{ dB}$$

c. The received carrier power level P_R is obtained from (7.69) as follows

$$2.667 \times 10^3 = CNR_{IN} = \frac{P_R}{N_o B} = \frac{P_R}{10^{-12} \times 4 \times 10^6}$$

$$P_R = 2.667 \times 10^3 \times 4 \times 10^{-6} = 10.67 \text{ mW}$$

Experiment 7.4   *Noise Performance of an FM System*

In this experiment, we expand the Simulink model of an FM system developed in Experiment 5.1 to measure its noise performance and compare it with the theory. The carrier frequency is 100Hz and the message signal is 1-Hz sine wave. The modulation index β is set at 10. In this experiment, we compute the postdetection SNR as a function of receiver's input CNR. The Simulink model is illustrated in Figure 7.22. The computation of postdetection SNR is performed by processing the FM modulator output along two paths as discussed in the context of Experiment 7.1. Along the **signal + noise path,** AWGN noise is added to the FM modulator output by using the **AWGN** block from the Communication Blockset Library. We need to set variance (σ^2) parameter of this block to establish a specific value of CNR_{IN} for simulation. From (7.69), the one-sided spectral density N_o for a given CNR_{IN} value is given by

$$N_o = \frac{A_c^2}{2CNR_{IN}B} \tag{7.104}$$

For carrier amplitude $A_c = 1$, the variance σ^2 of AWGN samples is given by using (7.104) and (6.344)

$$\sigma^2 = \frac{f_s}{4CNR_{IN}B} \tag{7.105}$$

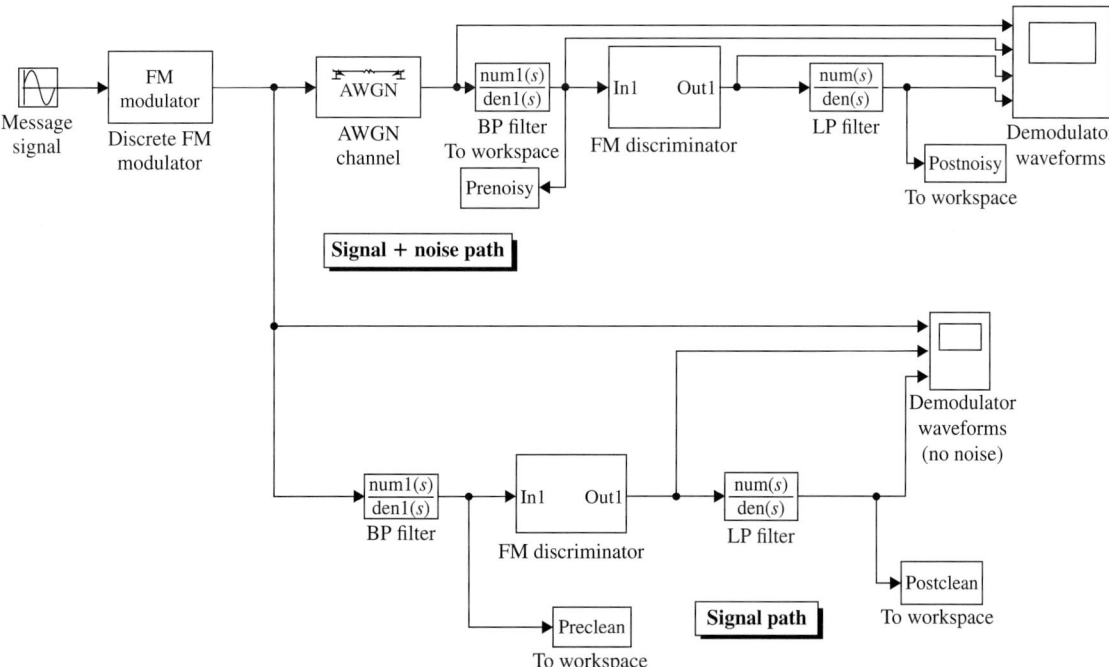

Figure 7.22 Simulink model for computing the SNR performance of an FM system.

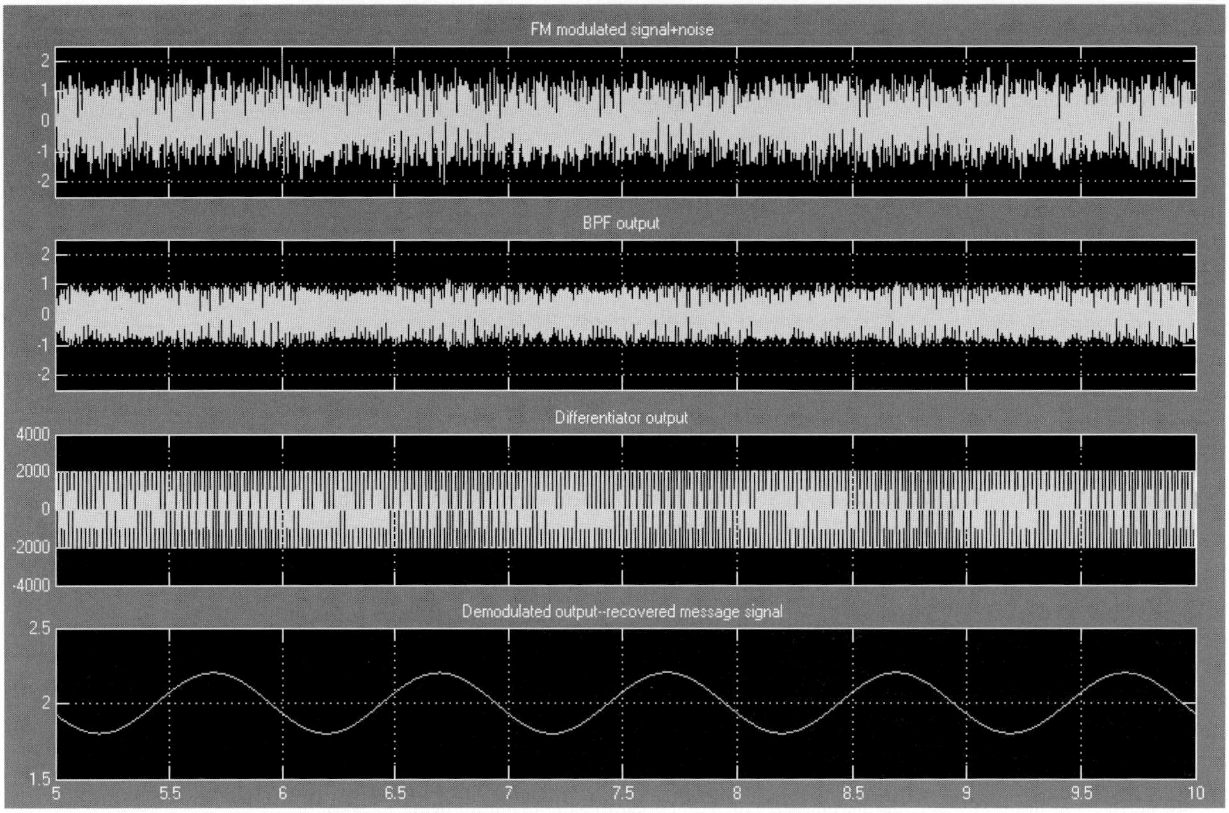

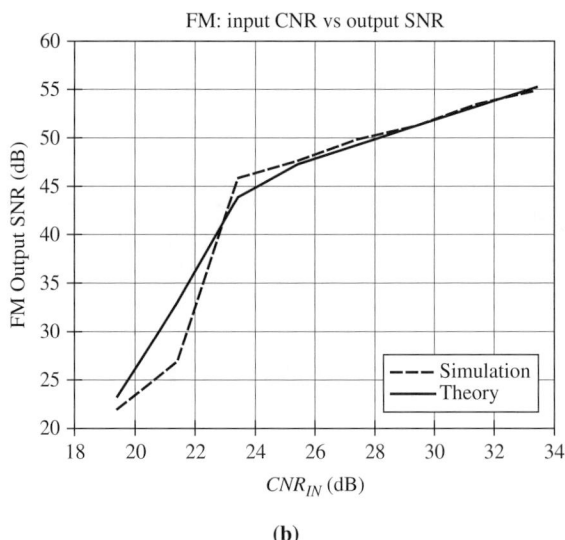

(a)

(b)

Figure 7.23 (a) Demodulator waveforms; (b) comparison of the simulated and theoretical SNR performance of an FM system.

The parameters of the simulation are set up by a companion MATLAB m-file. The m-file also computes the postdetection SNR by calculating signal and noise powers as discussed in Experiment 7.1. Figure 7.23(a) displays demodulator waveforms. The postdetection SNR performance comparison between simulation results and the theory is illustrated in Figure 7.23(b). As we can observe from Figure 7.23(b), there is close agreement between theory and simulation results. Note that the simulation confirms that the onset of threshold occurs when $CNR_{IN} \approx 23$ dB which for $\beta = 10$ corresponds to $CNR_{PD} \approx 10$ dB.

7.4   PREEMPHASIS AND DEEMPHASIS

The noise power at the output of an FM demodulator has a parabolic shape, that is, noise power increases as f^2. Therefore, an FM system exhibits better SNR performance for low-frequency components in the signal than for high-frequency components. The noise performance of an FM system can be improved by **preemphasizing** the high frequencies in the message signal at the FM modulator input and **deemphasizing** them at the output of the FM demodulator. The combination of preemphasis and deemphasis operations has no effect on the message signal. Deemphasis, however, attenuates high-frequency components in the parabolic-shaped noise spectrum, thereby yielding an improvement in the FM output SNR. The high-pass filter at the modulator, which emphasizes high-frequency components in the message signal frequency band, is called the **preemphasis filter.** The LP filter at the demodulator, which is the inverse of the preemphasis filter, is called the **deemphasis filter.** Figure 7.24 displays the use of preemphasis and deemphasis in an FM system.

SNR Improvement

The output signal power is the same with or without preemphasis/deemphasis because the overall frequency response of the system is flat over the message signal bandwidth, that is, B Hz. The noise power output at the discriminator output without deemphasis filtering is

$$P_{n_{FM}} = \int_{-B}^{B} G_{n_{FM}}(f)df \tag{7.106}$$

With deemphasis filtering, the output noise power is given by

$$P_{n_o} = \int_{-B}^{B} |H_{DE}(f)|^2 G_{n_{FM}}(f)df \tag{7.107}$$

Let us assume that the deemphasis filter is a single-pole LP filter with the transfer function

$$H_{DE}(f) = \frac{1}{1 + j(f/f_1)} \tag{7.108}$$

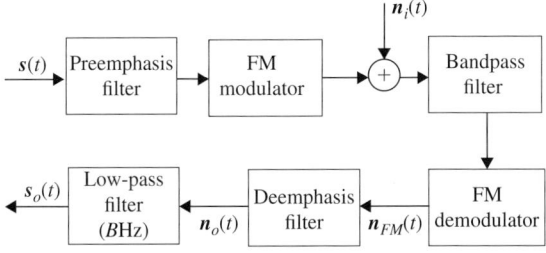

Figure 7.24 Preemphasis and deemphasis in an FM system.

where f_1 is the 3-dB frequency of the filter. In a single-pole RC filter, $f_1 = 1/2\pi\tau$, $\tau = RC$. τ is called the time constant of the filter. Substituting (7.108) and (7.88) into (7.107) yields

$$P_{n_o} = \int_{-B}^{B} \left| \frac{1}{1 + j(f/f_1)} \right|^2 \left(\frac{K_{FD}}{A_c} \right)^2 f^2 N_o \, df = \left(\frac{K_{FD}}{A_c} \right)^2 N_o f_1^2 \int_{-B}^{B} \frac{f^2}{f_1^2 + f^2} \, df$$

$$= 2 \left(\frac{K_{FD}}{A_c} \right)^2 N_o f_1^3 \left[\frac{B}{f_1} - \tan^{-1} \frac{B}{f_1} \right] \tag{7.109}$$

In a typical application, $B/f_1 >> 1$, and so $\tan^{-1}(B/f_1) \approx \pi/2$, which is usually small compared with B/f_1. For this case, (7.109) becomes

$$P_{n_o} = 2 \left(\frac{K_{FD}}{A_c} \right)^2 N_o f_1^2 B \tag{7.110}$$

The output SNR is given by

$$(SNR_{FM})_{DE} = \frac{\text{Signal power at the deemphasis filter output}}{\text{Noise power at the deemphasis filter output}} = \frac{P_{out}}{P_{n_o}} \tag{7.111}$$

Substituting (7.85) and (7.110) into (7.111) yields

$$(SNR_{FM})_{DE} = \frac{(K_{FD}\Delta f_{max})^2 \overline{s_n^2}}{2(K_{FD}/A_c)^2 N_o B f_1^2} = \left(\frac{\Delta f_{max}}{f_1} \right)^2 \overline{s_n^2} \left(\frac{A_c^2}{2N_o B} \right)$$

$$= \left(\frac{\Delta f_{max}}{f_1} \right)^2 \overline{s_n^2} CNR_{IN} \tag{7.112}$$

Equation (7.112) can be expressed by substituting $D = \dfrac{\Delta f_{max}}{B}$ as

$$(SNR_{FM})_{DE} = \left(\frac{\Delta f_{max}}{B} \right)^2 \left(\frac{B}{f_1} \right)^2 \overline{s_n^2} CNR_{IN}$$

$$= D^2 \left(\frac{B}{f_1} \right)^2 \overline{s_n^2} CNR_{IN} \tag{7.113}$$

Therefore, SNR improvement due to deemphasis is given by

$$\text{SNR improvement} = \frac{(SNR_{FM})_{DE}}{SNR_{FM}} = \frac{D^2 \left(\dfrac{B}{f_1} \right)^2 \overline{s_n^2} CNR_{IN}}{3D^2 \overline{s_n^2} CNR_{IN}} = \frac{(B/f_1)^2}{3} \tag{7.114}$$

In dB form, we have

$$\text{SNR improvement due to deemphasis} = 20\log_{10}(B/f_1) - 10\log_{10} 3$$

$$= 20\log_{10}(B/f_1) - 4.77 \, (\text{dB}) \tag{7.115}$$

Example 7.7

In commercial FM broadcasting, $B = 15$ kHz, $\tau = 75$ μsec. This yields $f_1 = 2.1$ kHz and $B/f_1 = 7.14$. Therefore, SNR improvement due to deemphasis $= 20\log_{10}(7.5) - 4.77 = 12.3$ dB

Preemphasis is particularly effective in improving the performance of FM systems that are used to transmit signals whose spectral energy is concentrated at low frequencies. In this case, the enhancement of high frequency components has little or no impact on the peak FM deviation and hence the bandwidth of the FM signal.

The human eye is less sensitive to high frequency components in the parabolic FM noise spectrum at the discriminator output. So an appropriate noise weighting is applied to measure the effective noise performance of an FM system. For video signals, if we use the EIA noise weighting and preemphasis spectrum shaping per CCIR-405 standard, the **weighted** SNR performance achieved using FM transmission is approximately 15 dB better than predicted by (7.96).

7.5   COMPARISON OF ANALOG MODULATION SYSTEMS

In this section, we compare various analog modulation systems on the following key performance metrics:

1. Bandwidth requirements
2. Postdetection (destination) SNR performance
3. Cost/complexity of implementing transmitter and receiver electronics

Table 7.1 summarizes the performance comparison of various amplitude and angle modulation schemes.

Bandwidth requirements. SSB-SC and VSB-AM are the most bandwidth-efficient modulation schemes. Before the advent of digital communications, SSB-SC was widely used for voice transmission over microwave and satellite FDM links.

Table 7.1 Performance Comparison of Analog Modulation Schemes

Type of Modulation	Transmission Bandwidth	SNR Advantage	Equipment Complexity	Comment
Baseband	B	1	Minor	Short point-to-point link
DSB-SC	$2B$	1	Moderate; coherent demodulator required	
Conventional AM	$2B$	$\eta \leq 1$	Minor; envelope detector is used	Low-cost receiver for broadcast application
SSB	B	1	Major; coherent demodulator required	
VSB	$B + f_v$, $f_v/B \approx 0.2 - 0.3$	1	Major; coherent demodulator required	Complex VSB filters
VSB + Carrier	$B + f_v$, $f_v/B \approx 0.2 - 0.3$	$\eta \leq 1$	Moderate; envelope detector is used	Low-cost receiver for broadcast application
PM	$2(\Delta\phi_{max} + 1)B$	$(\Delta\phi_{max})^2 \overline{s_n^2}$	Moderate	$\Delta\phi_{max} \leq \pi$ for certain modulation signal types
FM	$2(D + 1)B$	$3D^2\overline{s_n^2}$	Moderate	CNR_{IN} above threshold value
FM with preemphasis	$2(D + 1)B$	$D^2\overline{s_n^2}\left(\dfrac{B}{f_1}\right)^2$	Moderate; $f_1 = 3$ dB frequency of the deemphasis filter	CNR_{IN} above threshold value

VSB-AM is chosen as the standard transmission technology for analog TV broadcasting because it offers a practical compromise between bandwidth efficiency and equipment complexity.

Destination SNR performance. FM and PM systems offer significant SNR advantage over AM modulation schemes by trading the additional bandwidth. The best SNR performance is offered by FM systems that use wide deviation ratios and preemphasis/deemphasis. Threshold effects in FM systems set a limit on the minimum input CNR to obtain the SNR improvement in exchange for extra bandwidth. The increased noise immunity of FM led to its adoption for high-quality radio broadcasting. The SNR advantage in angle-modulation systems translates to a lower received power level requirement for a given SNR performance at the destination. Therefore, prior to the beginning of the digital era in telecommunications, FM was the transmission technology of choice for line-of-sight microwave, satellite, and first-generation cellular communication systems. The SNR performance improvement achievable in PM systems is limited because the maximum phase deviation $\Delta\phi$ is constrained to values $\leq \pi$ for modulating signals with jump discontinuities. Conventional AM and VSB+C are the worst in SNR performance and are not used where there is a link power budget constraint.

Equipment Complexity

AM and VSB+C are the least complex because receivers can use envelope detectors. VSB filtering at the receiver adds complexity and cost, although SAW filters are now a mature technology. This is why these modulation schemes are so widely used in broadcasting applications where hundreds of millions of receivers exist. DSB-SC

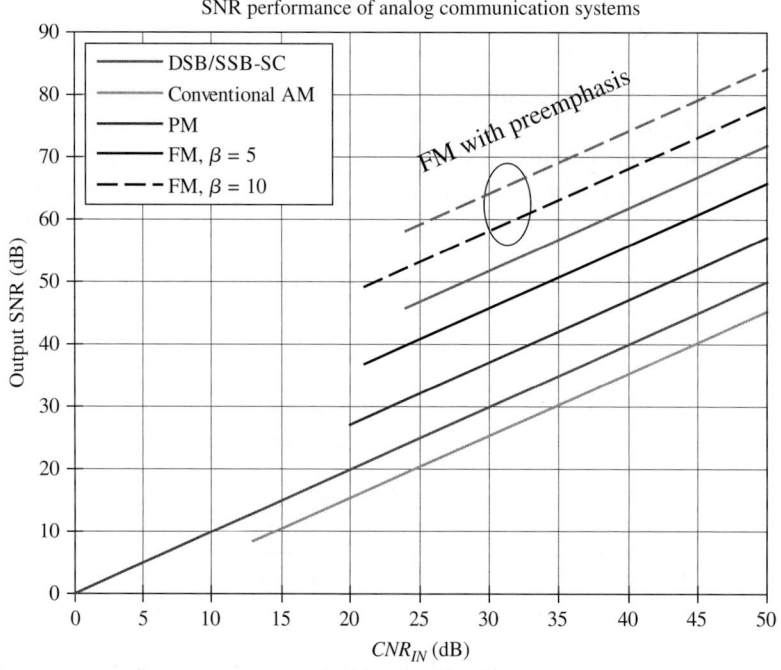

Figure 7.25 Output SNR for analog modulation schemes.

and SSB-SC require coherent demodulation, and therefore they are never used in a broadcasting environment. FM receivers are now implemented using a single IC and so complexity is not an issue.

For transmitting signals with significant low-frequency content and large bandwidth, VSB+C offers the best compromise in terms of the transmission bandwidth and ease of implementation. FM systems have good low-frequency response as well. If the increased bandwidth is an option, they provide the best SNR performance without any significant penalty in terms of equipment complexity.

Figure 7.25 displays the performance of various analog modulation schemes. In the figure, we have assumed $\eta = 1$ for conventional AM, and $\Delta\phi = \pi$ for PM. Further, $\overline{s_n^2} = 0.5$ applies in all cases.

7.6 LINK DESIGN

As discussed in Section 2.7, the signal in a communications system suffers attenuation and distortion as it propagates along a communications link. The distortion of the signal results from the frequency-selective characteristics of the transmission medium. Both attenuation and distortion increase as a function of the length of the link. An **amplifier** can be used to boost the received signal amplitude to compensate for the signal attenuation along the transmission link. However, the amplifier adds noise in the process of amplification. Thus, the attenuated and distorted signal is received in the presence of random noise, which has been modeled as AWGN added at the receiver front end in previous sections. The minimum value of received power level (P_R) is a function of the SNR performance specification and varies with the modulation scheme used in the communication link. The loss budget, also called the **system gain,** of a point-to-point link is given by

$$\text{System Gain (dB)} = P_T - P_R \tag{7.116}$$

where P_T is the transmitter output power level. Both P_T and P_R are specified in dBm or dBW. The system gain is allocated to transmission losses and link margin provided for temperature and aging effects. For wired media, the attenuation is a linear function of link length d. Therefore, we can write (7.116) as

$$\text{System Gain (dB)} = P_T - P_R = \alpha d + \text{link\_margin} \tag{7.117}$$

where α is link attenuation in dB/km. The maximum link length can now be calculated using

$$\text{Link length } d = \frac{P_T - P_R - \text{link\_margin}}{\alpha} \text{ km} \tag{7.118}$$

Example 7.8

Determine the span of a point-to-point video transmission link with attenuation of 2 dB/km using an FM modem with peak deviation $\Delta f_{\max} = 4$ MHz. The link should deliver a destination SNR of 50 dB. The one-sided spectral density of noise is $N_o = 10^{-12}$ W/Hz. Assume bandwidth of video signal $B = 4.2$ MHz, and transmitter output power $P_T = 1$ W.

Solution

The SNR of an FM system from (7.91) is given by

$$SNR_{FM} = 3D^2 \overline{s_n^2} CNR_{IN}$$

In dB form, it is given by

$$SNR_{FM} = CNR_{IN} + 10\log_{10}\left(D^2 \overline{s_n^2}\right) + 4.77 \text{ (dB)}$$

Now $D = \Delta f_{\max}/B = 4/4.2 \approx 1$. We will assume $\overline{s_n^2} = 0.5$. Substituting we get

$$SNR_{FM} = CNR_{IN} - 3 + 4.77 = CNR_{IN} + 1.77 \text{ (dB)}$$

To assure an output FM SNR = 50 dB, $CNR_{IN} = 48.23$ dB. From (7.69), we have

$$CNR_{IN} = \frac{P_R}{N_o B}$$

In dB form, it is given by

$$CNR_{IN} = P_R - 10\log_{10}(N_o B)$$

Therefore,

$$P_R = CNR_{IN} + 10\log_{10}(N_o B) = 48.23 + 10\log_{10}\left(10^{-12} \times 4.2 \times 10^6\right)$$

$$= 48.23 + 10\log_{10}\left(4.2 \times 10^{-6}\right)$$

$$= 48.23 - 53.767 = -5.54 \text{ dBW} = -24.46 \text{ dBm}$$

Substituting in (7.116), the system gain is given by

$$\text{System Gain} = P_T - P_R = 30 + 24.46 = 54.46 \text{ dB}$$

Because the attenuation of the transmission link is 2 dB/km, the span of the point-to-point link = 54.46/2 ~ 27 km. If the system span is longer than 27 km, we need to increase either the transmitter power P_T or add repeaters.

7.6.1 Analog Repeater

It is clear from (7.118) and Example 7.8 that attenuation and noise set a limit for the maximum link length. To transmit over longer distances, it is necessary to introduce **repeaters** periodically to compensate for the attenuation and distortion of the signal, as shown in Figure 7.26.

A repeater consists of an amplifier and an **equalizer** as shown in Figure 7.27. The amplifier boosts the signal level to make up for the attenuation of the signal in the previous repeater section. The equalizer attempts to compensate for the distortion introduced by the transmission medium. As discussed in Section 2.7, the distortion is caused by the frequency-selective characteristics of the transmission medium—that is, different frequency components in the signal are attenuated by different amounts. Most wire

Figure 7.26 Analog long-haul communications.

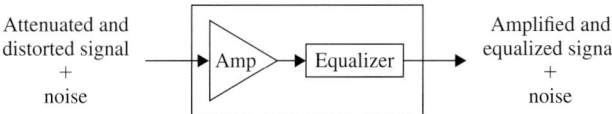

Figure 7.27 Analog repeater.

media exhibit high-frequency roll-off in amplitude response, so high-frequency components are attenuated more than low-frequency components in the signal. The equalizer thus has an inverse roll-off characteristic that accentuates high-frequency components. The second cause of distortion is that the group delay of the transmission medium is not constant over the passband of the signal. Thus different frequency components in the signal are delayed by different amounts as they propagate through the transmission link. This requires group delay equalization. All electronic amplifiers also add noise as discussed in Section 6.14. The output of the repeater consists of the amplified and equalized signal plus noise which is sent over the next repeater section.

Noise Contributed by Amplifiers

The noise contributed by an amplifier is characterized by the noise figure F defined in (6.306). As discussed in Section 6.14.1, the available noise output power of the amplifier with gain $\mathscr{G}$ is from (6.310) given by

$$N_{out} = F\mathscr{G}N_o B_N \text{ Watts}$$

or in dB form

$$N_{out} = NF + G + 10\log_{10}\left(N_o B_N\right) \text{ dBW} \tag{7.119}$$

where $G = 10\log_{10}\mathscr{G}$ is the amplifier gain in dB and $NF = 10\log_{10}F$ is the amplifier noise figure in dB. B_N is the equivalent noise bandwidth of the amplifier. Thus in a noiseless amplifier, the available noise output power is the noise input power increased by the gain of the amplifier and thus equals $G + 10\log_{10}(N_o B_N)$dBW. In a real amplifier, the noise output is further increased by the internal noise and is equal to $NF + G + 10\log_{10}(N_o B_N)$dBW.

7.6.2 Performance of Analog Communication System Using Cascade of Repeaters

We consider an analog communication system consisting of M repeater sections in cascade as shown in Figure 7.28. Note that the last repeater is part of the receiver at the destination. We assume that all repeater sections consist of identical cable sections, with each section producing attenuation of L dB. We further assume that each repeater's gain makes up for the loss introduced by the associated cable section. That is, $G = L$ dB.

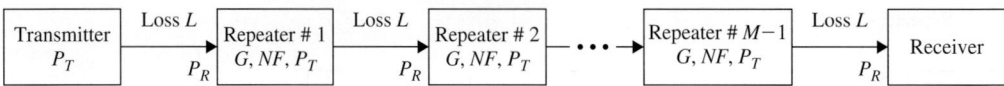

Figure 7.28 Analog communications system with repeaters.

We express the available noise output power of the first repeater from (7.119) as

$$\left(N_{out}\right)_1 = NF + G + 10\log_{10}\left(N_oB_N\right) \text{ dBW} \tag{7.120}$$

The CNR at the output of the first repeater is given by

$$\left(CNR_{out}\right)_1 = \frac{P_T}{\left(N_{out}\right)_1} = \frac{P_T}{FG_aN_oB_N} \tag{7.121}$$

where P_T is the transmitter output carrier power level. In dB form

$$P_R = P_T - L = P_T - G \tag{7.122}$$

where P_R is the input carrier power level at the first repeater. The CNR at the output of the first repeater in dB form can now be written from (7.121) using (7.120) and (7.122) as

$$\left(CNR_{out}\right)_1 = P_T - \left(N_{out}\right)_1 = P_R + G - \left[NF + G + 10\log_{10}\left(N_oB_N\right)\right]$$

$$= P_R - NF - 10\log_{10}\left(N_oB_N\right) \text{ dB} \tag{7.123}$$

The available noise power at the output of the second repeater consists of the contribution from the first repeater

$$F\mathscr{G}N_oB_N \times \underbrace{1/\mathscr{G}}_{\substack{\text{Line loss of 1st} \\ \text{repeater section}}} \times \underbrace{\mathscr{G}}_{\substack{\text{Gain of 2nd} \\ \text{repeater}}} = F\mathscr{G}N_oB_N$$

as well as the contribution originated by the second repeater

$$F\mathscr{G}N_oB_N$$

Therefore, the available noise power at the output of the second repeater is twice that at the output of the first repeater. It is given by

$$2F\mathscr{G}N_oB_N$$

In dB form, it is

$$\left(N_{out}\right)_2 = NF + G + 10\log_{10}\left(N_oB_N\right) + 10\log_{10}2 \text{ dBW} \tag{7.124}$$

This has the effect of deteriorating the CNR at the output of the second repeater by $10\log_{10} 2 = 3$ dB as shown below:

$$\begin{aligned}
\left(CNR_{out}\right)_2 &= P_T - \left(N_{out}\right)_2 = P_R + G - \left[NF + G + 10\log_{10}(N_o B_N) + \log_{10} 2\right]\\
&= P_R - NF - 10\log_{10}(N_o B_N) - 10\log_{10} 2\\
&= \left(CNR_{out}\right)_1 - 3
\end{aligned} \tag{7.125}$$

It is easy to extend this argument to conclude that each succeeding repeater contributes noise power exactly equal to that contributed by the first amplifier. Thus the noise power output from the last repeater is simply M times the noise power output of the first. That is,

$$\left(N_{out}\right)_M = M\left(N_{out}\right)_1 = MF \mathscr{G} N_o B_N \tag{7.126}$$

Expressed in dB form, we get

$$\left(N_{out}\right)_M = 10\log_{10} M + NF + G + 10\log_{10}(N_o B_N) \text{ dBW} \tag{7.127}$$

The output CNR of an analog communication system consisting of M repeater spans is, therefore, given by using (7.126) as

$$\left(CNR_{out}\right)_M = \frac{P_T}{MF \mathscr{G} N_o B_N} = \frac{\left(CNR_{out}\right)_1}{M} \tag{7.128}$$

or in dB form

$$\left(CNR_{out}\right)_M = \left(CNR_{out}\right)_1 - 10\log_{10} M \tag{7.129}$$

Equation (7.129) states that the output CNR in an analog communication system with M repeaters suffers a **penalty** of $10\log_{10} M$ dB. Doubling the repeaters in a system decreases the output SNR by 3 dB. It is interesting to observe the following trade-offs here:

1. Analog repeaters allow us to extend the system span by M times that is achievable with a direct link between a transmitter and receiver.
2. However, the span of each repeater section is reduced because we need to design each section for an output CNR that is $10\log_{10} M$ dB higher than the desired end-to-end system CNR_{SYS} specification. That is, we want to assure that $\left(CNR_{out}\right)_M \geq CNR_{SYS}$. For example, if a system uses four repeaters and the end-to-end output CNR_{SYS} requirement is 50 dB, each repeater section has to be designed for an output CNR of $50 + 10\log_{10} 4 = 56$ dB.

Example 7.9

The specifications of a CATV trunk amplifier for operation from 54 to 862 MHz are as follows:

$$\text{Noise Figure } NF = 9.5 \text{ dB}$$

$$\text{Gain} = 30 \text{ dB}$$

Assume transmitter output power $P_T = -6.75$ dBm/42 dBmV. National Cable Television Association (NCTA) standard specifies noise bandwidth $B_N = 4$ MHz for the measurement of CNR.

a. For the single amplifier section, calculate the power level required at the amplifier input to guarantee a demodulated output SNR of 48 dB using VSB+C AM with modulation index $m_a = 0.85$.

b. What is the amplifier span in (a) using a coaxial cable with an attenuation of 1.33 dB/100 ft @ 870 MHz.

c. Calculate the single amplifier span and total system span for a system using a 20-amplifier cascade.

Solution

a. For SNR performance analysis, the VSB+C AM system can be treated as a conventional AM system with noise bandwidth $B_N = 4$ MHz. The SNR of a conventional AM system is given by

$$SNR_{AM} = \eta CNR_{IN} \tag{7.51}$$

where η is given from (4.32) as

$$\eta = \frac{m_a^2 \overline{s_n^2}}{\left(1 + m_a^2 \overline{s_n^2}\right)} \tag{4.32}$$

Assuming $\overline{s_n^2} = 0.5$, $m_a^2 \overline{s_n^2} = 0.36$. Substituting into (4.32) yields

$$\eta = \frac{m_a^2 \overline{s_n^2}}{\left(1 + m_a^2 \overline{s_n^2}\right)} = \frac{0.36}{1 + 0.36} = 0.265 \tag{7.130}$$

The required CNR_{IN} in dB can be calculated from (7.51) as

$$CNR_{IN} = SNR_{AM} - 10\log_{10}\eta = 48 + 2.78 = 50.78 \text{ dB} \tag{7.131}$$

Because the amplifier in this case forms the front end of the VSB+C AM demodulator, we should have

$$\left(CNR_{out}\right)_1 = CNR_{IN} = 50.78 \text{ dB} \tag{7.132}$$

Substituting the values of NF and $N_o B_N$ into (7.123), we obtain

$$\left(CNR_{out}\right)_1 = P_R - 9.5 - 10\log_{10}\left(4 \times 10^{-21} \times 4 \times 10^6\right)$$

$$= P_R - 9.5 + 137.96 = P_R + 128.46 \tag{7.133}$$

The required P_R is given by substituting (7.132) into (7.133).

$$P_R = 50.78 - 128.46 = -77.68 \text{ dBW} = -47.68 \text{ dBm}$$

b. The system gain for an amplifier section is now obtained by applying (7.116) as

$$\text{System Gain} = P_T - P_R = -6.75 + 47.68 = 40.93 \text{ dB}$$

Thus the span length for a single amplifier section equals 40.93/1.33 = 3077 ft.

c. For a system using a 20-amplifier cascade, $CNR_{SYS} = CNR_{IN} = 50.78$ dB in order to meet end-to-end performance specification. The output CNR of 20-amplifier cascade from (7.129) must satisfy the following:

$$CNR_{SYS} = (CNR_{out})_{20} = (CNR_{out})_1 - 10\log_{10}20 \qquad (7.134)$$

Substituting (7.132) into (7.134) yields

$$50.78 = (CNR_{out})_1 - 10\log_{10}20 = P_R + 128.46 - 13$$

or

$$P_R = 50.78 - 128.46 + 13 = -64.68 \text{ dbW} = -34.68 \text{ dbm}$$

The system gain for an amplifier section from (7.116) is

$$\text{System Gain} = P_T - P_R = -6.75 + 34.68 = 27.93 \text{ dB}$$

Thus the span length for a single amplifier section equals 27.93/1.33 = 2100 ft.

CATV systems use an amplifier span of 2000 feet, which correlates nicely with our calculation. The total system length = $20 \times 2100 = 42,000$ ft = 8.4 miles. Note that the length of each amplifier section is decreased from 3070 ft to 2100 ft as a result of cascading. However, the total system now extends to 8.4 miles.

FINAL REMARKS

The performance of analog communication systems operating in the presence of additive white Gaussian noise was considered in this chapter. The SNR at the output of the system was used as a measure of overall signal quality. The output SNR in all AM schemes increases linearly with input CNR when coherent detection is used. Under low-input CNR conditions, an envelope detector exhibits a threshold effect, resulting in the mutilation of signal accompanied by rapid degradation of the output SNR. FM systems also exhibit a similar threshold effect under low-input CNR conditions. Angle-modulation systems operating above threshold offer improved noise immunity compared to AM schemes by trading the increased transmission bandwidth for the output SNR. The use of preemphasis and deemphasis offers further improvement in the output SNR of FM systems by taking advantage of the parabolic shape of the noise spectrum.

The design of long-haul analog transmission systems must take into account the accumulation of noise in repeaters. Analog link engineering guidelines developed here apply as well to the design of multi-wavelength, multi-gigabit fiber-optic communication systems using optical amplifiers to achieve longer system spans.

FURTHER READINGS

The noise performance of analog communication systems is covered in a number of undergraduate communication systems texts [1–5]. Rice [8] and Stumpers [9] are classic references on the analysis of noise in FM systems. Taub and Schilling [10] provide a nice tutorial presentation on the threshold phenomenon in FM systems.

1. Ziemer, R., and W. Tranter. *Principles of Communications: Systems, Modulation, and Noise,* 5th ed. New York: John Wiley, 2001.

2. Carlson, B., P. Crilly, and J. Rutledge. *Communication Systems,* 4th ed. New York: McGraw-Hill, 2002.

3. Proakis, J., and M. Salehi. *Fundamentals of Communication Systems.* Upper Saddle River, NJ: Prentice Hall, 2005.

4. Couch, L. *Digital and Analog Communication Systems,* 7th ed. Upper Saddle River, NJ: Prentice Hall, 2006.

5. Haykin, S. *Communication Systems,* 4th ed. New York: John Wiley, 2000.

6. Downing, J. *Modulation Systems and Noise.* Upper Saddle River, NJ: Prentice Hall, 1964.

7. National Cable & Telecommunications Association. *NCTA Recommended Practices for Measurements on Cable Television Systems,* 3rd ed. Washington, DC: 2002.

8. Rice, S. "Statistical Properties of a Sine-Wave Plus Random Noise." *Bell System Technical Journal* 27, no. 1 (1948): 109–157.

9. Stumpers, F. "Theory of Frequency-Modulation Noise." *Proceedings of IRE* 36, no. 9 (1948): 1081–1092.

10. Taub, H., and D. Schilling. *Principles of Communication Systems,* 2nd ed. New York: McGraw-Hill, 1986.

PROBLEMS

7.1. Consider the transmission of a 5-kHz message signal on a baseband communications channel which introduces attenuation of 30 dB. The channel noise is AWGN with $N_o/2 = 10^{-10}$ W/Hz. Calculate the minimum transmitted power P_T to achieve a baseband SNR_{BB} of at least 40 dB.

7.2. The message signal $s(t) = 10\cos(1000\pi t) + 5\cos(2000\pi t)$ modulates the carrier signal $c(t) = 10^{-3}\cos(100 \times 10^3 \pi t)$ using DSB-SC AM scheme. White Gaussian noise with power spectral density $N_o/2 = 10^{-7}$ W/Hz is added during transmission. The received signal is coherently demodulated after ideal BP filtering.

   a. Determine the receiver input CNR.

   b. Determine the output SNR.

   c. What degradation in postdetection SNR occurs if instead a fourth-order Butterworth filter with 3-dB bandwidth of 1.5 kHz is used as a postdetection filter. (Hint: ratio of noise-equivalent bandwidth to 3-dB bandwidth $B_N/f_{3dB} = 1.03$ for a fourth-order Butterworth filter.)

7.3. A message signal $s(t)$ with spectral density $G_s(f)$ is shown in Figure P7.1(a). It a modulates the carrier signal $c(t) = 10^{-3}\cos(2\pi f_c t)$ using a DSB-SC AM scheme. White Gaussian noise with power spectral density $N_o/2 = 10^{-8}$ W/Hz is added during transmission. The received signal is coherently demodulated.

   a. Assuming an ideal predetection BPF, determine the CNR at its output.

   b. Determine the output SNR assuming an ideal postdetection filter.

   c. Modify your calculations (a) and (b) for a predetection filter with amplitude response shown in Figure P7.1(b).

   d. How is the performance in (c) modified if a non-ideal postdetection filter with magnitude response in Figure P7.1(c) is used instead.

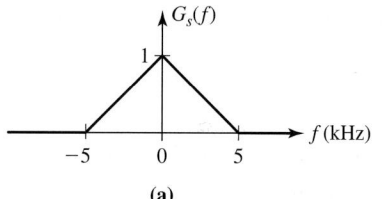

(a)

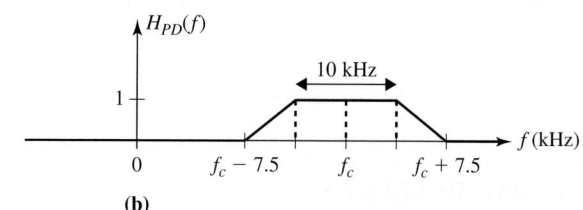

(b)

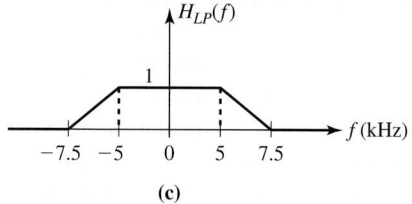

(c)

Figure P7.1

7.4. The message signal $s(t) = 5\cos(700\pi t) + 2\cos(7000\pi t)$ modulates the carrier signal $c(t) = \cos(2\pi f_c t)$ using SSB-AM scheme. White Gaussian noise with power spectral density $N_o/2 = 10^{-8}$ W/Hz is added during transmission. The channel attenuates the transmitted signal by 60 dB. The received signal is coherently demodulated.

   a. Assuming an ideal predetection BPF, determine the CNR at its output.

   b. Determine the output SNR.

7.5. A conventional AM system has a zero-mean Gaussian message signal whose spectrum is limited to B Hz. The peak value of the message signal is assumed to be $2.5\sigma_m$, where σ_m is standard deviation of its amplitude variations. Determine the output SNR in terms of receiver input carrier-to-noise ratio CNR_{IN}. Assume $m_a = 0.875$.

7.6 The message signal $s(t) = 1.0\cos(600\pi t) + 0.5\cos(6000\pi t)$ modulates the carrier signal $c(t) = 2\cos(100 \times 10^3 \pi t)$ using conventional AM scheme. The modulator operates with a modulation index $m_a = 0.85$. We assume that the channel adds white Gaussian noise with power spectral density $N_o/2 = 10^{-8}$ W/Hz during transmission. The received signal plus noise is demodulated using an envelope detector.

   a. Determine the receiver input CNR.

   b. Determine the output SNR.

   c. What degradation in postdetection SNR occurs if instead a fourth-order Butterworth filter with 3-dB bandwidth of 4.5 kHz is used as a postdetection filter.

7.7 A conventional AM system transmits speech signal with bandwidth 3.3 kHz and amplitude PDF given by $f_s(s) = 2.5e^{-5|s|}$. The peak value of the message signal is assumed to be $3.5\sigma_m$, where σ_m is standard deviation of its amplitude variations. The channel introduces white Gaussian noise with power spectral density $N_o/2 = 10^{-10}$ W/Hz added during transmission. Assume $m_a = 0.875$.

   a. Find the carrier power required so that the output SNR exceeds 45 dB.

   b. Determine the threshold value of carrier power.

7.8. Consider a message signal with bandwidth $B = 5$ kHz, and a normalized power $\overline{s_n^2} = 0.25$. It is required to transmit this signal via a channel that attenuates the transmitted signal by 30 dB. The channel noise is AWGN with $N_o/2 = 10^{-10}$ W/Hz. It is desirable to have an SNR of at least 40 dB at the receiver output.

   a. Find the required carrier power if DSB-SC modulation is used.

   b. Find the carrier power required if conventional AM with modulation index of $m_a = 0.75$ is used.

   c. With the carrier power calculated in part (b), what is the maximum SNR that one can obtain for conventional AM (assuming of course that we do not overmodulate the message signal)?

7.9. Consider an FM system with peak frequency deviation $\Delta f_{max} = 60$ kHz, message signal with bandwidth $B = 10$ kHz, and a normalized power $\overline{s_n^2} = 0.25$. The channel introduces AWGN with $N_o/2 = 10^{-9}$ W/Hz. Assuming received power level $P_R = 250$ mW, determine

   a. Output SNR.

   b. Required transmit power P_T for an output SNR = 45 dB when the channel introduces attenuation of 30 dB.

7.10. A PM system with transmission bandwidth $B_T = 140$ kHz is used to transmit a message signal with bandwidth $B = 10$ kHz, and a normalized power $\overline{s_n^2} = 0.25$. The channel introduces AWGN with $N_o/2 = 10^{-9}$ W/Hz. Assuming received power level $P_R = 250$ mW, determine

   a. Output SNR.

   b. Required transmit power P_T for output SNR = 45 dB when the channel introduces power attenuation of 30 dB.

   c. Repeat (a) and (b) if the peak phase deviation $\Delta\phi_{max}$ is limited to π radians. Calculate the required transmission bandwidth B_T.

7.11. A message signal with bandwidth $B = 15$ kHz, and normalized power $\overline{s_n^2} = 0.25$ is transmitted using an FM system. Assuming the deviation ratio $D = 3$, find the output SNR for input CNR values (i) 11 dB, (ii) 25, (iii) 35 dB. In which case is the system operating below threshold?

7.12. An RC filter with time constant 25 μsec is used for deemphasis in an FM system. Find the output SNR improvement in an FM system broadcasting signals with bandwidth 15 kHz. How much output SNR is improved if the signal bandwidth is increased to 53 kHz.

7.13. Consider a message signal with bandwidth $B = 5$ kHz and a normalized power $\overline{s_n^2} = 0.15$. It is required to transmit this signal via a channel that attenuates the transmitted signal by 30 dB. The channel noise is AWGN with spectral density $N_o/2 = 10^{-10}$ W/Hz. It is desirable to have an SNR of at least 60 dB at the receiver output.

   a. Find the minimum required transmit power P_T for a PM system with $\Delta\phi_{max} = 10$.

   b. Find the minimum required transmit power P_T for an FM system with $D = 10$.

   c. Find the minimum required transmit power P_T for an FM system utilizing preemphasis and deemphasis with $D = 10$ and $f_1 = 600$ Hz.

7.14. In a certain FM satellite communication system, the output SNR is found to be 40 dB with $D = 6$. The modulating signal has a bandwidth $B = 10$ kHz and a normalized power $\overline{s_n^2} = 0.15$. The system with $D = 6$ is not in threshold, but the output SNR is required to be at least 50 dB. The increase of the output SNR can be accomplished by either increasing (i) the transmitted power or (ii) D (that is, the transmission bandwidth) as much as possible.

   a. If option (i) is selected, what are the maximum values of D and the corresponding transmission bandwidth that can be used without running into threshold? What is the corresponding output SNR?

   b. If option (ii) is chosen instead, calculate the minimum increase in transmitted power required to attain an output SNR of 50 dB? What are the corresponding values of D and the transmission bandwidth?

7.15. The baseband frequency spectrum for stereo FM broadcasting is depicted in Figure 5.41.

   a. Calculate the noise output power without preemphasis.

   b. Calculate the same for monophonic transmission (the baseband spectral range for mono FM signal is 15 kHz).

c. How much noisier is stereo FM versus mono FM in dBs?

d. Repeat (a) through (c) taking preemphasis and deemphasis into consideration. Show that stereo FM is 22 dB noisier than mono FM.

7.16. In an FDM telephony system, 12 voice channels are frequency-division-multiplexed to form a **group** that occupies a frequency band from 60 to 108. Each 3.3-kHz voice signal is SSB-AM modulated and assigned a 4-kHz frequency slot to provide 0.7-kHz guardband between channels. The frequency-division-multiplexed group signal is then frequency modulated with a peak deviation Δf_{max} of 400 kHz.

a. Determine the transmission bandwidth of the FM signal.

b. Determine the degradation in output SNR of the 12th channel compared with the first.

7.17. A radio receiver block diagram is shown in Figure P7.2. Each block is impedance matched to the source of 50 ohms. The radio is designed to receive a signal with a bandwidth of 20 MHz centered at the BP filter frequency.

a. Calculate the noise figure of the overall receiver.

b. Calculate the input signal to the receiver to achieve the SNR of at least 25 dB at the input of baseband stage. Specify the answer in dBm and in volts.

c. Calculate the signal and noise power at each stage of the receiver chain for input signal level determined in part (b).

d. The baseband stage can only work with signals as large as 500 mV. What is the maximum signal that can be received?

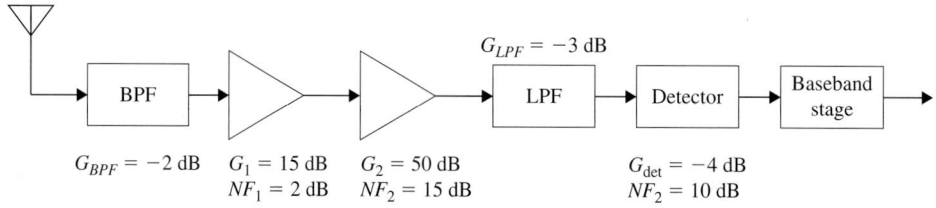

Figure P7.2

7.18. The message signal $s(t) = \cos(2\pi t)$ modulates a carrier $u(t) = \cos(40\pi t)$ to generate a DSB-AM signal $x(t)$.

a. Sample the DSB-AM signal $x(t)$ at 1000 Hz to generate N = 100,000 point sequence dsb.

b. Generate an N-point sequence of AWGN using the following statement

```
n = sigma*randn(1,N)
```

where sigma for a given value of CNR_{IN} is computed using (7.23) and (6.344) as

$$\sigma = \sqrt{\frac{f_s}{8 CNR_{IN}}}$$

The noisy signal at the receiver is given by

```
dsbn = dsb + n
```

c. Design an elliptic BP digital predetection filter with the passband edge frequencies [18–22] Hz using the following code segment:

```
Rs = 40;
wp = 2*Ts*[18 22]; % Ts = sampling
period
ws = 2*Ts*[15 25];
[N,Wn] = ellipord(wp,ws,Rp,Rs);
[b,a] = ellip(N,Rp,Rs,Wn);
```

d. Compute the BP filter output sequences using

```
Rxdsb = filter(b,a,dsb); % Noise-
free DSB signal

Rxdsbn = filter(b,a,dsbn); % Noisy
DSB signal
```

e. Demodulate Rxdsb and Rxdsbn sequences using the coherent detector. A fourth-order LP Butterworth digital filter with cutoff frequency of 2.5 Hz may be used to recover the message signal.

```
[num,den]=butter(N,2*fm*2.5*Ts) %
fm = message signal frequency

%clean demodulated signal

demod_sig = Coherent_Detector
(Rxdsb,num,den,u);

%noisy demodulated signal

demod_sign = Coherent_Detector
(Rxdsbn,num,den,u);

% u = coherent carrier sequence
```

f. Compute the postdetection SNR using

```
s = sum(demod_sig.^2);

noise_power = sum((demod_sign-demod_sig)
.^2);

SNR_Post=10*log10(s/noise_power);
```

g. For CNR_{IN} values 16–30 dB, plot the postdetection SNR (SNR_Post) values obtained using this simulation. Compute the corresponding theoretical postdetection SNR values using (7.19) and plot on the same graph for comparison.

7.19. The message signal $s(t) = \cos(2\pi t)$ modulates a carrier $u(t) = \cos(40\pi t)$ to generate a conventional AM signal $x(t)$. Use $m_a = 0.5$.

a. Sample the conventional AM signal $x(t)$ at 1000 Hz to generate N = 100,000 point sequence am.

b. Generate an N-point sequence of AWGN using the following statement

```
n = sigma*randn(1,N);
```

where sigma for a given value of CNR_{IN} is computed using (7.65) and (6.344) as

$$\sigma = \sqrt{\frac{N_o f_s}{2}}$$

The noisy signal at the receiver is given by

```
amn = am +n
```

c. Compute the BP filter output sequences using

```
Rx_am = filter(b,a,am); % Noise-free
AM signal
```

```
Rx_amn = filter(b,a,amn); % Noisy AM
signal
```

where vectors b and a are numerator and denominator coefficients of the BP filter designed in Problem 7.18(c).

d. Demodulate Rx_am and Rx_amn sequences using the envelope detector described in Problem 4.23. The fourth-order LP Butterworth digital filter designed in Problem 7.18(e) may be used to recover the message signal.

```
%clean demodulated signal

demod_sig = Envelope_Detector
(Rx_am,num,den,Ts,RC)

%noisy demodulated signal

demod_sign = Envelope_Detector
(Rx_amn,num,den,Ts,RC)
```

e. Compute the postdetection SNR as discussed in Problem 7.18(f).

f. For CNR_{IN} values 16–30 dB, plot the postdetection SNR (SNR_Post) values obtained using this simulation. Compute the corresponding theoretical postdetection SNR values using (7.50) and plot on the same graph for comparison.

7.20. The message signal $s(t) = \cos(2\pi t)$ modulates a carrier $u(t) = \cos(40\pi t)$ to generate an SSB-AM signal $x(t)$.

a. Sample the USB-AM signal $x(t)$ at 1000 Hz to generate N = 100,000 point sequence ssb.

b. Generate an N-point sequence of AWGN using the following statement:

```
n = sigma*randn(1,N);
```

where sigma for a given value of CNR_{IN} is computed using (7.38) and (6.344) as

$$\sigma = \sqrt{\frac{f_s}{16 CNR_{IN}}}$$

The noisy signal at the receiver is given by

```
ssbn = ssb + n
```

c. Design an elliptic BP digital predetection filter with the passband edge frequencies [20–22] Hz as discussed in Problem 7.18(c). Compute the BP filter output sequences using

```
Rx_ssb = filter(b,a,ssb); % Noise-
free SSB signal
```

```
Rx_ssbn = filter(b,a,ssbn); % Noisy
SSB signal
```

where vectors b and a are numerator and denominator coefficients of the BP filter.

d. Demodulate Rx_ssb and Rx_ssbn sequences using the coherent detector as described in Problem 7.18(e).

e. Compute the postdetection SNR as discussed in Problem 7.18(f).

f. For CNR_{IN} values 16 through 30 dB, plot the postdetection SNR (SNR_Post) values obtained using this simulation. Compute the corresponding theoretical postdetection SNR values using (7.35) and plot on the same graph for comparison.

7.21. The message signal $s(t) = \cos(2\pi t)$ modulates a carrier $u(t) = \cos(100\pi t)$ to generate an FM signal $x(t)$. Use $\beta = 5$.

a. Sample the FM signal $x(t)$ at 1000 Hz to generate N = 100,000 point sequence fm_s.

b. Generate an N-point sequence of AWGN using the following statement

```
n = sigma*randn(1,N);
```

where sigma for a given of CNR_{IN} is computed using (7.105) as

$$\sigma = \sqrt{\frac{f_s}{4 CNR_{IN} B}}$$

The noisy signal at the receiver is given by

```
fm_sn = fm_s + n
```

c. Design an elliptic BP digital predetection filter with the passband and stopband edge frequencies [43–57] and [38–62] Hz, respectively. Compute the BP filter output sequences using

```
fm_signal = filter(b,a,fm_s);%
Noise-free FM signal
```

```
fm_noisy = filter(b,a,fm_sn); %
Noisy FM signal
```

where vectors b and a are numerator and denominator coefficients of the BP filter.

d. The sequences `fm_signal` and `fm_noisy` are hard-limited to remove any amplitude variations.

```
fm_signal=fm_signal./abs(fm_signal);
% Noise-free FM signal

fm_noisy=fm_noisy./abs(fm_noisy); %
Noisy FM signal
```

e. Implement the differentiator by using the MATLAB command `diff`. Use the following code segment

```
y1 = diff(fm_signal); % Noise-free
FM signal

yd1 = [0 y1];

y_ signal = yd1 - mean(yd₁);

y2 = diff(fm_noisy); % Noisy FM signal

yd2 = [0 y2];

y_signaln = yd2 - mean(yd2);
```

Envelope detection can be accomplished by using the following code segment:

```
signal _env = abs(y_signal);

signaln _env = abs(y_signaln);
```

f. Recover the message using the eighth-order LP Butterworth filter with cutoff frequency of 2 Hz.

```
%clean demodulated signal

demod_sig = filter(num,den,signal_env)

%noisy demodulated signal

demod_sign = filter(num,den,signaln_env)
```

g. Compute the postdetection SNR as discussed in Problem 7.18(f).

h. For CNR_{IN} values 8 through 22 dB, plot the postdetection SNR (`SNR_Post`) values obtained using this simulation. Compute the corresponding theoretical postdetection SNR values using (7.91) and plot on the same graph for comparison.

An Interview with John M. Cioffi

Courtesy of John M. Cioffi

In your opinion what are the major innovations that have contributed to the phenomenal progress in digital and wireless communications? What has been the impact of semiconductor revolution? Internet? Optical fiber revolution?

This is a very broad question and does not specify time frame. If there were no time frame, obviously the invention of the telephone, digital switching, packet switching, Internet, transistor, semiconductors, optical transmission were all major contributions. Over the last two to three decades, the major items that have added new life and revenue to the industry have been:

a. The wireless phone (starting with GSM in Europe, CDMA in U.S., up to present) was a major shift and created opportunity.

b. DSL-enabled broadband around the world, essentially powering the Internet as we know it today with browsers and other higher-bandwidth applications that needed faster file transfers, and enabled video over phone lines as telecom-service-provider opportunity.

c. Smartphones (iPhone has to get the real credit here) also are a major advance.

You have been called "the father of DSL." What was your vision in founding Amati Corporation? Did you anticipate the level of success ADSL and the successor VDSL technologies have achieved?

I have never called myself "father of DSL," and do not know where the term originated but have heard that many times. The transmission at high-speed on twisted-pair requires a highly adaptive scheme where the format of information is adapted to each telephone line (there are over a billion telephone lines and no two are the same and they vary widely). This was not appreciated in the industry, nor accepted at the time, so Amati was started to prove it. Actually, yes I did hope that DSL would be applied to most telephone lines around the world from the beginning.

It can be said that some telephone companies have taken full advantage of your scientific contributions to squeeze more life ("profits") out of the TWP plant and postpone investment in the optical fiber–based infrastructure for the last mile. Do you think this lack of investment in the optical fiber–based infrastructure has been a significant drag towards creating effective competition in the broadband marketplace?

On the contrary, it has saved the telecommunications industry from bankruptcy. The copper asset is enormous and cannot be economically replaced within a lifetime. DSL created a new way to get much more revenue from that asset. (I'll note that several major telcos who've committed to fiber rollout over the past decade have all stopped because of cost, and those that commit now will also mostly find the cost prohibitive when DSL can provide the revenue they seek.) Further, smartphones will depend increasingly on Wifi-to-DSL backhaul to have good quality of service as they proliferate, so the wireless business will increasingly depend on DSL also. It's only if telcos are financially healthy because of DSL profits that they can think about very long-term uncertain commitments to items of questionable return like fiber investment.

Your professional career has been unique in the sense that it has spanned working and contributing on both sides of the isle: academic and industrial. How much of this dual relationship has been influential towards your outstanding success in solving so many practical problems in digital communications?

I am somewhat of a misfit in either world. In industry, I am viewed as extremist who pushes the edges too hard and in academia as too practical, so perhaps I needed to work both sides to survive.

Digital era started with the invention of transistor and Shannon's seminal papers on information theory. Are we doing enough fundamental research to drive the next round of major innovations?

Yes, there is always a lot of fundamental research, but the places (countries) it occurs may have widened. It is always good to see large corporations or governments fund such research, but there are many other smaller vehicles as well. It may well be that much of the research is funded now by many governments around the world, and this is a good thing.

What are the new frontiers of innovation in digital communications? Wireless communications?

My expertise is more physical-layer transmission. Some of the major research areas are the following: body-area networks where signals are transmitted from one device on a person to another for leisure or medical purposes, ensuring quality in last-link (DSL, WiFi, powerline, etc.) to customers, particularly under remote dynamic management, seamless wireless handoff from one system to another.

Who inspired you professionally the most?

It has been a collective of former teachers and bosses, with no single one completely standing above all the rest.

What made you choose a career in the communication field? Do you have any advice for new generation of students and entrepreneurs entering the communications field?

Communication is a basic human need. One could argue the most fundamental in that there is no need for food, clothing, or energy if one has no communication with others (including prayer to God, which is a form of communication). Without said communication, there is not much need to live. Thus, as an engineer, what better field in which to work?

The area is cyclical and goes from times of "we don't need you" to "we really need you" on this fundamental need of communication. If you are good at it, and like the communication area, stay with it, it all works well in the long term. For the entrepreneurs, "never give up unless you know you are wrong."

John M. Cioffi received a BS in 1978 from the University of Illinois and a PhD in 1984 from Stanford University, both in EE. He was awarded an Honorary Doctorate by the University of Edinburgh in 2010. Currently he is Hitachi Professor Emeritus at Stanford University where he held a tenured endowed professorship before retiring after 25 years. He worked at Bell Laboratories from 1978 to 1984 and IBM Research from 1984 to 1986. Cioffi founded Amati Communications Corporation in 1991 which was acquired by Texas Instruments in 1997 for its DSL technology. He designed the world's first ADSL and VDSL modems; the design today accounts for roughly 98% of the world's more than 350 million DSL connections. Dr. Cioffi is Chairman and CEO of ASSIA Inc., a Redwood City, CA-based company pioneering DSL management software sold to DSL service providers, specifically known for introducing Dynamic Spectrum Management (DSM). He currently is also on the board of directors of Alto Beam and ClariPhy.

Dr. Cioffi is a Fellow of IEEE and a recipient of many awards including IEEE Alexander Graham Bell Medal (2010), *Economist* magazine's 2010 Innovation Award, IEEE Kobayashi Medal (2001), IEEE Millennium Medal (2000), and IEE J J Thomson Medal (2000); He is an International Marconi Fellow (2006), a member of National Academy of Engineering (2001), an International Fellow United Kingdom's Royal Academy of Engineering (2009) and 1999 University of Illinois Outstanding Alumnus and 2010 Distinguished Alumnus. Cioffi has published several hundred technical papers and is the inventor named of more than 100 additional patents, many of which are heavily licensed in the communication industry.

CHAPTER 8

Conversion of Analog Signals to Digital Format

Most signals we encounter in the real world are analog, such as speech, music, video, and images. Rapid advances in digital signal processing, transmission, and consumer electronics technologies continue to tilt the balance overwhelmingly in favor of digital versus analog signal format. The popularity of the digital approach is evident in these applications that touch our lives every day: cellular/smart phones, CDs/DVDs, digital TVs, MP3 players. In all these applications, the original analog signal is first converted into digital format prior to being processed and then transmitted or stored as a digital data. The digital data, in turn, must then be converted to analog form before being delivered to the user as speech, music, image or full-motion video. The key factors driving transition to digital signal format include:

- **Superiority of digital transmission/storage.** Digital transmission is a more robust, flexible, and cost-effective approach to sending signals. Digital storage is more reliable, durable, and compact.
- **Advantages of digital signal processing.** Digital signal processing (DSP) continues to benefit from exponential improvements in the cost and performance of semiconductor devices, a phenomenon popularly known as Moore's law. DSP chip prices continue to decline while their capabilities (clock speeds and complexity) dramatically improve to penetrate all application scenarios. In addition, DSP provides tighter control of accuracy over an extended temperature range.
- **Flexibility in implementation of unique features.** Digital representation of signals permits the implementation of rich and powerful features that add value to existing applications and make new applications feasible. Examples include sophisticated compression, encryption, error correction, and detection algorithms.

In this chapter we will consider the conversion of analog signals for digital communication systems and networks. In this context we will study waveform coding techniques with which to obtain efficient digital representation of such signals. Chapter 14 considers compression techniques that reduce bit rate further by removing statistical and temporal redundancies in signals.

The chapter is organized into the following sections:

8.1   SAMPLING OF LOW-PASS SIGNALS.
   Sampling of an analog LP signal to obtain a discrete-time representation is explored in both time and frequency domains. The conditions for the recovery of the original analog signal from its discrete-time samples are then studied. We conclude the section with a discussion of practical sampling methods.

8.2   ALIASING.
   This section considers aliasing produced by undersampling. We analyze how out-of-band frequency components alias into the signal band, introducing distortion in the reconstruction process.

8.3   DIGITIZATION OF ANALOG SIGNALS.
   Quantization and encoding processes for the conversion of infinite precision discrete-time samples into digital codewords are described. This leads to the 6-dB law of quantization noise reduction for each additional bit used in the analog-to-digital (A/D) conversion scheme.

8.4   PULSE CODE MODULATION.
   This section describes the functional operation of a PCM system. The concepts of nonuniform quantization and companding are introduced to improve the quantization noise performance for low-amplitude signals.

8.5   DIFFERENTIAL PULSE CODE MODULATION.

We begin in this section our discussion of efficient waveform coding methods that exploit the correlation between adjacent samples of analog signals. The reduction in transmission bit rate achieved in differential pulse code modulation (DPCM) by sending the difference between the current sample and its prediction based on previous samples is explained.

8.6   OVERSAMPLING IN ANALOG-TO-DIGITAL CONVERSION.

We study oversampling technique which can be used to improve the resolution, or equivalently, noise performance of A/D conversion schemes.

8.7   DELTA MODULATION.

This section studies DM, in which oversampling is traded for a simple 1-bit A/D converter (comparator) for predicting the current sample from the previous samples. We next consider the performance of DM and explain methods that adaptively select the step size to mitigate the effect of slope overload while attempting to minimize the quantization noise.

8.8   SIGMA-DELTA MODULATION.

Sigma-delta modulation, which combines the technique of noise shaping with oversampling to allow high-resolution conversion using a 1-bit A/D converter, is considered. The performance improvement of sigma-delta modulation schemes is compared with classical A/D converters.

8.9   SAMPLING THEOREM FOR BANDPASS SIGNALS.

We introduce the undersampling approach, which deliberately takes advantage of aliasing effects, to obtain an efficient digital representation of BP analog signals. The section concludes with the discussion of BP sampling architecture employed in digital wireless receivers.

The chapter concludes with final remarks and a selected list of references.

8.1   SAMPLING OF LOW-PASS SIGNALS

Suppose we have an analog waveform $x(t)$ with the frequency spectrum shown in Figure 8.1 that is limited to B Hz. To convert the signal to digital format, we begin by taking instantaneous samples of the signal every T_s seconds. Let $x[n]$ denote the sample that results from the sampling of $x(t)$ at $t = nT_s$. That is,

$$x[n] = x(nT_s) = x(t)|_{t=nT_s}, \quad -\infty < n < \infty \qquad (8.1)$$

where T_s is the **sampling period,** and its reciprocal $(1/T_s)$ is called the **sampling frequency** f_s in Hz or samples/second. Again, we will use the notation $x[n]$ to denote the entire sequence as well as the nth sample in the sequence. The intended meaning will be obvious from the context.

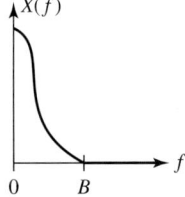

Figure 8.1 Spectrum of a LP signal.

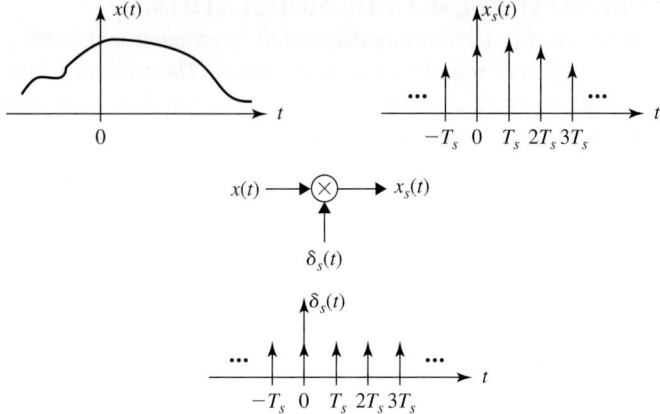

Figure 8.2 Sampling operation in the time domain.

We treat the sampling operation mathematically as a multiplication of the analog signal $x(t)$ by a periodic impulse train $\delta_s(t)$ as shown in Figure 8.2:

$$\delta_s(t) = \sum_{n=-\infty}^{\infty} \delta(t - nT_s) \tag{8.2}$$

where $\delta(t)$ is the unit impulse or delta function. The multiplication operation yields the sampled waveform $x_s(t)$

$$x_s(t) = x(t)\delta_s(t) = x(t)\sum_{n=-\infty}^{\infty} \delta(t - nT_s) = \sum_{n=-\infty}^{\infty} x(nT_s)\delta(t - nT_s) \tag{8.3}$$

$x_s(t)$ consists of a train of uniformly spaced impulses with the impulse at $t = nT_s$ weighted by the sampled value $x(nT_s)$ of the analog signal $x(t)$ at that instant.

It is not intuitively obvious how fast we should sample the analog signal so that we can recover it from the samples without any loss of information. The answer is provided by analyzing the sampling operation in the frequency domain. Applying the multiplication theorem of the Fourier transform (FT), the FT of $x_s(t)$ is given by

$$X_s(f) = X(f) \otimes \Delta_s(f) \tag{8.4}$$

where $\Delta_s(f)$ is the FT of the periodic impulse train $\delta_s(t)$. The FT of a periodic impulse train is also a periodic impulse train as discussed in Section 2.5.3. Specifically,

$$\Delta_s(f) = \Im\{\delta_s(t)\} = f_s \sum_{n=-\infty}^{\infty} \delta(f - nf_s) \tag{8.5}$$

Substituting (8.5) into (8.4), the spectrum of the sampled signal is given by

$$X_s(f) = f_s \sum_{n=-\infty}^{\infty} X(f) \otimes \delta(f - nf_s) = f_s \sum_{n=-\infty}^{\infty} X(f - nf_s) \tag{8.6}$$

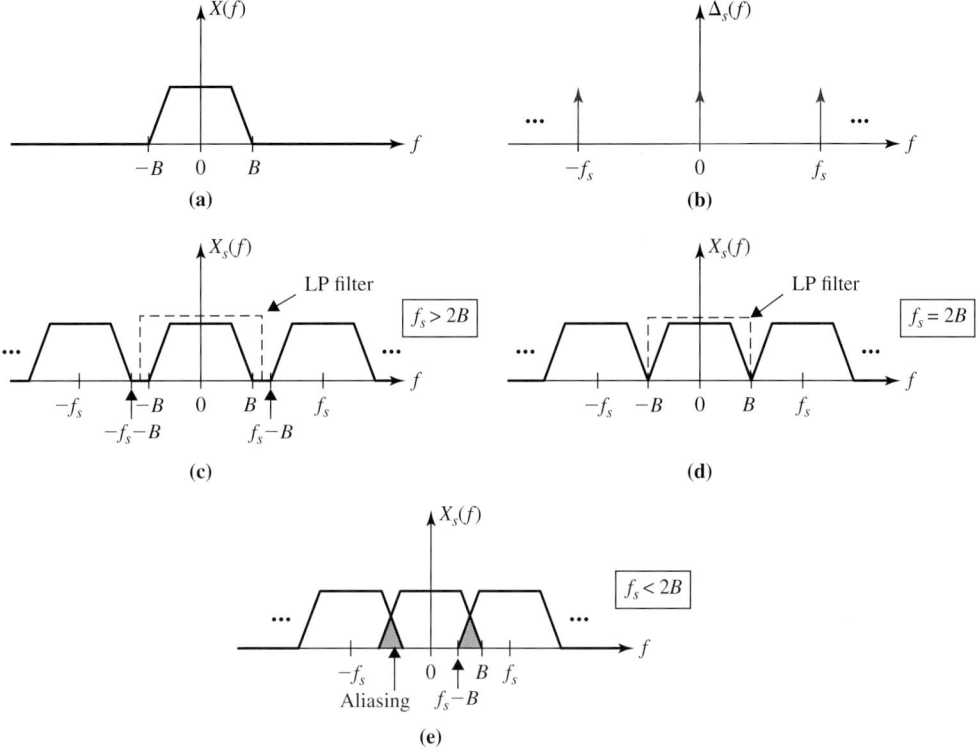

Figure 8.3 Sampling operation in the frequency domain.

We observe from (8.6) and Figure 8.3 that $X_s(f)$ consists of an infinite number of replicas of $X(f)$, each shifted by an integer multiple of f_s and scaled by f_s. Thus, $X_s(f)$ is a periodic function with period f_s. The term on the right-hand side of (8.6) for $n = 0$ is the spectrum of the original analog signal $x(t)$ (except for the scale factor f_s), and each of the remaining terms are the frequency translated versions of $X(f)$. Referring to Figure 8.3(c), it is evident that when $f_s - B > B$, or $f_s > 2B$ the copies of $X(f)$ do not overlap, and therefore when they are added together in (8.6), there remains (to within a scale factor) an undistorted replica of $X(f)$ at each integer multiple of the sampling frequency f_s. Consequently, $X(f)$ can be recovered from $X_s(f)$ with an ideal LP filter. On the other hand, if $f_s - B < B$, or $f_s < 2B$ the copies of $X(f)$ in (8.6) overlap as shown in Figure 8.3(e), so that when they are added together, there is no apparent way of recovering $X(f)$ by LP filtering $X_s(f)$. This is called **aliasing disortion.** As we shall see in Section 8.2, frequency components $f > f_s/2$ in the original analog signal cannot be recovered due to aliasing.

8.1.1   Nyquist-Shannon Sampling Theorem

Let $x(t)$ be a bandlimited signal with maximum frequency B Hz, that is, $X(f) = 0$ for $|f| > B$. Then $x(t)$ is uniquely determined by its samples $x(nT_s)$, $n = 0, \pm 1, \pm 2, \ldots$, if

$$f_s = 1/T_s \geq 2B \qquad (8.7)$$

Table 8.1 Typical Sampling Rates

	Bandwidth	Sampling Rate
Voice telephony	3.4 kHz	8 kHz
CD audio	20 kHz	44.1 kHz
Video	4.2 MHz	> 8.4 MHz. Usually $3f_{sc}$ = 10.7386 MHz or $4f_{sc}$ = 14.318 MHz is used, where f_{sc} = 3.579545 MHz is the color sub-carrier frequency in a color TV signal (Section 5.8.3)

The sampling theorem says that if a signal $x(t)$ contains no frequency components above B Hz, then it is completely described by instantaneous sample values uniformly spaced in time with period $T_s \leq 1/2B$ ($\Rightarrow$ sampling frequency $f_s \geq 2B$). The signal can be exactly reconstructed from these discrete-time samples by processing them through an ideal LP filter with cutoff frequency W Hz, where $B < W < f_s - B$. The frequency $2B$ is called the **Nyquist rate.** The frequency $f_s/2$ is called the **Nyquist** or **folding frequency.** It is the highest frequency that can be recovered by the reconstruction process. The frequency band from DC to $f_s/2$ is called the **Nyquist band.**

If the sampling is done at a rate higher than the Nyquist rate, it is called **oversampling.** On the other hand, if the sampling rate is lower than the Nyquist rate, it is called **undersampling.** Finally, if the sampling rate is exactly equal to the Nyquist rate, it is called **critical sampling.** Table 8.1 displays sampling rates for commonly used signals.

8.1.2   DFT of the Sampled Sequence

Another useful frequency domain description of the discrete-time samples $x[n]$ is obtained from its DTFT $X(e^{j\hat{\omega}})$. We want to investigate the relationship between $X(e^{j\hat{\omega}})$ and $X_s(f)$. Taking FT of both sides of (8.3), we get

$$X_s(\omega) = \int_{-\infty}^{\infty} \sum_{n=-\infty}^{\infty} x(nT_s)\delta(t - nT_s)e^{-j\omega t}dt = \sum_{n=-\infty}^{\infty} x(nT_s)e^{-j\omega nT_s} \qquad (8.8)$$

Now the DTFT of the sequence $x[n]$ can be written from (2.196) as

$$X(e^{j\hat{\omega}}) = \sum_{n=-\infty}^{\infty} x[n]e^{-j\hat{\omega}n} \qquad (8.9)$$

where

$$\hat{\omega} = \omega T_s \qquad (8.10)$$

is normalized angular frequency in radians/sample. The transforms (8.8) and (8.9) are of the same form and related as follows:

$$X(e^{j\hat{\omega}}) = X_s\left(\frac{\hat{\omega}}{T_s}\right) \qquad (8.11)$$

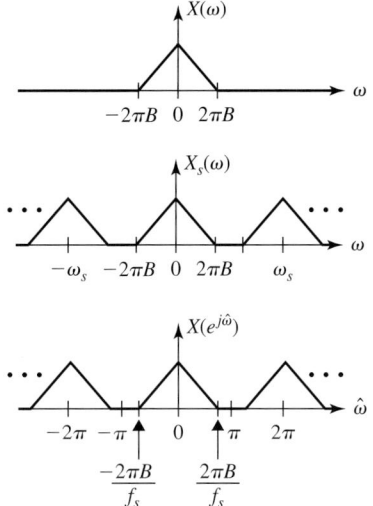

Figure 8.4 Spectral representations of the sampled signal.

Substituting (8.6) for $X_s(f)$ into (8.11) yields the important result

$$X(e^{j\hat{\omega}}) = \frac{1}{T_s} \sum_{n=-\infty}^{\infty} X\left(\frac{\hat{\omega} - 2\pi n}{T_s}\right) \tag{8.12}$$

Figure 8.4 illustrates $X_s(f)$ and $X(e^{j\hat{\omega}})$ representations for the sampled sequence $x[n]$ generated from the analog signal $x(t)$ with FT $X(\omega)$.

8.1.3 Reconstruction of the Analog Signal

The process of recovering analog signal $x(t)$ from the discrete-time sequence $x[n]$ is called **reconstruction.** The reconstruction process is basically one of interpolation as missing signal values between the sampling instants $\{nT_s\}$ need to be interpolated or "filled-in" to reconstruct the approximation $\hat{x}(t)$. We observed in Figure 8.3 that the analog signal spectrum $X(f)$ can be recovered from that of the sampled signal (that is, $X_s(f)$) with an ideal LP filter. Figure 8.5 illustrates the reconstruction using an ideal LP filter. The filter has a gain of T_s (to compensate for the factor f_s in (8.6)) and a cutoff frequency W between B and $f_s - B$. The transfer function $H_r(f)$ of the LP filter is given by

$$H_r(f) = \begin{cases} T_s, & |f| \leq W, B < W < f_s - B \\ 0, & \text{otherwise} \end{cases} \tag{8.13}$$

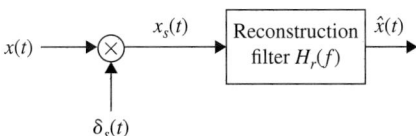

Figure 8.5 Reconstruction of the original analog signal.

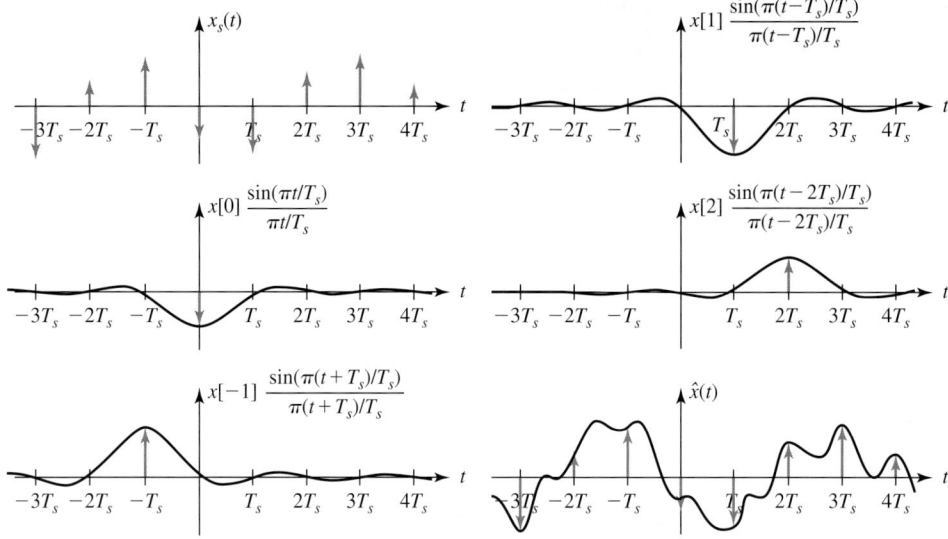

Figure 8.6 Interpolation of the original analog signal by an ideal LP filter.

The corresponding impulse response $h_r(t)$ is the inverse FT of $H_r(f)$, and is given by

$$h_r(t) = 2WT_s \operatorname{sinc}(2Wt), \qquad -\infty \le t \le \infty \qquad (8.14)$$

The output $\hat{x}(t)$ of the reconstruction filter to the sampled signal $x_s(t)$ is given by

$$\hat{x}(t) = x_s(t) \otimes h_r(t) = \left[\sum_{n=-\infty}^{\infty} x(nT_s)\delta(t - nT_s) \right] \otimes h_r(t) \qquad (8.15)$$

Substituting (8.14) into (8.15), we get

$$\hat{x}(t) = 2WT_s \sum_{n=-\infty}^{\infty} x(nT_s)\operatorname{sinc}\left[2W(t - nT_s)\right] \qquad (8.16)$$

A convenient and commonly used choice for the cutoff frequency is $W = f_s/2 = 1/2T_s$. Substituting in (8.16), we get

$$\hat{x}(t) = \sum_{n=-\infty}^{\infty} x(nT_s)\operatorname{sinc}(f_s t - n) \qquad (8.17)$$

Equation (8.17) provides an interpolation formula for reconstructing the original signal $x(t)$ from the sequence of sample values $x(nT_s)$. Equation (8.17) states that the reconstructed continuous-time signal $\hat{x}(t)$ is obtained by summing an infinite number of sinc pulses, each shifted in time by an amount nT_s and scaled in amplitude by the sample value $x(nT_s)$. Figure 8.6 illustrates the interpolation process by an ideal LP filter. Because $\operatorname{sinc}(0) = 1$ and $\operatorname{sinc}(m - n) = 0$ for $n \ne m$, it follows from (8.17) that

$$\hat{x}(mT_s) = x(mT_s), \text{ for all integer values of } m \qquad (8.18)$$

From (8.18), we can conclude that the values of reconstructed samples are exactly equal to those of the original continuous-time signal at sampling instants regardless of whether aliasing distortion occurred in the sampling process. However, if the condition $(f_s \geq 2B)$ of the sampling theorem is satisfied so there is no aliasing distortion, then $\hat{x}(t) = x(t)$ for all values of t. The ideal LP reconstruction filter is obviously unrealizable. Realizable filters require a nonzero transition bandwidth between the passband and the stop band as discussed in Section 2.8.2. This, in turn, requires oversampling to accommodate practical filter designs.

Example 8.1

The signal $x(t) = \cos(6\pi \times 10^3 t)$ is sampled at the rate of 10 kHz. The sampled signal is then applied to an ideal LP reconstruction filter. Find an expression for the output.

Solution

The FT of $x(t)$ is given from Table 2.2 as

$$X(f) = 0.5\big[\delta(f - 3 \times 10^3) + \delta(f + 3 \times 10^3)\big]$$

The sampling process generates the sampled signal $x_s(t)$, whose Fourier transform $X_s(f)$ can be written using (8.6) as

$$X_s(f) = 10^4 \sum_{n=-\infty}^{\infty} X(f - nf_s)$$

$X_s(f)$ is plotted in Figure 8.7, which also shows the frequency response of an ideal LP filter with a cutoff at $W = f_s/2 = 5$ kHz and a gain $T_s = 10^{-4}$. Because the sampling rate satisfies the Nyquist condition, the reconstructed output is precisely the original continuous-time signal $\cos(6\pi \times 10^3 t)$.

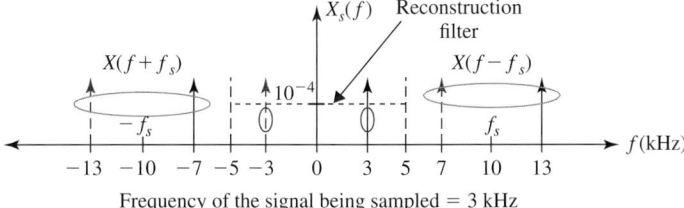

Figure 8.7 Spectrum of the sampled signal in Example 8.1.

8.1.4 Practical Sampling Techniques

The ideal sampling process considered thus far used a periodic impulse train to sample the continuous time signal. In practice, sampling is performed instead by using a pulse train. This leads to following two useful techniques of sampling a continuous time signal:

1. Natural sampling
2. Flat-top sampling

Natural Sampling

In natural sampling, the amplitude of the sampled signal takes the shape of the analog waveform for the duration of each sampling pulse. This is displayed in Figure 8.8. The sampled signal $x_s(t)$ in this case is given by

$$x_s(t) = x(t)g_{T_s}(t) \tag{8.19}$$

where $g_{T_s}(t) = \sum_{n=-\infty}^{\infty} \Pi\left[\dfrac{(t - nT_s)}{\tau}\right]$ is square wave with period T_s and duty cycle τ/T_s.

The FS expansion of $g_{T_s}(t)$ from Example 2.24 is given by

$$g_{T_s}(t) = \sum_{n=-\infty}^{\infty} C_n e^{j2\pi nf_s t} \tag{8.20}$$

where

$$C_n = \tau f_s \text{sinc}(nf_s\tau) \tag{8.21}$$

Substituting (8.20) and (8.21) into (8.19) yields

$$x_s(t) = x(t)\tau f_s \sum_{n=-\infty}^{\infty} \text{sinc}(nf_s\tau)e^{j2\pi nf_s t} = \tau f_s \sum_{n=-\infty}^{\infty} \text{sinc}(nf_s\tau)x(t)e^{j2\pi nf_s t} \tag{8.22}$$

Taking the FT of both sides of (8.22) and using the frequency translation property (2.78), we obtain

$$X_s(f) = \tau f_s \sum_{n=-\infty}^{\infty} \text{sinc}(nf_s\tau)\Im\left\{x(t)e^{j2\pi nf_s t}\right\} = \tau f_s \sum_{n=-\infty}^{\infty} \text{sinc}(nf_s\tau)X(f - nf_s) \tag{8.23}$$

Thus, as in the case of ideal sampling, the spectrum of the sampled signal consists of periodically repeated copies of $X(f)$. However, unlike ideal sampling where these copies are uniformly scaled by a factor f_s, the copies in the case of natural sampling

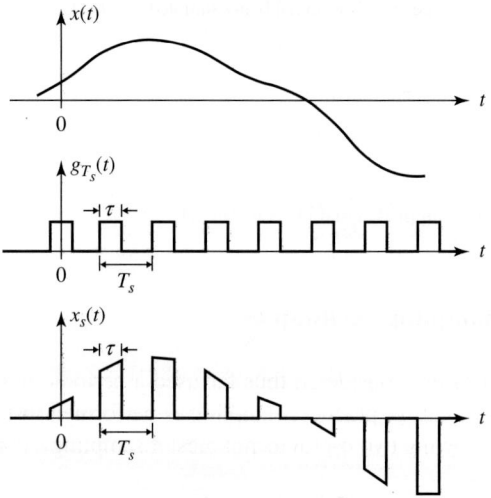

Figure 8.8 Natural sampling.

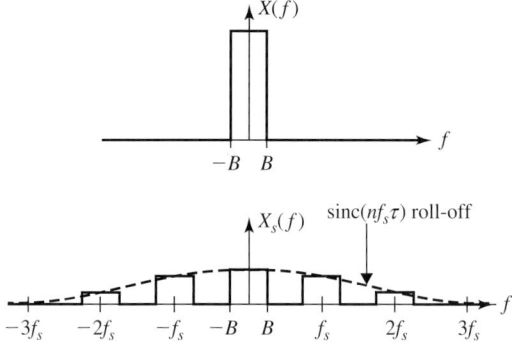

Figure 8.9 Spectrum of the naturally sampled signal.

are weighted by the sinc function $\text{sinc}(nf_s\tau)$. As a consequence, the magnitude of copies centered at higher multiples of the sampling frequency f_s are increasingly more attenuated in accordance with the envelope of the sinc function. This is illustrated in Figure 8.9. The original analog signal $x(t)$ can be reconstructed, without distortion, using an LP filter if the Nyquist criterion is satisfied.

Flat-Top Sampling

In flat-top sampling, the amplitude of the sampled signal is held constant for the duration of each sampling pulse. This constant amplitude is usually the value of the analog waveform at the beginning of the sampling pulse. This is displayed in Figure 8.10. The flat-top sampled signal is generated by a sample and hold circuit. Hence the sampled signal is given by

$$x_s(t) = \sum_{n=-\infty}^{\infty} x(nT_s)\Pi\left[\frac{(t - \tau/2 - nT_s)}{\tau}\right] \tag{8.24}$$

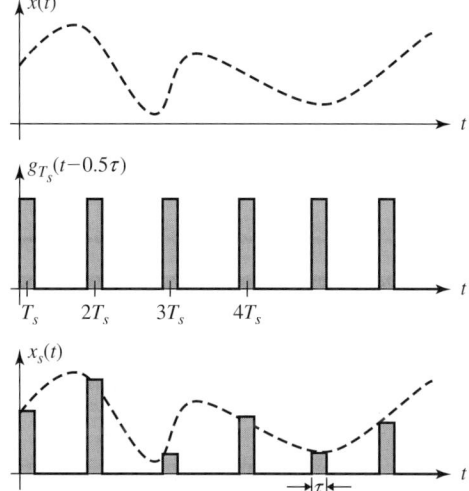

Figure 8.10 Flat-top sampling.

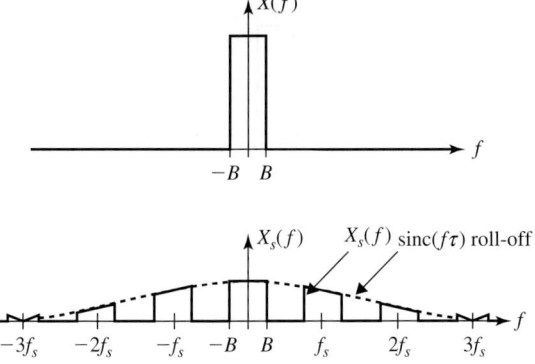

Figure 8.11 Spectrum of the flat-top sampled signal.

We can write (8.24) alternatively as

$$x_s(t) = \left[x(t) \sum_{n=-\infty}^{\infty} \delta(t - nT_s) \right] \otimes \Pi\left(\frac{t - \tau/2}{\tau} \right) \tag{8.25}$$

Taking the FT of both sides of (8.25) and using the convolution property, we obtain

$$X_s(f) = \left[f_s \sum_{n=-\infty}^{\infty} X(f - nf_s) \right] \Im\left\{ \Pi\left(\frac{t - \tau/2}{\tau} \right) \right\}$$

$$= \left[f_s \sum_{n=-\infty}^{\infty} X(f - nf_s) \right] \tau \mathrm{sinc}(f\tau) e^{-j\pi f\tau}$$

$$= \tau f_s \mathrm{sinc}(f\tau) e^{-j\pi f\tau} \sum_{n=-\infty}^{\infty} X(f - nf_s) \tag{8.26}$$

Equation (8.26) states that the spectrum of a flat-top sampled signal is equivalent to that of an ideally sampled signal weighted by $\tau f_s\, \mathrm{sinc}(f\tau) e^{-j\pi f\tau}$ term. The spectrum is illustrated in Figure 8.11. Even if the sampling rate satisfies Nyquist criterion, the reconstructed LP filter output suffers amplitude distortion because of the frequency-dependent weighting provided by the $\mathrm{sinc}(f\tau)$ function. The term $e^{-j\pi f\tau}$ results in time-shift of one-half the sampling pulse-width (that is, $\tau/2$) in the reconstructed output. The distortion in the recovered signal due to sinc function weighting is commonly referred to as the **aperture effect.** The amount of distortion depends on how much the analog signal changes during the holding time τ called the **aperture time.** In general, the aperture effect can be reduced if the duty cycle of the pulse train is less than 10%, that is $\tau/T_s \le 0.1$.

8.2 ALIASING

When the continuous-time signal $x(t)$ contains energy at frequencies greater than the folding frequency ($f_s/2$), then sampling at f_s samples per second causes that energy to appear at a lower frequency. We will consider two cases:

1. Frequency components in the range $f_s/2 < f \le f_s$

Let $x(t) = A\cos\left[2\pi(f_s/2 + f_o)t + \phi \right]$ represent a frequency component at $f = \dfrac{f_s}{2} + f_o$

where $0 < f_o \le f_s/2$. Now if we sample $x(t)$ at time intervals of $T_s = 1/f_s$, we get

$$x(nT_s) = A\cos\left[2\pi nT_s(f_s/2 + f_o) + \phi\right]$$

$$= A\cos\left\{2\pi nT_s\left[f_s(1 - 1/2) + f_o\right] + \phi\right\}$$

$$= A\cos\left[2\pi n + 2\pi nT_s(-f_s/2 + f_o) + \phi\right]$$

$$= A\cos\left[2\pi nT_s\left(\frac{f_s}{2} - f_o\right) - \phi\right]$$

$$= x_a(nT_s) \tag{8.27}$$

where $x_a(nT_s)$ is a sample of the aliased signal $x_a(t) = A\cos\left[2\pi t\left(\dfrac{f_s}{2} - f_o\right) - \phi\right]$.

Thus, if the sinusoidal waveform at frequency $f = \dfrac{f_s}{2} + f_o$ is sampled at f_s, it is aliased by the sinusoidal signal at lower frequency $f = \dfrac{f_s}{2} - f_o$ in the Nyquist band. Because the alias frequency is a mirror image of the input frequency about $\dfrac{f_s}{2}$, the phenomenon is called **folding.** Note also that the alias signal has undergone phase reversal; this is called **spectral inversion.** We can similarly derive a more general result that the frequency components in the bands $\left[(2k - 1)f_s/2, kf_s\right], k = 1, 2, 3, \ldots$ are all folded into the Nyquist band $\left[0, \dfrac{f_s}{2}\right]$.

2. Frequency components in the range $f_s < f \le 3f_s/2$

Let $x(t) = A\cos\left[2\pi(f_s + f_o)t + \phi\right]$ be a sinusoidal waveform where $0 < f_o \le \dfrac{f_s}{2}$. Now if we sample $x(t)$ at time intervals of $T_s = 1/f_s$, we obtain

$$x(nT_s) = A\cos\left[2\pi nT_s(f_s + f_o) + \phi\right]$$

$$= A\cos(2\pi nT_s f_s + 2\pi nT_s f_o + \phi)$$

$$= A\cos(2\pi n + 2\pi nT_s f_o + \phi)$$

$$= A\cos(2\pi nT_s f_o + \phi)$$

$$= x_a(nT_s) \tag{8.28}$$

where $x_a(nT_s)$ is a sample of the aliased signal $x_a(t) = A\cos(2\pi f_o t + \phi)$. We observe from (8.23) that if the sinusoidal waveform at frequency $f = f_s + f_o$ is sampled at f_s, it is aliased by the sinusoidal signal at lower frequency $f_o \le \dfrac{f_s}{2}$ in the Nyquist band. Note that there is no spectral inversion in this case. We can similarly derive a more general result that the frequency components in the bands $\left[kf_s, (2k + 1)f_s/2\right], k = 1, 2, 3, \ldots$ are all mapped into the Nyquist band $\left[0, \dfrac{f_s}{2}\right]$. The relationship between input and reconstructed frequencies is summarized in Table 8.2 and displayed in Figure 8.12.

Table 8.2 Reconstructed versus Input Frequencies

Frequency Band in which Input Frequency f Lies	Reconstructed Frequency f_a	Comments
Nyquist band: $[0, f_s/2]$	f	Conventional Nyquist sampling; no aliasing
$(f_s/2, f_s)$	$f_s - f$	Input frequency f is folded around the folding frequency $f_s/2$ to appear at f_a in the Nyquist band; spectral inversion occurs
$(f_s, 3f_s/2)$	$f - f_s$	No spectral inversion; input frequency f aliased by frequency f_a in the Nyquist band
$(3f_s/2, 2f_s)$	$2f_s - f$	Input frequency f aliased by frequency f_a in the Nyquist band; spectral inversion occurs
$(2f_s, 5f_s/2)$	$f - 2f_s$	No spectral inversion; input frequency f aliased by frequency f_a in the Nyquist band

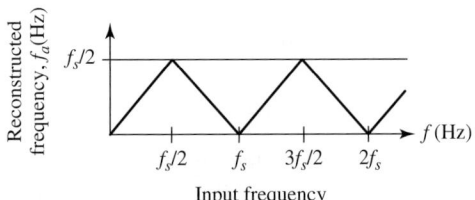

Figure 8.12 Relationship between input and reconstructed frequencies.

From Figure 8.12 and Table 8.2, we make an important observation that the effect of sampling will cause aliases of frequency components outside the Nyquist band to fall inside it (that is, between DC and the folding frequency $f_s/2$). Therefore, any frequency components that fall outside the Nyquist band, whether they be spurious tones or random noise, must be adequately filtered before sampling. If they are unfiltered, the sampling process will alias them back within the Nyquist band, where they can corrupt the desired signal. An LP filter that limits the bandwidth of an analog signal prior to sampling is called an **anti-aliasing filter** because it prevents the detrimental effect of aliasing that is otherwise produced. To minimize the system sample rate, we want the anti-aliasing filter to have a small transition bandwidth. Filter complexity and cost rise sharply with narrower transition bandwidths, so a trade-off is required between the cost of a small transition bandwidth and the costs of a higher sampling rate, which are the costs of more storage and higher transmission rates. In many applications, a sampling rate 10% higher than the Nyquist rate is used so that a provision of 10% transition bandwidth for the anti-aliasing filter can be accommodated.

Example 8.2

The signal $x(t) = \cos(14\pi \times 10^3 t)$ is sampled at the rate of 10 kHz. The sampled signal is then applied to an ideal LP reconstruction filter. Find an expression for the output.

Solution

The FT of $x(t)$ is given from Table 2.2 as

$$X(f) = 0.5\left[\delta(f - 7 \times 10^3) + \delta(f + 7 \times 10^3)\right]$$

The sampling process generates the sampled signal $x_s(t)$ whose Fourier transform $X_s(f)$ can be written using (8.6) as

$$X_s(f) = 10^4 \sum_{n=-\infty}^{\infty} X(f - nf_s)$$

$X_s(f)$ is plotted in Figure 8.13, which also shows the frequency response of an ideal LP filter with a cutoff at $W = f_s/2 = 5$ kHz and a gain $T_s = 10^{-4}$. Because the sampling rate does not satisfy the Nyquist condition,

$$x[n] = x(nT_s) = \cos(14\pi \times 10^3 nT_s) = \cos(1.4\pi n)$$

$$= \cos[(2 - 0.6)\pi n] = \cos(0.6\pi n) = \cos(0.6\pi n \times 10^4 T_s) \Rightarrow \cos(6\pi \times 10^3 t)$$

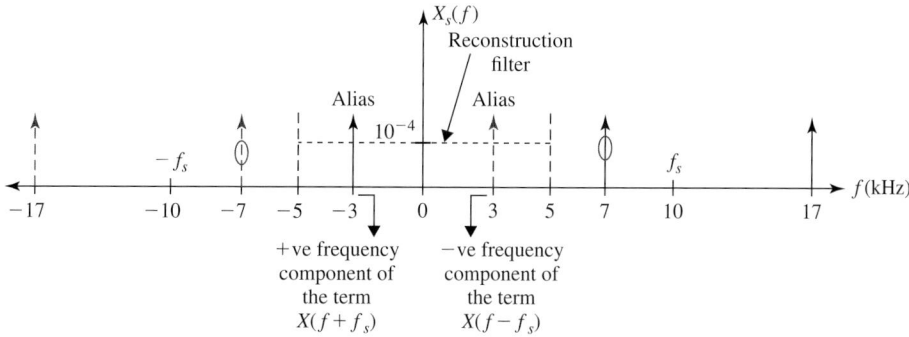

Figure 8.13 Spectrum of the sampled signal in Example 8.2.

Thus, the LP filter output signal is $\cos(6\pi \times 10^3 t)$, which aliases as $\cos(14\pi \times 10^3 t)$. It is instructive to look at the spectrum of the sampled signal and analyze the details of aliasing.

a. The impulse appearing at $f = 3$ kHz in the positive frequency band results from the negative frequency component in the $X(f - f_s)$ term of $X_s(f)$. Also, the impulse appearing at $f = -3$ kHz in the negative frequency band of the reconstruction filter results from the positive frequency component in the $X(f + f_s)$ term of $X_s(f)$. The alias components are accompanied by phase reversal as expected.

b. The reconstruction filter creates the output signal $\cos(6\pi \times 10^3 t)$ corresponding to the aliased spectral components that fall in the frequency range $(-f_s/2, f_s/2)$.

Example 8.3

The signal $x(t) = \cos(26\pi \times 10^3 t)$ is sampled at the rate of 10 kHz. The sampled signal is then applied to an ideal LP reconstruction filter. Find an expression for the output.

Solution

The FT of $x(t)$ is given from Table 2.2 as

$$X(f) = 0.5[\delta(f - 13 \times 10^3) + \delta(f + 13 \times 10^3)]$$

The sampling process generates the sampled signal $x_s(t)$, whose Fourier transform $X_s(f)$ can be written using (8.6) as

$$X_s(f) = 10^4 \sum_{n=-\infty}^{\infty} X(f - nf_s)$$

$X_s(f)$ is plotted in Figure 8.14, which also shows the frequency response of an ideal LP filter with a cutoff at $W = f_s/2 = 5$ kHz and a gain $T_s = 10^{-4}$. Because the sampling rate does not satisfy the Nyquist condition,

$$x[n] = x(nT_s) = \cos(26\pi nT_s) = \cos(2.6\pi n)$$

$$= \cos[(2 + 0.6)\pi n] = \cos(0.6\pi n) = \cos(0.6\pi n \times 10T_s) \Rightarrow \cos(6\pi t)$$

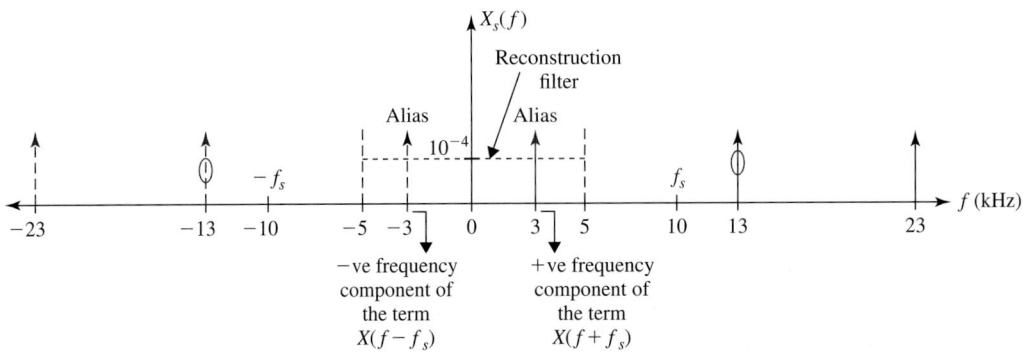

Frequency of the signal being sampled = 13 kHz

Figure 8.14   Spectrum of the sampled signal in Example 8.3.

Thus, the LP filter output signal is $\cos(6\pi \times 10^3 t)$, which aliases as $\cos(26\pi \times 10^3 t)$. It is instructive to look at the spectrum of the sampled signal and analyze the details of aliasing.

a. The impulse appearing at $f = 3$ kHz in the positive frequency band of the filter results from the positive frequency component in the $X(f + f_s)$ term of $X_s(f)$. The impulse appearing at $f = -3$ kHz in the negative frequency band of the reconstruction filter results from the negative frequency component in the $X(f - f_s)$ term of $X_s(f)$. There is no spectral inversion involved here.

b. The reconstruction filter creates the output signal $\cos(6\pi \times 10^3 t)$ corresponding to the aliased spectral components that fall in the frequency band $(-f_s/2, f_s/2)$.

Experiment 8.1   *Natural Sampling of a LP Random Signal*

In this experiment, we simulate natural sampling of an LP random signal using Simulink. The Simulink model is illustrated in Figure 8.15(a). The Random Number block (labeled Gaussian random signal) from the Simulink Sources library generates the sequence of normally distributed random numbers with a mean of 0 and a variance of 1. The anti-aliasing filter limits the bandwidth of the random signal to approximately 50 Hz. It is implemented as an elliptic filter of order 8. The sampling of the LP signal is accomplished by multiplying it with a 10% duty cycle rectangular pulse train with period $T_s = 1/125$.

Figure 8.15 (a) Simulink model to study natural sampling of a LP random signal; (b) waveforms; (c) simulated spectra of sampled and reconstructed waveforms.

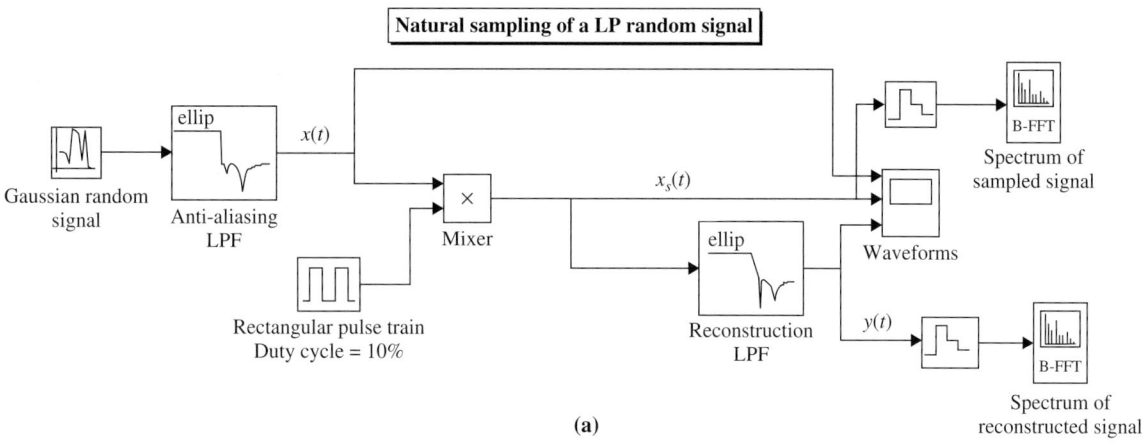

(a)

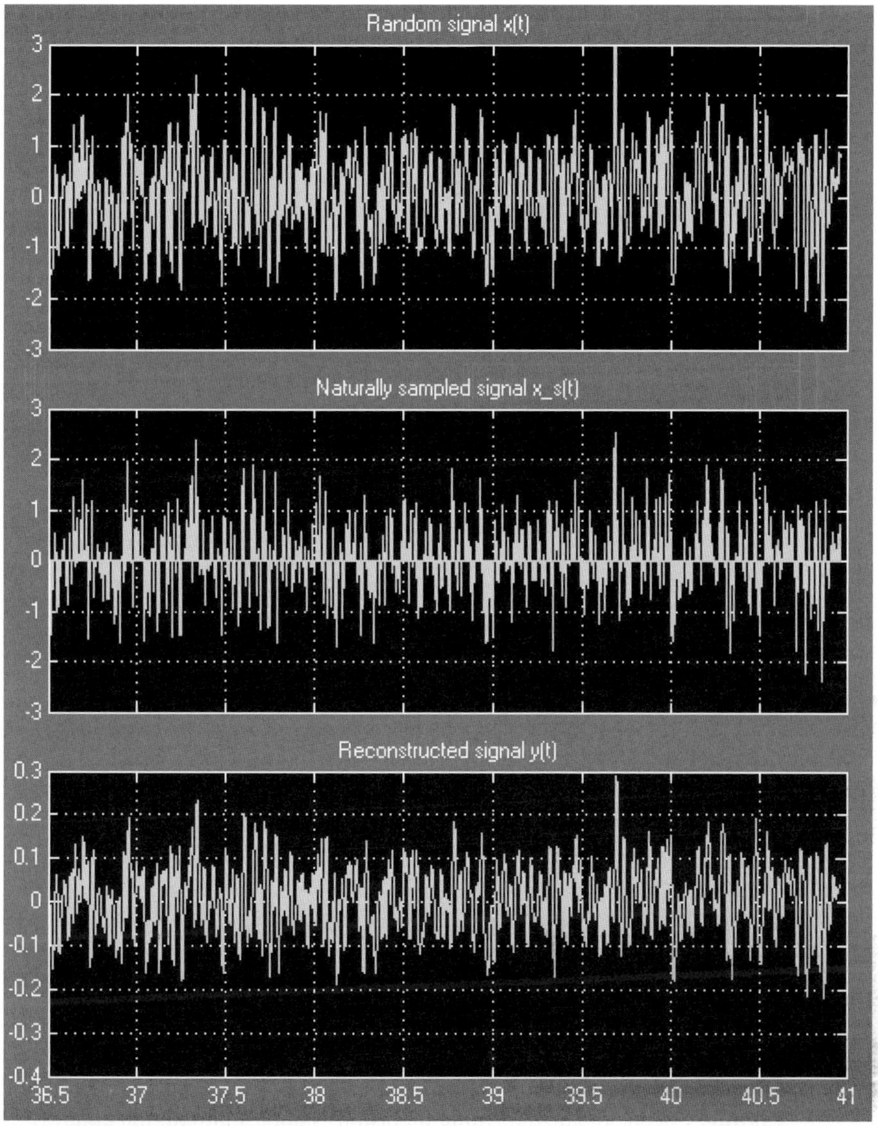

(b)

(*continued*)

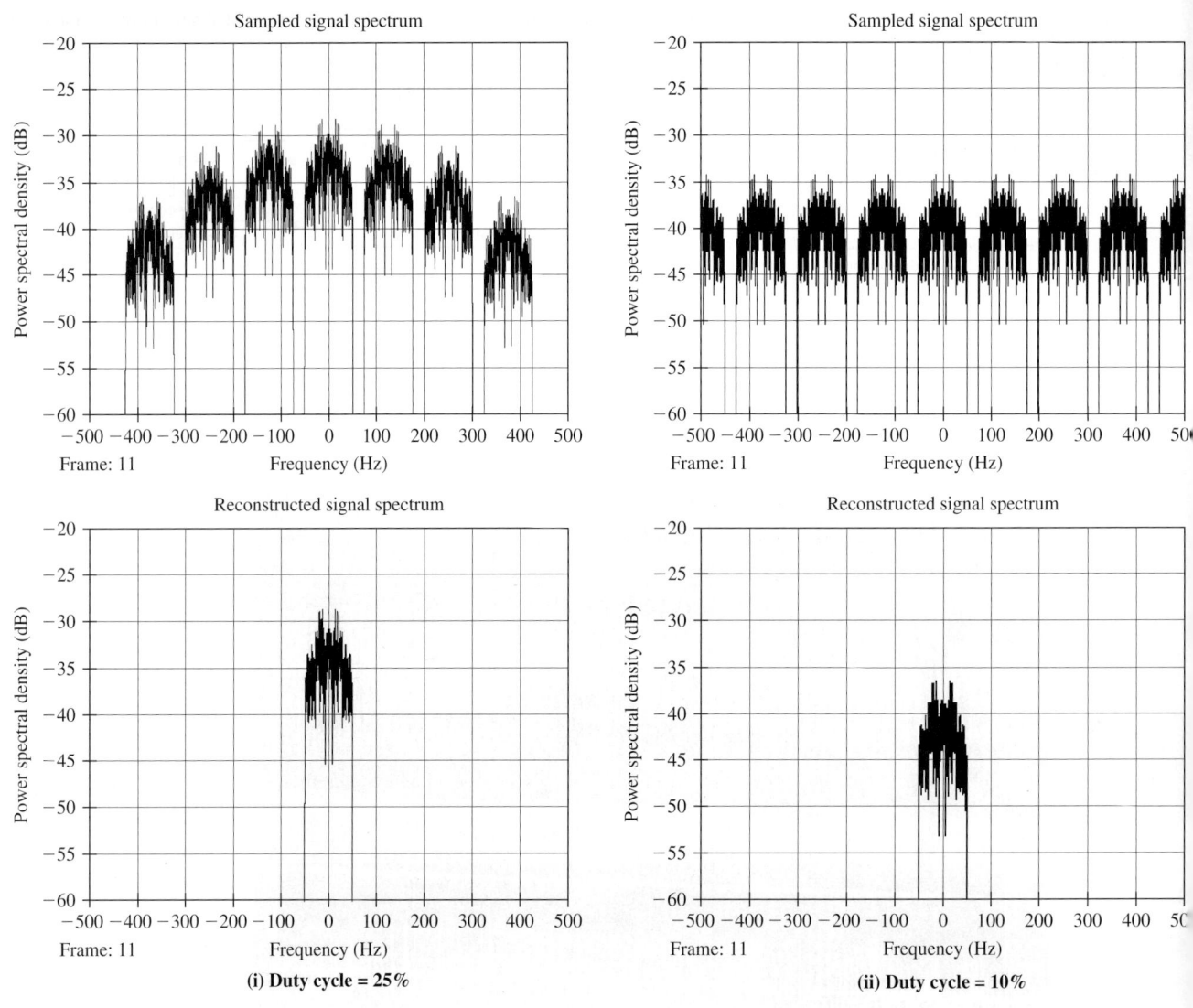

(i) Duty cycle = 25%   (ii) Duty cycle = 10%

(c)

The original random signal is reconstructed using an order 4 elliptic LP filter with 55-Hz passband edge frequency. The reconstructed waveform in Figure 8.15(b) appears to be a faithful reproduction of the original analog signal. Figure 8.15(c) displays simulated spectra of the sampled and reconstructed signals. For comparison we have also shown spectra for the case when a 25% duty-cycle rectangular pulse train is used to sample the random signal.

8.3   DIGITIZATION OF ANALOG SIGNALS

Conversion of an analog signal into digital format involves the following steps:

- **Sampling.** Obtain samples of $x(t)$ at uniformly spaced time intervals.
- **Quantization.** Map continuous-amplitude (infinite precision) samples into a finite number of amplitude levels.
- **Coding.** Encode quantized (finite precision) samples into digital codewords.

An **analog-to-digital converter (ADC)** incorporates all these functions to carry out digital conversion. The ADC is preceded by an anti-aliasing filter, as discussed in Section 8.2, to prevent the detrimental effect of aliasing produced in the sampling process. Because the analog-to-digital conversion takes a finite amount of time, it is often necessary to ensure that the analog signal at the input of the ADC remains constant until the conversion is complete to minimize the error in its digital representation. This is accomplished by a **sample and hold (S/H)** circuit in the ADC. It not only samples the input analog signal at periodic intervals but also holds the analog sampled values constant at its output for sufficient time to permit accurate conversion by the ADC. Next we consider quantization and coding processes that map discrete-time samples into digital codewords.

8.3.1 Quantization

A quantizer maps discrete-time, continuous-amplitude input sample $x[n]$ into one of a finite set of prescribed amplitudes (levels). We represent this operation as

$$y[n] = Q\big(x[n]\big) \tag{8.29}$$

where $y[n]$ represents the quantized sample corresponding to the input sample $x[n]$. The finite set of amplitudes is chosen with spacing between adjacent amplitude levels small enough so that the user cannot perceive the difference between the continuous-amplitude and quantized signals. Unlike sampling, quantization is a lossy and noninvertible process. That is, we *cannot* recover the original analog signal exactly from the quantized version. Figure 8.16 illustrates the quantization process. The peak-to-peak (full-scale) amplitude range of the input sequence $x[n]$ is partitioned by the quantizer into M **partition** or **threshold intervals,** where the kth interval denoted by I_k is determined by the partition or threshold levels x_k and x_{k+1}. That is,

$$I_k = \{x_k < x[n] \le x_{k+1}\}, \quad k = 1, 2, \ldots, M \tag{8.30}$$

The quantizer maps all input samples in the partition interval I_k into some amplitude y_k, called the **quantization** or **reconstruction level.** The spacing between adjacent partition levels is called the **step size.** If the full-scale range of the quantizer is divided into equal-length partition intervals, the quantizer is called a **uniform quantizer.** The quantization step size Δ for a uniform quantizer with $2V$ full-scale range is given by

$$\Delta = \frac{2V}{M} \tag{8.31}$$

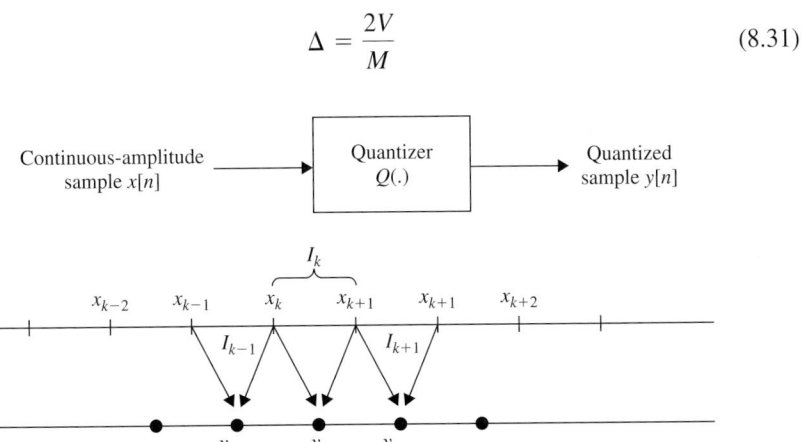

Figure 8.16 Quantization process.

where $2V$ = full-scale range of the ADC with bipolar inputs. Usually, the number of quantization levels M is chosen as power of 2. That is, $M = 2^m$. Substituting into (8.31) yields

$$\Delta = \frac{2V}{2^m} \tag{8.32}$$

In addition to equally spaced partition levels for a uniform quantizer, the quantization level is chosen to lie in the middle of the interval. That is,

$$y_k = \frac{x_k + x_{k+1}}{2} \tag{8.33}$$

Thus, a uniform quantizer has uniformly spaced quantization levels. Uniform quantization is the simplest and most widely used in DSP applications. However, in digital transmission and storage applications of signals such as speech, nonlinear and time-variant quantizers are frequently used. Figure 8.17 illustrates two types of eight-level uniform quantizers, called **midtread** and **midrise,** with full-scale voltage range of $2V$ volts.

8.3.2   Coding of Quantized Samples

The quantizer maps input sample $x[n]$ into the closest of $M = 2^m$ approximation values as illustrated in Figure 8.17. Thus, each quantization level can be represented by an m-bit codeword. **Coding** involves the process of assigning binary codewords to each of the finite number of quantization levels. The two's complement binary number system is the most commonly used representation in most computers and microprocessors. Thus, it is perhaps the most convenient way to label quantization levels. In the two's complement system, the leftmost, or MSB, is considered the sign bit, and we take the remaining bits as representing binary fractions. The sign bit a_0 is 0 for a positive number and 1 for a negative number.

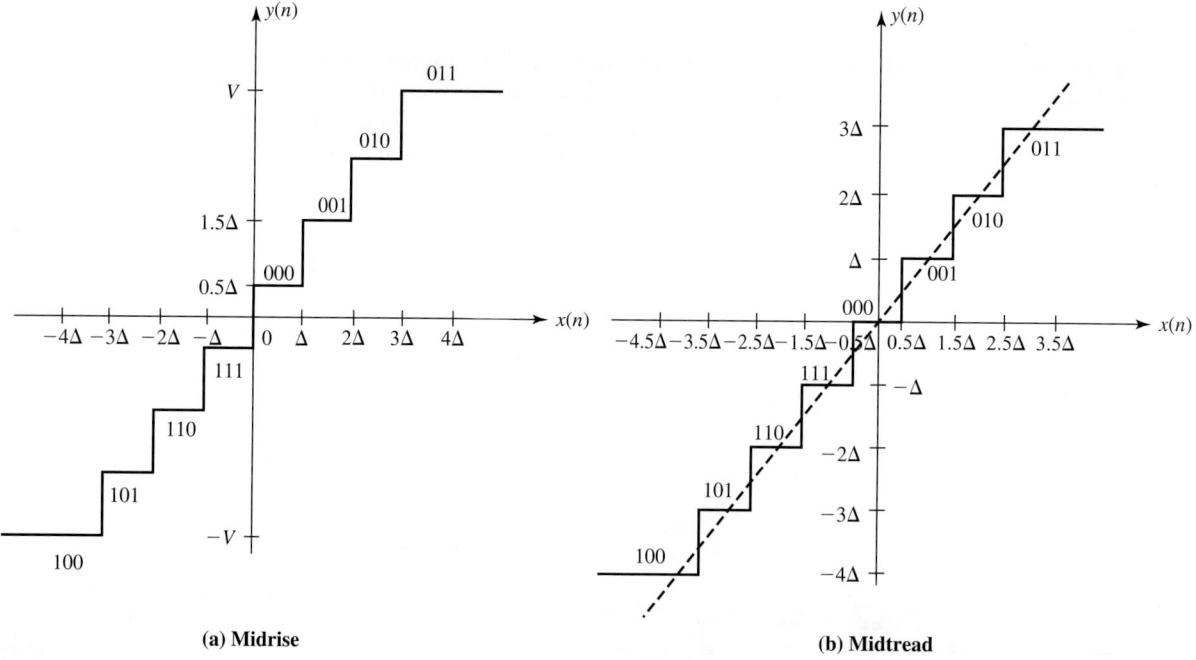

(a) Midrise   **(b) Midtread**

Figure 8.17 Two types of eight-level uniform quantizer.

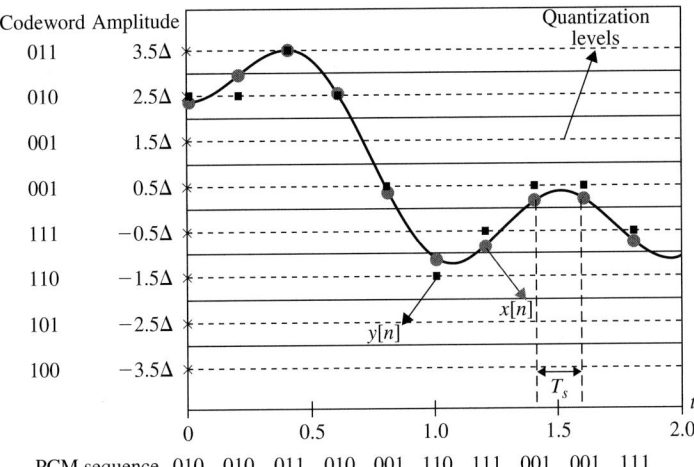

Figure 8.18 Quantization and coding operations.

We assume a binary fraction point ($\Diamond$) between the two most significant bits. In general, if we have an m-bit binary two's-complement fraction of the form $a_0 \Diamond a_1, a_2, \ldots, a_{m-1}$, then its value is

$$-a_0 + \sum_{i=1}^{m-1} a_i 2^{-i} = -a_0 + a_1 2^{-1} + a_2 2^{-2} + \ldots + a_{m-1} a_1 2^{-(m-1)}$$

For example, $1 \Diamond 011 = -1 + 0 \times 2^{-1} + 1 \times 2^{-2} + 1 \times 2^{-3} = -1 + 1/4 + 1/8 = -5/8$.

Thus for the two's complement numbering system, the binary codewords have following interpretation for $m = 3$:

Binary Word	Numeric Value
$0\Diamond11$	3/4
$0\Diamond10$	1/2
$0\Diamond01$	1/4
$0\Diamond00$	0
$1\Diamond11$	$-1/4$
$1\Diamond10$	$-1/2$
$1\Diamond01$	$-3/4$
$1\Diamond00$	-1

Figure 8.18 illustrates a simple example of quantization and coding of a sample waveform using the 8-level midrise quantizer in Figure 8.17(a). The unquantized samples $x[n]$ are illustrated by solid dots, and the quantized samples $y[n]$ are illustrated with solid squares.

Example 8.4

Quantize the sequence $\{1.2, -0.2, -0.5, 0.4, 0.89, 1.3\}$ using a uniform quantizer in the range of $(-1.5, 1.5)$ with eight levels, and write the quantized sequence.

Solution

The quantization step size Δ for a uniform quantizer with full-scale range of 3 Volts is given by

$$\Delta = \frac{3}{8} = 0.375$$

Figure 8.19 illustrates quantization and threshold levels for eight-level midrise type quantizer.

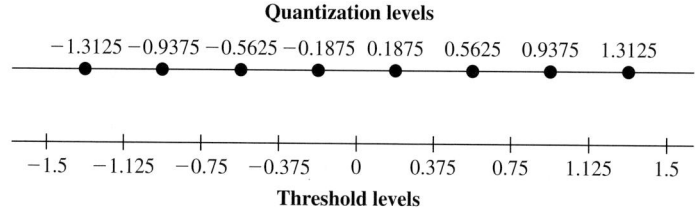

Figure 8.19 Quantization and threshold levels for Example 8.4.

Because 1.2 lies in the threshold interval [1.125, 1.5], it is quantized to 1.325. Similarly, we can show that the quantized sequence as

$$\{1.3125, -0.1875, -0.5625, 0.5625, 0.9375, 1.3125\}$$

8.3.3   Errors Introduced by Quantization Process

In general, the approximation value is not equal to the original signal value, so an error is introduced in the quantization operation. The quantization process introduces two forms of errors in the output:

- **Quantization noise.** Caused by rounding or truncation over the range of quantizer output levels; and
- **Saturation (peak clipping).** Due to the input exceeding the full-scale range of the ADC.

Quantization noise can be minimized by choosing a sufficiently small quantization step size Δ. Saturation can be avoided by carefully matching the full-scale range of an ADC to the anticipated input signal amplitude range.

Experiment 8.2   *Study of m-Bit Quantization Errors*

In this experiment, we simulate the quantization errors produced by *m*-bit quantizers using Simulink. The Simulink model is illustrated in Figure 8.20(a). A 1-Hz sine wave with peak amplitude of 1V is used as the input signal. The signal is sampled at 100 Hz using **zero-order hold** block from the Simulink library . We simulate 4- and 8-bit quantizers by selecting step sizes Δ of 0.125 and 1/128, respectively. Figure 8.20(b) displays the waveforms obtained using a step size of 0.125. Both quantization and saturation (peak clipping) errors can be observed. Quantization errors are significantly reduced in Figure 8.20(c) where a smaller quantization step size of 1/128 is used.

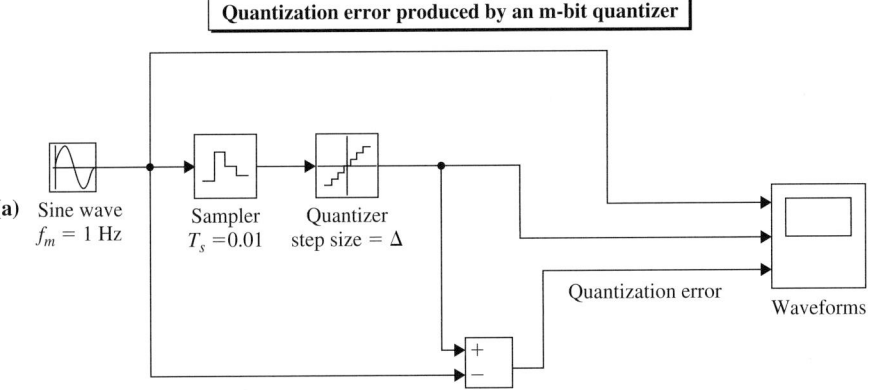

Quantization error produced by an m-bit quantizer

(a) Sine wave $f_m = 1$ Hz

Sampler $T_s = 0.01$

Quantizer step size = Δ

Subtract

Quantization error

Waveforms

Figure 8.20 (a) Simulink model for m-bit uniform quantizer; (b) 4-bit uniform quantizer waveforms; (c) 8-bit uniform quantizer waveforms.

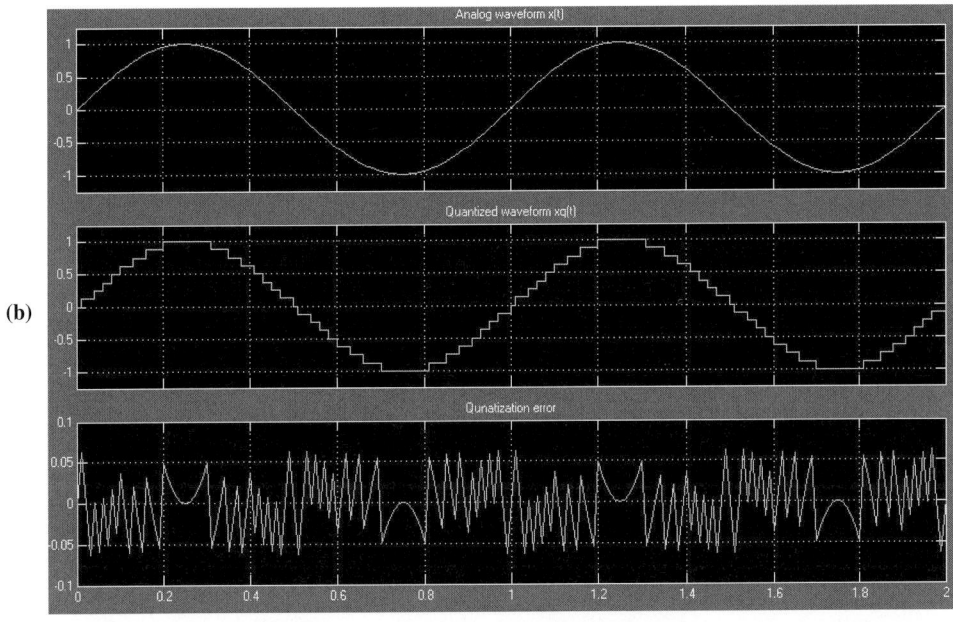

(b)

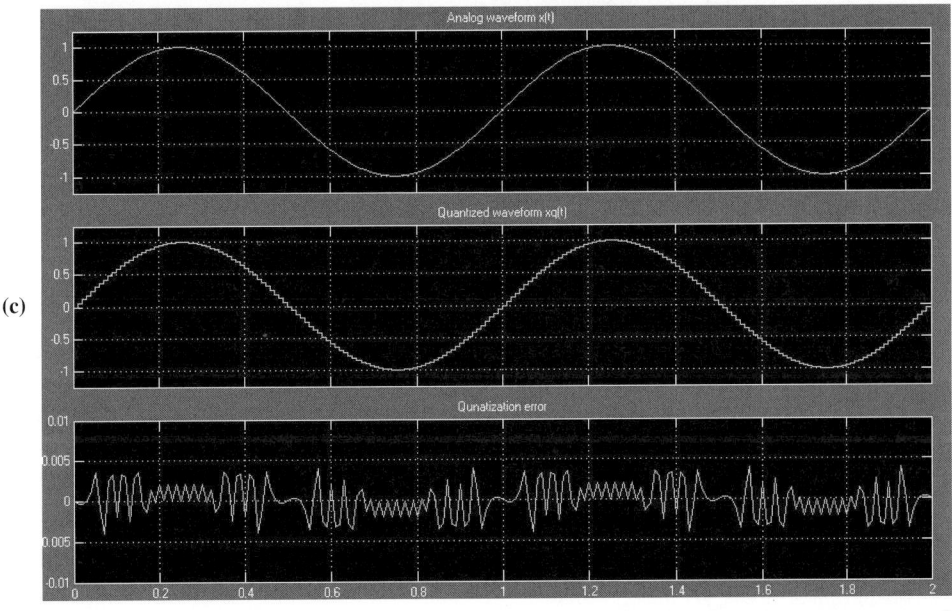

(c)

8.3.4   Quantization Noise

The quantized sample will generally be different from the true sample value because of truncation or rounding errors. The difference between them is the **quantization error,** defined as

$$e[n] = y[n] - x[n] \tag{8.34}$$

For an *m*-bit quantizer with Δ given by (8.32), the quantization error is always in the range $(-\Delta/2, \Delta/2]$ whenever

$$-V \le x[n] \le V \tag{8.35}$$

as shown in Figure 8.21.

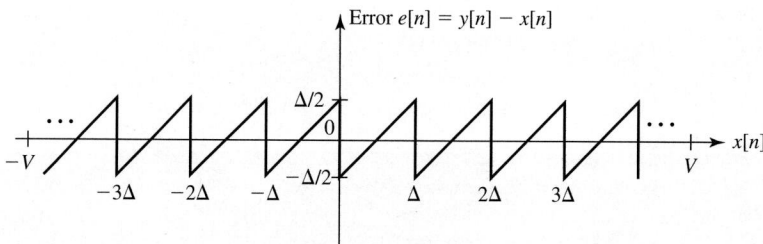

Figure 8.21 Quantizer error.

Example 8.5

Consider a 12-bit uniform quantizer with input range of ± 10V. Calculate the step size and maximum quantization error.

Solution

The quantization step size using (8.32) is given as

$$\Delta = 20/2^{12} \approx 4.9 \text{ mV}$$

Maximum quantization error $e[n] = \Delta/2 = 2.45$ mV

The least significant bit (LSB) of the ADC equals Δ. Thus, the maximum quantization error is approximately equal to one-half of an LSB.

Statistical Model of Quantization Errors

A simplified but useful model to analyze the effect of quantization errors is shown in Figure 8.22. In this model, the errors introduced by the quantizer are represented as an additive noise signal. In most cases, this statistical characterization of quantization errors yields useful results.

We make the following assumptions about the statistical properties of error sequence $e[n]$ to simplify our analysis:

- For rounding quantizers and small Δ (the number of levels *M* large), it is reasonable to assume that $e[n]$ is a uniformly distributed random variable with range $[-\Delta/2, \Delta/2]$.

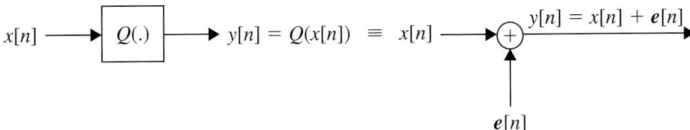

Figure 8.22 Additive noise model for quantizer.

- If truncation rather than rounding is used in implementing quantization, then the error will always be negative, and we will assume a uniform PDF from $-\Delta$ to 0.
- The successive noise samples $e[n]$ are uncorrelated ($\Rightarrow$ quantization errors constitute a white noise process).
- $e[n]$ is uncorrelated with random message signal $x[n]$.

The mean value of random variable $e[n]$ is zero, and its variance is given by

$$\sigma_e^2 = \int_{-\Delta/2}^{\Delta/2} e^2 \frac{1}{\Delta} de = \Delta^2/12 \qquad (8.36)$$

For an m-bit quantizer with full-scale range of $2V$, the noise variance, or average noise power, is

$$\sigma_e^2 = 2^{-2m} V^2/3 \qquad (8.37)$$

The figure of merit for an A/D converter is the **signal-to-quantization noise ratio (SQNR),** defined as

$$SQNR = 10 \log_{10} \frac{\text{Average signal power}}{\text{Average noise power}} = 10 \log_{10}\left(\frac{P_x}{P_e}\right) = 10 \log_{10}\left(\frac{\sigma_x^2}{\sigma_e^2}\right) \text{ dB } (8.38)$$

where σ_x^2 is the input signal variance representing the **signal power.**

Quantizer Performance: Arbitrary Message Signal

Consider an arbitrary message signal $|x[n]| \leq x_{\max}$ with power σ_x^2. We assume that the message signal covers the full-scale range of the quantizer. That is, $x_{\max} = V$. The SQNR of an m-bit quantizer is given by substituting (8.37) into (8.38) as

$$SQNR = 10 \log\left(3 \frac{\sigma_x^2}{V^2} 2^{2m}\right)$$

$$= 10 \log\left(3 \frac{\sigma_x^2}{x_{\max}^2} 2^{2m}\right) \qquad (8.39)$$

which simplifies to

$$SQNR = 6m + 4.77 - 20 \log\left(\frac{x_{\max}}{\sigma_x}\right) \text{ dB} \qquad (8.40)$$

Equation (8.40) is a very important result. It states that for an arbitrary message signal, **each additional bit in the ADC increases the SQNR by 6 dB.** The actual SQNR value for a given value of m depends on $\dfrac{x_{max}}{\sigma_x}$, which depends on the PDF of the message signal. σ_x is the rms value of the signal amplitude, and it would be necessarily less than the peak amplitude x_{max} of the signal. For random signals, such as music or speech, the PDF of the amplitude tends to be concentrated around zero and falls off rapidly with increasing amplitude. In such cases, the probability that the magnitude of the sample will exceed three or four times the rms value is low. For example, if the signal amplitude has Gaussian distribution, only 0.064% of the samples would have an amplitude greater than $4\sigma_x$. So if we choose $x_{max} \approx 4\sigma_x$, the probability that an analog sample stays within the range $[-x_{max}, x_{max}]$ is 0.9544. Thus to avoid clipping off the peaks of the signal, the input to the ADC should be adjusted so that full-scale range $2V = 2x_{max} \approx 8\sigma_x$. Using this value of x_{max} in (8.40), we obtain

$$SQNR = 6m - 7.25 \text{ dB} \tag{8.41}$$

Quantizer Performance: Sinusoidal Input Signal

For a sine wave input of peak amplitude x_{max}, the average signal power in a sine wave input is given by

$$\sigma_x^2 = x_{max}^2/2 \tag{8.42}$$

Substituting into (8.40) yields

$$SQNR = 6m + 4.77 - 20\log(\sqrt{2}) = 6m + 1.77 \text{ dB} \tag{8.43}$$

Again, **each additional bit in the ADC increases the SQNR by 6 dB.**

Example 8.6

For audio signals such as music, a high-quality representation means preserving frequencies up to 20 kHz. Although the Nyquist sampling rate is 40 kHz, sampling rates of 44.1 kHz in CD and 48 kHz in digital audio tape (DAT) standards are used. If an SQNR of around 96 dB is desired, calculate the number of bits required per sample.

Solution

The number of bits required can be computed using (8.41) as

$$SQNR = 96 = 6m - 7.25 \text{ dB}$$

$$m = (96 + 7.25)/6 \approx 17$$

Typically 16 or more bits are used to achieve the fine granularity required for high-quality audio. Thus the PCM bit rate per audio channel is given by

$$44,000 \text{ samples/second} \times 16 \text{ bit/sample} = 700 \text{ kbps}$$

For stereo audio, the PCM bit rate for CD-quality audio is given by 2×700 kbps $= 1.4$ Mbps.

Because of error mechanisms other than quantization noise (including thermal noise, sampling time jitter, etc.), the effective resolution achievable by an ADC is less than expected from its

Pioneers in the Field

Alec Harley Reeves was born March 2, 1902, at Redhill in Surrey, England. He attended Reigate Grammar School, won a scholarship to the City & Guilds Engineering College, and in 1921 went to Imperial College of Science and Technology in London. Reeves joined the International Western Electric Company in 1923, and was part of a team of engineers responsible for the first commercial transatlantic telephone link. In 1925 Western Electric's European operations were acquired by ITT, and in 1927 Reeves was transferred to ITT's research laboratories in Paris. He remained with the company for almost 50 years and was awarded 82 patents.

It was in Paris, in 1937, that Reeves formulated the principles of pulse code modulation (PCM). Since Alexander Graham Bell invented the telephone in 1876, voice had been converted into an analog electrical current waveform. Reeves recognized the major drawback that accompanies transmission of such analog signals in a repeater system: the noise is accumulative and amplified along with the original message signal. Reeves offered a radical alternative; he proposed that voice signal be sampled at regular intervals, with the values of these samples represented by binary numbers and transmitted as binary on–off pulses. The vacuum-tube based technology of the time was not up to the job. But Reeves's PCM patent of 1937 indicated the required circuit design principles. PCM was not used commercially until the invention of the transistor decades later, although the technique was first applied by Bell Labs for the complex and cumbersome secure radio system on which Churchill and Roosevelt talked for much of the Second World War.

After the war, Reeves returned to ITT's Standard Telecommunications Labs to work on ways to increase the capacity and reliability of communications systems. He was a pioneer of semiconductor devices and among the first to exploit the possibility of using light to carry information. Reeves inspired and managed the team led by Charles Kao and George Hockham who did pioneering work in the realization of optical fiber as a telecommunications medium. He was awarded the Stuart Ballantine Medal of the Franklin Institute in 1965 and also the CBE.

stated or nominal resolution specification ("m" bits). The actual resolution (known as **effective number of bits (ENOB)**) is given from (8.43) as

$$ENOB = (SNR - 1.77)/6 \quad \text{bits} \qquad (8.44)$$

where *SNR* is the actual measured SNR of the ADC in dB with a sinusoidal test signal.

8.4 PULSE CODE MODULATION

Pulse code modulation (PCM) is the most widely used method of analog-to-digital (A/D) conversion where the digital output is represented in a serial bit stream. PCM is very popular in digitizing all types of audio and video sources for telecommunications applications. Figure 8.23 is a block diagram representation of the transmission of analog signals end-to-end in a PCM system.

At the transmit end, an ADC converts the analog signal $x(t)$ into m-bit digital codewords as discussed in Section 8.3. We assume that the analog signal $x(t)$, bandlimited to B Hz by the anti-aliasing filter, is sampled at the $f_s \geq 2B$ rate, producing a sequence of f_s samples/second. The number of bits m/sample determines the accuracy with which the quantizer approximates analog samples. The digital output from the ADC consisting of m-bit codewords is first serialized into a bit stream at $f_s m$ bits/second, and then a digital modulator (Chapter 9) converts each bit into a physical waveform suitable for transmission or storage. The resultant PCM signal can be stored or transmitted any number of times without additional distortion so long as no additional transmission errors are introduced. Figure 8.18 illustrates the PCM sequence generated by digitizing a sample waveform segment.

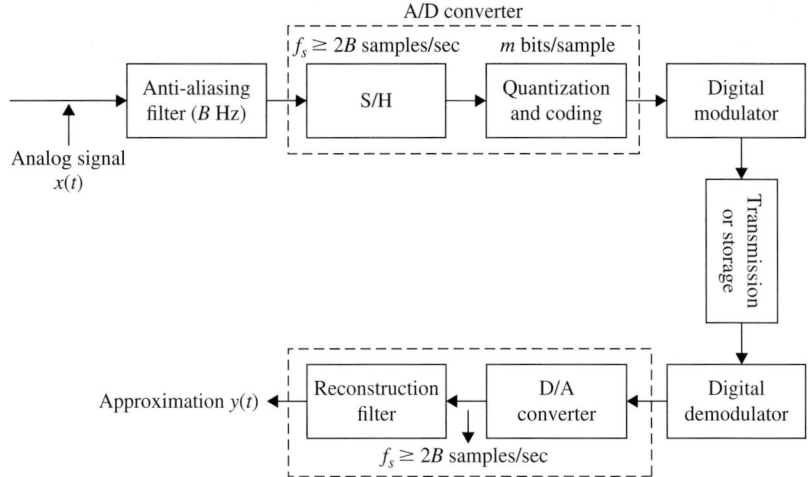

Figure 8.23 Pulse code modulation system.

At the receive end, an approximation to the original signal $x(t)$ is generated by the reverse process. A digital demodulator performs the detection of the serial bit stream from the received signal in the presence of noise. The **digital-to-analog converter (DAC)** then segregates the received bit stream into m-bit blocks and produces a staircase waveform approximation to the original signal in which amplitudes of pulses correspond to m-bit codewords. Finally, a **reconstruction (interpolation or smoothing)** LP filter recovers an approximation to the original analog signal from the staircase waveform with accuracy determined by the quantization process (in the absence of any transmission errors).

8.4.1 Nonuniform Quantization

Real audio signals—that is, speech and music—contain both small and large amplitudes, but small amplitudes are more likely. This is evident from the PDF of the speech signal amplitude illustrated in Figure 8.24. Although the dynamic range of the human voice is about 40 dB, the amplitude is typically 20 dB down from the peak value during conversation. Because the quantization noise for a uniform quantizer is independent of the signal amplitude, the resultant degradation of SQNR is 40 dB for amplitude levels near zero. An alternative to uniform quantization is to use variable step size Δ: small values of Δ for lower amplitude levels which are more likely and large values of Δ for higher amplitude levels which are less probable. Such a **nonuniform** quantizer characteristic can provide relatively constant SQNR compared with uniform quantization over a wide dynamic range using the same number of bits.

Nonuniform quantization can be accomplished by first compressing the samples of the input signal and then uniformly quantizing the compressed signal. This can be realized by passing the input signal through a **compressor** followed by a uniform quantizer as displayed in Figure 8.25. At the receiver, expansion (i.e., decompression) is used after digital-to-analog conversion to restore signals to their correct relative values. The **expander** characteristic is the inverse of the compression characteristic, and the combination of a compressor and an expander is called a **compander.**

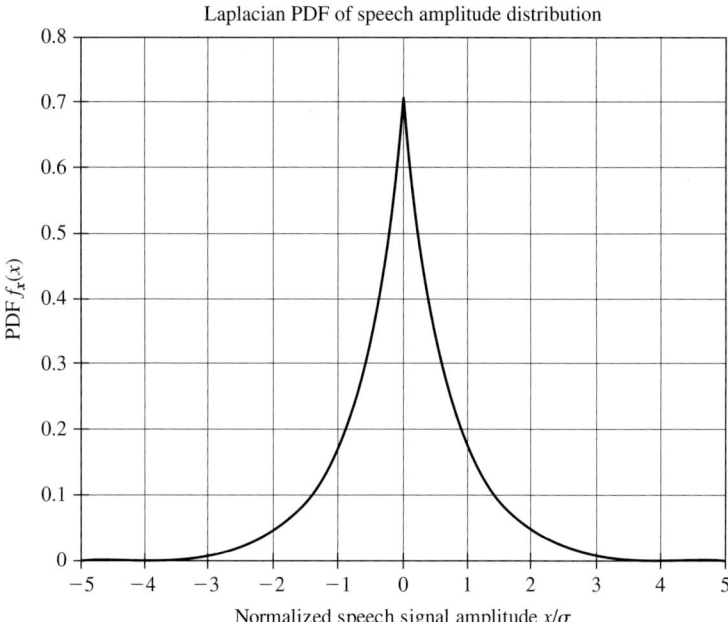

Figure 8.24 Laplacian PDF of speech signal amplitude distribution.

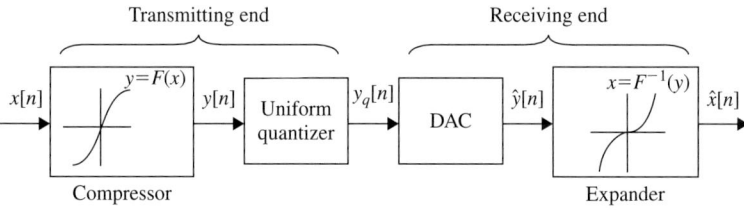

Figure 8.25 Nonuniform quantization.

Figure 8.26 illustrates the compression characteristics used in PCM voice telephony systems. In the United States, Canada, and Japan, a μ-law type of compression characteristic is used. It is defined by

$$y = F(x) = x_{\max} \frac{\log_e\left(1 + \mu \frac{|x|}{x_{\max}}\right)}{\log_e(1 + \mu)} \operatorname{sgn}(x) \tag{8.45}$$

where x and y are input and output voltages and μ is a positive constant. Note that $\mu = 0$ corresponds to the case of uniform quantization. The μ-law is neither strictly linear nor strictly logarithmic, but it is approximately linear at low input levels corresponding to $\mu|x| \ll x_{\max}$, and approximately logarithmic at high levels corresponding to $\mu|x| \gg x_{\max}$. In the United States, Canada, and Japan, the standard value for μ is 255.

In Europe and the **rest of the world (ROW),** another compression law, the A-law characteristic, is used. The case of uniform quantization corresponds to $A = 1$.

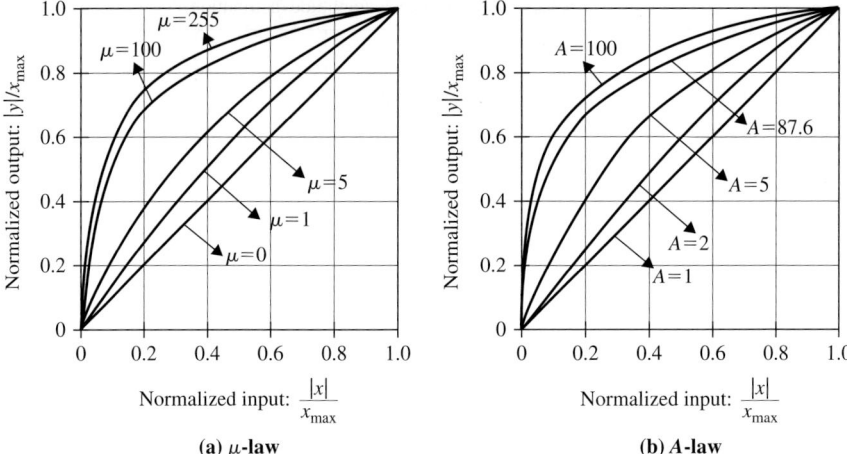

Figure 8.26 Compression characteristics for PCM telephony.

$$y = F(x) = \begin{cases} x_{\max} \dfrac{A(|x|/x_{\max})}{1 + \log_e A} \operatorname{sgn}(x), & 0 \leq |x|/x_{\max} \leq 1/A \\[3mm] x_{\max} \dfrac{1 + \log_e A(|x|/x_{\max})}{1 + \log_e A} \operatorname{sgn}(x), & 1/A \leq |x|/x_{\max} \leq 1 \end{cases} \qquad (8.46)$$

For PCM telephony in Europe and ROW, the standard value for A is 87.6.

Example 8.7

Develop the transfer characteristic of the nonuniform quantizer obtained by cascading $\mu = 40$ compander with a 3-bit uniform quantizer. Obtain the quantized output for the input sequence $\{0.8, -0.135, -0.35, 0.25, 0.45, 0.9\}$.

Solution

To develop the quantization table of nonuniform quantizer, we start with the partition and quantization levels of the 3-bit uniform quantizer obtained in Example 8.4. Next we apply inverse μ-law mapping to obtain the partition levels of the resulting nonuniform quantizer. The inverse μ-law mapping is obtained from (8.45) as

$$x = F^{-1}(y) = \frac{x_{\max}}{\mu}\left[(1 + \mu)^{\frac{|y|}{x_{\max}}} - 1\right]\operatorname{sgn}(y) \qquad (8.47)$$

Assuming $x_{\max} = 1$, the partition levels for the 3-bit uniform quantizer are

$$\underline{x}_{\text{uniform}} = (-1.0 \ -0.75 \ -0.5 \ -0.25 \ 0 \ 0.25 \ 0.5 \ 0.75 \ 1.0) \qquad (8.48)$$

Applying the mapping (8.47) to (8.48), the partition levels of nonuniform quantizer are obtained as

$$\underline{x}_{\text{nonuniform}} = (-1.0 \ -0.3801 \ -0.1351 \ -0.0383 \ 0.0 \ 0.0383 \ 0.1351 \ 0.3801 \ 1.0)$$

The quantization levels of the 3-bit uniform and non-uniform quantizer are

$$\underline{y} = (-0.875 \quad -0.625 \quad -0.375 \quad -0.125 \quad 0.125 \quad 0.375 \quad 0.625 \quad 0.875) \qquad (8.49)$$

Figure 8.27 displays the transfer characteristic of the 3-bit nonuniform quantizer along with $\mu = 40$ compander and 3-bit uniform quantizer.

The quantized sequence corresponding to input $\{0.8, -0.135, -0.35, 0.25, 0.45, 0.9\}$ is

$$\{0.875, -0.375, -0.625, 0.625, 0.875, 0.875\}$$

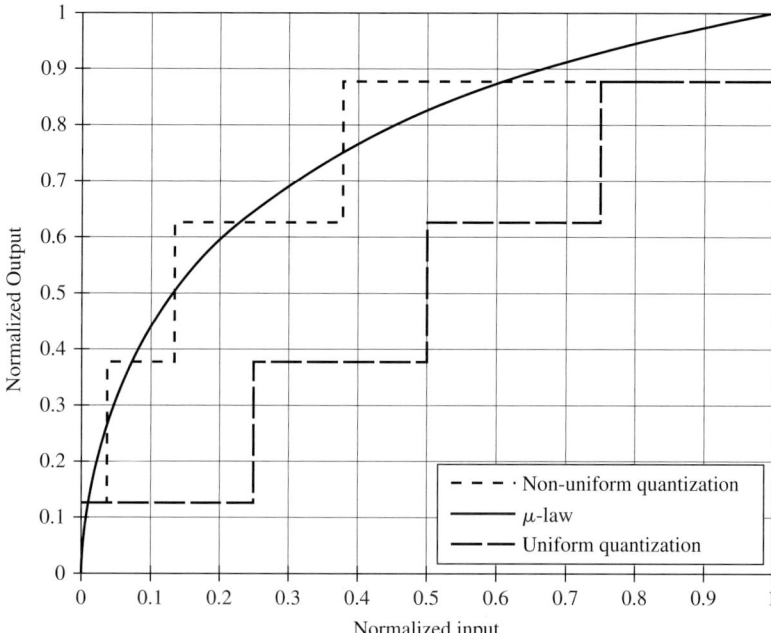

Figure 8.27 $\mu = 15$ law quantization.

Piecewise Linear Segment Companding

In an actual PCM system, the compression characteristic is implemented using a **piecewise linear** approximation to (8.45). The $\mu = 255$ compression characteristic is approximated by a set of eight straight line segments as shown in Figure 8.28.[1] It is seen that successively larger input signal segments are compressed into uniform output segments. Each segment is approximated by a 16-level uniform quantizer with step size doubling between successive segments. The 8-bit PCM codewords use sign-magnitude representation. The format of a PCM codeword is shown in Figure 8.29. The most significant bit is used as the sign bit. The next three bits represent the segment number. The last four bits identify a particular level in the 16-level uniform quantizer.

---

[1] C. Dammann, L. McDaniel, and C. Maddox, "D2 Channel Bank—Multiplexing and Coding," *Bell System Technical Journal* 51, (1972): 1675–1700.

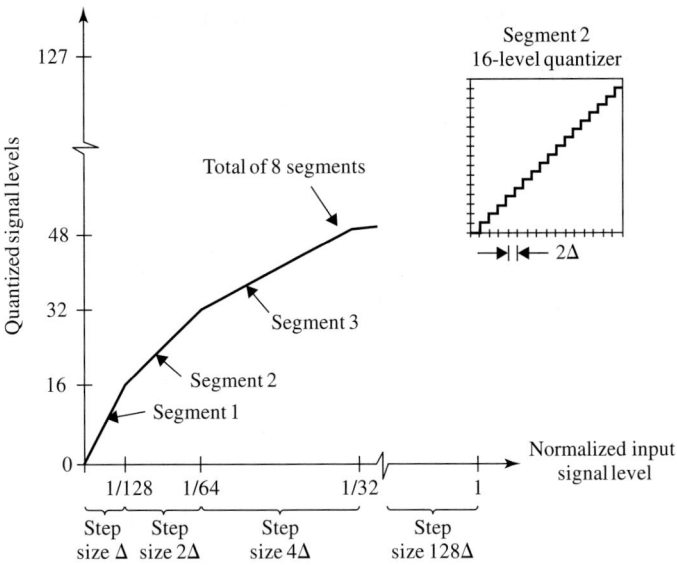

Figure 8.28 $\mu = 255$ compression characteristic per CCITT G.711 recommendation.

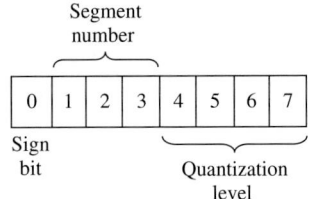

Figure 8.29 PCM codeword format.

Performance of Companded Systems

For the Laplacian distributed message source, the output SQNR using μ-law quantizer is given by[2]

$$SQNR = 6m + 4.77 - 20\log_{10}\left[\log_e(1 + \mu)\right]$$

$$- 10\log_{10}\left[1 + \left(\frac{x_{\max}}{\mu\sigma_x}\right)^2 + \sqrt{2}\left(\frac{x_{\max}}{\mu\sigma_x}\right)\right] \qquad (8.50)$$

Equation (8.50) when compared with (8.40) indicates that the SQNR for the μ-law quantizer does not have strong dependence upon the signal statistics (that is, $\dfrac{x_{\max}}{\sigma_x}$). We observe that as μ increases, the SQNR becomes less and less sensitive to the changes in $\dfrac{x_{\max}}{\sigma_x}$ even though $-20\log_{10}\left[\log_e(1 + \mu)\right]$ term reduces the SQNR. For $\mu >> 1$, the dependence of SQNR on message statistics is very small and SQNR can be approximated as

$$SQNR = 6m + 4.77 - 20\log_{10}\left[\log_e(1 + \mu)\right] \qquad (8.51)$$

Equation (8.51) states that μ-law quantization also follows the 6-dB law as in the case of uniform quantization. Substituting $\mu = 255$ in (8.51) yields

$$SQNR = 6m + 4.77 - 20\log_{10}\left[\log_e(1 + 255)\right]$$

$$= 6m + 4.77 - 14.87 \approx 6m - 10 \text{ dB} \qquad (8.52)$$

---

[2] B. Smith, "Instantaneous Companding of Quantized Signals," *Bell System Technical Journal* 36, no. 3 (1957): 653–709.

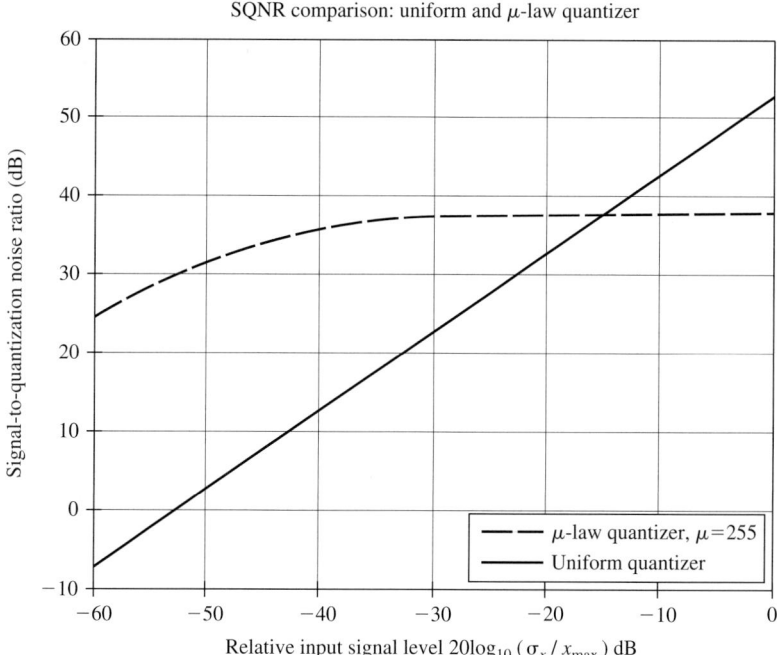

Figure 8.30 Performance comparison of uniform and μ-law quantizers.

Figure 8.30 illustrates the performance comparison of uniform and μ-law quantizers for the Laplacian distributed message source. We can see from the figure that the μ-law quantizer can maintain acceptable SQNR over a reasonably wide range on input signal power levels. On the other hand, the SQNR of a uniform quantizer decreases linearly as the input power drops.

It can be shown that the output SQNR for A-law quantization also follows the 6-dB law.[3] That is,

$$SQNR = 6m + 4.77 - 20\log_{10}(1 + \ln A) \tag{8.53}$$

Substituting $A = 87.6$ in (8.53) yields

$$SQNR = 6m + 4.77 - 20\log_{10}\big[1 + \ln(87.6)\big]$$

$$= 6m + 4.77 - 14.76 \approx 6m - 10 \text{ dB} \tag{8.54}$$

Example 8.8

In a landline public switched telephone network, the voice signal is LP filtered to preserve frequencies up to 3.4 kHz. The intent here is simply to achieve audio quality that allows the recognition of the speaker's voice at the other end of the line rather than high-quality audio reproduction. The resultant signal is sampled at 8 kHz. Telephony PCM equipment uses nonuniform quantizers. Calculate the number of bits required per sample to guarantee a SNR specification of 40 dB.

---

[3] Smith, "Instantaneous Companding of Quantized Signals," 653–709.

Solution

Assuming μ-law quantization, the number of bits required per sample is calculated using (8.52) as

$$40 = 6m - 10$$

Therefore, $m = (40 + 10)/6 \approx 8$.

Thus the PCM bit rate for telephony voice is given by

$$8{,}000 \text{ samples/second} \times 8 \text{ bit/sample} = 64 \text{ kbps}$$

It can be observed that high-quality audio signals require much higher data rates than are required for telephone voice, as discussed in Example 8.6.

The digitization of analog signals using PCM may result in unacceptably high bit rates for some applications because no attempt is made to reduce the number of bits required by taking advantage of statistical dependencies between samples. We now consider other waveform coding techniques that remove the redundancy present in the PCM format, thereby yielding more efficient digital representations of the original analog signal.

8.5   DIFFERENTIAL PULSE CODE MODULATION

When a voice or video signal is sampled at a rate slightly higher than the Nyquist rate, as is usually done in PCM, the resulting samples exhibit a high degree of statistical correlation. That is, consecutive samples will tend to have values that are close to each other in sections where the signal is changing slowly. As a result, **the dynamic range of differences between consecutive samples is substantially less than that of the original samples** as illustrated in Figure 8.31. In a PCM system, each sample is quantized independently, and previous sample values have no effect on the quantization of the current sample. Because of the memoryless nature of the quantization process, the resulting digital signal contains redundant information. In differential pulse code modulation

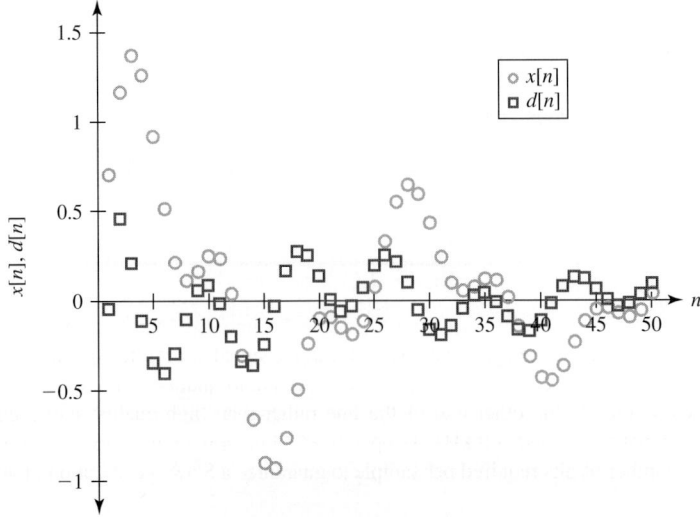

Figure 8.31 Dynamic range of differences between adjacent samples.

(DPCM), the correlation between adjacent signal samples is removed by subtracting from the current input sample an estimate based on previous samples and quantizing the difference instead of quantizing the input sample itself. This leads to a more efficient digital representation of the original analog signal when compared to PCM because it takes fewer bits to quantize the difference signal for the same SQNR performance.

Figure 8.32 displays the block diagram of a DPCM system. The input signal to the quantizer is the difference between the current sample value $x[n]$ and the predicted value $\hat{x}[n]$.

$$d[n] = x[n] - \hat{x}[n] \tag{8.55}$$

The signal $d[n]$ is called the **prediction error,** because it is the amount by which the prediction filter fails to predict the input exactly. The quantizer output may be expressed as

$$y[n] = d[n] + e[n] \tag{8.56}$$

where $e[n]$ is the quantization error. The quantizer output $y[n]$ is added to the predicted value $\hat{x}[n]$ to produce the prediction filter input

$$x_q[n] = \hat{x}[n] + y[n] \tag{8.57}$$

Substituting (8.56) into (8.57), we get

$$x_q[n] = \hat{x}[n] + d[n] + e[n]$$
$$= x[n] + e[n] \tag{8.58}$$

Thus $x_q[n]$ represents a quantized version of the input sample $x[n]$. The quantized sample $x_q[n]$ at the prediction filter input differs from the original input sample $x[n]$ by the quantization error $e[n]$, irrespective of the prediction filter complexity. Accordingly, if the prediction is good, the variance of the prediction error $d[n]$ will be smaller than the variance of $x[n]$. Therefore, a quantizer with fewer number of levels (compared to

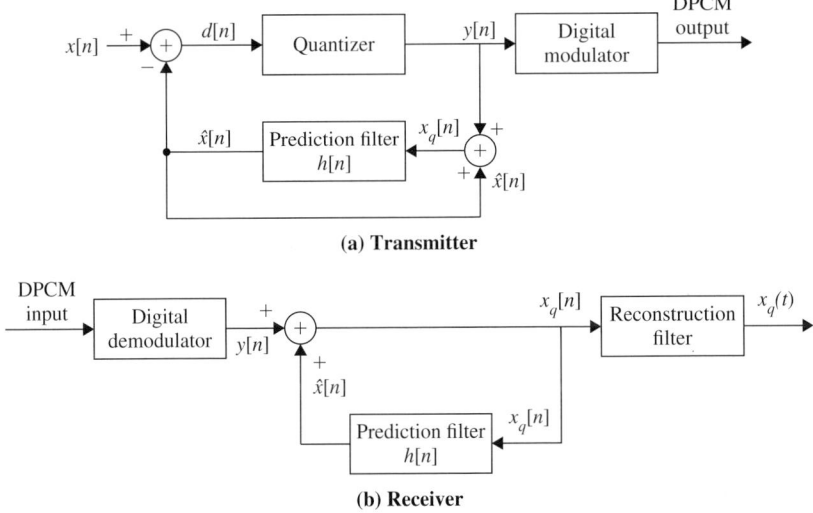

(a) Transmitter

(b) Receiver

Figure 8.32 Differential PCM system.

PCM) can be used to produce the same quantization error variance. The quantizer output $y[n]$ is converted into binary pulses by a digital modulator for transmission.

The receiver for reconstructing the quantized version of the input signal is shown in Figure 8.32(b). It consists of a digital demodulator that recovers the quantized error signal $y[n]$ in the absence of channel noise induced errors. The receiver reconstructs the quantized version of the input sample, $x_q[n]$, from the demodulator output $y[n]$ by adding to it the predicted value of the current sample, $\hat{x}[n]$, using the same prediction circuitry and data as is used in the transmitter. The receiver output is, therefore, given by

$$x_q[n] = \hat{x}[n] + y[n] \tag{8.59}$$

The receiver output $x_q[n]$ differs from the original input sample $x[n]$ by the quantization error $e[n]$ as indicated by (8.58). Because the error $e[n]$ depends only on the current prediction error value $d[n]$, there is no quantization error propagation in the DPCM system.

The prediction filter is usually implemented by a **finite impulse response (FIR)** design in which N previous reconstructed output samples are used to predict the value of the next sample. That is,

$$\hat{x}[n] = h_1 x_q[n-1] + h_2 x_q[n-2] + \ldots + h_N x_q[n-N] \tag{8.60}$$

In the simplest case, if a first-order prediction filter is used, the predicted value of current sample $\hat{x}[n]$ is given by $h_1 x_q[n-1]$. In general the prediction becomes more accurate as more terms are used in the prediction filter. We observe that the prediction is not in terms of the N previous input samples $x[n-1]$, $x[n-2]$, ..., $x[n-N]$, but rather in terms of the N previous reconstructed output samples $x_q[n]$. The reason is that the previous input sample values are not available at the receiver. By using the same data, the prediction filter at the transmitter and receiver generates the same sequence of prediction values $\hat{x}[n]$.

Prediction Gain

We assume the input signal sample sequence $x[n]$ is a discrete-time random process with zero mean and variance σ_x^2. The output signal-to-noise ratio of the DPCM system is defined as:

$$SNR_{\text{DPCM}} = \frac{\text{Average signal power}}{\text{Average noise power}} = \frac{\sigma_x^2}{\sigma_e^2} \tag{8.61}$$

where σ_e^2 is the variance of the quantization error $e[n]$. We express the right-hand side of (8.61) as the product of two factors as follows:

$$SNR_{\text{DPCM}} = \frac{\sigma_x^2 \sigma_d^2}{\sigma_d^2 \sigma_e^2} = G_p SQNR_{\text{PCM}} \tag{8.62}$$

where

$$\sigma_d^2 = \text{Variance of the prediction error}$$

$$SQNR_{\text{PCM}} = \frac{\sigma_d^2}{\sigma_e^2} = \text{SQNR of the quantizer} \tag{8.63}$$

$$G_p = \frac{\sigma_x^2}{\sigma_d^2} = \text{Prediction gain} \tag{8.64}$$

Note that $SQNR_{\text{PCM}}$ is the same as defined in (8.38) except that the signal term here refers to the difference signal $d[n]$ rather than the input signal $x[n]$. G_p is the **prediction gain** produced by the DPCM scheme. The quantity G_p, when greater than unity, represents the gain in SNR of a DPCM system. Now, for a given baseband (message) signal, the variance σ_x^2 is fixed, so that G_p is maximized by minimizing the variance σ_d^2 of the prediction error $d[n]$. Accordingly, the prediction filter should be designed to minimize σ_d^2 by proper choice of the filter order N and coefficients $\{h_1, h_2, \ldots, h_N\}$. In the case of voice signals, it is found that the optimum SNR advantage of the DPCM over PCM is in the neighborhood of 4 to 11 dB. The greatest improvement occurs in going from no prediction to first-order prediction, with some additional gain resulting from increasing the order of the prediction filter up to 4 or 5, after which little additional gain is obtained. Because each 6-dB reduction in the $SQNR_{\text{PCM}}$ requirement corresponds to 1 bit of saving per sample by virtue of (8.41), the advantage of DPCM may also be expressed in terms of bit rate. For the same SNR requirement, and assuming a sampling rate of 8 KHz, the use of DPCM may provide a saving of about 8 to 32 kbps (i.e., 1 to 4 bits of saving per sample) compared to the standard PCM. The CCITT has adopted the G.722 multirate DPCM standard (16/24/32/40 kbps) for voice encoding, which uses an adaptive quantizer as well as on-the-fly calculation of the FIR prediction filter coefficients to maximize the prediction gain. This is called **adaptive DPCM (ADPCM).**

8.6 OVERSAMPLING IN ANALOG-TO-DIGITAL CONVERSION

Oversampling means sampling the input analog signal at a rate f_s much higher than the Nyquist rate ($2B$). The ratio between the actual sampling rate and the Nyquist rate is referred to as the **oversampling ratio.**

$$\text{Oversampling ratio } K = \frac{f_s}{2B} \tag{8.65}$$

where B is the bandwidth of the analog signal. The main advantage of oversampling is the reduction in the quantization noise floor achieved by spreading it over a wider bandwidth. The mean-square quantization noise power for a uniform m-bit quantizer with $2V$ volt full-scale range is given from (8.36) as

$$\sigma_e^2 = \frac{\Delta^2}{12} = 2^{-2m} V^2/3 \tag{8.66}$$

The quantization noise for a Nyquist rate ADC is approximately Gaussian and spread more or less uniformly over the signal band $[-B, B]$ as shown by the unshaded rectangle in Figure 8.33. In this case the spectral density of the quantization noise is given by

$$G_e(f) = \frac{\sigma_e^2}{2B} \tag{8.67}$$

The quantization noise power σ_e^2 is fixed and independent of the sampling frequency. So if the signal is oversampled, say, at f_s Hz, the same noise power is spread over much wider bandwidth $[-f_s/2, f_s/2]$ as shown by the shaded rectangle in Figure 8.33. The spectral density of the quantization noise is, therefore, reduced to the value

$$G_e(f) = \frac{\sigma_e^2}{f_s}, \qquad -f_s/2 \le f \le f_s/2 \tag{8.68}$$

In the oversampled case, only a relatively small fraction of the total noise power falls in the band of interest $[-B, B]$. The noise power outside the signal band can be greatly attenuated with a digital LP filter following the ADC. After the LP filtering is performed, the signal can be downsampled to the Nyquist rate without any aliasing. This may be achieved by passing every Kth sample to the output and discarding the rest using a factor of K down-sampler. The collective operation of LP filtering and down-sampling is known as **decimation.**

The in-band noise power for the oversampled converter using (8.68) is given by

$$P_e = \int_{-B}^{B} \frac{\sigma_e^2}{f_s} df = \frac{2B\sigma_e^2}{f_s} = \frac{\sigma_e^2}{K} \tag{8.69}$$

Thus, when we oversample a bandlimited signal, the quantization noise power in the signal band is reduced by the factor K, where K is the oversampling ratio. This has the effect of increasing SQNR in (8.38) by $10\log_{10} K$ dB. Therefore, the SQNR of an oversampled converter is obtained from (8.41) and (8.43) as

$$SQNR = 6m - 7.25 + 10\log_{10}K \text{ dB} \qquad \text{Arbitrary message input signal} \tag{8.70}$$

$$SQNR = 6m + 1.77 + 10\log_{10}K \text{ dB} \qquad \text{Sinusoidal input signal} \tag{8.71}$$

Equations (8.70) and (8.71) state that the SQNR of an ADC can be increased by a factor of $10\log_{10}K$ when oversampling at K times the Nyquist rate. Let the oversampling ratio $K = 2^r$. Substituting into (8.70) yields

$$SQNR = 6m - 7.25 + 10\log_{10}2^r$$
$$= 6m - 7.25 + 3r \tag{8.72}$$

Thus, doubling the sampling frequency improves the SQNR by 3 dB, which is equivalent to increasing the ADC resolution by half a bit. Oversampling by a factor of $K = 2^{2r} = 4^r$ is required to achieve an r bit increase in the resolution or, equivalently, $6r$ dB

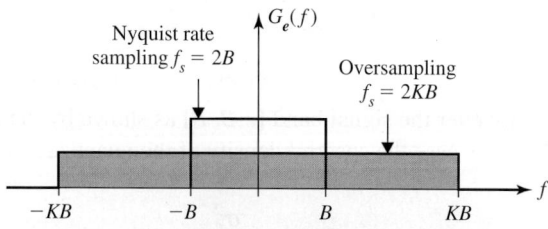

Figure 8.33 Quantization noise power spectral density for Nyquist rate versus oversampled conversion.

improvement in the SQNR of an ADC. This is not a favorable trade-off. For example, a 1-bit ADC with $4^3 = 64 \times$ oversampling achieves a resolution of four bits. To achieve 16-bit resolution, oversampling by a factor of 4^{15} is required, which is not practical.

Example 8.9

An audio system handles signals with a baseband that extends from 0 to 20 kHz. Determine the oversampling factor and the sampling frequency that will be necessary to achieve a performance that would be obtained with a 16-bit ADC using an 8-bit converter.

Solution

The SQNR achieved with 8- and 16-bit Nyquist-rate sampling ADCs are given using (8.41) as

$$\text{8-bit ADC: } SQNR = 6 \times 8 - 7.25 = 40.75 \text{ dB}$$

$$\text{16-bit ADC: } SQNR = 6 \times 16 - 7.25 = 88.75 \text{ dB}$$

Using (8.70), the performance of an oversampled 8-bit ADC is given by

$$SQNR = 40.75 + 10\log_{10}K \text{ dB}$$

For the SQNR of an 8-bit ADC with the oversampling ratio K to equal that of a Nyquist 16-bit ADC, we must have

$$88.75 = 40.75 + 10\log_{10}K$$

or

$$K = 10^{4.8} \approx 2^{16} = 65,536$$

Because the oversampling factor $K = \dfrac{f_s}{2B}$, the upsampling rate to achieve the same SQNR as for 16-bit ADC with an 8-bit ADC is given by

$$f_s = (65,536)(20000)(2) = 2.6214 \text{ GHz}$$

This is a very high sampling rate that cannot cost-effectively be implemented by current CMOS technology. The penalty is, however, not so high if a 12-bit ADC is used to achieve the performance of a 16-bit ADC as shown below. For the SQNR of a 12-bit ADC with the oversampling ratio K to equal that of a Nyquist 16-bit ADC, we must have

$$24 = 10\log_{10}K \text{ dB}$$

or

$$K = 10^{2.4} \approx 2^8 = 256$$

The upsampling rate to achieve the same SQNR as for 16-bit ADC with a 12-bit ADC is given by

$$f_s = (256)(20000)(2) = 10.24 \text{ MHz}$$

Another benefit of the oversampling is that it relaxes the requirements on the analog anti-aliasing filter. The anti-aliasing filter can have a transition band between B and $f_s/2$ as long as it provides very good attenuation beyond $f_s/2$, as shown in Figure 8.34. However, the digital LP filter must attenuate the remaining quantization noise power

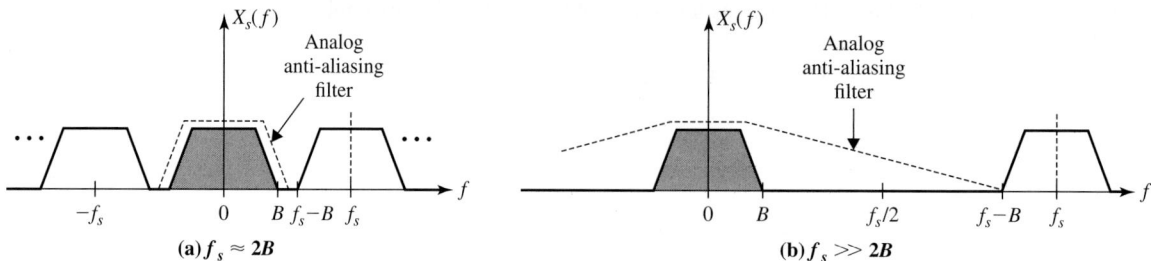

Figure 8.34 Anti-aliasing filter requirements in an oversampled system.

(beyond B) as much as possible. In the process of filtering out-of-band quantization noise, any other noise that existed in the transition band of the anti-aliasing filter prior to sampling will be attenuated further.

8.7 DELTA MODULATION

Delta modulation (DM) is a simplified version of the DPCM system: the prediction filter is first-order (a pure delay device) and the quantizer is two-level ($\pm\Delta$). By using a single bit to represent each sample, the sample rate and the output bit rate are equivalent. A block diagram of a DM system is shown in Figure 8.35. In delta modulation, because a 1-bit quantizer is employed, the quantization noise will be high unless the dynamic range of the difference ("error") signal $d(t)$ is much less than that of the input signal $x(t)$. This, in turn, means that the adjacent samples $x[n]$ and $x[n-1]$ must be highly correlated. Therefore, in DM, the input signal $x(t)$ is oversampled (i.e., at a rate usually much higher than the Nyquist rate) with the intent to increase the correlation between adjacent samples $x[n]$ and $x[n-1]$. Because the number of bits per sample is only one, the total number of bits per second required to transmit a waveform is consequently anticipated to be lower than that for a PCM system.

At the transmitter, the input sample $x[n] = x(nT_s)$ is compared with the predicted value $\hat{x}[n]$ and the difference

$$d[n] = x[n] - \hat{x}[n] \tag{8.73}$$

is applied to the quantizer. Because $\hat{x}[n] = x_q[n-1]$ in DM, (8.73) can be written as

$$d[n] = x[n] - x_q[n-1] \tag{8.74}$$

The output of the quantizer is given by

$$y[n] = \text{sgn}(d[n]) = \text{sgn}(x[n] - x_q[n-1]) \tag{8.75}$$

where $\text{sgn}(x)$ is defined in (2.18).

The quantizer functions like a comparator. When the input $d[n]$ exceeds zero, it outputs $+1$; when the input is less than zero, the output is -1. The output of the quantizer $y[n]$ is mapped into binary pulses by a digital modulator for transmission. At the receiver, the digital demodulator recovers the quantized difference signal sample $y[n]$. The current output sample is now reconstructed by adding $y[n]$ to the receiver output value during the previous sample period. That is,

$$x_q[n] = \Delta y[n] + x_q[n-1] \tag{8.76}$$

The recurrence relation in (8.76) for the reconstruction at the receiver can be expressed as

$$x_q[n] = \Delta y[n] + x_q[n-1] = \Delta y[n] + \Delta y[n-1] + x_q[n-2]$$

$$= \ldots = \Delta \sum_{i=1}^{n} y[i] + x_q[0]$$

$$= \Delta \sum_{i=1}^{n} y[i] \tag{8.77}$$

where we have assumed zero initial condition ($x_q[0] = 0$). Equation (8.77) states that to obtain $x_q[n]$, one only has to accumulate the values of $y[n]$. This simplifies the block diagram in Figure 8.35 to that of Figure 8.36.

The reconstructed signal $x_q(t)$ provides a **staircase approximation** to $x(t)$ from the quantized samples $x_q[n]$ as shown in Figure 8.37. Note that in the start-up phase, the

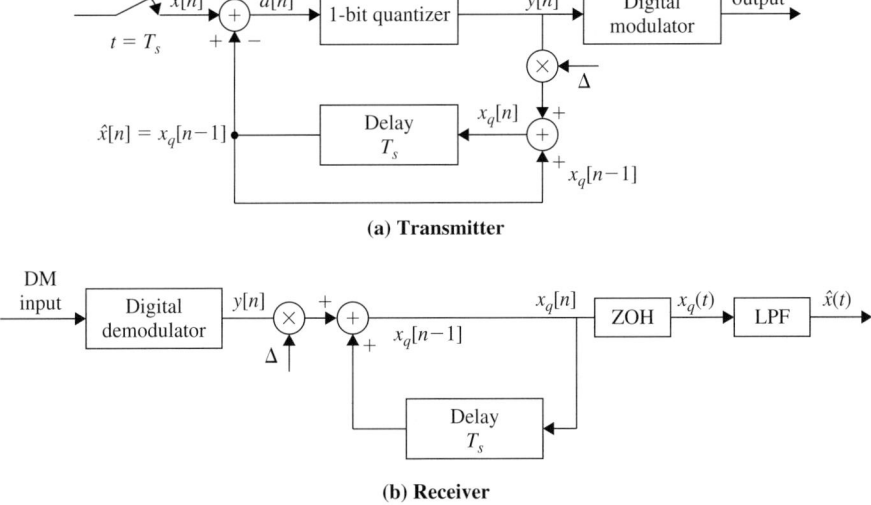

Figure 8.35 Delta modulation system: (a) transmitter; (b) receiver.

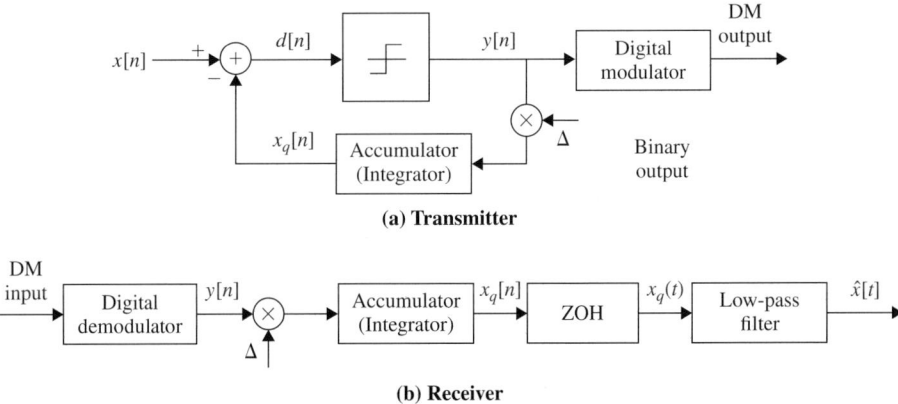

Figure 8.36 Practical implementation of DM system: (a) transmitter; (b) receiver.

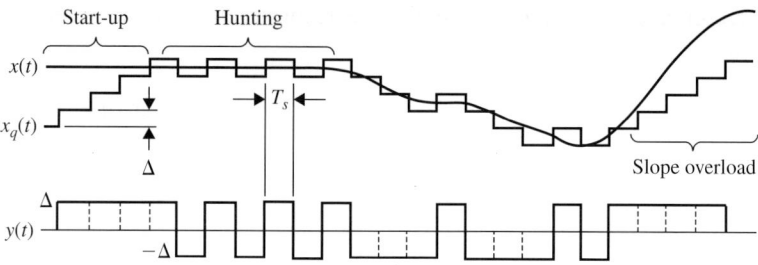

Figure 8.37 DM waveform.

staircase waveform $x_q(t)$ will differ considerably from the message signal $x(t)$. The transmitter outputs several positive pulses in the example illustrated in Figure 8.37 as $x_q(t)$ tries to catch up with $x(t)$. After the fourth pulse, the difference sample is negative, and the next pulse in the transmitter output is negative polarity. After the start-up period, $x_q(t)$ exhibits a **hunting** behavior during the slowly changing segment of $x(t)$. The transmitter output is a sequence of alternating positive and negative pulses, indicating that changes in the signal $x(t)$ are less than the step size. During the steep segment of $x(t)$, the staircase waveform $x_q(t)$ cannot follow the fast-changing input, resulting in **slope overload.** The latter is characterized by a succession of positive (or negative) pulses in the transmitter output.

8.7.1 Slope Overload and Granular Noise

Slope overload occurs when the step size Δ is not large enough to follow the rapid changes in the analog signal $x(t)$. During the sampling interval T_s, the staircase waveform $x_q(t)$ is capable of changing by the height of step size Δ. Thus, the maximum slope $x_q(t)$ can follow is Δ/T_s. If the input waveform's local slope exceeds this value, the staircase waveform cannot follow the changes, and this results in slope overload distortion as shown in Figure 8.38(a). Hence, slope overload occurs if

$$\Delta/T_s < \left|\frac{dx(t)}{dt}\right|_{max} \tag{8.78}$$

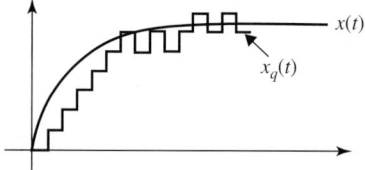

(a) Small Δ and slope overload distortion

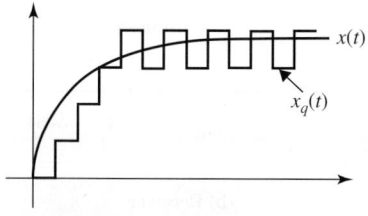

(b) Large Δ and granular noise

Figure 8.38 Slope overload and granular noise.

Let us consider the special case of a sinusoidal waveform $x(t) = A \cos(2\pi f_m t)$. The maximum signal slope is given by

$$\left| \frac{dx(t)}{dt} \right|_{\max} = A 2\pi f_m \tag{8.79}$$

In order to avoid slope overload, it follows from (8.78) that the maximum input signal slope must satisfy

$$\left| \frac{dx(t)}{dt} \right|_{\max} < \Delta/T_s$$

Substituting (8.79) yields

$$A 2\pi f_m < \Delta/T_s \tag{8.80}$$

The maximum amplitude at which the slope overload occurs is given by

$$A_{\max} = \frac{\Delta}{2\pi f_m T_s} = \frac{\Delta f_s}{2\pi f_m} \tag{8.81}$$

The overload amplitude of the modulating signal is inversely dependent on the frequency f_m. For higher modulating frequencies, the overload occurs for smaller amplitudes. For speech signals containing spectral components up to 4 kHz, it has been experimentally determined[4] that the DM will transmit them without noticeable overload if the signal amplitude in (8.81) is calculated with $f_m = 800$ Hz. Therefore, to avoid slope overload, the maximum amplitude for speech signals is given by

$$A_{\max} = \frac{\Delta f_s}{2\pi \times 800} = \frac{\Delta f_s}{1600\pi} \tag{8.82}$$

The slope overload can be alleviated by choosing a large value of step size Δ. On the other hand, if Δ is too large, considerable overshoot occurs during periods when the signal is not changing rapidly. In that case, we have significant quantization noise, called **granular noise,** as displayed in Figure 8.38(b). With random waveforms, such as speech, it is impossible to match the step size to the local input slope at all times. The slope-tracking problem with random waveforms can be alleviated by a strategy that detects the slope overload condition and increases the step size in an adaptive fashion.

8.7.2 Adaptive Delta Modulation

Granular noise and the slope overload distortion performance of DM can be dramatically improved by making dynamic adjustments to the quantizer step size. **Adaptive delta modulation (ADM)** algorithms[5] attempt to do this by selecting Δ in an adaptive fashion according to changes in the input waveform as shown in Figure 8.39. During a slowly varying segment of the input signal, the step size Δ is decreased to minimize the granular noise. However, the step size Δ is increased during a steep segment, so that the

---

[4] F. de Jager, "Delta Modulation, a Method of PCM Transmission Using the 1-Unit Code," *Philips Research Reports* 7 (1952): 442–466.

[5] J. Greefkes and F. de Jager, "Continuous Delta Modulation," *Philips Research Reports* 23 (1968).

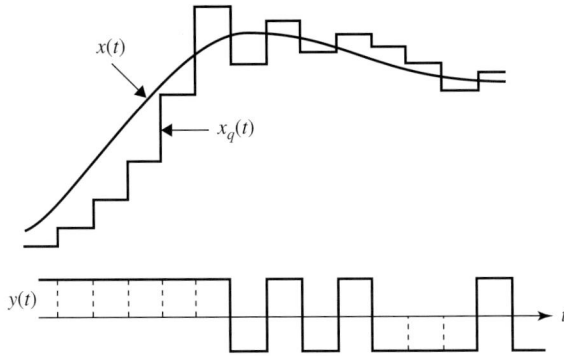

Figure 8.39 Adaptive delta modulation.

staircase waveform can follow the input quickly to reduce the slope overload distortion. To adaptively change the step size, we need to devise a mechanism to monitor the input slope. As discussed in the previous section, this can be accomplished by monitoring the transmitter output stream $y[n]$. If the input signal variation is small relative to the step size, the transmitter output stream alternates between positive and negative polarity pulses. This indicates that the granular noise is the dominant source of noise, and the step size needs to be decreased. The occurrence of slope overload distortion is indicated by a succession of positive or negative polarity transmitter output pulses. In this case, of course, the step size should be increased so that the staircase waveform can catch up with the input during a steep segment.

8.7.3 Continuously Variable Slope Delta Modulation

Continuously variable slope delta (CVSD) modulation is the most well-known ADM algorithm, and it was first proposed in Greefkes and Riemens.[6] Figure 8.40 displays block diagrams of the CVSD transmitter and receiver. The slope overload detection logic in the CVSD algorithm looks at the three most recent bits transmitted $\left(y[n], y[n-1], \text{and } y[n-2] \right)$ to compute the current step size value $\Delta[n]$. Practical implementations of ADM algorithms require appropriate limits on minimum ($\Delta_{\min}$) and maximum step size ($\Delta_{\max}$). That is,

$$\Delta_{\min} \leq \Delta[n] \leq \Delta_{\max} \tag{8.83}$$

$\Delta_{\max}$ controls the amount of slope overload distortion, while $\Delta_{\min}$ sets the amount of granular noise. The step-size adaptation rule within these constraints is described by

$$\Delta[n] = \beta \Delta[n-1] + \alpha[n]\Delta_{\max} \tag{8.84}$$

The value of parameter β in (8.84) is close to 1 and is chosen between 0.9 and 0.995. $\alpha[n]$ is computed by the logical expression

$$\alpha[n] = y[n]y[n-1]y[n-2] \oplus \bar{y}[n]\bar{y}[n-1]\bar{y}[n-2] \tag{8.85}$$

where $\oplus$ indicates logical XOR operations.

[6] J. A. Greefkes and K. Riemens, "Code Modulation with Digitally Controlled Companding for Speech Transmission," *Philips Technical Review* (1970): 335–353.

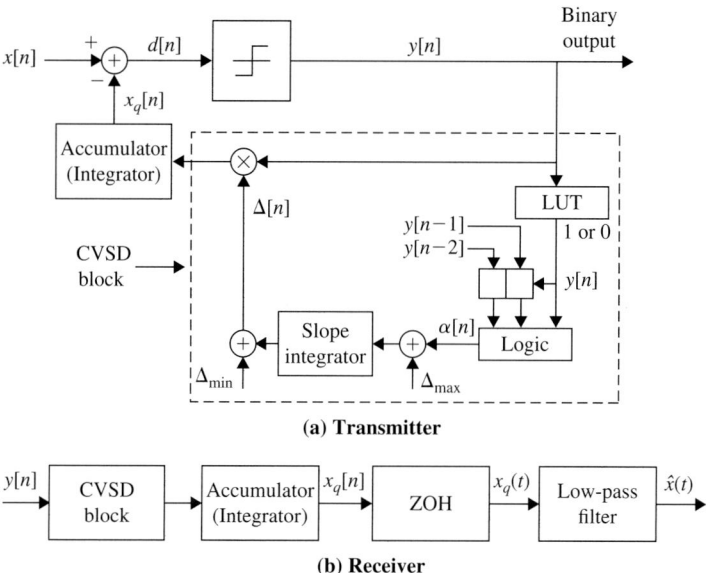

(a) Transmitter

(b) Receiver

Figure 8.40 CVSD transmitter and receiver.

The block labeled CVSD in Figure 8.40 implements (8.84) to calculate the current step size $\Delta[n]$. The **look-up table (LUT)** performs polar to unipolar translation $\big($that is, $y[n] = 1$, LUT outputs 1; $y[n] = -1$, LUT outputs $0\big)$. When three consecutive 1's or -1's occur at the transmitter output $\big(y[n]$'s$\big)$ indicating a steep segment, $\alpha[n] = 1$, the step size is increased to Δ_{max}. On the other hand, if strings of three consecutive 1's or -1's do not occur, $\alpha[n] = 0$. If this condition persists for a long enough period of time, the output of the slope integrator decays to near zero at the rate β, but never below the minimum step size Δ_{min}. When this size is reached, the system degenerates to DM, until the change in input causes the step size to increase again. Equation (8.84) is classified as an additive increase, multiplicative decrease algorithm. Jayant and Noll discuss many variants of (8.84) and other algorithms to adjust the step size and their performance for speech and image signals.[7] CVSD is used in tactical communications where good speech quality and security are required. MIL-STD-188-113 (16 kbps and 32 kbps), and Federal Standard 1023 (12 kbps) are examples of tactical communication systems using CVSD. CVSD is also available as an option in Bluetooth technology.

8.7.4 Quantization Noise

The quantization error in delta modulation is the difference between the original signal and the staircase approximation

$$\boldsymbol{e}[n] = \boldsymbol{x}[n] - \boldsymbol{x}_q[n] \tag{8.86}$$

We assume that the sampling rate and step size are chosen so as to avoid the slope overload condition. Under this assumption, the quantization error due to granular noise lies in the range $[-\Delta, \Delta]$. If we further assume that all signal amplitudes are equally

---

[7] N. Jayant and P. Noll, *Digital Coding of Waveforms: Principles and Applications to Speech and Video* (Upper Saddle River, NJ: Prentice-Hall, 1984).

likely, the quantization error is uniformly distributed over the range $[-\Delta, \Delta]$. Using the arguments leading to (8.36), the mean-square quantization noise is given by

$$\sigma_e^2 = \int_{-\Delta}^{\Delta} e^2 \frac{1}{2\Delta} de = \Delta^2/3 \tag{8.87}$$

It has been verified experimentally that the quantization noise is uniformly distributed over the frequency range $[-f_s, f_s]$. The bandwidth of the LP filter in the DM receiver is equal to the message bandwidth B. Therefore, the average noise power at the filter output is given by

$$N_Q = \frac{\Delta^2 B}{3f_s} = \frac{\Delta^2 B T_s}{3} \tag{8.88}$$

For a sinusoidal message signal, the maximum signal amplitude to avoid slope overload is given by (8.81). This corresponds to maximum output signal power

$$P_{max} = \frac{A_{max}^2}{2} = \frac{\Delta^2}{8\pi^2 (f_m T_s)^2} \tag{8.89}$$

Combining (8.88) and (8.89), we obtain the output SNR for a DM system with sinusoidal input as

$$SNR_{DM} = \frac{P_{max}}{N_Q} = \frac{3\Delta^2}{8\pi^2 (f_m T_s)^2 \Delta^2 B T_s} = \frac{3}{8\pi^2 f_m^2 T_s^3 B} \tag{8.90}$$

As discussed in Section 8.7.1, the maximum output signal power for speech signals is given by substituting (8.82) into (8.89) as

$$P_{max} = \frac{A_{max}^2}{2} = \frac{\Delta^2 f_s^2}{2(1600\pi)^2} \tag{8.91}$$

The output SNR at the output of a DM system for speech signals is given by combining (8.88) and (8.91) as

$$SNR_{DM} = \frac{P_{max}}{N_Q} = \frac{3f_s^3}{2(1600\pi)^2 B} \tag{8.92}$$

Equations (8.90) and (8.92) represent maximum achievable SNR values, because no slope overload distortion and minimum granular noise were assumed in deriving these expressions.

Example 8.10

Calculate the sampling frequency required in a DM to achieve the output SNR = 40 dB for speech signals. Assume that the demodulator LP filter bandwidth = 4 kHz.

Solution

The DM output SNR for speech signals is given from (8.92) as

$$SNR_{DM} = \frac{3f_s^3}{2(1600\pi)^2 B}$$

This yields

$$f_s^3 = \frac{2}{3}(1600\pi)^2 B \times SNR_{DM}$$

Substituting $B = 4 \times 10^3$ and $SNR = 10^4$, we obtain

$$f_s^3 = \frac{2}{3}(1600\pi)^2 \times 4 \times 10^3 \times 10^4 = \frac{80 \times 2.56 \times \pi^2}{3} \times 10^{12}$$

or

$$f_s = 87.67 \text{ kHz}$$

Because in DM transmission the bit rate equals the sampling rate, the bit rate required to send a speech signal using DM is 87.67 kbps. Recall from Example 8.8 that for the same SNR performance, PCM requires a serial bit rate of 64 kbps. Thus PCM is superior to DM in this case.

Example 8.11

Calculate the output SNR in a DM system for speech signals for sampling rates of 32 and 64 kHz. Compare the performance with equivalent bit-rate PCM systems. Assume a standard sampling rate of 8 kHz and speech signal bandwidth $B = 4$ kHz.

Solution

The DM output SNR for speech signals is given from (8.92) as

$$SNR_{DM} = \frac{3f_s^3}{2(1600\pi)^2 B}$$

In dB form

$$SNR_{DM} = 10\log_{10}\left(\frac{3f_s^3}{2(1600\pi)^2 B}\right) = 30\log_{10} f_s - 18.285 \text{ dB} \qquad (8.93)$$

where f_s is the sampling frequency in kHz. Thus SNR for $f_s = 32$ kHz is given from (8.93) as

$$SNR_{DM} = 30\log_{10} f_s - 18.285 = 30\log_{10} 32 - 18.285 = 26.9 \text{ dB}$$

Similarly for $f_s = 64$ kHz, the SNR for a DM system is

$$SNR_{DM} = 30\log_{10} f_s - 18.285 = 30\log_{10} 64 - 18.285 = 35.93 \text{ dB}$$

Thus doubling the sampling rate in a DM system increases output SNR by 9 dB. In the case of PCM systems, the output SNR is given from (8.41) as

$$SQNR = 6m - 7.25 \text{ dB}$$

For a 32-kbps PCM system, substituting $m = 4$ yields

$$SQNR = 6 \times 4 - 7.25 = 16.75 \text{ dB}$$

Similarly, for a 64-kbps PCM system, substituting $m = 8$ yields

$$SQNR = 6 \times 8 - 7.25 = 40.75 \text{ dB}$$

	Output SNR (dB)	
	32 kbps	64 kbps
DM	26.9	35.9
PCM	16.75	40.75

Thus, DM can outperform PCM at low bit rate, but it is inferior to PCM at the higher bit rate.

Experiment 8.3   *Delta Modulation*

In this experiment, we simulate a DM system using Simulink. A 1.5-Hz sine wave with peak amplitude 1V is used as a message signal. The Simulink model for the DM system is shown in Figure 8.41(a). The model implements block diagrams of delta modulator and demodulator in Figure 8.36. An LP digital filter recovers the original message signal from the reconstructed quantized staircase approximation $x_q[n]$. Figure 8.41(b) displays the waveforms obtained using a sampling rate of 96 Hz corresponding to $32 \times$ oversampling. A step size of 0.125 is selected. The waveforms obtained using a sampling rate of 96 Hz and a step size of 0.0625 are shown in Figure 8.41(c). Note the slope overload effect resulting from the choice of finer step size.

Figure 8.41 (a) Simulink model for the DM system; (b) DM waveforms: $32 \times$ oversampling, $\Delta = 0.125$; (c) DM waveforms: Slope overload with $32 \times$ oversampling, $\Delta = 0.0625$.

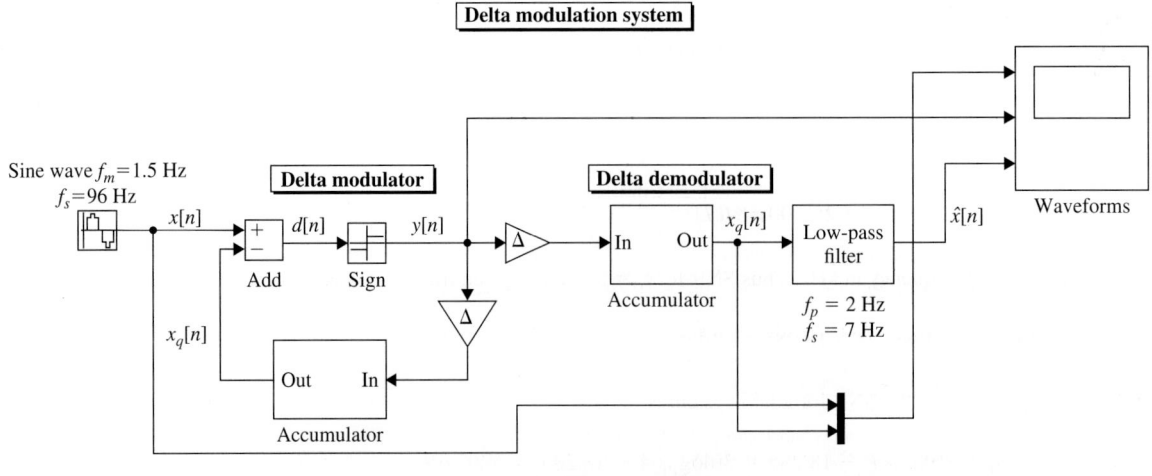

(a)

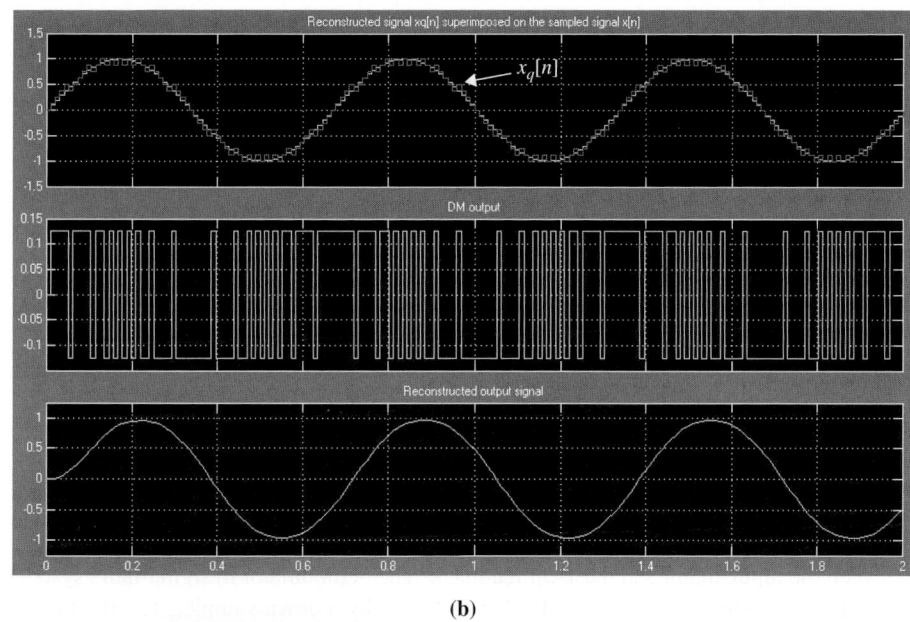

(b)

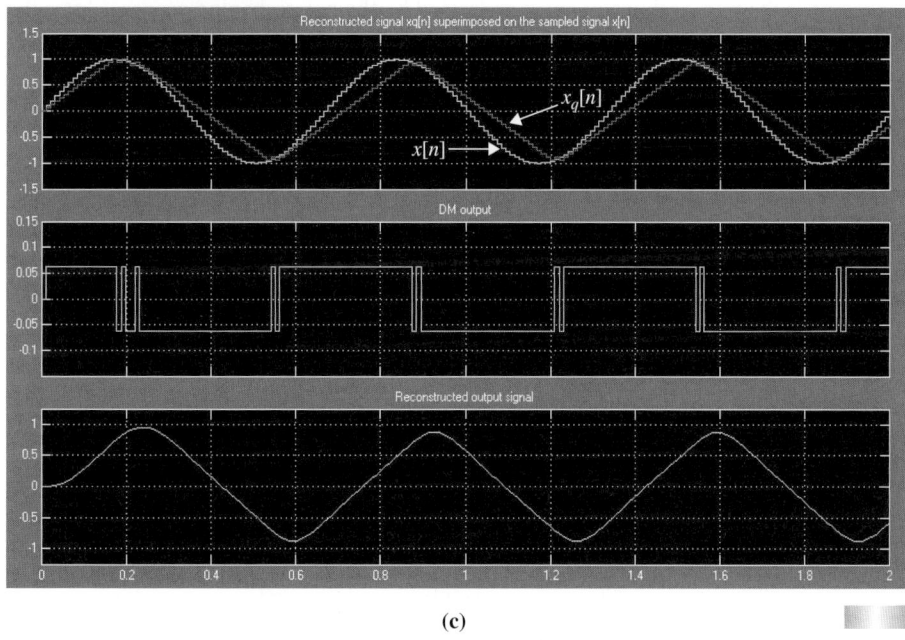

(c)

8.8 SIGMA-DELTA MODULATION

Sigma-delta modulation systems[8] also use a feedback modulator design as in DM systems. In a delta modulator, the feedback is used to generate a difference signal with smaller dynamic range, which can be quantized with a small step size and a commensurately small quantization error. In contrast, a sigma-delta modulator employs feedback

[8] S. R. Norsworthy, R. Schreier, and G. C. Temes, eds. *Delta–Sigma Data Converters, Theory, Design, and Simulation* (New York: IEEE Press, 1997); P. Aziz, H. V. Sorensen, and J. van der Spiegel, "An Overview of Sigma-Delta Converters," *IEEE Signal Processing Magazine*, January 1996, 61–84.

to implement **noise shaping** so that the quantization noise is pushed outside the signal band. Both systems employ oversampling to reduce the quantization noise power in the signal band by spreading it across the entire bandwidth to $f_s/2$, that is, above the band of interest. However, the effect of noise shaping in a sigma-delta modulator is to further redistribute the quantization noise so that most of it lies between B and $f_s/2$.

8.8.1 First-Order Sigma-Delta Modulation

The block diagram of a first-order sigma-delta modulator is shown in Figure 8.42. The modulator consists of an integrator, a 1-bit ADC or quantizer, and a 1-bit DAC or zero-order hold (ZOH) in the feedback path. Note that the integrator (accumulator) is moved from the feedback path (as in DM) to the forward path just before the 1-bit ADC.

To understand the operation of a sigma-delta modulator, it is convenient to consider the discrete-time equivalent circuit of Figure 8.43(a). The integrator has been replaced by a discrete-time version with transfer function $\dfrac{z^{-1}}{1-z^{-1}}$. It accumulates the difference between the input signal and the 1-bit feedback. The demodulator in sigma-delta system consists of a **decimator,** a digital LP filter followed by a down-sampler. The digital filter removes the high-frequency noise generated by the noise-shaping process. After the LP filtering is performed, the signal can be downsampled to the Nyquist rate by a factor of K down-sampler without any loss of information.

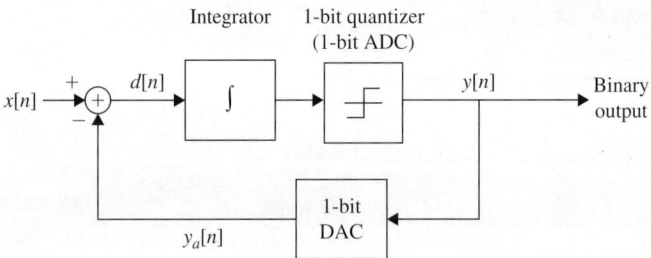

Figure 8.42 First-order sigma-delta modulator.

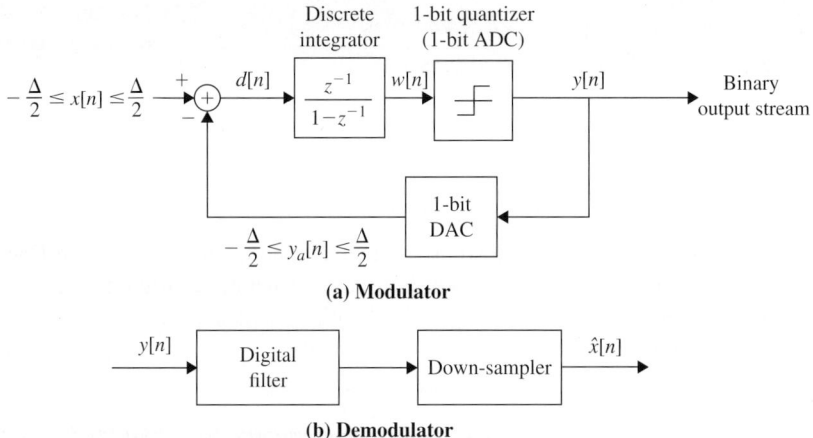

(a) Modulator

(b) Demodulator

Figure 8.43 Discrete-time model of first-order sigma-delta system.

8.8.2 Noise Performance

Figure 8.44 displays a linearized model of a first-order sigma-delta modulator where the 1-bit quantizer is replaced with a noise source $e[n]$. The signal that is quantized is a filtered version of the difference between the input $x[n]$ and the analog representation $y_a[n]$ of the quantized output $y[n]$. Now

$$y[n] = w[n] + e[n] \qquad (8.94)$$

where

$$w[n] = d[n-1] + w[n-1]$$
$$= x[n-1] - y_a[n-1] + w[n-1] \qquad (8.95)$$

If the DAC is ideal, it is replaced by a unity gain transfer function, and (8.95) can be expressed as

$$w[n] = x[n-1] - y[n-1] + w[n-1] = x[n-1] - e[n-1] \qquad (8.96)$$

Substituting (8.96) into (8.94) yields

$$y[n] = x[n-1] + e[n] - e[n-1] \qquad (8.97)$$

The output of the sigma-delta modulator is simply a delayed version of the signal plus quantization noise quantity $e[n] - e[n-1]$. The signal and noise transfer functions are obtained from (8.97) as

$$H_s = z^{-1} \qquad (8.98)$$

$$H_e = 1 - z^{-1} \qquad (8.99)$$

Note that the quantization noise has been shaped by a first-order discrete-time differentiator. The PSD of output noise due to sigma-delta modulation is given by

$$G_{n_{out}}(f) = G_e(f)|H_e(f)|^2 \qquad (8.100)$$

where $G_e(f)$ is a spectral density of the quantization noise. Substituting (8.36) into (8.68) yields

$$G_e(f) = \frac{\sigma_e^2}{f_s} = \frac{\Delta^2}{12 f_s} \qquad (8.101)$$

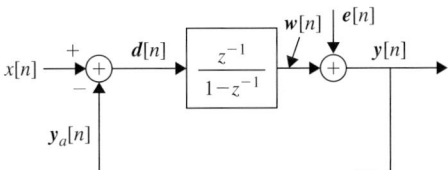

Figure 8.44 Linearized model of first-order sigma-delta modulator.

Now

$$|H_e(f)|^2 = \left|1 - z^{-1}\right|^2_{z=e^{j\omega T_s}} = \left|1 - e^{-j\omega T_s}\right|^2 = 4\sin^2\left(\frac{\omega T_s}{2}\right) = 4\sin^2\left(\frac{\pi f}{f_s}\right) \quad (8.102)$$

Substituting (8.101) and (8.102) into (8.100) yields

$$G_{n_{out}}(f) = \frac{\Delta^2}{3f_s}\sin^2\left(\frac{\pi f}{f_s}\right) \quad (8.103)$$

The magnitude spectrum of a first-order sigma-delta noise transfer function is plotted in Figure 8.45. Note that the quantization noise has been shaped in such a way that more of the noise power is outside the signal band than in the oversampling-only case, where the noise spectrum is flat. The output quantization noise power in the signal band is given by

$$N_{out} = \int_{-B}^{B} G_{n_{out}}(f)df = \frac{\Delta^2}{3f_s}\int_{-B}^{B}\sin^2\left(\frac{\pi f}{f_s}\right)df$$

$$= \frac{2\Delta^2}{3f_s}\int_{0}^{B}\sin^2\left(\frac{\pi f}{f_s}\right)df \quad (8.104)$$

For very large oversampling ratio K,

$$\sin^2(\pi f/f_s) \approx (\pi f/f_s)^2 \quad (8.105)$$

over the signal band. Substituting (8.105) into (8.104) yields

$$N_{out} = \frac{2\Delta^2}{3f_s}\int_{0}^{B}(\pi f/f_s)^2 df = \frac{2\pi^2\Delta^2 B^3}{9f_s^3} \quad (8.106)$$

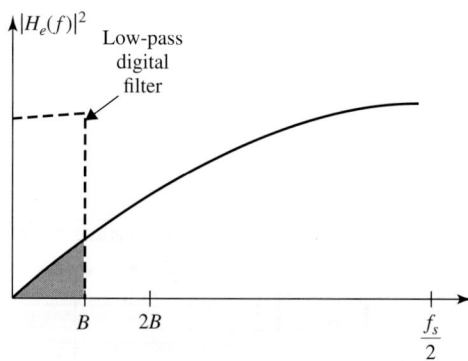

Figure 8.45 Noise shaping by the first-order sigma-delta system.

Because $K = f_s/2B$, (8.106) simplifies to

$$N_{out} = \frac{\pi^2 \Delta^2}{36 K^3} \tag{8.107}$$

Assuming a sinusoidal input of peak amplitude $\Delta/2$ as shown in Figure 8.43, the signal power is given by

$$P_{out} = \frac{1}{2}\left(\frac{\Delta}{2}\right)^2 \tag{8.108}$$

Combining (8.107) and (8.108), the output SNR of a first-order sigma-delta modulator is

$$SNR = \frac{P_{out}}{N_{out}} = \frac{1}{2}\left(\frac{\Delta}{2}\right)^2 \frac{36 K^3}{\pi^2 \Delta^2} = \frac{9 K^3}{2\pi^2} \tag{8.109}$$

or in dB form

$$SNR = 10\log_{10}\left(\frac{9}{2\pi^2}\right) + 10\log_{10}(K^3) = -3.41 + 30\log_{10} K \tag{8.110}$$

Let the oversampling ratio $K = 2^r$. Substituting into (8.110) we obtain

$$SNR = -3.41 + 30\log_{10}(2^r) = -3.41 + 9r \tag{8.111}$$

For every doubling of the oversampling ratio K, that is, for every increment in r, the SNR improves by 9 dB, or equivalently, the resolution improves by 1.5 bits.

Example 8.12

Calculate the sampling rate required using a first-order sigma-delta ADC to convert a 20-kHz bandwidth audio to CD-quality resolution of 16 bits. Compare the results with those obtained in Example 8.9.

Solution

From Example 8.9, the SQNR achieved with a 16-bit ADC using Nyquist-rate sampling is 88.75 dB. To achieve the performance of a 16-bit ADC, the oversampling ratio for a first-order sigma-delta ADC is obtained from (8.110) as

$$88.75 = -3.41 + 30\log_{10} K$$

or

$$\log_{10} K = 92.16/30 \Rightarrow K = 10^{3.072} = 1180$$

The oversampling rate to achieve the same SNR as for 16-bit ADC with a first-order sigma-delta ADC is given by

$$f_s = (1180)(20000)(2) = 47.21 \text{ MHz}$$

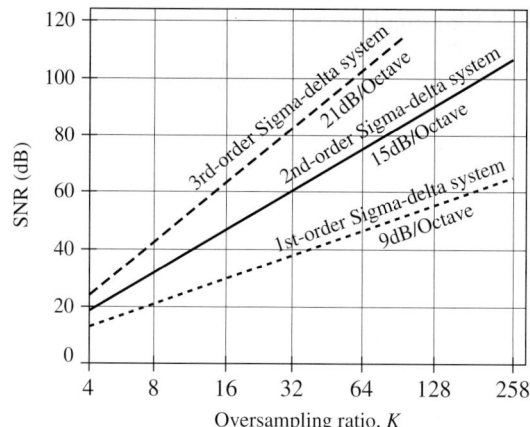

Figure 8.46 Performance of higher-order sigma-delta systems.

This is a much more reasonable sampling rate than obtained in Example 8.9, and can be implemented using current CMOS technology. The sigma-delta converter does not need as high an oversampling ratio as the oversampled PCM discussed in Section 8.6 because it not only spreads but also shapes the quantization noise so that most of it falls outside the signal passband as shown in Figure 8.45.

Higher-order sigma-delta modulators containing more than one integrator in the forward path can be used for increased resolution.[9] As shown in Figure 8.46, second-order sigma-delta modulators provide a 15-dB/octave improvement in SNR, which is equivalent to a 2.5-bit increase in resolution.

Experiment 8.4 *Sigma-Delta Modulation*

In this experiment, we simulate a sigma-delta modulation system using Simulink. A 1.5-Hz sine wave with peak amplitude 1V is used as the message signal. The Simulink model for the system is shown in Figure 8.47(a) which implements the discrete-time model in Figure 8.43. A fourth-order Butterworth digital filter with 2.25-Hz cutoff frequency recovers the original message signal from the modulator output binary stream. Figure 8.47(b) displays the waveforms obtained using a sampling rate of 48 Hz corresponding to 16 × oversampling. The modulator and reconstructed output waveforms for 32 × oversampling are displayed in Figure 8.47(c).

Figure 8.47 (a) Simulink model of first-order sigma-delta modulation system; (b) first-order sigma-delta modulator waveforms, 16 × oversampling; (c) first-order sigma-delta modulator waveforms, 32 × oversampling.

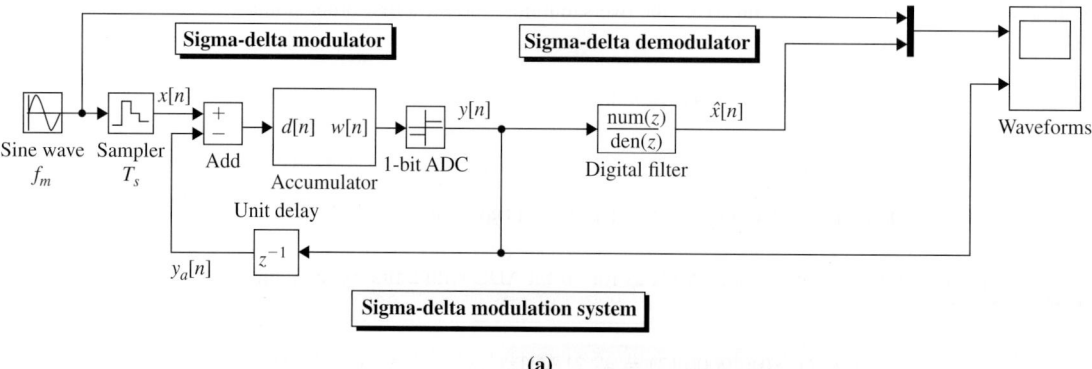

(a)

[9] J. Candy, "Decimation for Sigma Delta Modulation," *IEEE Transactions on Professional Communication* COM-34, (1986): 72–76.

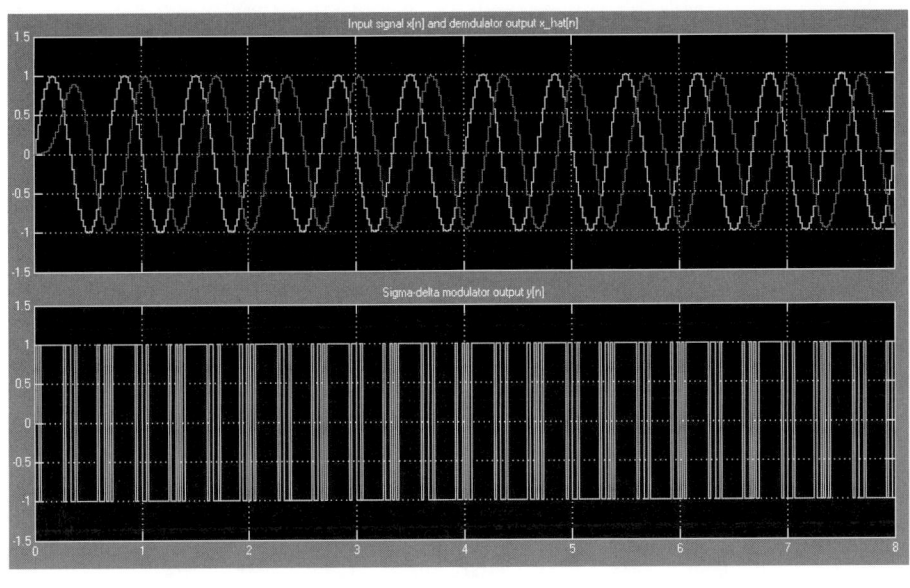

(b)

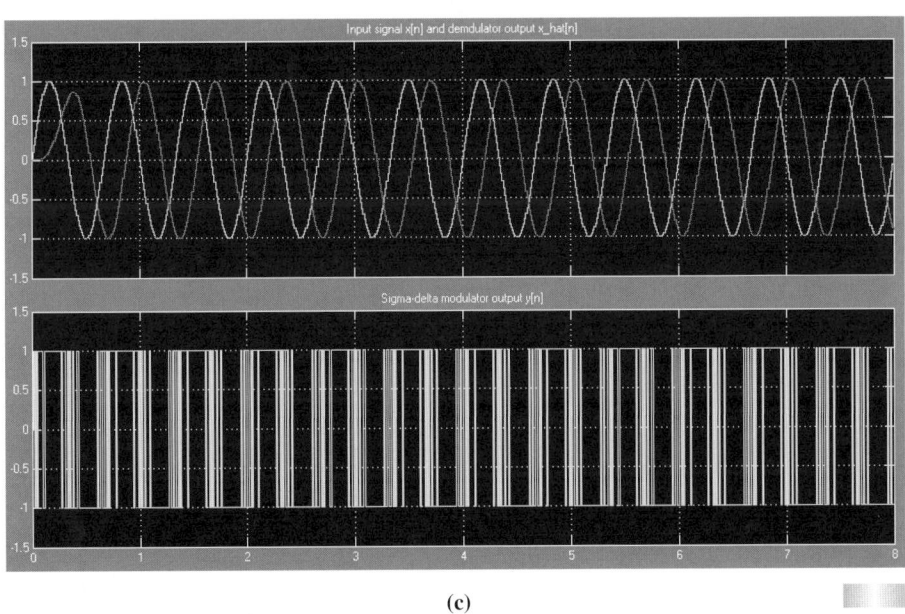

(c)

8.9   SAMPLING THEOREM FOR BANDPASS SIGNALS

The sampling theorem described in Section 8.1.2 tells us that the sampling rate must be at least twice the highest frequency in the signal to recover the original signal without any impairments due to aliasing. Consider a bandpass (BP) signal occupying the frequency band $[f_L, f_H]$ and bandwidth $B_{IF} = f_H - f_L$. Such a signal needs to be sampled at twice the highest frequency f_H to avoid aliasing, that is, $f_s \geq 2 f_H$. Bandpass signals used in many communication systems, such as cellular and satellite, are usually **narrowband,** that is, their bandwidths are a small fraction ($<<1$) of their carrier frequencies. So $f_H = f_c + B_{IF}/2$ is

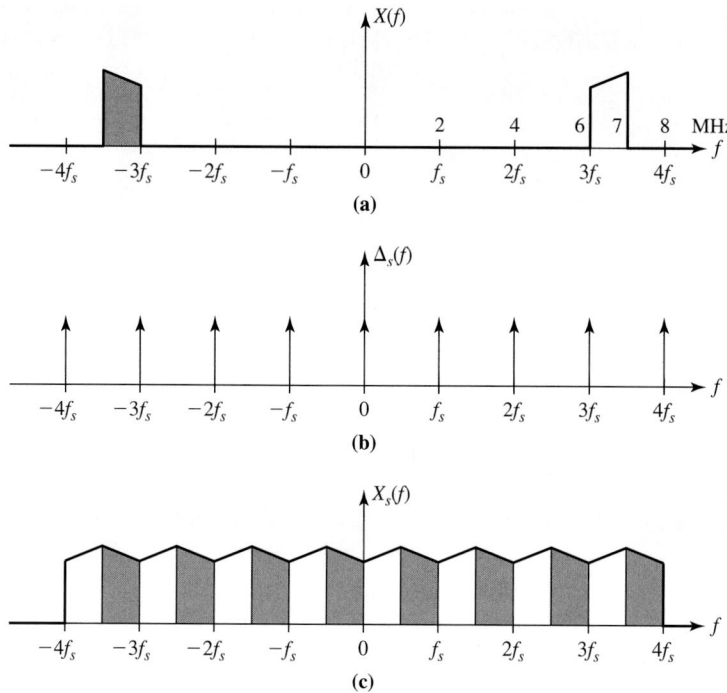

Figure 8.48 Spectrum of the sampled signal for the case $f_L/f_s = 3$.

very large, and consequently the sampling rate also has to be very large, which may not be practical in some situations. A more economical approach to digitizing BP signals therefore involves undersampling them and using the resultant aliasing to advantage.

Let us consider the case where a signal of 1-MHz bandwidth lies between 6 and 7 MHz as illustrated in Figure 8.48. Suppose the signal is sampled at *twice* the signal bandwidth, $f_s = 2$ MHz. Note that the lower bandedge frequency f_L is an odd integer multiple of the sampling frequency. Using (8.6), the spectrum of the sampled signal $X_s(f)$ is obtained by convolving the spectrum of the signal in Figure 8.48(a) with $\Delta_s(f)$ in Figure 8.48(b). That is,

$$X_s(f) = X(f) \otimes \Delta_s(f) = f_s \sum_{n=-\infty}^{\infty} X(f - nf_s) = f_s \sum_{n=-\infty}^{\infty} X(f - 2nB_{IF}) \qquad (8.112)$$

The sampled signal spectrum $X_s(f)$ consists of frequency-translated replicas of $X(f)$ centered at all harmonics of the sampling frequency f_s as shown in Figure 8.48(c). Although the signal is sampled at twice its bandwidth rather than the highest frequency in the signal, there is no aliasing, so any one of these replicas of $X(f)$ is an accurate representation of the original signal. Notice that in particular, the component of $X_s(f)$ lying in the baseband region between DC and 1 MHz is of special interest, as will be discussed later.

Next consider the case where a 1-MHz bandwidth signal occupies the frequency band between 7 and 8 MHz, as shown in Figure 8.49(a). The signal is again sampled at twice the signal bandwidth B_{IF}, that is, $f_s = 2$ MHz. Note that the upper bandedge frequency f_H is an even integer multiple of the sampling frequency. The spectrum of the sampled signal $X_s(f)$ is displayed in Figure 8.49(c). It consists of frequency-translated replicas of $X(f)$ centered at all harmonics of the sampling frequency f_s. Notice that there is no aliasing, so any one of these replicas of $X(f)$ is an accurate representation of the

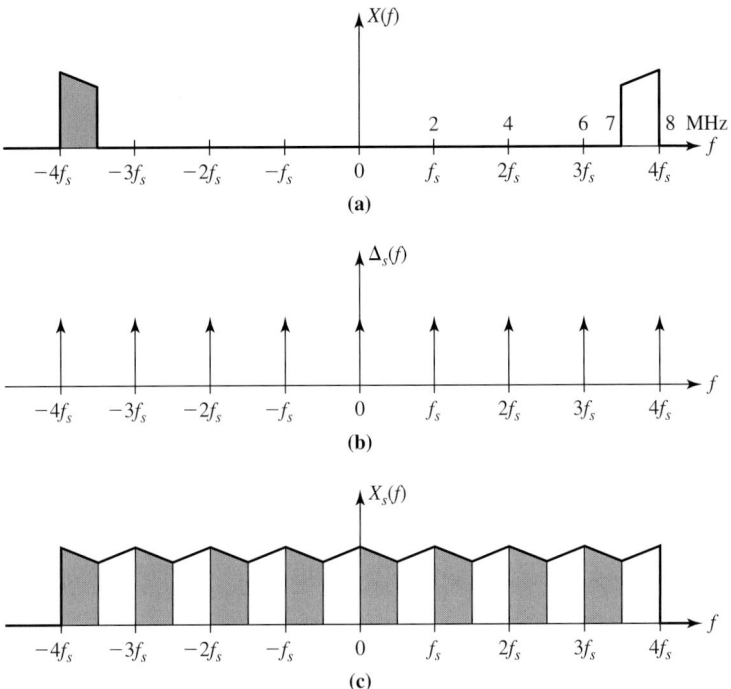

Figure 8.49 Spectrum of the sampled signal for the case $f_H/f_s = 4$.

original signal, except for frequency or spectral inversion. This implies, for example, that the baseband component of $X_s(f)$ lying between DC and 1 MHz has the shape of the negative half of the original signal spectrum. If the original signal spectrum $X(f)$ is symmetrical about the carrier frequency f_c, the spectral inversion does not offer any problem. The frequency inversion in the nonsymmetrical case can be removed by digital signal processing in software.

Finally, we consider the case where a 1-MHz bandwidth signal occupies the frequency band between 7.5 and 8.5 MHz as shown in Figure 8.50(a). The signal is again sampled at $f_s = 2$ MHz. The spectrum of the sampled signal $X_s(f)$ is displayed in Figure 8.50(c). Notice that positive and negative frequency bands of the original signal spectrum $X(f)$ overlap around each harmonic of the sampling frequency f_s and aliasing occurs. Thus the original signal cannot be recovered.

We can make an important observation from Figures 8.48 and 8.49; if one of the bandedge frequencies of the narrowband BP signal is an integer multiple of the bandwidth B_{IF}, it needs to be sampled at a much smaller rate $2B_{IF}$ to avoid aliasing. The choice of sampling frequency should ensure that the spectrum of the signal being sampled falls between integer multiples of 1/2 the sampling frequency. The spectrum of the BP signal in Figure 8.50 instead crosses the $4f_s$, and the resultant aliasing is evident. We are now ready to state the sampling theorem for BP signals as follows[10]:

If a BP signal is integer positioned, that is, one of the bandedge frequencies f_L or f_H is harmonic of the sampling frequency f_s, then the signal can be sampled at the minimum sampling rate of $2B_{IF}$ without any aliasing. That is,

$$f_s = 2 \times B_{IF} \qquad (8.113)$$

[10] R. Vaughan, N. Scott, and D. White, "The Theory of Bandpass Sampling," *IEEE Transactions on Signal Processing* 39, no. 9 (1991): 1973–1984.

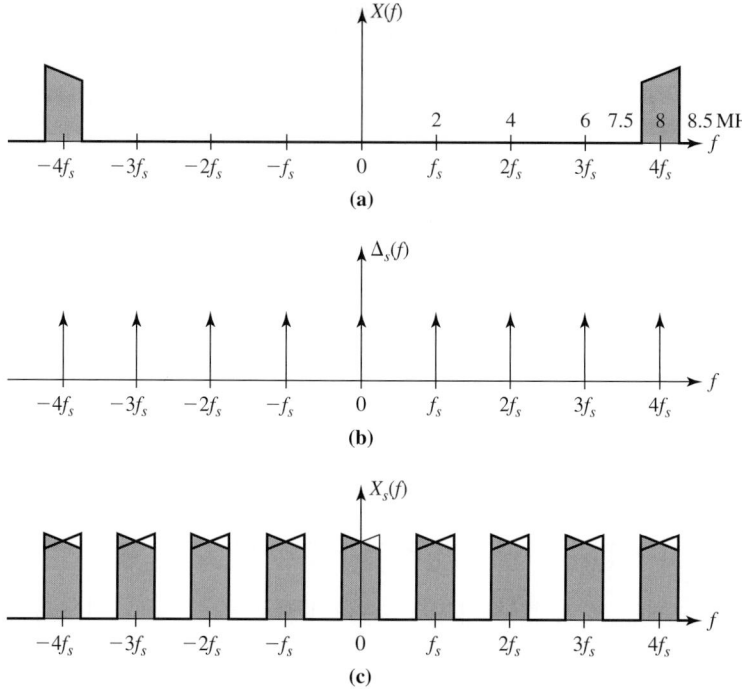

Figure 8.50 Spectrum of the sampled signal for the case $f_H/f_s = 4.25$.

Equation (8.113) is valid as long as either

$$\frac{f_H}{B_{IF}} = n \tag{8.114}$$

or

$$\frac{f_L}{B_{IF}} = n \tag{8.115}$$

For the case where the ratio is an even integer, spectral inversion in the sampled spectrum occurs.

To analyze the case when either f_L or f_H is not a harmonic of the sampling frequency f_s, we have reproduced the spectrum of the BP signal in Figure 8.51(a). Figure 8.51(b) displays a portion of the sampled BP signal spectrum illustrating the negative-frequency components shifted by the $(n-1)$st and the nth harmonics of the sampling frequency. It is clear from Figure 8.51(b) that there is no spectral overlapping if

$$(n - 1)f_s - f_L \leq f_L \tag{8.116}$$

and

$$nf_s - f_H \geq f_H \tag{8.117}$$

From (8.116) and (8.117), we conclude that the sampling frequency f_s for a BP signal must satisfy the following two inequalities in order to avoid aliasing

$$\frac{(n - 1)}{2}f_s \leq f_L \tag{8.118}$$

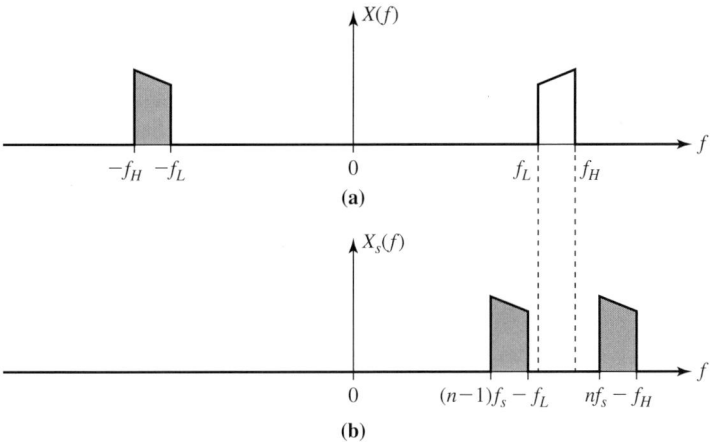

Figure 8.51 (a) Spectrum of the BP signal; (b) negative-frequency components shifted by the $(n-1)$st and the nth harmonics of f_s

and

$$f_H \leq nf_s - f_H$$

or

$$f_H \leq \frac{nf_s}{2} \tag{8.119}$$

From (8.119), we can write

$$f_s \geq 2\left(\frac{f_H}{n}\right) = 2B_{IF}\left(\frac{\left(\dfrac{f_H}{B_{IF}}\right)}{n}\right) \tag{8.120}$$

Because $f_s \geq 2B_{IF}$, it follows from (8.120) that

$$n \leq \frac{f_H}{B_{IF}} \tag{8.121}$$

We can now state the sampling theorem for BP signals as follows:

A BP signal occupying the frequency band $[f_L, f_H]$ and bandwidth $B_{IF} = f_H - f_L$ can be exactly reconstructed from its samples through BP filtering if the sampling frequency f_s satisfies

$$\frac{2f_H}{n} \leq f_s \leq \frac{2f_L}{n-1} \tag{8.122}$$

where the maximum value of integer n is given by

$$n_{\max} = \left\lfloor \frac{f_H}{B_{IF}} \right\rfloor, \quad \lfloor x \rfloor = \text{largest integer} \leq x \tag{8.123}$$

The choice of $n = n_{max}$ results in the smallest sampling rate

$$(f_s)_{min} = \frac{2f_H}{n_{max}} \approx 2B_{IF} \qquad (8.124)$$

Example 8.13

Determine the smallest possible sampling frequency to avoid aliasing in the example illustrated in Figure 8.44.

Solution

A 1-MHz bandwidth signal occupies the frequency band between $f_L = 7.5$ and $f_H = 8.5$ MHz. n_{max} is given from (8.123) as

$$n_{max} = \left\lfloor \frac{f_H}{B_{IF}} \right\rfloor = \left\lfloor \frac{8.5}{1} \right\rfloor = 8$$

Therefore, the smallest possible sampling frequency is obtained from (8.124) as

$$f_s = \frac{2f_H}{n_{max}} = \frac{2 \times 8.5}{8} = 2.125 \text{ MHz}$$

SNR Degradation Due to Undersampling

If the BP signal is sampled at sub-Nyquist rate, it results in the degradation of the SQNR. The SQNR of an undersampled ADC for the sinusoidal input signal can be estimated using (8.71) as

$$SQNR = 6m + 1.77 + 10 \log_{10}\left(\frac{f_s}{2f_H}\right)$$

$$= 6m + 1.77 - 10 \log_{10}\left(\frac{f_H}{f_s/2}\right) \qquad (8.125)$$

where $2f_H$ is Nyquist bandwidth of the BP signal. For example, if the ratio of the sampling frequency to the highest frequency in the signal $\frac{f_H}{f_s} = 3$, the SQNR degradation is approximately 7.8 dB, and the degradation increases to 13 dB for $\frac{f_H}{f_s} = 10$. It is thus obvious that the SQNR decreases by 3 dB for each doubling of the ratio $\frac{f_H}{f_s}$. From (8.124), it can be seen that the largest value of $\frac{2f_H}{f_s}$ corresponds to $n = n_{max}$. Substituting into (8.125) yields the worst-case SQNR degradation as

$$\text{Maximum SQNR degradation} = 10 \log_{10}(n_{max}) \text{ dB} \qquad (8.126)$$

Thus there is a trade-off involved between minimizing the sampling rate f_s and the resultant degradation in SQNR. Thus it is better to choose a higher sampling rate (that is, $n < n_{max}$) within the technology constraints to assure an acceptable SQNR degradation for a given application.

Example 8.14

Consider the cellular CDMA system operating in the band 869–894 MHz.

a. Determine the smallest possible sampling frequency to avoid aliasing. What is the corresponding SQNR degradation?
b. Determine the smallest value of the sampling frequency that results in SQNR loss no larger than 8 dB.

Solution

a. n_{max} is given from (8.123) as

$$n_{max} = \left\lfloor \frac{f_H}{B_{IF}} \right\rfloor = \left\lfloor \frac{894}{25} \right\rfloor = 35$$

Therefore, the smallest possible sampling frequency is given from (8.124) as

$$f_s = \frac{2f_H}{n_{max}} = \frac{2 \times 894}{35} = 51.0857 \text{ MHz}$$

The worst-case SQNR degradation $= 10\log_{10}(35) = 15.44$ dB

b. To keep SQNR degradation less than 8 dB, $10\log_{10}(n) \leq 8$. Therefore, $n \leq 6$. The smallest possible sampling frequency under this constraint is given from (8.124) as

$$f_s = \frac{2f_H}{6} = \frac{2 \times 894}{6} = 298 \text{ MHz}$$

Experiment 8.5   *Natural Sampling of a BP Random Signal*

In this experiment, we simulate natural sampling of a BP random signal using Simulink. The Simulink model is illustrated in Figure 8.52(a). The Random Number block from the Simulink Sources library generates the sequence of normally distributed random numbers with a mean of 0 and a variance of 1. The anti-aliasing filter limits the bandwidth of the random signal to a frequency band [80–120] Hz. It is implemented as a Chebyshev II BP filter of order 12. The sampling of the LP signal is accomplished by multiplying it with a 10% duty cycle rectangular pulse train with period $T_s = 1/125$. The original random signal is reconstructed using an order 8 elliptic BP filter with 70 and 130 Hz lower and upper passband edge frequencies, respectively. The reconstructed waveform in Figure 8.52(b) appears to be a faithful reproduction of the original analog BP signal. Figure 8.52(c) displays simulated spectra of the sampled and reconstructed signals.

Figure 8.52 (a) Simulink model to study natural sampling of a BP random signal; (b) waveforms; (c) simulated spectra.

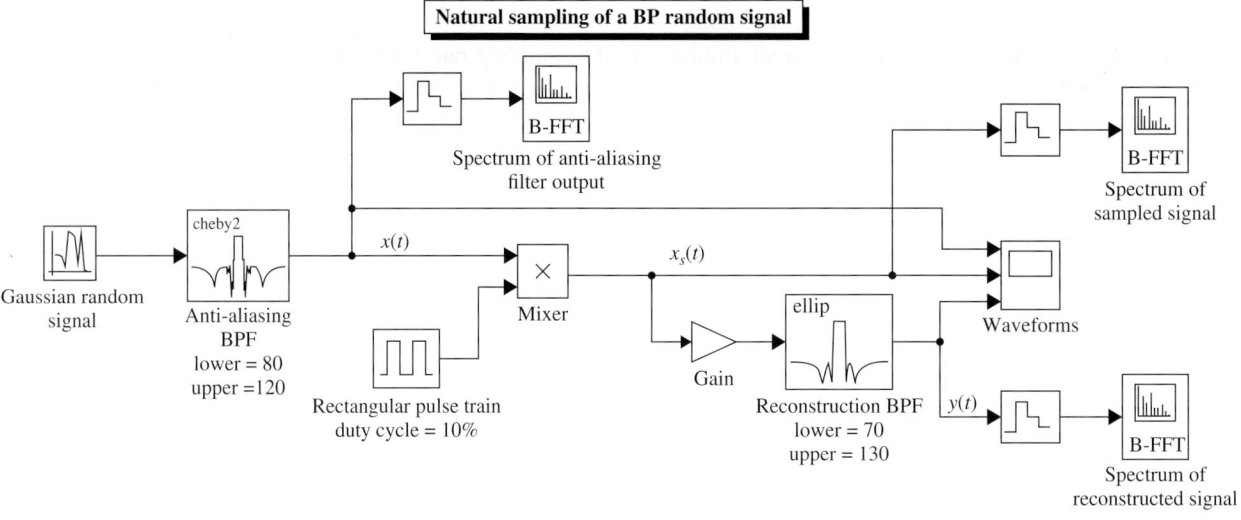

Natural sampling of a BP random signal
B-FFT
Spectrum of anti-aliasing filter output
B-FFT
Spectrum of sampled signal
cheby2
x(t)
x_s(t)
Gaussian random signal
Anti-aliasing BPF
lower = 80
upper =120
Mixer
Rectangular pulse train
duty cycle = 10%
Gain
ellip
Reconstruction BPF
lower = 70
upper = 130
Waveforms
y(t)
B-FFT
Spectrum of reconstructed signal

(a)

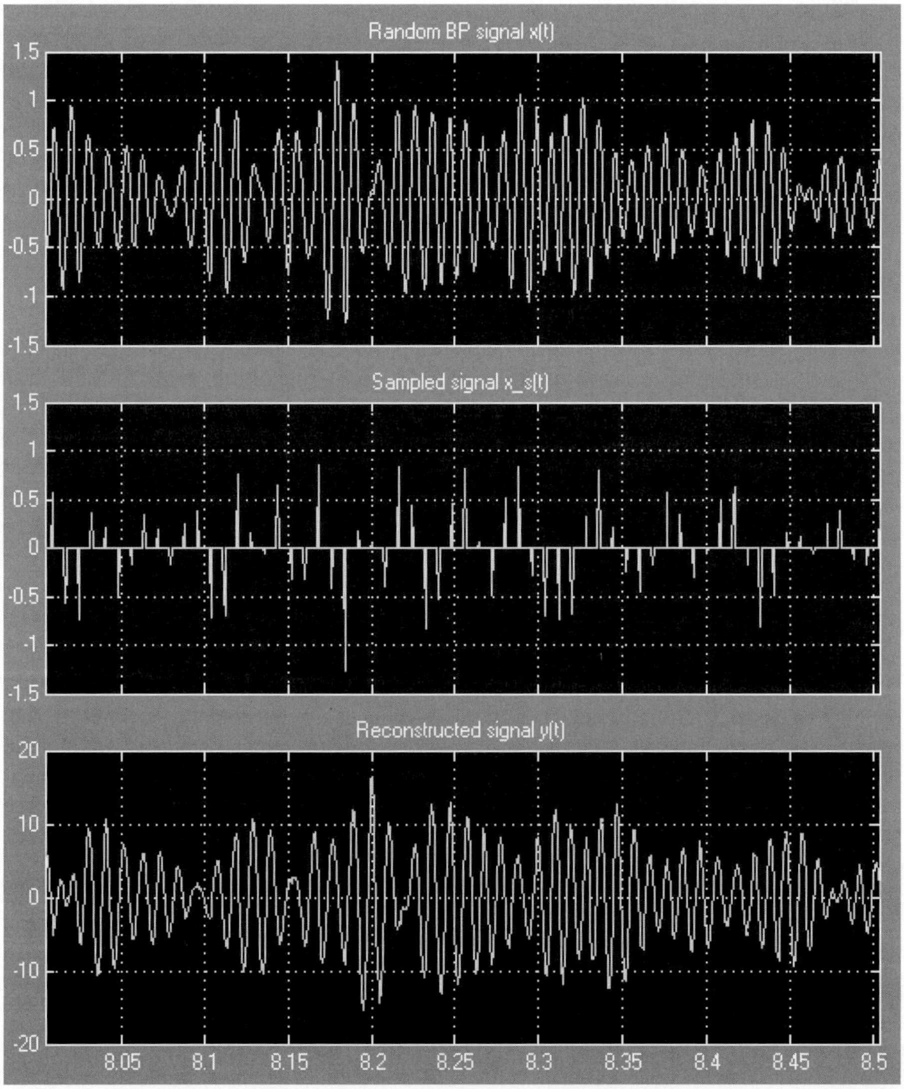

Random BP signal x(t)
Sampled signal x_s(t)
Reconstructed signal y(t)
1.5
1
0.5
0
-0.5
-1
-1.5
20
10
0
-10
-20
8.05
8.1
8.15
8.2
8.25
8.3
8.35
8.4
8.45
8.5

(b)

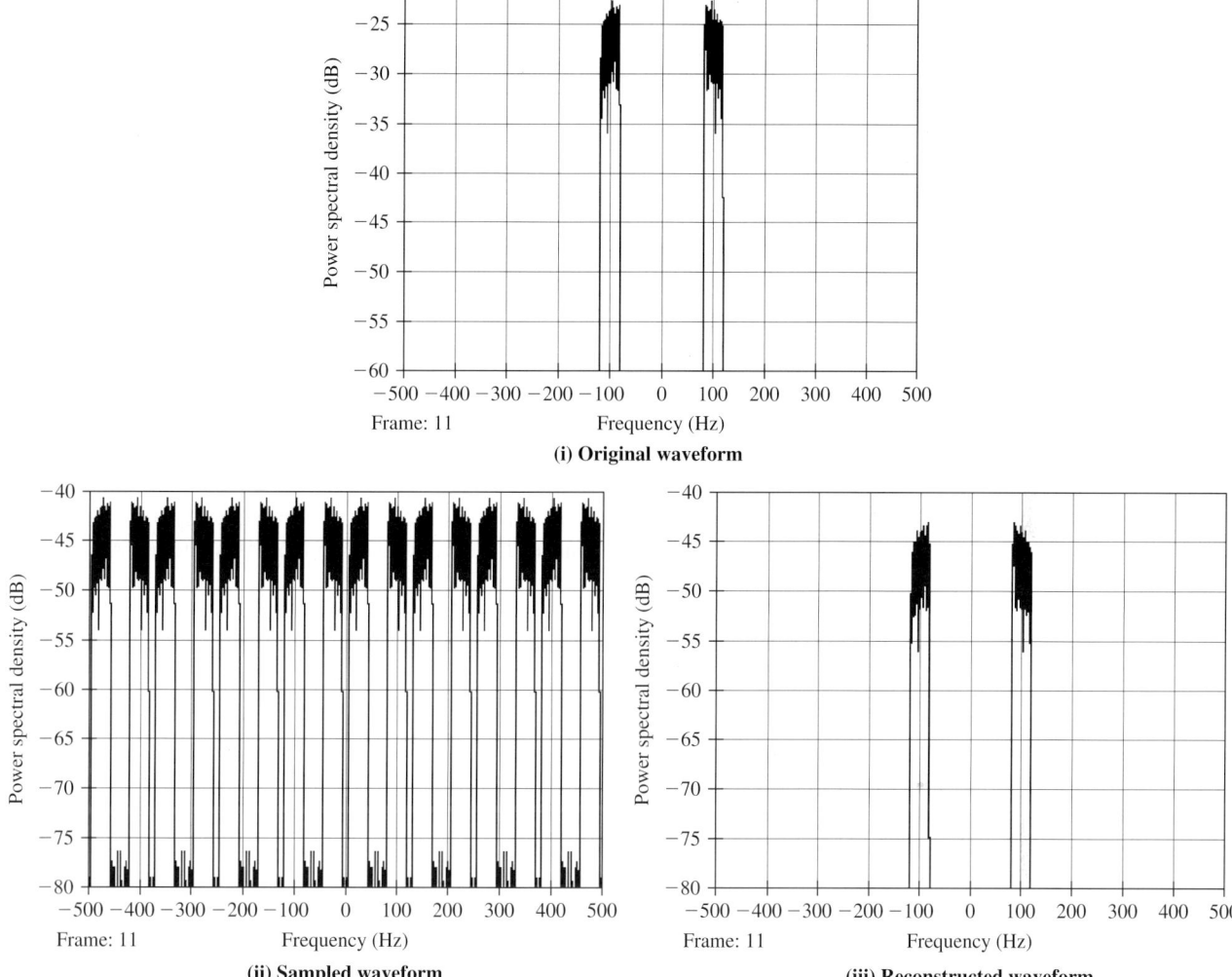

(i) Original waveform

(ii) Sampled waveform

(iii) Reconstructed waveform

(c)

8.9.1 BP Sampling in Digital Receivers

Bandpass sampling performs digitization and frequency translation in a single step. A popular application of undersampling is in digital receivers. A simplified block diagram of a traditional digital receiver using baseband sampling is shown in Figure 8.53(a). The RF and IF sections of the digital receiver are the same as those illustrated in Figure 4.36 for a superheterodyne receiver. The demodulator then recovers the baseband signal, which is converted into digital format by a baseband ADC for further digital processing. In a receiver that uses BP sampling, the IF signal is applied directly to a wide bandwidth ADC as shown in Figure 8.53(b). If we sample the IF signal at the proper rate as discussed in the previous section, it causes one of the copies of its spectrum to appear in the Nyquist bandwidth of the ADC output. DSP techniques can now be used to process the digital baseband signal. The demodulation can thus be performed in the DSP chip, thereby reducing the use of analog circuitry in the receiver. There is also more flexibility in this approach because the ADC sampling rate can be shifted to tune the desired BP channel (i.e., frequency slot of width B_{IF}) within the baseband. The obvious problem

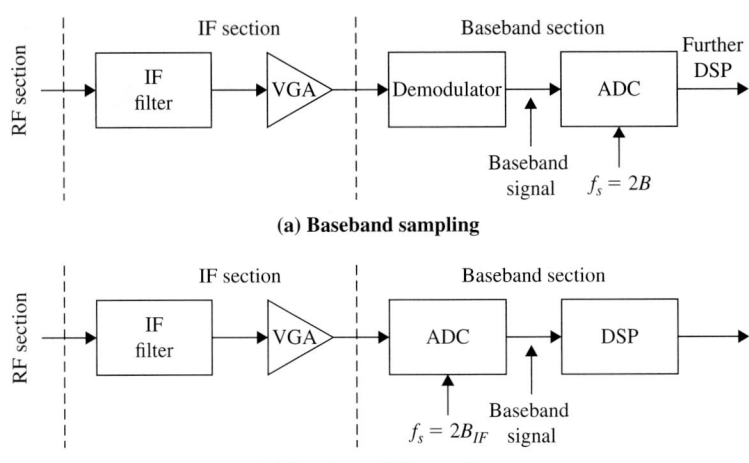

Figure 8.53 Digital receiver implementation using (a) baseband sampling (b) bandpass (IF) sampling.

with this approach is that the ADC must now be able to accurately digitize signals in the IF range. Technological advances have been made so that BP sampling ADCs are now available from many major vendors. The design of digital receivers employing BP subsampling represents the increasing trend to push the signal processing complexity from the analog into the digital domain. The resultant cost and performance benefits are then driven by Moore's law.

FINAL REMARKS

The introduction of PCM heralded the era of digital transmission and switching in public telecommunications networks. AT&T introduced the T-1 carrier system in 1962 to support long-haul voice transmission in PCM format. Before the advent of the optical fiber revolution, the bandwidth in telecommunications networks was a scarce resource. This led to more efficient predictive encoding schemes, such as DPCM and DM, for transmission over expensive links, such as satellite and intercontinental submarine cable systems. Now there is abundant bandwidth available in telecommunications networks as a result of widespread optical fiber deployment. The exception is wireless networks, where the scarce bandwidth resource is driving the development of efficient digital representations for various types of information media using advanced analog-to-digital conversion and compression technologies (see Chapter 14). Modern communication networks are designed to carry bits and therefore can handle all variety of multimedia applications in digital format.

FURTHER READINGS

Digital representation of analog signals is covered in a number of undergraduate communication systems texts [1–4]. Mitra [5] provides an excellent introduction to DSP systems. Jayant [11] is a comprehensive reference on waveform coding techniques.

1. Carlson, B., P. Crilly, and J. Rutledge. *Communication Systems,* 4th ed. New York: McGraw-Hill, 2002.

2. Proakis, J., and M. Salehi. *Fundamentals of Communication Systems.* Upper Saddle River, NJ: Prentice Hall, 2005.

3. Couch, L. *Digital and Analog Communication Systems,* 7th ed. Upper Saddle River, NJ: Prentice Hall, 2006.

4. Haykin, S, *Communication Systems,* 4th ed. Hoboken, NJ: John Wiley, 2000.

5. Mitra, S. *Digital Signal Processing: A Computer-Based Approach,* 3rd ed. New York: McGraw-Hill, 2006.

6. Dammann, C., L. McDaniel, and C. Maddox. "D2 Channel Bank—Multiplexing and Coding." *Bell System Technical Journal* 51, (1972): 1675–1700.

7. B. Smith. "Instantaneous Companding of Quantized Signals." *Bell System Technical Journal* 36, no. 3 (1957): 653–709.

8. de Jager, F. "Delta Modulation, a Method of PCM Transmission Using the 1-Unit Code." *Philips Research Reports* 7, (1952): 442–466.

9. Greefkes, J., and F. de Jager. "Continuous Delta Modulation." *Philips Research Reports* 23 (1968).

10. Greefkes, J. A., and K. Riemens. "Code Modulation with Digitally Controlled Companding for Speech Transmission." *Philips Technical Review* (1970): 335–353.

11. Jayant, N., and P. Noll. *Digital Coding of Waveforms: Principles and Applications to Speech and Video.* Upper Saddle River, NJ: Prentice-Hall, 1984.

12. Norsworthy, S. R., R. Schreier, and G. C. Temes, eds. *Delta–Sigma Data Converters, Theory, Design, and Simulation.* New York: IEEE Press, 1997.

13. Aziz, P., H. V. Sorensen, and J. van der Spiegel. "An Overview of Sigma-Delta Converters." *IEEE Signal Processing Magazine,* January 1996, 61–84.

14. Candy, J. "Decimation for Sigma Delta Modulation." *IEEE Transactions on Professional Communication* COM-34, no. 1 (1986): 72–76.

15. Vaughan, R., N. Scott, and D. White. "The Theory of Bandpass Sampling." *IEEE Transactions on Signal Processing* 39, no. 9 (1991): 1973–1984.

PROBLEMS

8.1. The signal $x(t) = 100[1 + 0.707\cos(100\pi t)]\cos(2000\pi t)$ is sampled by an impulse train.

    a. Determine the minimum sampling rate.

    b. What is the sampling rate if a guardband of 300 Hz is required.

    c. If the signal is sampled at $f_s = 1500$ Hz, write an expression for the reconstructed signal $\hat{x}(t)$. Display the spectra of original, sampled, and reconstructed signals in the same figure.

8.2. Suppose the reconstruction filter output signal $\hat{x}(t)$ is $\cos(30\pi t + \pi/6)$. If the sampling rate $f_s = 200$ Hz was used in obtaining it, determine two different input signals $x_1(t)$ and $x_2(t)$ that could have produced the above output signal. How many such input signals exist?

8.3. A sinusoidal signal $x(t) = 5\cos(10\pi t)$ is sampled by a 30% duty cycle square wave with period T_s.

    a. Determine the maximum value of the period T_s that allows the signal $x(t)$ to be reconstructed from the sampled signal.

    b. If the signal is sampled at twice the Nyquist frequency, plot the spectrum $X_s(f)$ of the sampled signal.

    c. Specify the transfer function of the reconstruction filter to recover $x(t)$ from the sampled signal generated in (b). Sketch its frequency response.

8.4. The signal with spectrum shown in Figure P8.1 is sampled by a 25% duty cycle square wave with period $T_s = \dfrac{1}{2.2B}$.

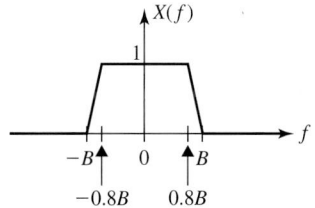

Figure P8.1

    a. Derive an expression for the spectrum $X_s(f)$ of the resultant sampled waveform and plot it.

    b. If the samples are instead generated by a sample and hold circuit, write an expression for the spectrum $X_s(f)$ of the sampled waveform and plot it.

    c. Specify the transfer function of the reconstruction filter in each case to recover the original signal without any distortion.

8.5. The samples of ± 1 volt peak-to-peak analog signal with bandwidth 3.3 kHz are to be transmitted using a PCM system.

    a. Determine the minimum sampling rate if 700-Hz guard band is required.

    b. Calculate the number of quantization levels and bits/sample required, if the peak amplitude signal is to be represented within 0.1% accuracy.

    c. What is the bit rate of the PCM signal?

8.6. For an m-bit ADC, show that peak SQNR is given by

$$\text{Peak } SQNR = 6m + 4.77 \text{ dB}$$

where peak SQNR is defined as the ratio of peak signal power (i.e., at the crest of the signal waveform) to the average quantization noise power.

8.7. Determine and illustrate the partition and quantization levels of a 4-bit, uniform midrise quantizer with ± 1 volt FS range. For the sequence $\{0.2, -0.3, -0.7, 0.08, 0.25, 0.5, 0.8, 0.95\}$,

    a. Determine the quantized sequence. Also determine the mean square quantization error and SNR.

    b. Determine the two's complement format binary stream corresponding to the quantized sequence.

8.8. 100 gigabyte hard disk is used to store PCM video signal. One volt peak-to-peak NTSC video signal is sampled at 10.73864

MHz. The quantizing scheme is selected so that peak signal-to-quantization noise ratio is at least 45 dB.

a. Calculate the number of quantization levels and bits/sample required.

b. What is the serial bit rate of the digital video signal?

c. How many minutes of video program can the hard disk store?

8.9. A video signal $x(t)$ of bandwidth 4.2 MHz is to be digitized.

a. Determine the Nyquist sampling rate.

b. Suppose that the video signal is sampled at $f_s = 10.73864$ MHz. Specify and draw the frequency response of a realizable LP filter that allows reconstruction of $x(t)$ from its samples.

c. A 10-bit ADC is used to digitize the video signal. What is the number of quantization levels? Assuming that the effective resolution of the ADC is 8.75 bits, calculate the ADC peak output SQNR.

d. What is the serial bit rate of the digital video signal.

e. What practical implementation factors cause the SQNR loss in (c)?

8.10. Determine and illustrate the partition and quantization levels of a μ-law quantizer in the range of $(-1, 1)$ with 16 levels and $\mu = 9$. For the same sequence as in Problem 8.7,

a. Determine the quantized sequence using the μ-law quantizer. Also determine the mean square quantization error and SNR.

b. For this sequence, which method (uniform vs. μ-law) gives the more accurate result?

8.11. Consider the performance of 8-bit, $\mu = 255$ companded PCM system for sinusoidal message signal with peak amplitude $x_{\max}$.

a. Write the expression for the output SQNR achievable with this companded system.

b. Plot the SQNR performance as a function of the relative RMS input level $20\log\left(\dfrac{\sigma_x}{x_{\max}}\right)$ and compare it with that for the PCM system without companding.

8.12. Suppose a message signal can be modeled as an LP stationary random process $x(t)$ with Laplacian first-order PDF

$$f_x(x) = \frac{1}{\sqrt{2}}e^{-\sqrt{2}|x|}$$

The bandwidth of the random signal is 5 kHz, and we desire to transmit it using a PCM system. Assume that the ADC FS range is set such that the analog sample stays within the range with probability 0.9965.

a. If sampling is done at the Nyquist rate and a uniform quantizer with 64 levels is utilized, what is the resulting SQNR?

b. What is the bit rate of the PCM signal?

c. If we need to increase the SQNR by 12 dB, what is the resultant bit rate increase?

8.13. Consider the μ-law compression characteristic. Assume $\mu = 255$. If the full-scale range is ± 1 volt and 256 uniformly-spaced quantization levels are used, what is the minimum and maximum effective separation between partition levels? If no compression is used, what is the spacing between partition levels?

8.14. The spectrum of a BP signal $x(t)$ is shown in Figure P8.2. Determine the smallest sampling frequency that allows perfect reconstruction of $x(t)$ from its samples $x[n]$ for each of the following cases:

a. $f_L = 60$, $f_H = 80$

b. $f_L = 47, f_H = 53$

c. $f_L = 50, f_H = 75$

Sketch the spectrum of the sampled signal and frequency response of the ideal BP filter in each case.

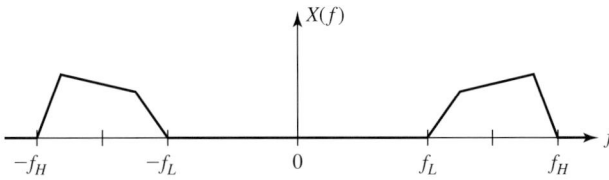

Figure P8.2

8.15. Consider an IF sampling base station receiver for CDMA cellular system operating at an IF of 70 MHz. The bandwidth of the IF channel is 1.25 MHz.

a. Determine the smallest sampling frequency to avoid aliasing. What is the corresponding SQNR degradation?

b. Determine the permissible sampling frequency range that results in SQNR loss no larger than 7 dB.

8.16. A linear DM system is tested with 1V peak-to-peak, 5-kHz sinusoidal test signal. The signal is sampled at 10 times the Nyquist rate.

a. Determine the step size required to prevent slope overload.

b. Calculate the quantization noise power in the test signal bandwidth?

c. Determine the demodulated SNR of the system.

8.17. A linear DM system is designed to transmit speech signals with 3.4 kHz bandwidth. The signal is sampled at 10 times the Nyquist rate and a step size of 100 mV is used.

a. The modulator is tested with a 1-kHz test signal. Determine the maximum amplitude of the test signal allowed to avoid slope overload.

b. Determine the demodulated SNR of the system.

8.18. Consider the first-order linear predictor defined by

$$\hat{x}[n] = h_1 x[n - 1]$$

where $x[n]$ is stationary random sequence with zero mean and h_1 is coefficient of first-order predictor filter. Let us define the variance of prediction error as $\sigma_d^2 = E\{(x[n] - \hat{x}[n])^2\}$.

a. Determine the optimal value of h_1 that minimizes σ_d^2 and calculate the minimum value of σ_d^2.

b. Determine the optimal prediction gain G_p.

8.19. Consider second-order sigma-delta modulator shown in Figure P8.3. Show that

$$y[n] = x[n-1] + (e[n] - 2e[n-1] + e[n-2])$$

$$Y(z) = z^{-1}X(z) + (1 - z^{-1})^2 E(z)$$

Prove the following:

a. The magnitude squared of the noise transfer function is given by

$$|H_e(f)|^2 = \left| (1 - z^{-1})^2 \right|^2_{z=e^{j\omega T_s}} = 4^2 \times \sin^4(\pi f/f_s)$$

b. The quantization noise power at the output is given by

$$N_{out} = \frac{\pi^4 \Delta^2}{60 K^5}$$

c. The output SNR of the second-order sigma-delta system is given by

$$SNR = 10\log_{10}\left(\frac{15}{2\pi^4}\right) + 10\log_{10}(K^5) = -11.135 + 50\log_{10} K$$

d. For the second-order sigma-delta system, every doubling of the oversampling ratio, the SNR improves by 15 dB and the resolution improves by 3.5 bits.

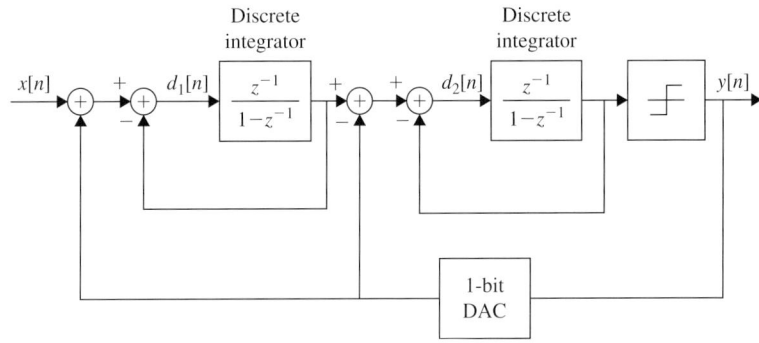

Figure P8.3

8.20. The signal $x(t) = \sin(1000\pi t) + 0.5\sin(1200\pi t) + 2\sin(1400\pi t)$ is sampled at the rate 2800 Hz.

a. Generate a sequence x[n] of length 4096. Plot the spectrum of x[n] using fft and fftshift functions.

b. Design a 7-pole elliptic LP filter as a reconstruction filter as illustrated in Example 2.34. Now use the function filter(num,den,x) to calculate the output y[n] of the filter. Plot the spectrum of y[n] using fft and fftshift functions.

c. Repeat (a) and (b) for a sampling rate of 1000Hz.

8.21. A Laplacian random variable is used to model amplitude of a speech signal. x is a zero mean, unit variance speech source defined by the PDF

$$f_x(x) = \frac{1}{\sqrt{2}} e^{-\sqrt{2}|x|}$$

a. Use the following MATLAB code segment to generate a Laplacian-distributed message sequence x[n] of length 10,000.

```
mu=0
sigma=1
u=rand(10000,1);
index1 = find(u < 0.5); index2 = find
(u >= 0.5);
```

```
x(index1) = log(2*u(index1));
x(index2) = -log(2*(1-u(index2)));
x = x*sigma + mu;
```

b. Quantize x[n] using an 8-bit, midrise type uniform quantizer. The uniformly quantized output is given by

```
magmax=max(abs(x));
xmin= - magmax, xmax=magmax;
delta=(xmax-xmin)/N;
y=floor((x-xmin)/ delta)* delta
+ delta /2+xmin;
```

c. The quantization error is given by

```
e[n] = y[n] - x[n]
```

Use the command hist(e,20) to generate 20-bit histogram for the error signal.

d. Calculate the mean-square error between the original and quantized sample values.

```
MSE=mean(e.^2)
```

e. Calculate the SQNR.

```
SQNR=10*log10(sigma^2/MSE)
```

f. Repeat (a) to (e) for 4-, 6-, 10-, and 12-bit uniform quantizers. Plot the SQNR as a function of number of quantization bits and compare it with theoretical values using (8.40).

8.22. In this problem, we apply nonuniform quantization to the Laplacian-distributed message sequence generated in problem 8.21.

a. Generate a Laplacian-distributed sequence x[n] of length 10,000. Apply $\mu = 255$ law companding to the sequence x[n].

```
xmin=min(x); xmax=max(x);
magmax=max(abs(x));
xmin=-magmax, xmax=magmax;
% mu-law companding
y=xmax*log10(1+abs(x)*(mu/xmax))/
log10(1+mu);
```

b. Use 8-bit uniform quantization to obtain yq[n] from the companded sequence y[n] obtained in part (a).

c. Apply inverse $\mu = 255$ law mapping to the quantized sequence yq[n] to recover the uncompressed sequence. Use the original sign.

```
xq=(xmax/mu)*(10.^((log10(1+mu)/
xmax)*yq)-1).*sign(x);
```

d. Calculate the mean-square error between the original and quantized sample values. Compare it with one obtained using uniform quantization.

8.23. The signal $x(t) = \sin(20\pi t) + 0.25\sin(10\pi t)$ is digitized using DM.

a. The signal is sampled at 1.28 kHz to obtain x[n]. Using step size step = 1/15, generate the delta-modulation representation y[n]. Plot it.

```
xq(1)=0; y(1)= 1;
for k = 2:N;
w1 = x(k) - xq(k-1) ;
y(k)=sign(w1);
xq(k) = xq(k-1)+y(k)*step;
end
```

b. Reconstruct xq[n] by accumulating y[n]. Recover the signal xhat by passing xq[n] through an LP filter. Plot x[n] and xhat[n] on the same figure and comment.

```
xq(n)= xq(n-1) + y(n)*step;
xhat = filter(b,a,xq);
```

c. Repeat (a) and (b) for step size $\Delta = 1/20$. Comment on your results

d. Calculate the mean-square error between the original and quantized sample values. Compare it with one obtained using uniform quantization.

8.24. The signal $x(t) = 10\sin(2\pi t)$ is digitized using Song ADM.

a. The signal is sampled at 128 Hz to obtain x[n]. The ADM step size $\Delta[n]$ is no longer constant; it is updated iteratively using the recurrence relation

$$\Delta[n] = \begin{cases} \dfrac{|\Delta[n-1]|}{y[n]}\big(y[n] + 0.5y[n-1]\big), & \Delta[n-1] \geq \Delta_{\min} \\ \Delta_{\min}, & \Delta[n-1] < \Delta_{\min} \end{cases}$$

Use $\Delta_{\min} = 0.125$. Initialize the algorithm with $y[1] = 0$ and $x_q[1] = 0$. Using step size $\Delta[n]$, generate the delta-modulation representation $y[n]$. Plot it.

b. Reconstruct xq[n] by accumulating y[n]. Recover the signal xhat by passing xq[n] through an LP filter. Plot x[n] and xhat[n] on the same figure and comment.

c. Repeat (a) and (b) for step size $\Delta = 1/20$. Comment on your results

d. Calculate the mean-square error between the original and quantized sample values. Compare it with one obtained using DM.

8.25. Consider the signal $x(t) = \sin(2\pi t)$ as input to a sigma-delta modulator.

a. The signal is 64 × oversampled at 128 Hz to obtain x[n]. The sigma-delta modulation representation yn[n] is obtained by using the following code segement.

```
wo = 0; y(1)=1
for k = 2:1:N+1;
w1 = x(k-1) - y(k-1) + wo;
y(k)=sign(w1);
wo = w1;
end
yn = y(2:N+1);
```

Plot it.

b. Recover the message signal xhat by passing yn[n] through a LP filter.

```
xhat = filter(b,a,yn);
```

Plot x[n] and xhat[n] on the same figure and comment.

c. Calculate the mean-square error between the original and quantized sample values. Compare it with the performance obtained using delta modulation.

CHAPTER 9

Digital Baseband Modulation

In the information processing world, we talk about information in terms of binary information-bearing symbols called **bits:** "0" and "1." Symbols, of course, are abstract entities; they need to be converted into **waveforms** before they can be transmitted or stored. The purpose of a digital transmission system is to transfer a sequence of 1's and 0's from a transmitter to a receiver as shown in Figure 9.1. In digital baseband communication systems, this is done by first encoding information bits into transmission symbols. The transmission system then assigns distinct pulses (e.g., square, Gaussian) to each of the transmission symbols. Because these pulses or waveforms have their spectral energy clustered in a band of frequencies at or near zero, they are called low-pass or **baseband** signals. The resulting sequence of pulses is then transmitted over a communication channel. At the receiver, these pulses are detected and converted back into bits.

Recall from Chapter 1 that the **digital modulator** is the interface device at the transmitter that maps the binary digital data into analog waveforms that match the characteristics of the communication channel. The **digital baseband modulator,** also called the **line encoder,** is shown in Figure 9.2. The **symbol mapping table** takes blocks of k bits at a time and uniquely maps them into sequence of transmission symbols. At T second intervals, the **pulse shaping filter** sequentially associates each transmission symbol with a basic pulse shape $v(t)$ for transmission over the channel. The purpose of the **spectral shaping filter** at the transmit end, in cooperation with the corresponding filter at the receive end of the system, is to minimize transmitted pulses from interfering with each other, a phenomenon known as **intersymbol interference (ISI).**

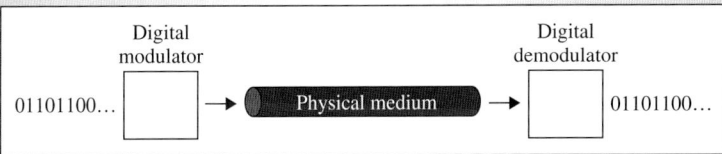

Figure 9.1 Digital transmission system.

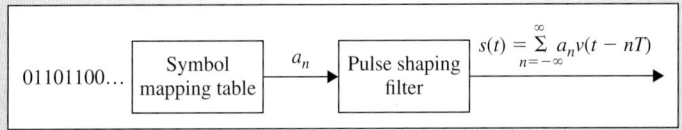

Figure 9.2 Digital baseband modulator.

This chapter considers key requirements and characteristics of various line-coding schemes. We also study design of pulse shapes to improve the spectral efficiency of digital baseband transmission systems. The chapter is organized into the following sections:

9.1 PULSE AMPLITUDE MODULATION.
We explain binary and multilevel baseband signals and introduce the concepts of symbol and bit rates of a digital transmission system.

9.2 BINARY LINE-CODING TECHNIQUES.
This section considers factors that need to be considered in selecting an appropriate line code for a digital baseband transmission scheme. Next we consider various bit-by-bit line-encoding formats for transmitting binary information.

9.3 SPECTRA OF DIGITAL BASEBAND SIGNALS.
The spectral density of a linearly modulated digital baseband signal is developed. It is then applied to obtain spectral density expressions for various line-coding schemes.

9.4   BANDWIDTH OF DIGITAL BASEBAND SIGNALS.

Various definitions of bandwidth for a digitally modulated baseband signal are reviewed. The spectral efficiency is defined as a figure of merit for a digital modulation scheme and then applied to compare various line-coding schemes.

9.5   SPECTRAL AND POWER OUT-OF-BAND PLOTS.

The spectral characteristics of various line-coding schemes are compared using normalized spectral and out-of-band plots.

9.6   BLOCK LINE CODES.

We study line codes, which map blocks of bits into codewords with desirable transmission properties. The latter include no DC component and strong timing content.

9.7   SCRAMBLING.

As an alternative to block line codes, this section considers scrambling techniques to achieve DC balance and accurate timing recovery.

9.8   PULSE SHAPING TO IMPROVE SPECTRAL EFFICIENCY.

The design of pulse shapes to improve the spectral efficiency of digital baseband transmission schemes is considered. In this context, we study **raised cosine (RC)** *pulses, which provide a strictly bandlimited spectrum as well as good time-domain characteristics.*

9.9   ESTIMATION OF ALLOWABLE BIT RATE.

We discuss the effect of channel bandwidth on the transmission of digital baseband signals and develop estimates of achievable bit rates in the absence of noise using different line-coding schemes and pulse formats.

The chapter concludes with final remarks and a selected list of references.

9.1   PULSE AMPLITUDE MODULATION

In the simplest line-coding scheme, the symbol mapping table assigns a distinct scalar symbol a_m to each block of k bits in the incoming data stream. The pulse shaping filter then produces waveforms that are pulses of some basic shape $v(t)$ with amplitude a_m from the M-level set $\mathscr{A}_M = \{a_1, a_2, \ldots, a_M\}$, where $M = 2^k$. Thus, it is called an M-ary or M-level **pulse amplitude modulation (PAM)** scheme. The M distinct waveforms are given by

$$s_m(t) = a_m v(t), m = 1, 2, \ldots, M \qquad (9.1)$$

The modulator outputs a pulse every T seconds, where T is called the **symbol period**. Let us consider the following examples:

- **Binary PAM.** The modulator maps each bit b_n into one of two possible signal waveforms, say $s_1(t)$ or $s_2(t)$.

  a. Polar or "antipodal" signaling. $\mathscr{A}_2 = \{1, -1\}$. A positive pulse $v(t)$ is transmitted to represent a binary 1, while a negative pulse $-v(t)$ represents a binary 0.

  $$s_1(t) = v(t) \text{ corresponding to binary 1}$$

  $$s_2(t) = -v(t) \text{ corresponding to binary 0}$$

  b. Unipolar signaling. $\mathscr{A}_2 = \{1, 0\}$. A positive pulse $v(t)$ is transmitted to represent a binary 1. No pulse is transmitted for a binary 0.

  $$s_1(t) = v(t) \text{ corresponding to binary 1}$$

  $$s_2(t) = 0 \text{ corresponding to binary 0}$$

Binary unipolar and antipodal waveforms using square pulses are shown in Figure 9.3.

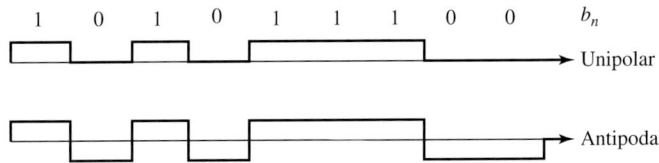

Figure 9.3 Binary unipolar and antipodal signaling with rectangular pulses.

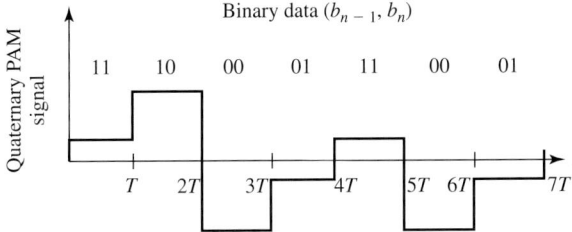

Figure 9.4 Quaternary PAM.

- **Quaternary PAM ($M = 4$).** The modulator transmits two bits at a time by employing four different amplitude pulses as shown in Figure 9.4. That is,

$$(b_{n-1}, b_n) \rightarrow a_n \in \mathscr{A}_4 = \{-3, -1, -1, 1\}$$

(b_{n-1}, b_n)	a_n
$(0, 0)$	-3
$(0, 1)$	-1
$(1, 1)$	1
$(1, 0)$	3

Thus for an *M*-ary PAM system, the modulator outputs a pulse every T seconds assuming one of M amplitude values from the alphabet set $\mathscr{A}_M$. Because the amplitude level is uniquely determined by k bits of random data it represents, the pulse amplitude during the nth symbol interval (i.e., $nT \leq t \leq (n + 1)T$) is a discrete random variable $a_n \in \mathscr{A}_M = \{a_1, a_2, \ldots, a_M\}$. Hence we can write the following expression for an *M*-ary PAM signal:

$$s(t) = \sum_{n=-\infty}^{\infty} a_n v(t - nT) \qquad (9.2)$$

Note that $s(t)$ is a random process because pulse amplitudes $\{a_n\}$ are discrete random variables assuming values from the finite set $\mathscr{A}_M$. The symbol period T for the transmission of each symbol a_n is related to the **symbol** or **pulse transmission rate** D by the reciprocal relationship:

$$\text{Symbol or Pulse period } (T) = \frac{1}{\text{Symbol or Pulse rate } (D)} \qquad (9.3)$$

The **bit interval** T_b is the time required to send a single data bit. Obviously,

$$\text{Bit interval } (T_b) = \frac{1}{\text{Bit rate } (R_b)} \qquad (9.4)$$

Because an *M*-ary modulator transmits pulses at the symbol rate (*D*) and each pulse conveys *k* bits of information, the equivalent bit or information rate R_b is related to the symbol or pulse rate by

$$R_b = kD = (\log_2 M)D \tag{9.5}$$

Equation (9.5) states that *the bit rate of the modulation scheme is improved by a factor of $log_2 M$ by using M-ary signaling.* The time devoted to transmitting a single bit can now be written by combining (9.3) and (9.5) as

$$T_b = \frac{1}{R_b} = \frac{1}{kD} = \frac{T}{k} = \frac{T}{\log_2 M} \tag{9.6}$$

Example 9.1

A modulator transmits 9600 pulses per second using binary signaling. What is the bit rate? What is the equivalent bit rate of the modulation scheme if quaternary pulses are used instead?

Solution

Using binary pulses, the bit rate of the modulation scheme is identical to the pulse or symbol rate. Therefore,

$$\text{Bit rate} = 9600 \text{ bits per second (bps)}$$

However, if quaternary signaling ($k = 2$) is used,

$$R_b = 2D = 2 \times 9600 = 19{,}200 \text{ bps}$$

9.2   BINARY LINE-CODING TECHNIQUES

The choice of a line-coding scheme for a digital baseband transmission system is critical to its performance. It is usually based on some of the following considerations:

- **Transparency.** Communication systems are designed to transfer user information transparently from the source to the destination. Transparency here implies that the system can convey any bit sequence without causing problems for correct data recovery at the receiver. For example, long strings of 1's and 0's, which occur frequently in practice, cause problems in clock recovery and may lead to loss of data. Transparency, in general, translates to strong bit timing content and no DC or low-frequency components in the line code spectrum.
- **Strong bit timing content.** Transitions in the transmitted signal allow simple clock recovery circuits to extract the clock for regenerating the digital signal at the receiver. A long string of binary 1's and 0's should not cause difficulty in clock recovery.
- **Low-frequency content.** AC-coupled electronics and transformer coupling commonly used in transmission systems block low frequencies. The long strings of 0's or 1's cause the signal to "droop" when AC coupling is used. It is desirable that the spectrum of the line code waveform should not have low-frequency content.

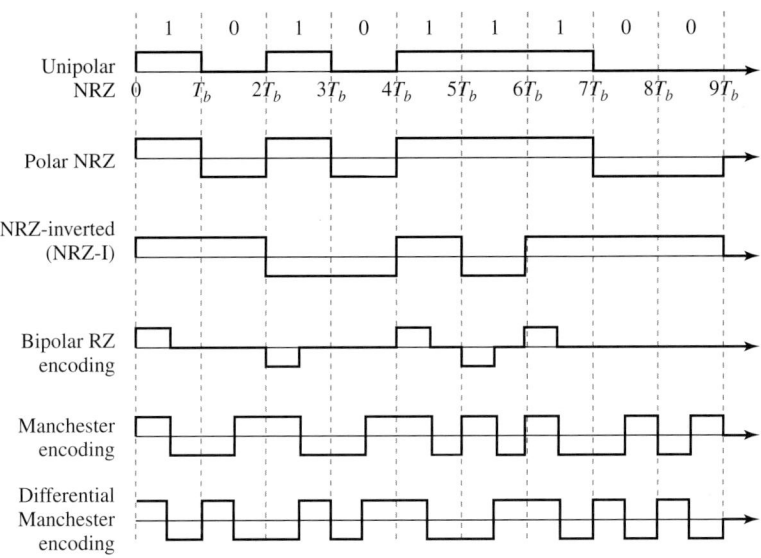

Figure 9.5 Binary line codes.

- **Spectral characteristics.** Wired transmission media exhibit significant spectral roll-off and crosstalk characteristics. Line codes can be designed to improve the system performance by controlling the transmitted signal spectrum.[1]
- **Bandwidth efficiency.** It is always desirable to maximize the bit rate over channels that have limited bandwidths.
- **Error detection capability.** If the line code provides simple error detection capability, it is quite helpful for remote fault monitoring in a repeatered system.
- **Power efficiency.** The transmitted power should be minimized for cost as well as equipment reliability considerations.

Figure 9.5 shows various bit-by-bit binary line codes that are used in practice. The figure shows the digital signals that are produced by the line codes for the binary sequence 101011100. Line-coding schemes can be classified as follows:

1. **Symbol mapping**
   - **Unipolar.** Binary 1 is represented by a positive amplitude pulse ($+A$ volts) and a binary 0 by the absence of a pulse (0 volts) during a bit interval.
   - **Polar.** Binary 1 is represented by a positive amplitude pulse ($+A$ volts) and a binary 0 by a negative amplitude pulse ($-A$ volts). It is also called **antipodal encoding.**
   - **Bipolar.** Binary 1 is alternately mapped into positive ($+A$ volts) and negative amplitude ($-A$ volts) pulses. The binary 0 is represented by no pulse (0 volts). That is why it is referred to as **alternate mark inversion (AMI)** encoding. Because it uses three voltage levels, is also called a **pseudoternary scheme.**
2. **Pulse shape**
   - **Non-return-to-zero (NRZ).** The pulse amplitude is held constant throughout the pulse or bit interval.
   - **Return-to-zero (RZ).** The pulse amplitude returns to a zero-volt level for a portion (usually one-half) of the pulse or bit interval.

---

[1] J. Lechleider, "Line Codes for Digital Subscriber Lines," *IEEE Communications Magazine* 27, no. 9 (1989): 24–25.

• **Manchester.** A binary 1 is denoted by a transition from a positive pulse to a negative pulse in the middle of the bit interval, and a binary 0 by a transition from a negative pulse to a positive pulse.

There is another set of coding schemes that transmit differences between successive data symbols. These are called **differential encoding methods.** A binary 1 causes toggling of the waveform transmitted during the previous symbol interval. No toggling is forced to transmit a binary 0. Figure 9.5 illustrates two such schemes: NRZ-I and differential Manchester encoding.

9.3   SPECTRA OF DIGITAL BASEBAND SIGNALS

It is important to study the spectra of digitally modulated baseband signals because it allows us to estimate the channel bandwidth required to transmit data using different line-coding or modulation schemes. We will consider the spectral characteristics of linearly modulated digital baseband signals. The term **linear modulation** is applied generally to signals that are made up from a linear superposition of baseband pulses. A linearly modulated digital baseband signal can be expressed as

$$s(t) = \sum_{n=-\infty}^{\infty} a_n v(t - nT) \tag{9.7}$$

where a_n are discrete identically distributed random variables. Pulse amplitude modulation is a special case of linear modulation.

9.3.1   Power Spectral Density of Random Pulse Trains

Using Wiener-Khinchin theorem discussed in Section 6.5, the spectrum of a WSS random signal is FT of its autocorrelation function. The linearly modulated signal $s(t)$, however, is a cyclostationary random process. To ensure the stationarity of $s(t)$, we, therefore, include a random delay in each of its sample functions. The autocorrelation function of $s(t)$ is defined as

$$R_s(\tau) = E\{s(t + \Delta)s(t + \tau + \Delta)\}$$

$$= E\left\{ \sum_{n=-\infty}^{\infty} \sum_{\ell=-\infty}^{\infty} a_n a_{n+\ell} v(t - nT - \Delta) v[t + \tau - (n + \ell)T - \Delta] \right\} \tag{9.8}$$

where Δ is a uniformly distributed random variable in $[0, T]$. Taking the expectation inside the double sum and noting that random variable Δ is statistically independent of the symbol sequence $\{a_n\}$, we obtain

$$R_s(\tau) = \sum_{n=-\infty}^{\infty} \sum_{\ell=-\infty}^{\infty} E\{a_n a_{n+\ell}\} E\{v(t - nT - \Delta) v[t + \tau - (n + \ell)T - \Delta]\}$$

$$= \sum_{\ell=-\infty}^{\infty} R(\ell) \sum_{n=-\infty}^{\infty} \frac{1}{T} \int_{-T/2}^{T/2} v(t - nT - \Delta) v[t + \tau - (n + \ell)T - \Delta] d\Delta \tag{9.9}$$

$R(\ell)$ is the autocorrelation function of the random data and is given by

$$R(\ell) = E\{a_n a_{n+\ell}\} \tag{9.10}$$

Making the change of variable $\alpha = t - nT - \Delta$ in (9.9) yields

$$R_s(\tau) = \sum_{\ell=-\infty}^{\infty} R(\ell) \sum_{n=-\infty}^{\infty} \frac{1}{T} \int_{t-(n+1/2)T}^{t-(n-1/2)T} v(\alpha)v(\alpha + \tau - \ell T)d\alpha$$

$$= \sum_{\ell=-\infty}^{\infty} R(\ell) \frac{1}{T} \int_{-\infty}^{\infty} v(\alpha)v(\alpha + \tau - \ell T)d\alpha \tag{9.11}$$

We can write (9.11) as

$$R_s(\tau) = \sum_{\ell=-\infty}^{\infty} R(\ell)r_v(\tau - \ell T) \tag{9.12}$$

where

$$r_v(\tau) = \frac{1}{T} \int_{-\infty}^{\infty} v(\alpha)v(\alpha + \tau)d\alpha \tag{9.13}$$

is the **pulse auto-correlation function.** Using Wiener-Khinchin theorem, the PSD of linearly modulated digital signal $s(t)$ is given by

$$G_s(f) = \Im\{R_s(\tau)\} = \Im\left\{\sum_{\ell=-\infty}^{\infty} R(\ell)r_v(\tau - \ell T)\right\}$$

$$= \sum_{\ell=-\infty}^{\infty} R(\ell)\Im\{r_v(\tau - \ell T)\}$$

$$= \sum_{\ell=-\infty}^{\infty} R(\ell)\Im\{r_v(\tau)\}e^{-j2\pi\ell fT} \tag{9.14}$$

Because $r_v(\tau) = \frac{1}{T}v(-\tau) \otimes v(\tau)$, we obtain

$$\Im\{r_v(\tau)\} = \frac{|V(f)|^2}{T} \tag{9.15}$$

where

$$v(t) \xleftrightarrow{\Im} V(f)$$

Substituting (9.15) into (9.14), we obtain the final result

$$G_s(f) = \frac{|V(f)|^2}{T} \sum_{\ell=-\infty}^{\infty} R(\ell)e^{-j2\pi\ell fT} \tag{9.16}$$

We can now apply the expression (9.16) to calculate the power spectral density of linearly modulated digital signals. We assume that M-ary PAM symbols a_n are equiprobable, statistically independent, and uncorrelated random variables with mean m_a and variance σ_a^2. For $\ell = 0$, we can write

$$R(0) = E\{a_n^2\} = \sigma_a^2 + m_a^2 \tag{9.17}$$

For $\ell \neq 0$, we can write

$$R(\ell) = E\{a_n a_{n+\ell}\} = E\{a_n\}E\{a_{n+\ell}\} = m_a^2 \tag{9.18}$$

We can summarize this as follows:

$$R(\ell) = \begin{cases} \sigma_a^2 + m_a^2, & \ell = 0 \\ m_a^2, & \ell \neq 0 \end{cases} \tag{9.19}$$

and

$$\sum_{\ell=-\infty}^{\infty} R(\ell)e^{-j2\pi\ell fT} = \sigma_a^2 + m_a^2 \sum_{\ell=-\infty}^{\infty} e^{-j2\pi\ell fT} \tag{9.20}$$

Substituting (9.20) into (9.16) yields

$$G_s(f) = \frac{|V(f)|^2}{T}\left[\sigma_a^2 + m_a^2 \sum_{\ell=-\infty}^{\infty} e^{-j2\pi\ell fT}\right] \tag{9.21}$$

It can be shown (Problem 9.10) that

$$\sum_{\ell=-\infty}^{\infty} e^{-j2\pi\ell fT} = \frac{1}{T}\sum_{\ell=-\infty}^{\infty} \delta\left(f - \frac{\ell}{T}\right)$$

Substituting into (9.21) yields

$$G_s(f) = \frac{|V(f)|^2}{T}\left[\sigma_a^2 + m_a^2 D \sum_{\ell=-\infty}^{\infty} \delta(f - \ell D)\right]$$

$$= |V(f)|^2 D\sigma_a^2 + (Dm_a)^2 \sum_{\ell=-\infty}^{\infty} |V(f)|^2\delta(f - \ell D)$$

$$= |V(f)|^2 D\sigma_a^2 + (Dm_a)^2 \sum_{\ell=-\infty}^{\infty} |V(\ell D)|^2\delta(f - \ell D) \tag{9.22}$$

The spectrum of the digital signal $s(t)$ contains impulses at harmonics of symbol rate D, unless $m_a = 0$ or $V(f) = 0$ at all values of $f = \ell D$, $\ell = 0, \pm 1, \pm 2, \dots$. Further, the spectrum of $s(t)$ depends on the statistical properties of the data (via m_a and σ_a^2) and the basic pulse shape (via $V(f)$). Next we apply (9.22) to two special cases.

1. Multilevel unipolar NRZ

$$a_n \in \{0, +A, +2A, \dots, +(M-1)A\} \tag{9.23}$$

$$m_a = E\{a_n\} = \frac{1}{M}\{0 + A + 2A + \ldots + (M-1)A\} = \frac{A(M-1)}{2} \qquad (9.24)$$

$$\sigma_a^2 = Var(a_n) = \frac{A^2(M^2-1)}{12} \qquad (9.25)$$

Substituting into (9.22), we get

$$G_s(f) = \frac{(M^2-1)A^2 D}{12}|V(f)|^2 + \frac{(M-1)^2}{4}(DA)^2 \sum_{\ell=-\infty}^{\infty} |V(\ell D)|^2 \delta(f - \ell D) \quad (9.26)$$

For a rectangular basic pulse shape,

$$v(t) = \Pi(t/T) \qquad (9.27)$$

$$V(f) = T\,\mathrm{sinc}(fT) \qquad (9.28)$$

Substituting (9.28) into (9.26) yields the expression for the spectral density of the *M*-ary unipolar NRZ signal as

$$G_s(f) = \frac{(M^2-1)A^2 T}{12}\mathrm{sinc}^2(fT) + \frac{(M-1)^2 A^2}{4} \sum_{\ell=-\infty}^{\infty} |\mathrm{sinc}(fT)|^2\,\delta(f - \ell D)$$

$$= \frac{(M^2-1)A^2}{12D}\mathrm{sinc}^2(f/D) + \frac{(M-1)^2 A^2}{4}\left[\delta(f) + \underbrace{\sum_{\substack{\ell=-\infty \\ \ell \neq 0}}^{\infty} |\mathrm{sinc}(\ell)|^2\,\delta(f - \ell D)}_{0}\right]$$

$$= \frac{(M^2-1)A^2}{12D}\mathrm{sinc}^2(f/D) + \frac{(M-1)^2 A^2}{4}\delta(f) \qquad (9.29)$$

We observe the presence of energy at DC in the spectrum of the *M*-ary unipolar NRZ signal as indicated by the presence of an impulse at $f = 0$. As discussed in Section 9.4, the frequency where the first null in the envelope of the spectral density $G_s(f)$ occurs is called the **first null bandwidth** (B_{null}) of a digital signal. From (9.29), we note that the first zero of $\mathrm{sinc}^2(f/D)$ occurs at $f = D$. Thus, the first null bandwidth of the *M*-ary unipolar NRZ signal is given by

$$B_{null} = D = \frac{R_b}{k} = \frac{R_b}{\log_2 M} \qquad (9.30)$$

2. Multilevel polar NRZ

$$a_n \in \{\pm A, \pm 3A, \ldots, \pm(M-1)A\} \qquad (9.31)$$

For a polar NRZ signal, it is obvious that $m_a = E\{a_n\} = 0$ and

$$\sigma_a^2 = Var(a_n) = (M^2-1)A^2/3 \qquad (9.32)$$

Substituting in (9.22), we obtain

$$G_s(f) = \frac{(M^2 - 1)A^2D}{3}|V(f)|^2 \tag{9.33}$$

For a rectangular basic pulse shape, substituting (9.28) into (9.33) yields the expression for the spectral density of the M-ary polar NRZ signal as

$$G_s(f) = \frac{(M^2 - 1)A^2T}{3} \operatorname{sinc}^2(fT)$$

$$= \frac{(M^2 - 1)A^2}{3D} \operatorname{sinc}^2(f/D) \tag{9.34}$$

It can be observed from (9.34) that the first null of $G_s(f)$ occurs at $f = D$. Therefore, the first null bandwidth of the of multilevel polar NRZ signal is given by

$$B_{null} = D = \frac{R_b}{k} = \frac{R_b}{\log_2 M} \tag{9.35}$$

It is important to note from (9.30) and (9.35) that the first null bandwidth of M-ary signaling is decreased by a factor $\log_2 M$ when compared to a binary scheme for the same information or bit rate.

9.3.2   Spectra of Binary Line Codes

Unipolar NRZ Code

For binary unipolar signaling, we substitute $M = 2$ and $D = R_b$ in (9.29) to obtain the following expression for its spectral density:

$$G_{\text{unipolarNRZ}}(f) = \frac{A^2}{4R_b}\left[\operatorname{sinc}^2\left(\frac{f}{R_b}\right) + R_b\delta(f)\right] \tag{9.36}$$

It follows from (9.36) that the first null bandwidth of a unipolar NRZ signal is equal to R_b Hz. The spectral density of a unipolar NRZ signal, as shown in Figure 9.6, contains an impulse at $f = 0$ corresponding to the presence of energy at DC. Transmission of a unipolar NRZ signal through AC-coupled circuits results in distortion of the pulse shapes. The effect is similar to that of passing the signal through a high-pass RC filter. The distortion takes the form of an exponential decay of the signal amplitude for a long string of 1's. This is commonly referred to as **signal droop.**

Polar NRZ Code

The spectral density for the binary polar NRZ line code is obtained by substituting $M = 2$ and $D = R_b$ in (9.34) as

$$G_{\text{polarNRZ}}(f) = \frac{A^2}{R_b}\operatorname{sinc}^2\left(\frac{f}{R_b}\right) \tag{9.37}$$

The first null bandwidth of a polar NRZ signal is equal to R_b Hz as shown in Figure 9.7. Although the polar NRZ signal does not have a spectral line at DC, it has

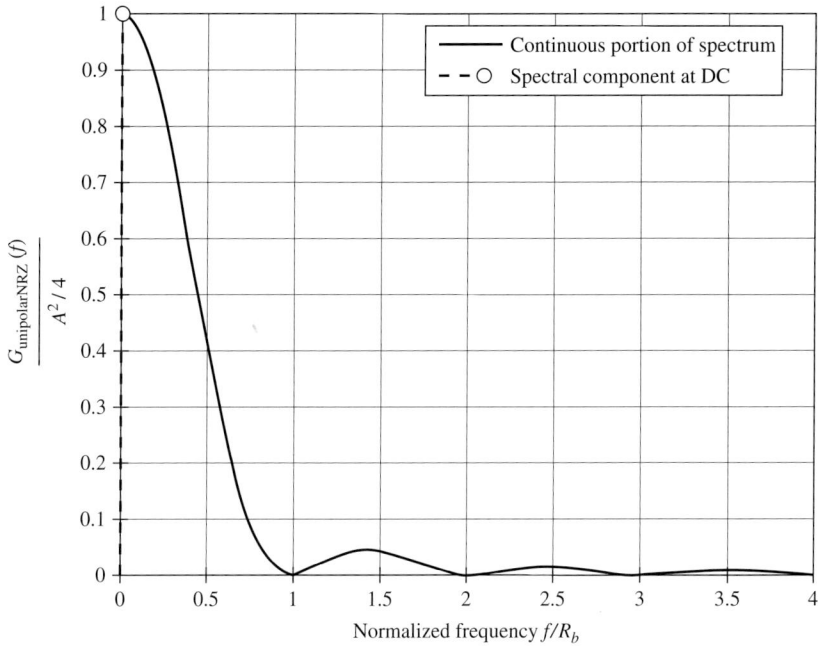

Figure 9.6 Spectral density of unipolar NRZ signal ($R_b = 1$).

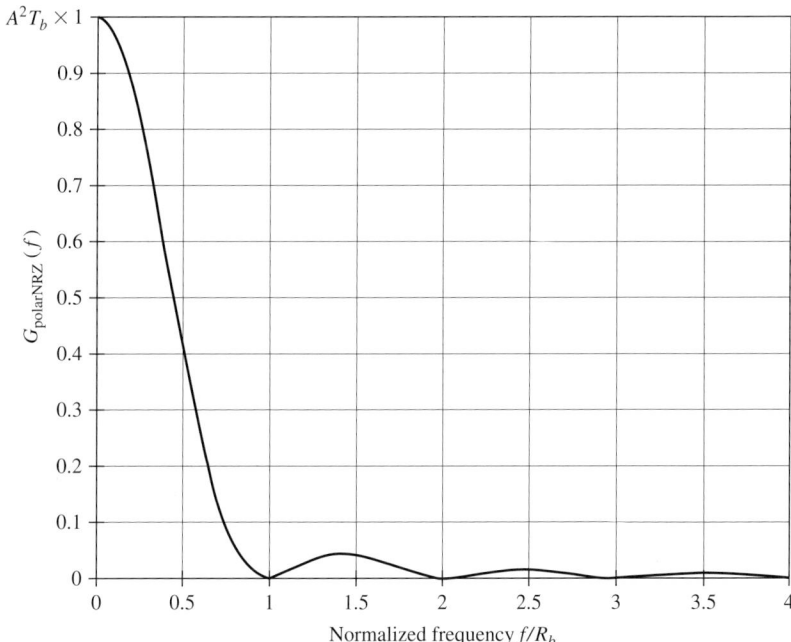

Figure 9.7 Spectral density of polar NRZ signal ($R_b = 1$).

significant spectral energy at the lower frequencies resulting from long strings of 1's and 0's. Because many communication channels do not pass low frequencies, it results in distortion of the transmitted pulses. For example, most telco local loop circuits cut off the frequencies below 200 Hz. As we shall determine in Chapter 10, the BER performance of polar NRZ signaling is superior to that of other signaling methods.

Unipolar RZ Code

Assuming 50% duty cycle pulses, the pulse duration is $T_b/2$ for binary unipolar RZ encoding. The FT of an RZ rectangular pulse is obtained from Table 2.2 as

$$V(f) = \frac{T_b}{2} \operatorname{sinc}(fT_b/2) \tag{9.38}$$

The spectral density for the unipolar RZ line code is given by substituting (9.38) into (9.26) as

$$G_{\text{unipolarRZ}}(f) = \frac{A^2 T_b}{16} \left\{ \operatorname{sinc}^2(fT_b/2) \left[1 + \frac{1}{T_b} \sum_{\ell=-\infty}^{\infty} \delta\left(f - \frac{\ell}{T_b} \right) \right] \right\}$$

$$= \frac{A^2 T_b}{16} \operatorname{sinc}^2(fT_b/2) + \frac{A^2}{16} \sum_{\ell=-\infty}^{\infty} \operatorname{sinc}^2(\ell/2) \delta\left(f - \frac{\ell}{T_b} \right) \tag{9.39}$$

Because $\operatorname{sinc}(\ell/2) = 0$ except for $\ell = \pm1, \pm3, \ldots$, this reduces to

$$G_{\text{unipolarRZ}}(f) = \frac{A^2 T_b}{16} \operatorname{sinc}^2(fT_b/2)$$

$$+ \frac{A^2}{16} \left\{ \begin{array}{l} \delta(f) + \operatorname{sinc}^2(1/2)\big[\delta(f - R_b) + \delta(f + R_b)\big] \\ \quad + \operatorname{sinc}^2(3/2)\big[\delta(f - 3R_b) + \delta(f + 3R_b)\big] + \ldots \end{array} \right\} \tag{9.40}$$

The spectral density of a unipolar RZ signal, as shown in Figure 9.8, contains impulses at $f = 0$ and $\pm R_b$, $\pm 3R_b$, ... The spectral component at DC represents a waste of power. Because the first zero of $\operatorname{sinc}(f/2R_b)$ occurs at $f = 2R_b$, the first null bandwidth of a unipolar RZ signal is equal to $2R_b$ Hz − twice that for the unipolar NRZ signaling. Obviously, it results from the pulse width being half as wide. Note that there is a spectral line at $f = R_b$. This can be used for the recovery of the clock signal, which is a periodic square wave at the bit rate. Another disadvantage of this scheme is that it also has significant spectral energy at lower frequencies.

Bipolar Code

For bipolar signaling, binary 1's are represented by pulses whose amplitudes alternate between $+A$ and $-A$. The binary 0 is represented by no pulse transmission during that bit interval. Therefore, the permissible values for the random variables a_n representing successive pulse amplitude values in time are $+A$, $-A$, and 0. If binary 1's and 0's are equally likely in the data, then the amplitude probabilities are $P\{a_n = 0\} = 1/2$, $P\{a_n = +A\} = 1/4$, and $P\{a_n = -A\} = 1/4$. Thus, the encoded amplitude level statistics are different than those of incoming random data bits. Also there is correlation between adjacent pulse amplitudes, so we need to use (9.16) to calculate the spectral density of bipolar signals. For $\ell = 0$, we have

$$R(0) = \sum_n a_n^2 P\{a_n = a_n, a_n = a_n\} = (A.A)\frac{1}{2} + 0.\frac{1}{2} = A^2/2 \tag{9.41}$$

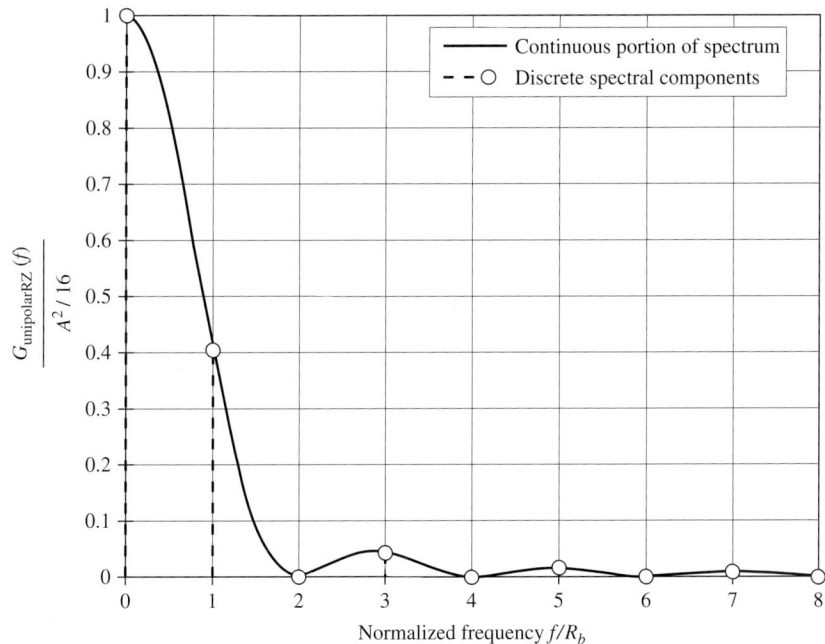

Figure 9.8 Spectral density of unipolar RZ signal ($R_b = 1$).

For $\ell = 1$ (the adjacent bit case) and the data sequences $(1, 1)$, $(1, 0)$, $(0, 1)$, and $(0, 0)$, the possible values of $a_n a_{n+1}$ products are $-A^2$, 0, 0, 0. Each of these sequences has a probability of $1/4$.

$$R(1) = \sum_n a_n a_{n+1} P\{\boldsymbol{a}_n = a_n, \boldsymbol{a}_{n+1} = a_{n+1}\} = (-A^2)\frac{1}{4} = \frac{-A^2}{4} \qquad (9.42)$$

For $\ell > 1$, the bits being considered are not adjacent, and the possible values of $a_n a_{n+\ell}$ products are:

- $(1, 1)$ maps to either A^2 with a probability of $1/8$ or $-A^2$ with a probability of $1/8$.
- Each of the data sequences $(1, 0)$, $(0, 1)$, and $(0, 0)$ maps to 0 with a probability of $1/4$.

$$R(\ell > 1) = \sum_n a_n a_{n+\ell} P\{\boldsymbol{a}_n, \boldsymbol{a}_{n+\ell}\} = (-A^2)\frac{1}{8} + (+A^2)\frac{1}{8} = 0 \qquad (9.43)$$

Combining (9.41) through (9.43) yields

$$R(\ell) = \begin{cases} A^2/2, & \ell = 0 \\ -A^2/4, & |\ell| = 1 \\ 0, & |\ell| > 1 \end{cases} \qquad (9.44)$$

Substituting (9.44) into (9.16), the spectral density for the bipolar line code is obtained as

$$G_{\text{bipolar}}(f) = \frac{|V(f)|^2 A^2}{2T_b}\left[1 - \cos(2\pi f T_b)\right] \qquad (9.45)$$

For a bipolar RZ signal with a rectangular basic pulse shape, substituting (9.38) into (9.45) yields

$$G_{\text{bipolarRZ}}(f) = \frac{A^2 T_b}{8} \, \text{sinc}^2(f T_b/2)\big[1 - \cos(2\pi f T_b)\big] \tag{9.46}$$

which simplifies to

$$G_{\text{bipolarRZ}}(f) = \frac{A^2}{4R_b} \, \text{sinc}^2(f/2R_b) \, \sin^2(\pi f/R_b) \tag{9.47}$$

Similarly, it can be shown that for bipolar NRZ signals, the spectral density is given by

$$G_{\text{bipolarNRZ}}(f) = \frac{A^2}{4R_b} \, \text{sinc}^2(f/R_b) \, \sin^2(\pi f/R_b) \tag{9.48}$$

The bipolar encoding was developed to produce a spectrum that is more amenable to channels that do not pass low frequencies. The spectral densities of both bipolar signals, as shown in Figure 9.9, contain a spectral null at $f = 0$. Because the spectral energy of the bipolar waveform is concentrated around $f = R_b/2$, signal droop on AC-coupled transmission circuits is avoided. The clock signal can be easily extracted from the bipolar waveform by converting it to a unipolar format by the use of full-wave rectification. The resulting unipolar signal has a frequency component at the bit rate. The first null bandwidth of both bipolar NRZ and RZ signals is equal to R_b Hz.

Bipolar signals have a built-in single-error detection capability because a single error will cause a violation of the alternating mark inversion rule. Any violation can be easily

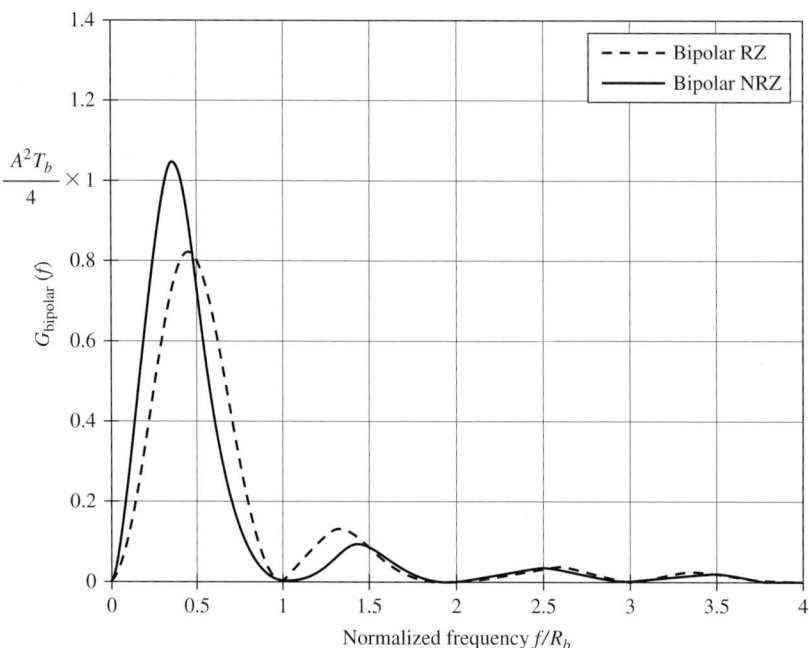

Figure 9.9 Spectral density of bipolar NRZ and RZ signals ($R_b = 1$).

detected by the receiver logic. Bipolar RZ is the standard line-coding scheme for the North American T1 carrier system.

Manchester Code

The Manchester coding is a form of binary antipodal signaling with the pulse shape

$$v(t) = \Pi\left(\frac{t + T_b/4}{T_b/2}\right) - \Pi\left(\frac{t - T_b/4}{T_b/2}\right) \tag{9.49}$$

The FT of this pulse shape is given by

$$V(f) = \frac{T_b}{2}\operatorname{sinc}(fT_b/2)e^{j\omega T_b/4} - \frac{T_b}{2}\operatorname{sinc}(fT_b/2)e^{-j\omega T_b/4}$$

$$= jT_b\operatorname{sinc}(fT_b/2)\sin(\omega T_b/4) \tag{9.50}$$

Substituting (9.50) into (9.33), the spectral density for the Manchester signal is given by

$$G_{\text{Manchester}}(f) = \frac{A^2}{R_b}\operatorname{sinc}^2(f/2R_b)\sin^2(\pi f/2R_b) \tag{9.51}$$

As expected, the first null bandwidth of the Manchester signal is equal to $2R_b$ Hz—twice that for unipolar NRZ signaling because the pulse width is half as wide. This is illustrated in Figure 9.10. However, the Manchester code has a zero DC level on

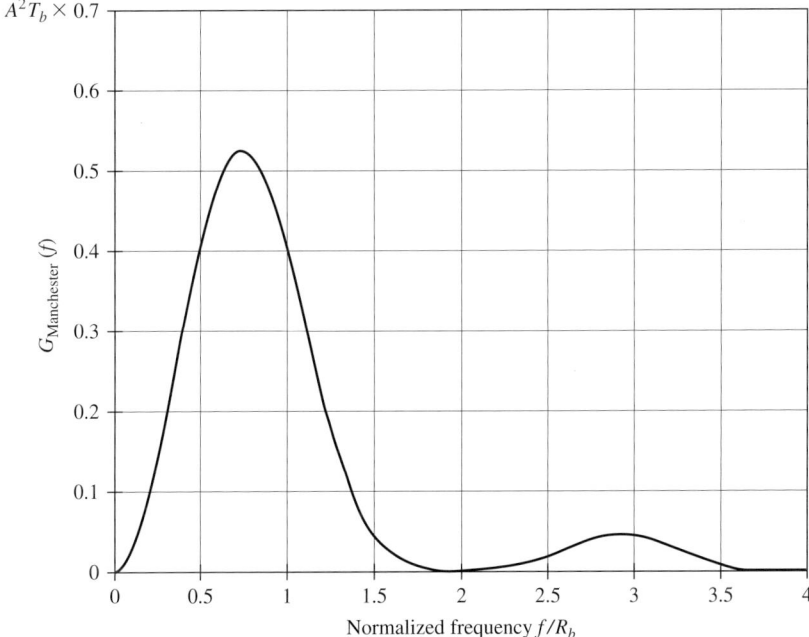

Figure 9.10 Spectral density of Manchester signal ($R_b = 1$).

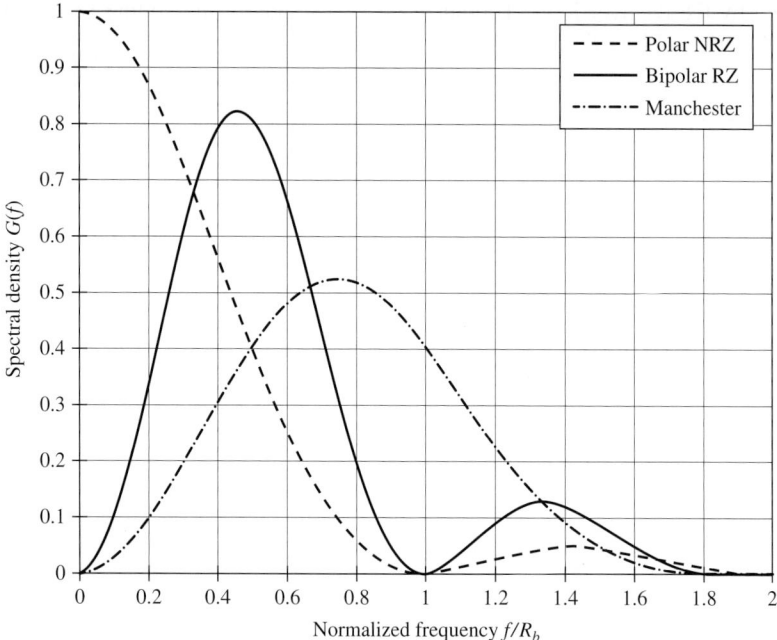

Figure 9.11 Comparison of spectra of popular line codes ($R_b = 1$).

a bit-by-bit basis. Moreover, a long string of 1's or 0's will not cause a loss of clock because there is pulse transition in each bit interval. Manchester line code is specified in the IEEE 802.3 10/100 Mbps Ethernet standard.

Figure 9.11 compares the spectral characteristics of three popular line codes: polar NRZ, bipolar RZ, and Manchester. For each line code, the pulse amplitude A was chosen so that the normalized average power is unity.

Experiment 9.1   *Waveforms and Spectra of Several Line-Coding Schemes*

In this experiment, we simulate the waveforms and spectra of various line-coding schemes. The Simulink model is illustrated in Figure 9.12(a). A **Polar Bernoulli Source,** discussed in Example 3.2, generates polar NRZ waveform. The mapping to unipolar signal is accomplished by the **Lookup Table block** from the **Lookup Tables** library of Simulink. Polar RZ waveform is generated by multiplying the polar NRZ waveform with a 50% duty cycle rectangular pulse train. The Manchester encoded waveform is generated by a custom Simulink block. The waveforms of different line codes are shown in Figure 9.12(b). Figure 9.12(c) displays simulated spectra of various line codes which confirm the theoretical results discussed earlier.

Figure 9.12 (a) Simulink model; (b) waveforms of various line codes; (c) simulated spectra of various line codes.

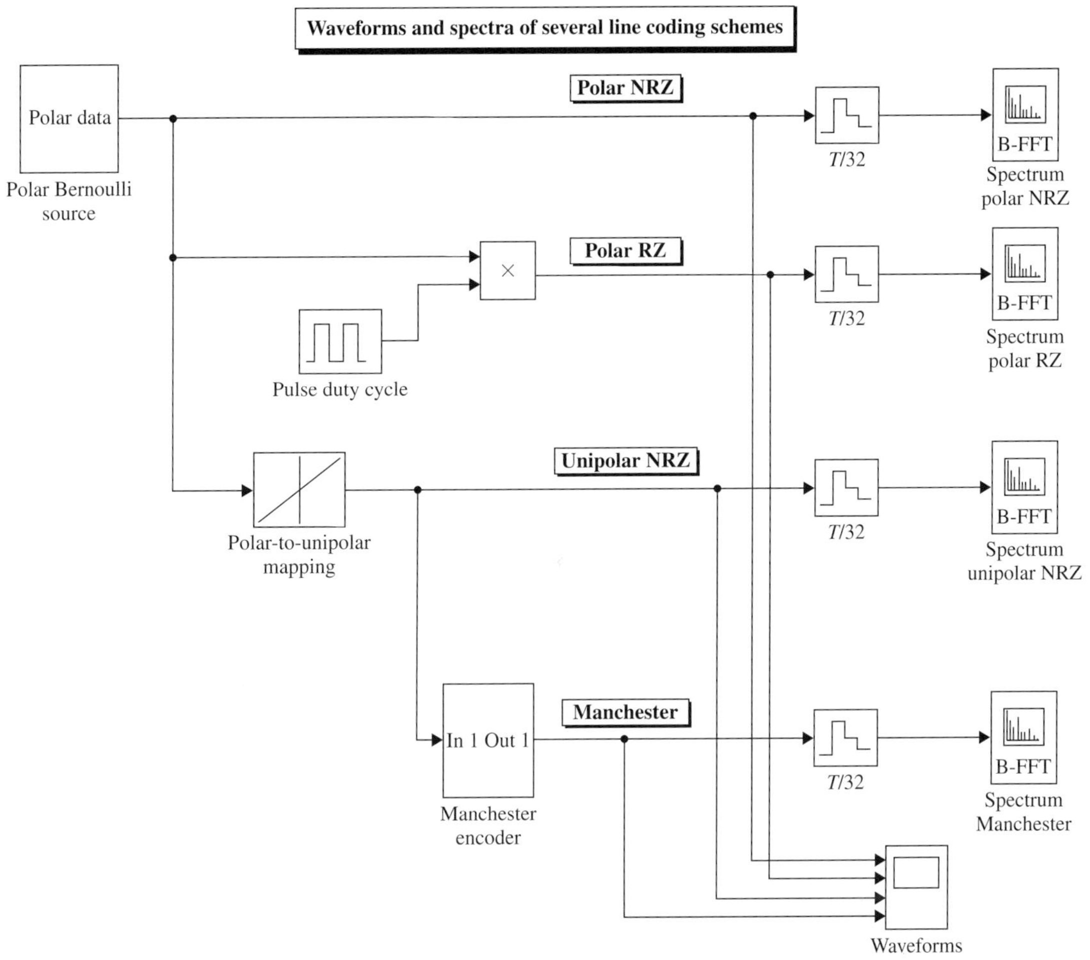

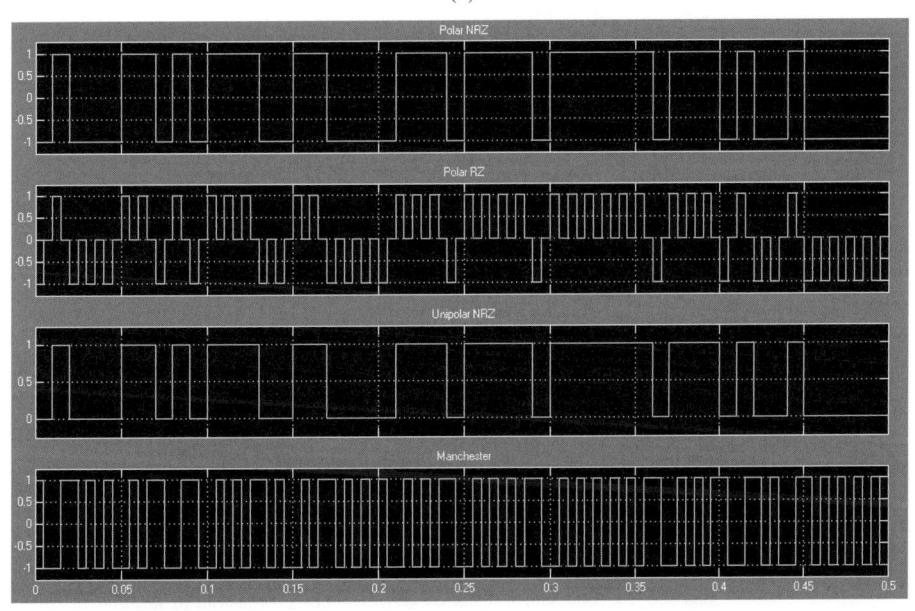

(a)

(b)

(continued)

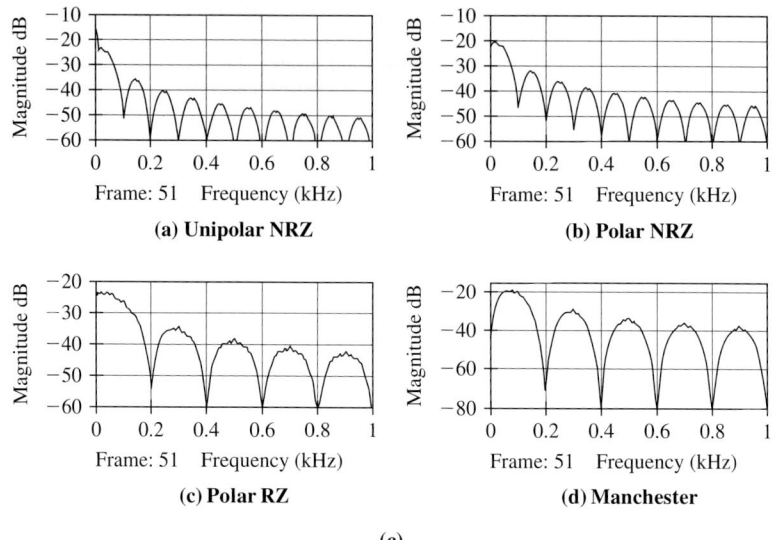

(a) Unipolar NRZ

(b) Polar NRZ

(c) Polar RZ

(d) Manchester

(c)

9.4 BANDWIDTH OF DIGITAL BASEBAND SIGNALS

All practical baseband signals have a frequency above which their spectral components may be considered negligible. The bandwidth of a digitally modulated baseband signal is defined as the width of the frequency band, from DC to a frequency B, which contains significant spectral components to represent the signal with acceptable distortion. The definition implies that the spectral components to be included in the "signal" are determined by its relevance in a given application. Thus there are many definitions of bandwidth, depending on the context.[2]

- **Half-power bandwidth (B_{3dB}).** It is the frequency where the spectral density $G_s(f)$ of a digital baseband signal has dropped to one-half of the peak value (i.e., 3 dB below).
- **First null bandwidth (B_{null}).** It is the frequency where the first null in the envelope of the spectral density $G_s(f)$ occurs. It represents the width of the main lobe of the spectral density function where most of the signal power resides. It is a very popular measure for the bandwidth of digital baseband signals.
- **Absolute bandwidth (B_{abs}).** It is the frequency beyond which the spectrum of a digital baseband signal is zero (i.e., $G_s(f) = 0$). This is a useful abstraction, except for the family of waveforms that includes RC pulses (to be discussed in Section 9.8), where the absolute bandwidth is well defined. However, for all other waveforms, the absolute bandwidth is infinite.
- **Fractional power bandwidth.** It is the range of frequencies that contains a specified percentage of the total signal power. The most popular version of this measure is the **99% power bandwidth** of a signal, which defines the frequency range within which lies 99% of the signal power.

Figure 9.13 displays popular definitions of bandwidth used in digital baseband transmission systems.

Spectral or Bandwidth Efficiency

The **spectral** or **bandwidth efficiency** of a digital modulation scheme that transmits data at rate R_b bps using B Hz of bandwidth is defined as

$$\eta = R_b/B \text{ bits/sec-Hz} \tag{9.52}$$

---

[2] F. Amoroso, "The Bandwidth of Digital Data Signals," *IEEE Communications Magazine* 18, no. 6 (1980): 13–24.

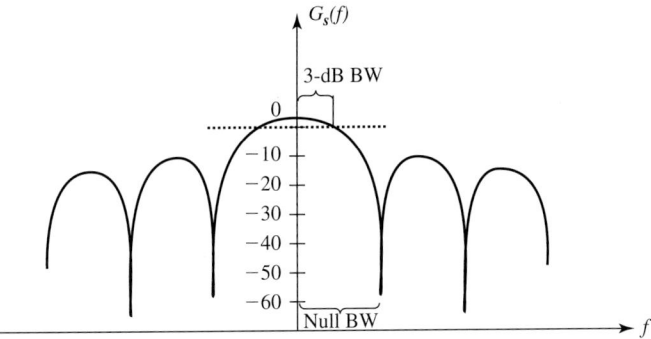

Figure 9.13 Definitions of bandwidth.

Table 9.1 Spectral Characteristics of Various Line Codes

Line Code	Null Bandwidth	Spectral Efficiency η_{null} bits/sec-Hz
NRZ unipolar	R_b	1
NRZ polar	R_b	1
RZ unipolar	$2R_b$	1/2
Bipolar RZ (AMI)	R_b	1
Manchester	$2R_b$	1/2
M-ary PAM	R_b/k	k

The spectral efficiency is a measure of how efficiently the allocated bandwidth is utilized by the digital transmission system. Table 9.1 summarizes the spectral characteristics of various line codes where $\eta_{null} = R_b/B_{null}$ definition of the spectral efficiency is used.

9.5 SPECTRAL AND POWER OUT-OF-BAND PLOTS

It is common practice to display spectra of line-encoding schemes by plotting the spectral density $G(f)$ in decibels, that is $10\log_{10} G(f)$, against the normalized frequency (i.e., f/R_b or f/D). Figure 9.14 displays the normalized spectral density plots of polar NRZ, bipolar RZ, and Manchester line codes. Such spectral plots make it much easier to visualize the side-lobe structure as well as their rate of decay. Another useful display of signal spectra is the **power out-of-band (POB)** plot. This plot exhibits at a given frequency f the total power lying outside f. That is,

$$P_{OB}(f) \equiv 10\log_{10} \frac{\int_f^\infty G(f)df}{\int_0^\infty G(f)df}, \quad f > 0 \tag{9.53}$$

The POB is used as a measure of the *compactness* of the power spectrum of a digital modulation scheme. When $P_{OB}(f) = 0.01(\sim -20$ dB$)$, the frequency f is called the 99% bandwidth of the signal. Figure 9.15 is a POB plot for the line codes in Figure 9.14. The POB provides a convenient estimate of the channel bandwidth required to achieve signal transmission with acceptable distortion. We observe from Figure 9.15 that the 99% bandwidth of NRZ signaling is around $7R_b$. Thus, NRZ signaling is not a viable solution for many practical bandlimited channels.

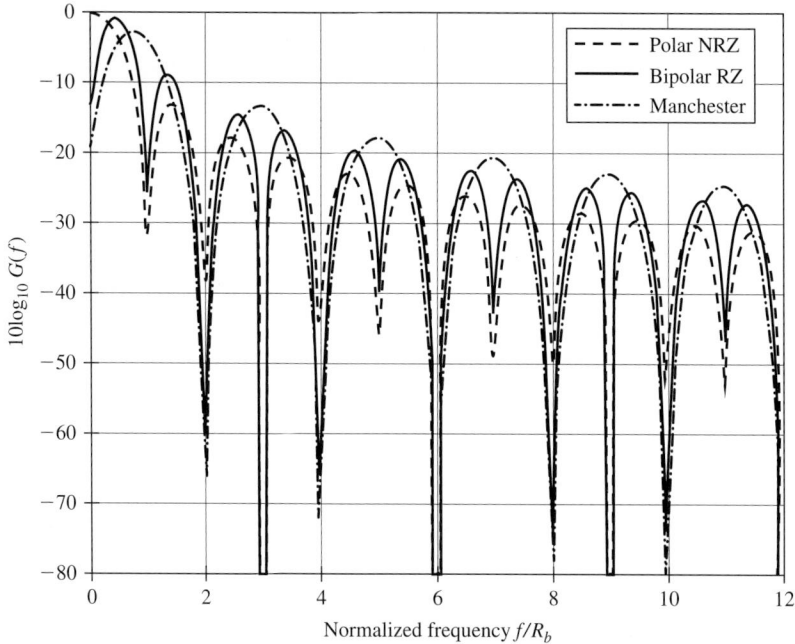

Figure 9.14 Decibel spectral plots of popular binary line codes. Normalized average power of line codes is assumed unity.

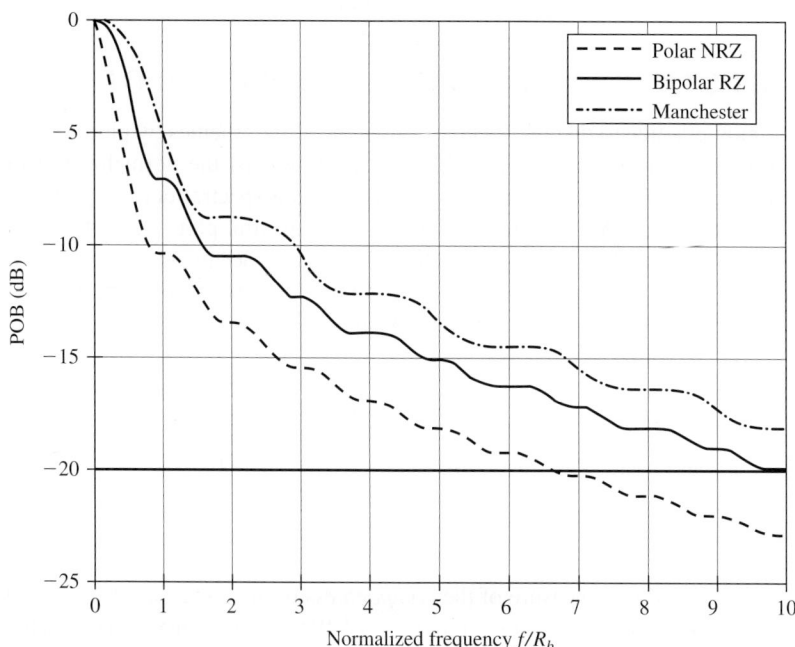

Figure 9.15 Power out-of-band plots of popular binary line codes.

9.6 BLOCK LINE CODES

In block encoding, the input stream is divided into blocks of k bits, each of which is mapped into a distinct n-symbol codeword $\underline{a} = [a_1, a_2, \ldots, a_n]$, where data symbols a_i can assume one of the M levels. The following constraint

$$2^k \leq M^n \qquad (9.54)$$

guarantees that each block of k bits is mapped into a unique n-symbol codeword. When the right-hand side of (9.54) is greater than the left-hand side, there are more codewords available than there are k-bit blocks. This redundancy can be used to select codewords with desirable properties, such as code transparency and DC balance. A line code is called **transparent** if it can transmit any bit pattern (e.g., long string of 1's and 0's) in the user data stream so that it can be recovered at the receiver without difficulty.

9.6.1 Binary Block Codes

kBnB Codes

In kBnB code, blocks of k information bits are mapped into n-bit codewords. Next we can use one of the binary line-coding techniques discussed in Section 9.2 to create the digital signal for transmission. Because $n > k$, the symbol rate for kBnB code exceeds the information bit rate as indicated in (9.55).

$$\text{Symbol rate}_{k\text{B}n\text{B}} = \frac{n}{k} \text{ Bit rate}_{k\text{B}n\text{B}}, n > k \qquad (9.55)$$

Redundancy in the code is used to provide the desired transmission features. In Table 9.2, the code conversion table of 4B5B code is given as an example of kBnB code. This code maps a block of four bits into a codeword containing five bits, according to Table 9.2. The 5-bit codes are normally line-coded using NRZ-I. Because $2^4 = 16$ 4-bit data blocks are mapped into a possible $2^5 = 32$ 5-bit codewords, the codewords are selected with at least two 1's. Because NRZ-I is used, this will force two transitions

Table 9.2 4B5B Code Conversion Table

Binary data input	Encoder binary output
0000	11110
0001	01001
0010	10100
0011	10101
0100	01010
0101	01011
0110	01110
0111	01111
1000	10010
1001	10011
1010	10110
1011	10111
1100	11010
1101	11011
1111	11101

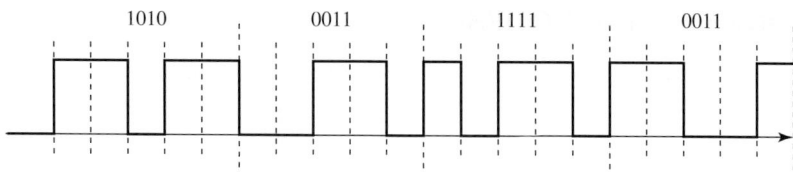

Figure 9.16 4B5B code example.

and no more than three 0's in a row. The signaling rate for 4B5B code is five-fourths of the information bit rate. The unused 5-bit combinations are used for encoding control and status information. The well-known $kBnB$ codes include 8B10B (gigabit Ethernet) and 64B66 (10-gigabit Ethernet). Figure 9.16 displays 4B5B encoding of the binary sequence 1010 0011 1111 0011.

HDBn *and* BnZS *Codes*

Bipolar coding has many desirable properties, including spectral null at DC and single-error detection capability. Long strings of 1's result in a square wave at $1/2T_b$ Hz that has good timing content. However, long strings of 0's still pose problems and can cause clock recovery circuits to lose synchronization. To make the bipolar code transparent, a continuous string of n 0's is replaced by a special bipolar code. That is why these block codes are called **substitution** codes. A well-known code of this type is called **high-density bipolar (HDB)** code. HDB3 is the code recommended in G.703 by ITU for European legacy digital multiplexing systems (Chapter 13). In HDB3 a string of four 0's is replaced by either 000V or B00V, where B represents a normal, nonzero bipolar pulse and V represents a nonzero bipolar pulse that violates the bipolar rule. This violation identifies the special sequence at the receiver so that the zero string will be reinserted into the data sequence. The choice of sequence 000V or B00V is made in such a way that consecutive V pulses alternate signs in order to avoid introducing a DC component. This implies that B00V is selected when there is an even number of 1's following the last special sequence and 000V is inserted when there is an odd number of 1's following the last substitution. Figure 9.17 displays HDB3 encoding of the binary sequence 0010 11110000000010101110101000001.

Bipolar with n Zero Substitution (BnZS) codes are similar to HDBn codes, where a string of n successive 0's is replaced with one of two special sequences containing some 1's to increase the timing content. As in the case of HDBn codes, the special sequences contain bipolar violations so they can be identified at the receiver. **Bipolar with 8 Zero Substitution (B8ZS)** code is used commonly in North American T1 (1.544 Mbps) and T1C (3.152 Mbps) legacy digital carrier systems. In B8ZS every string of eight 0's is substituted by a string 000VB0VB containing two bipolar violations. Thus

- If the immediately preceding nonzero bipolar pulse is of $-$ve polarity, then replace each group of eight 0's with the sequence $000-+0+-$.
- If the immediately preceding nonzero bipolar pulse is of $+$ve polarity, then replace each group of eight 0's with the sequence $000+-0-+$.

Figure 9.18 displays B8ZS encoding of the binary sequence in Figure 9.17.

In the B6ZS code used in North American T2 (6.3212 Mbps) legacy digital carrier systems, a string of 0's is replaced by the special sequence 0VB0VB. B3ZS code is used

User data stream:	0	0	1	0	1	1	1	1	0	0	0	0	0	0	0	0	1	0	1	0	1	1	1	0	1	0	1	0	0	0	0	1
Bipolar:	0	0	+	0	−	+	−	+	0	0	0	0	0	0	0	0	−	0	+	0	−	+	−	0	+	0	−	0	0	0	0	+
HDB3:	0	0	1	0	1	1	1	1	0	0	0	V	1	0	0	V	1	0	1	0	1	1	1	0	1	0	1	0	0	0	V	1
	0	0	+	0	−	+	−	+	0	0	0	+	−	0	0	−	+	0	−	0	+	−	+	0	−	0	+	0	0	0	+	−

Figure 9.17 HDB3 code example.

Userdatastream:	0	0	1	0	1	1	1	1	0	0	0	0	0	0	0	0	1	0	1	0	1	1	1	0	1	0	1	0	0	0	0	1
Bipolar:	0	0	+	0	−	+	−	+	0	0	0	0	0	0	0	0	−	0	+	0	−	+	−	0	+	0	−	0	0	0	0	+
B8ZS:	0	0	+	0	−	+	−	+	0	0	0	+	−	0	−	+	−	0	+	0	−	+	−	0	+	0	−	0	0	0	0	+

Figure 9.18 B8ZS code example.

in North American T3 (44.736 Mbps) legacy digital carrier systems. It replaces a string of three 0's with either B0V or 00V, with the choice being made to force an odd number of B pulses between consecutive V pulses.

9.6.2 Multilevel Block Codes

Multilevel block codes are used to control the spectrum of the digital signal for band-limited channels. Another important reason for spectral shaping is to minimize cross-talk between adjacent wire pairs in multipair cables.

k*B*n*T* (k *Binary,* n *Ternary) Codes*

kBnT codes map blocks of k information bits into codewords of n ternary symbols. The ternary output symbols take the values of $+A$, 0, and $-A$. This code achieves a symbol rate less than the information bit rate

$$\text{Symbol rate}_{kBnT} = \frac{n}{k} \text{ Bit rate}_{kBnT}, \, n < k \qquad (9.56)$$

Because this code stretches the transmitted symbol or pulse interval, it reduces the signal bandwidth. In kBnT coding, the encoder maintains a **running digital sum (RDS)** counter that keeps track of the cumulative DC balance of the transmitted digital signal. Each +ve pulse that is transmitted increases the RDS by 1, while a −ve pulse decreases it by 1. As an example, 4B3T code is shown in Table 9.3. The 16 possible 4-bit blocks are mapped into 27 possible combinations of three ternary symbols. The encoder selects the codeword with a positive or negative mean or bias for transmission, according to the current RDS counter value. That is, if RDS is between

- −3 and −1, select the code from the left-hand column (positive bias).
- 0 and 3, select the code from the right-hand column (negative bias).

4B3T is standardized as the line code in Europe and ROW for implementation of **basic rate interface (BRI)** in **Integrated Services Digital Network (ISDN).** Because the BRI bit rate is 160 kbps, the symbol rate using 4B3T is three-quarters of the bit rate, that is, 120 k symbols per second. Figure 9.19 displays 4B3T encoding of the binary sequence 1010 0011 1111 0011.

Table 9.3 4B3T Code Conversion Table

Data Bits	Line Encoder Output (Bias)	Line Encoder Output (Bias)
0000	+ 0 − (0)	+ 0 − (0)
0001	− + 0 (0)	− + 0 (0)
0010	0 + − (0)	0 + − (0)
0011	+ − 0 (0)	+ − 0 (0)
0100	0 0 + (1)	0 0 − (−1)
0101	0 + 0 (1)	0 − 0 (−1)
0110	+ 0 0 (1)	− 0 0 (−1)
0111	+ − + (1)	− + − (−1)
1000	− + + (1)	+ − − (−1)
1001	+ + − (1)	− − + (−1)
1010	+ + + (3)	− − − (−3)
1011	+ 0 + (2)	− 0 − (−2)
1100	0 + + (2)	0 − − (−2)
1101	+ + 0 (2)	− − 0 (−2)
1110	0 + − (0)	0 + − (0)
1111	− 0 + (0)	− 0 + (0)

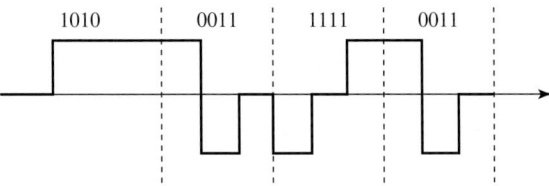

Figure 9.19 4B3T code example.

2B1Q (Two Binary, One Quaternary) Code

This code converts blocks of two consecutive information bits into a distinct quaternary amplitude (four-level) pulse for transmission. As such, this line-encoding scheme is a special case of *M*-ary PAM discussed in Section 9.1. Because the symbol rate using 2B1Q is half of the bit rate, it is more bandwidth efficient than 4B3T code. An example of 2B1Q code is displayed in Figure 9.4.

2B1Q coding is standardized in North America per ANSI T1.601 for ISDB basic rate U-interface. 2B1Q allows an information bit rate of 160 kbps using a line rate of 80 k symbols per second for distances up to about 18,000 feet (5.5 km) with attenuation up to 42 dB.

9.7   SCRAMBLING

Scrambling is an alternative method to remove long strings of 1's and 0's in a user bit stream to make the resultant binary data appear more random. The goal is to achieve bit transparency so that any arbitrary bit pattern can be transmitted without causing problems in data recovery at the receiver. Scrambling is used in all CCITT-standardized voiceband data modems as well as in SONET-based telecommunication networks.

There are two types of scramblers:

- Frame-synchronous
- Self-synchronous

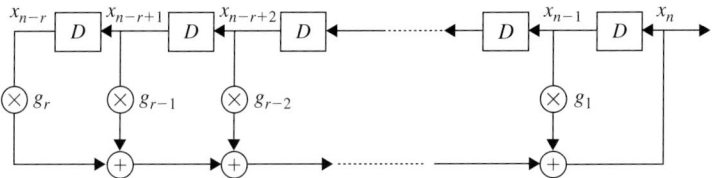

Figure 9.20 Linear feedback shift register implementation of a PN sequence generator.

Both types of scramblers use **pseudorandom noise (PN)** sequences to randomize the data. These are periodic sequences that eventually repeat, but they have characteristics that make them appear to be random. A PN sequence is generated by a **linear feedback shift register (LFSR)** shown in Figure 9.20. The feedback connections of the LFSR are determined by a generator polynomial

$$g(D) = 1 \oplus g_1 D \oplus g_2 D^2 \oplus \ldots \oplus g_r D^r \qquad (9.57)$$

The output binary sequence x_n is generated according to the recursive formula:

$$x_n = g_1 x_{n-1} \oplus g_2 x_{n-2} \oplus \ldots \oplus g_r x_{n-r} = \sum_{i=1}^{r} g_i x_{n-i} \qquad (9.58)$$

where the shift register coefficients $\{g_i\}$ are binary (0 or 1), and addition ($\oplus$) and multiplication are modulo-2.

A polynomial is said to be primitive if it has no factors other than 1 and itself. Only primitive generator polynomials can generate PN sequences with maximal length or period. The period of a PN sequence generated by a primitive polynomial of degree r is

$$N = 2^r - 1 \qquad (9.59)$$

Because the LFSR output sequence repeats itself with period N, PN sequences are also called **maximum-length (ML)** sequences. Table 9.4 displays primitive polynomials of all degrees up to 11 in octal format. The coefficient $g_o(=1)$ is on the right; the coefficient g_r is on the left. Numbers in the table indicated with [*] are trinomials (have only 2 feedback connections), and are better suited for some high-speed applications.

Table 9.4 Primitive Polynomials of Degrees Up to 11

Degree	Octal Representation of Generator Polynomial $g(D)$
2	7[*]
3	13[*]
4	23[*]
5	45[*], 75, 67
6	103[*], 147, 155
7	211, 217, 235, 367, 277, 325, 203[*], 313, 345
8	435, 551, 747, 453, 545, 537, 703, 543
9	1021[*], 1131, 1461, 1423, 1055, 1167, 1541, 1333, 1605, 1751, 1743, 1617, 1553, 1157
10	2011[*], 2415, 3771, 2157, 3515, 2773, 2033, 2443, 2461, 3023, 3543, 2745, 2431, 3177
11	4005[*], 4445, 4215, 4055, 6015, 7413, 4143, 4563, 4053, 5023, 5623, 4577, 6233, 667312

Example 9.2

Consider a three-stage LFSR ML sequence generator. The generator polynomial $g(D)$ from Table 9.4 in the octal form is 13. Therefore,

$$g_3 \quad g_2 \quad g_1 \quad g_0$$

$$1 \quad \ \ 1 \quad \ \ 0 \quad \ \ 1$$

$g(D)$ can now be written as

$$g(D) = 1 \oplus D^2 \oplus D^3$$

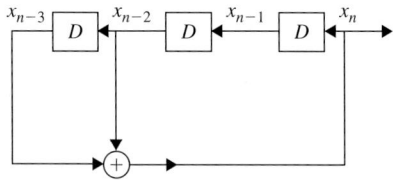

Figure 9.21 Three-stage LFSR.

Figure 9.21 displays the three-stage LFSR. The output sequence is generated according to the formula

$$x_n = x_{n-2} \oplus x_{n-3}$$

Let us consider the initial state to be $x_{n-2} = 0$, $x_{n-1} = 0$, $x_{n-3} = 1$. The output of the LFSR is $\{1011100, 1011100, 101 \ldots\}$. The sequence is periodic with period 7.

9.7.1 Frame-Synchronous Scrambler

In a frame-synchronous scrambler, the output of PN sequence generator x_n is added bit by bit to the user's data stream b_n to generate the scrambled bit sequence c_n. That is,

$$c_n = b_n \oplus x_n \tag{9.60}$$

The scrambled bit stream is transmitted to the descrambler using one of the line-encoding methods discussed in Section 9.2. Figure 9.22 illustrates the operation of frame-synchronous scrambling.

At the descrambler, the user data is recovered by adding the output of another PN generator to the scrambled bit stream c_n.

$$\text{Descrambler output} = c_n \oplus x_n = b_n \oplus x_n \oplus x_n = b_n \tag{9.61}$$

because

$$x_n \oplus x_n = 0.$$

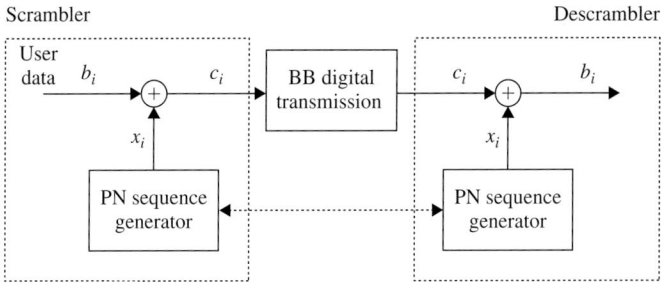

Figure 9.22 Frame-synchronous scrambling.

The challenge for proper operation of the frame-synchronized scrambling system is to maintain synchronization between PN sequence generators in the scrambler and the descrambler as emphasized by the dotted line in Figure 9.22. This is achieved by using frame synchronization techniques (Chapter 13).

9.7.2 SONET Scrambler

Synchronous Optical Network (SONET) is a digital data transmission standard for telecommunication infrastructure networks in North America and Japan. SONET uses a frame length of 125 μsec or a frame rate of 8000 frames per second. Each STS-1 frame can be viewed as a 9-row by 90-column structure, a total of 810 bytes (refer to Chapter 13 for details). Figure 9.23 displays a simplified representation of an STS-1 frame. Two bytes, A1 and A2, indicate the beginning of each STS-1 frame. The A1, A2 bytes pattern is F628 hex.

The SONET standard requires that all user data be scrambled by the output of a PN sequence generator specified by the generator polynomial $g(D) = 1 \oplus D^6 \oplus D^7$. Figure 9.24 displays the implementation of a SONET scrambler. Because the degree of the polynomial $r = 7$, the PN sequence repeats every $2^r - 1 = 127$ clock cycles. The framing bytes A1 and A2 and the STS-1 identification byte J0 are not scrambled. The generator is reset at the beginning of each STS-1 frame to a well-known state (1111111)

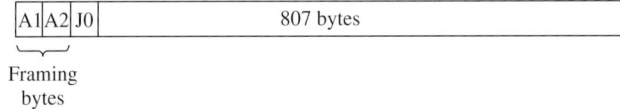

Figure 9.23 Simplified SONET STS-1 frame.

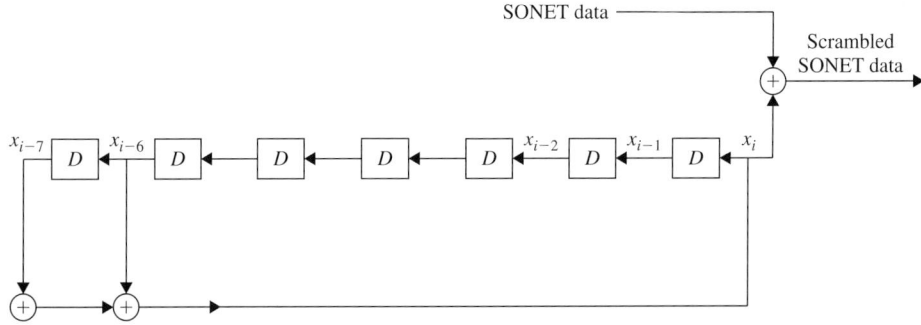

Figure 9.24 SONET scrambler.

by the first bit of the byte following the J0 byte. The descrambler similarly resets the generator to the well-known state at the beginning of each frame. The output of the PN generator after it is reset to 1111111 is given by

1111111000000010000011000010100 0111100100010110011101010001111

1010000111000100100110110101010 11110110001101001010111011100110

0101010 11111110000000100000110000101000111100100010110011101010 . . .

Note that the sequence repeats after 127 bits as shown by the underlined bits. Even if the data stream is all 0's, the scrambled data stream will appear as:

1111111000000010000011000010100 0111100100010110011101010001111 . . .

Although there are no transitions in the input bit stream, there are plenty of transitions in the output sequence. Therefore, a scrambler can perform the zero suppression function like a line code.

9.7.3 Self-Synchronous Scrambler

A self-synchronous scrambler does not XOR user data with a fixed PN sequence as in the case of frame-synchronous design. Instead, the input stream is added directly to the input of an LFSR as shown in Figure 9.25(a). The LFSR input c_n is also the scrambler's output.

$$c_n = b_n \oplus \sum_{i=1}^{r} g_i c_{n-i} \tag{9.62}$$

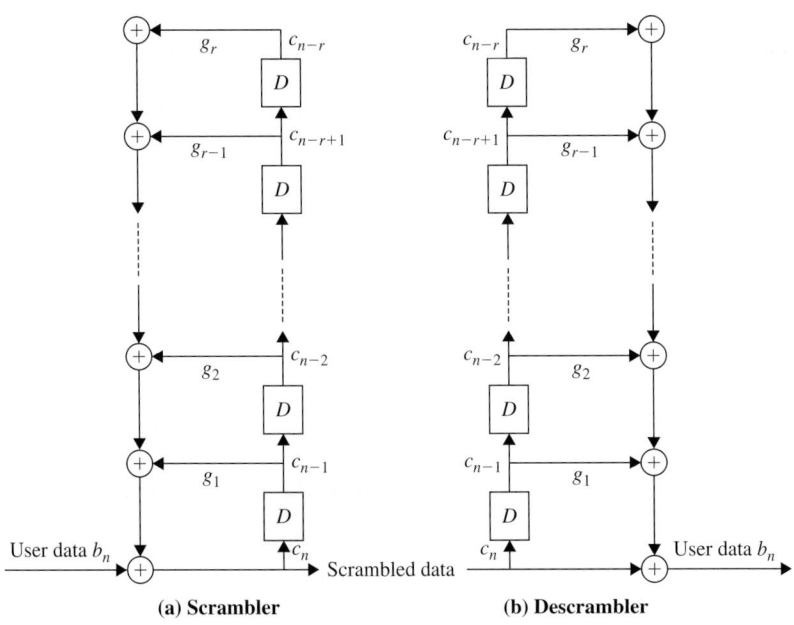

(a) Scrambler   **(b) Descrambler**

Figure 9.25 Self-synchronous scrambler and descrambler.

Note that the scrambler forms a feedback shift register. The descrambler, on the other hand, consists of a feedforward shift register. The scrambled data c_n forms input to an identical LFSR as illustrated in Figure 9.25(b). The descrambler output is obtained by XORing it with the output of the LFSR as follows:

$$\text{Descrambler output} = c_n \oplus \sum_{i=1}^{r} g_i c_{n-i} = b_n \oplus \sum_{i=1}^{r} g_i c_{n-i} \oplus \sum_{i=1}^{r} g_i c_{n-i} = b_n \quad (9.63)$$

Thus the input data stream is recovered by the descrambler.

Example 9.3

The sequence $b_n = \{100000000000\}$ is input to a self-synchronous scrambler. Assume that the LFSR is defined by degree 5 polynomial 45 octal from Table 9.4.

a. Sketch the scrambler.
b. Assuming that the initial state of the shift register is set to all zeros, determine the scrambled sequence c_n.

Solution

a. The generator polynomial corresponding to 45 octal is

$$g(D) = 1 \oplus D^2 \oplus D^5$$

That is,

g_5	g_4	g_3	g_2	g_1	g_0
1	0	0	1	0	1

The scrambler is illustrated in Figure 9.26.

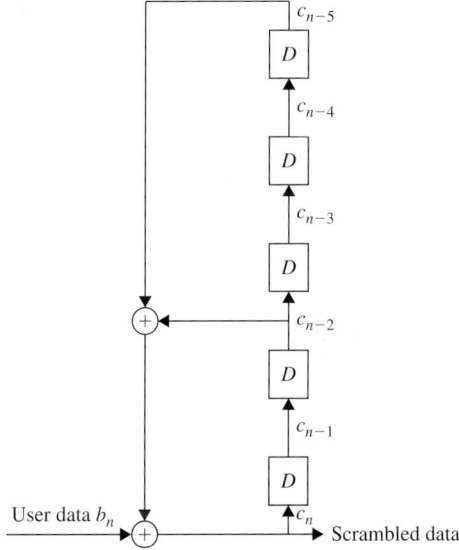

Figure 9.26 Self-synchronous scrambler: Example 9.3.

b. The scrambled data output can now be obtained from (9.62) as

$$c_n = b_n \oplus c_{n-2} \oplus c_{n-5}$$

Table 9.5 displays the calculation of scrambled bits. We observe that although the input bit sequence of length 12 contains a string of 11 0's, the scrambled sequence is well randomized.

Table 9.5 Calculation of Scrambled Bits

Data bits	b_n	1	0	0	0	0	0	0	0	0	0	0	0
	c_{n-1}	0	1	0	1	0	1	1	1	0	1	1	0
	c_{n-2}	0	0	1	0	1	0	1	1	1	0	1	1
Shift-register contents	c_{n-3}	0	0	0	1	0	1	0	1	1	1	0	1
	c_{n-4}	0	0	0	0	1	0	1	0	1	1	1	0
	c_{n-5}	0	0	0	0	0	1	0	1	0	1	1	1
Scrambled bits	c_n	1	0	1	0	1	1	1	0	1	1	0	0

9.7.4 ATM Scrambler

Asynchronous Transfer Mode (ATM) technology is widely deployed to transport Internet traffic in the form of data packets. The user data is scrambled by a self-synchronous scrambler whose LFSR is described by the polynomial $g(D) = 1 \oplus D^{43}$. The LFSR is initialized once, at the start of the operation, and may be set to any random 43-bit value. Subsequently, each bit of user data is XORed with a bit shifted out of the high order end of the register as illustrated in Figure 9.27(a). The scrambled data bit c_n resulting from this operation is transmitted to the descrambler as well as shifted back into the low order end of the register. The descrambler essentially operates by XORing each bit of incoming scrambled data with the (scrambled) incoming data bit received 43 bits previously as illustrated in Figure 9.27(b). At startup, the shift register may be initialized with the first 43 bits of data that arrive, after which it can begin descrambling.

The self-synchronous scrambler has a number of attractive properties. The state of the scrambler is transmitted to the descrambler in the scrambled data stream itself, avoiding the need for restarting the scrambler periodically to achieve synchronization between the scrambler and descrambler as in the case of the frame-synchronous scrambler. Another use of the self-synchronous scrambler is in encryption of the user data for security purposes. Because the state of the self-synchronous scrambler is set by a random number and changes dynamically with the user data, it is hard to predict. Thus it is more secure than the frame-synchronous scrambler where a fixed PN sequence is always combined with the user data.

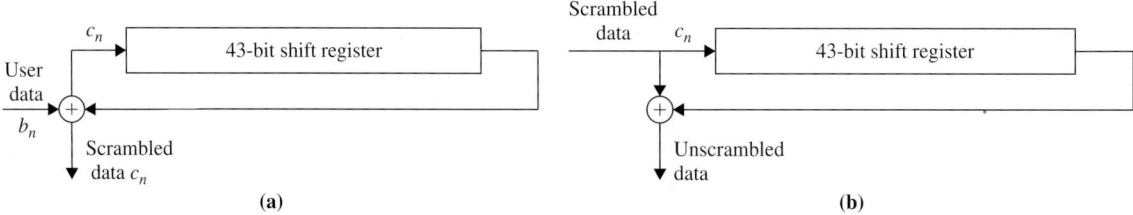

Figure 9.27 ATM: (a) scrambler; (b) descrambler.

9.8 PULSE SHAPING TO IMPROVE SPECTRAL EFFICIENCY

Recall from Section 9.2 that the spectral density of a linearly modulated digital signal depends on the spectrum of the underlying basic pulse shape (via $|V(f)|^2$). Although the simple, square NRZ pulse is an obvious way to send data, its short duration and sharp edges cause it to have a very wide bandwidth. With our insatiable demand for new and faster information delivery, data transmission requirements continue to rise at an exponential pace, resulting in the need for shorter and shorter pulse durations. The resultant need for higher bandwidth poses a challenge because of the limited spectrum available in cellular and other public telecommunication networks. As discussed in Section 2.6, a waveform cannot be both strictly duration limited and bandwidth limited. Two ways to reduce the bandwidth of any pulse are to round-off its corners and transitions and to lengthen the duration of the pulse beyond the symbol interval. The resultant overlapping pulses interfere with each other. The phenomenon of pulses interfering with each other is called **intersymbol interference (ISI).** We investigate two very interesting overlapping pulse shapes with finite bandwidth.

9.8.1 Sinc Pulse

The sinc pulse

$$v(t) = \text{sinc}(2Bt) = \frac{\sin(2\pi Bt)}{2\pi Bt} \tag{9.64}$$

is shown in Figure 9.28. Its Fourier transform is given from Table 2.2 by

$$V(f) = \frac{1}{2B}\Pi(f/2B) \tag{9.65}$$

Now if the digital baseband modulator sends M-ary information symbols a_n by transmitting sinc pulses $a_n \text{sinc}(2Bt)$ every $T = 1/2B$ seconds, the overlapping pulses do not interfere at $t = nT = n/2B$. Figure 9.29(a) shows the three sinc pulses corresponding to binary sequence 110 before they are added.

The composite signal $r(t)$ at the receiver input is the sum of the contributions from each bit:

$$r(0) = v(0) + v(-T) - v(-2T) = \text{sinc}(0) + \text{sinc}(-1) - \text{sinc}(-2) = 1 + 0 - 0 = 1$$

$$r(T) = v(T) + v(0) + v(-T) = \text{sinc}(1) + \text{sinc}(0) - \text{sinc}(-1) = 0 + 1 - 0 = 1$$

$$r(2T) = v(2T) + v(T) + v(0) = \text{sinc}(2) + \text{sinc}(1) - \text{sinc}(0) = 0 + 0 - 1 = -1$$

Because there is no ISI at exactly the center of each pulse interval, the receiver optimally makes the decision by sampling the composite signal at that instant for each transmitted symbol. That is, in the absence of noise, the receiver makes the decision about the symbol a_0 by sampling $r(0)$, which equals $a_0 v(0)$ because tails or precursors from all other pulses (symbols) have zero crossings at that instant. Thus we can transmit

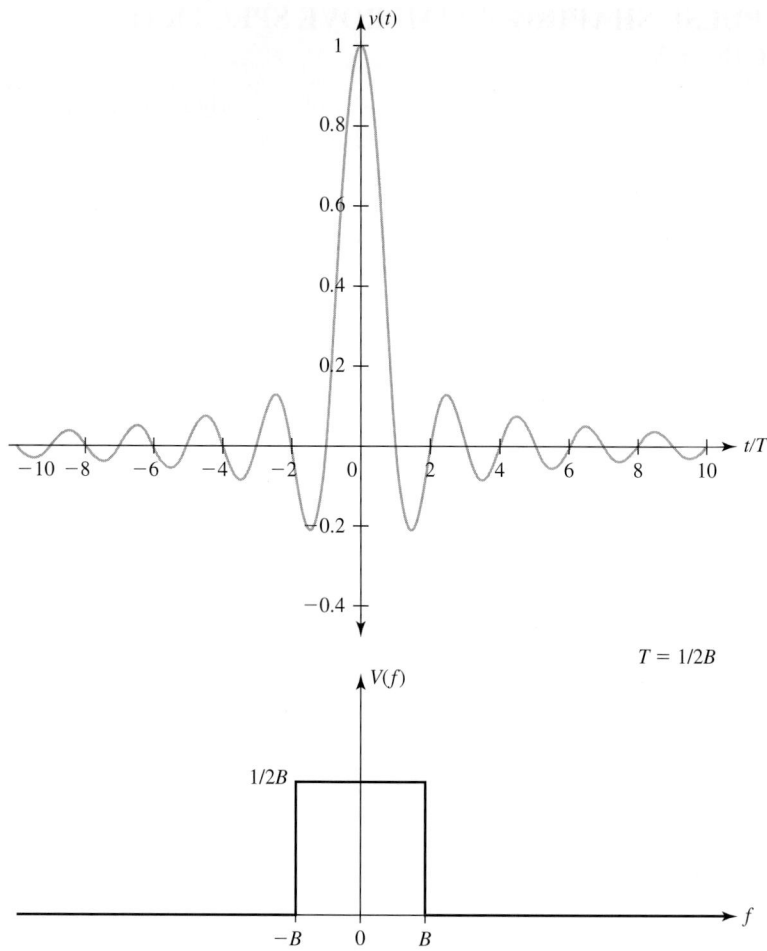

$$T = 1/2B$$

Figure 9.28 Sinc pulse and its Fourier transform.

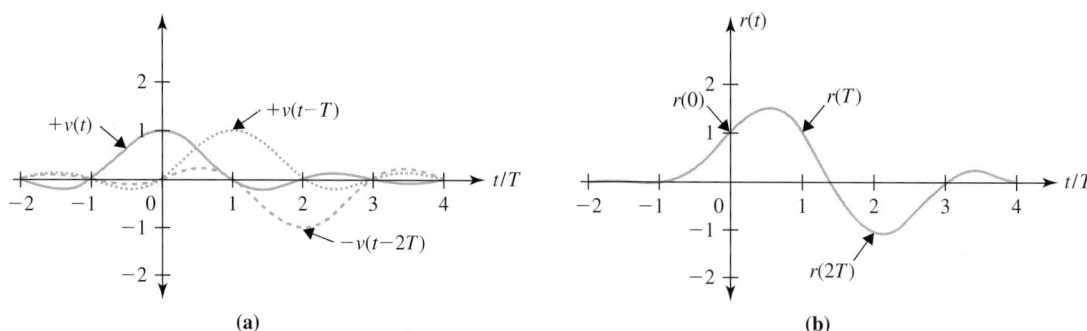

Figure 9.29 Receiver input corresponding to binary sequence 110: (a) three separate pulses; (b) composite signal.

symbols at rate $D = 2B$ symbols per second over an ideal low-pass channel of bandwidth B Hz using sinc pulses. As we shall see in Chapter 12, this is the maximum symbol rate that is achievable through an ideal low-pass channel without ISI. This is called the **Nyquist signaling rate.**

9.8.2 Raised Cosine Pulses

Although a sinc pulse has finite bandwidth, it corresponds to a "brick-wall" filter that is unrealizable. One widely used pulse is the raised cosine pulse, which is defined in the frequency domain by

$$
V_{RC}(f) = \begin{cases} T, & 0 \le |f| \le (1 - \alpha)/2T \\ \dfrac{T}{2}\left\{1 + \cos\left[\dfrac{\pi T}{\alpha}\left(|f| - \dfrac{1 - \alpha}{2T}\right)\right]\right\}, & (1 - \alpha)/2T \le |f| \le (1 + \alpha)/2T \\ 0, & |f| > (1 + \alpha)/2T \end{cases} \tag{9.66}
$$

The parameter α is called the **excess bandwidth factor.** It is also called the **roll-off factor** of the RC pulse. The time domain representation of the RC pulse is given by

$$
v_{RC}(t) = \operatorname{sinc}(t/T).\frac{\cos(\alpha\pi t/T)}{1 - 4\alpha^2 t^2/T^2} \tag{9.67}
$$

Observe that $v_{RC}(t)$ has zero-crossings at $t = \pm T, \pm 2T, \pm 3T, \pm 4T, \dots$. Thus, raised cosine pulses are also **Nyquist waveforms,** implying zero ISI at sampling instants. The time function corresponding to the special case $\alpha = 0$ (the ideal low-pass rectangular spectrum) is a sinc pulse just as expected. Figure 9.30 displays the RC pulse in time and frequency domains for various values of α.

The **absolute bandwidth** of the RC pulse from (9.66) is

$$
B_{abs} = \frac{(1 + \alpha)}{2T} = \frac{D(1 + \alpha)}{2} \tag{9.68}
$$

Because of the Nyquist property, we can transmit RC pulses every T seconds without any ISI over an ideal low-pass channel with bandwidth given by (9.68). The minimum value of bandwidth is $D/2$, corresponding to an ideal low-pass rectangular spectrum ($\alpha = 0$). The maximum value of bandwidth is D for the case $\alpha = 1$. The quantity $\alpha D/2$

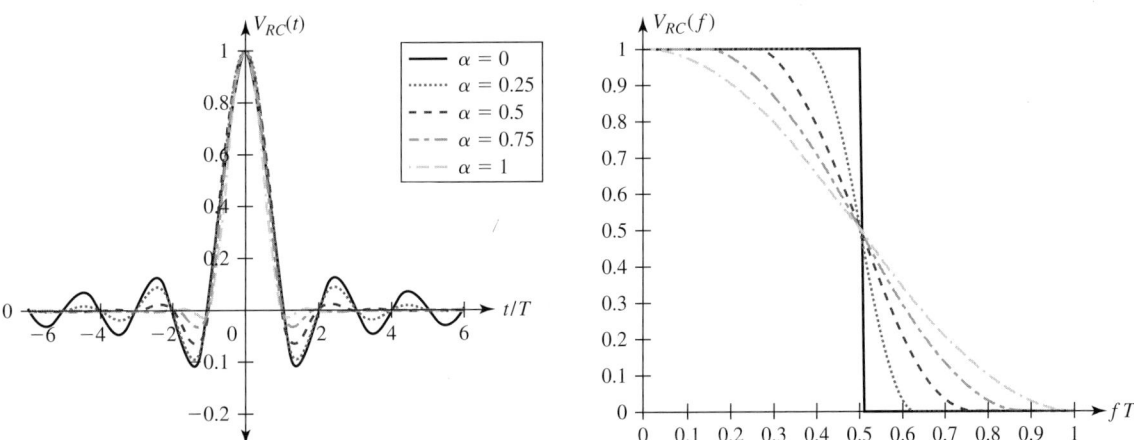

Figure 9.30 RC pulse in time and frequency domains.

Table 9.6 Spectral Characteristics of Various Line-Coding Schemes Using RC Pulses

Line Code	Absolute Bandwidth	Spectral Efficiency η_{rc} (bps)/Hz
NRZ Unipolar	$R_b(1 + \alpha)/2$	$2/(1 + \alpha)$
NRZ Polar	$R_b(1 + \alpha)/2$	$2/(1 + \alpha)$
RZ Unipolar	$R_b(1 + \alpha)$	$1/(1 + \alpha)$
Bipolar RZ (AMI)	$R_b(1 + \alpha)/2$	$2/(1 + \alpha)$
Manchester	$R_b(1 + \alpha)$	$1/(1 + \alpha)$
M-ary PAM	$R_b(1 + \alpha)/2k$	$2k/(1 + \alpha)$

is called the **excess bandwidth** required for RC signaling using roll-off factor α. Raised cosine pulses are a popular choice for line coding even with the bandwidth penalty of $\alpha D/2$ for a given symbol rate D. This is because larger values of α lead to faster sidelobe decay rates, which implies that the sampling clock jitter will not result in significant ISI. Further, the smooth roll-off characteristic of $V_{RC}(f)$ makes it easier to realize in practice.

The spectral efficiency of various line coding schemes using RC pulses is defined as

$$\eta_{rc} = R_b / B_{abs} \text{ bits/sec-Hz} \tag{9.69}$$

Note that we are using the absolute bandwidth in (9.69) for obvious reasons. Table 9.6 summarizes the spectral characteristics of various line-coding schemes using RC pulses.

Example 9.4

The RS-232 serial port on a PC is transmitting data at a rate of 38.4 kbps using a polar NRZ line code. Assume that binary 1's and 0's are equally likely to occur. Compute and plot the power spectral density for this RS-232 signal.

a. What is the first null bandwidth for this signal?
b. If the bandwidth is defined as the frequency beyond which the spectral components are attenuated at least 30 dB from the peak, estimate the bandwidth of the signal.
c. Estimate the 30-dB bandwidth of the RS-232 signal using RC pulses with roll-off factor $\alpha = 0.5$.

Solution

a. For polar NRZ signaling, $B_{null} = R_b = 38.4$kHz.
b. The spectral density of a polar NRZ signal with rectangular pulses is given from (9.37) as

$$G_{\text{polarNRZ}}(f) = A^2 T_b \big[\text{sinc}(f T_b)\big]^2$$

We are interested in the normalized spectrum to analyze spectral characteristics. So we will plot $10\log_{10}\big[\text{sinc}(f T_b)\big]^2$. The result is shown in Figure 9.31. This plot reveals that the spectrum is broad for this type of digital signaling with rectangular pulses. Although the null bandwidth is 38.4 kHz, this gives a false sense that the spectrum is relatively narrow because the

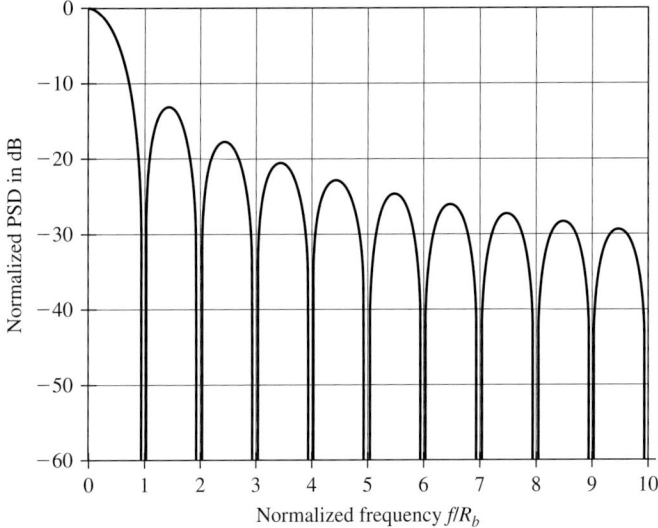

Figure 9.31 Normalized PSD of polar NRZ signaling using rectangular pulses.

first sidelobe peak (at $f = 57.6$ kHz $= 1.5R_b$) is down only 13.5 dB from the main lobe peak, and the second sidelobe peak (at $f = 96$ kHz $= 2.5R_b$) is down only 17.9 dB. The power spectrum (envelope) is falling off as $1/f^2$, which is only 6 dB/octave. From (9.37), the envelope of the PSD $G_{\mathrm{polarNRZ}}(f)$ is described by $(1/\pi f T_b)^2$. We can now calculate $f_{30\mathrm{dB}}$ as follows:

$$10^{-3} = (1/\pi f_{30\mathrm{dB}} T_b)^2$$

$$f_{30\mathrm{dB}}^2 = \left(\frac{R_b}{\pi}\right)^2 \times 10^3 \Rightarrow f_{30\mathrm{dB}} = 10.1 R_b$$

Therefore a bandwidth of $10.1 R_b = 386$ kHz is needed to pass the frequency components that are not attenuated by more than 30 dB.

c. Absolute bandwidth of RC pulses is given from (9.68) as $B_{abs} = 0.5(1 + \alpha)R_b$ for binary signaling where $\alpha = $ roll-off factor. Using $\alpha = 0.5$, the absolute bandwidth for polar NRZ signaling using RC pulses is

$$B_{abs} = 0.5(1 + 0.5)38.4 = 28.8 kHz = 0.75 R_b$$

The RC pulse frequency spectrum for roll-off factor $\alpha = 0.5$ is given by

$$V_{RC}(f) = \begin{cases} T_b, & 0 \leq |f| \leq 1/4T_b \\ \dfrac{T_b}{2}\left\{1 + \cos\left[2\pi T_b\left(|f| - \dfrac{1}{4T_b}\right)\right]\right\}, & 1/4T_b \leq |f| \leq 3/4T_b \\ 0, & |f| > 3/4T_b \end{cases}$$

To find the frequency $f_{30\mathrm{dB}}$ for polar NRZ signaling using RC pulses, we use the following:

$$\frac{G(f)}{G(0)} = \left.\left|\frac{V(f)}{V(0)}\right|^2\right|_{f=f_{30\mathrm{dB}}} = 10^{-3}$$

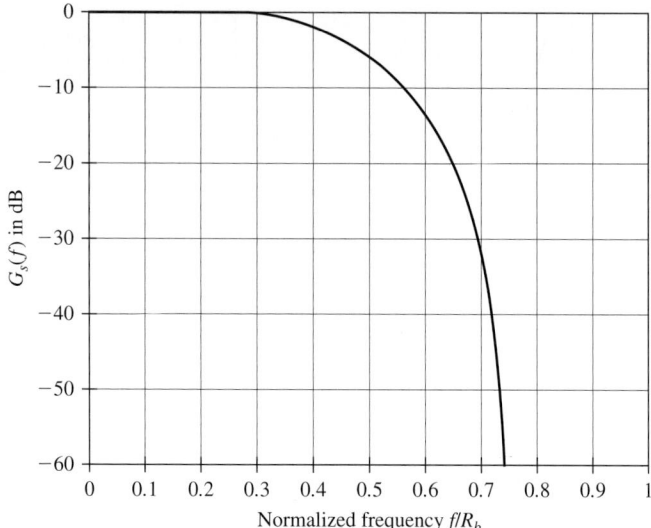

Figure 9.32 Normalized PSD of polar digital signal using RC pulse ($\alpha = 0.5$).

$$\frac{1}{2}\left\{1 + \cos\left(\frac{2\pi f_{30\text{dB}}}{R_b} - \frac{\pi}{2}\right)\right\} = 10^{-3/2}$$

$$\cos^2\left(\frac{\pi f_{30\text{dB}}}{R_b} - \frac{\pi}{4}\right) = 10^{-3/2}$$

$$\cos\left(\frac{\pi f_{30\text{dB}}}{R_b} - \frac{\pi}{4}\right) = 10^{-3/4}$$

$$\frac{\pi f_{30\text{dB}}}{R_b} - \frac{\pi}{4} = 1.392$$

$$\frac{f_{30\text{dB}}}{R_b} = 0.6931$$

$$\therefore \ f_{30\text{dB}} = 0.6931 \times 38.4 = 26.61 \text{ kHz}$$

This is verified in Figure 9.32 where the spectral density is down by 30 dB at $\dfrac{f_{30\text{dB}}}{R_b} = 0.7$.

Thus 30-dB bandwidth with RC pulses is 14.5 times smaller than that for the rectangular pulse signaling.

Experiment 9.2   *Effect of Channel on Baseband Digital Signals*

In this experiment we investigate the effect of the bandwidth of a communication channel on digital baseband signals using Simulink. Figure 9.33(a) displays the simulation model. The channel is simulated by an elliptic filter with passband edge frequency equal to the channel bandwidth W.

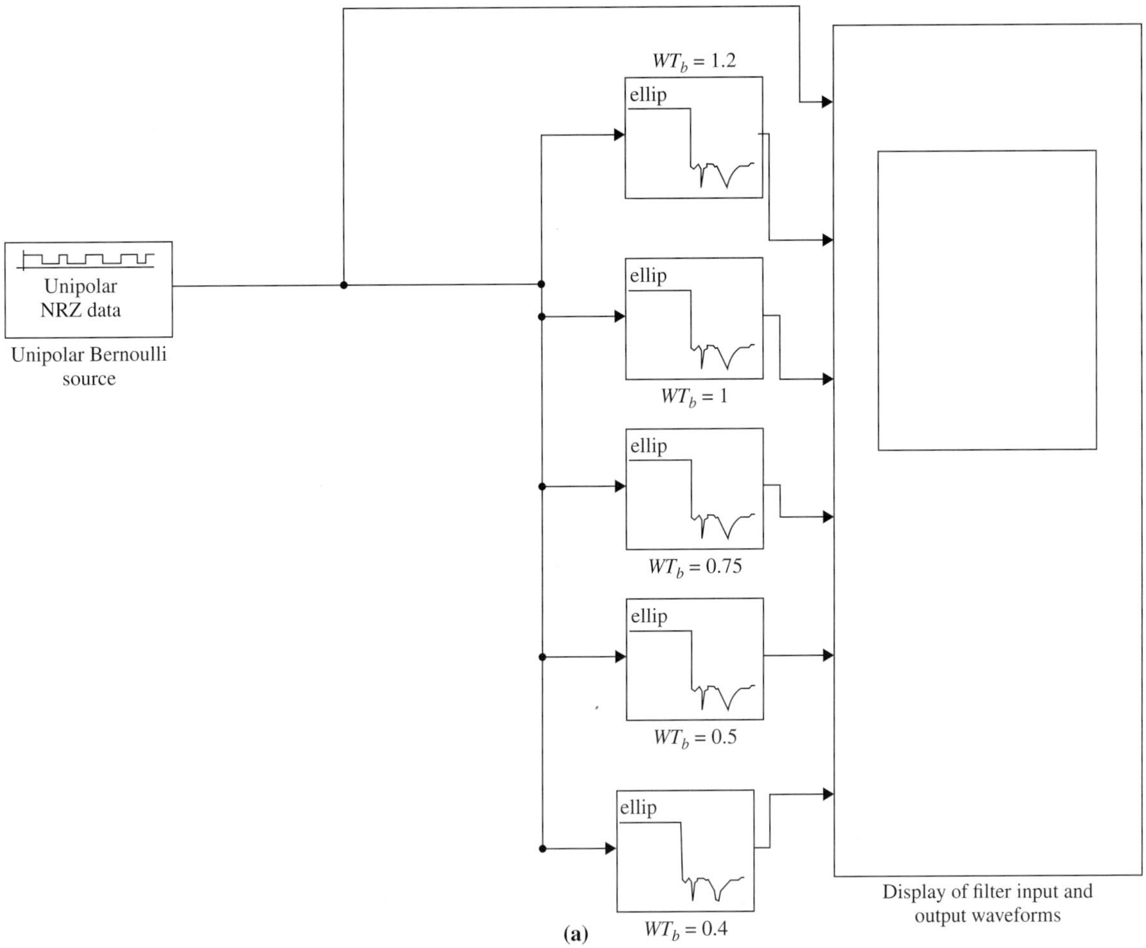

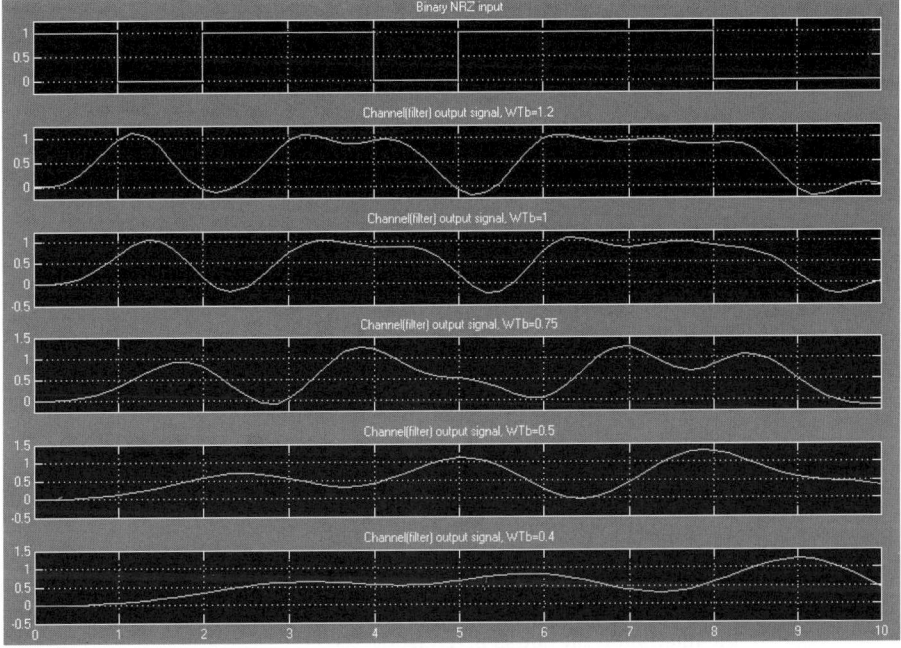

(a)

(b)

Figure 9.33 (a) Simulink model; (b) channel (filter) input and output waveforms.

Figure 9.33(b) displays the waveforms generated using this simulation for various values of WT_b products. The channel output waveforms show how the bandwidth of the channel affects the ability to transmit digital information in the form of baseband pulses.

As the bandwidth of the channel (filter) is decreased, the channel output is significantly distorted due to ISI. On the other hand as more of the spectral components of the input digital signal are passed, the output of the channel more closely approximates the input.

9.9   ESTIMATION OF ALLOWABLE BIT RATE

The quality of a digital transmission system is determined by the bit rate at which information can be transmitted reliably. Thus the quality is measured in terms of two parameters: **transmission speed,** or **bit rate,** in bits per second, and the **bit error rate (BER),** the fraction of bits that are received in error. These two parameters are determined by the bandwidth of the channel and by the noise. In this section, we will discuss the relationship between the transmission speed, channel bandwidth, and distortion of the transmitted waveform in the absence of noise. Clearly, as bandwidth is decreased, the precision with which the pulses can be identified at the receiver is reduced. We would now try to establish a quantitative relationship between maximum transmission speed and bandwidth of the transmission channel subject to specified criterion of accuracy.

Rectangular Pulses

From Figure 9.15 we note that the first null bandwidth of the polar NRZ, bipolar RZ, and Manchester signaling schemes (using square pulses) contains approximately 90% of the signal's average power. In many applications, the degree of accuracy provided by choosing the channel bandwidth W equal to the first null bandwidth of the signaling scheme may be sufficient. In this case, the maximum bit rate is given by applying (9.52) as

$$R_{max} = \eta_{null}W \qquad (9.70)$$

where η_{null} is the spectral efficiency of the line coding scheme from Table 9.1.

Example 9.5

Assuming that the TWP channel has a bandwidth of 4 kHz, calculate the maximum achievable bit rates using the following baseband signaling schemes with rectangular pulses:

a. NRZ polar
b. Bipolar RZ
c. Manchester
d. *M*-ary PAM

Solution

a. NRZ polar: $R_{max} = \eta_{null}W = 1 \times 4 = 4$ kbps
b. Bipolar RZ: $R_{max} = \eta_{null}W = 1 \times 4 = 4$ kbps
c. Manchester: $R_{max} = \eta_{null}W = 1/2 \times 4 = 2$ kbps
d. *M*-ary PAM: $R_{max} = \eta_{null}W = k \times 4 = 4k$ kbps

---

Raised Cosine Pulses

If we set the absolute bandwidth of RC pulses equal to the channel bandwidth (W Hz), the maximum bit rate is given from (9.69)

$$R_{max} = \eta_{rc}W \text{ bps} \qquad (9.71)$$

Example 9.6

Assuming that the TWP channel has a bandwidth of 4 kHz, calculate the maximum achievable bit rates using the following baseband signaling schemes using RC pulses with roll-off factor $\alpha = 0.5$:

a. NRZ polar
b. Bipolar RZ
c. Manchester
d. M-ary PAM

What is the maximum achievable bit rate in an M-ary PAM using sinc pulses?

Solution

a. NRZ polar: $R_{max} = \eta_{rc} W = \dfrac{2}{1 + 0.5} \times 4 = 5.34$ kbps

b. Bipolar RZ: $R_{max} = \eta_{rc} W = \dfrac{2}{1 + 0.5} \times 4 = 5.34$ kbps

c. Manchester: $R_{max} = \eta_{rc} W = \dfrac{1}{1 + 0.5} \times 4 = 2.67$ kbps

d. M-ary PAM: $R_{max} = \eta_{rc} W = \dfrac{2k}{1 + 0.5} \times 4 = 5.34k$ kbps

The maximum achievable bit rate in an M-ary PAM using sinc pulses is $8k$ bits per second.

Effect of Noise

As discussed in Section 9.8, sinc pulses are a special case of RC pulses ($\alpha = 0$). We observe from Table 9.6 that M-ary PAM signaling can achieve a maximum bit rate of $2kW = 2(\log_2 M)W$ bits per second over a channel bandwidth of W Hz using sinc pulses. One might conclude at this point that the bit rate can be increased without limit by increasing the number of levels M. This is not true because of the presence of noise in the system. Suppose we increase the number of levels while keeping the maximum amplitude levels $\pm A$ fixed. Each increase in the number of signal levels decreases the spacing between levels as illustrated in Figure 9.34. At some point these decreases will imply a significant increase in the probability of detection errors as the noise will be more likely to convert the transmitted amplitude level into a neighboring level. Thus, the presence of noise ultimately limits the number of levels that can be transmitted and hence the maximum achievable bit rate. This topic will be addressed in Chapters 10 and 11.

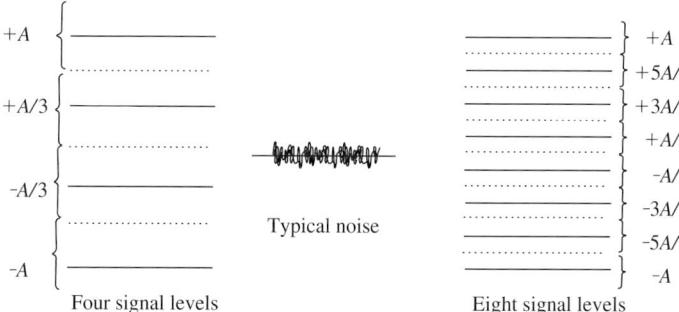

Figure 9.34 Effect of noise in multilevel transmission.

FINAL REMARKS

In this chapter we studied line-coding methods for converting a binary information stream into waveforms for transmission. Choosing a proper line code for a particular application requires the consideration of many interrelated factors. These include code transparency, spectrum management, error monitoring, and spectral efficiency. Therefore, line coding must be selected for compatibility with the characteristics of the transmission channel. When the bandwidth of the channel is not a consideration, NRZ, RZ, and Manchester codes can be used. If the channel is bandlimited and higher signaling rates are desired, multilevel signaling is codes are a common solution. Code transparency can be achieved by either scrambling the user data or using substitution codes to produce enough transitions in the transmitted data.

A big problem with the line codes is that they are not bandlimited. The power outside the first null bandwidth is nonnegligible, and the absolute bandwidth is infinite. If the channel is bandlimited, then high-frequency components will not be passed. High-frequency components correspond to sharp transitions in transmitted pulses. Thus the pulses will spread out into the adjacent symbol periods, causing ISI. Avoiding this requires the use of pulse shapes that have a well-defined bandlimited spectrum. We considered RC pulses, which have good time domain properties (zero ISI and fast decay) as well as finite absolute bandwidth. RC pulses, which can be easily implemented, achieve a maximum signaling rate very close to the maximum possible over a bandlimited channel.

The maximum transmission rate achievable over a channel of bandwidth of W Hz is given by $2(\log_2 M)W$ bits per second. This justifies the popularity of multilevel signaling in state-of-the art modem designs. However, the ultimate limit on the number of levels in a multilevel transmission scheme and hence the achievable bit rate is established by the unavoidable noise introduced by the communication channel and the receiver front end.

FURTHER READINGS

Although line coding is an area of significant practical importance, it is not as well covered in undergraduate communication systems texts. References [1–4] provide a good introduction to the subject.

1. Lee, E., and D. Messerschmitt. *Digital Communication,* 2nd ed. Leiden, The Netherlands: Kluwer, 1993.

2. Lathi, B. *Modern Digital and Analog Communication Systems,* 3rd ed. New York: Oxford, 1998.

3. Couch, L. W. *Digital and Analog Communication Systems,* 7th ed. Upper Saddle River, NJ: Prentice Hall, 2006.

4. Anderson, J. B., *Digital Transmission Engineering,* 2nd ed. Upper Saddle River, NJ: Prentice-Hall, 2006.

5. Lechleider, J. "Line Codes for Digital Subscriber Lines." *IEEE Communications Magazine* 27, no. 9 (1989) 24–25.

6. Amoroso, F. "The Bandwidth of Digital Data Signals." *IEEE Communications Magazine* 18, no. 6 (1980): 13–24.

PROBLEMS

9.1. What is the duration of a transmitted pulse or symbol for each of the following signals?

    a.   16-PAM signal at 200 kbps _____

    b.   Manchester coded data at 10 Mbps

          _____

    c.   Bipolar encoded data at 1.544 Mbps _____

    d.   2B1Q-encoded signal with a bit rate of 144 kbps

          _____

    What is the first-null bandwidth of signals in (a) and (d)?

    _____

9.2. An image is 1024×768 pixels is transmitted using 3 bytes/pixel coding.

    a. How long does it take to transmit it over a 56 kbps modem link? Over a 1.5 Mbps ADSL link? Over a 10 Mbps cable modem link?

    b. Compare the transmission times if JPEG compression is used prior to transmission. Assume that JPEG scheme achieves a compression ratio of 15:1.

9.3. Consider the random data signal consisting of binary 1's and 0's occurring with equal probability. Calculate the power spectral density $G_s(f)$ of 25% duty cycle unipolar RZ-encoded signal.

    a. Calculate the power spectral density $\mathcal{G}_s(f)$ of 25% duty cycle rectangular pulse train (Example 2.24).

    b. Plot both spectral densities on the same graph using the normalized frequency scale (i.e., f/R_b). What conclusions do you make?

9.4. Consider a random data signal consisting of binary 1's and 0's occurring with equal probability. Calculate the power spectral density $G_s(f)$ of polar NRZ-encoded signal.

    a. Calculate the power spectral density $\mathcal{G}_s(f)$ of the deterministic data pattern 101010 . . . with polar NRZ encoding.

    b. Repeat (a) for a test pattern consisting of six binary 1's followed by two binary 0's.

    c. Plot spectral densities on the same graph using the normalized frequency scale (i.e., f/R_b).

9.5. Optical fiber digital communication system uses unipolar Manchester pulses shown in Figure P9.1.

    a. Sketch the waveform for random data sequence 1011001.

    b. Derive an expression for the spectral density $G_s(f)$ assuming equiprobable binary data. How does this expression differ from Equation (9.51) and why?

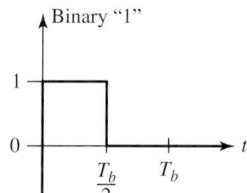 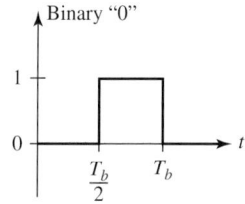

Figure P9.1

9.6. We want to design a digital communications link to transmit data at 1.544 Mbps. How much (first-null) bandwidth is required using the following signaling schemes?

    a. Bipolar RZ

    b. Polar RZ

    c. 4-ary PAM

    d. Manchester

9.7. Binary data is to be transmitted using M-ary PAM over the ideal bandlimited channel with a bandwidth $W = 4$ kHz. We use RC pulses with roll-off factor $\alpha = 0.5$ so that there is no ISI. If we want to achieve a bit rate of 56 kbps, determine

    a. the required size of signal set M.

    b. symbol rate and duration.

9.8. Consider the design of a digital communications link to transmit data at 1.544 Mbps. Compare the bandwidth required for following line-encoding schemes using RC pulses with roll-off factor $\alpha = 0.5$.

    a. Unipolar NRZ

    b. Bipolar RZ

    c. 4-ary PAM

    d. 16-ary PAM

9.9. Consider a random data signal consisting of binary 1's and 0's occurring with equal probability. We assume that the digital communication system uses polar NRZ encoding and the basic pulse shape described by

$$v(t) = \begin{cases} \cos\left(\dfrac{\pi t}{T_b}\right), & |t| < T_b/2 \\ 0, & \text{otherwise} \end{cases}$$

    a. Sketch the waveform for data sequence 1011001.

    b. Find an expression for the power spectral density $G_s(f)$.

    c. Compare the spectral efficiency with the system using rectangular pulses.

9.10. Consider the unit impulse train in time with period T.

$$\delta_p(t) = \sum_{n=-\infty}^{\infty} \delta(t - nT)$$

    a. Show that the FS expansion for this signal is given by

$$\sum_{n=-\infty}^{\infty} \delta(t - nT) = \sum_{n=-\infty}^{\infty} \frac{1}{T} e^{j2\pi nt/T}$$

    b. By taking FT of both sides, derive the identity

$$\sum_{n=-\infty}^{\infty} e^{-j2\pi nfT} = \frac{1}{T} \sum_{n=-\infty}^{\infty} \delta\left(f - \frac{n}{T}\right)$$

9.11. Consider a baseband channel with bandwidth 64 kHz.

    a. If bipolar RZ signaling with RC pulses is used, show that the spectrum of 64 kbps signal will fit into the channel when $\alpha = 1$. Find the absolute and 6-dB bandwidths.

    b. Repeat part (a) for the case of 144 kbps quaternary PAM signaling. Choose appropriate value of α as required.

9.12. A differential encoder is defined by the following Boolean expression

$$a_n = \overline{a_{n-1} \oplus b_n}$$

where b_n = current data bit into the differential encoder and a_n = current output bit.

    a. Assuming initial bit $a_0 = 0$, calculate the differential encoder output for the input bit sequence 011110101.

    b. Repeat (a) assuming initial bit $a_0 = 1$.

    c. What conclusions do you make from (a) and (b) regarding the action of the encoder?

9.13. Design the descrambler to recover the original data for the scrambler in Example 9.3. Verify that when the scrambled sequence c_n is applied to the input of the descrambler, the output is the original sequence 100000000000.

9.14. A scrambler is shown in Figure P9.2. Design the descrambler to recover the original data. If a data sequence 100000001111 is applied to the input of the scrambler, determine the scrambled output sequence. Verify that the output is the original data sequence when the scrambled sequence c_n is applied to the input of the descrambler.

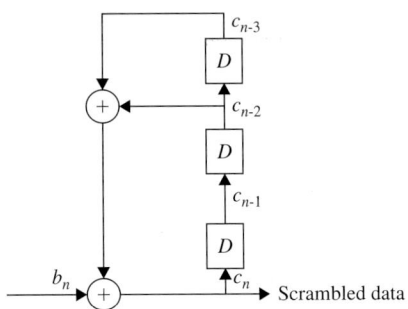

Figure P9.2

9.15. A 7-bit ADC samples video signal at 10.7386 MHz.

a. Find the serial bit rate of the resultant digital signal.

b. The digital signal is transmitted using RC pulses over a channel of bandwidth 12 MHz. If 16-ary PAM signaling is used, find the maximum roll-off factor α that can be used.

MATLAB PROBLEMS

9.16. Write an m-file to generate and display the following baseband signaling waveforms for the bit sequence [1 0 0 1 1 1 0 1 0 1 0 1]. Use `nsamp` = 16 samples/bit and bit period `Tb` = 1.

a. NRZ

b. Polar RZ

c. Polar NRZ

d. Bipolar RZ

e. Manchester

Next filter the above waveforms through a fourth-order Butterworth filter with 3-dB cutoff bandwidth B_{3dB} such that $B_{3dB}T_b = 1$. Repeat for $B_{3dB}T_b = 0.6$. Display the waveforms.

9.17. Generate a `Nbit`-length sequence u [n] of $\mathcal{U}[0,1]$ random variables. Use `Nbit` = 1024 and `nsamp` = 16 samples/bit in your simulation. Now a binary sequence can be produced by using the following:

```
u = rand(1,Nbit)

b = round(u)
```

a. For the bit sequence b [n], generate baseband waveforms x [n] for the following line-coding schemes:

(i) Polar RZ

(ii) Bipolar RZ

(iii) Manchester

b. Display the power spectral density estimates `gxx` of these waveforms using MATLAB command `pwelch`.

```
[gxx,w] = pwelch(x,Nbits,fs);
```

Compare them with theoretical results obtained in this chapter.

9.18. Write an m-file to generate and display the following baseband signaling waveforms for the bit sequence [1 0 1 0 0 1 0 1 0 1] using RC pulses with roll-off factor `alpha` = 0.5. Use `nsamp` = 16 samples/bit and bit period `Tb` = 1.

a. NRZ

b. Polar RZ

c. Polar NRZ

d. Bipolar RZ

e. Manchester

The RC pulse can be generated using the following function:

```
function y = rcpulse(alpha,t,Tb)

% t = -5Tb:delt:5Tb, where delt = Tb/
nsamp

t1 = pi/Tb;

t2 = t1*alpha;

con1 = 4.*alpha^2/Tb^2;

con2=sinc(t1*t)

y1 = cos(t2*t)./(1-con1*t.^2);

y= y1.*con2

y= y/sqrt(Tb)

end
```

Next, filter the above waveforms through a fourth-order Butterworth filter with 3-dB cutoff bandwidth B_{3dB} such that $B_{3dB}T_b = 0.6$. Display the waveforms.

9.19. Generate a `nbit`-length sequence u [n] of $\mathcal{U}[0,1]$ random variables. Use `Nbit` = 1024 and `nsamp` = 16 samples/bit in your simulation. Now a binary sequence can be produced by using the following:

```
u = rand(1,Nbit)

b = round(u)
```

a. For the bit sequence b[n], generate baseband waveforms x[n] using RC pulses (roll-off factor `alpha` = 0.5) for the following line-coding schemes:

   (i)   Polar RZ

   (ii) Bipolar RZ

   (iii) Manchester

b. Display the power spectral density estimates gxx of these waveforms using MATLAB command `pwelch`.

```
[gxx,w] = pwelch(x,Nbits,fs);
```

c. Compare them with theoretical results obtained in this chapter.

9.20. The impulse response of a certain telephone channel is given by

$$h(t) = -0.45h_{cheb}(t + 0.5T_b) + 0.7h_{cheb}(t) + 0.25h_{cheb}(t - 0.25T_b)$$

where $h_{cheb}(t)$ is impulse response of the 12-pole Chebyshev filter that can be designed by the following statement:

```
[num, den] = cheby2(12,40,2/nsamples);
```

a. Generate the bit sequence b[n]. Use Nbit = 16, bit period Tb = 1, and nsamp = 16 samples per bit in your simulation. For the bit sequence b[n], generate baseband waveforms x[n] for the following line-coding schemes:

   (i)   Polar RZ

   (ii) Bipolar RZ

   (iii) Manchester

b. Calculate the output of the channel in each case and display the waveforms.

c. Repeat (a) and (b) above for the baseband waveforms x[n] generated using RC pulses (alpha = 0.5).

CHAPTER 10

Detection of Baseband Signals in Noise

Digital modulation techniques considered in Chapter 9 involved mapping the block of k information bits at a time into one of M distinct waveforms for transmission over the communication channel. The set of waveforms $s_m(t)$, $m = 1, 2, \ldots, M$ used by the modulator are known to the **baseband demodulator.** In a digital communication system, the objective of the baseband demodulator is not to reproduce the transmitted waveform with fidelity as in the case of analog communication systems discussed in Chapters 4, 5, and 7. Instead, the function of the baseband demodulator or **detector** is to determine which one of the M transmission symbols is being conveyed in the received signal waveform during a symbol interval. Such a determination always involves uncertainty because the decision is made by observing the received signal, which is corrupted by the channel or receiver front-end noise. The detection or decision-making process, therefore, introduces occasional but unavoidable errors because of the presence of noise. In the binary case, this implies that the detector decides bit 1 when actually a bit 0 was transmitted. An appropriate performance objective in the design of optimum detection schemes is to minimize the probability that such errors will occur.

The optimum detection problem is studied here in the probability theory setting. The a priori probabilities (i.e., the probabilities before the received signal is observed) of the M transmission symbols are usually modeled as equiprobable. The detector uses the maximum a posteriori probability criterion to decide between M possible choices by observing the received signal during each symbol interval. We assume for simplicity that the transmission channel is not dispersive, so the detection of a symbol is not influenced by interference from other symbols. We further assume that the additive noise is white Gaussian with two-sided power spectral density $N_o/2$ W/Hz. The chapter is organized into the following sections:

10.1 BINARY SIGNAL DETECTION IN AWGN.

The simplest type of digital communication problem is considered in this section, namely, detection of binary signals in the presence of additive white Gaussian noise (AWGN).

10.2 THE MATCHED FILTER.

This section studies linear receivers that maximize SNR at the detector output. The resulting matched filter and correlation detector structures are then analyzed for various binary signaling schemes.

10.3 VECTOR SPACE CONCEPTS.

We review basic concepts of vector and inner product spaces. This is followed by a discussion of the Gram-Schmidt procedure to construct an orthonormal basis for a set containing a finite number of vectors.

10.4 VECTOR SPACE REPRESENTATION OF SIGNALS AND WGN.

We consider the representation of a finite set of signal waveforms encountered in digital communication systems as points or vectors in finite-dimensional spaces. Next we explain that it is sufficient to consider noise components along the signal space basis vectors for making a decision as to which signal was transmitted.

10.5 *M*-ARY SIGNAL DETECTION IN AWGN.

In this section, we study the detection of M-ary vectors in WGN such that the average probability of correct decision is maximized. The implementation of the optimum maximum likelihood (ML) detector as a bank of matched filters or correlators is then considered.

10.6 ERROR PERFORMANCE OF ML DETECTORS.

The union bound for the error performance of an M-ary communication system using the ML detection scheme is derived. We next obtain the relationship between symbol and bit error probabilities.

10.7 ERROR PERFORMANCE OF *M*-ARY PAM SIGNALS.

The error performance of M-ary PAM systems is investigated in this section. It is demonstrated that the nearest neighbor bound here provides the exact error rate for the system.

10.1   BINARY SIGNAL DETECTION IN AWGN

In a binary digital communication system, one of two possible signals, $s_1(t)$ or $s_2(t)$, is transmitted during each bit interval (T_b). The detector, therefore, makes a decision each bit interval whether a binary 1 or 0 was transmitted by processing the signal received only during that interval. The energies of $s_1(t)$ and $s_2(t)$, which are assumed to be finite, are denoted by E_1 and E_2, respectively. The general binary detection problem to be considered in this section is illustrated in Figure 10.1. Without loss of generality, consider the transmitted signal over the first signaling interval represented by

$$s(t) = \begin{cases} s_1(t), & 0 \le t \le T_b \quad \text{for binary 1} \\ s_2(t), & 0 \le t \le T_b \quad \text{for binary 0} \end{cases} \tag{10.1}$$

The transmitted signal is received in the presence of additive white Gaussian noise (AWGN) $n(t)$ with two-sided power spectral density $N_o/2$ W/Hz. The received signal can now be written as

$$r(t) = s(t) + n(t), \quad 0 \le t \le T_b \tag{10.2}$$

The detector consists of a linear, time-invariant filter with frequency response $H(f)$ followed by a sampler and threshold comparator. The initial conditions of the filter are set to 0 just prior to the arrival of each new pulse. The output of the linear filter is given by

$$r_o(t) = s_{o1}(t) \text{ or } s_{o2}(t) + n_o(t) \tag{10.3}$$

where

$$s_{o1}(t) = h(t) \otimes s_1(t) = \text{Receiver filter output to } s_1(t) \text{ pulse} \tag{10.4}$$

$$s_{o2}(t) = h(t) \otimes s_2(t) = \text{Receiver filter output to } s_2(t) \text{ pulse} \tag{10.5}$$

$$n_o(t) = n(t) \otimes h(t) = \text{Receiver filter output noise} \tag{10.6}$$

The receiver filter output $r_o(t)$ is sampled at time t_o during the bit interval $0 \le t \le T_b$. The resulting sample r_o is a random variable given by

$$r_o = \begin{cases} s_{o1} + n_o, & \text{for binary 1 sent} \\ s_{o2} + n_o, & \text{for binary 0 sent} \end{cases} \tag{10.7}$$

where s_{o1} and s_{o2} are values of $s_{o1}(t)$ and $s_{o2}(t)$, respectively, at the sampling instant $t = t_o$. n_o is the filter output noise sample at $t = t_o$. The random variable r_o is Gaussian with mean s_{o1} or s_{o2} (depending on whether $s_1(t)$ or $s_2(t)$ was transmitted). Its variance σ_o^2 is given by using (6.189) as

$$\sigma_o^2 = \overline{n_o^2} = \frac{N_o}{2} \int_{-\infty}^{\infty} |H(f)|^2 df \tag{10.8}$$

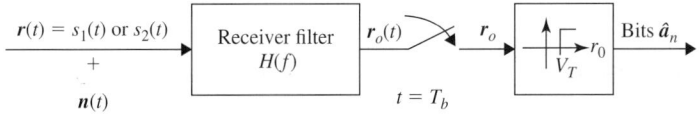

Figure 10.1 Binary signal detection.

We can write conditional PDFs of the random variable r_o as follows:

$$f_{r_o}(r_o | s_1(t) \text{ sent}) = f_{n_o}(r_o - s_{o1}) = \frac{1}{\sqrt{2\pi\sigma_o^2}} e^{-(r_o - s_{o1})^2/2\sigma_o^2} \qquad (10.9)$$

$$f_{r_o}(r_o | s_2(t) \text{ sent}) = f_{n_o}(r_o - s_{o2}) = \frac{1}{\sqrt{2\pi\sigma_o^2}} e^{-(r_o - s_{o2})^2/2\sigma_o^2} \qquad (10.10)$$

The conditional PDFs of r_o are shown in Figure 10.2. The threshold comparator makes the decision by comparing the output of the sampler r_o with threshold voltage V_T. The decision rule can be expressed as

$$r_o > V_T, \text{ declare that } s_1(t) \text{ was transmitted}$$

$$r_o < V_T, \text{ declare that } s_2(t) \text{ was transmitted}$$

We discuss the selection of optimum V_T next.

10.1.1 Probability of Bit Error

If the a priori probability that $s_1(t)$ was sent is p, and the a priori probability that $s_2(t)$ was sent is $1-p$, the average probability of bit error, BER, is given by

$$BER = P\{s_1(t) \text{ sent}\} \times P\{\text{error} | s_1(t) \text{ sent}\} + P\{s_2(t) \text{ sent}\} \times P\{\text{error} | s_2(t) \text{ sent}\}$$

$$= p \times P\{\text{error} | s_1(t) \text{ sent}\} + (1-p) \times P\{\text{error} | s_2(t) \text{ sent}\} \qquad (10.11)$$

The average probability of bit error is popularly known as **bit error rate (BER).** An error can occur in one of two ways:

1. $s_1(t)$ sent, and $r_o < V_T$
2. $s_2(t)$ sent, and $r_o > V_T$

The conditional probability of error can now be expressed as

$$P\{\text{error} | s_1(t) \text{ sent}\} = P\{r_o < V_T | s_1(t) \text{ sent}\} = \int_{-\infty}^{V_T} f_{r_o}(r_o | s_1(t) \text{ sent}) dr_o$$

$$= \int_{-\infty}^{V_T} \frac{1}{\sqrt{2\pi\sigma_o^2}} e^{-(r_o - s_{o1})^2/2\sigma_o^2} dr_o = Q\left(\frac{s_{o1} - V_T}{\sigma_o}\right) \qquad (10.12)$$

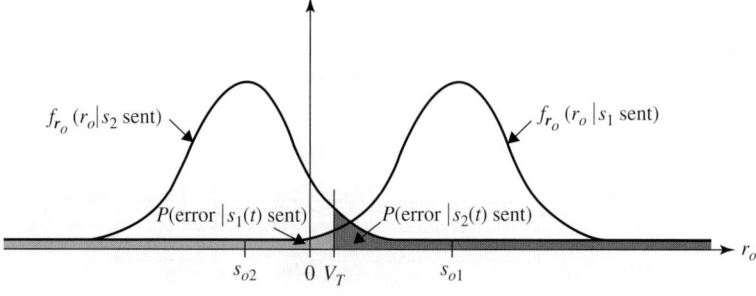

Figure 10.2 Calculation of probability of bit error for a binary communication system.

$$P\{\text{error}\,|\,s_2(t)\text{ sent}\} = P\{r_o > V_T\,|\,s_2(t)\text{ sent}\} = \int_{V_T}^{\infty} f_{r_o}(r_o\,|\,s_2(t)\text{ sent})dr_o$$

$$= \int_{V_T}^{\infty} \frac{1}{\sqrt{2\pi\sigma_o^2}}e^{-(r_o - s_{o2})^2/2\sigma_o^2}dr_o = Q\left(\frac{V_T - s_{o2}}{\sigma_o}\right) \quad (10.13)$$

where $Q(.)$ is defined by (6.55) as

$$Q(u) = \int_u^{\infty} \frac{1}{\sqrt{2\pi}}e^{-\frac{x^2}{2}}dx, \quad u > 0 \quad\quad (6.55)$$

Combining (10.11) through (10.13), we can write the probability of bit error expression as follows:

$$BER = pQ\left(\frac{s_{o1} - V_T}{\sigma_o}\right) + (1 - p)Q\left(\frac{V_T - s_{o2}}{\sigma_o}\right) \quad (10.14)$$

Assuming equally probable binary symbols, the expression (10.14) for the BER simplifies to

$$BER = \frac{1}{2}Q\left(\frac{s_{o1} - V_T}{\sigma_o}\right) + \frac{1}{2}Q\left(\frac{V_T - s_{o2}}{\sigma_o}\right) \quad (10.15)$$

Minimizing the Probability of Bit Error

The average probability of bit error BER can be minimized by optimum choices for

1. Comparator threshold voltage V_T
2. Linear filter $H(f)$

To find the optimum V_T, we need to take the derivative of BER with respect to V_T. To accomplish this, we calculate the derivative of Q-function using the Leibnitz's rule:

$$\frac{dQ(\phi(u))}{du} = \frac{d\left[\int_{\phi(u)}^{\infty} \frac{1}{\sqrt{2\pi}}e^{-\frac{x^2}{2}}dx\right]}{du} = \frac{1}{\sqrt{2\pi}}e^{-\frac{x^2}{2}}\Big|_{\phi(u)}^{\infty} = -\frac{1}{\sqrt{2\pi}}e^{-\frac{x^2}{2}}\Big|_{x=\phi(u)}\frac{d\phi(u)}{du}$$

$$= -\frac{1}{\sqrt{2\pi}}e^{-\frac{\phi^2(u)}{2}}\frac{d\phi(u)}{du} \quad (10.16)$$

We now apply (10.16) to compute the derivative of BER and set it equal to zero to obtain the following condition that optimum threshold V_{opt} must satisfy:

$$\frac{d(BER)}{dV_T}\Big|_{V_T = V_{opt}} = \frac{1}{2}\frac{1}{\sqrt{2\pi\sigma_o^2}}e^{-(V_{opt} - s_{o1})^2/2\sigma_o^2} - \frac{1}{2}\frac{1}{\sqrt{2\pi\sigma_o^2}}e^{-(V_{opt} - s_{o2})^2/2\sigma_o^2} = 0$$

Equivalently, V_{opt} is obtained by solving

$$e^{-(V_{opt} - s_{o1})^2} = e^{-(V_{opt} - s_{o2})^2}$$

or

$$(V_{opt} - s_{o1})^2 = (V_{opt} - s_{o2})^2$$

This yields

$$V_{opt} = \frac{s_{o1} + s_{o2}}{2} \tag{10.17}$$

Substituting the optimum value of threshold voltage V_{opt} into (10.15) yields

$$BER = Q\left(\frac{s_{o1} - s_{o2}}{2\sigma_o}\right) \tag{10.18}$$

where $s_{o1} > V_{opt} > s_{o2}$ has been assumed.

Example 10.1

For unipolar NRZ signaling, evaluate the BER performance of the detector that uses a RC low-pass filter in Example 2.33 as the receive filter.

Solution

The transfer function of the RC low-pass filter is given from (2.125) as

$$H(f) = \frac{1}{1 + j(f/f_{3dB})}$$

where f_{3dB} is its 3-dB cutoff frequency. The impulse response of the RC low-pass filter is given from (2.130) as

$$h(t) = 2\pi f_{3dB} e^{-2\pi f_{3dB} t} u(t)$$

For unipolar NRZ signaling, $s_1(t) = A$ and $s_2(t) = 0$, $0 \le t \le T_b$. The filter output to the $s_1(t)$ pulse is given by

$$s_{o1}(t) = \begin{cases} A[1 - e^{-2\pi f_{3dB} t}], & 0 \le t \le T_b \\ A[e^{2\pi f_{3dB} T_b} - 1]e^{-2\pi f_{3dB} t}, & t \ge T_b \end{cases} \tag{10.19}$$

The peak filter output occurs at $t = T_b$ as shown in Figure 10.3(a). It is given by

$$s_{o1} = s_{o1}(T_b) = A[1 - e^{-2\pi f_{3dB} T_b}] \tag{10.20}$$

Obviously, $s_{o2} = 0$. From (6.249), the noise power at the output of RC low-pass filter can be written as

$$\sigma_o^2 = N_o B_N \tag{10.21}$$

where the noise-equivalent bandwidth B_N of the RC low-pass filter from (6.253) is

$$B_N = \frac{\pi f_{3dB}}{2}$$

Substituting into (10.21) yields

$$\sigma_o^2 = \frac{N_o \pi f_{3dB}}{2} \tag{10.22}$$

Combining (10.20) and (10.22), we obtain

$$\frac{(s_{o1} - s_{o2})^2}{4\sigma_o^2} = \frac{A^2[1 - e^{-2\pi f_{3dB}T_b}]^2}{N_o 2\pi f_{3dB}} = \frac{2(A^2 T_b/2)[1 - e^{-2\pi f_{3dB}T_b}]^2}{(N_o 2\pi f_{3dB}T_b)} = \frac{2E_b[1 - e^{-z}]^2}{N_o z} \quad (10.23)$$

where

$$z = 2\pi f_{3dB}T_b$$

$$E_b = \text{Average energy/bit} = \frac{1}{2}A^2 T_b + \frac{1}{2} \times 0 = \frac{A^2 T_b}{2}$$

Note that z is the product of the transmitted pulse duration and the filter bandwidth. It is commonly called the **bandwidth time (BT) product** and is a very useful design parameter. Substituting (10.23) into (10.18), we obtain

$$BER = Q\left(\sqrt{\frac{s_{o1}^2}{4\sigma_o^2}}\right) = Q\left(\sqrt{\frac{2E_b(1 - e^{-z})^2}{N_o z}}\right) \quad (10.24)$$

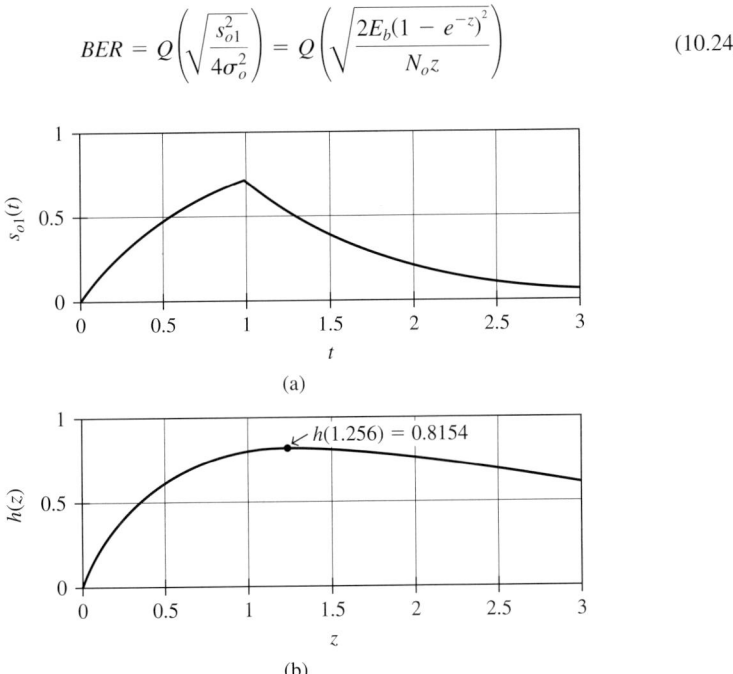

Figure 10.3 (a) RC low-pass filter output waveform; (b) plot of function $h(z) = \dfrac{2(1 - e^{-z})^2}{z}$.

We observe from (10.24) that the BER is a function of the BT product z. For a given bit rate, the BER performance can be optimized by choosing the appropriate value of z, that is, the receiver filter bandwidth f_{3dB}. Figure 10.3(b) displays a plot of $h(z) = \dfrac{2(1 - e^{-z})^2}{z}$ as a function of the BT product z. The maximum value of $h(z)$ is 0.8154, and it occurs at $z = 1.256$. This corresponds to the RC low-pass filter bandwidth $f_{3dB} = \dfrac{0.2}{T_b} = 0.2R_b$ Hz. Substituting the maximum value of $h(z)$ in the expression for BER yields

$$BER_{RC} = Q\left(\sqrt{0.8154\frac{E_b}{N_o}}\right) \quad (10.25)$$

In the next section, we will compare the performance of this simpler filter with the optimal design.

10.2   THE MATCHED FILTER

We consider the design of the linear filter $H(f)$ in Figure 10.1 that minimizes the average probability of bit error expression (10.18) for a binary detection scheme. Because the Q-function is a monotonically decreasing function of its argument, we need to solve the following optimization problem in order to find the optimal filter transfer function $H_{opt}(f)$:

$$\underset{H(f)}{\text{Max}}\left(\frac{s_{o1} - s_{o2}}{2\sigma_o}\right) \tag{10.26}$$

In the special case when $s_2(t) = 0$, the preceding optimization problem simplifies to

$$\underset{H(f)}{\text{Max}}\left(\frac{s_{o1}}{2\sigma_o}\right) = \underset{H(f)}{\text{Max}}\left(\frac{s_{o1}^2}{2\sigma_o^2}\right) \tag{10.27}$$

The quantity inside the brackets defines **peak signal-to-rms noise power ratio (SNR)** at the output of the sampler. The filter output signal at the sampling time t_o is obtained from (10.4) as

$$s_{o1} = s_1(t) \otimes h(t)|_{t=t_o} = \int_{-\infty}^{\infty} S_1(f)H(f)e^{j2\pi ft}df\Big|_{t=t_o}$$

$$= \int_{-\infty}^{\infty} S_1(f)H(f)e^{j2\pi ft_o}\, df \tag{10.28}$$

Using (10.8) and (10.28), we can write

$$\frac{s_{o1}^2}{\sigma_o^2} = \frac{\left|\int_{-\infty}^{\infty} S_1(f)H(f)e^{j2\pi ft_o}\, df\right|^2}{\dfrac{N_o}{2}\int_{-\infty}^{\infty} |H(f)|^2\, df} \tag{10.29}$$

The optimization problem in (10.27) seeks an $H(f)$ that maximizes the expression on the RHS of (10.29). This can be accomplished by maximizing the numerator of (10.29) using Cauchy-Schwarz inequality,[1] which is

$$\left|\int_{-\infty}^{\infty} X(f)Y(f)df\right|^2 \leq \int_{-\infty}^{\infty} |X(f)|^2 df \int_{-\infty}^{\infty} |Y(f)|^2 df \tag{10.30}$$

where $X(f)$ and $Y(f)$ may be complex functions of real variable f. Furthermore, equality is obtained only when

$$X(f) = KY^*(f) \tag{10.31}$$

---

[1] Note that Cauchy-Schwarz inequality is a generalization of the inequality involving the dot product of two finite-dimensional vectors $\underline{x}$ and $\underline{y}$. That is,

$$|\underline{x} \bullet \underline{y}| = \|\underline{x}\|\, \|\underline{y}\|\, |\cos\theta| \leq \|\underline{x}\|\, \|\underline{y}\|$$

where θ is the angle between them and $\|\underline{x}\|$ denotes the length or norm of the vector $\underline{x}$.

where K is an arbitrary constant. To apply Cauchy-Schwarz inequality, let us choose

$$X(f) = H(f) \qquad (10.32)$$

and

$$Y(f) = S_1(f)e^{j2\pi f t_o} \qquad (10.33)$$

Substituting (10.32) and (10.33) into (10.30), we obtain

$$\left| \int_{-\infty}^{\infty} H(f)S_1(f)e^{j2\pi f t_o}df \right|^2 \leq \int_{-\infty}^{\infty} |H(f)|^2 df \int_{-\infty}^{\infty} |S_1(f)|^2 df \qquad (10.34)$$

Replacing the numerator of (10.29) with the right-hand side of (10.34) yields the inequality

$$\frac{s_{o1}^2}{\sigma_o^2} \leq \frac{\displaystyle\int_{-\infty}^{\infty} |H(f)|^2 df \int_{-\infty}^{\infty} |S_1(f)|^2 df}{\displaystyle\frac{N_o}{2} \int_{-\infty}^{\infty} |H(f)|^2 df} = \frac{2}{N_o} \int_{-\infty}^{\infty} |S_1(f)|^2 df \qquad (10.35)$$

The maximum of s_{o1}^2/σ_o^2 is obtained when $H(f)$ is chosen according to (10.31). Substituting (10.32) and (10.33) into (10.31), the optimum filter response is obtained as

$$H_{opt}(f) = S_1^*(f)e^{-j2\pi f t_o} \qquad (10.36)$$

By taking the inverse FT of both sides of (10.36), the impulse response of the optimum filter can be expressed as

$$h_{opt}(t) = s_1^*(t_o - t) \qquad (10.37)$$

The impulse response $h_{opt}(t)$ of the optimum filter is the time reverse of the input signal $s_1(t)$, and thus it is referred to as the **matched filter.** Note that the filter response function (10.37) is independent of the white noise spectral density level $N_o/2$. Because the matched filter solution maximizes the output SNR (10.27), this property is used for time-delay estimation in radar systems. The invention of the matched filter by D. O. North resulted from the World War II development of radar systems. The SNR for the matched filter detector at the sampler output is obtained from (10.35) as

$$SNR_{MF} = \left(\frac{s_{o1}^2}{\sigma_o^2} \right)_{max} = \frac{2}{N_o} \int_{-\infty}^{\infty} |S_1(f)|^2 df = \frac{2}{N_o} \int_{-\infty}^{\infty} s_1^2(t)dt = \frac{2E_1}{N_o} \qquad (10.38)$$

where E_1 is energy of the pulse $s_1(t)$. Equation (10.38) is a very interesting result. It states that the matched filter output SNR depends on the signal energy but not on the signal waveform shape. Of course, the signal energy can be increased by increasing the pulse amplitude or duration.

If $s_2(t) \neq 0$, the optimization (10.26) can be similarly carried using Cauchy-Schwarz inequality. The transfer function of the matched filter in this case is given by

$$H_{opt}(f) = \left[S_1^*(f) - S_2^*(f) \right]e^{-j2\pi f t_o} \qquad (10.39)$$

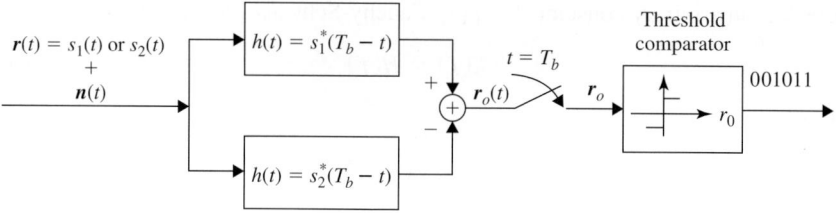

Figure 10.4 Realization of the matched filter detector.

From (10.39), the impulse response of the matched filter can be written as

$$h_{opt}(t) = s_1^*(t_o - t) - s_2^*(t_o - t) \qquad (10.40)$$

The matched filter can be realized as two filters in parallel matched to $s_1(t)$ and $s_2(t)$, respectively, as illustrated in Figure 10.4. The difference of their outputs at the sampling time t_o is compared with the threshold given by (10.17). How to choose t_o? We note that if $t_o < T_b$, the filter will be unrealizable, because it will have nonzero impulse response for $t < 0$. From now on we will take $t_o = T_b$. The response of the matched filter to $s_1(t)$ and $s_2(t)$ at $t = T_b$ is given by

$$s_{o1} = s_1(t) \otimes h_{opt}(t)|_{t=T_b} = \int_{-\infty}^{\infty} |s_1(t)|^2 dt - \int_{-\infty}^{\infty} s_1(t)s_2^*(t)dt \qquad (10.41)$$

$$s_{o2} = s_2(t) \otimes h_{opt}(t)|_{t=T_b} = -\int_{-\infty}^{\infty} |s_2(t)|^2 dt + \int_{-\infty}^{\infty} s_2(t)s_1^*(t)dt \qquad (10.42)$$

Example 10.2

Determine the impulse response function of the filter matched to the pulse shown in Figure 10.5(a).

a. Display the output pulse.
b. What is the peak value of the output?

Solution

The impulse response of the matched filter is given by

$$h_{opt}(t) = s_1(T_b - t)$$

Figure 10.5(b) illustrates $h_{opt}(t)$.

a. The output of the matched filter is given by

$$s_{o1}(t) = s_1(t) \otimes h_{opt}(t) = \int_{-\infty}^{\infty} s_1(\tau)h_{opt}(t - \tau)d\tau$$

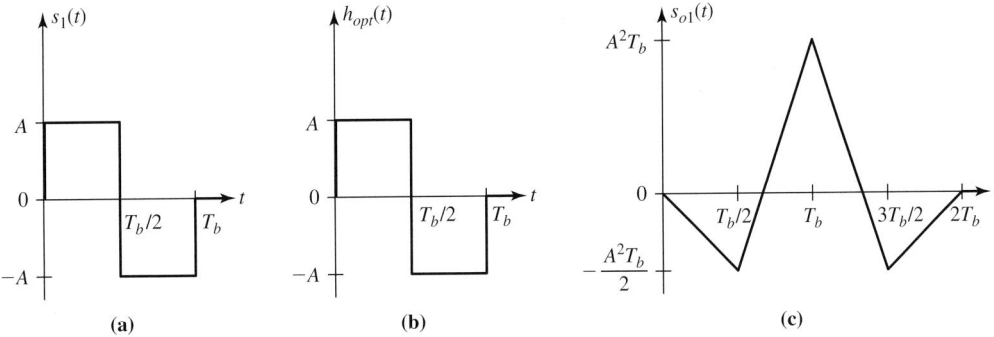

Figure 10.5 Matched filter waveforms.

The matched filter output is displayed in Figure 10.5(c).

b. We note that the peak of the filter output occurs at the sampling instant $t = T_b$ and is equal to the energy of the signal $s_1(t)$. This is a very important property of the matched filter: the value of the output at the sampling instant is equal to the energy of the transmitted pulse. It is independent of the shape of the waveform for $s_1(t)$.

Let us define the **distance** d between two matched filter output signal sample values by

$$d^2 \triangleq s_{o1} - s_{o2} \tag{10.43}$$

Substituting (10.41) and (10.42) into (10.43), we obtain the following expression for a matched-filter detector

$$d^2 = \int_{-\infty}^{\infty} |s_1(t)|^2 dt - \int_{-\infty}^{\infty} s_1(t)s_2^*(t)dt + \int_{-\infty}^{\infty} |s_2(t)|^2 dt - \int_{-\infty}^{\infty} s_2(t)s_1^*(t)dt$$

$$= \int_{-\infty}^{\infty} |s_1(t) - s_2(t)|^2 dt \tag{10.44}$$

By combining (10.40) and (10.44), we can write

$$d^2 = \int_{-\infty}^{\infty} |h_{opt}(t)|^2 dt = \int_{-\infty}^{\infty} |H_{opt}(f)|^2 df \tag{10.45}$$

The noise at the output of the matched filter can now be obtained by substituting (10.45) into (10.8) as

$$\sigma_o^2 = \frac{N_o}{2} \int_{-\infty}^{\infty} |H_{opt}(f)|^2 df = \frac{N_o}{2} d^2 \tag{10.46}$$

The BER of a matched detector filter is given by substituting (10.44) and (10.46) into (10.18) as

$$BER_{MF} = Q\left(\sqrt{\frac{d^2}{2N_o}}\right) \tag{10.47}$$

10.2.1 Correlation Detectors

The matched filter can also be realized by an alternative scheme shown in Figure 10.6. The output signal from the matched filter is given by

$$\boldsymbol{r}_o(t) = \boldsymbol{r}(t) \otimes h_{opt}(t) = \int_{-\infty}^{\infty} h_{opt}(t - \tau)\boldsymbol{r}(\tau)d\tau \tag{10.48}$$

Substituting $h_{opt}(t) = s(T_b - t)$, we get

$$\boldsymbol{r}_o(t) = \int_{-\infty}^{\infty} s\big[T_b - (t - \tau)\big]\boldsymbol{r}(\tau)d\tau \tag{10.49}$$

At the sampling instant $t = T_b$, we have

$$\boldsymbol{r}_o(T_b) = \int_{-\infty}^{\infty} s(\tau)\boldsymbol{r}(\tau)d\tau \tag{10.50}$$

Because $s(t)$ is of finite duration ($0 \le t \le T_b$) waveform, the matched filter output is given by

$$\boldsymbol{r}_o(T_b) = \int_{0}^{T_b} s(\tau)\boldsymbol{r}(\tau)\boldsymbol{d\tau} \tag{10.51}$$

Equation (10.51) can be implemented using the multiplier integrator structure shown in Figure 10.6(a). Such a realization is referred to as a **correlation detector,** because it evaluates correlation or similarity between the received signal and the transmitted signal waveforms. Further, if the transmitted waveform is a rectangular pulse, it becomes unnecessary to multiply by $s(t)$ at the detector. The resulting structure is called an **integrate** and **dump detector;** it is displayed in Figure 10.6(b).

10.2.2 Performance of Binary Signaling Systems

We will now compare the performance of various binary signaling systems using matched filter detection.

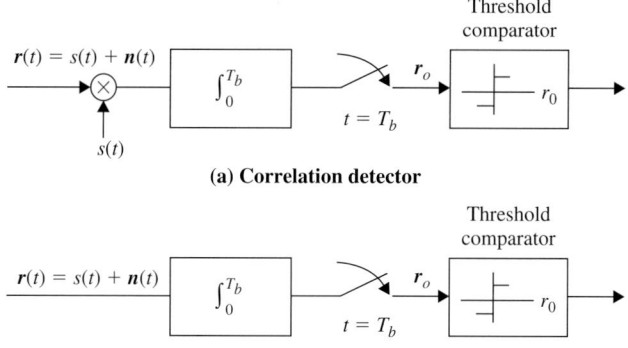

(a) Correlation detector

(b) "Integrate and dump" version of the correlation detector

Figure 10.6 Correlation detector implementation.

Unipolar NRZ or On-Off Signaling

In this case, $s_1(t) = A$ and $s_2(t) = 0$ for $0 \leq t \leq T_b$. Substituting into (10.44) yields

$$d^2 = \int_{-\infty}^{\infty} |s_1(t) - s_2(t)|^2 dt = \int_0^{T_b} A^2 dt = A^2 T_b = 2E_b \qquad (10.52)$$

where

$$E_b = \text{Average energy/bit} = \frac{1}{2}A^2 T_b + \frac{1}{2} \cdot 0 = \frac{A^2 T_b}{2}$$

Substituting (10.52) into (10.47) yields

$$BER_{MF} = Q\left(\sqrt{\frac{2E_b}{2N_o}}\right) = Q\left(\sqrt{\frac{E_b}{N_o}}\right) \qquad (10.53)$$

The parameter E_b/N_o, called **SNR/bit,** appears in the BER expression of every digital communications system. For unipolar NRZ signaling, we conclude by comparing (10.53) with (10.25) that the nonoptimal RC low-pass filter detector requires $10\log_{10} 0.8154 = 0.89$ dB additional SNR/bit versus the matched filter detector for the same error performance.

Polar or Antipodal NRZ Signaling

In this case, $s_1(t) = -s_2(t)$. Therefore $s_1(t) - s_2(t) = 2A$ for $0 \leq t \leq T_b$. Substituting into (10.44) yields

$$d^2 = \int_{-\infty}^{\infty} |s_1(t) - s_2(t)|^2 dt = 4 \int_0^{T_b} A^2 dt = 4A^2 T_b = 4E_b \qquad (10.54)$$

where

$$E_b = \text{Average energy/bit} = \frac{1}{2}A^2 T_b + \frac{1}{2}A^2 T_b = A^2 T_b$$

Substituting (10.54) into (10.47) yields

$$BER_{MF} = Q\left(\sqrt{\frac{4E_b}{2N_o}}\right) = Q\left(\sqrt{\frac{2E_b}{N_o}}\right) \tag{10.55}$$

We observe by comparing (10.55) with (10.53) that the polar NRZ signaling requires 3 dB less SNR/bit for the same BER performance when compared with the unipolar NRZ encoding. By using a procedure similar to the one described in Example 10.1, we can show that the BER performance achieved with the nonoptimal RC low-pass filter detector is given by

$$BER_{RC} = Q\left(\sqrt{1.63\frac{E_b}{N_o}}\right) \tag{10.56}$$

This represents an SNR penalty of 0.89 dB when compared with the matched filter detector for binary polar signaling.

Orthogonal Signaling

In orthogonal signaling, $s_1(t)$ and $s_2(t)$ are chosen to be orthogonal over the bit interval $0 \leq t \leq T_b$. That is,

$$\int_0^{T_b} s_1(t)s_2(t)dt = 0 \tag{10.57}$$

There are many choices for orthogonal signals. As an example, consider the signal set

$$s_1(t) = \begin{cases} A, & 0 \leq t \leq T_b/2 \\ 0, & \text{otherwise} \end{cases} \tag{10.58}$$

and

$$s_2(t) = \begin{cases} A, & T_b/2 \leq t \leq T_b \\ 0, & \text{otherwise} \end{cases}$$

Substituting into (10.44) yields

$$d^2 = \int_{-\infty}^{\infty} |s_1(t) - s_2(t)|^2 dt = \int_0^{T_b} A^2 dt = A^2 T_b = 2E_b \tag{10.59}$$

where

$$E_b = \text{Average energy/bit} = \frac{1}{4}A^2T_b + \frac{1}{4}A^2T_b = \frac{A^2T_b}{2}$$

Substituting (10.59) into (10.47) yields

$$BER_{MF} = Q\left(\sqrt{\frac{2E_b}{2N_o}}\right) = Q\left(\sqrt{\frac{E_b}{N_o}}\right) \tag{10.60}$$

By comparing (10.60) with (10.53), we observe that the orthogonal baseband signaling requires 3 dB more SNR/bit than antipodal scheme for the same BER performance. The performance of orthogonal signaling is identical to that of unipolar NRZ or on-off waveforms, which are also orthogonal.

Bipolar NRZ Signaling

In this case, $s_1(t)$ alternates between $v(t)$ and $-v(t)$ for binary 1 and $s_2(t) = 0$ for binary 0. The impulse response of the matched filter for bipolar signaling is given by

$$h_{opt}(t) = v(T_b - t)$$

For a rectangular basic pulse shape $v(t)$ of amplitude A and duration T_b, its energy is given by

$$E_1 = \int_0^{T_b} v(t)^2 dt = A^2 T_b$$

Because bipolar signaling uses three pulses, the average energy per bit E_b is

$$E_b = \frac{1}{4}E_1 + \frac{1}{2} \times 0 + \frac{1}{4}E_1 = \frac{E_1}{2} \tag{10.61}$$

The variance of noise at the matched filter output is obtained by substituting

$$\sigma_o^2 = \frac{N_o}{2}\int_{-\infty}^{\infty} |H_{opt}(f)|^2 df = \frac{N_o}{2}\int_0^{T_b} v(t)^2 dt = \frac{N_o E_1}{2} \tag{10.62}$$

The probability of bit error is given by

$$BER = P[\text{error}|v(t) \text{ sent}]P[v(t) \text{ sent}] + P[\text{error}|-v(t) \text{ sent}]$$

$$P[-v(t) \text{ sent}] + P[\text{error}|s_2(t) \text{ sent}]P[s_2(t) \text{ sent}] \tag{10.63}$$

Substituting the pulse probabilities $P\{s_2(t)\} = 1/2$ and $P\{v(t)\} = P\{-v(t)\} = 1/4$ into (10.63), we get

$$BER = \frac{1}{4}P[\text{error}|v(t) \text{ sent}] + \frac{1}{4}P[\text{error}|-v(t) \text{ sent}] + \frac{1}{2}P[\text{error}|s_2(t) \text{ sent}] \tag{10.64}$$

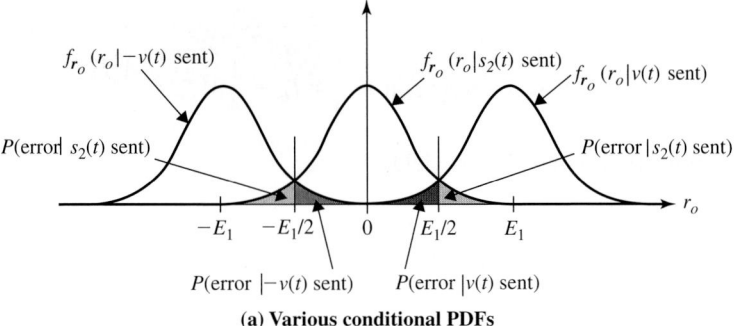

(a) Various conditional PDFs

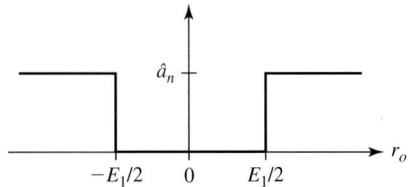

(b) Transfer characteristic of the threshold comparator

Figure 10.7 Bipolar signaling error performance calculation.

Figure 10.7(a) displays the conditional PDFs of r_o. There are two thresholds set at $-E_1/2$ and $E_1/2$. The comparator transfer characteristic is shown in Figure 10.7(b). From Figure 10.7(a), the conditional probability of error, $P[\text{error}|-v(t)\text{ sent}]$, can be expressed as

$$P[\text{error}|-v(t)\text{ sent}] = P\{r_o > -E_1/2| - v(t)\text{ sent}\} = \int_{-E_1/2}^{\infty} f_{r_o}(r_o| - v(t)\text{ sent})dr_o$$

$$= \int_{-E_1/2}^{\infty} \frac{1}{\sqrt{2\pi\sigma_o^2}} e^{-(r_o+E_1)^2/2\sigma_o^2} dr_o = \int_{\frac{E_1}{2\sigma_o}}^{\infty} \frac{1}{\sqrt{2\pi}} e^{-x^2/2} dx = Q\left(\frac{E_1}{2\sigma_o}\right)$$

$$(10.65)$$

Similarly, it can be shown that

$$P[\text{error}|v(t)\text{ sent}] = P\{r_o < E_1/2|v(t)\text{ sent}\} = Q\left(\frac{E_1}{2\sigma_o}\right) \qquad (10.66)$$

Further,

$$P[\text{error}|s_2(t)\text{ sent}] = P\{(r_o < -E_1/2)\cup(r_o > E_1/2)|s_2(t)\text{ sent}\}$$

$$= \int_{-\infty}^{-E_1/2} f_{r_o}(r_o|s_2(t)\text{ sent})dr_o + \int_{E_1/2}^{\infty} f_{r_o}(r_o|s_2(t)\text{ sent})dr_o$$

$$= 2\int_{E_1/2}^{\infty} \frac{1}{\sqrt{2\pi\sigma_o^2}} e^{-r_o^2/2\sigma_o^2} dr_o$$

$$= 2\int_{\frac{E_1}{2\sigma_o}}^{\infty} \frac{1}{\sqrt{2\pi}} e^{-x^2/2} dx = 2Q\left(\frac{E_1}{2\sigma_o}\right) \qquad (10.67)$$

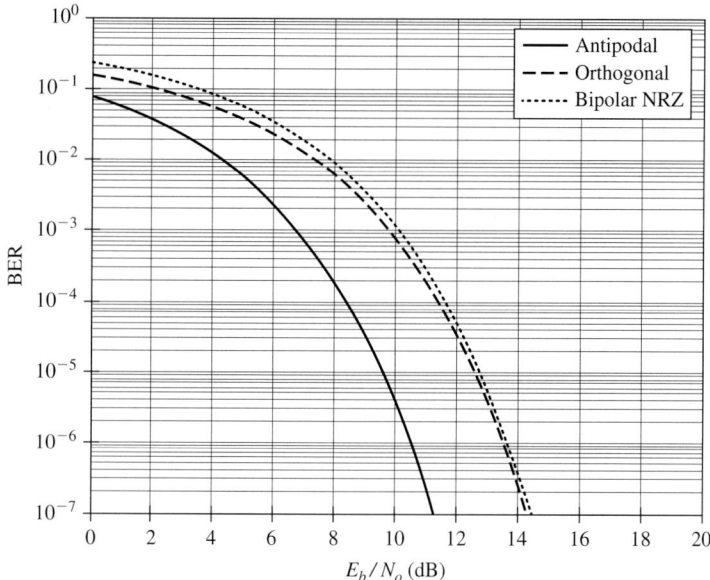

Figure 10.8 BER performance of binary signaling schemes.

Combining (10.64) through (10.67) yields

$$BER = \frac{1}{4}Q\left(\frac{E_1}{2\sigma_o}\right) + \frac{1}{4}Q\left(\frac{E_1}{2\sigma_o}\right) + \frac{1}{2}\left\{2 \times Q\left(\frac{E_1}{2\sigma_o}\right)\right\} = \frac{3}{2}Q\left(\frac{E_1}{2\sigma_o}\right) \quad (10.68)$$

Substituting (10.61) and (10.62) into (10.68) yields

$$BER = \frac{3}{2}Q\left(\sqrt{\frac{E_b}{N_o}}\right) \quad\quad (10.69)$$

Figure 10.8 displays the BER performance of three binary signaling schemes versus SNR/bit (E_b/N_o). Antipodal signaling performs the best, with a 3-dB advantage over orthogonal and bipolar schemes. To achieve a BER of 10^{-6}, the antipodal signaling requires an E_b/N_o of approximately 10.5 dB.

Example 10.3

Suppose that binary data is transmitted over an AWGN channel with a power spectral density $N_o/2 = 10^{-10}$ W/Hz. Determine the signal amplitude A required to achieve a BER $= 10^{-6}$ when the data rate is (a), 10 kbps, (b), 100 kbps, and (c), 1.55 Mbps. Evaluate for bipolar NRZ and Manchester line coding. What is the signal bandwidth (based on the first spectral null) in each case?

Solution

For bipolar NRZ signaling,

$$BER = \frac{3}{2}Q\left(\sqrt{\frac{E_b}{N_o}}\right) \text{ using an MF receiver}$$

$$N_o/2 = 10^{-10} \Rightarrow N_o = 2 \times 10^{-10}$$

Using Table 6.1, we get $x = 4.7535$ for $BER = 10^{-6}$.

$$\therefore \frac{E_b}{N_o} = (4.7535)^2 = 23.377 \Rightarrow E_b = 4.675 \times 10^{-9}$$

Now $E_b = \dfrac{A^2 T_b}{2}$

a. $R = 10$ kbps, $\therefore T_b = 10^{-4}$

$$A^2 = \frac{4.675 \times 10^{-9} \times 2}{10^{-4}} \Rightarrow A = 9.67 \text{ mV}$$

b. $R = 100$ kbps, $\therefore T_b = 10^{-5}$

$$A^2 = \frac{4.675 \times 10^{-9} \times 2}{10^{-5}} \Rightarrow A = 30.58 \text{ mV}$$

c. $R = 1.55$ Mbps, $\therefore T_b = 6.45 \times 10^{-7}$

$$A^2 = \frac{4.675 \times 10^{-9} \times 2}{6.45 \times 10^{-7}} \Rightarrow A = 120.38 \text{ mV}$$

For Manchester encoding (antipodal), $E_b = A^2 T_b$ and $BER = Q\left(\sqrt{\dfrac{2E_b}{N_o}}\right)$ using an MF receiver. From Table 6.1, we get $x = 4.7535$ for $BER = 10^{-6}$.

$$\therefore \frac{2E_b}{N_o} = (4.7535)^2 = 22.5625 \Rightarrow E_b = 2.25625 \times 10^{-9}$$

Now

a. $R = 10$ kbps, $\therefore T_b = 10^{-4}$

$$A^2 = \frac{2.25625 \times 10^{-9}}{10^{-4}} \Rightarrow A = 4.75 \text{ mV}$$

b. $R = 100$ kbps, $\therefore T_b = 10^{-5}$

$$A^2 = \frac{2.25625 \times 10^{-9}}{10^{-5}} \Rightarrow A = 15 \text{ mV}$$

c. $R = 1.55$ Mbps, $\therefore T_b = 6.45 \times 10^{-7}$

$$A^2 = \frac{2.25625 \times 10^{-9}}{6.45 \times 10^{-7}} \Rightarrow A = 59.14 \text{ mV}$$

The following table summarizes the results.

Bit Rate (kbps)	Bipolar NRZ		Manchester	
	A (mV)	BW (kHz)	A (mV)	BW (kHz)
10	9.67	10	4.75	20
100	30.58	100	15	200
1550	120.38	1550	59.14	3100

Experiment 10.1 *Binary Antipodal System with Correlation Detector*

In this experiment, we model a binary polar NRZ digital communication system with correlation detector. Figure 10.9(a) illustrates the Simulink model for the system. The parameters of simulation are set up by a companion MATLAB m-file. The m-file also computes the theoretical BER and plots simulated and theoretical BER performance. The **Polar Bernoulli source,** discussed in Example 3.2, is used to generate a polar NRZ signal. AWGN is added by using the **AWGN channel** block illustrated in Figure 10.9(a). The correlation detector is implemented by a discrete-time integrator which is reset at the beginning of each bit interval. The output of the integrator is sampled at $t = kT_b$ in the **symbol-rate sampling** block. The **sign** block then produces regenerated output pulses based on the comparison of these sample values with threshold level (0 volts in this case). The regenerated polar signal is next compared with the transmitted polar signal in **Error-rate meter** block. The simulated BER values are transmitted to MATLAB workspace to generate the

Figure 10.9 (a) Simulink model for binary antipodal communication system; (b) binary antipodal signaling waveforms; (c) comparison of theoretical and simulated BER performance.

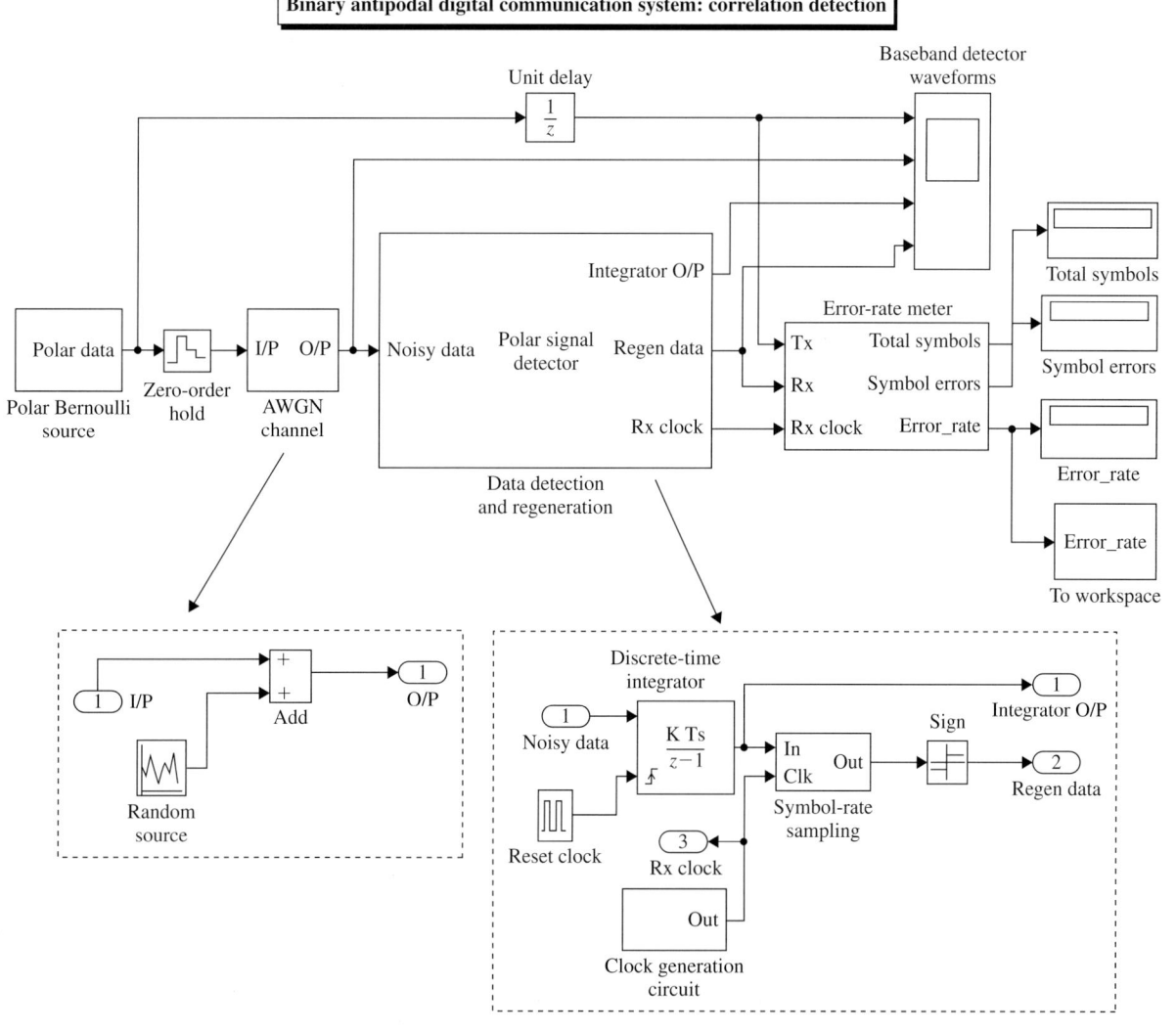

(a)   (*continued*)

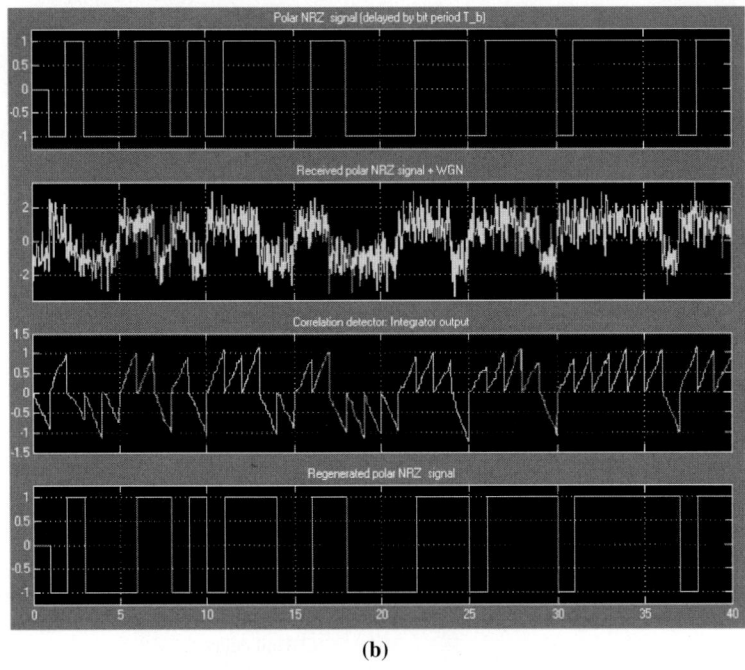

(b)

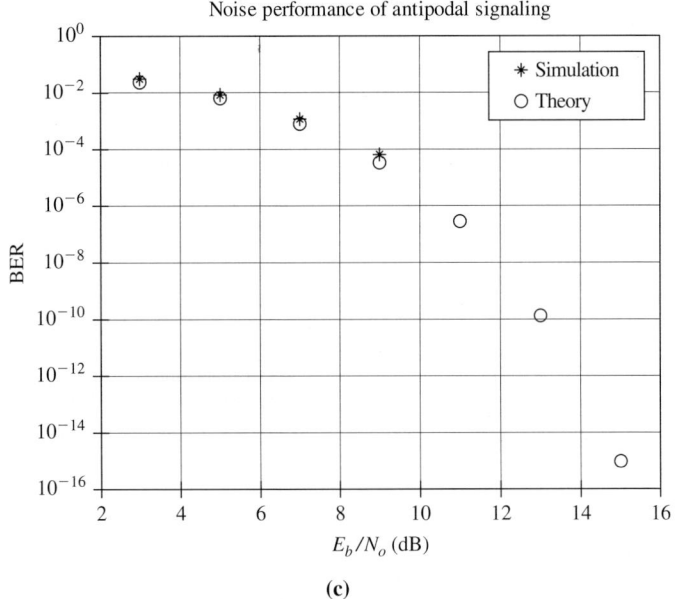

(c)

BER performance curve. Figure 10.9(b) displays various waveforms generated using this simulation. Figure 10.9(c) provides a comparison of theoretical and simulated BER performance.

Experiment 10.2 *Binary Antipodal Signaling System with Matched-Filter Detection*

In this experiment, we model a binary antipodal digital communication system with MF detector. Figure 10.10(a) illustrates the Simulink model for the system. The parameters of simulation are set up by a companion MATLAB m-file. The m-file also computes the theoretical BER and plots simulated and theoretical BER performance. The Polar Bernoulli source, discussed in

Figure 10.10 (a) Simulink model for binary antipodal communication system; (b) RRC antipodal signaling waveforms; (c) comparison of theoretical and simulated BER performance.

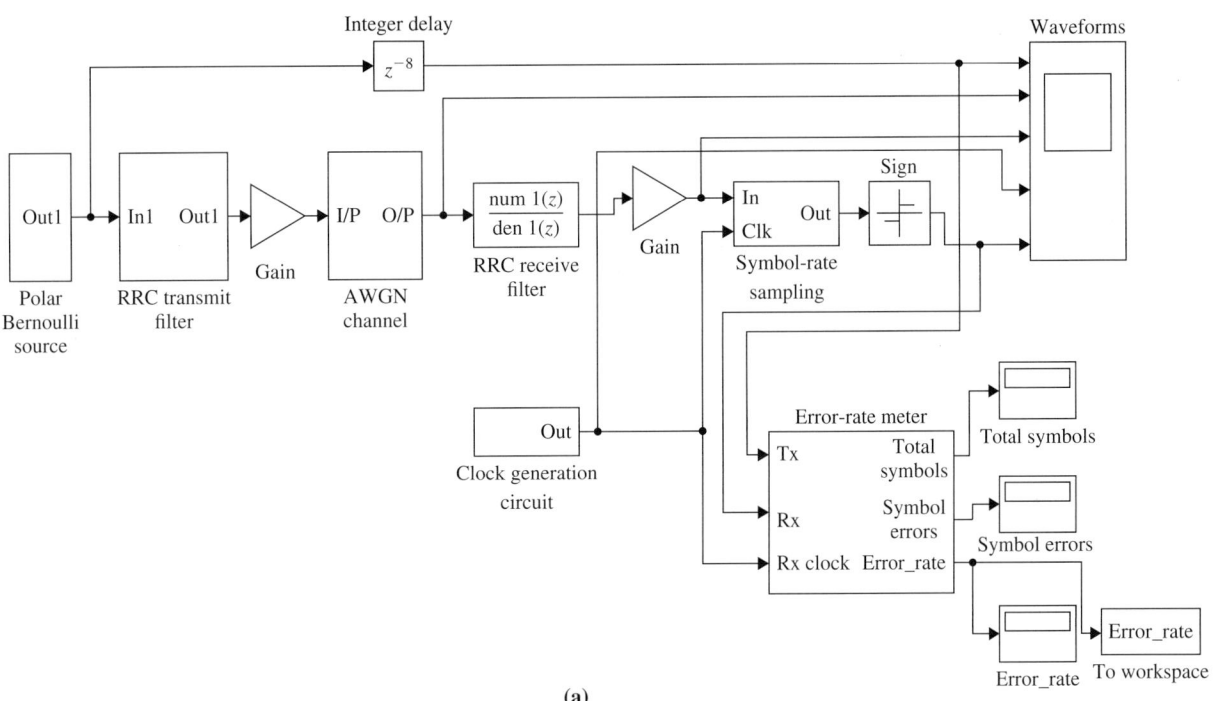

(a)

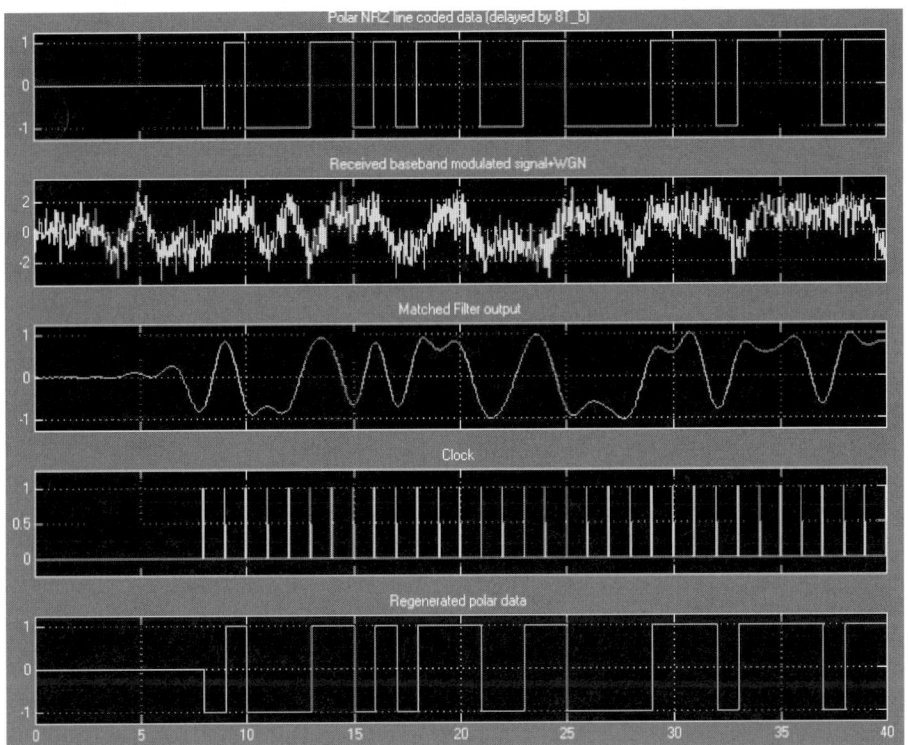

(b)

(*continued*)

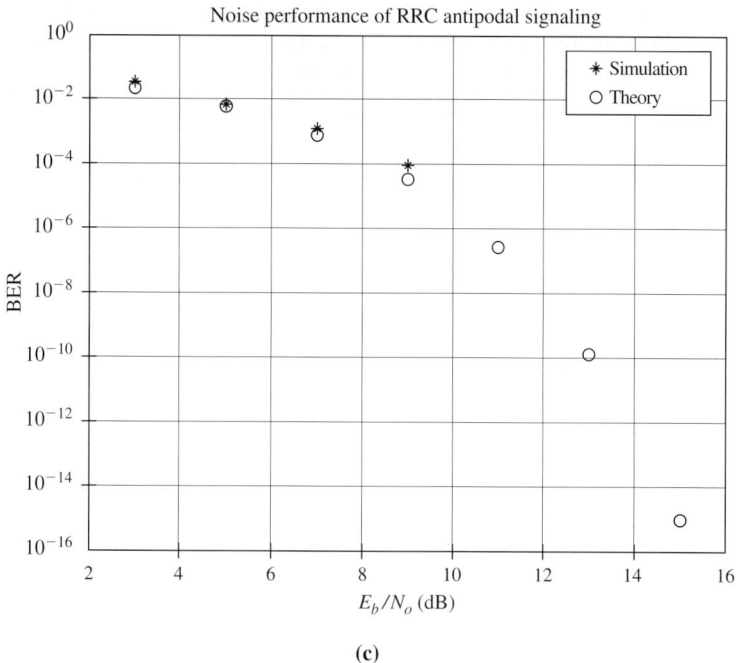

Noise performance of RRC antipodal signaling

(c)

Example 3.2, is used to generate a polar NRZ signal. The transmit pulse shaping is implemented by a **root raised cosine (RRC)** filter with roll-off factor $\alpha = 0.5$. AWGN is added by using the AWGN channel block illustrated in Figure 10.9(a). The receiver filter is also RRC type matched to the transmit filter. The output of the MF is sampled at $t = kT_b$ in the symbol-rate sampling block. The **sign** block then produces regenerated output pulses based on the comparison of these sample values with threshold level (0 volts in this case). The regenerated polar signal is next compared with the transmitted signal in Error-rate meter block. The simulated BER values are transmitted to MATLAB workspace to generate the BER performance curve. Figure 10.10(b) displays various waveforms generated using this simulation. Figure 10.10(c) provides a comparison of theoretical and simulated BER performance.

10.3   VECTOR SPACE CONCEPTS

We are familiar with vectors in two- and three-dimensional Euclidean space. A vector in a two-dimensional Euclidean space represents a point in the plane; it is specified by an ordered pair of real numbers (u_1, u_2). Similarly, a vector or point in a three-dimensional Euclidean space is specified by an ordered 3-tuple of real numbers (u_1, u_2, u_3). This concept can be generalized to define an *n*-dimensional vector as an ordered *n*-tuple of numbers $\underline{u} = (u_1, u_2, \ldots, u_n)$. The components of the vector are elements of the field of complex numbers $\mathbb{C}$ (or its subset $\mathbb{R}$). In Chapter 14, we will study vector spaces defined on the binary field $\mathbb{F} = \{0, 1\}$ in the context of developing coding schemes for reliable communications.

A **vector** or **linear space** V is a set or collection of vectors with the property that if $\underline{u}$ and $\underline{v}$ are in V, then the linear combination $\alpha\underline{u} + \beta\underline{v}$ is also in V for any scalars $\alpha, \beta \in \mathbb{C}$. This is called the **superposition property.** All vector spaces include the zero vector $(\underline{0})$ because multiplying any vector by the scalar zero yields the zero vector. Probably the most familiar example of a vector space is $\mathbb{R}^n$ − the set of all *n*-tuples of real numbers. Addition and scalar multiplication operations in $\mathbb{R}^n$ are defined component wise.

In this chapter, our focus is primarily on the vector space $\mathbb{L}_2$ that is collection of finite-energy complex waveforms (functions) defined over the interval $(t_o, t_o + T)$. For any vector $u(t)$ in $\mathbb{L}_2$

$$\int_T |u(t)|^2 \, dt < \infty$$

where $\int_T$ denotes integration over the interval $(t_o, t_o + T)$. To prove that $\mathbb{L}_2$ is a vector space, we need to show that it satisfies the superposition property. That is, if $u(t)$ and $v(t)$ are two finite-energy complex waveforms, $\alpha u(t) + \beta v(t)$ is also finite-energy (that is, in $\mathbb{L}_2$) for any complex numbers α and β. Using the inequality $\|\underline{u} + \underline{v}\|^2 \leq 2\|\underline{u}\|^2 + 2\|\underline{v}\|^2$, we can write

$$\int_T |\alpha u(t) + \beta v(t)|^2 dt \leq 2|\alpha|^2 \int_T |u(t)|^2 dt + 2|\beta|^2 \int_T |v(t)|^2 dt < \infty \qquad (10.70)$$

Thus, the set of finite-energy complex waveforms $\mathbb{L}_2(t_o, t_o + T)$ constitutes a vector space with complex addition and scalar multiplication operations. Similarly, the set of finite-energy real waveforms forms a vector space with real addition and scalar multiplication. We will interchangeably use the notation $\underline{u}$ to denote the vector $u(t)$ in $\mathbb{L}_2$.

A subspace S of a vector space V is a subset of V such that the vectors in S also satisfy the superposition property. For example, $\mathbb{R}^2$ is a subset but not a subspace of $\mathbb{C}^2$. The vector $\underline{u} = (2, 3)$ is an element of $\mathbb{R}^2$ as well as $\mathbb{C}^2$. But the scalar product $2j\underline{u} = (4j, 6j)$ is not a real 2-tuple, and therefore not in $\mathbb{R}^2$.

10.3.1 Finite Dimensional Vector Spaces

A set of vectors $\underline{v}_1, \underline{v}_2, \ldots, \underline{v}_n \in V$ is said to span V if every vector $\underline{u} = (u_1, u_2, \ldots, u_n) \in V$ is a linear combination of $\underline{v}_1, \underline{v}_2, \ldots, \underline{v}_n$. That is,

$$\underline{u} = u_1 \underline{v}_1 + u_2 \underline{v}_2 + \ldots + u_n \underline{v}_n \qquad (10.71)$$

A vector space V is finite dimensional if there is a finite set of vectors $\underline{v}_1, \underline{v}_2, \ldots, \underline{v}_n$ that span V. If it is not finite dimensional, it is called infinite dimensional. As an example, consider the vector space $\mathbb{R}^n$. Let $\underline{e}_i, 1 \leq i \leq n$ be the vector containing 1 in position i and 0s elsewhere, that is, $\underline{e}_1 = (1, 0, \ldots, 0, 0)$, $\underline{e}_2 = (0, 1, 0 \ldots, 0)$, and so on. The vectors $\underline{e}_1, \underline{e}_2, \ldots, \underline{e}_n$ are called the **unit vectors** of $\mathbb{R}^n$. Note that every vector $\underline{u} = (u_1, u_2, \ldots, u_n)$ can be expressed as a linear combination of the unit vectors. That is,

$$\underline{u} = u_1 \underline{e}_1 + u_2 \underline{e}_2 + \ldots + u_n \underline{e}_n \qquad (10.72)$$

The set of vectors $\underline{e}_1, \underline{e}_2, \ldots, \underline{e}_n$, therefore, spans the vector space $\mathbb{R}^n$.

A set of vectors $\underline{v}_1, \underline{v}_2, \ldots, \underline{v}_n$ is said to be **linearly independent** if none of the vectors in this set can be expressed as a linear combination of the remaining vectors in the set. That is, it is impossible to find scalars $\alpha_1, \alpha_2, \ldots, \alpha_n$ not all zero such that

$$\sum_{i=1}^{n} \alpha_i \underline{v}_i = \underline{0} \qquad (10.73)$$

for a linearly independent set of vectors $\underline{v}_1, \underline{v}_2, \ldots, \underline{v}_n$.

A set of vectors $\underline{v}_1, \underline{v}_2, \ldots, \underline{v}_n$ in V is a basis for V if the set both spans V and is linearly independent. The basis of a vector space is *not* unique. $\underline{e}_1, \underline{e}_2, \ldots, \underline{e}_n$ is a basis for $\mathbb{R}^n$ but not the only one. The dimension of a vector space V is the number of vectors in any basis of V. Given any basis $\underline{v}_1, \underline{v}_2, \ldots, \underline{v}_n$ for a finite dimensional vector space V, any vector $\underline{u}$ in V can be represented as

$$\underline{u} = \sum_{i=1}^{n} \alpha_i \underline{v}_i \tag{10.74}$$

where $\alpha_1, \alpha_2, \ldots, \alpha_n$ are unique scalars. In terms of the given basis, each vector $\underline{u}$ in V can be represented by the n-tuple of coefficients $(\alpha_1, \alpha_2, \ldots, \alpha_n)$.

The simplest example of a basis is the standard basis in $\mathbb{R}^3$ consisting of the unit vectors $\underline{e}_1 = (1, 0, 0)$, $\underline{e}_2 = (0, 1, 0)$, and $\underline{e}_3 = (0, 0, 1)$. Therefore, the dimension of $\mathbb{R}^3$ is 3.

10.3.2   Inner-Product Vector Spaces

A vector space does not in itself contain any notion of distance or angle, although such notions are clearly present for vectors in two- and three-dimensional Euclidean spaces. An **inner product** is a generalization of the dot product. A vector space equipped with an inner product is called an **inner-product space.** Examples of inner-product spaces include:

1. The vector space $\mathbb{R}^n$, where the inner product is given by the **dot product.** For any two vectors $\underline{u}, \underline{v}$ in $\mathbb{R}^n$, the dot product is defined as

$$(\underline{u} \bullet \underline{v}) = \sum_{i=1}^{n} u_i v_i \tag{10.75}$$

2. The vector space $\mathbb{L}_2(t_o, t_o + T)$ of finite-energy complex waveforms defined over the interval $(t_o, t_o + T)$. For any two vectors $u(t)$, $v(t)$ in $\mathbb{L}_2$, the inner product is defined as

$$(\underline{u} \bullet \underline{v}) = \int_T u(t) v^*(t) dt \tag{10.76}$$

The **norm** or **length** $\|\underline{v}\|$ of a vector $\underline{v}$ is defined as

$$\|\underline{v}\| = \sqrt{(\underline{v} \bullet \underline{v})} \tag{10.77}$$

In the vector space $\mathbb{R}^n$, the norm of a vector $\underline{v} = [v_1, v_2, \ldots, v_n]$ is given by

$$\left\|\underline{v}\right\| = \sqrt{\sum_{i=1}^{n} v_i^2} \tag{10.78}$$

The norm of a vector $u(t)$ in the space $\mathbb{L}_2(t_o, t_o + T)$ of finite-energy complex waveforms is similarly given by

$$\left\|\underline{u}\right\| = \sqrt{\int_T |u(t)|^2 dt} \tag{10.79}$$

The distance d($\underline{u}$, $\underline{v}$) between two vectors $\underline{u}$, $\underline{v}$ in an inner-product space V is defined as the norm of the difference of the vectors. That is,

$$d(\underline{u}, \underline{v}) = \|\underline{u} - \underline{v}\| \tag{10.80}$$

In the vector space $\mathbb{R}^n$, the distance between two vectors $\underline{u}$, $\underline{v}$ would be

$$d(\underline{u}, \underline{v}) = \left\|\underline{u} - \underline{v}\right\| = \sqrt{\sum_{i=1}^{n}(u_i - v_i)^2} \tag{10.81}$$

which agrees with the Euclidean or Cartesian notion of distance. The distance $d(\underline{u}, \underline{v})$ between two vectors $u(t)$ and $v(t)$ in the space $\mathbb{L}_2$ of finite-energy complex waveforms follows from the definition as

$$d(\underline{u}, \underline{v}) = \left\|u(t) - v(t)\right\| = \sqrt{\int_T |u(t) - v(t)|^2 dt} \tag{10.82}$$

Orthogonal and Orthonormal Vectors

Two vectors $\underline{u}$ and $\underline{v}$ are defined to be **orthogonal** if $(\underline{u} \cdot \underline{v}) = 0$. In an inner-product space, a set of vectors $\underline{\phi}_1, \underline{\phi}_2, \ldots$ is **orthonormal** if

$$(\underline{\phi}_j \cdot \underline{\phi}_k) = \begin{cases} 1, & j = k \\ 0, & j \neq k \end{cases} \tag{10.83}$$

In other words, an orthonormal set is a set of orthogonal vectors in which each vector is *normalized* in the sense of having unit length. It can be seen that if a set of vectors $\underline{v}_1, \underline{v}_2, \ldots, \underline{v}_n$ is orthogonal, then the set

$$\underline{\phi}_j = \frac{\underline{v}_j}{\|\underline{v}_j\|}, j = 1, \ldots, n \tag{10.84}$$

is orthonormal. Note that if two vectors are orthogonal, then any scaling (including normalization) of a vector maintains the orthogonality. The projection of a vector $\underline{u}$ onto another vector $\underline{v}$ is the component of $\underline{u}$ along $\underline{v}$ axis. It is defined as

$$\text{Projection of } \underline{u} \text{ onto } \underline{v} = (\underline{u} \cdot \underline{v})\underline{v} \tag{10.85}$$

If two vectors are orthogonal, the projection of one onto the other results in a zero vector.

We conclude this section with a very important result that orthonormal bases always exist for finite-dimensional subspaces of infinite-dimensional vector spaces such as $\mathbb{L}_2$. Gram-Schmidt orthogonalization is a constructive procedure that takes a finite set of vectors $s_1(t), s_2(t), \ldots, s_m(t)$ and constructs an orthonormal basis $\{\phi_i(t), i = 1, \ldots, N\}$, where $N \leq M$. The procedure is not only useful in actually finding orthonormal bases, but is also important theoretically, because it proves their existence.

10.3.3   Gram-Schmidt Orthonormalization Procedure

Gram-Schmidt procedure builds a set of orthonormal vectors, one by one, from a set of vectors that need not be either orthogonal or normalized.

1. The first basis function may be any of the $s_i(t)$, $i = 1, 2, \ldots, M$. Let us take $s_1(t)$. The unit energy function $\phi_1(t)$ is obtained by dividing $s_1(t)$ by $\sqrt{E_1}$.

$$\phi_1(t) = \frac{s_1(t)}{\left\| s_1(t) \right\|} = \frac{s_1(t)}{\sqrt{E_1}} \tag{10.86}$$

where

$$\left\| s_1(t) \right\| = \sqrt{\int_T |s_1(t)|^2 dt} = \sqrt{E_1}$$

2. To find the second basis function $\phi_2(t)$, we subtract from $s_2(t)$ its projection onto $\phi_1(t)$ to form the function

$$\theta_2(t) = s_2(t) - \phi_1(t)\big(s_2(t) \bullet \phi_1(t)\big) \tag{10.87}$$

where

$$\big(s_2(t) \bullet \phi_1(t)\big) = \int_T s_2(t)\phi_1(t)dt$$

$\theta_2(t)$ is orthogonal to $\phi_1(t)$, because we removed the component of $s_2(t)$ along the $\phi_1(t)$ axis. The second basis function is

$$\phi_2(t) = \frac{\theta_2(t)}{\left\| \theta_2(t) \right\|} = \frac{\theta_2(t)}{\sqrt{E_{\theta_2}}}$$

where

$$\left\| \theta_2(t) \right\| = \sqrt{\int_T |\theta_2(t)|^2 dt} = \sqrt{E_{\theta_2}}$$

3. The procedure in step 2 can be extended to calculate any basis function $\phi_k(t)$ for $k \geq 2$. To accomplish this, we form the function $\theta_k(t)$ from $s_k(t)$ as follows:

$$\theta_k(t) = s_k(t) - \sum_{i=1}^{k-1} c_{ki}\phi_i(t), \quad 2 \leq k \leq M \tag{10.88}$$

where

$$c_{ki} = \big(s_k(t) \bullet \phi_i(t)\big) \tag{10.89}$$

We observe that $\theta_k(t)$ is orthogonal to every previous basis function $\phi_j(t), j = 1, \ldots,$ $k-1$ as shown below:

$$\left(\theta_k(t) \bullet \phi_j(t)\right) = \left(s_k(t) \bullet \phi_j(t)\right) - \sum_{i=1}^{k-1} c_{ki}\left(\phi_i(t) \bullet \phi_j(t)\right)$$

$$= c_{kj} - c_{kj}\left(\phi_j(t) \bullet \phi_j(t)\right) = c_{kj} - c_{kj} = 0$$

The kth basis function can now be expressed as

$$\phi_k(t) = \frac{\theta_k(t)}{\left\|\theta_k(t)\right\|} = \frac{\theta_k(t)}{\sqrt{E_{\theta_k}}} \tag{10.90}$$

where

$$\left\|\theta_k(t)\right\| = \sqrt{\int_T |\theta_k(t)|^2 dt} = \sqrt{E_{\theta_k}}$$

If we start with a set of vectors that are not linearly independent, then the algorithm finds any vector, say $s_m(t)$, that is a linear combination of the existing orthonormal basis (indicated by $\theta_m(t) = 0$), excludes it from inclusion into the basis, and proceeds to find the next basis vector.

The G-S process thus produces $N \leq M$ orthonormal basis functions for representing M distinct finite-energy signals $s_1(t), s_2(t), \ldots, s_M(t)$.

Example 10.4

Determine an orthonormal basis for the signal set displayed in Figure 10.11 by applying the Gram-Schmidt procedure.

Solution

We take $s_1(t)$ as the first basis function.

$$E_1 = \int_T s_1^2(t)dt = \int_0^3 s_1^2(t)dt = \int_0^2 1 dt = 2$$

The unit energy function $\phi_1(t)$ is obtained by dividing $s_1(t)$ by $\sqrt{E_1}$. That is,

$$\phi_1(t) = \begin{cases} \dfrac{s_1(t)}{\sqrt{2}}, & 0 \leq t \leq 2 \\ 0, & \text{otherwise} \end{cases} \tag{10.91}$$

Next we compute the function $\theta_2(t)$ by using (10.88).

$$\theta_2(t) = s_2(t) - c_{21}\phi_1(t)$$

where

$$c_{21} = \left(s_2(t) \bullet \phi_1(t)\right) = \int_0^3 s_2(t)\phi_1(t)dt = \frac{1}{\sqrt{2}}\int_0^1 1 dt + \frac{1}{\sqrt{2}}\int_1^2 -1\, dt = 0$$

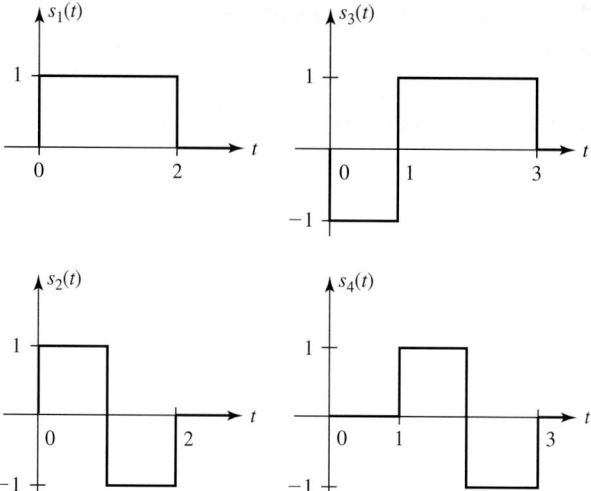

Figure 10.11 Signal set for Example 10.4.

This implies that $s_2(t)$ is orthogonal to $s_1(t)$. Therefore,

$$\theta_2(t) = s_2(t)$$

Because

$$\left\| \theta_2 \right\| = \sqrt{E_2} = \sqrt{\int_0^2 s_2^2(t)dt} = \sqrt{1 + 1} = \sqrt{2}$$

the second orthonormal function is obtained from (10.90) as

$$\phi_2(t) = \frac{\theta_2(t)}{\sqrt{2}} = \frac{s_2(t)}{\sqrt{2}} \tag{10.92}$$

To obtain the next orthonormal function, the function $\theta_3(t)$ is computed using (10.89) as

$$\theta_3(t) = s_3(t) - c_{31}\phi_1(t) - c_{32}\phi_2(t)$$

where

$$c_{31} = \left(s_3(t) \bullet \phi_1(t)\right) = \int_0^3 s_3(t)\phi_1(t)dt = \frac{1}{\sqrt{2}}\int_0^1 -1\, dt + \frac{1}{\sqrt{2}}\int_1^2 1\, dt = 0$$

$$c_{32} = \left(s_3(t) \bullet \phi_2(t)\right) = \int_0^3 s_3(t)\phi_2(t)dt = \frac{1}{\sqrt{2}}\int_0^1 -1\, dt + \frac{1}{\sqrt{2}}\int_1^2 -1\, dt = -\sqrt{2}$$

Substituting the values of c_{31} and c_{32}, we obtain

$$\theta_3(t) = s_3(t) + \sqrt{2}\phi_2(t) \tag{10.93}$$

or

$$\theta_3(t) = \begin{cases} 0, & 0 \le t \le 2 \\ 1, & 2 \le t \le 3 \end{cases}$$

Pioneers in the Field

Vladimir Aleksandrovich Kotelnikov was born on September 6, 1908, in Kazan into a family with a long academic tradition. Both his father and aunt were mathematics professors, and his grandfather had been Dean of Physics and Mathematics at the University of Kazan. After graduating from secondary school in Moscow in 1925, Kotelnikov began to study radio engineering as an undergraduate at what subsequently became the Moscow Power Engineering Institute (MEI), and he remained there to do his postgraduate work. While still a postgraduate student, he wrote the classic paper in 1933 on the sampling of continuous-time, bandlimited signals. There is little doubt that Kotelnikov was the first to derive the sampling theorem in the context of signal transmission, even though the mathematical basis of sampling had been considered earlier by a number of mathematicians. Claude Shannon was unaware of Kotelnikov's work when he published the sampling theorem 16 years later in his 1949 paper. In his 1947 thesis for the Doctorate of Sciences degree, Kotelnikov pioneered the representation of finite energy signal waveforms as vectors ("points") in finite-dimensional signal space. He then used this concept to derive the optimal receiver structures for radar and communication systems. His 1947 dissertation was published in the United States in 1959 as *The Theory of Optimum Noise Immunity,* which was a translation of the 1956 Russian monograph. Kotelnikov subsequently worked on scrambling, cryptography, and planetary radar (including the radar-assisted cartography of Venus). He was awarded the prestigious Lenin Prize in 1964 for his leading role in development of the Soviet space program. He also received the German Eduard Rhein Prize in 1999 and the IEEE Alexander Graham Bell Medal in 2000.

Because $\|\theta_3(t)\| = 1$, $\phi_3(t) = \theta_3(t)$. Substitution into (10.93) yields

$$\phi_3(t) = s_3(t) + \sqrt{2}\phi_2(t) \qquad (10.94)$$

To check for another orthonormal function, we calculate the function $\theta_4(t)$ by using (10.88). That is,

$$\theta_4(t) = s_4(t) - c_{41}\phi_1(t) - c_{42}\phi_2(t) - c_{43}\phi_3(t)$$

where

$$c_{41} = \left(s_4(t) \bullet \phi_1(t)\right) = \int_0^3 s_4(t)\phi_1 dt = \frac{1}{\sqrt{2}}\int_1^2 1\, dt = \frac{1}{\sqrt{2}}$$

$$c_{42} = \left(s_4(t) \bullet \phi_2(t)\right) = \int_0^3 s_4(t)\phi_2 dt = \frac{1}{\sqrt{2}}\int_1^2 -1\, dt = -\frac{1}{\sqrt{2}}$$

$$c_{43} = \left(s_4(t) \bullet \phi_3(t)\right) = \int_0^3 s_4(t)\phi_3 dt = \int_2^3 -1\, dt = -1$$

Substituting the values of c_{41}, c_{42}, and c_{43}, we have

$$\theta_4(t) = s_4(t) - \frac{1}{\sqrt{2}}\phi_1(t) + \frac{1}{\sqrt{2}}\phi_2(t) + \phi_3(t) = 0$$

or

$$s_4(t) = \frac{1}{\sqrt{2}}\phi_1(t) - \frac{1}{\sqrt{2}}\phi_2(t) - \phi_3(t) \qquad (10.95)$$

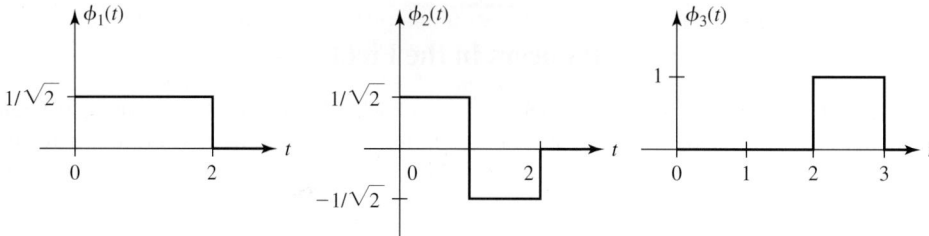

Figure 10.12 Basis functions for the signal set in Figure 10.11.

Thus $\phi_1(t)$, $\phi_2(t)$, and $\phi_3(t)$ form a complete orthonormal basis. Therefore $N = 3$. The set of orthonormal functions is displayed in Figure 10.12.

10.4   VECTOR SPACE REPRESENTATION OF SIGNALS AND WGN

In this section we consider the representation of finite energy signal waveforms as vectors ("points") in finite-dimensional vector spaces. Although this concept was independently invented and applied by Kotenikov and Shannon, credit for popularizing it is often given to the classic text of Wozencraft and Jacobs.[2] This geometric viewpoint forms one of the foundations of modern digital communication systems analysis and design.

10.4.1   Vector Space Representation of Waveforms

Suppose that we have a set of M finite energy signal waveforms $\{s_i(t), i = 1, \ldots, M\}$ defined over the interval $(t_o, t_o + T)$. It is easy to verify that these waveforms form a finite-dimensional subspace of vector space $\mathbb{L}_2$ of all finite energy waveforms. Using the Gram-Schmidt orthogonalization procedure, we can find an orthonormal basis $\{\phi_i(t), i = 1, 2, \ldots, N, N \leq M\}$ such that each of the M waveforms $s_i(t)$ can be represented exactly as

$$s_i(t) = \sum_{j=1}^{N} s_{ij}\phi_j(t) \tag{10.96}$$

where

$$s_{ij} = \left(s_i(t) \bullet \phi_j(t)\right) = \int_T s_i(t)\phi_j(t)dt \tag{10.97}$$

Thus, the waveforms $\{s_i(t), i = 1, \ldots, M\}$ can be represented as N-tuples

$$\underline{s}_i = (s_{i1}, s_{i2}, \ldots, s_{iN}), i = 1, \ldots, M \tag{10.98}$$

in the subspace spanned by the orthonormal basis $\{\phi_i(t), i = 1, 2, \ldots, N\}$. We call this subspace the **signal space.** This representation allows us to view signals as vectors or points in N-dimensional signal space instead of waveforms in infinite-dimensional function space $\mathbb{L}_2$. The concepts of length and distance for vector spaces prove quite useful in developing the optimal signal detection strategies as well as in performance analysis. We call the set of waveforms $\{s_i(t), i = 1, \ldots, M\}$ the **signal set** for the digital modulation scheme. The set of M vectors $\{\underline{s}_i, i = 1, \ldots, M\}$ is called the **signal constellation.** It is a unique representation for the signal set $\{s_i(t), i = 1, \ldots, M\}$ in the signal space determined by the basis $\{\phi_i(t), i = 1, 2, \ldots, N\}$. We observe that the representation of a signal set by a specific constellation is unique with respect to a particular signal space. The same constellation, however, may represent a differ signal set in a different signal space defined by another set of basis vectors.

Example 10.5

Determine the vector space representation for the signal set in Figure 10.11 by using the orthonormal basis found in Example 10.4.

Solution

Because the dimensionality N of the signal space in Example 10.4 is 3, each signal in Figure 10.11 can be expressed using (10.96) as a linear combination of the three basis functions $\phi_1(t)$, $\phi_2(t)$, and $\phi_3(t)$ found in Example 10.4. That is,

$$s_i(t) = s_{i1}\phi_1(t) + s_{i2}\phi_2(t) + s_{i3}\phi_3(t), \ i = 1, 2, 3, 4 \tag{10.99}$$

From (10.91) and (10.99), we can obtain signal vector corresponding to the signal $s_1(t)$.

$$s_1(t) = s_{11}\phi_1(t) + s_{12}\phi_2(t) + s_{13}\phi_3(t) = \sqrt{2}\phi_1(t) \Rightarrow \underline{s}_1 = (s_{11}, s_{12}, s_{13}) = (\sqrt{2}, 0, 0)$$

Similarly, we can obtain vector space representation for the signals $s_2(t)$, $s_3(t)$, and $s_4(t)$ using (10.92), (10.94), (10.95), and (10.99) as follows:

$$s_2(t) = s_{21}\phi_1(t) + s_{22}\phi_2(t) + s_{23}\phi_3(t) = \sqrt{2}\phi_2(t) \Rightarrow \underline{s}_2 = (s_{21}, s_{22}, s_{23}) = (0, \sqrt{2}, 0)$$

$$s_3(t) = s_{31}\phi_1(t) + s_{32}\phi_2(t) + s_{32}\phi_3(t) = -\sqrt{2}\phi_2(t) + \phi_3(t) \Rightarrow \underline{s}_3 = (s_{31}, s_{32}, s_{33}) = (0, -\sqrt{2}, 1)$$

$$s_4(t) = s_{41}\phi_1(t) + s_{42}\phi_2(t) + s_{43}\phi_3(t) = \frac{1}{\sqrt{2}}\phi_1(t) - \frac{1}{\sqrt{2}}\phi_2(t) - \phi_3(t) \Rightarrow \underline{s}_4$$

$$= (s_{41}, s_{42}, s_{43}) = (1/\sqrt{2}, -1/\sqrt{2}, -1)$$

The vector space representation of the signal set in Figure 10.11 is displayed in Figure 10.13.

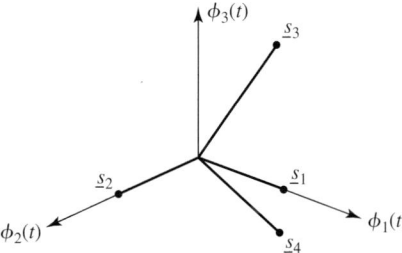

Figure 10.13 Signal vectors for the signal set in Figure 10.11.

The occurrence of a particular transmission symbol determines the probability $P(\underline{s}_i)$ of the ith vector $\underline{s}_i$ in the constellation. The power available in any physical communication system limits the average amount of energy required to transmit each successive transmission symbol. Thus, an important concept for a signal constellation is its average energy. The average energy of a signal constellation (also called average energy/symbol) E_s is defined by

$$E_s = \sum_{i=1}^{M} \|\underline{s}_i\|^2 P(\underline{s}_i) \tag{10.100}$$

Assuming equally likely symbols, the average energy/symbol is given by

$$E_s = \frac{1}{M} \sum_{i=1}^{M} \|\underline{s}_i\|^2 \tag{10.101}$$

The average energy/bit, E_b, is related to E_s by

$$E_b = \frac{E_s}{\log_2 M} \tag{10.102}$$

The average energy of a signal constellation is also closely related to the concept of average power, which is

$$P_s = \frac{E_s}{T} \tag{10.103}$$

where T is the symbol interval. The minimization of E_s places signal-constellation points near the origin; however, the error performance of a modulation scheme in the presence of noise is determined by the distance between points, as discussed in Section 10.6.

10.4.2 Examples of Signal Constellations

Binary Antipodal Signaling

In this case,

$$s_1(t) = -s_2(t) = A\Pi(t/T_b) \tag{10.104}$$

If we choose the basis function

$$\phi_1(t) = \frac{1}{\sqrt{T_b}}\Pi(t/T_b), \tag{10.105}$$

it is possible to express the signal set in (10.104) in one-dimensional space spanned by $\phi_1(t)$ as

$$s_1(t) = A\sqrt{T_b}\phi_1(t) = \sqrt{E_b}\phi_1(t)$$

$$s_2(t) = -A\sqrt{T_b}\phi_1(t) = -\sqrt{E_b}\phi_1(t) \tag{10.106}$$

The constellation points are given from (10.106) as

$$s_1 = \sqrt{E_b}$$

$$s_2 = -\sqrt{E_b} \tag{10.107}$$

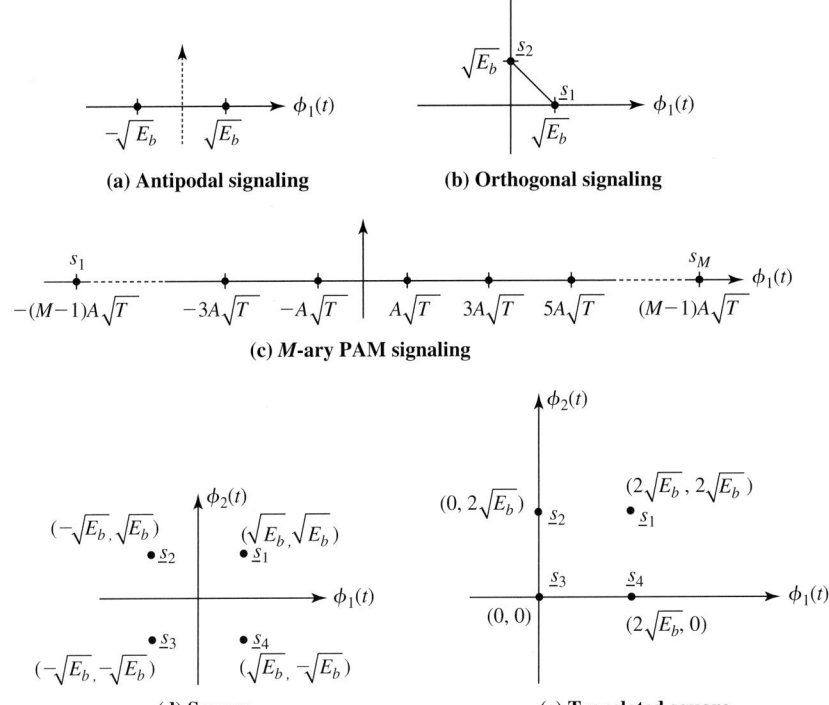

Figure 10.14 Various signal constellations.

Figure 10.14(a) illustrates the signal constellation for antipodal waveforms.

Binary Orthogonal Signaling

Consider the orthogonal signal set described by (10.58).

$$s_1(t) = \begin{cases} A, & 0 \le t \le T_b/2 \\ 0, & \text{otherwise} \end{cases}$$

and

$$s_2(t) = \begin{cases} A, & T_b/2 \le t \le T_b \\ 0, & \text{otherwise} \end{cases}$$

Because the functions $s_1(t)$ and $s_2(t)$ are nonoverlapping in time, a simple application of G-S procedure indicates that we need two basis functions. If we choose the basis functions as

$$\phi_1(t) = \sqrt{\frac{2}{T_b}}\Pi\left(\frac{t - T_b/4}{T_b/2}\right)$$

$$\phi_2(t) = \sqrt{\frac{2}{T_b}}\Pi\left(\frac{t - 3T_b/4}{T_b/2}\right) \tag{10.108}$$

it is possible to express the orthogonal signal set in the two-dimensional space spanned by $\phi_1(t)$ and $\phi_2(t)$ as

$$s_1(t) = A\sqrt{\frac{T_b}{2}}\phi_1(t) = \sqrt{E_b}\phi_1(t)$$

$$s_2(t) = A\sqrt{\frac{T_b}{2}}\phi_2(t) = \sqrt{E_b}\phi_2(t) \tag{10.109}$$

The constellation points are given from (10.109) as

$$\underline{s}_1 = \left(\sqrt{E_b}, 0\right)$$

$$\underline{s}_2 = \left(0, \sqrt{E_b}\right) \tag{10.110}$$

Figure 10.14(b) displays the constellation for the orthogonal signaling.

M-ary PAM

The *M*-ary PAM signal set is given by

$$s_m(t) = a_m A\Pi(t/T), \quad m = 1, 2, \ldots, M \tag{10.111}$$

where $a_m \in \{\pm 1, \pm 3, \ldots, \pm (M-1)\}$. If we choose the basis function

$$\phi_1(t) = \frac{1}{\sqrt{T}}\Pi(t/T), \tag{10.112}$$

it is possible to express the signal set (10.111) in one-dimensional space spanned by $\phi_1(t)$ as

$$s_m(t) = a_m A\sqrt{T}\phi_1(t), \quad m = 1, 2, \ldots, M \tag{10.113}$$

The constellation points are given from (10.113) as

$$s_m - a_m A\sqrt{T}, \quad m - 1, 2, \ldots, M \tag{10.114}$$

Figure 10.14(c) displays the signal constellation for an *M*-ary PAM signal set.

Square Constellation

Figure 10.14(d) illustrates the signal constellation which appears widely in digital transmission systems. It can be viewed as obtained by combining two antipodal signal sets formed from two orthogonal basis functions. Figure 10.14(e) is a translation of 10.14(d), diagonally upward by $\sqrt{2E_b}$. By application of (10.101), the average energy of the constellation in Figure 10.14(e) is

$$E_s = \frac{1}{4}\sum_{i=1}^{4}\|s_i\|^2$$

From Figure 10.14(e), we can write

$$\|\underline{s_1}\|^2 = \left(2\sqrt{E_b}\right)^2 + \left(2\sqrt{E_b}\right)^2 = 8E_b$$

$$\|\underline{s_2}\|^2 = 0 + \left(2\sqrt{E_b}\right)^2 = 4E_b$$

$$\|\underline{s_3}\|^2 = 0$$

$$\|\underline{s_4}\|^2 = \left(2\sqrt{E_b}\right)^2 + 0 = 4E_b$$

Therefore,

$$E_s = \frac{1}{4}\left[8E_b + 4E_b + 0 + 4E_b\right] = 4E_b$$

This is twice that of the average energy/symbol for the constellation in Figure 10.14(d). Energy efficient constellations are thus centered about the origin in the signal space.

Example 10.6

Consider the two basis functions shown in Figure 10.15(a). Sketch the waveforms corresponding to the points in the constellation shown in Figures 10.15(b) and (c).

Solution

The dimensionality N of the signal set in Figure 10.15(b) is 1. If we choose $\phi_1(t)$ as the basis function, the waveforms corresponding to the points in the constellation can be expressed as:

$$s_1(t) = s_{11}\phi_1(t) = A\phi_1(t)$$

$$s_2(t) = s_{21}\phi_1(t) = -A\phi_1(t)$$

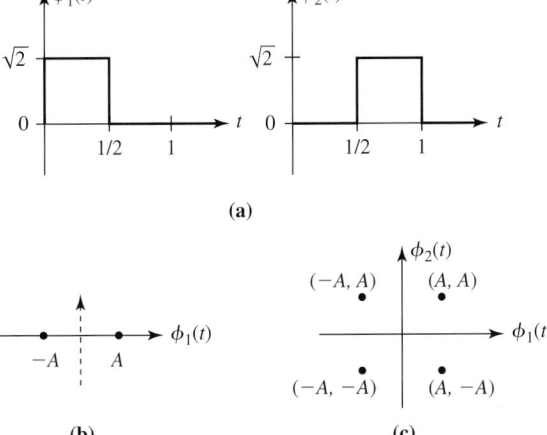

Figure 10.15 Basis functions and signal constellations for Example 10.6.

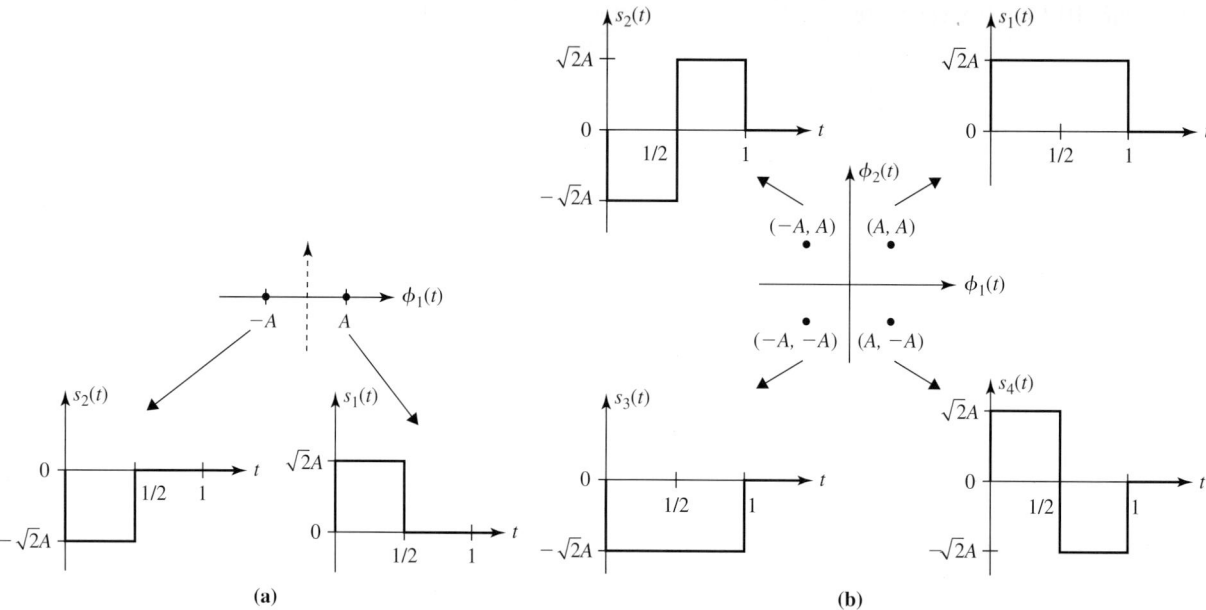

Figure 10.16 Signal sets corresponding to constellations in Figures 10.15(b) and (c).

Figure 10.16(a) displays the signals $s_1(t)$ and $s_2(t)$.

The dimensionality N of the signal set in Figure 10.15(c) is 2. The waveforms corresponding to the points in the constellation can be expressed as:

$$s_1(t) = s_{11}\phi_1(t) + s_{12}\phi_2(t) = A\phi_1(t) + A\phi_2(t)$$

$$s_2(t) = s_{21}\phi_1(t) + s_{22}\phi_2(t) = -A\phi_1(t) + A\phi_2(t)$$

$$s_3(t) = s_{31}\phi_1(t) + s_{32}\phi_2(t) = -A\phi_1(t) - A\phi_2(t)$$

$$s_4(t) = s_{41}\phi_1(t) + s_{42}\phi_2(t) = A\phi_1(t) - A\phi_2(t)$$

Figure 10.16(b) displays the signals $s_1(t)$, $s_2(t)$, $s_3(t)$, and $s_4(t)$.

10.4.3 Vector Space Representation of WGN

We demonstrated in Section 10.4.2 that a set of M finite energy waveforms $\{s_i(t), i = 1, \ldots, M\}$ can be represented as vectors in an N-dimensional vector space spanned by the orthonormal basis $\{\phi_i(t), i = 1, 2, \ldots, N\}$. The representation of a random process requires an orthonormal basis of infinite dimension. Consider the representation of the white Gaussian noise $\boldsymbol{n}(t)$ with spectral density $N_o/2$ W/Hz by the sum

$$\boldsymbol{n}(t) = \sum_{i=1}^{N} \boldsymbol{n}_i \phi_i(t) + \boldsymbol{n}'(t) \tag{10.115}$$

where $\boldsymbol{n}_j = \big(\boldsymbol{n}(t) \bullet \phi_j(t)\big)$ is a projection of $\boldsymbol{n}(t)$ onto the axis $\phi_j(t)$. The component $\boldsymbol{n}'(t)$ defined by

$$\boldsymbol{n}'(t) = \boldsymbol{n}(t) - \sum_{i=1}^{N} \boldsymbol{n}_i \phi_i(t) \tag{10.116}$$

represents the difference between the white Gaussian noise and its finite-dimensional representation in the vector space spanned by $\{\phi_i(t), i = 1, 2, \ldots, N\}$. It can be shown[3] that $n'(t)$ is irrelevant in the decision about which signal was transmitted. Next we investigate the properties of Gaussian random variables n_j.

The mean values of Gaussian random variables n_j are given by

$$E\{n_j\} = E\{n(t) \bullet \phi_j(t)\} = E\left\{\int_T n(t)\phi_j(t)dt\right\} = \int_T E\{n(t)\}\phi_j(t)dt = 0 \qquad (10.117)$$

for all j because $E\{n(t)\} = 0$. The covariances of random variables n_j can be expressed as

$$E\{n_i n_j\} = E\left\{\int_T n(t)\phi_i(t)dt\left\{\int_T n(u)\phi_j(u)du\right\}\right\}$$

$$= \int_T \int_T E\{n(t)n(u)\}\phi_i(t)\phi_j(u)dt = \int_T \int_T \frac{N_o}{2}\delta(t - u)\phi_i(t)\phi_j(u)dt$$

$$= \frac{N_o}{2}\int_T \phi_i(u)\phi_j(u)du = \frac{N_o}{2}\delta_{ij} \qquad (10.118)$$

Therefore, the random variables $\{n_j\}$ are uncorrelated, and each has a mean-square value $N_o/2$. Because $n(t)$ is a Gaussian, this implies that $\{n_j\}$ are jointly Gaussian and statistically independent. In summary, we can represent the white Gaussian noise $n(t)$ as a Gaussian random vector $\underline{n} = (n_1, n_2, \ldots, n_N)$ in the signal space spanned by $\{\phi_i(t), i = 1, 2, \ldots, N\}$, where the components n_j are iid Gaussian random variables with mean zero and variance $N_o/2$. The random vector $\underline{n} = (n_1, n_2, \ldots, n_N)$ appears as a spherical cloud in the signal space centered at the origin. Each point in the cloud represents a realization in the ensemble of sample functions for the random process. The density of points in the cloud, indicated by the intensity of shading, is directly proportional to the probability of observing $\underline{n}$ in a given region. Figure 10.17 displays Gaussian noise and signal plus noise vectors in three-dimensional space.

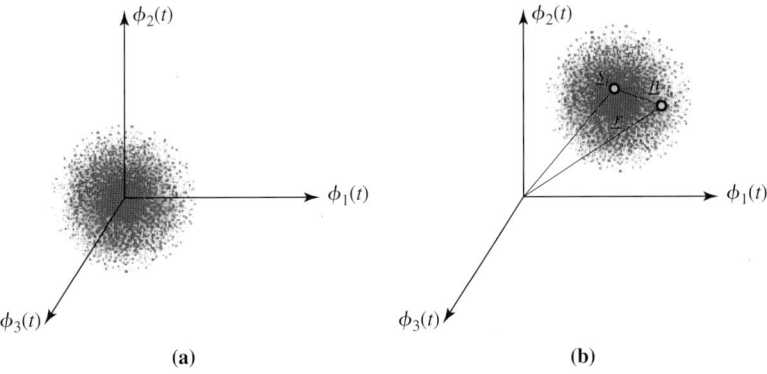

(a) **(b)**

Figure 10.17 (a) Gaussian noise; (b) signal plus noise vectors.

[3] J. Wozencraft and I. Jacobs, *Principles of Communication Engineering* (Hoboken, NJ: John Wiley, 1965).

10.5   *M*-ARY SIGNAL DETECTION IN AWGN

We now consider an *M*-ary communication system in which the modulator sends one of the *M* waveforms $\{s_i(t), i = 1, \ldots, M\}$ every symbol period *T*. The transmitted waveform $s_i(t)$ is received in the presence of AWGN $\boldsymbol{n}(t)$.

$$\boldsymbol{r}(t) = s_i(t) + \boldsymbol{n}(t), \quad 0 \leq t \leq T \tag{10.119}$$

We are interested in the optimal detection schemes to determine which signal $s_i(t)$ from the set $\{s_i(t), i = 1, \ldots, M\}$ was sent by observing a sample function of the random signal $\boldsymbol{r}(t)$ over the interval $0 \leq t \leq T$. In Section 10.4, we showed that signals in the set $\{s_1(t), s_2(t), \ldots, s_M(t)\}$ as well as AWGN can be represented as vectors in *N*-dimensional signal space, where $N \leq M$. Thus we can convert the problem of determining which signal $s_i(t)$ (or equivalently the constellation point $\underline{s}_i$) was sent during the interval $0 \leq t \leq T$ into the following vector detection problem:

$$\underline{r} = \underline{s}_i + \underline{n} \tag{10.120}$$

where $\underline{r}$, $\underline{s}_i$, and $\underline{n}$ are *N*-dimensional vectors corresponding to the dimension of the signal space. Based on the observation of a particular realization $\underline{r}$ of the received signal vector $\underline{r}$, we wish to design a detector that is optimum in the sense that it minimizes the probability of symbol error, or equivalently, maximizes the probability of making a correct decision. Given the observation $\underline{r}$ of the received signal vector $\underline{r}$, the conditional probability that the detector makes the correct decision $\hat{\underline{s}} = \underline{s}_i$ is given by

$$P\{\text{correct decision}|\underline{r} = \underline{r}\} = P\{\underline{s}_i \text{ sent}|\underline{r} = \underline{r}\} \tag{10.121}$$

$P\{\underline{s}_i \text{ sent}|\underline{r} = \underline{r}\}$ is the conditional probability that the signal $\underline{s}_i$ was transmitted given $\underline{r} = \underline{r}$. Therefore, it is referred to as the **a posteriori probability** of $\underline{s}_i$. We observe from (10.121) that maximizing the probability of correct decision is to choose $\hat{\underline{s}}$ from the set $\{\underline{s}_i, i = 1, \ldots, M\}$ that maximizes the a posteriori probability $P\{\underline{s}_i \text{ sent}|\underline{r} = \underline{r}\}$. Thus, the detector that minimizes the probability of symbol error is the **maximum a posteriori (MAP) detector.**

10.5.1   The Maximum a Posteriori Detector

The MAP detector is defined as the detector that observes the received signal vector $\underline{r} = \underline{r}$ and chooses the signal vector $\underline{s}_k$ that maximizes the a posteriori probability $P\{\underline{s}_i \text{ sent}|\underline{r} = \underline{r}\}$. The detector declares that the signal $\underline{s}_k$ was transmitted if

$$P\{\underline{s}_k|\underline{r} = \underline{r}\} \geq P\{\underline{s}_i|\underline{r} = \underline{r}\} \text{ for all } i \neq k \tag{10.122}$$

If equality holds in (10.122) for some $j \neq k$, then the decision can be assigned to either $\underline{s}_k$ or $\underline{s}_j$ without changing the probability of error. This decision criterion is called the **maximum a posteriori probability (MAP) criterion.** Using Baye's rule (6.146), the a posteriori probability may be expressed as

$$P\{\underline{s}_i|\underline{r} = \underline{r}\} = \frac{f_{\underline{r}}(\underline{r}|\underline{s} = \underline{s}_i)P(\underline{s}_i)}{f_{\underline{r}}(\underline{r})} \tag{10.123}$$

where

$f_r(r|s = s_i)$ = conditional PDF of the received signal vector r given that s_i was sent

$P(s_i)$ = a priori probability that s_i was sent

Because the denominator $f_r(r)$ in (10.123) does not depend on s_i, it can be ignored in maximizing $P\{s_i|r = r\}$. We can, therefore, state the MAP detection rule as follows:
Declare that the signal $\hat{s} = s_k$ was transmitted if

$$f_r(r|s = s_k)P(s_k) \geq f_r(r|s = s_i)P(s_i) \quad \text{for all } i \neq k \tag{10.124}$$

If equality holds in (10.124), for some $j \neq k$, then the decision can be assigned to interchangeably either s_k or s_j without changing the probability of error.

10.5.2 The Maximum Likelihood Detector

If all M transmitted signals s_i are equally likely—that is, if

$$P(s_i) = \frac{1}{M},$$

then the MAP detection rule becomes the maximum likelihood detection rule

$$\underset{i}{\text{Max}}\, P\{s_i|r = r\} = \underset{i}{\text{Max}}\, f_r(r|s = s_i) \tag{10.125}$$

The conditional PDF $f_r(r|s = s_i)$ or any monotonic function of it is usually called the **likelihood function.** The ML detection rule can now be stated as follows:
Declare that the signal $\hat{s} = s_k$ was transmitted if

$$f_r(r|s = s_k) \geq f_r(r|s = s_i) \quad \text{for all } i \neq k \tag{10.126}$$

Equation (10.126) is called the **maximum likelihood (ML)** criterion. Again, if equality holds in (10.126) for some $j \neq k$, then the decision can be assigned to either s_k or s_j without changing the probability of error.

Recall from Section 10.4.3 that components of $\boldsymbol{n}$ are independent and identically distributed Gaussian random variables with mean zero and variance $N_o/2$. The joint PDF of $\boldsymbol{n}$ can be written from (6.173) as

$$f_{\boldsymbol{n}}(\boldsymbol{n}) = \prod_{j=1}^{N} f_{n_j}(n_j) = \frac{1}{(\pi N_o)^{N/2}} e^{-\sum_{j=1}^{N} \frac{n_j^2}{N_o}} \tag{10.127}$$

Because $\boldsymbol{r} = s_i + \boldsymbol{n}$, we can write the following expression for the conditional PDF $f_r(r|s_i)$

$$f_r(r|s = s_i) = f_{\boldsymbol{n}}(r - s_i) = \frac{1}{(\pi N_o)^{N/2}} e^{-\sum_{j=1}^{N} \frac{(r_j - s_{ij})^2}{N_o}} \tag{10.128}$$

Because exp(.) is a monotonic function of its argument, maximizing $f_{\underline{r}}(\underline{r}|\underline{s} = \underline{s}_k)$ is equivalent to minimizing the **log likelihood function,** defined as

$$\mathcal{L}(\underline{s}_i) \triangleq \log_e\left\{(\pi N_o)^{N/2} f_{\underline{r}}(\underline{r}|\underline{s} = \underline{s}_i)\right\} = \frac{1}{N_o}\sum_{j=1}^{N}(r_j - s_{ij})^2 \tag{10.129}$$

The sum in (10.129) is related to the *Euclidean distance*

$$d(\underline{r}, \underline{s}_i) = \left\|\underline{r} - \underline{s}_i\right\| = \sqrt{\sum_{j=1}^{N}(r_j - s_{ij})^2} \tag{10.130}$$

between the vectors $\underline{r}$ and $\underline{s}_i$. The ML detector thus makes the optimal decision by seeking $\underline{s}_k$ that achieves the minimum value of $\|\underline{r} - \underline{s}_i\|^2$ over all points in the signal contstellation. That is, the ML detector selects the signal constellation point $\underline{s}_k$ **closest** in Euclidean distance to the received vector $\underline{r}$. The ML detection rule (10.126) can now be stated in terms of the Euclidean distance as follows:
Declare that the signal $\hat{\underline{s}} = \underline{s}_k$ was transmitted if

$$\|\underline{r} - \underline{s}_k\|^2 \le \|\underline{r} - \underline{s}_i\|^2 \text{ for all } i \ne k \tag{10.131}$$

We can similarly state the MAP detection rule in terms of the Euclidean norm as follows: Declare that the signal $\hat{\underline{s}} = \underline{s}_k$ was transmitted if

$$\|\underline{r} - \underline{s}_k\|^2 - N_o \log_e\{P(\underline{s}_k)\} \le \|\underline{r} - \underline{s}_i\|^2 - N_o \log_e\{P(\underline{s}_i)\} \text{ for all } i \ne k \tag{10.132}$$

10.5.3 MAP and ML Detector Implementations

The ML detector makes decisions by simply measuring the Euclidean distance between the received vector $\underline{r}$ and all members of the signal set $\{\underline{s}_i, i = 1, \ldots, M\}$, and declaring that $\underline{s}_k$ was transmitted if $i = k$ minimizes

$$\|\underline{r} - \underline{s}_i\|^2 = \|\underline{r}\|^2 - 2(\underline{r} \bullet \underline{s}_i) + \|\underline{s}_i\|^2 = \|\underline{r}\|^2 - 2(\underline{r} \bullet \underline{s}_i) + E_i \tag{10.133}$$

where $E_i = \int_T |s_i(t)|^2 dt$ is the energy of the ith signal $s_i(t)$. The first term on the right-hand side of (10.133) is constant during the minimization and can therefore be dropped. Because minimizing (10.133) is equivalent to maximizing the quantity $2(\underline{r} \bullet \underline{s}_i) - E_i$, the optimization problem for the ML detector can be expressed as

$$\underset{i}{\text{Max}}\left\{(\underline{r} \bullet \underline{s}_i) - \frac{E_i}{2}\right\} \tag{10.134}$$

The observation vector $\underline{r}$ can be computed by passing the received signal $r(t), 0 \le t \le T$ through a bank of correlators matched to the orthogonal basis functions $\{\phi_i(t), i = 1, 2, \ldots, N\}$. The detector then calculates inner products $(\underline{r} \bullet \underline{s}_i) - \frac{E_i}{2}$ for each vector $\underline{s}_i$ in

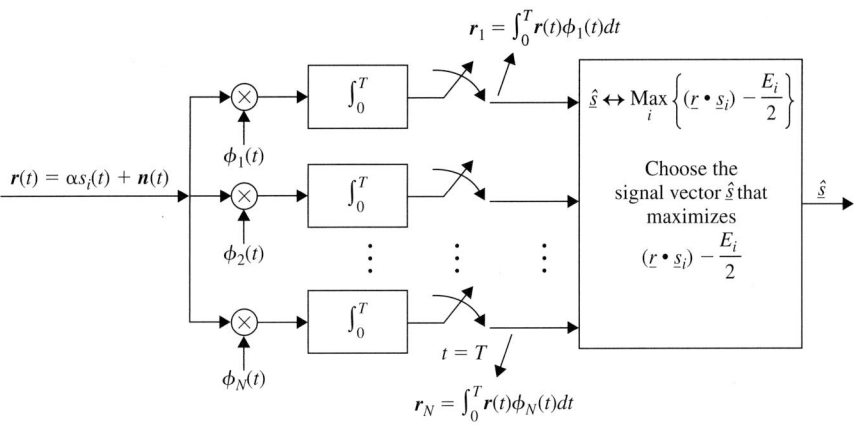

Figure 10.18 ML detector implementation using a bank of correlators.

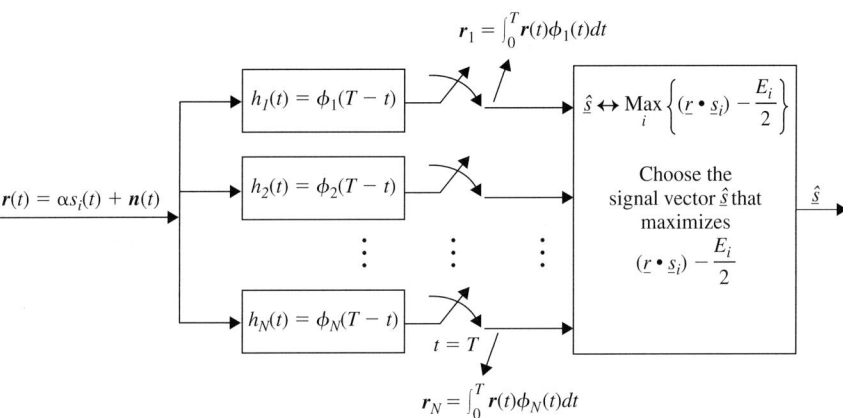

Figure 10.19 ML detector implementation using a bank of matched filters.

the signal set and declares that $\underline{s}_k$ was transmitted if $i = k$ achieves the largest inner product value. Figure 10.18 displays the implementation of the ML detector using correlators. If all the signals have the same energy, then the E_i term in (10.134) is constant over i and can, therefore, be dropped.

Alternatively, the ML detector can be implemented using a bank of N matched filters as shown in Figure 10.19. As discussed in Section 10.2, if we choose the jth matched filter with impulse response $h_j(t) = \phi_j(T - t)$, the output of the matched filter r_j at the sampling instant $t = T$ is identical to that obtained in the correlation implementation. That is,

$$r_j = r(t) \otimes h_j(t)\Big|_{t=T} = \int_T r(u)h_j(t - u)du\Big|_{t=T} = \int_T r(u)\phi_j(t - T + u)du\Big|_{t=T}$$

$$= \int_T r(u)\phi_j(u)du \qquad (10.135)$$

10.5.4 Decision Regions

The MAP or ML detection can be viewed as partitioning the signal space into M non-overlapping or disjoint regions $D_1, D_2, \ldots, D_M$. In the case of ML detection, decision regions are assigned using the detection rule (10.131) as follows:

$$D_i = \{\underline{r}: \|\underline{r} - \underline{s}_i\| < \|\underline{r} - \underline{s}_j\| \text{ for all } j \neq i\} \tag{10.136}$$

That is, if the received signal vector $\underline{r}$ falls in the region D_i, it is closest to the signal $\underline{s}_i$ in the signal space. The ML detection rule (10.136) can now be stated as:

$$\text{If } \underline{r} \text{ in } D_i \Rightarrow \underline{s}_i \text{ was transmitted} \tag{10.137}$$

The following geometrical procedure can be used to partition the signal space into ML decision regions.

- Connect all adjacent pairs of signal points by lines.
- Draw the perpendicular bisector for each line.

The boundaries of the decision regions are formed by bisectors of lines joining the signal points. Figure 10.20 illustrates decision regions constructed using this procedure for two signal constellations.

We observe from Figure 10.20(a) that the signals $\underline{s}_2$ and $\underline{s}_3$ are closest to $\underline{s}_1$, so they are most likely to be easily mistaken for $\underline{s}_1$. Therefore the shortest noise vector $\boldsymbol{n}$ will throw $\underline{s}_1 + \boldsymbol{n}$ into the decision region D_2 or D_3. The distance between the closest signal pair in the constellation is called the **minimum distance** $d_{\min}$ of the constellation. In the example illustrated in Figure 10.20(a), we have

$$d_{\min} = \|\underline{s}_1 - \underline{s}_2\| \text{ or } \|\underline{s}_1 - \underline{s}_3\| \text{ or } \|s_3 - s_4\| \tag{10.138}$$

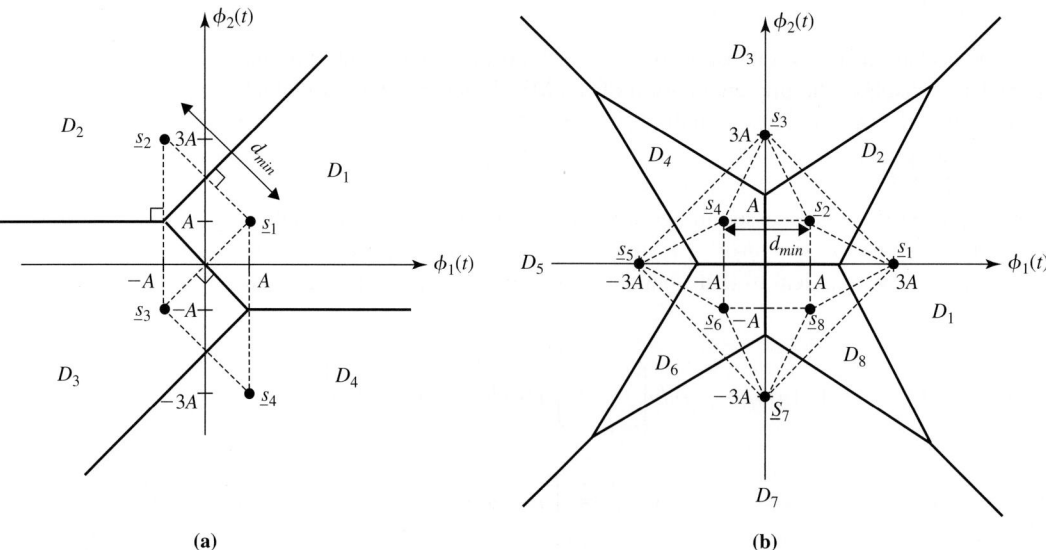

(a)   **(b)**

Figure 10.20 ML decision regions.

10.6   ERROR PERFORMANCE OF ML DETECTORS

The fundamental measure of ML detector performance is its error probability. For an *M*-ary communication system with complex constellation, it is difficult to derive the symbol error probability expression in a closed form. In this case, we seek an upper-bound to the probability of error and use simulation to validate it. We begin our discussion with the ML detector error performance for two-signal constellations.

10.6.1   Two-Signal Error Probability

Consider the signal constellation with two signals $\underline{s}_i$ and $\underline{s}_k$ as shown in Figure 10.21. Let us select the signal basis so that the first orthonormal function $\phi_1(t)$ lies along the vector connecting $\underline{s}_i$ and $\underline{s}_k$; thus the dimension of signal space is 1. As discussed in Section 10.4.3, we need consider only the projection $\boldsymbol{n}_1$ of the WGN onto $\phi_1(t)$ in determining the ML detector performance. $\boldsymbol{n}_1$ is a Gaussian random variable with mean zero and variance $N_o/2$. If $\underline{s}_i$ is transmitted, the ML detector decides $\underline{s}_k$ if the received signal $\boldsymbol{r} = \underline{s}_i + \boldsymbol{n}_1$ lies beyond the perpendicular bisector of the line $\underline{s}_k - \underline{s}_i$. This event occurs if $\boldsymbol{n}_1$ exceeds $d/2$, where d is the distance $\|\underline{s}_k - \underline{s}_i\|$. The **two-signal probability** $P_2\{\underline{s}_k \text{ decided}|\underline{s}_i \text{ sent}\}$ can, therefore, be expressed as

$$P_2\{\underline{s}_k \text{ decided}|\underline{s}_i \text{ sent}\} = P\{\boldsymbol{r} \text{ lies on line segment } D_k\} = P\{\boldsymbol{n}_1 > d/2\}$$

$$= \int_{d/2}^{\infty} f_{\boldsymbol{n}_1}(n_1)dn_1 = \frac{1}{\sqrt{\pi N_o}}\int_{d/2}^{\infty} e^{-\frac{n_1^2}{N_o}}dn_1$$

$$= Q\left(\frac{d/2}{\sqrt{N_o/2}}\right) = Q\left(\frac{\|\underline{s}_k - \underline{s}_i\|}{\sqrt{2N_o}}\right) \qquad (10.139)$$

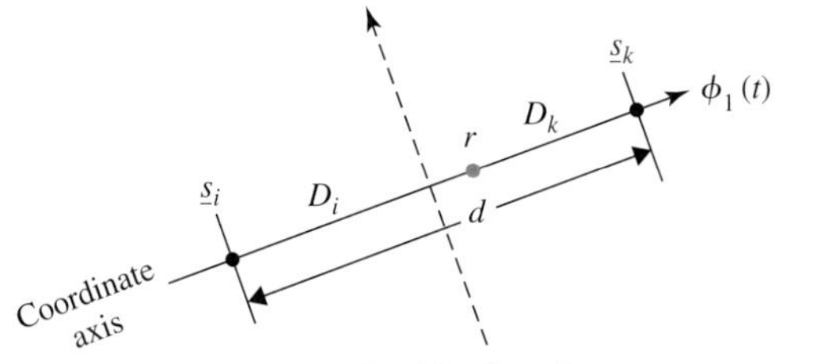

Figure 10.21 Calculation of two-signal error probability.

Example 10.7

Determine the BER of an ML detector for the following binary signal sets illustrated in Figure 10.13:

a. Antipodal signaling
b. Orthogonal signaling

Solution

For binary signals, assuming equally probable signals, we can write the BER expression from (10.11) as

$$BER = \frac{1}{2}P\{\underline{s}_2 \text{ decided}|\underline{s}_1 \text{ sent}\} + \frac{1}{2}P\{\underline{s}_1 \text{ decided}|\underline{s}_2 \text{ sent}\} \qquad (10.140)$$

a. **Antipodal signaling**

Referring to the constellation of antipodal signals in Figure 10.14(a), we can write

$$d = 2\sqrt{E_b} \tag{10.141}$$

Substituting (10.141) into (10.139), the BER is then obtained from (10.140) as

$$BER = P\{\underline{s}_2 \text{ decided}|\underline{s}_1 \text{ sent}\} = P\{\underline{s}_1 \text{ decided}|\underline{s}_2 \text{ sent}\} = Q\left(\sqrt{\frac{2E_b}{N_o}}\right) \tag{10.142}$$

This is the performance of an optimum ML detector for antipodal signals. Because (10.142) is identical to the performance of an MF detector (10.55), we observe that the MF not only maximizes the output SNR but is also optimum in the ML sense.

b. **Orthogonal signaling**

Referring to the constellation of orthogonal signals in Figure 10.14(b), we obtain

$$d = \sqrt{2E_b} \tag{10.143}$$

Substituting (10.143) into (10.139), the BER then follows from (10.140) as

$$BER = P_e = Q\left(\sqrt{\frac{E_b}{N_o}}\right) \tag{10.144}$$

We note that the performance of the ML detector for orthogonal signals is identical to that of an MF detector. Again, the MF is also optimum in the ML sense.

10.6.2 *M*-Signal Error Probability

For an *M*-ary communication system, the ML detection rule partitions the signal space into *M* decision regions $D_1, D_2, \ldots, D_M$. Assuming that the signal $\underline{s}_i$ was transmitted, the probability of a correct decision is given by

$$P\{\text{correct decision}|\underline{s}_i \text{ sent}\} = P\{\underline{r} \text{ lies in } D_i|\underline{s}_i \text{ sent}\} \tag{10.145}$$

This is because the ML detector decides $\underline{s}_i$ if the received vector $\underline{r}$ lies in D_i. On the other hand, an error event occurs if the received vector $\underline{r}$ lands outside D_i in one of the other decision regions $D_k, k \neq i$. Therefore, the probability of symbol error can be expressed as

$$P\{\text{error}|\underline{s}_i \text{ sent}\} = P\{\underline{r} \text{ not in } D_i|\underline{s}_i \text{ sent}\} = P\left\{\bigcup_{k \neq i}[\underline{r} \text{ in } D_k|\underline{s}_i \text{ sent}]\right\} \tag{10.146}$$

Because the decision regions are nonoverlapping or mutually exclusive,

$$P\left\{\bigcup_{k \neq i}[\underline{r} \text{ in } D_k|\underline{s}_i \text{ sent}]\right\} = \sum_{k \neq i}P\{\underline{r} \text{ in } D_k|\underline{s}_i \text{ sent}\} \tag{10.147}$$

Substituting (10.147) into (10.146), we obtain

$$P\{\text{error}|\underline{s}_i \text{ sent}\} = \sum_{k \neq i} P\{\underline{r} \text{ in } D_k|\underline{s}_i \text{ sent}\} \tag{10.148}$$

Now

$$P\{\underline{r} \text{ in } D_k|\underline{s}_i \text{ sent}\} = \int_{D_k} f_{\underline{r}}(\underline{r}|\underline{s}_i \text{ sent})d\underline{r} = \int_{D_k} f_{\underline{n}}(\underline{r} - \underline{s}_i)d\underline{r} \tag{10.149}$$

where $f_{\underline{n}}(\underline{n})$ is n-dimensional joint Gaussian PDF given by (10.127). It is evident from (10.149) that it is necessary to integrate $f_{\underline{n}}(\underline{n})$ over a different region $D_k \subset \mathbb{R}^N$ to compute each term in the sum (10.148). For many signal constellations implemented in practice, decision regions D_k tend to have complex geometries as evident from Figure 10.20(b). It is difficult to solve integral (10.149) in such cases. This leads us to investigate a union bound that provides a tight estimate of the probability of symbol error for an arbitrary signal constellation. To accomplish this, we replace $P\{\underline{r} \in D_k|\underline{s}_i \text{ sent}\}$ with the two-signal error probability $P_2\{\underline{s}_k \text{ decided}|\underline{s}_i \text{ sent}\}$. Let us consider the effect of this step in the case of square constellation in Figure 10.22. The conditional probability of symbol error $P\{\text{error}|\underline{s}_1 \text{ sent}\}$ from Figure 10.22(a) is given by

$$P\{\text{error}|\underline{s}_1 \text{ sent}\} = P\{\underline{r} \text{ not in } D_1|\underline{s}_1 \text{ sent}\} = P\{\underline{r} \text{ in } D_2 \cup D_3 \cup D_4|\underline{s}_1 \text{ sent}\}$$

$$= P\{\underline{r} \text{ in } D_2|\underline{s}_1 \text{ sent}\} + P\{\underline{r} \text{ in } D_3|\underline{s}_1 \text{ sent}\} + P\{\underline{r} \text{ in } D_4|\underline{s}_1 \text{ sent}\}$$

$$\tag{10.150}$$

If we now substitute $P_2\{\underline{s}_2 \text{ decided}|\underline{s}_1 \text{ sent}\}$ for $P\{\underline{r} \text{ in } D_2|\underline{s}_1 \text{ sent}\}$, the calculation involves integration over the half-plane R_2 instead of quadrant D_2 as shown in Figure 10.22(b). Therefore, $P_2\{\underline{s}_2 \text{ decided}|\underline{s}_1 \text{ sent}\} \geq P\{\underline{r} \text{ in } D_2|\underline{s}_1 \text{ sent}\}$. Similarly, the last two terms in (10.150) are upper-bounded by the corresponding two-signal error probabilities as evident from Figures 10.22(c) and (d). Note that R_2, R_3, and R_4 are overlapping. We can, therefore, add these two-signal error probabilities to produce a union bound to (10.150) as follows:

$$P\{\text{error}|\underline{s}_1 \text{ sent}\} \leq \sum_{k=2,3,4} P_2\{\underline{s}_k \text{ decided}|\underline{s}_1 \text{ sent}\} \tag{10.151}$$

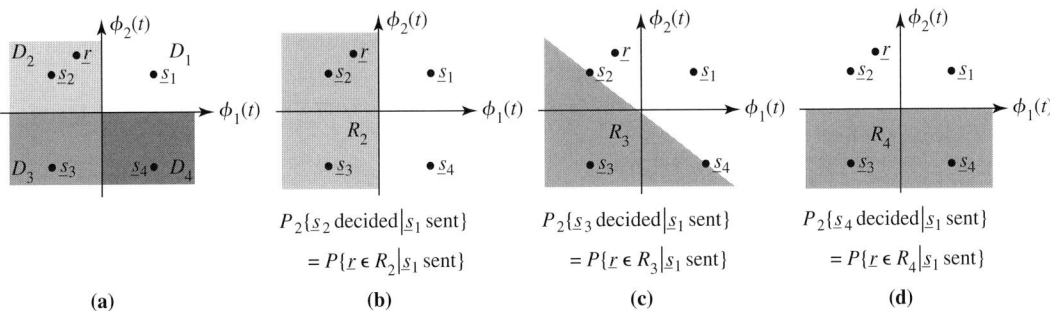

Figure 10.22 (a) Decision regions for square constellation; (b) through (d) Integration regions for the union bound.

Equation (10.151) provides a tight bound because the two-dimensional joint Gaussian PDF of $\underline{n}$ about $\underline{s}_1$ decays rapidly, especially for large values of E_b/N_o, and only the circular region closest to $\underline{s}_1$ contributes in the integration.

We now return to (10.148). The $P\{\text{error}|\underline{s}_i \text{ sent}\}$ can be upper-bounded by replacing each term in the summation by the corresponding two-signal error probability as

$$P\{\text{error}|\underline{s}_i \text{ sent}\} \leq \sum_{k \neq i} P_2\{\underline{s}_k \text{ decided}|\underline{s}_i \text{ sent}\} = \sum_{k \neq i} Q\left(\frac{\|\underline{s}_k - \underline{s}_i\|}{\sqrt{2N_o}}\right) \quad (10.152)$$

The average probability of symbol error for an M-signal set is given by

$$P_e = \sum_{i=1}^{M} P(\underline{s}_i) P\{\text{error}|\underline{s}_i \text{ sent}\} \quad (10.153)$$

For equally likely signals in the signal set, we have

$$P_e = \frac{1}{M} \sum_{i=1}^{M} P\{\text{error}|\underline{s}_i \text{ sent}\} \quad (10.154)$$

Substituting (10.152) into (10.154) yields the union bound on the average probability of symbol error as

$$P_e \leq \frac{1}{M} \sum_{i=1}^{M} \sum_{k \neq i} Q\left(\frac{\|\underline{s}_k - \underline{s}_i\|}{\sqrt{2N_o}}\right) \quad (10.155)$$

A closer look at (10.155) reveals that it contains $M(M-1)$ exponentials that decay rapidly as the distance argument $\|\underline{s}_k - \underline{s}_i\|$ grows. The terms with the least distance, $d_{\min}$, will dominate the sum. There are usually several minimum-distance signal pairs in the constellation, and the double sum counts each pair twice. We can thus write the following approximation to the average probability of symbol error from (10.155):

$$P_e \approx \frac{2K}{M} Q\left(\frac{\|d_{\min}\|}{\sqrt{2N_o}}\right) \quad (10.156)$$

in which K is the number of distinct signal pairs that lie at the least distance $d_{\min}$. Equation (10.156) is called the **nearest neighbor approximation** to P_e, reflecting the dominance of adjacent signal points in determining the symbol error probability.

Example 10.8

Consider the QPSK (square) constellation in Figure 10.23. Calculate the symbol error rate and compare it with the nearest neighbor bound.

Solution

The decision region D_i for each constellation point $\underline{s}_i$ is the quadrant that contains it as displayed in Figure 10.23. Because the conditional probability error $P\{\text{error}|\underline{s}_i \text{ sent}\}$ is the same for each constellation point as a result of symmetry, we will consider $P\{\text{error}|\underline{s}_1 \text{ sent}\}$. The probability

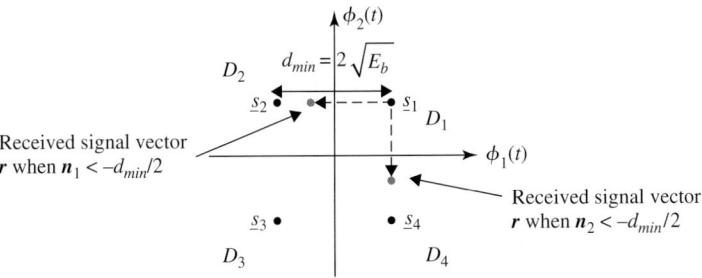

Figure 10.23 Decision regions for QPSK probability of error calculation.

of a correct decision requires that noise components along both coordinate axes fall within the quadrant D_1. That is,

$$P\{\text{correct decision}|\underline{s}_1 \text{ sent}\} = P\{\boldsymbol{n}_1 > -d_{\min}/2 \text{ and } \boldsymbol{n}_2 > -d_{\min}/2\}$$

$$= P\{\boldsymbol{n}_1 > -d_{\min}/2\}P\{\boldsymbol{n}_2 > -d_{\min}/2\}$$

$$= \left(1 - Q\left(\frac{d_{\min}}{\sqrt{2N_o}}\right)\right)\left(1 - Q\left(\frac{d_{\min}}{\sqrt{2N_o}}\right)\right)$$

$$= 1 - 2Q\left(\frac{d_{\min}}{\sqrt{2N_o}}\right) + Q^2\left(\frac{d_{\min}}{\sqrt{2N_o}}\right) \qquad (10.157)$$

This allows us to write the conditional probability of error as

$$P\{\text{error}|s_i \text{ sent}\} = 1 - P\{\text{correct decision}|\underline{s}_1 \text{ sent}\} = 2Q\left(\frac{d_{\min}}{\sqrt{2N_o}}\right) - Q^2\left(\frac{d_{\min}}{\sqrt{2N_o}}\right) \qquad (10.158)$$

The average probability of symbol error is given by substituting (10.158) into (10.154) as

$$P_e = 2Q\left(\frac{d_{\min}}{\sqrt{2N_o}}\right) - Q^2\left(\frac{d_{\min}}{\sqrt{2N_o}}\right) \qquad (10.159)$$

For acceptable error rates (i.e., $P_e \leq 10^{-3}$), the second term on the right-hand side of (10.159) is negligible. Therefore,

$$P_e \approx 2Q\left(\frac{d_{\min}}{\sqrt{2N_o}}\right) \qquad (10.160)$$

Let us compare (10.160) with the nearest neighbor bound obtained using (10.156). The number of minimum distance pairs for the constellation equals 4. Substituting $K = 4$ into (10.156), we obtain

$$P_e \approx \frac{2 \times 4}{4}Q\left(\frac{d_{\min}}{\sqrt{2N_o}}\right) = 2Q\left(\sqrt{\frac{2E_b}{N_o}}\right) \qquad (10.161)$$

Note that the nearest neighbor bound (10.161) equals the *exact* symbol error rate for QPSK signaling.

Example 10.9

A binary digital communication system uses antipodal signaling. The signal $s_1(t)$ corresponding to binary "1" is displayed in Figure 10.24(a). The channel introduces AWGN with power spectral density $N_o/2$ Watts/Hz.

a. Sketch the impulse response of the filter matched to $s_1(t)$. Sketch its output to the input $s_1(t)$.
b. Draw the signal constellation. What is the d_{min} for the signal set?
c. Write an expression for BER in terms of A and N_o.

Solution

a. Binary antipodal signals $s_1(t)$ and $s_2(t)$ can be represented in one-dimensional signal space by using the basis function as

$$\phi_1(t) = \sqrt{\frac{3}{2T_b}} \frac{s_1(t)}{A}$$

b. The impulse response of the filter matched to $s_1(t)$ is given from Figure 10.19 as

$$h(t) = \phi_1(T_b - t) = \sqrt{\frac{3}{2T_b}} \frac{s_1(T_b - t)}{A}$$

Figure 10.24(b) and (c) display impulse response of the matched-filter and its output to the input pulse $s_1(t)$. Using the basis function $\phi_1(t)$, $s_1(t)$ and $s_2(t)$ can be expressed as

$$s_1(t) = A\sqrt{\frac{2T_b}{3}}\phi_1(t)$$

$$s_2(t) = -A\sqrt{\frac{2T_b}{3}}\phi_1(t)$$

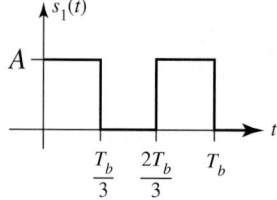

(a) Transmitted pulse $s_1(t)$

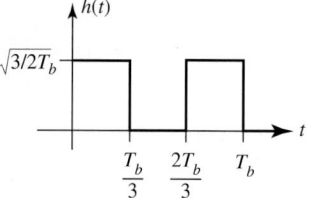

(b) Matched filter impulse response $h(t)$

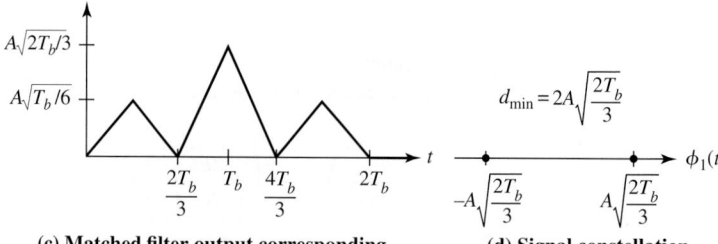

(c) Matched filter output corresponding to input pulse $s_1(t)$

(d) Signal constellation

Figure 10.24 Waveforms and signal constellation for Example 10.9.

Figure 10.24 (d) displays the constellation for the antipodal signal set. The minimum distance $d_{\min}$ for the constellation is given by

$$d_{\min} = 2A\sqrt{\frac{2T_b}{3}}$$

c. The average probability of bit error is now obtained from (10.47) by substituting for $d_{\min}$ as

$$BER = Q\left(\sqrt{\frac{d_{\min}^2}{2N_o}}\right) = Q\left(\sqrt{\frac{4A^2T_b}{3N_o}}\right)$$

10.6.3 Relationship Between Bit and Symbol Error Rates

For M-ary transmission schemes, we have used the average probability of symbol error P_e as the figure of merit. For comparing various digital transmission schemes, it is usually more meaningful to compare them by their bit error rate performance. The relationship between bit and symbol probabilities depends upon (1) the structure of the signal space, and (2) the mapping of the signal space points into binary sequences.

In many practical M-ary communication systems, the mapping between M constellation points and k-bit sequences ($M = 2^k$) is accomplished using **Gray coding** so that only one bit changes in going from a signal point to an adjacent signal point in the constellation. Figure 10.25 displays the signal constellations for QPSK, 8-PSK, and 8-PAM modulation schemes where the signal points are identified by 2-bit and 3-bit Gray codes, respectively. Because the probability of mistaking to an adjacent signal point is the most likely symbol error event, the choice of Gray coding ensures a single-bit error when the most frequent symbol errors occur. Thus, the choice of Gray-code mapping of the data bits minimizes the number of bits in error when the most common

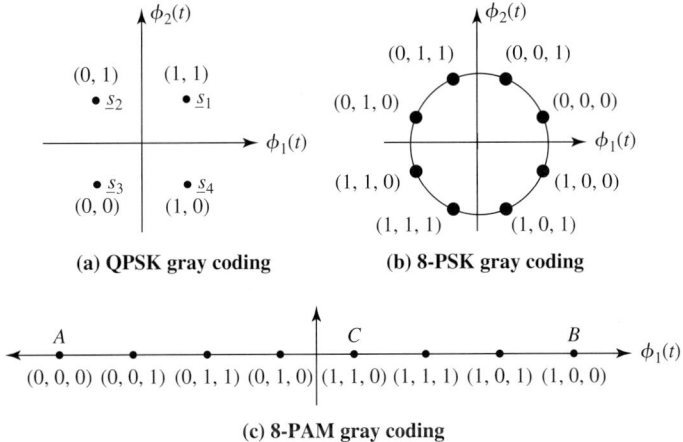

(a) QPSK gray coding

(b) 8-PSK gray coding

(c) 8-PAM gray coding

Figure 10.25 Gray coding examples.

decision errors occur. Because each transmission symbol represents $\log_2 M$ bits, we obtain the following relationship between bit and symbol error rates:

$$P_e = \frac{\text{Symbols decided in error}}{\text{Total number of transmitted symbols}}$$

$$\approx \frac{\text{Bits in error}}{\text{Total number of bits transmitted}/(\log_2 M)}$$

$$= (\log_2 M)BER \tag{10.162}$$

Alternatively, we can write (10.162) as

$$BER = \frac{P_e}{\log_2 M} \tag{10.163}$$

10.7 ERROR PERFORMANCE OF *M*-ARY PAM SIGNALS

The *M*-ary PAM signal set is given from (10.113) as

$$s_m(t) = a_m \sqrt{T} \phi_1(t), \ m = 1, 2, \ldots, M \tag{10.164}$$

where $a_m \in \{\pm 1, \pm 3, \ldots, \pm(M-1)\}$. It is convenient to express the signal set in (10.164) as follows:

$$s_m(t) = \sqrt{E_s} C_o a_m \phi_1(t), \ m = 1, 2, \ldots, M \tag{10.165}$$

where the normalization constant C_o is introduced to make the average energy of the signal set equal to E_s. The average energy of an *M*-ary PAM constellation is

$$E_s = \frac{1}{M}\sum_{i=1}^{M}\left\|s_i\right\|^2 = \frac{8C_o^2 E_s}{M}\sum_{i=1}^{M/2}\left(\frac{2i-1}{2}\right)^2$$

$$= \frac{C_o^2 E_s(M^2-1)}{3} \tag{10.166}$$

This yields

$$C_o = \sqrt{\frac{3}{(M^2-1)}} \tag{10.167}$$

The *M*-ary PAM minimum distance can be expressed in terms of the energy and size of the constellation as follows:

$$d_{\min} = 2C_o\sqrt{E_s} = \sqrt{\frac{12E_s}{M^2-1}} \tag{10.168}$$

The *M*-ary PAM probability of correct symbol detection is

$$P_c = \sum_{i=1}^{M} P(\underline{s}_i) P[\text{correct decision} | \underline{s}_i \text{ sent}]$$

$$= \frac{1}{M} \sum_{i=1}^{M} P[\text{correct decision} | \underline{s}_i \text{ sent}] \text{ for equally likely symbols} \quad (10.169)$$

The probability of symbol error can be exactly computed for *M*-ary PAM by noting that the conditional probability of a correct decision falls into one of two categories:

- Two end points with only one nearest neighbor (points *A* and *B* in Figure 10.25(c))

$$P[\text{correct decision} | \underline{s}_i \text{ sent}]|_{\text{end point } A} = P\{\boldsymbol{n}_1 > d_{\min}/2\} = \left(1 - Q\left(\frac{d_{\min}}{\sqrt{2N_o}}\right)\right) \quad (10.170)$$

$$P[\text{correct decision} | \underline{s}_i \text{ sent}]|_{\text{end point } B} = P\{\boldsymbol{n}_1 < d_{\min}/2\} = \left(1 - Q\left(\frac{d_{\min}}{\sqrt{2N_o}}\right)\right) \quad (10.171)$$

- $(M - 2)$ inner points with two nearest neighbors each (e.g., point *C* in Figure 10.25(c))

$$P[\text{correct decision} | \underline{s}_i \text{ sent}]|_{\text{interior point}} = P\{-d_{\min}/2 < \boldsymbol{n}_1 < d_{\min}/2\}$$

$$= \left(1 - 2Q\left(\frac{d_{\min}}{\sqrt{2N_o}}\right)\right) \quad (10.172)$$

Substituting (10.170) through (10.172) into (10.169), we obtain

$$P_c = \frac{M - 2}{M}\left(1 - 2Q\left(\frac{d_{\min}}{\sqrt{2N_o}}\right)\right) + \frac{2}{M}\left(1 - Q\left(\frac{d_{\min}}{\sqrt{2N_o}}\right)\right)$$

$$= 1 - 2\left(\frac{M - 1}{M}\right)Q\left(\frac{d_{\min}}{\sqrt{2N_o}}\right) \quad (10.173)$$

Thus, the *M*-ary PAM probability of symbol error is

$$P_e = 1 - P_c = 2\left(\frac{M - 1}{M}\right)Q\left(\frac{d_{\min}}{\sqrt{2N_o}}\right) \quad (10.174)$$

Note that this is the *exact* probability of symbol error for *M*-ary PAM signaling. Let us compare (10.174) with the nearest neighbor bound obtained using (10.156). The number of minimum distance pairs for the constellation is $M - 1$. Substituting $K = M - 1$ into (10.156) yields

$$P_e \approx 2\left(\frac{M - 1}{M}\right)Q\left(\frac{d_{\min}}{\sqrt{2N_o}}\right) \quad (10.175)$$

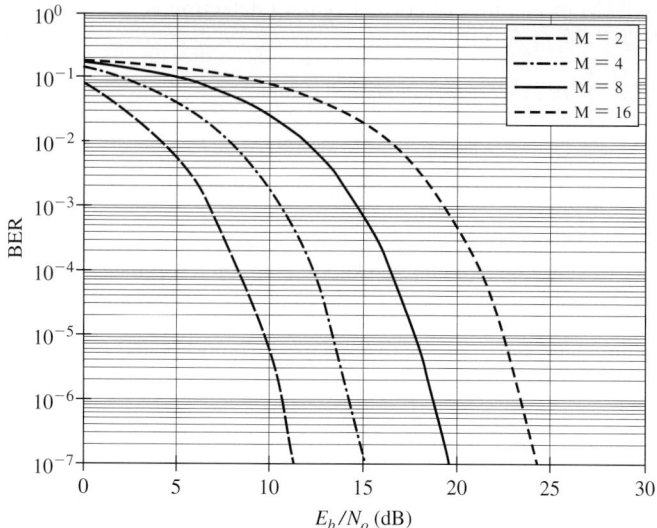

Figure 10.26 Bit error rate performance *M*-ary PAM.

Comparing (10.175) with (10.174), we can conclude that the nearest neighbor bound is exact for *M*-ary PAM. By substituting (10.168) in (10.174) or (10.175), we obtain

$$P_e = \frac{2(M-1)}{M} Q\left(\sqrt{\frac{12E_s}{2N_o(M^2-1)}}\right) = \frac{2(M-1)}{M} Q\left(\sqrt{\frac{6E_s}{N_o(M^2-1)}}\right) \quad (10.176)$$

The BER for *M*-ary PAM signaling can now be written from (10.176) by using (10.102) and (10.163) as

$$BER_{M-PAM} = \frac{2(M-1)}{M \log_2 M} Q\left(\sqrt{\frac{6 \log_2 M}{(M^2-1)} \frac{E_b}{N_o}}\right) \quad (10.177)$$

Figure 10.26 displays the bit error rate performance of *M*-ary PAM systems. The case $M = 2$ corresponds to the BER for binary antipodal signals. As *M* increases, each transmission symbol conveys $\log_2 M$ bits of information. However, it is accompanied with an SNR/bit penalty of $10 \log_{10} \frac{(M^2-1)}{3 \log_2 M}$dB. For the same BER performance, approximately 4 dB additional SNR/bit is required for every doubling of the amplitude levels (*M*). That is, each 4 dB increase in E_b/N_o buys us an additional information bit per transmission symbol. Thus, if we increase the number of amplitude levels by a factor of 4, the bit rate of the system can be increased to three times the original value while requiring an additional 8 dB in E_b/N_o for the same error rate performance. To increase E_b/N_o by 8 dB, the modulator power must be increased by a factor of $10^{0.8} = 6.3$. This trade-off may not always be feasible in low-SNR environments. This important issue in communication systems design will be further explored in Chapters 11 and 13.

Experiment 10.3 *Noise Performance of 4-PAM Signaling System*

In this experiment, we model a 4-PAM digital communication system. Figure 10.27(a) illustrates the Simulink model for the system. The parameters of simulation are set up by a companion MATLAB m-file. The m-file also computes the theoretical BER and plots simulated and theoretical BER performance. The **M-PAM source,** discussed in Example 3.2, is used to generate quaternary polar NRZ signal. AWGN is added by using the AWGN channel block illustrated in Figure 10.9(a). The correlation detector is implemented by a discrete-time integrator which is reset at the beginning of each symbol interval. The output of the integrator is sampled at $t = kT$ in the **Symbol-rate sampling** block. These sample values are compared in **4-Level threshold comparator**, and output pulses are then generated by 4-PAM look up table. The regenerated quaternary polar signal is next compared with the transmitted signal in Error-rate meter block. The simulated BER values are transmitted to a MATLAB workspace to generate the BER

Figure 10.27 (a) Simulink model for 4-PAM communication system; (b) 4-PAM signaling waveforms; (c) Comparison of theoretical and simulated BER performance.

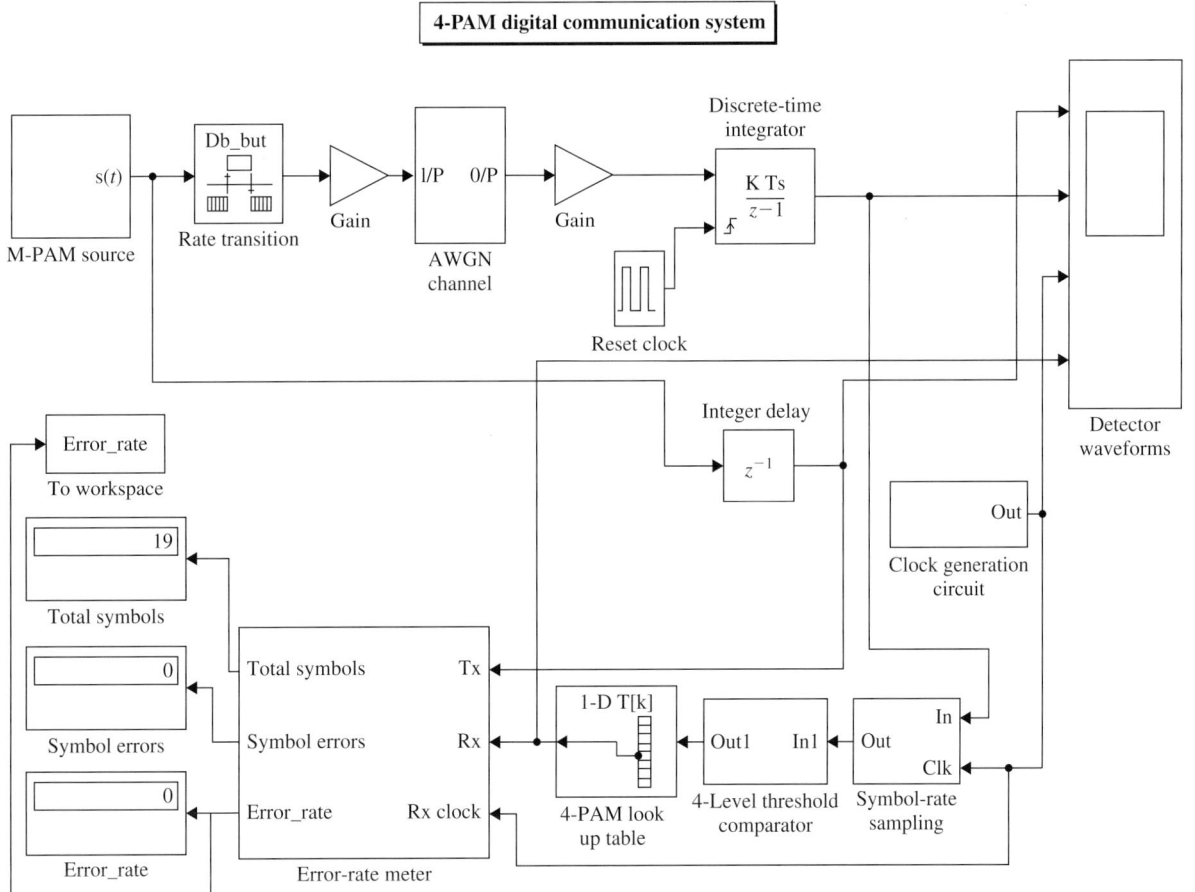

(a)

(continued)

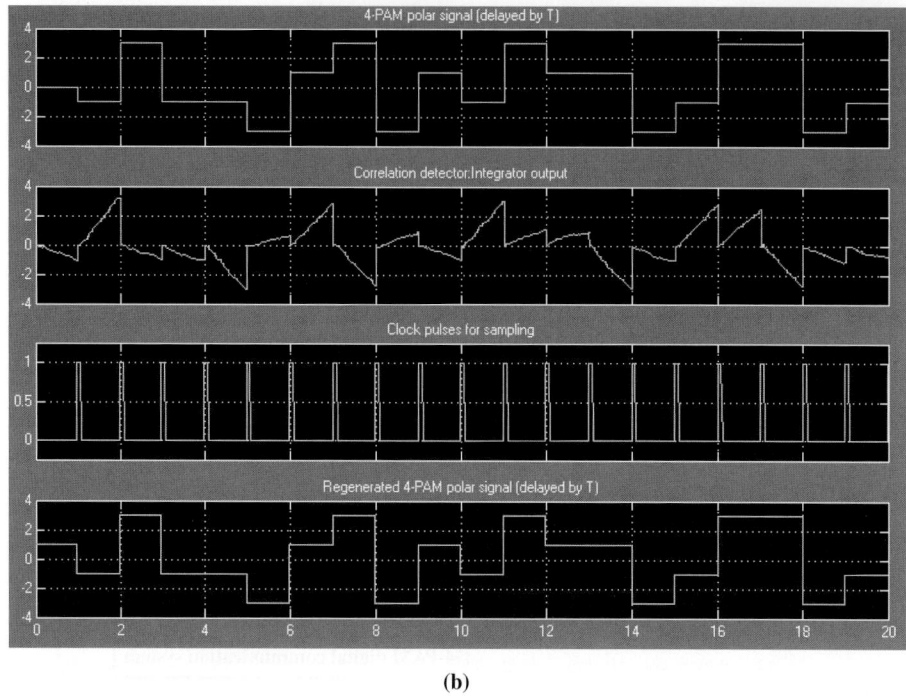

(b)

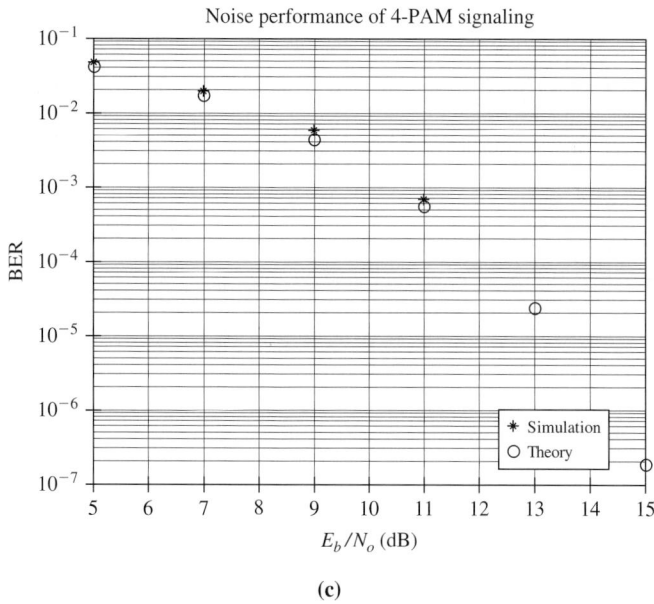

(c)

performance curve. Figure 10.27(b) displays various waveforms generated using this simulation. Figure 10.27(c) provides a comparison of theoretical and simulated BER performance.

FINAL REMARKS

We investigated the detection of digital signals corrupted by white Gaussian noise in this chapter. In this context, we found it extremely useful to represent signals and noise as vectors in finite-dimensional spaces. The optimum detector structures that minimize the average probability of symbol error select the signal point closest to the noisy received vector in the signal space. Such detectors can be implemented as banks of correlators or matched filters. The probability of symbol error for these detectors is dominated by mistaking adjacent signal points for the transmitted signal vector due to the presence of noise. In high SNR environment, this leads to a simple calculation to obtain a reasonably tight and useful estimate for the error rate performance of digital communication systems.

Many different signal sets generate identical constellations by the appropriate choice of the basis set. The calculations of bit and symbol error rates depend solely on the configuration of constellation independent of the choice of basis function set. This decoupling is quite useful in analyzing the performance of digital communication systems.

FURTHER READINGS

Detection of digital signals in the presence of noise is covered in a number of undergraduate communication systems texts [1–5]. Wozencraft and Jacobs [6] is an excellent reference on the geometrical representation of digital signals and noise as vectors. Ziemer [7], Anderson [8], and Proakis [9] provide a more advanced and comprehensive treatment of the material covered in this chapter.

1. Proakis, J., and M. Salehi. *Fundamentals of Communication Systems.* Upper Saddle River, NJ: Prentice Hall, 2005.

2. Couch, L. *Digital and Analog Communication Systems,* 7th ed. Upper Saddle River, NJ: Prentice Hall, 2006.

3. Haykin, S. *Communication Systems,* 4th ed. Hoboken, NJ: John Wiley, 2000.

4. Carlson, B., P. Crilly, and J. Rutledge. *Communication Systems,* 4th ed. New York: McGraw-Hill, 2002.

5. Ziemer, R., and W. Tranter. *Principles of Communications: Systems, Modulation, and Noise,* 5th ed. Hoboken, NJ: John Wiley, 2001.

6. Wozencraft, J., and I. Jacobs. *Principles of Communication Engineering.* Hoboken, NJ: John Wiley, 1965.

7. Ziemer, R., and R. Peterson. *An Introduction to Digital Communication,* 2nd ed. Upper Saddle River, NJ: Prentice Hall, 2001.

8. Anderson, J. *Digital Transmission Engineering,* 2nd ed. Upper Saddle River, NJ: Prentice Hall, 2005.

9. Proakis, J., and M. Salehi. *Digital Communications,* 5th ed. New York: McGraw-Hill, 2008.

PROBLEMS

10.1. Binary data is transmitted over an AWGN channel with a power spectral density $N_o/2 = 10^{-9}$ W/Hz. Determine the signal amplitude A required to achieve a BER $= 10^{-6}$, when the data rate is (a) 1 Mbps, (b) 10 Mbps, and (c) 100 Mbps. Evaluate for Unipolar NRZ and RZ line coding schemes. What is the first-null signal bandwidth in each case?

10.2. Consider a binary signaling system using sinusoidal pulses

$$s_1(t) = A \sin\left(\frac{\pi t}{T_b}\right), \ 0 \le t \le T_b$$

$$s_2(t) = 0$$

A correlation receiver is used for the detection of transmitted symbols at the output of an AWGN channel with noise spectral density $N_o/2 = 2.8 \times 10^{-11}$ W/Hz.

a. Determine an expression for the average probability of bit error assuming equiprobable binary data.

b. Evaluate the bit error rate for $A = 50$ mV and the bit rate of 1 Mbps.

c. How much the received pulse amplitude A has to increase for the same BER performance when the bit rate is doubled?

10.3. A binary signaling system uses pulses $s_1(t)$ and $s_2(t), 0 \le t \le T_b$ to transmit binary data occurring with

probabilities p and $1 - p$, respectively. A matched filter receiver is used for the detection of transmitted symbols at the output of an AWGN channel with noise spectral density $N_o/2$ W/Hz.

a. Show that the optimum threshold value V_{opt} is given by

$$V_{opt} = \frac{N_o}{2} \log_e \frac{p}{1 - p} + \frac{s_{o1} + s_{o2}}{2}$$

where s_{o1} and s_{o2} are given by (10.41) and (10.42), respectively.

b. What is the optimum threshold value when the binary signals are equiprobable?

c. Show that the average probability of error for the system is given by

$$BER = pQ\left(\frac{\dfrac{s_{o1} - s_{o2}}{2} - \dfrac{N_o}{2} \log_e \dfrac{p}{1 - p}}{\sqrt{\dfrac{N_o(s_{o1} - s_{o2})}{2}}}\right)$$

$$+ (1 - p)Q\left(\frac{\dfrac{N_o}{2} \log_e \dfrac{p}{1 - p} + \dfrac{s_{o1} - s_{o2}}{2}}{\sqrt{\dfrac{N_o(s_{o1} - s_{o2})}{2}}}\right)$$

10.4. The binary signaling system in Problem 10.3 uses antipodal pulses $s_1(t) = A\Pi(t/T_b) = -s_2(t)$.

a. Show that the optimum threshold value V_{opt} is given by

$$V_{opt} = \frac{N_o}{2}\log_e\frac{p}{1-p}$$

b. Calculate the value of optimum threshold V_{opt} for following a priori bit probabilities:

(i) $p = 0.5, 1 - p = 0.5$

(ii) $p = 0.3, 1 - p = 0.7$

(iii) $p = 0.8, 1 - p = 0.2$

c. Show that the average probability of error for the system is given by

$$BER = pQ\left(\frac{2E_b - \dfrac{N_o}{2}\log_e\dfrac{p}{1-p}}{\sqrt{2N_oE_b}}\right)$$

$$+ (1-p)Q\left(\frac{\dfrac{N_o}{2}\log_e\dfrac{p}{1-p} + 2E_b}{\sqrt{2N_oE_b}}\right)$$

where E_b is average energy/bit.

10.5. The binary signaling system in Problem 10.3 uses unipolar NRZ pulses $s_1(t) = A\Pi(t/T_b)$ and $s_2(t) = 0$.

a. Show that the optimum threshold value V_{opt} is given by

$$V_{opt} = E_b + \frac{N_o}{2}\log_e\frac{p}{1-p}$$

where E_b is average energy/bit.

b. Calculate the value of optimum threshold V_{opt} for following a priori bit probabilities:

(i) $p = 0.5, 1 - p = 0.5$

(ii) $p = 0.3, 1 - p = 0.7$

(iii) $p = 0.8, 1 - p = 0.2$

c. Write an expression for the average probability of error at the detector output.

10.6. Consider the binary digital communication system using antipodal signaling. The received signal corresponding to binary "1" is given by

$$r(t) = s_1(t) + n(t)$$

where $s_1(t)$ is shown in Figure P10.1 and $n(t)$ is AWGN with power spectral density $N_o/2$ Watts/Hz.

a. Sketch the impulse response of the filter matched to $s_1(t)$.

b. Sketch the output of the filter in (a) to the input $s_1(t)$.

c. Draw the signal constellation. What is the d_{min} for the signal set?

d. Write an expression for BER in terms of A and N_o.

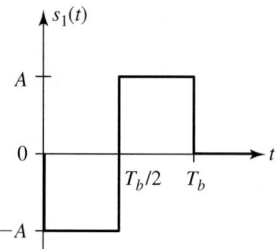

Figure P10.1

10.7. A binary digital communication system uses orthogonal pulses shown in Figure P10.2. The channel noise is white Gaussian with a power spectral density $N_o/2$ W/Hz.

a. Draw block diagram of the ML detector. Sketch impulse response functions of matched filters.

b. Plot the output of the filter matched to $s_1(t)$ when the input is $s_1(t)$. Repeat when the input is instead $s_2(t)$.

c. Plot the output of the filter matched to $s_2(t)$ when the input is $s_2(t)$. Repeat when the input is instead $s_1(t)$. What do you conclude from (b) and (c)?

d. Draw the signal constellation. What is the d_{min} for the signal set?

e. Write an expression for BER in terms of A and N_o.

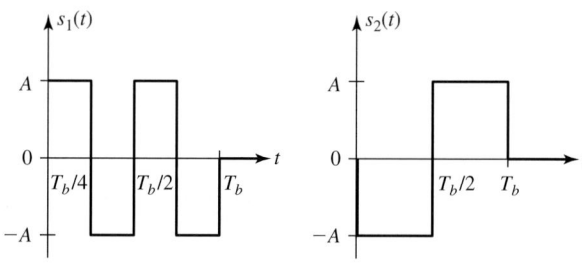

Figure P10.2

10.8. Consider the signal set displayed in Figure P10.3.

a. Apply the Gram-Schmidt procedure to determine an orthonormal basis for the signal set.

b. Plot the signal constellation corresponding to the signal set.

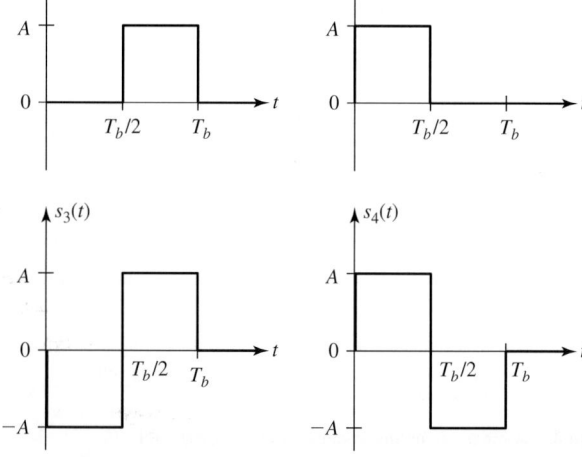

Figure P10.3

10.9. Consider the signal set

$$s_i(t) = \sqrt{\frac{2E_s}{T}} \cos[2\pi f_c t + \psi_i], 0 \le t \le T \quad i = 1, \dots, 8$$

where

$$\psi_i \in \left\{0, \frac{\pi}{4}, \frac{\pi}{2}, \frac{3\pi}{4}, \pi, \frac{5\pi}{4}, \frac{3\pi}{2}, \frac{7\pi}{4}\right\}$$

a. What is the dimensionality of signal space?

b. Determine the basis vectors for the signal set.

c. Draw the constellation diagram of the signal set.

10.10. Consider the two basis functions shown in Figure 10.4(a). Sketch the waveforms corresponding to the points in the constellation shown in Figures P10.4(b) and (c).

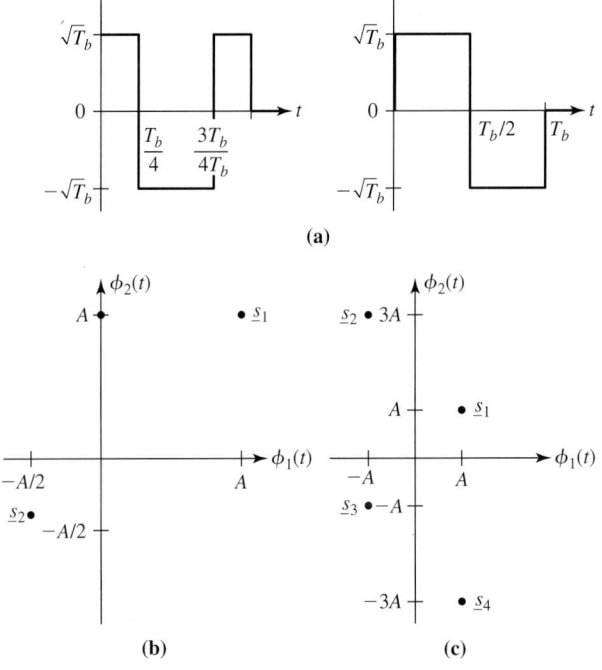

(a)

(b) **(c)**

Figure P10.4

10.11. Using the basis function in Figure P10.5(a), sketch the waveforms corresponding the points of the constellation shown in Figure P10.5(b).

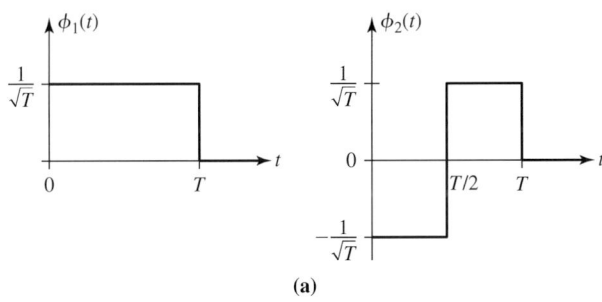

(a)

Figure P10.5

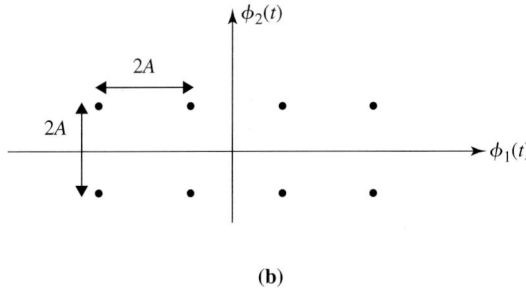

(b)

Figure P10.5 (continued)

10.12. Consider the signal constellation shown in Figure P10.5(b).

a. Derive the exact average probability of symbol error for the constellation.

b. Compute the average probability of symbol error using the nearest neighbor bound. Comment.

10.13. Consider the signal sets shown in Figure P10.6.

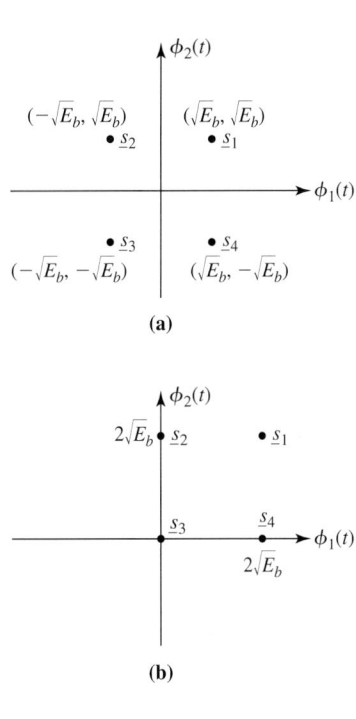

(a)

(b)

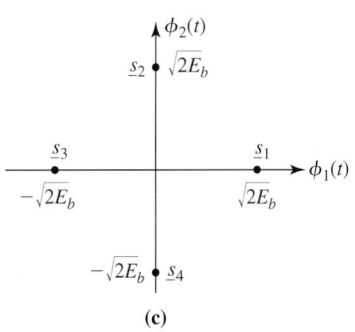

(c)

Figure P10.6

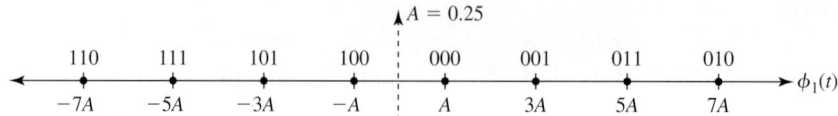

Figure P10.7

a. Determine the average energy of each signal constellation.

b. Sketch decision regions in each case.

c. Write the average probability of symbol error for each constellation using the nearest neighbor bound

d. From this example, what conclusions can you make about the constellation rotation and translation on the error performance of the signal set.

10.14. Consider the 8-PAM signal with constellation in Figure P10.7.

a. Draw the block diagram of the correlation detector.

b. Sketch the transfer characteristic of the threshold comparator.

c. Determine the estimated symbol sequence and corresponding bit sequence for the correlator output samples $\{+0.12, -0.201, +0.71, -1.55, -0.6, 1.25\}$.

10.15. Consider the 8-point signal constellation shown in Figure P10.8.

a. Determine the symbol rate if the desired bit rate is 45 Mbps.

b. Calculate the average energy of the signal set.

c. What is the $d_{\min}$ for the signal set?

d. Use the nearest neighbor bound to estimate the probability of bit error. Can you improve the estimate by including additional terms?

10.16. Consider the 8-point signal constellation shown in Figure P10.9.

a. Assign the bits to each point in the signal constellation using Gray coding.

b. Calculate the average energy of the signal set.

c. Sketch ML decision regions D_i for the signal set.

d. Use the nearest neighbor bound to estimate the probability of bit error.

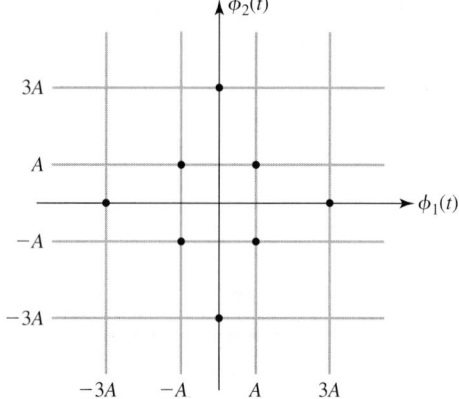

Figure P10.8

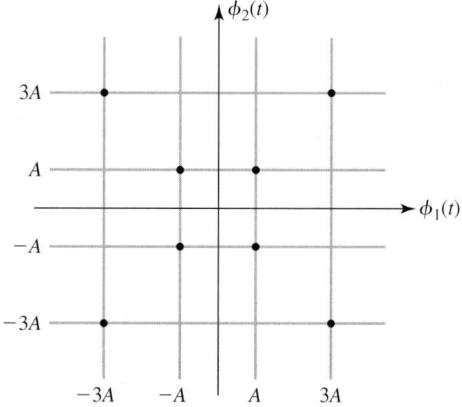

Figure P10.9

MATLAB PROBLEMS

10.17. Consider the transmission of binary unipolar NRZ pulses over an AWGN channel.

a. Generate the random bit sequence b[n] of length Nbits = 10.

b. Generate the unipolar NRZ pulse sequence x[n] corresponding to the above random bit sequence. Use nsamp =16 samples/pulse. Display x[n].

c. AWGN is simulated by a sequence of Gaussian random variables with zero mean and variance σ^2. For a value of SNR/bit EbNo in dB, the one-sided spectral density N_o is given by

$$N_o = E_b 10^{-\text{EbNo}/10}$$

For unipolar NRZ signaling with $T_b = 1$, $E_b = 1/2$. The variance of Gaussian random samples to simulate AWGN of one-sided spectral density N_o is now obtained from (6.344) as

$$\sigma^2 = \frac{N_o f_s}{2} = \frac{10^{-\text{EbNo}/10} f_s}{4}$$

where f_s = number of samples/bit (nsamp) for $T_b = 1$.

The sequence r[n] at the detector input is given by

r(n) = x(n) +sigma*randn(1, Nbits*nsamp)

where sigma =sqrt(nsamp*(10^(−0.1 *EbNo))/4).

Display the received signal sequence r[n] for EbNo = 13 dB.

d. The sequence r[n] is processed by an integrate-and-dump filter. Display the output waveform y[n].

```
for n = 1:Nbits

m1 = (n-1)*nsamples+1

for j = 1:nsamples

m2=m1+j-1

y(m2) = sum(r(m1:m2))/nsamples

end

end
```

e. The sequence y[n] is sampled and detected using a threshold comparator.

```
ro=y(n*nsamples) % Bit-rate sampler
output

% Threshold comparator

If ro <= 0.5

bhat(n) = 0;

else

bhat(n) = 1;

end
```

f. Regenerate the unipolar NRZ sequence xhat[n] and display it.

```
% Regenerated Unipolar NRZ

xhat = [];

for i=1:Nbits

xhat = [xhat bhat(i)*ones(1,nsamples)];

end
```

10.18. We simulate the BER performance of unipolar NRZ signaling over an AWGN channel for E_b/N_o values of 3–13 dB.

a. Generate the random bit and unipolar NRZ pulse sequences of length Nbits = 20,000. Use nsamp = 16 samples/pulse.

b. For a given value of E_b/N_o, add AWGN to the transmitted sequence x[n] as discussed in Problem 10.17(c) to generate the received sequence r[n].

c. The sequence r[n] is processed by an integrate-and-dump filter. It is then sampled and detected using a threshold comparator. The simulated BER is calculated using the following code segment:

```
error = 0; % Error counter

% Count errors

for n = 1:Nbits

if bhat(n) ~= b(n)

error = error+1;

end;

ber = error/Nbits;

EbNo
```

d. Calculate the theoretical BER performance using (10.53) and compare it with the simulated values for the specified values of E_b/N_o in a plot.

10.19. Repeat Problem 10.17 for binary polar signaling.

10.20. Repeat Problem 10.18 for binary polar signaling.

10.21. Consider the transmission of 4-PAM pulses over an AWGN channel.

a. Generate the random symbol sequence a[n] of length Nsymbols = 10.

```
M = 4

M1=M-1;

a = 2*fix(M*rand(1,Nsymbols))- M1;
% Symbol stream
```

b. Generate the polar 4-PAM sequence x[n] corresponding to the above random symbol sequence. Use nsamp = 16 samples/pulse. Display x[n].

c. AWGN is simulated by a sequence of Gaussian random variables with zero mean and variance σ^2. For a given value of EsNo of E_s/N_o in dB, the one-sided spectral density N_o is given by

$$N_o = E_s 10^{-\text{EsNo}/10}$$

For the 4-PAM signal set $\{-3, -1, 1, 3\}$ and $T = 1$, $E_s = 5$. The variance of Gaussian random samples to simulate AWGN of one-sided spectral density N_o is now obtained from (6.344) as

$$\sigma^2 = \frac{N_o f_s}{2} = \frac{5 \times 10^{-\text{EsNo}/10} f_s}{2}$$

where f_s = number of samples/pulse (nsamp) for $T = 1$.

The sequence r[n] at the detector input is given by

```
r(n) = x(n) +sigma*randn(1, Nbits*nsamp)
```

where sigma =sqrt(5*nsamp*(10^(-0.1 *EsNo))/2).

Display the received signal sequence r[n] for EsNo = 16 dB.

d. The sequence r[n] is processed by an integrate-and-dump filter. Display the output waveform y[n].

```
for n = 1:Nsymbols

m1 = (n-1)*nsamples+1

for j = 1:nsamples

m2=m1+j-1

y(m2) = sum(r(m1:m2))/nsamples

end

end
```

e. The sequence y[n] is sampled and detected using a threshold comparator.

```
ro=y(n*nsamples) % Symbol-rate
sampler output

% Threshold comparator
```

```
if ((ro <= 0) & (ro > -2))

bhat(n) = -1;

elseif(ro <= -2)

bhat(n) = -3;

elseif((ro > 0) & (ro < 2))

bhat(n) = 1;

else

bhat(n) = 3;

end
```

f. Regenerate the 4-PAM polar waveform xhat[n] and display it.

```
% Regenerated 4-PAM polar waveform

xhat = [];

for i=1: Nsymbols

xhat = [xhat
bhat(i)*ones(1,nsamples)];

end
```

10.22. We simulate the error rate performance of polar 4-PAM signaling over an AWGN channel for E_s/N_o values of 6–16 dB.

a. Generate the random symbol and 4-PAM pulse sequences of length Nsymbols = 20,000. Use nsamp = 16 samples/pulse.

b. For a given value of E_s/N_o, add AWGN to the transmitted sequence x[n] as discussed in Problem 10.21(c) to generate the received sequence r[n].

c. The sequence r[n] is processed by an integrate-and-dump filter. It is then sampled and detected using a threshold comparator. The simulated probability of symbol error ser is calculated using the following code segment:

```
error = 0; % Error counter

% Count errors

for n = 1: Nsymbols

if bhat(n) ~= a(n)

error = error+1;

end;

ser = error/ Nsymbols;
```

Calculate the theoretical probability of symbol error P_e using (10.176) and compare it with the simulated values for the specified values of E_s/N_o in a plot.

An Interview with Vince Poor

Courtesy of Vince Poor

Why did you choose a career in the communication field?

I began graduate school to study electromagnetics, but after a course in statistical communications, I decided to switch fields. The book for that course was written by John Thomas of Princeton, who eventually became my Ph.D. advisor.

In your opinion what are the major innovations that have contributed to the phenomenal progress in digital and wireless communications? What has been the impact of the semiconductor revolution? The Internet?

There's no doubt that progress in semiconductor technology, including processors, memories, and displays, has been the single most important enabler of advances in wireless communications. However, it has been the algorithms, codes, modulation techniques, protocols, etc., that have been made practicable by these advances in semiconductors that have given us the wireless networks we have today. There have also been countless other innovations, in radio circuits, batteries, software, etc., that have contributed greatly to the field. The cell phone is one of the most innovation-rich devices that human ingenuity has produced.

MIMO space-time processing is an important part of modern wireless communication standards such as IEEE 802.11n (Wi-Fi), 4G, 3GPP Long Term Evolution, and WiMAX. What are the fundamental limits and trade-offs involved here?

MIMO has really transformed wireless networks. Without it, we would have hit a capacity wall that would have limited the technology significantly. The theoretical limits of MIMO are well understood, but the fundamental limits may be due more to less well-understood physical limitations, such as antenna coupling, nonideal characteristics of radio components, etc.

Tell us about the performance of multiuser detection (MUD) schemes, which has been an area of significant contributions by you? Is it ready for prime time? A mandatory feature for 4G cellular communications standards?

The basic idea of multiuser detection is that interference can be well modeled and mitigated accordingly. In other words, it's not the same as entropic noise, which isn't amenable to such treatment and thus gives a fundamental limit on performance. In some ways, multiuser detection is already in prime time, as MIMO systems such as BLAST-type systems make use of multiuser detection to separate the transmissions of different antennas. Prototype multiuser detection receivers for user separation have also been implemented by many OEMs; these particularly use successive interference cancellation, which does a good job of providing many of the gains of optimal multiuser detection but with much lower complexity.

What are the new frontiers of innovation in wireless communications?

It's always very difficult to predict technological progress. History shows very clearly how wrong we can be about what will happen in the future. But, that said, certainly there is much to do in wireless communications. While great progress has been made thus far, the performance, quality, and reliability of mobile communications are still far from ideal. Until these reach the level of their wire-line counterparts, researchers and designers in the wireless field will still have plenty of room for innovation.

Who inspired you professionally the most?

My Ph.D. advisor, John Thomas, was a great inspiration to me. He was very good at motivating students to do their best, and he taught me a lot about how to work with students. I've also learned a lot from Tom Kailath of Stanford, who has been a great role model for many people in our field. I also greatly admire Andy Viterbi and Irwin Jacobs for their ability to turn fundamental ideas into a very successful technological enterprise. These are just a few of the many names I could cite. We're fortunate in our field to have many people to look up to.

Do you have any advice for new generations of students and researchers entering the communications field?

I think it's very important for students to focus on fundamental subjects. My own education was largely in the areas of random processes, detection and estimation theory, information theory, etc. Although these subjects are rather abstract, understanding the fundamentals has allowed me to move with the field as it has changed, which it has done dramatically over the course of my career to date. If I had focused as a student on something that was very topical at the time, it might have been at the expense of the ability to be more nimble later.

H. Vincent Poor (Ph.D., Princeton 1977) is Dean of the School of Engineering and Applied Science (SEAS) at Princeton University, where he is also the Michael Henry Strater University Professor of Electrical Engineering. He joined Princeton's faculty in 1990, and has served as dean of SEAS since 2006. Prior to joining the Princeton faculty, he was a faculty member at the University of Illinois, and he has held visiting appointments at a number of other institutions, including Harvard, Stanford, and Imperial College (London).

Dr. Poor has authored or coauthored more than 1,000 publications primarily in the area of wireless networking and related fields, including a dozen books. Dr. Poor is a member of the U.S. National Academy of Engineering, and is a Fellow of the Institute of Electrical and Electronics Engineers (IEEE), the American Academy of Arts & Sciences, and the Royal Academy of Engineering of the United Kingdom. He received a Guggenheim Fellowship in 2002, and the IEEE Education Medal in 2005. Recent recognition of his work includes the 2009 Edwin Howard Armstrong Award of the IEEE Communications Society, and the 2010 Ambrose Fleming Medal of the Institution of Engineering & Technology. In 2011, he will receive the IEEE's Eric E. Sumner Award and an honorary D.Sc. degree from the University of Edinburgh.

CHAPTER 11

Digital Information Transmission Using Carrier Modulation

Digital carrier modulation is the process by which a user bit stream is converted into bandpass (BP) waveforms that are compatible with transmission characteristics of many important communication channels such as radio, satellite, and cellular. Information bit stream is embedded into the carrier waveform by varying, or modulating, some attribute of the carrier, such as its amplitude, frequency, phase, or a combination thereof. The resultant BP signal contains the user information and occupies a frequency slot centered about a carrier frequency f_c in the available spectrum of a radio, satellite, or cable channel. At the destination, carrier demodulation process recovers the underlying baseband waveform from the received signal in the presence of noise. Transmitted data can now be regenerated using the techniques for baseband signal detection discussed in Chapter 10.

Radio, satellite, and cellular communication systems use free space channels to transmit digital information. These systems use a scarce frequency spectrum that is licensed by government regulatory agencies worldwide. Carrier modulation enables **channelization,** whereby the bandwidth of a wideband channel is divided into many smaller bandwidth channels that are assigned to different subcarriers.

- Digital cellular telephones use carrier frequencies in the 900 MHz (as well as 1800 and 1900 MHz) bands, but they have nonzero energy over a narrowband that is typically only 200 kHz (GSM) to 1.25 MHz (CDMA) wide.
- Digital satellite transmission uses carriers in the 12- and 17-GHz bands with transponder bandwidths of about 26 MHz.
- Digital transmission in CATV systems uses 6-MHz channels with downstream carrier frequencies in the range 550–875 MHz.

Digital transmission by a carrier is a key enabling technology that makes cellular/wireless, satellite, telco dial-up, and cable modem communications possible. In this chapter we present the fundamental concepts and techniques of digital carrier modulation and demodulation. As in the case of baseband signals, the geometric representation of carrier modulated digital signals is used in assessing their performance in the presence of additive Gaussian noise. The chapter is organized into the following sections:

11.1 BASIC CONCEPTS.
The basic digital carrier modulation techniques are introduced in this section. Alternative representations of digitally modulated BP signals are considered, and various demodulation options are reviewed.

11.2 BINARY AMPLITUDE-SHIFT KEYING.
This section presents BASK where the carrier is gated on and off by the information sequence to be transmitted. We consider its implementation and analyze the performance.

11.3 BINARY PHASE-SHIFT KEYING.
Transmission of digital information by toggling the phase of a carrier is considered in this section. We consider the implementation of BPSK and evaluate its performance.

11.4 BINARY FREQUENCY-SHIFT KEYING.
After considering two options for embedding the digital information sequences in the frequency of a carrier, we study Sunde's frequency-shift keying in detail.

11.5 DIFFERENTIAL BINARY PHASE-SHIFT KEYING.
In this section we consider a variant of BPSK whereby differentially encoded data is transmitted. A partially coherent demodulation scheme that detects phase changes is used to decode the data bits.

11.6 NONCOHERENT DEMODULATION OF BINARY DIGITAL CARRIER SIGNALS.
Noncoherent techniques for demodulation of BASK and BFSK signals are considered, and their performance is compared with that of their coherent counterparts.

11.7 QUADRATURE MODULATION SCHEMES.

We introduce the concept of digitally modulating orthogonal carriers by M-ary pulse trains. Recovery of M-ary information sequences also requires coherent demodulation using orthogonal carriers. The implementation and performance of quadrature phase-shift keying (QPSK) and offset quadrature phase-shift keying (OQPSK) are then considered.

11.8 MINIMUM SHIFT KEYING.

We study this most popular implementation of continuous-phase frequency-shift keying and consider its performance.

11.9 QUADRATURE AMPLITUDE MODULATION.

The popularity of this quadrature modulation scheme, implemented in many dial-up and cable modems, is due to its high spectral efficiency. We consider its implementation and performance analysis.

11.10 SPECTRA OF QUADRATURE MODULATED SIGNALS.

By using the concept of complex envelope, the computation of the spectrum of a carrier modulated signal is converted into the sum of the spectra of its quadrature LP components. We then study and compare the spectra and bandwidth requirements of various digital carrier modulation schemes.

11.11 COMPARISON OF CARRIER MODULATION SCHEMES.

This section compares the carrier modulation schemes for a given bit rate and BER performance based on two competing requirements: bandwidth and SNR/bit.

The chapter concludes with final remarks and a selected list of references.

11.1 BASIC CONCEPTS

The modulation of a carrier by digital data is two-step process as illustrated in Figure 11.1. First, the line encoder maps a block of k bits ($\underline{b}$) at a time into a distinct baseband waveform $\boldsymbol{a}_n v(t - nT)$ as in digital baseband modulation schemes discussed in Chapter 9. The symbols $\{\boldsymbol{a}_n\}$ can assume one of the M amplitude levels, where $M = 2^k$. The **carrier modulator** then generates a distinct carrier modulated waveform by varying amplitude, frequency, or phase of a sinusoidal carrier in accordance with baseband

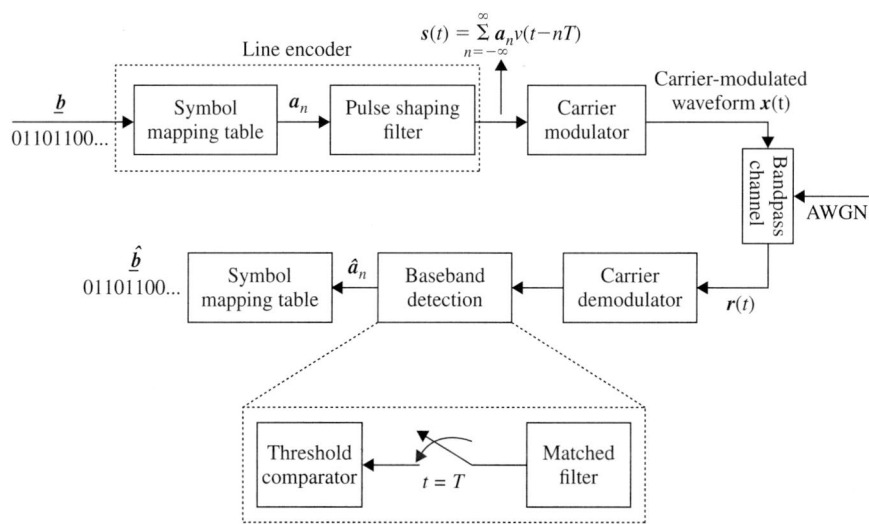

Figure 11.1 Digital carrier transmission system.

Pioneers in the Field

Library of Congress Prints
& Photographs Division
[LC-USZ62-39702]

Guglielmo Marconi, the great pioneer of radio telegraphy, was born on April 25, 1874, in Bologna, Italy, of an Irish mother and an Italian father. He was educated privately at Bologna, Florence, and Leghorn. As a young man, still in his teens, he was inspired to think that one could use electromagnetic waves to send telegraph signals over large distances through space. He was influenced particularly by the work of Scottish physicist James Maxwell, who predicted the existence of electromagnetic waves and German physicist Heinrich Hertz who demonstrated that rapid variations of electric current could be projected into space in the form of electromagnetic waves similar to those of light. To prove the feasibility of radio communication, Marconi began laboratory experiments in 1895 at his father's country estate at Pontecchio. He succeeded in ringing a bell two rooms away in his attic workshop purely by striking a telegraph key that created electromagnetic waves. He began producing this effect at longer and longer distances, eventually moving outside and sending the signals several hundred yards. He realized the limitation of his approach for long-distance wireless communications because it depended on using more powerful electrical charges to travel farther. Marconi eventually found that if the antenna was grounded, the signal would travel much farther. Thus, Marconi invented the grounded antenna and began sending telegraph signals up to 2 miles, even through hills and other obstacles.

In 1896, Marconi took his apparatus to England, where he was introduced to William Preece, engineer-in-chief of the post office, and later that year was granted the world's first patent for a system of wireless telegraphy. He demonstrated his system successfully in London, on Salisbury Plain, and across the Bristol Channel, and in July 1897 formed the Wireless Telegraph & Signal Company Ltd. (renamed Marconi's Wireless Telegraph Company Ltd. in 1900). By 1899, he had established wireless communication between France and England across a 32-mile link along the English Channel. Marconi used spark gap transmitters, which worked by keying a spark to jump across the gap and generating electromagnetic waves in the process. The resultant signal produced a very broad spectrum, thus preventing multiple simultaneous transmissions. Marconi then developed a system of tuned multiplex telegraphy in 1900, which allowed multiple messages to be sent on the same transmitter simultaneously without significant interference. Next Marconi challenged the widely held belief that electromagnetic waves would not be able to follow the curvature of the earth and could, therefore, never transmit signals across the vastness of an ocean. Convinced that the wireless signals could span the ocean, he set out to prove it. Marconi had a powerful transmitting station built in Poldu, Cornwall, on the English coast and set sail for St. John's, Newfoundland. Pretending to be working on contacting passing ships on their transatlantic voyages, he launched a kite with a receiving wire 400 feet into the air. On December 12, 1901, he received the letter "S" several times and had an assistant verify the reception. Marconi had achieved the first transatlantic wireless transmission.

Marconi's invention of the digital modulation of the electromagnetic waves and the discovery of the grounded waves that could bend to the curvature of the earth overcoming hills and obstacles, inaugurated the new revolutionary age in communication in the twentieth century. He received many international awards in recognition of his contributions, including the Nobel Prize for Physics in 1909, which he shared with Karl Braun.

pulse $a_n v(t - nT)$. We explain this operation in the context of common binary carrier modulation schemes:

- **Binary amplitude-shift keying (BASK).** The digitally modulated baseband signal modulates the amplitude of the carrier. If the digital signal is a positive pulse (e.g., corresponding to a binary 1), the carrier is turned on for the duration of a bit interval. No carrier burst is transmitted during a bit interval for a binary 0 (corresponding to absence of a pulse).
- **Binary phase-shift keying (BPSK).** The digitally modulated baseband signal modulates the phase of the carrier. In the case of BPSK, the carrier phase is toggled to represent a binary digital signal. If the digital signal is a positive pulse (e.g., corresponding to a binary 1), $\cos(2\pi f_c t)$ is transmitted, and if it is a negative pulse

(corresponding to a binary 0), the carrier burst $\cos(2\pi f_c t + \pi) = -\cos(2\pi f_c t)$ is transmitted.

- **Binary frequency-shift keying (BFSK).** The digitally modulated baseband signal modulates the frequency of the carrier. In the case of BFSK, the carrier frequency is toggled to represent a binary digital signal. If the digital signal is a positive pulse (e.g., corresponding to a binary 1), the carrier has the frequency $f_1 = f_c + \Delta f/2$, and if it is a negative pulse (corresponding to a binary 0), the carrier has the frequency $f_2 = f_c - \Delta f/2$, where Δf is called the **frequency deviation.**

Figure 11.2 displays waveforms for three binary carrier modulation systems.

At the destination, a **carrier demodulator** recovers the baseband signal from the received digitally modulated carrier waveform in the presence of noise added by the channel and/or the receiver front-end. A coherent demodulator uses the carrier signal, which is phase and frequency synchronized to the received signal for recovering the underlying baseband digital signal. This requires a carrier recovery circuit at the demodulator. Coherent demodulation may neither be desirable nor feasible in many practical applications. Noncoherent or partially coherent implementations are used in such cases to recover the baseband signal. This is followed by baseband signal detection to produce decisions on the transmitted symbols using techniques considered in Chapter 10. The symbol mapping function then decodes the transmission symbols into a sequence of data bits as discussed in Chapter 9.

11.1.1 Representations of Digitally Modulated Carrier Signals

As discussed in Section 4.4, a BP waveform can be expressed either in amplitude and phase form

$$x(t) = A(t)\cos\big[2\pi f_c t + \psi(t)\big] \tag{11.1}$$

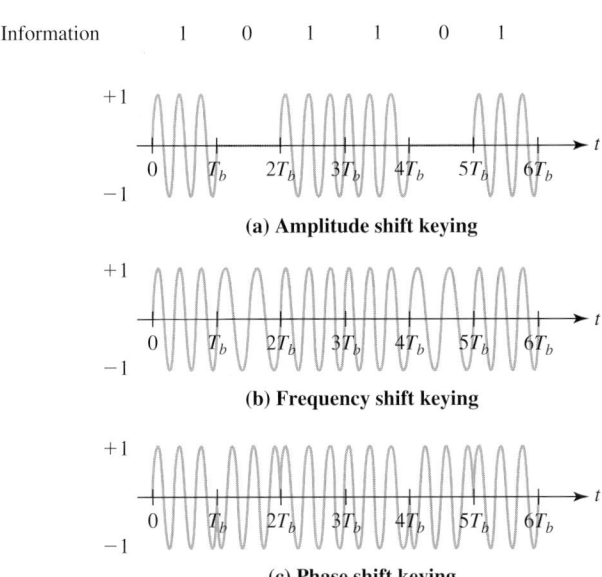

(a) Amplitude shift keying

(b) Frequency shift keying

(c) Phase shift keying

Figure 11.2 Binary carrier modulation schemes.

or in quadrature form

$$x(t) = I(t)\cos(2\pi f_c t) - Q(t)\sin(2\pi f_c t) \tag{11.2}$$

where $A(t) \geq 0$ is the time-varying amplitude or envelope of the modulated signal and $\psi(t)$ is the time-varying phase. $I(t)$ and $Q(t)$ are called **in-phase** and **quadrature components,** respectively. They are related to $A(t)$ and $\psi(t)$ by

$$I(t) = A(t)\cos\psi(t)$$

$$Q(t) = A(t)\sin\psi(t) \tag{11.3}$$

The carrier frequency f_c is chosen sufficiently large compared with the amplitude and phase variations of $x(t)$ so that its spectrum does not have significant energy at $f = 0$.

In many popular digital communication systems, $I(t)$ and $Q(t)$s are statistically independent, linearly modulated random pulse trains as discussed in Section 9.3. That is,

$$\boldsymbol{I}(t) = \sum_n \boldsymbol{a}_n^I v(t - nT)$$

$$\boldsymbol{Q}(t) = \sum_n \boldsymbol{a}_n^Q w(t - nT) \tag{11.4}$$

where $\boldsymbol{a}_n^I$ and $\boldsymbol{a}_n^Q$ are M-ary transmission symbols; $v(t)$ and $w(t)$ are basic pulse shapes of symbol duration T seconds. Such modulation methods are called **quadrature schemes. Phase-shift keying (PSK)** and **quadrature amplitude modulation (QAM)** are prime examples of these widely used carrier modulation schemes. In some carrier modulation schemes, the BP signal is a nonlinear function of the independent pulse train; an example is frequency-shift keying (FSK). It is more convenient to describe this type in terms of the amplitude and phase format.

The digitally modulated BP random signal $x(t)$ can be expressed in terms of its quadrature components as

$$\boldsymbol{x}(t) = A_c\big[\boldsymbol{I}(t)\cos(2\pi f_c t) - \boldsymbol{Q}(t)\sin(2\pi f_c t)\big] \tag{11.5}$$

As discussed in Section 4.4, the complex envelope $\tilde{\boldsymbol{x}}(t)$ of the BP signal $\boldsymbol{x}(t)$ can be written as

$$\tilde{\boldsymbol{x}}(t) = \boldsymbol{I}(t) + j\boldsymbol{Q}(t) \tag{11.6}$$

Combining (11.5) and (11.6), we obtain an alternative representation for the random signal $\boldsymbol{x}(t)$ in terms of its complex envelope as

$$\boldsymbol{x}(t) = A_c\mathrm{Re}\big\{\tilde{\boldsymbol{x}}(t)e^{j2\pi f_c t}\big\} \tag{11.7}$$

11.2 BINARY AMPLITUDE-SHIFT KEYING

In BASK, every T_b seconds the modulator transmits a carrier burst only if the binary information bit is 1. There is no transmission if the information bit is 0. The symbol mapping function is trivial here in the sense that it maps information bits (b_n) 1 and 0 to transmission symbols (a_n) 1 and 0, respectively. The two waveforms corresponding to the information bit being a 1 or 0 are given by

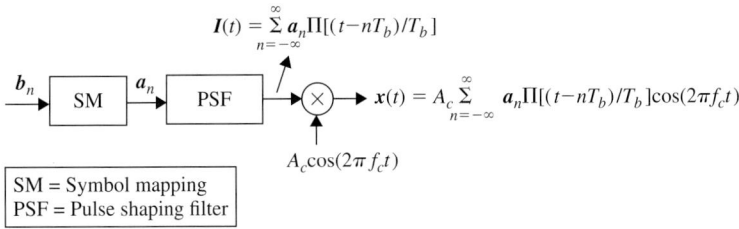

Figure 11.3 BASK modulator.

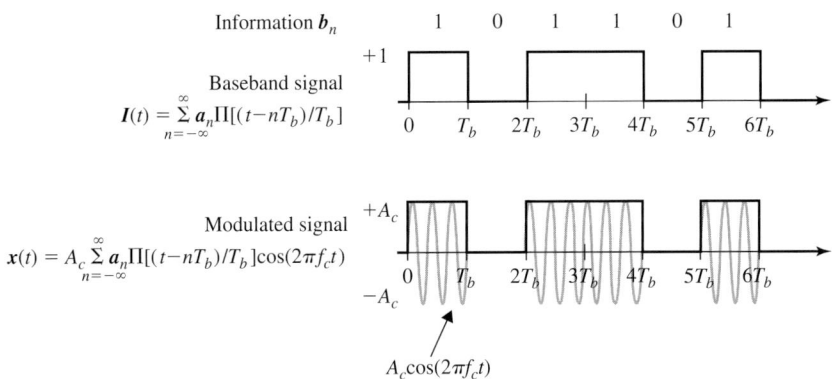

Figure 11.4 BASK modulator waveforms.

$$\text{Binary 1: } s_1(t) = \begin{cases} A_c\cos(2\pi f_c t), & 0 \leq t \leq T_b \\ 0, & \text{otherwise} \end{cases}$$

$$\text{Binary 0: } s_2(t) = 0, \quad 0 \leq t \leq T_b \tag{11.8}$$

Using (11.8), the BASK signal can be expressed as

$$x(t) = A_c \sum_{n=-\infty}^{\infty} a_n \Pi\big[(t - nT_b)/T_b\big]\cos(2\pi f_c t), \quad a_n \in \mathscr{A}_2 = \{1, 0\} \tag{11.9}$$

where A_c is the amplitude of the carrier signal. The underlying baseband digital signal $I(t) = \sum_{n=-\infty}^{\infty} a_n \Pi\big[(t - nT_b)/T_b\big]$ in (11.9) is a random pulse train because amplitudes $\{a_n\}$ of the transmitted pulse sequence are binary random variables. Note that the BP random process $x(t)$ contains only the in-phase component $I(t)$; the quadrature component $Q(t)$ is zero. The block diagram of a BASK modulator is shown in Figure 11.3. Figure 11.4 illustrates waveforms in the binary ASK modulation process.

11.2.1 Coherent Demodulation of BASK Signals

The coherent demodulation process illustrated in Figure 11.5 consists of multiplying the modulated signal $x(t)$ by a reference carrier $2\cos(2\pi f_c t)$, which is frequency and phase synchronized with the carrier at the modulator. This implies that the carrier

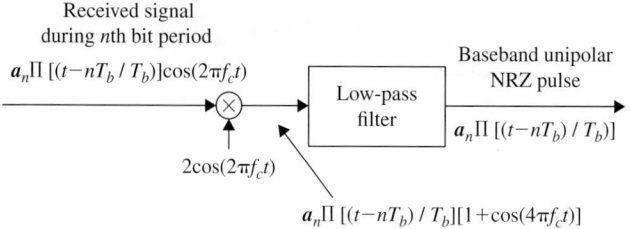

Figure 11.5 BASK demodulator.

recovery loop at the demodulator needs to accurately track the phase of the modulator. The resultant signal

$$x(t) \times 2\cos(2\pi f_c t) = \left\{ A_c \sum_{n=-\infty}^{\infty} a_n \Pi\big[(t - nT_b)/T_b\big] \cos(2\pi f_c t) \right\} \times 2\cos(2\pi f_c t)$$

$$= \left\{ A_c \sum_{n=-\infty}^{\infty} a_n \Pi\big[(t - nT_b)/T_b\big] \right\} \big[1 + \cos(4\pi f_c t) \big] \qquad (11.10)$$

is shown in Figure 11.6. By low-pass filtering it, the underlying baseband NRZ signal $\sum_{n=-\infty}^{\infty} a_n \Pi\big[(t - nT_b)/T_b\big]$ can be recovered.

In the presence of noise, the structure of the BASK receiver in Figure 11.7 includes a front-end BP filter to remove out-of-band noise. The LP filtering is implemented by

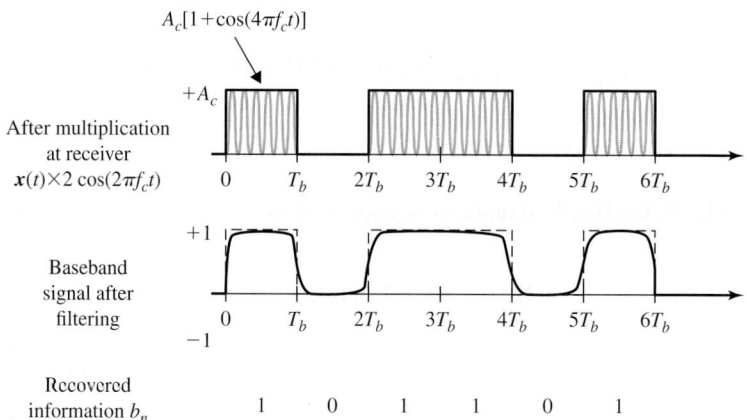

Figure 11.6 BASK demodulator waveforms.

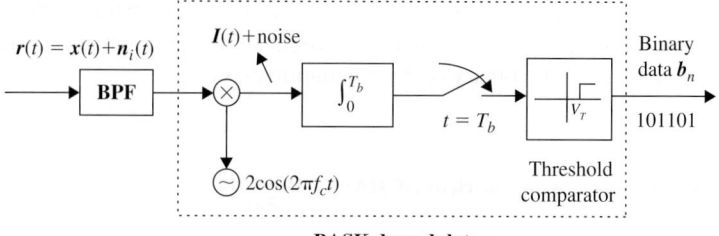

Figure 11.7 BASK receiver.

an integrate-and-dump filter discussed in Section 10.2.1. The unipolar NRZ pulse train, recovered by the coherent demodulation, is now processed to detect $\{a_n\}$ in the presence of noise using a sampler followed by a threshold comparator.

Error Performance

The BASK signal at the receiver in the presence of noise is given by

$$r(t) = \alpha x(t) + n_i(t) \tag{11.11}$$

where α represents the attenuation introduced by the transmission channel. We assume $\alpha = 1$ without any loss of generality. $n_i(t)$ is AWGN with the double-sided power spectral density of $N_o/2$ W/Hz. The BP filter passes the ASK carrier burst without distortion while rejecting out-of-band noise. Assuming $s_1(t)$ is transmitted during the bit interval $0 \le t \le T_b$, the output of the multiplier is given by

$$
\begin{aligned}
\left[s_1(t) + n(t) \right] \times 2\cos(2\pi f_c t) &= A_c \cos(2\pi f_c t) \times 2\cos(2\pi f_c t) + n(t) \times 2\cos(2\pi f_c t) \\
&= A_c \left[1 + \underbrace{\cos(4\pi f_c t)}_{\text{Filtered out}} \right] + n_c(t)
\end{aligned} \tag{11.12}
$$

where $n_c(t)$ is the in-phase component of the BP filter output noise $n(t)$. Its spectral density is N_o W/Hz as discussed in Section 6.12.1. From (11.12), the output of the integrate-and-dump filter $r_o(t)$ at the sampling instant $t = T_b$ can be written as

$$r_o = \begin{cases} A_c T_b + n_1(T_b), & \text{Binary 1} \\ n_1(T_b), & \text{Binary 0} \end{cases} \tag{11.13}$$

where

$$n_1(T_b) = \int_0^{T_b} n_c(t)dt \tag{11.14}$$

$n_1(T_b)$ is a Gaussian random variable with zero mean and variance given by

$$\sigma^2 = \overline{n_1^2(T_b)} = E\left\{ \int_0^{T_b}\int_0^{T_b} n_c(t)n_c(u)dtdu \right\} = \int_0^{T_b}\int_0^{T_b} N_o\delta(t-u)dtdu = \int_0^{T_b} N_o du = N_o T_b \tag{11.15}$$

Thus, input to the threshold comparator, r_o, is a Gaussian random variable with the variance σ^2 given by (11.15) and the mean $A_c T_b$ or 0, depending on whether a binary 1 or 0 was transmitted. Consequently, the optimum threshold V_T is $A_c T_b/2$ volts. The comparator declares that a binary 1 was transmitted if $r_o > A_c T_b/2$, and a binary 0 decision is made if $r_o < A_c T_b/2$. Assuming equally likely binary symbols, the BER of a binary communication system is obtained from (10.11) as

$$BER = 0.5 \times P\{\text{error} | s_1(t) \text{ sent}\} + 0.5 \times P\{\text{error} | s_2(t) \text{ sent}\} \tag{11.16}$$

From Section 10.1.1, we can write following expression for $P\{\text{error}|s_1(t)\text{ sent}\}$:

$$P\{\text{error}|s_1\text{ sent}\} = \int\limits_{-\infty}^{A_cT_b/2} f_{r_o}(r_o|s_1)dr_o = \frac{1}{\sqrt{2\pi\sigma^2}}\int\limits_{-\infty}^{A_cT_b/2} e^{-(r_o-A_cT_b)^2/2\sigma^2}dr_o$$

$$= \frac{1}{\sqrt{2\pi}}\int\limits_{A_cT_b/2\sigma}^{\infty} e^{-\frac{u^2}{2}}du = Q\left(\frac{A_cT_b}{2\sigma}\right) \qquad (11.17)$$

where $f_{r_o}(r_o|s_1)$ is a conditional pdf of the random variable r_o assuming that $s_1(t)$ was transmitted. Because both $f_{r_o}(r_o|s_1)$ and $f_{r_o}(r_o|s_2)$ are symmetric pdfs, it follows that

$$BER = P\{\text{error}|s_1\text{ sent}\} = P\{\text{error}|s_2\text{ sent}\} = Q\left(\frac{A_cT_b}{2\sigma}\right) \qquad (11.18)$$

The average energy per bit in BASK signaling is given by

$$E_b = P\{s_1(t)\text{ sent}\} \times E_1 + P\{s_2(t)\text{ sent}\} \times E_2 \qquad (11.19)$$

where

$$E_1 = \text{Energy in } s_1(t) = \int\limits_0^{T_b} s_1^2(t)dt = \int\limits_0^{T_b} A_c^2\cos^2(2\pi f_c t)dt = \frac{A_c^2 T_b}{2}$$

$$E_2 = \text{Energy in } s_2(t) = 0$$

For equiprobable binary signals, the average energy per bit is given by

$$E_b = \frac{A_c^2 T_b}{4} \qquad (11.20)$$

Substituting (11.15) and (11.20) into (11.18) yields

$$BER_{BASK} = Q\left(\sqrt{\frac{E_b}{N_o}}\right) \qquad (11.21)$$

Alternatively, the BER performance of the BASK system can be evaluated in a simpler fashion by using the techniques developed in Section 10.6. If we choose the basis function

$$\phi_1(t) = \sqrt{\frac{2}{T_b}}\cos(2\pi f_c t), \quad 0 \le t \le T_b, \qquad (11.22)$$

we can write signals in (11.8) as

$$s_1(t) = A_c\sqrt{\frac{T_b}{2}}\phi_1(t) = \sqrt{2E_b}\phi_1(t)$$

$$s_2(t) = 0 \qquad (11.23)$$

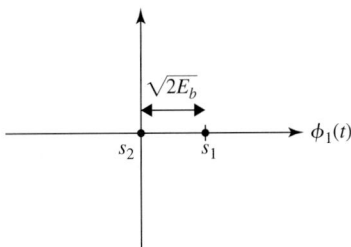

Figure 11.8 BASK constellation.

The signal constellation for BASK is shown in Figure 11.8. It is identical to that of unipolar signaling with $d = \sqrt{2E_b}$. The BER performance of BASK is, therefore, the same as that of unipolar NRZ signaling. Using (10.139), it is given by

$$BER_{BASK} = Q\left(\frac{d}{\sqrt{2N_o}}\right) = Q\left(\sqrt{\frac{E_b}{N_o}}\right) \tag{11.24}$$

Example 11.1

Binary data is transmitted using ASK through a channel that adds white Gaussian noise with power spectral density $N_o = 10^{-11}$ W/Hz. Determine the amplitude of a received carrier burst to provide a $BER = 10^{-5}$ for the following data rates: (a) 300 bps; (b) 3 kbps; (c) 9.6 kbps.

Solution

The BER of the ASK system is given from (11.24) by

$$BER_{BASK} = Q\left(\sqrt{\frac{E_b}{N_o}}\right)$$

To achieve a $BER = 10^{-5}$, $\sqrt{\frac{E_b}{N_o}} = 4.27$ or $\frac{E_b}{N_o} = (4.27)^2 = 18.233$.
Substituting $N_o = 10^{-11}$ W/Hz yields

$$E_b = 18.233 \times 10^{-11}$$

From (11.20), we have

$$E_b = \frac{A_c^2 T_b}{4} = \frac{A_c^2}{4R_b}$$

The amplitude of the received carrier pulse is, therefore, given by

$$A_c = 2\sqrt{E_b R_b} \text{ Volts}$$

a. 300 bps, $A_c = 2\sqrt{E_b R_b} = 2\sqrt{18.233 \times 10^{-11} \times 300} = 466.7 \; \mu V$
b. 3000 bps, $A_c = 2\sqrt{E_b R_b} = 2\sqrt{18.233 \times 10^{-11} \times 3000} = 1479 \; \mu V$
c. 9600 bps, $A_c = 2\sqrt{E_b R_b} = 2\sqrt{18.233 \times 10^{-11} \times 9600} = 2646 \; \mu V$

Experiment 11.1   *BASK Simulation and Performance Comparison*

In this experiment, we model a binary ASK digital communication system using Simulink and MATLAB. Figure 11.9(a) illustrates the Simulink model for the system. The parameters of simulation including bit rate, carrier frequency, and sampling rate are set up by a companion MATLAB m-file. The m-file also computes the theoretical BER and plots simulated and theoretical BER performance. The **unipolar Bernoulli source** block generates a sequence of bits (0's and 1's) which appears as a unipolar NRZ signal. The ASK signal is produced by the **BASK modulator** block which multiplies the unipolar NRZ pulse train with the output of a discrete-time sinusoidal source. AWGN is added to the ASK signal by using the AWGN channel block illustrated in Figure 10.9(a). At the receiver, the **BASK demodulator** block multiplies the received signal with the carrier waveform synchronized to the one in the modulator block. The underlying unipolar NRZ signal is recovered using the correlation detector. The latter is implemented by a discrete-time integrator which is reset at the beginning of each bit period. The output of the integrator is sampled at the end of each bit period in the **bit-rate sampling** block. The **threshold comparator** block then generates output unipolar NRZ pulses based on the comparison of received signal samples with the threshold value.

Figure 11.9 (a) Simulink model for ASK system; (b) binary BASK signaling waveforms; (c) comparison of theoretical and simulated BER performance.

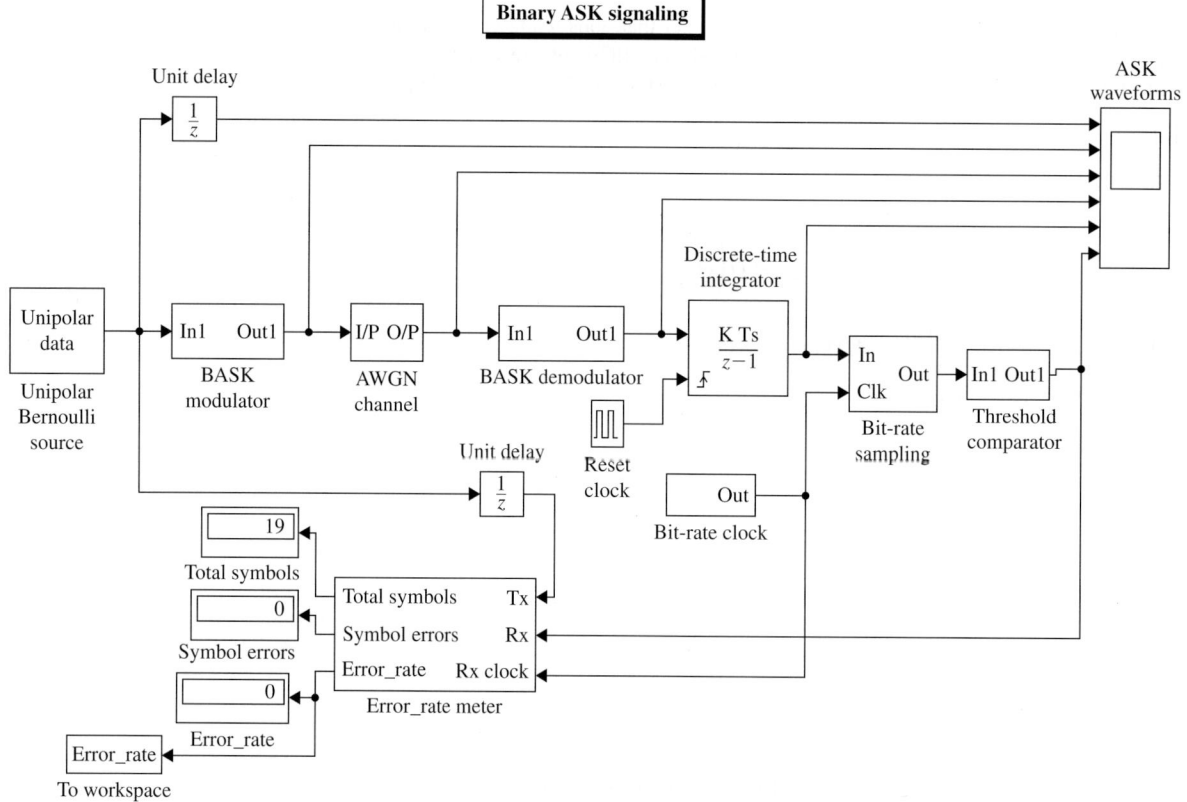

(a)

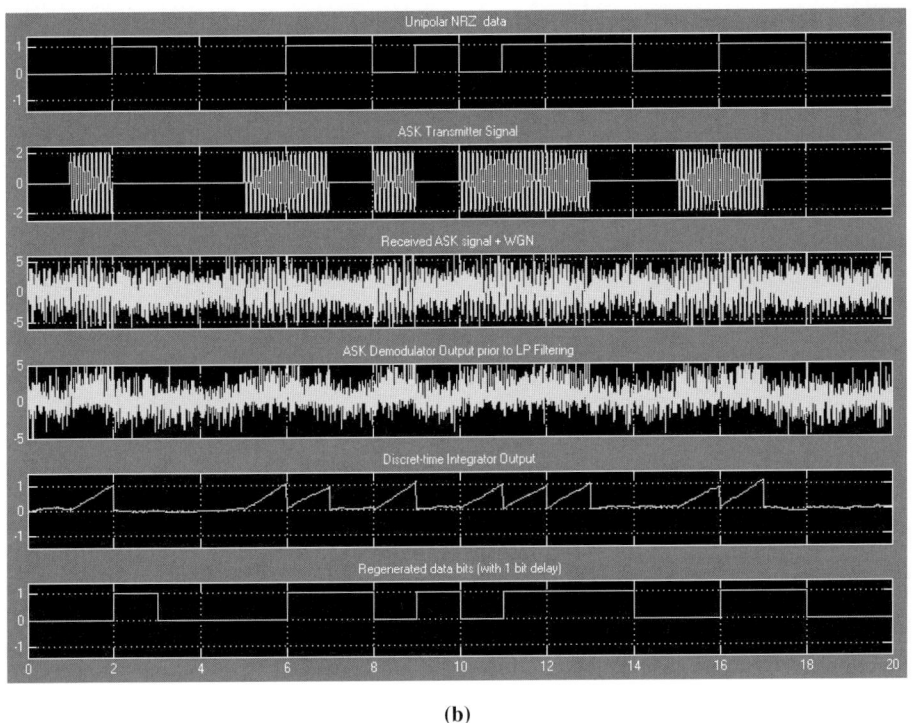

(b)

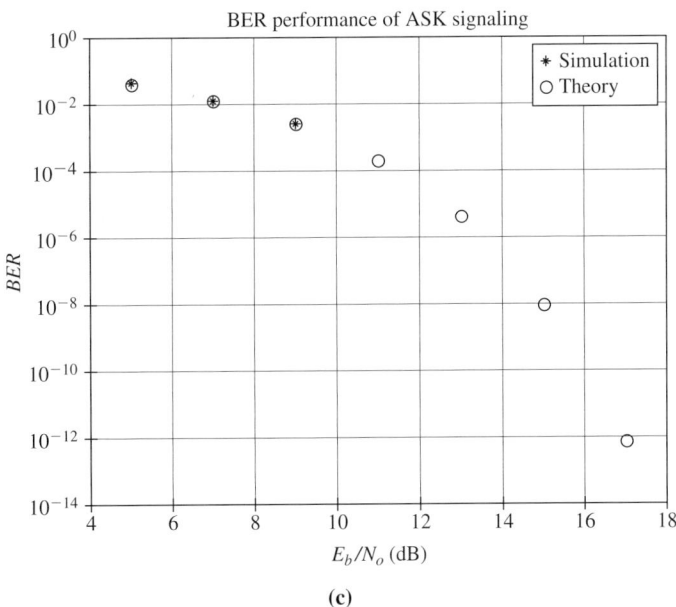

(c)

The regenerated unipolar NRZ signal is then compared with the transmitted sequence in the Error-rate meter block. The simulated BER value is transmitted to MATLAB workspace to generate the BER performance curve. Figure 11.9(c) provides a comparison of theoretical and simulated BER performance. Figure 11.9(b) displays various waveforms generated using this simulation.

11.3   BINARY PHASE-SHIFT KEYING

In BPSK, the symbol mapping table encodes information bits (b_n) 1 and 0 to transmission symbols (a_n) 1 and -1, respectively. The resultant output of the pulse shaping filter is a polar NRZ pulse train which then amplitude modulates the carrier. Every T_b seconds the modulator transmits one of the two carrier bursts that corresponds to the binary information bit being a 1 or 0.

$$\text{Binary 1: } s_1(t) = A_c\cos(2\pi f_c t),\ 0 \le t \le T_b$$

$$\text{Binary 0: } s_2(t) = A_c\cos(2\pi f_c t + \pi) = -A_c\cos(2\pi f_c t) \qquad (11.25)$$

The resultant BPSK signal can be expressed as

$$\boldsymbol{x}(t) = A_c \sum_{n=-\infty}^{\infty} \boldsymbol{a}_n \Pi\big[(t - nT_b)/T_b\big]\cos(2\pi f_c t),\ \ \boldsymbol{a}_n \in \mathscr{A}_2 = \{1 - 1\} \qquad (11.26)$$

Again, the underlying baseband digital signal $\boldsymbol{I}(t) = \displaystyle\sum_{n=-\infty}^{\infty} \boldsymbol{a}_n \Pi\big[(t - nT_b)/T_b\big]$ in (11.26) is a random pulse train because amplitudes $\{\boldsymbol{a}_n\}$ of the transmitted pulse sequence are binary random variables. The BP random process $\boldsymbol{x}(t)$ contains only the in-phase component $\boldsymbol{I}(t)$; the quadrature component $\boldsymbol{Q}(t)$ is zero. Figure 11.10 depicts the BPSK modulation process; the resultant modulation waveforms are illustrated in Figure 11.11.

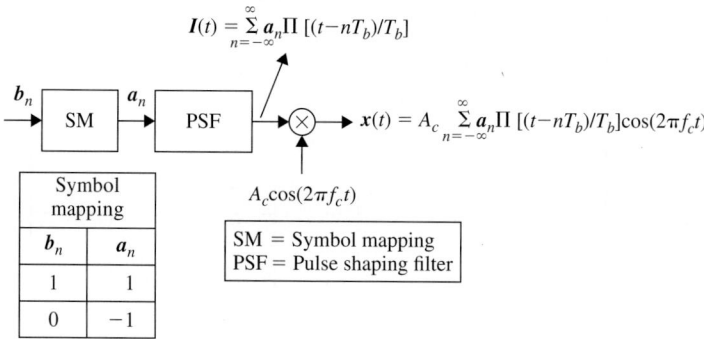

Figure 11.10 BPSK modulator.

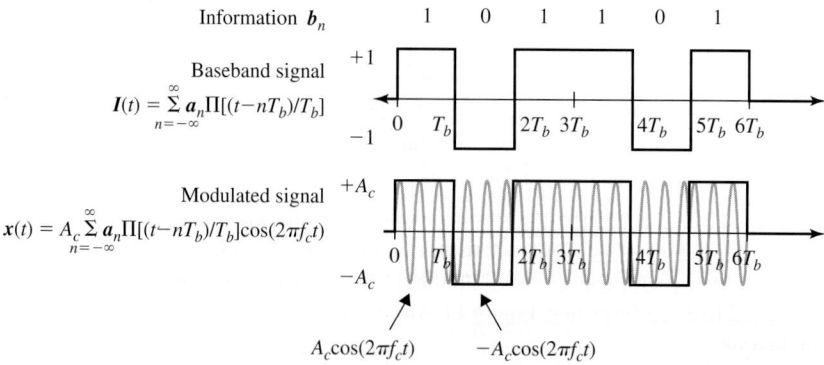

Figure 11.11 BPSK modulator waveforms.

11.3.1 Coherent Demodulation of BPSK Signals

The demodulation process consists of multiplying the modulated signal $x(t)$ by $2\cos(2\pi f_c t)$ as shown in Figure 11.12. The resultant signal,

$$x(t) \times 2\cos(2\pi f_c t) = \left\{ A_c \sum_{n=-\infty}^{\infty} a_n \Pi\left[(t - nT_b)/T_b\right]\cos(2\pi f_c t) \right\} \times 2\cos(2\pi f_c t)$$

$$= A_c \sum_{n=-\infty}^{\infty} a_n \Pi\left[(t - nT_b)/T_b\right]\left[1 + \cos(4\pi f_c t)\right] \qquad (11.27)$$

is shown in Figure 11.13. By low-pass filtering it, the underlying baseband polar NRZ signal $\sum_{n=-\infty}^{\infty} a_n \Pi\left[(t - nT_b)/T_b\right]$ can be recovered.

In the presence of noise, the structure of the BPSK receiver in Figure 11.14 includes a front-end BP filter to remove out-of-band noise. Coherent demodulation of the BP filter output recovers the underlying polar NRZ pulse train, which is now processed to detect $\{a_n\}$ in the presence of noise using a sampler followed by a threshold comparator.

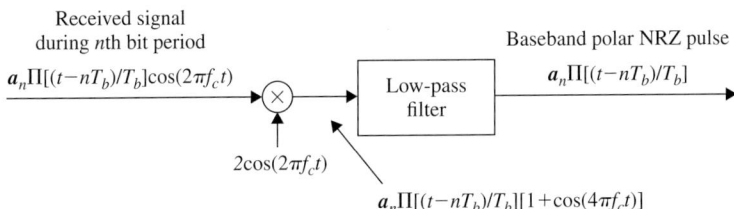

Figure 11.12 BPSK demodulator.

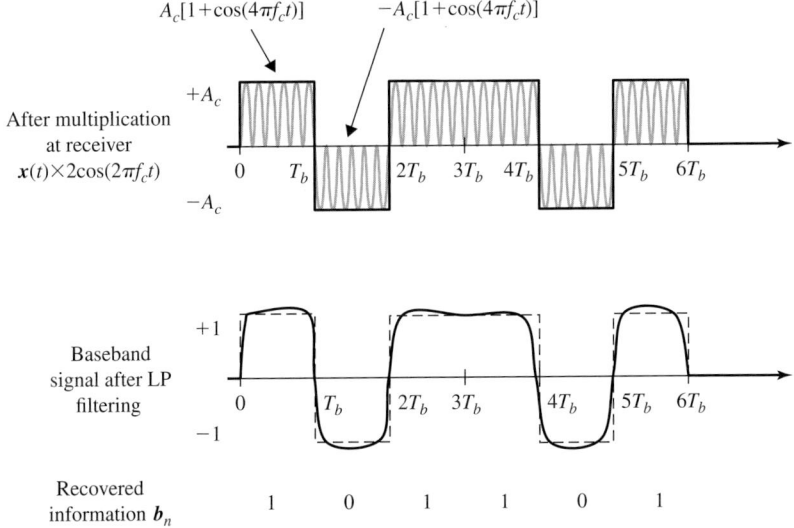

Figure 11.13 BPSK demodulator waveforms.

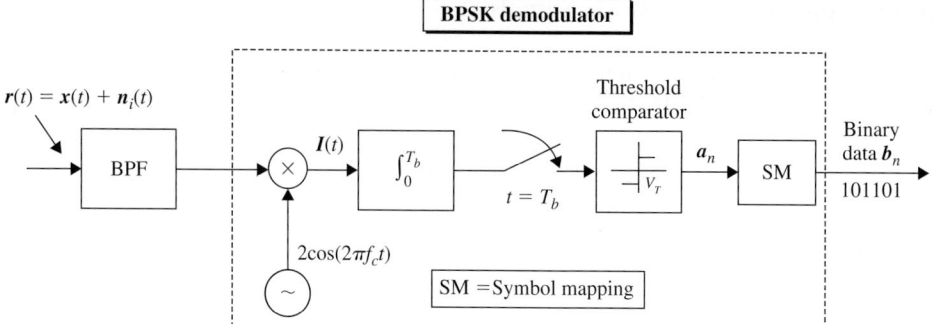

Figure 11.14 BPSK receiver.

Error Performance

The received BPSK signal in the presence of noise is given by

$$r(t) = \alpha x(t) + n_i(t) \tag{11.28}$$

where α represents the attenuation introduced by the transmission channel. Again, we assume $\alpha = 1$ without any loss of generality. $n_i(t)$ is AWGN with the double-sided power spectral density of $N_o/2$ Watts/Hz. The BP filter passes BPSK carrier bursts without distortion while rejecting out-of-band noise. Using an approach similar to that described in Section 11.2.1, the output of the integrate-and-dump filter $r_0(t)$ at the sampling instant $t = T_b$ can be written as

$$r_o = \begin{cases} A_c T_b + n_1(T_b), & \text{Binary 1} \\ -A_c T_b + n_1(T_b), & \text{Binary 0} \end{cases} \tag{11.29}$$

where $n_1(T_b) = \displaystyle\int_0^{T_b} n_c(t)dt$ from (11.14). Thus input to the threshold comparator, r_o, is a Gaussian random variable with variance σ^2 given by (11.15) and mean $A_c T_b$ or $-A_c T_b$ depending on whether a binary 1 or 0 was transmitted. Consequently, the optimum threshold V_T is 0 volts. The comparator declares that a binary 1 was transmitted if $r_o > 0$, and a binary 0 decision is made if $r_o < 0$. Assuming equally likely binary symbols, the BER of a BPSK system is given by using (11.16) as

$$BER_{BPSK} = P\{\text{error} | s_1 \text{ sent}\} = \int_{-\infty}^{0} f_{r_o}(r_o|s_1)dr$$

$$= \frac{1}{\sqrt{2\pi\sigma^2}} \int_{-\infty}^{0} e^{-\frac{(r_o - A_c T_b)^2}{2\sigma^2}} dr_o = Q\left(\frac{A_c T_b}{\sigma}\right) \tag{11.30}$$

Using (11.19), the average energy per bit in BPSK signaling is given by

$$E_b = P\{s_1(t) \text{ sent}\} \times E_1 + P\{s_2(t) \text{ sent}\} \times E_2$$

where

$$E_1 = \text{Energy in } s_1(t) = \int_0^{T_b} s_1^2(t)dt = \int_0^{T_b} A_c^2 \cos^2(2\pi f_c t)dt = \frac{A_c^2 T_b}{2}$$

$$E_2 = \text{Energy in } s_2(t) = \int_0^{T_b} s_2^2(t)dt = \int_0^{T_b} A_c^2 \cos^2(2\pi f_c t)dt = \frac{A_c^2 T_b}{2}$$

For equiprobable binary signals, the average energy per bit is given by

$$E_b = \frac{A_c^2 T_b}{2} \tag{11.31}$$

Substituting (11.15) and (11.31) into (11.30) yields

$$BER_{BPSK} = Q\left(\sqrt{\frac{2E_b}{N_o}}\right) \tag{11.32}$$

Alternatively, the BER performance of the BPSK system can be evaluated by using the techniques developed in Section 10.6. If we choose the same basis function as in (11.22), that is,

$$\phi_1(t) = \sqrt{\frac{2}{T_b}} \cos(2\pi f_c t), \quad 0 \le t \le T_b$$

we can write signals in (11.25) as

$$s_1(t) = A_c\sqrt{\frac{T_b}{2}}\phi_1(t) = \sqrt{E_b}\phi_1(t)$$

$$s_2(t) = -A_c\sqrt{\frac{T_b}{2}}\phi_1(t) = -\sqrt{E_b}\phi_1(t) \tag{11.33}$$

The signal constellation for BPSK is shown in Figure 11.15; BPSK is thus antipodal signaling with $d = 2\sqrt{E_b}$. Using (10.139), the BER of BPSK is given by

$$BER_{BPSK} = Q\left(\frac{d}{\sqrt{2N_o}}\right) = Q\left(\sqrt{\frac{2E_b}{N_o}}\right) \tag{11.34}$$

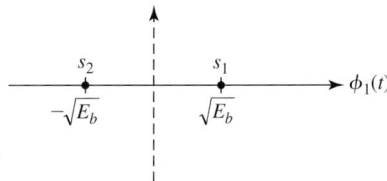

Figure 11.15 BPSK constellation.

Comparing (11.34) with (11.24), it is obvious that for the same BER performance, BPSK is 3 dB more efficient than BASK in terms of required SNR/bit (E_b/N_o).

Example 11.2

Compare the average power level required at the demodulator to maintain a $BER = 10^{-6}$ using BPSK and BASK signaling schemes for data transmission over a radio channel at 4800 bps. Assume that the channel adds white Gaussian noise with power spectral density $N_o = 10^{-10}$ W/Hz.

Solution

From (11.24) and (11.34), we have

$$BER_{BASK} = Q\left(\sqrt{\frac{E_b}{N_o}}\right)$$

$$BER_{BPSK} = Q\left(\sqrt{\frac{2E_b}{N_o}}\right)$$

From Table 6.1, $Q(x) = 10^{-6}$ if $x = 4.75$.
For BASK, $E_b = (4.75)^2 \times 10^{-10} = 2.256 \times 10^{-9}$
For BPSK, $E_b = \dfrac{(4.75)^2}{2} \times 10^{-10} = 1.128 \times 10^{-9}$

For BASK, the required average power P_{av} is obtained as

$$P_{av} = \frac{E_b}{T_b} = E_b R_b = 2.256 \times 10^{-9} \times 4800 = 10.83 \ \mu W = -19.65 \text{ dBm}$$

For BPSK, the required average power P_{av} is obtained as

$$P_{av} = \frac{E_b}{T_b} = E_b R_b = 1.128 \times 10^{-9} \times 4800 = 5.415 \ \mu W = -22.66 \text{ dBm}$$

The average power required at the demodulator is 3 dB less for BPSK than BASK.

Experiment 11.2   *BPSK Simulation and Performance Comparison*

In this experiment, we model a BPSK digital communication system using Simulink and MATLAB. Figure 11.16(a) illustrates the Simulink model for the system. The parameters of simulation including bit rate, carrier frequency, and sampling rate are set up by a companion MATLAB m-file. The m-file also computes the theoretical BER and plots simulated and theoretical BER performance. The **Polar Bernoulli source** block generates the polar NRZ signal. The BPSK signal is produced by the **BPSK modulator** block, which multiplies the polar NRZ pulse train with the output of a discrete-time sinusoidal source. AWGN is added to the BPSK signal by using the AWGN channel block illustrated in Figure 10.9(a). At the receiver, the **BPSK demodulator** block multiplies the received signal with the carrier waveform synchronized to the one in the modulator block. The underlying polar NRZ signal is recovered using the correlation detector. The latter is implemented by a discrete-time integrator, which is reset at the beginning of each bit period. The output of the integrator is sampled at the end of each bit period in the bit-rate sampling block.

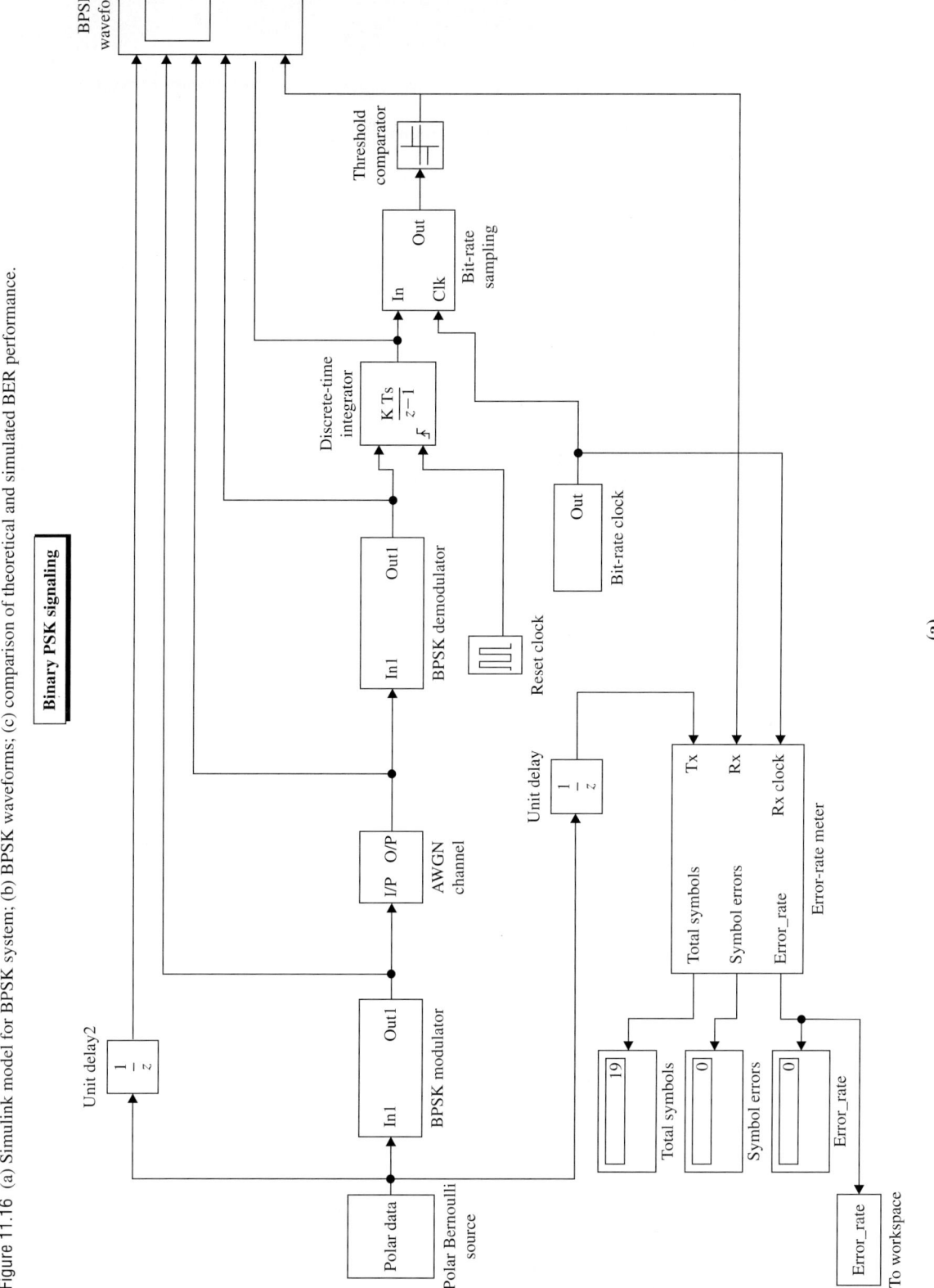

Figure 11.16 (a) Simulink model for BPSK system; (b) BPSK waveforms; (c) comparison of theoretical and simulated BER performance.

(a)

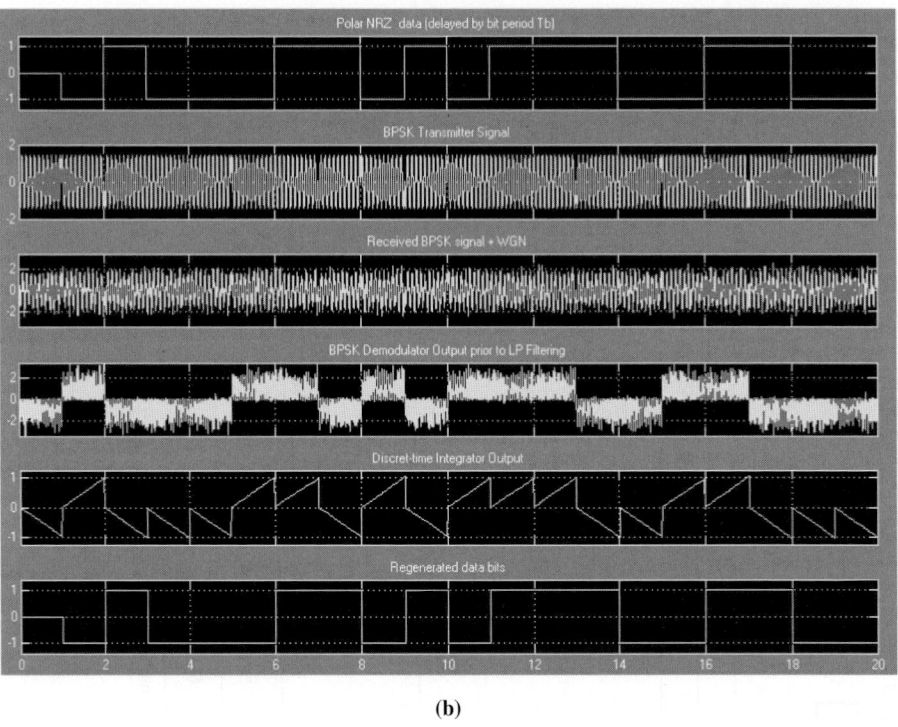

(b)

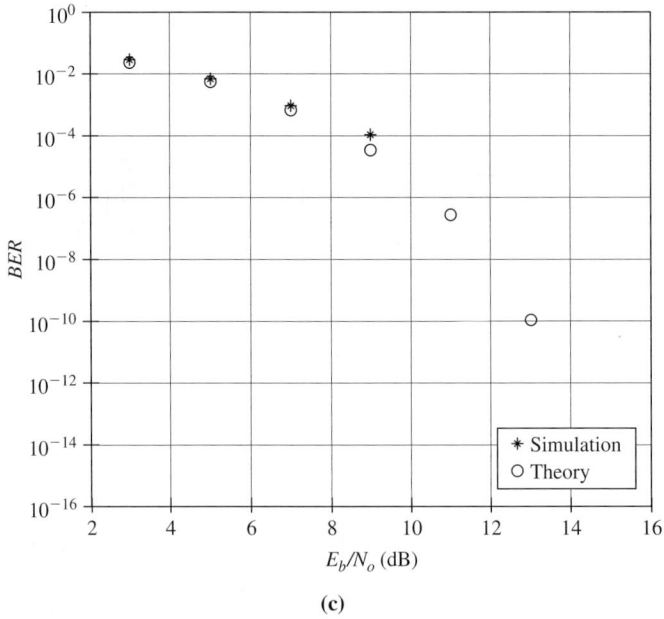

(c)

The threshold comparator block then generates output polar NRZ pulses based on the comparison of received signal samples with the threshold value. The regenerated polar NRZ signal is then compared with the transmitted signal in the Error-rate meter block. The simulated BER value is transmitted to MATLAB workspace to generate the BER performance curve. Figure 11.16(b) displays various waveforms generated using this simulation. Figure 11.16(c) provides a comparison of theoretical and simulated BER performance.

11.4 BINARY FREQUENCY-SHIFT KEYING

Frequency-shift keying (FSK) encodes information bits into the frequency of the carrier waveform. One significant advantage of all FSK systems is that the transmitted signal has a constant envelope. The simplest scheme of this kind is BFSK, where we employ two different frequencies, say $f_1 = f_c + \Delta f/2$ and $f_2 = f_c - \Delta f/2$, to transmit binary data. The two FSK carrier bursts may be expressed as

$$\text{Binary 1: } s_1(t) = A_c\cos(2\pi f_1 t + \phi_1), \quad 0 \le t \le T_b$$
$$\text{Binary 0: } s_2(t) = A_c\cos(2\pi f_2 t + \phi_2), \quad 0 \le t \le T_b \qquad (11.35)$$

Because the frequency deviation $\Delta f = f_1 - f_2$ determines the degree to which we can discriminate between the signal waveforms $s_1(t)$ and $s_2(t)$, we rewrite (11.35) as

$$\text{Binary 1: } s_1(t) = A_c\cos(2\pi f_c t + \pi\Delta f t + \phi_1), \quad 0 \le t \le T_b$$
$$\text{Binary 0: } s_2(t) = A_c\cos(2\pi f_c t - \pi\Delta f t + \phi_2), \quad 0 \le t \le T_b \qquad (11.36)$$

A simple way to generate a BFSK signal is to use two separate oscillators tuned to frequencies f_1 and f_2 and switch between their outputs in accordance with the amplitude of the random data bit during that bit interval. ϕ_1 and ϕ_2 are arbitrary phases of two frequency bursts generated by separate oscillators. Figure 11.17(a) displays the BFSK modulation process. Because there is no requirement for the phase to be continuous in the BFSK signal, it results in discontinuous phase transitions at switching times. This leads to undesirable broadening of the BFSK signal spectrum. Figure 11.17(b) displays the BFSK waveform.

Continuous-phase FSK (CPFSK) avoids these phase discontinuities at symbol switching times because the digital baseband signal modulates the frequency of a single oscillator as shown in Figure 11.18(a). The VCO oscillates at an instantaneous frequency that is linearly proportional to the digital baseband signal $I(t) = \sum_n a_n\Pi\big[(t - nT_b)/T_b\big]$.

From (5.14) and (5.15), the VCO instantaneous frequency is given by

$$f_{inst}(t) = f_c + k_f\sum_n a_n\Pi\big[(t - nT_b)/T_b\big]$$

$$= f_c + \frac{\Delta f}{2}\sum_n a_n\Pi\big[(t - nT_b)/T_b\big]$$

where k_f is frequency sensitivity of the FM modulator in Hz/Volt. We observe that the binary antipodal NRZ pulse train produces the maximum frequency deviation

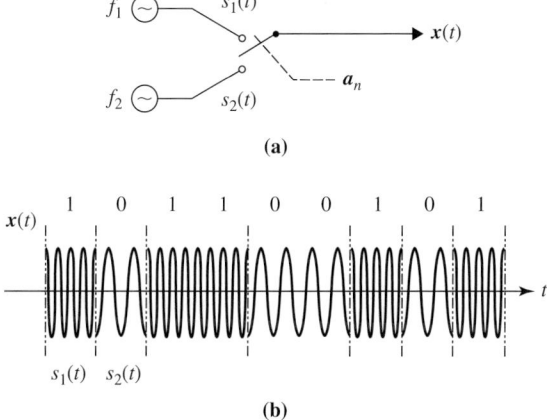

(a)

(b)

Figure 11.17 (a) BFSK modulation; (b) BFSK waveform.

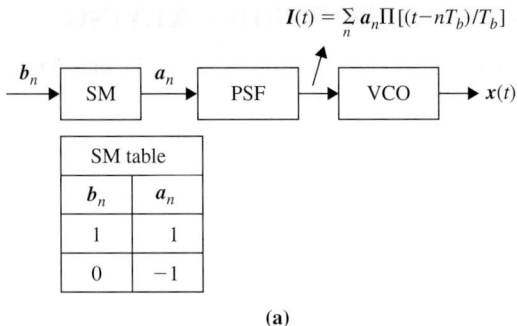

$$I(t) = \sum_n a_n \Pi[(t - nT_b)/T_b]$$

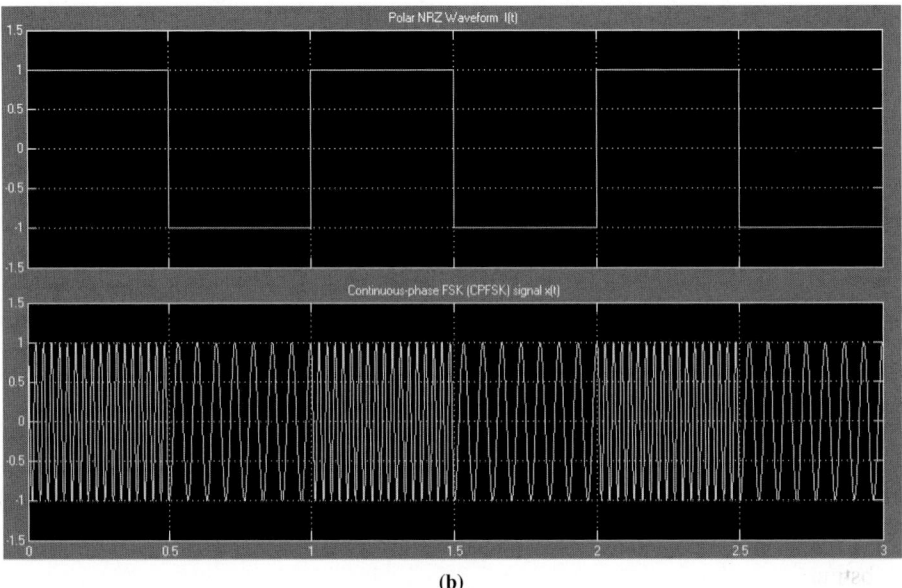

Figure 11.18 (a) CPFSK modulation; (b) CPFSK waveform.

$\Delta f_{\max} = \dfrac{\Delta f}{2}$. The CPFSK waveform sketched in Figure 11.18(b) illustrates the frequency changes at symbol transitions. At these transitions, the phase is continuous as the CPFSK signal shifts from one frequency to another. The CPFSK, therefore, has much lower side-lobe energy than the BFSK.

11.4.1   Orthogonality of BFSK Signals

To facilitate detection of BFSK signals, we want to choose frequencies f_1 and f_2 so that $s_1(t)$ and $s_2(t)$ in (11.36) are orthogonal. We initially consider the case where a single VCO is used to generate two carriers, that is, $\phi_1 = \phi_2 = \phi$. Using the definition of orthogonality from Section 10.3.3, we can write

$$\int_0^{T_b} s_1(t)s_2(t)dt = A_c^2 \int_0^{T_b} \cos(2\pi f_c t + \pi \Delta f t + \phi)\cos(2\pi f_c t - \pi \Delta f t + \phi)dt$$

$$= \frac{A_c^2}{2}\int_0^{T_b} \cos(2\pi \Delta f t)dt + \frac{A_c^2}{2}\int_0^{T_b} \cos(4\pi f_c t + 2\phi)dt \qquad (11.37)$$

The second integral is zero if the carrier frequency f_c is chosen so that it is an integral multiple of the bit rate R_b, that is, $f_c T_b = N$. Therefore,

$$\int_0^{T_b} s_1(t)s_2(t)dt = \frac{A_c^2}{2}T_b\frac{\sin(2\pi\Delta f T_b)}{2\pi\Delta f T_b} = \frac{A_c^2}{2}T_b \text{sinc}(2\Delta f T_b) \tag{11.38}$$

The function $\text{sinc}(2\Delta f T_b)$ in (11.38) is zero when $2\Delta f T_b$ is a nonzero integer. This implies that the frequency separation Δf between BFSK waveforms in (11.36) should be an integer multiple of $1/2T_b$ for orthogonality. That is,

$$\Delta f_{coherent} = \frac{k}{2T_b}, \quad k = 1, 2, \ldots \tag{11.39}$$

The two FSK carriers $s_1(t)$ and $s_2(t)$ with the same phases and satisfying (11.39) are said to be **coherently orthogonal.** We observe from (11.39) that the minimum frequency separation between BFSK frequencies f_1 and f_2 for orthogonality is $1/2T_b$. That is,

$$\text{Coherent FSK signaling: } \Delta f_{\min} = \frac{1}{2T_b} = \frac{R_b}{2} \tag{11.40}$$

The **modulation index** for a BFSK signal is defined as

$$\text{Modulation index } h = \frac{\text{Frequency deviation}}{\text{Bit rate}} = \frac{\Delta f}{T_b} \tag{11.41}$$

Substituting (11.40) into (11.41), the minimum value of h for coherent FSK signaling is given by

$$\text{Coherent FSK signaling: } h_{\min} = 0.5 \tag{11.42}$$

The phases of two FSK bursts $s_1(t)$ and $s_2(t)$ do not have to be same (i.e., $\phi_1 \neq \phi_2$). In this case, it can be shown that BFSK waveforms are orthogonal if frequency separation Δf is an integer multiple of R_b.

$$\Delta f_{noncoherent} = k/T_b, \quad k = 1, 2, \ldots \tag{11.43}$$

We note from (11.43) that for an arbitrary phase relationship between FSK carriers, the minimum carrier spacing for orthogonality is given by

$$\text{Noncoherent FSK signaling: } \Delta f_{\min} = \frac{1}{T_b} = R_b \tag{11.44}$$

This corresponds to $h = 1.0$. Equation (11.44) represents a more conservative approach to the BFSK system design for achieving orthogonality of transmitted waveforms, and is most frequently used in practice. The BFSK system where the spacing between two carrier frequencies is exactly equal to the bit rate R_b is called **Sunde's FSK** after its inventor. Sunde's FSK exhibits a continuous-phase characteristic at bit-switching times, assuming there is no starting phase variation for each bit interval. We will consider Sunde's BFSK for further analysis in this section.

11.4.2 Coherent Demodulation of BFSK Signals

A binary FSK waveform can be viewed as consisting of two interleaved ASK signals with the same amplitude but different carrier frequencies, $f_1 = f_c + \Delta f/2$ and $f_2 = f_c - \Delta f/2$, where $\Delta f = R_b$ is assumed. Because the signal waveforms in (11.36) with this frequency spacing are orthogonal, the interleaved ASK signals can be detected without mutual interference using a coherent demodulator structure displayed in Figure 11.19. As expected, each branch of the demodulator replicates the demodulator structure for ASK signaling in Figure 11.7. Assuming perfect phase estimates by carrier recovery loops, the reference carriers in the upper and lower branches are $\cos(2\pi f_1 t + \phi_1)$ and $\cos(2\pi f_2 t + \phi_2)$, respectively. The received BFSK signal in the presence of noise is given by

$$r(t) = \alpha x(t) + n_i(t), \quad 0 \le t \le T_b \tag{11.45}$$

where $x(t)$ is one of two possible signals $s_1(t)$ and $s_2(t)$ in (11.36). α represents the attenuation introduced by the transmission channel. Again, we assume $\alpha = 1$ without any loss of generality. $n_i(t)$ is AWGN with the double-sided power spectral density of $N_o/2$ W/Hz. The BP filter passes FSK signals without distortion while rejecting out-of-band noise. Assuming $s_1(t)$ is transmitted during the bit interval $0 \le t \le T_b$, the output of the multipliers in the upper and lower branches is

$$\left[s_1(t) + n(t)\right] \times 2\cos(2\pi f_1 t + \phi_1) = A_c \cos(2\pi f_1 t + \phi_1) \times 2\cos(2\pi f_1 t + \phi_1) + n(t) \times 2\cos(2\pi f_1 t + \phi_1)$$

$$= A_c\left[1 + \underbrace{\cos(4\pi f_1 t + 2\phi_1)}_{\text{Filtered out}}\right] + n_c(t)$$

$$\left[s_1(t) + n(t)\right] \times 2\cos(2\pi f_2 t + \phi_2) = A_c \cos(2\pi f_1 t + \phi_1) \times 2\cos(2\pi f_2 t + \phi_2) + n(t) \times 2\cos(2\pi f_2 t + \phi_2)$$

$$= \underbrace{A_c \cos(2\pi f_1 t + \phi_1)] \times 2\cos(2\pi f_2 t + \phi_2)}_{\text{Orthogonal}} + n_c'(t) \tag{11.46}$$

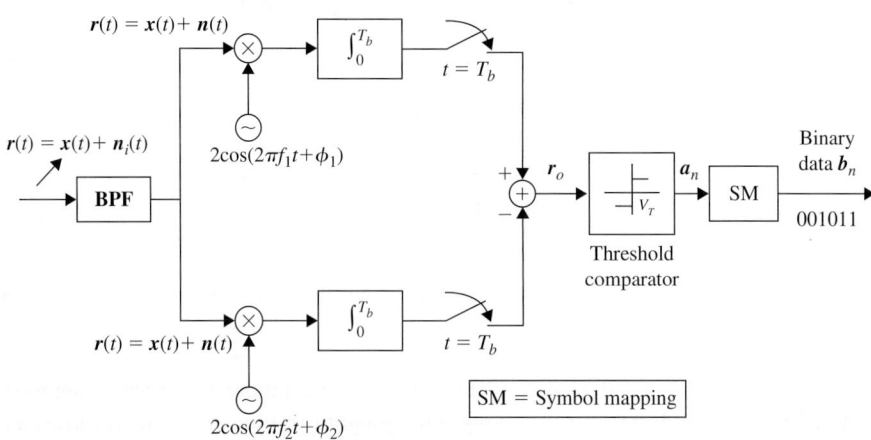

Figure 11.19 Coherent BFSK demodulator.

Similarly, when $s_2(t)$ is transmitted during the bit interval $0 \leq t \leq T_b$, the output of the upper and lower branches is given by

$$\left[s_2(t) + n(t)\right] \times 2\cos(2\pi f_1 t + \phi_1) = A_c\cos(2\pi f_2 t + \phi_2) \times 2\cos(2\pi f_1 t + \phi_1) + n(t) \times 2\cos(2\pi f_1 t + \phi_1)$$

$$= A_c\underbrace{\left[\cos(2\pi f_1 t + \phi_1) \times 2\cos(2\pi f_2 t + \phi_2)\right]}_{\text{Orthogonal}} + n_c(t)$$

$$\left[s_2(t) + n(t)\right] \times 2\cos(2\pi f_2 t + \phi_2) = A_c\cos(2\pi f_2 t + \phi_2) \times 2\cos(2\pi f_2 t + \phi_2) + n(t) \times 2\cos(2\pi f_2 t + \phi_2)$$

$$= A_c\left[1 + \underbrace{\cos(4\pi f_2 t + 2\phi_2)}_{\text{Filtered out}}\right] + n_c'(t) \tag{11.47}$$

where $n_c(t)$ and $n_c'(t)$ are, respectively, the in-phase components of the BP filter output noise $n(t)$ in the upper and lower branches. Both have spectral density of N_o W/Hz. From (11.46) and (11.47), the outputs of integrate-and-dump filters at the sampling instant $t = T_b$ can be expressed as

$$\text{Upper branch:} \quad r_1(T_b) = \begin{cases} A_c T_b + n_1(T_b), & \text{Binary } 1\left(s_1(t) \text{ transmitted}\right) \\ n_1(T_b), & \text{Binary } 0\left(s_2(t) \text{ transmitted}\right) \end{cases} \tag{11.48}$$

$$\text{Lower branch:} \quad r_2(T_b) = \begin{cases} n_2(T_b), & \text{Binary } 1\left(s_1(t) \text{ transmitted}\right) \\ A_c T_b + n_2(T_b), & \text{Binary } 0\left(s_2(t) \text{ transmitted}\right) \end{cases} \tag{11.49}$$

where

$$n_1(T_b) = \int_0^{T_b} n_c(t)dt$$

$$n_2(T_b) = \int_0^{T_b} n_c'(t)dt \tag{11.50}$$

Now

$$\overline{n_1^2(T_b)} = E\left\{\int_0^{T_b}\int_0^{T_b} n_c(t)n_c(u)dtdu\right\} = \int_0^{T_b}\int_0^{T_b} N_o\delta(t - u)dtdu = \int_0^{T_b} N_o du = N_o T_b$$

$$\overline{n_2^2(T_b)} = N_o T_b \tag{11.51}$$

The input $r_o = r_1 - r_2$ to the threshold comparator can be expressed by combining (11.48) and (11.49) as

$$r_o = \begin{cases} A_c T_b + n_o(t), & \text{Binary } 1 \\ -A_c T_b + n_o(t), & \text{Binary } 0 \end{cases} \tag{11.52}$$

where $n_o(t) = n_1(t) - n_2(t)$. The variance of $n_o(t)$ is given by

$$\sigma_o^2 = \overline{n_o^2(t)} = \overline{n_1^2(t)} + \overline{n_2^2(t)} = N_o T_b + N_o T_b = 2N_o T_b \tag{11.53}$$

We observe that r_o is a Gaussian random variable with variance $2N_oT_b$ and mean A_cT_b or $-A_cT_b$ depending on whether a binary 1 or 0 was transmitted. Consequently, the optimum threshold V_T is 0 volts. The comparator declares that a binary 1 was transmitted if r_o is positive, and a binary 0 decision is made if r_o is negative. Therefore,

$$P(\text{error}|s_1 \text{ sent}) = \int_{-\infty}^{0} f_{r_o}(r_o|s_1(t) \text{ was sent})dr_o$$

$$= \frac{1}{\sqrt{2\pi\sigma_o^2}} \int_{-\infty}^{0} e^{-\frac{(r_o - A_cT_b)^2}{2\sigma_o^2}} dr = Q\left(\frac{A_cT_b}{\sigma_o}\right) = Q\left(\sqrt{\frac{E_b}{N_o}}\right) \quad (11.54)$$

where $E_b = \dfrac{A_c^2 T_b}{2}$ is energy per bit. The BER of a coherent BFSK system can now be obtained using (11.16) as

$$BER_{BFSK} = Q\left(\sqrt{\frac{E_b}{N_o}}\right) \quad (11.55)$$

Alternatively, the BER can be calculated by using the constellation diagram for a BFSK system. If we choose the basis functions

$$\phi_1(t) = \sqrt{\frac{2}{T_b}} \cos(2\pi f_1 t + \phi_1)$$

$$\phi_2(t) = \sqrt{\frac{2}{T_b}} \cos(2\pi f_2 t + \phi_2) \quad (11.56)$$

where $\Delta f = R_b$, the binary FSK waveforms in (11.35) can be represented as orthogonal vectors

$$\underline{s}_1 = \left(\sqrt{E_b}, 0\right)$$

$$\underline{s}_2 = \left(0, \sqrt{E_b}\right)$$

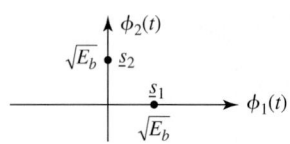

Figure 11.20 BFSK constellation.

in the $\phi_1 - \phi_2$ plane. The signal constellation for binary FSK is shown in Figure 11.20; BFSK is thus orthogonal signaling with $d = \sqrt{2E_b}$. The BER performance of BFSK is, therefore, given from (10.139) as

$$BER_{BFSK} = Q\left(\frac{d}{\sqrt{2N_o}}\right) = Q\left(\sqrt{\frac{E_b}{N_o}}\right) \quad (11.57)$$

Experiment 11.3   *BFSK Simulation and Performance Comparison*

In this experiment, we model a BFSK digital communication system using Simulink and MAT-LAB. Figure 11.21(a) illustrates the Simulink model for the system. The parameters of the simulation including bit rate, FSK frequencies, and sampling rate are set up by a companion MATLAB m-file. The m-file also computes the theoretical BER and plots simulated and theoretical BER performance. The Polar Bernoulli source block in the BFSK modulator block generates the polar NRZ signal. The BFSK modulator consists of a two-way switch fed by two oscillators tuned to

Figure 11.21 (a) BFSK simulation and performance comparison; (b) BFSK signaling waveforms; (c) comparison of theoretical and simulated BER performance.

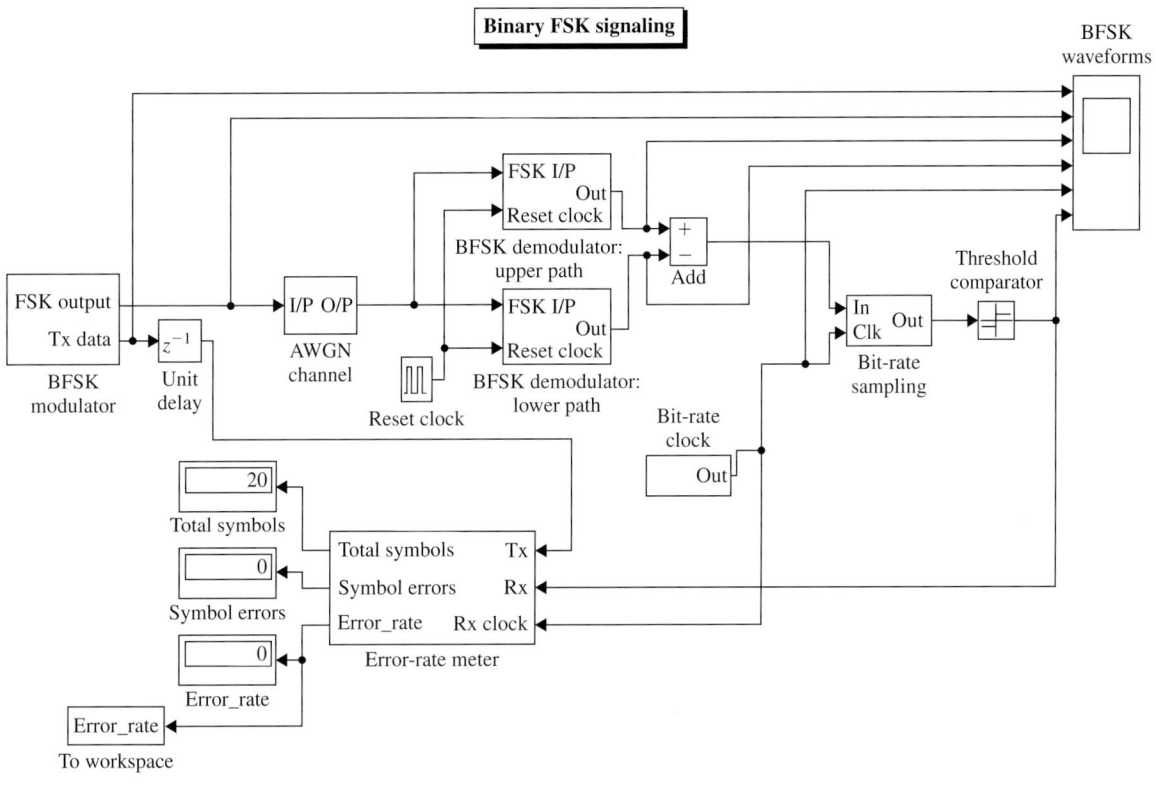

(a)

(b)

(*continued*)

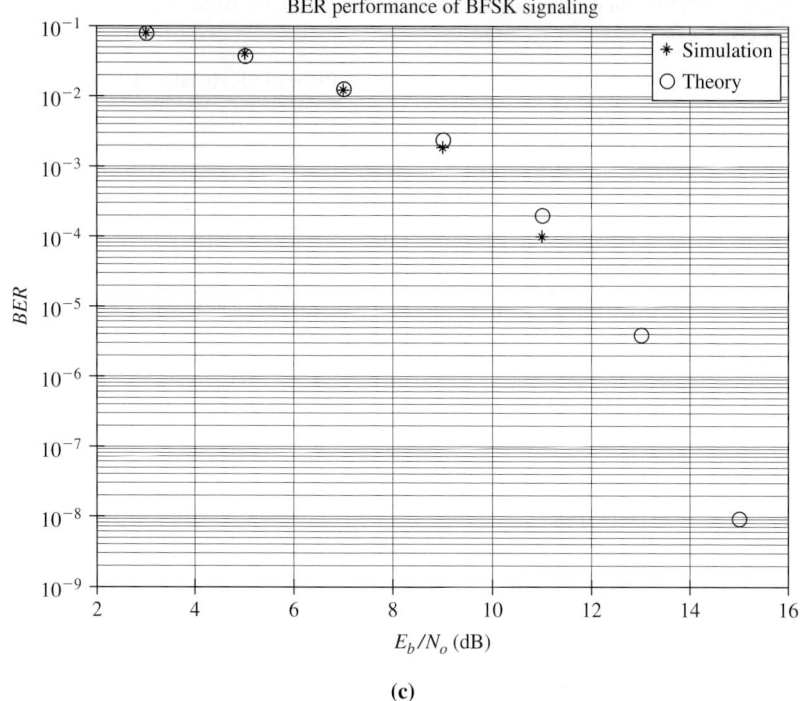

(c)

frequencies 8 and 12 Hz, respectively. The switch is controlled by the polar NRZ signal. If the NRZ pulse amplitude in a bit interval is positive, 12-Hz oscillator output is selected. On the other hand, output is switched to 8 Hz oscillator for the negative NRZ pulse. AWGN is added to the BFSK signal by using the AWGN channel block. The BFSK demodulator processes the received noisy BFSK signal along two branches to recover the underlying polar NRZ signal. The upper and lower branches implement coherent ASK demodulators with carrier frequencies of 12- and 8-Hz, respectively. The output of BFSK demodulator is sampled at the end of each bit period in the bit-rate sampling block. The threshold comparator block then generates output polar NRZ pulses based on the comparison of received signal samples with the threshold value. The regenerated polar NRZ signal is then compared with the transmitted sequence in the Error-rate meter block. The simulated BER value is transmitted to MATLAB workspace to generate the BER performance curve. Figure 11.21(b) displays various waveforms generated using this simulation. Figure 11.21(c) provides a comparison of theoretical and simulated BER performance. ▓░

11.5 DIFFERENTIAL BINARY PHASE-SHIFT KEYING

Although a coherent demodulator yields the best performance in AWGN channels, it may not be the most desirable or robust option for rapidly time-varying channels. In many applications, the following suboptimal approaches, which do not require coherent phase reference, may be used:

- **Differentially coherent demodulator.** Uses the carrier phase of the previous symbol as a phase reference for the demodulation of the current symbol.
- **Noncoherent demodulator.** Recovers the underlying digital pulse train without using the carrier phase information.

The performance of a modulation scheme using either a differential or a noncoherent demodulator is, in general, inferior to the coherent approach. In this section, we will

Table 11.1 Example of Differential Encoding of BPSK Data

Data bits b_n		0	1	1	1	1	0	1	0	1
Differentially encoded bits d_n	1	1	0	1	0	1	1	0	0	1
Transmission symbols a_n	1	1	-1	1	-1	1	1	-1	-1	1
Carrier phase (radians) ψ_n	0	0	π	0	π	0	0	π	π	0

study **differential binary phase-shift keying (DBPSK)** as an example of differential modulation schemes. Differential PSK involves the following two concepts:

- **Differential encoding.** The data are differentially encoded, as discussed in Section 9.2, prior to being mapped into the standard BPSK signals.
- **Differential detection.** The demodulator uses the carrier phase of the previous signaling interval as the phase reference for the demodulation of the current symbol.

A differentially encoded modulator transmits the difference between successive data bits. Differential coding starts with an arbitrary initial bit, say $d_o = 1$. Subsequent differential bits are determined by the data bits b_n according to the rule:

$$d_n = d_{n-1} \oplus b_n \qquad (11.58)$$

The effect is to leave the differential bit d_n unchanged from the previous bit if the incoming bit b_n is 0, and to toggle d_n if b_n is 1. The encoded bit d_n is mapped by the symbol mapping table into polar transmission symbol $a_n \in \mathscr{A}_2 = \{1, -1\}$. Table 11.1 illustrates the encoding process in DBPSK. The first row is a binary data stream and the second row shows the differential encoding of the data. The third row is the sequence of transmission symbols, and the last row displays the resultant carrier phase shifts. Figure 11.22 displays the block diagram of a DBPSK modulator.

The output of a DBPSK modulator is given by

$$x(t) = \sqrt{\frac{2E_b}{T_b}} \sum_n v(t - nT_b)\cos(2\pi f_c t + \psi_n)$$

$$= \sqrt{\frac{2E_b}{T_b}} \sum_n a_n v(t - nT_b)\cos(2\pi f_c t) \qquad (11.59)$$

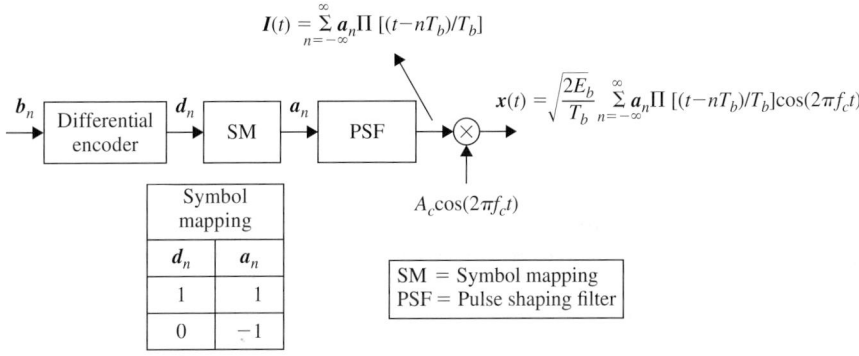

Figure 11.22 DBPSK modulator.

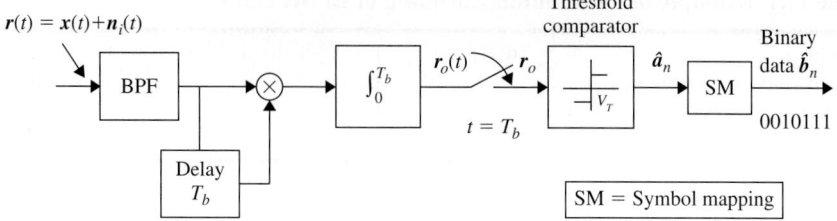

Figure 11.23 DBPSK receiver.

where $a_n \in \mathcal{A}_2 = \{1, -1\}$ are binary random variables representing amplitudes of pulses in the underlying polar pulse train. The carrier frequency f_c is chosen so that it is an integer multiple of the bit rate R_b, that is, $f_c T_b = N$.

The block diagram of a differential PSK receiver is shown in Figure 11.23. It uses the received signal carrier burst from the previous bit interval as the reference carrier for the current bit interval. In the absence of noise, the multiplier output during the nth bit interval is given by

$$x(t) \times x(t - T_b) = \frac{2E_b}{T_b} a_n a_{n-1} \cos[2\pi f_c t] \cos[2\pi f_c (t - T_b)]$$

$$= \frac{E_b}{T_b} a_n a_{n-1} \{\cos(4\pi f_c t) + 1\} \qquad (11.60)$$

The output of the integrate-and-dump filter at the sampling instant $t = nT_b$ is $E_b a_n a_{n-1}$. In the presence of receiver noise, the output of the sampler is

$$r_o = a_n a_{n-1} E_b + n(T_b)$$

where $n(t)$ is non-Gaussian noise. The input sample fed to the threshold comparator is given by

$$r_o = \begin{cases} E_b + n(T_b), & a_n = a_{n-1} \\ -E_b + n(T_b), & a_n \neq a_{n-1} \end{cases} \qquad (11.61)$$

Because r_o exhibits polar symmetry, the threshold voltage should be set at $V_T = 0$. We can now write the following decision rule for decoding the differential bit.

$$r_o > 0 \Rightarrow \hat{a}_n = \hat{a}_{n-1} \Rightarrow \hat{b}_n = 0, \text{ and}$$

$$r_o < 0 \Rightarrow \hat{a}_n \neq \hat{a}_{n-1} \Rightarrow \hat{b}_n = 1$$

Table 11.2 illustrates the decoding process. The first row is differentially encoded bits from Table 11.1. The second row shows the output of the threshold comparator. The

Table 11.2 Example of Differential Decoding of BPSK

Differentially encoded bits d_n	1	1	0	1	0	1	1	0	0	1
Threshold-comparison sign		+	−	−	−	−	+	−	−	−
Decoded differential bits $\hat{d}_n$	1	1	0	1	0	1	1	0	0	1
Regenerated data bits $\hat{b}_n$		0	1	1	1	1	0	1	0	1

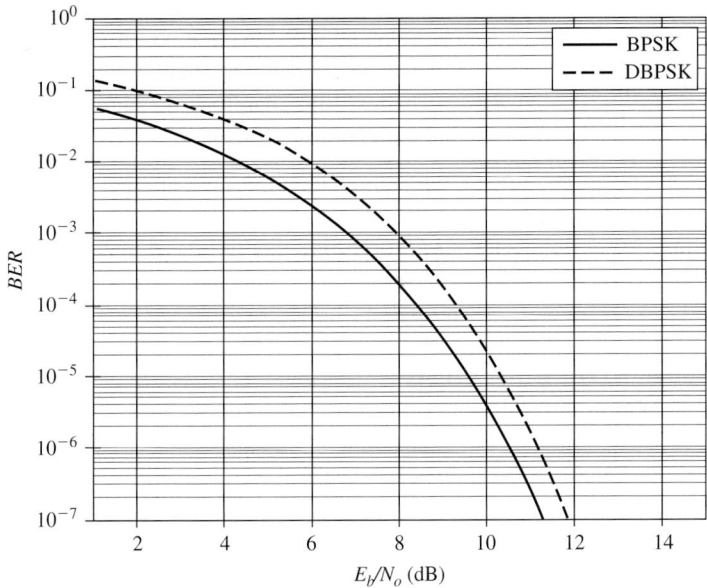

Figure 11.24 BER performance comparison of BPSK and DBPSK.

third row illustrates decoded differential bits at the demodulator. The last row displays the regenerated data bits at the demodulator.

Error Performance

The BER of a DBPSK system is given by[1]

$$BER_{BDPSK} = \frac{1}{2}e^{-\frac{E_b}{N_o}} \tag{11.62}$$

The proof is lengthy because the noise $n(t)$ is not simply Gaussian. The error performance of DBPSK is similar to that of BPSK and QPSK, suffering less than 1dB E_b/N_o penalty as evident from Figure 11.24. DBPSK has about a 2-dB SNR/bit advantage over the noncoherent systems discussed in Section 11.6. With such a good BER performance and no need for carrier recovery circuitry, DBPSK has been an attractive modulation scheme when its wide bandwidth ($2R_b$ Hz) is acceptable.

11.6 NONCOHERENT DEMODULATION OF BINARY DIGITAL CARRIER SIGNALS

Coherent demodulation may neither be desirable nor feasible in many practical applications.

- The propagation delay on some radio channels changes too rapidly to permit accurate tracking of the carrier phase at the demodulator, and noncoherent detection becomes the only viable recourse.

[1] R. Ziemer and W. Tranter, *Principles of Communications: Systems, Modulation, and Noise,* 6th ed. (Hoboken, NJ: John Wiley, 2009).

- Tracking the incoming signal's carrier phase and synchronizing the demodulator to it requires additional hardware complexity with cost and power efficiency ramifications. Consumers prefer the convenience of small handheld communication devices (e.g., cell phones, PDAs) and long battery life. Therefore, the complexity of coherent design is traded away for simplicity and power efficiency.

In a noncoherent demodulator, the demodulator does not attempt to recover and use the carrier phase information. While digital communication is possible without knowing the carrier phase, it will be shown in this section that there is a penalty in the required E_b/N_o in comparison to corresponding coherent demodulators.

11.6.1   Noncoherent Binary ASK

Noncoherent binary ASK is the most widely used signaling technique in optical fiber communication systems. During the bit interval $0 \leq t \leq T_b$, the ASK signal may be expressed using (11.8) as

$$\begin{aligned}
&\text{Binary 1}: s_1(t) = A_c\cos(2\pi f_c t + \phi_o)\\
&\text{Binary 0}: s_2(t) = 0
\end{aligned} \tag{11.63}$$

where ϕ_o represents the phase offset between the modulator and the demodulator. We assume f_c to be an integer multiple of R_b, that is, $f_c T_b = N$. The received BASK signal in the presence of noise is given by

$$r(t) = \alpha x(t) + n_i(t) = \alpha A_c \sum_{n=-\infty}^{\infty} a_n \Pi\big[(t - nT_b)/T_b\big]\cos(2\pi f_c t + \phi_o) + n_i(t) \tag{11.64}$$

where $a_n \in \mathscr{A}_2 = \{1, 0\}$ are binary random variables representing amplitudes of pulses in the unipolar NRZ pulse train as discussed in Section 11.1. α represents the attenuation introduced by the transmission channel. Again, we assume $\alpha = 1$ without any loss of generality. $n_i(t)$ is AWGN with the double-sided power spectral density of $N_o/2$ W/Hz.

The design of a noncoherent ASK demodulator follows the concept of envelope detection for the demodulation of AM signals discussed in Section 4.3.2. A properly designed envelope detector attempts to recover the underlying baseband pulse train by tracking the amplitude or envelope of the input carrier signal embedded in the receiver noise. A noncoherent ASK receiver consists of a BP filter followed by an envelope detector as shown in Figure 11.25. The BP filter centered at frequency f_c passes the ASK signal without distortion while rejecting out-of-band noise. The input to the envelope detector during the bit interval $0 \leq t \leq T_b$ is given by

$$r_1(t) = \begin{cases} A_c\cos(2\pi f_c t + \phi_o) + n(t), & \text{Binary 1}\\ n(t), & \text{Binary 0} \end{cases} \tag{11.65}$$

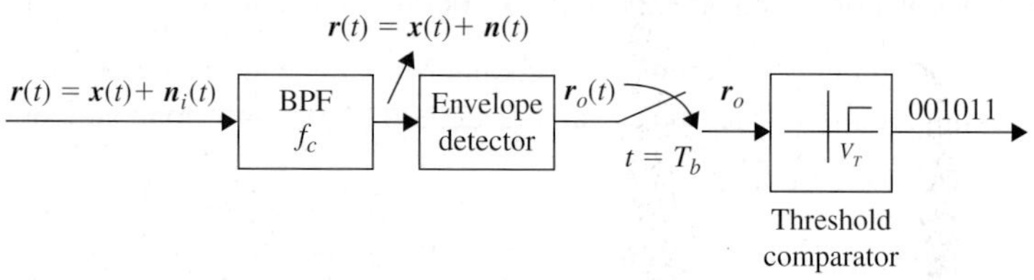

Figure 11.25 Noncoherent ASK receiver.

The narrowband Gaussian noise $n(t)$ at the envelope detector input can be expanded into its direct and quadrature components as follows:

$$n(t) = n_c(t)\cos(2\pi f_c t + \phi_o) - n_s(t)\sin(2\pi f_c t + \phi_o) \qquad (11.66)$$

where $n_c(t)$ and $n_s(t)$ are LP Gaussian noise processes with mean zero and variance $2N_o B$ as discussed in Section 6.12.1. The envelope detector output $r_o(t)$ is sampled and compared with a threshold V_T. The comparator decides $s_1(t)$ was transmitted if the output of the sampler $r_o > V_T$ and $s_2(t)$ was transmitted if $r_o < V_T$.

We now derive the statistics of the sampler output r_o. When $s_2(t)$ is transmitted, the input $r_1(t)$ to the envelope detector consists of the narrowband Gaussian noise as stated in (11.65). From Section 6.12.2, the conditional pdf of the envelope r_o has Rayleigh distribution and is given by

$$f_{r_o}(r_o|s_2) = \begin{cases} \dfrac{r_o}{\sigma^2} e^{-\frac{r_o^2}{2\sigma^2}}, & r_o \geq 0 \\ 0, & r_o < 0 \end{cases} \qquad (11.67)$$

where σ^2 is variance of noise at the output of the BP filter. It is given by

$$\sigma^2 = \frac{N_o}{2}2B_N = N_o B_N \qquad (11.68)$$

where B_N equals the noise bandwidth of the BP filter. Also if $s_1(t)$ was transmitted, the input $r_1(t)$ to the envelope detector consists of a sine wave of peak amplitude A_c and narrowband Gaussian noise $n(t)$ as stated in (11.65). From Section 6.12.2, the conditional pdf of envelope r_o has a Rician distribution and is given by

$$f_{r_o}(r_o|s_1) = \begin{cases} \dfrac{r_o}{\sigma^2} e^{-\frac{r_o^2 + A_c^2}{2\sigma^2}} I_0\left(\dfrac{r_o A_c}{\sigma^2}\right), & r_o \geq 0 \\ 0, & r_o < 0 \end{cases} \qquad (11.69)$$

BER is minimized by choosing the optimum threshold value. For the case of high SNR ($A_c/\sigma \gg 1$), which is the usual mode of operation for a noncoherent demodulator, the point of intersection of two conditional pdfs in Figure 11.26 defines the

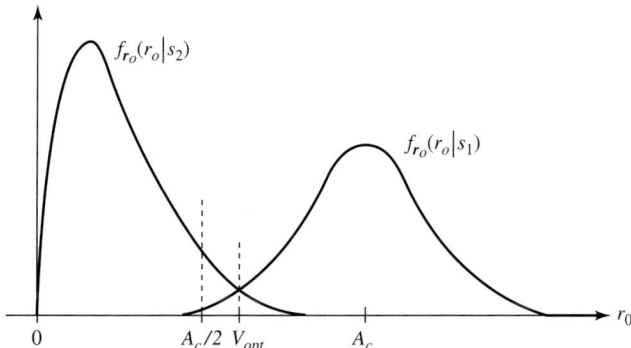

Figure 11.26 Optimum threshold definition.

optimum threshold. It is given by $V_{opt} \sim A_c/2$. The modified Bessel function $I_o\left(\dfrac{r_o A_c}{\sigma^2}\right)$ for $A_c/\sigma \gg 1$ can be approximated by

$$I_o\left(\frac{r_o A_c}{\sigma^2}\right) = \frac{e^{r_o A_c/\sigma^2}}{\sqrt{2\pi r_o A_c/\sigma^2}} \tag{11.70}$$

From Figure 11.26, we can write following expression for $P(\text{error}|s_1 \text{ sent})$:

$$P(\text{error}|s_1 \text{ sent}) = \int_0^{V_T} f_{r_o}(r_o|s_1)dr_o = \int_0^{A_c/2} \frac{r_o}{\sigma^2} e^{-\frac{r_o^2 + A_c^2}{2\sigma^2}} I_o\left(\frac{r_o A_c}{\sigma^2}\right)dr_o$$

$$= \int_0^{A_c/2} \frac{r_o}{\sigma^2} e^{-\frac{r_o^2 + A_c^2}{2\sigma^2}} \frac{e^{r_o A_c/\sigma^2}}{\sqrt{2\pi r_o A_c/\sigma^2}} dr_o \tag{11.71}$$

Because $(A_c/\sigma \gg 1)$, the integrand in (11.71) is negligible except for values of r_o in the vicinity of A_c. Therefore, the lower limit in (11.71) can be extended to $-\infty$, and $\sqrt{\dfrac{r_o}{2\pi A_c \sigma^2}}$ can be replaced by $\sqrt{\dfrac{1}{2\pi\sigma^2}}$ without significant error. This yields

$$\int_0^{V_T} f_{r_o}(r_o|s_1)dr_o \approx \frac{1}{\sqrt{2\pi\sigma^2}} \int_{-\infty}^{A_c/2} e^{-\frac{(r_o - A_c)^2}{2\sigma^2}} dr_o = Q\left(\frac{A_c}{2\sigma}\right) \tag{11.72}$$

Similarly, we can write the following expression for $P(\text{error}|s_2 \text{ sent})$ from Figure 11.26 as

$$P(\text{error}|s_2 \text{ sent}) = \int_{A_c/2}^{\infty} f_{r_o}(r_o|s_2)dr_o = \int_{A_c/2}^{\infty} \frac{r_o}{\sigma^2} e^{-\frac{r_o^2}{2\sigma^2}} dr_o = e^{-\frac{A_c^2}{8\sigma^2}} \tag{11.73}$$

Substituting (11.72) and (11.73) into (11.16) yields

$$BER = \frac{1}{2}Q\left(\frac{A_c}{2\sigma}\right) + \frac{1}{2}e^{-\frac{A_c^2}{8\sigma^2}} \tag{11.74}$$

For $x \gg 1$, using the approximation for the Q function

$$Q(x) \approx e^{-x^2/2}/\sqrt{2\pi x^2}$$

the first term in (11.74) can be written as

$$\frac{1}{2}Q\left(\frac{A_c}{2\sigma}\right) \approx \frac{1}{\sqrt{2\pi(A_c/\sigma)}} e^{-\frac{A_c^2}{8\sigma^2}}$$

Consequently, under high SNR conditions $(A_c/\sigma \gg 1)$, the second term in the (11.74) dominates. Therefore, the BER for the noncoherent ASK signaling can be approximated as

$$BER \approx \frac{1}{2}e^{-\frac{A_c^2}{8\sigma^2}}, \quad A_c/\sigma \gg 1 \tag{11.75}$$

Although the null-to-null bandwidth of the ASK signal is $2R_b$, it is appropriate to choose the noise-equivalent bandwidth for the BP filter $B_N = R_b$. Substituting (11.68) into (11.75), the BER achievable with noncoherent ASK signaling is given by

$$BER_{N-BASK} \approx \frac{1}{2}e^{-\frac{A_c^2}{8\sigma^2}} = \frac{1}{2}e^{-\frac{A_c^2}{8N_oR_b}} = \frac{1}{2}e^{-\frac{E_b}{2N_o}} \tag{11.76}$$

where the average energy per bit from (11.20) is $E_b = \dfrac{A_c^2T_b}{4}$.

11.6.2 Noncoherent Binary FSK

As binary FSK can be viewed as consisting of two interleaved ASK signals with the same carrier amplitude A_c but different carrier frequencies, $f_1 = f_c + \Delta f/2$ and $f_2 = f_c - \Delta f/2$, noncoherent demodulation can be implemented with a pair of BP filters and envelope detectors, as shown in Figure 11.27. The frequencies f_1 and f_2 are selected so that spacing $\Delta f = R_b$ (Sunde's FSK). This ensures that the BPFs effectively separate the two frequencies and that the two narrowband noise waveforms are uncorrelated.

The BFSK signal at the receiver in the presence of noise is given by

$$r(t) = \alpha s(t) + n_i(t), \qquad 0 \le t \le T_b \tag{11.77}$$

where $s(t)$ is one of two possible signals $s_1(t)$ and $s_2(t)$ in (11.36). α represents the attenuation introduced by the transmission channel. Again, we assume $\alpha = 1$ without any loss of generality. $n_i(t)$ is AWGN with the double-sided power spectral density of $N_o/2$ W/Hz. We shall now develop the statistics of envelope detector outputs in upper and lower branches.

Binary 1: $s_1(t)$ Transmitted

The input to the envelope detector in the upper branch consists of a carrier burst at frequency f_1 plus narrowband Gaussian noise $n_1(t)$. From Section 6.12.2, the conditional pdf of the envelope detector output sample r_1 has a Rician distribution given by

$$f_{r_1}(r_1|s_1) = \begin{cases} \dfrac{r_1}{\sigma^2}e^{-\frac{r_1^2+A_c^2}{2\sigma^2}} I_o\left(\dfrac{r_1A_c}{\sigma^2}\right), & r_1 \ge 0 \\ 0, & r_1 < 0 \end{cases} \tag{11.78}$$

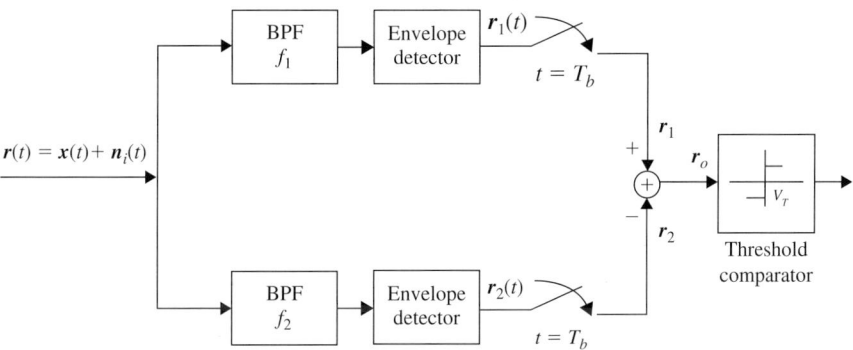

Figure 11.27 Noncoherent FSK demodulator.

The input to the envelope detector in the lower branch consists of narrowband Gaussian noise $n_2(t)$ From Section 6.12.2, the conditional pdf of the envelope detector output sample r_2 is Raleigh distributed.

$$f_{r_2}(r_2|s_1) = \begin{cases} \dfrac{r_2}{\sigma^2}e^{-\frac{r_2^2}{2\sigma^2}}, & r_2 \geq 0 \\ 0, & r_2 < 0 \end{cases} \tag{11.79}$$

Binary 0: $s_2(t)$ Transmitted

The input to the envelope detector in the lower branch consists of a carrier burst of frequency f_2 (i.e., $s_2(t)$) plus narrowband Gaussian noise $n_2(t)$. The conditional pdf of the envelope detector output sample r_2 has a Rician distribution given by

$$f_{r_2}(r_2|s_2) = \begin{cases} \dfrac{r_2}{\sigma^2}e^{-\frac{r_2^2+A_c^2}{2\sigma^2}}I_0\left(\dfrac{r_2A_c}{\sigma^2}\right), & r_2 \geq 0 \\ 0, & r_2 < 0 \end{cases} \tag{11.80}$$

The input to the envelope detector in the upper branch consists of narrowband Gaussian noise $n_1(t)$. The conditional pdf of the envelope detector output sample r_1 is Raleigh distributed.

$$f_{r_1}(r_1|s_2) = \begin{cases} \dfrac{r_1}{\sigma^2}e^{-\frac{r_1^2}{2\sigma^2}}, & r_1 \geq 0 \\ 0, & r_1 < 0 \end{cases} \tag{11.81}$$

In Equations (11.78) through (11.81), σ^2 is the variance of narrowband Gaussian noise processes $n_1(t)$ and $n_2(t)$. It is given by

$$\sigma^2 = \frac{N_o}{2}2B_N = N_oB_N \tag{11.82}$$

where B_N = noise-equivalent bandwidth of BP filters in Figure 11.27.

Error Performance

When $s_2(t)$ is transmitted, the demodulator makes an error whenever the envelope sample obtained from the upper channel r_1 (due to noise alone) exceeds r_2 obtained from the lower channel (due to signal plus noise).

$$P_e = P\{r_1 > r_2|s_2\} \tag{11.83}$$

Thus, the probability of this error can be obtained by integrating $f_{r_1}(r_1|s_2)$ with respect to r_1 from r_2 to infinity, then averaging over all possible values of r_2.

$$BER = \int_0^\infty f_{r_2}(r_2|s_2)\left[\int_{r_2}^\infty f_{r_1}(r_1|s_2)dr_1\right]dr_2$$

$$= \int_0^\infty \frac{r_2}{\sigma^2}e^{-\frac{r_2^2+A_c^2}{2\sigma^2}}I_0\left(\frac{r_2A_c}{\sigma^2}\right)\left[\int_{r_2}^\infty \frac{r_1}{\sigma^2}e^{-\frac{r_1^2}{2\sigma^2}}dr_1\right]dr_2 \tag{11.84}$$

The inner integral equals $e^{-\frac{r_2^2}{2\sigma^2}}$. Substituting into (11.84), we obtain

$$BER = e^{-\frac{A_c^2}{2\sigma^2}} \int_0^\infty \frac{r_2}{\sigma^2} e^{-\frac{r_2^2}{\sigma^2}} I_0\left(\frac{r_2 A_c}{\sigma^2}\right) dr_2 \qquad (11.85)$$

The BER for the noncoherent FSK signaling, using the integral in Appendix A, can now be written as

$$BER_{N-BFSK} = \frac{1}{2} e^{-\frac{A_c^2}{4\sigma^2}} \qquad (11.86)$$

Although the null-to-null bandwidth of an FSK signal is $3R_b$ as discussed in Section 11.10, it is appropriate to choose the noise-equivalent bandwidth for the BP filter $B_N = R_b$. Substituting (11.82) into (11.86), the BER achievable with noncoherent FSK signaling is given by

$$BER_{N-BFSK} = \frac{1}{2} e^{-\frac{A_c^2}{4N_o B_N}} = \frac{1}{2} e^{-\frac{A_c^2}{4N_o R_b}} = \frac{1}{2} e^{-\frac{E_b}{2N_o}} \qquad (11.87)$$

where the average energy per bit $E_b = \frac{A_c^2 T_b}{2}$. A comparison of (11.87) and (11.76) indicates that the same value of SNR/bit is required in both noncoherent BASK and BFSK schemes for a given BER performance. However, BFSK requires 3 dB less carrier level to deliver the same average energy per bit. Noncoherent BFSK is much more rugged than BASK in a hostile environment, and so it is popular in low bit-rate modem applications. Figure 11.28 displays a BER performance comparison of various coherent and noncoherent binary carrier modulation schemes. As observed in Section 11.5, noncoherent schemes

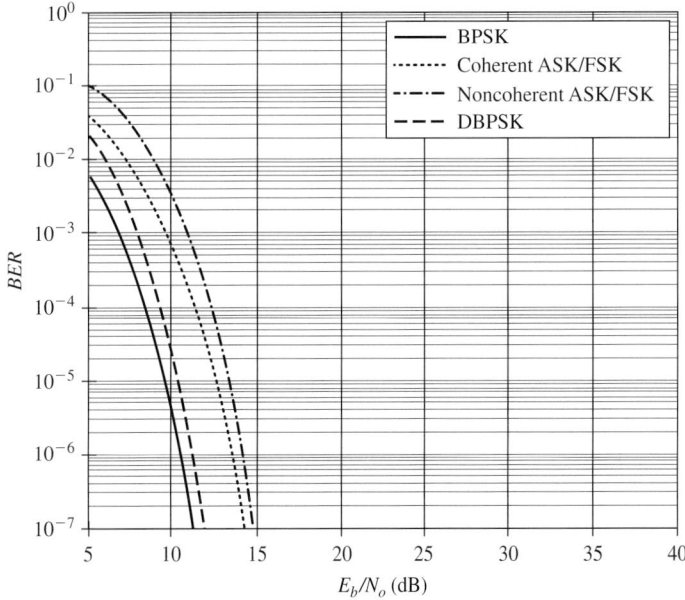

Figure 11.28 BER performance comparison of coherent and noncoherent binary carrier modulation schemes.

suffer approximately a 1-dB penalty when compared to coherent implementations. Thus noncoherent and differential schemes offer very attractive alternatives in many applications where the cost and equipment complexity may be traded for performance.

Example 11.3

Compare the SNR/bit and average power P_{av} required at the demodulator to maintain a $BER = 10^{-6}$ using BPSK, DBPSK, coherent BFSK, and noncoherent BFSK signaling schemes for data transmission over a radio channel at 56 kbps. Assume that the channel adds white Gaussian noise with power spectral density $N_o = 10^{-10}$ W/Hz.

Solution

From Table 6.1, $Q(x) = 10^{-6}$ if $x = 4.75$
For BPSK,

$$BER_{BPSK} = Q\left(\sqrt{\frac{2E_b}{N_o}}\right)$$

$\sqrt{\dfrac{2E_b}{N_o}} = 4.75$. This implies that SNR/bit $= \dfrac{E_b}{N_o} = \dfrac{4.75^2}{2} = 11.28 = 10.53$ dB

Also, $E_b = \dfrac{(4.75)^2}{2} \times 10^{-10} = 1.128 \times 10^{-9}$

For DBPSK,

$$BER_{DBPSK} = \frac{1}{2}e^{-\frac{E_b}{N_o}}$$

Taking the natural log of both sides, we get

$$\log_e 10^{-6} = \log_e \frac{1}{2} - \frac{E_b}{N_o}$$

$$-13.815 = -0.693 - \frac{E_b}{N_o}$$

$$\frac{E_b}{N_o} = 13.122$$

That is, SNR/bit $= \dfrac{E_b}{N_o} = 13.122 = 11.18$ dB

Also, $E_b = 13.122 \times 10^{-10} = 1.3122 \times 10^{-9}$
For coherent BFSK,

$$BER_{BFSK} = Q\left(\sqrt{\frac{E_b}{N_o}}\right)$$

$\sqrt{\dfrac{E_b}{N_o}} = 4.75$. This implies that SNR/bit $= \dfrac{E_b}{N_o} = 4.75^2 = 22.56 = 13.53$ dB

Also, $E_b = (4.75)^2 \times 10^{-10} = 2.256 \times 10^{-9}$
For noncoherent BFSK,

$$BER_{N-BFSK} = \frac{1}{2}e^{-\frac{E_b}{2N_o}}$$

Taking the natural log of both sides, we get

$$\log_e 10^{-6} = \log_e \frac{1}{2} - \frac{E_b}{2N_o}$$

$$-13.815 = -0.693 - \frac{E_b}{2N_o}$$

$$\frac{E_b}{2N_o} = 13.122$$

That is, SNR/bit $= \dfrac{E_b}{N_o} = 2 \times 13.122 = 26.244 = 14.19$ dB

Also, $E_b = 26.244 \times 10^{-10} = 2.644 \times 10^{-9}$

Average power $P_{\text{av}} = \dfrac{E_b}{T_b} = E_b R_b$.

BPSK: $P_{\text{av}} = 1.128 \times 10^{-9} \times 56 \times 10^3 = 63.17\ \mu\text{W} = -12$ dBm
DBPSK: $P_{\text{av}} = 1.3122 \times 10^{-9} \times 56 \times 10^3 = 73.48\ \mu\text{W} = -11.34$ dBm
BFSK: $P_{\text{av}} = 2.256 \times 10^{-9} \times 56 \times 10^3 = 126.34\ \mu\text{W} = -9$ dBm
Noncoherent BFSK: $P_{\text{av}} = 2.644 \times 10^{-9} \times 56 \times 10^3 = 148.06\ \mu\text{W} = -8.3$ dBm

Modulation Scheme	SNR/bit (dB)	Average Power $P_{\text{av}}\ \mu$W (dBm)
BPSK	10.53	63.17 (-12)
DBPSK	11.18	73.48 (-11.34)
BFSK	13.53	126.34 (-9)
Noncoherent BFSK	14.19	148.06 (-8.3)

11.7   QUADRATURE MODULATION SCHEMES

In BPSK the phase of the carrier burst is shifted 0 or 180 degrees every bit period, depending on the information bit being a 1 or 0. Thus each modulated carrier pulse transmits 1 bit of information. If, on the other hand, the modulation scheme can use phase shifts of 45, 135, 225, or 315 degrees, each modulated carrier pulse transmits two bits of information. This technique is called **quadrature phase-shift keying (QPSK).** Using QPSK, we can *double* the data rate when compared to BPSK over a channel of the same bandwidth. QPSK is one of the modulation methods in the family known as **quadrature modulation schemes** that are popular in satellite, cellular, and telco dial-up/cable modem applications.

Suppose we have an information source that is generating M-ary random symbols at the rate of $2D$ symbols per second. We split the original symbol stream into two sequences that consist of odd and even symbols, say, a_n^I and a_n^Q, respectively. The arrival rate of sequences $\{a_n^I\}$ and $\{a_n^Q\}$ therefore, is D symbols per second.

Let the sequence $\{a_n^I\}$ modulate in-phase carrier $A_c \cos(2\pi f_c t)$ to produce the signal

$$A_c \sum_{n=-\infty}^{\infty} a_n^I v(t - nT)\cos(2\pi f_c t) = A_c I(t)\cos(2\pi f_c t) \qquad (11.88)$$

where

$$I(t) = \sum_{n=-\infty}^{\infty} a_n^I v(t - nT) \tag{11.89}$$

$\dfrac{v(t)}{\sqrt{T}}$ is a unit energy pulse of the symbol duration $T = 1/D$ seconds. As an example, $v(t)$ is a rectangular pulse, that is, $v(t) = \prod (t/T)$. Because $\{a_n^I\}$ are M-ary random variables, $I(t)$ is a random pulse train. The signal in (11.88) is identical to the BPSK signal in (11.26) if $\{a_n^I\}$ is a polar binary symbol sequence. Similarly, let the sequence $\{a_n^Q\}$ modulate the quadrature carrier $A_c \sin(2\pi f_c t)$ to produce the signal

$$A_c \sum_{n=-\infty}^{\infty} a_n^Q w(t - nT) \sin(2\pi f_c t) = A_c Q(t) \sin(2\pi f_c t) \tag{11.90}$$

where

$$Q(t) = \sum_{n=-\infty}^{\infty} a_n^Q w(t - nT) \tag{11.91}$$

This modulated signal will also have its power located within the same frequency band of the BP channel. Because $\{a_n^Q\}$ are M-ary random variables, $Q(t)$ is a random pulse train, where $\dfrac{w(t)}{\sqrt{T}}$ is a unit energy pulse of width T seconds. The composite modulated signal $x(t)$ is now obtained by combining the in-phase and quadrature components in (11.88) and (11.90) as shown in Figure 11.29.

$$\begin{aligned} x(t) &= A_c\big[I(t)\cos(2\pi f_c t) - Q(t)\sin(2\pi f_c t)\big] \\ &= A_c \sum_{n=-\infty}^{\infty} \big[a_n^I v(t - nT)\cos(2\pi f_c t) - a_n^Q w(t - nT)\sin(2\pi f_c t)\big] \end{aligned} \tag{11.92}$$

Equation (11.92) represents a quadrature multiplexed signal similar in concept to that discussed in Section 4.7. The composite BP signal will pass through the linear BP channel without mutual interference as long as the orthogonality of carriers is maintained.

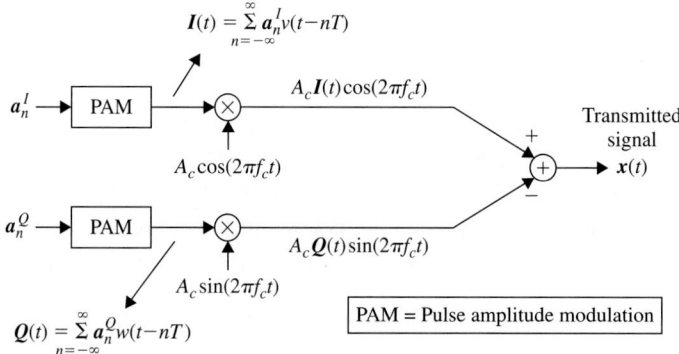

Figure 11.29 Quadrature modulation scheme.

11.7.1 Demodulation of Quadrature-Modulated Signals

Because the in-phase and quadrature pulse trains $I(t)$ and $Q(t)$ modulate orthogonal carriers $\cos(2\pi f_c t)$ and $\sin(2\pi f_c t)$, respectively, they can be recovered from the composite signal $x(t)$ by coherent demodulation as shown in Figure 11.30. By multiplying $x(t)$ with $2\cos(2\pi f_c t)$ and then LP filtering the resulting signal, we recover the in-phase component $I(t)$ as shown:

$$
\begin{aligned}
x(t) \times 2\cos(2\pi f_c t) &= A_c\{I(t)\cos(2\pi f_c t) - Q(t)\sin(2\pi f_c t)\} \times 2\cos(2\pi f_c t) \\
&= 2A_c I(t)\cos^2(2\pi f_c t) - 2A_c Q(t)\sin(2\pi f_c t)\cos(2\pi f_c t) \\
&= A_c I(t)\big[1 + \cos(4\pi f_c t)\big] - A_c Q(t)\sin(4\pi f_c t) \\
&= A_c I(t) + \text{double frequency } (2f_c) \text{ terms} \qquad (11.93)
\end{aligned}
$$

$I(t)$ is the baseband M-ary PAM pulse train from which the M-ary sequence $\{a_n^I\}$ is detected.

Similarly, the M-ary sequence $\{a_n^Q\}$ is recovered from the M-ary PAM quadrature component $Q(t)$ obtained by multiplying $x(t)$ with $2\sin(2\pi f_c t)$ and then LP filtering the output. Thus, a quadrature modulation scheme is a two-dimensional signaling system that effectively doubles the symbol rate achievable ($2D$ versus D symbols/sec) over a BP channel.

11.7.2 QPSK

QPSK is a quadrature modulation scheme: each orthogonal carrier is modulated by a statistically independent binary polar NRZ pulse train. QPSK is the most common form of phase-shift keying. The block diagram of a QPSK modulator, illustrated in Figure 11.31, is a simplification of the generic implementation in Figure 11.29. Binary data arriving at rate R_b is split by a serial-to-parallel converter into two data streams, one containing even bits $\{b_{2n}\}$ and other odd bits $\{b_{2n+1}\}$. The symbol mapping tables in

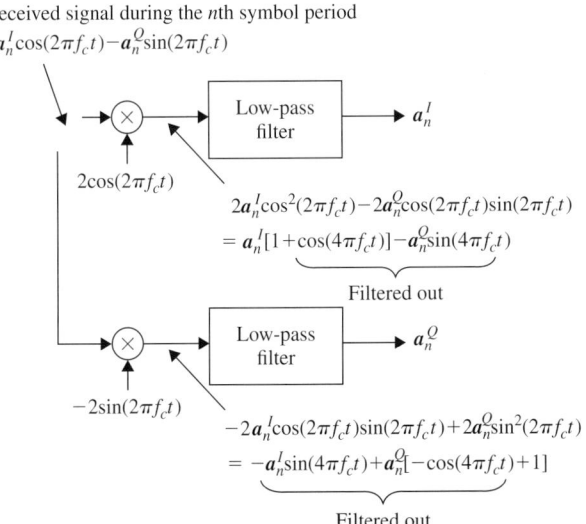

Figure 11.30 Quadrature demodulation of the received signal during nth symbol period.

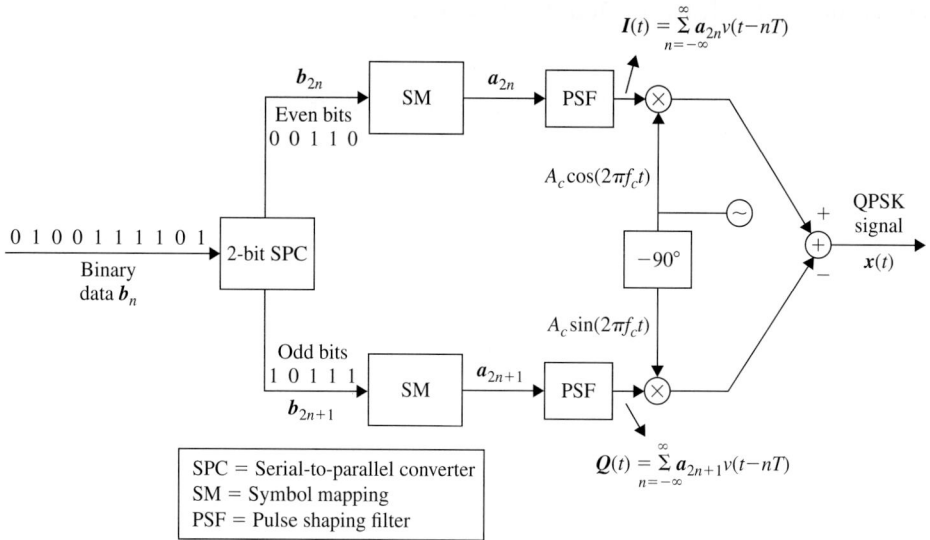

Figure 11.31   QPSK modulator.

the upper and lower branches of the modulator encode even and odd bits into polar transmission symbols $\{a_{2n}\}$ and $\{a_{2n+1}\}$, respectively. The output of the pulse shaping filter in the upper branch is a binary polar NRZ pulse train $I(t)$ that modulates the in-phase carrier $A_c \cos(2\pi f_c t)$. Similarly, a binary polar NRZ pulse train $Q(t)$ generated by the pulse shaping filter in the lower branch modulates the quadrature carrier $A_c \sin(2\pi f_c t)$. The QPSK signal $x(t)$ is now obtained by combinning the in-phase and quadrature components. The QPSK signal can be expressed using (11.92) as

$$x(t) = A_c\big[I(t)\cos(2\pi f_c t) - Q(t)\sin(2\pi f_c t)\big] \tag{11.94}$$

where

$$I(t) = \sum_{n=-\infty}^{\infty} a_{2n} v(t - nT)$$

$$Q(t) = \sum_{n=-\infty}^{\infty} a_{2n+1} v(t - nT) \tag{11.95}$$

We assume that $v(t)/\sqrt{T}$ is a unit-energy pulse in (11.95). Figure 11.32 illustrates QPSK modulation waveforms. We observe $180°$ phase transitions at $t = 4T_b$ (i.e., $2T$) and $6T_b$ (i.e., $3T$) in the QPSK signal when polar transmission symbols change from $(1, 1)$ to $(-1, -1)$ and vice versa.

Without loss of generality, we consider the carrier-modulated pulse during the first symbol interval. It is given from (11.94) and (11.95) as

$$s(t) = A_c v(t)\big[a_0 \cos(2\pi f_c t) - a_1 \sin(2\pi f_c t)\big], \quad 0 \le t \le T \tag{11.96}$$

Using the symbol mapping in Table 11.3, (11.96) can be expressed in the amplitude and phase form as

$$s(t) = A_c v(t)\cos(2\pi f_c t + \psi_0), \quad 0 \le t \le T \tag{11.97}$$

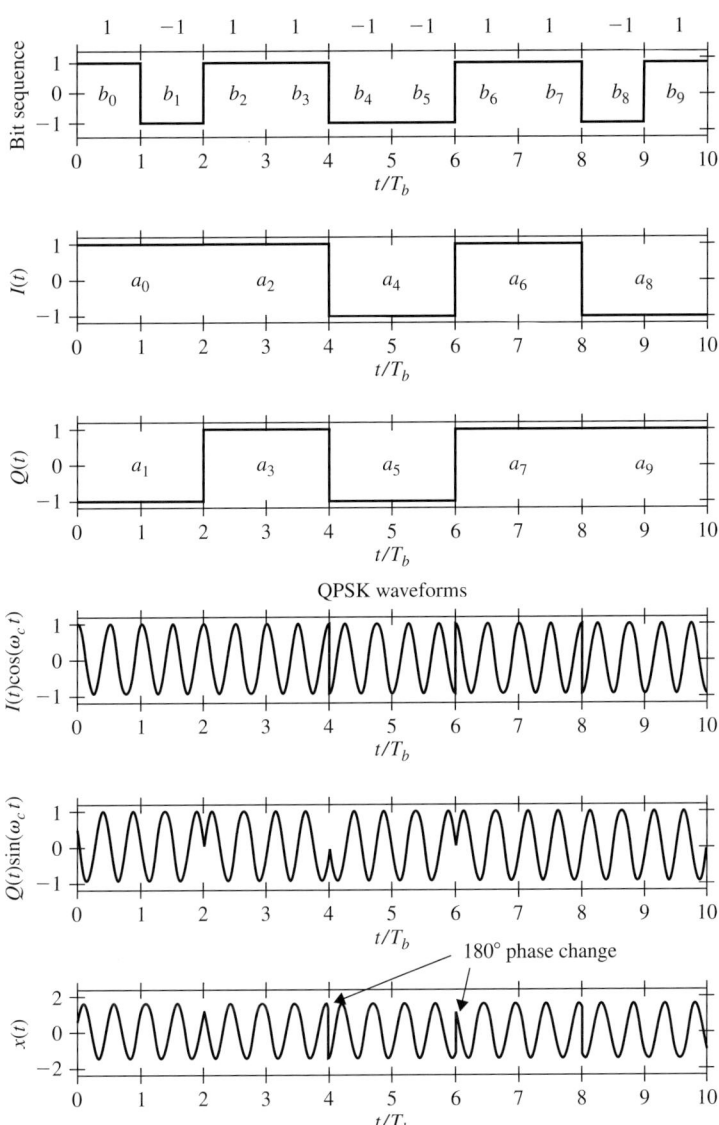

Figure 11.32 QPSK waveforms.

Table 11.3 Mapping of Odd and Even Bits into Transmission Symbols and Waveforms

Odd and Even Bits (b_0, b_1)	(a_0, a_1)	Transmitted Carrier Burst $s_i(t)$, $0 \le t \le T$
11	$(1/\sqrt{2}, 1/\sqrt{2})$	$s_1(t) = A_c v(t) \cos(2\pi f_c t + \pi/4)$
01	$(-1/\sqrt{2}, 1/\sqrt{2})$	$s_2(t) = A_c v(t) \cos(2\pi f_c t + 3\pi/4)$
00	$(-1/\sqrt{2}, -1/\sqrt{2})$	$s_3(t) = A_c v(t) \cos(2\pi f_c t + 5\pi/4)$
10	$(1/\sqrt{2}, -1/\sqrt{2})$	$s_4(t) = A_c v(t) \cos(2\pi f_c t + 7\pi/4)$

The phase of the transmitted carrier burst ψ_0 during the first symbol interval is a discrete random variable whose value is determined by symbols a_0 and a_1 according to the following relation:

$$\psi_0 = \tan^{-1}\frac{a_1}{a_0} \tag{11.98}$$

ψ_0 assumes one of four possible values $\{\pi/4, 3\pi/4, 5\pi/4, 7\pi/4\}$ depending on the values of a_0 and a_1 that, in turn, are determined by even and odd bits (b_0, b_1) being transmitted during the first symbol interval. Every symbol interval QPSK transmits the pair of even and odd bits (b_{2n}, b_{2n+1}) as one of the four distinct carrier bursts shown in the right-hand column of the Table 11.3.

The carrier modulated pulses $\{s_i(t), i = 1, \ldots, 4\}$ in Table 11.3 constitute the signal set of QPSK modulation scheme. The average energy per symbol in QPSK is given by

$$E_s = \sum_{i=1}^{4} P\{s_i(t) \text{ sent}\} \int_0^T s_i^2(t)dt = A_c^2 T \sum_{i=1}^{4} P\{s_i(t) \text{ sent}\} \int_0^T \frac{v^2(t)}{T}\cos^2(2\pi f_c t)dt$$

$$= A_c^2 T \sum_{i=1}^{4} P\{s_i(t) \text{ sent}\}\frac{1}{2}\int_0^T \frac{v^2(t)}{T}dt = \frac{A_c^2 T}{2} \tag{11.99}$$

As each symbol represents two bits, the average energy per bit in QPSK is given by

$$E_b = E_s/2 \tag{11.100}$$

It is convenient to write the QPSK signal $x(t)$ by substituting (11.99) into (11.94) as

$$x(t) = \sqrt{\frac{2E_s}{T}}\left[I(t)\cos(2\pi f_c t) - Q(t)\sin(2\pi f_c t)\right] \tag{11.101}$$

The coherent reception of the QPSK signal is shown in Figure 11.33. The input QPSK signal at the receiver in the presence of noise is given by

$$r(t) = \alpha x(t) + n_i(t) \tag{11.102}$$

where α represents the attenuation introduced by the transmission channel. Again, we assume $\alpha = 1$ without any loss of generality. $n_i(t)$ is AWGN with the double-sided power spectral density of $N_o/2$ W/Hz. The BP filter passes the QPSK carrier burst without distortion while rejecting out-of-band noise. Note that each branch of the demodulator is a BPSK demodulator, except for the use of orthogonal demodulating carriers. The in-phase NRZ polar pulse train $I(t)$ is recovered in the upper branch by multiplying the output of the BP filter by a coherent in-phase carrier and LP filtering the output. Similarly, the quadrature NRZ polar pulse train $Q(t)$ is recovered in the lower branch by multiplying the output of the BP filter by a coherent quadrature carrier

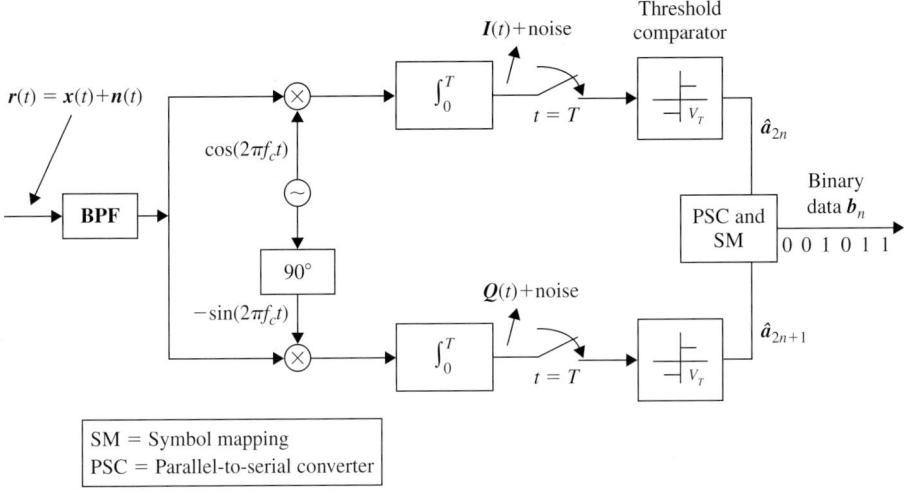

Figure 11.33 QPSK demodulator.

and LP filtering the output. The detection of transmission symbols a_{2n} and a_{2n+1} is then performed by comparing the output of each sampler in a threshold comparator with $V_T = 0$.

Error Performance

If we choose basic pulse shape $v(t) = \Pi\left(\dfrac{t - T/2}{T}\right)$, the carrier-modulated pulse during the nth symbol interval can be written from (11.94) and (11.95) as

$$s(t) = \sqrt{\frac{2E_s}{T}}\left[a_{2n}\cos(2\pi f_c t) - a_{2n+1}\sin(2\pi f_c t)\right], \quad nT \leq t \leq (n + 1)T \quad (11.103)$$

By choosing the basis functions

$$\phi_1(t) = \sqrt{\frac{2}{T}}\cos(2\pi f_c t)$$

$$\phi_2(t) = \sqrt{\frac{2}{T}}\sin(2\pi f_c t) \quad (11.104)$$

and using (11.103), it is possible to express the four possible carrier-modulated pulses in the signal set (Table 11.3) as vectors in the plane spanned by ϕ_1 and ϕ_2. That is,

$$\underline{s} = \left(a_{2n}\sqrt{E_s}, a_{2n+1}\sqrt{E_s}\right) = \left(\pm\sqrt{\frac{E_s}{2}}, \pm\sqrt{\frac{E_s}{2}}\right) = \left(\pm\sqrt{E_b}, \pm\sqrt{E_b}\right) \quad (11.105)$$

Figure 11.34 QPSK signal constellation.

These are shown as the four points in the signal constellation in Figure 11.34. The constellation can be viewed as a two-dimensional BPSK constellation.

From Figure 11.34, $d_{\min} = 2\sqrt{E_b}$. Therefore, the probability of symbol error for QPSK is obtained from (10.156) by substituting $K = 4, M = 4$ as

$$P_e \approx \frac{2K}{M} Q\left(\frac{d_{\min}}{\sqrt{2N_o}}\right) = 2Q\left(\sqrt{\frac{2E_b}{N_o}}\right) \qquad (11.106)$$

Recall from Example 10.8 that the nearest neighbor estimate in (11.106) represents the exact symbol error rate for QPSK. Thus, the BER of QPSK is obtained from (11.106) and (10.163) as

$$BER_{QPSK} = \frac{P_e}{2} = Q\left(\sqrt{\frac{2E_b}{N_o}}\right) \qquad (11.107)$$

Note that the QPSK BER performance is identical to that of the BPSK. That is, $E_b/N_o \sim 11$ dB is required for a $BER = 10^{-6}$.

Experiment 11.4 *QPSK Simulation and Performance Comparison*

In this experiment, we model a QPSK digital communication system using Simulink and MATLAB. Figure 11.35(a) illustrates the Simulink model for the system. The parameters of the simulation including bit rate, carrier frequency, and sampling rate are set up by a companion MATLAB m-file. The m-file also computes the theoretical BER and plots simulated and theoretical BER performance. The **QPSK data** block generates in-phase and quadrature polar NRZ pulse trains $I(t)$ and $Q(t)$ corresponding to sequences of odd- and even-numbered bits, respectively. The **in-phase modulator** block produces a BPSK signal by multiplying the polar NRZ pulse train $I(t)$ with the output of a sinusoidal source. The **quadrature modulator** block produces another BPSK signal by multiplying the polar NRZ pulse train $Q(t)$ with the output of a quadrature sinusoidal source. The QPSK signal is now obtained by adding the in-phase and quadrature BPSK signals. AWGN is added to the QPSK signal by using the AWGN channel block. At the receiver, the noisy QPSK signal serves as input to **in-phase** and **quadrature demodulator** blocks that utilize orthogonal carriers to coherently demodulate the in-phase and quadrature BPSK signals. The output of the in-phase demodulator block is polar NRZ pulse train $I(t)$, whereas the quadrature demodulator block regenerates polar NRZ pulse train $Q(t)$. The original bit stream is obtained by a **parallel-to-serial conversion** block which multiplexes the in-phase and quadrature signals. This signal is then compared with the transmitted sequence in the Error-rate meter block. The simulated BER value is transmitted to MATLAB workspace

Figure 11.35 (a) Simulink model for QPSK system; (b) QPSK modulator waveforms; (c) QPSK demodulator waveforms; (d) comparison of theoretical and simulated BER performance.

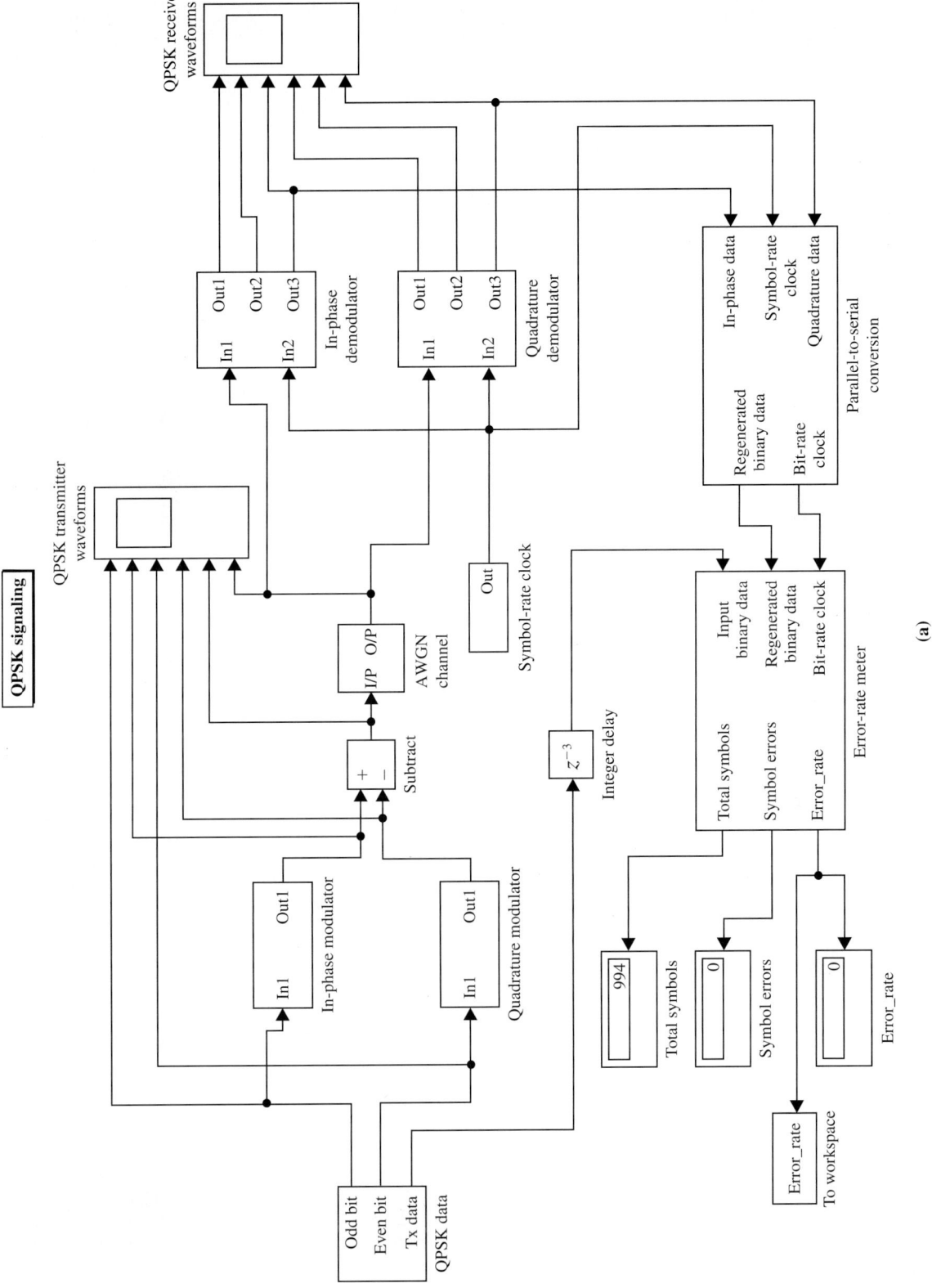

(a)

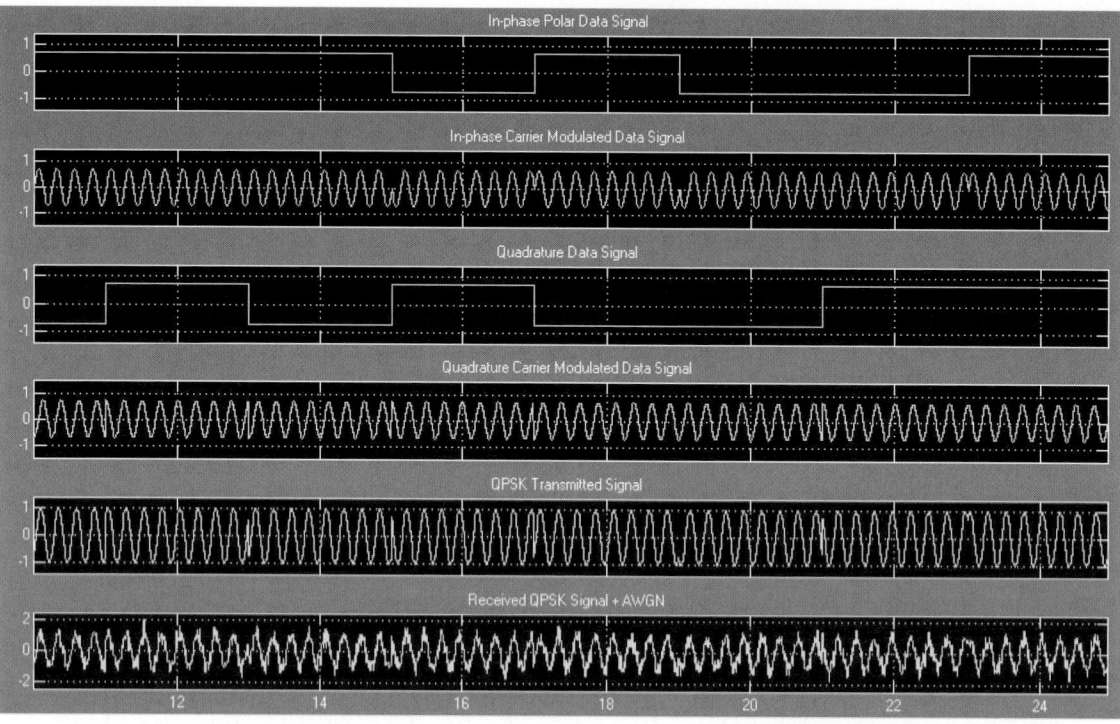

(b)

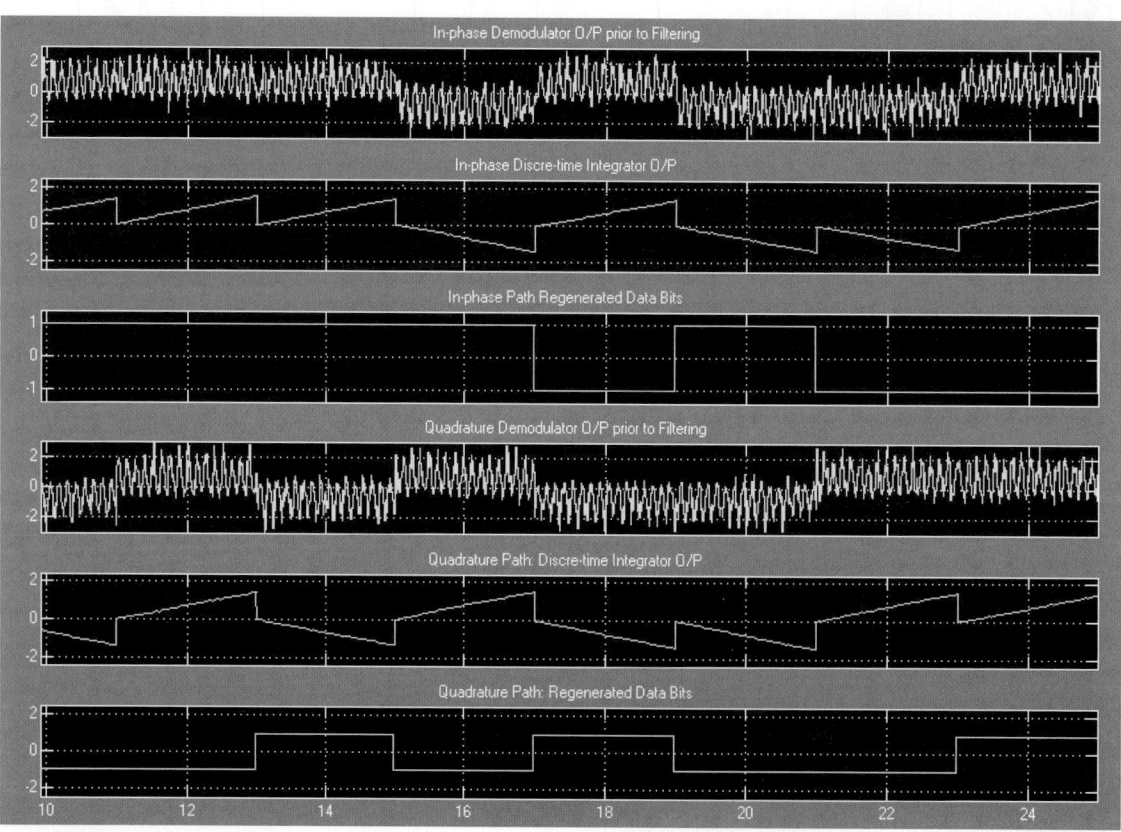

(c)

(*continued*)

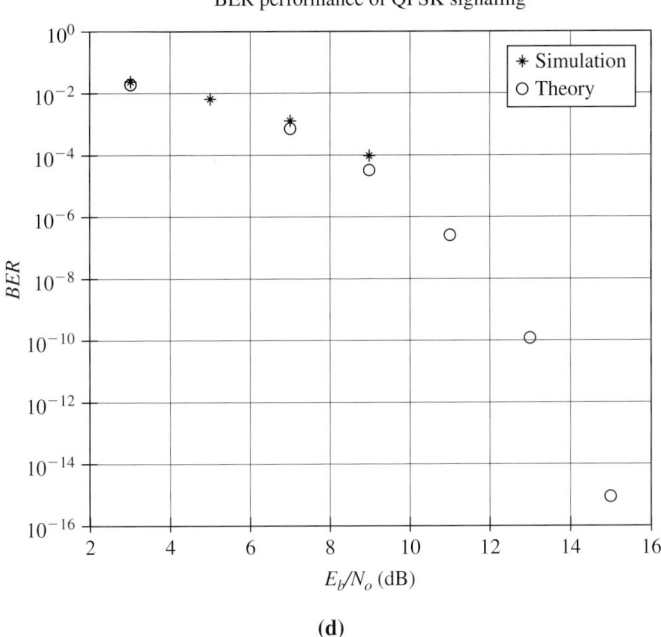

(d)

to generate the BER performance curve. Figure 11.35(b) and (c) displays various modulator and demodulator waveforms generated using this simulation. Figure 11.35(d) provides a comparison of theoretical and simulated BER performance.

11.7.3 Offset QPSK

Offset QPSK (OQPSK) is a minor but important variation on QPSK. In QPSK, there is no constraint on allowed phase transitions (0, 90, or 180 degrees) as illustrated by the dotted lines in Figure 11.36(a). Because the quadrature modulation waveforms $I(t)$ and $Q(t)$ in QPSK can switch signs simultaneously (e.g., if 11 is followed by 00), the data-bearing phase $\psi(t)$ correspondingly changes by $180°$. The QPSK waveform has a constant envelope even with $180°$ phase transitions when rectangular pulses are used. However, the spectrum produced by rectangular pulses has large and slowly decaying sidelobes, as discussed in Chapter 9. These sidelobes can be reduced by using filtered pulses like RC instead. Unfortunately, this destroys the constant envelope nature of the QPSK signal in the process because the filtered waveform cannot change instantaneously from one peak to another when $180°$ phase transitions occur. Most mobile radio and satellite products are designed with Class-C power amplifiers, which provide

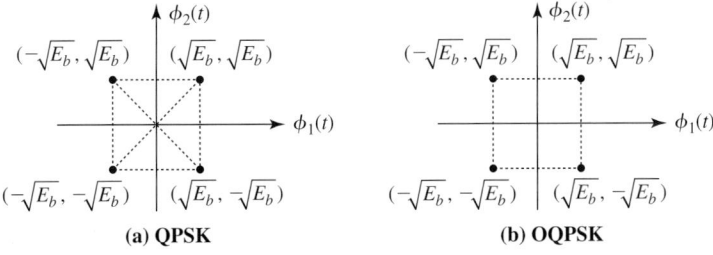

Figure 11.36 Allowed phase transitions in QPSK and OQPSK.

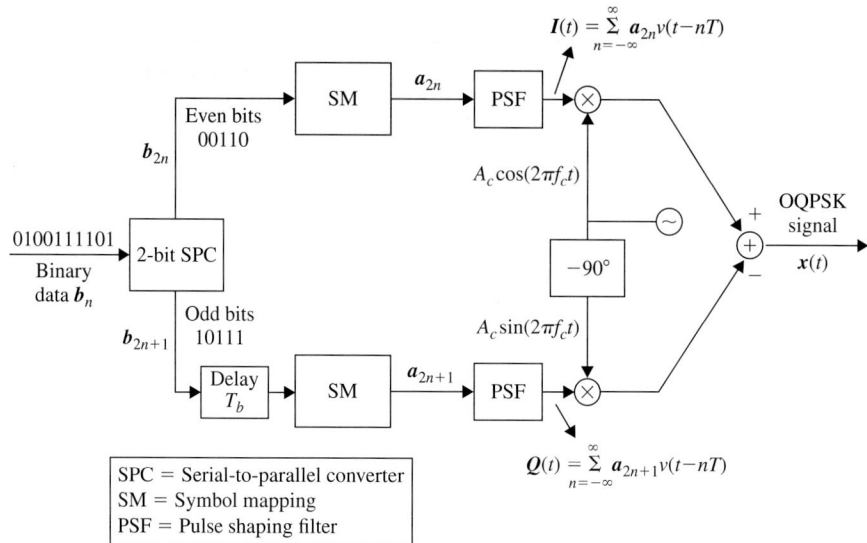

Figure 11.37 OQPSK modulator.

the highest power efficiency among the common types of power amplifiers. However, Class-C amplifiers are highly nonlinear and restore the filtered sidelobes, causing adjacent channel interference when amplifying a waveform with envelope variation.

OQPSK has been designed to combat this problem. The OQPSK modulator, shown in Figure 11.37, delays the quadrature signal $Q(t)$ by T_b seconds. Thus by modifying (11.95), we obtain following expression for the OQPSK signal from (11.94):

$$x(t) = \sqrt{\frac{2E_b}{T_b}} \left[I(t)\cos(2\pi f_c t) - Q(t)\sin(2\pi f_c t) \right] \tag{11.108}$$

where

$$I(t) = \sum_{n=-\infty}^{\infty} a_{2n} v(t - 2nT_b)$$

$$Q(t) = \sum_{n=-\infty}^{\infty} a_{2n+1} v\left[t - (2n+1)T_b \right] \tag{11.109}$$

Because $I(t)$ and $Q(t)$ waveforms in OQPSK do not switch at the same time (due to a single bit delay in the quadrature path), phase transitions occur every $T_b = T/2$ seconds, caused by a change in either a_{2n} or a_{2n+1} but not both. Thus the symbol transitions in OQPSK occur only to neighbors in the constellation diagram, and they never exceed $\pm 90°$ as shown in Figure 11.36(b). Cutting the maximum phase shift in half results in much smaller envelope variation after BP filtering. Figure 11.38 illustrates OQPSK modulation waveforms. We observe 90° phase transitions at $t = 4T_b$ (i.e., $2T$) and $6T_b$ (i.e., $3T$) in the OQPSK signal when binary transmission symbols change from $(1, 1)$ to $(-1, 1)$ and $(-1, -1)$ to $(1, -1)$, respectively.

The structure of an OQPSK demodulator, shown in Figure 11.39, is identical to that of a QPSK demodulator except for a single bit delay in the in-phase path. This is to compensate for the similar delay in the quadrature path in OQPSK modulator. Because the OQPSK constellation is identical to that of QPSK, its BER performance is identical to that of QPSK.

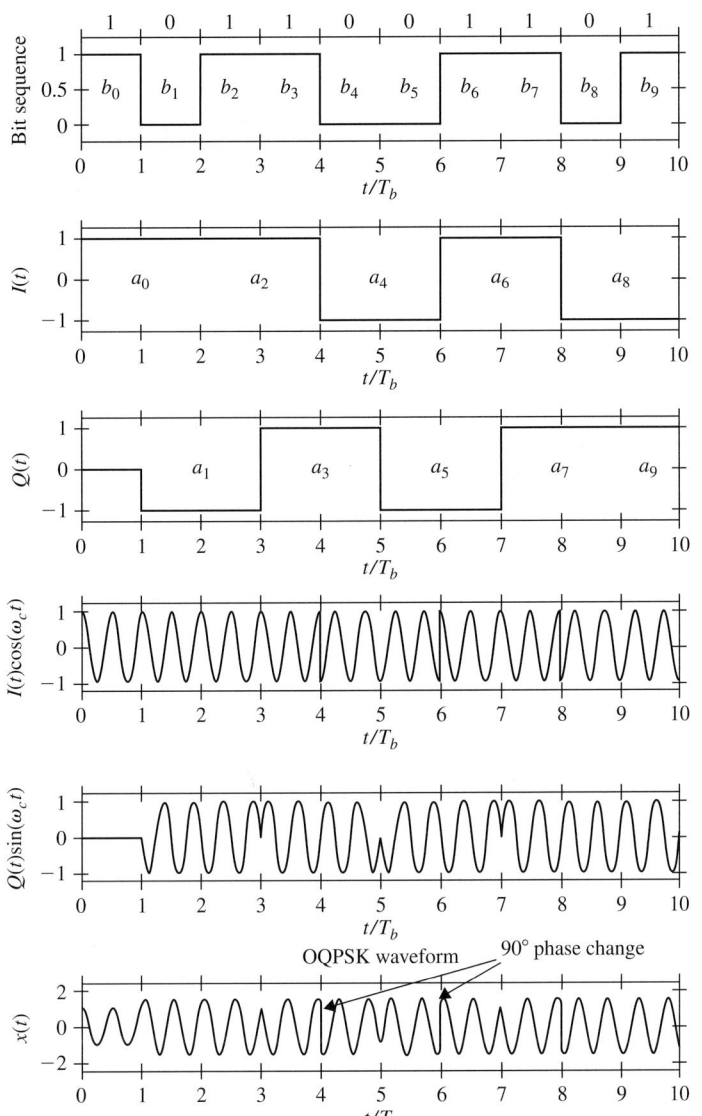

Figure 11.38 OQPSK waveforms.

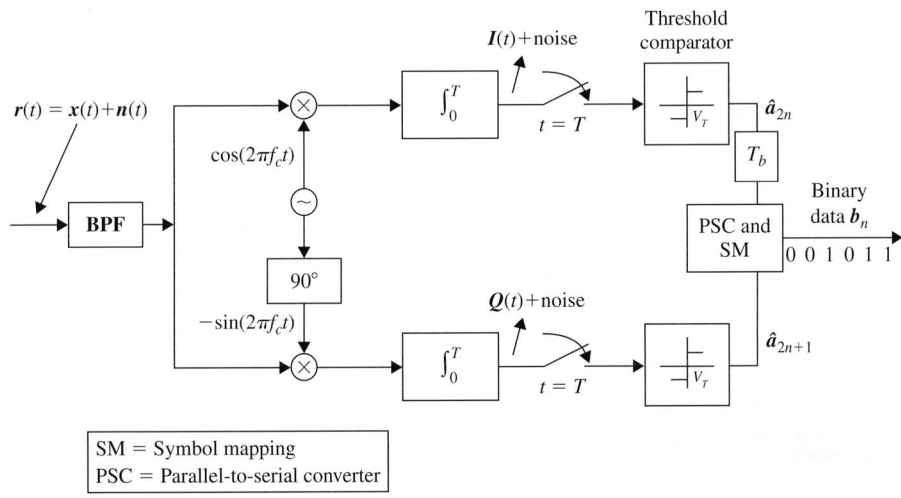

SM = Symbol mapping
PSC = Parallel-to-serial converter

Figure 11.39 OQPSK demodulator.

Experiment 11.5   *OQPSK Simulation and Performance Comparison*

In this experiment, we model an OQPSK digital communication system using Simulink and MATLAB. The Simulink model of the OQPSK system is virtually identical to that of the QPSK simulation as illustrated in Figure 11.34(a). The quadrature modulator and in-phase

Figure 11.40 (a) OQPSK modulator waveforms; (b) OQPSK demodulator waveforms; (c) comparison of theoretical and simulated BER performance.

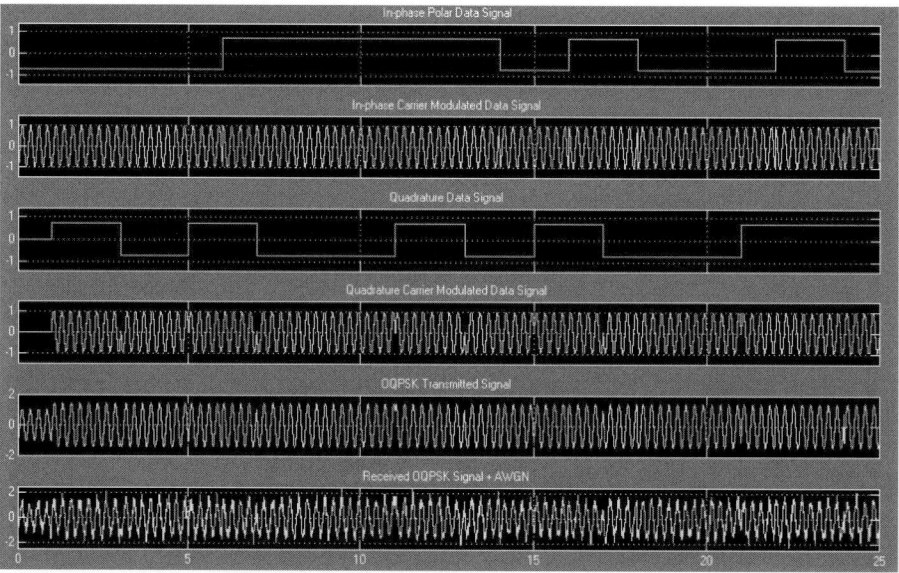

(a)

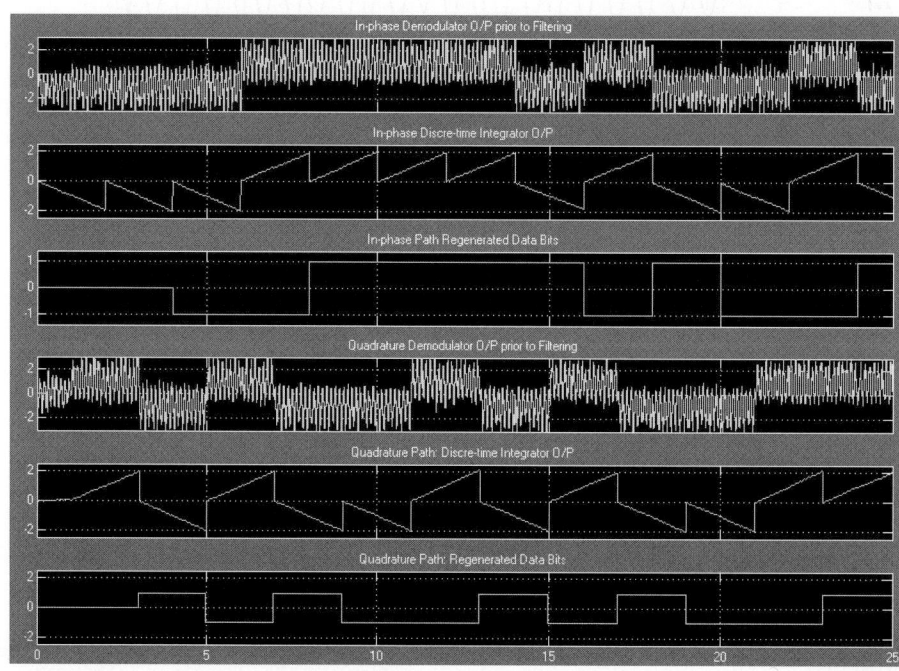

(b)

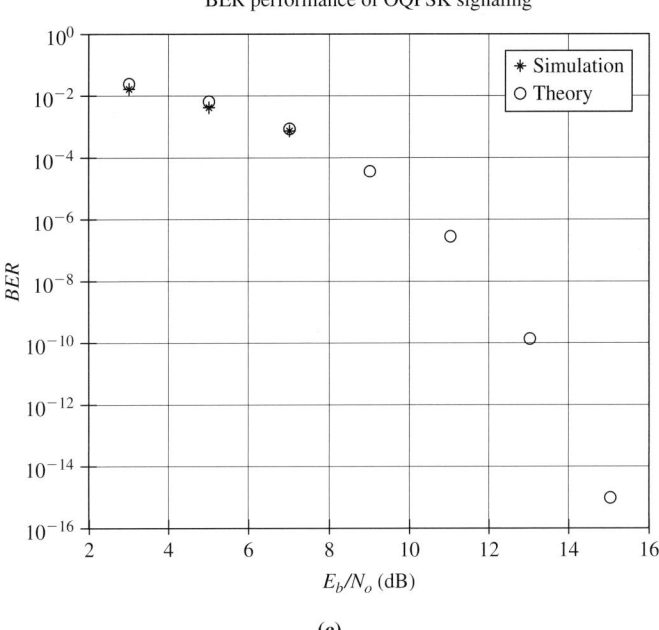

BER performance of OQPSK signaling

(c)

demodulator blocks, however, incorporate single bit delay as shown in Figures 11.37 and 11.39. Figure 11.40(a) and (b) displays OQPSK modulator and demodulator waveforms generated using this simulation. Figure 11.40(c) provides a comparison of theoretical and simulated BER performance.

11.7.4 *M*-ary Phase-Shift Keying

In *M*-ary PSK, *M* different phase shifts of the carrier are used to convey the information. The $M = 2^k$ signal waveforms, each representing k information bits, are represented as

$$s_i(t) = A_c v(t)\cos[2\pi f_c t + \psi_i + \varphi], 0 \leq t \leq T, \ i = 1, \ldots, M \qquad (11.110)$$

where

$$\varphi = 0 \text{ or } \frac{\pi}{M} = \text{fixed phase offset}$$

$$\psi_i = \frac{2\pi(i - 1)}{M}, i = 1, 2, \ldots, M \qquad (11.111)$$

$v(t)/\sqrt{T}$ is a unit-energy pulse of symbol duration *T*. We observe that the carrier phase ψ_i assumes one of *M* possible values, corresponding to *k* information bits being conveyed during that symbol interval. All *M*-ary PSK waveforms in (11.110) have equal energy $E_s = \dfrac{A_c^2 T}{2}$. We can now write an expression for an *M*-ary PSK signal from (11.110) as

$$x(t) = \sqrt{\frac{2E_s}{T}} \sum_{n=-\infty}^{\infty} v(t - nT) \cos[2\pi f_c t + \psi_n + \varphi] \qquad (11.112)$$

ψ_n is M-ary random variable representing the phase of the carrier during the nth symbol interval. It assumes values in the set $\left\{ \dfrac{2\pi(i-1)}{M}, i = 1, 2, \ldots, M \right\}$ with equal probability. Equation (11.112) can be expanded to obtain the quadrature form representation for the M-ary PSK signal as

$$x(t) = \sqrt{\frac{2E_s}{T}} \big[I(t)\cos(2\pi f_c t) - Q(t)\sin(2\pi f_c t) \big] \tag{11.113}$$

where

$$I(t) = \sum_{n=-\infty}^{\infty} a_n^I v(t - nT)$$

$$Q(t) = \sum_{n=-\infty}^{\infty} a_n^Q v(t - nT) \tag{11.114}$$

$$a_n^I = \cos(\psi_n + \varphi)$$

$$a_n^Q = \sin(\psi_n + \varphi) \tag{11.115}$$

By choosing the basis functions in (11.104), it is possible to express all waveforms in the M-PSK signal set (11.112) as vectors in the plane spanned by ϕ_1 and ϕ_2 as

$$\underline{s} = \left(a_n^I \sqrt{E_s}, a_n^Q \sqrt{E_s} \right) \tag{11.116}$$

The signal vectors lie around a circle of radius $\sqrt{E_s}$. The constellation for 8-PSK ($M = 8$) is shown in Figure 11.41(a).

Error Performance

An accurate estimate for the symbol error probability can be obtained from the nearest neighbor approximation (10.156). As illustrated in Figure 11.41(b), the minimum distance between two adjacent signal points is

$$d_{\min} = 2D = 2\sqrt{E_s}\sin\left(\frac{\pi}{M}\right) \tag{11.117}$$

Substituting (11.117) into (10.156) and noting that the factor $2K/M = 2$, we obtain the following estimate of the symbol error rate for M-ary PSK:

$$P_e \approx 2Q\left[\sqrt{\frac{2E_s}{N_o}\sin^2\left(\frac{\pi}{M}\right)} \right] = 2Q\left[\sqrt{\frac{2E_b \log_2 M}{N_o}\sin^2\left(\frac{\pi}{M}\right)} \right] \tag{11.118}$$

We observe from (11.118) that the additional energy required for M-ary PSK compared to BPSK signaling is $10\log_{10}\left[\log_2 M \sin^2\left(\frac{\pi}{M}\right) \right]$. From (11.118), the BER of an M-ary PSK system is given by

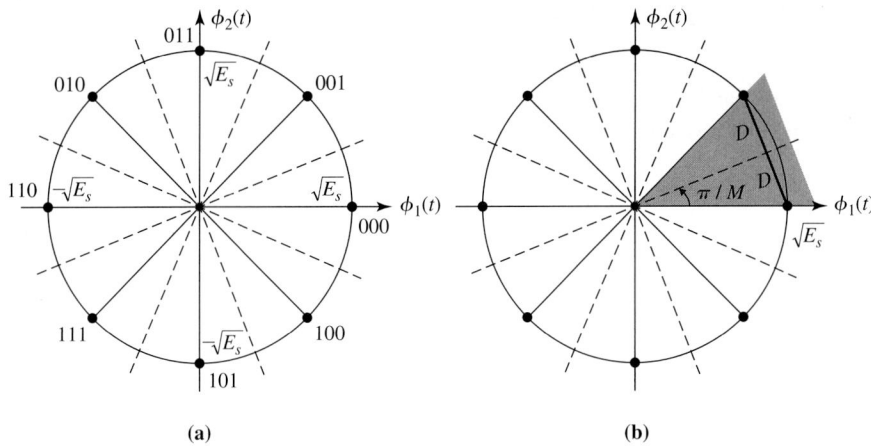

Figure 11.41 8-PSK: (a) constellation; (b) error performance calculation.

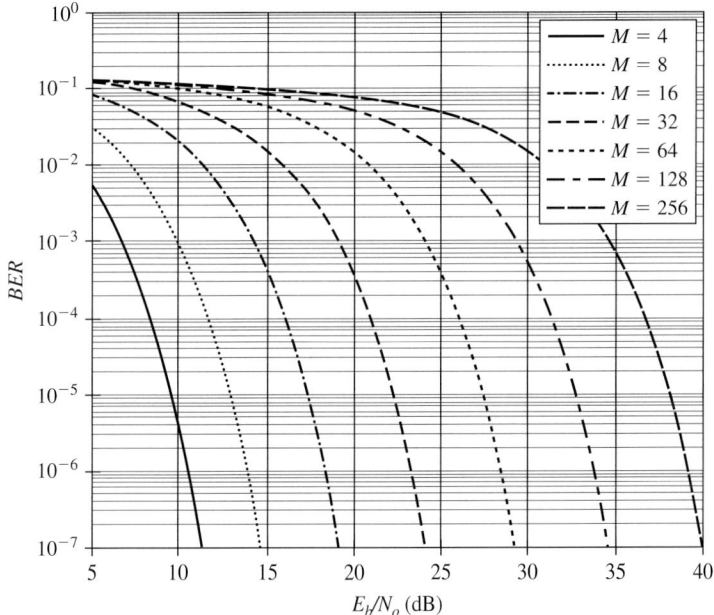

Figure 11.42 BER performance of *M*-ary PSK schemes.

$$BER_{MPSK} \approx \frac{1}{\log_2 M} 2Q\left[\sqrt{\frac{2E_b \log_2 M}{N_o} \sin^2\left(\frac{\pi}{M}\right)}\right] \qquad (11.119)$$

The modulator and demodulator structures for *M*-ary PSK are very similar to those illustrated in Figures 11.48 and 11.49, respectively. Figure 11.42 shows the BER performance of *M*-ary PSK as a function of E_b/N_o. As the *M*-ary PSK constellation can expand only along the circumference of a circle of radius $\sqrt{E_s}$, $d_{\min}$ suffers a severe penalty as a result of an increase in *M*. Thus for large values of *M*, doubling the number of phases requires an additional 6 dB of SNR/bit to achieve the same BER performance.

11.8   MINIMUM SHIFT KEYING

In Section 11.4, we noted that Sunde's FSK exhibits a continuous phase characteristic by using two carriers with frequency spacing Δf exactly equal to the bit rate R_b. The **minimum shift keying (MSK)** is a binary CPFSK scheme with $\Delta f = R_b/2$. That is,

$$\Delta f = f_1 - f_2 = \frac{R_b}{2} = \frac{1}{2T_b} \tag{11.120}$$

Equation (11.120) corresponds to modulation index $h = \Delta f T_b = 0.5$. The two carrier frequencies used in the MSK system are given by

$$\text{Binary 1:} f_1 = f_c + \Delta f/2 = f_c + \frac{1}{4T_b}$$

$$\text{Binary 0:} f_2 = f_c - \Delta f/2 = f_c - \frac{1}{4T_b} \tag{11.121}$$

We recall from Section 11.4.1 that the frequency spacing in MSK is the minimum value required for two FSK signals to be coherently orthogonal, hence the name minimum shift keying. We further observe that the frequency spacing in (11.120) is only half as much as the conventional $1/T_b$ spacing required for noncoherent orthogonal FSK carriers.

It is interesting to consider the amplitude-phase representation for the MSK signal. That is,

$$x(t) = \sqrt{\frac{2E_b}{T_b}} \cos\left[2\pi f_c t + \boldsymbol{\psi}(t)\right], \quad 0 \le t \le T_b \tag{11.122}$$

where $\boldsymbol{\psi}(t)$ is the excess phase of an angle-modulated waveform discussed in Section 5.1. From Section 11.4, we know that the polar binary modulating signal $I(t)$ produces a maximum frequency deviation $\Delta f_{\max} = \dfrac{\Delta f}{2}$. Substituting into (5.19), $\boldsymbol{\psi}(t)$ for the MSK signal is given by

$$\boldsymbol{\psi}(t) = \psi(0) + 2\pi\frac{\Delta f}{2}\int_0^t I(\alpha)d\alpha = \psi(0) + \frac{\pi}{2T_b}\int_0^t I(\alpha)d\alpha \tag{11.123}$$

The phase $\psi(0)$, denoting the value of phase at time $t = 0$, represents the accumulated phase ("phase history") up to time $t = 0$. For the polar NRZ pulse $a_0\Pi\left(\dfrac{t - T_b/2}{T_b}\right)$ during $0 \le t \le T_b$, the phase of the MSK signal over the first bit interval is given by

$$\boldsymbol{\psi}(t) = \psi(0) + \frac{\pi}{2T_b}a_0\int_0^t \Pi\left(\frac{\alpha - T_b/2}{T_b}\right)d\alpha, \quad 0 \le t \le T_b$$

$$= \psi(0) + \frac{\pi t}{2T_b}a_0 = \psi(0) \pm \frac{\pi t}{2T_b} \tag{11.124}$$

Note that the phase $\boldsymbol{\psi}(t)$ changes linearly over the bit interval. Substituting (11.124) into (11.122) yields the following expression for an MSK signal

$$x(t) = \sqrt{\frac{2E_b}{T_b}} \cos\left[2\pi f_c t \pm \frac{\pi t}{2T_b} + \psi(0)\right], \quad 0 \le t \le T_b \tag{11.125}$$

The sign of the frequency shift $\pm \dfrac{\pi t}{2T_b}$ in (11.125) is determined by the polarity of the modulating pulse during the bit period. Thus, the phase changes over the bit period $0 \le t \le T_b$ are given from (11.124) by

$$\text{Binary 1: } \psi(T_b) - \psi(0) = \frac{\pi T_b}{2T_b} = \frac{\pi}{2}$$

$$\text{Binary 0: } \psi(T_b) - \psi(0) = -\frac{\pi T_b}{2T_b} = -\frac{\pi}{2} \tag{11.126}$$

Equation (11.126) states that sending a binary 1 increases the phase of an MSK signal by $\pi/2$ radians over a bit interval, whereas sending a binary 0 decreases the phase by an equal amount over the same interval. Because the phase of a carrier is unique in the range 0 to 2π or, equivalently, from $-\pi$ to π, it is instructive to examine the evolution of $\psi(t)$ (modulo 2π) as a function of time t. Such a plot is called the **phase trellis.** Because the phase change over each bit interval in the MSK is either $\pi/2$ or $-\pi/2$, the phase $\psi(t)$ (modulo 2π) = 0 or π for even multiples of bit interval ($t = 2nT_b$), and $\psi(t) = \pm\pi/2$ for odd multiples of bit interval ($t = (2n + 1)T_b$), assuming $\psi(0) = 0$. Figure 11.43 illustrates the MSK phase trellis for binary information sequence 1101000101, under the assumption that $\psi(0) = 0$. We observe that the (modulo 2π) phase is continuous (that is, no jump discontinuities) at bit switching times.

MSK can be viewed as a special case of OQPSK with sinusoidal pulse weighting. By combining (11.108) and (11.109), we can write following expression for an OQPSK signal with such a weighting:

$$x(t) = A_c \left[\underbrace{\cos(\pi t / 2T_b) \sum_{n=-\infty}^{\infty} a_{2n} v(t - 2nT_b) \cos(2\pi f_c t)}_{I(t)} + \underbrace{\sin(\pi t / 2T_b) \sum_{n=-\infty}^{\infty} a_{2n+1} v[t - (2n + 1)T_b] \sin(2\pi f_c t)}_{Q(t)} \right] \tag{11.127}$$

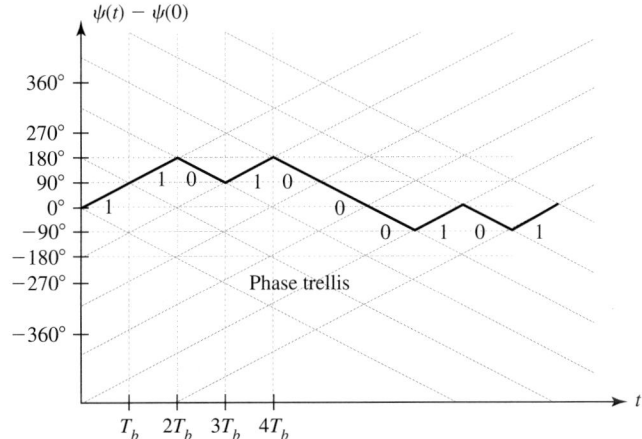

Figure 11.43 MSK phase trellis.

where

$$v(t) = \Pi\left(\frac{\pi t}{2T_b}\right) \tag{11.128}$$

Equation (11.127) states that even bits $\{a_{2n}\}$ modulate the in-phase carrier $\cos(2\pi f_c t)$ every $2T_b$ seconds. Further, odd bits $\{a_{2n+1}\}$, delayed by the bit period T_b, modulate the quadrature carrier $\sin(2\pi f_c t)$ every $2T_b$ seconds. This form of MSK wherein the weighting function for symbols in the in-phase and quadrature channels, respectively, are alternating half-cycles of cosine and sine waveforms, is referred to as **MSK type I.** The waveforms of MSK generated using OQPSK approach are illustrated in Figure 11.44. We now consider the weighted OQPSK signal in (11.127) over the bit period $(n-1)T_b \le t \le nT_b$. That is,

$$x(t) = \sqrt{\frac{2E_b}{T_b}}\left[a_{2n}\cos(\pi t/2T_b)\cos(2\pi f_c t) + a_{2n+1}\sin(\pi t/2T_b)\sin(2\pi f_c t)\right] \tag{11.129}$$

Using well-known trigonometric identities, (11.129) can be expressed as

$$x(t) = \sqrt{\frac{2E_b}{T_b}}a_{2n}\cos\left[2\pi f_c t - \zeta\right] \tag{11.130}$$

where

$$\zeta = \tan^{-1}\left[\frac{a_{2n+1}\sin(\pi t/2T_b)}{a_{2n}\cos(\pi t/2T_b)}\right] = \tan^{-1}\left[\frac{a_{2n+1}}{a_{2n}}\tan\left(\frac{\pi t}{2T_b}\right)\right] = \frac{a_{2n+1}}{a_{2n}}\left(\frac{\pi t}{2T_b}\right) \tag{11.131}$$

Now $a_{2n+1} = \pm 1$ and $a_{2n} = \pm 1$. So we can write $\dfrac{a_{2n+1}}{a_{2n}} = a_{2n+1}a_{2n}$. Substituting (11.131) into (11.130) yields

$$x(t) = \sqrt{\frac{2E_b}{T_b}}a_{2n}\cos\left(2\pi f_c t - a_{2n}a_{2n+1}\frac{\pi t}{2T_b}\right)$$

$$= \sqrt{\frac{2E_b}{T_b}}\cos\left(2\pi f_c t - a_{2n}a_{2n+1}\frac{\pi t}{2T_b} + \varphi_{2n}\right) \tag{11.132}$$

where $\varphi_{2n} = 0$ or π corresponds to $a_{2n} = 1$ or -1, respectively. Because $a_{2n}a_{2n+1} = \pm 1$, (11.132) can be expressed as

$$x(t) = \cos\left(2\pi f_c t \mp \frac{\pi t}{2T_b} + \varphi_{2n}\right) \tag{11.133}$$

We observe from (11.133) that $x(t)$ is an FSK signal with signaling frequencies $f_1 = f_c + \dfrac{1}{4T_b}$ and $f_2 = f_c - \dfrac{1}{4T_b}$. We will now show that $x(t)$ is continuous phase as well. The term $a_{2n}a_{2n+1}$ in (11.132) may change sign at bit switching time producing a frequency shift of magnitude Δf. However in OQPSK either a_{2n} or a_{2n+1} can change but not both at bit switching times.

- a_{2n} may change at $t = (2n-1)T_b$ producing a phase change of magnitude $|2\pi\Delta f(2n-1)T_b| = |(2n-1)\pi| = \pi$. Further, the change in a_{2n} produces an additional phase change of π in φ_{2n}. Because the total phase change at bit switching time $t = (2n-1)T_b$ is 2π, no phase discontinuity is caused due to a change in a_{2n}.
- a_{2n+1} may change at $t = 2nT_b$ producing a phase change of magnitude $|2\pi\Delta f 2nT_b| = |2n\pi|$. Because the total phase change at bit switching time $t = 2nT_b$ is $2n\pi$, it is equivalent to no phase change.

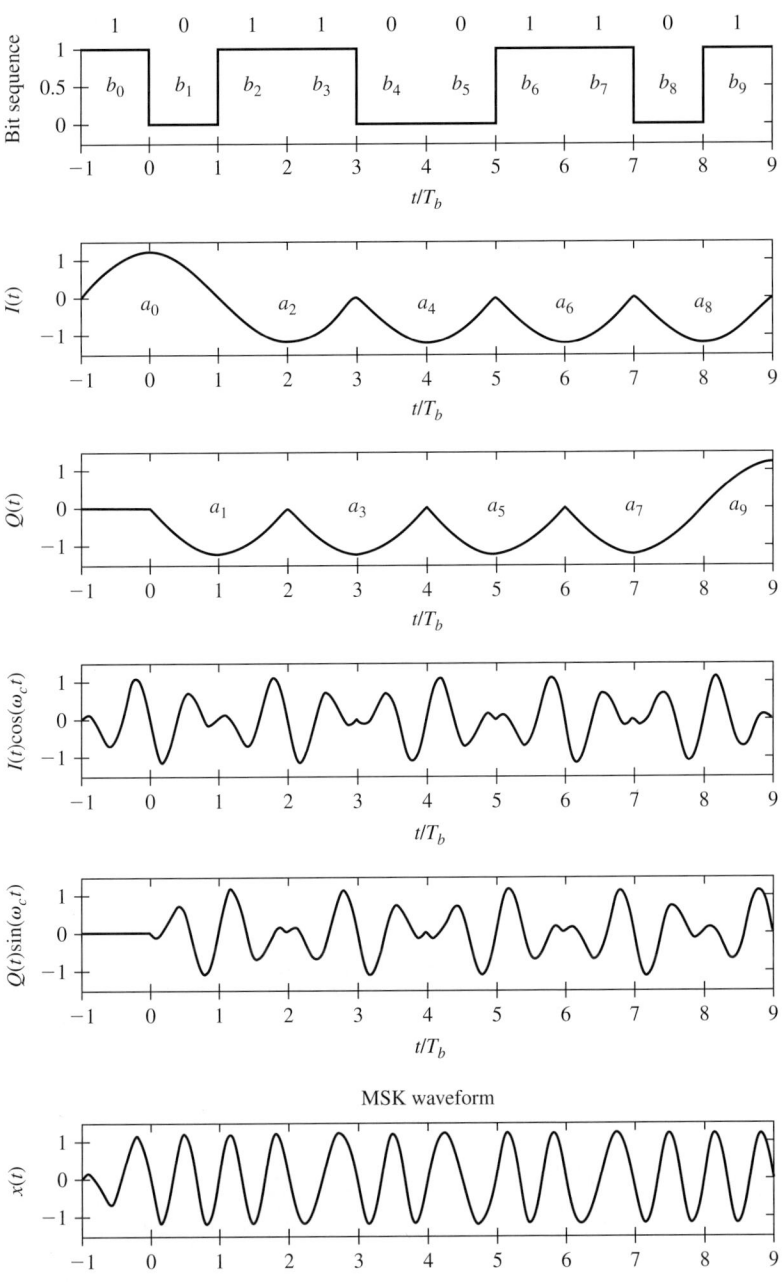

Figure 11.44 MSK waveforms.

Because MSK is a form of OQPSK with sinusoidal pulse weighting, the BER performance for MSK is identical to that of QPSK/OQPSK. It is given by

$$BER_{MSK} = Q\left(\sqrt{\frac{2E_b}{N_o}}\right) \tag{11.134}$$

Figure 11.45 compares the performance of MSK with QPSK and OQPSK.

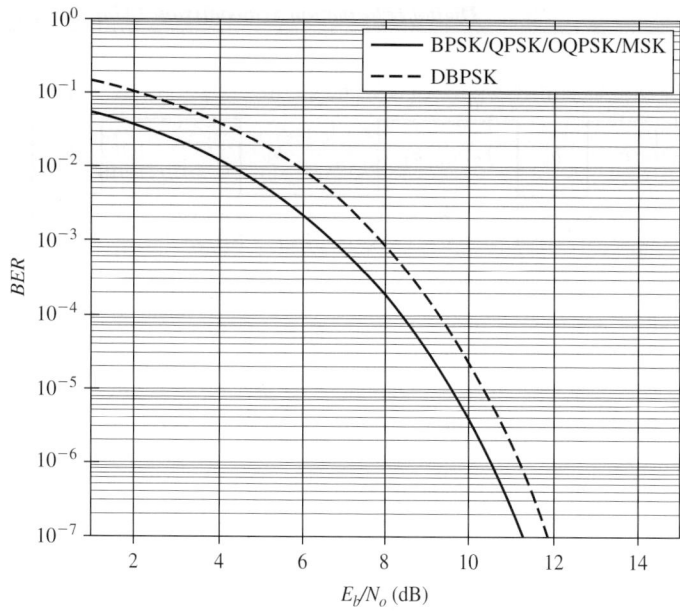

Figure 11.45 MSK performance comparison.

Experiment 11.6 *MSK Simulation and Performance Comparison*

In this experiment, we model an MSK digital communication system using Simulink and MAT-LAB. The Simulink model for an MSK system is identical to that shown in Figure 11.35 for QPSK. The details of in-phase and quadrature modulator blocks are, however, different because of sinusoidal weighting. Figure 11.46(a) and (b) display MSK modulator and demodulator

Figure 11.46 (a) MSK modulator waveforms; (b) MSK demodulator waveforms; (c) comparison of theoretical and simulated BER performance.

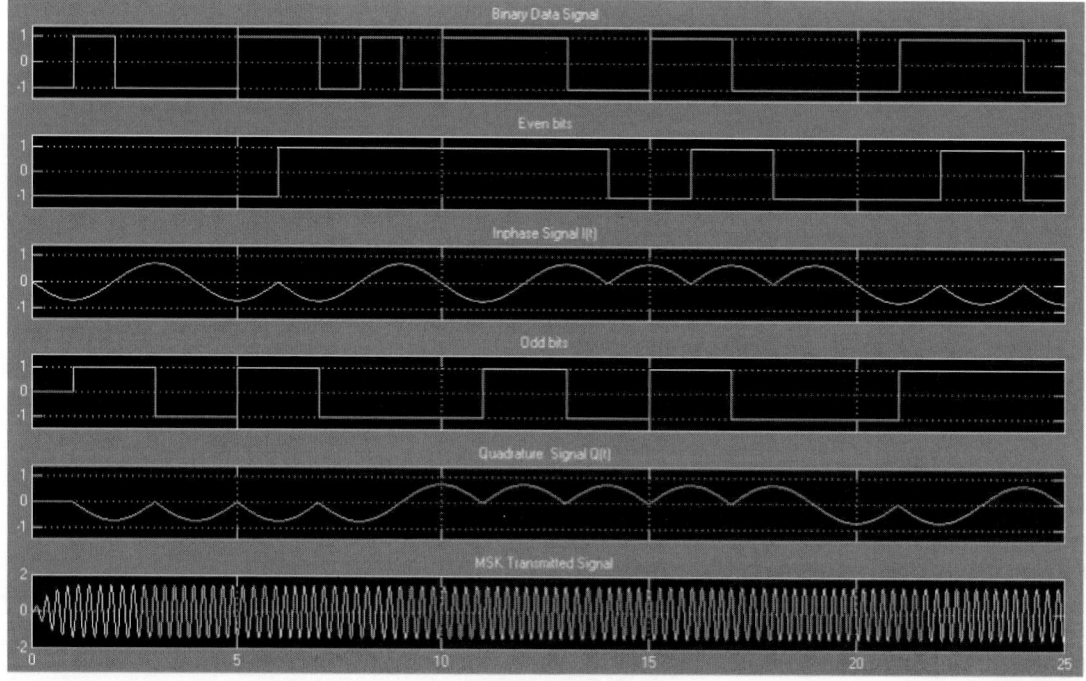

(a)

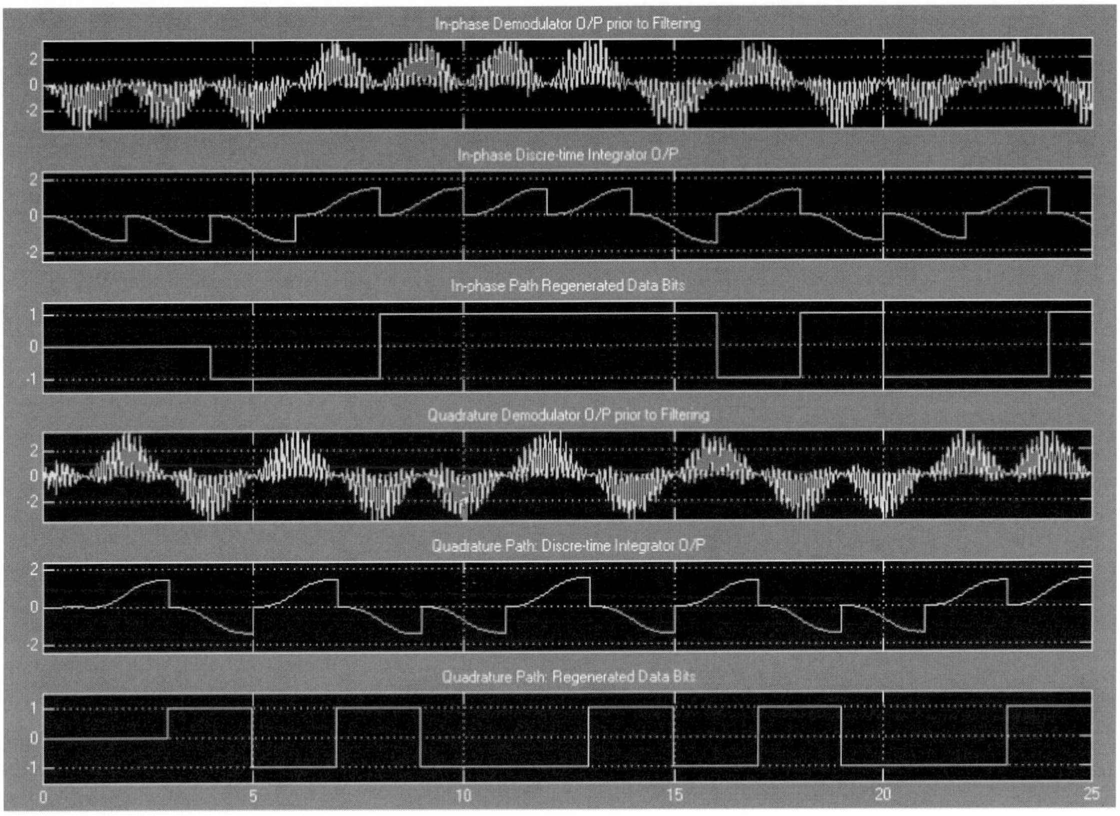

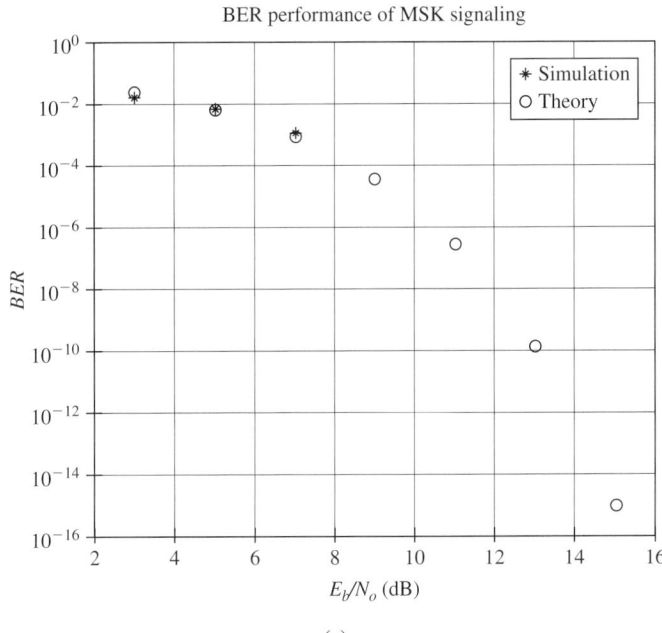

(b)

BER performance of MSK signaling

(c)

waveforms generated using this simulation. Figure 11.46(c) provides a comparison of theoretical and simulated BER performance.

11.9 QUADRATURE AMPLITUDE MODULATION

QAM is one of the most widely used quadrature modulation schemes. Binary information arriving at R_b bits per second is split into two sequences that consist of even and odd bits. For an M-QAM system, the symbol mapping table in the upper branch maps each block of $k/2$ even bits into transmission symbol a_n^I, where $M = 2^k$. Similarly each block of $k/2$ odd bits entering the lower branch is encoded into transmission symbol a_n^Q. a_n^I and a_n^Q are $\sqrt{M}$-ary random variables assuming values in the set $\{\pm 1, \pm 3, \ldots, \pm(\sqrt{M} - 1)\}$. For a 16-QAM system, as an example, a_n^I and a_n^Q assume values in the alphabet set $\{-3, -1, 1, 3\}$. The output of the pulse shaping filter in the upper branch is a $\sqrt{M}$-ary polar pulse train $I(t) = \displaystyle\sum_{n=-\infty}^{\infty} a_n^I v(t - nT)$ that modulates the in-phase carrier $A_c\cos(2\pi f_c t)$. Similarly, a $\sqrt{M}$-ary polar pulse train $Q(t) = \displaystyle\sum_{n=-\infty}^{\infty} a_n^Q v(t - nT)$ generated by the pulse shaping filter in the lower branch modulates the quadrature carrier $A_c\sin(2\pi f_c t)$. M-QAM, therefore, can be viewed as sending two $\sqrt{M}$-ary PAM waveforms over quadrature carriers, where $M = 4^n$. This implementation leads to rectangular signal constellations as illustrated in Figure 11.47. QPSK is the simplest QAM scheme ($M = 4$) where binary polar pulse trains modulate quadrature carriers. The block diagram of an M-QAM modulator in Figure 11.48 is similar to a QPSK modulator.

The block diagram of an M-QAM demodulator in Figure 11.49 is similar to a QPSK demodulator except that the symbol mapping outputs $k/2$ bits for each detected transmission symbol $\hat{a}_n^I$ and $\hat{a}_n^Q$.

The general form of rectangular M-QAM signal is given by

$$x(t) = \sqrt{\frac{2E_s}{T}}\big[I(t)\cos(2\pi f_c t) - Q(t)\sin(2\pi f_c t)\big] \tag{11.135}$$

$$I(t) = C_o \sum_{n=-\infty}^{\infty} a_n^I v(t - nT)$$

$$Q(t) = C_o \sum_{n=-\infty}^{\infty} a_n^Q v(t - nT) \tag{11.136}$$

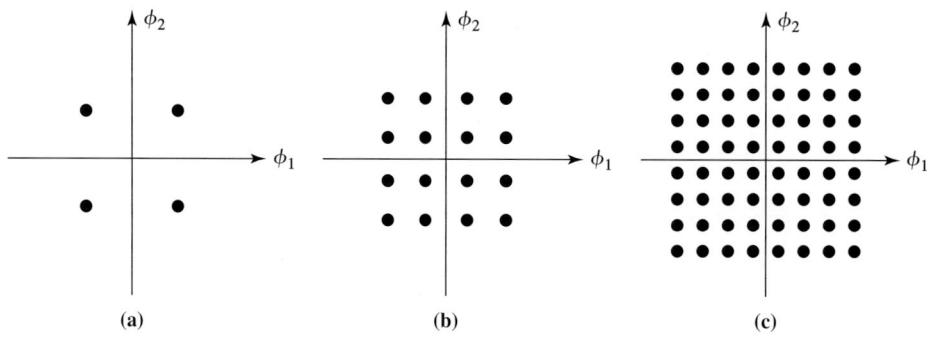

Figure 11.47 QAM constellations: (a) 4-QAM; (b) 16-QAM; (c) 64-QAM.

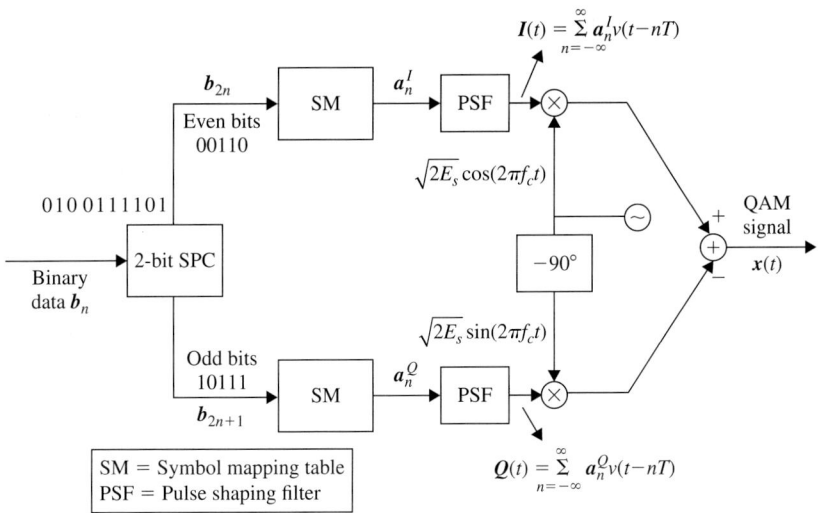

Figure 11.48 *M*-QAM modulator.

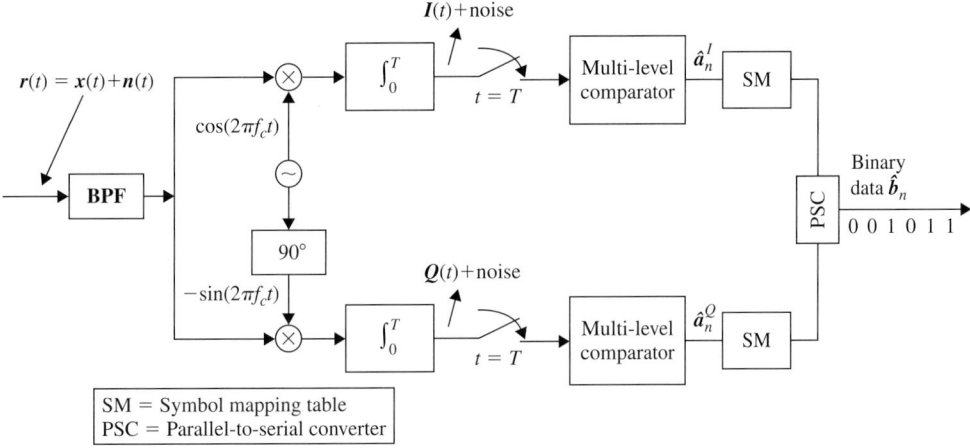

Figure 11.49 *M*-QAM demodulator.

where $\dfrac{v(t)}{\sqrt{T}}$ is the usual unit-energy pulse. The constant C_o is introduced in order to make the average energy of the signal set equal to E_s. The average symbol energy, E_s, is given by

$$E_s = \sum_{m=1}^{\sqrt{M}} \sum_{n=1}^{\sqrt{M}} E\{a_m^I, a_n^Q\} \int_0^T |s_{mn}(t)|^2 dt \qquad (11.137)$$

where $s_{mn}(t)$ is the transmitted waveform corresponding to the constellation point (a_m^I, a_n^Q).

$$s_{mn}(t) = \sqrt{\frac{2E_s}{T}} C_o \big[a_m^I v(t) \cos(2\pi f_c t) - a_n^Q v(t) \sin(2\pi f_c t) \big] \qquad (11.138)$$

Substituting (11.138) into (11.137), we get

$$E_s = \frac{2E_s C_o^2}{M} \sum_{m=1}^{\sqrt{M}} \sum_{n=1}^{\sqrt{M}} \left[(a_m^I)^2 + (a_n^Q)^2 \right] \frac{1}{2} \int_0^T \left| \frac{v(t)}{\sqrt{T}} \right|^2 dt = \frac{E_s C_o^2}{M} \sum_{m=1}^{\sqrt{M}} \sum_{n=1}^{\sqrt{M}} \left[(a_m^I)^2 + (a_n^Q)^2 \right]$$

$$\Rightarrow C_o^2 = \frac{M}{\displaystyle\sum_{m=1}^{\sqrt{M}} \sum_{n=1}^{\sqrt{M}} \left[(a_m^I)^2 + (a_n^Q)^2 \right]} \tag{11.139}$$

For example, $M = 16$, $a_n^I, a_n^Q \in \{\pm 3, \pm 1\}$

$$C_o^2 = \frac{16}{\displaystyle\sum_{m=1}^{4} \sum_{n=1}^{4} \left[(a_m^I)^2 + (a_n^Q)^2 \right]} = \frac{16}{160} = \frac{1}{10}$$

For a rectangular M-QAM constellation, it can be shown using (11.139) that

$$C_o = \sqrt{\frac{3}{2(M-1)}} \tag{11.140}$$

By choosing the basis functions in (11.104), it is possible to express all the M-QAM waveforms in the nth symbol interval as vectors in the plane spanned by ϕ_1 and ϕ_2 as

$$\underline{s} = \left(a_n^I C_o \sqrt{E_s},\, a_n^Q C_o \sqrt{E_s} \right) \tag{11.141}$$

It is obvious from (11.141) that

$$d_{\min} = 2 C_o \sqrt{E_s} \tag{11.142}$$

Substituting (11.140) into (11.142), we get

$$d_{\min} = 2 \sqrt{\frac{3E_s}{2(M-1)}} \tag{11.143}$$

The details of 4-QAM and 16-QAM constellations are illustrated in Figure 11.50.

Error Performance

The probability of receiving correct symbol P_c in an M-QAM system is given by

$$
\begin{aligned}
P_c ={} & \text{Probability of correct reception on } I \text{ path} \\
& \times \text{Probability of correct reception on } Q \text{ path} \\
={} & (1 - P_o) \times (1 - P_o)
\end{aligned}
\tag{11.144}
$$

where

$$P_o = \text{Probability of incorrect decision on } I \text{ and } Q \text{ paths, individually}$$

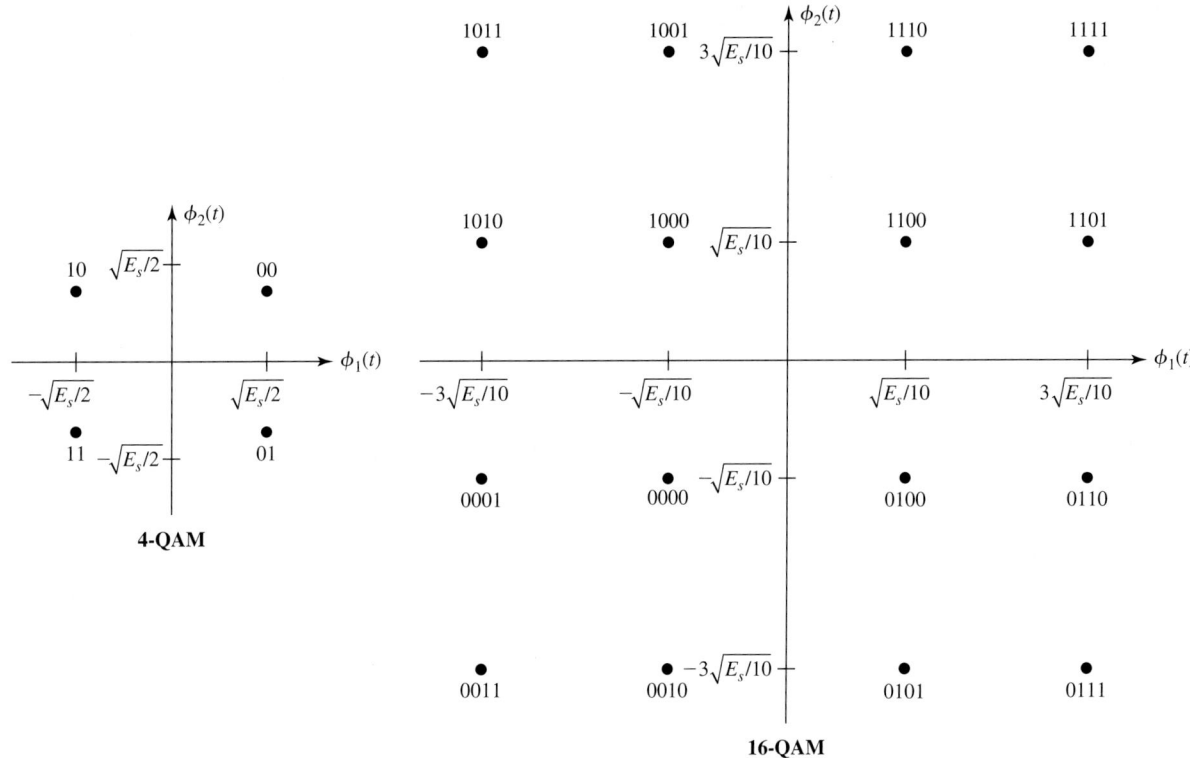

Figure 11.50 Details of 4-QAM and 16-QAM constellations.

The probability of symbol error P_e in an M-QAM system can now be obtained from (11.144) as

$$P_e = 1 - P_c = 1 - (1 - P_o)^2 = 2P_o - P_o^2 \approx 2P_o, \quad P_o << 1$$
$$P_e \approx 2P_o, \quad P_o << 1 \tag{11.145}$$

P_o is the probability of symbol error in an $\sqrt{M}$-ary PAM system given by (10.175) as

$$P_o = \frac{2\left(\sqrt{M} - 1\right)}{\sqrt{M}} Q\left(\frac{d_{\min}}{\sqrt{2N_o}}\right) \tag{11.146}$$

Now if we substitute $d_{\min}$ from (11.142) into (11.146), we obtain

$$P_o = \frac{2\left(\sqrt{M} - 1\right)}{\sqrt{M}} Q\left(\sqrt{\frac{3E_s}{(M - 1)N_o}}\right) \tag{11.147}$$

The probability of symbol error for the M-QAM system is now given by combining (11.145) and (11.147) as

$$P_e = \frac{4\left(\sqrt{M} - 1\right)}{\sqrt{M}} Q\left(\sqrt{\frac{3E_s}{(M - 1)N_o}}\right) \tag{11.148}$$

The BER of an *M*-QAM system is obtained from (11.148) and (10.163) by substituting $E_s = kE_b = \log_2 M \times E_b$.

$$BER_{MQAM} = \frac{P_e}{\log_2 M} = \frac{4\left(\sqrt{M} - 1\right)}{(\log_2 M)\sqrt{M}} Q\left(\sqrt{\frac{3E_b(\log_2 M)}{(M - 1)N_o}}\right) \tag{11.149}$$

Equation (11.149) simplifies for specific values of *M* as follows:

1. $M = 4$

$$BER_{4-QAM} = \frac{4\left(\sqrt{4} - 1\right)}{2\sqrt{4}} Q\left(\sqrt{\frac{3E_b(\log_2 4)}{(4 - 1)N_o}}\right) = Q\left(\sqrt{\frac{2E_b}{N_o}}\right)$$

Note that the expression for BER_{4-QAM} is the same as that for a QPSK system. This is not surprising because they have identical constellations.

2. $M = 16$

$$BER_{16-QAM} = \frac{4(4 - 1)}{16} Q\left(\sqrt{\frac{3E_b(\log_2 16)}{(16 - 1)N_o}}\right) = \frac{3}{4} Q\left(\sqrt{\frac{0.8E_b}{N_o}}\right)$$

Figure 11.51 displays the BER performance of *M*-QAM as a function of E_b/N_o. One concludes by comparing Figures 11.42 and 11.51 that *M*-QAM is significantly more efficient than *M*-ary PSK in terms of SNR/bit required to achieve the same BER performance.

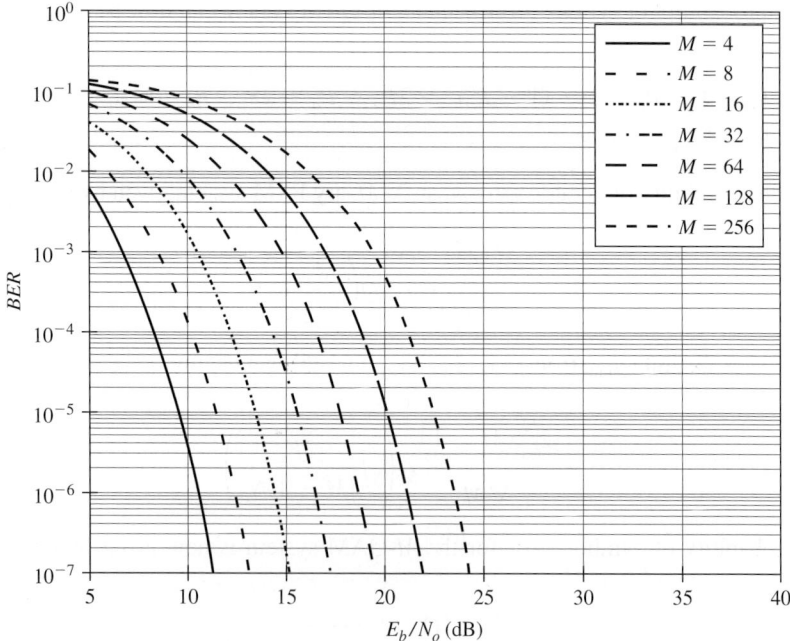

Figure 11.51 BER performance of *M*-QAM system.

Example 11.4

Compare the SNR/bit required for a data rate of 1 Mbps and $BER = 10^{-6}$ over a radio channel using (a) BPSK/QPSK/OQPSK; (b) 8-PSK; (c) 16-PSK; (d) 16-QAM; and (e) 64-QAM. Assume that the channel introduces AWGN with one-sided spectral density $N_o = 10^{-10}$ Watts/Hz.

Solution

a. BPSK/QPSK/OQPSK/MSK

$$BER_{BPSK} = Q\left(\sqrt{\frac{2E_b}{N_o}}\right)$$

From Table 6.1, $Q(x) = 10^{-6}$ for $x = 4.75$.

$$\sqrt{\frac{2E_b}{N_o}} = 4.75. \text{ This implies that SNR/bit} = \frac{E_b}{N_o} = \frac{4.75^2}{2} = 11.28 = 10.53 \text{ dB}$$

b. 8-PSK

$$BER_{MPSK} \approx \frac{1}{\log_2 M} 2Q\left[\sqrt{\frac{2E_b \log_2 M}{N_o}} \sin\left(\frac{\pi}{M}\right)\right]$$

$$1.5 \times 10^{-6} \approx Q\left[\sqrt{\frac{6E_b}{N_o}} \sin\left(\frac{\pi}{8}\right)\right]$$

From Table 6.1, $Q(x) = 1.5 \times 10^{-6}$ for $x = 4.67$.

$$4.67^2 = \frac{6E_b}{N_o} \sin^2\left(\frac{\pi}{8}\right)$$

$$\frac{E_b}{N_o} = \frac{21.8}{6 \times 0.146} = 24.8 = 13.94 \text{ dB}$$

c. 16-PSK

Substituting $M = 16$ in the BER_{MPSK} expression, we get

$$2 \times 10^{-6} \approx Q\left[\sqrt{\frac{8E_b}{N_o}} \sin\left(\frac{\pi}{16}\right)\right]$$

From Table 6.1, $Q(x) = 2 \times 10^{-6}$ for $x = 4.61$.

$$4.61^2 = \frac{8E_b}{N_o} \sin^2\left(\frac{\pi}{16}\right)$$

$$\frac{E_b}{N_o} = \frac{21.252}{8 \times 0.038} = 69.8 = 18.44 \text{ dB}$$

d. 16-QAM

Substituting $M = 16$ into (11.149), BER_{16-QAM} is given by

$$BER_{16-QAM} = \frac{3}{4}Q\left(\sqrt{\frac{0.8E_b}{N_o}}\right)$$

$$\frac{4}{3} \times 10^{-6} = Q\left(\sqrt{\frac{0.8E_b}{N_o}}\right)$$

From Table 6.1, $Q(x) = 1.333 \times 10^{-6}$ for $x = 4.7$.

$$4.7^2 = \frac{0.64 \times E_b}{N_o}$$

$$\frac{E_b}{N_o} = \frac{22.09}{0.64} = 34.51 = 15.38 \text{ dB}$$

e. 64-QAM
   Substituting $M = 64$ into (11.149), we get

$$BER_{64-QAM} = \frac{7}{12}Q\left(\sqrt{\frac{18E_b}{63N_o}}\right)$$

$$\frac{12}{7} \times 10^{-6} = Q\left(\sqrt{\frac{0.2857E_b}{N_o}}\right)$$

From Table 6.1, $Q(x) = 1.714 \times 10^{-6}$ for $x = 4.64$.

$$4.64^2 = \frac{0.2857E_b}{N_o}$$

$$\frac{E_b}{N_o} = \frac{21.53}{0.2857} = 75.357 = 18.77 \text{ dB}$$

Experiment 11.7   *16-QAM System Simulation and Performance Comparison*

In this experiment, we model a 16-QAM digital communication system using Simulink and MATLAB. Figure 11.52(a) illustrates the Simulink model for the system. The parameters of the simulation including bit rate, carrier frequency, and sampling rate are set up by a companion MATLAB m-file. The m-file also computes the theoretical BER and plots simulated and theoretical BER performance. The **16-QAM data** block generates in-phase and quadrature polar 4-PAM pulse trains $I(t)$ and $Q(t)$ corresponding to sequences of odd- and even-numbered bits, respectively. The in-phase modulator block produces a carrier-modulated 4-PAM signal by multiplying pulse train $I(t)$ with the output of sinusoidal source. The quadrature modulator block produces another carrier-modulated 4-PAM signal by multiplying the pulse train $Q(t)$ with the output of a quadrature sinusoidal source. The 16-QAM signal is now obtained by adding the in-phase and quadrature carrier waveforms. AWGN is added to the 16-QAM signal by using the AWGN channel block. At the receiver, the noisy 16-QAM signal serves as input to in-phase and quadrature demodulator blocks that utilize orthogonal carriers to coherently demodulate the in-phase and quadrature carrier-modulated 4-PAM signal. Both demodulator blocks incorporate 4-level threshold comparators to regenerate respective 4-PAM signals trains $I(t)$ and $Q(t)$. The original symbol stream is produced by a parallel-to-serial conversion block which multiplexes the in-phase and quadrature signals. This signal is then compared with the transmitted sequence in the Error-rate meter block. The simulated BER value is transmitted to MATLAB workspace to generate the

Figure 11.52 (a) 16-QAM system Simulink model; (b) 16-QAM modulator waveforms; (c) 16-QAM demodulator waveforms; (d) comparison of theoretical and simulated BER performance.

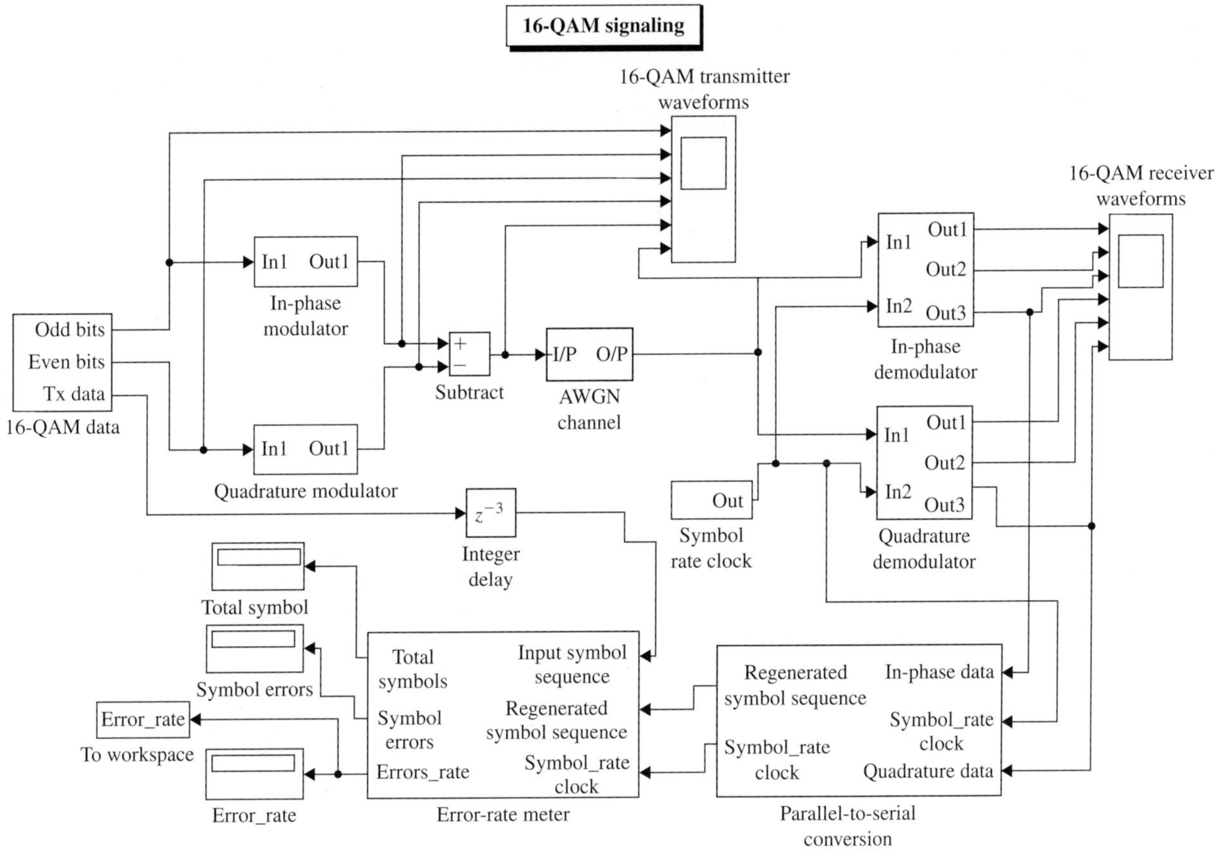

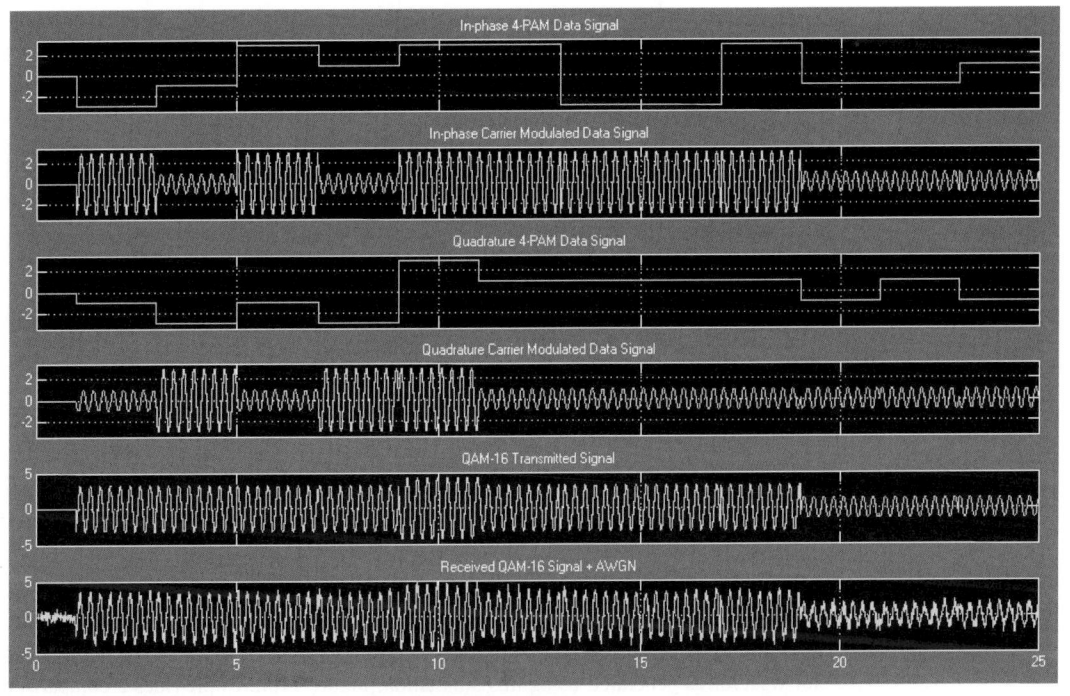

(a)

(b)

(*continued*)

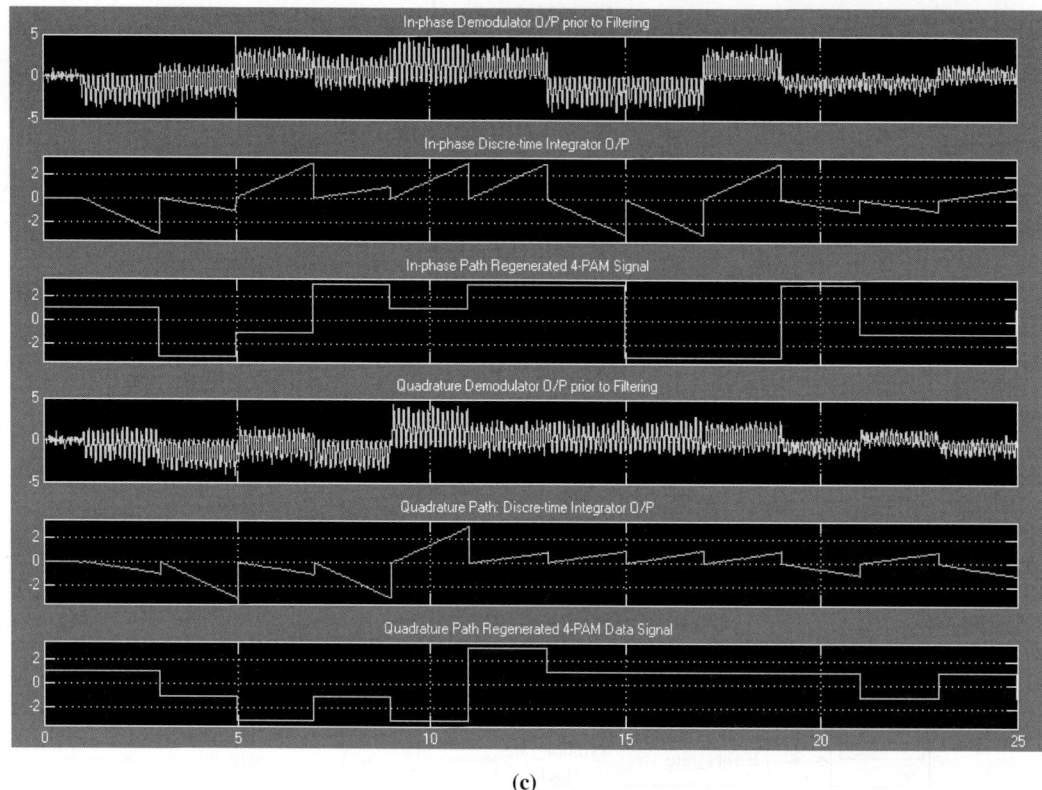

(c)

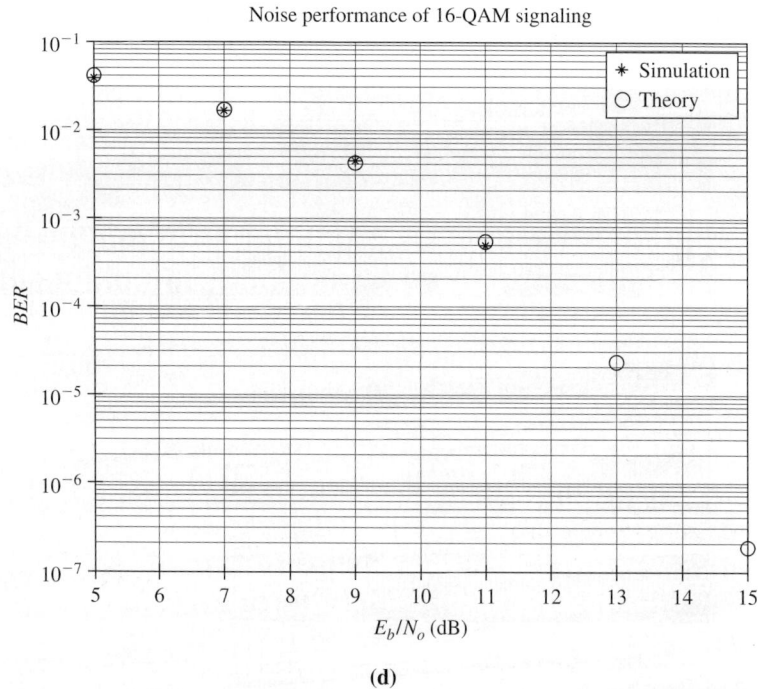

(d)

BER performance curve. Figures 11.52(b) and 11.52(c) display various modulator and demodulator waveforms generated using this simulation. Figure 11.52(d) provides a comparison of theoretical and simulated BER performance.

11.10 SPECTRA OF QUADRATURE MODULATED SIGNALS

We consider quadrature multiplexed BP random signal

$$x(t) = A_c\big[I(t)\cos(2\pi f_c t + \theta) - Q(t)\sin(2\pi f_c t + \theta)\big]$$

where

$$I(t) = \sum_{n=-\infty}^{\infty} a_n^I v(t - nT) \tag{11.89}$$

$$Q(t) = \sum_{n=-\infty}^{\infty} a_n^Q w(t - nT) \tag{11.91}$$

$x(t)$ here is identical to (11.5) except for the introduction of random phase θ. θ is a uniformly distributed random variable in $[0, 2\pi]$, and is included to ensure the stationarity of $x(t)$. As discussed in Section 11.1.1, $x(t)$ can be expressed in terms of its complex envelope $\tilde{x}(t)$ as

$$x(t) = A_c \mathrm{Re}\big\{\tilde{x}(t)e^{j(2\pi f_c t + \theta)}\big\}$$

where

$$\tilde{x}(t) = I(t) + jQ(t)$$

$v(t)$ and $w(t)$ are unit energy pulses of duration T seconds. Let $G_{\tilde{x}}(f)$ be the spectral density of the complex envelope $\tilde{x}(t)$. The spectral density $G_x(f)$ of the BP signal $x(t)$ is obtained from $G_{\tilde{x}}(f)$ by simple frequency translation. That is,

$$G_x(f) = \frac{A_c^2}{4}\big[G_{\tilde{x}}(f - f_c) + G_{\tilde{x}}(f + f_c)\big] \tag{11.150}$$

where $G_{\tilde{x}}(f)$ is the spectral density of the complex envelope $\tilde{x}(t)$. Assuming $I(t)$ and $Q(t)$ are statistically independent signals and at least one has zero mean, the autocorrelation function of the complex envelope $\tilde{x}(t)$ is given by

$$R_{\tilde{x}}(\tau) = E\big\{\tilde{x}(t)\tilde{x}^*(t + \tau)\big\} = E\big\{I(t)I^*(t + \tau)\big\} + E\big\{Q(t)Q^*(t + \tau)\big\}$$

$$= R_I(\tau) + R_Q(\tau) \tag{11.151}$$

Taking the Fourier transform of both sides in (11.151), we can write

$$G_{\tilde{x}}(f) = G_I(f) + G_Q(f) \tag{11.152}$$

Substituting (11.152) into (11.150), the spectral density of $x(t)$ is obtained as

$$G_x(f) = \frac{A_c^2}{4}\big[G_I(f - f_c) + G_Q(f - f_c) + G_I(f + f_c) + G_Q(f + f_c)\big] \tag{11.153}$$

where

$$G_I(f) = \text{power spectral density of in-phase component } \mathbf{I}(t)$$

$$G_Q(f) = \text{power spectral density of quadrature component } \mathbf{Q}(t)$$

This is a very significant result: the spectral density of quadrature-modulated BP signal is the sum of the frequency-translated versions of the spectra of its LP in-phase and quadrature components. Thus we can apply the techniques developed for calculating the spectra of digitally modulated baseband signals in Section 9.3 to determine the frequency spectra of digitally modulated BP signals. We will use null-null bandwidth as a measure of spectral occupancy in comparing various digital carrier modulation schemes. The **null-null bandwidth** $(\mathbf{B}_{null-null})$ is defined as width of the main lobe (that is, from the first null below the carrier frequency to the first null above it) in the spectral density plot of a digitally modulated carrier signal.

BASK

The BASK signal can be expressed using (11.9) as

$$x(t) = A_c \sum_{n=-\infty}^{\infty} a_n^I v(t - nT_b)\cos(2\pi f_c t) = A_c I(t)\cos(2\pi f_c t) \tag{11.154}$$

where $v(t) = \prod(t/T_b)$ is rectangular pulse shape, and $T_b = 1/R_b$.

$I(t) = \sum_{n=-\infty}^{\infty} a_n^I v(t - nT_b)$ is a binary unipolar NRZ pulse train whose spectral density $G_I(f)$ is given from (9.36) as

$$G_I(f) = \frac{T_b}{4}\left[\text{sinc}^2(f/R_b) + R_b\delta(f)\right] \tag{11.155}$$

The spectral density of the complex envelope $\tilde{x}(t)$ of the ASK signal is given by substituting (11.155) into (11.152) as

$$G_{\tilde{x}}(f) = G_I(f) = \frac{T_b}{4}\left[\text{sinc}^2(f/R_b) + R_b\delta(f)\right] \tag{11.156}$$

The spectrum of BP signal $x(t)$ can now be written by substituting (11.156) into (11.153) as

$$G_{ASK}(f) = \frac{A_c^2 T_b}{16}\left\{\text{sinc}^2\left[(f - f_c)/R_b)\right] + R_b\delta(f - f_c)\right.$$

$$\left. + \text{sinc}^2\left[(f + f_c)/R_b)\right] + R_b\delta(f + f_c)\right\} \tag{11.157}$$

The spectral density of ASK signal $x(t)$ contains a discrete carrier component. The PSD for the ASK signal is shown in Figure 11.53. The null-to-null bandwidth of the ASK signal transmitting data at a bit rate of R_b bits per second is $2R_b$ Hz. Note that it is twice the transmission bandwidth required to transmit the underlying baseband NRZ signal.

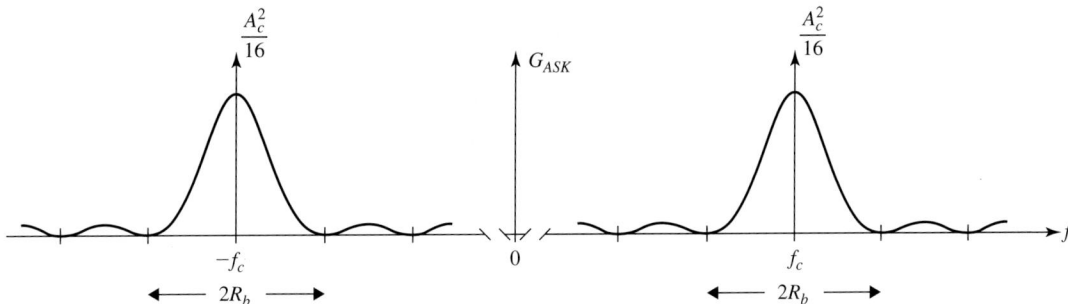

Figure 11.53 ASK spectral density.

M-*ary PSK signals.*

The *M*-ary PSK signal for a symbol rate of *D* symbols per second is given from (11.113) through (11.115) as

$$x(t) = \sqrt{\frac{2E_s}{T}}\left[I(t)\cos 2\pi f_c t - Q(t)\sin 2\pi f_c t\right]$$

where

$$I(t) = \sum_{n=-\infty}^{\infty} a_n^I v(t - nT)$$

$$Q(t) = \sum_{n=-\infty}^{\infty} a_n^Q v(t - nT)$$

$$a_n^I = \cos(\psi_n + \varphi)$$

$$a_n^Q = \sin(\psi_n + \varphi)$$

Now

$$E\{a_n^I\} = E\{a_n^Q\} = 0$$

$$\sigma_a^2 = Var(a_n^I) = Var(a_n^Q) = 1/2 \qquad (11.158)$$

Substituting (11.158) into (9.22), we obtain

$$G_I(f) = \frac{1}{2}D|V(f)|^2 = G_Q(f) \qquad (11.159)$$

Substituting (11.159) into (11.152) yields

$$G_{\tilde{x}}(f) = D|V(f)|^2 \qquad (11.160)$$

Let *v*(*t*) be a rectangular pulse of duration *T* seconds. That is,

$$v(t) = \Pi(t/T)$$

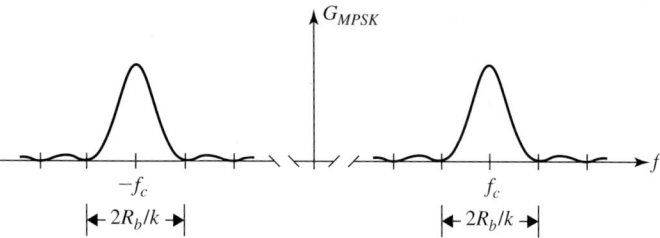

Figure 11.54 *M*-PSK spectral density.

Then $V(f) = T\mathrm{sinc}(fT)$. Substituting into (11.160) yields

$$G_{\tilde{x}}(f) = DT^2\mathrm{sinc}^2(fT) = T\mathrm{sinc}^2(f/D) \qquad (11.161)$$

The spectral density of the *M*-ary PSK signal is given by substituting $A_c = \sqrt{\dfrac{2E_s}{T}}$ and (11.161) into (11.153) as

$$G_x(f) = \frac{E_s}{2}\left\{\mathrm{sinc}^2\left[(f - f_c)/D\right] + \mathrm{sinc}^2\left[(f + f_c)/D\right]\right\}$$

Substituting $D = R_b/k$ yields

$$G_{MPSK}(f) = \frac{E_s}{2}\left\{\mathrm{sinc}^2\left[k(f - f_c)/R_b\right] + \mathrm{sinc}^2\left[k(f + f_c)/R_b\right]\right\} \qquad (11.162)$$

From (11.162), the null-to-null bandwidth for the *M*-ary PSK signal is $2R_b/k$ as shown in Figure 11.54.

BPSK

For $M = 2$, substituting $k = 1$ and $E_s = E_b$ in (11.162), we get

$$G_{BPSK}(f) = \frac{E_b}{2}\left\{\mathrm{sinc}^2\left[(f - f_c)/R_b\right] + \mathrm{sinc}^2\left[(f + f_c)/R_b\right]\right\} \qquad (11.163)$$

The spectrum of BPSK signaling is plotted in Figure 11.55 along with that of QPSK/OQPSK and MSK. The null-to-null bandwidth for BPSK is also $2R_b$, the same as that of ASK. However, the BPSK spectrum does not have the carrier-frequency impulse. The absence of a discrete carrier component makes BPSK more power efficient. Note that the bandwidth of the BPSK signal is twice that of the underlying baseband signal.

QPSK/OQPSK

For the QPSK signal, $M = 4, k = 2$. Substituting in (11.162) yields

$$G_{QPSK}(f) = \frac{E_s}{2}\left\{\mathrm{sinc}^2\left[2(f - f_c)/R_b\right] + \mathrm{sinc}^2\left[2(f + f_c)/R_b\right]\right\} \qquad (11.164)$$

The null-to-null bandwidth for the QPSK signal is R_b, which is one-half that for BPSK as shown in Figure 11.55. The power spectrum of OQPSK is identical to that of QPSK. OQPSK and QPSK illustrate two schemes that look alike from a theoretical point of

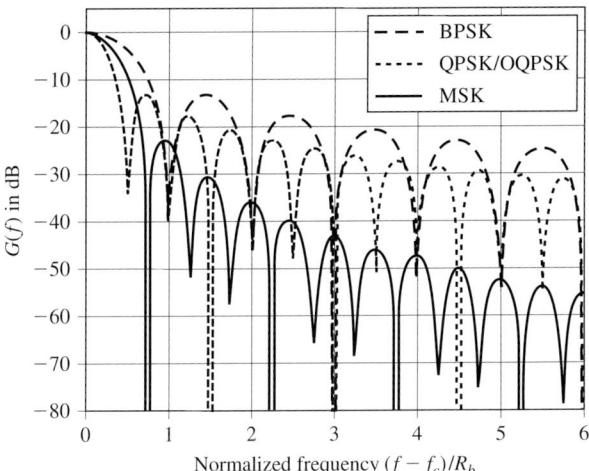

Figure 11.55 MSK, BPSK, and QPSK/OQPSK spectra.

view but can behave quite differently in practice. The bandlimited OQPSK system retains its spectral shaping under hard limiting (as in a nonlinear satellite transponder), while the QPSK spectrum is spread out again.

MSK

We consider the MSK as an OQPSK signal in (11.127) where $I(t)$ and $Q(t)$ are random polar NRZ pulse trains. The spectral density of $I(t)$ and $Q(t)$ is now given by using (9.33) with $M = 2$ as

$$G_I(f) = G_Q(f) = D|P(f)|^2 = \frac{R_b}{2}|P(f)|^2 \qquad (11.165)$$

where $P(f)$ is FT of the half-sinusoidal pulse $p(t)$ defined by

$$p(t) = \Pi\left(\frac{\pi t}{2T_b}\right)\cos\left(\frac{\pi t}{2T_b}\right) \longleftrightarrow \frac{4T_b}{\pi}\frac{\cos(2\pi f T_b)}{1 - (4fT_b)^2} = P(f) \qquad (11.166)$$

Substituting (11.165) and (11.166) into (11.152), we obtain

$$G_{\tilde{x}}(f) = G_I(f) + G_Q(f) = R_b|P(f)|^2 = \frac{16T_b\cos^2(2\pi T_b f)}{\pi^2\left[1 - (4T_b f)^2\right]^2} \qquad (11.167)$$

The spectral density of MSK signal $x(t)$ is now given by substituting (11.167) into (11.153) as

$$G_{MSK}(f) = \frac{E_b}{2T_b}\left[G_{\tilde{x}}(f - f_c) + G_{\tilde{x}}(f + f_c)\right]$$

$$= \frac{8E_b}{\pi^2}\left\{\frac{\cos^2[2\pi T_b(f - f_c)]}{\left[1 - (4T_b(f - f_c))^2\right]^2} + \frac{\cos^2[2\pi T_b(f + f_c)]}{\left[1 - (4T_b(f + f_c))^2\right]^2}\right\} \qquad (11.168)$$

It can be seen from Figure 11.55 that the null-to-null bandwidth for the MSK signal is 1.5 R_b. While the main lobe of the MSK spectrum is broader than the main lobe of the QPSK or OQPSK spectrum, the side lobes decrease much more rapidly for the former than for the latter. This is a very desirable characteristic for avoiding adjacent channel interference when channels are densely packed to efficiently utilize the scarce spectrum.

M-*ary QAM*

The rectangular *M*-QAM signal for a symbol rate *D* is given from (11.135) as

$$x(t) = \sqrt{\frac{2E_s}{T}}\big[I(t)\cos(2\pi f_c t) - Q(t)\sin(2\pi f_c t)\big]$$

The in-phase and quadrature baseband signals $I(t)$ and $Q(t)$ in (11.136) are statistically independent $\sqrt{M}$-ary polar NRZ pulse trains. Using (9.22), the spectral densities of quadrature signals are given by

$$G_I(f) = C_o^2 \sigma_a^2 D|V(f)|^2 = G_Q(f) \qquad (11.169)$$

For $\sqrt{M}$-ary polar sequence $\{a_n\} \in \{\pm 1, \pm 3, \ldots, \pm\sqrt{M} - 1\}$

$$\sigma_a^2 = \frac{2}{\sqrt{M}}\sum_{i=1}^{\sqrt{M}/2}(2i - 1)^2 = \frac{M - 1}{3} \qquad (11.170)$$

Substituting (11.40) and (11.170) into (11.169) yields

$$G_I(f) = \frac{D}{2}|V(f)|^2 = G_Q(f) \qquad (11.171)$$

The spectral density of the complex envelope of an *M*-QAM signal is now given by substituting (11.171) into (11.152) as

$$G_{\tilde{x}}(f) = D|V(f)|^2 \qquad (11.172)$$

Substituting $A_c = \sqrt{\frac{2E_s}{T}}$ and (11.172) into (11.153) yields the spectral density of the *M*-ary QAM signal $x(t)$ as

$$G_x(f) = \frac{E_s D}{T2}\big\{|V(f - f_c)|^2 + |V(f + f_c)|^2\big\} \qquad (11.173)$$

Let $v(t)$ be a rectangular pulse of width *T* seconds. Then

$$v(t) = \Pi(t/T)$$

$$V(f) = T\text{sinc}(fT)$$

Substituting into (11.173), we get

$$G_x(f) = \frac{E_s}{2}\big\{\text{sinc}^2[(f - f_c)/D] + \text{sinc}^2[(f + f_c)/D]\big\}$$

Substituting $D = R_b/k$, we get

$$G_{MQAM}(f) = \frac{E_s}{2}\left\{\text{sinc}^2\left[k(f - f_o)/R_b\right] + \text{sinc}^2\left[k(f + f_o)/R_b\right]\right\} \qquad (11.174)$$

The null-to-null bandwidth of an *M*-ary QAM signal is $2R_b/k = 2R_b/\log_2 M$, which is the same as that for an *M*-ary PSK signal.

Sunde's FSK

Using (11.36), the BFSK signal can be written as

$$x(t) = \sqrt{\frac{2E_b}{T_b}} \sum_{n=-\infty}^{\infty} \Pi\left(\frac{t - nT_b}{T_b}\right)\cos\left[2\pi f_c t + a_n\pi\Delta ft\right] \qquad (11.175)$$

where $a_n \in \mathscr{A}_2 = \{1, -1\}$ is a binary random variable. $x(t)$ can be written after trigonometric expansion as

$$x(t) = \sqrt{\frac{2E_b}{T_b}} \sum_{n=-\infty}^{\infty} \Pi\left(\frac{t - nT_b}{T_b}\right)\left\{\cos(2\pi f_c t)\cos(a_n\pi\Delta ft) - \sin(2\pi f_c t)\sin(a_n\pi\Delta ft)\right\} \qquad (11.176)$$

Now

$$\cos(a_n\pi\Delta ft) = \cos(\pi\Delta ft)$$

$$\sin(a_n\pi\Delta ft) = a_n\sin(\pi\Delta ft) \qquad (11.177)$$

Because $\Delta f = R_b$ for Sunde's FSK, we can express the quadrature components of $x(t)$ using (11.176) and (11.177) as

$$I(t) = \sum_{n=-\infty}^{\infty} \Pi\left(\frac{t - nT_b}{T_b}\right)\cos(\pi R_b t) = \cos(\pi R_b t) \qquad (11.178)$$

$$Q(t) = \sum_{n=-\infty}^{\infty} \Pi\left(\frac{t - nT_b}{T_b}\right)a_n\sin(\pi R_b t) = \sum_{n=-\infty}^{\infty} a_n^Q p(t - nT_b) \qquad (11.179)$$

where

$$a_n^Q = (-1)^n a_n$$

$$p(t) = \Pi(t/T_b)\sin(\pi R_b t)$$

The complex envelope of $x(t)$ can now be written by combining (11.178) and (11.179) as

$$\tilde{x}(t) = I(t) + jQ(t) = \cos(\pi R_b t) + j\sum_n a_n^Q p(t - nT_b) \qquad (11.180)$$

The quadrature components are statistically independent. The $I(t)$ component is deterministic and its spectral density is given by

$$G_I(f) = \frac{1}{4}\left[\delta\left(f - \frac{R_b}{2}\right) + \delta\left(f + \frac{R_b}{2}\right)\right] \qquad (11.181)$$

$G_I(f)$ contributes spectral impulses at $\pm R_b/2$. The spectral density of $Q(t)$ is obtained by substituting $E(a_n^Q) = 0$, $Var(a_n^Q) = 1$ into (9.22) as

$$G_Q(f) = R_b|P(f)|^2 \tag{11.182}$$

where

$$|P(f)|^2 = \frac{4}{(\pi R_b)^2}\left[\frac{\cos(\pi f/R_b)}{(2f/R_b)^2 - 1}\right]^2 \tag{11.183}$$

Combining (11.181) through (11.183) yields the spectral density of the complex envelope $\tilde{x}(t)$ of the FSK signal as

$$G_{\tilde{x}}(f) = G_I(f) + G_Q(f) = \frac{1}{4}\left[\delta\left(f - \frac{R_b}{2}\right) + \delta\left(f + \frac{R_b}{2}\right)\right] + \frac{4R_b}{(\pi R_b)^2}\left[\frac{\cos(\pi f/R_b)}{(2f/R_b)^2 - 1}\right]^2 \tag{11.184}$$

Sunde's FSK spectrum is now obtained by substituting (11.184) into (11.153) as

$$G_{BFSK}(f) = \frac{E_b R_b}{8}\left\{\delta\left[f - \left(f_c - \frac{R_b}{2}\right)\right] + \delta\left[f - \left(f_c + \frac{R_b}{2}\right)\right] + \delta\left[f + \left(f_c - \frac{R_b}{2}\right)\right] + \delta\left[f + \left(f_c + \frac{R_b}{2}\right)\right]\right\}$$
$$+ \frac{E_b}{2\pi^2}\left(\frac{\cos[\pi(f - f_c)/R_b]}{[2(f - f_c)/R_b]^2 - 1}\right)^2 + \frac{E_b}{2\pi^2}\left(\frac{\cos[\pi(f + f_c)/R_b]}{[2(f + f_c)/R_b]^2 - 1}\right)^2 \tag{11.185}$$

Figure 11.56 displays the spectrum of Sunde's BFSK. Observe that the impulses correspond to the keyed frequencies $f_c \pm \dfrac{\Delta f}{2} = f_c \pm \dfrac{R_b}{2}$, and that the spectrum has fourth-order roll-off. The rapid roll-off means that Sunde's FSK has very little adjacent channel spillover for $|f - f_c| > R_b$. Although the null-to-null bandwidth of Sunde's BFSK is $3R_b$, some authors recommend that a bandwidth of R_b is sufficient instead of $3R_b$.

11.10.1 Other Bandwidth Definitions

So far we have considered the null-null bandwidth definition of the digitally modulated BP signals. As discussed in Section 9.4, the following alternative measures of the useful frequency content of these signals are widely used.

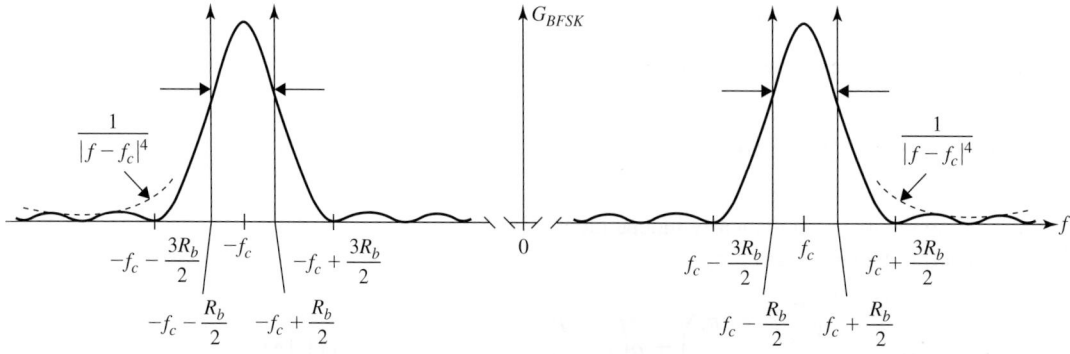

Figure 11.56 Sunde's FSK spectrum.

- **Absolute-absolute bandwidth** ($B_{abs-abs}$). It is defined as the width of the frequency band around the carrier frequency beyond which the spectrum of a digitally modulated BP signal is zero. This measure is meaningful when RC (or Nyquist) pulses are used in the underlying baseband signal.
- **Fractional power bandwidth.** It is the band of frequencies around the carrier frequency that contains a specified percentage of the total signal power. The most popular version of this measure is B_{99} (called the **99% power bandwidth**), which defines the frequency band inside which lies 99% of the signal power. This bandwidth criterion has been adopted by the Federal Communications Commission (FCC Rules and Regulations Section 2.202) and states that the occupied bandwidth is the band that excludes exactly 0.5% of the signal power above the upper band limit and exactly 0.5% of the signal power below the lower band limit.

Table 11.4 summarizes both null-null and absolute-absolute bandwidths for various carrier modulation schemes. Note that in each case, the bandwidth of various quadrature modulation schemes is twice that of the underlying baseband digital signal. As an example, the underlying baseband digital signal in the ASK is a unipolar NRZ pulse train. For a bit rate equal to R_b bps, the bandwidth requirements for transmitting the unipolar NRZ pulse train from Tables 9.1 and 9.6 are

$$\text{Rectangular pulse shape: } B_{null} = R_b \text{ Hz}$$

$$\text{Raised cosine (RC) pulse shape: } B_{abs} = (1 + \alpha)R_b/2 \text{ Hz}$$

where α is the roll-off factor of the RC pulse (Section 9.8). To transmit the data at the same rate of R_b bps using ASK, the bandwidth requirements are

$$\text{Rectangular pulse shape: } B_{null-null} = 2R_b \text{ Hz}$$

$$\text{Raised cosine (RC) pulse shape: } B_{abs-abs} = (1 + \alpha)R_b \text{ Hz}$$

Following our discussion in Section 9.4, the spectral or bandwidth efficiency of a digital carrier modulation scheme is the ratio of data rate R_b bits per second to the required transmission bandwidth B_T Hz. From (9.52), we can write

$$\eta = R_b/B_T \text{ bits/sec-Hz}$$

where B_T can be either $B_{nul-nulll}$ or $B_{abs-abs}$ or B_{99} as justified by the application. For example, the spectral efficiency for ASK signaling using null-null and absolute-absolute bandwidth definitions, respectively, are $1/2$ and $1/(1 + \alpha)$.

Example 11.5

Digital data is to be transmitted over a microwave link with a bandwidth of 100 kHz. Determine the maximum bit rate that can be transmitted over the link using BPSK, (a) QPSK/OQPSK, (b) MSK, and (c) Sunde's FSK. Repeat parts (a) and (b) for an RC pulse shape with $\alpha = 0.5$. Ignore noise.

Solution

a. BPSK
   The null-null bandwidth is related to the bit rate (Table 11.4) by

$$B_{null-null} = 2R_b$$

Table 11.4 Comparison of Carrier Modulation Schemes

Binary Bandpass Signaling	Null-to-Null RF Bandwidth (Hz)	Abs-Abs Bandwidth (Hz)	BER with Coherent Detection	BER with Noncoherent Detection
ASK	$2R_b$	$R_b(1+\alpha)$	$Q\left(\sqrt{E_b/N_o}\right)$	$0.5e^{-E_b/2N_o}$
BPSK	$2R_b$	$R_b(1+\alpha)$	$Q\left(\sqrt{2E_b/N_o}\right)$	Requires coherent detection
Sunde's FSK	$3R_b$		$Q\left(\sqrt{E_b/N_o}\right)$	$0.5e^{-E_b/2N_o}$
DBPSK	$2R_b$	$R_b(1+\alpha)$	$Q\left(\sqrt{2E_b/N_o}\right)$	$0.5e^{-E_b/N_o}$
M-ary Bandpass Signaling				
QPSK/OQPSK	R_b	$R_b(1+\alpha)/2$	$Q\left(\sqrt{2E_b/N_o}\right)$	Requires coherent detection
MSK	$1.5R_b$	$3R_b(1+\alpha)/4$	$Q\left(\sqrt{2E_b/N_o}\right)$	Requires coherent detection
M-PSK ($M>4$)	$2R_b/\log_2 M$	$R_b(1+\alpha)/\log_2 M$	$\dfrac{2}{\log_2 M}Q\left(\sqrt{2\log_2 M \sin^2(\pi/M)E_b/N_o}\right)$	Requires coherent detection
M-DPSK ($M>4$)	$2R_b/\log_2 M$	$R_b(1+\alpha)/2\log_2 M$		$\dfrac{2}{\log_2 M}Q\left(\sqrt{4\log_2 M \sin^2(\pi/2M)E_b/N_o}\right)$
M-QAM (Square constellation)	$2R_b/\log_2 M$	$R_b(1+\alpha)/\log_2 M$	$\dfrac{4}{\log_2 M}\left(1-\dfrac{1}{\sqrt{M}}\right)Q\left(\sqrt{\dfrac{3\log_2 M}{M-1}E_b/N_o}\right)$	Requires coherent detection
M-FSK Coherent	$(M+3)\,R_b/2\log_2 M$		$\dfrac{M-1}{\log_2 M}Q\left(\sqrt{(\log_2 M)E_b/N_o}\right)$	
Noncoherent	$2M\,R_b/\log_2 M$			$\dfrac{M-1}{2\log_2 M}\,0.5\,e^{-(\log_2 M)E_b/2N_o}$

Therefore, $R_b = B_{null-null}/2 = 100/2 = 50$ kb/s.

Using an RC basic pulse shape with $\alpha = 0.5$, the absolute bandwidth is related to the bit rate (Table 11.4) by

$$B_{abs-abs} = (1 + \alpha)R_b = 1.5R_b.$$

Therefore, $R_b = B_{abs-abs}/1.5 = 100/1.5 = 66.7$ kb/s.

b. QPSK

From Table 11.4, $B_{null-null} = R_b$.

Therefore, $R_b = B_{null-null} = 100$ kb/s.

Using an RC basic pulse shape with $\alpha = 0.5$, $B_{abs-abs} = (1 + \alpha)R_b/2 = 0.75R_b$.

Therefore, $R_b = B_{abs-abs}/0.75 = 100/0.75 = 133.4$ kb/s.

c. MSK

From Table 11.4, $B_{null-null} = 1.5R_b$.

Therefore, $R_b = B_{null-null}/1.5 = 100/1.5 = 66.667$ kb/s.

Using an RC basic pulse shape with $\alpha = 0.5$, $B_{abs-abs} = 3(1 + \alpha)R_b/4 = 1.125R_b$.

Therefore, $R_b = B_{abs-abs}/1.125 = 100/1.125 = 88.9$ kb/s.

d. Sunde's FSK

If a more conservative null-to-null bandwidth definition for the required bandwidth is used, $B_{null-null} = 3R_b$.

Therefore, $R_b = B_{null-null}/3 = 100/3 = 33.4$ kb/s.

However, if the $B_{null-null} = R_b$ definition is used, $R_b = B_{null-null} = 100$ kb/s.

Modulation Scheme	Bit Rate	Bit Rate (RC pulses, $\alpha = 0.5$)
BPSK	50 kbps	66.7 kbps
QPSK	100 kbps	133.4 kbps
MSK	66.7 kbps	88.9 kbps
Sunde's FSK	33.4 kbps	
	100 kbps	

Example 11.6

A channel of bandwidth 150 kHz is available. We wish to transmit through it at a data rate of 500 kbps.

a. What is required M for M-ary PSK, DPSK, and QAM? (Note that M should be 2^n for PSK and DPSK and 4^n for a QAM square constellation, where n is an integer.)

b. Compare the modulation schemes of part (a) on the basis of E_b/N_o required to achieve $BER = 10^{-6}$.

Solution

a. The null-null bandwidth for each of the linear modulation schemes (PSK, DPSK, and 4^n for QAM) is given by

$$B_{null-null} = 2D = 2R_b/k \text{ Hz}$$

$$150 = 2 \times 500/k \Rightarrow k = 20/3 = 6.67$$

For M-PSK, M-DPSK, the closest allowed value of M is 128, corresponding to the choice of $k = 7$. For M-QAM, $k = 8$, and $M = 256$ for a square constellation.

b. To give $BER = 10^{-6}$, we calculate E_b/N_o using Table 11.4.

	E_b/N_o(dB)
128-PSK	33.8
128-DPSK	37
256-QAM	23.5

11.11   COMPARISON OF CARRIER MODULATION SCHEMES

For a given bit rate, the design of a digital communication system involves seeking the best trade-off between SNR/bit (E_b/N_o) and the transmission bandwidth required to achieve a specified bit error rate performance. There are a number of other application-related considerations that affect the selection of a carrier modulation/demodulation technique. These include spectral compactness to avoid the adjacent channel interference, hardware complexity, and power consumption. Table 11.4 summarizes transmission bandwidth and SNR/bit requirements for digital carrier transmission systems discussed in this chapter. For a bit rate of R_b bps, QPSK systems require a transmission bandwidth of R_b Hz, which is one-half the value required for BPSK/BASK systems. Although the null-to-null bandwidth of MSK is $1.5R_b$ compared with R_b Hz for QPSK/OQPSK, the energy in its sidelobes decays more rapidly, causing less spectral interference in adjacent channels.

Now let us consider *M*-ary quadrature modulation schemes further. For a given bit rate R_b, the transmission bandwidth is reduced by a factor of $\log_2 M$. However, the SNR/bit required in an *M*-ary system to guarantee a specified BER performance also increases as a nonlinear function of *M*. In high-SNR environments, the available SNR/bit can be traded for improved bandwidth efficiency by using a modulation scheme with large *M*. Because telephone and cable channels offer high SNR/bit, the use of large *M* modulation schemes is quite common to squeeze more bits per second for every Hz of bandwidth. However, in low-SNR channels, such as cellular and satellite, it is not

Table 11.5 SNR/bit Penalty versus Bandwidth Efficiency for Quadrature Modulation Schemes

Carrier Modulation Scheme	Relative Transmission Bandwidth vs. BPSK	E_b/N_o Penalty vs. BPSK (dB)	E_b/N_o for $BER = 10^{-4}$ (dB)
BPSK	1	0	8.4
M-ary PSK	$1/\log_2 M$	$-10\log_{10}\left[\log_2 M \sin^2\left(\dfrac{\pi}{M}\right)\right]$	
4 (QPSK/MSK)	1/2	0	8.4
8	1/3	3.57	11.97
16	1/4	8.17	16.57
M-ary DPSK	$1/\log_2 M$	$-10\log_{10}\left[2\log_2 M \sin^2\left(\dfrac{\pi}{2M}\right)\right], M \geq 4$	
4(DQPSK)	1/2	2.32	10.72
8	1/3	6.41	14.81
16	1/4	11.14	19.54
M-QAM	$1/\log_2 M$	$10\log_{10}\left[2\,(M-1)/3\log_2 M\right]$	
8	1/3	1.92	10.32
16	1/4	3.98	12.38
64	1/6	8.45	16.85
256	1/8	13.27	21.67

possible to exchange the SNR/bit for bandwidth efficiency. Thus, OQPSK and MSK are widely used in satellite and cellular communication systems. Table 11.5 illustrates this trade-off between SNR/bit and transmission bandwidth for a fixed bit rate R_b.

It is important to note the difference in the SNR/bit penalty for different modulation schemes. *M*-ary QAM is significantly more power efficient for large values of *M*. For example, 16-QAM has a 4-dB advantage over 16-PSK, and this increases to ~15 dB for $M = 256$. This explains the popularity of the *M*-QAM modulation scheme and its adoption in cable as well as dial-up modem standards.

FINAL REMARKS

In this chapter we discussed the transmission of digital signals over BP channels using carrier modulation. Carrier modulation involves embedding data-bearing polar or unipolar NRZ pulse trains in the carrier waveform by varying, or modulating, some of its attribute, such as amplitude, phase, or frequency. This has the effect of transferring the signal spectral energy into a specified frequency slot of the BP channel. The recovery of the underlying baseband signal at the demodulator is achieved by coherent or noncoherent demodulation techniques. Now the transmitted data can be detected using the techniques for baseband signals discussed in Chapter 10.

The most popular carrier modulation schemes use quadrature carriers that achieve twice the transmission rate by sending digital signals over in-phase and quadrature channels without any interference. The two-dimensional nature of this modulation scheme was explained using the concept of signal constellation. A modem standard uniquely specifies the signal constellation deployed in its implementation.

The error rate performance calculations for many carrier modulation systems were performed using the techniques developed for the underlying baseband signals in Chapter 10. It is extremely interesting and useful to note that many different signal sets will generate identical constellations by the appropriate choice of the basis set. For example, antipodal and BPSK signaling schemes have the same constellations and consequently have the same BER performance. The calculations of bit and symbol error rates depend solely on the configuration of constellation independent of the choice of basis function set. This decoupling is quite useful in analyzing the performance of digital communication systems.

We observed that the spectra for many carrier modulation schemes can be specified as frequency translated versions of the spectra of the underlying baseband signals discussed in Chapter 9. Finally, we compared the performance of various carrier modulation schemes in terms of trade-off between bandwidth and SNR.

FURTHER READINGS

Transmission of digital data by carrier modulation schemes is covered in a number of undergraduate communication systems texts [1–6]. Ziemer [7] and Anderson [8] provide a more advanced and comprehensive treatment of the material covered in this chapter. The discussion of MSK is benefited from references [9, 10].

1. Ziemer, R., and W. Tranter. *Principles of Communications: Systems, Modulation, and Noise,* 6th ed. Hoboken, NJ: John Wiley, 2009.

2. Proakis, J., and M. Salehi. *Fundamentals of Communication Systems,* 1st ed., Upper Saddle River, NJ: Prentice Hall, 2005.

3. Carlson, B, P. Crilly, and J. Rutledge. *Communication Systems,* 4th ed. New York: McGraw-Hill, 2002.

4. Couch, L. *Digital and Analog Communication Systems,* 7th ed. Upper Saddle River, NJ: Prentice Hall, 2006.

5. Haykin, S. *Communication Systems,* 4th ed. Hoboken, NJ: John Wiley, 2000.

6. Proakis, J., M. Salehi, and G. Bauch. *Contemporary Communication Systems Using MATLAB,* 3rd ed. Stamford, CT: Brooks-Cole, 2004.

7. Ziemer, R., and R. Peterson. *An Introduction to Digital Communication,* 2nd ed. Upper Saddle River, NJ: Prentice Hall, 2001.

8. Anderson, J. *Digital Transmission Engineering,* 2nd ed. Upper Saddle River, NJ: Prentice-Hall, 2005.

9. Pasupathy, S. "Minimum Shift Keying: A Spectrally Efficient Modulation." *IEEE Communications Magazine* 17 (1979): 14–22.

10. Proakis, J., and M. Salehi. *Digital Communications,* 5th ed. New York: McGraw-Hill, 2008.

PROBLEMS

11.1. Digital data at 100 kbps is transmitted over an AWGN channel with a power spectral density $N_o/2 = 10^{-10}$ W/Hz. Calculate the average received power level required to achieve a $BER = 10^{-6}$ for the following modulation schemes:

   a. Coherent binary ASK

   b. Coherent binary PSK

   c. Coherent binary FSK

11.2. A binary digital carrier system with average transmitted power 100 mW has to be designed for the worst-case transmission loss of 60 dB, and $N_o = 10^{-12}$ W/Hz. Find the maximum allowable bit rate for a $BER = 10^{-5}$ using: (a) BPSK; (b) DBPSK; (c) noncoherent BFSK.

11.3. Binary data 01001011101 is to be transmitted using DBPSK. Assume that the carrier frequency $f_c = 2R_b$ and the pulse shape is unipolar NRZ.

   a. Sketch the differential encoder and modulator output waveforms.

   b. Show that the DBPSK demodulator reconstructs the original data in the absence of noise.

11.4. Binary string 01001011101 is to be transmitted using a QPSK signal. Assume that the carrier frequency $f_c = R_b$ and the pulse shape is unipolar NRZ.

   a. Sketch in-phase and quadrature baseband waveforms $I(t)$ and $Q(t)$.

   b. Sketch in-phase and quadrature carrier modulated waveforms $I(t) \cos(2\pi f_c t)$ and $Q(t)\cos(2\pi f_c t)$.

   c. Sketch QPSK waveform.

11.5. Binary string 01001011101 is to be transmitted using an OQPSK signal. Assume that the carrier frequency $f_c = R_b$ and the pulse shape is unipolar NRZ.

   a. Sketch in-phase and quadrature baseband waveforms $I(t)$ and $Q(t)$.

   b. Sketch in-phase and quadrature carrier modulated waveforms $I(t) \cos(2\pi f_c t)$ and $Q(t)\cos(2\pi f_c t)$.

   c. Sketch OQPSK waveform.

11.6. Binary string 01001011101 is to be transmitted using an MSK signal. Assume that the carrier frequency $f_c = R_b$ and the pulse shape is unipolar NRZ.

   a. Sketch in-phase and quadrature baseband waveforms $I(t)$ and $Q(t)$

   b. Sketch in-phase and quadrature carrier modulated waveforms $I(t) \cos(2\pi f_c t)$ and $Q(t)\cos(2\pi f_c t)$

   c. Sketch MSK waveform.

   d. Plot the phase trellis for the bit sequence.

11.7. A channel with a bandwidth of 4 kHz is available. What data rates can be supported by the following modulation schemes?

   a. BPSK

   b. QPSK

   c. MSK

   d. 8-PSK

   e. 64-QAM

   f. 256-QAM

   Assume that the modulator uses RC pulse shaping with a roll-off factor $\alpha = 0.5$. Ignore noise.

11.8. Repeat Problem 11.6 assuming that the modulator uses unipolar NRZ pulse shaping.

11.9. Consider a telephone line channel that is equalized to allow bandpass data transmission over a frequency range of 300 to 3300 Hz. The available channel bandwidth is 3000 Hz with the mid-channel frequency of 1800 Hz. Assume that the modulator uses RC pulse shaping.

   a. For QPSK transmission at 4,800 bps with $f_c = 1,800$ Hz, show that the spectrum of this signal will fit into the channel with roll-off factor $\alpha = 0.25$. Find the absolute and 6-dB bandwidths of the QPSK signal.

   b. Repeat part (a) for the case of 6000 bps 8-PSK signaling. Choose the appropriate value of α.

11.10. A digital cellular system transmits data using QPSK over a BP channel with center frequency 1.93 GHz and bandwidth of 1.25 MHz. The modulator uses RC pulse shaping with a roll-off factor $\alpha = 0.5$. Assume that the channel introduces AWGN of one-sided spectral density $N_o = 10^{-9}$

   a. Determine the maximum bit rate R_b of the system.

   b. Calculate the average power required at the receiver in order to guarantee a BER less than or equal to 10^{-6}.

11.11. Binary data is to be transmitted at 4 Mbps on a radio channel having 1.25 MHz bandwidth.

   a. Select the modulation method that minimizes the signal energy, and calculate E_b/N_o in dB needed for a $BER = 10^{-6}$.

   b. Suppose that we are willing relax the data rate requirement to limit our choice to 4-point signal constellations. What bit rate is achievable with a modulation scheme that ensures constant envelope modulated signal? Determine E_b/N_o in dB needed for a $BER = 10^{-6}$.

11.12. Consider the 8-ary PSK constellation shown in Figure 11.41(a).

   a. Sketch the modulated waveform corresponding to the sequence 100101111010. The carrier frequency is $f_c = 2D$, and the pulse shape is unipolar NRZ.

   b. Draw the block diagram of the modulator and specify the appropriate symbol mapping table assuming the average energy/symbol $E_s = 5$ Joules.

c. Draw the block diagram of the demodulator.

d. Specify the threshold comparator characteristic for in-phase and quadrature branches.

11.13. A QAM system operates on an AWGN channel with $E_s/N_o = 28$ dB and symbol rate $D = 10^6$.

a. Select a square QAM constellation and specify a corresponding integer number of bits per symbol, k, for a modem with the highest bit rate such that $P_e < 10^{-6}$.

b. Compute the bit rate for part (a).

c. Repeat part (a) if $E_b/N_o = 22$ dB.

d. Compute the bit rate for part (c).

11.14. Consider the transmission of digital data using QAM over 6-MHz cable channel which introduces AWGN. We assume that the modem uses RC-shaped pulses with $\alpha = 0.5$.

a. Determine the required E_b/N_o to achieve a symbol error probability of 10^{-6} at 8 Mbps.

b. Repeat part (a) for a bit rate of 16 Mbps.

c. Repeat part (a) for a bit rate of 32 Mbps.

d. Comment on these results?

11.15. Consider the 8-QAM signal constellation shown in Figure P11.1.

a. Assign the bits to each point in the signal constellation using Gray coding.

b. Sketch the modulated waveform corresponding to the sequence 100101111010. The carrier frequency is $f_c = 2D$, and the pulse shape is unipolar NRZ.

c. Determine the symbol rate if the desired bit rate is 45 Mbps.

d. Specify the appropriate symbol mapping table and threshold comparator characteristic for in-phase and quadrature branches.

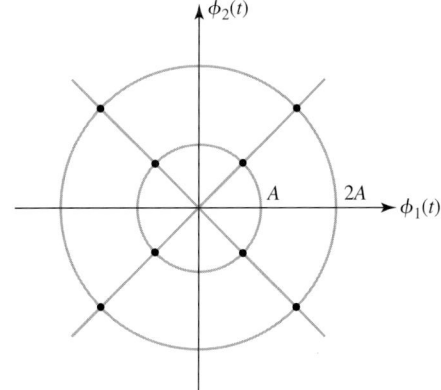

Figure P11.1

11.16. Consider the 8-QAM signal constellation shown in Figure P11.1.

a. Use the nearest neighbor bound to estimate the probability of symbol error.

b. Sketch the decision region boundaries for each point in the constellation.

c. Compare the SNR required for the 8-QAM with that required for the 8-PSK to achieve the same symbol error probability.

d. Which of the two signaling schemes is more vulnerable to phase errors? Comment.

11.17. Consider the 16-QAM signal constellation shown in Figure 11.50.

a. Sketch the modulated waveform corresponding to the sequence 0111100110101101. The carrier frequency is $f_c = 2D$, and the pulse shape is unipolar NRZ.

b. Sketch the decision region boundaries for each point in the constellation.

c. Specify the appropriate symbol mapping table and the threshold comparator characteristic for in-phase and quadrature branches.

11.18. It is desired to transmit data at the rate of 500 kbps over a channel of bandwidth 200 kHz. Assume that the channel introduces AWGN of one-sided spectral density $N_o = 10^{-9}$. The modulator uses RC pulse shaping with roll-off factor $\alpha = 0.5$.

a. Consider PSK, DPSK, and QAM digital modulation schemes. Choose the constellation size $M = 2^n$, where n is an integer. For QAM restrict to a square constellation.

b. Select the most efficient modulation scheme on the basis of average power required to achieve a $BER = 10^{-6}$ or better.

c. Discuss the relative advantages and disadvantages of the modulation schemes considered here.

11.19. The CCITT V.2916-QAM signal constellation shown in Figure P11.2. Assume that the pulse shape is unipolar NRZ and average energy per symbol is 2 Watts/sec.

a. Draw a bock diagram of the modulator and specify the contents of symbol mapping tables.

b. Sketch the modulated waveform corresponding to the sequence 0111100110101101. The carrier frequency is $f_c = 2D$, and the pulse shape is unipolar NRZ.

c. Sketch the decision boundaries for the ML detector.

d. Determine the estimated symbol sequences $\hat{a}_n^I$ and $\hat{a}_n^Q$ and corresponding bit sequences for the following outputs of symbol-rate samplers.

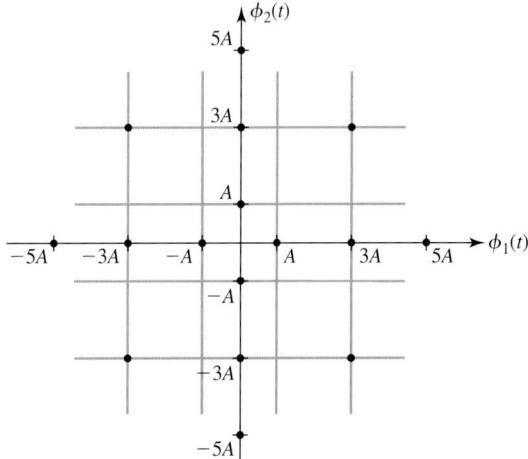

Figure P11.2

n	1	2	3	4	5	6
In-phase sampler O/P	0.93	−2	−1.97	−0.052	2.1	−0.95
Quadrature sampler O/P	−0.56	0.015	2	0.95	−1.95	−0.015

11.20. For MSK signaling, show that the carriers in (11.125) are orthogonal.

  a. Sketch the constellation diagram and determine the decision regions.

  b. Draw the block diagrams of the modulator and the demodulator.

MATLAB PROBLEMS

A digital carrier modulated system typically uses a carrier frequency which is much larger than the bandwidth of the signal. Complex envelope representation requires significantly fewer samples to represent such signals and process them through BP systems. Therefore, we will carry simulations in terms of complex envelopes for computational efficiency, wherever justified.

11.21. Consider the simulation of a QPSK system to display waveforms and estimate the spectral density of a QPSK signal.

  a. Generate in-phase and quadrature symbol sequences `ai[n]` and `aq[n]` of length `Nsymbols`.

```
ai = sign(rand(1, Nsymbols)-0.5);

aq = sign(rand(1, Nsymbols)-0.5);

a = complex(ai , aq);
```

  Use `Nsymbols = 1024`.

  b. Generate polar NRZ waveforms `In[n]` and `Qn[n]` corresponding to symbol sequences `ai[n]` and `aq[n]`. Use `nsamp` = 32 samples / symbol interval (T) in your simulation.

```
In= [];

Qn= [];

for j=1: Nsymbols

In = [In ai(j)*ones(1,nsamples)];

Qn = [Qn aq(j)*ones(1,nsamples)];

end
```

  The complex envelope `xwave[n]` of the QPSK signal is given by

```
xwave = complex(In, Qn)
```

  Plot in-phase and quadrature waveforms `I[n]` and `Q[n]`.

  c. The QPSK signal sequence `x[n]` is given by

```
Ntotal=Nbits*nsamples

nn = 1:1:Ntotal;

wo =i*2*pi*fc*t;

w_n= exp(wo);

x=real(xwave.*w_n)
```

  Choose $f_c = 4T$. Plot [n] for 10 symbol periods.

  d. Display the power spectral density estimates `gxx` of these waveforms using MATLAB command `pwelch`.

```
[gxx,w]= pwelch(xwave, Nsymbols, nsamples);
```

  Compare it with the display obtained from the theoretical expression obtained in this chapter.

11.22. Repeat 11.21 assuming that the modulator uses RC pulse shaping with $\alpha = 0.5$.

11.23. Consider the transmission of QPSK signals over an AWGN channel.

  a. Generate the complex envelope `xwave[n]` of the QPSK signal as discussed in Problem 11.21. Use `Nsymbols = 20,000`.

```
xwave = complex(In, Qn)
```

  b. AWGN is simulated by a sequence of Gaussian random variables with zero mean and variance σ^2. For a given value `EsNo` of E_s/N_o in dB, the one-sided spectral density N_o is given by

$$N_o = E_s 10^{-\text{EsNo}/10}$$

  c. For the QPSK signal with $T = 1$, $E_s = 2$. The variance of Gaussian random samples to simulate AWGN of one-sided spectral density N_o is now obtained from (6.344) as

$$\sigma^2 = \frac{N_o f_s}{2} = \frac{2 \times 10^{-\text{EsNo}/10} f_s}{2} = 10^{-\text{EsNo}/10} f_s$$

  where f_s = number of samples/pulse (`nsamp`) for $T = 1$.

  d. The in-phase and quadrature components of the received sequence `r[n]` are given by

```
ri= In +sigma*(randn(1, Ntotal)

rq= Qn +sigma*(randn(1, Ntotal)
```

  where

```
sigma =SQRT(nsamp*(10^(-0.1*EsNo))
```

  and

```
Ntotal= Nsymbols*nsamples.
```

  e. The sequence `ri[n]` and `rq[n]` are processed by integrate-and-dump filters in the in-phase and quadrature paths. The outputs of symbol-rate samplers `rio` and `rqo` are detected using threshold comparators.

```
for n = 1: Nsymbols

m1=(n-1)*nsamples+1;

m2=n*nsamples;

rio = sum(ri(m1:m2))/nsamples;
```

```
rqo = sum(rq_n(m1:m2))/nsamples;

% Threshold comparator

if(rio < 0 & rqo < 0)

ahat(n) = -1-1j;

elseif(rio >= 0 & rqo >=  0)

ahat(n) = 1+1j;

elseif(rio < 0 & rqo >=  0)

ahat(n) = -1 + 1j;

else

ahat(n) = 1-1j;

end

end
```

f. Calculate the simulated average probability of error for
    E_s/N_o values of 6–16 dB and compare it with the nearest
    neighbor bound.

11.24. Consider the simulation of a 16-QAM system to display waveforms and estimate the spectral density of a 16-QAM signal.

a. Generate in-phase and quadrature symbol sequences
    ai[n] and aq[n] of length Nsymbols.

    ```
    M = 16

    rootm = sqrt(M)

    M1= rootm-1;

    ai = 2*fix(rootm*rand(1,Nsymbols))-
    M1; % In-phase symbol stream

    aq = 2*fix(rootm*rand(1,Nsymbols))-
    M1; %Quadrature symbol stream
    ```

    Use Nsymbols = 1024.

b. Generate polar NRZ waveforms In[n] and Qn[n]
    for the symbol sequences ai[n] and aq[n]. Use
    nsamp =16 samples/symbol interval (T) in your simu-
    lation. Plot the in-phase and quadrature waveforms
    In[n] and Qn[n].

c. Display the power spectral density estimates gxx of these
    waveforms using MATLAB command pwelch.

    ```
    [gxx,w]= pwelch(xwave, Nsymbols,
    nsamples);
    ```

    Compare it with the display obtained from the theoretical
    expression obtained in this chapter.

11.25. Repeat 11.24 assuming that the modulator uses RC pulse
shaping with $\alpha = 0.5$.

11.26. Consider the transmission of QAM-16 signals over an AWGN
channel.

a. Generate in-phase and quadrature baseband waveforms
    In[n] and Qn[n] of the QAM-16 signal as discussed in
    Problem 11.24. Use Nsymbols = 20,000.

    ```
    xwave = complex(In, Qn);
    ```

b. AWGN is simulated by a sequence of Gaussian random
    variables with zero mean and variance σ^2. For a given
    value esno of E_s/N_o in dB, the one-sided spectral density
    N_o is given by

    $$N_o = E_s 10^{-\text{EsNo}/10}$$

c. For the QAM-16 signal with $T = 1$, $E_s = 10$. The variance
    of Gaussian random samples to simulate AWGN of one-
    sided spectral density N_o is now obtained from (6.344) as

    $$\sigma^2 = \frac{N_o f_s}{2} = \frac{10 \times 10^{-\text{EsNo}/10} f_s}{2} = 5 \times 10^{-\text{EsNo}/10} f_s$$

    where f_s = number of samples/pulse (nsamp) for $T = 1$.

d. The in-phase and quadrature components of the received
    sequence r[n] are given by

    ```
    ri= In +sigma*(randn(1, Ntotal)

    rq= Qn +sigma*(randn(1, Ntotal)
    ```

    where

    ```
    sigma =SQRT(nsamp*(5*(10^(-0.1*EsNo)))
    ```

    and

    ```
    Ntotal= Nsymbols*nsamples.
    ```

e. The sequence ri[n] and rq[n] are processed by
    integrate-and-dump filters in the in-phase and quadrature
    paths. The outputs of symbol-rate samplers rio and rqo
    are detected using threshold comparators.

    ```
    % Threshold comparator

    if((rio <=  0) & (rio > -2))

    areal = -1;

    elseif(rio <= -2)

    areal = -3;

    elseif((rio > 0) & (rio < 2))

    areal = 1;

    else

    areal = 3;

    end

    if ((rqo <=  0) & (rqo > -2))

    aimag = -1;

    elseif(rqo <= -2)

    aimag = -3;

    elseif((rqo > 0) & (rqo < 2))

    aimag = 1;

    else

    aimag = 3;

    end

    ahat = complex(areal, aimag);
    % Detector estimate
    ```

f. Calculate the simulated average probability of error for
    E_s/N_o values of 6–19 dB and compare it with the nearest
    neighbor estimate.

An Interview with Henry Samueli

Courtesy of Henry Samueli

Why did you choose a career in the communication field?

I was fascinated with electronics as a youngster and in the seventh grade I built a short-wave radio out of vacuum tubes from a Heathkit project, and that set me on my career path to become an electrical engineer in the communications field. I developed a deep curiosity about how wireless communications worked, and I made it my mission in life to figure out how that radio worked. It took me until graduate school to finally figure it out.

In your opinion what are the major innovations that have contributed to the phenomenal progress in broadband and wireless communications? What has been the impact of semiconductor revolution? Optical fiber revolution? Internet?

The semiconductor revolution has been the primary driver behind the exponential growth of the broadband and wireless communications industries. The capabilities of communications chips double roughly every two years in accordance with Moore's law, so over the last 20 years we have seen a thousand-fold increase in functionality of these communications devices which has enabled the amazing devices we all use today.

To what extent is Moore's law relevant to improvements in the integrated circuits for broadband communications?

In addition to increasing functionality of chips, Moore's law has enabled much higher communications speeds over the Internet and wireless channels. Higher speed communications requires much more sophisticated algorithms and signal processing techniques which are now practical to implement on a single integrated circuit. Twenty years ago these algorithms could only be run on mainframe computers, but today they run in the palm of your hand.

What is the next big thing in broadband communications? Wireless communications?

Broadband and wireless communications have been evolving steadily over the last 20 years and will continue to do so. Every few years, the telecommunications carriers upgrade their networks to run at higher and higher speeds. In the wireless space, the next big transition is to a technology known as LTE (Long Term Evolution of 3G). Initial LTE rollouts have begun with several carriers worldwide, and the technology should become mainstream by the middle of this decade. It will enable wireless download speeds of up to 100 Mbps over the cellular networks. There are many advances in wired networks as well, with optical and cable access networks pushing data rates up to 1 Gbps to the home. In addition, in-home networking is becoming more popular for sharing multimedia content between users and devices, and there are many new technologies to enable this such as WiFi wireless, MoCA over coax cables, and HomePlug over power lines.

Who inspired you professionally the most?

The list is too long to enumerate. There were so many pioneers in the communications and semiconductor industries, especially in the early days of Bell Labs. They all were great inspirations to current generation communications engineers.

What was your vision for the young high-tech start-up when you and Henry Nicholas founded Broadcom? What environmental and other factors contributed to its phenomenal success?

Both of us came out of the defense industry, having worked at TRW on military broadband communications systems. Our vision when we started Broadcom was to take the knowledge we gained from defense applications and find a way to evolve this technology and apply it to commercial applications. Our phenomenal success was largely due to the luck of our timing. We started the company just in time to get caught up in the Internet revolution.

Do you have any advice for the new generation of students and entrepreneurs entering the communications field?

The simplest advice to students and entrepreneurs is to just follow your passions. Being an entrepreneur takes an enormous amount of hard work and self-sacrifice. Unfortunately, success is most often due to factors which are out of your control such as timing and market conditions, so don't worry too much about things you can't control, just focus and be passionate about things you can control.

Dr. Henry Samueli received a B.S., M.S., and Ph.D. in Electrical Engineering from UCLA in 1975, 1976, and 1980, respectively. Since 1985 Dr. Samueli has been a professor in the Electrical Engineering Department at the University of California, Los Angeles, where he has supervised research programs in broadband communications circuits and digital signal processing. He has published more than 100 technical papers in these areas, and he is a named inventor in 62 patents. He was elected a Fellow of the Institute of Electrical and Electronics Engineers (IEEE) in 2000, a member of the National Academy of Engineering in 2003, and a Fellow of the American Academy of Arts and Sciences in 2004. Dr. Samueli serves on the UC President's Board on Science and Innovation, and the Chancellor's Advisory Council at both UCLA and UC Irvine.

Dr. Samueli co-founded Broadcom Corporation in 1991 and currently serves as Chief Technical Officer of the company. Broadcom is a global leader in providing semiconductor solutions for wired and wireless communications. He helps drive the vision of Broadcom's research and development activities and he also helps coordinate corporate-wide engineering development initiatives. In 2009 Broadcom had revenues of 4.5 billion and employed more than 7500 people worldwide at year-end. He was the chief scientist and one of the founders of PairGain Technologies, Inc., a telecommunications equipment manufacturer in the digital subscriber line (DSL) industry, and he consulted for PairGain from 1988 to 1994.

CHAPTER 12

Digital Signal Transmission Through Time Dispersive Channels

In Chapters 10 and 11, we studied the transmission of digital signals through an idealized channel model where the only signal impairment mechanism considered was additive white Gaussian noise. Because the channel bandwidth was assumed to be much greater than the signal bandwidth, the detection of a transmitted symbol was not influenced by interference from other symbols. In this chapter we consider the problem of digital signaling at symbol rates such that the channel introduces **intersymbol interference (ISI).** The cause of ISI is different depending on the channel type:

- In telephone channels, the mechanism of ISI is the magnitude and delay distortion caused by the nonideal frequency response characteristic $H_c(f)$ of the TWP. Because the bandwidth of these channels is limited, this implies that the output signal pulses are not duration-limited as discussed in Section 2.6. A succession of pulses transmitted through the channel at rates comparable to or greater than the channel bandwidth are smeared to the extent that they cannot be identified as distinct pulses resulting in ISI.
- In cellular channels, the signal from the base station arrives at the mobile via many paths with randomly varying time delays causing spreading of transmitted pulses. This is characterized statistically by the **RMS delay spread** parameter of the cellular channel. Symbol periods on the order of the channel's rms delay spread cause ISI, and a mitigation scheme is required.

The term **equalization** refers to the signal processing that is done at the receiver to mitigate the effects of ISI. An important characteristic of the channels in this category is that their impulse or frequency response is either not known in advance or varies over time. As a consequence, the cancellation of ISI requires that the equalizer measure the impulse or frequency response of the channel (**training**) and adapt its response as the channel changes (**tracking**). That is, the equalizer must be adaptive.

This chapter considers signal design and equalization schemes for the mitigation of ISI. Equalizers that make symbol-by-symbol decisions can be classified as either linear or nonlinear designs. Linear equalization techniques usually enhance noise in the process of compensating for the channel roll-off characteristics. Thus, most widely used equalizer designs attempt to balance ISI cancellation with noise enhancement.

Although this chapter limits consideration to transmission of M-ary PAM signals over channels which introduce AWGN and ISI, the results can be generalized to other linear modulation schemes such as M-PSK and M-QAM by using the complex envelope representation of signals and systems. This chapter is organized into following sections:

12.1 TRANSMISSION OF PAM SIGNALS THROUGH BANDLIMITED CHANNELS.

We model the transmission of digital data using amplitude-modulated pulse waveforms over a channel, which introduces ISI in addition to additive white Gaussian noise.

12.2 NYQUIST'S CRITERION FOR ZERO ISI.

This section considers the design of the pulse shape so that symbol detection will not suffer from ISI. The resulting Nyquist criterion specifies the maximum symbol rate achievable through such a channel in the absence of noise.

12.3 TRANSMIT AND RECEIVE FILTERS FOR BANDLIMITED AWGN CHANNELS.

In this section, optimum transmitter pulse shaping and receive filter responses for nonideal bandlimited channels are derived.

12.4 PARTIAL RESPONSE (DUOBINARY) SIGNALING.

We study duobinary waveform shapes that allow controlled amounts of ISI to achieve Nyquist rate transmission over bandlimited channels using practically realizable transmit and receive filters.

12.5   LINEAR EQUALIZERS.

Because real-life communication channels either are not known in advance or change with time, we describe the design of optimum linear receiver structures that are easily amenable to adaptation required for compensating ISI variations. Minimum mean-square error and zero-forcing criteria are used to compute optimum equalizer coefficients.

12.6   ADAPTIVE EQUALIZATION.

This section introduces adaptive techniques for optimizing equalizer performance when channel characteristics are not known or subject to temporal variations. We study an algorithm for dynamically adjusting equalizer coefficients to optimize its performance in such an environment.

12.7   DECISION FEEDBACK EQUALIZERS.

This section describes a nonlinear equalizer structure that uses decision feedback to cancel the ISI from symbols that have already been detected. Such equalizers provide improved ISI cancellation without significant noise enhancement.

12.8   PERFORMANCE OF LINEAR AND DECISION FEEDBACK EQUALIZERS.

We analyze the performance of various equalizers for representative channel models.

The chapter concludes with final remarks and a selected list of references.

12.1   TRANSMISSION OF PAM SIGNALS THROUGH BANDLIMITED CHANNELS

For our purposes, a bandlimited channel is characterized as a linear filter having frequency response characteristic $H_c(f) = 0$ for $|f| > W$. This, of course, implies that if the transmitted signal has frequency components outside the channel band (i.e., $|f| > W$ Hz), they are completely attenuated by the channel. The system model for signaling through a bandlimited channel is shown in Figure 12.1. We assume that the M-ary PAM data signal is given by

$$s(t) = \sum_{n=-\infty}^{\infty} a_n \delta(t - nT) \tag{12.1}$$

where a_n is the M-ary pulse amplitude in the nth symbol interval. We assume that $a_n \in \{\pm A, \pm 3A, \ldots, \pm(M-1)A\}$ are iid discrete random variables. The transmitted waveform is generated by passing $s(t)$ through a pulse-shaping transmit filter with impulse response $h_T(t)$.

$$x(t) = \sum_{n=-\infty}^{\infty} a_n h_T(t - nT) \tag{12.2}$$

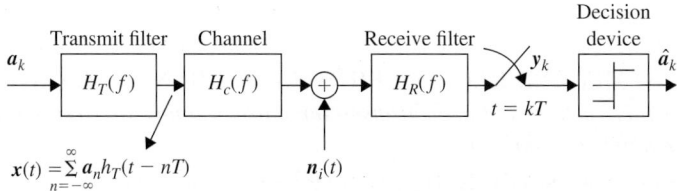

Figure 12.1 System model for PAM signaling through a bandlimited channel.

We assume that $h_T(t)$ is an orthogonal pulse in the sense that

$$\int_{-\infty}^{\infty} h_T(t - mT)h_T(t - nT)dt = 0, \quad m \neq n \tag{12.3}$$

Equation (12.3) implies that copies of $h_T(t)$ shifted by integer multiples of the symbol interval are orthogonal. An example of a widely implemented orthogonal pulse is the **root raised cosine (RRC)** waveform which is discussed in Section 12.2. When the signal in (12.2) is transmitted over a bandlimited channel, it results in an overlap of the individual transmitted symbol waveforms (i.e., $a_n h_T(t - nT)$) at the receiver, creating ISI. The channel output is further corrupted by the addition of white Gaussian noise $n_i(t)$ at the receiver front-end. The received signal is given by

$$\boldsymbol{r}(t) = \boldsymbol{x}(t) \otimes h_c(t) + \boldsymbol{n}_i(t)$$

$$= \sum_{n=-\infty}^{\infty} a_n p_c(t - nT) + \boldsymbol{n}_i(t) \tag{12.4}$$

where $p_c(t)$ is the combined impulse response of the transmit filter and the channel.

$$p_c(t) = h_T(t) \otimes h_c(t) \tag{12.5}$$

Alternatively, the channel output pulse $p_c(t)$ can be represented in the frequency domain as

$$P_c(f) = H_T(f)H_c(f) \tag{12.6}$$

where

$$p_c(t) \stackrel{\mathfrak{I}}{\longleftrightarrow} P_c(f)$$

$$h_c(t) \stackrel{\mathfrak{I}}{\longleftrightarrow} H_c(f)$$

$$h_T(t) \stackrel{\mathfrak{I}}{\longleftrightarrow} H_T(f) \tag{12.7}$$

Let us assume that the received signal $\boldsymbol{r}(t)$ is first passed through a filter with frequency response function $H_R(f)$ and then sampled at symbol rate $D = 1/T$. We express the output of the receive filter as

$$\boldsymbol{y}(t) = \sum_{n=-\infty}^{\infty} a_n p_r(t - nT) + \boldsymbol{n}(t) \tag{12.8}$$

where

$$p_r(t) = p_c(t) \otimes h_R(t) = h_T(t) \otimes h_c(t) \otimes h_R(t) \tag{12.9}$$

is the combined impulse response of the transmit filter, channel, and the receive filter. In the frequency domain, the overall response of the system can be represented as

$$P_r(f) = H_T(f)H_c(f)H_R(f) \tag{12.10}$$

$n(t)$ is the noise component at the receive filter output. Now if $y(t)$ is sampled at times $t = kT, k = 0, 1, \ldots$, we have

$$y(kT) = \sum_{n=-\infty}^{\infty} a_n p_r(kT - nT) + n(kT) \tag{12.11}$$

Defining $y_k = y(kT)$, $n_k = n(kT)$, and $p_r[k] = p_r(kT)$, we can write (12.11) as

$$y_k = \sum_{n=-\infty}^{\infty} a_n p_r[k - n] + n_k \tag{12.12}$$

The receive filter output sample values can, equivalently, be represented as

$$y_k = a_k p_r[0] + \sum_{\substack{n=-\infty \\ n \neq k}}^{\infty} a_n p_r[k - n] + n_k$$

$$= a_k p_r[0] + \underbrace{\sum_{\substack{n=-\infty \\ n \neq 0}}^{\infty} a_{k-n} p_r[n]}_{\text{ISI}} + n_k \tag{12.13}$$

The first term on the right-hand side of (12.13) is the desired signal because it can be used to identify the transmitted symbol a_k, while the middle sum is the interference from the neighboring pulses. Each interference term is proportional to a sample of the receiver output pulse $p_r(t)$ associated with other symbols a_n, $n \neq k$. The maximum value of ISI occurs when each symbol a_{k-n} has the largest magnitude $(M - 1)A$ and the same algebraic sign as $p_r[n]$. The **peak distortion** D_{peak} is given by

$$D_{peak} = (M - 1)A \sum_{\substack{n=-\infty \\ n \neq 0}}^{\infty} |p_r[n]| \tag{12.14}$$

The ISI is zero if and only if the overall impulse response $p_r(t)$ has zero crossings at T-spaced intervals. That is,

$$p_r[k] = \begin{cases} 1, & k = 0 \\ 0, & k \neq 0 \end{cases} \tag{12.15}$$

12.1.1 Eye Diagrams

An eye diagram is a simple and convenient tool for studying the effects of ISI and other channel impairments in digital transmission. It is obtained by displaying multiple sweeps of the signal of interest, for example $p_r(t)$, on an oscilloscope triggered at the symbol rate. It is superposition of T-second segments of the signal obtained by slicing it at the symbol rate as shown in Figure 12.2. In practice, an eye diagram is viewed using a pseudorandom signal of sufficiently long period to simulate the random data in a given application. The eye diagram derives its name from the fact that it resembles the human eye for binary signals. For an *M*-PAM signal, the eye diagram looks like a group of (*M* − 1) binary eyes stacked vertically.

Eye diagrams conveniently provide a great deal of useful information about the quality of the signal being observed. The interior region of the eye diagram is called the **eye opening.** Referring to Figure 12.3, the height of the eye opening, at a specified sampling time, defines the **noise margin** of the system. If the eye is closing because of severe ISI or noise, errors will occur due to poor noise margin at the sampling instant. The width of the eye opening determines sensitivity to the sampling time offset. A narrow eye opening width implies that a small error in the sampling clock could result in sampling at time instants when the noise margin is small, and thus errors would be more likely. It is apparent that the preferred time for sampling is the instant of time at which the eye is open the widest.

The slope of the inner eye indicates sensitivity to timing jitter, or variance in the timing offset. A very steep slope implies that the eye closes rapidly as the timing offset increases. In this case, a significant amount of jitter in the sampling time considerably

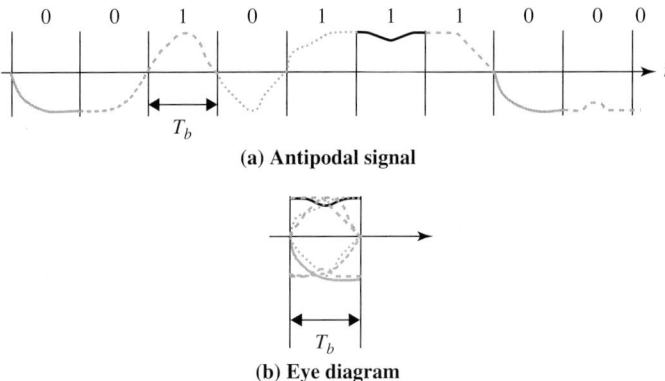

Figure 12.2 Distorted antipodal signal and its eye diagram display.

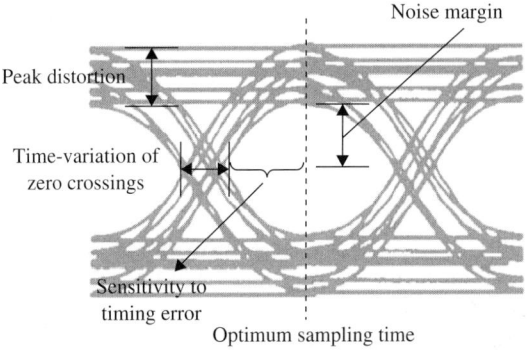

Figure 12.3 Interpretation of eye diagram.

Figure 12.4 Eye diagrams for antipodal *M*-PAM signaling

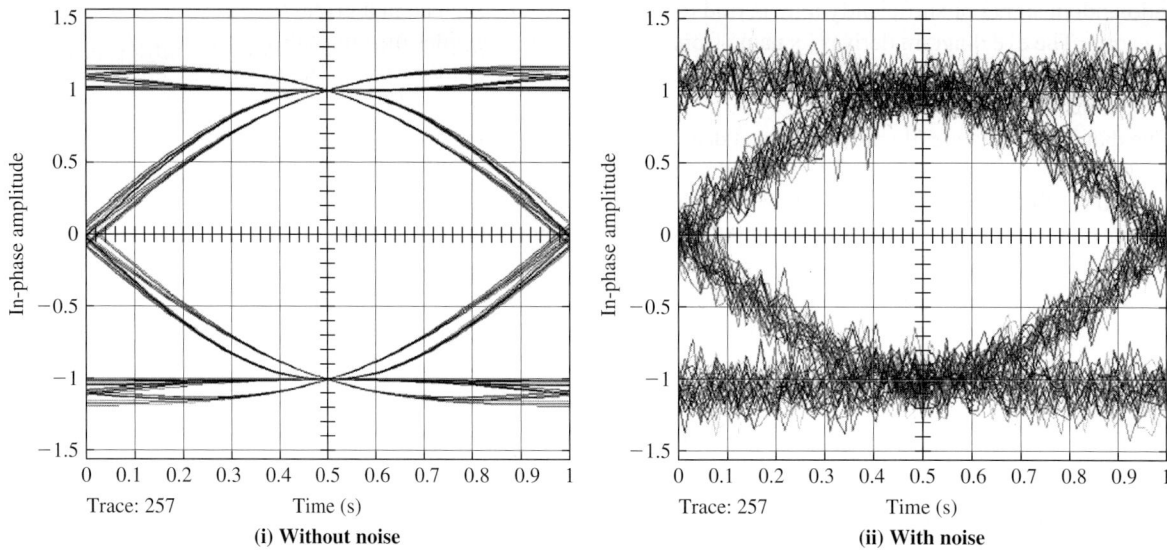

(i) Without noise | (ii) With noise

(a) Antipodal signaling, *M* = 2, α = 0.8

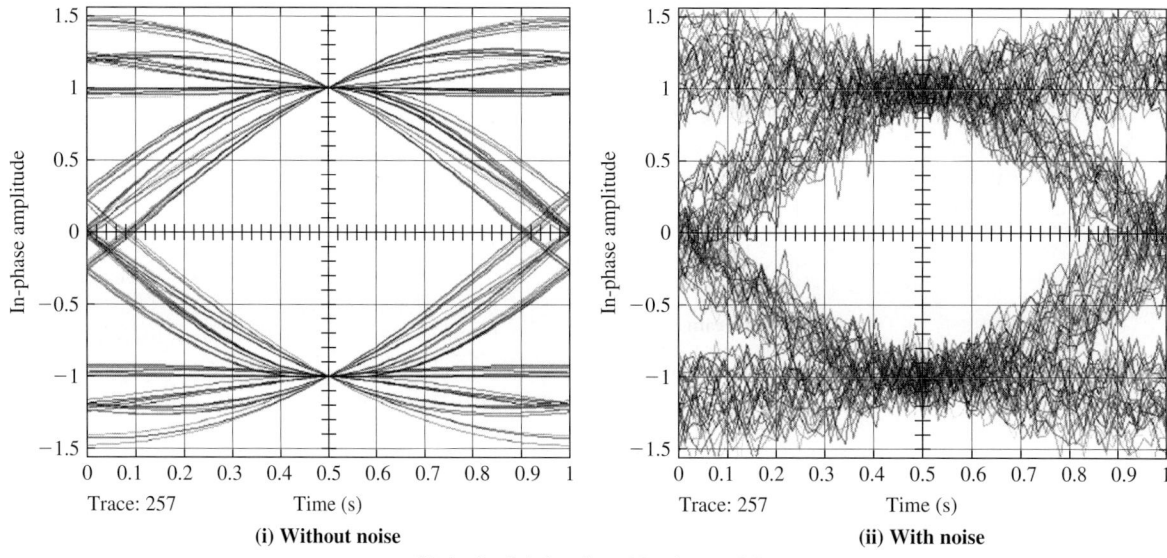

(i) Without noise | (ii) With noise

(b) Antipodal signaling, *M* = 2, α = 0.5

increases the probability of error. Figure 12.4 illustrates eye diagrams for RC pulse signaling with various roll-off factor (i.e., α) values. For binary transmission on this channel, there is a significant eye opening in the center of the plot as displayed in Figures 12.4(a) to (c). As the roll-off factor α is decreased implying reduced excess bandwidth

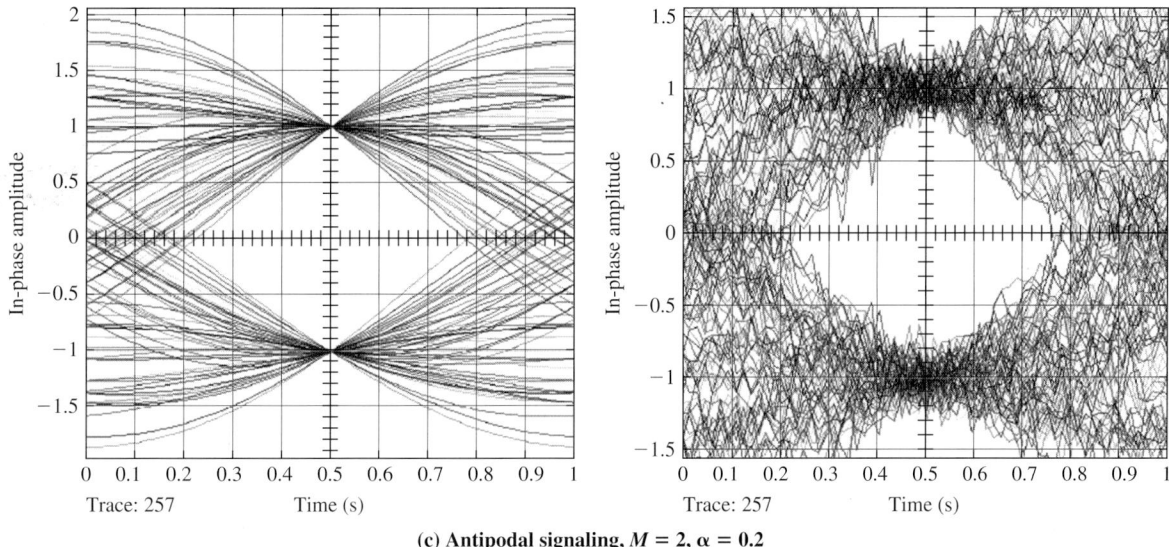

(c) Antipodal signaling, $M = 2$, $\alpha = 0.2$

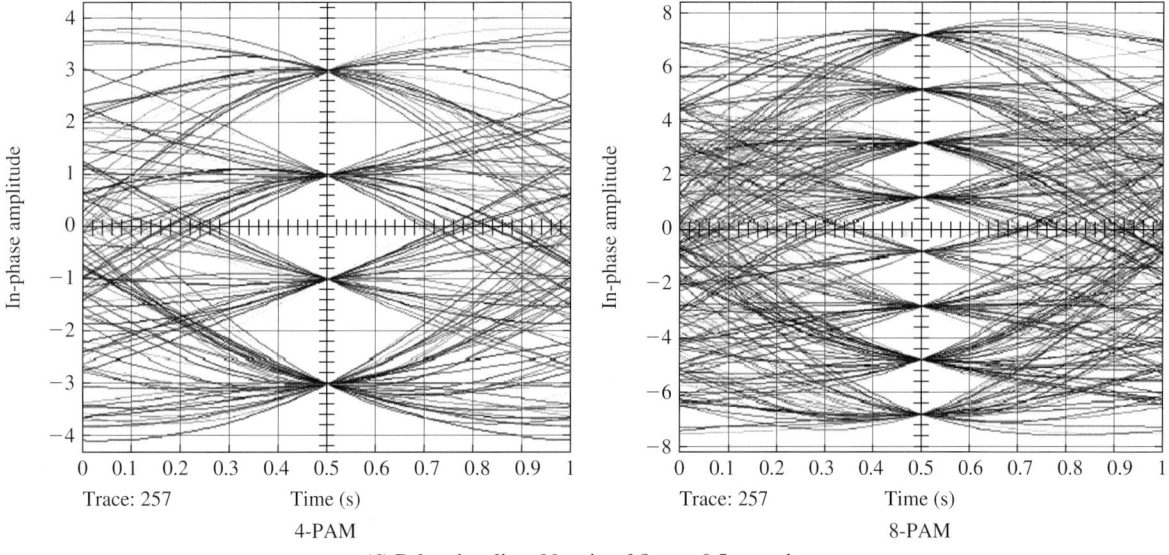

4-PAM

8-PAM

(d) Polar signaling, $M = 4$ and 8, $\alpha = 0.5$, no noise

signaling, the ISI increases, resulting in a narrower eye opening. Note that the eye also closes as more noise is added.

As M is increased, the eye opening is reduced leading to less noise margin. We can see from Figure 12.4(d) that eye openings are proportionately smaller for 4- and 8-PAM RC pulses.

Pioneers in the Field

Harry Nyquist was born on February 7, 1889, in Nilsby, Sweden, and moved to the United States in 1907. He attended the University of North Dakota, Grand Forks, from 1912 to 1915 and received B.S. and M.S. degrees in electrical engineering in 1914 and 1915, respectively. He then attended Yale University, New Haven, Connecticut, from 1915 to 1917, and was awarded a Ph.D. degree in 1917.

Nyquist worked at AT&T's Department of Development and Research from 1917 to 1934, when it became Bell Telephone Laboratories, and remained there until his retirement in 1954. During his 37 years with the Bell System, he acquired 138 patents and published 12 technical articles. His work ranged from thermal noise to signal transmission. Some of Nyquist's best-known work in signal transmission area occurred in the 1920s, inspired by telegraph communication problems of the time. Nyquist determined the number of pulses that can be transmitted in a telegraph channel is limited to twice the bandwidth of the channel. This is known as Nyquist's criterion for zero ISI. Nyquist also established the characteristics that pulse shapes must satisfy to comply with his criterion and proposed raised-cosine pulse as an example. In 1927, Nyquist provided a mathematical explanation of thermal noise experimentally studied by his colleague J. B. Johnson. Thermal noise is also called Johnson or Nyquist noise because of their pioneering work in the field. In 1932, Nyquist discovered the stability criterion for negative feedback control systems. During World War II, this work enabled the design of control systems for artillery employing electromechanical feedback. In addition, Nyquist is credited for the invention of the vestigial sideband transmission system which is widely used in digital television broadcasting and cable TV systems.

Before his death in 1976, Nyquist received many honors for his outstanding work in the communications field. He was awarded the National Academy of Engineering's Founder's Medal in recognition of his many fundamental contributions to engineering. In 1960, he received the IEEE Medal of Honor. Nyquist was also awarded the Stuart Ballantine Medal of the Franklin Institute in 1960 and the Mervin J. Kelly award in 1961.

12.2   NYQUIST'S CRITERION FOR ZERO ISI

Recall from Section 2.6 that a waveform cannot be both duration- and bandwidth-limited. As a consequence, transmitted pulses bandlimited by the shaping filter at the transmitter or by the channel are lengthened beyond the symbol interval, resulting in ISI. A very interesting result by Nyquist, however, proved the existence of pulses that simultaneously achieve the objectives of zero ISI and narrow bandwidth. These waveforms, called **Nyquist pulses,** have a unique characteristic in that they undergo zero crossings where the peaks of other pulses in the pulse train occur. According to Nyquist, if the FT $P_r(f)$ of the pulse $p_r(t)$ satisfies

$$\sum_{n=-\infty}^{\infty} P_r\left(f + \frac{n}{T}\right) = T, \quad |f| \leq 1/2T \tag{12.16}$$

then

$$p_r(kT) = \begin{cases} 1, & k = 0 \\ 0, & k \neq 0 \end{cases} \tag{12.15}$$

Proof

The sampled overall impulse response $p_r(kT)$ can be expressed in terms of inverse FT of $p_r(t)$ as

$$p_r(kT) = p_r(t)|_{t=kT} = \int_{-\infty}^{\infty} P_r(f)e^{j2\pi ft}df\bigg|_{t=kT} = \int_{-\infty}^{\infty} P_r(f)e^{j2\pi fkT}df \tag{12.17}$$

If we now break the integral on the right-hand side of (12.17) into contiguous intervals of length $1/T$, we obtain

$$p_r(kT) = \sum_{n=-\infty}^{\infty} \int_{(2n-1)/2T}^{(2n+1)/2T} P_r(f) e^{j2\pi fkT} df \qquad (12.18)$$

By making a change of variable $f' = f - \dfrac{n}{T}$, we can write (12.18) as

$$p_r(kT) = \sum_{n=-\infty}^{\infty} \int_{-1/2T}^{1/2T} P_r\left(f' + \frac{n}{T}\right) e^{j2\pi(f' + \frac{n}{T})kT} df'$$

$$= \int_{-1/2T}^{1/2T} \left[\sum_{n=-\infty}^{\infty} P_r\left(f + \frac{n}{T}\right) \right] e^{j2\pi fkT} df$$

$$= \int_{-1/2T}^{1/2T} P_r^{folded}(f) e^{j2\pi fkT} df \qquad (12.19)$$

where

$$P_r^{folded}(f) = \sum_{n=-\infty}^{\infty} P_r\left(f + \frac{n}{T}\right) \qquad (12.20)$$

$P_r^{folded}(f)$ is a periodic function of f with period $1/T$. It is often called the **folded** (aliased or overlapped) **spectrum** of $P_r(f)$ because the sampling process causes the frequency response outside of the fundamental interval $(-1/2T, 1/2T)$ to be added or folded in. By comparing (12.19) with the inverse **discrete-time Fourier transform (DTFT)** definition (12.22),[1] we observe that $P_r^{folded}(f)$ is related to the DTFT $P_r(e^{j2\pi fT})$ of the sampled sequence $p_r[k] = p_r(kT)$ by

$$P_r^{folded}(f) = TP_r(e^{j2\pi fT}) \qquad (12.23)$$

The zero ISI condition (12.15) can be expressed in the frequency domain as

$$P_r(e^{j2\pi fT}) = \sum_{k=-\infty}^{\infty} p_r(kT) e^{-j2\pi fkT} = p_r(0)e^{-j0} = 1 \qquad (12.24)$$

---

[1] By substituting $\hat{\omega} = 2\pi fT$ into (2.196), the DTFT of a sequence $x[k]$ can be expressed as

$$X(e^{j2\pi fT}) = \sum_{k=-\infty}^{\infty} x[k] e^{-j2\pi kfT} \qquad (12.21)$$

$x[k]$ can be recovered from $X(e^{j2\pi fT})$ by using the **inverse DTFT** defined as

$$x[k] = T \int_{-1/2T}^{1/2T} X(e^{j2\pi fT}) e^{j2\pi fkT} df \qquad (12.22)$$

Combining (12.23) and (12.24), we obtain

$$P_r^{folded}(f) = T, \quad |f| \le 1/2T \tag{12.25}$$

or equivalently

$$\sum_{n=-\infty}^{\infty} P_r\left(f + \frac{n}{T}\right) = T, \quad |f| \le 1/2T \tag{12.26}$$

This is called Nyquist's criterion for zero ISI. For a channel of bandwidth W, $H_c(f) = 0$ for $|f| > W$. Because $P_r(f) = H_T(f)H_c(f)H_R(f)$, it follows, therefore, that $P_r(f) = 0$ for $|f| > W$. We now investigate the following three cases of signaling at symbol rate D over a channel of bandwidth W Hz:

1. **$D > 2W$.** That is, we want to send data at a rate greater than $2W$ symbols/second over a channel of bandwidth W Hz. As $W < D/2 = 1/2T$, it is impossible to find a $P_r(f)$ that satisfies (12.26) as illustrated in Figure 12.5(a). In this case it is not possible to design a system with zero ISI at sampling instants (i.e., at $t = kT$).

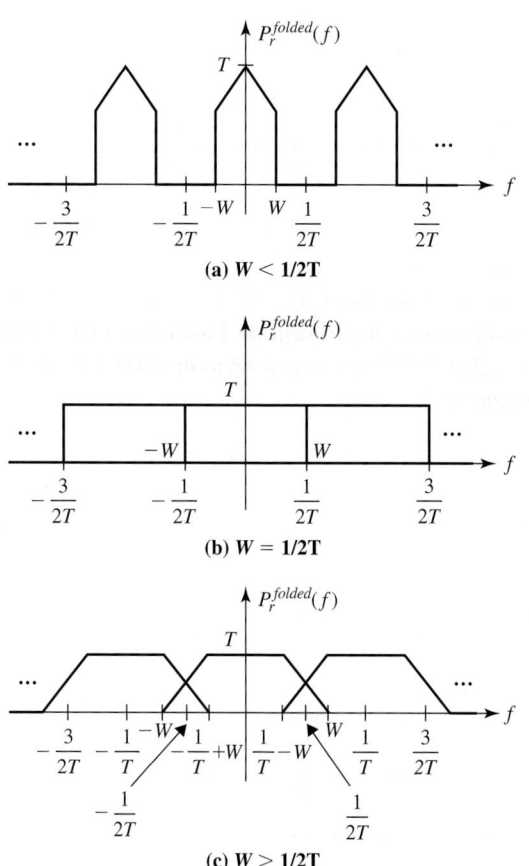

Figure 12.5 Folded spectrum $P_r^{folded}(f)$.

2. $D = 2W$. That is, we want to send data at $2W$ symbols/second over a channel of bandwidth W Hz. As displayed in Figure 12.5(b), there exists only one $P_r(f)$ with bandwidth $W = D/2 = 1/2T$ that satisfies (12.26). It is given by

$$P_r(f) = \begin{cases} T, & |f| \le W = 1/2T \\ 0, & \text{otherwise} \end{cases} \qquad (12.27)$$

The existence of $P_r(f)$ in (12.27) implies that $D = 2W$ is the *highest* symbol rate at which we can transmit data through a channel of bandwidth W Hz and achieve zero ISI. It is called the **Nyquist rate.** Alternatively, the *minimum* bandwidth of $1/2T$ Hz is required to accomplish zero ISI signaling at $1/T$ symbols or pulses per second. It is called the **Nyquist bandwidth** $B_{Nyquist}$. The overall impulse response of the system is inverse FT of $P_r(f)$ in (12.27). It is given by

$$p_r(t) = \text{sinc}(t/T) \qquad (12.28)$$

Equation (12.28) states that communication at the Nyquist rate requires the use of sinc pulses. As discussed later, this type of signaling has serious practical implementation issues.

3. $D < 2W$. That is, we want to send data at a rate less than the Nyquist limit of $2W$ symbols/second over a channel of bandwidth W Hz. In this case, there exist many choices for $P_r(f)$ that have smoother transitions at spectral band edges while satisfying the Nyquist criterion for zero ISI.

As an example, consider the important case when $P_r(f) = 0$ for $|f| > 1/T$. That is, the channel has no response beyond twice the Nyquist bandwidth. The Nyquist criterion, in this case, simplifies to

$$P_r\left(f + \frac{1}{T}\right) + P_r(f) + P_r\left(f - \frac{1}{T}\right) = T, \quad |f| \le 1/2T \qquad (12.29)$$

Figure 12.5(c) displays such a pulse spectrum. Note the odd (or vestigial) symmetry exhibited by $P_r(f)$ around $1/2T$ Hz. Several pulse spectra that satisfy (12.29) have been devised. A popular pulse spectrum $P_r(f)$ that satisfies the condition (12.29) and has desirable spectral and other properties is the raised cosine (RC) frequency characteristic considered in Section 9.8.2.

12.2.1 RC Pulse Signaling

The absolute bandwidth of RC-shaped pulses with zero-crossings at $t = \pm T, \pm 2T, \pm 3T, \pm 4T, \ldots$ is given from (9.61) as

$$B_{abs} = \frac{(1 + \alpha)}{2T} \qquad (12.30)$$

where α is a roll-off factor of the frequency characteristic. Because $B_{abs} > 1/2T$, RC pulses require channel bandwidth W in excess of Nyquist bandwidth. The **excess bandwidth** is given by

$$\text{Excess bandwidth} = B_{abs} - B_{Nyquist} = \frac{(1 + \alpha)}{2T} - \frac{1}{2T} = \frac{\alpha}{2T}$$

For RC pulses, the roll-off factor α equals the excess bandwidth expressed as a fraction or percentage of the Nyquist bandwidth. That is,

$$\frac{\text{Excess bandwidth}}{B_{Nyquist}} = \frac{B_{abs} - B_{Nyquist}}{B_{Nyquist}} = \frac{\dfrac{\alpha}{2T}}{\dfrac{1}{2T}} = \alpha \qquad (12.31)$$

The data rate achieved using NRZ unipolar encoding with RC-shaped pulses over a channel bandwidth W Hz is obtained from (9.61) as

$$W = B_{abs} = \frac{(1 + \alpha)}{2T} \Rightarrow D = \frac{2W}{(1 + \alpha)} \qquad (12.32)$$

For $\alpha = 0.5$, $D = 4/3W$ which amounts to a 33% reduction in symbol rate versus the Nyquist rate. The penalty is a 50% reduction in signaling speed (i.e., $D = W$) for $\alpha = 1$. In this case, RC signaling transmits 1 symbol/Hz of channel bandwidth versus two symbols/Hz achievable *only* with sinc-pulse signaling.

For bandpass signals generated using linear modulation schemes, such as M-PSK and M-QAM, $B_{abs-abs} = (1 + \alpha)D$ from Table 11.4. The data rate achieved over a channel bandwidth W Hz is now given by

$$W = B_{abs-abs} = (1 + \alpha)D \Rightarrow D = \frac{W}{(1 + \alpha)} \text{ symbols/second} \qquad (12.33)$$

In summary, Nyquist's criterion states that for zero ISI we can transmit no more than $2W$ symbols per second over a channel of bandwidth W Hz using baseband pulses. However, if we reduce the symbol rate D below the Nyquist rate of $2W$ symbols per second, it is possible to achieve zero ISI using practical transmitting and receiving filters. For bandpass systems, using linear modulation schemes over a channel of bandwidth W Hz, we can transmit no more than W symbols/sec to achieve zero ISI. However, practical filter design constraints limit the transmission speed to less than W symbols/sec.

Example 12.1

Let $P_r(f)$ be the trapezoidal spectrum given by

$$P_r(f) = \begin{cases} 1, & |f| < 2500 \\ 3 - \dfrac{|f|}{1250}, & 2500 \le |f| < 3750 \\ 0, & \text{otherwise} \end{cases}$$

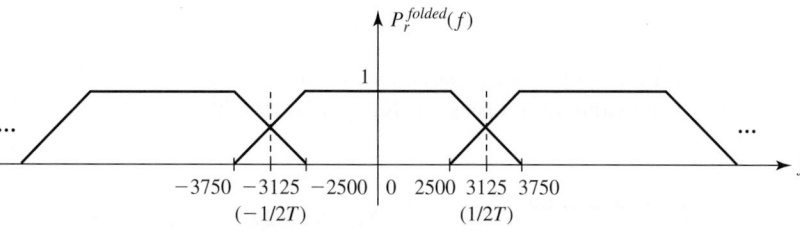

Figure 12.6 Folded spectrum $P_r^{folded}(f)$ for Example 12.1.

a. For what symbol rate is $p_r(t)$ a Nyquist pulse?
b. At this symbol rate, what is the excess bandwidth of the pulse and roll-off factor?

Solution

a. The folded spectrum $P_r^{folded}(f)$ is shown in Figure 12.6. If we choose $1/2T = 3125$, that is symbol rate $D = 6250$ symbols/second, then $P_r(f)$ satisfies Nyquist criterion for ISI free transmission.
b. Excess bandwidth $= B_{abs} - B_{Nyquist} = 3750 - 3125 = 625$

$$\text{Roll-off factor } \alpha = \frac{625}{3125} = 0.2$$

The ideal Nyquist signaling, however, has serious practical consequences. First, sinc pulses are noncausal and of infinite duration. They can be approximated in practice by introducing an appropriate delay and truncating the pulse. However, the pulse decays very slowly $(1/|t|)$ so the truncation period must be long. The second issue is that this type of signaling is extremely sensitive with respect to timing jitter in the sampler. A small sampling offset ε, for instance, produces the output sample

$$y_k = a_k \operatorname{sinc}(\varepsilon/T) + \sum_{\substack{n=-\infty \\ n \neq k}}^{\infty} a_n \operatorname{sinc}(k - n + \varepsilon/T) \tag{12.34}$$

The sum on the right-hand side of (12.34) can generate very large values of ISI for some transmitted symbol sequences no matter how small the timing offset ε.

Example 12.2

Design an M-ary PAM system that transmits digital data using RC pulses at 12,000 bps over an ideal channel with bandwidth $W = 2400$ Hz. Specify the number of levels required for excess bandwidth of 50%.

Solution

The symbol rate achievable using RC pulses ($\alpha = 0.5$) over a channel of bandwidth $W = 2400$ Hz is given from (12.32) as

$$D = \frac{2 \times 2400}{(1 + 0.5)} = 3200 \text{ symbols/second}$$

Because $D = R_b/k$, the bit rate R_b achievable using M-ary PAM is given by

$$R_b = k \times 3200 \text{ bits/second}$$

Substituting $R_b = 12,000$ bps yields

$$12,000 = k \times 3200 \Rightarrow k = 3.75 \approx 4$$

Thus

$$M = 2^k = 2^4 = 16$$

12.3   TRANSMIT AND RECEIVE FILTERS FOR BANDLIMITED AWGN CHANNELS

In Section 10.2 it was demonstrated that the matched filter is the optimum detector for M-ary PAM signals transmitted through AWGN channels that introduce no ISI. In this section, we consider the design of optimum transmit and receive filters for M-ary PAM signals transmitted through bandlimited AWGN channels. It is assumed here that the frequency response $H_c(f)$ of the channel is known. We consider the following cases.

1. Ideal Bandlimited Channel

For an ideal bandlimited channel, the frequency response can be expressed as

$$H_c(f) = \begin{cases} 1, & |f| \le W \\ 0, & |f| > W \end{cases} \tag{12.35}$$

Substituting into (12.10), we obtain

$$P_r(f) = H_T(f)H_R(f), \quad |f| \le W \tag{12.36}$$

We select transmit and receive filters to satisfy the following requirements:

- Nyquist criterion to guarantee zero ISI at sampling instants
- Matched receive filter to maximize peak signal to rms noise power ratio (SNR) at sampling instants

As discussed in Section 12.2, a widely implemented choice for $P_r(f)$ to yield zero ISI at the sampler output is the RC spectrum. That is,

$$H_T(f)H_R(f) = P_{RC}(f) \tag{12.37}$$

Now if the transfer functions of the transmit and receive filters are selected to satisfy the matched filter property, we obtain the following decomposition:

$$H_T(f) = \sqrt{P_{RC}(f)}\,e^{-j2\pi f t_o} \tag{12.38}$$

$$H_R(f) = H_T^*(f) = \sqrt{P_{RC}(f)}\,e^{j2\pi f t_o} \tag{12.39}$$

where t_o is the time delay necessary to ensure the physical realizability of the transmit and receive filters. Thus, the overall RC spectral characteristic is split evenly between the transmit and receive filters. This is called **root raised cosine (RRC)** signaling. RRC transmit and receive filters satisfy both Nyquist and matched filter optimization criteria for ideal bandlimited channels.

The RRC frequency characteristic can be obtained from (9.66) as

$$P_{RRC}(f) = \sqrt{P_{RC}(f)} = \begin{cases} \sqrt{T}, & |f| \le (1-\alpha)/2T \\ \sqrt{\dfrac{T}{2}}\left\{\cos\left[\dfrac{\pi T}{2\alpha}\left(|f| - \dfrac{1-\alpha}{2T}\right)\right]\right\}, & (1-\alpha)/2T \le |f| \le (1+\alpha)/2T \\ 0, & \text{elsewhere} \end{cases} \tag{12.40}$$

We can now obtain an expression for the RRC pulse by taking inverse FT of (12.40) as

$$p_{RRC}(t) = 4\alpha \frac{\cos\left[(1 + \alpha)\pi t/T\right] + \dfrac{\sin\left[(1 - \alpha)\pi t/T\right]}{(4\alpha t/T)}}{\pi\left[1 - (4\alpha t/T)^2\right]} \tag{12.41}$$

where α is the roll-off factor.

Figure 12.7 displays RRC pulse in both time and frequency domains. We observe from Figure 12.7(a) that the RRC pulse is *not* a Nyquist pulse. That is, $p_{RRC}(nT) \neq 0$ for integer values of $n \neq 0$. Due to the smooth characteristic of the RRC frequency response, it is possible to design practical filters for the transmitter and the receiver that approximate the overall RC characteristic.

2. Nonideal bandlimited channel

The channel frequency response $H_c(f)$ is not ideal, but it is known for $|f| \leq W$ and $H_c(f) = 0$ for $|f| > W$. We seek to jointly optimize the transmit and receive filters so that SNR is maximized with zero ISI at the sampling instants. For zero ISI, we require

$$H_T(f)H_c(f)H_R(f) = P_{RC}(f) \tag{12.42}$$

Although we have assumed RC frequency response for the combination of transmit filter, channel, and receive filter in (12.42), it can be any other response that satisfies the Nyquist criterion. For fixed $H_T(f)$ and $H_c(f)$, the optimum receive filter is matched to the channel output pulse $p_c(t)$ to maximize the SNR at sampling instants. The frequency response of the matched filter is obtained from (10.36) as

$$H_R(f) = H_T^*(f)H_c^*(f) \tag{12.43}$$

Combining (12.42) and (12.43) yields

$$|H_T(f)H_c(f)|^2 = P_{RC}(f)$$

or

$$|H_T(f)| = \frac{\sqrt{P_{RC}(f)}}{|H_c(f)|} \tag{12.44}$$

Substituting (12.44) into (12.43), we obtain

$$|H_R(f)| = \sqrt{P_{RC}(f)} \tag{12.45}$$

Alternatively, we can obtain the optimum design by splitting the channel compensation equally between the transmit and receive filters, that is

$$|H_T(f)| = \sqrt{\frac{P_{RC}(f)}{|H_c(f)|}}, \quad |f| \leq W \tag{12.46}$$

$$|H_R(f)| = \sqrt{\frac{P_{RC}(f)}{|H_c(f)|}}, \quad |f| \leq W \tag{12.47}$$

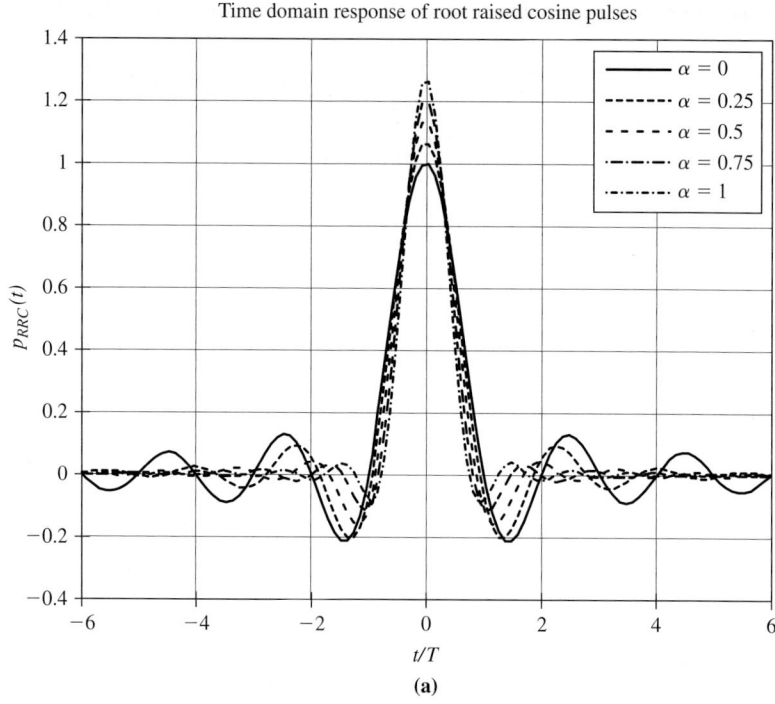

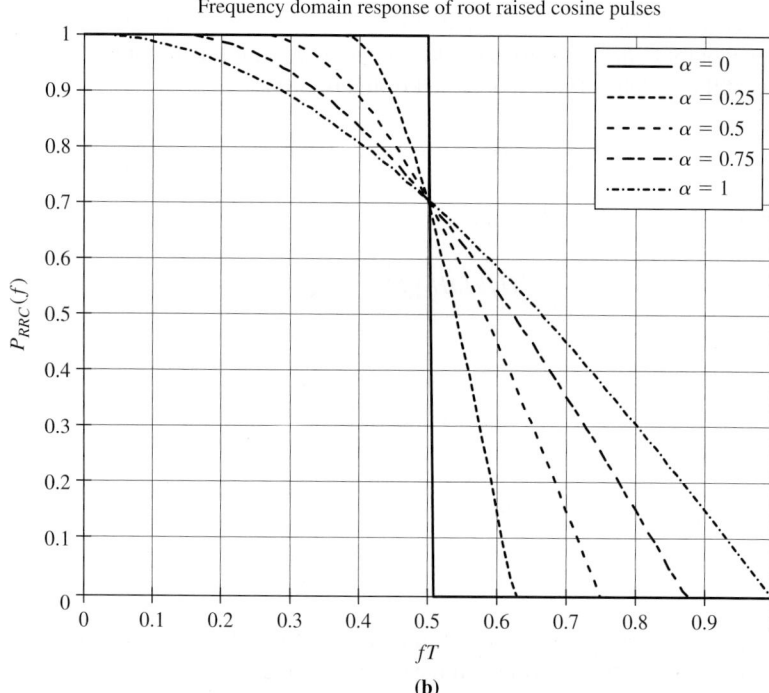

Figure 12.7 (a) RRC pulse in time domain; (b) RRC pulse in frequency domain.

12.3.1 Probability of Error Performance

Because the overall impulse response is the RC characteristic as indicated in (12.42), the sampler output sequence is given from (12.13) as

$$y_k = a_k + n_k \qquad (12.48)$$

n_k is a Gaussian random variable with mean zero and variance

$$\sigma^2 = \overline{n_k^2} = \frac{N_o}{2} \int_{-\infty}^{\infty} |H_R(f)|^2 df = \frac{N_o}{2} \int_{-W}^{W} \left| \frac{P_{RC}(f)}{H_c(f)} \right| df \qquad (12.49)$$

The average probability of bit error is given by

$$BER = P(a_k = A) \times P\{y_k < 0 \,|\, a_k = A\} + P(a_k = -A) \times P\{y_k > 0 \,|\, a_k = -A\}$$

$$= \frac{1}{2} \left[P\{n_k < -A\} + P\{n_k > A\} \right]$$

$$= Q\left(\frac{A}{\sigma} \right) \qquad (12.50)$$

The energy of the transmitted pulse with amplitude A is given by

$$E_b = A^2 \int_{-\infty}^{\infty} |H_T(f)|^2 df = A^2 \int_{-W}^{W} \left| \frac{P_{RC}(f)}{H_c(f)} \right| df \qquad (12.51)$$

This allows us to write A in terms of E_b as

$$A = \sqrt{ \frac{E_b}{\displaystyle\int_{-W}^{W} \left| \frac{P_{RC}(f)}{H_c(f)} \right| df} } \qquad (12.52)$$

Substituting (12.49) and (12.52) into (12.50), we obtain

$$BER = Q\left(\left[\int_{-W}^{W} \left| \frac{P_{RC}(f)}{H_c(f)} \right| df \right]^{-1} \sqrt{\frac{2E_b}{N_o}} \right) \qquad (12.53)$$

The quantity $10\log_{10}\left[\left(\int_{-W}^{W} \left| \frac{P_{RC}(f)}{H_c(f)} \right| df \right)^{-2} \right]$ represents the loss in SNR/bit due to noise enhancement. For an ideal bandlimited channel, $\int_{-W}^{W} \left| \frac{P_{RC}(f)}{H_c(f)} \right| df = \int_{-W}^{W} |P_{RC}(f)| df = 1.$

Substituting into (12.53) yields the following simplified expression for the probability of bit error

$$BER = Q\left(\sqrt{\frac{2E_b}{N_o}}\right) \tag{12.54}$$

The performance in (12.54) is identical to that of antipodal signaling over an infinite bandwidth channel considered in Section 10.2.

Example 12.3

Binary data is transmitted through a bandlimited channel at 4.8kbps. The channel is modeled by

$$H_c(f) = 0.5 + 0.5 \cos(\pi f/3600), \quad |f| \leq 3600 \text{ Hz}$$

The channel introduces AWGN noise with spectral density $N_o/2$ W/Hz. Find the transfer functions of optimum transmit and receive filters to deliver RC output pulse ($\alpha = 0.5$) at the receiver.

Solution

Because $1/T = 4800$, the RC pulse spectrum for $\alpha = 0.5$ is given from (9.66) as

$$P_{RC}(f) = \begin{cases} 1/4800, & 0 \leq |f| \leq 1200 \\ \dfrac{1}{2400}\left[1 + \cos\left(\dfrac{\pi}{2400}(|f| - 1200)\right)\right], & 1200 \leq |f| \leq 3600 \\ 0, & \text{elsewhere} \end{cases} \tag{12.55}$$

Substituting (12.55) into (12.46) and (12.47), the optimum transmit and receive filter characteristics are given by

$$|H_T(f)| = |H_R(f)| = \begin{cases} \sqrt{\dfrac{1}{4800[0.5 + 0.5\cos(\pi f/3600)]}}, & 0 \leq |f| \leq 1200 \\ \sqrt{\dfrac{\cos\left[\dfrac{\pi}{4800}(|f| - 1200)\right]}{2400[0.5 + 0.5\cos(\pi f/3600)]}}, & 1200 \leq |f| \leq 3600 \\ 0, & \text{elsewhere} \end{cases}$$

12.4   PARTIAL RESPONSE (DUOBINARY) SIGNALING

To achieve communication at symbol rate $D = 2W$, Nyquist's zero ISI criterion mandates the use of sinc pulses that cannot be implemented in practice. **Partial response (PR) signaling** techniques allow a controlled amount of ISI to obtain practically realizable pulse shapes for signaling at the Nyquist rate of $2W$ symbols per second. Because the ISI is deterministic and introduced, by design, from a few preceding symbols, its effect on the symbol detection can be canceled at the receiver.

In the simplest of PR schemes, called **duobinary signaling,** interference from the immediately preceding symbol is allowed. In this case, Nyquist criterion (12.15) is replaced by the condition

$$p_r[k] = \begin{cases} 1, & k = 0, 1 \\ 0, & \text{otherwise} \end{cases} \tag{12.56}$$

where $p_r[k]$ is a T-spaced sampled sequence of the overall impulse response function $p_r(t)$. The condition (12.56) can be expressed in the frequency domain as

$$P_r(e^{j2\pi fT}) = \sum_{k=-\infty}^{\infty} p_r[k]e^{-j2\pi fkT} = p_r[0] + p_r[1]e^{-j2\pi fT}$$

$$= 1 + e^{-j2\pi fT} = 2e^{-j\pi fT}\cos(\pi fT) \tag{12.57}$$

Substituting (12.57) into (12.23), we obtain the following relationship between the DTFT of $p_r[k]$ in (12.56) and its folded spectrum $P_r^{folded}(f)$

$$P_r^{folded}(f) = 2Te^{-j\pi fT}\cos(\pi fT) \tag{12.58}$$

The minimum bandwidth $P_r(f)$ satisfying (12.58) is given by

$$P_r(f) = \begin{cases} 2Te^{-j\pi fT}\cos(\pi fT), & |f| \leq 1/2T \\ 0, & \text{otherwise} \end{cases} \tag{12.59}$$

The corresponding duobinary pulse, $p_r(t)$, is given by

$$p_r(t) = \text{sinc}(t/T) + \text{sinc}\big[(t - T)/T\big] \tag{12.60}$$

Figure 12.8 displays $p_r(t)$ along with its magnitude spectrum. Unlike the ideal Nyquist signaling case, the frequency response function $P_r(f)$ in (12.59) is continuous, and it is therefore easily approximated by physically realizable transmit and receive filters. It follows further from (12.59) that the duobinary signaling at symbol rate $D = 1/T$ requires a channel bandwidth $W = 1/2T$ Hz. Duobinary PR signaling was first proposed by Lender, and later generalized by Kretzmer.[2] The main advantage of the duobinary pulse relative to the RC pulse is that signaling at the Nyquist symbol rate is feasible with zero excess bandwidth. Because tails of the duobinary pulse decay much more rapidly $(1/|t|^2)$ than those of the ideal Nyquist pulse $(1/|t|)$, it is robust with respect to sampling jitter.

In another PR scheme, called **modified duobinary signaling,** the overall impulse response function $p_r(t)$ satisfies the condition

$$p_r[k] = \begin{cases} 1, & k = -1 \\ -1, & k = 1 \\ 0, & \text{otherwise} \end{cases} \tag{12.61}$$

[2] A. Lender, "Correlative Level Coding for Binary Data Transmission," *IEEE Spectrum* 3 (1966): 104–115; E. Kretzmer, "Generalization of a Technique for Binary Data Communication," *IEEE Transactions on Communications Technology* COM-14 (1966): 67–68.

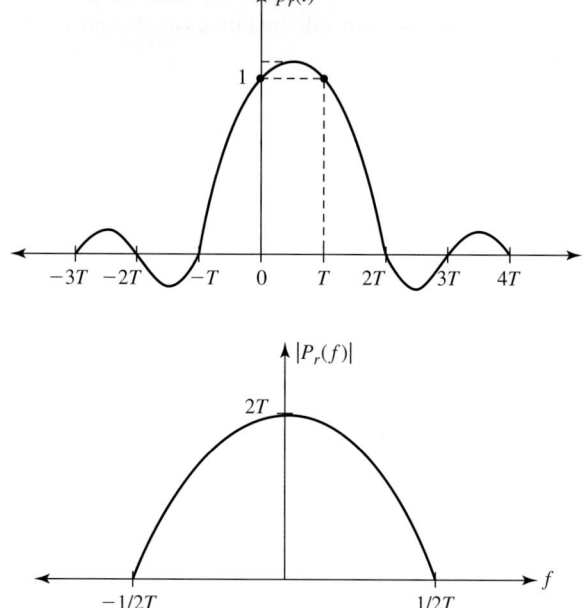

Figure 12.8 Duobinary pulse in time and frequency domains.

The condition (12.61) can be expressed in the frequency domain as

$$P_r(e^{j2\pi fT}) = \sum_{k=-\infty}^{\infty} p_r[k]e^{-j2\pi fkT} = p_r[-1]e^{j2\pi fT} + p_r[1]e^{-j2\pi fT}$$

$$= e^{j2\pi fT} - e^{-j2\pi fT} = 2j\sin(2\pi fT) \qquad (12.62)$$

Substituting (12.62) into (12.23), we obtain the following relationship between the DTFT of $p_r[k]$ in (12.61) and its folded spectrum $P_r^{folded}(f)$

$$P_r^{folded}(f) = j2T\sin(2\pi fT) \qquad (12.63)$$

The minimum bandwidth $P_r(f)$ satisfying (12.63) is given by

$$P_r(f) = \begin{cases} j2T\sin(2\pi fT), & |f| \le 1/2T \\ 0, & \text{otherwise} \end{cases} \qquad (12.64)$$

The corresponding pulse $p_r(t)$ is given by

$$p_r(t) = \text{sinc}\big[(t + T)/T\big] - \text{sinc}\big[(t - T)/T\big] \qquad (12.65)$$

This pulse and its amplitude are illustrated in Figure 12.9. It is called a **modified duobinary pulse.** Note that the spectrum of this pulse has a zero at $f = 0$, making it suitable for transmission over a channel that does not pass DC. This is often the case for TWP links where the transmitted signal is coupled to the line through a transformer. Like duobinary pulse, modified duobinary pulse allows signaling at symbol rate $D = 1/T$ over a channel bandwidth $W = 1/2T$ Hz. In other words, both duobinary and modified

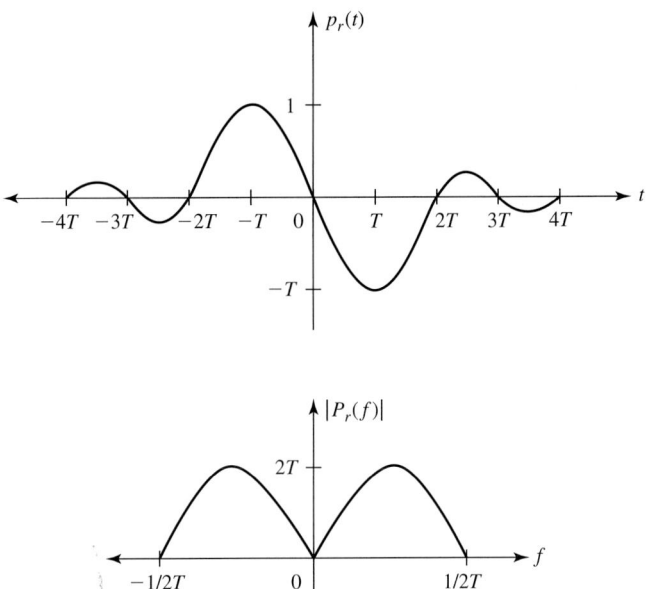

Figure 12.9 Modified duobinary pulse in time and frequency domains.

duobinary schemes achieve Nyquist rate signaling rates (i.e., $D = 2W$ symbols per second) over an ideal channel of bandwidth W Hz.

12.4.1 Detection of Duobinary Signals

Figure 12.10 illustrates the block diagram of a duobinary communication system. The polar encoder maps the binary data b_k into polar levels $a_k = \pm A$. We assume that the desired spectral characteristic (12.59) is split evenly between the transmit and receive filters, that is,

$$|H_T(f)| = |H_R(f)| = \sqrt{|P_r(f)|} = \begin{cases} \sqrt{|2T\cos(\pi f T)|}, & |f| \leq 1/2T \\ 0, & \text{otherwise} \end{cases} \quad (12.66)$$

We consider symbol-by-symbol detection, although it is not an optimum strategy for duobinary signals. For the duobinary pulse, $p_r(kT) = 1$, for $k = 0, 1$ and zero otherwise. Hence, samples of the receive filter output at the sampling instant $t = kT$ have the form

$$y_k = a_k + a_{k-1} + n_k \quad (12.67)$$

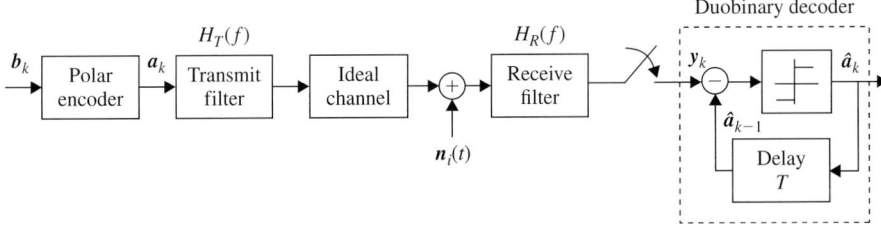

Figure 12.10 Duobinary signaling.

where a_k and a_{k-1} are transmitted levels from the kth and $(k-1)$th symbol intervals, respectively. Observe the correlation between received signal samples. Now

$$a_k + a_{k-1} = \begin{cases} 2A, & \text{with probability } \tfrac{1}{4} \; (a_k = a_{k-1} = A) \\ 0, & \text{with probability } \tfrac{1}{2} \; (a_k = -a_{k-1}) \\ -2A, & \text{with probability } \tfrac{1}{4} \; (a_k = a_{k-1} = -A) \end{cases} \qquad (12.68)$$

Ignoring the noise, y_k takes on one of three possible levels, $-2A$, 0, $2A$ with corresponding probabilities $1/4$, $1/2$, $1/4$, respectively. Note that duobinary signaling results in an increased number of amplitude levels at the receiver. Considering the binary case, $\hat{a}_k$ can be detected by subtracting the previously detected symbol $\hat{a}_{k-1}$ from the current receive filter output sample y_k.

$$\hat{a}_k = y_k - \hat{a}_{k-1} \qquad (12.69)$$

This procedure can be repeated sequentially for every received symbol. Note that the duobinary decoder requires knowledge of previously detected symbol $\hat{a}_{k-1}$ to estimate the transmitted symbol $\hat{a}_k$ in the kth signaling interval. Hence error propagation occurs if the previously detected symbol $\hat{a}_{k-1}$ is in error due to additive noise. Error propagation can be avoided by **precoding** the data at the transmitter. The precoding is performed on the binary data sequence prior to transmit filter pulse shaping.

Data Precoding

Let $\{b_k\}$ denote the data sequence of 1's and 0's that is to be transmitted. A new sequence $\{d_k\}$, called the **precoded sequence,** is generated by the operation.

$$d_k = b_k \oplus d_{k-1} \qquad (12.70)$$

where $\oplus$ denotes modulo-2 addition. Thus

$$d_k = \begin{cases} d_{k-1}, & b_k = 0 \\ \overline{d}_{k-1}, & b_k = 1 \end{cases} \qquad (12.71)$$

where $\overline{a}$ denotes the logical complement of a. The sequence $\{d_k\}$ is then mapped to the sequence of polar transmitted signal levels $\{a_k\}$ according to relationship

$$a_k = A(2d_k - 1) \qquad (12.72)$$

That is, $a_k = -A$ if $d_k = 0$ and $a_k = A$ if $d_k = 1$. Figure 12.11 displays a duobinary communication system utilizing precoding. The noise-free samples at the output of the receive filter are given as

$$y_k = a_k + a_{k-1} = A\big[(2d_k - 1) + (2d_{k-1} - 1)\big] \qquad (12.73)$$

or

$$y_k = \begin{cases} 2A, & \text{with probability } \tfrac{1}{4} \; (d_k = d_{k-1} = 1) \\ 0, & \text{with probability } \tfrac{1}{2} \; (d_k \neq d_{k-1}) \\ -2A, & \text{with probability } \tfrac{1}{4} \; (d_k = d_{k-1} = 0) \end{cases} \qquad (12.74)$$

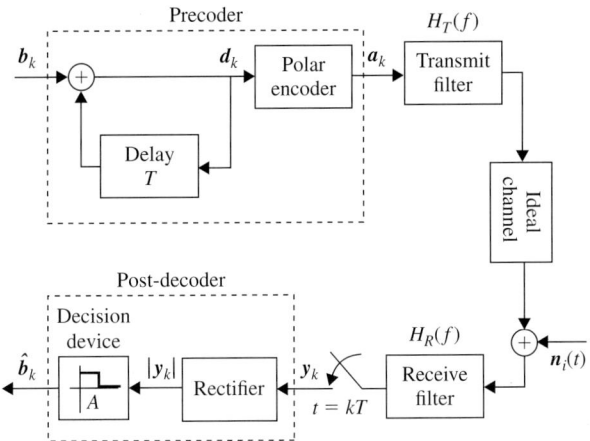

Figure 12.11 Duobinary signaling with data precoding.

Combining (12.71) and (12.74) yields

$$y_k = \begin{cases} \pm 2A, & b_k = 0 \\ 0, & b_k = 1 \end{cases} \qquad (12.75)$$

It follows from (12.75) that if $y_k = \pm 2A \Rightarrow b_k = 0$, $y_k = 0 \Rightarrow b_k = 1$. In the presence of additive noise, the sampled outputs from the receiving filters are given by

$$y_k = \begin{cases} \pm 2A + n_k, & b_k = 0 \\ n_k, & b_k = 1 \end{cases} \qquad (12.76)$$

where n_k is a Gaussian random variable with mean zero and variance

$$\sigma^2 = \overline{n_k^2} = \frac{N_o}{2} \int_{-\infty}^{\infty} |H_R(f)|^2 df = N_o T \int_{-1/2T}^{1/2T} |\cos(\pi f T)| df = \frac{2N_o}{\pi} \qquad (12.77)$$

The detected data symbols are generated by comparing $|y_k|$ with the threshold set at A and using the decoding rule

$$\hat{b}_k = \begin{cases} 1, & |y_k| < A \\ 0, & |y_k| > A \end{cases} \qquad (12.78)$$

It is evident from (12.78) that the detector makes decision $\hat{b}_k$ based on the current receive filter output sample y_k without requiring the knowledge of previously detected symbols. Hence error propagation does not occur.

Table 12.1 illustrates various operations involved in duobinary signaling. The precoding initialization bit (d_0) is selected to be 0. In the absence of noise, the original binary data sequence is decoded correctly as indicated by the last row of the table.

Table 12.1 Binary Signaling with Duobinary Pulses

Data bits b_k		1	0	0	1	1	1	0	0	1	0
Precoded sequence d_k	0	1	1	1	0	1	0	0	0	1	1
Transmitted sequence a_k	$-A$	A	A	A	$-A$	A	$-A$	$-A$	$-A$	A	A
Received sequence y_k		0	$2A$	$2A$	0	0	0	$-2A$	$-2A$	0	$2A$
Decoded sequence $\hat{b}_k$		1	0	0	1	1	1	0	0	1	0

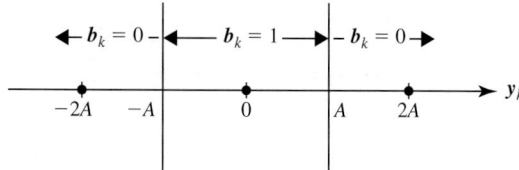

Figure 12.12 Decision regions.

12.4.2 Probability of Error Performance

To calculate the probability of error, it is useful to consider Figure 12.12, which shows the received signal diagram with decision boundaries. The detector makes an error if

1. $|y_k| < A$, assuming $b_k = 0$ was transmitted. This error is caused by the occurrence of one of the following events:
   - $y_k < A$ when $a_k = a_{k-1} = 1$ (with probability 1/4) $\Rightarrow n_k < -A$
   - $y_k > -A$ when $a_k = a_{k-1} = -1$ (with probability 1/4) $\Rightarrow n_k > A$
2. $|y_k| > A$, assuming $b_k = 1$ was transmitted with probability 1/2.

   $b_k = 1 \Rightarrow d_k \neq d_{k-1} \Rightarrow a_k + a_{k-1} = 0$. Thus the event $|y_k| > A \Rightarrow |n_k| > A$

The average probability of bit error is given by

$$BER = \frac{1}{2} \times P\{|y_k| > A|b_k = 1\} + \frac{1}{4} \times P\{y_k < A|b_k = 0\} + \frac{1}{4} \times P\{y_k > -A|b_k = 0\}$$

$$= \frac{1}{2}\left[P\{n_k < -A\} + P\{n_k > A\}\right] + \frac{1}{4} \times P\{n_k < -A\} + \frac{1}{4} \times P\{n_k > A\}$$

$$= \frac{3}{4}\left[P\{n_k < -A\} + P\{n_k > A\}\right]$$

$$= \frac{3}{2}Q\left(\frac{A}{\sigma}\right) \tag{12.79}$$

The energy of the transmitted pulse with amplitude A is given by

$$E_b = A^2 \int_{-\infty}^{\infty} |P_r(f)|df = A^2 2T \int_{-1/2T}^{1/2T} |\cos(\pi fT)|df = A^2 \frac{4}{\pi} \tag{12.80}$$

This allows us to write A in terms of E_b as

$$A = \sqrt{\frac{\pi E_b}{4}} \tag{12.81}$$

Substituting (12.77) and (12.81) into (12.79), we obtain

$$BER = \frac{3}{2}Q\left(\sqrt{\frac{\pi^2 2E_b}{16N_o}}\right) = \frac{3}{2}Q\left(\frac{\pi}{4}\sqrt{\frac{2E_b}{N_o}}\right) \tag{12.82}$$

Comparing (12.82) with (10.55) for a binary antipodal encoding scheme, we note that duobinary signaling requires $(4/\pi)^2$ or 2.1 dB additional SNR/bit to achieve the same

BER performance. This is because symbol-by-symbol detection of duobinary signals does not take advantage of the correlation between received signal samples for the detection of transmitted symbols. The correlation is used, however, to achieve ISI cancellation.

Example 12.4

How fast can data be transmitted using duobinary signaling over an ideal channel with bandwidth $W = 1.5$ MHz? Specify the SNR/bit required to achieve a BER of 10^{-6}. Assume that AWGN has a power spectral density 10^{-10} W/Hz.

Solution

Because duobinary signaling achieves transmission at the Nyquist rate using minimum bandwidth, data can be transmitted at $D = 2W = 2 \times 1.5 = 3$ Mb/s.

Using (12.82), we have

$$BER = \frac{3}{2} Q\left(\frac{\pi}{4} \sqrt{\frac{2E_b}{N_o}} \right)$$

Using Table 6.1, the argument of Q-function $= 4.835$ for $10^{-6} \times 2/3$. That is,

$$\frac{\pi^2}{16} \frac{2E_b}{N_o} = (4.835)^2 = 23.52$$

Solving for E_b/N_o, we obtain

$$\frac{E_b}{N_o} = 19.06 = 12.8 \text{ dB}$$

12.5   LINEAR EQUALIZERS

In Section 12.3, we discussed the design of transmit and receive filters to achieve ISI-free transmission assuming that the channel frequency response $H_c(f)$ is known. In practice we often encounter channels whose frequency response characteristics are either not known or change with time. We consider linear equalizers to mitigate ISI distortion produced as a result of nonideal magnitude and phase response characteristics of the channel.

The purpose of an equalizer is to process T-spaced[3] samples of the receive filter output to reduce the ISI as much as possible so that the probability of correct decision is maximized. The block diagram of the system including the equalizer is illustrated in Figure 12.13. We assume that the transmit filter is RRC type. Because the channel

---

[3] A **fractionally spaced equalizer (FSE),** which processes samples obtained at a fraction of the symbol period (typically, $T/2$), compensates delay distortion much more effectively. Another important property of an FSE is the insensitivity of its performance to the choice of sampler phase. The analysis of the FSE, however, is more complicated than a T-spaced equalizer and therefore is not considered here.

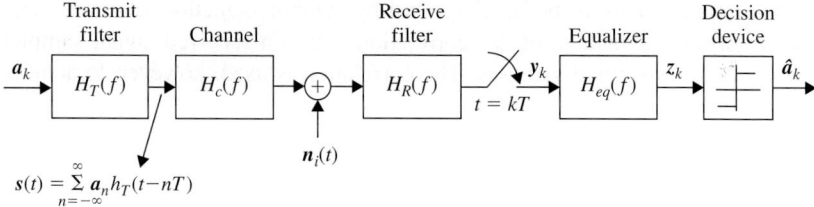

Figure 12.13 PAM system with equalizer.

frequency response is usually unknown or varies with time, we select the receive filter $h_R(t)$ so it is SRRC type and matched to the transmit filter. Using (10.39), we obtain

$$H_R(f) = H_T^*(f) \tag{12.83}$$

For $h_T(t)$ real, (12.83) corresponds to

$$h_R(t) = h_T(-t) \tag{12.84}$$

The purpose of the matched filter is to maximize the SNR of T-spaced output samples prior to their processing by the equalizer. The output of the matched receive filter is obtained from (12.8) as

$$y(t) = \sum_{n=-\infty}^{\infty} a_n p_r(t - nT) + n(t) \tag{12.85}$$

where $p_r(t) = h_T(t) \otimes h_c(t) \otimes h_R(t) = h_T(t) \otimes h_c(t) \otimes h_T(-t)$ is the composite impulse response of the transmit filter, channel and the matched filter. We assume that M-ary transmission symbols $a_n \in \{\pm 1, \pm 3, \ldots, \pm(M - 1)\}$ are iid random variables with mean 0 and variance σ_a^2. It is convenient to express (12.85) as

$$y(t) = \|p_r\| \sum_{n=-\infty}^{\infty} a_n q(t - nT) + n(t) \tag{12.86}$$

where $q(t)$ is the composite impulse response normalized to unit energy. That is,

$$q(t) = \frac{p_r(t)}{\|p_r\|} \tag{12.87}$$

where

$$\|p_r\| = \sqrt{\int_{-\infty}^{\infty} |p_r(t)|^2 dt} \tag{12.88}$$

We observe that for binary polar signaling $\|p_r\|^2$ equals average energy per bit E_b at the receive filter output. In the case of M-ary signaling, the average energy per symbol $E_s = \|p_r\|^2 \sigma_a^2$. The output of the receive filter is now sampled at the symbol rate $D = 1/T$. The T-spaced samples of the receive filter output are given by

$$y_k = \|p_r\| \sum_{n=-\infty}^{\infty} a_n q(kT - nT) + n(kT) = \|p_r\| \sum_{n=-\infty}^{\infty} a_n q_{k-n} + n_k \tag{12.89}$$

where

$$q_{k-n} = q[k - n] = q(kT - nT).$$

Because the receiver input noise $n_i(t)$ is AWGN with spectral density $N_o/2$, the MF output noise samples $\{n_k\}$ are Gaussian random variables with mean zero and autocorrelation function given by

$$
\begin{aligned}
E\{n_k n_\ell\} &= E\left\{ \int_{-\infty}^{\infty} n_i(\alpha)h_R(kT - \alpha)d\alpha \int_{-\infty}^{\infty} n_i(\beta)h_R(\ell T - \beta)d\beta \right\} \\
&= \int_{-\infty}^{\infty}\int_{-\infty}^{\infty} E\{n_i(\alpha)n_i(\beta)\}h_R(kT - \alpha)h_R(\ell T - \beta)d\alpha d\beta \\
&= \int_{-\infty}^{\infty}\int_{-\infty}^{\infty} E\{n_i(\alpha)n_i(\beta)\}h_R(kT - \alpha)h_R(\ell T - \beta)d\alpha d\beta \\
&= \frac{N_o}{2}\int_{-\infty}^{\infty}\int_{-\infty}^{\infty} \delta(\alpha - \beta)h_R(kT - \alpha)h_R(\ell T - \beta)d\alpha d\beta \\
&= \frac{N_o}{2}\int_{-\infty}^{\infty} \underbrace{h_R(kT - \beta)h_R(\ell T - \beta)d\beta}_{\substack{\text{orthogonal in the}\\\text{sense of (12.3)}}} \\
&= \frac{N_o}{2}\delta_{kl}
\end{aligned}
\tag{12.90}
$$

Equation (12.90) implies that $Var(n_k) = N_o/2$. Because random variables n_k are Gaussian and uncorrelated, they are statistically independent.

The samples $\{y_k\}$ are processed by the equalizer to minimize ISI in the output sample z_k. z_k is next passed through a threshold comparator device that produces an estimate $\hat{a}_k$ of the transmitted symbol. In our performance calculations for channels which introduce ISI and AWGN, we define the SNR/bit to be E_b/N_o, where E_b and N_o are defined at the receive filter output. As discussed earlier, $E_b = ||p_r||^2$ for binary antipodal signaling.

A linear equalizer is a discrete-time LTI filter with impulse response $\{h_{eq}[k]\}$ defined by

$$\{h_{eq}[k]\} = \{c_{-N}, \ldots, c_{-1}, c_0, c_1, \ldots, c_N\} \tag{12.91}$$

Figure 12.14 displays a tapped delay line or transversal filter implementation of a linear equalizer. The length or **span** of the equalizer is determined by the number of unit delay elements in the tapped delay line. The impulse or frequency response characteristics of an equalizer can be adjusted by dynamically updating its tap gains or coefficients c_i based on an estimate of the channel response. From Figure 12.14, it can be observed that the $2N + 1$ T-spaced receive filter output samples are linearly weighted by coefficients c_i and summed to produce the equalizer output sample z_k. The recurring relationship is given by

$$z_k = \sum_{i=-N}^{N} c_i y_{k-i} \tag{12.92}$$

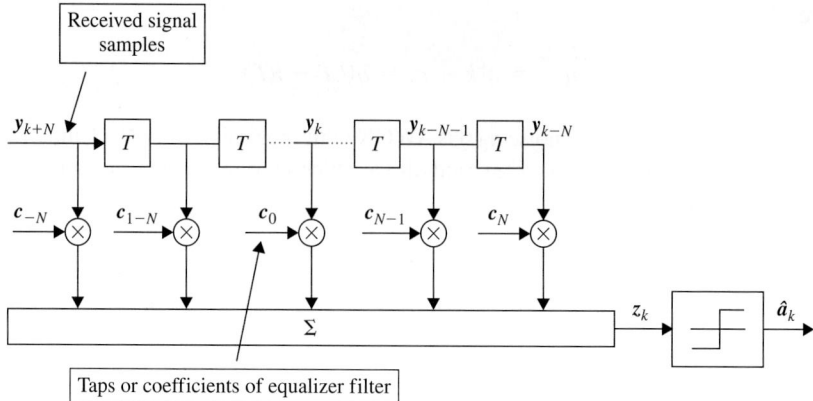

Figure 12.14 Transversal filter with $2N + 1$ filter taps.

Substituting (12.89) into (12.92) yields

$$z_k = \sum_{i=-N}^{N} c_i \left\{ \|p_r\| \sum_{n=-\infty}^{\infty} a_n q_{k-i-n} + n_{k-i} \right\}$$

$$= \|p_r\| a_k \sum_{i=-N}^{N} c_i q_{-i} + \|p_r\| \sum_{n\neq k} a_n \sum_{i=-N}^{N} c_i q_{k-i-n} + \sum_{i=-N}^{N} c_i n_{k-i}$$

$$= \|p_r\| a_k p_{eq}[0] + \|p_r\| \sum_{n\neq k} a_n p_{eq}[k-n] + \sum_{i=-N}^{N} c_i n_{k-i} \qquad (12.93)$$

where

$$p_{eq}[k] = q[k] \otimes h_{eq}[k] = \sum_{i=-N}^{N} c_i q_{k-i} \qquad (12.94)$$

is the response of the equalizer to the normalized overall impulse response sequence $q[k]$. The first term $\|p_r\| a_k p_{eq}[0]$ on the right-hand side of (12.93) is the desired signal because it can be used to identify the transmitted symbol during the kth symbol interval, while the middle sum $\|p_r\| \sum_{n\neq k} a_n p_{eq}[k-n]$ represents the residual ISI at the output of the equalizer. The term $\sum_{i=-N}^{N} c_i n_{k-i}$ is the noise component of the equalizer output. For the remainder of this section, we assume $\|p_r\| = 1$ without any loss of generality.

The equalizer coefficients c_i, $i = 0, \pm 1, \pm 2, \ldots, \pm N$ can be selected to optimize various performance criteria. These include:

- **Zero-forcing (ZF) criterion.** Forces ISI to be zero.
- **Minimum mean square error (MMSE) criterion.** Minimizes the expected value of squared error between the transmitted symbol and the equalizer output.

12.5.1 Zero-Forcing Equalizer

The equalizer coefficients c_i, $i = 0, \pm 1, \pm 2, \ldots, \pm N$ are chosen to force the samples of the equalizer output to zero at all but one of the $2N + 1$ T-spaced instants in the span of the equalizer. That is, we want to choose coefficients c_i such that

$$p_{eq}[k] = \begin{cases} 1, & k = 0 \\ 0, & k = \pm 1, \pm 2, \ldots, \pm N \end{cases} \qquad (12.95)$$

If we let the number of coefficients of a **zero-forcing equalizer (ZFE)** increase to infinity, we would obtain an infinite-length equalizer with zero ISI at its output. The condition (12.95) for zero ISI at the equalizer output can be expressed in the frequency domain as

$$P_{eq}\left(e^{j2\pi fT}\right) = H_{eq}^{ZF}\left(e^{j2\pi fT}\right)Q\left(e^{j2\pi fT}\right) = 1, \quad |f| \le 1/2T \qquad (12.96)$$

or

$$H_{eq}^{ZF}\left(e^{j2\pi fT}\right) = \frac{1}{Q\left(e^{j2\pi fT}\right)}, \quad |f| \le 1/2T \qquad (12.97)$$

where

$$h_{eq}^{ZF}[k] \xleftarrow{\ DTFT\ } H_{eq}^{ZF}\left(e^{j2\pi fT}\right)$$

$$q[k] \xleftarrow{\ DTFT\ } Q\left(e^{j2\pi fT}\right)$$

We observe from (12.97) that an infinite-length, zero-forcing equalizer is simply an inverse filter. That is, the frequency response of the ZFE is the inverse of the overall frequency response $Q\left(e^{j2\pi fT}\right)$. The spectral density of noise at the output of the equalizer is given by

$$N_{eq}\left(e^{j2\pi fT}\right) = \frac{N_o}{2}|H_{eq}^{ZF}\left(e^{j2\pi fT}\right)|^2 = \frac{N_o}{2}\left|\frac{1}{Q\left(e^{j2\pi fT}\right)}\right|^2 \qquad (12.98)$$

If the spectrum $Q\left(e^{j2\pi fT}\right)$ has severe attenuation at some frequencies within the Nyquist band of the signal, ZFE greatly enhances noise power at those frequencies as it attempts to make the overall frequency response (including equalizer) flat over $|f| \le 1/2T$. In this case, although the equalizer eliminates all the ISI, the equalized system will deliver poor BER performance because of the accompanying noise enhancement. This is of special concern in cellular channels that exhibit spectral nulls in the Nyquist band due to fading. It is frequently convenient to work with (12.97) in z-transform format obtained by substituting $z = e^{j2\pi fT}$. That is

$$H_{eq}^{ZF}(z) = \frac{1}{Q(z)} \qquad (12.99)$$

Example 12.5

Consider the composite impulse response

$$q(t) = \begin{cases} e^{-t/T}, & t \ge 0 \\ 0, & \text{otherwise} \end{cases}$$

a. Write the discrete-time impulse response $q[k]$.
b. Calculate the peak ISI distortion at the equalizer input.
c. Calculate the coefficients of a linear equalizer that completely eliminates the ISI.

Solution

a. The discrete-time overall channel impulse response is given by

$$q[k] = e^{-k}, k \geq 0$$

b. Using (12.14), the peak ISI distortion is given as

$$D_{peak} = \sum_{\substack{k=-\infty \\ k \neq 0}}^{\infty} |q[k]| = \sum_{k=1}^{\infty} e^{-k} = \frac{1}{e-1} \approx \frac{1}{1.7} = 0.582$$

Worst-case eye opening $= 1 - 0.582 = 0.418$ (41.8%)

c. The z-transform of the channel impulse response can be written as

$$Q(z) = \sum_{k=0}^{\infty} q[k]z^{-k} = \sum_{k=0}^{\infty} e^{-k}z^{-k} = \frac{1}{1-(ze)^{-1}} = \frac{z}{z-e^{-1}}$$

The z-transform of the equalizer is given from (12.99) as

$$H_{eq}^{ZF}(z) = \frac{1}{Q(z)} = \frac{z-e^{-1}}{z} = 1 - e^{-1}z^{-1}$$

By inspection, the discrete-time impulse response of the equalizer is obtained as

$$h_{eq}^{ZF}[k] = \{1, -e^{-1}\}$$

Note that the ZFE equalizer has 2 taps.

We next find the coefficients c_i of finite-length ZFE that approximates the inverse filter in (12.97). Combining (12.94) and (12.95), we obtain

$$\sum_{i=-N}^{N} c_i q_{k-i} = \begin{cases} 1, & k = 0 \\ 0, & k = \pm 1, \pm 2, \ldots, \pm N \end{cases} \tag{12.100}$$

Equation (12.100) can be expressed in the matrix form as

$$\underline{p}_{eq} = \underline{Q} \, \underline{c} \tag{12.101}$$

where $\underline{p}_{eq}$ and $\underline{c}$ are $(2N + 1)$ column vectors given by

$$\underline{p}_{eq} = (0 \; \ldots \; 0 \; 1 \; 0 \; \ldots \; 0)^T \tag{12.102}$$

$$\underline{c} = (c_{-N}, c_{-N+1}, \ldots, c_0, c_1, \ldots, c_N)^T \tag{12.103}$$

respectively, and $\underline{Q}$ is the $(2N + 1) \times (2N + 1)$ matrix of the normalized overall impulse response samples $\{q[k]\}$.

$$Q = \begin{pmatrix} q[0] & q[-1] & \cdots & q[-2N] \\ q[1] & q[0] & \cdots & q[-2N+1] \\ q[2] & q[1] & \cdots & q[-2N+2] \\ \vdots & \vdots & \vdots & \vdots \\ q[2N] & q[2N-1] & \cdots & q[0] \end{pmatrix} \qquad (12.104)$$

Thus the $4N + 1$ sample values $\{q[k]\}$ can be used to determine the $2N + 1$ unknown coefficients c_i, $i = 0, \pm1, \pm2, \ldots, \pm N$ by solving (12.101). Because there are $2N + 1$ equations in (12.101), the optimum coefficient vector $\underline{c}_{opt}$ is given by

$$\underline{c}_{opt} = \underline{Q}^{-1}\underline{p}_{eq} \qquad (12.105)$$

It is obvious from the definition (12.102) that a ZFE of span $2N + 1$ will force exactly N zeros at the sampling instants on either side of the peak pulse response. It has been shown[4] that the zero-forcing solution minimizes the peak ISI distortion if the eye is initially open.

Example 12.6

Given the overall impulse response

$$\{q[k]\} = \{0.0434, -0.0543, 0.0760, -0.2279, -0.4341, 0.7814, 0.2822,$$
$$0.0, 0.2279, 0.0326, 0.0760\}$$

determine the tap coefficients of a 5-tap ZFE. Plot the equalized output pulse sequence. Compare the performance with a 31-tap equalizer.

Solution

The optimum coefficient vector for ZFE is given by

$$\underline{c}_{opt} = \underline{Q}^{-1}\underline{p}_{eq}$$

where

$$Q = \begin{pmatrix} q[0] & q[-1] & q[-2] & q[-3] & q[-4] \\ q[1] & q[0] & q[-1] & q[-2] & q[-3] \\ q[2] & q[1] & q[0] & q[-1] & q[-2] \\ q[3] & q[2] & q[1] & q[0] & q[-1] \\ q[4] & q[3] & q[2] & q[1] & q[0] \end{pmatrix} = \begin{pmatrix} 0.7814 & -0.4341 & -0.2279 & 0.0760 & -0.0543 \\ 0.2822 & 0.7814 & -0.4341 & -0.2279 & 0.0760 \\ 0.0 & 0.2822 & 0.7814 & -0.4341 & -0.2279 \\ 0.2279 & 0.0 & 0.2822 & 0.7814 & -0.4341 \\ 0.0326 & 0.2279 & 0.0 & 0.2822 & 0.7814 \end{pmatrix}$$

and

$$\underline{p}_{eq} = (0\ 0\ 1\ 0\ 0)^T$$

---

[4] R. Lucky, J. Salz, and E. Weldon, *Principles of Data Communication*, (New York: McGraw-Hill, 1968).

The inverse of $\underline{Q}$ matrix is obtained using MATLAB as

$$
\underline{Q}^{-1} = \begin{pmatrix}
1.0910 & 0.3624 & 0.4615 & 0.1606 & 0.2644 \\
-0.4429 & 0.9020 & 0.2351 & 0.3788 & 0.1606 \\
0.0726 & -0.4443 & 0.9692 & 0.2351 & 0.4615 \\
-0.2482 & -0.0831 & -0.4443 & 0.9020 & 0.3624 \\
0.1733 & -0.2482 & 0.0726 & -0.4429 & 1.0910
\end{pmatrix}
$$

Using matrix multiplication, the optimum tap weights are obtained as

$$
\underline{c}_{opt} = \begin{pmatrix}
0.4615 \\
0.2351 \\
0.9692 \\
-0.4443 \\
0.0726
\end{pmatrix}
$$

The equalizer output pulse sequence is given by

$$
p_{eq}[k] = q[k] \otimes h_{eq}[k] = \{0.0200, -0.0148, 0.0644, -0.1592, -0.1531, 0.0, 0.0, 1.0, 0.0, 0.0,
$$
$$
0.2841, -0.0518, 0.0757, -0.0314, 0.0055\}
$$

Figure 12.15 displays the equalizer input and output pulse sequence. As expected there two zeros on each side of the peak. However, zero forcing has not eliminated ISI at points further out. In general, with an equalizer of length $(2N + 1)$, we can control only $(2N + 1)$ sampled values of equalizer output $\{p_{eq}[k]\}$.

Figure 12.16(a) displays the frequency response of the transmit filter, the channel, and the matched receive filter cascade. Over the normalized frequency range $0 \leq \omega T \leq \pi$, corresponding to $0 \leq f \leq 1/2T$, the gain varies by about 10 dB. Figure 12.16(b) shows

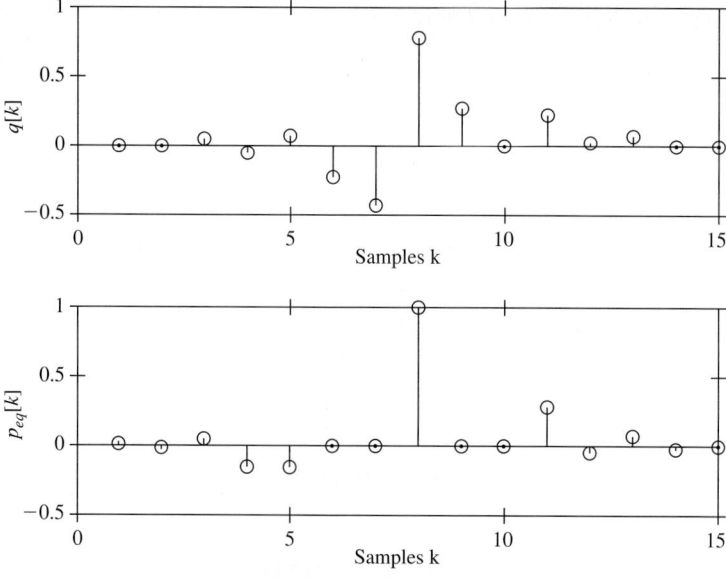

Figure 12.15 5-tap ZFE input and output samples.

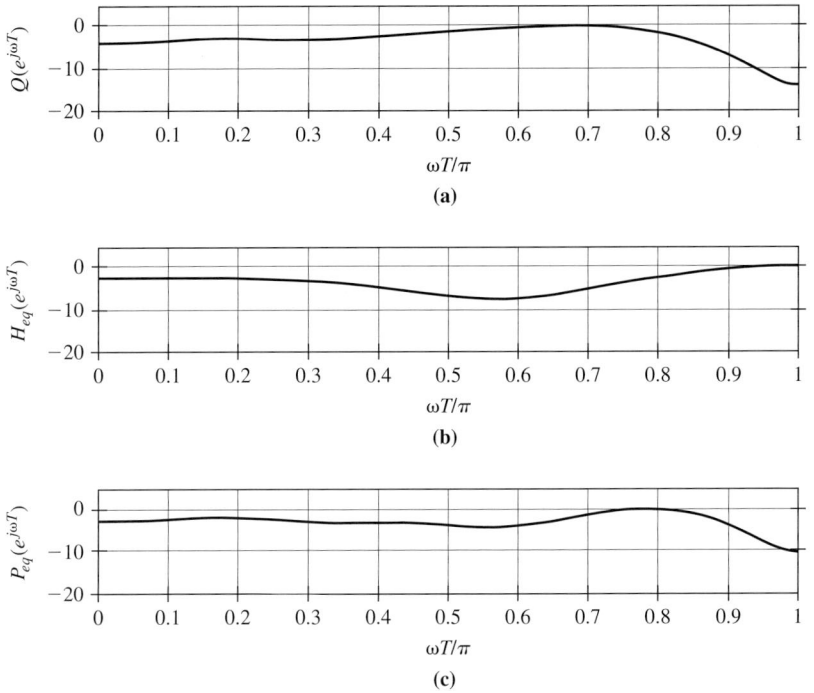

Figure 12.16 Frequency response characteristics of the 5-tap ZFE solution: (a) transmit filter-channel-MF cascade; (b) equalizer; and (c) combined response.

the frequency response of the 5-tap ZFE. Note that in combating the channel effect, the equalizer provides gain where the channel attenuates and attenuation where the channel has gain. Figure 12.16(c) shows the combined channel/equalizer frequency response. We see that the equalizer is not very successful at equalizing the channel attenuation at high frequencies.

Next we check by increasing the number of taps in the ZFE to determine if it is more effective in equalizing the channel. The performance of a 31-tap equalizer for the channel is illustrated in Figures 12.17 and 12.18. It is evident from Figures 12.17(b) and 12.18(c) that 31-tap equalizer is successful in combating the ISI by effectively equalizing the channel.

12.5.2 Minimum Mean-Square Error Equalizer

A MMSE equalizer minimizes the expected value of the mean-square error between the transmitted symbol a_k and the equalizer output sample z_k. We define the mean-square error at the equalizer output as

$$J = E\{e_k^2\} = E\{[z_k - a_k]^2\} \tag{12.106}$$

The equalizer output sample in (12.92) can be expressed in the vector form as

$$z_k = \sum_{i=-N}^{N} c_i y_{k-i} = \underline{c}^T \underline{y}_k = \underline{y}_k^T \underline{c} \tag{12.107}$$

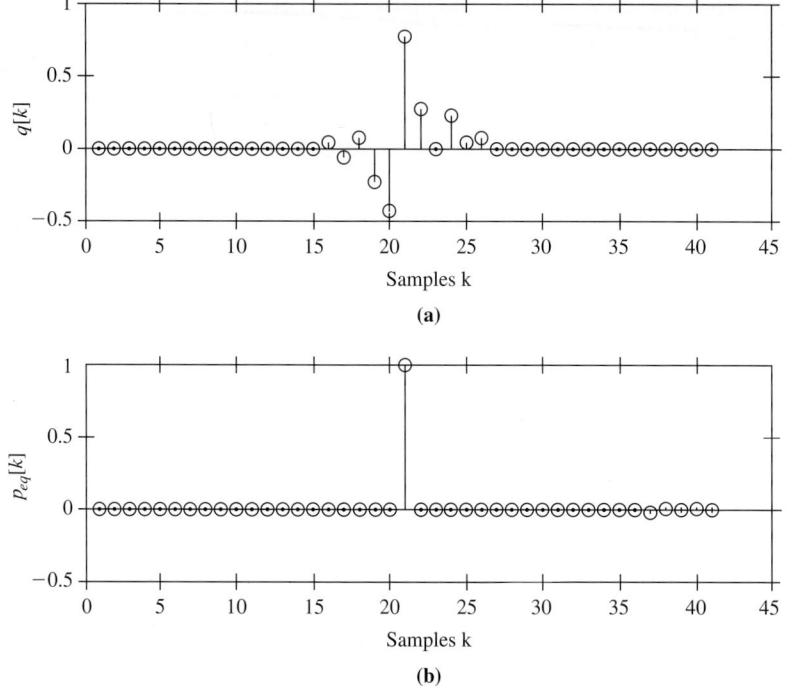

Figure 12.17 31-tap ZFE input and output samples.

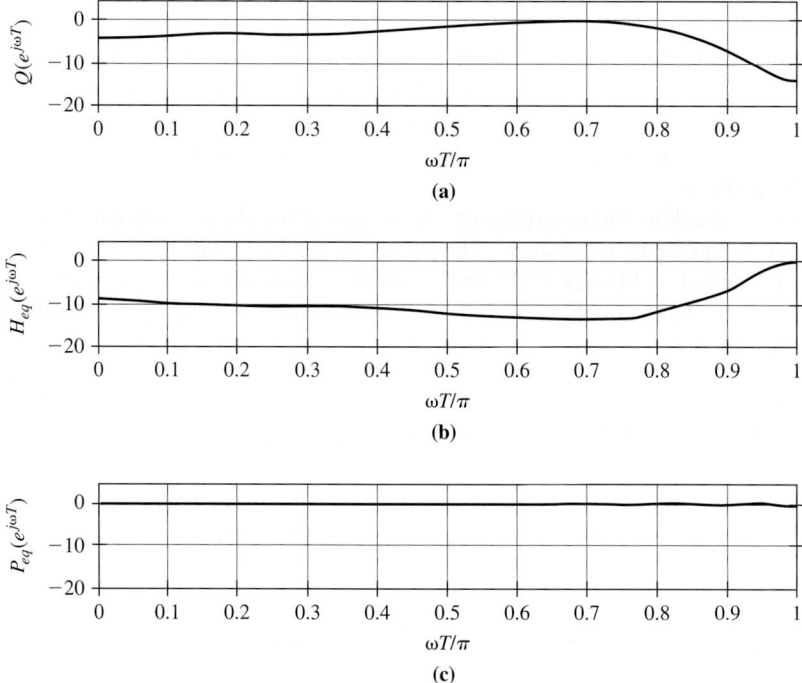

Figure 12.18 Frequency response characteristics of the 31-tap ZFE solution: (a) transmit filter-channel-MF cascade; (b) equalizer; and (c) combined response.

where $\underline{y}_k$ is a vector of $2N + 1$ samples contained in the equalizer delay line at the time of deciding $\hat{a}_k$. That is,

$$\underline{y}_k = (y_{k-N}, y_{k-N+1}, \ldots, y_k, y_{k+1}, \ldots, y_{k+N})^T \tag{12.108}$$

We seek the equalizer coefficients c_i, $i = 0, \pm 1, \pm 2, \ldots, \pm N$ that minimize the mean-square error in (12.106). This is a linear MMSE estimation problem. The coefficients $\underline{c}_{opt}$ of the MMSE equalizer can be calculated by making use of the orthogonality principle which states that the error $e_k = z_k - a_k = \underline{y}_k^T \underline{c} - a_k$ must be orthogonal to the samples contained in the equalizer delay line. That is,

$$E\{\underline{y}_k e_k\} = E\{\underline{y}_k[\underline{y}_k^T \underline{c}_{opt} - a_k]\} = 0$$

or

$$E\{\underline{y}_k \underline{y}_k^T \underline{c}_{opt}\} = E\{\underline{y}_k a_k\} \tag{12.109}$$

We can express (12.109) as

$$\underline{R}_{yy} \underline{c}_{opt} = \underline{r}_{ay} \tag{12.110}$$

where $\underline{R}_{yy} = E\{\underline{y}_k \underline{y}_k^T\}$ is the covariance matrix of $\underline{y}_k$ and $\underline{r}_{ay} = E\{a_k \underline{y}_k\}$ is the cross-correlation vector between a_k and $\underline{y}_k$. Because the covariance matrix $\underline{R}_{yy}$ is positive definite, $\underline{R}_{yy}^{-1}$ exists. The MMSE equalizer coefficient are, therefore, given by

$$\underline{c}_{opt} = \underline{R}_{yy}^{-1} \underline{r}_{ay} \tag{12.111}$$

Substituting (12.107) into (12.106), mean-square error at the equalizer output can be expressed as

$$\begin{aligned}
J(\underline{c}) = E\{[z_k - a_k]^2\} &= E\{\underline{c}^T \underline{y}_k \underline{y}_k^T \underline{c} - 2\underline{c}^T a_k \underline{y}_k + a_k^2\} \\
&= \underline{c}^T E\{\underline{y}_k \underline{y}_k^T\} \underline{c} - 2\underline{c}^T E\{a_k \underline{y}_k\} + E\{a_k^2\} \\
&= \underline{c}^T \underline{R}_{yy} \underline{c} - 2\underline{c}^T \underline{r}_{ay} + \sigma_a^2
\end{aligned} \tag{12.112}$$

The minimum mean-square corresponding to the optimum coefficient vector $\underline{c}_{opt}$ is obtained by substituting (12.111) into (12.112) as

$$J_{\min} = \sigma_a^2 - \underline{c}_{opt}^T \underline{r}_{ay} \tag{12.113}$$

The elements of the $(2N + 1) \times (2N + 1)$ matrix $\underline{R}_{yy}$ are given by

$$R_{yy}[i,j] = E\{y_{k-i} y_{k-j}\}, \quad -N \leq i, j \leq N \tag{12.114}$$

Substituting (12.89) into (12.114) yields

$$\underline{R}_{yy}[i,j] = E\left\{ \sum_{\ell=-\infty}^{\infty} \sum_{m=-\infty}^{\infty} a_\ell a_m q_{k-i-\ell} q_{k-j-m} + n_{k-i} n_{k-j} \right\} \tag{12.115}$$

For iid transmission symbols $\{a_n\}$

$$E\{a_\ell a_m\} = \begin{cases} \sigma_a^2, & \ell = m \\ 0, & \text{otherwise} \end{cases} \tag{12.116}$$

We know from (12.90) that noise samples at the MF output are statistically independent. Therefore,

$$E\{n_{k-i} n_{k-j}\} = \frac{N_o}{2} \delta_{ij} \tag{12.117}$$

Substituting (12.116) and (12.117) into (12.115) we obtain

$$\underline{R}_{yy}[i,j] = \sigma_a^2 \sum_{l=-\infty}^{\infty} q_{k-i-\ell} q_{k-j-\ell} + \frac{N_o}{2} \delta_{ij} \tag{12.118}$$

Making the change of variable $n = k - i - \ell$, we can write (12.118) as

$$\underline{R}_{yy}[i,j] = \sigma_a^2 \sum_{n=-\infty}^{\infty} q_n q_{n+(i-j)} + \frac{N_o}{2} \delta_{ij} = \underline{R}_{yy}[j,i] \tag{12.119}$$

For a finite-length overall impulse response sequence q_k of length $2L + 1$, (12.119) simplifies to

$$\underline{R}_{yy}[i,j] = \sigma_a^2 \sum_{n=-L}^{L-|i-j|} q_n q_{n+|i-j|} + \frac{N_o}{2} \delta_{ij} = \underline{R}_{yy}[j,i] \tag{12.120}$$

The elements of the crosscorrelation vector $\underline{r}_{ay}$ are given by

$$\underline{r}_{ay}[i] = E\{a_k y_{k-i}\}, \qquad -N \le i \le N \tag{12.121}$$

Substituting (12.89) and (12.116) into (12.121) yields

$$\underline{r}_{ay}[i] = E\left\{a_k \left[\sum_{\ell=-\infty}^{\infty} a_\ell q_{k-i-\ell} + n_{k-i}\right]\right\} = \sum_{\ell=-\infty}^{\infty} E\{a_k a_\ell\} q_{k-i-\ell} + E\{a_k n_{k-i}\} = \sigma_a^2 q_{-i} \tag{12.122}$$

If the overall impulse response sequence is finite-length, that is, $q_k = 0$ for $|k| > L$, and $L < N$, the vector $\underline{r}_{ay}$ can be expressed from (12.122) as

$$\underline{r}_{ay} = \sigma_a^2 \, (\underbrace{0, \ldots, 0}_{N-L}, \underbrace{q[L], q[L-1], \ldots, q[0], \ldots, q[-L+1], q[-L]}_{2L+1}, \underbrace{0, \ldots, 0}_{N-L})^T \tag{12.123}$$

Infinite-Length MMSE Equalizer

For an infinite-length equalizer, the equalizer output sample in (12.92) becomes

$$z_k = \sum_{i=-\infty}^{\infty} c_i y_{k-i}$$

Substituting into (12.106) and after some further manipulation, we can write the mean-square error $J(\underline{c})$ as

$$J(\underline{c}) = \sum_{i=-\infty}^{\infty} \sum_{j=-\infty}^{\infty} c_i c_j \underline{R}_{yy}[i,j] - 2 \sum_{i=-\infty}^{\infty} c_i \underline{r}_{ay}[i] + E\{a_k^2\} \qquad (12.124)$$

Now substituting (12.119) and (12.122) into (12.124), we obtain

$$J(\underline{c}) = \sum_{i=-\infty}^{\infty} \sum_{j=-\infty}^{\infty} c_i c_j \left\{ \sigma_a^2 \sum_{n=-\infty}^{\infty} q_n q_{n+(i-j)} + \frac{N_o}{2} \delta_{ij} \right\} - 2\sigma_a^2 \sum_{i=-\infty}^{\infty} c_i q_{-i} + \sigma_a^2$$

or

$$\frac{J(\underline{c})}{\sigma_a^2} = \sum_{i=-\infty}^{\infty} \sum_{j=-\infty}^{\infty} c_i c_j \left\{ \sum_{n=-\infty}^{\infty} q_n q_{n+(i-j)} + \frac{N_o}{2\sigma_a^2} \delta_{ij} \right\} - 2 \sum_{i=-\infty}^{\infty} c_i q_{-i} + 1 \qquad (12.125)$$

Taking the DTFT of both sides yields

$$\frac{J(\underline{c})}{\sigma_a^2} = |H_{eq}(e^{j2\pi fT})|^2 \left[|Q(e^{j2\pi fT})|^2 + \frac{N_o}{2\sigma_a^2} \right] - 2H_{eq}(e^{j2\pi fT}) Q^*(e^{j2\pi fT}) + 1 \qquad (12.126)$$

If we now differentiate (12.126) with respect to $H_{eq}(e^{j2\pi fT})$ and set the resultant derivative to zero, the optimum equalizer filter is given by

$$H_{eq}^{MMSE}(e^{j2\pi fT}) = \frac{Q^*(e^{j2\pi fT})}{\left[|Q(e^{j2\pi fT})|^2 + \dfrac{N_o}{2\sigma_a^2} \right]} \qquad (12.127)$$

The difference between $H_{eq}^{MMSE}(e^{j2\pi fT})$ in (12.127) and the one obtained for the zero-forcing criterion in (12.97) is the presence of SNR term $2\sigma_a^2/N_o$. For high SNR values, the MMSE equalizer transfer function approaches the inverse filter. That is,

$$H_{eq}^{MMSE}(e^{j2\pi fT}) \approx \frac{1}{Q(e^{j2\pi fT})} \qquad (12.128)$$

Thus both optimization criteria yield the same solution for the tap weights. When the SNR is low, the MMSE solution, however, determines tap weights that try to achieve the optimum trade-off between minimizing the ISI and noise enhancement at the equalizer output.

Example 12.7

For the overall impulse response sequence $q[k]$ in Example 12.6 determine the tap coefficients of a 5-tap MMSE equalizer. Assume that SNR/bit at the sampler output = 10 dB. Plot the equalized output waveform. Compare the performance with a 31-bit equalizer.

Solution

Because $E_b = 1$ has been assumed, the SNR/bit at prior to equalization is given by $\dfrac{1}{N_o}$. Therefore, $N_o = 1/10$. Also, for binary polar signaling, $\sigma_a^2 = 1$. The optimum coefficient vector for the
MMSE equalizer is given by

$$\underline{c}_{opt} = \underline{R}_{yy}^{-1} \underline{r}_{ay}$$

$\underline{R}_{yy}$ is obtained by using (12.120) as

$$\underline{R}_{yy} = \begin{pmatrix} 1.0500 & -0.0337 & -0.2363 & 0.1960 & -0.0919 \\ -0.0337 & 1.0500 & -0.0337 & -0.2363 & 0.1960 \\ -0.2363 & -0.0337 & 1.0500 & -0.0337 & -0.2363 \\ 0.1960 & -0.2363 & -0.0337 & 1.0500 & -0.0337 \\ -0.0919 & 0.1960 & -0.2363 & -0.0337 & 1.0500 \end{pmatrix}$$

Using (12.123), $\underline{r}_{ay}$ can be expressed as

$$\underline{r}_{ay} = \begin{pmatrix} 0.0 \\ 0.2822 \\ 0.7814 \\ -0.4341 \\ -0.2279 \end{pmatrix}$$

The inverse of the $\underline{R}_{yy}$ matrix is obtained using MATLAB as

$$\underline{R}_{yy}^{-1} = \begin{pmatrix} 1.0602 & -0.0288 & 0.2657 & -0.1910 & 0.1518 \\ -0.0288 & 1.0392 & -0.0086 & 0.2328 & -0.1910 \\ 0.2657 & -0.0086 & 1.0714 & -0.0086 & 0.2657 \\ -0.1910 & 0.2328 & -0.0086 & 1.0392 & -0.0288 \\ 0.1518 & -0.1910 & 0.2657 & -0.0288 & 1.0602 \end{pmatrix}$$

Using matrix multiplication, the optimum tap weights are obtained as

$$\underline{c}_{opt} = \begin{pmatrix} 0.2478 \\ 0.2289 \\ 0.7780 \\ -0.3856 \\ -0.0754 \end{pmatrix}$$

The equalizer output pulse sequence is given by

$$p_{eq}[k] = q[k] \otimes h_{eq}[k] = \{0.0108, -0.0035, 0.0402, -0.0980, -0.0830, -0.1083, -0.0067, 0.8571$$
$$0.0074, -0.1075, 0.1823, -0.0452, 0.0294, -0.0318, -0.0057\}$$

Figure 12.19 displays samples of the 5-tap MMSE equalizer input and output pulse sequence.
It does not do a very good job of mitigating the ISI and inverting the channel as illustrated by
Figures 12.19(b) and 12.20(c), respectively. The 31-tap equalizer does a much better job of
minimizing the ISI as displayed in Figure 12.21(b). This is confirmed in Figure 12.22(c) where
we note that the channel is equalized to within about 3 dB of Nyquist criterion requirement.

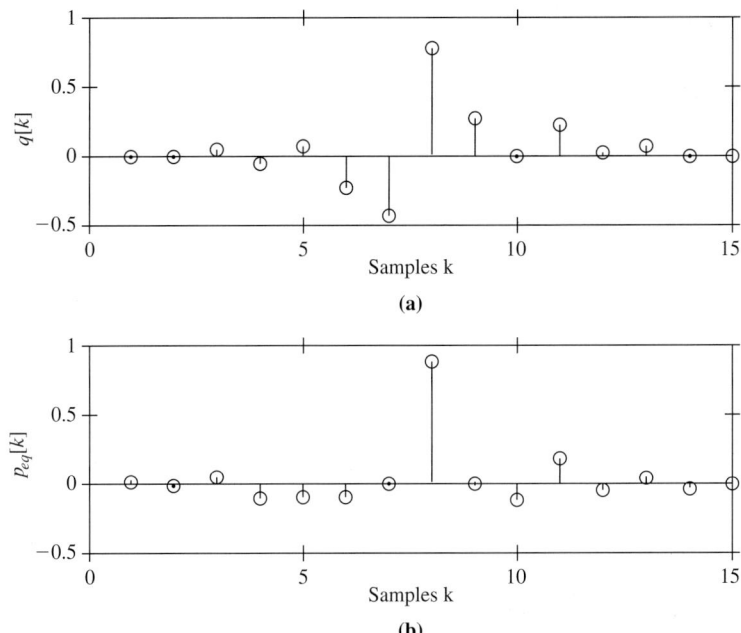

Figure 12.19 5-tap MMSE equalizer input and output samples.

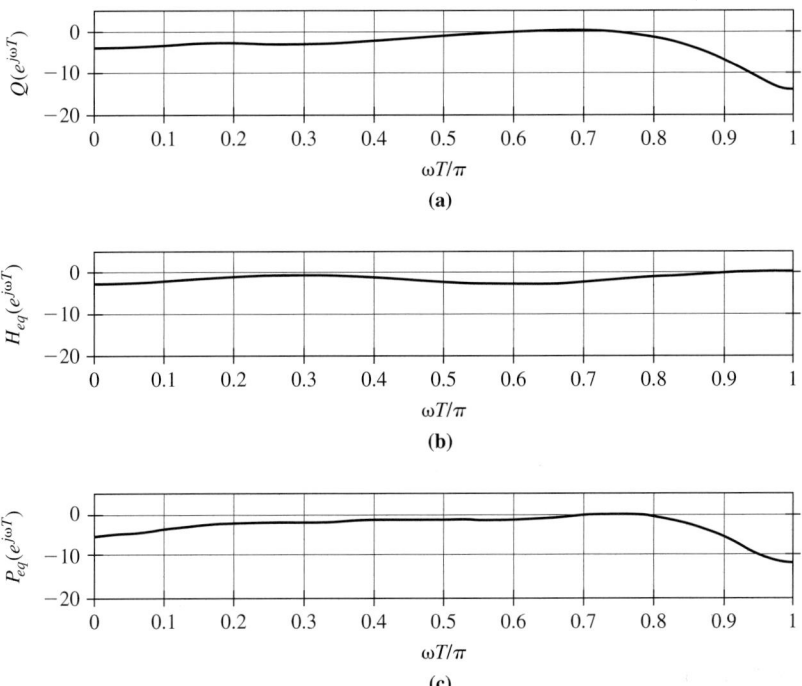

Figure 12.20 Frequency response characteristics of the 5-tap MMSE solution: (a) transmit filter-channel-MF cascade; (b) equalizer; and (c) combined response.

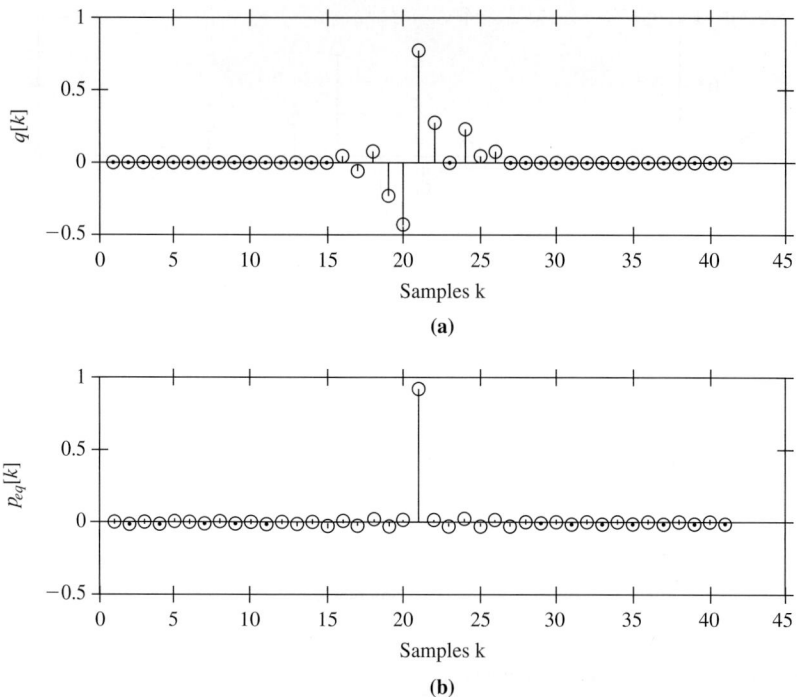

Figure 12.21 31-tap MMSE equalizer input and output samples.

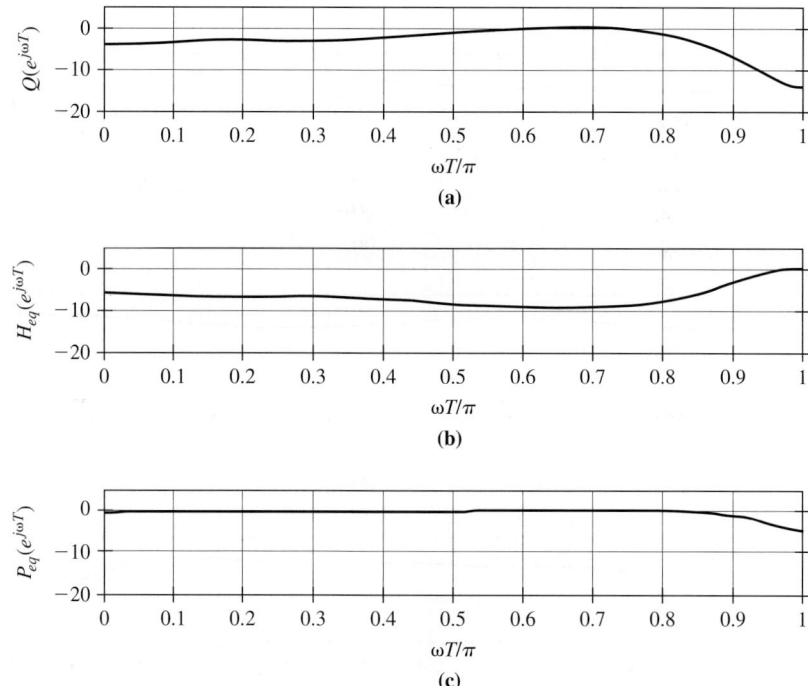

Figure 12.22 Frequency response characteristics of the 31-tap MMSE equalizer solution: (a) transmit filter-channel-MF cascade; (b) equalizer; and (c) combined response.

12.6 ADAPTIVE EQUALIZATION

In most real-life communication channels, the channel response is usually not known in advance or varies with time. Consequently, adaptive algorithms are required to compute the equalizer coefficients for compensating time-varying ISI introduced by the channel. The equalizer, therefore, must periodically estimate the channel response $(h_C(t))$ and update its coefficients accordingly. Depending on the channel characteristics, the coefficient updating can be done in one of the following ways:

- During the modem/system initialization (with possible reinitialization when the system performance is detected to be unsatisfactory).
- At regular intervals, for example, once for each transmission burst in burst-mode communications. An example is GSM cellular system.
- Continuously during normal operation.

An adaptive equalizer can be designed to operate in one of the following modes:

- **Training (data-aided, DA).** Short, known training symbol sequences are transmitted and used as the reference in the equalizer adaptation. This process is called **equalizer training.**
- **Decision-directed (DD).** The detected symbols are used as the reference in the equalizer adaptation.
- **Blind equalization.** No training sequences are used. The equalizer learns the channel using the detected data and utilizes advanced statistical signal processing techniques for equalization.

Most practical adaptive schemes use the training mode during the initialization phase and DD mode to adjust the equalizer coefficients during normal operation ("equalizer tracking"). The DD implementation works reliably only in reasonably good SNR/BER environments.

In Section 12.5, it was shown that the $2N + 1$ coefficients $\underline{c}_{opt}$ of an MMSE equalizer are given by (12.111) as

$$\underline{c}_{opt} = \underline{R}_{yy}^{-1}\underline{r}_{ay} \tag{12.111}$$

where $\underline{R}_{yy}$ is a $(2N + 1) \times (2N + 1)$ autocorrelation matrix of the equalizer input samples, and $\underline{r}_{ay}$ is a $(2N + 1)$-dimensional crosscorrelation vector between the transmitted symbol and the equalizer input samples. In practical implementations of equalizers, the optimum coefficient vector $\underline{c}_{opt}$ in (12.111) is usually obtained by an iterative search procedure that avoids the explicit computation of the inverse of the matrix $\underline{R}_{yy}$. Instead we use the **steepest-descent** or **gradient** method for iteratively searching the unconstrained minimum of the real-valued function $f(\underline{x})$ of n variables. The steepest-descent method is based on the observation that the gradient vector $\Delta_{\underline{x}} f = \left(\dfrac{\delta f}{\delta x_1}, \dfrac{\delta f}{\delta x_2}, \ldots, \dfrac{\delta f}{\delta x_n}\right)$ points locally in the direction of the *greatest* rate of increase of $f(\underline{x})$. Hence $-\Delta_{\underline{x}} f$ points locally in the direction of greatest decrease of $f(\underline{x})$. Thus starting with initial guess $\underline{x}_0$ corresponding to a point on $f(\underline{x})$, the successive values $\underline{x}_k$ generated using

$$\underline{x}_{k+1} = \underline{x}_k - \mu \Delta_{\underline{x}} f \tag{12.129}$$

satisfy the property $f(\underline{x}_0) \geq f(\underline{x}_1) \geq f(\underline{x}_2) \geq \ldots$ It can be shown that the sequence of values $\underline{x}_k$ generated by the algorithm (12.129) converge to a local minimum of $f(\underline{x})$. μ is called the **step size,** and its choice is critical in determining the speed of convergence of the algorithm to the optimum value. The mean-square error function in (12.112) is hyperparaboloid (i.e., a "quadratic" surface in $(2N + 1)$-dimensional space) and has a unique minimum. Thus, the local minimum resulting from a steepest-descent search is a true or global minimum.

Applying the steepest-descent search algorithm to solve the optimization problem $\underset{\underline{c}}{\text{Min}}\, J(\underline{c})$, the coefficient vector $\underline{c}(k)$ is updated at the kth iteration according to the recursive relation

$$\underline{c}(k + 1) = \underline{c}(k) - \mu \underline{g}_k, \quad k = 0, 1, \ldots \tag{12.130}$$

where $\underline{g}_k = \Delta_{\underline{c}} J$ denotes the gradient vector computed at the kth iteration. $\underline{c}(k + 1)$ is the new coefficient vector that is at least as close to the optimum $\underline{c}_{opt}$ as $\underline{c}(k)$. μ is chosen to be a small positive step size to ensure the convergence of the iterative procedure. Figure 12.23 displays the convergence of the gradient algorithm in two dimensions. By taking the partial derivative of $J(\underline{c})$ in (12.112) with respect to c_i, $i = 0, \pm 1, \pm 2, \ldots, \pm N$, the gradient $\nabla_{\underline{c}} J(\underline{c})$ can be expressed in the vector form as

$$\nabla_{\underline{c}} J(\underline{c}) = 2(\underline{R}_{yy}\underline{c} - \underline{r}_{ay}) \tag{12.131}$$

Substituting (12.131) into (12.130), we obtain

$$\underline{c}(k + 1) = \underline{c}(k) - 2\mu[\underline{R}_{yy}\underline{c}(k) - \underline{r}_{ay}]$$
$$= (I - 2\mu\underline{R}_{yy})\underline{c}(k) + 2\mu\underline{r}_{ay} \tag{12.132}$$

The gradient vector $\underline{g}_k \to 0$ as $k \to \infty$, and the coefficient vector $\underline{c}(k) \to \underline{c}_{opt}$. The iteration process is stopped after the difference between the values of the equalizer coefficients calculated during successive iterations is below a preset threshold value, such as 10^{-6}. In practice, the algorithm converges after a few hundred iterations.

12.6.1   Least Mean Square Error Algorithm

The computation of the gradient vector in (12.131) requires a knowledge of the autocorrelation matrix $\underline{R}_{yy}$ and crosscorrelation vector $\underline{r}_{ay}$. As discussed earlier, $\underline{R}_{yy}$ and $\underline{r}_{ay}$ may not always be available (i.e., computationally feasible) if the channel is not known in

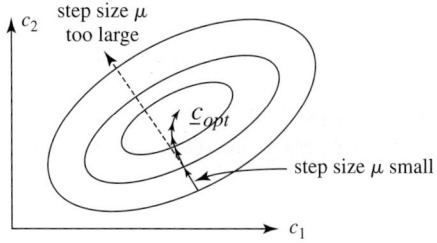

Figure 12.23 Convergence of 2-tap equalizer.

advance or varies with time. As an alternative approach to computing the gradient vector $\Delta_c J$, we write the MMSE objective function $J(\underline{c})$ from (12.112) as

$$J(\underline{c}) = E\{[z_k - a_k]^2\} = E\{\underline{c}^T \underline{y}_k \underline{y}_k^T \underline{c} - 2\underline{c}^T a_k \underline{y}_k + a_k^2\}$$

The gradient vector $\Delta_c J$ can now be obtained by exchanging the order of expectation and partial differentiation as

$$\Delta_c J = \Delta_c \left[E\{\underline{c}^T \underline{y}_k \underline{y}_k^T \underline{c} - 2\underline{c}^T a_k \underline{y}_k + a_k^2\} \right]$$
$$= E\{\Delta_c [\underline{c}^T \underline{y}_k \underline{y}_k^T \underline{c} - 2\underline{c}^T a_k \underline{y}_k + a_k^2]\} = -2E\{\underline{y}_k [\underline{y}_k^T \underline{c} - a_k]\} \quad (12.133)$$

Substituting

$$e_k = z_k - a_k = \underline{y}_k^T \underline{c} - a_k \quad (12.134)$$

into (12.133) yields

$$\Delta_c J = -2E\{e_k \underline{y}_k\} \quad (12.135)$$

The **least mean square error (LMSE)** algorithm is based on the significant observation by Woodrow[5] that the *instantaneous* value of the gradient vector $-e_k \underline{y}_k$ can be used in place of $\Delta_c J = -2E\{e_k \underline{y}_k\}$ in a modified version of the steepest-descent iterative algorithm described previously. The instantaneous value of the gradient vector $\hat{\underline{g}}_k$ at the kth iteration can be written from (12.135) as

$$\hat{\underline{g}}_k = -e_k \underline{y}_k \quad (12.136)$$

where e_k denotes the difference between the transmitted symbol a_k and the actual equalizer output z_k during the kth iteration. $\underline{y}_k$ is the vector of $2N + 1$ samples contained in the equalizer delay line at the time of computing $\hat{\underline{c}}(k + 1)$. Thus, the algorithm for adjusting the equalizer tap coefficients may be expressed by substituting (12.136) into (12.130) as

$$\hat{\underline{c}}(k + 1) = \hat{\underline{c}}(k) - \mu \hat{\underline{g}}_k = \hat{\underline{c}}(k) + \mu e_k \underline{y}_k \quad (12.137)$$

where $\hat{\underline{c}}(k)$ denotes an estimate of the coefficient vector at the kth iteration. Because an estimate of the gradient vector is used in (12.137), the algorithm is also called a **stochastic gradient algorithm.** The block diagram of an adaptive equalizer that adapts its tap coefficients according to (12.137) is illustrated in Figure 12.24. The adaptive equalizer is trained by the transmission of a known pseudorandom sequence $\{a_k\}$ over the channel. At the receiver, the equalizer employs the known sequence to adjust its coefficients. In the **training mode,** the difference between the training sequence symbol a_k and the actual equalizer output z_k is used to form the error signal e_k. Upon initial adjustment, the adaptive equalizer switches from the training mode to a **decision-directed mode,** in which case the decisions at the output of the detector are sufficiently reliable so that the error signal is formed by using $e_k = z_k - \hat{a}_k$. This error is scaled by the step size μ, and

[5] B. Woodrow, "Adaptive Filters, I: Fundamentals," Stanford Electronics Laboratory Report No. 6764-6 (Stanford University, Stanford, CA: 1966).

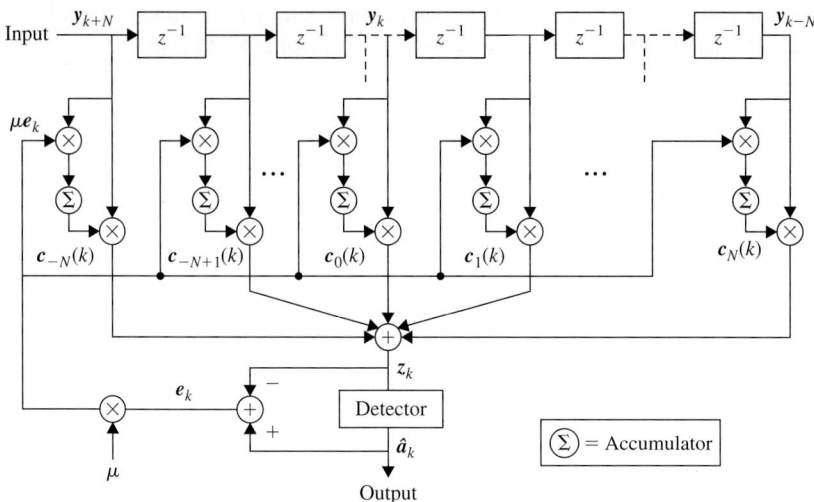

Figure 12.24   Adaptive LMS equalizer.

the scaled error signal μe_k multiplies the received signal samples y_k at the $2N + 1$ taps. The products $\mu e_k y_{k-j}$, $j = 0, \pm 1, \ldots, \pm N$ at the $2N + 1$ taps are then added to the previous values of the equalizer coefficients to obtain the updated tap coefficients as follows:

$$c_j(k + 1) = c_j(k) + \mu e_k y_{k-j}, \quad -N \le j \le N \tag{12.138}$$

where $c_j(k)$ is the jth component of the coefficient vector $\hat{\underline{c}}(k)$ at the kth iteration. This computation is repeated as each new signal sample is received in the equalizer delay line. Thus, the equalizer coefficients are updated at the symbol rate.

Because the instantaneous estimate of the gradient in the LMS algorithm is a random vector, the trajectory of the coefficient vector is random as well. However, if an average trajectory is defined by taking expectations, it converges in the stationary case toward the optimum given that the step size μ is sufficiently small. The trajectory doesn't converge all the way to the optimum, but after the convergence it remains fluctuating randomly around the optimum point. It is clear that the amount of random variation is proportional to the step size μ. To make the random variation reasonably small, the value of μ should be chosen much smaller than in the steepest-descent algorithm. On the other hand, with a larger value of μ, the algorithm can follow faster changes in the channel characteristics. Hence, a trade-off must be made between these two scenarios in choosing the value of μ.

12.7   DECISION FEEDBACK EQUALIZERS

Linear equalizers perform satisfactorily on well-behaved channels such as telephone lines, whose frequency response characteristics do not exhibit severe spectral attenuation or nulls. As discussed in Section 12.6, linear ISI cancellation cannot always be accomplished successfully without significant noise enhancement. The key idea in using decision feedback equalization is to cancel ISI that is contributed by previous symbols before detecting the current symbol. Figure 12.25 displays the sampled

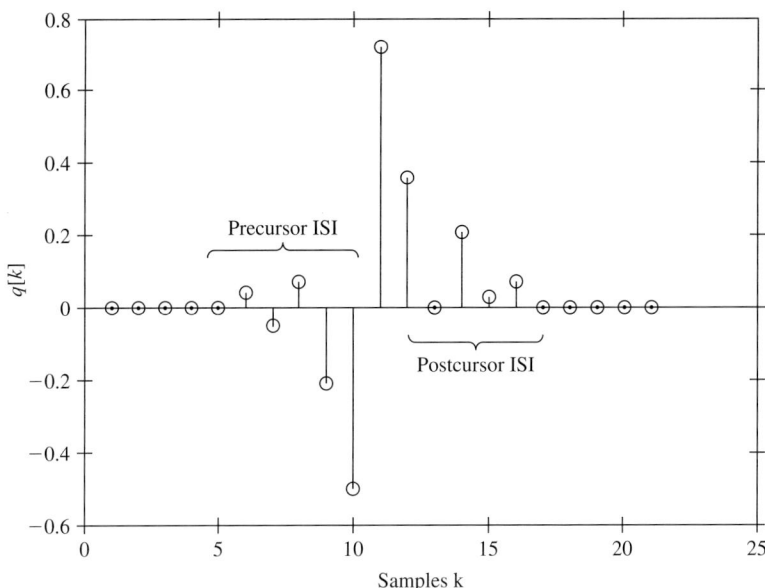

Figure 12.25 Pre- and post-cursor ISI.

impulse response $\{q_k\}$ of the transmit filter, channel, and matched receive filter cascade. The sampled output of the receive matched filter is obtained from (12.89) as

$$y_k = \sum_{n=-\infty}^{\infty} a_n q_{k-n} = a_k q_0 + \sum_{\substack{n=-\infty \\ n \neq k}}^{\infty} a_n q_{k-n} + n_k \qquad (12.139)$$

where we have assumed $\|p_r\| = 1$ without any loss of generality. For a finite-length impulse response $\{q_k\}$ of length $(2L + 1)$, (12.139) simplifies to

$$y_k = a_k q_0 + \underbrace{\sum_{n=1}^{L} a_{k-n} q_n}_{\substack{\text{ISI due to postcursors} \\ \text{of past symbols}}} + \underbrace{\sum_{n=1}^{L} a_{k+n} q_{-n}}_{\substack{\text{ISI due to precursors} \\ \text{of future symbols}}} + n_k \qquad (12.140)$$

The second term in (12.140) represents ISI contribution due to postcursors (q_k, $k > 0$) associated with symbols that occur prior to the desired symbol a_k. The third term is due to precursors (q_k, $k < 0$) associated with symbols that occur after the desired symbol a_k. The **decision feedback equalizer (DFE),** as shown in Figure 12.26, consists of two transversal filters, a **feed forward equalizer (FFE)** and a **feedback equalizer (FBE).** The DFE is assumed to have the length $N_1 + 1$ in the FFE section and N_2 in its FBE section. The function of the FFE is to cancel ISI due to precursors, while the FBE is responsible for canceling the ISI caused by postcursors of previously detected symbols. The FFE is a linear transversal equalizer of the type discussed in Section 12.5 whose coefficients c_i, $i = -N_1, \ldots, 1, 0$ are selected to minimize precursor ISI at the threshold detector input. The FFE output sequence, assuming complete precursor ISI cancellation, can be written from (12.93) as

$$z_k = \sum_{i=-N_1}^{0} c_i y_{k-i} = a_k p_{eq}[0] + \sum_{n=1}^{M} a_{k-n} p_{eq}[n] + n_k^{eq} \qquad (12.141)$$

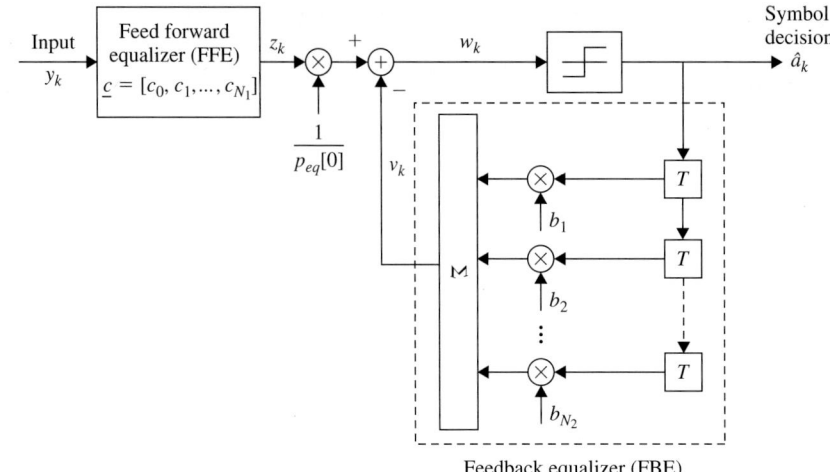

Figure 12.26 Decision feedback equalizer.

where M is the number of postcursor samples in the FFE output pulse sequence $p_{eq}[n]$, and

$$n_k^{eq} = \sum_{i=-N_1}^{0} c_i n_{k-i} \tag{12.142}$$

is the FFE output noise sequence.

Because the past decisions $\hat{a}_{k-1}$, $\hat{a}_{k-2}$, . . . are available for the detection of a_k at $t = kT$, they can be fed back through the FBE to cancel the effect of postcursor ISI at the threshold detector input. To accomplish this, the FBE output v_k is subtracted from that of the FFE to form the input to the detector. From Figure 12.26, the input to the detector can be expressed using (12.141) as

$$w_k = \frac{z_k}{p_{eq}[0]} - v_k = a_k + \sum_{n=1}^{M} a_{k-n} \frac{p_{eq}[n]}{p_{eq}[0]} + \frac{n_k^{eq}}{p_{eq}[0]} - v_k \tag{12.143}$$

The FBE coefficients b_n, $n = 1, 2, \ldots, N_2$ are determined by noting that the FBE output v_k at the time of decision making instant $t = kT$ must equal the postcursor ISI. That is,

$$v_k = \sum_{n=1}^{N_2} \hat{a}_{k-n} b_n = \sum_{n=1}^{M} a_{k-n} \frac{p_{eq}[n]}{p_{eq}[0]} \tag{12.144}$$

It is easy to see from (12.144) that the coefficients b_n equal normalized postcursor samples of the FFE output pulse $p_{eq}(t)$.

$$b_n = \frac{p_{eq}[n]}{p_{eq}[0]}, \quad n = 1, \ldots, N_2 \tag{12.145}$$

We observe from (12.143) and (12.144) that the FBE output cancels ISI from previously detected symbols, provided that previous decisions are correct and the number of taps in the equalizer $N_2 \geq M$. The DFE is referred to as nonlinear because of the nonlinear characteristic of the detector that provides the input to the feedback equalizer.

Example 12.8

Consider a channel with overall impulse response sequence

$$\{q_k = \{1, \ 0, \ 0.5\}$$

A DFE is used at the receiver to correct the postcursor ISI introduced by the channel.

a. Write expressions for input to the equalizer y_k and the threshold comparator z_k assuming correct decisions are fed.
b. Draw the block diagram of the equalizer.
c. Calculate the noise amplification produced by the equalizer and probability of bit error.

Solution

a. Because the channel doesn't introduce any precursor ISI, the DFE doesn't have any FFE. In this case, the receive filter output samples form input to the FBE. That is,

$$z_k = y_k = a_k q_0 + a_{k-2} q_2 + n_k = a_k + 0.5 a_{k-2} + n_k$$

The feedback coefficient is given from (12.145) as

$$b_2 = q[2] = 0.5$$

The threshold comparator input w_k is given by

$$w_k = y_k - b_2 \hat{a}_{k-2} = y_k - 0.5 \hat{a}_{k-2} = a_k + 0.5 a_{k-2} - 0.5 \hat{a}_{k-2} + n_k$$

Assuming correct decisions are fed, the feedback term cancels the postcursor ISI term. That is

$$w_k = a_k + 0.5 a_{k-2} - 0.5 a_{k-2} + n_k = a_k + n_k$$

b. The block diagram of the DFE is shown in Figure 12.27.

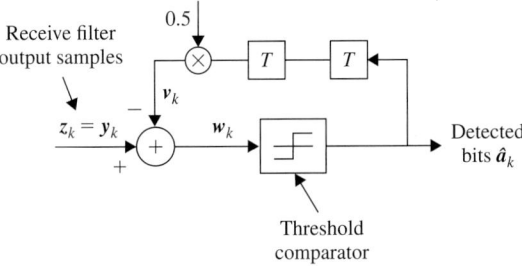

Figure 12.27 DFE for Example 12.8.

c. In the absence of FFE, there is no noise enhancement and with accurate ISI cancellation, the BER is given by

$$BER = Q\left(\sqrt{\frac{2E_b}{N_o}}\right)$$

for antipodal signaling. However, for low values of E_b/N_o, more erroneous decisions are fed back, and BER will be substantially higher than predicted by the white noise limit above due to error propagation.

12.7.1   Coefficient Optimization

We can use the MMSE criterion to obtain optimum coefficient vectors $\underline{c} = (c_{-N_1}, \ldots, c_1, c_0)$ and $\underline{b} = (b_1, b_2, \ldots, b_{N_2})$ for a DFE. Such an equalizer design is called **MMSE-DFE equalizer.** Adaptive versions of such equalizers are very attractive for time-varying dispersive channels. The mean-square error at the detector input is defined as

$$J(\underline{c}, \underline{b}) = E\{[\boldsymbol{w}_k - \boldsymbol{a}_k]^2\} \tag{12.146}$$

We can express the detector input sample by combining (12.141) and (12.144) as

$$\boldsymbol{w}_k = \sum_{i=-N_1}^{0} c_i \boldsymbol{y}_{k-i} - \sum_{i=1}^{N_2} b_i \hat{\boldsymbol{a}}_{k-i} \tag{12.147}$$

Substituting (12.147) into (12.146), the mean-square error at the detector input is obtained as

$$J(\underline{c}, \underline{b}) = E\left\{\left[\sum_{i=-N_1}^{0} c_i \boldsymbol{y}_{k-i} - \sum_{i=1}^{N_2} b_i \hat{\boldsymbol{a}}_{k-i} - \boldsymbol{a}_k\right]^2\right\} \tag{12.148}$$

We observe from (12.148) that $J(\underline{c}, \underline{b})$ is a nonlinear function of vectors $\underline{c}$ and $\underline{b}$, because the symbol estimates $\underline{\hat{a}}_k = (\hat{a}_{k-1}, \hat{a}_{k-2}, \ldots, \hat{a}_{k-N_2})$ are generated by the threshold detector from the samples $\boldsymbol{w}_k$. Minimization of the mean-square error of (12.148) requires significant computational effort. The optimization problem is considerably simplified if we assume that previously detected symbols fed to the FFB are correct. In this case, we can replace the vector $\underline{\hat{a}}_k$ with $\underline{a}_k = (a_{k-1}, a_{k-2}, \ldots, a_{k-N_2})$ in (12.148). Now the MSE $J(\underline{c}, \underline{b})$ is a linear function of vectors $\underline{c}$ and $\underline{b}$. The optimal coefficient vector $\underline{c}_{opt}$ is obtained by solving $\nabla_{\underline{c}} J(\underline{c}, \underline{b}) = \underline{0}$. That is

$$\frac{\partial J}{\partial c_j} = E\left\{2\boldsymbol{y}_{k-j}\left[\sum_{i=-N_1}^{0} c_i \boldsymbol{y}_{k-i} - \sum_{i=1}^{N_2} b_i a_{k-i} - a_k\right]\right\} = 0, \quad j = -N_1, \ldots, 1, 0 \tag{12.149}$$

Because the expectation is a linear operator as discussed in Section 6.6.2, we can express (12.149) as

$$\sum_{i=-N_1}^{0} c_i E\{\boldsymbol{y}_{k-i} \boldsymbol{y}_{k-j}\} - \sum_{i=1}^{N_2} b_i E\{a_{k-i} \boldsymbol{y}_{k-j}\} - E\{a_k \boldsymbol{y}_{k-j}\} = 0, \quad j = -N_1, \ldots, 1, 0$$
$$\tag{12.150}$$

The optimum tap coefficients of the FFE can now be obtained by solving the following set of $N_1 + 1$ linear equations.

$$\sum_{i=-N_1}^{0} c_i \underline{R}_{yy}[i, j] - \sum_{i=1}^{N_2} b_i \underline{r}_{ay}[j - i] - \underline{r}_{ay}[j] = 0, \quad j = -N_1, \ldots, 1, 0 \tag{12.151}$$

where $\underline{R}_{yy}[i, j]$ and $\underline{r}_{ay}[j]$ are defined by (12.120) and (12.122), respectively. Similarly, the optimal coefficient vector $\underline{b}_{opt}$ can be obtained by solving the N_2 linear equations $\nabla_{\underline{b}} J(\underline{c}, \underline{b}) = \underline{0}$. That is

$$\frac{\partial J}{\partial b_j} = E\left\{-2a_{k-j}\left[\sum_{i=-N_1}^{0} c_i \boldsymbol{y}_{k-i} - \sum_{i=1}^{N_2} b_i a_{k-i} - a_k\right]\right\} = 0, \quad j = 1, \ldots, N_2 \tag{12.152}$$

Again exchanging the order of expectation and summation, we can express (12.152) as

$$\sum_{i=-N_1}^{0} c_i E\{\boldsymbol{y}_{k-i}\boldsymbol{a}_{k-j}\} - \sum_{i=1}^{N_2} b_i E\{\boldsymbol{a}_{k-i}\boldsymbol{a}_{k-j}\} - E\{\boldsymbol{a}_k\boldsymbol{a}_{k-j}\} = 0, \quad j = 1, \dots, N_2$$

(12.153)

Substituting (12.116) and (12.122) into (12.153), we obtain

$$\sum_{i=-N_1}^{0} c_i r_{ay}[i - j] - b_j \sigma_a^2 = 0, \quad j = 1, \dots, N_2$$

(12.154)

The optimum tap coefficients of the FBE are now determined by solving the following set of N_2 linear equations.

$$b_j = \frac{1}{\sigma_a^2} \sum_{i=-N_1}^{0} c_i r_{ay}[i - j], \quad j = 1, \dots, N_2$$

(12.155)

In adaptive implementation of the DFE, the forward and feedback coefficients may be adjusted simultaneously to minimize the mean-square error. The update equation for the forward coefficients is the same as that for the linear equalizer. The feedback coefficients are adjusted according to the following iteration rule:

$$b_m(k + 1) = b_m(k) + \mu e_k \hat{a}_{k-m}, \quad m = 1, \dots, N_2$$

(12.156)

where $b_m(k)$ is the mth feedback coefficient at the kth iteration. μ is the step size of the iterative algorithm. Note that because the output of the feedback section of the DFE is a weighted sum of noise-free past decisions, the feedback coefficients play no part in determining the noise power at the equalizer output.

12.7.2 Channel Estimation

If the channel is time-varying, the transmitter sends training sequence at regular intervals to estimate the channel. Figure 12.28 illustrates the channel estimation and equalizer circuits in a DFE. In the training mode, a known training sequence is used to estimate the composite impulse response. The detected symbols are used as the reference in the tracking mode.

We consider the estimation of an FIR channel of length $L + 1$. The channel estimation circuit which produces an MMSE estimate $\{\hat{q}_m, m = 0, \dots, L\}$ of the composite

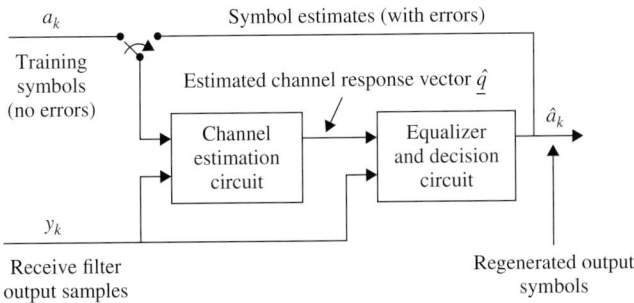

Figure 12.28 Channel estimation in a DFE.

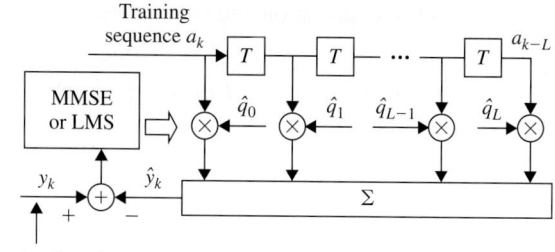

Figure 12.29 Channel estimation circuit.

impulse response is shown in Figure 12.29. It is similar in design to a linear equalizer considered in Section 12.5.2 with tap gains $\{\hat{q}_m, m = 0, \ldots, L\}$ to be determined during the training period. In order to obtain an optimum estimate $\{\hat{q}_m\}$, a sequence of known training symbols a_i, $i = 1, \ldots, N_{train}$ is used. The estimation circuit produces following estimates the receive filter output:

$$\hat{y}_k = \sum_{n=0}^{L} \hat{q}_n a_{k-n}, \quad k = L + 1, \ldots, N_{train} \tag{12.157}$$

This can be written in the matrix form as

$$\underline{\hat{y}} = \underline{A}\,\underline{\hat{q}} \tag{12.158}$$

where

$$\underline{\hat{y}} = (\hat{y}_{L+1}, \hat{y}_{L+2}, \ldots, \hat{y}_{Ntrain})^T \tag{12.159}$$

$$\underline{\hat{q}} = (\hat{q}_0, \hat{q}_1, \ldots, \hat{q}_L)^T \tag{12.160}$$

and

$$\underline{A} = \begin{pmatrix} a_{L+1} & a_L & \cdots & a_2 & a_1 \\ a_{L+2} & a_{L+1} & \cdots & a_3 & a_2 \\ \vdots & \vdots & \cdots & \vdots & \vdots \\ a_{Ntrain} & a_{Ntrain-1} & \cdots & a_{Ntrain-L+1} & a_{Ntrain-L} \end{pmatrix} \tag{12.161}$$

Note that $\underline{\hat{q}}$ is a column vector of length $L + 1$ and $\underline{A}$ is a $(N_{train} - L) \times (L + 1)$ matrix. To obtain an MMSE estimate of the overall impulse response vector $\hat{q}$, we form the following objective function

$$J(\underline{\hat{q}}) = \frac{1}{N_{train} - L} \sum_{k=L+1}^{N_{train}} (y_k - \hat{y}_k)^2 = \frac{1}{N_{train} - L} \sum_{k=L+1}^{N_{train}} \left(y_k - \sum_{n=0}^{L} \hat{q}_n a_{k-n} \right)^2 \tag{12.162}$$

where y_k is matched receive filter output sample given by (12.89) corresponding to the transmission of known training bits by the transmitter. The objective function (12.162) can be expressed as

$$J(\underline{\hat{q}}) = \underline{\hat{q}}^T \underline{A}^T \underline{A}\,\underline{\hat{q}} - 2\underline{\hat{q}}^T \underline{A}^T \underline{y} + \underline{y}^T \underline{y} \tag{12.163}$$

where

$$\underline{y} = (y_{L+1}, y_{L+2}, \ldots, y_{Ntrain})^T \tag{12.164}$$

As discussed in Section 12.5.2, the MMSE solution to the optimization problem Min $J(\hat{\underline{q}})$ is given by
$\hat{\underline{q}}$

$$\hat{\underline{q}} = (\underline{A}^T\underline{A})^{-1}\underline{A}^T\underline{y} \tag{12.165}$$

12.8 PERFORMANCE OF LINEAR AND DECISION FEEDBACK EQUALIZERS

The performance of a linear equalizer is degraded by the residual ISI and noise enhancement at the equalizer output. For binary polar signaling, the sampled output of the linear equalizer is given from (12.93) after substituting $\|p_r\| = \sqrt{E_b}$ as

$$z_k = \sqrt{E_b}a_k p_{eq}[0] + \sqrt{E_b}\sum_{n \neq k}a_n p_{eq}[k - n] + n_k^{eq} \tag{12.166}$$

where

$$n_k^{eq} = \sum_{i=-N}^{N} c_i n_{k-i} \tag{12.167}$$

is the equalizer output noise sequence. Using (12.90), the variance of noise at the equalizer output is given by

$$\begin{aligned} \sigma_{eq}^2 &= Var(n_k^{eq}) = E\{(n_k^{eq})^2\} = E\left\{\sum_{i=-N}^{N}\sum_{j=-N}^{N}c_i c_j n_{k-i}n_{k-j}\right\} \\ &= \sum_{i=-N}^{N}\sum_{j=-N}^{N}c_i c_j E\{n_{k-i}n_{k-j}\} = \sum_{i=-N}^{N}\sum_{j=-N}^{N}c_i c_j \frac{N_o}{2}\delta_{ij} \\ &= \frac{N_o}{2}\sum_{i=-N}^{N}c_i^2 \end{aligned} \tag{12.168}$$

The quantity

$$\eta_{NE} = \sum_{i=-N}^{N} c_i^2 \tag{12.169}$$

represents the enhancement of noise at the equalizer output. η_{NE} is called the **noise enhancement factor** of the linear equalizer.

For an equalizer with $2N + 1$ taps and an overall impulse response $\{q[n]\}$ of length $2L + 1$, the residual ISI is determined by $2N + 2L + 1$ symbols corresponding to the extent of $\{p_{eq}[n]\}$. It is given by

$$D_k = \sum_{n \neq k}a_n p_{eq}[k - n] \tag{12.170}$$

Note that $\boldsymbol{D}_k$ is a random variable whose value D_k is determined by a particular sequence of $2N + 2L$ random information symbols $\{a_{k-N-L}, \ldots, a_{k-1}, a_{k+1}, \ldots, a_{k+N+L}\}$. For polar transmission symbols $\boldsymbol{a}_k \in \{1, -1\}$, the conditional probability of bit error for a fixed D_k is given by

$$P\{\text{error}|\boldsymbol{D}_k = D_k\} = \frac{1}{2}P\{\text{error}|\boldsymbol{D}_k = D_k, \boldsymbol{a}_k = 1\} + \frac{1}{2}P\{\text{error}|\boldsymbol{D}_k = D_k, \boldsymbol{a}_k = -1\}$$

$$= \frac{1}{2}P\{\boldsymbol{n}_k^{eq} + \sqrt{E_b}D_k < -\sqrt{E_b}p_{eq}[0]\} + \frac{1}{2}P\{\boldsymbol{n}_k^{eq} + \sqrt{E_b}D_k > \sqrt{E_b}p_{eq}[0]\}$$

$$= Q\left(\sqrt{\frac{E_b(p_{eq}[0] - D_k)^2}{\sigma_{eq}^2}}\right)$$

$$= Q\left(\sqrt{\frac{2E_b(p_{eq}[0] - D_k)^2}{N_o\eta_{NE}}}\right) = Q\left(\sqrt{\frac{2E_b}{N_o}\frac{(p_{eq}[0] - D_k)^2}{\eta_{NE}}}\right) \qquad (12.171)$$

We observe that $p_{eq}[0] - D_k$ equals eye opening in the presence of ISI resulting from a particular symbol sequence. The probability of bit error can be calculated by averaging (12.171) over 2^{2N+2L} possible symbol sequences, $\{a_{k-N-L}, \ldots, a_{k-1}, a_{k+1}, \ldots, a_{k+N+L}\}$, of length $(2N + 2L)$ in a Monte Carlo simulation. This can be done either in the Simulink or MATLAB environment. A simple but loose upper bound on the BER is given by replacing D_k in (12.171) with peak ISI distortion $D_{peak} = \sum_{n \neq 0}|p_{eq}[n]|$. That is,

$$BER \leq Q\left(\sqrt{\frac{2E_b(p_{eq}[0] - D_{peak})^2}{\eta_{NE}N_o}}\right) = Q\left(\sqrt{\frac{2E_b\xi_{ISI}^2}{\eta_{NE}N_o}}\right) \qquad (12.172)$$

where

$$\xi_{ISI} = p_{eq}[0] - D_{peak} = p_{eq}[0] - \sum_{n \neq 0}|p_{eq}[n]| \qquad (12.173)$$

is the worst-case eye opening at the equalizer output due to ISI. Thus the quantity $10 \log_{10}(\xi_{ISI}^2/\eta_{NE})$ characterizes the worst-case SNR/bit penalty of the equalized system compared to antipodal signaling over an ideal AWGN channel.

For purpose of illustration, we compare the BER results by Monte Carlo simulation for three different channel models introduced by Proakis.[6] Figure 12.30 illustrates the error performance of the channel model considered in Examples 12.6 and 12.7. This channel is well-behaved in the sense that it does not have significant loss (or null) in the Nyquist band, as is evident from Figure 12.22(a). The equalized response obtained in Figure 12.22(c) confirms that a linear equalizer does a good job in compensating the roll-off produced by the channel. The linear equalizer achieves the BER performance within about 2.5 dB of the ideal AWGN antipodal signaling.

Next we consider the channel in Figure 12.31(a) that has a high frequency null near the Nyquist bandedge as evident from Figure 12.31(b). This makes it difficult to equalize with a linear equalizer as displayed in Figure 12.31(c). The equalizer tries to provide

---

[6] J. Proakis, and M. Salehi, *Digital Communications*, 5th ed. (New York: McGraw-Hill, 2007).

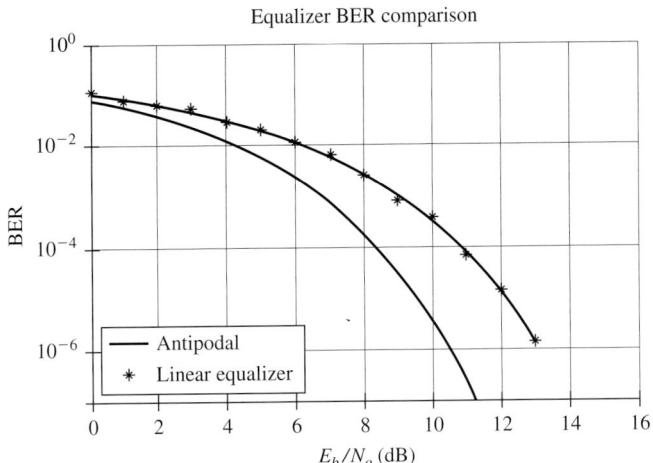

Figure 12.30 Linear equalizer performance for a well-behaved channel.

Figure 12.31 Linear and decision feedback equalizer performance comparison for a channel with high-frequency null.

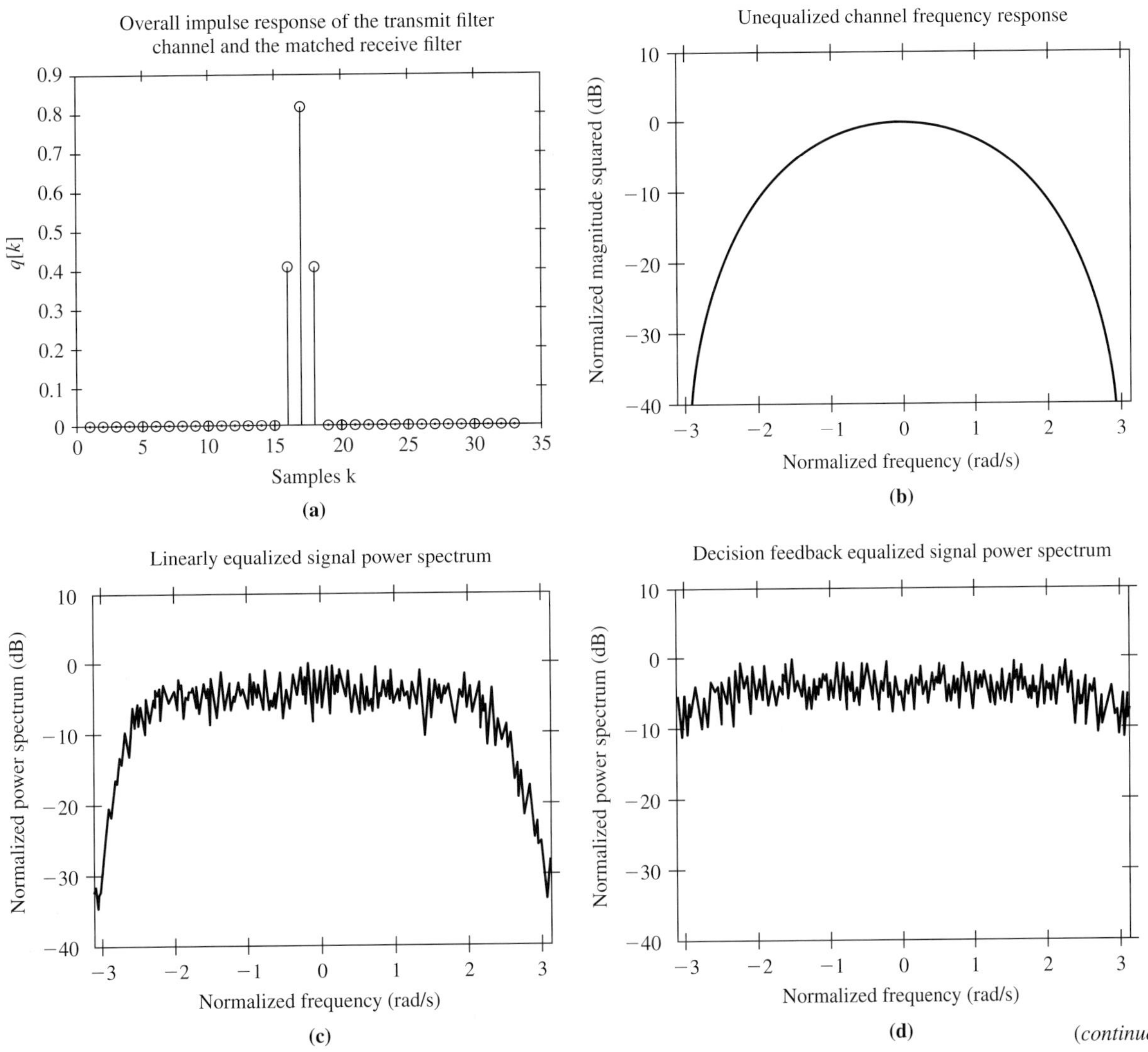

(*continued*)

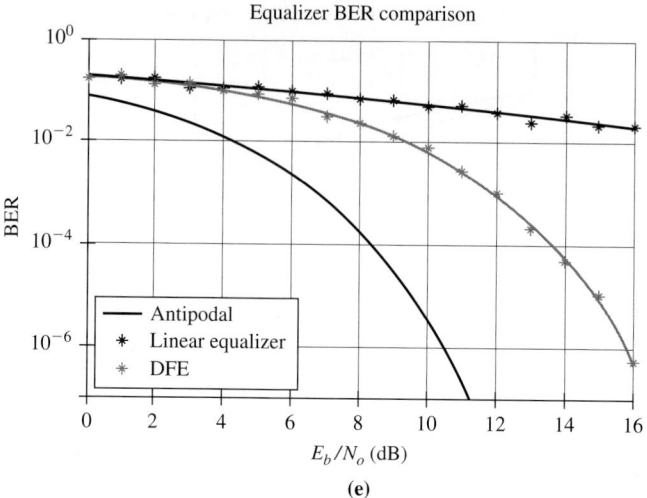

(e)

gain at higher frequencies, but it is unsuccessful in compensating without significant amplification of the noise. The BER performance of a 31-tap linear equalizer hits an **error floor** in the sense that further increase in the SNR/bit does not improve the error performance significantly. The performance of a DFE ($N_1 = N_2 = 15$) for the same channel is illustrated in Figure 12.31(e). Note that the DFE is very effective in compensating this challenging channel. At $BER = 10^{-6}$, the SNR penalty versus the ideal case is less than 6 dB.

As a final example, we consider a channel with deep null in the Nyquist band as illustrated by its frequency response in Figure 12.32(b). Again the linear equalizer is unsuccessful in compensating the channel as displayed in Figure 12.32(c). However, the DFE is effective in dealing with the null as shown in Figure 12.32(d). It yields a significant improvement in performance when compared to the linear equalizer having the same number of taps as shown in Figure 12.32(e). The DFE achieves the BER performance within ~10 dB of the ideal AWGN antipodal signaling.

It can be concluded from Figures 12.30 and 12.31 that the DFE is more effective in compensating the ISI without as much noise enhancement as a linear equalizer. The coefficients of a linear transversal equalizer are selected to force the combined channel and equalizer impulse response to approximate a unit sample sequence. In a DFE, the ability of the FBE to cancel the ISI due to past symbols allows more freedom in the choice of the coefficients for the FFE. The combined impulse response of the channel and the FFE may have postcursor ISI. That is, the FFE need not approximate the inverse of the channel characteristics, and so it avoids excessive noise enhancement. When a particular incorrect decision is fed back, the DFE output reflects this error during the next few symbols because the incorrect decision traverses the feedback delay line. Thus, there is a greater likelihood of more incorrect decisions following the first one, that is, error propagation. Fortunately, the error propagation in a DFE is not catastrophic. On typical channels, errors occur in short bursts that degrade performance only slightly. The penalty for incorrect decision errors being fed back on the BER performance of a DFE is approximately 2 dB in terms of SNR/bit.[7]

---

[7] J. Proakis and M. Salehi, *Digital Communications*, 5th ed. (New York: McGraw-Hill, 2007).

Figure 12.32 Linear and decision feedback equalizer performance comparison for a channel with deep null in the Nyquist band.

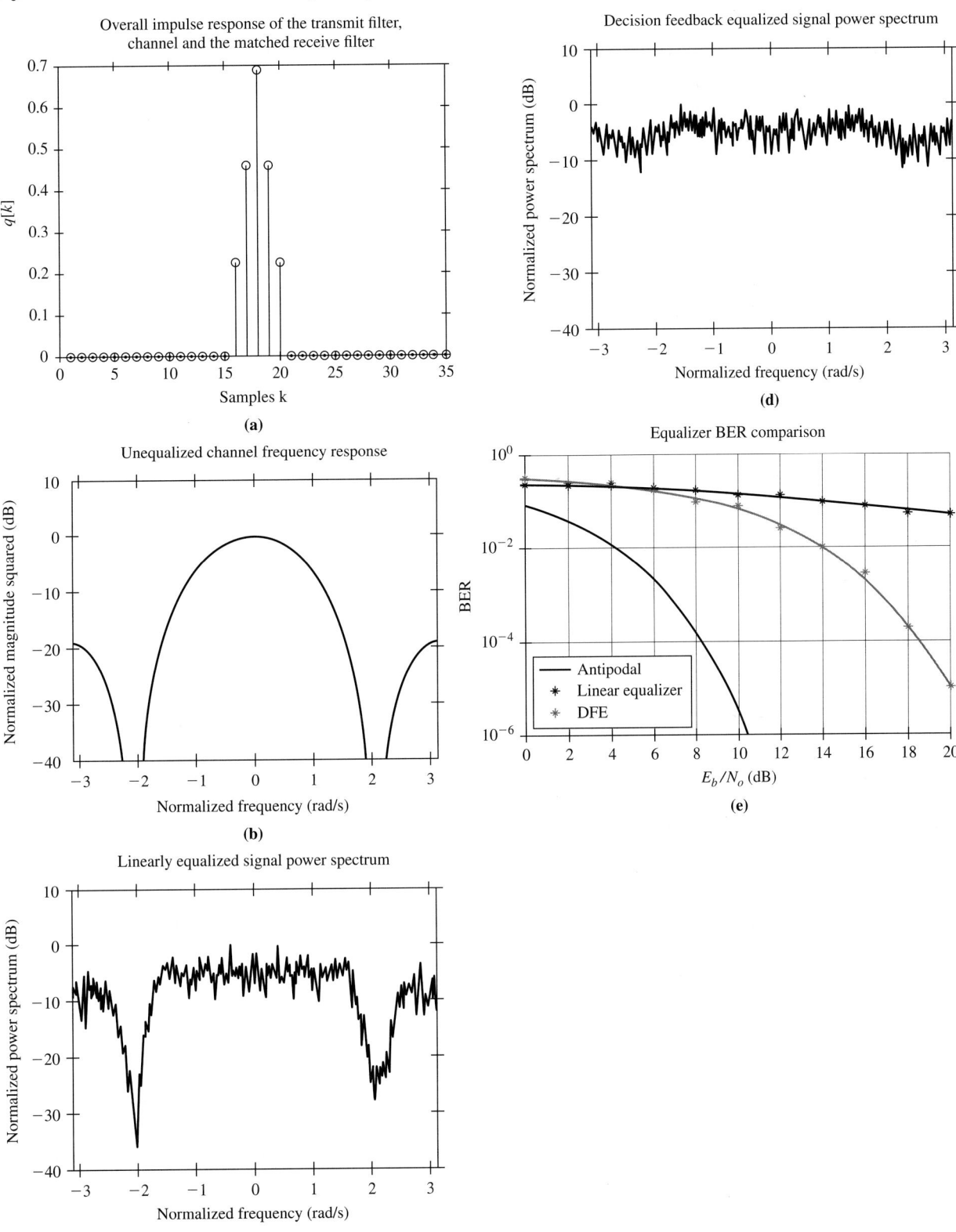

FINAL REMARKS

ISI is a major problem in many real-life channels. Although channel output pulses may overlap due to linear distortion, they can be designed to not interfere with one another, or to interfere in controlled ways. One popular approach to mitigate ISI is by adaptive equalization, as the channel response is usually not known in advance or varies with time in a random fashion. For channels with severe ISI, considerable gain in performance can be achieved compared to the linear equalizer by the inclusion of the decision-feedback section, which eliminates the ISI from previously detected symbols. Adaptive compensation is also effective in mitigating the ISI caused by other types of channel distortion (e.g., random multipath in a cellular channel).

FURTHER READINGS

Digital communications over bandlimited channels is covered in texts [1–4]. Proakis [2] is the most comprehensive and up-to-date treatment of the material in the field. Lucky [1] is a classic reference in channel equalization for digital communications. Lender [6] and Pasupathy [8] provide excellent introductions to duobinary and generalized partial response signaling techniques, respectively. Qureshi [9] is an extensive and tutorial reference on adaptive equalization.

1. Lucky, R., J. Salz, and E. Weldon. *Principles of Data Communication.* New York: McGraw-Hill, 1968.

2. Proakis, J., and M. Salehi. *Digital Communications,* 5th ed. New York: McGraw-Hill, 2007.

3. Proakis, J., and M. Salehi. *Communication Systems Engineering,* 2nd ed. Upper Saddle River, NJ: Prentice Hall, 2002.

4. Anderson, J. *Digital Transmission Engineering,* 2nd ed. Upper Saddle River, NJ: Prentice-Hall, 2005.

5. Lender, A. "The Duobinary Technique for High Speed Data Transmission." *IEEE Transactions on Communications Electronics* 82, (1963): 214–218.

6. Lender, A. "Correlative Level Coding for Binary Data Transmission." *IEEE Spectrum* 3, (1966): 104–115.

7. Kretzmer, E. "Generalization of a Technique for Binary Data Communication." *IEEE Transactions on Communications Technology* COM-14 (1966): 67–68.

8. Pasupathy, S. "Correlative Coding: A Bandwidth Efficient Signaling Scheme." *IEEE Transactions on Communications Technology* 15 (1977): 4–11.

9. Qureshi, S. "Adaptive Equalization." *Proceedings of the IEEE* 53 (1985): 1349–1387.

10. Woodrow, B. "Adaptive Filters, I: Fundamentals." Stanford Electronics Laboratory, Stanford University, Stanford, CA: Tech Report No. 6764-6, December 1966.

PROBLEMS

12.1. Let $P_r(f)$ be the triangular spectrum given by

$$P_r(f) = \begin{cases} 2.5 \times 10^{-4}\left(1 - \dfrac{|f|}{4000}\right), & |f| < 4000 \\ 0, & \text{otherwise} \end{cases}$$

a. For what symbol rate, $p_r(t)$ is a Nyquist pulse?

b. Determine $p_r(t)$ and verify the conclusion from (a).

c. At this symbol rate, what is the excess bandwidth of the pulse and roll-off factor?

12.2. Consider an M-ary PAM system to transmit data at 50 kbps over an ideal bandlimited channel with bandwidth $W = 7500$ Hz. Assume RRC pulse signaling with a roll-off factor $\alpha = 0.5$.

a. Determine the required size of the signal set, M.

b. Determine E_b/N_o required to achieve $P_e = 10^{-6}$.

12.3. Binary data is transmitted using polar RC pulses with spectrum displayed in Figure P12.1.

a. Calculate the roll-off factor.

b. What is the maximum signaling rate to avoid ISI?

c. The channel distorts the signal pulses and the sample values of the matched filter output pulse are given by

$$\{q[k]\} = \{0.0194, -0.1452, 0.9677, 0.2032, 0.029\}$$

List the bit sequence that will generate the worst-case ISI and the corresponding value of peak distortion.

d. How likely is such a sequence assuming that data bits are equiprobable and statistically independent?

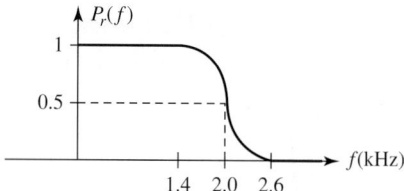

Figure P12.1

12.4. Consider a 4-PAM system to transmit data through a bandlimited channel at 8.4 kbps. The channel is characterized by the frequency response

$$H_c(f) = \frac{1}{1 + j(f/4200)}$$

The channel introduces AWGN noise with spectral density $N_o/2 = 10^{-12}$ W/Hz.

a. Write transfer functions of transmit and receive filters to deliver RC output pulse ($\alpha = 1$) at the receiver.

b. Estimate the average energy per bit, E_b, required to achieve a $BER = 10^{-6}$.

12.5. The binary data 001011100 is applied to the input of a duobinary encoder.

a. Construct the precoder output assuming initialization bit $d_o = 1$.

b. What is the corresponding received sequence?

c. Derive the decoding rule at the receiver to reconstruct the data.

d. Assume that due to noise, the sampler output produced by the fourth bit is reduced to zero. Construct the decoded output sequence $\hat{b}_k$. How many errors are there in the decoded sequence?

12.6. The binary data 101100011 is applied to the input of a modified duobinary encoder.

a. Construct the precoder output assuming initialization bits = (0, 0).

b. What is the corresponding received sequence?

c. Derive the decoding rule at the receiver to reconstruct the data.

d. Assume that due to noise, the sampler output produced by the fifth bit is reduced to zero. Construct the decoded output sequence $\hat{b}_k$. How many errors are there in the decoded sequence?

12.7. Consider a channel with overall impulse response

$$q[k] = \begin{cases} \alpha^k, & k \geq 0 \\ & \qquad\qquad \alpha < 1 \\ 0, & \text{otherwise} \end{cases}$$

a. Calculate the peak ISI distortion at the equalizer input.

b. Calculate the coefficients of a linear equalizer that completely eliminates the ISI.

c. Calculate the noise variance at the equalizer output.

d. Derive an upper-bound expression for the bit error rate of the system.

12.8. Consider a binary antipodal system with overall impulse response

$$\{q[k]\} = \{1, 0.7\}$$

The channel introduces AWGN noise with spectral density $N_o/2$ W/Hz.

a. Design a 5-tap linear equalizer to eliminate ISI.

b. Calculate the noise variance at the equalizer output.

c. Derive an expression for the bit error rate of the system.

d. Plot the BER curves of the system (i) without equalizer and (ii) with the equalizer designed in (a). Compare with AWGN performance with no ISI.

12.9. Consider a binary digital communication system with overall impulse response

$$\{q[k]\} = \{0.0105, -0.0542, 0.1570, 0.9710, -0.1698, 0.0220, 0.0107\}$$

The channel introduces AWGN noise with spectral density $N_o/2 = 0.05$ W/Hz.

a. Calculate the worst-case eye opening at the equalizer input.

b. Determine the coefficients of a 5-tap ZFE. Plot the equalized output waveform.

c. Calculate the noise enhancement and a worst-case estimate of BER at the equalizer output. Compare with AWGN performance with no ISI.

12.10. Consider a binary digital communication system with overall impulse response

$$\{q[k]\} = \{0.0101, -0.0891, 0.5752, 0.7423, 0.2714, 0.1762, 0.074\}$$

The channel introduces AWGN noise with spectral density $N_o/2 = 0.05$ W/Hz.

a. Design a 7-tap MMSE equalizer for the channel. Plot the equalized output waveform.

b. Calculate the worst-case eye opening at the equalizer output.

c. Calculate the noise enhancement at the equalizer output.

d. Plot DTFTs of the overall channel, equalizer, and combined responses.

e. Repeat (a) through (d) for 31-tap MMSE equalizer. Comment about the performance improvement versus 7-tap equalizer.

12.11. Consider a binary digital communication system with overall impulse response

$$\{q[k]\} = \{0.8729, 0.4364, 0.2182\}$$

The channel introduces AWGN noise with spectral density $N_o/2 = 0.025$ W/Hz.

a. Design a 5-tap MMSE equalizer for the channel. Plot the equalized output waveform.

b. Calculate the worst-case eye opening at the equalizer output.

c. Calculate the noise enhancement at the equalizer output.

d. Plot DTFTs of the overall channel, equalizer, and combined responses.

e. Repeat (a) through (d) with a 5-tap ZFE.

12.12. Show that the gradient vector of the mean-square error objective function

$$J(\underline{c}) = \underline{c}^T R_{yy} \underline{c} - 2\underline{c}^T r_{ay} + \sigma_a^2$$

is given by $\nabla_{\underline{c}} J(\underline{c}) = 2(R_{yy}\underline{c} - r_{ay})$.

12.13. The overall channel model of a digital transmission system is described by the impulse response

$$\{q[k]\} = \{0.743, 0.667\}$$

A DFE is used at the receiver to correct postcursor ISI.

a. Draw the block diagram of the equalizer.

b. Write expressions for input to the equalizer y_k and the threshold comparator z_k assuming correct decisions are fed.

c. Calculate the noise amplification produced by the equalizer and probability of bit error.

12.14. The overall channel model of a digital transmission system is described by the impulse response

$$\{q[k]\} = \{1, -0.45, 0.3, -0.05\}$$

A DFE is used at the receiver to correct postcursor ISI.

a. What are the equalizer coefficients?

b. Draw the block diagram of the equalizer.

c. For an input data bit $a_k = 1$, calculate the equalizer input assuming previous data bits have values $a_{k-1} = 1, a_{k-2} = -1, a_{k-3} = 1$. Assuming correct decisions are fed, calculate the threshold comparator input.

d. Repeat (c) assuming that the previous decision is incorrect.

e. Repeat (d) assuming that errors were made in both previous bits. Compare the noise margin in all three cases and comment.

12.15. Consider a binary antipodal system with overall channel impulse response

$$\{q[k]\} = \{0.58, 0.813\}$$

a. Design a 1-tap DFE for the channel. What is the feedback coefficient value?

b. Due to additive white Gaussian noise, the corrupted samples at the input to the equalizer for time instants $k = 1, \ldots, 6$ are is given by

$$\{y[k]\} = \{-0.116, 0.29, -0.174, 1.508, 0, -1.16\}$$

Assuming the correct previous decision value $\hat{a}_0 = -1$ is fed back, calculate the detected values of bits corresponding the input sequence $y[k]$.

c. Assuming instead that the wrong previous decision value $\hat{a}_0 = 1$ is fed back, calculate the detected values of bits corresponding the input sequence $y[k]$. How many incorrect decisions are made assuming that decisions in (b) are correct.

d. In both cases (b) and (c), calculate the mean-square error at the threshold comparator input assuming that decisions in (b) are correct.

MATLAB PROBLEMS

12.16. Consider the transmission of polar RRC pulses through a bandlimited channel with an impulse response given by

$$h_c(t) = \begin{cases} e^{-t/\tau}, & t \geq 0 \\ 0, & \text{otherwise} \end{cases}$$

where $\tau = 0.5$

a. Generate $\mathtt{Nbits} = 10000$ random bits and map them to binary polar symbols a[n]. Assume symbol (bit) period $T = 1$. Upsample the random data sequence a[n] by oversampling factor $\mathtt{nsamples} = 8$.

```
Nbits = 10000          % Number of
bits

bit_sequence= rand(1,Nbits);

a =sign(bit_sequence-0.5);

a_up= upsample(a, nsamples);
```

b. Generate the RRC pulse shape `prrcos` with roll-off factor $\alpha = 0.25$ using the following m-file over the interval $[-5T : \text{delt} : 5T]$ where $\text{delt} = 1/\text{nsamples}$.

```
delt=T/nsamples

pulse_duration = 10*T;      % RRC
pulse duration

t = [-pulse_duration/2 : delt :
pulse_duration/2];

Function prrcos = rootrcos(alpha,t,T)

% function roorcos(alpha,t,T)

% T = symbol period
```

```
% alpha = roll-off factor

% t = [-pulse_duration/2 : delt :
pulse_duration/2]

t = t +.0000001;

tpi = pi/T;

amtpi=tpi*(1-alpha);

aptpi=tpi*(1+alpha);

ac = 4.*alpha/T;

at = 16.*alpha^2/T^2;

prrcos =(sin(amtpi*t)+(ac*t).*cos
(aptpi*t))./(tpi*t.*(1-at*t.^2));

prrcos =prrcos/sqrt(T);

end
```

Alternatively, the RRC pulse may be generated using MATLAB function `rcosflt`. Plot `rootrcos`. Note that the RRC pulse has a delay of 5T.

```
delay_rrc = 5*T

delay_rc = 2* delay_rrc
```

c. Generate RRC pulse sequence x after normalizing `prrcos`.

```
x =conv(prrcos, a_up);
```

d. Use Matlab function `eyediagram` to plot the eye diagram of the sequence x .

```
eyediagram(x,nsamples,T)
```

e. Pass the pulse sequence x through a filter matched to the prrcos pulse shape. Plot the eye diagram with the MF output signal xmf_out.

```
hmatch=prrcos(end:-1:1);

xmf_out=conv(hmatch, x);
```

Why is the eye in part (e) more open than in (d)? Explain.

f. Now pass the RRC pulse sequence x through the channel followed by RRC matched filter.

```
t = [0 : delt : 5*T]

tel_channel =exp(-t/tau);

xchan_out=conv(tel_channel, x);

xmf_out=conv(hmatch, xchan_out);
```

Plot the eye diagram of the signal xmf_out at the MF output.

12.17. Repeat Problem 12.16 for $\alpha = 0.5, 0.75$, and 1. Determine the eye opening for $\alpha = 0.5, 0.75$, and 1. Compare with worst-case eye opening in all three cases in tabular form.

12.18. Consider the system model in Figure 12.13. We analyze the performance of ZFE in mitigating the effect of ISI. Assume 100,000 random data bits.

a. Calculate the overall impulse response qpulse of the system (that is, transmit filter, channel, and matched filter) using the channel model in problem 12.16. Plot qpulse. Sample the qpulse to generate the overall discrete-time impulse response qvector of the system.

```
qpulse=conv(conv(tel_channel, prr-
cos), hmatch);

qvector = qpulse(delay_rc:nsamples:
end-delay_rc);

qvector_norm = norm(qvector)

q_norm = qvector/qvector_norm %
Normalized qvector
```

Plot the vector q_norm by using stem function.

b. Add Gaussian noise to the signal xmf_out generated in Problem 12.16(f). Given SNR/bit EbNo(in dB) at the receiver output, the one-sided spectral density N_o is given by

$$N_o = E_b 10^{-EbNo/10}$$

where E_b is the energy of receive filter output pulse. The variance of Gaussian noise samples at the matched filter input is given by

$$\sigma^2 = \frac{N_o}{2}$$

```
Eb = qvector_norm^2

No = Eb*10^(-EbNo/10); % SNR = Eb/No

sigma= sqrt(No/2); % Standard devia-
tion of the AWGN samples
```

```
noise_in =sigma*randn(1,Nbits*nsamp
les);

noise_out =conv(noise_in, hmatch); %
Noise samples at MF output
```

c. Sample MF output to generate *T*-spaced samples for further processing by ZFE.

```
samp_offset= (2*delay_rc)*nsamples;

equ_input_sig=xmf_out(samp_
offset:nsamples:Nbits *nsamples)

equ_input_noise=noise_out(samp_
offset:nsamples:Nbits *nsamples);

equ_input= equ_input_sig +
equ_input_noise;
```

d. Design ZFE of length 7 using the m-file function zfequalizer.

```
leq = 7

ceq = zfequalizer(q_norm, leq); %
ZFE equalizer taps

peq = conv(ceq',q_norm); % equalized
output pulse
```

Display on the same plot qvector and peq. Such a plot shows the effectiveness of the equalizer in mitigating the ISI.

e. Pass the MF output through the equalizer.

```
equ_output=filter(ceq,1,equ_input);

equ_out = equ_output(ceil(leq/2):
end);
```

f. Perform transmitted bit sequence detection from *T*-spaced equalizer output samples using a threshold comparator. Calculate the BER.

```
ahat = sign(equ_out);

LL=length(equ_out);

ber= sum(a(1:LL)~=ahat(1:LL))/LL;
```

g. In the absence of equalization, the BER performance is given by

```
ahat_uneq = sign(equ_input);

ber_uneq = sum(a(1:LL)~= ahat_uneq
(1:LL))/LL;
```

h. Repeat BER calculations with and without equalization for EbNo values from 1 to 20 dB and plot them. For comparison, plot also polar AWGN signaling performance in the absence of ISI.

12.19. Repeat Problem 12.18 and plot the BER performance using an MMSE equalizer. Compare it with that obtained using a ZFE equalizer.

12.20. Consider the design of an LMS equalizer for the two-ray channel

$$h_c(t) = \delta(t) - 0.65\delta(t - T)$$

We assume RRC signaling as discussed in Problem 12.18. The following parameters are used during simulation:

Number of training symbols = 200

Number of taps in the equalizer = 9

Step size = 0.01 to 0.1 in steps of 0.02

Initial estimate of tap vector $\underline{c} = (0\ 0\ 0\ 0\ 1\ 0\ 0\ 0\ 0)$

a. Calculate the optimum tap vector and the resultant mean-square error for EbNo values from 1 to 20 dB and plot MMSE versus EbNo.

b. Use the optimum tap vector obtained in part (a) to calculate the BER performance using simulation procedure described in Problem 12.18. Compare the BER performance with that obtained using an MMSE equalizer.

12.21. Consider the transmission of polar RRC pulses through a bandlimited channel with the impulse response given by

$$h_c(t) = 0.815\delta(t) + 0.575\delta(t - T) + 0.575\delta(t + T)$$

a. Determine the overall impulse response sequence qvector ($q[k]$). Design MMSE-DFE equalizer for the channel. Plot qvector and equalizer output pulse peq. Also plot the DTFTs of qvector and peq.

b. Design MMSE equalizer for the channel. Plot qvector and equalizer output pulse peq. Also plot the DTFTs of qvector and peq.

c. Perform BER calculations with MMSE-DFE and MMSE equalization for EbNo values from 1 to 20 dB and plot them. For comparison, plot also polar AWGN signaling performance in the absence of ISI. Comment on the effectiveness of nonlinear MMSE-DFE versus linear MMSE equalization for this channel.

12.22. Consider the transmission of polar RRC pulses through a bandlimited channel with the impulse response given by

$$h_c(t) = \delta(t) - 0.75\delta(t - T)$$

We want to design DFE for this system. We assume, however, that the overall channel response qvector ($q[k]$) is not known to the DFE. Instead the DFE uses the MMSE estimate of the overall impulse response sequence obtained using training symbols as discussed in Section 12.7.2.

a. Design a DFE equalizer for the channel. Plot qvector and peq vectors and their DTFTs.

b. Design MMSE equalizer for the channel. Display on the same plot qvector and equalizer output pulse peq. Also plot the DTFTs of qvector and peq.

c. Perform BER calculations with MMSE and DFE equalization for EbNo values from 1 to 20 dB and plot them. For comparison, plot also polar AWGN signaling performance in the absence of ISI. Comment on the effectiveness of DFE versus linear MMSE equalization for this channel.

An Interview with Robert Lucky

Courtesy of Robert Lucky

Why did you choose a career in the communication field? Do you feel nostalgic about the 1960s at Bell Labs?

In my youth I was always fascinated with electricity and electronics. I loved to build Heathkits and other gadgets. And I liked math and science, so becoming an engineer was a natural choice. I don't even remember considering anything else. Like a lot of the choices in life, getting into communications in graduate school was mostly happenstance. I much preferred mathematical fields as opposed to experimental or physics-related specialties. Besides, I liked very much the names of seminal papers like "A Mathematical Theory of Information" and "A Mathematical Theory of Noise." As for feeling nostalgic about the 1960s at Bell Labs, well of course! All of us who were there feel a deep nostalgia about those "golden years" at Bell Labs. I always remind myself that at the time we didn't know how good we had it. I thought then that this was the way the world would always be—there would be a seemingly inexhaustible source of funds for research, intellectual curiosity would abound, and you would be surrounded by the best and brightest. Whatever subject in which you might have an interest, there would be a world-class expert down the hall from your office. Today when I drive by the deserted Bell Labs laboratory in Holmdel, New Jersey, and see the grass growing up through the asphalt of the once-busy parking lot, I feel a terrible sense of loss. Camelot is no more.

In your opinion what are the major innovations that have contributed to the phenomenal progress in digital and wireless communications? What has been the impact of semiconductor revolution? The optical fiber revolution? The Internet?

First and foremost, everything evolved from the transistor and the integrated circuit. This permitted undreamed of complexity, so that, quite literally, our dreams of what could be done were completely overturned. They say that necessity is the mother of invention, but inspiration, challenge, and possibility can't be ignored. In particular, when you know that something might be possible, then you can set out to do it, and the power of integrated circuits gave us those possibilities. The Internet, computers, wireless, and optics all in a sense meld together. They all depend on each other and used that synergy to grow and evolve. I take a great vicarious pride in the fact that my friends invented the Internet. They changed the world, and I feel a part of that change simply from being an engineer in the field at that time. But also, the Internet is a social invention, and today many of the world-changing ideas are less technical than they are social and business-related—Google, Facebook, Wikipedia, eBay, and so forth. When I joined Bell Labs, the two big developments that were ongoing were the millimeter waveguide transmission system and Picturephone. Together, they would be the future of communications. I remember when we first heard that Corning had produced optical fiber with only a 20 dB per kilometer loss. I give the Bell Labs management great credit for almost immediately stopping the development of the millimeter waveguide system and throwing resources onto optical fiber transmission. As for the Picturephone, I had one in my office for a few years. One day there was no one left to call. I think I had the last one. The unanticipated exponential growth of Internet traffic led to enormous emphasis and progress in optical transmission in the years that followed. At the same time, there was a revolution in wireless access, which was partly technical and partly social. As an engineer in the field, I am thankful for the rise in wireless, because it opened up a plethora of new technical problems, just as wireline access was becoming largely a "solved" problem.

1948 was the year of "double big bang": the invention of transistor and publication of Shannon's seminal papers. With the disappearance of the Bell system research model, are we doing enough fundamental research to drive the next round of major innovations?

No, we are not doing enough fundamental research in communications. The entire business model has changed dramatically. Twenty-five or so years ago there were great industrial labs that invested in fundamental research. Besides Bell Labs, there were IBM research, RCA, GE, Texas Instruments, and many others. As long as everyone in the business was investing in research, everyone could bear the expense without competitive penalty. But when some began opting out, research became a drag on the bottom line without an obvious return on investment. Today there is very little investment in industrial research. It is largely recognized that the return on investment from fundamental research is mostly a social return that is difficult to capture by the original funder. It is now something that government

must fund, and that must be done at universities. When I graduated, long ago, Bell Labs was the Mecca for communications research. It was the place to be. Today it is the universities. The problem with this model is that many, though not all, universities have little sense of what problems are practically important and what problems are simply exercises in the seeking of academic tenure. The system would be better led by a modicum of industrial research that would gently steer the academic research in fruitful directions.

Your invention of the adaptive equalizer implied the use of DSP and/or processor to solve a challenging digital transmission problem. Was it the first time? Tell us about your thought process at that time. How long before the technology caught up with the solution for wide-scale deployment of adaptive equalizers in modems?

When I worked on the first adaptive equalizers in the mid-1960s, the limitations on complexity were foremost on my mind. My first adaptive equalizer used about a hundred mechanical relays in a man-sized rack of equipment. I loved to hear the relays click as the equalizer adjusted. At first the clicks would be a constant buzz, like the sound of a waterfall. But as the equalizer got closer to its steepest-descent goal, the clicks would first become more individually distinct, and then reduce to a trickle. Soon after that first implementation, the adjustment was done by transistors, and not too long after that, by software in DSPs. The limitations on the allowable complexity were essentially removed, so that the only questions were about the optimality of the algorithms themselves. Today, like everything else, equalizers are only a piece of software embedded in a processor somewhere, virtually indistinguishable from other system processing.

What are the new frontiers of innovation in digital communications? Wireless communications?

Good question! If I were still doing or managing research, I would worry about this a lot. In recent years most communications research has been in two fields—optics and wireless. Both of these fields have advanced enormously. The question would be whether they have reached diminishing returns. There have been enough recent significant contributions that I wouldn't call either one dead or dying, but I would worry. Perhaps we need to open up some new fruitful avenue of research, but I don't know what it will be.

Who inspired you professionally the most?

Claude Shannon inspired me the most. Yet I only met him once or twice and never really had a substantive conversation with him. But he spoke to me through his written words. His paper on information theory was truly inspirational. Even today, more than a half century later, I am in awe of this work. What genius! When I first went to work at Bell Labs, I was so proud of being in the place where

Shannon worked. Then I found that he wasn't actually there, but at MIT. Nevertheless, his inspiration still lived at Bell Labs, and there were others in the field there like Dave Slepian, Steve Rice, Sid Darlington, and Bill Bennett whose very presence lent a sense of destiny to those hallowed halls.

Do you have any advice for the new generation of students and researchers entering the communications field?

I do think that things are harder today than they were at my time. The world is much more complex and much of communications has become mature technology pushing against fundamental physical limitations. We need a new Claude Shannon, and hopefully some young student out there can be that new Shannon. My advice is to dream big and not be discouraged by any sense of inferiority. I've seen famous people make mistakes and ordinary people blossom. A lot of life is being in the right place at the right time, having luck, and taking advantage. I wish that I were one of the new generation myself, but alas, I can only wish you well.

Robert Lucky received his doctorate in electrical engineering from Purdue University in 1961. He has since been honored with four honorary doctorates, and has received a number of major awards, including the prestigious Marconi Prize and the IEEE Edison Medal. He has been elected a fellow of the IEEE and to membership in the National Academy of Engineering, and to both the American and European Academies of Arts and Sciences. He has led premier research laboratories in telecommunications over the last several decades, first at Bell Labs and then at Telcordia Technologies, where he was corporate vice president, applied research. Early in his career he invented the adaptive equalizer, the key enabler for all high-speed modems today. He co-authored a textbook on data communications that was the most cited reference in the field over the period of a decade. He is the author of many technical papers and of several books, including *Silicon Dreams* and *Lucky Strikes Again*. He has been the editor of a series of books in communications and of several technical journals. However, most engineers know him best because of the monthly columns he has written for IEEE *Spectrum Magazine* over the last 20 years offering philosophical and sometimes humorous observations on engineering, life, and technology.

Digital Multiplexing and Synchronization

In this chapter, we address two major topics in digital communications: digital multiplexing and synchronization. **Digital multiplexing** is the process of combining multiple user digital signals into a composite signal such that individual signals can be separated at the receiving end without any errors. **Synchronization** (*syn* meaning "together" and *chronous* meaning "time") refers to the process of achieving a common time reference between two or more periodic processes that are occurring at the transmitter and receiver. In digital communications, a hierarchy of synchronization tasks needs to be handled. First, assuming that a coherent digitally modulated carrier transmission system is involved, there is the task of **carrier synchronization,** which concerns the generation of a carrier at the receiver that is frequency- and phase-locked with the carrier embedded in the incoming signal. This locally generated carrier is used in the digital communication receiver for the coherent detection of the underlying baseband signal. It is followed by the task of synchronizing locally generated symbol-rate clock at the receiver with the one embedded in the demodulated baseband signal. This is commonly called **symbol** or **bit synchronization.** The recovered clock is used to define the timing of regenerated data pulses. The next level in the synchronization hierarchy is **frame synchronization.** It involves inserting framing words or patterns in the data stream to mark the beginning of a frame that is normally formed in the process of digital multiplexing. For a receiver to properly segregate constituent digital signals in the multiplexed bit stream, it must successfully detect the framing pattern marking the beginning of each frame. Figure 13.1 displays how this hierarchy of synchronization functions is implemented in a digital communications receiver.

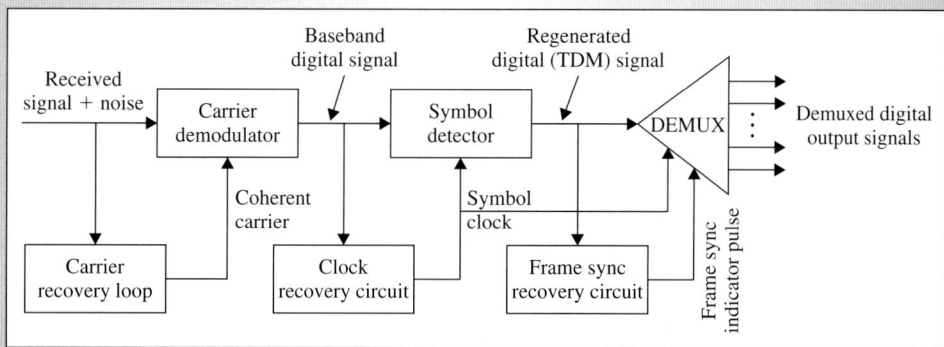

Figure 13.1 Synchronization function blocks in a digital communications receiver.

We have seen from the spectral analysis of digital carrier-modulated signals in Chapter 11 that the most efficient modulation techniques suppress the carrier completely; all transmitted power is devoted exclusively to information symbols and none is wasted on a spectral energy component at the carrier frequency. Similarly, efficient line codes considered in Chapter 9 give rise to data streams not containing spectral lines at the symbol rate. In this case, the synchronizers must regenerate a carrier and clock from a signal that contains neither in explicit form. Nonlinear devices are necessary to regenerate a discrete spectral line from a signal in which carrier and symbol-rate frequency components have been suppressed. This is followed by a narrowband circuit (typically a tuned filter or a phase-locked loop) that separates the regenerated carrier or clock from background disturbances.

The chapter is organized into the following sections:

13.1   DIGITAL MULTIPLEXING.

This section explains the concepts of time-division-multiplexing and demultiplexing of signals in a digital communication system. We then discuss multiplexing hierarchies for plesiochronous digital signals and synchronization problems involved in combining them.

13.2   SONET.

In this section we consider synchronous multiplexing aspects of the SONET standard, which is a global framework for the telecommunications infrastructure. We discuss line rates, frame formats, and unique multiplexing features of signals in the SONET hierarchy.

13.3   CARRIER SYNCHRONIZATION.

We consider techniques for generating a carrier at the receiver, which is synchronized in frequency and phase with the carrier embedded in the incoming signal. We discuss both raised power and Costas closed-loop carrier recovery schemes. The effect of AWGN on the performance of carrier synchronizers is considered next.

13.4   SYMBOL SYNCHRONIZATION.

This section studies the problem of extracting the clock signal from the baseband received signal when it does not contain a discrete spectral line at the signal's bit (or symbol) rate. We discuss special characteristics of phase-locked loops (PLLs) designed to generate the clock signal synchronized to transitions of the baseband-received signal. A Simulink simulation model is then used to study the operation of a PLL-based clock recovery circuit.

13.5   FRAME SYNCHRONIZATION.

This section addresses the problem of frame synchronization in a time-division-multiplexed system. Various aspects of frame alignment procedure and its key performance parameters are then explained. The section concludes with a discussion of considerations in the selection of frame alignment word.

The chapter concludes with final remarks and a selected list of references.

13.1   DIGITAL MULTIPLEXING

Digital multiplexing refers to the sharing of a communication channel by several digital signals from one point in a network to another. In **time-division multiplexing (TDM),** the low-speed digital signals (**tributary signals**) are interleaved in time into a high-speed output signal. This task is performed by a **multiplexer** at the transmit end in a digital communication system. The receiving terminal, or **demultiplexer,** performs the inverse operation of separating the high-speed signal into its component parts and thus recovering several low-speed tributary signals. Figure 13.2 illustrates multiplexing of three input data streams and their demultiplexing at the receive end. Each input information source generates a unit of data (e.g., a bit or a byte or a fixed-size packet of bits) every T seconds. The output of the multiplexer is organized into **frames.** If all n input data rates are equal, each frame has n equal-sized time slots. The output of the multiplexer runs n times faster so it can serve all inputs in the time it takes one input data unit to arrive. In the example of Figure 13.2, the multiplexer sends one data unit every $T/3$ seconds. The resultant frames are **bit-interleaved** if the data is clocked bit-by-bit from each of the tributary inputs. On the other hand, the multiplexed frames are **byte-interleaved** if the data is clocked on a byte basis.

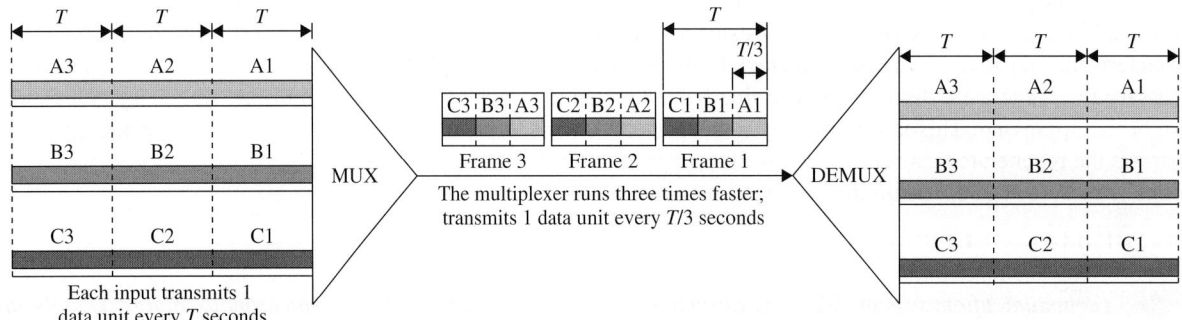

Figure 13.2 Time-division multiplexing.

Due to variation in delay and clock frequency on the incoming lines, various tributary signals at the multiplexer input are not perfectly aligned in time with each other. Therefore, they cannot be time-division multiplexed by simply interleaving them as displayed in Figure 13.2. We need a mechanism to synchronize each tributary digital signal so that it can be placed in its allocated time slot in the multiplexer output frame. In this context, we now consider two different cases:

- **Plesiochronous tributaries.** N tributaries have the same nominal bit rate value, but actual values lie within a specified tolerance range.
- **Synchronous tributaries.** N tributaries have the same instantaneous clock frequencies. Here each tributary signal's associated clock is derived from the same master clock source, as in a PCM multiplexer. Alternatively, each tributary signal can be generated by a terminal whose internal clock is relatively stable for a long period of time, and it is synchronized to the master network clock, as in a SONET multiplexer (Section 13.2).

Further, framing bits need to be added into the high-speed multiplexer output so that various component digital signals may be properly identified at the demultiplexer.

Example 13.1

A PCM T1 multiplexer accepts 24 analog telephone signals, digitizes them, and outputs a time-division multiplexed (TDM) signal. As discussed in Example 8.8 each voice channel is sampled at the 8-kHz rate and digitized to a 64 kbps PCM signal. This is called **digital signal 0 (DS0)** in the telco universe. Thus, digitization of 24 analog telephone signals produces a total of $24 \times 8 = 192$ bits every 1/8000 second. Because all circuits in the transmit end equipment derive timing signals from the same master clock, 24 bytes can be interleaved to generate the time-division multiplexed (TDM) output signal. This group of 192 bits plus a framing bit that marks the beginning of the group is called the **digital signal 1 (DS1)** frame. Figure 13.3 displays the DS1 frame where

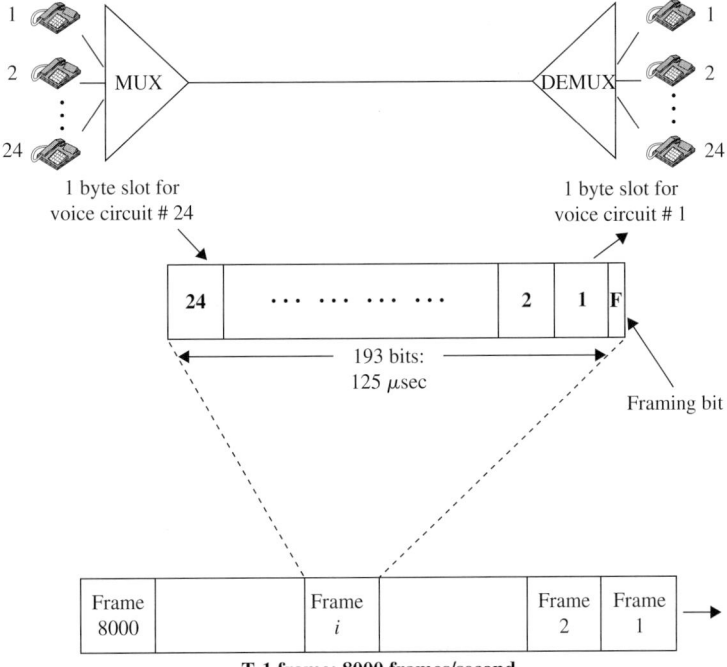

Figure 13.3 T1 Carrier system.

each slot carries a 1-byte sample for one of 24 voice channels. The total number of bits in the frame is 193. The framing bit F follows a certain periodic pattern (010101 . . .) to help identify the beginning of each frame at the demultiplexer. The resulting speed of the TDM signal is 193 bits/frame $\times$ 8000 frames/second = 1.544 Mbps.

13.1.1   Plesiochronous Digital Hierarchies

The PCM T1 multiplexer forms part of the digital communication system in Figure 13.3, known as **T1 carrier system,** introduced by the Bell System in the United States in 1961 to carry traffic between central offices in the telephone network. The continued growth of network traffic and the advances in digital transmission technologies have led to the development of various standard digital multiplexing hierarchies. Figure 13.4 displays the **plesiochronous digital hierarchies (PDH)** that were developed in North America and Europe. In North American PDH, the DS1 signal, which corresponds to the output of a T-1 multiplexer, forms the basic building block. The DS2 signal is obtained by combining four DS1 signals and then adding 136 kilobits of synchronization information. The DS3 signal is obtained by combining seven DS2 signals and then adding 552 kilobits of synchronization information. The DS3 signal, with a speed of 44.736 Mbps, is widely used in providing high-speed connections to corporate users in the access part of the network.

The PDH in Europe, developed by CCITT, uses the CEPT-1 (also called E1) signal as the basic building block. The CEPT-1 signal at 2.048 Mbps multiplexes 32 64-kbps channels. One of the 32 channels is reserved for signaling, while another one is used for frame alignment and link maintenance. Thus, 30 out of 32 channels are used to carry user traffic. The second, third, and fourth levels of the PDH are obtained by combining four of the signals in the lower level.

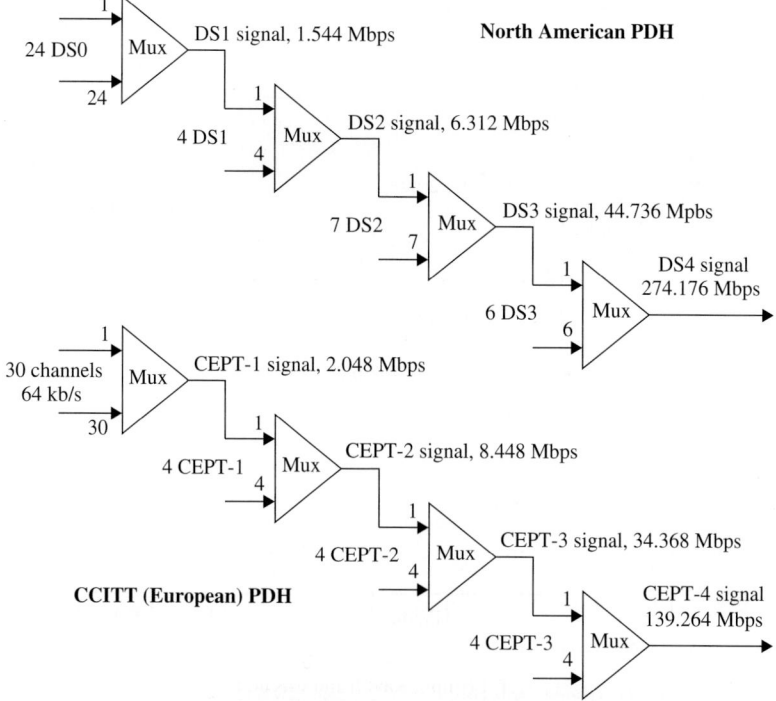

Figure 13.4 Plesiochronous digital hierarchies.

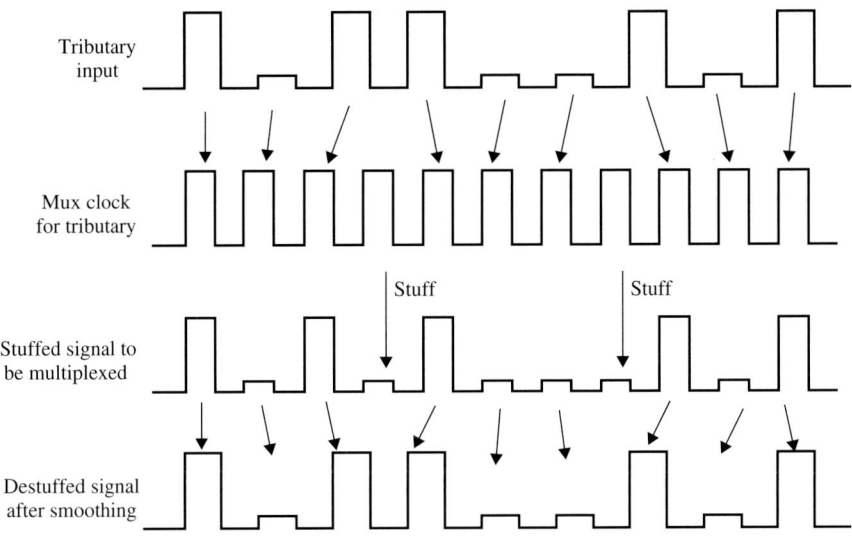

Figure 13.5 Bit stuffing.

13.1.2 Synchronization of PDH Signals

The input tributary signals here have the same nominal bit rate value f_t, but actual values f_i differ slightly from one another owing to the stability and tolerance of their individual clock sources. Further, the multiplexer has its own independent clock. This points to the need to synchronize each tributary to the clock of the multiplexer so they can be bit-interleaved to produce the TDM output. This can be accomplished by the **stuffing synchronization** technique. The idea is based on running the multiplexer output at a slightly faster rate than the sum of the maximum instantaneous rates of all incoming tributary signals. The extra capacity is now used to stuff extra pulses into each incoming tributary signal until its rate is equal to that of a multiplexer-generated clock signal. Figure 13.5 illustrates the concept of pulse stuffing synchronization.

13.1.3 M12 Multiplexer: DS2 Frame

The M12 multiplexer combines four DS1 signals by bit interleaving them in a DS2 frame as displayed in Figure 13.6. The DS2 frame is composed of four subframes, designated M1 through M4. Each subframe consists of six blocks, and each block contains 49 bits. The first bit in each block is an overhead (OH) bit inserted by the multiplexer to facilitate synchronization and demultiplexing functions. Each DS2 frame contains 24 of these OH bits (1 OH bit/block $\times$ 6 blocks/ subframe $\times$ 4 subframes/DS2 frame). The remaining 48 bits in a block are information bits.

> Total number of information bits in a DS2 frame
>
> = 48 bits/block $\times$ 6 blocks/subframe $\times$ 4 subframes/DS2 frame
>
> = 1152 bits

The four subframes do not represent each of the separate DS1 signals. Rather, the DS2 frame is formed by bit-by-bit interleaving the four DS1 signals as shown in the figure. Here $DS1_i$, $i = 1, \ldots, 4$ designates the time slot devoted to the ith DS1 tributary input.

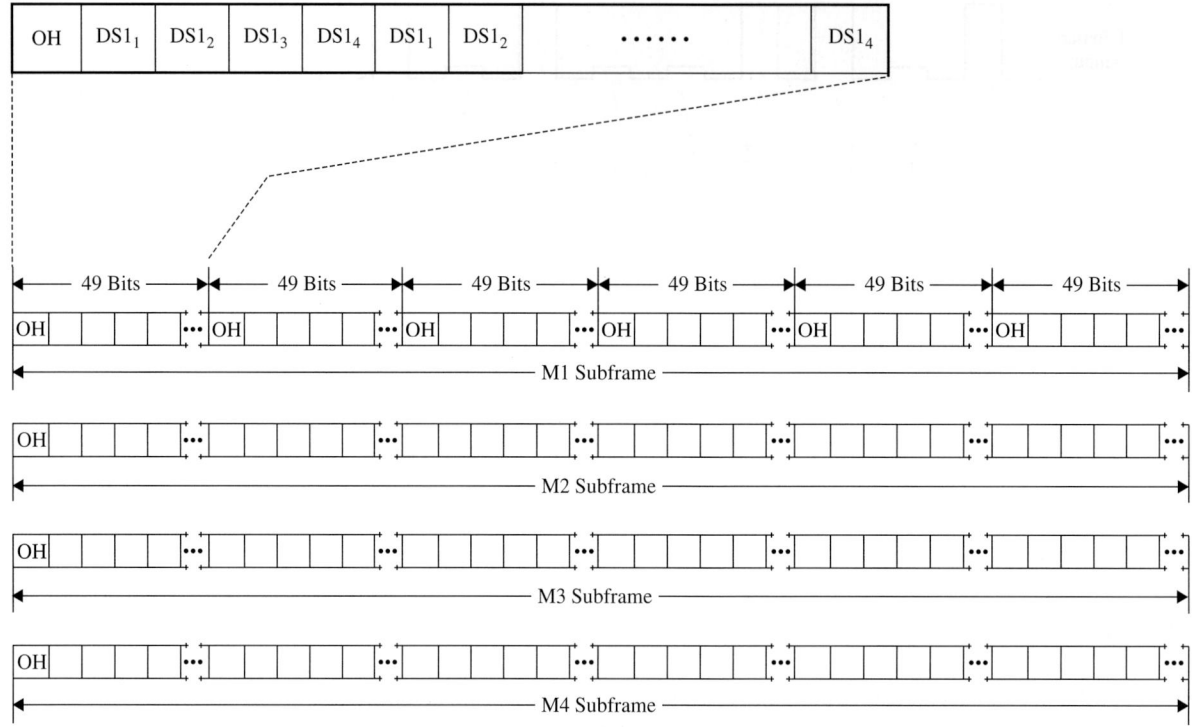

Figure 13.6 DS2 frame format.

13.1.4 DS2 OH Bits

Although $4 \times DS1$ nominal rate $= 4 \times 1.544$ Mbps $= 6.176$ Mbps, the overall rate chosen for DS2 signal is 6.312 Mbps. The reason this rate is chosen is to provide extra capacity for DS2 bit stuffing and OH bits. The DS2 OH bits provide frame alignment and bit stuffing control. The OH bits are located in the first bit position of every block. Figure 13.7 shows the location of various DS2 overhead bits designated F, M, and C.

- **F-bits (framing bits).** There are eight F-bits per DS2 frame. The F-bits are located in the first bit position in blocks 3 and 6 of each subframe. The frame alignment pattern, which is repeated every subframe, is 01.
- **M-bits (multiframing bits).** There are four M-bits per DS2 frame. The M-bits are located in the first bit position in each subframe. M12 demultiplexer uses the M-bit pattern, 0111, to identify the four subframes.
- **C-bits.** These bits are used as bit stuffing indicators. There are three C-bits per subframe, designated C_{ij}, where i corresponds to the subframe number and j refers to the position number of the C-bit in a particular subframe.

In each DS2 frame, one bit can be stuffed for each of the four DS1 signals. Specifically, the state of the three C-bits in the ith subframe indicates whether or not bit stuffing occurs for the ith DS1 input during the multiplexing process. The state of the C-bits is determined by the synchronization hardware in the multiplexer. If all three C-bits are set to 1, it indicates that the stuffing has occurred. The location of the stuffed bit is the first data bit position associated with the $DS1_i$ signal in block 6 of the ith subframe. If all three C-bits are set to zero, no stuffing has occurred, and the associated "stuffable" bit position is merely treated as a normal DS1 data bit. During the demultiplexing process,

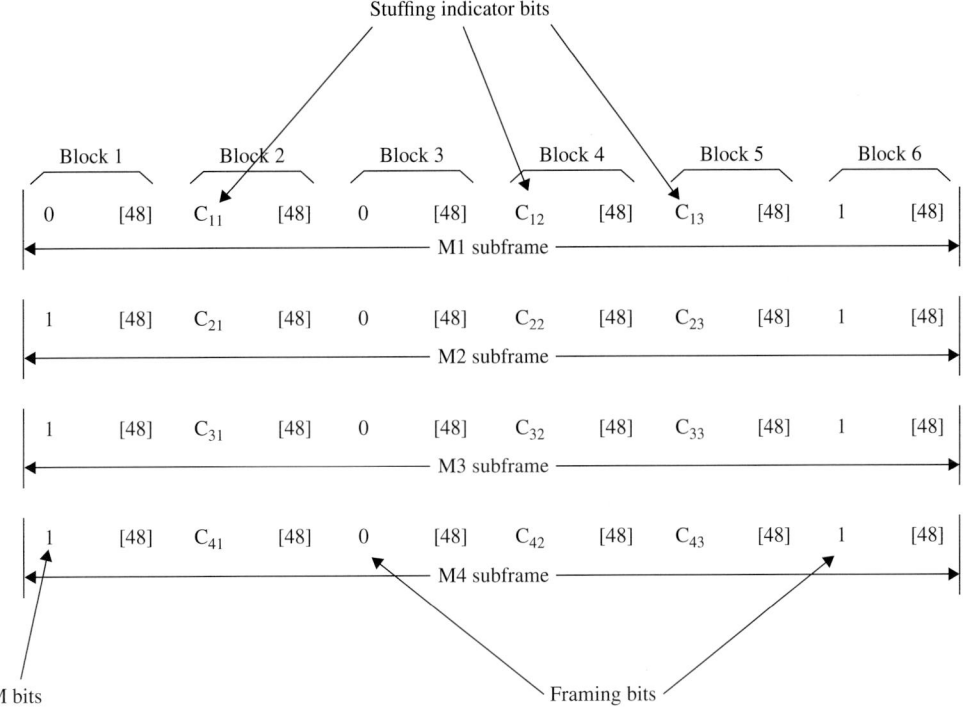

Figure 13.7　DS2 frame overhead bits.

the C-bits are used to determine if the "stuffable" bit is to be included in the recon-structed DS1 signal. For example, if $C_{21} = C_{22} = C_{23} = 0$, then bit 02 of block 6 in the M2 subframe is a data bit and therefore is included in the reconstruction of the second DS1 signal. If $C_{21} = C_{22} = C_{23} = 1$, then bit 02 of block 6 in the M2 subframe is a stuff bit and therefore is not included in the reconstruction of the second DS1 signal. The three C-bits constitute a (3, 1) single-error-correcting code to minimize the probability of stuff position error.

The ability to handle small variations in the input DS1 signal rates can be calculated from the DS2 framing format. Because each DS2 frame allows for the stuffing of one bit in each of the four DS1 signals, the maximum stuffing rate for each DS1 signal is equal to the DS2 frame rate. A DS2 frame contains $49 \times 6 \times 4 = 1176$ bits as shown in Figure 13.7. Therefore,

$$\text{Frame rate} = 6.312 \text{ Mbps}/1176 \text{ bits/frame} = 5367.35 \text{ frames per sec}$$

Hence, each input DS1 signal can be incremented by 5.367 kbps.

Example 13.2

For the M12 frame format, compute the number of overhead bits per second added by the multi-plexer. Also, calculate the minimum and maximum allowable rates for input DS1 signals.

Solution

Number of OH bits = 5367.35 frames per sec $\times$ 24 OH bits per frame = 128.816 kbps
Maximum allowable DS1 bits = 6.312 Mbps $-$ 128.816 kbps = 6.183184 Mbps.

This capacity is allocated evenly across the four DS1 signals. Therefore,

$$\text{Maximum allowable DS1 rate} = 6.183184/4 = 1.545796 \text{ Mbps} \qquad (13.1)$$

The bit stuffing rate for a DS1 signal operating at the maximum limit is 0 b/s. Because one stuffing opportunity is available per DS2 frame, the maximum stuff rate is limited to the DS2 frame rate, that is, 5.367 kbps. Therefore, the minimum allowable DS1 rate into the M12 multiplexer is the difference between the maximum allowable DS1 rate and maximum stuff rate. That is,

$$\text{Minimum allowable DS1 rate} = 1.545796 \text{ Mbps} - 5.367 \text{ kbps} = 1.540429 \text{ Mbps} \quad (13.2)$$

Therefore, a DS1 signal may be input to the M12 multiplexer at the minimum rate of 1.540429 Mbps. The bit stuffing rate for a DS1 signal operating at this rate is 5.367 kbps.

If DS1 inputs lie between the maximum and minimum limits stated in (13.1) and (13.2), the synchronizing circuits in the multiplexer add the necessary stuff bits to bring each input to the intermediate rate of 1.545796 Mbps prior to interleaving.

Example 13.3

Suppose the actual bit rates of DS1 tributaries input to an M12 multiplexer are given as

DS1 tributary no. 1 1.545796 Mbps
DS1 tributary no. 2 1.544600 Mbps
DS1 tributary no. 3 1.544450 Mbps
DS1 tributary no. 4 1.540429 Mbps

What are the stuff rates for each of the DS1 signals?

Solution

Stuff rate for DS1 tributary No. 1 $= 1.545796 \times 10^6 - 1.545796 \times 10^6 = 0$ kbps
Stuff rate for DS1 tributary No. 2 $= 1.545796 \times 10^6 - 1.544600 \times 10^6 = 1.196$ kbps
Stuff rate for DS1 tributary No. 3 $= 1.545796 \times 10^6 - 1.544450 \times 10^6 = 1.346$ kbps
Stuff rate for DS1 tributary No. 4 $= 1.545796 \times 10^6 - 1.540429 \times 10^6 = 5.367$ kbps

Figure 13.8 displays four DS1 tributary signals and corresponding stuff rates.

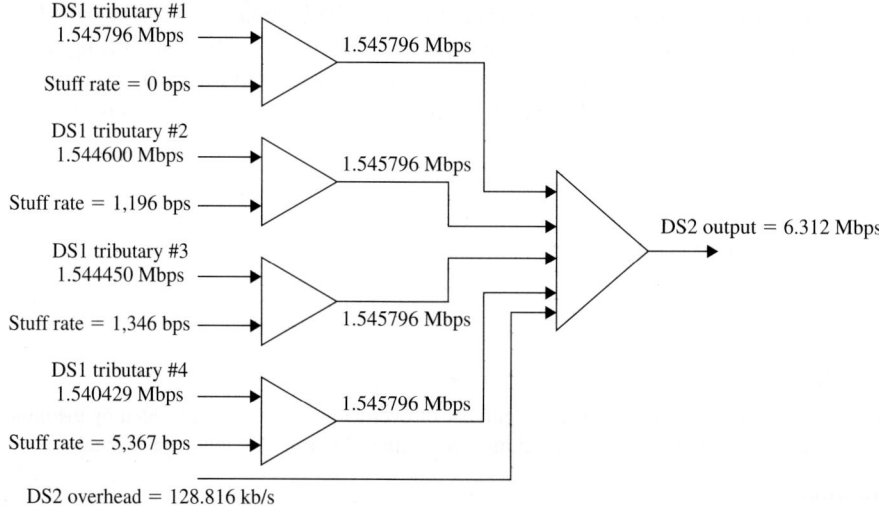

Figure 13.8 Multiplexing of DS1 signals in M12 multiplexer.

13.2 SONET

The **synchronous optical network (SONET)** and its variant **synchronous digital hierarchy (SDH)** are global standards for synchronous multiplexing of high-speed digital signals and their transmission over telecommunication networks. In this section, we concentrate on the multiplexing aspects of SONET. The SONET standard defines a hierarchy of high-speed signals to extend the digital transmission hierarchy into the multi-gigabit per second range as displayed in Table 13.1.

The frame formats of various hierarchical-level signals are called **synchronous transport signals (STS).** SONET uses a 51.84-Mbps electrical signal, known as **STS-1,** as the basic building block. Higher-level SONET signals are produced by interleaving bytes from the lower-level SONET signals. For example, an STS-N signal is formed by byte-interleaving N STS-1 signals. Each STS-N electrical signal has a corresponding **optical carrier level-N (OC-N)** signal. The optical OC-N signal is formed by scrambling the electrical STS-N signal using the standardized polynomial (Figure 9.24) and then modulating an optical source. The frame format used by SDH is called **synchronous transport module (STM),** with STM-1 being the base-level signal at 155.52 Mbps. The STM-1 signal is converted to an OC-3 optical signal for transmission. We observe from Table 13.1 that the rate of an STS-N or STM-N signal is simply N times the rate of an STS-1 or STM-1 signal, respectively.

STS-1 Frame

SONET uses a frame structure that has the same 8-kHz repetition rate as traditional telephone TDM systems. Figure 13.9 illustrates the structure of the SONET STS-1 frame. SONET uses a frame length of 125 μsec or a frame rate of 8000 frames per second. Each STS-1 frame can be viewed as a 9-row by 90-column structure, a total of 810 bytes. The STS-1 line rate = 8 bits/byte $\times$ 9 rows $\times$ 90 columns $\times$ 8000 frames/sec = 51.84 Mbps. The order of transmission of bytes is row by row from top to bottom, left to right (the most significant bit first).

The STS-1 frame is divided into two main areas: **transport overhead** and the **synchronous payload envelope (SPE).** The first three columns constitute the transport overhead: a total of 27 bytes. These bytes are devoted to specific functions, such as frame recovery, synchronous multiplexing, performance monitoring, alarm reporting, and various maintenance and administrative functions. For example, bytes A1 and A2 indicate the beginning of each STS-1 frame and are used for frame recovery. The A1, A2 bytes' pattern is F628 hex. Bytes H1, H2, and H3, called **pointer bytes,** are used for synchronous multiplexing. SPE column 1 (nine bytes) contains the **path overhead (POH).** These bytes are used for identification and performance monitoring of the user payload contained in the SPE. Two columns in SPE (columns 30 and 59)

Table 13.1 SONET/SDH Digital Hierarchy

SONET Electrical Signal STS-N	Optical Signal OC-N	Bit Rate (Mbps)	SDH Electrical Signal STM-N
STS-1	OC-1	51.84	N/A
STS-3	OC-3	155.52	STM-1
STS-12	OC-12	622.08	STM-4
STS-48	OC-48	2488.32	STM-16
STS-192	OC-192	9953.28	STM-64
STS-768	OC-768	39813.12	STM-256

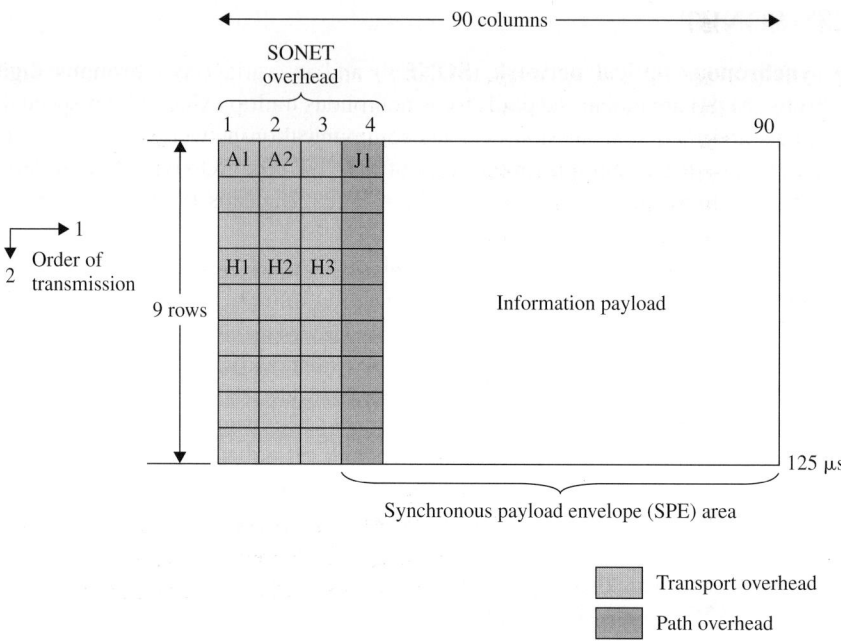

Figure 13.9 SONET STS-1 frame.

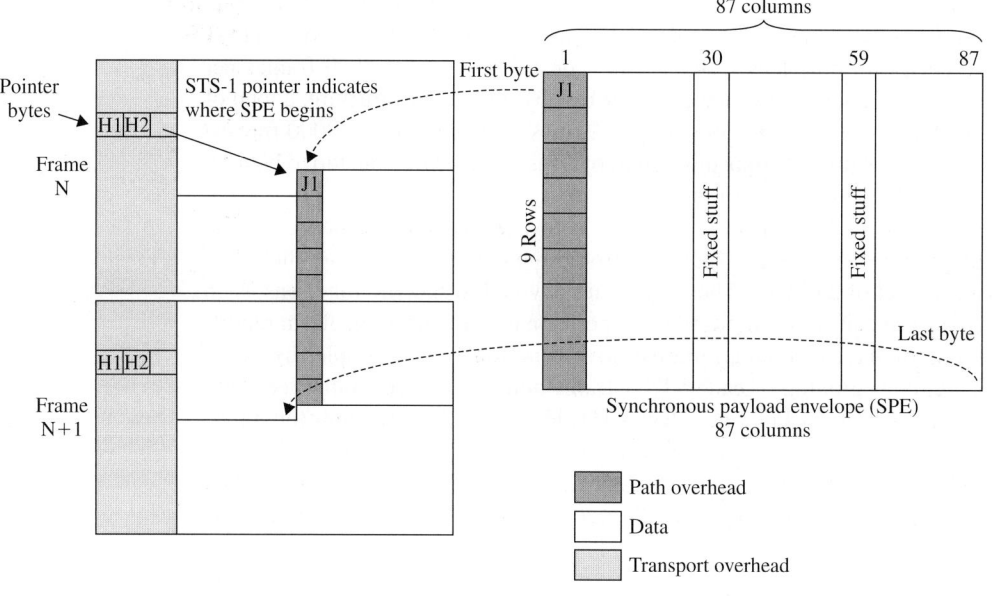

Figure 13.10 Floating of SPE in two consecutive STS-1 frames.

are not used for payload but are designated as the fixed stuff columns. The 756 bytes in the remaining 84 columns are designated to carry the user data payload. The bit rate of the STS-1 payload is 8 bits/byte × 9 rows × 84 columns × 8000 frames/sec = 48.384 Mbps.

The SPE may start anywhere within the remaining 87 columns of the STS-1 frame. Unless the SPE happens to start at the fourth column of the first row (which is rare), it occupies a portion of two consecutive frames as displayed in Figure 13.10.

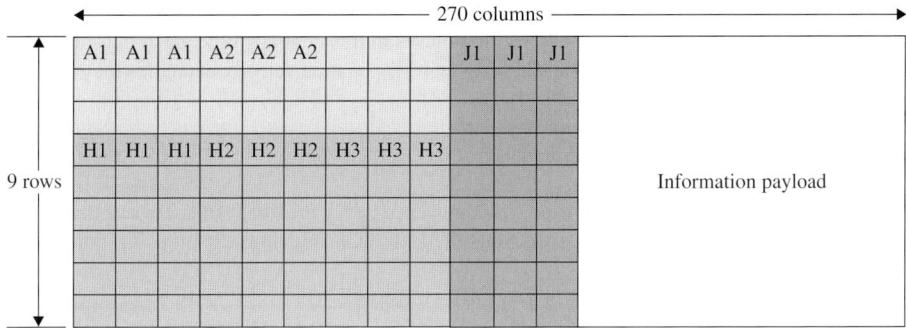

Figure 13.11 STS-3 frame.

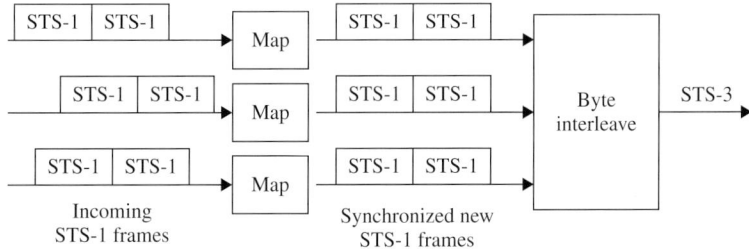

Figure 13.12 Multiplexing of SONET signals.

13.2.1 Multiplexing of SONET Signals

Recall from Section 13.1.2 that a PDH multiplexer interleaves bits from individual lower-speed tributary signals into a higher-speed aggregate signal. Higher-level SONET signals, on the other hand, are produced by interleaving bytes from lower-level SONET signals. The STS-N frame is an array of N × 810 bytes. The STS-N frame is produced by interleaving bytes of the N synchronized STS-1 signals, in effect producing a frame that has nine rows, 3 × N transport overhead columns, and 87 × N SPE columns. Figure 13.11 displays the STS-3 frame.

Before N STS-1 signals can be interleaved, each incoming STS-1 signal first needs to be synchronized to the local STS-1 clock of the multiplexer. This is accomplished by terminating the section and line overhead of each incoming STS-1 signal and then mapping its SPE into a new STS-1 frame that is synchronized to the local clock as shown in Figure 13.12. The pointer in the new STS-1 frame is adjusted as necessary, and the mapping is done on the fly. This procedure ensures that all of the incoming STS-1 frames are mapped into STS-1 frames that are synchronized with respect to each other.

Example 13.4

Consider a SONET OC-48 optical fiber link consisting of 20 sections of 50 km each. Assuming the velocity of propagation in optical fiber is 2×10^8 m/sec, calculate the number of extra pulses that will arrive at the multiplexer because of the 0.0008% increase in propagation velocity due to temperature and wavelength variations.

Solution

Total link length = 20 × 50 = 1000 km
Propagation delay = $1000 \times 10^3/(2 \times 10^8)$ = 5 msec

The number of SONET OC-48 pulses in 1000 km link is 5 msec $\times$ 2.48 $\times$ 10^9 b/s = 12.4416 $\times$ 10^6. Thus there are about 12 million pulses in transit at any time, each pulse occupying about 0.08 meter of cable. A 0.0008% increase in propagation velocity decreases the propagation delay by the same amount.

$$\text{Change in propagation delay} = 0.000008 \times 5 \text{ msec} = 40 \text{ nsec}$$

Thus there are 2.48 $\times$ 10^9 bps $\times$ 40 nsec = 100 fewer pulses in the fiber cable. These extra pulses need to be absorbed by the multiplexer. SONET deals with this problem by using pointers as discussed in the next section.

13.2.2 Synchronization of SONET Signals

Although SONET/SDH network elements are synchronous timed—that is, they derive their clocks from the same master clock—slight timing differences exist between them. Data can come into a device more slowly or more quickly than it is transmitted out at the other side, as discussed in Example 13.4. So something needs to be done to adjust the differences between the transmit and receive clocks. This is accomplished by decoupling the SPE from the incoming STS-1 frame. The SPE can now float between two locally generated STS-1 frames to compensate for the timing differences. This is made possible by pointer bytes (H1 and H2) in the SONET overhead. The pointer bytes perform two functions: (1) locate the first byte (i.e., J1 byte) of the STS-1 SPE (that is, where the SPE begins) and (2) indicate the need for frequency justification. The 16 bits of the STS-1 pointer bytes are classified into three fields as shown in Figure 13.13. A description of the fields follows:

- **New data flag (NDF).** 4 bits. NDF = 0110 $\Rightarrow$ normal operation, NDF = 1001 $\Rightarrow$ New pointer value.
- **Spare field.** 2 bits.
- **Pointer (offset) value field.** 10 bits. Indicates the offset in bytes from the H3 byte location to the first byte of the STS-1 SPE. A value of 0 means that the SPE starts in row 4, column 4. The pointer bits are alternately labeled as IDIDIDIDID, where I = increment bit, D = decrement bit. The I and D bit designations have additional meaning for positive and negative justification.

The new pointer value is repeated in at least 3 frames with the NDF bit pattern 1001.

Positive Frequency Justification

When input payload stream is slower than the locally generated frame rate ("clock"), a stuff byte is required from time to time so that the SPE payload catches up with the locally generated frame. The additional (dummy) byte is always stuffed in location right after the H3 byte as shown in Figure 13.14(a). This is known as **positive stuffing** or **justification.** At the receiver, the byte after H3 is ignored. This operation is indicated to the receiver by

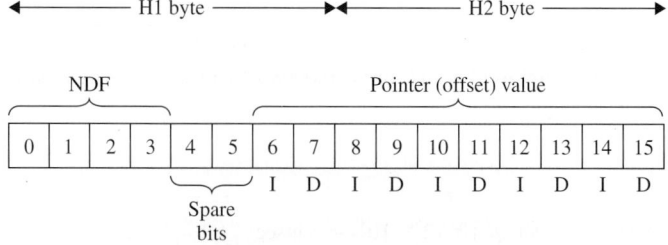

Figure 13.13 Definition of H1 and H2 bytes.

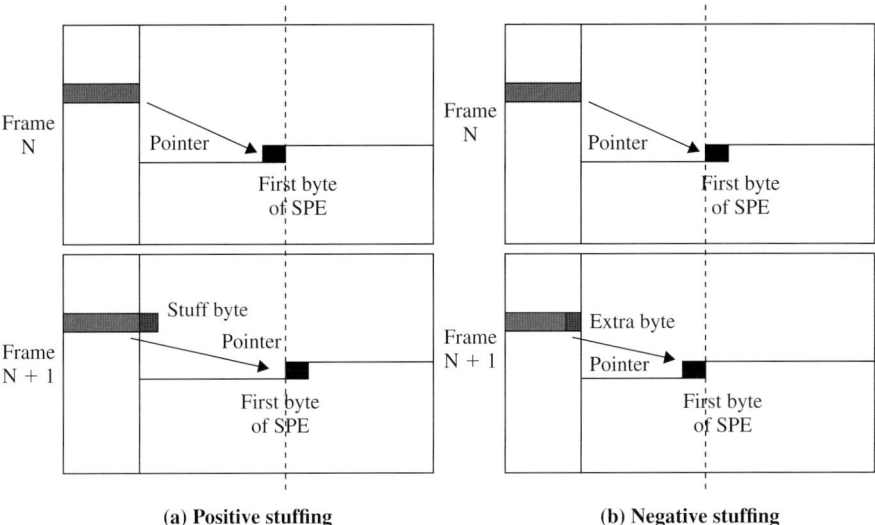

(a) Positive stuffing   (b) Negative stuffing

Figure 13.14 Frequency justification.

inverting the I bits of the pointer value. The pointer is incremented by 1 in the next frame (to indicate that the SPE now starts one byte later), and the subsequent pointers contain the new value. Table 13.2 illustrates how the pointer field bits are manipulated in a specific example to indicate to the receiver the forthcoming positive stuffing operation.

Negative Frequency Justification

If the SPE payload stream is faster than the locally generated frame rate, an extra SPE byte is transmitted from time to time to enable the frame to catch up. The extra byte, which is always written in the H3 byte location as shown in Figure 13.14(b), is known as **negative stuffing** or justification. This operation is indicated to the receiver by inverting the D bits of the pointer value. Whenever the extra byte is inserted, the pointer is decremented by 1 in the next frame (to indicate that the SPE now starts one byte earlier), and the subsequent pointers contain the new value. Table 13.3 illustrates how the pointer field bits are manipulated in a specific example to indicate to the receiver the forthcoming negative stuffing operation.

Table 13.2 Positive Stuffing

Status/Actions	NDF Bits	I D I D I D I D I D	Pointer Value	Frame #
Normal operation	0110	0 0 0 1 0 1 1 0 0 1	89	N − 1
Positive stuff required	0110	1 0 1 1 1 1 0 0 1 1	undefined	N
New pointer value assigned	1001	0 0 0 1 0 1 1 0 1 0	90	N + 1
	1001	0 0 0 1 0 1 1 0 1 0	90	N + 2
	1001	0 0 0 1 0 1 1 0 1 0	90	N + 3

Table 13.3 Negative Stuffing

Status/Actions	NDF Bits	I D I D I D I D I D	Pointer Value	Frame #
Normal operation	0110	0 0 0 1 0 1 1 0 1 0	90	M − 1
Negative stuff required	0110	0 1 0 0 0 0 1 1 1 1	undefined	M
New pointer value assigned	1001	0 0 0 1 0 1 1 0 0 1	89	M + 1
	1001	0 0 0 1 0 1 1 0 0 1	89	M + 2
	1001	0 0 0 1 0 1 1 0 0 1	89	M + 3

13.3 CARRIER SYNCHRONIZATION

For coherent demodulation, the receiver in a digital communications system generates a carrier waveform that is synchronized in both frequency and phase with the incoming carrier signal. Note that the frequency or phase of the carrier generated by the LO at the transmitter would, in general, drift over time and temperature to some degree. The purpose of a carrier synchronizer, also called a **carrier recovery loop,** is to produce a pure sine wave at the receiver that is frequency- and phase-locked with the embedded carrier in the received signal. For suppressed-carrier digital modulation schemes, carrier recovery circuits incorporate some technique to regenerate a discrete spectral component at the carrier frequency or a harmonic thereof. This is then followed by a PLL that tracks the regenerated component and in the process produces the synchronized (in the absence of noise) carrier at the voltage-controlled oscillator (VCO) output. The raised-power and Costas loops implement such closed-loop carrier recovery schemes using the PLL as a key element.

13.3.1 Raised-Power Loops

Raised-power loops utilize Mth-order nonlinearity to generate a spectral line at the harmonic frequency of the carrier embedded in the incoming signal. A PLL then generates the coherent carrier waveform by locking onto the harmonic of the carrier produced by the Mth-order nonlinearity. It also adaptively tracks and removes frequency/phase offsets between incoming and locally generated carrier waveforms. We begin our discussion with binary phase-shift keying (BPSK) signaling. We observed in Figure 11.54 that the BPSK signal does not contain a spectral line at the carrier frequency f_c. Figure 13.15 displays the block diagram of a squaring loop carrier synchronizer for BPSK systems. The BPSK signal can be written from (11.26) as

$$x(t) = A_c I(t) \cos(2\pi f_c t + \phi_o) \tag{13.3}$$

where $I(t) = \sum_{n=-\infty}^{\infty} a_n \Pi[(t - nT_b)/T_b]$ and $a_n \in \mathscr{A}_2 = \{1 - 1\}$ are binary random variables. ϕ_o is a slowly varying phase offset. Now if we apply a squaring operation to $x(t)$, we obtain

$$x^2(t) = A_c^2 I^2(t) \cos^2(2\pi f_c t + \phi_o) = A_c^2 \cos^2(2\pi f_c t + \phi_o)$$

$$= \frac{A_c^2}{2}[1 + \cos(4\pi f_c t + 2\phi_o)] \tag{13.4}$$

because $I^2(t) = 1$. It is clear from (13.4) that modulation of the BPSK signal has been removed; the squared signal contains a DC component and a pure sine wave at frequency $2f_c$. The input to the PLL phase detector is BP filter output $\frac{A_c^2}{2} \cos(4\pi f_c t + 2\phi_o)$ and the VCO-generated carrier signal. The VCO oscillates close to a frequency $2f_c$ and produces the output $-2\sin(4\pi f_c t + 2\hat{\phi}_o)$, which has its own slowly varying phase offset $\hat{\phi}_o$. The multiplication of this with the PLL input produces the phase difference signal $\frac{A_c^2}{2} \sin[2(\phi_o - \hat{\phi}_o)]$ plus some other higher-frequency terms, which are removed by the low-pass filter (LPF). This difference (or error) signal forces the VCO offset $\hat{\phi}_o$ to match the input signal offset ϕ_o so that the VCO output has the same frequency and phase as the incoming carrier signal. Observe that the PLL itself runs at twice

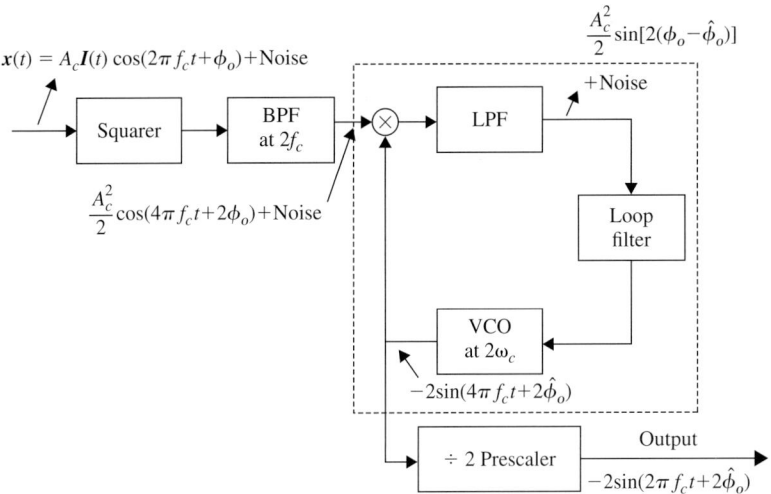

Figure 13.15 Squaring loop synchronizer.

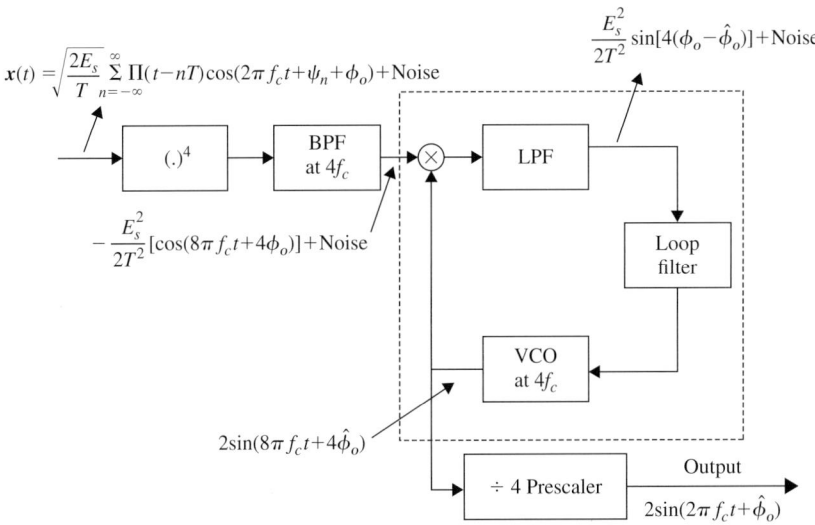

Figure 13.16 Quadrupling loop synchronizer.

the carrier frequency. The locally generated carrier is obtained as the output of a ÷ 2 frequency divider (called ÷ 2 **prescaler**).

Quadrupling Loop

The squaring loop synchronizer structure can be easily extended to more complex modulation schemes. For M-ary PSK signal sets, the squarer can be replaced with an Mth-law device, and the ÷ 2 prescaler can be replaced by a ÷ M prescaler. Figure 13.16 displays the fourth-power or quadrupling carrier recovery loop for a QPSK signal. We express the QPSK signal using (11.112) as

$$\boldsymbol{x}(t) = \sqrt{\frac{2E_s}{T}} \sum_{n=-\infty}^{\infty} \Pi(t - nT)\cos[2\pi f_c t + \boldsymbol{\psi}_n + \phi_o] \tag{13.5}$$

where the data-bearing phase ψ_n in the nth symbol period assumes one of the four values from the set $\left\{\psi_n = \dfrac{2\pi(i-1)}{4} + \dfrac{1}{4}\pi, i = 1, \ldots, 4\right\}$. The output of a fourth-power device during a symbol interval can be expressed as

$$
\begin{aligned}
x^4(t) &= \frac{4E_s^2}{T^2}\cos^4(2\pi f_c t + \psi_n + \phi_o) \\
&= \frac{4E_s^2}{T^2}\left\{\frac{3}{8} + \frac{1}{2}\cos(4\pi f_c t + 2\psi_n + 2\phi_o) + \frac{1}{8}\cos(8\pi f_c t + 4\psi_n + 4\phi_o)\right\} \\
&= \frac{4E_s^2}{T^2}\left\{\frac{3}{8} + \frac{1}{2}\cos(4\pi f_c t + 2\psi_n + 2\phi_o) + \frac{1}{8}\cos(8\pi f_c t + \pi + 4\phi_o)\right\} \\
&= \frac{4E_s^2}{T^2}\left\{\frac{3}{8} + \frac{1}{2}\cos(4\pi f_c t + 2\psi_n + 2\phi_o) - \frac{1}{8}\cos(8\pi f_c t + 4\phi_o)\right\}
\end{aligned}
\tag{13.6}
$$

From (13.6), we conclude that the output of the bandpass filter centered at $4f_c$ is a sinusoidal waveform at four times the carrier frequency. The input to PLL is, therefore, given by $-\dfrac{E_s^2}{2T^2}\{\cos(8\pi f_c t + 4\phi_o)\} + \text{noise}$. Note that a quadrupling operation followed by BP filtering has removed the modulation. The VCO oscillates close to a frequency $4f_c$ and produces the output $2\sin(8\pi f_c t + 4\hat{\phi}_o)$, which has its own slowly varying phase offset $\hat{\phi}_o$. The multiplication of this with the PLL input produces the phase difference signal $\dfrac{E_s^2}{2T^2}\sin\left[4(\phi_o - \hat{\phi}_o)\right]$ plus some other higher-frequency terms, which are removed by the LPF. The PLL attempts to force this difference (or error) signal to zero and in so doing matches its phase offset $4\hat{\phi}_o$ to the $4\phi_o$ offset of the incoming signal carrier. Because the VCO runs at $4f_c$, the locally generated carrier is obtained as output of the $\div\,4$ prescaler.

13.3.2 Costas Loop

Costas loop is the most common implementation of a closed-loop carrier recovery system when the received signal does not contain a spectral line at the carrier frequency. Figure 13.17 illustrates the block diagram of a Costas loop synchronizer. The upper branch signal $i(t)$ is obtained by multiplying the received BPSK signal $x(t)$ by the VCO output $2\cos(2\pi f_c t + \hat{\phi}_o)$ and low-pass filtering the output.

$$
\begin{aligned}
i(t) &= A_c I(t)\cos(2\pi f_c t + \phi_o) \times 2\cos(2\pi f_c t + \hat{\phi}_o) \\
&= A_c I(t)\big[\underbrace{\cos(4\pi f_c t + \phi_o + \hat{\phi}_o)}_{\text{filtered out by LPF}} + \cos(\phi_o - \hat{\phi}_o)\big] \\
&= A_c I(t)\cos(\phi_o - \hat{\phi}_o)
\end{aligned}
\tag{13.7}
$$

Similarly, the lower branch signal $q(t)$ is obtained by multiplying the input signal $x(t)$ by the output of quadrature carrier waveform $-2\sin(2\pi f_c t + \hat{\phi}_o)$ and low-pass filtering the output.

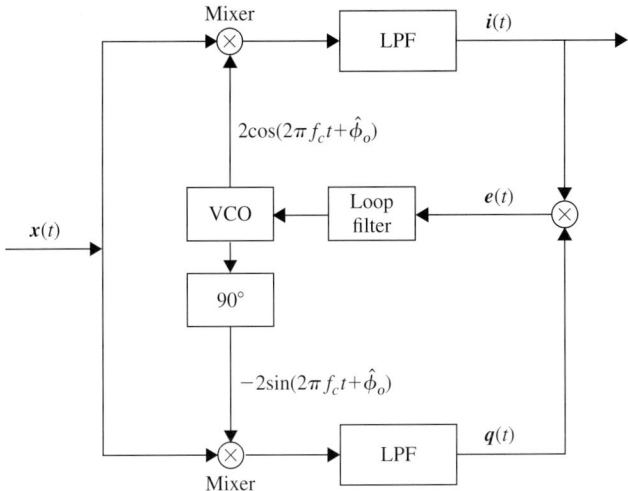

Figure 13.17 Costas loop.

$$q(t) = A_c \mathbf{I}(t)\cos(2\pi f_c t + \phi_o) \times -2\sin(2\pi f_c t + \hat{\phi}_o)$$

$$= A_c \mathbf{I}(t)\Big[\underbrace{-\sin(4\pi f_c t + \phi_o + \hat{\phi}_o)}_{\text{filtered out by LPF}} + \sin(\phi_o - \hat{\phi}_o)\Big]$$

$$= A_c \mathbf{I}(t)\sin(\phi_o - \hat{\phi}_o) \tag{13.8}$$

These two signals are multiplied to produce the error signal $e(t)$, which is given by

$$e(t) = A_c^2 \mathbf{I}^2(t)\big[\cos(\phi_o - \hat{\phi}_o)\sin(\phi_o - \hat{\phi}_o)\big] = \frac{A_c^2}{2}\mathbf{I}^2(t)\big\{\sin(0) + \sin[2(\phi_o - \hat{\phi}_o)]\big\}$$

$$= \frac{A_c^2}{2}\mathbf{I}^2(t)\sin(2\Delta\phi) = \frac{A_c^2}{2}\sin(2\Delta\phi) \tag{13.9}$$

where $\Delta\phi = \phi_o - \hat{\phi}_o$ denotes the phase difference between the incoming signal and VCO-generated carriers. Note that the BPSK signal modulation has been removed in the error signal $e(t)$ because $\mathbf{I}^2(t) = 1$. It easy to see that the error signal $e(t)$ plays the same role as the PLL control voltage in forcing the phase error between incoming and locally generated carriers to zero. Note that the upper branch output $i(t) = A_c\mathbf{I}(t)$ $\cos\Delta\phi \approx A_c\mathbf{I}(t)$ as $\Delta\phi \approx 0$, when the loop is phase-locked ($e(t) \approx 0$). That is, $i(t)$ is proportional to the underlying baseband data signal $\mathbf{I}(t)$ with additive noise and can be detected using a sampler and threshold comparator as discussed in Section 11.3. Thus, Costas loop not only provides a convenient mechanism for carrier recovery but also fully demodulates the received signal. Therefore, Costas loop is also called Costas demodulator or Costas receiver.

13.3.3   Effect of Noise on the Carrier Phase Estimation

Because the input signal in a communication receiver is always embedded in noise, the PLL adds jitter to the phase of the local VCO output in the process of tracking the incoming carrier phase. The design trade-offs involved in minimizing the effect of noise (i.e., phase error) versus the tracking capabilities of the PLL are considered here.

PLL Output Phase Jitter Variance

The input to the PLL is assumed to be an unmodulated carrier signal embedded in the narrowband white Gaussian noise as displayed in Figure 13.18.

$$r(t) = A_c \cos[2\pi f_c t + \phi_o] + n(t) \tag{13.10}$$

where ϕ_o is an input carrier phase. The narrowband white Gaussian noise $n(t)$ can be expanded in the quadrature components as

$$n(t) = n_c(t)\cos(2\pi f_c t) - n_s(t)\sin(2\pi f_c t) \tag{13.11}$$

$n_c(t)$ and $n_s(t)$ are lowpass Gaussian noise processes with mean zero and variance $N_o B$ where B is the bandwidth of $n(t)$. The input to PLL is multiplied with the VCO output $-\sin[2\pi f_c t + \hat{\phi}_o]$ and low-pass filtered. Note that the VCO phase $\hat{\phi}_o$ tracks random variations of the received carrier phase owing to the presence of noise at the PLL input. The PD output can now be written as

$$v_e(t) = K_{PD}\{r(t) \times -\sin[2\pi f_c t + \hat{\phi}_o]\}_{LP}$$

$$= K_{PD}\{[A_c \cos[2\pi f_c t + \phi_o] + n_c(t)\cos(2\pi f_c t) - n_s(t)\sin(2\pi f_c t)]$$

$$\times -\sin[2\pi f_c t + \hat{\phi}_o]\}_{LP} \tag{13.12}$$

where K_{PD} is PD gain constant. After simple trigonometric manipulations, (13.12) can be simplified to

$$v_e(t) = K_{PD}[\sin(\phi_o - \hat{\phi}_o) + n_1(t)] \tag{13.13}$$

where

$$n_1(t) = -\frac{n_c(t)}{A_c}\sin(\hat{\phi}_o) + \frac{n_s(t)}{A_c}\cos(\hat{\phi}_o) \tag{13.14}$$

To simplify our analysis, we assume that the VCO phase $\hat{\phi}_o$ is slowly varying compared with input noise $n(t)$. Under this condition, $n_1(t)$ is also Gaussian because it is the linear combination of $n_c(t)$ and $n_s(t)$. The spectral density of $n_1(t)$ is given by

$$G_{n_1}(f) = \frac{N_o}{A_c^2}, \ |f| \le \frac{B}{2} \tag{13.15}$$

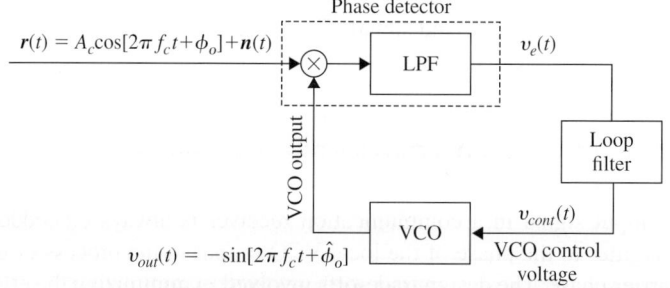

Figure 13.18 PLL with unmodulated carrier and narrowband white Gaussian noise input.

The variance of $n_1(t)$ is obtained from (13.15) as

$$\sigma_{n_1}^2 = \frac{N_o B}{A_c^2} \tag{13.16}$$

If the input noise is sufficiently small, the loop successfully tracks the input phase and the phase error $\phi_o - \hat{\phi}_o$ is small with probability ≈ 1. Under this condition, $\sin(\phi_o - \hat{\phi}_o) \approx \phi_o - \hat{\phi}_o$, and we can use the linear model of the PLL in the presence of noise as shown in Figure 13.19. Note that in this model the output of the second adder represents the phase error.

Because the PLL model in Figure 13.19 represents a linear system, we consider signal and noise components separately. This allows us to obtain the simplified noise model of the PLL as shown in Figure 13.20. So with just the noise input, the spectral density of the VCO output phase $G_{\hat{\phi}_o}(f)$ is related to the spectral density of $n_1(t)$ through the PLL phase transfer function $H(f)$. That is,

$$G_{\hat{\phi}_o}(f) = G_{n_1}(f)|H(f)|^2 \tag{13.17}$$

where from (5.92), we have

$$H(s) = \frac{KF(s)}{s + KF(s)}$$

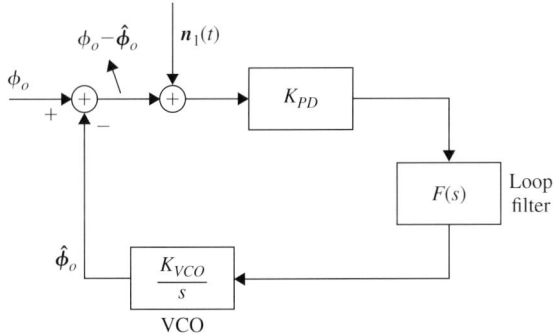

Figure 13.19 Linear model of PLL with noise.

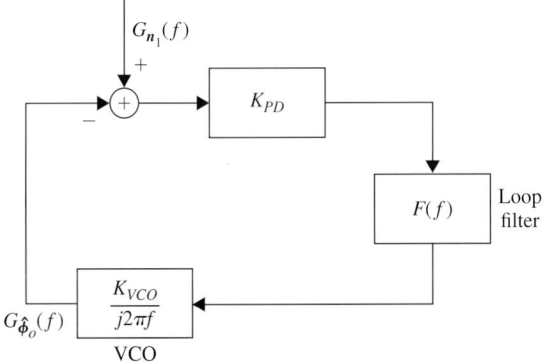

Figure 13.20 Equivalent noise model of PLL.

where K is an open-loop gain of the PLL and $F(s)$ is a transfer function of the loop filter. The variance of the VCO output phase $\hat{\boldsymbol{\phi}}_o$ is obtained from (13.17) as

$$
\sigma^2_{\boldsymbol{\phi}_o} = \int\limits_{-\infty}^{\infty} G_{\hat{\boldsymbol{\phi}}_o}(f)\,df = \int\limits_{-\infty}^{\infty} G_{\boldsymbol{n}_1}(f)|H(f)|^2 df
$$

$$
= \frac{N_o}{A_c^2} \int\limits_{-\infty}^{\infty} |H(f)|^2 df = \frac{2N_o}{A_c^2} \int\limits_{0}^{\infty} |H(f)|^2 df = \frac{2N_o B_N}{A_c^2} \tag{13.18}
$$

where B_N is the one-sided equivalent noise bandwidth of the PLL defined in (5.122). We note that the loop phase error variance is same as the variance of the VCO output phase $\hat{\boldsymbol{\phi}}_o$. In terms of SNR/symbol $\rho_L = \dfrac{E_s}{N_o} = \dfrac{A_c^2 T}{2N_o}$, $\sigma^2_{\hat{\phi}_o}$ can be expressed as

$$
\sigma^2_{\hat{\boldsymbol{\phi}}_o} = \frac{B_N T}{\rho_L} \tag{13.19}
$$

Thus the phase error variance $\sigma^2_{\hat{\phi}_o}$ is inversely proportional to the loop SNRρ_L. Decreasing the loop bandwidth B_N minimizes the phase error variance. Therefore, the phase error variance can be reduced by either increasing the loop SNR or decreasing its noise bandwidth. However, the second option is at the cost of the PLL's ability to track an incoming signal's phase variation. A large value of the loop bandwidth increases the tracking range of the loop. The optimum choice of loop bandwidth ensures that the VCO adequately tracks the signal phase changes while not being overly responsive to noise-induced perturbations.

13.3.4 Effect of Noise on the Performance of Carrier Synchronizers

We first consider the squaring loop and analyze the effect of noise on the VCO output phase jitter. The output of the squarer in the presence of narrowband white Gaussian noise is given by

$$
\begin{aligned}
x^2(t) &= [A_c\boldsymbol{I}(t) + \boldsymbol{n}_c(t)]^2\cos^2(2\pi f_c t + \phi_o) + \boldsymbol{n}_s^2(t)\sin^2(2\pi f_c t + \phi_o) \\
&\quad -2[A_c\boldsymbol{I}(t) + \boldsymbol{n}_c(t)]\boldsymbol{n}_s(t)\cos(2\pi f_c t + \phi_o)\sin(2\pi f_c t + \phi_o) \\
&= [A_c\boldsymbol{I}(t) + \boldsymbol{n}_c(t)]^2\left[\frac{1}{2} + \frac{1}{2}\cos(4\pi f_c t + 2\phi_o)\right] + \boldsymbol{n}_s^2(t)\left[\frac{1}{2} - \frac{1}{2}\cos(4\pi f_c t + 2\phi_o)\right] \\
&\quad -[A_c\boldsymbol{I}(t) + \boldsymbol{n}_c(t)]\boldsymbol{n}_s(t)\sin(4\pi f_c t + 2\phi_o)
\end{aligned} \tag{13.20}
$$

As illustrated in Figure 13.15, the input to the PLL is output of the BPF which retains components in (13.20) centered around the frequency $2f_c$. That is,

$$
\begin{aligned}
x^2(t)|_{BPF} &= \frac{[A_c\boldsymbol{I}(t) + \boldsymbol{n}_c(t)]^2}{2}\cos(4\pi f_c t + 2\phi_o) - \frac{\boldsymbol{n}_s^2(t)}{2}\cos(4\pi f_c t + 2\phi_o) \\
&\quad -[A_c\boldsymbol{I}(t) + \boldsymbol{n}_c(t)]\boldsymbol{n}_s(t)\sin(4\pi f_c t + 2\phi_o)
\end{aligned} \tag{13.21}
$$

The PLL input in (13.21) is multiplied with the VCO output $-2\sin(4\pi f_c t + 2\hat{\boldsymbol{\phi}}_o)$ and then LP filtered to remove the sum-frequency terms. Thus we can express the PD output as

$$
\begin{aligned}
\{x^2(t)|_{BPF} \times -2\sin(4\pi f_c t + 2\hat{\boldsymbol{\phi}}_o)\}_{LP} = &\underbrace{-[A_c \boldsymbol{I}(t) + \boldsymbol{n}_c(t)]^2 \cos(4\pi f_c t + 2\phi_o)\sin(4\pi f_c t + 2\hat{\boldsymbol{\phi}}_o)}_{\sin(8\pi f_c t + 2\phi_o + 2\hat{\boldsymbol{\phi}}_o) \text{ term filtered out}} \\
&\underbrace{+\boldsymbol{n}_s^2(t)\cos(4\pi f_c t + 2\phi_o)\sin(4\pi f_c t + 2\hat{\boldsymbol{\phi}}_o)}_{\sin(8\pi f_c t + 2\phi_o + 2\hat{\boldsymbol{\phi}}_o) \text{ term filtered out}} \\
&\underbrace{+2[A_c \boldsymbol{I}(t) + \boldsymbol{n}_c(t)]\boldsymbol{n}_s(t)\sin(4\pi f_c t + \phi_o)\sin(4\pi f_c t + 2\hat{\boldsymbol{\phi}}_o)}_{\cos(8\pi f_c t + 2\phi_o + 2\hat{\boldsymbol{\phi}}_o) \text{ term filtered out}} \\
= &\frac{1}{2}\left[A_c^2 + 2A_c \boldsymbol{I}(t)\boldsymbol{n}_c(t) + \boldsymbol{n}_c^2(t) - \boldsymbol{n}_s^2(t)\right]\sin\left[2(\phi_o - \hat{\boldsymbol{\phi}}_o)\right] \\
&+ \left[A_c \boldsymbol{I}(t)\boldsymbol{n}_s(t) + \boldsymbol{n}_c(t)\boldsymbol{n}_s(t)\right]\cos\left[2(\phi_o - \hat{\boldsymbol{\phi}}_o)\right]
\end{aligned}
\tag{13.22}
$$

The term $\dfrac{A_c^2}{2}\sin[2(\phi_o - \hat{\boldsymbol{\phi}}_o)]$ in (13.22) is the desired error signal term which forces the VCO phase offset $\hat{\boldsymbol{\phi}}_o$ to match the input signal offset ϕ_o. Other terms on the right-hand side of (13.22) represent the noise $\times$ signal and noise $\times$ noise distortion. These noise terms cause jitter in the VCO output phase. For a squaring loop, the resultant phase error variance $\sigma_{\hat{\phi}_o}^2$ is given by[1]

$$
\sigma_{\hat{\phi}_o}^2 = \frac{B_N T}{S_L \rho_L}
\tag{13.23}
$$

where S_L is called the **squaring loss** and is given by

$$
S_L = \frac{1}{1 + \dfrac{0.5}{\rho_L}}
\tag{13.24}
$$

Note that $S_L < 1$. As such, the squaring loss term in (13.24) accounts for the increase in the loop phase error variance as a result of noise $\times$ signal and noise $\times$ noise components generated in the process of squaring operation.

If a Costas loop is used to recover the carrier phase in a BPSK system, the variance of the loop phase error is also given by (13.23) provided that the loop filter is identical to that used in the squaring loop. For QPSK signaling, the squaring loss for the quadrupling loop is given by[2]

$$
S_L = \frac{1}{1 + \left[\dfrac{4.5}{\rho_L} + \dfrac{6}{\rho_L^2} + \dfrac{1.5}{\rho_L^3}\right]}
\tag{13.25}
$$

[1] J. Stiffler, *Theory of Synchronous Communications* (Upper Saddle River, NJ: Prentice Hall, 1971).

[2] Stiffler, *Theory of Synchronous Communications*.

Table 13.4 Tracking Performance of Various Carrier Recovery Loops

Carrier Recovery Loop	Squaring Loss S_L	Loop Phase Error Variance $\sigma^2_{\hat{\phi}_o}$	Comment
PLL	Not applicable	$\sigma^2_{\hat{\phi}_o} = \dfrac{B_N T}{\rho_L}$	Phase error due to BP AWGN
Squaring loop Costas loop	$S_L = \dfrac{1}{1 + \dfrac{0.5}{\rho_L}}$	$\sigma^2_{\hat{\phi}_o} = \dfrac{B_N T}{S_L \rho_L}$	BPSK signaling; Phase error due to BP AWGN
Quadrupling loop	$S_L = \dfrac{1}{1 + \left[\dfrac{4.5}{\rho_L} + \dfrac{6}{\rho_L^2} + \dfrac{1.5}{\rho_L^3}\right]}$	$\sigma^2_{\hat{\phi}_o} = \dfrac{B_N T}{S_L \rho_L}$	QPSK signaling; Phase error due to BP AWGN

Table 13.4 summarizes the tracking performance of different carrier recovery loops for BPSK and QPSK signaling.

Example 13.5

Consider the squaring loop carrier acquisition circuit for a BPSK system with following parameters:

Bit rate = 1 Mbps
Loop filter noise bandwidth B_N = 50 kHz
Loop SNRρ_L = 10 dB

a. Calculate the squaring loss.
b. Calculate the loop phase error variance.

Solution

a. The squaring loss is

$$S_L = \frac{1}{1 + \dfrac{0.5}{\rho_L}} = \frac{1}{1 + \dfrac{0.5}{10}} = \frac{1}{1 + 0.05} = \frac{1}{1.05} = 0.952$$

b. The loop phase error variance is

$$\sigma^2_{\hat{\phi}_o} = \frac{B_N T}{S_L \rho_L} = \frac{5 \times 10^3 \times 1 \times 10^{-6}}{0.952 \times 10} = 5.25 \times 10^{-4} \text{ rad}^2$$

Example 13.6

Consider the squaring loop carrier acquisition circuit for a BPSK system with the following parameters:

Bit rate = 1.2 kbps
Loop SNR ρ_L = 10 dB

Assuming that the carrier frequency of the received signal undergoes transients of ± 200 Hz, design a two-pole PLL so that the total loop phase error does not exceed 0.5 radians after $\div 2$ prescaler.

Solution

The phase error is made of two parts:

a. Phase error due to AWGN
b. Steady-state phase error due to frequency step of ± 200 Hz

The phase error variance due to AWGN is obtained from (13.23) as

$$\sigma_{\hat{\phi}_o}^2 = \frac{B_N T}{S_L \rho_L} = \frac{B_N T}{0.952 \times 10} = 0.105 B_N T \ \text{rad}^2$$

$$\text{RMS phase error} = \sigma_{\hat{\phi}_o} = 0.324 \sqrt{B_N T} \ \text{rad} \tag{13.26}$$

The steady-state phase error $\theta_e(\infty)$ of a two-pole PLL due to a frequency-step $\Delta\omega$ is given from Table 5.5 as

$$\theta_e(\infty) = \frac{\Delta\omega}{K} \tag{13.27}$$

For the two-pole PLL, we note the following relationship between K, ζ, and ω_n from Table 5.4:

$$K = \frac{\omega_n}{2\zeta} \tag{13.28}$$

Substituting (13.28) into (13.27) yields

$$\theta_e(\infty) = \frac{2\zeta \Delta\omega}{\omega_n} \tag{13.29}$$

The noise bandwidth of the two-pole PLL is given from Table 5.4 as

$$B_N = \frac{\omega_n}{8\zeta} \tag{13.30}$$

Substituting (13.30) into (13.29), the steady-state phase error $\theta_e(\infty)$ can be expressed in terms of $B_N T$ product as

$$\theta_e(\infty) = \frac{\Delta\omega}{4B_N} = \frac{\Delta\omega T}{4B_N T} \tag{13.31}$$

In the present example, $\Delta\omega T = \frac{2\pi(\pm 200)}{1200} = \pm\frac{\pi}{3}$ rad/symbol. However, because of the squaring operation, the PLL has to deal with twice this value, that is, $\pm\frac{2\pi}{3}$ rad/symbol.

Therefore, the steady-state phase error at the VCO output is given by

$$\theta_e(\infty) = \frac{2\pi/3}{4B_N T} = \frac{\pi}{6B_N T} \tag{13.32}$$

A reasonable estimate[3] of the total phase error is the sum of the two errors given by (13.26) and (13.32). Because the phase error at the prescaler output is not to exceed 0.5 radian, the

[3] J. Anderson, *Digital Transmission Engineering,* 2nd ed. (Hoboken, NJ: Wiley-Interscience, 2005).

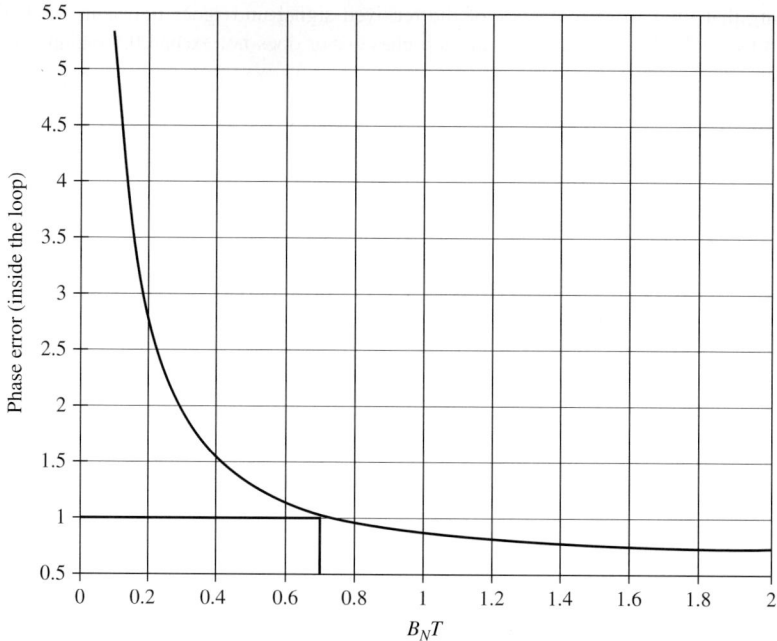

Figure 13.21 Total phase error versus $B_N T$.

corresponding error inside the loop should be less than 1 radian. Therefore, we want to find $B_N T$ value such that total phase error

$$0.324\sqrt{B_N T} + \frac{\pi}{6B_N T} \le 1.0 \qquad (13.33)$$

A plot of total phase error in (13.33) versus $B_N T$ is shown in Figure 13.21. We can observe that the choice of $B_N T \ge 0.72$ will result in the total phase error to be ≤ 1 rad. We choose damping constant $\zeta = 1$ to prevent an overshoot of the phase error. From Table 5.4, we obtain

$$\omega_n = 8\zeta B_N = 8 \times 1 \times 0.72 \times 1.2 \times 10^3 = 6.912 \times 10^3 \text{ radians/sec}$$

The closed-loop transfer function of the PLL is given from Table 5.4 as

$$H(s) = \frac{\omega_n^2}{s^2 + 2s\zeta\omega_n + \omega_n^2} = \frac{47.776 \times 10^6}{s^2 + 2s \times 6.912 \times 10^3 + 47.776 \times 10^6}$$

From Table 5.4, the open loop gain K and time-constant τ_1 are given by

$$K = 4B_N = 4 \times 0.72 \times 1.2 \times 10^3 = 3.456 \times 10^3$$

$$\tau_1 = \frac{1}{4K\zeta^2} = \frac{1}{4 \times 3.456 \times 10^3} = 72 \ \mu\text{sec}$$

The loop filter is given by

$$F(s) = \frac{K}{1 + \tau_1 s} = \frac{3.456 \times 10^3}{1 + 72 \times 10^{-6}s}$$

Figure 13.22 displays a possible implementation of the PLL loop filter.

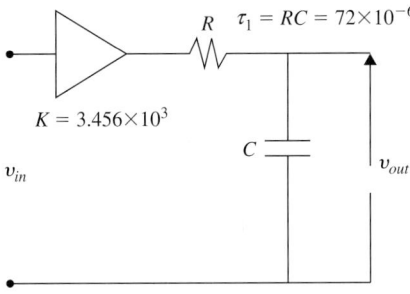

Figure 13.22 Loop filter for two-pole PLL.

13.4 SYMBOL SYNCHRONIZATION

The most important advantage of a digital transmission system is its ability to reconstruct the transmitted digital signal almost perfectly even after it has been impaired by the transmission medium (attenuation + distortion) and noise. The process of reconstruction involves three basic functions:

1. Filtering (matched filter or correlator) and/or equalization
2. Clock recovery
3. Regeneration

Figure 13.23 illustrates these functions in a digital communications receiver.

As discussed in Chapters 10 through 12, the MF/equalizer block optimally receives and reshapes (i.e., equalizes) incoming pulses so that a decision can be made about the transmitted symbols. The decisions are made based on the samples produced by periodically sampling the reshaped pulses at the symbol rate. To perform the periodic sampling, a clock signal is required at the receiver. A **clock** or **timing signal** is a signal that alternates between a logical high and a logical low value, normally with a 50% duty cycle, and is usually in the form of a square wave as illustrated in Figure 13.24.

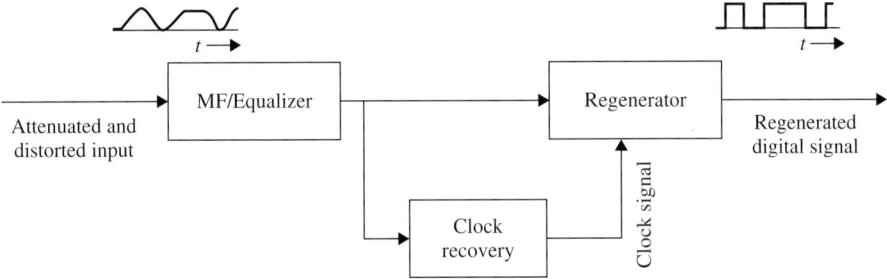

Figure 13.23 Reconstruction in a digital communications receiver.

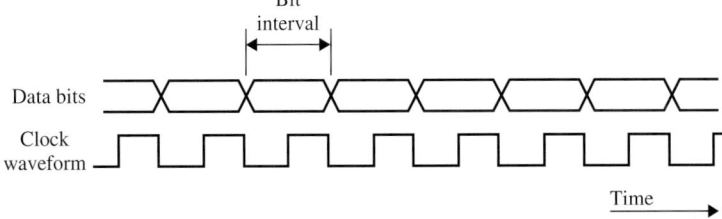

Figure 13.24 Digital signal and its associated clock.

The frequency of the square wave is called the **clock frequency** or **speed.** The process of extracting such a clock signal from the random data is called **symbol timing synchronization** (also called **symbol clock recovery**). The circuit block in the digital communications receiver which recovers clock from the reshaped pulses is called the **clock recovery circuit (CRC).** Symbol clock recovery is relatively independent of the carrier phase recovery, and it is usually obtained from the demodulated baseband signal. Symbol clock recovery is one of the most critical functions performed at the receiver of a synchronous digital communication system.

For optimum error performance, it is important that the frequency of the recovered clock tracks not only the symbol rate, but also where the waveform is sampled within each symbol interval. The choice of sampling instant τ_o within the symbol interval of duration T is called the **timing phase.** It is obvious from the eye diagram in Figure 13.25 that the best timing phase corresponds to the time instant within the symbol interval where the eye opening is a maximum. In a practical communication system, the receiver clock must be continuously adjusted in frequency and in timing phase τ_o to compensate for frequency drifts between the oscillators used in the transmitter clock generation and receiver clock recovery circuits and, thus, to optimize the sampling time instants of the receiving filter output. In practice, a repeating feature in the clock pulses, such as a rising edge, marks the sampling instants.

The regenerator consists of a threshold comparator followed by a pulse generator. The threshold comparator samples reshaped pulses at time instants defined by the clock signal (e.g., at rising edges). The pulse generator will produce a clean pulse whenever the magnitude of the reshaped pulse sample exceeds the threshold. The width of the regenerated pulse is controlled by the clock signal.

13.4.1   Clock Recovery from NRZ Data

Binary data is commonly transmitted in the NRZ format because of its bandwidth efficiency compared to RZ signaling. Two characteristics of NRZ data make clock recovery difficult:

*   The data may exhibit long strings of 1's or 0's. Under this condition, the CRC must not only continue to produce the clock signal, but also incur acceptable variation or drift in the clock frequency.

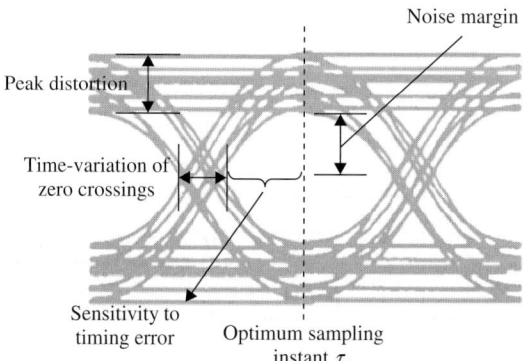

Figure 13.25 Optimum sampling point.

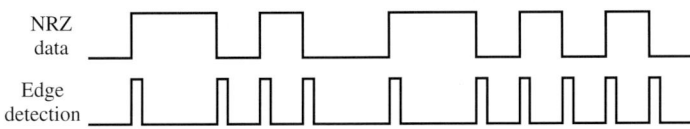

Figure 13.26 Edge detection.

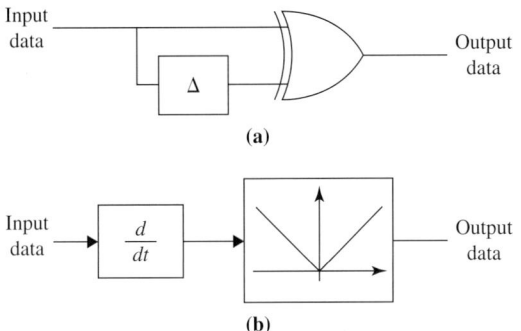

Figure 13.27 Edge detectors.

- As illustrated in Figure 9.6, NRZ data contains spectral nulls at frequencies that are integer multiples of the bit rate R_b. For example, the spectrum of an OC-48 SONET signal with a bit rate of 2.488 Gbps has no discrete spectral component at 2.488 GHz.

Owing to the absence of a discrete spectral line at the bit rate in the NRZ format, nonlinear processing is required to create a frequency component at R_b. This is accomplished by detecting the rising and falling edge ("transition") of each pulse in the data signal and generating a pulse corresponding to it, as displayed in Figure 13.26. This is called **edge detection.** The edge detector can be implemented by an XOR gate with a delay on one input as shown in Figure 13.27(a). Alternatively, it can be realized using a differentiator followed by a full-wave rectifier as illustrated in Figure 13.27(b).

The edge detector can be implemented by an XOR gate with a delay on one input as shown in Figure 13.27(a). Alternatively, it can be realized using a differentiator by a full-wave rectifier as illustrated in Figure 13.27(b).

It can be concluded from the preceding discussion that a CRC should have the following key functional blocks:

- Edge detector that generates pulses corresponding to input data transitions.
- An oscillator circuit that generates a periodic output pulse stream at a frequency that converges to the input symbol rate but incurs negligible drift when some data transitions are missing.

Figure 13.28 shows a conceptual realization of a CRC where an edge detector output drives a high-Q oscillator that continues to oscillate in the absence of data transitions. In practice, a PLL is used as an oscillator synchronized with input data transitions. Because the PLL is a closed-loop feedback system, it constantly tracks slowly varying changes in the symbol rate of the incoming data.

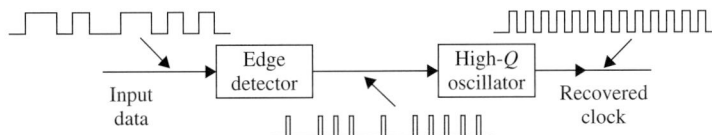

Figure 13.28 Conceptual implementation of CRC.

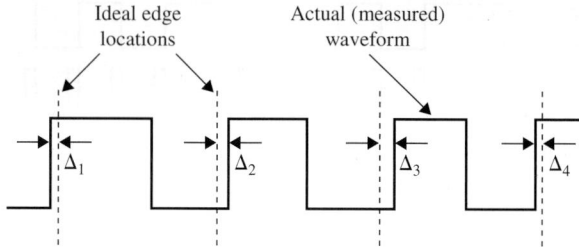

Figure 13.29 Definition of jitter.

Jitter

In practice, timing edges of the recovered clock signal deviate from their ideal locations as displayed in Figure 13.29. This is called **jitter.** Generally, output jitter of a CRC based on the PLL technique can be caused by two kinds of sources: (1) additive noise that accompanies the input signal and (2) noise generated in the CRC (e.g., due to VCO phase fluctuations). Jitter in the clock signal, in turn, causes jitter in the reconstructed signal. Although jitter can be measured in several ways (e.g., peak-peak, RMS), **time interval error (TIE)** representation of the jitter is widely used in practice. TIE expresses the deviation in time between the actual clock and an ideal clock with the same frequency. Either a falling (or rising) edge of signals can be used for measurement. Figure 13.30 displays the piecewise linear plot of TIE versus time (in clock periods). Note that in this example, TIE is initially zero and the actual clock's rising edge is at its ideal position. However, TIE decreases linearly as the actual rising edge leads the ideal rising edge until the error reaches a negative peak value of -11 ps. Then the error decreases in linear fashion until it becomes zero (ideal and actual edge areas aligned). Next, the actual edge lags the ideal as TIE increases linearly, reaching a positive peak value of 11 ps. This TIE pattern is repeated. The TIE waveform in Figure 13.30 represents a jitter model that introduces 22 ps peak-to-peak error.

13.4.2   PLL for Clock Recovery

As discussed in Section 5.5, a PLL consists of a phase detector, a low-pass filter, and a voltage-controlled oscillator (VCO) as illustrated in Figure 13.31. However, the components of a PLL for extracting the clock from random data bits have somewhat different operating characteristics:

The basic requirement of a PD is to produce an output signal that is proportional to the difference between the phases of two input signals. Because input to the PLL consists of two digital signals, an XOR gate can be used as the PD. The transfer characteristic of

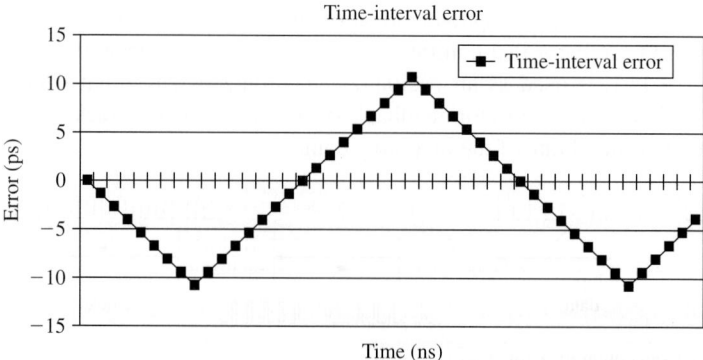

Figure 13.30 Time interval error.

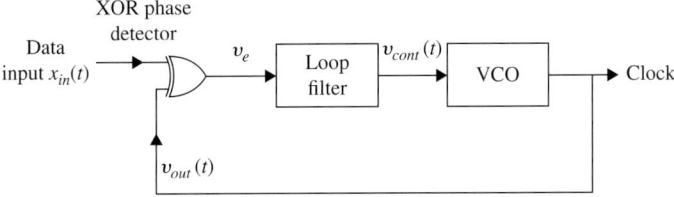

Figure 13.31 PLL for clock recovery.

the XOR gate as a PD is displayed in Figure 13.32(a). Note that the PD output $v_e = 0$ if the input digital signal $x_{in}(t)$ and the VCO output $v_{out}(t)$ are in phase (that is, phase difference $\theta_e = 0$), and that it reaches the maximum value $K_{PD}\pi$ when the two signals are exactly out of phase ($\theta_e = \pi$). It is easy to see from Figure 13.32(a) that for $\theta_e < \pi$, v_e increases, and for $\theta_e > \pi$, v_e decreases. Of course, the characteristic is periodic in θ_e with period 2π. The range $0 \leq \theta_e \leq \pi$ is the range where the PLL can operate in the locked condition. Figure 13.32(b) illustrates the operation of the XOR PD when the PLL is in the locked condition. The digital signals $x_{in}(t)$ and $v_{out}(t)$ are two 50% duty cycle, phase-shifted periodic square-wave signals at the same frequency $f_{in} = f_{out} = 1/T$. The output of the PD is a periodic square-wave signal $v_e(t)$ at the frequency $2f_{in}$, and with the duty cycle D_{θ_e} that depends on the phase difference θ_e between $x_{in}(t)$ and $v_{out}(t)$.

$$D_{\theta_e} = \frac{\theta_e}{\pi}$$

The operation of the PLL can now be summarized as follows. Suppose that initially there is no incoming signal at all, $x_{in}(t) = 0$. The VCO output $v_{out}(t)$ is a square-wave signal with 50% duty cycle. For $x_{in}(t) = 0$, the output of the XOR PD is exactly the same

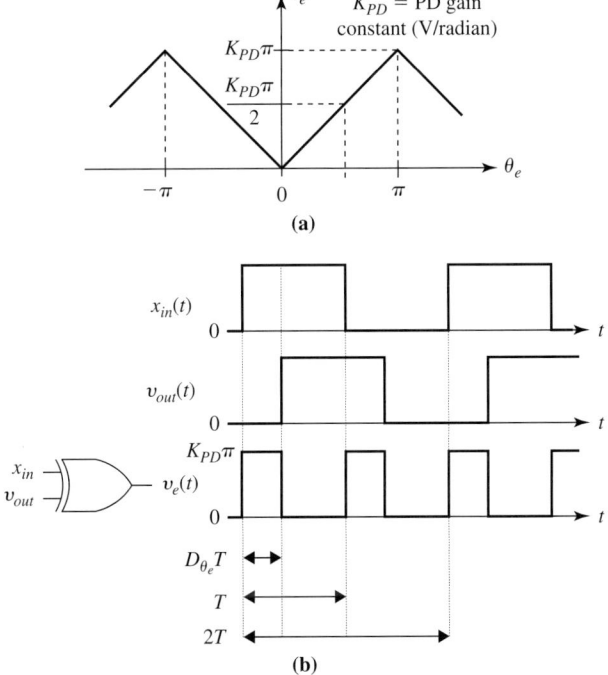

Figure 13.32 XOR detector: (a) transfer characteristic; (b) operation.

as the VCO output. That is, $v_e(t) = v_{out}(t)$. The LP loop filter attenuates AC components of $v_e(t)$ so that the filter output is approximately equal to the DC component of $v_e(t)$. In this case, the DC component is equal to $\dfrac{K_{PD}\pi}{2}$ because $v_e(t)$ is $K_{PD}\pi$ for one-half of the period and 0 for the other half of the period. The filter output voltage $v_{cont}(t)$ is input to the VCO. Therefore, we conclude that the VCO operates at the frequency that corresponds to the voltage $v_{cont}(t) = \dfrac{K_{PD}\pi}{2}$ at the VCO input. That is, $f_{out} = f_o$, where f_o is the free-running frequency of the PLL. Suppose now that the incoming signal $x_{in}(t)$ at frequency f_{in} is applied to one of the two inputs of the XOR PD. If the frequency f_{in} is sufficiently close to the free-running frequency f_o, (that is, within the capture range of the PLL), the PLL will lock onto the incoming signal. During the acquisition process, the phase difference between $x_{in}(t)$ and $v_{out}(t)$ and therefore $v_{cont}(t)$ varies with time, until it reaches the value required to lock the VCO frequency f_{out} to the frequency f_{in} of the incoming signal. In the locked condition, $f_{out} = f_{in}$, and $x_{in}(t)$ and $v_{out}(t)$ are phase shifted by some value θ_e between 0 and π. The phase difference θ_e between $x_{in}(t)$ and $v_{out}(t)$ depends on the value of the incoming signal frequency f_{in}. If $f_{in} = f_o$, the phase difference must be exactly $\theta_e = \pi/2$ so that $v_e = \dfrac{K_{PD}\pi}{2}$, from Figure 13.32(a) and the VCO indeed operates at f_o. If, for example, $f_{in} = f_{\max}$, where $f_{\max}$ is maximum frequency in the capture range of the PLL, the phase difference θ_e must be equal to π in order to obtain $v_e = K_{PD}\pi$ that results in the VCO output frequency equal to $f_{\max}$. It is important to note here that in order to keep $f_{out} = f_{in}$ in the locked condition, the filter output voltage $v_{cont}(t)$ must track the frequency f_{in} of the incoming signal. Therefore, a change in f_{in} causes a proportional change in $v_{cont}(t)$, as long as the PLL stays in the locked condition with $f_{out} = f_{in}$.

PLL Design

From Section 5.5, if an active lead-lag LP filter with the transfer function

$$F(s) = \frac{1 + s\tau_2}{1 + s\tau_1} \tag{13.34}$$

is used as a loop filter, the phase transfer function of the resulting second-order PLL is given from Table 5.4 as

$$H(s) = \frac{\omega_n^2 + s\left(2\zeta\omega_n - \dfrac{\omega_n^2}{K}\right)}{s^2 + 2s\zeta\omega_n + \omega_n^2} \tag{13.35}$$

where

$$K = K_{VCO}K_{PD} = \text{open-loop gain} \tag{13.36}$$

$$\omega_n = \sqrt{\frac{K}{\tau_1}} = \text{natural frequency} \tag{13.37}$$

$$\zeta = \frac{1}{2}\omega_n\left(\tau_2 + \frac{1}{K}\right) = \text{damping factor} \tag{13.38}$$

The choice of PLL parameters K, ω_n, and ζ affects its performance as a clock recovery circuit (CRC). We follow the design method described in Kishine[4] for determining the parameters of a PLL-based CRC. The **jitter transfer function** of a CRC is a key design requirement. It represents the output jitter as the input jitter is varied at different rates. This characteristic is indeed the same as the phase transfer function (13.35) of the PLL. We expect that if the input jitter varies slowly, that is, if the edges wander from the ideal locations slowly, then the output tracks the input. On the other hand, if the input jitter varies rapidly, the CRC must filter the jitter, that is, the output must follow the input to a lesser extent. Thus, the jitter transfer exhibits an LP characteristic, as is the case with PLLs. The magnitude of jitter transfer function (13.35) can be expressed in terms of $Z_w \triangleq \zeta\omega_n$ as

$$|H(j\omega)| = \sqrt{\frac{(Z_w/\zeta)^2 + 4(Z_w\omega)^2}{[(Z_w/\zeta)^2 - \omega^2]^2 + 4(Z_w\omega)^2}} \qquad (13.39)$$

where we have assumed that $2\zeta\omega_n > > \dfrac{\omega_n^2}{K}$, that is, $\dfrac{\omega_n^2}{K} \cong 0$. At $\omega = \omega_n$

$$|H(j\omega)|_{\omega=\omega_n} = \sqrt{1 + \frac{1}{4\zeta^2}} \qquad (13.40)$$

Equation (13.40) describes ζ dependence of the peaking characteristics of the jitter transfer function. In the case of backbone telecommunications networks, many digital regenerators or repeaters may be cascaded in order to transport information over long distances. Jitter, introduced by the CRC during the regeneration of data at each repeater, accumulates when a digital signal traverses over a cascade of repeaters in the long-haul transmission system. The variance of the accumulated timing jitter is directly proportional to the number of repeaters in the cascade. So the longer the cascade, the more jitter is accumulated. In order to keep the jitter from growing exponentially as the number of digital repeaters in the cascade increases, it is recommended that jitter peaking be lower than 0.1 dB. That is,

$$20\log_{10}|H(j\omega)|_{\omega=\omega_n} = 20\log_{10}\sqrt{1 + \frac{1}{4\zeta^2}} < 0.1 \qquad (13.41)$$

Solving for ζ, we obtain

$$\zeta > 4.6 \qquad (13.42)$$

In practice, damping factor values in the range of $\zeta = 4 - 10$ are used.[5] With the minimum value of $\zeta = 4.6$, the jitter transfer function for various values of Z_w is displayed in Figure 13.33. For comparison, we have also plotted the jitter transfer function template for SONET OC-48 stipulated in ITU-T recommendation G.783. As illustrated, in order to meet the specification, $Z_w \leq 6$ MHz has to be implemented.

---

[4] K. Kishine, K. Ishii, and H. Ichino, "Loop-Parameter Optimization of a PLL for a Low-jitter 2.5-Gbps One-chip Optical Receiver IC with 1:8 DEMUX," *IEEE Journal on Solid-state Circuits*-1 (2002): 38–50.

[5] Members of Technical Staff, Bell Telephone Laboratories, *Transmission Systems for Communications,* 5th ed., Bell Telephone Laboratories, 1982.

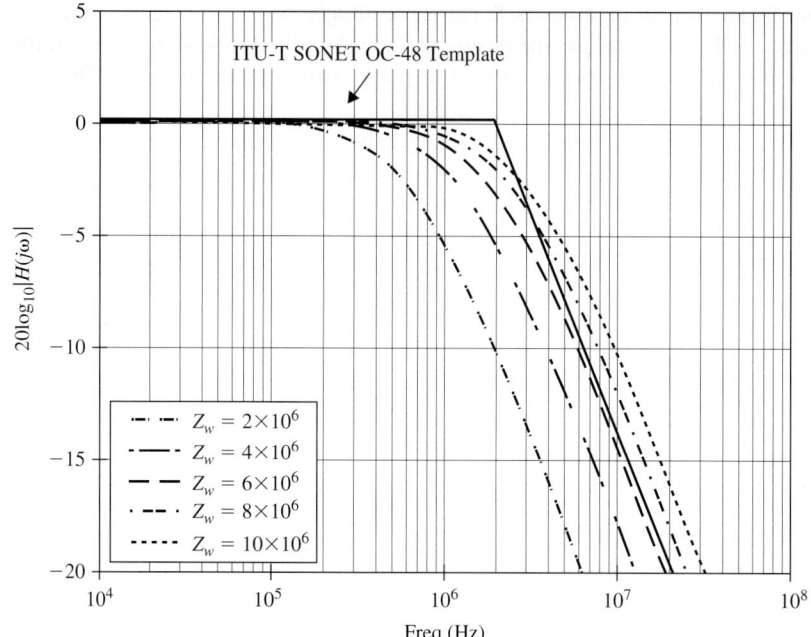

Figure 13.33 Dependence of jitter transfer curve on Z_w.

From Table 5.4, the noise bandwidth B_N of an active lead-lag PLL is given by

$$B_N = \frac{\omega_n}{8\zeta}\left[1 + \left(2\zeta - \frac{\omega_n}{K}\right)^2\right]$$

$$= \frac{\omega_n}{8\zeta}(1 + 4\zeta^2) \quad \text{for } K >> \omega_n \tag{13.43}$$

For values of ζ specified by (13.42), we obtain the following expression for B_N:

$$B_N \approx \frac{\zeta\omega_n}{2} = \frac{Z_w}{2}$$

or

$$Z_w = 2B_N \tag{13.44}$$

Thus jitter transfer function specification set a lower limit on ζ and an upper limit on Z_w (that is, twice the noise bandwidth of the PLL). Next we derive the relationship between PLL parameters K, ω_n, and ζ and loop filter parameters τ_1 and τ_2. Multiplying both sides of (13.38) by ω_n, we obtain

$$Z_w = \zeta\omega_n = \frac{1}{2}\omega_n^2\left(\tau_2 + \frac{1}{K}\right)$$

$$\cong \frac{1}{2}\omega_n^2\tau_2 \quad \text{when } \tau_2 >> \frac{1}{K} \tag{13.45}$$

Substituting (13.37) into (13.45) yields

$$Z_w = \frac{K}{2}\frac{\tau_2}{\tau_1}$$

or

$$K = 2Z_w \frac{\tau_1}{\tau_2} \tag{13.46}$$

Multiplying both sides of (13.45) by ζ^2, ζ can be expressed in terms of loop filter constant τ_2 as

$$\zeta^2 Z_w = \frac{1}{2}\zeta^2 \omega_n^2 \tau_2 = \frac{1}{2}Z_w^2 \tau_2$$

or

$$\zeta = \sqrt{\frac{Z_w \tau_2}{2}} \tag{13.47}$$

Because the lower limit on ζ and Z_w are fixed, the loop filter constant τ_2 for SONET OC-48 PLL design is obtained from (13.47) as

$$\tau_2 = \frac{2\zeta^2}{Z_w} > \frac{2 \times 4.6^2}{6 \times 10^6} = 7.05 \ \mu sec$$

The capture (pull-in) range of a PLL is given by[6]

$$\Delta \omega_P = K\sqrt{2F(0)F(\infty)} \tag{13.48}$$

For lead-lag filter in (13.34), we have

$$F(0) = 1$$

$$F(\infty) = \frac{\tau_2}{\tau_1} \tag{13.49}$$

Substituting (13.46) and (13.49) into (13.48), the capture range of the PLL can be expressed as

$$\Delta \omega_P = 2Z_w \frac{\tau_1}{\tau_2}\sqrt{2\frac{\tau_2}{\tau_1}} = 2\sqrt{2}Z_w \sqrt{\frac{\tau_1}{\tau_2}} \tag{13.50}$$

Equation (13.50) states that the capture range of the PLL can be increased by making $\dfrac{\tau_1}{\tau_2}$ as large as possible, because Z_w is fixed based on jitter transfer considerations. The ratio $\dfrac{\tau_1}{\tau_2}$ is, however, limited by (13.46), because the open-loop gain K is limited by the technology and circuit design constraints. Using a value of $K = 2 \times 10^8$ Hz/s, we obtain

$$\frac{\tau_1}{\tau_2} = \frac{K}{2Z_w} = \frac{2 \times 10^8}{2 \times 6 \times 10^6} = \frac{100}{6} = 16.67$$

Therefore, if we choose $\tau_2 = 8 \ \mu sec$, $\tau_1 = 16.67\tau_2 \approx 135 \ \mu sec$.

---

[6] F. Gardner, *Phaselock Techniques*, 3rd ed., (Hoboken, NJ: Wiley-Interscience, 2005).

Experiment 13.1 *SONET OC-48 Clock and Data Recovery Using PLL*

In this experiment, we model the **clock and data recovery (CDR)** circuit for SONET OC-48 (2.488 Gbps) receiver using Simulink. Figure 13.34 illustrates the Simulink model for the system. We assume the following PLL simulation parameters:

$$\tau_2 = 8\ \mu\text{sec} \tag{13.51}$$

$$\tau_1 = 135\ \mu\text{sec} \tag{13.52}$$

$$K = 2 \times 10^8\ \text{Hz/s} \tag{13.53}$$

Substituting (13.51) and (13.52) into (13.34), the transfer function of the loop filter is obtained as

$$F(s) = \frac{1 + s\tau_2}{1 + s\tau_1} = \frac{1 + s \times 8 \times 10^{-6}}{1 + s \times 135 \times 10^{-6}} \tag{13.54}$$

The **Unipolar NRZ source** block produces binary NRZ data at 2.488 Gbps as illustrated in Figure 13.35(a). The edge detector is implemented by the combination of an XOR block and a 200 ps delay element. This produces 200 ps wide pulses at the rising and falling edges of the NRZ data. Figure 13.35(b) displays the edge detector output. A pulse of varying width is generated at the output of the PD depending on the phase difference between the two inputs. This is displayed in Figure 13.35(c). The LPF block displays the transfer function for this model that is designed to optimally suppress the transfer of jitter that may be present in the input data signal. Figure 13.35(d) illustrates the LPF output. The VCO block produces a sine wave that varies from its quiescent frequency value as determined by the control signal produced by the LPF. The quiescent frequency for the VCO in this project is 2.5 GHz to synchronize with the incoming data rate with open-loop gain K of 0.2 GHz/s. The convert to square wave block is used to produce a clock signal in the form of a square wave to be sent out to the decision circuit as well as

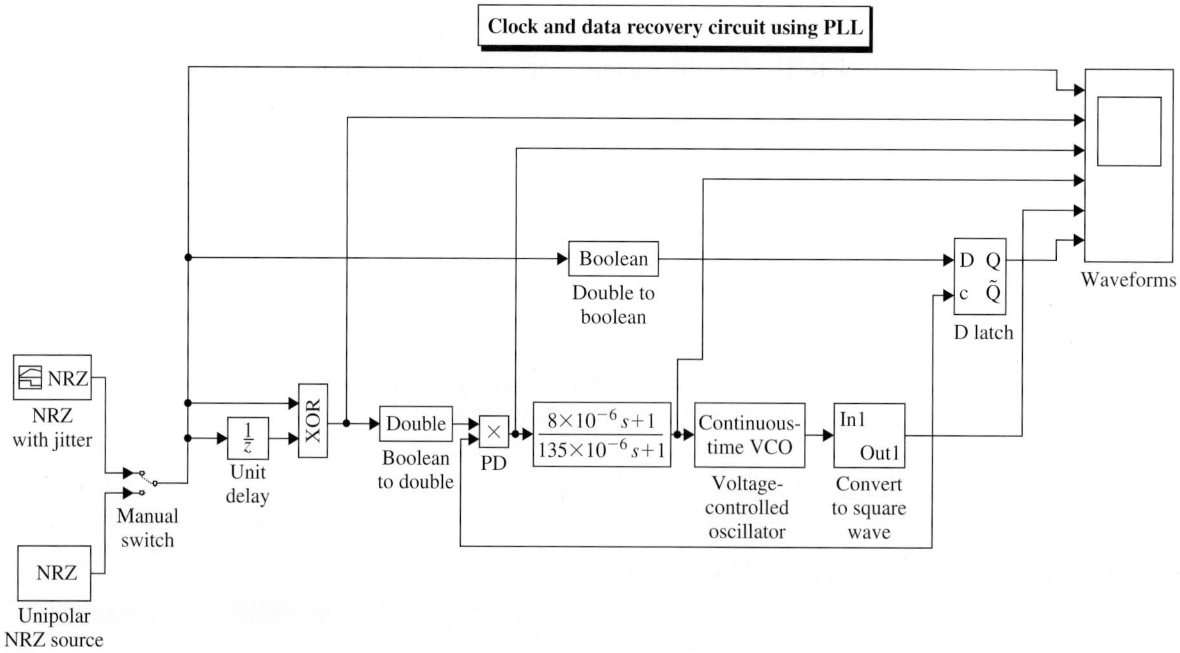

Figure 13.34 Simulink model for CDR.

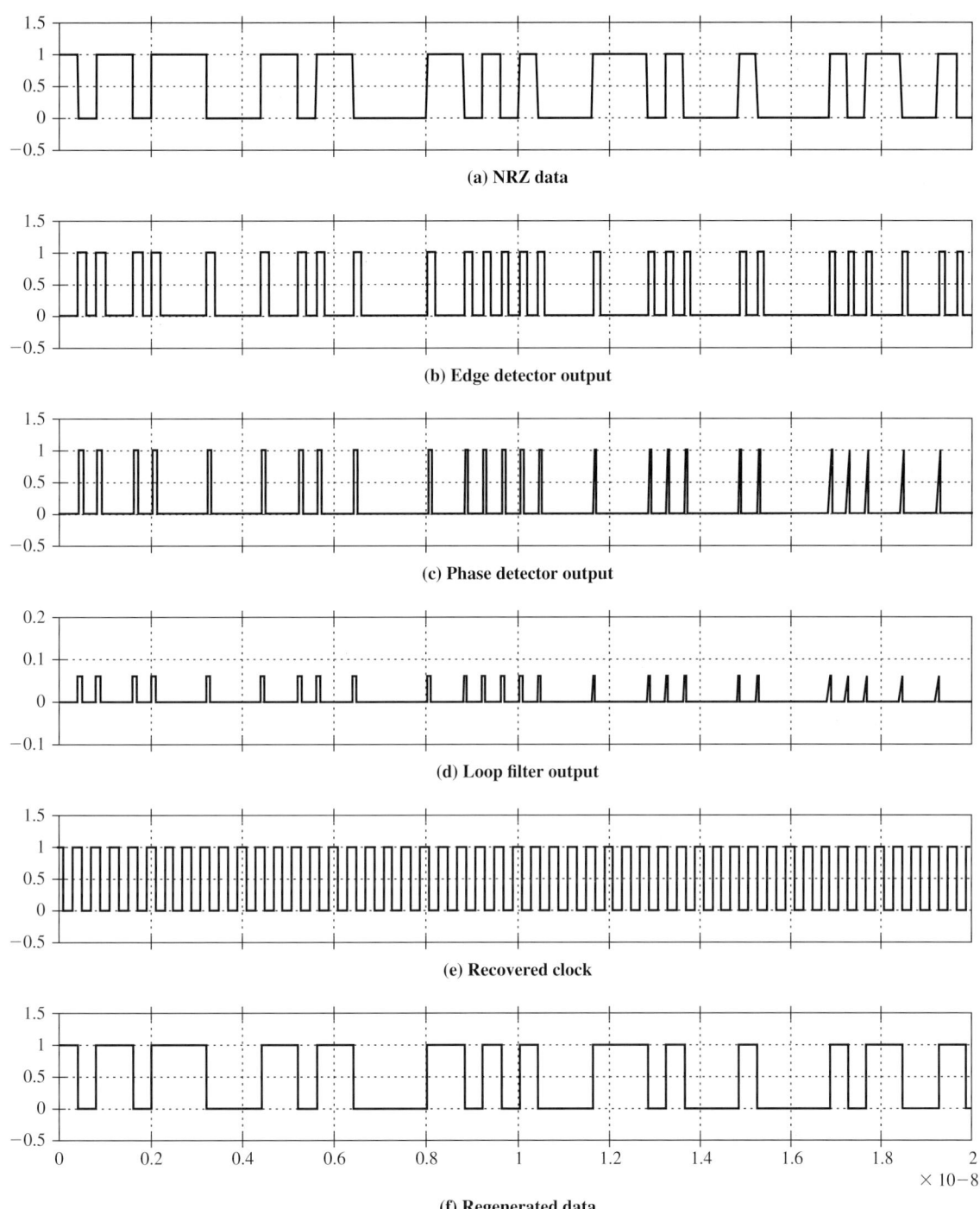

(a) NRZ data

(b) Edge detector output

(c) Phase detector output

(d) Loop filter output

(e) Recovered clock

(f) Regenerated data

Figure 13.35 CDR waveforms: NRZ data without jitter.

fed back to the PD. Figure 13.35(e) displays the clock signal. The simple regenerator circuit for this Simulink model is implemented by a D-latch flip-flop which has as its two inputs the original NRZ data and the clock signal produced by the CRC. The output of the D-latch flip-flop is the retimed data as shown in Figure 13.34(f). It is evident from Figure 13.35(f) that the VCO output is initially not in phase with the input signal, but phase lock is reached within 12 ns.

Next we consider the operation of CRC with jittered NRZ data.

Figure 13.36(a) illustrates the NRZ data with jitter entering the CRC. The jitter illustrated by the TIE waveform in Figure 13.30 is injected into the output of the unipolar NRZ source block. The waveforms in Figures 13.36(b) through 13.36(f) illustrate the operation of the CRC in the presence of jitter. It is clear from Figures 13.36(e) through 13.36(f) that the PLL is able to clean the jitter. This is verified by the comparison of the retimed output with the original jitter-free NRZ signal.

Figure 13.36 CDR waveforms: NRZ data with jitter.

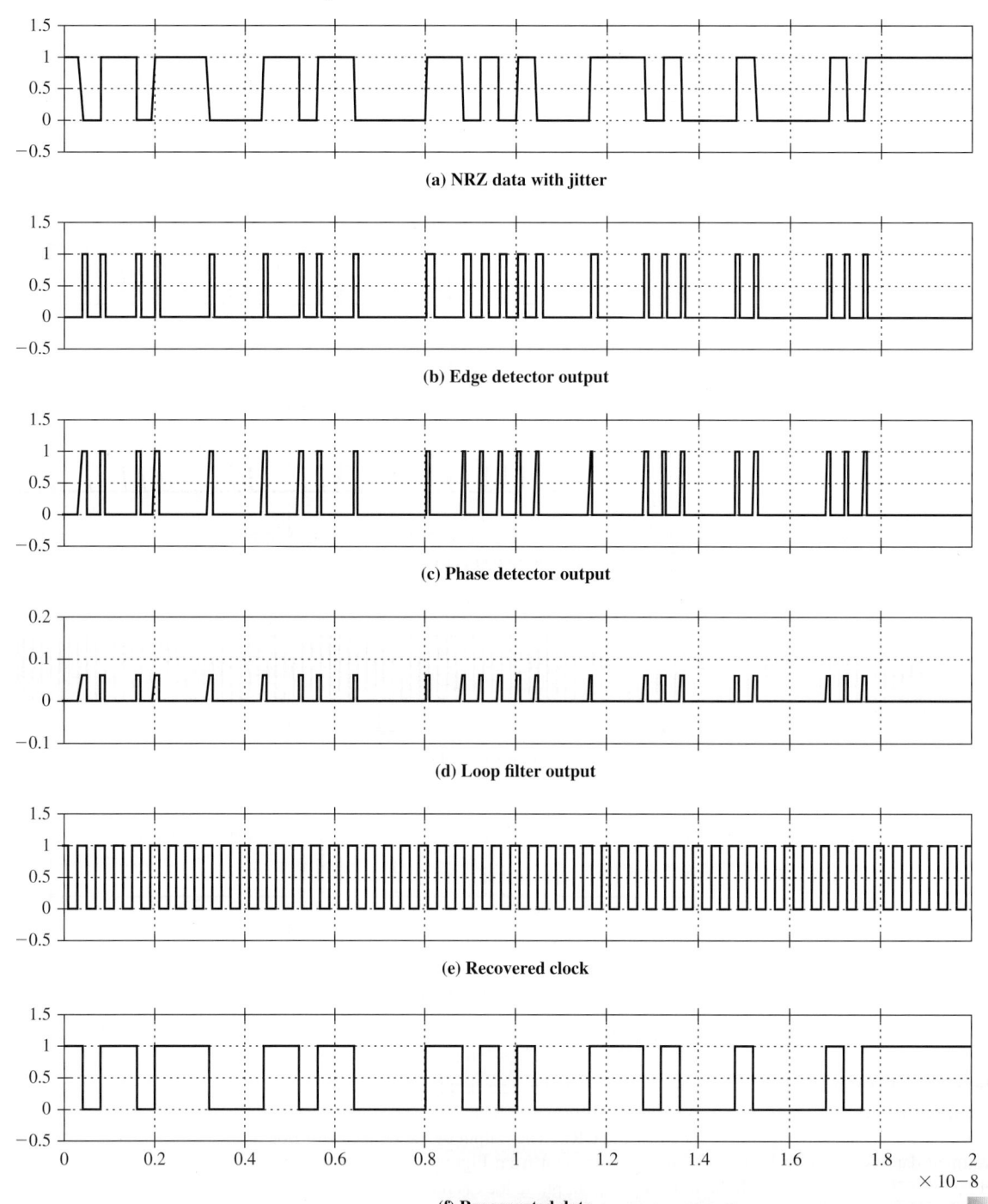

(a) NRZ data with jitter

(b) Edge detector output

(c) Phase detector output

(d) Loop filter output

(e) Recovered clock

$\times 10^{-8}$

(f) Regenerated data

13.5   FRAME SYNCHRONIZATION

The purpose of frame synchronization is to identify a specific marker (e.g., beginning of the frame) in the received data stream. In the case of TDM, framing synchronization is needed so that the received multiplexed data can be sorted and directed to the appropriate output channel by the demultiplexer. Frame synchronization is usually accomplished by the detection of a unique **frame alignment word (FAW),** which is a known pattern of 1's and 0's that is periodically sent into the data stream by the multiplexer. The FAW is frequently appended at the beginning of a block of data (i.e., in the **header**). Examples include SONET STS-1 and IEEE 802.3 Ethernet frames. In some other implementations, the FAW is sent in a distributed fashion in a number of frames constituting a **superframe.** Examples include the DS1 and DS2 frames discussed in Section 13.1. To ensure that the data itself doesn't contain the FAW, the process of **bit stuffing** is used. For example, if the FAW is 01111110, the data sequence at the transmitter is examined, and if a sequence of five 1's occurs, a 0 is "stuffed" at the transmitter. The receiver looks for five consecutive 1's in the received sequence. Five 1's followed by a 0 indicate that the 0 is a stuffing bit, and the receiver removes it.

The framing subsystem in the demultiplexer has two operating modes: in-frame and out-of-frame. Its operation is conveniently explained by the state transition diagram in Figure 13.37. Let us assume the demultiplexer is in in-frame mode and the frame synchronization circuit is tracking the FAW correctly. The system is then said to be in SYNC state. In this state, the receiver looks for the FAW only in the time slots where the word is supposed to be. Because of transmission errors, the FAW is likely to be corrupted once in a while, and this causes the framing subsystem to transition to PREALARM state. After arriving in PREALARM state, the system will again look at the position assigned for the FAW in the next frame. If the receiver finds the proper word, it will go back to SYNC state. However, if α successive tests fail to confirm the presence of the FAW, the framing system moves to out-of-frame mode and the demultiplexer stops sending data to output channels. At this point, the framing system enters the SEARCH state (out-of-frame mode). The search process sequentially

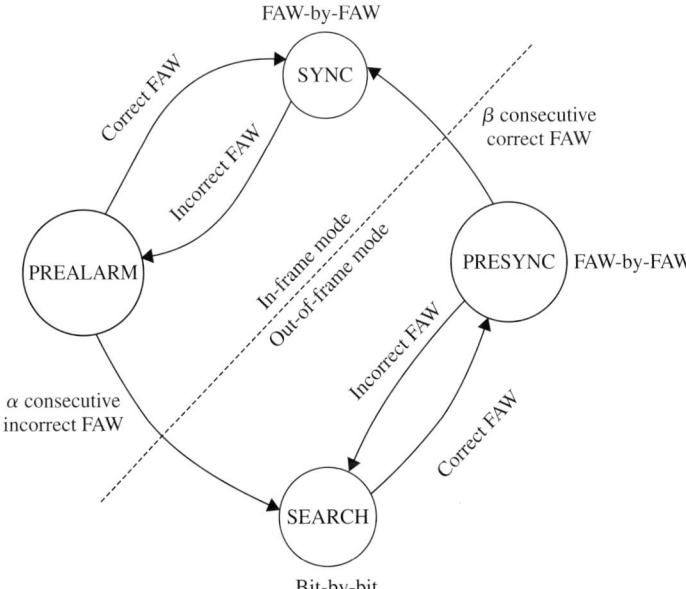

Figure 13.37 State transition diagram of frame alignment procedure.

shifts one bit position in the frame for a match with the FAW. If there is a match, the position is provisionally accepted as a candidate and the system immediately moves to PRESYNC state. The problem in acquiring the frame synchronization is that the system does not know if the data pattern at the candidate position is the actual FAW or a replica formed by the random information bits. So the system has to confirm that what it has found is the real FAW. If the comparison shows a match for a β number of frames, frame alignment is declared and the system moves to the SYNC state. If not, a search process is reinitiated at the next bit position, followed by a confirmation process, and so on.

13.5.1   Performance of a Frame Synchronizer

One important requirement for any frame synchronization subsystem is that it must be able to keep the communication system in its synchronous state under high error rate conditions. That is, it must keep the framing system in SYNC state as long as possible, even when the number of channel errors increases. This is measured by the average holding time of the frame synchronization subsystem. The design objective is to maximize the average holding time, which increases in direct proportion to the probability of correctly detecting a FAW P_D. Assuming that bit errors are statistically independent, P_D is given by

$$P_D = \{\text{FAW of length } N \text{ is received correctly}\} = (1 - p)^N \qquad (13.55)$$

where $p = BER$ of the transmission link. The failure to detect the true FAW results from the corrupted bits in the FAW caused by the random transmission errors. A simple way to improve P_D is to accept a less-than-perfect match by allowing all incoming FAWs with a Hamming distance less than or equal to ε from the correct FAW. That is, a received N-bit FAW may be accepted as correct even if it contains a small number, ε or fewer, errors.

In this case, the probability of correctly detecting a FAW P_D obeys the binomial distribution and is given by

$$P_D = P\{i \leq \varepsilon \text{ errors in the FAW of length } N\} = \sum_{i=0}^{\varepsilon} \binom{N}{i} p^i (1 - p)^{N-i} \qquad (13.56)$$

where $\binom{n}{i} = \dfrac{N!}{i!(N - i)!}$ is the binomial coefficient. If the received FAW, due to bit errors, does not match the locally stored FAW in $\varepsilon + 1$ places or more, it will be not be detected (i.e., it will be missed).

When the frame synchronization is lost (i.e., when the system is in the out-of-frame mode), the process leading to the frame reacquisition may involve several search and confirmation steps. This reframing process is characterized by the **maximum average reframe time** of the frame alignment procedure. The maximum average reframe time consists of two components:

- Time to find the true frame alignment word (or position) by the search process. This is inversely related to the probability of false simulation of the FAW P_{FS}.
- Time to confirm the true frame alignment word (or position) by the PRESYNC process. This is directly related to the probability of correctly detecting a FAW P_D given by (13.56).

The probability of false simulation of the FAW P_{FS} is given by the probability that random bits match the true FAW of length N with ε or fewer errors. There are 2^N possible binary N-tuples of random data, but only one of them is the true FAW with probability $1/2^N$. For a given value of ε, the total number of random data N-tuples with Hamming distance less than or equal to ε from the true FAW is

$$\sum_{i=0}^{\varepsilon}\binom{N}{i} \tag{13.57}$$

Thus, the probability that N data bits will match the true FAW with ε or fewer errors is given by

$$P_{FS} = \frac{1}{2^N}\sum_{i=0}^{\varepsilon}\binom{N}{i} \tag{13.58}$$

Note that this is independent of the link BER. The system designer would like to maximize P_D and minimize P_{FS}. P_D is increased by choosing short frame alignment words (i.e., N is small), whereas P_{FS} improves with longer FAWs (i.e., N is large). These, however, are conflicting objectives. Figure 13.38 displays the probabilities of miss $(1 - P_D)$ and false simulation (P_{FS}) as a function of the number of bits (N) in the FAW. Figure 13.38(a) is plotted for the transmission system $BER = 10^{-3}$. In frame synchronizer design, (13.58) may be used to determine the length of the FAW (N) required so that the false simulation probability will meet specifications. From Figure 13.38(b), if $P_{FS} = 2 \times 10^{-5}$ is allowed, $N = 20$ may be required.

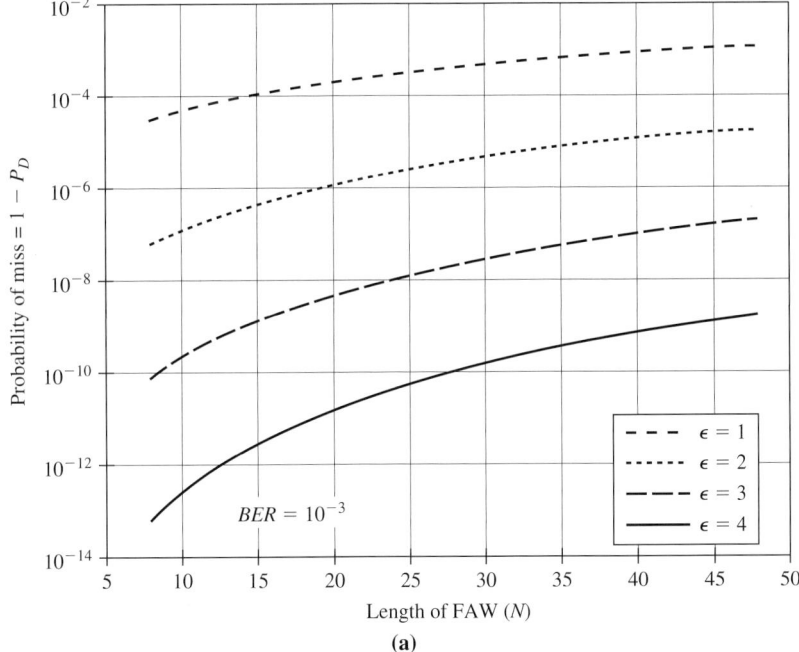

Figure 13.38 (a) Probability of miss and (b) probability of FAW false simulation. *(continued)*

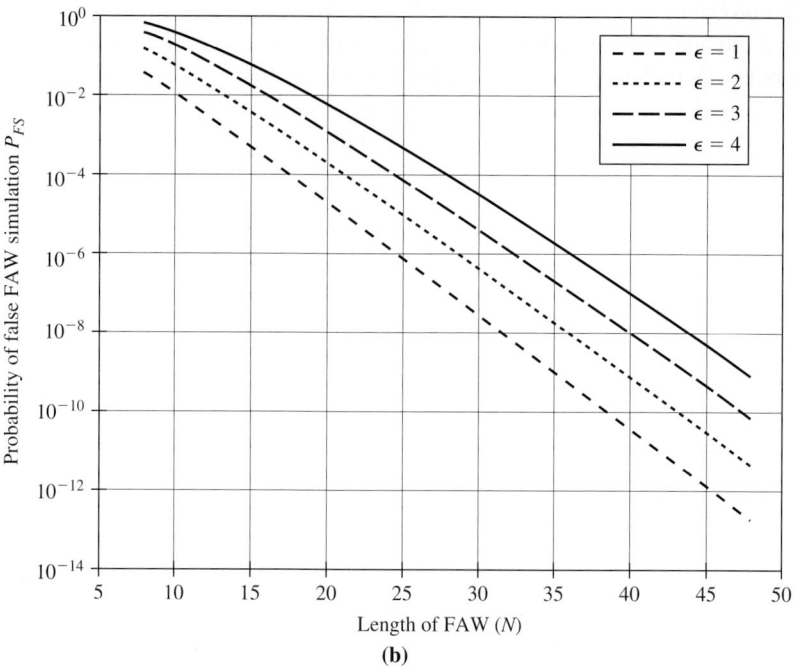

Probability of false FAW simulation P_{FS}

Length of FAW (N)

(b)

Example 13.7

The T1 PCM multiplexer uses alternating bit pattern for frame synchronization. Frame alignment strategy requires the presence of the correct FAW without error. The information bits are equally likely to be 0 or 1.

a. Assuming a random starting position in the search mode, calculate the average number of tests required for rejection of that position for false alignment.
b. Calculate the average number of bits that elapse until the frame synchronizer locks onto the true FAW.

Solution

a. Let the random variable x denote the number of tests required for rejection of an arbitrary position for false alignment. Each test involves observing the bit position for the alternating bit pattern 010101. . . until it is violated. Without loss of generality assume first observed bit is zero. Because at least two tests are required to determine a violation, we can write

$$P\{x \leq 1 \,|\, \text{First bit} = 0\} = 0$$

Further,

$$P\{x = 2 \,|\, \text{First bit} = 0\} = P\{\text{Second bit is zero}\} = p = 1/2$$

$$P\{x = 3 \,|\, \text{First bit} = 0\} = P\{11 \text{ pattern} \,|\, \text{First bit} = 0\} = p^2 = 1/4$$

$$P\{x = 4 \,|\, \text{First bit} = 0\} = P\{100\text{pattern} \,|\, \text{First bit} = 0\} = p^3 = 1/8$$

The probability of performing n tests before observing the alternating bit pattern violation is, therefore, given by

$$P\{x = n \,|\, \text{First bit} = 0\} = p^{n-1} = \left(\frac{1}{2}\right)^{n-1}$$

The average number of tests required before observing the alternating bit pattern violation is obtained as

$$E\{x\} = E\{x \mid \text{First bit} = 0\} = \sum_{i=2}^{\infty} iP\{x = i \mid \text{First bit} = 0\}$$

$$= \sum_{i=2}^{\infty} ip^{i-1} = \frac{d}{dp} \sum_{i=2}^{\infty} p^i = \frac{d}{dp}\left[-1 - p + \sum_{i=0}^{\infty} p^i\right]$$

$$= \frac{d}{dp}\left[-1 - p + \frac{1}{1-p}\right] = \frac{1}{(1-p)^2} - 1 = \frac{1}{\left(1 - \dfrac{1}{2}\right)^2} - 1 = 3$$

That is, it takes 3 tests, on average, for the rejection of an incorrect framing bit location. This corresponds to $(2 \times 193) + 1$ bit times to make such a determination.

b. On average, if the frame synchronizer starts at a random bit location in T-1 frame (contains 193 bits), it will have to examine $193/2 = 96.5$ incorrect bit locations before locking onto the framing bit. For each such incorrect bit location, on average, a nonalternating pattern will be discovered on the third observation at which time the synchronizer will move one bit forward to the next bit. Because the synchronizer spends $(2 \times 193) + 1$ bit times in rejecting each incorrect bit location, the average number of bits elapsed until the frame synchronizer locks onto the framing bit = $96.5 \times [(2 \times 193) + 1] = 37{,}345$ bits

At this point, the synchronizer moves to PRESYNC state. It continues to observe the framing bit location until an alternating pattern has been observed for a sufficient number of bits, say β. If the alternating pattern is verified for β number of frames, frame alignment is declared and the synchronizer moves to the SYNC state.

13.5.2 Choice of Frame Alignment Word

The frame synchronization circuit constantly "looks" for the FAW in the data stream. A digital correlator, shown in Figure 13.39, can be used to detect the position of the N-bit FAW in the data. The output of the digital correlator is

$$v_k = \sum_{i=0}^{N-1} a_{k-i} c_i \qquad (13.59)$$

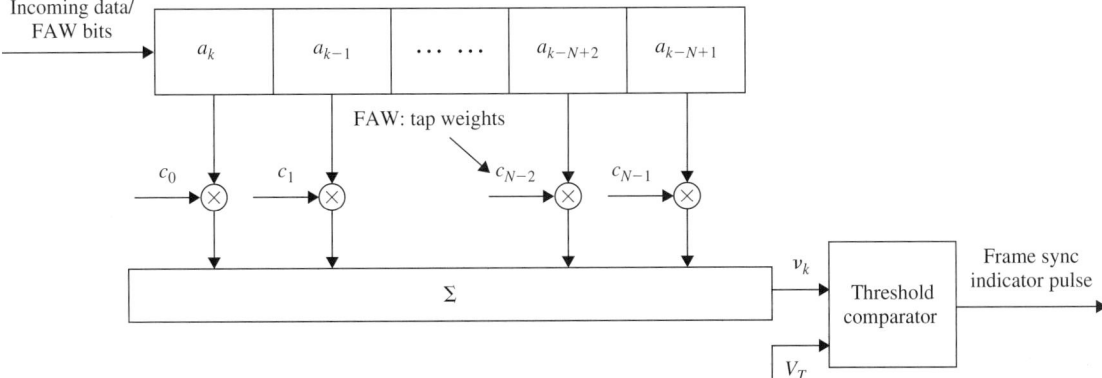

Figure 13.39 FAW detection by correlation detector.

where $\underline{c} = (c_0, c_1, \ldots, c_{N-1})$ is the FAW represented by the tap gains and a_i are input data and/or FAW bits in the shift register. We assume that both a_i and c_i assume values in $\mathscr{A}_2 = \{1, -1\}$. From (13.59), it follows that the digital correlator calculates the crosscorrelation between the bit stream passing through the shift register and the FAW.

As the received data slides by the N-bit FAW, v_k takes on different values. There comes a time when the N-bit FAW fills the N-stage shift register. In this case $a_{k-i} = c_i$, v_k achieves its maximum value given by

$$v_k = \sum_{i=0}^{N-1} c_i c_i = N \tag{13.60}$$

The digital correlator thus correlates consecutive N-bit segments of the received data with the N-bit FAW. The segment that yields the maximum correlation value, as determined by (13.60), is declared as the FAW and therefore the location of the FAW is identified. If the shift register word differs from the FAW in one bit position, then $v_k = N - 2$. Therefore, we set the threshold voltage V_T slightly below $N - 2$ to detect FAWs with zero or one bit error.

The correlation properties of the FAW are quite important because as the successive bits of the FAW pass through the shift register, $v(k)$ traces out the shape of its autocorrelation function. The periodic autocorrelation function $R_c(k)$ of the FAW is given by

$$R_c(k) \equiv \sum_{i=0}^{N-1} c_i c_{(i+k)_{\mathrm{mod}\,N}} \tag{13.61}$$

Good FAWs have the property that their autocorrelation function magnitude is uniformly small for all time-shifts other than zero-shift. Another important property of good framing words is that they exhibit low-crosscorrelation values with random data. Barker and Neuman-Hofman sequences exhibit such good correlation properties. The autocorrelation function of Barker sequences (assuming bipolar values) is given by

$$R(k) = \begin{cases} N, & k = 0 \\ 0, & k \neq 0, \text{odd} \\ -1, & k \neq 0, \text{even} \end{cases} \tag{13.62}$$

Note that the magnitude of the largest side-lobe (that is, nonzero shift correlation) is at most 1 for these sequences. Table 13.5 displays all the Barker sequences in existence.

Table 13.5 Barker Sequences

N	Barker Sequence
1	+
2	+ + or + −
3	+ + −
4	+ + + − or + + − +
5	+ + + − +
7	+ + + − − + −
11	+ + + − − − + − − + −
13	+ + + + + − − + + − + − +

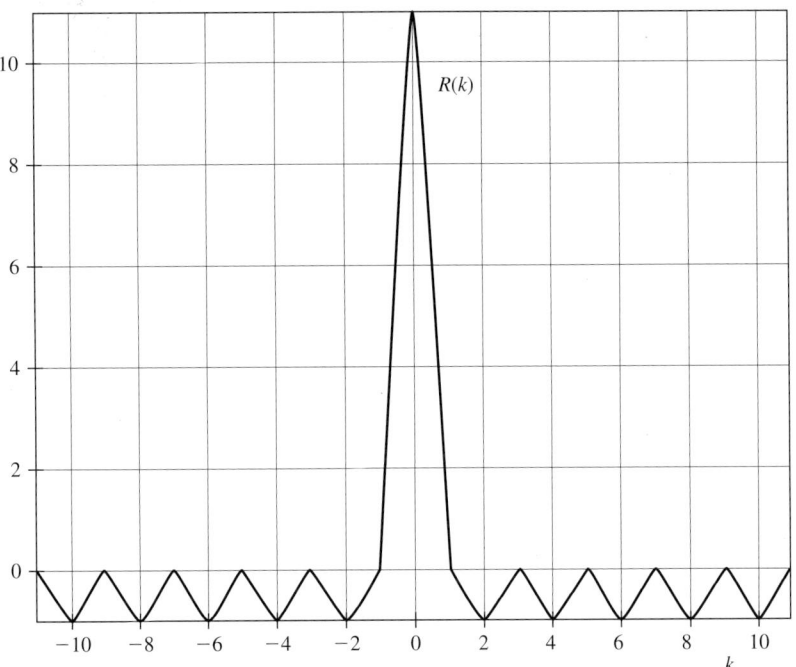

Figure 13.40 Autocorrelation function ($N = 11$).

Figure 13.40 illustrates the autocorrelation function of the Barker sequence of length 13. In many cases, however, there is a need for longer sequences to improve performance. Neuman-Hofman sequences[7] were specifically designed to maximize performance when correlation detection is used. As such they perform somewhat better than Barker sequences. More important, Neuman-Hofman sequences of longer lengths exist.

FINAL REMARKS

Digital multiplexing plays a key role in exploiting the tremendous bandwidth made available by optical fiber transmission technology. At the terabit-per-second transmission rate, this implies that one hair-thin fiber can support multiplexing of over half a million data connections at 1.554 Mbps, 20 million digital voice telephony channels, or half a million compressed digital TV channels. Synchronization, as required in the context of modern digital communications, consists of estimating two parameters of the received signal, that is, frequency and time. Frame synchronization allows frame boundaries to be recovered from the received multiplexed signal. This enables proper demultiplexing of thousands of data streams carried in a multi-gigabit TDM signal. Carrier synchronization produces a local carrier reference that agrees closely in frequency and phase with the received carrier for the operation of a phase-coherent demodulator. Bit synchronization produces a local clock that is accurately time-aligned with the received pulses for proper detection of the data symbols. Carrier and bit synchronization are crucial operations in the design of digital transmission systems that are efficient in power and bandwidth requirements.

[7] F. Neuman and L. Hofman, "New Pulse Sequences with Desirable Correlation Properties," *Proceedings of the National Telemetry Conference* (1971): 272–282.

FURTHER READINGS

Although digital multiplexing and synchronization problems are of paramount significance in digital communications, there is a scarcity of readable and practically useful material in some areas. Smith [1], Anderson [2], and Ziemer et al. [3] provide good introductions to selected topics covered here. Ballart et al. [4] is a good reference on SONET. Gardner [5] is an excellent reference on PLLs. Stiffler [6] is a comprehensive reference on various synchronization topics. Razavi [7, 8] provides an extensive treatment of clock recovery circuits, especially practical implementation at high speeds. Choi [11] and Scholtz [13] provide good tutorials on frame synchronization.

1. Smith, D. *Digital Transmission Systems,* 3rd ed. Berlin, Germany: Springer, 2003.

2. Anderson, J. *Digital Transmission Engineering,* 2nd ed. Hoboken, NJ: Wiley-Interscience, 2005.

3. Ziemer, R., and R. Peterson. *An Introduction to Digital Communication,* 2nd ed. Upper Saddle River, NJ: Prentice Hall, 2001.

4. Ballart, R., and Y. Ching. "SONET: Now It's the Standard Optical Network." *IEEE Communications Magazine,* March 1989, 8–15.

5. Gardner, F. *Phaselock Techniques,* 3rd ed. Hoboken, NJ: Wiley-Interscience, 2005.

6. Stiffler, J. *Theory of Synchronous Communications.* Upper Saddle River, NJ: Prentice Hall, 1971.

7. Razavi, B., ed., *Monolithic Phase-Locked Loops and Clock Recovery Circuits.* New York: IEEE Press, 1997.

8. Razavi, B. *Design of Integrated Circuits for Optical Communications.* New York: McGraw-Hill, 2003.

9. Members of Technical Staff, Bell Telephone Laboratories. *Transmission Systems for Communications,* 5th ed., Bell Telephone Laboratories, 1982.

10. Kishine, K., K. Ishii, and H. Ichino. "Loop-Parameter Optimization of a PLL for a Low-jitter 2.5-Gbps One-chip Optical Receiver IC with 1:8 DEMUX." *IEEE Journal on Solid-state Circuits* 1 (2002): 38–50.

11. Choi, D. "Frame Alignment in a Digital Carrier System: A Tutorial." *IEEE Communications Magazine* 2 (1990): 48–54.

12. Neuman, F., and L. Hofman. "New Pulse Sequences with Desirable Correlation Properties." *Proceedings of the National Telemetry Conference* (1971): 272–282.

13. Scholtz, R. "Frame Synchronization Techniques." *IEEE Transactions on Communications* 8 (1980): 1204–1213.

PROBLEMS

13.1. Consider the synchronous time-division-multiplexing of 8 1-Mbps digital signals. The output frame is composed of 64 blocks of user data and each block is formed by interleaving one bit from each input line. Assume that the multiplexer adds 1 framing byte to each frame to facilitate demultiplexing operation at the receiver.

    a. Illustrate the TDM output frame format.

    b. Determine the input bit duration.

    c. Determine the output bit duration.

    d. Determine the output frame rate.

    e. Determine the output bit rate.

13.2. Consider the synchronous time-division-multiplexing of 16 2-Mbps digital signals. The output frame is composed of 256 blocks of user data and each block is formed by interleaving bytes from each input line. Assume that the frame synchronization circuitry adds 2 framing bytes to each frame. Illustrate the TDM output frame format.

    a. Determine the input bit and byte durations.

    b. Determine the output bit and byte durations.

    c. Determine the output frame rate.

    d. Determine the output bit rate.

13.3. The E-1 (CEPT-1) carrier system multiplexes 30 voice channels. The E-1 frame consists of 32 bytes. Byte 0 carries the frame alignment word 0011011. Bytes 1-15 and 17-31 carry PCM words corresponding to voice channels. Byte 16 carries the signaling information. The frame transmission rate is 8000 frames per second.

    a. Sketch E-1 frame format.

    b. What is the duration of each E-1 frame?

    c. What bit rate is assigned to each voice channel? Signaling channel?

    d. Suppose 32 kbps DPCM is used instead of PCM to digitize each voice channel. How many voice calls can be carried by E-1 carrier using this compressed format. Suggest the new format of E-1 frame.

13.4. Suppose a multiplexer combines four input streams each operating at a nominal rate of 1 Mbps. The multiplexer frame format is shown in Figure P13.1. The frame is composed of a framing byte and 256 bit-multiplexed data bits. To facilitate stuffing synchronization, 4 flag and 4 stuffable bits are provided, one for each input channel. The flag bit for each channel indicates whether the corresponding stuffable bit location contains a stuffing or user data bit.

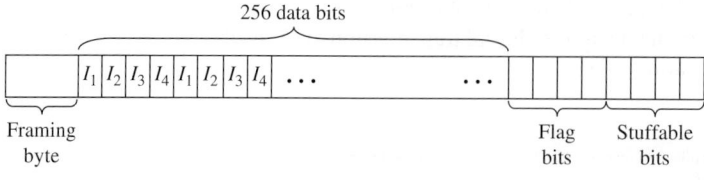

Figure P13.1

a. Calculate the multiplexer output bit rate.

b. Determine the acceptable tolerance on input signal rates.

c. What is the maximum stuffing rate per channel?

13.5. The M12 multiplexer described in ITU-T Rec. G.473 combines four DS1 signals using stuffing synchronization. The multiplexer output frame format is shown in Figure 13.6. A tolerance of 50 ppm on nominal DS1 signal rates is allowed in the ITU-T standard.

a. What is the duration of a subframe? A frame?

b. Determine the maximum and minimum input DS1 signal rates.

c. Determine the multiplexer synchronous rate per channel.

13.6. The frame format for a M23 multiplexer which combines 7 DS2 signals to form the DS3 signal is displayed in Figure P13.2. In each DS3 frame one bit can be stuffed for each of the seven DS2 signals. Specifically, the state of the three C-bits in the ith subframe indicates whether or not bit stuffing occurs for the ith DS2 input during the multiplexing process.

a. What is the number of bits in a DS3 frame?

b. How many frames per second are produced by the multiplexer?

c. Calculate the number of overhead bits per second added by the multiplexer.

d. How many bits are available for stuffing per second?

e. Specify minimum and maximum allowable rates for DS2 input signals.

13.7. The actual bit rates of 7 DS2 tributary signals input to a M23 multiplexer are given in the following table. Calculate the bit stuffing rate required for each of the DS2 signal for multiplexing them in a DS3 frame. Display the tributary and corresponding stuffing rates in a multiplexer block diagram.

DS2 Tributary	Bit Rate (Mbps)
1	6.307500
2	6.306272
3	6.315671
4	6.310775
5	6.313225
6	6.314450
7	6.312000

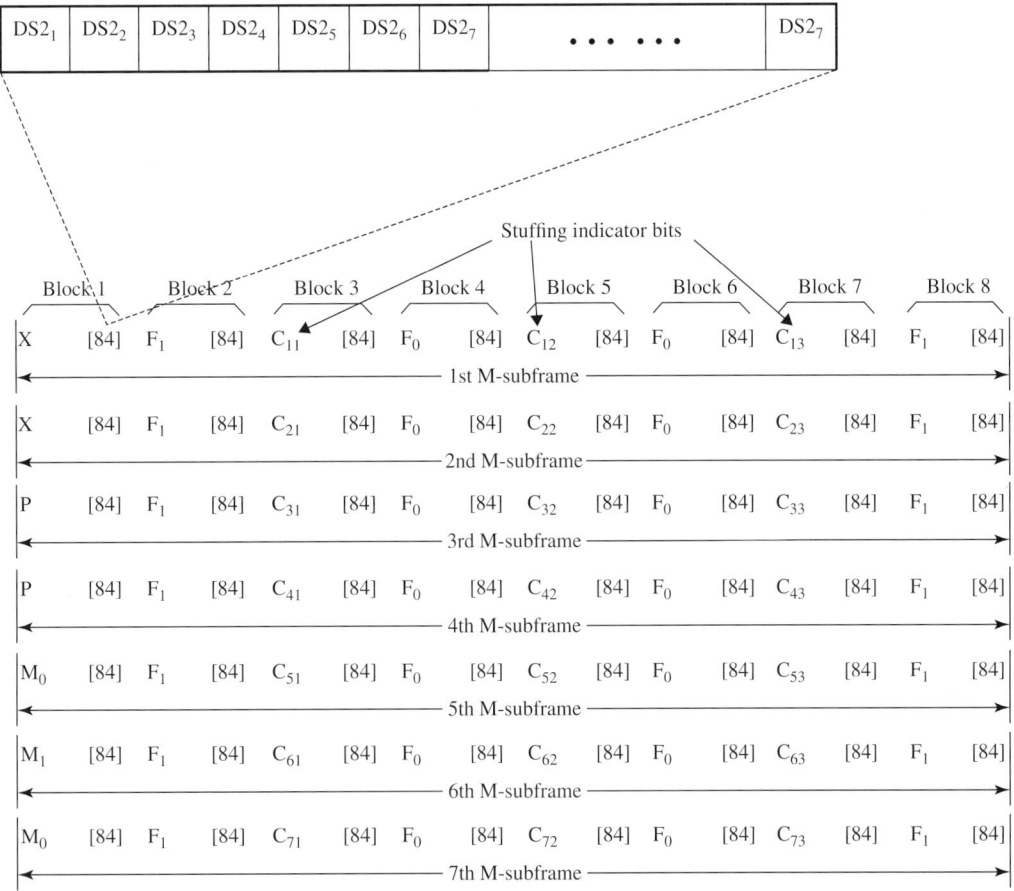

Figure P13.2

13.8. Consider the M12 multiplexer with frame format illustrated in Figure 13.6.

     a. What is the probability of accepting false FAW in the search mode, assuming random data from tributaries, if a perfect match is required with 8 framing (F) bits of the framing pattern?

     b. What is the probability of rejecting true FAW in the search mode for a link *BER* = 10^{-3}?

13.9. The 8.448 Mbps second-level multiplexer based on ITU-T Rec. G.742 combines four E1 (CEPT-1) signals at 2.048 Mbps. A 10-bit framing word is used at the beginning of each 848-bit frame. Frame alignment strategy requires the presence of the correct FAW without error.

     a. What is the probability of accepting a false FAW word in the in-frame mode assuming random binary data?

     b. Assuming a random starting position in the search mode, calculate the average number of tests required for rejection of that position for false alignment?

     c. Calculate the average number of bits that elapse until the frame synchronizer locks onto the true FAW.

13.10. Consider a QPSK system operating at 1 Mbps. Calculate the phase error variance if a quadrupling loop is used to recover the carrier. Assume that the received signal E_b/N_o is 11 dB and the PLL noise bandwidth = 5 kHz.

13.11. A squaring loop is used for carrier recovery in a BPSK system. Calculate the normalized loop $B_N T_b$ needed so that the output phase error variance after the prescaler is 0.04 rad^2. Assume that the received signal E_b/N_o is 11 dB.

     a. Write an expression for the closed-loop transfer function of the two-pole PLL that meets the above phase error specification.

     b. Sketch an implementation of the squaring loop.

13.12. A Costas loop is used for carrier recovery in a BPSK system with the following parameters:

Bit rate = 1 Mbps

Loop filter noise bandwidth B_N = 50 kHz

Loop SNR ρ_L = 10 dB

     a. Calculate the squaring loss.

     b. Calculate the loop phase error variance.

13.13. PLLs used in clock recovery circuits are characterized by very small bandwidth ($\omega_{3dB}T \ll 1$) and damping factor $\zeta \geq 5$.

     a. Show that the closed loop transfer function of the PLL in (13.35) can be approximated to that of a single-pole filter

$$H(s) \approx \frac{2\zeta\omega_n}{s + 2\zeta\omega_n}$$

     b. What is the 3-dB bandwidth of the loop ?

13.14. Consider length 13 Neuman-Hofman sequence {1, 1, 1, 1, 1, 1, −1, −1, 1, 1, −1, 1, −1}.

     a. Compute and sketch its autocorrelation function.

     b. What is the magnitude of its maximum side-lobe values?

     c. Comment on its correlation properties versus that of length-13 Barker sequence.

13.15. Consider length 15 PN sequence {−1, 1, 1, 1, −1, −1, −1, −1, 1, −1, 1, −1, −1, 1, 1}.

     a. Compute and sketch its autocorrelation function.

     b. What is the magnitude of its maximum side-lobe values?

     c. Comment on its correlation properties versus that of length-13 Barker sequence.

MATLAB PROBLEMS

13.16. Consider a frame consisting of *N*-bit FAW and *L* data bits. Scholtz[8] has derived a bound on the probability for frame synchronization in one pass $P_{one\text{-}pass}$. $P_{one\text{-}pass}$ is the probability that the FAW is detected (with ε or fewer errors) in one-pass through a frame (one bit position at time). It is

$$P_{one\text{-}pass} \geq [1 - (L + M - 1)P_{FS}]P_D$$

where P_D and P_{FS} are given by (13.55) and (13.58), respectively.

     a. Write an m-file to compute $P_{one\text{-}pass}$ with following parameters:

p = *BER* of the link

ε = Number of errors allowed

L = Number of data bits in the frame

N = length of FAW

     b. Assuming $L = 1800$ bytes, calculate and plot $P_{one\text{-}pass}$ as a function of $N = 8 - 32$ with ε as parameter. Use values of ε = 0, 1, 2, 3, 4.

     c. What is the length of FAW required to achieve $P_{one\text{-}pass}$ of at least 99.94%?

---

[8] R. Scholtz, "Frame Synchronization Techniques," *IEEE Transactions on Communications* August (1980): 1204–1213.

CHAPTER 14

Information Theory and Compression Techniques

T he fundamental goal of a communication system is to transfer information reliably from the source to the destination. The invention of information theory by Shannon in his seminal paper provided the concepts, insights, and mathematical foundation for modern communication systems.[1] Before Shannon's paper, it was not precisely clear what the information content of a message was. There was some elementary understanding of how to transmit a waveform and process a received waveform, but there was essentially no understanding of how to convert a message into bits and transmit it. There was some basic understanding of various modulation techniques, such as AM, FM, and PCM. However, there was little conceptual understanding of the basis upon which to compare their relative performance.

One of the fundamental results of the Shannon's paper was his demonstration that the problem of transmitting an information source through some channel can be separated, without any loss of optimality, into the independent problems of representing that source by a sequence of binary digits and of transmitting a random binary sequence through that channel. This implies that all types of communications, whether inherently analog or digital in nature, are equivalent to the generation, transmission, and reception of random binary data. Shannon then posed two fundamental problems of information transmission:

- What is the minimum rate (bits/symbol) required to represent a source that corresponds to a measure of fidelity? (i.e., the ultimate data compression achievable). This is called the **source coding** problem.
- What is the ultimate transmission rate of reliable communication achievable in the presence of ubiquitous noise? This is called the **channel coding** problem.

In this chapter we will study the answers Shannon provided to these questions. In his source coding theorem, Shannon proved that there exists an ultimate minimum rate, for every information source, beyond which it cannot be compressed. This minimum rate, according to Shannon, can not be less than the **entropy** H of the source. Shannon's most surprising result is his channel coding theorem, which states that a communication channel is characterized by a parameter, called the **channel capacity** C, such that random binary data at rate $R < C$ can be transmitted over the channel with an arbitrary low error rate. The most unexpected result of the channel coding theorem is that the ultimate limit of performance set by the channel noise is not the accuracy, but the rate at which data can be reliably transmitted.

To focus attention on the information theoretic concepts, we will consider the simplified block diagram of a digital communication system illustrated in Figure 14.1.

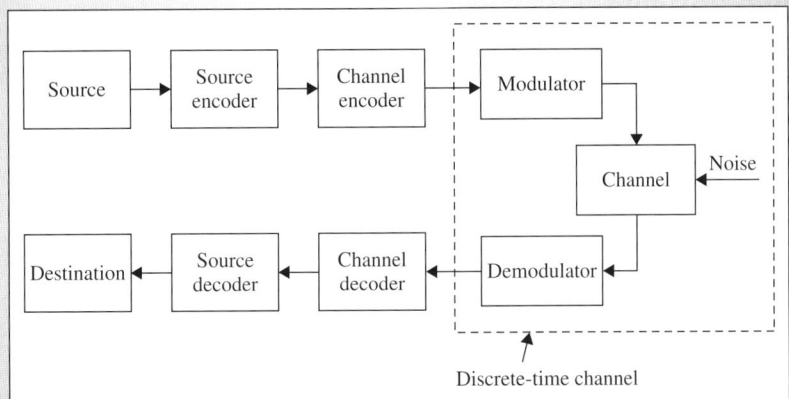

Figure 14.1 Simplified model of a digital communication system.

[1] C. Shannon, "A Mathematical Theory of Communication," *Bell System Technical Journal* 27 (1948): 379–423.

The term **discrete-time channel** refers to the cascade of modulator, physical channel, and demodulator. Note that the source and channel coding functions have been separated without any loss of optimality according to Shannon.[2] Thus the optimal channel coding and source compression schemes can be designed independent of each other. In this chapter, we also study compression methods for text, image, and digital TV signals. Channel coding is the subject of Chapter 15.

The chapter is organized into the following sections:

14.1   BASIC CONCEPTS OF INFORMATION THEORY.

> *This section introduces the concept of entropy as a measure of the information content of a discrete random variable. We define joint and conditional entropy and establish the chain rule for entropy. The section concludes with a discussion of the differential entropy concept and mutual information between two random variables.*

14.2   SOURCE CODING.

> *In this section, we consider the information content of a discrete memoryless source. We then derive Shannon's source coding theorem, which establishes the ultimate limit on the amount of compression that can be achieved in representing the source.*

14.3   CHANNEL CODING.

> *This section introduces the concepts of discrete memoryless channel, mutual information, and channel capacity. We next study Shannon's channel coding theorem, which specifies the fundamental limit on the amount of information that can be transmitted through a noisy channel.*

14.4   CAPACITY OF AWGN CHANNELS.

> *The information capacity of an AWGN channel is derived subject to an average power constraint. Next we derive the limiting value of SNR/bit below which there can be no communication at any bit rate. The section concludes with a discussion of the trade-off between SNR/bit and spectral efficiency in various digital carrier transmission schemes versus the capacity-achieving system.*

14.5   LOSSLESS COMPRESSION TECHNIQUES.

> *This section presents lossless techniques that reduce the number of bits required to represent a file of information under the condition that the original file must be reconstructed exactly. After studying variable-length coding schemes, such as Huffman and run-length coding, the section concludes with a description of Lempel-Ziv compression algorithms.*

14.6   IMAGE COMPRESSION: JPEG.

> *Lossy compression techniques, where decoding yields an imperfect reconstruction of the original image, are considered in this section. We study two-dimensional discrete cosine transform, variable-length coding, and color subsampling techniques that are used in many image and video compression standards. The section concludes with a discussion of the JPEG standard.*

14.7   DIGITAL VIDEO COMPRESSION: MPEG.

> *This section discusses interframe coding to reduce the temporal redundancy in a digital video signal. We then explain the motion-compensated prediction technique and its implementation in MPEG standards. We conclude with a discussion of MPEG standards and their performance features.*

The chapter concludes with final remarks and a selected list of references.

14.1   BASIC CONCEPTS OF INFORMATION THEORY

Before the publication of Shannon's paper, the concepts of message and its information content were not precisely understood or defined. According to Shannon, messages should be thought of as choices between alternatives. An example of the set of alternatives is the English language alphabet that we use every day in conveying information

---

[2] Shannon, "A Mathematical Theory of Communication," 379–423.

to each other. Shannon further proposed that the **information content** of a message is determined by the probabilities associated with the set of alternatives rather than what they may represent. To formalize this probabilistic model of information, we consider the information content of a discrete random variable x that takes on values from an alphabet $\mathscr{A}_x = \{x_1, x_2, \ldots, x_K\}$ with PMF $p_x(x_i) = P\{x = x_i\}$, $x_i \in \mathscr{A}_x$. In the present context, x may represent output of an information source or a communication channel. The **entropy** of the random variable x is defined as

$$H(x) = -\sum_{x_i \in \mathscr{A}_x} p_x(x_i) \log_2 p_x(x_i) \tag{14.1}$$

$H(x)$ is a measure of our uncertainty about the value of random variable x. Alternatively, entropy can be interpreted as the amount of information obtained by observing a realization of x. Note that $H(x)$ is always a function of the PMF of x!

$$H(x) = H\big(\{p_x(x_i)\}\big) \tag{14.2}$$

The entropy of a random variable x is expressed in bits when the base of the logarithm is 2 in (14.1).

Example 14.1

Consider a random variable x with probabilities $\{0.5, 0.2, 0.15, 0.10, 0.05\}$. Calculate the entropy of x.

Solution

$$H(x) = -0.5 \log_2(0.5) - 0.2 \log_2(0.2) - 0.15 \log_2(0.15) - 0.1 \log_2(0.1)$$

$$-0.05 \log_2(.05) = 1.923 \text{ bits}$$

Example 14.2

x assumes values 0 and 1 with probabilities p and $1 - p$, respectively. Discuss the entropy of x as a function of p.

Solution

The entropy of x is given from (14.1) as

$$H(x) = -p \log_2 p - (1 - p) \log_2(1 - p) \text{ bits}$$

Because we encounter binary random variables quite frequently, we define the **binary entropy function** $\mathscr{H}(p)$ as

$$\mathscr{H}(p) \triangleq -p \log_2 p - (1 - p) \log_2(1 - p) \tag{14.3}$$

Figure 14.2 displays the binary entropy function $\mathscr{H}(p)$. The entropy of a binary random variable is zero when $p = 0$ or $p = 1$. In either case, the random variable values are predictable, so

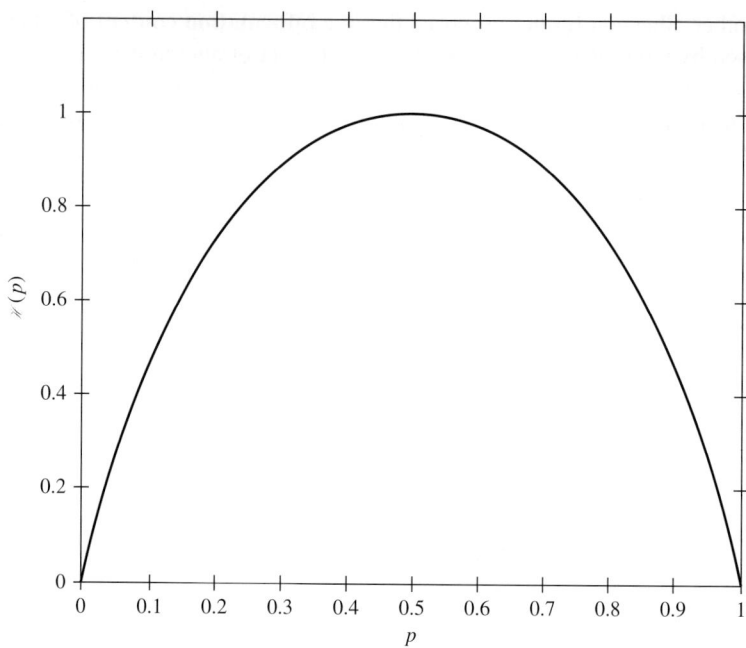

Figure 14.2 The binary entropy function $\mathscr{H}(p)$.

there is no uncertainty and no information gained by observing the realization of a random variable. The maximum value of $\mathscr{H}(p)$ occurs when $p = 1/2$, that is, when both values are equally unpredictable.

It follows from the discussion in Example 14.2 that maximum information is obtained by observing the realization of a random variable if it assumes all values with equal probability. This is formalized in the following statement: The uncertainty $H(\boldsymbol{x})$ of a discrete random variable $\boldsymbol{x}$ with K alternatives or outcomes $\{x_1, x_2, \ldots, x_K\}$ is bounded as

$$0 \leq H(\boldsymbol{x}) \leq \log_2 K \tag{14.4}$$

with equality on the left if and only if $p_i = 1$ for some i, and with equality on the right if and only if $p_i = 1/K$ for all i. The proof is given in Cover and Thomas.[3]

We now extend the definition of entropy to a pair of random variables.

14.1.1 Joint and Conditional Entropy

The **joint entropy** of a pair of discrete random variables $(\boldsymbol{x}, \boldsymbol{y})$ is defined as

$$H(\boldsymbol{x}, \boldsymbol{y}) = -\sum_{x_i \in \mathscr{X}} \sum_{y_j \in \mathscr{Y}} p_{\boldsymbol{xy}}(x_i, y_j) \log_2 p_{\boldsymbol{xy}}(x_i, y_j) \tag{14.5}$$

---

[3] T. Cover and J. Thomas, *Elements of Information Theory* (Hoboken, NJ: John Wiley, 1991).

Pioneers in the Field

Reprinted with permission of Alcatel-Lucent USA Inc.

Claude Elwood Shannon was born in Petoskey, Michigan, on April 30, 1916. As a boy, Shannon showed an inclination toward things mechanical. His best subjects in school were science and mathematics, and at home he constructed such devices as model planes, a radio-controlled model boat, and a telegraph system to a friend's house half a mile away. The telegraph made opportunistic use of two barbed wires around a nearby pasture. He earned spending money from a paper route and delivering telegrams, as well as repairing radios for a local department store. His childhood hero was Edison, who he later learned was a distant cousin. He graduated from the University of Michigan in 1936 with bachelor's degrees in mathematics and electrical engineering. He then went to Massachusetts Institute of Technology (MIT), and after spending the summer of 1937 at Bell Labs, he wrote one of the greatest master's theses ever, published in 1938 as *A Symbolic Analysis of Relay and Switching Circuits* in which he showed that the Boolean algebra provided the perfect mathematical model for switching theory and indeed for the subsequent design of digital circuits and computers. This work was awarded the prestigious Alfred Noble Prize in 1940. In 1940 he earned both a master's degree in electrical engineering and a Ph.D. in mathematics from MIT.

The year after graduating from MIT, Shannon took a job at Bell Labs, where he became known for keeping to himself by day and riding his unicycle down the halls at night. In 1948,

Shannon published his landmark paper, *A Mathematical Theory of Communication,* where he defined the concept of information and proposed a precise way to quantify it. According to Shannon, the fundamental unit of information is the *bit.* He showed that all information sources—speech, audio, video, images, and text files—have a source rate associated with them which can be measured in bits per second. Communication channels have a capacity measured in the same units. The information can be transmitted reliably over the channel if and only if the source rate does not exceed the channel capacity. Few other works of this century have had greater impact on science and engineering. In 1990, Scientific American called this paper, "The Magna Carta of the Information Age." Shannon stayed with Bell Labs for 15 years and left in 1956 to join MIT as Donner Professor of Science. He continued to serve on the MIT faculty until 1978.

Shannon published many more provocative and influential articles in a variety of disciplines. One example is Shannon's 1949 paper entitled *Communication Theory of Secrecy Systems.* This work is now generally credited with transforming cryptography from an art to a science. Shannon was renowned for his eclectic interests and capabilities. A favorite story describes him juggling while riding a unicycle down the halls of Bell Labs. He designed and built chess-playing, maze-solving, juggling, and mind-reading machines. These activities bear out Shannon's claim that he was more motivated by curiosity than usefulness. Shannon was the recipient of numerous awards in recognition of his monumental contributions to the creation of the information age, including the IEEE Medal of Honor (1966) and the National Medal of Science (1966), presented by President Johnson.

---

where x and y assume values in alphabets $\mathscr{A}_x = \{x_1, x_2, \ldots, x_K\}$ and $\mathscr{A}_y = \{y_1, y_2, \ldots, y_L\}$, respectively. If x and y are statistically independent, $p_{xy}(x_i, y_j) = p_x(x_i)p_y(y_j)$. Substituting into (14.5) yields

$$
\begin{aligned}
H(x, y) &= -\sum_{x_i \in \mathscr{A}_x}\sum_{y_j \in \mathscr{A}_y} p_x(x_i)p_y(y_j)\log_2 p_x(x_i)p_y(y_j) \\
&= -\sum_{x_i \in \mathscr{A}_x}\sum_{y_j \in \mathscr{A}_y} p_x(x_i)p_y(y_j)\log_2 p_x(x_i) - \sum_{x_i \in \mathscr{A}_x}\sum_{y_j \in \mathscr{A}_y} p_x(x_i)p_y(y_j)\log_2 p_y(y_j) \\
&= -\sum_{x_i \in \mathscr{A}_x} p_x(x_i)\log_2 p_x(x_i) - \sum_{y_j \in \mathscr{A}_y} p_y(y_j)\log_2 p_y(y_j) \\
&= H(x) + H(y)
\end{aligned}
\tag{14.6}
$$

The **conditional entropy** of the random variable x conditioned on the event $\{y = y_j\}$ is defined as

$$
H(x \mid y = y_j) = -\sum_{x_i \in \mathscr{A}_x} p_x(x_i \mid y = y_j)\log_2 p_x(x_i \mid y = y_j)
\tag{14.7}
$$

$H(x|y = y_j)$ represents our uncertainty about x after observing the event $\{y = y_j\}$. Similarly, we can define

$$H(y|x = x_i) = -\sum_{y_j \in \mathscr{S}_y} p_y(y_j|x = x_i)\log_2 p_y(y_j|x = x_i) \tag{14.8}$$

The **equivocation** or **average conditional entropy** $H(x|y)$ of the random variable x given the random variable y is defined as

$$H(x|y) = \sum_{y_j \in \mathscr{S}_y} p_y(y_j)H(x|y = y_j)$$

$$= -\sum_{x_i \in \mathscr{S}_x} \sum_{y_j \in \mathscr{S}_y} p_y(y_j)p_x(x_i|y = y_j)\log_2 p_x(x_i|y = y_j)$$

$$= -\sum_{x_i \in \mathscr{S}_x} \sum_{y_j \in \mathscr{S}_y} p_{xy}(x_i, y_j)\log_2 \frac{p_{xy}(x_i, y_j)}{\displaystyle\sum_{x_\ell \in \mathscr{S}_x} p_{xy}(x_\ell, y_j)} \tag{14.9}$$

$H(x|y)$ is a measure of the remaining uncertainty about x after observing the random variable y. Note that $H(x|y = y_j)$ is an entropy conditioned on an event, whereas the equivocation $H(x|y)$ is an entropy conditioned on a random variable. Strictly speaking, $H(x|y)$ is not entropy but rather an average entropy. We now show that the joint entropy, $H(x, y)$, of a pair of random variables is the entropy of one plus the conditional entropy of the other. That is,

$$H(x, y) = H(x) + H(y|x) \tag{14.10}$$

Proof

$H(x, y)$ can be expressed by expanding (14.5) and applying (14.9) as

$$H(x, y) = -\sum_{x_i \in \mathscr{S}_x} \sum_{y_j \in \mathscr{S}_y} p_{xy}(x_i, y_j)\log_2 p_{xy}(x_i, y_j) = -\sum_{x_i \in \mathscr{S}_x} \sum_{y_j \in \mathscr{S}_y} p_{xy}(x_i, y_j)\log_2[p_x(x_i)p_y(y_j|x = x_i)]$$

$$= -\sum_{x_i \in \mathscr{S}_x} \sum_{y_j \in \mathscr{S}_y} p_{xy}(x_i, y_j)\log_2 p_x(x_i) - \sum_{x_i \in \mathscr{S}_x} \sum_{y_j \in \mathscr{S}_y} p_{xy}(x_i, y_j)\log_2 p_y(y_j|x = x_i)$$

$$= -\sum_{x \in \mathscr{S}_x} p_x(x_i)\log_2 p_x(x_i) - \sum_{x_i \in \mathscr{S}_x} \sum_{y_j \in \mathscr{S}_y} p_{xy}(x_i, y_j)\log_2 p_y(y_j|x = x_i)$$

$$= H(x) + H(y|x)$$

Equation (14.10) states that the uncertainty of the pair (x, y) equals the uncertainty of x plus the uncertainty remaining about y after x has been observed. Similarly, it can be shown that

$$H(x, y) = H(y) + H(x|y) \tag{14.11}$$

We can now write the following expressions for average conditional entropies in terms of the joint entropy $H(x, y)$:

$$H(x|y) = H(x, y) - H(y) \tag{14.12}$$

$$H(y|x) = H(x, y) - H(x) \tag{14.13}$$

When x and y are statistically independent, it can be easily shown using (14.9) that

$$H(x|y) = H(x) \tag{14.14}$$

$$H(y|x) = H(y) \tag{14.15}$$

Equations (14.14) and (14.15) state that if x and y are statistically independent random variables, knowledge of one does not reduce our uncertainty about the other. It can be shown that the average conditional entropy satisfies the following inequality:

$$H(x|y) \leq H(x) \tag{14.16}$$

$$H(y|x) \leq H(y) \tag{14.17}$$

with equality if and only if x and y are statistically independent random variables. Inequalities (14.16) and (14.17) state that conditioning can never increase uncertainty.

Chain Rule for Entropy

Equations (14.10) and (14.11) can be generalized by induction for the case of n random variables $x_1, x_2, \ldots, x_n$ as follows:

$$H(x_1, x_2, \ldots, x_n) = H(x_1) + H(x_2|x_1) + H(x_3|x_1, x_2) + \ldots$$
$$+ H(x_n|x_1, x_2, \ldots, x_{n-1}) \tag{14.18}$$

$H(x_n|x_1, x_2, \ldots, x_{n-1})$ denotes our uncertainty about the random variable x_n after observing $x_1, x_2, \ldots, x_{n-1}$. If the random variables $x_1, x_2, \ldots, x_n$ are statistically independent, (14.18) simplifies to

$$H(x_1, x_2, \ldots, x_n) = H(x_1) + H(x_2) + H(x_3) + \ldots + H(x_n) = \sum_{i=1}^{n} H(x_i) \tag{14.19}$$

Example 14.3

The joint PMF $p_{xy}(x_i, y_j)$ of random variables x and y is given in the following table:

x \ y	y_1	y_2	y_3	y_4
x_1	1/8	1/16	1/32	1/32
x_2	1/32	1/8	1/16	1/32
x_3	1/32	1/32	1/8	1/16
x_4	1/16	1/32	1/32	1/8

Find $H(x)$, $H(y)$, $H(x, y)$, $H(x|y)$, $H(y|x)$.

Solution

The joint entropy $H(x, y)$ is obtained by substituting $p_{xy}(x_i, y_j)$ entries from the table into (14.5).

$$H(x, y) = -\sum_{x_i \in \mathscr{A}_x} \sum_{y_j \in \mathscr{A}_y} p_{xy}(x_i, y_j) \log_2 p_{xy}(x_i, y_j)$$

$$= 4\left(\frac{1}{8} \log_2 8 + \frac{1}{16} \log_2 16 + \frac{2}{32} \log_2 32 \right)$$

$$= \frac{4}{\log_e 2}(0.26 + 0.1733 + 0.2166) = 3.75 \text{ bits}$$

The marginal PMFs $p_x(x_i)$ and $p_y(y_j)$ are obtained by summing the rows and columns, respectively, as

$$p_x(x_i) = \{1/4, 1/4, 1/4, 1/4\}$$

$$p_y(y_j) = \{1/4, 1/4, 1/4, 1/4\}$$

Because x and y are equiprobable, their entropies are given by

$$H(x) = \log_2 4 = 2 \text{ bits}$$

$$H(y) = \log_2 4 = 2 \text{ bits}$$

Now we can compute the average conditional entropies using (14.12) and (14.13) as

$$H(x|y) = H(x, y) - H(y) = 3.75 - 2 = 1.75 \text{ bits}$$

$$H(y|x) = H(x, y) - H(x) = 3.75 - 2 = 1.75 \text{ bits}$$

14.1.2   Differential Entropy

We now introduce the concept of differential entropy for a continuous random variable x. The **differential entropy** $h(x)$ of a continuous random variable x with PDF $f_x(x)$ is defined as

$$h(x) = -\int_{-\infty}^{\infty} f_x(x) \log f_x(x) dx \tag{14.20}$$

As in the discrete case, the differential entropy depends only on the PDF of the random variable. Although the concept of differential entropy is similar in many ways to the entropy of a discrete random variable, it cannot be interpreted as the uncertainty of a continuous random variable x. As a matter of fact, it will require an infinite number of bits to represent the infinite values assumed by the continuous random variable x.

Example 14.4

Consider a continuous random variable x uniformly distributed between a and b, so that its PDF is

$$f_x(x) = \begin{cases} \dfrac{1}{b-a}, & a \leq x \leq b \\ 0, & \text{otherwise} \end{cases}$$

Its differential entropy is

$$h(x) = -\int_{a}^{b} \frac{1}{b-a} \log \frac{1}{b-a} dx = \log(b-a) \tag{14.21}$$

Note that for $b - a < 1$, $\log(b - a) < 0$, and the differential entropy is negative. Hence, unlike the entropy of a discrete random variable, differential entropy can be negative.

Example 14.5

Consider a Gaussian random variable $x \sim \mathcal{N}(0, \sigma_x^2)$. Its PDF is

$$f_x(x) = \frac{1}{\sqrt{2\pi\sigma_x^2}} e^{-x^2/2\sigma_x^2}$$

$$h(x) = -\int_{-\infty}^{\infty} f_x(x) \log_2 f_x(x) dx = -\int_{-\infty}^{\infty} f_x(x) \log_2 \frac{1}{\sqrt{2\pi\sigma_x^2}} e^{-x^2/2\sigma_x^2} dx$$

$$= -\int_{-\infty}^{\infty} f_x(x) \log_2 \left(\frac{1}{\sqrt{2\pi\sigma_x^2}} \right) dx - \int_{-\infty}^{\infty} f_x(x) \log_2 e^{-x^2/2\sigma_x^2} dx$$

$$= \log_2 \left(\sqrt{2\pi\sigma_x^2} \right) + \frac{\log_2 e}{2\sigma_x^2} \int_{-\infty}^{\infty} x^2 f_x(x) dx$$

$$= \frac{1}{2} \log_2(2\pi\sigma_x^2) + \frac{1}{2} \log_2 e = \frac{1}{2} \log_2(2\pi e \sigma_x^2) \text{ bits} \tag{14.22}$$

For discrete random variables, we observed in (14.4) that entropy was maximum when all the outcomes were equally likely. That is, a discrete random variable has maximum entropy if it has uniform PMF. For continuous random variables, we can obtain a similar result subject to either mean-square value or peak amplitude constraint.

- For a continuous random variable x with $\overline{x^2} = \sigma_x^2$, the Gaussian PDF maximizes the entropy. That is,

$$h(x) \le \frac{1}{2} \log_2(2\pi e \sigma_x^2) \text{ bits} \tag{14.23}$$

where the equality is achieved if $x \sim \mathcal{N}(0, \sigma_x^2)$. The proof is left as an exercise in Problem 14.6.
- For a continuous random variable x with $|x| \le a$, the entropy is maximum if x is uniformly distributed over $[-a, a]$. The proof is left as an exercise in Problem 14.5.

14.1.3 Mutual Information

The **mutual information** between two discrete random variables x and y, denoted by $I(x; y)$, is defined as

$$I(x; y) = H(x) - H(x|y) \tag{14.24}$$

The uncertainty about random variable x is $H(x)$ prior to observing y. $H(x|y)$ represents the remaining uncertainty about x after observation of y. The difference between these uncertainties, $I(x; y)$, is a measure of the information gained (or uncertainty removed) about random variable x by observing the random variable y. Substituting (14.1) and (14.9) into (14.24) yields

$$
\begin{aligned}
I(x; y) = H(x) - H(x|y) &= -\sum_{x \in \mathcal{X}_x} p_x(x_i)\log_2 p_x(x_i) + \sum_{x_i \in \mathcal{X}_x}\sum_{y_j \in \mathcal{X}_y} p_{xy}(x_i, y_j)\log_2 p_x(x_i|y = y_j) \\
&= -\sum_{x_i \in \mathcal{X}_x}\sum_{y_j \in \mathcal{X}_y} p_{xy}(x_i, y_j)\log_2 p_x(x_i) + \sum_{x_i \in \mathcal{X}_x}\sum_{y_j \in \mathcal{X}_y} p_{xy}(x_i, y_j)\log_2 p_x(x_i|y = y_j) \\
&= \sum_{x_i \in \mathcal{X}_x}\sum_{y_j \in \mathcal{X}_y} p_{xy}(x_i, y_j)\log_2 \frac{p_x(x_i|y = y_j)}{p_x(x_i)} \\
&= \sum_{x_i \in \mathcal{X}_x}\sum_{y_j \in \mathcal{X}_y} p_{xy}(x_i, y_j)\log_2 \frac{p_{xy}(x_i, y_j)}{p_x(x_i)p_y(y_j)} \qquad (14.25)
\end{aligned}
$$

$I(x; y)$ has many other interesting properties:

1. $I(x; y) \geq 0$ with equality if x and y are statistically independent
2. $I(x; y) = I(y; x)$ $\qquad\qquad$ (14.26)
3. $I(x; y) \leq \min\{H(x), H(y)\}$

The relationship between $H(x)$, $H(y)$, $H(x, y)$, $H(x|y)$, $H(y|x)$, and $I(x; y)$ is expressed in a Venn diagram illustrated in Figure 14.3. Notice that the mutual information $I(x; y)$ corresponds to the intersection of the information in x with the information in y.

We now extend the definition of mutual information to continuous random variables. The mutual information $I(x; y)$ between two continuous random variables x and y is defined as

$$
I(x; y) = h(x) - h(x|y) = h(y) - h(y|x) \qquad (14.27)
$$

By using a derivation similar to the one we used to obtain (14.25), we can express $I(x; y)$ as

$$
I(x; y) = \int_{-\infty}^{\infty} f_{xy}(x, y)\log\frac{f_{xy}(x, y)}{f_x(x)f_y(y)}dxdy \qquad (14.28)
$$

where $f_{xy}(x, y)$ is the joint PDF of random variables x and y.

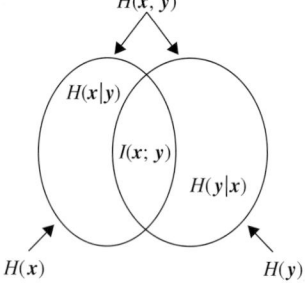

Figure 14.3 Relationship between various entropies and mutual information.

Example 14.6

The joint PMF $p_{xy}(x_i, y_j)$ of random variables x and y is given by

x \ y	y_1	y_2	y_3	y_4
x_1	1/32	1/32	1/8	1/16
x_2	1/32	1/32	1/16	1/8
x_3	1/16	1/16	1/16	1/16
x_4	0	0	1/4	0

Find $I(x; y)$.

Solution

$I(x; y)$ is given from (14.24) as

$$I(x; y) = H(x) - H(x|y)$$

The marginal PMFs $p_x(x_i)$ and $p_y(y_j)$ are obtained by summing, respectively, the columns and rows as

$$p_x(x_i) = \{1/4, 1/4, 1/4, 1/4\}$$

$$p_y(y_j) = \{1/8, 1/8, 1/2, 1/4\}$$

Because x is equiprobable, its entropy is given by

$$H(x) = \log_2 4 = 2 \text{ bits} \qquad (14.29)$$

Now

$$H(x|y) = \sum_{y_j \in \mathscr{Y}} p_y(y_j) H(x|y = y_j)$$

and

$$H(x|y = y_j) = -\sum_{x_i \in \mathscr{X}} p_x(x_i|y = y_j) \log_2 p_x(x_i|y = y_j)$$

Using $p_x(x_i|y = y_j) = \dfrac{p_x(x_i, y = y_j)}{p_y(y_j)}$, the conditional PMF matrix is given by

x \ y	y_1	y_2	y_3	y_4
x_1	1/4	1/4	1/4	1/4
x_2	1/4	1/4	1/8	1/2
x_3	1/2	1/2	1/8	1/4
x_4	0	0	1/2	0

$$H(x|y = y_1) = -\sum_{x_i \in \mathscr{X}} p_x(x_i|y = y_1) \log_2 p_x(x_i|y = y_1)$$

$$= \frac{1}{2} \log_2 2 + \frac{1}{4} \log_2 4 + \frac{1}{4} \log_2 4 = \frac{1}{2} + \frac{1}{2} + \frac{1}{2} = 1.5$$

Similarly,

$$H(x|y = y_2) = H(x|y = y_4) = 1.5 \text{ bits}$$

$$H(x|y = y_3) = -\sum_{x_i \in \mathscr{X}} p_x(x_i|y = y_1) \log_2 p_x(x_i|y = y_1)$$

$$= \frac{1}{2} \log_2 2 + \frac{1}{4} \log_2 4 + \frac{2}{8} \log_2 8 = \frac{1}{2} + \frac{1}{2} + \frac{3}{4} = 1.75$$

$$H(x|y) = \sum_{y_j \in \mathscr{Y}} p_y(y_j) H(x|y = y_j) = \frac{2}{8} \times 1.5 + \frac{1}{2} \times 1.75 + \frac{1}{4} \times 1.5 = 1.625 \text{ bit} \qquad (14.30)$$

Substituting (14.29) and (14.30) into (14.24) yields

$$I(x; y) = H(x) - H(x|y) = 2 - 1.625 = 0.375 \text{ bit}$$

14.2   SOURCE CODING

The source coding deals with efficient representation of different source types such as speech, images, and text files as sequences of bits for transmission through a digital network. The source encoder has the function of converting the input from its original form into a sequence of bits as efficiently as possible, that is, utilizing as few bits as possible, subject to the need to reconstruct the input with negligible loss of information. In this case source encoding is often called **data compression.** For example, modern speech compression schemes can encode telephone-quality speech at bit rates on the order of 8 to 16 kbps versus 64 kbps achievable using PCM as discussed in Section 8.4. In 1948 Shannon addressed the question of determining the best performance attainable in terms of encoded bits/symbol for any code of any block length. He found that the best performance achievable by any source encoding procedure was given by the entropy of the source. Shannon proved that no code can attain an average number of bits/symbol smaller than the entropy.

14.2.1   Discrete Memoryless Sources

A discrete information source generates messages at discrete-time instants that can be modeled as a discrete-time random process. That is, the source output is a sequence of identically distributed random variables $x_1, x_2, \ldots, x_n, \ldots$ as illustrated in Figure 14.4. The discrete random variables x_i assume values from a finite set of symbols $\mathscr{A}_x = \{a_1, a_2, \ldots, a_K\}$, called the **source alphabet,** according to PMF $p_x(a_i) = P\{x = a_i\} = p_i$. A source is called a **discrete memoryless source (DMS)** if the source output random variables $x_1, x_2, \ldots, x_n, \ldots$ are statistically independent. A discrete memoryless source x is completely specified by the source alphabet $\mathscr{A}_x$ and the associated PMF $p_x(a_i) = P\{x = a_i\} = p_i, i = 1, 2, \ldots, K$.

For a DMS x with alphabet $\mathscr{A}_x$, which generates the sequence $x_1, x_2, \ldots, x_n, \ldots$ of iid random variables, the entropy is given by

$$H(x) = -\sum_{a_i \in \mathscr{A}_x} p_x(a_i) \log_2 p_x(a_i) \quad = -\sum_{i=1}^{K} p_i \log_2 p_i \quad \text{bits/symbol} \qquad (14.31)$$

The entropy of a source is a measure of its average information content.

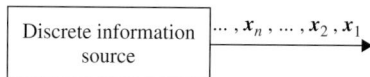

Figure 14.4 Discrete-time information source.

Example 14.7

Calculate the entropy of a DMS x with M equiprobable symbols.

Solution

$$H(x) = -\sum_{i=1}^{M} \frac{1}{M} \log_2 \frac{1}{M} = \log_2 M \qquad (14.32)$$

As a special case, if the number of source symbols is a power of 2, that is, $M = 2^k$, (14.32) simplifies to

$$H(x) = -\sum_{i=1}^{2^k} \frac{1}{2^k} \log_2 \frac{1}{2^k} = \log_2 2^k = k \text{ bits/symbol} \tag{14.33}$$

Equation (14.33) states that when $M = 2^k$ source output symbols are equiprobable, we can assign each symbol a k-bit codeword and achieve the entropy of the source. As we shall see next, this simple code achieves the best possible performance.

If the discrete-time source is not memoryless, the **entropy rate** $H'(x)$ of the source x is defined by the conditional entropy

$$H'(x) = \lim_{n \to \infty} H(x_n | x_1, x_2, \ldots, x_{n-1}) \tag{14.34}$$

$H(x_n | x_1, x_2, \ldots, x_{n-1})$ represents the fresh information provided by the source output x_n at time n given the previous outputs $x_1, x_2, \ldots, x_{n-1}$. The entropy rate plays the role of entropy for sources with memory.

14.2.2 Shannon's Source Coding Theorem

The source coding theorem, introduced by Shannon in his seminal paper in 1948, is one of the fundamental results of information theory.[4] The source coding theorem establishes a fundamental limit on the rate at which the output of an information source can be compressed without causing significant loss of information. Because the entropy of a source is a measure of its information content, it is therefore not surprising that the entropy of a source plays a key role in this theorem.

Consider a DMS x that generates statistically independent and identically distributed random variables $x_1, x_2, \ldots, x_n, \ldots$. The discrete-time random variables x_i assume values from the finite alphabet $\mathscr{A}_x = \{a_1, a_2, \ldots, a_K\}$ with probabilities $\{p_1, p_2, \ldots, p_K\}$. If we observe the source output sequences $\underline{x} = (x_1, x_2, \ldots, x_n)$ as n gets very large, the symbol a_1, on the average, will appear approximately np_1 times, symbol a_2 is repeated approximately np_2 times, and symbol a_j is repeated np_j times with high probability (i.e., close to 1). We call such sequences **typical sequences.** All other sequences are referred to as **nontypical sequences.**

Example 14.8

Consider a source with alphabet $\mathscr{A} = \{a, b, c, d, e, f, g, h\}$ with symbol probabilities $\left\{\frac{1}{4}, \frac{1}{4}, \frac{1}{8}, \frac{1}{8},\right.$ $\left.\frac{1}{16}, \frac{1}{16}, \frac{1}{16}, \frac{1}{16}\right\}$. If we examine output sequences of length $n = 16$, we would expect a to appear approximately $16 \times 1/4 = 4$ times, c to appear $16 \times 1/8 = 2$ times, d to appear $16 \times 1/16 = 1$ time and so on. Examples of length 16 typical sequences are $\{a, d, b, b, e, a, f, a, c, a, g, b, b, c, d, h\}$ and $\{a, d, b, f, a, g, a, h, b, e, c, b, a, c, b, d\}$. Examples of nontypical sequences of length 16 are $\{d, b, a, h, h\,b, c, c, a, b, d, c, e, e, f, f\}$ and $\{c, h, h, d, c, c, b, c, c, a, e, e, a, f, g, g\}$.

[4] Shannon, "A Mathematical Theory of Communication," 379–423.

By invoking the DMS assumption, we can write the probability of a typical sequence as

$$P\{\text{typical sequence } \underline{x}\} \approx \underbrace{p_1 p_1 \cdots p_1}_{np_1 \text{ times}} \times \underbrace{p_2 p_2 \cdots p_2}_{np_2 \text{ times}} \times \cdots \times \underbrace{p_K p_K \cdots p_K}_{np_K \text{ times}}$$

$$= p_1^{np_1} p_2^{np_2}, \ldots, p_K^{np_K} = \prod_{k=1}^{K} p_k^{np_k}$$

$$= \prod_{k=1}^{K} 2^{\log_2(p_k^{np_k})} = \prod_{k=1}^{K} 2^{(np_k \log_2 p_k)}$$

$$= 2^{n \sum_{k=1}^{K} (p_k \log_2 p_k)}$$

$$= 2^{-nH(x)} \tag{14.35}$$

where $p_i = P\{x_j = a_i\}$ for all j and for all i. $H(x)$ is the entropy of the DMS x. For large n, all output sequences of the source are typical with probability almost 1. Equation (14.35) states that these sequences are equiprobable with probability $\approx 2^{-nH(x)}$. Therefore,

$$\sum_{\text{typical sequences } \underline{x}} 2^{-nH(x)} \approx 1 \quad \text{for large } n \tag{14.36}$$

There are K^n possible output sequences of length n for a source with alphabet of size K. However, the number of typical sequences from (14.36) is almost $2^{nH(x)}$. Because the probability of a typical sequence is almost 1, the probability of nontypical sequences is negligible. The essence of source coding or data compression is that as $n \to \infty$, nontypical sequences never appear as the output of the source. Therefore, one only needs to be able to represent typical sequences as binary codes and ignore nontypical sequences. Because there are only $2^{nH(x)}$ typical sequences of length n, it takes $nH(x)$ bits to represent them on the average. This implies that, on the average, it takes $H(x)$ bits per source output to represent a simple source that produces independent and identically distributed outputs.

Example 14.9

For the DMS in Example 14.8, calculate the number of typical and nontypical sequences of length 16.

Solution

The entropy of the source is given by

$$H(x) = -\sum_{i=1}^{K} p_i \log_2 p_i = -0.25 \log_2(0.25) - 0.25 \log_2(0.25) - 0.125 \log_2(0.125) - 0.125 \log_2(0.125)$$

$$-0.0625 \log_2(0.0625) - 0.0625 \log_2(0.0625) - 0.0625 \log_2(0.0625) - 0.0625 \log_2(0.0625)$$

$$= 2.75 \text{ bits/symbol}$$

Total number of sequences of length 16 is $8^{16} = 2^{48}$
The number of typical sequences of length 16 is $2^{(16 \times 2.75)} = 2^{44}$
The number of nontypical sequences is $2^{48} - 2^{44} = 15 \times 2^{44}$

A formal statement of Shannon's source coding theorem follows.

Theorem 14.1 (Source coding theorem). The output sequence of a DMS x consisting of n independent and identically distributed random variables $x_1, x_2, \ldots, x_n$ can be encoded into no less than $nH(x)$ bits with negligible risk of information loss as $n \to \infty$. Conversely, if the source output sequence $x_1, x_2, \ldots, x_n$ is compressed into fewer than $nH(x)$ bits, it is virtually certain that information will be lost, irrespective of the complexity of encoder and decoder.

The source coding theorem proves the existence of source coding techniques that achieve compressed data rates close to the entropy of the source but does not provide any algorithms or ways to construct such codes. If the source is not memoryless, but it is stationary with memory, then a similar theorem applies with the entropy replaced by the entropy rate. In the case of a source with memory, the more one knows about the source's previous outputs, the more one can compress.

Example 14.10

Calculate the entropy of the English language.

Solution

The English language has 26 letters, and with the spaces between words it becomes an alphabet of size 27. If it is modeled as a memoryless source (no dependency between letters in a word), then the entropy is $H(x) = \log_2(27) = 4.75$ bits/letter.

If the dependency between letters in a text is captured in a model, the entropy rate can be derived to be $H(x) = 1.3$ bits/letter. Note that a noninformation theoretic representation of a text may require 5 bits/letter because 2^5 is the closest power of 2 to 27. Shannon's results indicate that there may be a compression algorithm with the rate of 1.3 bits/letter.

Although Shannon's results are not constructive, there are a number of source coding algorithms for discrete-time, discrete-valued sources that come close to Shannon's entropy bound. One such algorithm is the Huffman source coding algorithm. Another is the Lempel-Ziv algorithm. Huffman and Lempel-Ziv compression schemes apply to sources which produce discrete-time and discrete-valued outputs.

14.3   CHANNEL CODING

In this section, we consider the fundamental possibilities and limitations of error-free communication through a noisy channel. Shannon addressed this problem in his famous channel coding theorem. His result that noise in the channel sets the ultimate limit on the rate and not the accuracy at which data can be reliably transmitted came as a total surprise to communication engineers. We begin our discussion with modeling of communication channels.

14.3.1   Modeling of Communication Channels

All communication channels can be modeled as discrete-time channels by invoking the sampling theorem. Figure 14.5 displays a discrete-time channel where the channel input symbol is a discrete random variable x taking on values from the finite alphabet

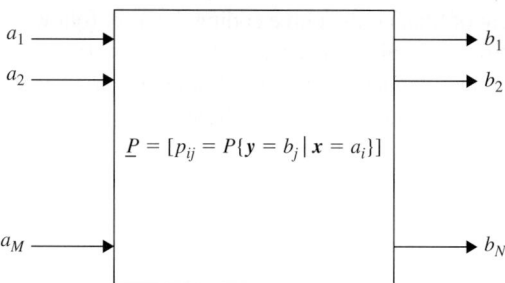

Figure 14.5 Discrete-time, finite-alphabet communication channel model.

$\mathscr{A}_x = \{a_1, a_2, \ldots, a_M\}$ according to PMF $p_x(a_i) = P\{x = a_i\}$. We assume that the channel output symbol y is also a discrete random variable taking on values from the finite alphabet $\mathscr{A}_y = \{b_1, b_2, \ldots, b_N\}$ according to PMF $p_y(b_j) = P\{y = b_j\}$. Because of the noise added by the channel, there is uncertainty at the receiver about the input symbol x after observing the channel output y. That is, the mapping of channel input symbols into output symbols is probabilistic and is described by the set of conditional or **transition probabilities** $p_{ij} = P\{y = b_j | x = a_i\}$, where $b_j \in \mathscr{A}_y$ and $a_i \in \mathscr{A}_x$. Accordingly, the channel in Figure 14.5 is often specified by the matrix of various transition probabilities as follows:

$$\underline{P} = \begin{pmatrix} p_{11} & p_{12} & \cdots & p_{1N} \\ p_{21} & p_{22} & \cdots & p_{21N} \\ \vdots & \vdots & \cdots & \vdots \\ p_{M1} & p_{M2} & \cdots & p_{MN} \end{pmatrix} \tag{14.37}$$

The channel matrix $\underline{P}$ can be used to calculate the output probabilities $p_y(b_j) = P\{y = b_j\}$.

$$p_y(b_j) = P\{y = b_j\} = \sum_{i=1}^{M} P\{x = a_i, y = b_j\}$$

$$= \sum_{i=1}^{M} P\{x = a_i\} P\{y = b_j | x = a_i\}, \quad j = 1, 2, \ldots, N \tag{14.38}$$

Equation (14.38) can be expressed in the matrix form as

$$\underline{p}_y = \underline{p}_x \underline{P} \tag{14.39}$$

where vectors

$$\underline{p}_x = \begin{pmatrix} p_x(a_1) & p_x(a_2) & \cdots & p_x(a_M) \end{pmatrix} \tag{14.40}$$

and

$$\underline{p}_y = \begin{pmatrix} p_y(b_1) & p_y(b_2) & \cdots & p_y(b_N) \end{pmatrix} \tag{14.41}$$

are PMFs of channel input and output random variables x and y, respectively.

Discrete Memoryless Channels

In general the channel output symbol $\mathbf{y}_\ell$ at time ℓ depends not only on the current input symbol $\mathbf{x}_\ell$ but on previous and, sometimes, future inputs as well (for example, storage channels). That is, a channel can have a memory. An important class of discrete-time channels is **discrete memoryless channels (DMCs)** in which the output symbol $\mathbf{y}_\ell$ at time ℓ depends only on the current channel input $\mathbf{x}_\ell$. If $\underline{x} = (x_1, x_2, \ldots, x_n)$ and $\underline{y} = (y_1, y_2, \ldots, y_n)$ represent channel input and output vectors for a DMC, we can write

$$P(\underline{y}|\underline{x}) = \prod_{\ell=1}^{n} P(\mathbf{y}_\ell|\mathbf{x}_\ell) \tag{14.42}$$

An example of a DMC is the **binary symmetric channel (BSC)** in which the input and output symbols assume values from the binary alphabet, that is, $\mathscr{A}_x = \mathscr{A}_y = \{0, 1\}$. When an error occurs, a 0 is received as a 1 with probability $p = P(1|0)$ and vice versa as shown in Figure 14.6. The probability $p = P(1|0) = P(0|1)$ is called the **crossover probability.** The probability of receiving 0 and 1 correctly is given by $1 - p$. That is, $P(1|1) = P(0|0) = 1 - p$. The channel matrix for a BSC is given by

$$\underline{P} = \begin{pmatrix} 1-p & p \\ p & 1-p \end{pmatrix} \tag{14.43}$$

Another widely used DMC model is the **binary erasure channel (BEC)** in which a fraction ε of the bits are lost or erased (rather than corrupted as in the BSC). Binary 1 and 0 are received correctly with probability $1 - \varepsilon$. The binary erasure channel has two inputs and three outputs as shown in Figure 14.7. The receiver knows which bits have been erased. The channel matrix for a BEC is given by

$$\underline{P} = \begin{pmatrix} 1-\varepsilon & \varepsilon & 0 \\ 0 & \varepsilon & 1-\varepsilon \end{pmatrix} \tag{14.44}$$

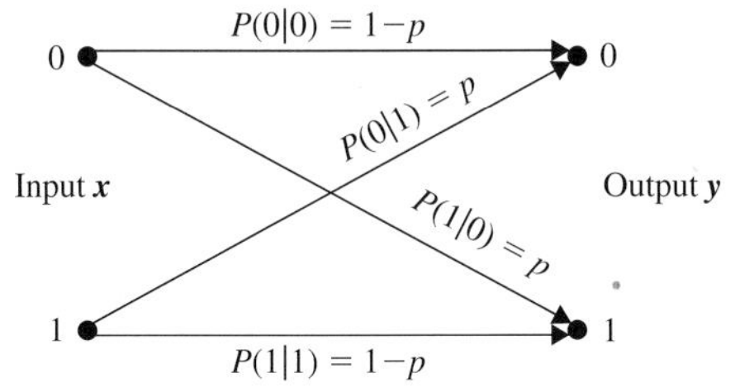

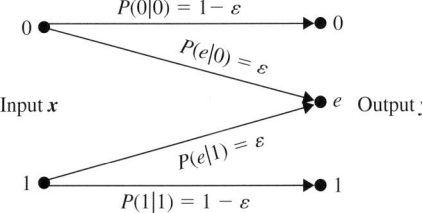

Figure 14.6 Binary symmetric channel model.

Figure 14.7 Binary erasure channel model.

14.3.2   Capacity of a Communication Channel

The mutual information $I(x; y)$ between channel input (x) and output (y) random variables is given from (14.24) as

$$I(x; y) = H(x) - H(x|y)$$

If the channel is noise-free, $H(x|y)$ should be zero, and the average amount of information gained by the receiver after observing the channel output y equals $H(x)$ bits. In the presence of channel noise, $H(x|y)$ represents the residual uncertainty about x after observing the channel output y. Because the mutual information $I(x; y)$ is the average amount of information conveyed to the receiver per transmitted symbol, its units are bits/channel use or bits/symbol transmitted. Using (14.25), we can write

$$I(x; y) = \sum_{a_i \in \mathscr{A}_x} \sum_{b_j \in \mathscr{A}_y} p_{xy}(a_i, b_j) \log_2 \frac{p_{xy}(a_i, b_j)}{p_x(a_i) p_y(b_j)} \tag{14.45}$$

Applying Bayes's rule in (14.45), $I(x; y)$ can be expressed as

$$
\begin{aligned}
I(x; y) &= \sum_{a_i \in \mathscr{A}_x} \sum_{b_j \in \mathscr{A}_y} p_x(a_i) p_y(b_j | x = a_i) \log_2 \frac{p_y(b_j | x = a_i)}{p_y(b_j)} \\
&= \sum_{a_i \in \mathscr{A}_x} \sum_{b_j \in \mathscr{A}_y} p_x(a_i) p_y(b_j | x = a_i) \log_2 \frac{p_y(b_j | x = a_i)}{\displaystyle\sum_{a_k \in \mathscr{A}_x} p_{xy}(a_k, b_j)} \\
&= \sum_{a_i \in \mathscr{A}_x} \sum_{b_j \in \mathscr{A}_y} p_x(a_i) p_y(b_j | x = a_i) \log_2 \frac{p_y(b_j | x = a_i)}{\displaystyle\sum_{a_k \in \mathscr{A}_x} p_x(a_k) p_y(b_j | x = a_k)}
\end{aligned}
\tag{14.46}
$$

From (14.46) it can be seen that $I(x; y)$ is a function of the channel input PMF $\underline{p}_x$ and transition probabilities of the channel $p_y(b_j | x = a_i)$. For a given channel, $I(x; y)$ will be maximized for some choice of PMF $\underline{p}_x$ on the input alphabet $\mathscr{A}_x$. This maximum value is called the **capacity** C of the channel. It is defined as

$$C = \underset{\underline{p}_x}{\text{Max}} \ I(x; y) \ \text{bits/channel use} \tag{14.47}$$

Thus, the capacity C represents the maximum information that can be transmitted over the channel per channel use.

Example 14.11

Consider the noiseless binary channel illustrated in Figure 14.8 with $\mathscr{A}_x = \mathscr{A}_y = \{0, 1\}$. Calculate the capacity C of the channel.

Solution

Because each transmitted bit is received without error, there is no uncertainty about input x after observing the output y. Therefore, $H(x|y) = 0$, and

$$I(x; y) = H(x) - H(x|y) = H(x)$$

Figure 14.8 Noiseless binary channel model.

Now $H(x) \le 1$. The maximum value of $H(x) = 1$ occurs when x is equiprobable. Therefore,

$$C = \underset{p_x}{\text{Max}}\, I(x; y) = 1 \text{ bit/channel use}$$

For a noiseless channel with q-ary alphabet $\mathscr{A}_x = \mathscr{A}_y = \{0, 1, \ldots, q - 1\}$, the channel capacity is given by

$$C = \underset{p_x}{\text{Max}}\, I(x; y) = \log_2 q \text{ bits/channel use} \tag{14.48}$$

because $H(x) \le q$ with equality if all q channel symbols are equiprobable.

Example 14.12

Consider the noisy four-symbol channel illustrated in Figure 14.9 with $\mathscr{A}_x = \mathscr{A}_y = \{0, 1, 2, 3\}$. Calculate the capacity C of the channel.

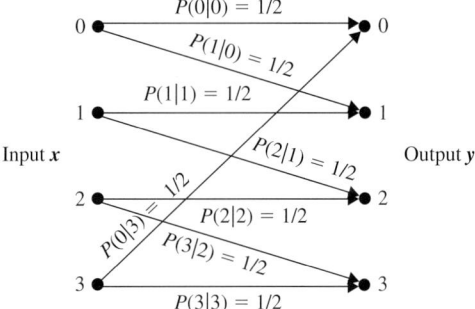

Figure 14.9 Noisy four-symbol channel model.

Solution

In this channel, each input letter is received either as the same letter with probability 1/2 or as the next letter with probability 1/2. If we use all four input symbols, then observation of the output does not reveal with certainty which input symbol was sent. If, on the other hand, we use only two of the inputs (1 and 3 say), then we can immediately tell from the output which input symbol was sent. This channel then acts like the noiseless channel of Example 14.11, and we can send 1 bit per transmission over this channel with no errors. The channel capacity, therefore, is equal to 1 bit per/channel use.

Capacity of Symmetric Channels

A channel is said to be **symmetric** if the rows of the channel transition probability matrix $\underline{P}$ are permutations of one another and so are the columns. A channel is said to be **weakly symmetric** if every row of the channel matrix $\underline{P}$ is a permutation of every other row and all column sums $\sum_{a_i \in \mathscr{A}_x} p_y(b_j | \boldsymbol{x} = a_i)$ are equal. Let $\underline{p} = (p_{i1}, p_{i2}, \ldots, p_{iN})$ be the probability vector corresponding to a row of the channel transition probability matrix $\underline{P}$. Then

$$I(\boldsymbol{x}; \boldsymbol{y}) = H(\boldsymbol{y}) - H(\boldsymbol{y} | \boldsymbol{x})$$

$$= H(\boldsymbol{y}) - \sum_{a_i \in \mathscr{A}_x} p_x(a_i) H(\boldsymbol{y} | \boldsymbol{x} = a_i) \tag{14.49}$$

Because each row of the matrix $\underline{P}$ is a permutation of every other row, we can say that $H(\boldsymbol{y} | \boldsymbol{x} = a_i) = H(\underline{p})$ is same for all i. That is, $H(\boldsymbol{y} | \boldsymbol{x} = a_i)$ is independent of the value assumed by $\boldsymbol{x}$. Therefore,

$$I(\boldsymbol{x}; \boldsymbol{y}) = H(\boldsymbol{y}) - H(\underline{p}) \tag{14.50}$$

where

$$H(\underline{p}) = H(p_{i1}, p_{i2}, \ldots, p_{iN}) = \sum_{j=1}^{N} p_{ij} \log_2 p_{ij} \tag{14.51}$$

For a symmetric or weakly symmetric channel, if the input PMF $\underline{p}_x$ is uniformly distributed, it follows from (14.39) that the output PMF $\underline{p}_y$ is also uniformly distributed because each row of the channel matrix $\underline{P}$ is a permutation of every other row. Therefore, $\underset{p_x}{\text{Max}} H(\boldsymbol{y}) = \log_2 N$, where N is number of elements in the channel output alphabet $\mathscr{A}_y = \{b_1, b_2, \ldots, b_N\}$. The channel capacity of a symmetric or weakly symmetric channel can now be expressed as

$$C = \underset{p_x}{\text{Max}} I(\boldsymbol{x}; \boldsymbol{y}) = \underset{p_x}{\text{Max}} [H(\boldsymbol{y}) - H(\underline{p})] = \underset{p_x}{\text{Max}} H(\boldsymbol{y}) - H(\underline{p})$$

$$= \log_2 N - H(\underline{p}) \tag{14.52}$$

Example 14.13

Calculate the capacity of a BSC with $p_x(0) = \alpha$ and $p_x(1) = 1 - \alpha$.

Solution

We note from (14.43) that the channel matrix for a BSC is symmetric. Therefore, the capacity of a BSC is given by applying (14.51) and (14.52) as

$$C = \log_2(2) - H(p, 1 - p)$$

$$= 1 - \mathscr{H}(p) \text{ bits/channel use} \tag{14.53}$$

The capacity of a BSC is displayed in Figure 14.10. We observe that the channel capacity C is function of the channel error probability p. It assumes the maximum value of 1 bit/channel use when the channel bit error probability $p = 0$ or 1. When $p = 0$, the channel is noiseless, and it is obvious that C is maximum. However, it is not so obvious that C is maximum when $p = 1$. In that case, because the channel consistently makes errors—that is, a 1 is always received as 0 and vice versa—we can flip the decision each time and have error-free reception. The channel capacity is minimum, that is, zero, when $p = 1/2$ The received symbol is equally likely to be 0 or 1 when either symbol is transmitted. This implies that the transmitted and received bits are statistically independent. That is, $H(\boldsymbol{x} | \boldsymbol{y}) = H(\boldsymbol{x})$, and $I(\boldsymbol{x}; \boldsymbol{y}) = H(\boldsymbol{x}) - H(\boldsymbol{x}) = 0$. Thus, no information is transmitted.

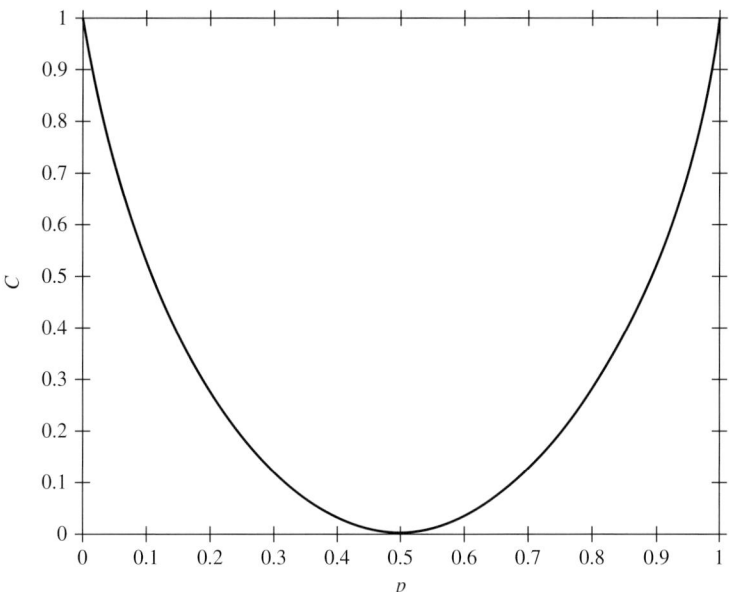

Figure 14.10 Capacity of a binary symmetric channel.

Example 14.14

A channel has the transition matrix

$$\underline{P} = \begin{pmatrix} 1/2 & 1/3 & 1/6 \\ 1/6 & 1/2 & 1/3 \\ 1/3 & 1/6 & 1/2 \end{pmatrix}$$

a. Sketch the channel diagram showing transition probabilities.
b. Determine the channel output probabilities assuming that the input probabilities are
$\underline{p}_x = (1/2 \quad 1/4 \quad 1/4)$.
c. Find the channel capacity.

Solution

a.

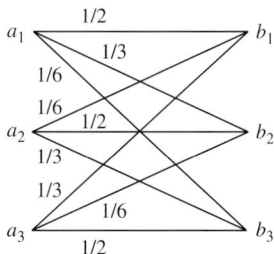

Figure 14.11 Channel model.

b. From (14.39), we have

$$\underline{p}_y = \underline{p}_x \underline{P} = (1/2 \ 1/4 \ 1/4) \begin{pmatrix} 1/2 & 1/3 & 1/6 \\ 1/6 & 1/2 & 1/3 \\ 1/3 & 1/6 & 1/2 \end{pmatrix} = (9/24 \ 8/24 \ 7/24)$$

c. Because the channel is symmetric, the channel capacity is obtained by applying (14.51) and (14.52) as

$$C = \log_2(3) - H(1/2, 1/3, 1/6)$$

$$= 1.5849 - 1.4591 = 0.1258 \text{ bits/channel use}$$

Example 14.15

Calculate the capacity of a BEC with $p_x(0) = \alpha$ and $p_x(1) = 1 - \alpha$.

Solution

We use $C = \underset{p_x}{\text{Max}} I(x; y) = \underset{p_x}{\text{Max}} \{H(x) - H(x|y)\}$ to calculate the channel capacity because it is easier to calculate $H(x|y)$ for a BEC. If $y = 0$ (or 1), we know with certainty that $x = 0$ (or 1). Therefore,

$$H(x|y = 0) = 0$$

$$H(x|y = 1) = 0$$

For a BEC, $H(x|y)$ can therefore be expressed using (14.9) as

$$H(x|y) = \sum_{y_j \in \mathcal{Y}} p_y(y_j) H(x|y = y_j) = p_y(e) H(x|y = e)$$

The conditional entropy $H(x|y = e)$ is obtained from (14.7) as

$$H(x|y = e) = -\sum_{x_i \in \mathcal{X}} p_x(x_i|y = e) \log_2 p_x(x_i|y = e) \tag{14.54}$$

From Figure 14.7, we have

$$p_y(e|x = 0) = p_y(e|x = 1) = \varepsilon \tag{14.55}$$

Using the law of total probability (6.16) and (14.55), we can write

$$p_y(e) = p_x(0) p_y(e|x = 0) + p_x(1) p_y(e|x = 1) = \alpha\varepsilon + (1 - \alpha)\varepsilon \tag{14.56}$$

Using Bayes's rule, (14.55), and (14.56), we obtain

$$p_x(0|y = e) = \frac{p_y(e|x = 0) p_x(0)}{p_y(e)} = \frac{\varepsilon\alpha}{\varepsilon\alpha + (1 - \alpha)\varepsilon} = \frac{\varepsilon\alpha}{\varepsilon} = \alpha \tag{14.57}$$

$$p_x(1|y = e) = \frac{p_y(e|x = 1) p_x(1)}{p_y(e)} = \frac{\varepsilon(1 - \alpha)}{\varepsilon\alpha + (1 - \alpha)\varepsilon} = \frac{\varepsilon(1 - \alpha)}{\varepsilon} = 1 - \alpha \tag{14.58}$$

Substituting (14.57) and (14.58) into (14.54) yields

$$H(x|y = e) = -\{(1 - \alpha) \log_2(1 - \alpha) + \alpha \log_2 \alpha\} = \mathcal{H}(\alpha) \tag{14.59}$$

where $\mathcal{H}(\alpha)$ is the binary entropy function. We can now write the following expression for the average conditional entropy $H(x|y)$ by substituting (14.56) and (14.59) into (14.9).

$$H(x|y) = p_y(e) H(x|y = e) = \varepsilon \mathcal{H}(\alpha) \tag{14.60}$$

For a binary random variable x with $p_x(0) = \alpha$ and $p_x(1) = 1 - \alpha$, we have from (14.3)

$$H(x) = \mathscr{H}(\alpha)$$

Combining (14.3) and (14.60), the mutual information $I(x; y)$ can now be expressed as

$$I(x; y) = \mathscr{H}(\alpha) - \varepsilon \mathscr{H}(\alpha) = (1 - \varepsilon)\mathscr{H}(\alpha) \tag{14.61}$$

Because $\mathscr{H}(\alpha) \leq 1$, taking the maximum over all input PMF $p_x(x)$ yields

$$C = \underset{p_x(a_i)}{\mathrm{Max}}\, I(x; y) = 1 - \varepsilon \text{ bits/channel use} \tag{14.62}$$

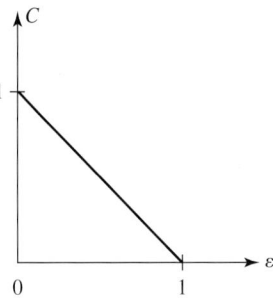

Figure 14.12 Capacity of a binary erasure channel.

The capacity of a BEC is displayed in Figure 14.12. The expression for capacity in (14.61) intuitively makes sense. Because a portion ε of the bits are lost in the channel, we can recover (at most) a portion $1 - \varepsilon$ of the bits. Hence the capacity cannot be greater than $1 - \varepsilon$.

Example 14.16

Calculate the capacity of the noisy typewriter where $\mathscr{A}_x = \mathscr{A}_y = \{A, B, C, \ldots, Z, -\}$ is assumed as illustrated in Figure 14.13.

Solution

The input and output alphabets consist of 26 characters of English language and the space character "$-$". The channel input is either received unchanged at the output with probability 1/3 or is transformed into one of two adjacent letters with probability 1/3 as illustrated in Figure 14.13. For example, when the character B is sent, either B, C, or D is received with probability 1/3 for each. If we use 9 out of 27 as input characters (e.g., $B, E, H, K, N, Q, T, W, Z$), we can transmit 1 character without error with each transmission. The capacity of this channel is given by

$$C = \underset{p_x}{\mathrm{Max}}\{H(y) - H(y|x)\}$$

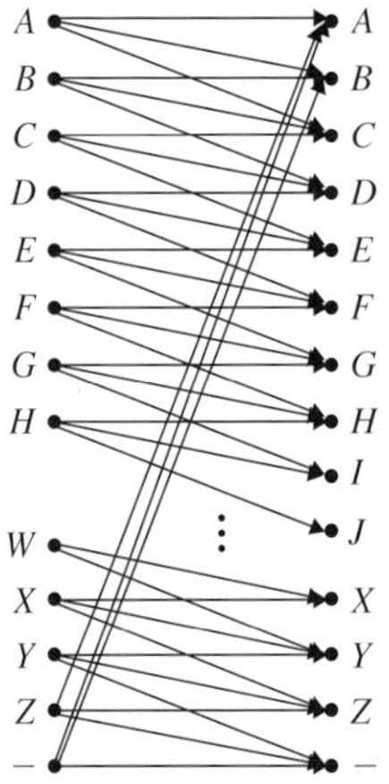

Using (14.8), the conditional entropy $H(y|x = B)$ can be expressed as

$$
\begin{aligned}
H(y|x = B) &= -\sum_{y_j = B,\, C,\, \text{or } D} p_y(y_j | x = B) \log_2 p_y(y_j | x = B) \\
&= -(1/3)\log_2(1/3) - (1/3)\log_2(1/3) - (1/3)\log_2(1/3) \\
&= -\log_2(1/3) = \log_2 3
\end{aligned}
$$

Therefore, we can say that $H(y|x) = \log_2 3$. Because this is a symmetric channel, $\underset{p_x}{\mathrm{Max}}\{H(y)\} = \log_2 27 = \log_2 9 + \log_2 3$ is achieved by using PMF p_x uniformly distributed over all the inputs. The channel capacity is now given by $C = \log_2 9 + \log_2 3 - \log_2 3 = \log_2 9$ bits/channel use.

Figure 14.13 Noisy typewriter channel.

14.3.3 Shannon's Channel Capacity Theorem

Now we consider the fundamental limit for the amount of information that can be transmitted through a noisy channel and discuss practical methods to approach it. We assume that the channel encoder divides the binary information sequence into message blocks $\underline{m} = (m_0, m_1, \ldots, m_{k-1})$ of k data bits each. The encoder maps each message block into an n-bit unique **codeword** $\underline{x} = (x_0, x_1, \ldots, x_{n-1})$ using an **(n, k) block code** $\mathscr{C}$. There are $M = 2^k$ different codewords of length n in $\mathscr{C}$. The **code rate** of the (n, k) block code is defined as

$$R_c = \frac{k}{n} = \frac{\log_2 M}{n} \tag{14.63}$$

It measures **bits transmitted per use** of the communication channel. We can write an alternative expression for the number of codewords in $\mathscr{C}$ in terms of the code rate R_c as

$$M = 2^{nR_c} \tag{14.64}$$

Prior to Shannon's paper, it was widely believed that reliability (i.e., arbitrary low probability of error) could be achieved over noisy channels by trading the speed of transmission. However, Shannon's remarkable channel coding theorem says that reliable transmission is possible over noisy channels as long as the rate R_c is less than the channel capacity C.

Theorem 14.2 (Channel coding theorem). For any $\varepsilon > 0$ and sufficiently large n, there exists a code of length n such that we can transmit information at rate $R_c < C$ with maximum probability of codeword error $< \varepsilon$. Conversely, if $R_c > C$, then it is not possible to transmit information without errors.

Shannon's coding theorem is an existence theorem, and as such it does not specify practical methods of generating "good" codes. Instead, it says that such "good" codes exist. The key result of Shannon's theorem is that the ultimate limit of performance set by the noise on the communication channel is not the **accuracy** (i.e., arbitrary low error probability), but the **rate** at which data can be reliably transmitted.

The proof of the channel coding theorem is provided in Shannon's original paper as well as in several excellent texts.[5] We shall here consider only an intuitive preview of the proof. The key idea is that, for sufficiently long codewords or sequences, every channel looks like the noisy typewriter channel. That is, we can identify a subset of the input sequences (i.e., the codewords) that produce essentially disjoint or nonoverlapping sets of possible output sequences. The transmitted codeword can, therefore, be identified virtually without error by ML decoding. To transmit information at channel capacity, we need to develop a method of generating such a distinguishable set of codewords of length n. This is illustrated in Figure 14.14.

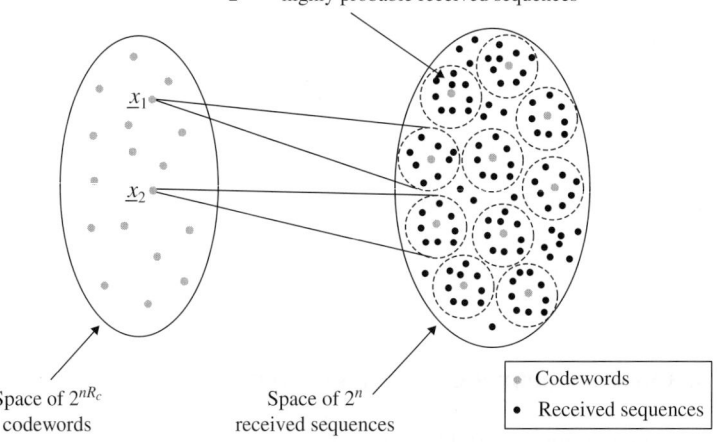

Figure 14.14 Partitioning of typical output sequences for error-free ML decoding.

[5] C. Shannon, "A Mathematical Theory of Communication," *Bell System Technical Journal* 27 (1948): 379–423; R. Gallager, *Information Theory and Reliable Communication* (Hoboken, NJ: John Wiley, 1968); T. Cover, and J. Thomas, *Elements of Information Theory* (Hoboken, NJ: John Wiley, 1991).

For a BSC, the output channel sequence $\underline{y}$, for sufficiently large n, differs from the transmitted codeword $\underline{x}$ typically in np bit positions, where p is channel cross-over probability. That is,

$$\underline{y} = \underline{x} \oplus \underline{e} \qquad (14.65)$$

where $\underline{e}$ is the corresponding error sequence that will typically contain np 1's and $n(1-p)$ 0's. The probability of occurrence of $\underline{e}$ is given by

$$P\{\text{Error sequence } \underline{e} \text{ with } np \text{ 1's and } n(1-p) \text{ 0's.}\} = (p)^{np}(1-p)^{n(1-p)} = 2^{np\log_2 p}2^{n(1-p)\log_2(1-p)}$$

$$= 2^{n[p\log_2 p + (1-p)\log_2(1-p)]} = 2^{-n\,\mathscr{H}(p)} \qquad (14.66)$$

For sufficiently large n, there are $2^{n\,\mathscr{H}(p)}$ such error sequences, equally likely. Hence, each input codeword is mapped into one of $2^{n\,\mathscr{H}(p)}$ typical channel output sequences. For a BSC with $p = 0.01$, $\mathscr{H}(0.01) = 0.0808$, and hence there are $2^{n0.08}$ noisy output sequences in the subset corresponding to each transmitted codeword. In order to ensure that we can achieve vanishingly low probability of decoding error, we need to choose input codewords so that subsets of highly probable output sequences corresponding to different codewords are disjoint as illustrated in Figure 14.14. Now we know from (14.64) that there are 2^{nR_c} n-bit codewords in code $\mathscr{C}$ with code rate R_c. Therefore, the total number of typical output sequences contained in 2^{nR_c} subsets must not exceed 2^n sequences for virtually error-free decoding. That is, we require

$$2^{nR_c}2^{n\,\mathscr{H}(p)} \leq 2^n \qquad (14.67)$$

or

$$2^{nR_c} \leq 2^{n[1-\mathscr{H}(p)]}$$

(14.67) can, equivalently, be expressed as

$$R_c \leq 1 - \mathscr{H}(p) = C \text{ bits/channel use} \qquad (14.68)$$

That is, the code rate R_c cannot exceed the capacity of a channel if we wish to ensure virtually error-free transmission. The **information transmission rate R,** measured in bits per second, is related to the code rate R_c by

$$R = \frac{R_c}{T} \text{ bits/second} \qquad (14.69)$$

where $T =$ Transmission period to convey R_c information bits

14.3.4 Another Channel Coding Theorem

The noisy-channel coding theorem from the previous section says that reliable communication with error probability ε and rate $R_c < C$ can be achieved by using codes with sufficiently large block length n. The theorem does not say, however, how large n needs to be to achieve given values of R_c and ε. The following version of the channel coding theorem due to Gallager[6] shows an explicit relationship between the codeword probability of error and the length n.

---

[6] R. Gallager, *Information Theory and Reliable Communication* (Hoboken, NJ: John Wiley, 1968).

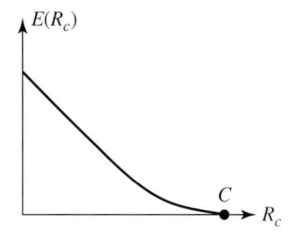

Figure 14.15 Gallager's error exponent.

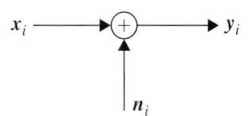

Figure 14.16 AWGN channel.

Theorem 14.3 (Channel coding theorem: Gallager) For a DMC, there is a code whose average probability of error decreases exponentially as a function of codeword length n and rate R_c.

$$P_{cw}(e) \cong e^{-nE(R_c)} \tag{14.70}$$

where the **error exponent** $E(R_c)$ is greater than zero for all rates R_c less than the capacity C. Figure 14.15 displays typical behavior of the Gallager error exponent $E(R_c)$.

14.4   CAPACITY OF AWGN CHANNELS

Many real-world channels have continuous, rather than discrete, inputs and outputs. The most important example of a discrete-time, continuous amplitude channel is the additive white Gaussian noise (AWGN) channel. The output y_i at time i is the sum of the input x_i and the noise n_i as shown in Figure 14.16.

$$y_i = x_i + n_i \tag{14.71}$$

where x_i and y_i are real numbers and n_i is a Gaussian random variable with mean zero and variance $N_o/2$. The capacity of this channel may be infinite if no additional constraints are placed on the input. If the channel input alphabet is chosen as an infinite subset of real numbers arbitrarily far apart, the channel outputs are distinguishable with no error even after having been corrupted by the noise. Although this scheme has infinite information capacity, it requires an infinite energy input symbol set. We can avoid this unrealistic scenario by placing an average power constraint on the input symbol set. For any codeword of n symbols $\underline{x} = (x_0, x_1, \ldots, x_{n-1})$ transmitted over the channel, we require

$$\frac{1}{n} \sum_{i=0}^{n-1} x_i^2 \le P_{av} \tag{14.72}$$

where P_{av} is the average power of the input symbol set.

The capacity of the AWGN channel is maximum of the mutual information $I(\boldsymbol{x}; \boldsymbol{y})$ over all input PDFs $f_{\boldsymbol{x}}(x)$.

$$C = \underset{f_{\boldsymbol{x}}(x)}{\text{Max}}\, I(\boldsymbol{x}; \boldsymbol{y}) \tag{14.73}$$

subject to the average power constraint in (14.72).

14.4.1   Shannon's Capacity Theorem for AWGN Channels

Theorem 14.4. The capacity of an AWGN channel with input power constraint P_{av} and noise variance $N_o/2$ is

$$C = \frac{1}{2} \log_2 \left(1 + \frac{P_{av}}{N_o/2} \right) \text{ bits/channel use} \tag{14.74}$$

The proof of the theorem is given in Appendix A. We shall present here a geometrical argument, originally used by Shannon,[7] to derive the result. Using the

---

[7] C. Shannon, "Communication in the Presence of Noise," *Proceedings of the Institute of Radio Engineers* 37 (1949): 10–21.

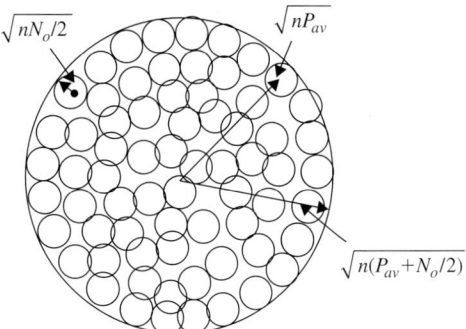

Figure 14.17 Sphere packing for the AWGN channel.

approach discussed in Section 10.5, we can view codewords $\underline{x} = (x_0, x_1, \ldots, x_{n-1})$ of length n as vectors or points in n-dimensional space. The received vector appears as a spherical cloud in the n-dimensional space centered on $\underline{x}$. For large n, the power of the n-dimensional Gaussian noise vector is close, with high probability, to $nN_o/2$. Consequently, the received vector with high probability is inside a sphere of radius $\sqrt{nN_o/2}$ around the transmitted codeword $\underline{x}$. Because of the average power constraint, all received vectors, with high probability, will be contained in a hypersphere of radius $\sqrt{n(P_{av} + N_o/2)}$.

We would like to pack the n-dimensional hypersphere with nonoverlapping spheres—one for each codeword as illustrated in Figure 14.17. In this case, the ML decoder makes the correct decision as the received vector falls inside the sphere corresponding to the transmitted codeword with high probability. How many such codewords can exist that will be distinguishable at the output of an AWGN channel? The question can be answered by recalling that the volume of an n-dimensional sphere is given by

$$V = \frac{\pi^{n/2}}{(n/2)!} r^n \tag{14.75}$$

where r is the radius of the sphere. The maximum number of nonintersecting decoding spheres that can be packed into the volume of a hypersphere is at most

$$M = \left(\frac{\sqrt{n(P_{av} + N_o/2)}}{\sqrt{nN_o/2}} \right)^n = \left(\frac{P_{av} + N_o/2}{N_o/2} \right)^{n/2}$$

$$= \left(1 + \frac{P_{av}}{N_o/2} \right)^{n/2} \tag{14.76}$$

and the rate of the code is

$$R_C \leq \frac{\log_2 M}{n} = \frac{1}{n} \log_2 \left(1 + \frac{P_{av}}{N_o/2} \right)^{n/2} = \frac{1}{2} \log_2 \left(1 + \frac{P_{av}}{N_o/2} \right) \tag{14.77}$$

This sphere-packing argument indicates that we cannot send information with low probability of error at rates greater than $C = \frac{1}{2} \log_2 \left(1 + \frac{P_{av}}{N_o/2} \right)$ bits/channel use.

14.4.2 Capacity of Bandlimited AWGN Channels

In this section we consider communication over a bandlimited AWGN channel. Because the frequency spectrum is usually a shared resource, this model applies to many real-world channels, such as telephone, radio, and satellite links. We model the bandlimited channel as an ideal LP filter with frequency response function

$$|H(f)| = \begin{cases} 1, & -W \leq f \leq W \\ 0, & \text{otherwise} \end{cases} \tag{14.78}$$

The output $y(t)$ of such a channel can be written as

$$y(t) = [x(t) + n(t)] \otimes h(t) \tag{14.79}$$

where $x(t)$ is the channel input signal waveform, $n(t)$ is AWGN, and $h(t)$ is the impulse response of the ideal LP filter described in (14.78). Because the channel is bandlimited to W Hz, we can represent the channel output by samples taken $1/2W$ seconds apart (sampling theorem, Section 8.1). Suppose the channel is used over a time interval of T seconds. We can, therefore, view the bandlimited, time-limited output waveforms of the channel as vectors in the $2TW$ dimensional space. If P_s denotes the average power of the bandlimited output signal waveform, the power per signal sample is given by

$$P_{av} = \frac{P_s T}{2WT} = \frac{P_s}{2W} \tag{14.80}$$

Because the channel output noise is bandlimited WGN with power spectral density $N_o/2$ and bandwidth W, the total output noise power is given by $\frac{N_o 2W}{2} = N_o W$. The $2WT$ output noise samples are independent, identically distributed Gaussian random variables of zero mean and variance given by

$$\frac{N_o WT}{2WT} = \frac{N_o}{2} \tag{14.81}$$

Substituting (14.80) and (14.81) into (14.74) yields the capacity per sample as

$$C = \frac{1}{2} \log_2\left(1 + \frac{P_s/2W}{N_o/2}\right) = \frac{1}{2} \log_2\left(1 + \frac{P_s}{N_o W}\right) \text{ bits/channel use} \tag{14.82}$$

Because there are $2W$ samples per second, the capacity of the channel is given by

$$C = W \log_2\left(1 + \frac{P_s}{N_o W}\right) \text{ bits/second} \tag{14.83}$$

The quantity

$$SNR = \frac{P_s}{N_o W} \tag{14.84}$$

is called the **signal-to-noise power ratio (SNR)**. Substituting (14.84) into (14.83), the capacity of the bandlimited AWGN channel can be expressed as

$$C = W \log_2(1 + SNR) \text{ bits/second} \tag{14.85}$$

Equation (14.85) is one of the most famous results of information theory. It states that the values of channel SNR and bandwidth W set a limit on the transmission rate, not on the error

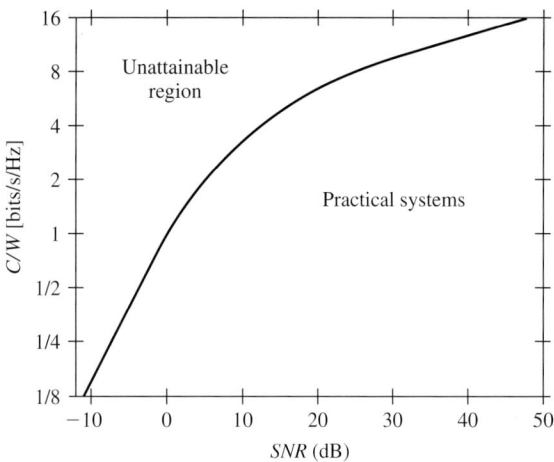

Figure 14.18 Normalized channel capacity versus channel SNR.

performance. Figure 14.18 displays the normalized channel capacity of an AWGN channel as a function of the channel SNR. Practical systems operate below the ideal capacity curve.

Example 14.17

What is the maximum rate at which information can be sent on a telephone channel of bandwidth 3.3 kHz assuming a channel SNR of 30 dB? Calculate the value of SNR required to achieve a bit rate of 53.3 kbps.

Solution

Substituting the values of bandwidth and SNR into (14.85), we get

$$C = 3.3\log_2(1 + 10^3) = 32.9 \text{ kb/s}$$

Next we calculate the SNR required for transmission at 53.3 kbps.

$$53.3 = 3.3\log_2(1 + SNR)$$

$$\log_2(1 + SNR) = 53.3/3.3 = 16.15$$

$$SNR = 2^{16.15} - 1 \approx 2^{16.15}$$

$$SNR(\text{dB}) = 10\log_{10}2^{16.15} = 161.5\log_{10}2 \approx 48$$

Thus an SNR of 48 dB is required to achieve a maximum bit rate of 53.3 kbps.

14.4.3   Implications of Capacity Theorem for Bandlimited AWGN Channels

We observe from (14.83) that the increase in channel capacity as a function of SNR is logarithmic. So while we can increase the capacity to any desired value by increasing the signal power, it requires a lot more power to achieve a small increase in capacity. The effect of bandwidth on the capacity is more complicated because of two competing effects. On the one hand, the capacity increases linearly as a function of bandwidth. On the other hand, however, a higher bandwidth means higher input noise at the receiver which, in turn, decreases the SNR. It is interesting to obtain the limiting value of channel capacity as bandwidth increases to infinity. This can be accomplished by expressing (14.83) as

$$C = \frac{P_s}{N_o}\left(\frac{WN_o}{P_s}\right)\log_2\left(1 + \frac{P_s}{N_oW}\right)$$

$$= \frac{P_s}{N_o}\log_2\left(1 + \frac{P_s}{N_oW}\right)^{\frac{WN_o}{P_s}} = \frac{P_s}{N_o}\log_2(1 + x)^{1/x} \tag{14.86}$$

where $x = \dfrac{P_s}{N_oW}$. As $W \to \infty$, $x \to 0$, and $\lim\limits_{x\to 0}(1 + x)^{1/x} = e$. Substituting into (14.86), we obtain the limit

$$\lim_{W\to\infty} C = \lim_{x\to 0}\frac{P_s}{N_o}\log_2(1 + x)^{1/x} = \frac{P_s}{N_o}\log_2 e = 1.44\frac{P_s}{N_o} \tag{14.87}$$

Equation (14.87) states that the channel capacity cannot be increased to any desired value by increasing the bandwidth only. It is upper-bounded by the limit expressed in (14.87).

Shannon Limit

We next want to determine the limiting value of SNR/bit, E_b/N_o, below which there can be no error-free communication at any information rate. For this purpose, we rewrite (14.83) in terms of E_b/N_o as

$$\frac{C}{W} = \log_2\left(1 + \frac{E_bC}{N_oW}\right) \tag{14.88}$$

where $E_b = P_s/C$ is signal energy/bit. From (14.88), the SNR/bit can be expressed in terms of C/W as

$$\frac{E_b}{N_o} = \frac{2^{C/W} - 1}{C/W} \tag{14.89}$$

Substituting $\eta_{\text{ideal}} = C/W$ into (14.89), we obtain

$$\frac{E_b}{N_o} = \frac{2^{\eta_{\text{ideal}}} - 1}{\eta_{\text{ideal}}} \tag{14.90}$$

Note that η_{ideal} is spectral efficiency (bit/sec-Hz) of the capacity-achieving system. Figure 14.19 displays the plot of spectral efficiency η_{ideal} versus E_b/N_o.

Let us consider the limiting value of E_b/N_o as $W \to \infty$. That is,

$$\lim_{W\to\infty}\frac{E_b}{N_o} = \lim_{W\to\infty}\left(\frac{2^{C/W} - 1}{C/W}\right) \tag{14.91}$$

Now

$$2^{C/W} = e^{\log_e 2^{C/W}} = e^{(C/W)\log_e 2} \tag{14.92}$$

Substituting (14.92) into (14.91) and using the approximation $\lim\limits_{x\to 0} e^x \cong 1 + x$, we obtain

$$\lim_{W\to\infty}\frac{E_b}{N_o} = \lim_{W\to\infty}\left(\frac{e^{(C/W)\log_e 2} - 1}{C/W}\right) \xrightarrow{W\to\infty} \left(\frac{1 + (C/W)\log_e 2 - 1}{C/W}\right) \to \log_e 2 = 0.693 \tag{14.93}$$

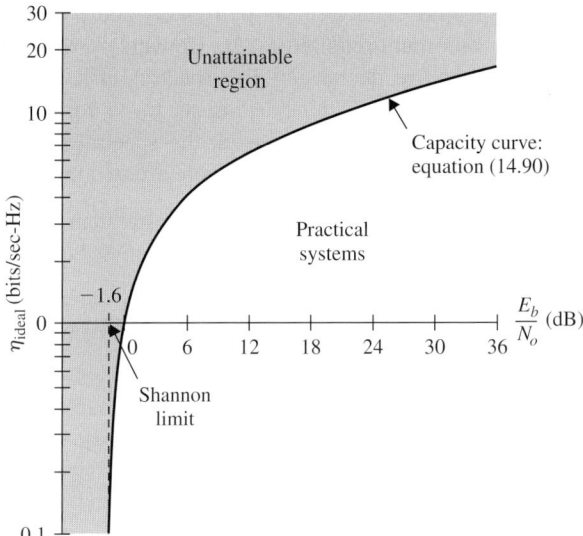

Figure 14.19 η_{ideal} versus E_b/N_o.

In dB form, this limiting value of E_b/N_o in (14.93) is called the **Shannon limit.**

$$\left(\frac{E_b}{N_o}\right)_{\text{Shannon\_limit}} = 10\log_{10}0.693 = -1.6 \text{ dB} \qquad (14.94)$$

Equation (14.94) states that for reliable communication, we must have $\dfrac{E_b}{N_o} > -1.6$ dB.

Comparing with binary PSK, which requires $E_b/N_o = 9.6$ dB for a $BER = 10^{-5}$, Shannon's work promises performance improvement of $9.6 + 1.6 = 11.2$ dB through the use of sophisticated coding techniques. Today, almost all of that promised improvement is realizable with turbo and LDPC codes. Figure 14.19 displays the Shannon limit on the plot of η_{ideal} versus E_b/N_o.

14.4.4 Power-Bandwidth Trade-Offs

For any practical communication system ($R < C$), (14.88) can be expressed as

$$\frac{R}{W} < W \log_2\left(1 + \frac{E_b R}{N_o W}\right) \qquad (14.95)$$

Equation (14.95) implies that, for reliable communication, the SNR/bit required must exceed the threshold value given by

$$\frac{E_b}{N_o} > \frac{2^\eta - 1}{\eta} \qquad (14.96)$$

where $\eta = R/W =$ spectral efficiency of the system (bits/sec-Hz). Equation (14.96) describes a fundamental trade-off between two key parameters in a communication system. The spectral efficiency is a measure of how efficiently the bandwidth of the system is being utilized. The SNR/bit E_b/N_o, on the other hand, measures the power efficiency of a system. Increased spectral efficiency can be reliably achieved only with a corresponding increase in the minimum required E_b/N_o. Conversely, the minimum required E_b/N_o can only be reduced by decreasing the spectral efficiency of the system. Figure 14.20 displays the spectral efficiency η versus E_b/N_o for various digital modulation schemes without coding. For comparison, the spectral efficiency η_{ideal} for a capacity-achieving system has also been plotted. There are two regions of interest.

1. **Bandwidth-limited** ($\eta \gg 1$). Here bit rate is much greater than the system bandwidth.
2. **Power-limited** ($\eta \ll 1$). Here bit rate is much less than the system bandwidth.

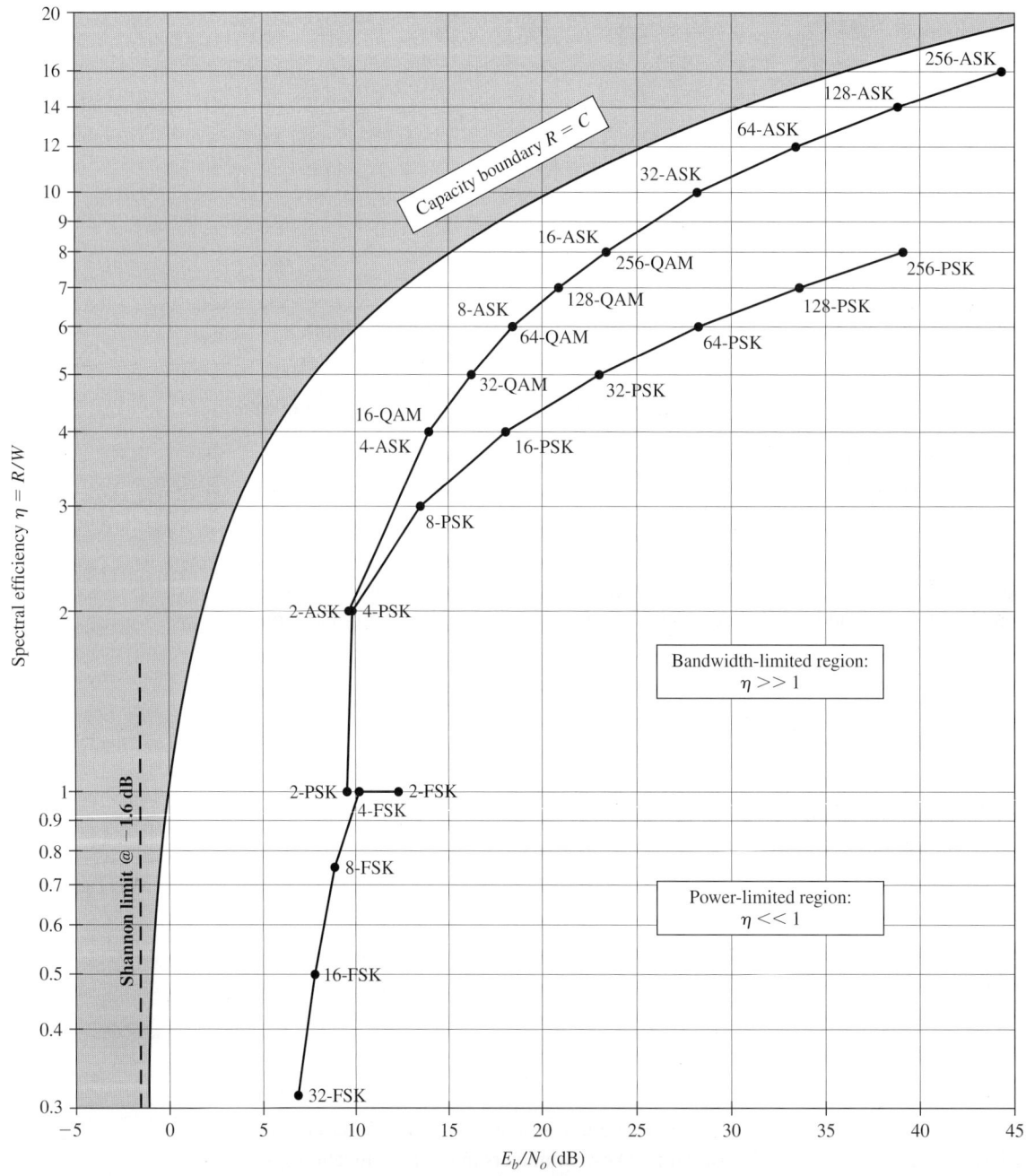

Figure 14.20 Power-bandwidth trade-offs.

In the bandwidth-limited region, the capacity curve flattens out, and thus increasing amounts of E_b/N_o are required to achieve an improvement in the spectral efficiency η. As an example, we can observe that a capacity-achieving system operating at an E_b/N_o of 1.8 dB and using a spectral efficiency η of 2 bits/s/Hz would have to increase E_b/N_o to 20 dB to increase the spectral efficiency to 10 bits/s/Hz. In the power-limited region the capacity boundary curve is very steep, and to achieve a small reduction in E_b/N_o requires a large increase in bandwidth. All modulation schemes operate about 10 dB away in terms E_b/N_o requirement from the channel capacity curve. Therefore, the channel coding offers the potential of considerable performance improvement.

14.5   LOSSLESS COMPRESSION TECHNIQUES

Shannon's source coding theorem tells us that an information source x with entropy $H(x)$ can be encoded or represented with negligible risk of information loss using $H(x)$ bits per source output. **Data compression** is the process of reducing the number of bits required to represent the information conveyed in such forms as text, speech, audio, image, and video. In most cases, there is redundancy within the "raw" data representing various information types. The basis for compression is redundancy removal. The development of compression algorithms for efficient representation of information has been a hot area of research and development activity since Shannon's prediction over six decades ago. Two different classes of compression techniques have emerged according to the type of information they are designed to compress.

- **Lossless compression.** Allows the original data to be reconstructed exactly from the compressed data.
- **Lossy compression.** Allows an approximation of the original data to be reconstructed in exchange for a higher degree of compression.

Compressed data is stored or transmitted, depending on the application.

Lossless compression is used in applications where it is important that the original and the decompressed data be identical. Typical examples are text and data files, such as financial records and spreadsheets. Lossless data compression is used by modems and facsimile machines to reduce the file sizes prior to transmission and by operating systems and utility programs to optimize disk space. The popular zip file format is an example. Lossy compression is used for multimedia (speech, audio, image, and video) signals for which some loss of quality can be tolerated to achieve significant savings in data or file size. The lossy data compression methods take advantage of the limitations of the human sensory system so that impairments are almost imperceptible.

14.5.1   Lossless Compression Techniques

In lossless data compression, a sequence of information symbols is encoded into a sequence of bits so that the average number of bits/ information symbol is minimized and the original information stream can be recovered exactly from the encoded binary sequence.

Figure 14.21 illustrates the principle of lossless compression. Next we describe three popular techniques that are quite effective in compressing different types of data.

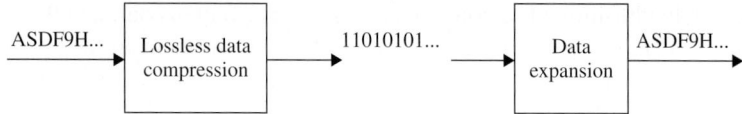

Figure 14.21   Principle of lossless compression.

14.5.2   Huffman Coding

In 1952 Huffman invented an algorithm for source encoding that is optimal in the sense of minimizing the average number of bits/source symbol.[8] A Huffman code segments the original sequence of symbols into a sequence of fixed-length blocks. Each block is assigned a variable-length binary sequence called a codeword. More frequently occurring blocks are assigned shorter codewords, and less frequently occurring blocks are mapped to longer codewords. The codewords are selected so that *no codeword is a prefix of another codeword*.

    The Huffman code for a set of symbols may be generated by constructing a binary tree with nodes containing the symbols to be encoded and their probabilities of occurrence. The tree may be constructed as follows:

1. List each source symbol in descending order of its probability of occurrence.
    a. Create a box for each symbol with its probability of occurrence listed above it.
2. While there are two or more uncombined nodes
    a. Select two uncombined nodes (e.g., *d* and *e*) of minimum probabilities.
    b. Combine these nodes by creating a new intermediate node (*de*) whose probability is the sum of the two probabilities (i.e., $p_d + p_e$).
3. Label the inverse tree branches: top branches with 0, bottom branches with 1.
4. The code of each symbol is the binary sequence labeling the path from the root down to the corresponding terminal node.

The encoding procedure is illustrated in Figure 14.22.

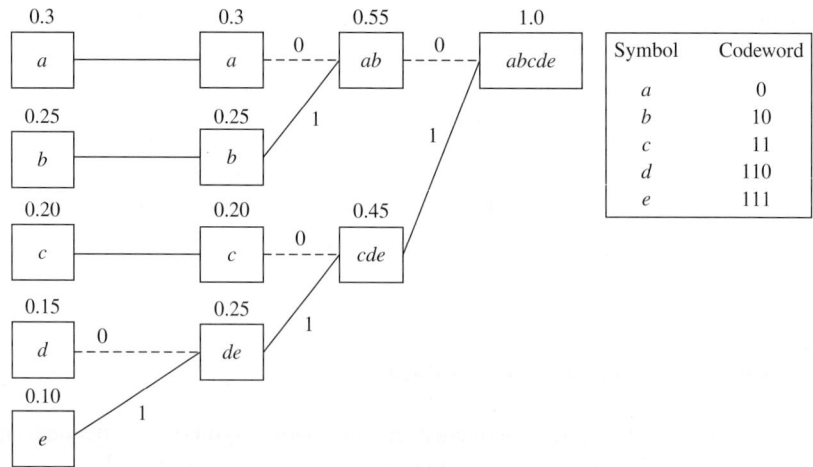

Figure 14.22   Building a Huffman tree.

[8] D. Huffman, "A Method for the Construction of Minimum Redundancy Codes," *Proceedings of the Institute of Radio Engineers* 40, no. 9 (1952): 1098–1101.

The average length $\bar{l}$ of a Huffman code is defined as

$$\bar{l} = \sum_{a_i \in \mathcal{A}_x} p_x(a_i) l(a_i) \tag{14.97}$$

where $l(a_i)$ is the length of the codeword corresponding to the source output $x = a_i$.

Example 14.18

Consider a source x assuming values from the alphabet $\mathcal{A}_x = \{a, b, c, d, e\}$ and associated probabilities $\{0.3, 0.25, 0.2, 0.15, 0.1\}$.

a. Use the Huffman coding procedure to assign binary codewords to all symbols.
b. Determine the entropy of the source.
c. What is the average length of the Huffman code and how does it compare with the volume of an n-dimensional sphere entropy of the source?

Solution

a. The Huffman tree for the source is illustrated in Figure 14.22.
b. The entropy of this source is

$$H(x) = -\sum_{x \in \mathcal{A}_x} p_x(x) \log_2 p_x(x) = -0.3 \log_2(0.3) - 0.25 \log_2(0.25) - 0.2 \log_2(0.2)$$

$$-0.15 \log_2(0.15) - 0.1 \log_2(0.1) = 2.23 \text{ bits/symbol}$$

c. The average number of bits/symbol for this code is given by using (14.97) as

$$\bar{l} = \sum_{a_i \in \mathcal{A}_x} p_x(a_i) l(a_i) = 2 \times 0.3 + 2 \times 0.25 + 2 \times 0.2 + 3 \times 0.15 + 3 \times 0.1 = 2.25 \text{ bits/symbol}$$

In other words, this code attains the best possible performance, and no increase in block length will yield any improvements. The simplest code to use for this information source would assign codewords of equal length to each symbol. Because the number of codewords is five, 3-bit codewords would be required. The performance of such a code is 3 bits/symbol. Thus, for example, a file consisting of 64,000 symbols would produce 192 kbits using 3-bit codewords versus an average of 144 kbits using the Huffman code.

It can be shown[9] that the average length $\bar{l}$ of a Huffman code satisfies the inequality

$$H(x) \le \bar{l} \le H(x) + 1 \tag{14.98}$$

A useful measure of goodness of a source code is the **efficiency** ρ, which is defined as the ratio of entropy of the source to the average length of the code. That is,

$$\text{Efficiency } \rho = \frac{H(x)}{\bar{l}} \tag{14.99}$$

Substituting (14.99) into the left-hand side of the inequality (14.98), we note that $\rho \le 1$.

---

[9] T. Cover and J. Thomas, *Elements of Information Theory* (Hoboken, NJ: John Wiley, 1991).

If we design the Huffman code for length-n symbol blocks $\underline{x} = (x_1, x_2, \ldots, x_n)$, where each source symbol x_i assumes values in the alphabet $\mathscr{A}_x$, we would have

$$H(\underline{x}) \leq \bar{l}_n \leq H(\underline{x}) + 1 \tag{14.100}$$

where $\bar{l}_n$ denotes the average length of the codeword corresponding to the source output sequence $\underline{x} = \underline{x}$. That is,

$$\bar{l}_n = \sum_{\underline{x}} p_{\underline{x}}(\underline{x}) l(\underline{x}), \quad \underline{x} = (a_1, \ldots, a_n), a_i \in \mathscr{A}_x \tag{14.101}$$

If the source is memoryless, we can easily show[10] that

$$H(\underline{x}) = n H(x) \tag{14.102}$$

Substituting (14.102) into (14.100) and dividing by n yields

$$H(x) \leq \bar{l} \leq H(x) + \frac{1}{n} \tag{14.103}$$

where the two average lengths are related by $\bar{l} = \dfrac{\bar{l}_n}{n}$. Thus, if we make n large enough, the average code length $\bar{l}$ of a Huffman code can be made as close to the entropy $H(x)$ as desired for a discrete memoryless source. It can also be shown that for a discrete source with memory the average code length $\bar{l}$ of a Huffman code approaches the entropy rate of the source.

Example 14.19

Consider a source x that produces symbols from the alphabet $\mathscr{A}_x = \{a, b, c\}$ with probabilities $\{0.6, 0.1, 0.3\}$. Find the Huffman code for x. Compare it with the entropy of the source x. Next design the Huffman code for pairs of source symbols. Compare its average length with the entropy of the source x.

Solution

The Huffman tree for the source is illustrated in Figure 14.23.

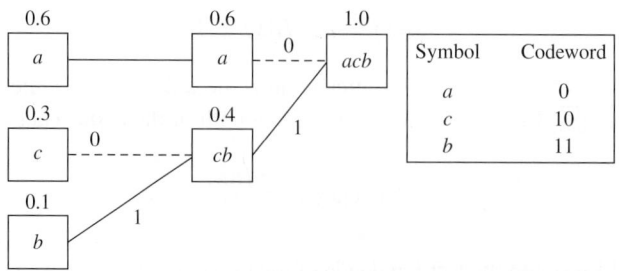

Figure 14.23 Huffman tree for the source coding.

[10] T. Cover and J. Thomas, *Elements of Information Theory* (Hoboken, NJ: John Wiley, 1991).

The average length of the Huffman code is

$$\bar{l} = \sum_{a_i \in \mathscr{A}_x} p_x(a_i) l(a_i) = 0.6 \times 1 + 0.3 \times 2 + 0.1 \times 2 = 1.4 \text{ bits/symbol}$$

The entropy of the source is

$$H(x) = -\sum_{a_i \in \mathscr{A}_x} p_x(a_i) \log_2 p_x(a_i) = -0.6 \log_2(0.6) - 0.3 \log_2(0.3) - 0.1 \log_2(0.1)$$

$$= 1.295 \text{ bits/symbol}$$

If we now encode pairs of source symbols, we will have the alphabet

$$\mathscr{A}_x^2 = \{aa, ab, ac, ba, bb, bc, ca, cb, cc\}$$

with probabilities

$$\{0.36, 0.06, 0.18, 0.06, 0.01, 0.03, 0.18, 0.03, 0.09\}.$$

A Huffman tree for this source is developed in Figure 14.24. The Huffman code is displayed in Table 14.1.

The average code length is

$$\bar{l}_2 = \sum_x p_{\underline{x}}(\underline{x}) l(\underline{x}) = 0.36 \times 1 + 0.18 \times 3 + 0.18 \times 3 + 0.09 \times 4 + 0.06 \times 4 + 0.06 \times 4$$

$$+ 0.03 \times 5 + 0.03 \times 6 + 0.01 \times 6 = 2.67 \text{ bits/pair of source symbols}$$

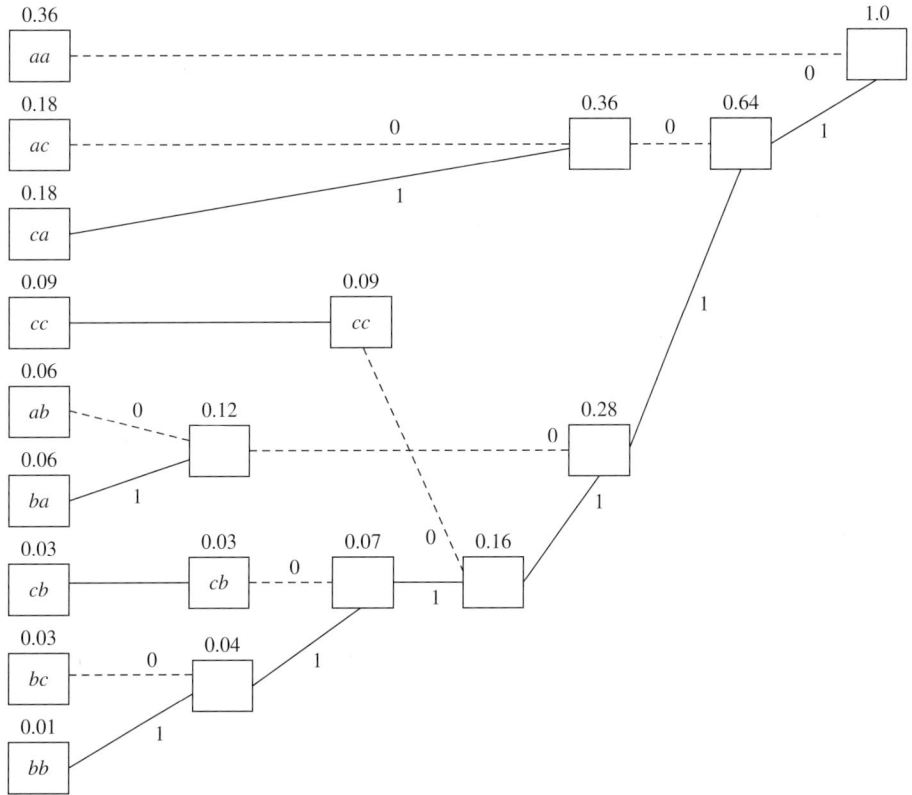

Figure 14.24 Huffman tree for encoding pairs of symbols.

**Table 14.1 Huffman Code
for Pairs of Symbols**

Symbol Pair	Codeword
aa	0
ac	100
ca	101
cc	1110
ab	1100
ba	1101
cb	11110
bc	111110
bb	111111

Therefore, the average code length = 1.335 bits/symbol. This is closer to the entropy of the source (1.295 bits/symbol).

The extent to which compression can be achieved depends on the probabilities of various symbols. For example, suppose that a source produces symbols with equal probability. Clearly the best way to code the symbols is to give them codewords of equal length to the extent possible. In particular, if the source produces equiprobable symbols from an alphabet of size $M = 2^k$, then the best code simply assigns a k-bit codeword to each symbol. No other code can produce further compression! The design of the Huffman code requires knowledge of the probabilities of the various symbols. In certain applications these probabilities are known ahead of time, so the same Huffman code can be used repeatedly. If the probabilities are not known, codes that can adapt to the symbol statistics "on the fly" are preferred. Later in this chapter we present the Lempel-Ziv adaptive codes.

14.5.3   Run-Length Encoding

The sequences of symbols produced by information sources in many applications consist of long strings (called **runs**) of a small number of symbols or characters. In such cases it is more efficient to encode the run lengths (or counts) of symbols and transmit the symbols and their associated run lengths. For example, in facsimile transmission, the raster scanning process produces very long runs of white pixels separated by short runs of black pixels as displayed in Figure 14.25. In this case, **run-length encoding (RLE)** consists of a binary symbol representing each pixel type followed by its run length to convey information about alternating runs of white and black pixels. RLE is a very effective means of achieving lossless data compression for these types of information sources. Run-length codes work as follows:

○○○○○●○○○○○○○○○○○●○

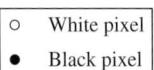

○	White pixel
●	Black pixel

Figure 14.25 White and black pixels in facsimile.

- Parse the source symbol sequence into variable-length strings consisting of consecutive occurrences of the frequent symbol followed by the other symbol.
- Apply Huffman or similar code to encode the lengths of the run, followed by a string that specifies the terminating symbol.

Now if very short binary codewords are used to specify the length of very long runs, then it is clear that very high compression factors are achieved using this scheme.

Example 14.20

Consider the run-length coding of the black-and-white pixel sequence.

Note that white pixels occur much more frequently than black pixels.

The above pixel sequence can alternatively be written as

$$00000000000010000000000010001000000000010000001 \qquad (14.104)$$

where white and black pixels are, respectively, represented as 0 and 1.

Using the run-length code in Table 14.2, we encode the length-41 binary sequence in (14.104) into four-bit codewords as follows:

$$\underline{000000000000}1\underline{00000000000}1\underline{000}1\underline{000000000}1\underline{000000}$$

Run	12	11	3	9	6
	↓	↓	↓	↓	↓
Code	1100	1011	0011	1001	1010

Table 14.2 Run-Length Code for Example 14.20

Run	Length	Codeword
1	0	0000
01	1	0001
001	2	0010
0001	3	0011
00001	4	0100
000001	5	0101
0000001	6	0110
00000001	7	0111
⋮		
⋮		
00000...01	14	1110
00000...00	>14	1111

In this example, the 41 original binary symbols are compacted into 20 bits.

Run-length encoding does not work well for messages without repeated sequences of the same symbol. For example, it may work well for drawings and even black-and-white scanned images, but it does not work well for photographs because small changes in shading from one pixel to the next would require that many symbols be defined.

14.5.4 Lempel-Ziv Coding

In many types of data, there are recurring patterns of information symbols. The family of data compression algorithms, based on landmark papers[11] by Abraham Lempel and Jacob Ziv in 1977 and 1978, identify and take advantage of this repetition. The key idea of the various Lempel-Ziv algorithms is to store patterns in an adaptive dictionary and to transmit

[11] J. Ziv and A. Lempel, "A Universal Algorithm for Sequential Data Compression," *IEEE Transactions on Information Theory* 23 (1977): 337–343; J. Ziv and A. Lempel, "Compression of Individual Sequences via Variable-rate Coding," *IEEE Transactions on Information Theory* 24 (1978): 530–536.

pointers to the patterns in the dictionary rather than the actual patterns. The dictionary is built "on the fly" while the data is being encoded. As we will see, it is not necessary to explicitly transmit the dictionary because the decoder can build up the dictionary in the same way as the encoder while decompressing the data. Lempel-Ziv algorithms belong to the class of so-called **universal** compression algorithms that do not require the knowledge of the source statistical model to apply them. They are widely used in compression utilities such as zip and gzip, GIF image compression, and the V.42 modem standard. The performance of LZ algorithms approaches the entropy of the source for long sequences. We next consider LZ78 and LZW algorithms for lossless data compression.

LZ78

The basic idea in the LZ78 algorithm is to replace a phrase or substring of source symbols with a `pointer` in a dictionary where that substring occurred previously. As illustrated in Figure 14.26, the encoder scans the string of source symbols until it encounters a phrase that is not in the dictionary. The just-identified phrase is a concatenation of a substring called `prefix` already in the dictionary and the new symbol `s`. The new phrase `prefix.s` is added to the dictionary. The encoder outputs the codeword (`pointer`, `s`) and repeats the process beginning with the next symbol after `s`.

The symbols in the source alphabet are added to the dictionary when encountered, and they are assigned the pointer value 0 as there is no match in the dictionary. A description of the algorithm is summarized as follows:

- Initialize `pointer = 1`.
- Find the longest matching substring `prefix` in the dictionary (at the location `pointer`) among the next source symbols to be encoded.
- Transmit the codeword (`pointer`, new symbol `s`).
- Store the new phrase `prefix.s` in the dictionary at `pointer+1` location.

The pseudocode for the encoding process follows:

```
prefix = [];
while (there is input)
 s = next symbol from input;
 new_phrase = prefix.s
 if (new_phrase exists in the dictionary)
      prefix = new_phrase ;}

 else

      output (pointer(prefix), s);
 add new_phrase to the dictionary;
 prefix = [];
 end
end
```

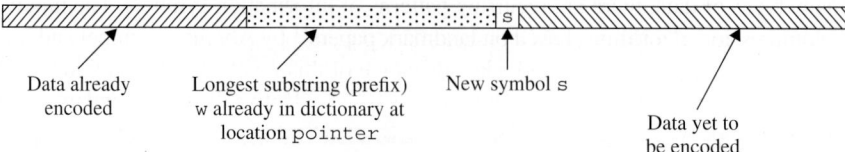

Figure 14.26 LZ78 encoding.

Example 14.21

Encode the string 0012121031013321033331 using the LZ78 algorithm.

Solution

In the first step, 0 is encountered and added to the dictionary. The output is (0, 0) as discussed previously. The encoder then proceeds to the second position, encountering 0, which is already in the dictionary. It is followed by 1, and 01 is not yet in the dictionary. The encoder adds the string 01 to the dictionary and outputs (1, 1). The process continues until the end of the input string is reached.

Table 14.3 LZ78 Encoding Process

| Dictionary | | Transmitted Codeword |
pointer	New Phrase w.s	(pointer, new symbol s)
1	0	(0, 0)
2	01	(1, 1)
3	2	(0, 2)
4	1	(0, 1)
5	21	(3, 1)
6	03	(1, 3)
7	10	(4, 0)
8	13	(4, 3)
9	3	(0, 3)
10	210	(5, 0)
11	33	(9, 3)
12	331	(11, 1)

It is evident from Table 14.3 that the LZ78 encoding sequentially parses the input string into phrases that have not appeared before. These phrases are entered into the dictionary. Thus, the string '0012121031013321033331' is parsed into phrases '0', '01', '2', '1', '21', '03', '10', '13', '3', '210', '33', '331'.

The decoding process is shown in Table 14.4. It starts with the codeword (0, 0), where the pointer 0 indicates that the new symbol 0 is from the source alphabet and needs to be added to the dictionary. The next codeword is (1, 1) resulting in the entry 01 being added to the dictionary because the pointer 1 corresponds to the source symbol 0 followed by the new symbol 1. The decoder output is 01. The decoder thus builds an identical dictionary at the receiving end. The decoding continues this way until all codewords have been decoded.

Lempel-Ziv-Welch (LZW) Algorithm

Lempel-Ziv-Welch (LZW) is a universal lossless data compression algorithm created by Abraham Lempel, Jacob Ziv, and Terry Welch. It was published by Welch in 1984 as an improved implementation of the LZ78 algorithm.[12] The main difference between LZW and LZ78 is that the encoder output consists of a string of pointers to the dictionary,

[12] T. Welch, "A Technique for High-performance Data Compression," *IEEE Computer* 17 (1984): 8–19.

Table 14.4 LZ78 Decoding Process

Received Codeword (pointer, new symbol s)	Decoded Output	Dictionary	
		pointer	Phrase
(0, 0)	0	1	0
(1, 1)	01	2	01
(0, 2)	2	3	2
(0, 1)	1	4	1
(3, 1)	21	5	21
(1, 3)	03	6	03
(4, 0)	10	7	10
(4, 3)	13	8	13
(0, 3)	3	9	3
(5, 0)	210	10	210
(9, 3)	33	11	33
(11, 1)	331	12	331

and the new symbol is not part of the codeword. This requires initializing the dictionary with all symbols of the source alphabet at both the encoder and the decoder.

Encoding

- The dictionary is initialized with symbols from the source alphabet $\mathscr{A}$. One popular LZW implementation initializes the dictionary with values 0 to 255, where the first 128 entries are pointers to ASCII characters. For example, the character E is assigned the pointer 69.
- The encoder then examines the string of source output symbols until a phrase occurs that is *not* in the dictionary. Each new phrase is a concatenation of a previously encountered phrase called `prefix` and a new symbol `s` that caused the just-identified new phrase `prefix.s` to differ from those already in the dictionary.
- The new phrase is added to the dictionary along with its associated pointer, and the encoder outputs the pointer corresponding to the `prefix` of the just-identified new phrase. Note that codeword here is pointer to the new phrase in the dictionary.
- The new symbol becomes the initial symbol of the next substring to be added to the dictionary.

The LZW encoding algorithm can be summarized as follows:

```
Initialize dictionary with characters of alphabet;
prefix = first input symbol;
while (there is input)
s = next symbol from input;
new_phrase = prefix.s
if new_phrase exists in the dictionary
prefix = new_phrase;
else
add new_phrase to the dictionary;
output the pointer for prefix;
prefix = s;
end
end
```

Example 14.22

Encode using the LZW algorithm the string
TO_BE_OR_NOT_TO_BE_THAT_IS_TO_BE

Solution

The LZW encoding process is illustrated in Table 14.5. The first character is T and it is already in the dictionary. So the next character is appended to the prefix (T in this case), and the result is TO, which is not in the dictionary. Therefore, the encoder transmits the prefix T and adds the new phrase TO to the dictionary. It is assigned the pointer 256. The prefix is reset to the new last character, which was not sent, so it is O. The next character _ is appended, and the result is O_, which is not in the dictionary. So the encoder transmits the code for O, and the phrase O_ is added to the dictionary with pointer 257. The process repeats until the end of the string is reached.

In this example the new phrases added to the dictionary in the beginning are two characters long, and each time the code for a single character from the alphabet is transmitted. As one of

Table 14.5 LZW Encoding Example

Prefix w	Input	Dictionary		Output	
		Pointer	New Phrase	Phrase	Pointer
nil	T				
T	O	256	TO	T	84
O	_	257	O_	O	79
_	B	258	_B	_	45
B	E	259	BE	B	66
E	_	260	E_	E	69
_	O	261	_O	_	45
O	R	262	OR	O	79
R	_	263	R_	R	82
_	N	264	_N	_	45
N	O	265	NO	N	78
O	T	266	OT	O	79
T	_	267	T_	T	84
_	T	268	_T	_	45
T	O	-	-	-	-
TO	_	269	TO_	TO	256
_	B	-	-	-	-
_B	E	270	_BE	_B	258
E	_	-	-	-	
E_	T	271	E_T	E_	260
T	H	272	TH	T	84
H	A	273	HA	H	72
A	T	274	AT	A	65
T	_	-	-	-	
T_	I	275	T_I	T_	267
I	S	276	IS	I	73
S	_	277	S_	S	83
_	T	-	-	-	-
_T	O	278	_TO	_T	268
O	_	-	-	-	
O_	B	279	O_B	O_	257
B	E	-	-	-	
BE	-	-	-	BE	259

those two-character phrases is repeated, its code gets sent (using fewer bits than would be required for two characters sent separately) and a new three-character dictionary entry is defined. In this example it happens with the string TO_. Later in this example, the code for a three-character string gets transmitted. As the encoding process builds up, codes for longer phrases are transmitted, leading to improved compression.

Decoding

The dictionary is initialized with single character strings corresponding to the source alphabet $\mathscr{A}$ as in the encoding operation. The first received pointer (codeword) always represents a character in the source alphabet. So the decoder outputs the character corresponding to the received pointer and also initializes the prefix with it. For subsequent pointers (codewords) received, the LZW decoder operates as follows:

- It appends the first character of the string represented by the received pointer to the prefix and inserts the result in the dictionary.
- It outputs the string for the received pointer and also places it in the prefix to start the next dictionary entry.

An exception occurs when the received pointer has not yet been added by the decoder to the dictionary. In this case, it appends to the prefix the first character of the prefix. The decoder outputs and inserts the result in the dictionary.

The LZW decoding algorithm then proceeds as follows:

```
Initialize dictionary with characters of alphabet;
read first pointer;
output character s corresponding to the pointer;
prefix = s;
while (read next pointer)
 If next pointer in the dictionary
        phrase = dictionary entry corresponding to next
        pointer;
 output phrase;
 add prefix.1st character of phrase to dictionary;
 prefix = phrase;
 else
 phrase = prefix;
 new_phrase = phrase.1st character of prefix;
     output new_phrase;
 add new_phrase to dictionary;
 prefix = new_phrase;
 end
end
```

Example 14.23

Decode using the LZW algorithm the string
TO_BE_OR_NOT_TO_BE_THAT_IS_THE_ QUESTION

Solution

The LZW decoding process is illustrated in Table 14.6.

Table 14.6 LZW Decoding Example

	Input		Dictionary		Output
Prefix w	Pointer	Phrase	Pointer	New Phrase	Phrase
nil	84	T			T
T	79	O	256	TO	O
O	45	_	257	O_	_
_	66	B	258	_B	B
B	69	E	259	BE	E
E	45	_	260	E_	_
_	79	O	261	_O	O
O	82	R	262	OR	R
R	45	_	263	R_	_
_	78	N	264	_N	N
N	79	O	265	NO	O
O	84	T	266	OT	T
T	45	_	267	T_	_
_	256	TO	268	_T	TO
TO	258	_B	269	TO_	_B
_B	260	E_	270	_BE	E_
E_	84	T	271	E_T	T
T	72	H	272	TH	H
H	65	A	273	HA	A
A	267	T_	274	AT	T_
T_	73	I	275	T_I	I
I	83	S	276	IS	S
S	268	_T	277	S_	_T
_T	257	O_	278	_TO	O_
O_	259	BE	279	O_B	BE

14.6 IMAGE COMPRESSION: JPEG

A digital image (or a frame of digital video) is a representation of a two-dimensional image using a rectangular array of pixels. For a gray-tone digital image, each pixel holds an integer-valued sample corresponding to the brightness of the picture at a spatial location. In the case of a color digital image, each pixel is represented by a triplet of integer-valued samples, one for each of the three components of a color representation, such as RGB. A digital image can be obtained either by sampling a raster scan (Section 5.8) or by directly using a digital camera. At present, all digital cameras use CCD sensor arrays. The pixel frame produced by a digital camera consists of output values from a CCD array, which is by nature discrete both horizontally and vertically.

In an attempt to standardize different digital video formats, the International Telecommunications Union-Radio Sector (ITU-R) developed the BT.601 recommendation. It specifies a new component format for color images and video, known as YC_bC_r. Y is the luminance component and represents the brightness. The two chroma components C_b and C_r represent the extent to which the color deviates from gray toward blue and red, respectively. The amplitude of each component is typically represented with 8-bit precision per sample for consumer-quality video. Digital representation of images requires huge numbers of bits, as illustrated by the following example.

Example 14.24

Calculate the number of bits required to represent a color image with a resolution of 1024 × 1024.

Solution

Total number of pixels in the color image = 1024 × 1024 = 1.048576 million pixels.

As discussed in Section 5.8.3, a color image is composed of red, green, and blue component images. Usually each of the color components is represented by one byte, resulting in 3 bytes/ pixel. Therefore, a total of 1.048576 million pixels × 3 bytes/pixel = 3.145728 Mbytes ($\approx$ 25.16 Mbits) is required to represent the color image.

Uncompressed image and video data requires considerable storage capacity and transmission bandwidth. The recent growth of data-intensive, multimedia-based web applications has not only sustained the need to find more efficient ways to encode images and video signals but has made compression of such signals central to storage and communication technologies. The compression techniques utilize **redundancy** and **irrelevancy** reduction to obtain a more efficient representation of an image. In general, two types of redundancy can be identified in a digital image:

- **Spatial.** Neighboring pixels are often correlated with each other. So, to some extent, the value of a pixel is predictable given the values of nearby pixels.
- **Color space.** RGB components are correlated among themselves.

Figure 14.27 displays an example of a gray-tone image where nearby pixels have very similar values in portions of the picture with gradual intensity change. Irrelevancy refers to perceptually unimportant information in the image as a result of limitations of the **human visual system (HVS).** The human eye has a limited response to fine spatial detail and is less sensitive to detail near object edges or around shot-changes. Consequently, controlled impairments introduced into the decoded picture by the bit rate reduction process should not be visible to a human observer.

Most applications in image or video processing do not require the original data to be reconstructed exactly. Lossy compression is acceptable as long as there is little or no perceptible degradation in image quality. Much higher compression ratios are achieved with lossy versus lossless image compression systems. An example of a lossless image compression scheme is **graphical interchange format (GIF).** GIF is used primarily for simple images such as line drawings and images containing simple geometrical shapes. A lossy compression system for static images implements the following three key functions as illustrated in Figure 14.28:

- Reduction of spatial redundancy by removing correlation between pixels.
    - Concentrate image information into an alternative format that lends itself to efficient quantization and coding

Figure 14.27 Image with smooth portions.

© Ingram Publishing/SuperStock

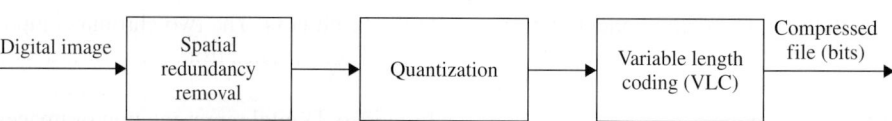

Figure 14.28 Functional blocks of a digital image compression scheme.

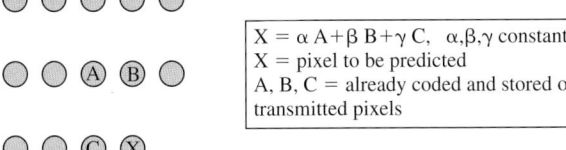

X = α A + β B + γ C, α,β,γ constants
X = pixel to be predicted
A, B, C = already coded and stored or
transmitted pixels

Figure 14.29 Predictive coding of pixels.

- Quantization of coefficients or data produced in the alternative image format.
- Variable-length coding of quantized data.

Spatial Redundancy Removal

Predictive or **differential coding techniques** encode the error or difference between the current pixel and its predicted value computed from already coded and transmitted (or stored) adjacent pixel values. Figure 14.29 displays the predictive coding of image pixels. The decoder can perform the same prediction from the already decoded pixels and reconstruct the new pixel value based on the predicted value and decoded prediction error. As discussed in Section 8.5, the prediction error pixel values exhibit significantly lower dynamic range when compared to the original pixel values. Consequently, the predicted-error image can be coded using a lower number of bits/pixel.

Transform coding techniques take a block of pixel values and transform into another domain so that most of the information (energy) is concentrated into only a small fraction of transform coefficients. After appropriate quantization, the block of transform coefficients lends itself to efficient encoding through the use of Huffman and run-length codes. The most popular and well-established transform techniques are

- **Two-dimensional discrete cosine transform (2-D DCT)**
  - Used in **Joint Photographic Expert Group (JPEG)** and **Motion Picture Expert Group (MPEG)** standards
- **Discrete wavelet transform (DWT)**
  - Standardized in MPEG-4 and JPEG 2000

The DCT is applied in JPEG and MPEG standards on blocks of 8 × 8 pixels. The DWT on the other hand is as a frame-based approach; it is applied to entire images as in JPEG 2000 and MPEG-4 standards.

Quantization

The purpose of quantization is to achieve compression by representing DCT coefficients with no greater precision than is necessary to achieve the desired image quality, that is, to discard information that is not visually significant. In this context, the choice of appropriate quantization step size for each DCT coefficient takes into consideration the HVS characteristics.

Variable-Length Coding

The encoding stage further compresses the quantized values losslessly to give a better overall compression ratio. It uses variable-length encoding to obtain a compressed output bit stream. In JPEG, a combination of run-length and Huffman codes are used as further explained in Section 14.6.2.

Now we will discuss in detail how these functions are implemented in the widely used JPEG image compression scheme.

14.6.1 Discrete Cosine Transform

The 2-D DCT provides a way to separate the spatial frequencies contained in an image. For the block-based DCT transform approach, the image is partitioned into disjoint blocks of $N \times N$ pixels (e.g., 8×8 pixels in JPEG) as indicated in Fig. 14.30. For an $N \times N$ pixel block $f(i, j)$, the 2-D DCT coefficients $F(k, \ell)$ are given by

$$F(k, \ell) = \frac{\alpha(k, \ell)}{N} \sum_{i=0}^{N-1} \sum_{j=0}^{N-1} f(i, j) \cos\left(\frac{(2i + 1)k\pi}{2N}\right) \cos\left(\frac{(2j + 1)\ell\pi}{2N}\right),$$
$$k, \ell = 0, 1, \dots, N - 1 \tag{14.105}$$

where

$$\alpha(k, \ell) = \begin{cases} 1, & k, \ell = 0 \\ 2, & \text{otherwise} \end{cases}$$

The 2-D DCT expresses each $N \times N$ pixel block in terms of a set of basis waveforms each corresponding to a particular spatial frequency pair. The set of basis waveforms for 2-D 64-point DCT are displayed in Figure 14.31. The output of the DCT is the set of 8×8 basis-signal amplitudes or **DCT coefficients** whose values are uniquely determined by the particular 8×8 input pixel values. DCT coefficient values can thus be regarded as the relative amount of the 2-D spatial frequencies contained in the 8×8 input pixel block. The coefficient $F(0, 0)$ with zero frequency in both dimensions is called the **DC coefficient.** It is a measure of the average energy of the block. The remaining 63 coefficients are **AC coefficients.** DCT has significant values concentrated at the low frequencies that correspond to the upper-left corner of the transformed block. The coefficients corresponding to high frequencies tend to be zero or near zero for most images. This is called the energy compaction property of the DCT.

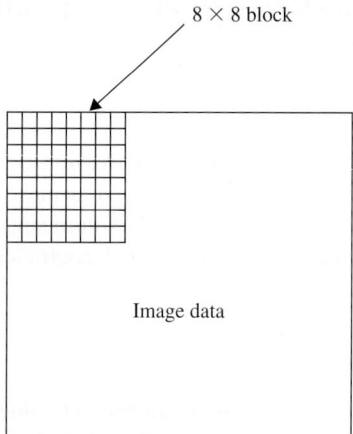

Figure 14.30 Partition of digital image into 8×8 pixel blocks.

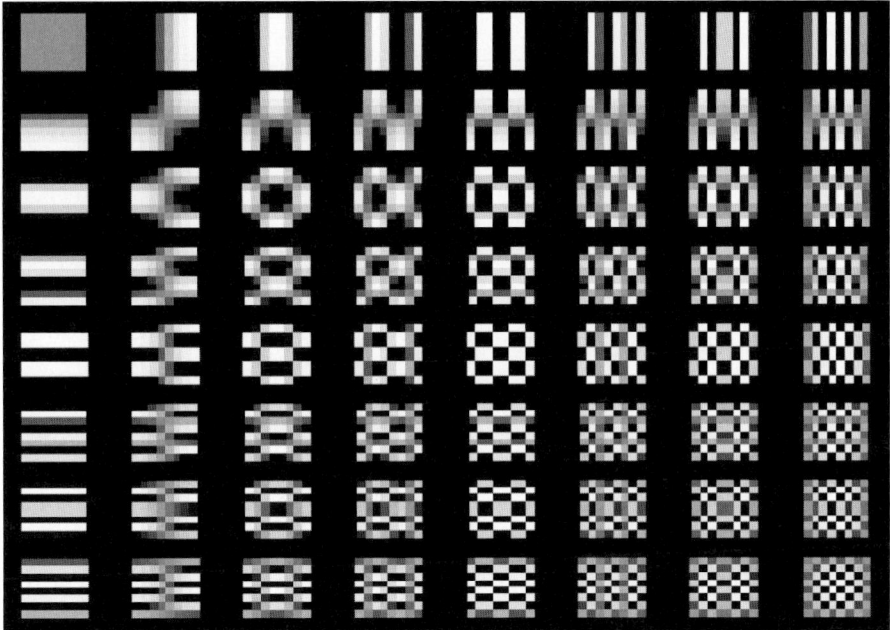

Figure 14.31 Basis functions for two-dimensional 8-point DCT.

From (14.105) and the orthogonality property of the DCT, the *N*-point **inverse DCT (IDCT)** is given by

$$f(i, j) = \alpha(i, j) \sum_{k=0}^{N-1} \sum_{\ell=0}^{N-1} F(k, \ell) \cos\left(\frac{(2i + 1)k\pi}{2N}\right) \cos\left(\frac{(2j + 1)\ell\pi}{2N}\right),$$
$$i, j = 0, 1, \ldots, N - 1 \tag{14.106}$$

Thus the original $N \times N$ pixel block values, $f(i, j)$, can be reconstructed by adding N^2 basis waveforms scaled by corresponding DCT coefficients $F(k, \ell)$. The DCT introduces no loss to the source image samples; it merely transforms them to a domain in which they can be more efficiently encoded.

14.6.2   JPEG Compression Standard

JPEG is the image compression standard developed by the Joint Photographic Experts Group. We will consider JPEG compression of grayscale images in this section. For color images, each (RGB or alternative representation) color component is coded separately as discussed in the next section.

JPEG Encoding

Figure 14.32 shows a block diagram of a JPEG encoder. The pixel values are level-shifted, prior to DCT operation, from unsigned integers with range $[0, 2^p - 1]$ to signed

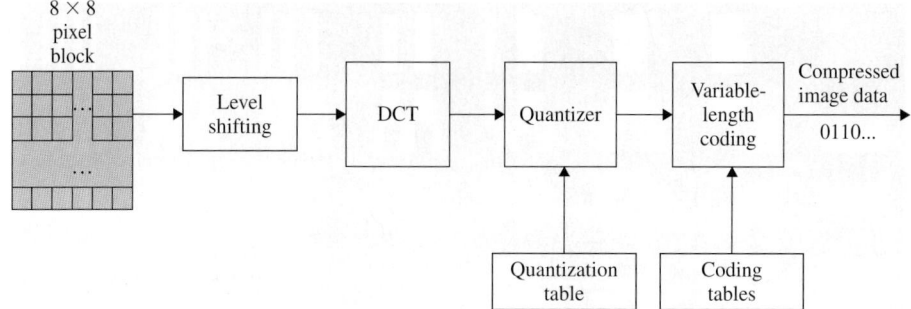

Figure 14.32 JPEG encoder block diagram.

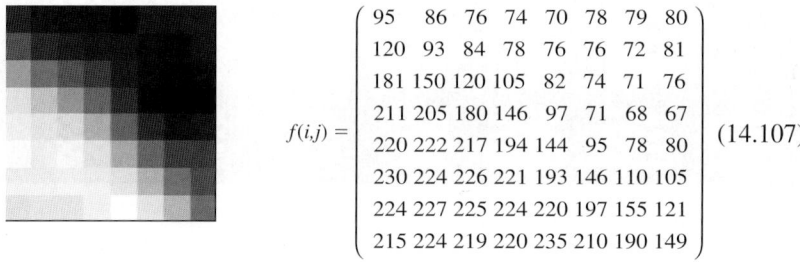

$$f(i,j) = \begin{pmatrix} 95 & 86 & 76 & 74 & 70 & 78 & 79 & 80 \\ 120 & 93 & 84 & 78 & 76 & 76 & 72 & 81 \\ 181 & 150 & 120 & 105 & 82 & 74 & 71 & 76 \\ 211 & 205 & 180 & 146 & 97 & 71 & 68 & 67 \\ 220 & 222 & 217 & 194 & 144 & 95 & 78 & 80 \\ 230 & 224 & 226 & 221 & 193 & 146 & 110 & 105 \\ 224 & 227 & 225 & 224 & 220 & 197 & 155 & 121 \\ 215 & 224 & 219 & 220 & 235 & 210 & 190 & 149 \end{pmatrix} \quad (14.107)$$

Figure 14.33 8×8 pixel block and its luminance values.

integers with range $[-2^{p-1}, 2^{p-1} - 1]$, where $p =$ input bits/pixel. For example, if the pixel values are generated by an 8-bit A/D converter (i.e., $p = 8$), 2^{8-1} is subtracted from the input image samples prior to DCT operation. The DCT stage now applies 2-D DCT to 8×8 blocks of the pixel values. This process generates 64 DCT coefficients for each 8×8 pixel block. As an example, consider an 8×8 pixel block and its luminance values displayed in Figure 14.33.

The DCT coefficients of the level-shifted image samples in (14.107) are given by

$$F(k, \ell) = \begin{pmatrix} 123.75 & 261.430 & -22.96 & 3.77 & 10.75 & 2.07 & -1.86 & -0.64 \\ -377.34 & -52.59 & 88.19 & -9.2 & 8.4 & 6.75 & 7.94 & -6.67 \\ -1.96 & -147.61 & -18.08 & 42.39 & -11.53 & -3.45 & -1.50 & 4.29 \\ 4.44 & 8.24 & -32.95 & -15.53 & 7.25 & -1.82 & 5.24 & -2.15 \\ 1.00 & 12.61 & 3.19 & -18.49 & -11.00 & 0.24 & -8.63 & 2.02 \\ 7.04 & 12.93 & 4.39 & 5.42 & -10.19 & 1.25 & -1.23 & -4.90 \\ 7.03 & 0.62 & 5.75 & 1.43 & 6.13 & 0.14 & -2.17 & -0.31 \\ 2.29 & 0.58 & -1.09 & 2.39 & -0.62 & 0.52 & -0.66 & -1.63 \end{pmatrix}$$

$$(14.108)$$

We observe from (14.108) that the DCT coefficients representing low-frequency components have significant values. The coefficients in each DCT block are

$$Q(k, \ell) = \begin{pmatrix} 16 & 11 & 10 & 16 & 24 & 40 & 51 & 61 \\ 12 & 12 & 14 & 19 & 26 & 58 & 60 & 55 \\ 14 & 13 & 16 & 24 & 40 & 57 & 69 & 56 \\ 14 & 17 & 22 & 29 & 51 & 87 & 80 & 62 \\ 18 & 22 & 37 & 56 & 68 & 109 & 103 & 77 \\ 24 & 35 & 55 & 64 & 81 & 104 & 113 & 92 \\ 49 & 64 & 78 & 87 & 103 & 121 & 120 & 101 \\ 72 & 92 & 95 & 98 & 112 & 100 & 103 & 99 \end{pmatrix}$$

Figure 14.34 JPEG luminance component quantization table.

then quantized. Typically, a different quantizer is used for each distinct frequency pair because of the differences in perceptual importance. An 8×8 quantization table determines the step size for uniform quantization of each DCT component in JPEG. Figure 14.34 displays a JPEG luminance component quantization table.

The quantized DCT coefficients are obtained by division of each coefficient by its corresponding quantizer step size $Q(k, \ell)$ as follows:

$$G(k, \ell) = \text{sgn}[F(k, \ell)] \left\lfloor \frac{|F(k, \ell)|}{Q(k, \ell)} + 0.5 \right\rfloor \tag{14.109}$$

Substituting (14.108) into (14.109) and applying the corresponding quantizer step size from the table in Figure 14.34, we obtain the following quantized DCT coefficients:

$$G(k, \ell) = \begin{pmatrix} 8 & 24 & -2 & 0 & 0 & 0 & 0 & 0 \\ -31 & -4 & 6 & 0 & 0 & 0 & 0 & 0 \\ 0 & -11 & -1 & 2 & 0 & 0 & 0 & 0 \\ 0 & 0 & -1 & -1 & 0 & 0 & 0 & 0 \\ 0 & 1 & 0 & 0 & 0 & 0 & 0 & 0 \\ 0 & 0 & 0 & 0 & 0 & 0 & 0 & 0 \\ 0 & 0 & 0 & 0 & 0 & 0 & 0 & 0 \\ 0 & 0 & 0 & 0 & 0 & 0 & 0 & 0 \end{pmatrix} \tag{14.110}$$

Note that a great majority of coefficients are quantized to zero in (14.110); the energy of the signal is concentrated in the first few low-frequency coefficients in the upper-left corner. JPEG incorporates run-length coding to take advantage of this. To accomplish this, JPEG scans DCT coefficients in the zigzag pattern shown in Figure 14.35 to produce a one-dimensional sequence or block of 64 consecutive values for variable-length encoding. The zigzag scanning is used to increase the run length of zero coefficients found in the block.

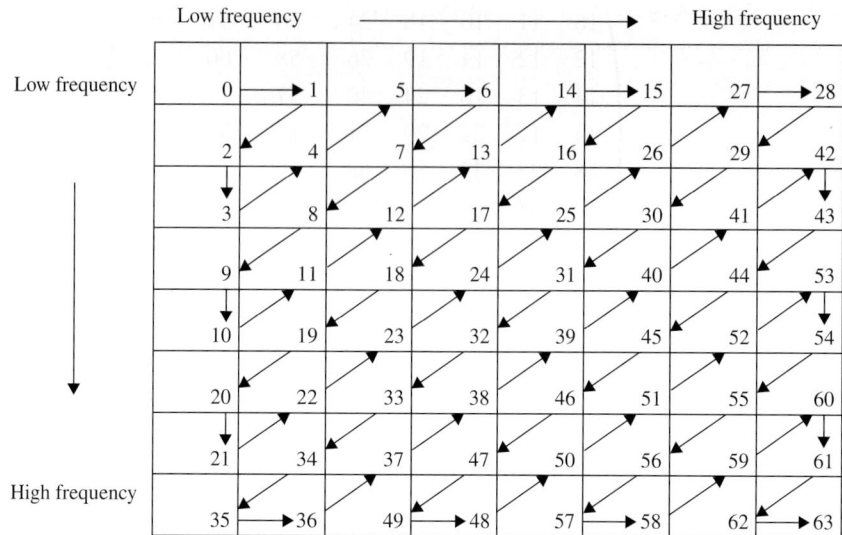

Figure 14.35 Zigzag scanning DCT coefficients.

Example 14.25

Find the one-dimensional sequence that results after zigzag scanning quantized DCT AC coefficients in (14.110). Use the EOB (end of block) symbol to indicate that the remaining coefficients are all 0.

Solution

The one-dimensional sequence that results after zigzag scanning quantized DCT AC coefficients in (14.110) is

$$24 \; -31 \; 0 \; -4 \; -2 \; 0 \; 6 \; -1 \; 1 \; 0 \; 0 \; 0 \; -1 \; 0 \; 0 \; 0 \; 0 \; 2 \; -1 \; 1 \; 0 \; 0 \; 0 \; 0 \; -1 \; \text{EOB} \qquad (14.111)$$

Because the DC coefficients exhibit significant correlation among adjacent blocks, differential coding is used in which the value to be coded is the difference between the current DC coefficient (DC_i) and that of the previous block (DC_{i-1}). For 8-bit/pixel data, the prediction error $DC_i - DC_{i-1}$ can take values in the range $\pm(255 \times 8) = \pm 2040$ if the input pixels assume values in the range -128 to $+127$ (the DCT has a gain of 8 at very low frequencies). Hence the Huffman code table would have to be quite large. JPEG adopts a much more efficient coding by using a (size, amplitude) pair representation to describe the prediction error values, where size defines the number of bits required to represent the amplitude, and the amplitude is simply the magnitude of the DC prediction error. Given a DC prediction error value, its amplitude is computed as follows:

- If the DC prediction error is positive, then the amplitude is simply a binary representation with size bits of precision.
- If the DC prediction is negative, then the amplitude is the 1's complement of its absolute value.

For example, if the DC prediction error has amplitude 14, then from Table 14.7, size = 4. Thus 14 is described by (4, 01110). The Huffman codeword for size = 4 is 101, so 14 is coded as 10101110. Similarly, -14 is coded as 10110001.

Table 14.7 Variable-Length Coding of DC Prediction Error

			Huffman Coder	Amplitude	
DC Prediction Error		Size	for Size	1's Complement	Binary
-1	1	1	010	0	1
$-3, -2$	2, 3	2	011	00, 01	10, 11
$-7, -6, -5, -4$	4, 5, 6, 7	3	100	000, 001, 010, 011	100, 101, 110, 111,
$-15, \ldots, -8$	8, \ldots, 15	4	101	0000, \ldots, 0111	1000, \ldots, 1111
\vdots	\vdots	\vdots	\vdots	\vdots	\vdots
$-1023, \ldots, -512$	512, \ldots, 1023	10	1111 1110	00 0000 0000, \ldots	\ldots, 11 1111 1111
$-2047, \ldots, -1024$	1024, \ldots, 2047	11	1111 1111 0	000 0000 0000, \ldots	\ldots, 111 1111 1111

The quantized AC coefficients are coded by the pair {Run/Size, Amplitude} where

- **Run.** The run length (number) of zeros before a nonzero AC coefficient
- **Size.** Number of bits required to represent the amplitude of the nonzero AC coefficient
- **Amplitude.** Amplitude of the nonzero AC coefficient

Size and amplitude are defined just as for DC coefficients. The values of run and size are Huffman coded. This is efficient because there is a strong correlation between the size of a coefficient and the expected run of zeros that precedes it—small coefficients usually follow long runs; larger coefficients tend to follow shorter runs. The value of the amplitude is appended to the codeword. For example, assume the AC coefficient is preceded by six zeros and has a value -18. For -18, size $= 5$. The one's complement of -18 is 101101. Hence, this coefficient is represented by (6/5, 101101). If the Huffman codeword for (6/5) is 1101, then the codeword for this coefficient is 1101101101.

Example 14.26

Encode the AC coefficients in (14.111) using JPEG's variable-length encoding scheme.

Solution

(0/5, 24), (0/5, -31), (1/3, -4), (0/2, -2), (1/3, 6), (0/4, -11), (3/1, -1), (4/2, 2), (0/1, -1), (0/1, 1), (4/1, -1), (EOB)

Because the JPEG standard provides for various encoding options, an interchange format is defined for exchanging JPEG bit streams between a wide variety of platforms and applications.

JPEG Decoding

Figure 14.36 illustrates the block diagram of a JPEG decoder. After the compressed bit stream passes through a variable-length decoder, the DCT coefficients are first dequantized and then transformed to the spatial domain via a 2-D IDCT. After a block-to-raster translation, the image is fully decoded.

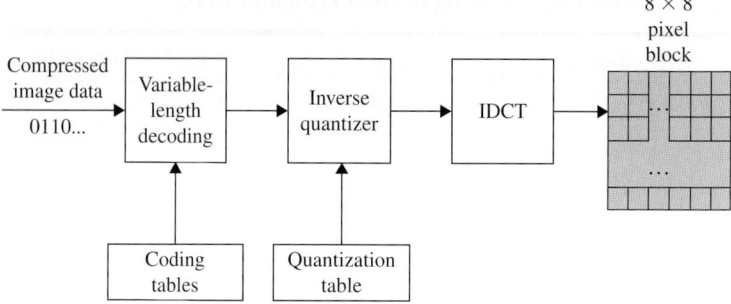

Figure 14.36 JPEG decoder block diagram.

14.6.3 Subsampling of Chrominance Components

The RGB components of a color image discussed in Section 5.8.3 have significant correlation. From a compression viewpoint, the RGB space is, therefore, not an efficient representation. So we convert the color image from RGB to either YC_bC_r or YUV space to reduce the correlation. Y is the luminance component, whereas (C_b, C_r) and (U, V) are chrominance components in these alternative component representations of the color image. Figure 14.37 illustrates how we can obtain the YC_bC_r or YUV pixel values from the RGB image samples.

It is widely known that the HVS perceives the luminance in higher resolution than the chrominance. That is, the human eye is much more sensitive to the details of luminance than color. Image compression systems take advantage of this difference in sensitivity by downsampling the chrominance components. Chroma subsampling is the process whereby the color information in the image is downsampled at a lower resolution than the original to improve the compression. Figure 14.38 illustrates various chroma subsampling schemes and the notation used to denote them.

- **4:4:4** means no downsampling of the chroma pixels.
- **4:2:2** means 2:1 horizontal downsampling with no vertical downsampling. That is, 1/2 of the horizontal resolution in the chroma components is dropped, while the full resolution is retained in the vertical direction, with respect to the luminance. Each scan line contains four Y pixels for two (C_b or U) and (C_r or V) pixels. This is also known as 2×1 chroma subsampling, and is quite common for digital cameras.
- **4:2:0** means 2:1 horizontal downsampling, with 2:1 vertical downsampling. That is, the chrominance resolution in both the horizontal and vertical directions is cut in half

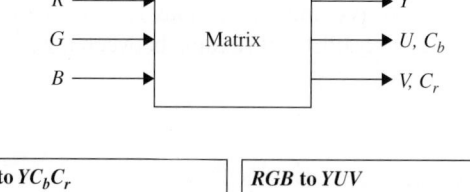

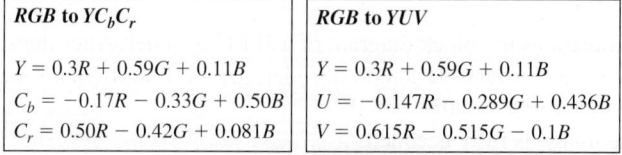

RGB to YC_bC_r	**RGB to YUV**
$Y = 0.3R + 0.59G + 0.11B$	$Y = 0.3R + 0.59G + 0.11B$
$C_b = -0.17R - 0.33G + 0.50B$	$U = -0.147R - 0.289G + 0.436B$
$C_r = 0.50R - 0.42G + 0.081B$	$V = 0.615R - 0.515G - 0.1B$

Figure 14.37 Alternative component representations of the color image.

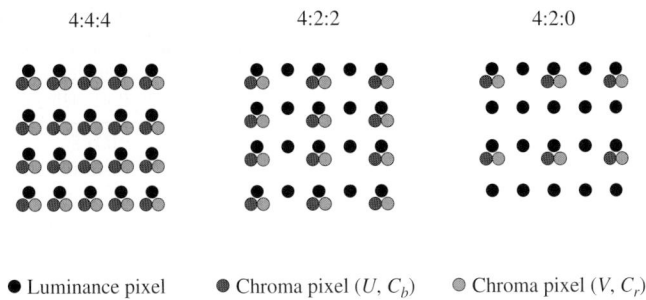

Figure 14.38 Chroma subsampling.

Table 14.8 JPEG Picture Quality versus Compression Ratios for Various Video Standards

Bits/pixel	CGA 320 × 200	VGA 640 × 480	SVGA 800 × 600
0.5	poor	fair	good
1.0	fair	good	excellent
2.0	good	excellent	excellent

with respect to the luminance. For every four Y pixels, there is one C_b (or U) pixel and one C_r (or V) pixel. This form is also known as 2 × 2 chroma subsampling and is used in JPEG and MPEG.

For color images with moderately complex scenes, Table 14.8 illustrates the levels of picture quality produced by JPEG codecs for the indicated ranges of compression. These levels are only a guideline—quality and compression can vary significantly according to source image characteristics and scene content. The units "bits/pixel" here mean the total number of bits in the compressed image, including the chrominance components, divided by the number of pixels in the luminance component. Perceptually, at rates of 1.5-2 bits/pixel, the resulting image is practically lossless.

14.7   DIGITAL VIDEO COMPRESSION: MPEG

A digital video signal consists of a sequence of digital images generated at a specified frame rate as discussed in Section 5.8.2. The frame rate should be high enough to avoid flicker when the full-motion video is displayed on the user's device. The two basic video formats are **progressive** and **interlaced.** In interlaced video, each frame of video pixels contains two interleaved fields, a top field and a bottom field. The top field contains the even-numbered rows 0, 2, $N_v - 2$ (with 0 being the top row number for a frame and N_v being its total number of rows) of pixels, and the bottom field contains the odd-numbered rows 1, 3, $N_v - 1$ (starting with the second row of the frame) of pixels. In progressive video, there is no concept of a field. A frame begins at the top left corner and continues through scanning of successive lines to the bottom of the frame. Table 14.9 displays digital video formats specified in CCIR BT-601 standard.

For a **standard definition TV (SDTV)** frame consisting of 720 × 480 pixels at 25 frames/second, the bit rate for the uncompressed video signal is 24 × 720 × 480 × 25 = 207.36 Mbits/s. Using 4:2:0 color subsampling, the uncompressed bit rate reduces to (8 × 720 × 480 + 8 × 360 × 240 + 8 × 360 × 240) × 25 = 103.68 Mbps. As another example, consider one of the **high definition TV (HDTV)** frames that has a resolution of 1920 × 1080 pixels/frame at 30 frames/second. The uncompressed bit rate

Table 14.9 CCIR BT.601 Standard for Uncompressed Digital Video

Video Format	Luminance Resolution	Color Subsampling	Frame Rate	Uncompressed Bit Rate (Mbps)	Remarks
SDTV NTSC	720×480	4:2:0	25I	103.68	
PAL	720×576	4:2:0	30I	124.416	
HDTV	1280×720	4:2:0	24P/30P/60P	265/332/664	
	1920×1080	4:2:0	24P/30P/60I	597/746/746	
SIF NTSC	352×240	4:2:0	25P	30	
CIF PAL	352×288	4:2:0	30P	37	
QCIF	176×144	4:2:0	30P	9.1	

I = interlaced, P = Progressive

for this HDTV signal is $24 \times 1920 \times 1080 \times 30 = 1.5$ Gbps. Using 4:2:0 color subsampling, the uncompressed bit rate reduces to $(8 \times 1920 \times 1080 + 8 \times 960 \times 540 + 8 \times 960 \times 540) \times 30 = 746$ Mbps. Clearly, effective compression algorithms are desirable for these signals.

In the JPEG digital image compression scheme, we used **intraframe** coding that exploited the spatial redundancies in the image to achieve compression. That is, each image is encoded independently of all other images. For video compression, JPEG can be applied to the sequence of images, compressing each individually. This is called **motion JPEG.** For the 720×480 TV frame described previously, the motion JPEG algorithm can produce digital video with high quality at bit rates of about 20 Mbps. For video signals, however, it is reasonable to anticipate that pixels in consecutive images or frames are also correlated. Moving objects and parts of the background in a scene then appear in a number of consecutive video frames, even though possibly displaced in horizontal and vertical directions and even distorted. Therefore, temporal redundancy among adjacent frames exists. **Interframe** video coding methods exploit this redundancy to achieve higher compression ratios. In scenes with little or no motion, the consecutive frames differ in very small ways. In this case the notion of predictive coding suggests that we encode the differences between consecutive frames. The pixels in these difference frames will predominantly consist of zeros and will cover a narrow dynamic range. Using variable-rate coding schemes, we know that such signals will be highly compressible.

Figure 14.39 illustrates the block diagram of a video encoder where transform and predictive coding are used to remove spatial and temporal redundancies. The encoding

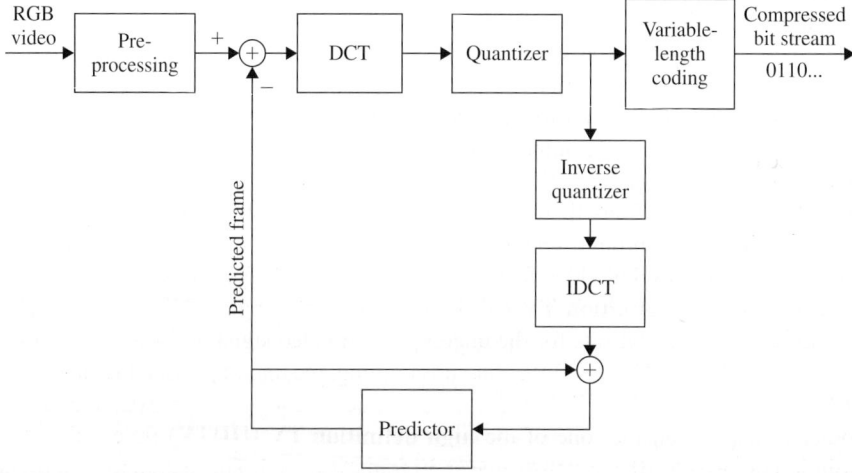

Figure 14.39 Block diagram of a predictive video encoder.

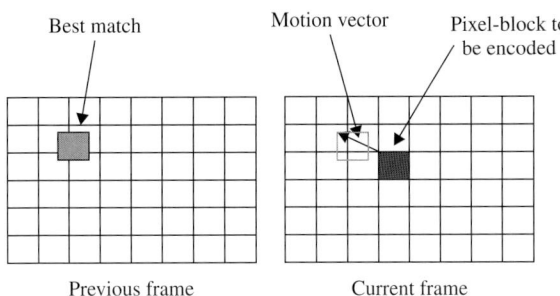

A displaced block in the previous frame is used as the prediction of the block being encoded in the current frame.

Figure 14.40 Block-based motion estimation.

process usually begins with some preprocessing. This may include subsampling, format translation (interlaced to progressive), and color conversion to YC_bC_r. Next, each prediction error block is DCT coded, and the DCT coefficients are quantized and coded using a variable-length encoder. The quantized blocks are also inverse quantized and translated into the spatial domain by an IDCT. The reconstructed prediction error block is now added to the pixel block from the previous frame stored in the predictor to replicate a copy of the encoded image as seen by the decoder. This copy is then stored in local memory within the predictor block for predictive encoding the next frame.

The encoder in Figure 14.39 encodes the difference between blocks in the same spatial location between successive frames. However, in scenes that contain a significant amount of motion, this strategy fails to capture the temporal relation between the successive frames. Motion compensation algorithms have been developed to address this problem.

Motion-Compensated Interframe Prediction

Motion compensation refers to the process of correcting the prediction frame for motion between the successive video source frames. All digital video compression methods use a block-based motion compensation approach. The pixel-block to be encoded in the current frame is matched with a large number of displaced blocks of the same size in the previous frame using the luminance component of the picture. The block in the previous frame that best matches the block being coded is used as the **prediction block.** The **best matching** is determined on the basis of minimum error between the block being coded and the prediction block. The location of the prediction block is indicated by a **motion vector (MV)** that represents the horizontal and vertical offset from the block being coded to the prediction block. The transform-coded prediction error block and motion vector are transmitted by the encoder after variable-length coding. Figure 14.40 illustrates the process.

14.7.1 MPEG

MPEG-1 and MPEG-2 are widely used international standards for digital compression of video and audio signals. The MPEG video compression algorithm relies on two basic techniques:

- Block-based motion compensation for the reduction of temporal redundancy. In the MPEG standards, the motion compensation algorithm attempts to find the best match for **macro** blocks that consist of 16×16 pixel blocks of luminance symbols. The motion vector that results from this process is then used for the associated 8×8 chrominance pixel blocks.

- DCT-based compensation for the reduction of spatial redundancy.

Video on demand and related applications require that the encoded video signal accommodate capabilities associated with VCR controls. These include the ability to fast forward, reverse, and access a specific frame in a video sequence. The MPEG standards encode three different types of frames that offer the choice of trading compression efficiency for fast access capability in support of VCR functionality. I-frames are encoded with intra-frame coding—no temporal compression. Because their decoding is independent of all other frames, I-frames facilitate fast-forward, reverse, and random-access capabilities. I-frames have the lowest compression, but they can be encoded and decoded faster than the other frame types. P-frames (predictive) are encoded by using motion compensation relative to the most recent I- or P-frame. P-frames have better compression levels than I-frames. B-frames (bidirectional) use motion compensation relative to both the preceding and the following I- or P-frames. The motion vector for a given block can refer to either or both of these two frames. B-frames achieve the highest compression of the three frame types, but they also take the longest time to encode. In addition, they cause significant delay at the encoder, because they require the availability of the following I- or P-frame. The encoded frames in MPEG are arranged in groups of pictures as shown in Figure 14.41. I-frames are inserted into the sequence at regular intervals to provide VCR capabilities as well as to limit the propagation of errors associated with predictive coding. The remainder of the frames consist of P-frames and B-frames.

MPEG Video Encoder

Figure 14.42 displays a block diagram of an MPEG video encoder. It is similar to Figure 14.39 except for the additional motion compensation circuitry. After preprocessing, the encoder selects the coding type (I, P, or B). For I-frame, there is no motion compensation, and it is intraframe coded like a JPEG image. If the input image data is coded as a P- or B-frame, the encoder does not code the macroblocks directly. Rather it codes the prediction error between each macroblock in the current frame and the motion-compensated prediction frame. For P-frame, the motion-compensated prediction frame is generated from the reconstructed previous frame using motion vector data. In the case of B-frames, the motion-compensated prediction frame is generated from the reconstructed previous and future frames using motion vector data.

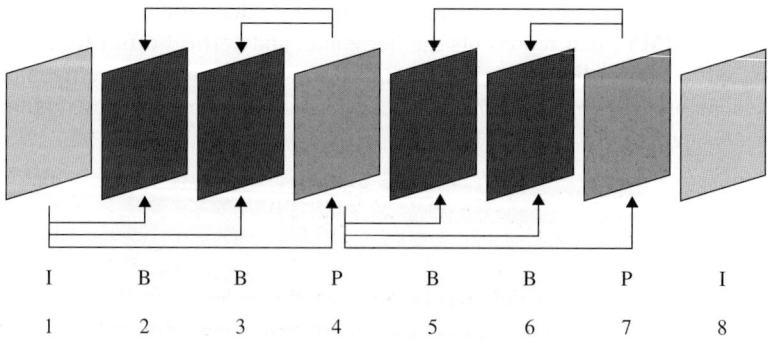

Camera/display order: 1 2 3 4 5 6 7 8
Encoding/decoding order: 1 4 2 3 7 5 6 8

Figure 14.41 Group of frames in MPEG.

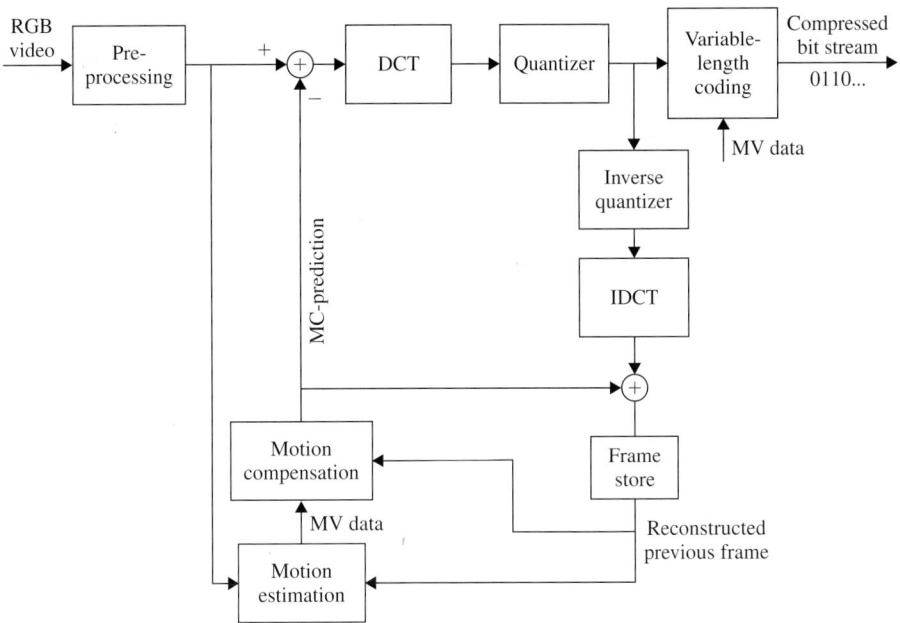

Figure 14.42 MPEG video encoder.

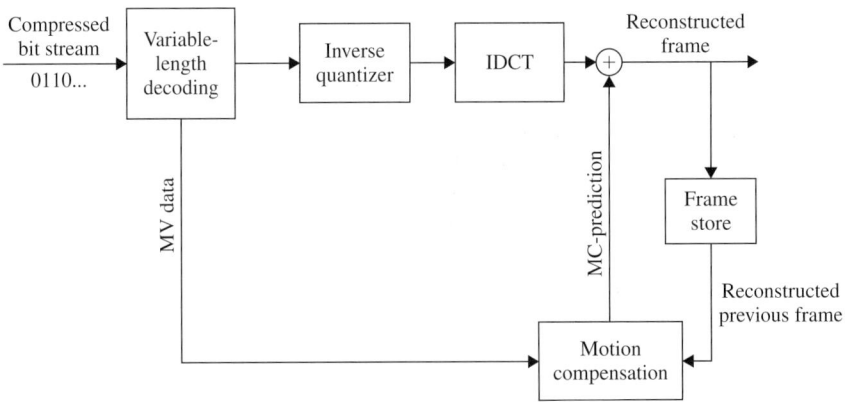

Figure 14.43 MPEG video decoder.

MPEG Video Decoder

Figure 14.43 displays a block diagram of an MPEG video decoder. As expected, the functionality of the video decoder is very similar to the feedback loop of the video encoder. The input compressed bit stream is Huffman decoded and the frame type (I, P, or B) is then determined from the header information. For each macroblock, the decoded coefficients are dequantized and translated into the spatial domain by IDCT. Further decoding proceeds as follows:

- **I-frames.** No motion compensation is performed. The IDCT output is a reconstructed macroblock.
- **P-frames.** The motion vector data is used to generate motion-compensated prediction macroblocks from the reconstructed previous frame. The decoder output is

reconstructed by adding the prediction error to the MC-prediction frame on a macroblock basis.

- **B-frames.** The motion vector data is used to generate motion-compensated prediction macroblocks from the reconstructed previous and future frames. The decoder output is reconstructed by adding the prediction error to the MC-prediction frame on a macroblock basis.

The MPEG-1 standard was developed to produce VCR-quality compressed digital video and associated audio at rates up to 1.5 Mbps. If video is coded at about 1.2 Mbps and stereo audio is coded at 128 kbps, the combined digital video and audio signal makes storage possible in CD-ROMs and transmission possible over T-1 rate telephone lines. Originally, the MPEG-2 standard was meant to code CCIR-601 SDTV video for a large number of consumer applications. Very good-quality video is attainable using bit rates in the range of 4 to 6 Mbps. However, the scope of the MPEG-2 standard includes CCIR-601 HDTV formats at 1280 × 720 and 1920 × 1080 resolutions. MPEG-2 can produce high-quality compressed HDTV signals at bit rates in the range 20 to 40 Mbps.

FINAL REMARKS

The 1948 paper by Shannon, "A Mathematical Theory of Communication," laid the foundations for the **Information Age** as we know it today. Shannon showed how information could be quantified, and he profoundly observed that the representation and transmission of all information types is essentially digital in nature. One of the most significant results from his paper is that the problem of transmitting information from a source through some channel can be separated, with no loss of optimality, into the independent problems of representing that source by a sequence of binary digits and of transmitting a random binary sequence through that channel. He then posed two fundamental problems of information theory and also, to a large extent, answered them: what is the ultimate data compression rate (entropy of the source) and what is the ultimate transmission rate of communication (channel capacity). His channel coding theorem result—that if the information rate is below the capacity of the channel, there is no rate-reliability trade-off—came as a total surprise to engineers at the time. Until then it was universally accepted that increasing the transmission rate of information over a communication channel increased the probability of error. It is not surprising, then, that the channel coding theorem was not readily accepted by practicing communications engineers at the time. It was treated as a mathematical curiosity that was of little practical value. The noisy channel coding theorem is what gave rise to the entire field of channel coding (Chapter 15). Five decades of research and invention have finally produced coding schemes that closely approach Shannon's channel capacity limit on memoryless communication channels. The performance of Turbo and LDPC codes approaches the Shannon limit within an astonishing 1/2 dB. It would be fair to say that without channel coding, the digital media, broadband, and mobile revolutions would not have been technically feasible.

Shannon's source coding theorem argued that every information source, such as music, speech, and video, is completely characterized by a single number—the entropy of the source. This theorem has also proved to be prophetic as evidenced by the proliferation of compression technologies in our daily lives: speech (cell phones), audio (MP3 players), images (JPEG and digital cameras), and video (HDTV and DVD players).

FURTHER READINGS

Shannon's landmark papers [1, 4] are very readable and still provide the best introduction to the theory of information transmission. Gallager's text [2] is an excellent and comprehensive treatment of the field. Cover and Thomas [3] provide a readable and thorough coverage of information theory. Good introductory treatment of information theory is also available in several digital communications texts [5, 6]. Gallager [7] reviews Shannon's life and his remarkable contributions in many fields, including information theory. The paper by Massey [8] makes an interesting analysis and comparison of Shannon's main results.

1. Shannon, C. "A Mathematical Theory of Communication." *Bell System Technical Journal* 27 (1948): 379–423.

2. Gallager, R. *Information Theory and Reliable Communication.* Hoboken, NJ: John Wiley, 1968.

3. Cover, T., and J. Thomas. *Elements of Information Theory.* Hoboken, NJ: John Wiley, 1991.

4. Shannon, C. "Communication in the Presence of Noise." *Proceedings of the Institute of Radio Engineers* 37 (1949): 10–21.

5. Ziemer, R., and R. Peterson. *An Introduction to Digital Communication,* 2nd ed. Upper Saddle River, NJ: Prentice Hall, 2001.

6. Proakis, J., and M. Salehi. *Digital Communications,* 5th ed. New York: McGraw-Hill, 2007.

7. Gallager, R. "Claude E. Shannon: A Retrospective on His Life, Work, and Impact." *IEEE Transactions on Information Theory* 47 (2001): 2681–2695.

8. Massey, J. "Information Theory: The Copernican System of Communications, " *IEEE. Communications Magazine* 22 (1984): 26–28.

9. Huffman, D. "A Method for the Construction of Minimum Redundancy Codes." *Proceedings of the Institute of Radio Engineers* 40 (1952): 1098–1101.

10. Ziv, J., and A. Lempel. "A Universal Algorithm for Sequential Data Compression." *IEEE Transactions on Information Theory* 23 (1977): 337–343.

11. Ziv, J., and A. Lempel. "Compression of Individual Sequences via Variable-rate Coding." *IEEE Transactions on Information Theory* 24 (1978): 530–536.

12. Berrou, C., M. Glavieux, and P. Thitimajshima. "Near Shannon Limit Error-correcting Coding and Decoding: Turbo Codes." *Proceedings of IEEE International Conference on Communications,* Geneva, Switzerland, May (1993): 1064–1070.

13. Berrou, C., and M. Glavieux. "Near Optimum Error-correcting Coding and Decoding: Turbo Codes." *IEEE Transactions on Communications* 44 (1996): 1261–1271.

PROBLEMS

14.1. A discrete memoryless source emits symbols from the alphabet set $\mathscr{A} = \{a, b, c, d, e\}$ with probabilities $\{0.5, 0.3, 0.1, 0.05, 0.05\}$ respectively.

   a. Determine the information content of the source in bits/symbol.

   b. What is the maximum information content of the source? Specify the corresponding source PMF.

   c. Determine the number of bits per symbol required to transmit the source with simple binary coding.

14.2. A discrete memoryless source emits symbols every 125 μsec from the alphabet set $\mathscr{A} = \{-1, -3/4, -1/2, -1/4, 1/4, 1/2, 3/4, 1\}$ with respective probabilities $\{1/16, 1/16, 1/8, 1/4, 1/4, 1/8, 1/16, 1/16\}$.

   a. Determine the entropy of the source.

   b. What is the minimum bit rate required to transmit the source?

14.3. A discrete memoryless source emits symbols from the alphabet set $\mathscr{A} = \{0, 1/8, 1/4, 1/2, 3/4, 7/8, 15/16, 1\}$ with respective probabilities $\{1/16, 1/8, 1/8, 1/4, 5/32, 1/8, 3/32, 1/16\}$.

   a. Determine the entropy of the source.

   b. Assume that the source is quantized according to the following quantization table

Input Symbol	Quantizer Output Symbol
0, 1/8, 1/4	1/8
1/2, 3/4	5/8
7/8, 15/16, 1	15/16

Find the entropy of the quantized source.

14.4. Consider a discrete-time, continuous amplitude source x characterized by the Laplacian PDF

$$f_x(x) = \frac{1}{\sqrt{2}\sigma_x} e^{-\frac{\sqrt{2}|x|}{\sigma_x}}$$

   a. Calculate the differential entropy of x.

   b. Assume that the source x is uniformly quantized with a quantization step size Δ. Calculate the probability $P(i\Delta)$ that x is quantized to $i\Delta$, where $i = 0, \pm 1, \pm 2, \ldots$.

   c. Determine the entropy of the quantized source.

14.5. For a continuous random variable x with $|x| \le a$, prove that the differential entropy is maximum if x is uniformly distributed over $[-a, a]$. Show that the maximum entropy is given by $\log_2 2a$.

14.6. For a continuous random variable x with $\overline{x^2} = \sigma_x^2$, prove that the Gaussian PDF maximizes the differential entropy. Show that

$$h(x) \leq \frac{1}{2}\log_2(2\pi e \sigma_x^2) \text{ bits}$$

where the equality is achieved if $x \sim \mathcal{N}(0, \sigma_x^2)$.

14.7. A Gaussian random signal with zero mean, variance σ^2 and bandwidth B Hz is sampled at the Nyquist rate. The sampled signal is then applied to a quantizer with the following quantization table.

Quantizer Input	Quantizer Output
$(-\infty, -4\sigma)$	y_0
$(-4\sigma, -3\sigma)$	y_1
$(-3\sigma, -2\sigma)$	y_2
$(-2\sigma, -\sigma)$	y_3
$(-\sigma, \sigma)$	y_4
$(\sigma, 2\sigma)$	y_5
$(2\sigma, 3\sigma)$	y_6
$(3\sigma, 4\sigma)$	y_7
$(4\sigma, \infty)$	y_8

a. Determine the entropy of the quantizer output.

b. Calculate the minimum bit rate required to transmit the quantized source.

14.8. A discrete memoryless source has the alphabet $\mathscr{A}_x = \{a, b, c, d\}$ with respective probabilities $\{1/2, 1/4, 1/8, 1/8\}$.

a. Determine the number of typical sequences of length 8.

b. Determine the number of nontypical sequences of length 8.

c. Write two examples each of typical and nontypical sequences of length 8.

14.9. A discrete memoryless source emits symbols every 1 ms from the alphabet $\mathscr{A}_x = \{x_1, x_2, \ldots, x_8\}$ with respective probabilities

$$\{0.35, 0.2, 0.15, 0.12, 0.08, 0.05, 0.03, 0.02\}.$$

a. Determine the entropy of the source.

b. Use the Huffman coding procedure to assign binary codewords to all symbols.

c. What is the average length of the Huffman code and how does it compare with the entropy of the source?

d. Calculate the minimum bit rate required to transmit the source.

14.10. A discrete memoryless source emits symbols from the alphabet $\mathscr{A}_x = \{a, b, c, d\}$ with respective probabilities $\{0.2, 0.5, 0.15, 0.15\}$.

a. Design a Huffman code to assign binary codewords to all symbols.

b. Now design a Huffman code for encoding pairs of symbols at a time.

c. Compare the performance of the two codes. How do they compare with the entropy of the source?

14.11. Let a binary channel be described by the transition probabilities matrix

$$\underline{P} = \begin{pmatrix} 2/3 & 1/3 \\ 1/8 & 7/8 \end{pmatrix}$$

Assume the source probabilities are $P(x_1) = \frac{3}{4}$ and $P(x_2) = \frac{1}{4}$.

a. Determine the output symbol probabilities.

b. Calculate the $H(x)$, $H(x|y)$, and mutual information $I(x; y)$.

14.12. Consider the channel illustrated in Figure P14.1.

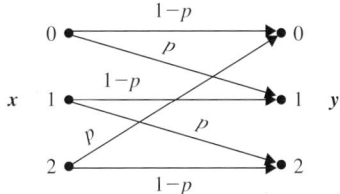

Figure P14.1

a. Write the matrix $\underline{P}$ of the channel transition probabilities.

b. Calculate the capacity of the channel. For what input distribution is this capacity achieved?

14.13. A channel is described by the transition probabilities matrix

$$\underline{P} = \begin{pmatrix} 3/8 & 1/8 & 3/8 & 1/8 \\ 1/8 & 3/8 & 1/8 & 3/8 \end{pmatrix}$$

Find the capacity of the channel. For what input distribution is this capacity achieved?

14.14. Two binary symmetric channels are connected in cascade as shown in Figure P14.2.

a. Determine the transition probabilities matrix for the cascaded channel.

b. Calculate $P(z_1)$ and $P(z_2)$ when $P(x_1) = P(x_2) = 0.5$.

c. Determine the capacity of each channel.

d. Determine the capacity of the cascaded channel.

Output

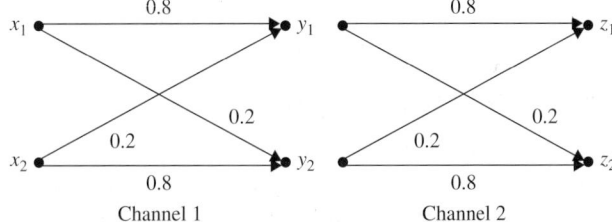

Figure P14.2

14.15. The Z-channel input alphabet is $\{0, 1\}$, and output alphabet is $\{0, 1\}$, like the BSC. However, the Z-channel is asymmetrical. The 0 symbol is always transmitted correctly, but the 1 symbol is received incorrectly (as 0) with probability ε.

a. Sketch the channel diagram showing all transition probabilities.

b. Find the capacity of the channel and the input channel PMF that achieves it.

c. Discuss the special cases of (b) when $\varepsilon = 0$ and $\varepsilon = 1$.

d. Evaluate the channel input probabilities that achieve the capacity for the case $\varepsilon = 1/2$.

14.16. Encode the following string using the LZW algorithm

abracadabra

Assume that the LZW implementation initializes the dictionary with values 0 to 255, where the first 128 entries are ASCII characters.

14.17. Encode the following string using the LZW algorithm:

This_love_ This_love _is_ a_strange_love_ A_faded_ kind_ of_day_love _This_love

14.18. Decode the following LZW-encoded string

1213346176889

The source encoder alphabet is binary. List the complete dictionary.

14.19. Consider a CATV channel with a bandwidth 6 MHz. Assume that the channel can be modeled as an AWGN channel.

a. What is the capacity of the channel for an SNR of 35 dB?

b. Calculate the minimum SNR required for a data rate of 43 Mbps.

c. Compare the bit rate calculated in (a) with that achievable using 256-QAM. The modulator uses RRC pulses with roll-off factor $\alpha = 0.5$.

14.20. Calculate the maximum information rate that can be transmitted over an AWGN channel of bandwidth 200 kHz. Assume that the received power level is 1 mW and the one-sided noise spectral density is 10^{-9} watts/Hz.

a. How much is the capacity increased by doubling the received power?

b. How much is the capacity increased by doubling the bandwidth instead?

c. Comment on the power-bandwidth trade-off in (a) and (b).

14.21. Find the channel capacity of the DMC shown in Figure P14.3:

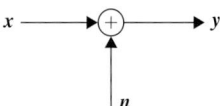

Figure P14.3

The output y of the channel is given by

$$y = x + n$$

where $P\{n = 0\} = P\{n = \varepsilon\} = 1/2$ and x is a binary random variable with alphabet $\mathcal{x} = \{-1, 1\}$. Assume that x and n are statistically independent. Calculate the capacity of channel for values of $\varepsilon = \pm1$, and 0.5.

14.22. The DCT coefficients corresponding to an 8×8 block of pixels are given below:

$$\begin{pmatrix} 1260 & -1 & -12 & -5 & 2 & -2 & -3 & 1 \\ -23 & -17 & -6 & -3 & -3 & 0 & 0 & -1 \\ -11 & 9 & -2 & 2 & 0 & -1 & -1 & 0 \\ -7 & -2 & 0 & 1 & 1 & 0 & 0 & 0 \\ -1 & -1 & 1 & 2 & 0 & -1 & 1 & 1 \\ 2 & 0 & 2 & 0 & -1 & 1 & 1 & -1 \\ -1 & 0 & 0 & -1 & 0 & 2 & 1 & -1 \\ -3 & 2 & -4 & -2 & 2 & 1 & -1 & 0 \end{pmatrix}$$

a. Using JPEG luminance quantization table, find the resulting block of quantized DCT coefficients.

b. Find the one-dimensional sequence that results after zig-zag scanning.

14.23. Consider a black-and-white HDTV picture with the frame rate of 60 Hz. Each frame is made up of 1080 scan lines × 1920 pixels/line. We assume that pixels can occupy 1 of 16 brightness levels with equal probability and independent of others.

a. Calculate the information content of the black-and-white HDTV image. What is the minimum bit rate required to transmit the signal?

b. Repeat (a) for color HDTV if the pixels can additionally occupy one of 256 colors with equal probability and independent of others.

MATLAB PROBLEMS

14.24. Consider a DMS whose output is generated from an alphabet $\mathcal{x} = \{a, b, c, d, e, f, g, h\}$ with respective probabilities $\{0.2, 0.05, 0.03, 0.1, 0.3, 0.02, 0.22, 0.08\}$.

a. Design a Huffman code and sketch the corresponding code tree. Specify the codewords for the letters in the alphabet.

b. Determine the average codeword length of the Huffman code.

c. Calculate the entropy of the source and compare it with the average codeword length calculated in (b).

d. Encode the sequence aaabdbceefghddca.

14.25. For the DMS in problem 14.23, we now consider Huffman encoding blocks of 2 source symbols at a time.

a. List all length-2 source output sequences (total of 64) and their probabilities.

b. Specify the codewords. Calculate the average length of the Huffman code.

c. Compare the efficiency of this code with that calculated in problem 14.24 as well as the entropy of the source. Comment.

d. Encode the sequence aaabdbceefghddca.

14.26. **Huffman code for English language.** The probabilities of the letters in the English language character set are given In Table P14.1.

    a. Design a Huffman code for the English language character set.

    b. Specify the codewords. Calculate the average length of the code.

    c. Compare the efficiency of this code with the entropy of the English language. Comment.

Table P14.1 Probability of Occurrence of Letters in English Language

Letter	Probability	Letter	Probability	Letter	Probability
Space	0.187	H	0.04305	P	0.01623
E	0.1073	D	0.03100	W	0.01620
T	0.0856	L	0.02775	B	0.01179
A	0.0668	F	0.02395	V	0.00752
O	0.0654	C	0.02260	K	0.00344
N	0.0581	M	0.02075	X	0.00136
R	0.0559	U	0.02010	J	0.00108
I	0.0519	G	0.01633	Q	0.00099
S	0.0499	Y	0.01623	Z	0.00063

14.27. Use LZW encoding algorithm to compress the string "It is better to have loved and lost than never to have loved at all." Display the results in the format of Table 14.5.

14.28. Use LZW decoding algorithm to recover the ASCII string from the following compressed code below. Display the results in the format of Table 14.6.

    69 97 114 108 121 32 116 111 32 98 101 100 32 97 110 267 101 257 259 261 263 114 105 115 101 32 109 97 107 101 115 268 281 269 32 104 272 108 116 104 121 44 32 119 292 294 260 269 267 119 278 101 46

14.29. For the AWGN channel in Figure 14.16, the channel capacity is achieved if the input x has Gaussian PDF. In this problem, we investigate the average information per symbol transmitted through the channel (that is, mutual information $I(x; y)$) when the input x is a discrete random variable assuming values from a finite symbol alphabet $\mathscr{X}$. An example is M-ary PAM scheme with $\mathscr{X} = \{\pm 1, \pm 3, \ldots, \pm(M - 1)\}$. The mutual

information between the input and output is obtained by combining (A.2) and (A.1) as

$$I(x; y) = h(y) - \log_2 \sqrt{\pi e N_o} \text{ bits/channel use}$$

where the differential entropy $h(y)$ from (14.20) is

$$h(y) = -\int_{-\infty}^{\infty} f_y(y) \log f_y(y) dy$$

The PDF of channel output y can be expressed as

$$f_y(y) = \sum_{x \in \mathscr{X}} f_{xy}(x, y) = \sum_{x \in \mathscr{X}} f_{y|x}(y|x = x) p_x(x)$$

$$= \sum_{x \in \mathscr{X}} \frac{1}{\sqrt{2\pi \sigma_n^2}} e^{-(y - x)^2/N_o} p_x(x)$$

where $p_x(x)$ is the PMF of the channel input x. For the PMF of a discrete random variable, it is difficult to calculate the entropy $h(y)$ analytically. So we will use MATLAB to numerically calculate it.

    a. Assume 8-PAM with $\mathscr{X} = \{\pm 1, \pm 3, \pm 5, \pm 7\}$. Each symbol is equiprobable, that is, $p_x(x) = 1/8$ for each x in $\mathscr{X}$. Calculate $\sigma_x^2 = P_{av}$.

    b. Determine noise variance $\sigma_n^2 = N_o/2$ for $SNR = 10\log_{10}(\sigma_x^2/\sigma_n^2) = 20$ dB.

```
hn = log2(sqrt(pi*2.7182*No));
```

    c. Calculate $f_y(y)$ at a dense set of values of y in the range $[-100, 100]$.

```
y = -100:0.01:100;
```

    d. Calculate entropy $h(y)$ by numerical integration

```
hy = -trapz(y, fy.*log2(fy));
```

    e. Compute mutual information.

```
mi = hy - hn
```

    f. Repeat steps (b) through (e) for SNR values in the range 0–25 dB. Plot mutual information (bits/symbol transmitted) versus SNR.

14.30. Repeat 14.29 for 4-PAM and 16-PAM. Display mutual information (bits/symbol transmitted) versus SNR for 4-PAM, 8-PAM, and 16-PAM schemes on the same plot along channel capacity for comparison purposes. Comment.

Appendix A

Capacity of AWGN Channel: Alternative Proof

The capacity of the AWGN channel from (14.73) is

$$C = \underset{f_x(x)}{\text{Max}} I(x; y) \qquad (14.73)$$

subject to the average power constraint on the input symbol set. That is,

$$\frac{1}{n}\sum_{i=0}^{n-1} x_i^2 \leq P_{av} \qquad (14.72)$$

for any codeword of n symbols $\underline{x} = (x_{n-1}, \ldots, x_1, x_0)$. For a discrete-time, continuous-amplitude channel, the mutual information is given from (14.27) as

$$I(x; y) = h(y) - h(y|x)$$

$$= h(y) - h(x + n|x)$$

$$= h(y) - h(n) \qquad (14A.1)$$

because n is statistically independent of x. From Example 14.5, the entropy of a Gaussian random variable is given by

$$h(n) = \frac{1}{2}\log_2(\pi e N_o) \text{ bits for } n \sim \mathcal{N}(0, N_o/2) \qquad (14A.2)$$

Substituting (14A.1) and (14A.2) into (14.73), we obtain

$$C = \underset{f_x(x)}{\text{Max}} I(x; y) = \underset{f_x(x)}{\text{Max}}\{h(y) - h(n)\}$$

$$= \underset{f_x(x)}{\text{Max}}\{h(y)\} - \log_2\sqrt{\pi e N_o} \text{ bits/channel use} \qquad (14A.3)$$

Also

$$\overline{y^2} = E\{(x + n)^2\} = E\{x^2\} + 2\underbrace{E\{xn\}}_{0} + E\{n^2\}$$

$$= P_{av} + \frac{N_o}{2} \qquad (14A.4)$$

For a continuous random variable y with $\overline{y^2} = P_{av} + \dfrac{N_o}{2}$, the Gaussian PDF maximizes the entropy. That is,

$$h(y) \leq \frac{1}{2}\log_2\left[2\pi e\left(P_{av} + \frac{N_o}{2}\right)\right] = \log_2\sqrt{2\pi e\left(P_{av} + \frac{N_o}{2}\right)} \qquad (14A.5)$$

where the equality is achieved if $y \sim \mathcal{N}\left(0, P_{av} + \dfrac{N_o}{2}\right)$. Substituting (14A.5) and (14A.2) into (14A.3), the capacity of an AWGN is obtained as

$$C = \frac{1}{2}\log_2\left(1 + \frac{P_{av}}{N_o/2}\right) \text{ bits/channel use}$$

Because n is Gaussian, y will be Gaussian if x is Gaussian. That is, $x \sim \mathcal{N}(0, P_{av})$.

An Interview with Robert G. Gallager

Courtesy of Robert G. Gallager.

Why did you choose a career in the communication field? How did your close association with Claude Shannon influence your many achievements?

It was partly good luck and partly a natural affinity for the field. When I graduated from Penn with a bachelor's degree in electrical engineering, I had no thought of graduate school and started to work at Bell Labs in the switching area. They had an educational program called Kelly College and their new engineers spent a significant part of their time taking classes taught by some of the best researchers (Dave Slepian, Bill Bennett, Tukey, and a number of others). It was probably a better education than at the best universities then. It was there that I was introduced to Information Theory and expanded my love of probability theory. When I was drafted into the U.S. Army, I was assigned to a group doing communications work, and I applied to graduate school primarily to get out of the army three months early. With my background, it was natural to get a research assistantship at MIT in the communications area. Information Theory was a very exciting area at MIT at the time. Claude Shannon was in the process of moving from Bell Labs to MIT. He, along with Bob Fano, Peter Elias, Jack Wozencraft, Dave Huffman, and a number of other faculty, were attracting the brightest graduate students at the time. I felt a little dim-witted in the presence of all that intellectual talent, but managed to survive because of my early start at Bell Labs.

You are quoted to have called Shannon one of the greatest scientists of the 20th century. Are geniuses like Einstein and Shannon born or is their genius cultivated by proper nurturing and external environment?

It is clearly a combination of genes and environment, plus the way they interact. Shannon had a natural talent for building creatively simple things, plus a natural talent for cutting through all the complications of research and focusing on the central core. He was encouraged in both of these by mentors and colleagues at MIT and Bell Labs. He was never interested in scholasticism, that is, cataloging what each person has done in a research field and adding small increments. Rather, he made contributions to fields that were not at all developed, finding the right models and creating ideas that were unimaginable before and almost obvious afterwards. He created information theory by developing a small set of very simple (but very unexpected) ideas that in retrospect fit together perfectly and created the architecture for the coming revolution.

In your opinion what are the major innovations that have contributed to the phenomenal progress in digital and wireless communications? What has been the impact of the semiconductor revolution? Optical fiber revolution? Software technologies?

The semiconductor revolution, coming after the theory was ready and waiting, jump started the whole process, and, of course, also led to phenomenal progress in the computer industry. The computer and communication industries each created the need for rapid growth in the other. As the field grew, the need for high speed backbones created the need for optical fibers, which were ready for the task due to some very far-sighted research at a number of leading laboratories.

Tell us about your simple and elegant proof of the channel coding theorem.

I was teaching the information theory course at MIT. The channel coding theorem was the crown jewel of the theory, and the topics around it were the subject of much student research. I couldn't stand going through the awful proofs of the time, some insightful but not quite correct, and others correct but totally obscure. Finding a better way of looking at the coding theorem became a passion for me, and finally, on waking up one morning it was there. It was not that it came in a dream or something, but for me, when I sleep, all the details go away and I see the principles more clearly.

You invented LDPC codes as part of your doctoral dissertation at MIT in 1960. Why were they forgotten for about 30 years before it was discovered that they are capable of achieving Shannon limit-like Turbo codes? You must feel great pride today that an LDPC code has been selected for DVB-S2 standard over seven other turbo code-based candidates because of its more efficient implementation as well as better performance. Also for 10GBase-T Ethernet, which sends data at 10 Gbps over TWP cables. Any comment?

LDPC codes were unsuccessful in applications for many years because they required very large block lengths to be useful, and the computational complexity was too great and too slow for the technology of the day. They were rightfully forgotten because they were far from being cost effective. As computation became cheaper and faster, LDPC codes became effective and thus stimulated a great deal of new research which brought them to where they are today. The pace of research is very different from the pace of technology, but fortunately research often runs ahead so as to be ready when needed.

You have been vocal in your concerns about the teaching methods used in our education system and research models pursued at major universities and major industrial organizations. Are we doing enough fundamental and/or Shannon style research to drive the next round of major innovations?

The two research models that seem to be most popular in universities and industrial research labs are, first, the practically motivated research that is more development than research, and, second, the very mathematical pursuit of small extensions or gaps in the theory. The papers arising from each of these models tend to have many authors, many references, and tend to be deadly dull. Shannon's style of research was to look at very simple models of real-life problems and say something both new and simple. Today's technology is becoming increasingly complex and overblown. The ideas that make it simpler and understandable are critical for the future.

Who inspired you professionally the most?

Peter Elias, Claude Shannon, my many students who often seemed to be one step ahead of me, and many colleagues in the information theory field. Information theory attracted so many first-rate talents in the 50s and 60s that the mentoring of new generations was always first rate. It was not just brilliance, but also dedication and generosity of spirit.

Do you have any advice for the new generation of students and researchers entering the communications field?

Be kind and patient with yourself. Learning important ideas has always been difficult. It requires more effort, but has more reward than is apparent. Be kind and patient with your colleagues and your students. They also learn new ideas more slowly than is apparent, but your help clarifies things as much for you as for them.

Robert G. Gallager is well-known for his fundamental work on Information Theory over the last 50 years, including the noisy channel coding theorem, the invention of Low Density Parity Check codes, and his pioneering textbook, *Information Theory and Reliable Communication*, John Wiley, 1968. He is also well known for his pioneering work on data networks, focusing on distributed algorithms, routing, congestion control, and random access techniques.

He is the recipient of the Claude Shannon Award (1983), the IEEE Medal of Honor (1990), the Technion Harvey prize (1999), the Eduard Rhein prize (2002), the Marconi prize (2003), and many other awards. He is a Fellow of the IEEE, a member of the U.S. National Academy of Engineering, the U.S. National Academy of Sciences, and the American Academy of Arts and Sciences. He has been a faculty member of EECS at MIT since 1960, and is proud of the achievements of his many students. He is now retired but is still active in research and teaching.

CHAPTER 15

Channel Coding Techniques

In digital communication systems, transmission errors are unavoidable due to the presence of noise and other channel impairments. For example, typical bit error rates for systems using TWPs are on the order of 10^{-5}. Optical fiber links achieve outstanding error rate performance as low as 10^{-12} or better. On the other hand, digital cellular systems can experience error rates as high as 10^{-2} or worse during deep fades. The acceptable error rate is, of course, determined by the application. Certain types of applications, such as speech compression algorithms, are tolerant of high bit error rates during digital transmission. On the other hand, applications such as file transfers and financial transactions require 100% reliability.

The advent of channel coding in digital communication systems effectively started in 1948 with Shannon's seminal paper as discussed in Chapter 14. According to Shannon's channel coding theorem, errors induced by the noisy channel or storage medium can be reduced to any desired level by proper encoding of the information as long as the information rate is less than the capacity of the channel. A tremendous amount of effort has been expended toward designing good codes and efficient decoding techniques since the early contributions by Hamming, Golay, Elias, and others. For AWGN channels, Shannon's work promised that reliable transmission could be achieved at the desired bit error rate with a SNR/bit as low as -1.6 dB through the use of channel coding techniques. Today, most of that promised improvement is realizable with capacity-approaching turbo and LDPC codes. This has led to the realization that coding can be exploited as a system design technique that can fundamentally change the trade-offs in the design of digital communication and storage systems.

The fundamental idea of channel coding is to add redundancy in the transmitted bit stream which can be used at the receiver to overcome the effects of noise and other channel impairments. To focus attention on the channel encoding and decoding techniques, we will consider the simplified block diagram of a digital communication system shown in Figure 15.1. The channel encoder accepts data bits from the source encoder and

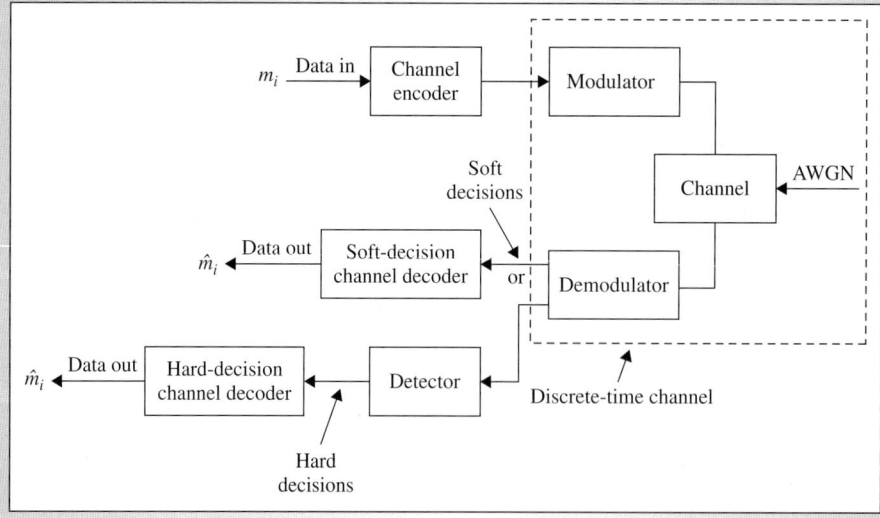

Figure 15.1 Simplified model of a digital communication system.

introduces redundancy according to a prescribed rule. The encoded data passes through a discrete-time channel comprised of modulator, transmission channel, and demodulator. In the hard-decision decoding, the detector at the receiver provides "hard" decisions (i.e., 0 or 1 in the case of binary signaling) to the channel decoder. Alternatively, the decoder may process "soft decisions" comprising the symbol-rate sample values from the demodulator without any binary quantization. In either case, the channel decoder utilizes the redundancy contained in the received signal and attempts error detection and correction to reconstruct the transmitted bit sequence.

The chapter is organized into the following sections:

15.1 BLOCK CODES.

This section covers in detail the fundamental concepts of linear block codes. We explain generator and parity check matrices for systematic linear block codes and their minimum distance characterization.

15.2 HARD-DECISION DECODING OF BLOCK CODES.

We review the concepts of maximum likelihood (ML) hard-decision decoding for block codes. We then discuss syndrome decoding of linear block codes and Hamming bound.

15.3 CYCLIC CODES.

In this section we discuss the representation of cyclic codes by generator polynomials. This is followed by a review of encoding and decoding methods for systematic cyclic codes. Some well-known cyclic codes are then introduced. We conclude this section with a discussion of CRC codes for error detection.

15.4 ERROR CORRECTION PERFORMANCE OF HARD-DECISION DECODED BLOCK CODES.

We define the probability of codeword error as a performance measure to characterize the error correction performance of linear block codes. Upper bounds for the probability of codeword error and the probability of decoded bit error are next derived for maximum likelihood (ML) hard-decision decoding scheme.

15.5 SOFT-DECISION DECODING OF BLOCK CODES.

The ML soft-decision decoding for block codes is considered here. We next introduce the concept of coding gain as another useful performance measure and compare the advantage of soft-decision versus hard-decision decoding. The performance of some popular block codes is then presented.

15.6 CONVOLUTIONAL CODES.

This section is devoted to the presentation of the fundamentals of convolutional codes. We consider the generation of convolutional codes by linear shift register encoders and their representation in terms of state transition and trellis diagrams. Next we discuss maximum likelihood hard- and soft-decision decoding for convolutional codes. This is followed by a description of the Viterbi algorithm as an efficient implementation for ML decoding.

15.7 ERROR PERFORMANCE OF CONVOLUTIONAL CODES.

We define the probability of decoding an incorrect path through trellis as a performance measure to characterize the error correction performance of convolutional codes. Using the union bounding technique, we next derive upper bounds on the probability of decoding an erroneous path and the probability of decoded bit error for both hard- and soft-decision ML decoding schemes. The performance of some popular convolutional codes is then presented along with a discussion of coding gain.

15.8 TURBO CODES.

This section introduces turbo codes, which can achieve performance within a fraction of a dB of the Shannon limit. We discuss the key concepts of parallel concatenation and iterative decoding. Decoding of turbo codes using the BCJR algorithm is then presented along with a performance comparison in terms of the probability of decoded bit error.

15.9   TRELLIS-CODED MODULATION.

A combined coding and modulation technique that achieves significant coding gain without bandwidth expansion is introduced in this section. We explain how this performance is achieved by emphasizing the key concepts of expanded signal constellations, signal constellation partitioning, and the selection of partitions by convolutional encoders.

The chapter concludes with final remarks and a selected list of references.

15.1   BLOCK CODES

The encoder in a block code divides the binary information sequence into blocks of k data bits each. A message block is represented by the binary k-tuple $\underline{m} = (m_0, m_1, \ldots, m_{k-1})$. There are a total of 2^k different possible such message blocks. The encoder maps each block of k data bits into an n-bit unique **codeword** $\underline{x} = (x_0, x_1, \ldots, x_{n-1})$ by adding n-k redundant bits, called **parity** or **check bits.** Therefore, there are 2^k different codewords generated by the encoder corresponding to 2^k different messages $\underline{m}$. The set $\mathcal{C}$ of 2^k different codewords is called an **(n, k) binary block code.** Figure 15.2 displays the block encoding and decoding process. The **code rate** of the code is defined as $R_c = k/n$, and n is called the **block length.** If we assume that the codewords are transmitted across a transmission channel at the rate of R bits/second, then the information transfer rate achieved with an (n, k) binary block code is RR_c bits/second. It can therefore be concluded that the block coding reduces the effective information transfer rate by a factor of $(1 - R_c)$. Because the n-bit codeword depends on the corresponding k-bit input message, the encoder has no memory and can, therefore, be implemented using digital combinatorial circuits.

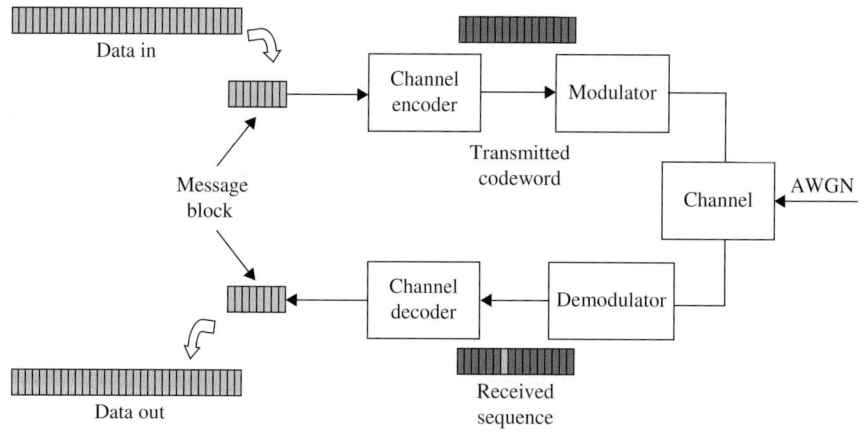

Figure 15.2   Block encoding and decoding.

Example 15.1

The simplest example of a block code is a single-parity bit code that takes k data bits and appends one parity bit to form a codeword. The parity bit is computed using the modulo-2 sum of the data bits.

Message block. $\underline{m} = (m_0, m_1, \ldots, m_{k-1})$

Parity bit. $b = \sum_{i=0}^{k-1} m_i$

Codeword. $\underline{x} = (m_0, m_1, \ldots, m_{k-1}, b)$

Obviously, if the data bits contain an even number of 1's, then the parity bit will be 0; the parity bit will be 1 if the data bits contain an odd number of 1's. This simple code assigns a parity bit such that all codewords have an even number of 1's. If a single-bit error occurs during transmission, then the received word will have an odd number of 1's and the parity bit computed at the receiver will be different from the one appended at the transmitter. Consequently, the single error is detected.

Block codes extend this concept by adding a larger number of parity or check bits to either detect more than one error or correct for one or more errors.

Example 15.2

A simple error-correcting code is a binary repetition code of length 3. It repeats each bit three times so that a binary 0 is encoded into a codeword (0 0 0) and a binary 1 is encoded into a codeword (1 1 1). Figure 15.3 is a pictorial representation of this code. The three-dimensional binary space contains 2^3 binary 3-tuples corresponding to 8 vertices of the cube.

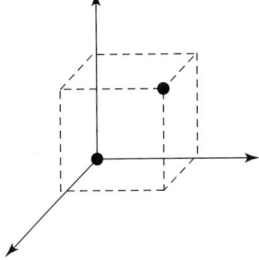

Figure 15.3 Binary repetition code (3, 1).

15.1.1 Linear Block Codes

Before we discuss linear block codes, it is useful to revisit concepts of vector spaces discussed in Section 10.3. Consider the set $\mathbb{F}_2^n$ of all binary n-tuples or vectors $\underline{v} = (v_1, v_2, \ldots, v_n)$ defined over the binary field $\mathbb{F}_2 = \{0, 1\}$ with modulo-2 addition and standard multiplication operations. $\mathbb{F}_2^n$ is a **binary linear vector space.** That is, if $\underline{u}, \underline{v}$ are in $\mathbb{F}_2^n$, then the linear combination $\alpha \underline{u} + \beta \underline{v}$ is also in $\mathbb{F}_2^n$, where $\alpha, \beta \in \mathbb{F}_2$ ("superposition property"). A **subspace** V of a binary linear vector space $\mathbb{F}_2^n$ is a subset of $\mathbb{F}_2^n$ such that the vectors in V also satisfy the superposition property.

The binary (n, k) block code $\mathscr{C}$ is **linear** if its 2^k codewords form a subspace of $\mathbb{F}_2^n$. It follows from the superposition property that

- The sum of any two codewords in $\mathscr{C}$ is also a codeword.
- Because the sum of a codeword and itself is a valid codeword and is equal to all-zero vector ($\underline{0}$), the zero vector is a codeword in every linear block code.

Example 15.3

Consider (7, 4) linear block code invented by R.W. Hamming. Table 15.1 displays codewords of the code. The (7, 4) Hamming code maps $2^k = 2^4 = 16$ message vectors into 16 unique codewords. Note that there are 128 7-tuples in the linear vector space $\mathbb{F}_2^7$. It is easy to see that the 16 codewords form a subspace of $\mathbb{F}_2^7$. The all-zero vector ($\underline{0}$) is present, and the sum of any two codewords yields another codeword member of the subspace $\mathscr{C}$. Therefore these codewords represent a linear block code.

Pioneers in the Field

Richard W. Hamming was born February 11, 1915, in Chicago, Illinois. He obtained a B.S. in 1937 from the University of Chicago, an M.A. in 1939 from the University of Nebraska, and a Ph.D. in 1942 from the University of Illinois; all in mathematics. His early experience was obtained at Los Alamos where he joined the Manhattan Project providing key modeling and computing support to the group of scientists developing the first atomic bomb.

In 1946 Hamming joined Bell Labs and stayed there until 1976. Hamming invented Hamming codes in 1950 while working contemporarily with Claude Shannon at Bell Labs. He realized that, by the appending of a parity check (an extra bit or block of bits) to each transmitted sequence of data bits, transmission errors could be corrected automatically, without having to resend the message. This work was originally prompted by a failure in a computer that had been running calculations over a weekend—Hamming arrived on Monday morning expecting to see the results but found that the computer had ground to a halt very early in the calculation. He reasoned that if the computer could recognize an error then it could also correct it. His paper on error-correcting codes published in 1950 started the new field of error-correcting codes. He is famous for saying, "The purpose of computation is insight, not numbers."

Although Hamming is best known for his pioneering work on error-correcting codes, he made significant contributions in various aspects of computing, numerical analysis, and management of computing. Hamming has received a number of awards which include: Fellow, IEEE, 1968; the ACM Turing Prize, 1968; the IEEE Emanuel R. Piore Award, 1979; Member, National Academy of Engineering, 1980; and the Harold Pender Award, University of Pennsylvania, 1981. In 1987 a major IEEE award was named after him, namely the Richard W. Hamming Medal.

Table 15.1 (7, 4) Linear Block Code

Information Bits	Codeword	Weight
0 0 0 0	0 0 0 0 0 0 0	0
0 0 0 1	0 0 0 1 0 1 1	3
0 0 1 0	0 0 1 0 1 1 0	3
0 0 1 1	0 0 1 1 1 0 1	4
0 1 0 0	0 1 0 0 1 1 1	4
0 1 0 1	0 1 0 1 1 0 0	3
0 1 1 0	0 1 1 0 0 0 1	3
0 1 1 1	0 1 1 1 0 1 0	4
1 0 0 0	1 0 0 0 1 0 1	3
1 0 0 1	1 0 0 1 1 1 0	4
1 0 1 0	1 0 1 0 0 1 1	4
1 0 1 1	1 0 1 1 0 0 0	3
1 1 0 0	1 1 0 0 0 1 0	3
1 1 0 1	1 1 0 1 0 0 1	4
1 1 1 0	1 1 1 0 1 0 0	4
1 1 1 1	1 1 1 1 1 1 1	7

Minimum Distance of a Block Code

The **Hamming weight** $w_H(\underline{x})$ of a codeword $\underline{x}$ is the number of 1's it contains. The **Hamming distance** $d_H(\underline{x}_1, \underline{x}_2)$ between two codewords $\underline{x}_1$ and $\underline{x}_2$ is the number of positions in which they differ. For example, let

$$\underline{x}_1 = (1\ 0\ 0\ 1\ 0\ 1\ 1\ 0\ 1)$$

$$\underline{x}_2 = (0\ 1\ 1\ 1\ 1\ 0\ 1\ 0\ 0)$$

The modulo-2 sum of $\underline{x}_1$ and $\underline{x}_2$ is given by

$$\underline{x}_1 \oplus \underline{x}_2 = (1\ 1\ 1\ 0\ 1\ 1\ 0\ 0\ 1)$$

The Hamming distance $d_H(\underline{x}_1, \underline{x}_2)$ between $\underline{x}_1$ and $\underline{x}_2$ is the Hamming weight of the vector $\underline{x}_1 \oplus \underline{x}_2$.

$$d_H(\underline{x}_1, \underline{x}_2) = w_H(\underline{x}_1 \oplus \underline{x}_2) = 6$$

Because the sum of any two codewords is another codeword for a linear code, it follows that the Hamming distance between any two codewords $\underline{x}_1, \underline{x}_2$ in $\checkmark$ equals the weight of a third codeword $\underline{x}_3$ in $\checkmark$. That is,

$$d_H(\underline{x}_1, \underline{x}_2) = w_H(\underline{x}_1 \oplus \underline{x}_2) = w_H(\underline{x}_3) \tag{15.1}$$

The **minimum distance** $d_{\min}$ for a block code $\checkmark$ is defined as the minimum Hamming distance between any two codewords. That is,

$$d_{\min} = \text{Min}\{d_H(\underline{x}_1, \underline{x}_2): \underline{x}_1, \underline{x}_2 \in \checkmark, \underline{x}_1 \neq \underline{x}_2\} \tag{15.2}$$

Therefore, the minimum distance $d_{\min}$ for a linear block code equals the minimum weight of one of its nonzero codewords. For the $(7, 4)$ code in Table 15.1, the minimum distance $d_{\min}$ is 3. The minimum distance of a block code is an important parameter that determines its error-detecting and error-correcting capabilities.

Generator Matrix

Because an (n, k) block code forms a k-dimensional subspace of $\mathbb{F}_2^n$, all 2^k codewords can be generated by linear combinations of the k linearly independent vectors of the subspace. The k basis vectors are called the **generator vectors** of the code. Let $\underline{g}_0, \underline{g}_1, \ldots, \underline{g}_{k-1}$ be the set of k linearly independent $1 \times n$ vectors used to generate the linear block code $\checkmark$. Each of the 2^k codewords in $\checkmark$ can now be expressed as

$$\underline{x} = m_0 \underline{g}_0 + m_1 \underline{g}_1 + \ldots + m_{k-1} \underline{g}_{k-1} \tag{15.3}$$

where $\underline{m} = (m_0, m_1, \ldots, m_{k-1})$ is the message row vector. It is convenient to define the following $k \times n$ **generator matrix** $\underline{G}$ for the code

$$\underline{G} = \begin{pmatrix} \underline{g}_0 \\ \underline{g}_1 \\ \vdots \\ \underline{g}_{k-1} \end{pmatrix} = \begin{pmatrix} g_{00} & g_{01} & \cdots & g_{0, n-1} \\ g_{10} & g_{11} & \cdots & g_{1, n-1} \\ \vdots & \vdots & \cdots & \vdots \\ g_{k-1, 0} & g_{k-1, 1} & \cdots & g_{k-1, n-1} \end{pmatrix} \tag{15.4}$$

The codeword $\underline{x}$ can now be written be as a matrix product of the message vector $\underline{m}$ with the generator matrix $\underline{G}$.

$$\underline{x} = \underline{m}\,\underline{G} \tag{15.5}$$

The components of the codeword $\underline{x}$ are described by

$$x_j = \sum_{i=0}^{k-1} m_i g_{ij}, \; j = 0, \ldots, n - 1 \tag{15.6}$$

Example 15.4

The generator matrix for the Hamming code in Table 15.1 is

$$\underline{G} = \begin{pmatrix} \underline{g_0} \\ \underline{g_1} \\ \underline{g_2} \\ \underline{g_3} \end{pmatrix} = \begin{pmatrix} 1 & 0 & 0 & 0 & 1 & 0 & 1 \\ 0 & 1 & 0 & 0 & 1 & 1 & 1 \\ 0 & 0 & 1 & 0 & 1 & 1 & 0 \\ 0 & 0 & 0 & 1 & 0 & 1 & 1 \end{pmatrix} \tag{15.7}$$

and the codeword corresponding to the message vector (1 1 0 0) is

$$\underline{x} = (1 \ 1 \ 0 \ 0) \begin{pmatrix} 1 & 0 & 0 & 0 & 1 & 0 & 1 \\ 0 & 1 & 0 & 0 & 1 & 1 & 1 \\ 0 & 0 & 1 & 0 & 1 & 1 & 0 \\ 0 & 0 & 0 & 1 & 0 & 1 & 1 \end{pmatrix} = (1 \ 1 \ 0 \ 0 \ 0 \ 1 \ 0)$$

15.1.2 Systematic Linear Block Codes

Systematic linear block codes are codes in which the message vector appears directly in the codeword as illustrated in Figure 15.4. Systematic codes are a subset of linear block codes. For a systematic linear block code,

$$\underline{x} = (x_0, x_1, \ldots, x_{n-1}) = (\underline{m} : \underline{b}) = (\underbrace{m_0, m_1, \ldots, m_{k-1}}_{k \text{ message bits}}, \underbrace{b_0, b_1, \ldots, b_{n-k-1}}_{n-k \text{ parity bits}}) \tag{15.8}$$

A systematic linear block code will have a generator matrix of the form

$$\underline{G} = (\underline{I_k} : \underline{P}) = \begin{pmatrix} 1 & 0 & 0 & \cdots & 0 & \vdots & p_{00} & p_{01} & \cdots & p_{0,\,n-k-1} \\ 0 & 1 & 0 & \cdots & 0 & \vdots & p_{10} & p_{11} & \cdots & p_{1,\,n-k-1} \\ \vdots & \vdots & & \cdots & \vdots & \vdots & \vdots & \vdots & \vdots & \vdots \\ 0 & 0 & \cdots & 1 & 0 & \vdots & p_{k-2,\,0} & p_{k-2,\,1} & \cdots & p_{k-2,\,n-k-1} \\ 0 & 0 & 0 & \cdots & 1 & \vdots & p_{k-1,\,0} & p_{k-1,\,1} & \cdots & p_{k-1,\,n-k-1} \end{pmatrix}$$

$$\underbrace{\qquad\qquad\qquad}_{k \times k \text{ Identity matrix}} \qquad \underbrace{\qquad\qquad\qquad\qquad}_{k \times (n-k) \text{ Parity submatrix}}$$

$$\tag{15.9}$$

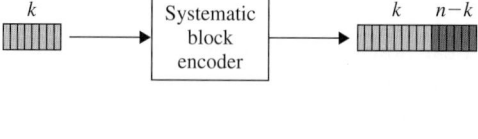

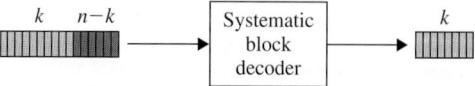

Figure 15.4 Systematic block codes.

The codeword $\underline{x}$ can now be written as

$$\underline{x} = \underline{m}\,\underline{G} = \underline{m}(\underline{I_k} \vdots \underline{P}) = (\underline{m}\,\underline{I_k} \vdots \underline{m}\,\underline{P}) = (\underline{m} \vdots \underline{b}) \tag{15.10}$$

where

$$\underline{b} = \underline{m}\,\underline{P} = (b_0, b_1, \ldots, b_{n-k-1}) \tag{15.11}$$

We observe from (15.11) that parity bits are linear combinations of the message bits as determined by the columns of the parity submatrix $\underline{P}$. That is,

$$b_j = \sum_{i=0}^{k-1} m_i p_{ij}, \quad j = 0, \ldots, n - k - 1 \tag{15.12}$$

In summary, the components of the codeword $\underline{x} = (x_0, x_1, \ldots, x_{n-1})$ can be written as

$$x_j = \begin{cases} m_j, & j = 0, \ldots, k - 1 \\ b_{j-k}, & j = k, k + 1, \ldots, n - 1 \end{cases} \tag{15.13}$$

Because the generator matrix performs a linear mapping of the message vector to generate the corresponding codeword, each row of the generator matrix is itself a codeword. For example, the first row of (15.9) is a codeword corresponding to the message vector $(1, 0, 0, \ldots, 0)$.

For the (7, 4) code in Example 15.4, the components of codewords are related to message vectors as follows:

$$\underline{x} = \underline{m}\,\underline{G} = (m_0 \ m_1 \ m_2 \ m_3) \begin{pmatrix} 1 & 0 & 0 & 0 & \vdots & 1 & 0 & 1 \\ 0 & 1 & 0 & 0 & \vdots & 1 & 1 & 1 \\ 0 & 0 & 1 & 0 & \vdots & 1 & 1 & 0 \\ 0 & 0 & 0 & 1 & \vdots & 0 & 1 & 1 \end{pmatrix}$$

$$= (m_0 \ m_1 \ m_2 \ m_3 \ m_0 + m_1 + m_2 \ m_1 + m_2 + m_3 \ m_0 + m_1 + m_3)$$

Parity-Check Matrix

The **parity-check matrix** $\underline{H}$ is an $(n - k) \times n$ matrix such that its rows are orthogonal to the rows of the generator matrix $\underline{G}$, that is,

$$\underline{G}\,\underline{H}^T = \underline{0} \tag{15.14}$$

For a systematic code, the parity-check matrix is given by

$$\underline{H} = (\underline{P}^T \vdots \underline{I}_{n-k}) \tag{15.15}$$

It is easy to prove (15.14) by combining (15.9) and (15.15) and noting that multiplication of any matrix with an identity matrix yields the matrix itself.

$$\underline{G}\,\underline{H}^T = (\underline{I_k} \vdots \underline{P}) \begin{pmatrix} \underline{P} \\ \cdots \\ \underline{I}_{n-k} \end{pmatrix} = \underline{P} + \underline{P} = \underline{0}$$

where

$$\underline{H}^T = \begin{pmatrix} \underline{P} \\ \cdots \\ \underline{I}_{n-k} \end{pmatrix} = \begin{pmatrix} p_{00} & p_{01} & \cdots & p_{0,\,n-k-1} \\ p_{10} & p_{11} & \cdots & p_{1,\,n-k-1} \\ \vdots & \vdots & \cdots & \vdots \\ p_{k-1,\,0} & p_{k-1,\,1} & \cdots & p_{k-1,\,n-k-1} \\ \cdots\cdots\cdots\cdots\cdots\cdots\cdots\cdots\cdots \\ 1 & 0 & \cdots & 0 \\ 0 & 1 & \cdots & 0 \\ \vdots & \vdots & \cdots & \vdots \\ 0 & 0 & \cdots & 1 \end{pmatrix} \tag{15.16}$$

As an example, the parity-check matrix for the Hamming (7, 4) code is obtained from (15.7) as

$$\underline{H} = \begin{pmatrix} 1 & 1 & 1 & 0 & \vdots & 1 & 0 & 0 \\ 0 & 1 & 1 & 1 & \vdots & 0 & 1 & 0 \\ 1 & 1 & 0 & 1 & \vdots & 0 & 0 & 1 \end{pmatrix}$$

If $\underline{x}_i$ is a codeword, substituting (15.14) yields

$$\underline{x}_i\underline{H}^T = \underline{m}_i\,\underline{G}\,\underline{H}^T = \underline{0}$$

Thus, a vector $\underline{x}_i$ is a codeword if and only if

$$\underline{x}_i\underline{H}^T = \underline{0} \tag{15.17}$$

This property is used to determine whether the received vector is a valid codeword or corrupted.

15.1.3   Error and Syndrome Vectors

Errors can be classified as **random bit** or **burst errors.** In the random bit error model, the bit errors occur independently of each other. A burst error refers to a contiguous sequence of bits that are received in error. The length of the burst is measured from the first corrupted bit to the last corrupted bit. Some bits in between may not have been corrupted, as displayed in Figure 15.5.

Suppose we transmit an n-bit codeword $\underline{x} = (x_0, x_1, \ldots, x_{n-1})$. The errors resulting from the transmission of the codeword are represented by an **error vector** or **error pattern** $\underline{e} = (e_0, e_1, \ldots, e_{n-1})$, where $e_i = 1$ if an error occurs in the ith transmitted bit

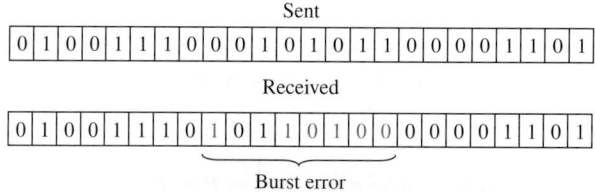

Figure 15.5 Burst error.

and $e_i = 0$ otherwise. For a binary linear (n, k) block code, there are a total of $2^n - 1$ potential nonzero error patterns. The received vector $\underline{y}$ resulting from the transmission of a codeword $\underline{x}$ is given by

$$\underline{y} = \underline{x} + \underline{e} \tag{15.18}$$

The **syndrome** of the received vector $\underline{y}$ is defined as

$$\underline{s} = \underline{y}\,H^T \tag{15.19}$$

Example 15.5

For the $(7, 4)$ code in Example 15.4, calculate the syndrome for the received vector $(1\,0\,0\,1\,0\,1\,0)$.

Solution

$$\underline{s} = \underline{y}\,H^T = (1\,0\,0\,1\,0\,1\,0)\begin{pmatrix} 1 & 0 & 1 \\ 1 & 1 & 1 \\ 1 & 1 & 0 \\ 0 & 1 & 1 \\ \cdots & \cdots & \cdots \\ 1 & 0 & 0 \\ 0 & 1 & 0 \\ 0 & 0 & 1 \end{pmatrix} = (1\,0\,0)$$

The syndrome table for all single-error patterns for the $(7, 4)$ Hamming code is displayed in Table 15.2.

We observe from (15.17) that if $\underline{y}$ is a valid member of the code $\mathscr{C}$, then $\underline{s} = \underline{y}\,H^T = \underline{0}$. Thus, the syndrome equals the zero vector $(\underline{0})$ if the transmitted codeword is received without error or is corrupted in a manner that results in the received vector being another valid codeword. The nonzero error pattern in the second case is undetectable by the syndrome test. Substituting (15.17) and (15.18) into (15.19) yields

$$\underline{s} = (\underline{x} + \underline{e})H^T = \underline{x}\,H^T + \underline{e}\,H^T = \underline{e}\,H^T \tag{15.20}$$

Table 15.2 Single-Error Pattern Syndrome Vectors for (7, 4) Hamming Code

Error Pattern	Syndrome
0000001	001
0000010	010
0000100	100
0001000	011
0010000	110
0100000	111
1000000	101

It is obvious from (15.19) and (15.20) that the syndrome test, when performed either on a corrupted codeword or on the error pattern that caused it, yields the same syndrome vector. If the received vector $\underline{y}$ contains detectable errors, the syndrome is a nonzero vector, that is, $\underline{s} \neq \underline{0}$. Unfortunately, knowledge of syndrome $\underline{s}$ does not provide sufficient information to uniquely identify the error pattern $\underline{e}$. This is because $\underline{s} = \underline{e}\,\underline{H}^T$ is a system of n-k equations with n unknowns. Therefore, there are 2^k solutions, that is, 2^k different error patterns generate the same syndrome. For example, if $\underline{s}_1$ is syndrome corresponding to error pattern $\underline{e}_1$, then $\underline{e}_1 + \underline{x}_i$ yields the same syndrome, where $\underline{x}_i$ is one of 2^k codewords in $\mathscr{C}$.

$$(\underline{e}_1 + \underline{x}_i)\underline{H}^T = \underline{e}_1\underline{H}^T + \underline{x}_i\underline{H}^T = \underline{s}_1 + \underline{0} = \underline{s}_1, \quad i = 1, 2, \ldots, 2^k \qquad (15.21)$$

Thus 2^k error patterns corresponding to syndrome $\underline{s}_1$ are obtained by modulo-2 addition of 2^k codewords to the error pattern $\underline{e}_1$.

Example 15.6

Calculate all the possible error vectors that yield the syndrome vector (0 1 1).

Solution

From Table 15.2, the single-error vector corresponding to the syndrome (0 1 1) is (0 0 0 1 0 0 0). The other error sequences are obtained by modulo-2 addition of $2^k - 1$ nonzero codewords to the error sequence (0 0 0 1 0 0 0). For example, the modulo-2 sum of the error vector (0 0 0 1 0 0 0) and the codeword (0 0 0 1 0 1 1) yields another error vector (0 0 0 0 0 1 1) with the same syndrome. Table 15.3 displays error vectors corresponding to the syndrome (0 1 1).

Table 15.3 Error Patterns Corresponding to the Syndrome Vectors (0 1 1)

Error Vector $\underline{e}$	Weight $w_H(\underline{e})$
0 0 0 1 0 0 0	1
0 0 0 0 0 1 1	2
0 0 1 1 1 1 0	4
0 0 1 0 1 0 1	3
0 1 0 1 1 1 1	5
0 1 0 0 1 0 0	2
0 1 1 1 0 0 1	4
0 1 1 0 0 1 0	3
1 0 0 1 1 0 1	4
1 0 0 0 1 1 0	3
1 0 1 1 0 1 1	5
1 0 1 0 0 0 0	2
1 1 0 1 0 1 0	4
1 1 0 0 0 0 1	3
1 1 1 1 1 0 0	5
1 1 1 0 1 1 1	6

It is easy to verify that 2^k error patterns in Table 15.3 generate the same syndrome vector (0 1 1). Therefore, it is not possible to earmark a unique error pattern from the syndrome.

15.2 HARD-DECISION DECODING OF BLOCK CODES

In hard-decision decoding, the threshold device in the detector makes a hard decision about each transmitted symbol. For example, in the case of binary signaling, the threshold comparator decides whether a 0 or 1 was transmitted based on the received signal sample. The channel decoder operates on these binary quantized outputs of the receiver. From the perspective of the channel decoder, the cascade of transmitter, channel, and receiver can be represented by a BSC with crossover probability p equal to the transmission link BER. Figure 15.6 displays a digital communication system with hard-decision decoding.

The channel decoder makes **maximum likelihood (ML)** decisions on the threshold detector output vector $\underline{y} = (y_0, y_1, \ldots, y_{n-1})$. As discussed in Section 10.5, a maximum likelihood decoder seeks the codeword $\underline{x}_\ell = (x_{\ell 0}, x_{\ell 1}, \ldots, x_{\ell, n-1})$ that was most likely to have been transmitted given the received vector $\underline{y}$. That is, the ML decoder decides that the codeword $\underline{x}_\ell$ was transmitted if

$$P(\underline{y}|\underline{x}_\ell) \geq P(\underline{y}|\underline{x}_m), \quad \ell \neq m \tag{15.22}$$

Because $\log_e(.)$ is a monotonic function of its argument, the maximization of the likelihood function $P(\underline{y}|\underline{x}_m)$ is equivalent to maximizing its log-likelihood function $\log_e\{P(\underline{y}|\underline{x}_m)\}$. Invoking the memoryless assumption for a BSC, we obtain

$$P(\underline{y}|\underline{x}_m) = \prod_{j=0}^{n-1} P(y_j|x_{mj}) \tag{15.23}$$

Taking logarithm of the both sides of (15.23) yields

$$\log_e\{P(\underline{y}|\underline{x}_m)\} = \log_e\left\{\prod_{j=0}^{n-1} P(y_j|x_{mj})\right\} = \sum_{j=0}^{n-1} \log_e\{P(y_j|x_{mj})\} \tag{15.24}$$

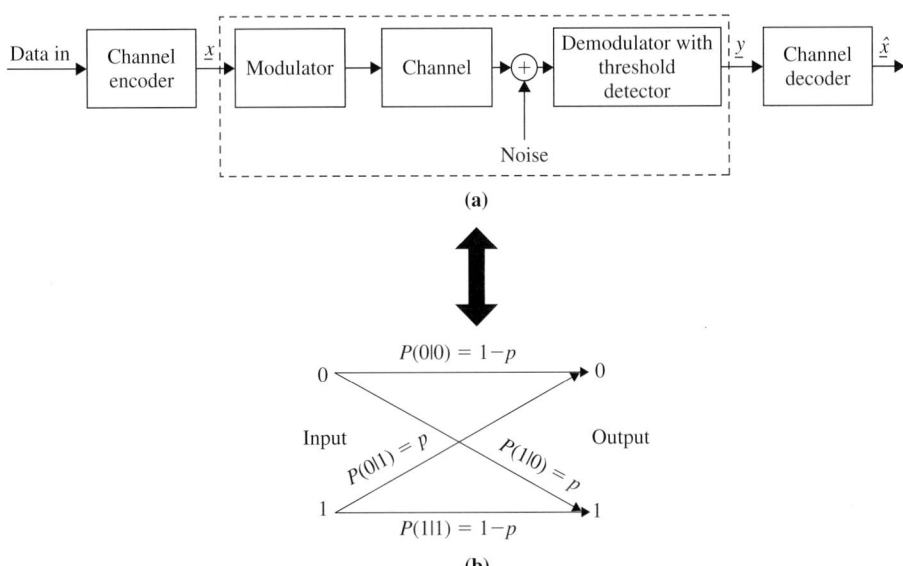

(a)

(b)

Figure 15.6 (a) Digital communication system with hard-decision decoding; (b) equivalent BSC model of the transmission link.

For a BSC, the $P(y_j|x_{mj})$ is related to the crossover probability p as follows:

$$P(y_j|x_{mj}) = \begin{cases} p, & y_j \neq x_{mj} \\ 1 - p, & y_j = x_{mj} \end{cases} \tag{15.25}$$

If the received vector $\underline{y}$ and the codeword $\underline{x}_m$ being considered differ in d_H positions, substitution of (15.25) into (15.24) yields

$$\log_e\{P(\underline{y}|\underline{x}_m)\} = d_H \log_e(p) + (n - d_H)\log_e(1 - p)$$

$$= d_H \log_e\left(\frac{p}{1 - p}\right) + n\log_e(1 - p) \tag{15.26}$$

where n is the length of the codeword. Because $\log_e(p/1 - p) < 0$ for $p < 0.5$, maximizing (15.26) is equivalent to minimizing the Hamming distance d_H between the received vector $\underline{y}$ and the codeword $\underline{x}_m$. Therefore, the ML decoding implies minimum distance decoding in the Hamming sense. For the BSC, the ML decoder will choose as its estimate $\hat{x}$ the codeword that is closest to the received vector $\underline{y}$ in terms of the Hamming distance.

Example 15.7

Consider (7, 4) Hamming code in Example 15.2. If the received vector is (1 1 0 1 0 0 0), determine the transmitted codeword.

Solution

The ML decoder picks the codeword that is closest to $\underline{y}$ = (1 1 0 1 0 0 0) in the Hamming distance. The following table displays Hamming distance between the received vector $\underline{y}$ and every codeword in the (7, 4) Hamming code.

$\underline{x}_i \oplus \underline{y}$	$d_H(\underline{x}_i, \underline{y}) = w_H(\underline{x}_i \oplus \underline{y})$
(0 0 0 0 0 0 0) $\oplus$ (1 1 0 1 0 0 0) = (1 1 0 1 0 0 0)	3
(0 0 0 1 0 1 1) $\oplus$ (1 1 0 1 0 0 0) = (1 1 0 0 0 1 1)	4
(0 0 1 0 1 1 0) $\oplus$ (1 1 0 1 0 0 0) = (1 1 1 1 1 1 0)	6
(0 0 1 1 1 0 1) $\oplus$ (1 1 0 1 0 0 0) = (1 1 1 0 1 0 1)	5
(0 1 0 0 1 1 1) $\oplus$ (1 1 0 1 0 0 0) = (1 0 0 1 1 1 1)	5
(0 1 0 1 1 0 0) $\oplus$ (1 1 0 1 0 0 0) = (1 0 0 0 1 0 0)	2
(0 1 1 0 0 0 1) $\oplus$ (1 1 0 1 0 0 0) = (1 0 1 1 0 0 1)	4
(0 1 1 1 0 1 0) $\oplus$ (1 1 0 1 0 0 0) = (1 0 1 0 0 1 0)	3
(1 0 0 0 1 0 1) $\oplus$ (1 1 0 1 0 0 0) = (0 1 0 1 1 0 1)	4
(1 0 0 1 1 1 0) $\oplus$ (1 1 0 1 0 0 0) = (0 1 0 0 1 1 0)	3
(1 0 1 0 0 1 1) $\oplus$ (1 1 0 1 0 0 0) = (0 1 1 1 0 1 1)	5
(1 0 1 1 0 0 0) $\oplus$ (1 1 0 1 0 0 0) = (0 1 1 0 0 0 0)	2
(1 1 0 0 0 1 0) $\oplus$ (1 1 0 1 0 0 0) = (0 0 0 1 0 1 0)	2
(1 1 0 1 0 0 1) $\oplus$ (1 1 0 1 0 0 0) = (0 0 0 0 0 0 1)	**1**
(1 1 1 0 1 0 0) $\oplus$ (1 1 0 1 0 0 0) = (0 0 1 1 1 0 0)	3
(1 1 1 1 1 1 1) $\oplus$ (1 1 0 1 0 0 0) = (0 0 1 0 1 1 1)	4

The decoded codeword is (1 1 0 1 0 0 1).

15.2.1 Syndrome Decoding of Block Codes

Now we can apply the minimum distance rule to resolve the uncertainty about which error pattern is most likely from the set of 2^k error sequences corresponding to a given syndrome vector. Given the syndrome associated with the received vector $\underline{y}$, the ML decoding scheme selects the error vector with minimum weight. For the (7, 4) code in Example 15.3, this can be accomplished by using Table 15.2, which associates each possible syndrome with the minimum weight error vector that generated it. If $\underline{y}$ contains correctable errors, the syndrome has some nonzero value that can earmark the particular error pattern $\underline{e}_j$ in the table. The error pattern would then be added by modulo-2 to the received vector to produce the transmitted codeword

$$\hat{\underline{x}} = \underline{y} + \underline{e}_j \qquad (15.27)$$

The decoding of block codes can be facilitated by constructing a table called the **standard array** of the code. It contains all possible 2^n received vectors in 2^{n-k} rows $\times$ 2^k column format. Each row, called a **coset,** consists of a correctable error pattern in the first column, called the **coset leader,** followed by the codewords perturbed by that error pattern. The first row lists all the 2^k codewords, starting with the all-zero codeword. The last column lists syndromes corresponding to the error patterns in the first column. The standard array for the (7, 4) Hamming code is displayed in Table 15.4. The decoding is performed by searching the column in which the received vector $\underline{y}$ lies. The codeword at the head of the column is picked as the transmitted codeword. Note that the received vector is decoded correctly if the corrupting error pattern is the coset leader. If the error pattern is not a coset leader, an erroneous decoding will result.

Example 15.8

Suppose that the codeword $\underline{x} = (1\ 1\ 0\ 0\ 0\ 1\ 0)$ in the (7, 4) Hamming code is transmitted and $\underline{y} = (0\ 1\ 0\ 0\ 0\ 1\ 0)$ is received. Show that the syndrome decoding can identify the correct error pattern.

Solution

We calculate the syndrome of $\underline{y}$ as (1 0 1). From Table 15.4 we note that (1 0 1) is the syndrome corresponding to the correctable error pattern $\underline{e} = (1\ 0\ 0\ 0\ 0\ 0\ 0)$. Thus $\underline{y} + \underline{e} = (0\ 1\ 0\ 0\ 0\ 1\ 0) + (1\ 0\ 0\ 0\ 0\ 0\ 0) = (1\ 1\ 0\ 0\ 0\ 1\ 0)$ is identified as the transmitted codeword.

15.2.2 Error-Detecting and Error-Correcting Capabilities

The error-detecting and error-correcting capability of a block code are related to the minimum Hamming distance $d_{\min}$ of the code. The errors introduced during transmission can transform a transmitted codeword into another valid codeword or not depending on the error pattern. An error-detection scheme will fail to detect transmission error patterns that convert a valid codeword into another valid codeword. For example, consider the error detection strategy using the single-parity bit code discussed in Example 15.1. All error patterns that introduce an even number of errors fail to be detected because the corrupted received vector $\underline{y}$ satisfies the parity condition and hence qualifies as a legitimate codeword. Now a code with minimum Hamming distance $d_{\min}$ implies that all legitimate codewords differ in at least $d_{\min}$ positions. Therefore, the number of transmission errors must be at least $d_{\min}$ to transform a transmitted codeword into

Table 15.4 Standard Array for (7, 4) Hamming Code

Coset Leaders	Codewords															Syndrome
0000000	0001011	0010110	0011101	0100111	0101100	0110001	0111010	1000101	1001110	1010011	1011000	1100010	1101001	1110100	1111111	000
0000001	0001010	0010111	0011100	0100110	0101101	0110000	0111011	1000100	1001111	1010010	1011001	1100011	1101000	1110101	1111110	001
0000010	0001001	0010100	0011111	0100101	0101110	0110011	0111000	1000111	1001100	1010001	1011010	1100000	1101011	1110110	1111101	010
0000100	0001111	0010010	0011001	0100011	0101000	0110101	0111110	1000001	1001010	1010111	1011100	1100110	1101101	1110000	1111011	100
0001000	0000011	0011110	0010101	0101111	0100100	0111001	0110010	1001101	1000110	1011011	1010000	1101010	1100001	1111100	1110111	011
0010000	0011011	0000110	0001101	0110111	0111100	0100001	0101010	1010101	1011110	1000011	1001000	1110010	1111001	1100100	1101111	110
0100000	0101011	0110110	0111101	0000111	0001100	0010001	0011010	1100101	1101110	1110011	1111000	1000010	1001001	1010100	1011111	111
1000000	1001011	1010110	1011101	1100111	1101100	1110001	1111010	0000101	0001110	0010011	0011000	0100010	0101001	0110100	0111111	101

another valid codeword at the receiver. This implies that all error patterns with Hamming weight $d_{min} - 1$ are detectable because the resultant received vector y will not be a valid codeword. An (n, k) block code can detect s errors if d_{min} of the code satisfies

$$d_{min} \geq s + 1 \tag{15.28}$$

Thus a code with $d_{min} = 3$ allows all two-bit errors to be detected. A minimum distance of 4 allows three-bit errors to be detected as well.

The effectiveness of an error-detection code is measured by the probability that the system fails to detect an error pattern. For an (n, k) linear block code, there are a total of $2^n - 1$ potential nonzero error patterns. The $2^k - 1$ of these patterns are identical to the $2^k - 1$ nonzero codewords. If any of these error patterns occurs, it converts the transmitted codeword into another valid codeword. Thus, the probability of undetected error $P_u(e)$ for a BSC model is the probability that the error pattern is one of $2^k - 1$ nonzero codewords. Now the probability that an error pattern e has Hamming weight $w_H(e)$ is given by

$$P\{w_H(e) \text{ errors in error pattern } e\} = p^{w_H(e)}(1 - p)^{n - w_H(e)} \tag{15.29}$$

where p is a crossover probability of the BSC. Using (15.29), we can write the following expression for the probability of undetected error $P_u(e)$

$$P_u(e) = P\{\text{error pattern is a nonzero codeword } x\}$$

$$= \sum_{2^k - 1 \text{ nonzero codewords } x} p^{w_H(x)}(1 - p)^{n - w_H(x)} \tag{15.30}$$

Example 15.9

Consider single-parity bit code considered in Example 15.1. Find an expression for the probability of undetected error $P_u(e)$. Compare values of $P_u(e)$ for $p = 10^{-3}$ and $n = 8, 16,$ and 24.

Solution

The single-parity bit code will fail if the error pattern has an even number of 1's. Therefore, the probability of undetected error $P_u(e)$ is given by

$$P_u(e) = P\{\text{error pattern with even number of 1's}\} = P\{w_H(e) \text{ is even}\}$$

$$= \binom{n}{2}p^2(1 - p)^{n-2} + \binom{n}{2}p^4(1 - p)^{n-4} + \ldots \tag{15.31}$$

where the number of terms in (15.31) extends up to the maximum possible even number of errors. In all cases of practical interest, the probability of single-bit error p is much less than 1. We can then use the approximation $p^i(1 - p)^{n-i} \approx p^i$. For $p = 10^{-3}$, $p^2(1 - p)^{n-2} \approx 10^{-6}$ and $p^4(1 - p)^{n-4} \approx 10^{-12}$. Thus the probability of undetected error $P_u(e)$ is dominated by the first term in (15.31). The following table compares $P_u(e)$ for various values of p and n.

n	$P_u(e)$	
	$p = 10^{-3}$	$p = 10^{-4}$
8	2.8×10^{-5}	2.8×10^{-7}
16	1.2×10^{-4}	1.2×10^{-6}
24	2.76×10^{-4}	2.76×10^{-6}

To investigate the error-correction capability of an (n, k) block code, let us draw nonoverlapping hyperspheres of radius t around all codewords. This can be assured if the minimum Hamming distance $d_{\min}$ of the code satisfies

$$d_{\min} \geq 2t + 1 \tag{15.32}$$

as shown in Figure 15.7(a). The hypersphere centered around $\underline{x}_\ell$ will encapsulate all received vectors $\underline{y}$ containing t or less errors, that is, at Hamming distance $d_H(\underline{y}, \underline{x}_\ell) \leq t$. If the received vector $\underline{y}$ lies inside the hypersphere centered around $\underline{x}_\ell$, the ML decoder picks $\underline{x}_\ell$ as the transmitted codeword because it is the codeword closest to $\underline{y}$. The code can, therefore, correctly decode a received vector containing up to t errors as these spheres are disjoint. For the case $d_{\min} < 2t$ illustrated in Figure 15.7(b), if $\underline{x}_\ell$ is transmitted, the decoder may erroneously choose $\underline{x}_m$ as $d_H(\underline{y}, \underline{x}_\ell) = d_H(\underline{y}, \underline{x}_m)$.

It follows from (15.32) that an (n, k) block code with minimum Hamming distance $d_{\min}$ can correct $t = \lfloor (d_{\min} - 1)/2 \rfloor$ errors, where $\lfloor x \rfloor$ denotes the largest integer less than or equal to x. That is,

$$t = \begin{cases} \dfrac{d_{\min} - 1}{2}, & d_{\min} \text{ odd} \\[2ex] \dfrac{d_{\min}}{2} - 1, & d_{\min} \text{ even} \end{cases} \tag{15.33}$$

Thus a code with $d_{\min} = 3$ allows all one-bit errors to be corrected. A minimum distance of 5 allows double-bit errors to be corrected as well.

To highlight the significance of $d_{\min}$ in determining the error performance, we will use the notation $(n, k, d_{\min})$ to specify a linear block code. In general, a code that can correct t errors may correct some error patterns containing $t + 1$ or more errors. A code that can correct exactly t errors or less is called a **perfect code.** The $(7, 4)$ Hamming code is an example of a perfect code.

Hamming Bound

Because $d_{\min}$ determines the error-detecting and error-correcting capability of a block code, it is meaningful to determine the highest value of $d_{\min}$ achievable for an (n, k)

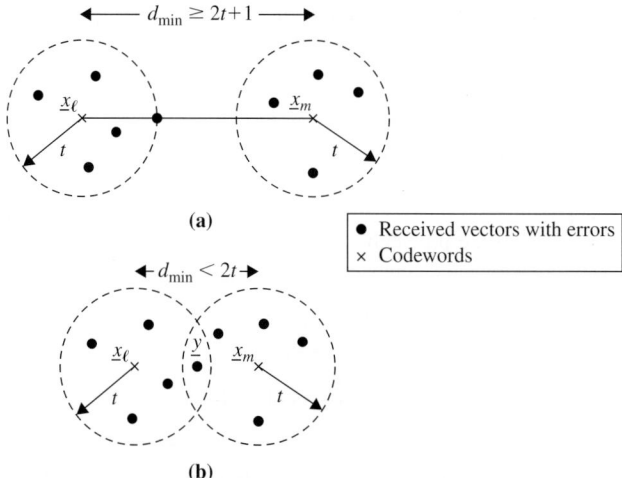

Figure 15.7 Decision regions for ML decoding.

block code. This assures that the maximum use of the available redundancy has been achieved. To obtain such a relationship, we note that an (n, k) block code assigns 2^k codewords out of a total of 2^n n-tuples or vectors in the n-dimensional vector space $\mathbb{F}_2^n$. Therefore, $2^n - 2^k$ n-tuples or vectors are unused. The number of n-tuples that lie within a hypersphere of radius t (that is, differing in t or fewer positions) is given by $\sum_{i=1}^{t}\binom{n}{i}$.

Because there are 2^k codewords in an (n, k) block code, we must have $2^k \sum_{i=1}^{t}\binom{n}{i}$ n-tuples unused to ensure t-error correction capability. Hence the total number of n-tuples in the code must be at least

$$2^k + 2^k \sum_{i=1}^{t}\binom{n}{i} = 2^k \sum_{i=0}^{t}\binom{n}{i}$$

However, the total number of available n-tuples in $\mathbb{F}_2^n$ is 2^n. Hence

$$2^n \geq 2^k \sum_{i=0}^{t}\binom{n}{i} \tag{15.34}$$

or

$$2^{n-k} \geq \sum_{i=0}^{t}\binom{n}{i}$$

Note that $n - k$ is the number of parity bits in the codeword of an (n, k) block code. Equation (15.34) is known as the **Hamming bound.** Note that the Hamming bound is a necessary condition for a code that can correct t errors. It is not a sufficient condition. For a perfect code, Hamming bound is satisfied with equality.

Example 15.10

Show that a linear block code with the parameters $n = 23$, $k = 12$, $d_{min} = 7$ can exist.

Solution

The number of errors that can be corrected with $d_{min} = 7$ is given from (15.33) as

$$t = \frac{d_{min} - 1}{2} = \frac{7 - 1}{2} = 3$$

Using the Hamming bound (15.34), we obtain

$$2^{23-12} \geq \sum_{i=0}^{3}\binom{23}{i} = \binom{23}{0} + \binom{23}{1} + \binom{23}{2} + \binom{23}{3}$$

$$2048 \overset{?}{\geq} 1 + 23 + 253 + 1771 = 2048$$

Thus Hamming bound is satisfied with equality. Therefore, (23, 12, 7) code exists and is a perfect code. It is a very special code named after its inventor M. Golay as (23, 12, 7) Golay code.

15.3   CYCLIC CODES

An (n, k, d_{min}) linear block code is a **cyclic code** if every cyclic shift of a codeword in $\mathscr{C}$ is also a codeword in $\mathscr{C}$. Thus if $\underline{x} = (x_0, x_1, \ldots, x_{n-1})$ is a codeword in a cyclic code $\mathscr{C}$, then $\underline{x}' = (x_{n-1}, x_0, x_1, \ldots, x_{n-2})$ obtained by shifting $\underline{x}$ cyclically one place to the right, is also a codeword. Cyclic codes are an important subclass of linear block codes. One of the reasons for their popularity is ease of implementation with the use of high-speed shift registers with feedback. Further, because of their inherent algebraic structure, the decoding is simplified in practice.

Cyclic codes can be described using a generator matrix $\underline{G}$ or parity-check matrix $\underline{H}$; however, they are usually described using the concept of a **generator polynomial.** In cyclic codes, message vectors, codewords, and error vectors are represented by polynomials with binary coefficients. Let $\underline{m} = (m_0, m_1, \ldots, m_{k-1})$ be the message vector. Then $\underline{m}$ is represented by the **message polynomial** as

$$m(D) = m_0 D^{k-1} + m_1 D^{k-2} + \ldots + m_{k-1} \tag{15.35}$$

Similarly, the **code polynomial** $x(D)$ corresponding to the codeword $\underline{x} = (x_0, x_1, \ldots, x_{n-1})$ is expressed as

$$x(D) = x_0 D^{n-1} + x_1 D^{n-2} + \ldots + x_{n-1} \tag{15.36}$$

A cyclic code is specified by its generator polynomial $g(D)$. It is known to both the encoder and the decoder. The degree of the generator polynomial $g(D)$ for an (n, k, d_{min}) code is n-k. A generator polynomial $g(D) = 1 + g_1 D + \ldots + g_{n-k} D^{n-k}$ generates an (n, k, d_{min}) cyclic code if it is a factor of $D^n + 1$. That is,

$$D^n + 1 = g(D)h(D) \tag{15.37}$$

where polynomial multiplication uses modulo-2 arithmetic. Equation (15.37) implies that $D^n + 1$ is divisible by $g(D)$.

Every code polynomial in the (n, k, d_{min}) cyclic code can be expressed as the product of the generator polynomial and the message polynomial.

$$x(D) = m(D)g(D) \tag{15.38}$$

Equation (15.38) states that $x(D)$ is a valid codeword of a cyclic code if and only if $g(D)$ divides into $x(D)$ without a remainder.

Example 15.11

The polynomial $D^7 + 1$ can be factored as

$$D^7 + 1 = (D^3 + D^2 + 1)(D^4 + D^2 + D + 1)$$

Using $g(D) = D^3 + D^2 + 1$ as a generator polynomial of degree $n - k = 3$, we can generate an $(n, k) = (7, 4)$ cyclic code. Similarly, using $g(D) = D^4 + D^2 + D + 1$ as a generator polynomial of degree $n - k = 4$, we can generate an $(n, k) = (7, 3)$ cyclic code.

The simple encoding algorithm in (15.38) does not generate a systematic code, as verified in Example 15.12.

Example 15.12

The (7, 4) Hamming code has the generator polynomial $g(D) = D^3 + D + 1$. Determine the codeword corresponding to the message vector (1 1 0 1).

Solution

The message polynomial corresponding to the vector (1 1 0 1) is given by

$$m(D) = D^3 + D^2 + 1$$

Now

$$x(D) = m(D)g(D) = (D^3 + D^2 + 1)(D^3 + D + 1)$$

$$= D^6 + D^5 + D^4 + D^3 + D^2 + D + 1 \leftrightarrow (1\ 1\ 1\ 1\ 1\ 1\ 1)$$

The code is not systematic because (1 1 0 1) is not part of the codeword (1 1 1 1 1 1 1).

15.3.1 Encoding of Systematic Cyclic Codes

The encoding algorithm in (15.38) can be modified to get codewords of the systematic cyclic code $(n, k, d_{\min})$ generated by the polynomial $g(D)$.

1. Multiply the message polynomial $m(D)$ by D^{n-k}. This has the effect of placing zeros in $(n - k)$ lowest order positions.
2. Divide $D^{n-k}m(D)$ by $g(D)$. This gives

$$D^{n-k}m(D) = g(D)\underbrace{q(D)}_{\text{quotient}} + \underbrace{b(D)}_{\text{remainder}} \tag{15.39}$$

   Notice that $b(D)$ must have a degree $n - k - 1$ or less because the degree of $g(D)$ is $n - k$.
3. Add remainder $b(D)$ to $D^{n-k}m(D)$. This puts parity bits in the $n - k$ lowest significant positions.

$$x(D) = D^{n-k}m(D) + b(D) \tag{15.40}$$

We can easily show that (15.40) represents the valid code polynomial by substituting (15.39) into (15.40).

$$x(D) = g(D)q(D) + b(D) + b(D) = g(D)q(D) \tag{15.41}$$

We conclude from (15.41) that $x(D)$ given by (15.40) is a polynomial of degree $n - 1$ or less and a multiple of $g(D)$. Therefore, it is a code polynomial in the cyclic code generated by $g(D)$. The code polynomial $x(D)$ in (15.40) can be written as

$$x(D) = m_0 D^{n-1} + m_1 D^{n-2} + \ldots + m_{k-1}D^{n-k} + b_0 D^{n-k-1} + \ldots + b_{n-k-1}$$

$$\underline{x} = (\underline{m}, \underline{b}) = (\underbrace{m_0, m_1, \ldots, m_{k-1}}_{k \text{ message bits}}, \underbrace{b_0, b_1, \ldots, b_{n-k-1}}_{n - k \text{ parity bits}}) \tag{15.42}$$

Because the codeword in (15.42) contains k information bits followed by $n - k$ parity bits, the code is systematic. Note that the parity bits in the codeword (15.42) correspond to the remainder polynomial $b(D)$ obtained in step 2 above.

Example 15.13

Use the generator polynomial $g(D) = D^3 + D + 1$ to determine the codeword corresponding to the message vector (1 1 0 0).

Solution

Generator polynomial: $g(D) = D^3 + D + 1 \Rightarrow n - k = 3$ Information: $(1\,1\,0\,0) \Rightarrow m(D) = D^3 + D^2$

$$D^3 m(D) = D^6 + D^5$$

Next we divide $D^3 m(D) = D^6 + D^5$ by $g(D) = D^3 + D + 1$.

$$
\begin{array}{r}
D^3 + D^2 + D \\
\hline
D^3 + D + 1)\overline{D^6 + D^5 \quad\quad\quad} \\
D^6 + D^4 + D^3 \\
\hline
D^5 + D^4 + D^3 \\
D^5 + D^3 + D^2 \\
\hline
D^4 + D^2 \\
D^4 + D^2 + D \\
\hline
D \Leftrightarrow \underline{b} = (0\ 1\ 0) \\
\end{array}
$$

$b(D)$

The transmitted codeword $x(D)$ is given by using (15.42) as

$$x(D) = D^3 m(D) + b(D) = D^6 + D^5 + D \Leftrightarrow \underline{x} = (1\,1\,0\,0\,0\,1\,0)$$

Note that the codeword is identical to the one assigned in Table 15.1.

15.3.2 Decoding of Cyclic Codes

Suppose that the code polynomial $x(D)$ is transmitted over a noisy channel. The received polynomial $y(D)$ can be described as

$$y(D) = x(D) + e(D) \tag{15.43}$$

where $e(D)$ is the error polynomial corresponding to the error vector $\underline{e} = (e_0, e_1, \ldots, e_{n-1})$. Dividing $y(D)$ by the generator polynomial $g(D)$ yields

$$y(D) = u(D)g(D) + s(D) \tag{15.44}$$

The remainder $s(D)$ in (15.44) is a polynomial of degree $n - k - 1$ or less. It is called the **syndrome polynomial.** Note that $s(D)$ serves the same function as the syndrome vector $\underline{s}$ in (15.19). If $g(D)$ divides into $y(D)$ without a remainder (i.e., $s(D) = 0$),

$y(D)$ is a valid code polynomial. This implies either no error or an undetectable error pattern. On the other hand, if $s(D) \neq 0$, $y(D)$ has been corrupted by a detectable error pattern. Thus error detection can be accomplished by simply checking the remainder of the division of the received polynomial $y(D)$ by $g(D)$. Substituting (15.41) and (15.44) into (15.43), the error polynomial $e(D)$ can be expressed as

$$e(D) = y(D) + x(D) = \left[u(D) + q(D)\right]g(D) + s(D) \qquad (15.45)$$

Equation (15.45) shows that $s(D)$ is also the syndrome of $e(D)$. The decoding procedure can now be summarized as follows: On receipt of $y(D)$ (possibly corrupted), the decoder calculates $s(D)$ (remainder) as a result of modulo-2 division by $g(D)$.

- If $s(D) = 0$, no detectable error.
- For a nonzero $s(D)$ polynomial, the error pattern corresponding to the syndrome polynomial or vector can be obtained from the Table 15.2.

Example 15.14

For the cyclic code (7, 4) with $g(D) = D^3 + D + 1$, assume a received vector $\underline{y} = (1\,1\,0\,0\,0\,0\,0)$. Derive the syndrome $s(D)$ and find the ML estimate of the transmitted codeword.

Solution

The received vector $\underline{y} = (1\,1\,0\,0\,0\,0\,0)$ corresponds to the polynomial $y(D) = D^6 + D^5$.
Let us first derive the syndrome $s(D)$ by long division.

$$
\begin{array}{r}
D^3 + D^2 + D \qquad\qquad\qquad \\
\hline
D^3 + D + 1\,)\,D^6 + D^5 \qquad\qquad\quad \\
D^6 + D^4 + D^3 \qquad\quad \\
\hline
D^5 + D^4 + D^3 \\
D^5 + D^3 + D^2 \\
\hline
D^4 + D^2 \\
D^4 + D^2 + D \\
\hline
D
\end{array}
$$

Because $s(D) = D$, the syndrome vector is $s = (0\,1\,0)$. This corresponds to the error pattern $(0\,0\,0\,0\,0\,1\,0)$ from Table 15.2. The decoded codeword is therefore $\underline{y} = (1\,1\,0\,0\,0\,0\,0) + (0\,0\,0\,0\,0\,1\,0) = (1\,1\,0\,0\,0\,1\,0)$.

15.3.3 Important Families of Block Codes

Hamming Codes

Hamming codes are designed to correct single-bit errors. They can detect all double errors. The key parameters of this family of (n, k) block codes include:

Block length: $n = 2^m - 1, m \geq 3$
Number of data bits: $k = 2^m - m - 1$

Number of parity bits: $n - k = m$

Minimum distance: $d_{min} = 3$

An important property of Hamming codes is that they are single-error correcting binary perfect codes. The $(n - k) \times n$ parity-check matrix $\underline{H}$ for Hamming codes has special structure: its columns consist of all nonzero binary sequences of length $n - k$. The parity-check matrix for the Hamming (7, 4) code from Example 15.4 is

$$\underline{H} = \begin{pmatrix} 1 & 1 & 1 & 0 & \vdots & 1 & 0 & 0 \\ 0 & 1 & 1 & 1 & \vdots & 0 & 1 & 0 \\ 1 & 1 & 0 & 1 & \vdots & 0 & 0 & 1 \end{pmatrix}$$

Golay Code

This is a very special three-error correcting (23, 12) cyclic code with minimum distance 7. The code has been widely used as a (24, 12) **extended Golay code** with minimum distance 8 by adding an extra parity bit, which is a parity check over the other 23 bits. Unfortunately, the Golay code does not generalize to other combinations of n and k.

Bose-Chaudhuri-Hocquenghem Codes

For a channel that introduces random errors, Bose-Chaudhuri-Hocquenghem (BCH) codes provide some of the best performance among known codes for a given block length and code rate. For positive pair of integers $m \geq 3$ and $t < (2^m - 1)/2$, an (n, k) BCH code has the following parameters:

Block length: $n = 2^m - 1$

Number of parity bits: $n - k \leq mt$

Minimum distance: $d_{min} \geq 2t + 1$

This code can correct up to t random errors in a codeword of length n bits. Hamming codes can be viewed as single-error correcting BCH codes. Generator polynomials for these codes are listed in many texts, including Lin and Costello.[1] These polynomials have a degree less than or equal to mt.

Reed-Solomon Codes

Reed-Solomon (R-S) codes are nonbinary BCH codes defined over $\mathbb{F}_q = \{0, 1, 2, \ldots, q - 1\}$, where $q = 2^m$. This code, therefore, processes data in chunks of m bits, called symbols. An (n, k) R-S code has the following parameters:

Symbol length: m bits per symbol

Block length: $n = 2^m - 1$ symbols $= m(2^m - 1)$ bits

Data length: k symbols $= km$ bits

Number of parity symbols: $n - k = 2t$ symbols $= m(2t)$ bits

Minimum distance: $d_{min} = 2t + 1$ symbols

In general, a t-symbol error correcting R-S code can correct t bursts (of m bits each) per codeword. That is why R-S codes are extremely popular for burst error correction and are used in applications ranging from CD players to cellular and deep-space applications.

---

[1] S. Lin and D. Costello, *Error Control Coding,* 2nd ed. (Upper Saddle River, NJ: Prentice Hall, 2004).

15.3.4 Cyclic Redundancy Check Codes

Cyclic redundancy check (CRC) codes are a broad class of cyclic codes that are generated by either a **primitive**[2] polynomial $p(D)$ or a polynomial $g(D) = (D + 1) p(D)$. These codes are widely used for error detection in communication networks. Figure 15.8 illustrates the operation of the error detection scheme. At the transmitter, parity bits (also called **checksum**) are computed and sent along with information bits in a data frame or packet. At the receiver, the checksum is recalculated, based on the received data frame. The received and recalculated checksums are compared, and if they do not match, an error condition is declared. The receiver has the option to request a retransmission of the frame.

Table 15.5 provides generator polynomials that are incorporated in various international standards. For example, the IEEE 802.3 standard specifies that Ethernet frames must incorporate a 4-byte checksum generated using a CCITT-32 polynomial for error detection purposes.

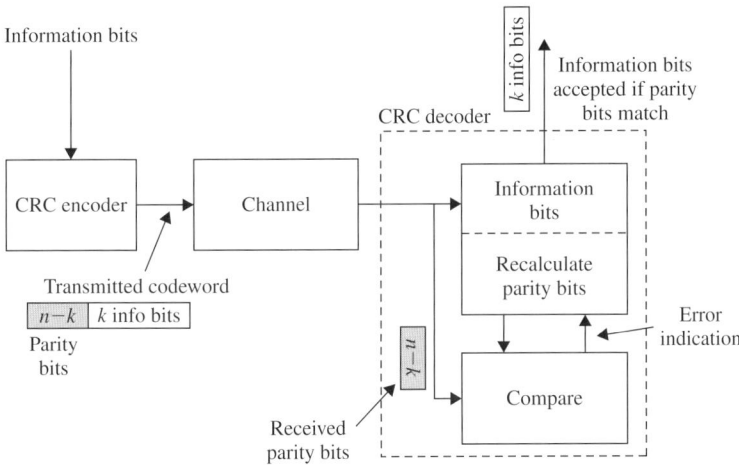

Figure 15.8 Error detection using checksum.

Table 15.5 Standard Generator Polynomials

Name	Polynomial $g(D)$	Used In
CRC-8	$D^8 + D^2 + D + 1$	Asynchronous transfer mode (ATM) protocol
CRC-10	$D^{10} + D^9 + D^5 + D^4 + D + 1$	Asynchronous transfer mode (ATM) protocol
CRC-12	$D^{12} + D^{11} + D^3 + D^2 + D + 1 = (D + 1)(D^{11} + D^2 + 1)$	IBM bisync protocol
CRC-16	$D^{16} + D^{15} + D^2 + 1 = (D + 1)(D^{15} + D + 1)$	IBM bisync protocol
CCITT-16	$D^{16} + D^{12} + D^5 + 1$	CCITT HDLC protocol
CCITT-32	$D^{32} + D^{26} + D^{23} + D^{22} + D^{16} + D^{12} + D^{11} + D^{10} D^8 + D^7 + D^5 + D^4 + D^2 + D + 1$	IEEE 802.3 (Ethernet) protocol

---

[2] A polynomial $p(D)$ of degree m is **irreducible** if $p(D)$ is not divisible by any polynomial of degree less than m but greater than zero. An irreducible polynomial $p(D)$ of degree m is said to be **primitive** if the smallest positive integer n for which $p(D)$ divides $D^n + 1$ is $n = 2^m - 1$. For example, $P(D) = D^4 + D + 1$ divides $D^{15} + 1$ but does not divide any $D^n + 1$ for $1 \leq n < 15$.

15.4   ERROR CORRECTION PERFORMANCE OF HARD-DECISION DECODED BLOCK CODES

The probability of codeword error, $P_{cw}(e)$, is defined as the probability that a transmitted codeword is decoded in error. Under hard-decision decoding, an $(n, k, d_{\min})$ block code can correct t or fewer errors if $d_{\min} \geq 2t + 1$. Thus a received vector may be decoded in error if it contains more than t errors. The probability of codeword error $P_{cw}(e)$ can, therefore, be expressed as

$$P_{cw}(e) = P\{t + 1 \text{ or more errors in codeword of length } n\}$$

$$= P\left\{ \bigcup_{j=t+1}^{n} \{j \text{ errors in codeword of length } n\} \right\} \tag{15.46}$$

By the application of union bound (6.11), we can write (15.46) as

$$P_{cw}(e) \leq \sum_{j=t+1}^{n} P\{j \text{ errors in codeword of length } n\} \tag{15.47}$$

Now

$$P\{j \text{ errors in codeword of length } n\} = \binom{n}{j} p^j (1 - p)^{n-j} \tag{15.48}$$

Substituting (15.48) into (15.47) yields

$$P_{cw}(e) \leq \sum_{j=t+1}^{n} \binom{n}{j} p^j (1 - p)^{n-j} \tag{15.49}$$

where p is the BER associated with the transmission of bits in the codeword. For binary antipodal signaling over an AWGN channel, we can write from (10.55)

$$p = Q\left(\sqrt{\frac{2E_{cb}}{N_o}} \right) = Q\left(\sqrt{\frac{R_c 2E_b}{N_o}} \right) \tag{15.50}$$

where $E_{cb} = kE_b/n = R_c E_b$ is the energy of the coded bit and $N_o/2$ is the noise power spectral density. Equation (15.49) holds with equality for perfect codes. In most applications of interest, p is small enough so that the first term in the sum (15.49) dominates, yielding

$$P_{cw}(e) \approx \binom{n}{t + 1} p^{t+1} (1 - p)^{n-t-1} \tag{15.51}$$

Next we shall derive a useful upper bound for the probability of codeword error $P_{cw}(e)$ in terms of the weights of codewords. For any linear code on a BSC,

$$P_{cw}(e) = P_{cw}(e | \underline{x}_m), \quad m = 0, 1, 2, \ldots, 2^k - 1 \tag{15.52}$$

That is, the codeword error probability for the mth codeword $\underline{x}_m$ is the same for all m. Therefore, we assume without loss of generality that the all-zero codeword $\underline{x}_0$ is transmitted. Consider the event that the received vector $\underline{y}$ is decoded as a codeword $\underline{x}_m$ of Hamming weight $w_H(\underline{x}_m) = d$. Transmission errors in bit positions, where the two codewords $\underline{x}_0$ and $\underline{x}_m$ are identical, increase the Hamming distance between the received vector $\underline{y}$ and either of the codewords equally. However, an error in the bit position where the codewords are different results in an increment of $d_H(\underline{y}, \underline{x}_0)$ accompanied by a corresponding decrement in $d_H(\underline{y}, \underline{x}_m)$. Therefore, the ML decoder makes an error when $\left\lfloor \dfrac{d}{2} + 1 \right\rfloor$ or more transmission errors occur in bit positions where $\underline{x}_m$ has 1's. In this case, the received vector $\underline{y}$ is closer to $\underline{x}_m$ than $\underline{x}_0$. The probability $P_2(d)$ of selecting the codeword $\underline{x}_m$ with Hamming weight $w_H(\underline{x}_m) = d$ instead of the all-zero codeword is given by

$$P_2(d) = P\{\underline{x}_m \text{ decoded} \,|\, \underline{x}_0 \text{ sent}\} = P\{d_H(\underline{y}, \underline{x}_m) \leq d_H(\underline{y}, \underline{x}_0) | \underline{x}_0 \text{ transmitted}\}$$

$$= P\left\{ \left\lfloor \frac{d}{2} + 1 \right\rfloor \text{ or more transmission errors in bit positions where } \underline{x}_m \text{ has 1's} \right\}$$

$$= \sum_{j=\lfloor 0.5d + 1 \rfloor}^{d} \binom{d}{j} p^j (1 - p)^{n-j} \tag{15.53}$$

It can be shown[3] that

$$P_2(d) \leq \left(2\sqrt{p(1 - p)} \right)^d = \left(2\sqrt{p(1 - p)} \right)^{w_H(\underline{x}_m)} \tag{15.54}$$

An upper bound on the probability of codeword error is now obtained by invoking the union bound and then applying (15.54).

$$P_{cw}(e) = P_{cw}(e|\underline{x}_0) = P\{\underline{x}_1 \text{ or } \underline{x}_2 \text{ or } \ldots \text{ or } \underline{x}_{2^k-1} \text{ decoded} | \underline{x}_0 \text{ transmitted}\}$$

$$\leq \sum_{m=1}^{2^k-1} P_2(\underline{x}_m|\underline{x}_0) \leq \sum_{m=1}^{2^k-1} \left(2\sqrt{p(1 - p)} \right)^{w_H(\underline{x}_m)} \tag{15.55}$$

A simpler but looser upper bound is obtained by substituting the minimum weight of the code $d_{\min}$ for $w_H(\underline{x}_m)$ in (15.55).

$$P_{cw}(e) \leq (2^k - 1)\left(2\sqrt{p(1 - p)} \right)^{d_{\min}} < 2^k \left(2\sqrt{p(1 - p)} \right)^{d_{\min}} \tag{15.56}$$

By rearranging terms in the summation, the bound in (15.55) can be expressed as

$$P_{cw}(e) \leq \sum_{d=d_{\min}}^{n} A_d P_2(d) \leq \sum_{d=d_{\min}}^{n} A_d \left(2\sqrt{p(1 - p)} \right)^d \tag{15.57}$$

where A_d is the number of codewords with the Hamming weight d in the $(n, k, d_{\min})$ code. MacWilliams and Sloane[4] contain extensive discussions of the weight distributions of block codes. Table 15.6 displays the weights for Golay codes, the (7, 4)

Table 15.6 Weight Distribution of Various Block Codes

Code	Weights A_d
Hamming (7, 4)	$A_3 = 7, A_4 = 7, A_7 = 1$
Hamming (15, 11)	$A_3 = 35, A_4 = 105, A_5 = 168, A_6 = 280, A_7 = 435, A_8 = 435, A_9 = 280,$ $A_{10} = 168, A_{11} = 105, A_{12} = 35, A_{15} = 1$
Golay (23, 12)	$A_7 = 253, A_8 = 506, A_{11} = 1288, A_{12} = 1288, A_{15} = 506, A_{16} = 253, A_{23} = 1$
Extended Golay (24, 12)	$A_8 = 759, A_{12} = 2576, A_{16} = 759, A_{24} = 1$

[3] Lin and Costello, *Error Control Coding.*

[4] F. MacWilliams and N. Sloane, *The Theory of Error-Correcting Codes* (Amsterdam: Elsevier, 1977).

Hamming code, and the (15, 11) Hamming code. For p small, the first term in the sum (15.57) dominates, yielding

$$P_{cw}(e) \approx A_{d_{\min}} \left(2\sqrt{p(1-p)} \right)^{d_{\min}} \tag{15.58}$$

Next we relate the average **probability of decoded bit error** P_b with the probability of codeword error $P_{cw}(e)$. The decoder delivers an erroneous codeword when at least $(t+1)$ errors occur in the transmitted codeword. The decoded codeword differs in at least $d_{\min} = 2t + 1$ bits from the actual transmitted codeword. That is, the erroneously decoded codeword has a minimum of $2t + 1$ errors in n bits. Therefore,

$$P_b = \frac{\text{Average number of bits decoded in error}}{\text{Total number of bits}}$$

$$\approx \frac{d_{\min} \times \text{Average number of codewords decoded in error}}{n \times \text{Total number of codewords}} = \frac{d_{\min}}{n} P_{cw}(e) \quad (15.59)$$

Substituting (15.58) into (15.59), we obtain the following approximation for the probability of decoded bit error for p small:

$$P_b \approx \frac{d_{\min}}{n} A_{d_{\min}} \left(2\sqrt{p(1-p)} \right)^{d_{\min}} \tag{15.60}$$

Example 15.15

Compare the probability of bit error performance for (7, 4) Hamming code with uncoded binary antipodal signaling system. Compute the estimates of P_b using upper bounds (15.56) through (15.58) and display alongside the exact plot. Assume E_b/N_o values in the range of 4 to 14 dB.

Solution

For binary antipodal signaling, the bit error rate of the uncoded system is given from (10.55) as

$$BER = Q\left(\sqrt{\frac{2E_b}{N_o}} \right)$$

For the coded system, the bit error rate for binary antipodal signaling is given from (15.50) as

$$p = Q\left(\sqrt{\frac{R_c 2E_b}{N_o}} \right)$$

Observe that p is crossover probability associated with the BSC model of the hard-decision coded system. Because Hamming codes are perfect codes, the exact probability of decoded bit error P_b is obtained by substituting (15.49) into (15.59) as

$$P_b = \frac{d_{\min}}{n} \sum_{j=t+1}^{n} \binom{n}{j} p^j (1-p)^{n-j} \tag{15.61}$$

Substituting the parameters of (7, 4) Hamming code, we get

$$P_b = \frac{3}{7} \sum_{j=2}^{7} \binom{7}{j} p^j (1-p)^{n-j} \tag{15.62}$$

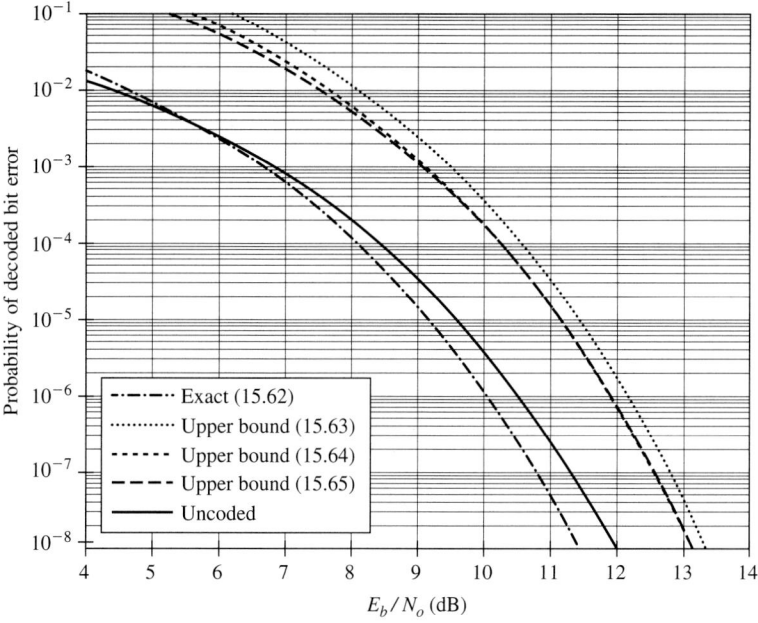

Figure 15.9 (7, 4, 3) Hamming code error performance.

Combining upper bounds in (15.56) through (15.58) with (15.59), the following estimates of probability of decoded bit error P_b are obtained:

$$P_b \le \frac{d_{\min}}{n}(2^k - 1)\left(2\sqrt{p(1-p)}\right)^{d_{\min}} = \frac{3 \times 15}{7}\left(2\sqrt{p(1-p)}\right)^3 = \frac{45}{7}x^3 \quad (15.63)$$

$$P_b \le \frac{d_{\min}}{n}\sum_{d=d_{\min}}^{n} A_d\left(2\sqrt{p(1-p)}\right)^d = \frac{3}{7}\sum_{d=3}^{7} A_d\left(2\sqrt{p(1-p)}\right)^d = \frac{3}{7}(7x^3 + 7x^4 + x^7) \quad (15.64)$$

$$P_b \approx \frac{d_{\min}}{n}A_{d_{\min}}\left(2\sqrt{p(1-p)}\right)^{d_{\min}} = \frac{3 \times 7}{7}x^3 = 3x^3 \quad (15.65)$$

where $x = 2\sqrt{p(1-p)}$.

Figure 15.9 compares the performance of uncoded and (7, 4) Hamming coded systems. For $P_b = 10^{-8}$, the coded system requires approximately 0.5 dB less SNR/bit. We have also plotted various upper bounds for decoded bit error rate. It can be verified that the tightest bounds given by (15.64) and (15.65) differ by about 1.75 dB from the exact value at $P_b = 10^{-8}$. For longer block length codes, these bounds provide useful error-rate estimates when exact calculation is impractical.

15.5 SOFT-DECISION DECODING OF BLOCK CODES

For the ideal soft-decision decoding as shown in Figure 15.1, the symbol-rate sampler values of the demodulator output are directly used in the channel decoder rather than quantizing them to 0 or 1 in the detector. Because the channel decoder uses the additional information contained in the unquantized received samples to determine the transmitted codeword, soft-decision decoding provides better performance than hard-decision decoding. Let $\underline{s}_m = \sqrt{E_{cb}}\,(s_{m0}, s_{m1}, \ldots, s_{m, n-1})$ be the vector in the signal space corresponding to the codeword $\underline{x}_m = (x_{m0}, x_{m1}, \ldots, x_{m, n-1})$, where $E_{cb} = kE_b/n$ is the energy of the coded bit. For binary antipodal signaling, $s_{mj} = 2x_{mj} - 1$. If $x_{mj} = 1$, then $s_{mj} = 1$ and it equals -1 for $x_{mj} = 0$. The jth component $\underline{r}_j$ of the received vector $\underline{r}$ is given by

$$\boldsymbol{r}_j = \sqrt{E_{cb}}s_{mj} + \boldsymbol{n}_j \tag{15.66}$$

where $\boldsymbol{n}_j$ is a Gaussian random variable with mean 0 and variance $\sigma_o^2 = N_o/2$. As discussed in Section 10.5, the ML soft decoding rule uses Euclidean distance rather than Hamming distance as the decoding metric. The Euclidean distance $d_E(\underline{r}, \underline{s}_m)$ between vectors $\underline{r}$ and $\underline{s}_m = \sqrt{E_{cb}}(s_{m0}, s_{m1}, \ldots, s_{m, n-1})$ is given from (10.130) as

$$d_E(\boldsymbol{r}, \underline{s}_m) = \sqrt{\sum_{j=1}^{n}\left(r_j - \sqrt{E_{cb}}s_{mj}\right)^2} \tag{15.67}$$

The ML soft decoding rule decodes $\underline{x}_\ell$ as the transmitted codeword if $\underline{s}_\ell$ is closest to the received vector $\underline{r}$ in the Euclidean distance

$$d_E(\underline{r}, \underline{s}_\ell) < d_E(\underline{r}, \underline{s}_m), \quad \ell \neq m$$

Now

$$d_E^2(\boldsymbol{r}, \underline{s}_m) = \sum_{j=0}^{n-1}\left[\boldsymbol{r}_j - \sqrt{E_{cb}}s_{mj}\right]^2 = \sum_{j=0}^{n-1}\left[\boldsymbol{r}_j^2 - 2\sqrt{E_{cb}}\boldsymbol{r}_j s_{mj} + E_{cb}s_{mj}^2\right]$$

$$= \sum_{j=0}^{n-1}(\boldsymbol{r}_j^2 + E_{cb}) - 2\sqrt{E_{cb}}\sum_{j=0}^{n-1}\boldsymbol{r}_j s_{mj} = K - 2\sqrt{E_{cb}}\sum_{j=0}^{n-1}\boldsymbol{r}_j s_{mj} \tag{15.68}$$

The quantity $K = E_{cb} + \sum_{j=0}^{n-1}\boldsymbol{r}_j^2$ is a positive number that remains constant during the minimization and can therefore be dropped. Thus, minimizing the Euclidean distance $d_E(\boldsymbol{r}, \underline{s}_m)$ in (15.68) is equivalent to maximizing the correlation sum

$$c(\boldsymbol{r}, \underline{s}_m) = \sum_{j=0}^{n-1}\boldsymbol{r}_j s_{mj} \tag{15.69}$$

The correlation sum $c(\underline{r}, \underline{s}_m)$ conditioned on the transmitted codeword $\underline{x}_m$ is a Gaussian random variable. Its expected value is $n\sqrt{E_{cb}}$ for the actual transmitted codeword. For all other codewords, $c(\underline{r}, \underline{s}_m)$ will have smaller mean values. The ML decoding is accomplished by selecting $\underline{x}_m$ for which $c(\underline{r}, \underline{s}_m)$ is the largest. Although the computation of (15.69) involves only n **multiply and accumulate (MAC)** operations, it becomes impractical to implement this algorithm because of the exponential growth of code size (2^k) with block length k.

15.5.1   Soft-Decision Decoding Error Performance

Again, we derive an upper bound assuming that the all-zero codeword $\underline{x}_0$ is transmitted. The probability $P_2(d)$ of selecting the codeword $\underline{x}_m$ with Hamming weight $w_H(\underline{x}_m) = d$ is given by

$$P_2(d) = P\{\underline{x}_m \text{ decoded}|\underline{x}_0 \text{ sent}\} = P\{d_E(\underline{r}, \underline{s}_m) < d_E(\underline{r}, \underline{s}_0)|\underline{x}_0 \text{ transmitted}\} \tag{15.70}$$

As discussed in Section 10.5, the pairwise error probability $P_2(d)$ can be written from (10.144) as

$$P_2(d) = Q\left(\frac{d_E(\underline{s}_m, \underline{s}_0)}{\sqrt{2N_o}}\right) \tag{15.71}$$

The Hamming distance $d_H(\underline{x}_m, \underline{x}_0)$ between codewords $\underline{x}_m$ and $\underline{x}_0$ is

$$d_H(\underline{x}_m, \underline{x}_0) = w_H(\underline{x}_m \oplus \underline{x}_0) = w_H(\underline{x}_m) = d \tag{15.72}$$

The Euclidean distance between polar sequences $\underline{s}_m$ and $\underline{s}_0$ is related to the Hamming distance $d_H(\underline{x}_m, \underline{x}_0)$ by

$$d_E^2(\underline{s}_m, \underline{s}_0) = E_{cb}\sum_{j=1}^{n}(s_{mj} - s_{0j})^2 = 4E_{cb}d_H(\underline{x}_m, \underline{x}_0) = 4E_{cb}d \tag{15.73}$$

Substituting (15.73) into (15.71) yields

$$P_2(d) = Q\left(\sqrt{\frac{4E_{cb}d}{2N_o}}\right) = Q\left(\sqrt{\frac{2E_{cb}w_H(\underline{x}_m)}{N_o}}\right) \tag{15.74}$$

An upper bound on the probability of codeword error is obtained by invoking the union bound as done in deriving (15.55). Therefore,

$$P_{cw}(e) \le \sum_{m=1}^{2^k-1}P_2(\underline{x}_m|\underline{x}_0) = \sum_{m=1}^{2^k-1}Q\left(\sqrt{\frac{2E_{cb}w_H(\underline{x}_m)}{N_o}}\right) \tag{15.75}$$

A simpler but looser upper bound is obtained by substituting the minimum weight of a codeword $d_{\min}$ for $w_H(\underline{x}_m)$ in (15.75)

$$P_{cw}(e) \le (2^k - 1)Q\left(\sqrt{\frac{2E_{cb}d_{\min}}{N_o}}\right) < 2^k Q\left(\sqrt{\frac{2E_{cb}d_{\min}}{N_o}}\right) \tag{15.76}$$

By rearranging terms on the right-hand side of (15.75), the upper bound on $P_{cw}(e)$ can be expressed in the alternate form as

$$P_{cw}(e) \le \sum_{d=d_{\min}}^{n}A_dP_2(d) \le \sum_{d=d_{\min}}^{n}A_dQ\left(\sqrt{\frac{2E_{cb}d}{N_o}}\right) \tag{15.77}$$

where A_d is the number of codewords with the Hamming weight d in the $(n, k, d_{\min})$ code. Substituting (15.77) into (15.59), we obtain the following upper bound on the probability of decoded bit error

$$P_b \approx \frac{d_{\min}}{n}P_{cw}(e) \le \frac{d_{\min}}{n}\sum_{d=d_{\min}}^{n}A_dQ\left(\sqrt{\frac{2E_{cb}d}{N_o}}\right) \tag{15.78}$$

For high E_b/N_o values, $d = d_{\min}$ term dominates the sum yielding the following approximation for P_b

$$P_b \approx \frac{d_{\min}}{n}A_{d_{\min}}Q\left(\sqrt{\frac{2E_{cb}d_{\min}}{N_o}}\right) \tag{15.79}$$

15.5.2   Coding Gain

One important performance measure of the channel coding is power efficiency achievable in a coded digital communication system. This advantage of a coded versus an uncoded system is characterized in terms of its coding gain. The **coding gain** of a code is defined as the difference in the SNR/bit (E_b/N_o) required to achieve a specified codeword error rate when compared to an uncoded binary antipodal system. Another commonly used measure to evaluate the performance of code is its coding gain for large SNR values, called the **asymptotic coding gain.** It is defined as

$$\text{Asymptotic coding gain } G = 10\log_{10} \frac{(E_b/N_o)_{\text{uncoded}}}{(E_b/N_o)_{\text{coded}}} \qquad (15.80)$$

where $(E_b/N_o)_{\text{uncoded}}$ and $(E_b/N_o)_{\text{coded}}$ are assumed to be large. We next calculate the asymptotic coding gain for a block code with hard- and soft-decision ML decoding.

For an uncoded system, the probability of error for a word or packet of k bits is given by

$$P_w(e) = 1 - (1 - p)^k \approx kp \qquad (15.81)$$

where $p =$ BER of the transmission link. Substituting $p = Q\left(\sqrt{2\left(\dfrac{E_b}{N_o}\right)_{\text{uncoded}}}\right)$ into (15.81) yields

$$P_w(e) \approx kp = kQ\left(\sqrt{2\left(\frac{E_b}{N_o}\right)_{\text{uncoded}}}\right) \qquad (15.82)$$

Applying Chernoff bound on the Q-function $Q\left(\sqrt{2x}\right) \leq \dfrac{e^{-x}}{2}$ to (15.82) yields

$$P_w(e) \approx \frac{k}{2}e^{-\left(\frac{E_b}{N_o}\right)_{\text{uncoded}}} \qquad (15.83)$$

Taking the logarithm of both sides of (15.83) yields

$$\log_e P_w(e) \approx \log_e\left(\frac{k}{2}\right) - \left(\frac{E_b}{N_o}\right)_{\text{uncoded}} \qquad (15.84)$$

For the hard-decision ML decoding case, we shall use the approximation (15.56) for the probability of codeword error

$$P_{cw}(e) \leq (2^k - 1)\left(2\sqrt{p(1-p)}\right)^{d_{\min}} < 2^k\left(2\sqrt{p(1-p)}\right)^{d_{\min}} \qquad (15.56)$$

For p small, we can write (15.56) as

$$P_{cw}(e) \approx 2^k(4p)^{d_{\min}/2} \qquad (15.85)$$

Now substituting $p = Q\left(\sqrt{2R_c\left(\dfrac{E_b}{N_o}\right)_{\text{coded}}}\right)$ into (15.85) and applying the Chernoff bound on the Q-function, we obtain

$$P_{cw}(e) \approx 2^{k+\frac{d_{\min}}{2}} e^{-\frac{R_c}{2}d_{\min}\left(\frac{E_b}{N_o}\right)_{\text{coded}}} \tag{15.86}$$

Taking the logarithm of both sides of (15.86) yields

$$\log_e P_{cw}(e) \approx \left(k + \frac{d_{\min}}{2}\right)\log_e 2 - \frac{R_c d_{\min}}{2}\left(\frac{E_b}{N_o}\right)_{\text{coded}} \tag{15.87}$$

To achieve the same probability of error, the right-hand sides of (15.84) and (15.87) must be equal. That is,

$$\log_e\left(\frac{k}{2}\right) - \left(\frac{E_b}{N_o}\right)_{\text{uncoded}} = \left(k + \frac{d_{\min}}{2}\right)\log_e 2 - \frac{R_c d_{\min}}{2}\left(\frac{E_b}{N_o}\right)_{\text{coded}} \tag{15.88}$$

Now for large SNR/bit values, we can approximate (15.88) as

$$\left(\frac{E_b}{N_o}\right)_{\text{uncoded}} \approx \frac{R_c d_{\min}}{2}\left(\frac{E_b}{N_o}\right)_{\text{coded}}$$

or

$$\frac{(E_b/N_o)_{\text{uncoded}}}{(E_b/N_o)_{\text{coded}}} \approx \frac{R_c d_{\min}}{2} \tag{15.89}$$

For the hard-decision ML decoding, the asymptotic coding gain of the block code is obtained by substituting (15.89) into (15.80) as

$$G_{hd} = 10\log_{10}\frac{(E_b/N_o)_{\text{uncoded}}}{(E_b/N_o)_{\text{coded}}} \approx 10\log_{10}\frac{R_c d_{\min}}{2} \tag{15.90}$$

In the case of soft-decision decoding, we shall use the upper bound (15.76) for the probability of codeword error

$$P_{cw}(e) < 2^k Q\left(\sqrt{2d_{\min}\left(\frac{E_{cb}}{N_o}\right)_{\text{coded}}}\right) = 2^k Q\left(\sqrt{2R_c d_{\min}\left(\frac{E_b}{N_o}\right)_{\text{coded}}}\right)$$

$$\approx 2^{k-1}e^{-R_c d_{\min}\left(\frac{E_b}{N_o}\right)_{\text{coded}}} \approx 2^k e^{-R_c d_{\min}\left(\frac{E_b}{N_o}\right)_{\text{coded}}} \tag{15.91}$$

Taking the logarithm of both sides of (15.91) yields

$$\log_e P_{cw}(e) \approx k\log_e 2 - R_c d_{\min}\left(\frac{E_b}{N_o}\right)_{\text{coded}} \tag{15.92}$$

To achieve the same probability of error, the right-hand sides of (15.84) and (15.92) must be equal. That is,

$$\log_e\left(\frac{k}{2}\right) - \left(\frac{E_b}{N_o}\right)_{\text{uncoded}} = k\log_e 2 - R_c d_{\min}\left(\frac{E_b}{N_o}\right)_{\text{coded}} \tag{15.93}$$

Now for large SNR/bit values, we can write (15.93) as

$$\left(\frac{E_b}{N_o}\right)_{\text{uncoded}} \approx R_c d_{\min}\left(\frac{E_b}{N_o}\right)_{\text{coded}}$$

or

$$\frac{(E_b/N_o)_{\text{uncoded}}}{(E_b/N_o)_{\text{coded}}} \approx R_c d_{\min} \tag{15.94}$$

For the soft-decision ML decoding, the asymptotic coding gain of the block code is obtained by substituting (15.94) into (15.80) as

$$G_{sd} = 10\log_{10}\frac{(E_b/N_o)_{\text{uncoded}}}{(E_b/N_o)_{\text{coded}}} \approx 10\log_{10}R_c d_{\min} \tag{15.95}$$

We observe from (15.90) and (15.95) that the asymptotic coding gain depends only on the code rate R_c and the minimum Hamming distance $d_{\min}$ of the code. Further comparing (15.90) and (15.95), we note that the soft-decision ML decoding offers a **3-dB advantage** over the hard-decision ML decoding. The 3-dB coding gain is obtained only for very large SNR values. For moderate values of SNR, the real coding gain is less than 3 dB.

Example 15.16

For the (7, 4) Hamming code, compare the error performance using hard- and soft-decision decoding schemes. What is the coding gain advantage of soft-decision decoding for $P_b = 10^{-8}$? Assume binary antipodal signaling.

Solution

The hard-decision decoding performance for the (7, 4) Hamming code is plotted using (15.62). For soft-decision decoding, the probability of decoded bit error P_b using the upper bound in (15.78) is given by

$$P_b \approx \frac{d_{\min}}{n}\sum_{d=d_{\min}}^{n} A_d Q\left(\sqrt{\frac{2E_{cb}d}{N_o}}\right) = \frac{3}{7}\sum_{d=3}^{7} A_d Q\left(\sqrt{\frac{2\times 4E_b d}{7N_o}}\right)$$

$$= 3Q\left(\sqrt{\frac{6\times 4E_b}{7N_o}}\right) + 3Q\left(\sqrt{\frac{8\times 4E_b}{7N_o}}\right) + \frac{3}{7}Q\left(\sqrt{\frac{14\times 4E_b}{7N_o}}\right) \tag{15.96}$$

For soft-decision decoding, we have plotted probability of bit error performance (15.96) in Figure 15.10. The exact error performance for hard-decision decoded (7, 4) Hamming code is also displayed in the figure. It can be observed that soft-decision decoding offers a coding gain of 1.75 dB at $P_b = 10^{-8}$.

Pioneers in the Field

Courtesy MIT Museum

Peter Elias was born on November 23, 1923, in New Brunswick, NJ, the son of an engineer in Thomas A. Edison's laboratory. He attended Swarthmore College for two years before transferring to MIT in 1942. Upon receiving the S.B. in business and engineering management in 1944, he enlisted in the U.S. Navy and served as a radio technician instructor. After he was discharged in 1946 with the rank of Electronic Technician's Mate first class, he earned an M.A., a M.Eng and Sci., and a Ph.D. from Harvard University. Professor Elias joined the MIT faculty in 1953 as an assistant professor. He became an associate professor in 1956 and a full professor in 1960, the year he became the youngest person to head EECS. He was a member of the MIT faculty from 1953 to 1991, at which time he assumed emeritus rank and became a senior lecturer.

One of Elias's most remarkable papers is "Coding for Noisy Channels," which he published in the 1955 IRE Convention Record where among other significant results he introduced and named *convolutional* codes. His motivation was to show that it was in principle possible, by using a convolutional code with infinite constraint length, "to transmit information at a rate equal to channel capacity with probability one that no decoded symbol will be in error." In his error-free coding, he exploited the fact that the codewords in a convolutional code have a tree structure that allows the decoder to use as much or as little of the code length as it wishes to reduce decoding effort to what is needed for a desired error probability. This realization led directly to the invention of sequential decoding by J. M. Wozencraft. Sequential decoding of convolutional codes became the first coding system used on a deep-space mission (Pioneer 9 in 1969) and soon became the NASA standard coding system for deep space. Elias was also the inventor of product codes and interactive decoding of such codes which can obtain error probability arbitrarily close to zero with practical decoding effort. Elias used iterative decoding in a single-pass fashion, but this provided the starting point for other developments such as LDPC codes, developed by R. G. Gallager in his 1960 MIT doctoral thesis which Elias supervised, that iterate over multiple passes. Berrou and Glavieux's turbo codes is a further evolution of Elias's basic idea: convolutional codes and iterative decoding are again used with a clever interleaving scheme. Elias also contributed fundamental new concepts and techniques to source coding and communication networks.

Elias received the highest honor of the IEEE Information Theory Society, the Shannon Award, in 1977. He was a Fellow of the IEEE, the American Association for the Advancement of Science, the American Academy of Arts and Sciences, the National Academy of Sciences and the National Academy of Engineering. He also served on the President's Science Advisory Committee panel on Computers in Higher Education.

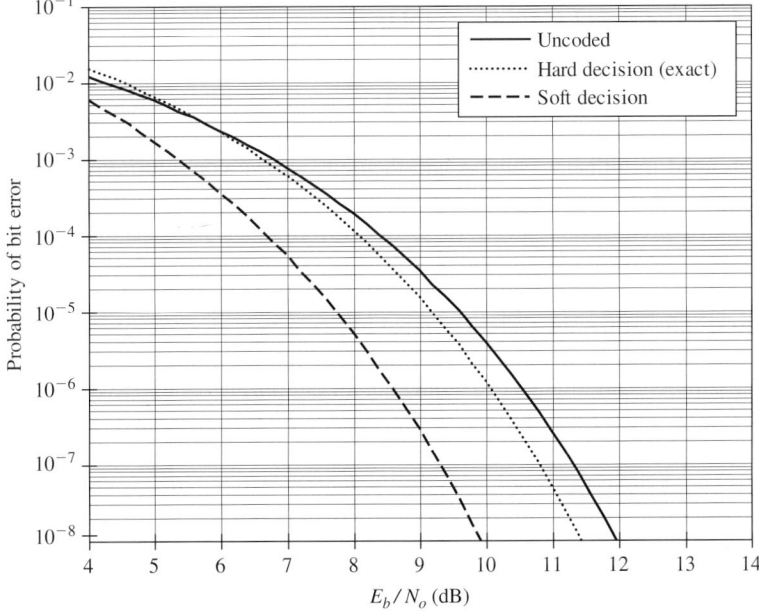

Figure 15.10 (7, 4) Hamming code: hard versus soft decoding coding gain.

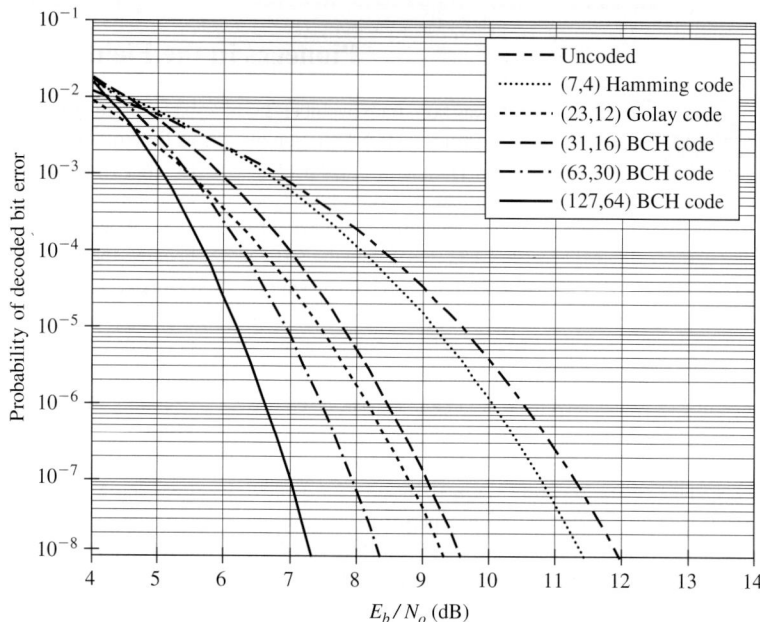

Figure 15.11 Probability of decoded bit error performance of various block codes.

We conclude the section by displaying the error performance of several block codes in Figure 15.11. Hard-decision decoding and BPSK signaling are assumed. The coding gain of (127, 64) BCH code is approximately 5 dB when compared to uncoded BPSK at an error rate of 10^{-8}.

15.6   CONVOLUTIONAL CODES

Block codes take a block of k bits at a time and map it into an n-bit codeword irrespective of the previous inputs to the encoder. Thus, a block coding system is **memoryless.** Convolutional codes are fundamentally different from block codes. Information bits are not grouped into distinct blocks and then encoded; a **convolutional encoder** continuously encodes an input bit sequence into an output bit sequence. Other important characteristics of convolutional codes, different from block codes, is that each input bit influences several successive output bits. That is, convolutional codes have memory.

A convolutional encoder consists of a shift register of length $L - 1$, where L is called the **constraint length** of the code. The input binary data is clocked into the shift register each bit period. The encoder output is a linear combination of the input bits and the content of the shift register. Figure 15.12 illustrates a sample encoder consisting of a 2-stage shift register ($L = 3$). Every bit period, the coder output is generated by the outputs of the two modulo-2 adders. For this code, two output bits are generated for each input bit so that the code rate is 1/2. Observe that a particular input bit influences the output during its own period as well as during the next two bit periods.

A convolutional code is specified by three integers n, k, and L; however, n does not define the codeword length as it does for block codes.

- n = number of output bits per k input bits
- Rate of convolutional code $R_c = k/n$ for an (n, k) convolutional code
- Constraint length L = number of output bits that a given input bit influences

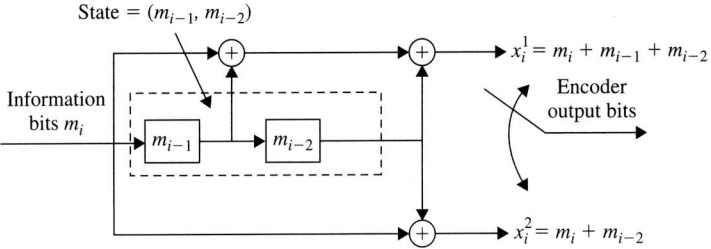

State $= (m_{i-1}, m_{i-2})$

Information bits m_i

m_{i-1} m_{i-2}

$x_i^1 = m_i + m_{i-1} + m_{i-2}$

Encoder output bits

$x_i^2 = m_i + m_{i-2}$

Encoder output $x_1^1 x_1^2 x_2^1 x_2^2 x_3^1 x_3^2 x_4^1 x_4^2 x_5^1 x_5^2 \ldots$

Figure 15.12 Rate 1/2 ($n = 2$, $k = 1$) convolutional encoder example.

The following shorthand notation is used to specify convolutional codes:

- (n, k, L) convolutional code
- (R_c, L) convolutional code

The state of convolutional encoder is defined by the contents of the shift register. The state of the encoder in Figure 15.12 is completely determined by the two previous information bits. Therefore, there are four different possible states: $S_0 = (0, 0)$, $S_1 = (0, 1)$, $S_2 = (1, 0)$, $S_3 = (1, 1)$.

15.6.1   Representation of Convolutional Codes

Convolutional codes can be represented in several different ways. These include:

- Sets of generator polynomials
- State transition diagrams
- Trellis diagrams

Generator Polynomial Representation

A convolutional code is completely specified by a set of n generator polynomials $\{g_1(D), g_2(D), \ldots, g_n(D)\}$ − one polynomial for each of the n outputs. The length of the shift register for the encoder is equal to the degree of the highest-degree generator polynomial. The polynomials define the number of modulo-2 adders and connections to them. The output polynomials are represented by

$$x_j(D) = m(D)g_j(D), \quad j = 1, \ldots, n \tag{15.97}$$

where $m(D) = m_0 + m_1 D + m_2 D^2 + \ldots$ is message polynomial corresponding to the input binary sequence $m_0, m_1, m_2, \ldots$.

Example 15.17

The convolutional encoder in Figure 15.12 is specified by two polynomials.

Upper branch: $g_1(D) = 1 + D + D^2$
Lower branch: $g_2(D) = 1 + D^2$

Determine the output sequence of the encoder for the input sequence 0 1 1 0 1 assuming that the encoder's initial state is $S_0 = (0, 0)$.

Solution

The polynomial corresponding to the input bit sequence 0 1 1 0 1 is given by

$$m(D) = D + D^2 + D^4$$

The output of the upper branch is the product of the polynomial $g_1(D)$ and the input binary sequence $m(D)$. That is,

$$x_1(D) = (D + D^2 + D^4)(1 + D + D^2) = D + (D^2 + D^2) + (D^3 + D^3) + (D^4 + D^4) + D^5 + D^6$$

$$= D + D^5 + D^6 \Leftrightarrow 0\,1\,0\,0\,0\,1\,1 \tag{15.98}$$

The output of the lower branch is the product of the polynomial $g_2(D)$ and the input binary sequence $m(D)$.

$$x_2(D) = (D + D^2 + D^4)(1 + D^2) = D + D^2 + D^3 + (D^4 + D^4) + D^6$$

$$= D + D^2 + D^3 + D^6 \Leftrightarrow 0\,1\,1\,1\,0\,0\,1 \tag{15.99}$$

Using (15.98) and (15.99), we can write the output sequence of the encoder as 00 11 01 01 00 10 11. Note that the message sequence of length M produces an encoded sequence of length $n(M + L - 1) = 14$.

A convolutional code is called **systematic** if the incoming message bits are transmitted unaltered in the output code sequence. Otherwise, it is called a **nonsystematic convolutional code.** The convolutional code generated by the encoder in Example 15.17 is nonsystematic. For an encoder to be systematic, one of the generator polynomials for the code must be of degree 0 (for example, $g_1(D) = 1$).

Generator polynomials are often specified as **generator sequences** in binary format or equivalent octal representation as discussed in Section 9.7. The generator polynomials in Example 15.17 can therefore be represented as

$$g_1(D) = 1 + D + D^2 \Leftrightarrow \underbrace{(1\ 1\ 1)}_{\underline{g}_1} \Leftrightarrow 7$$

$$g_2(D) = 1 + D^2 \Leftrightarrow \underbrace{(1\ 0\ 1)}_{\underline{g}_2} \Leftrightarrow 5$$

Using the generator sequences in binary format, the generator matrix $\underline{G}$ of a convolutional code can be expressed as

$$\underline{G} = \begin{pmatrix} \underline{g}_1 \\ \underline{g}_2 \\ \vdots \\ \underline{g}_n \end{pmatrix}$$

For an example, the generator matrix of (2, 1, 4) convolutional code with generator polynomials (17, 15) is given by

$$\underline{G} = \begin{pmatrix} 1 & 1 & 1 & 1 \\ 1 & 1 & 0 & 1 \end{pmatrix}$$

State Transition Diagram

Because the convolutional encoder is a **finite state machine (FSM),** the convolutional code can also be represented by a state transition diagram. Figure 15.13 illustrates such a diagram for the encoder in Figure 15.12. The nodes in this transition diagram are the states of the FSM, and the branches represent the possible transitions between states caused by specified inputs. Each solid arrow denotes the encoder state transition generated by an input bit 1, and a dashed line denotes the state change caused by an input bit 0. Each branch is labeled with the encoder input/output pair associated with a particular state transition. For example, if the encoder is in state S_0, an input bit 1 causes a transition to state S_2 and encoder output 11.

Trellis Diagram

A trellis diagram is an extension of the state diagram; it captures state transitions of the encoder with time for a given input sequence. Figure 15.14 depicts the trellis for the convolutional encoder in Figure 15.12. As in the state transition diagram, nodes and branches of the trellis represent the encoder states and state transitions, respectively. A solid line denotes the encoder state transition generated by an input bit 1, whereas

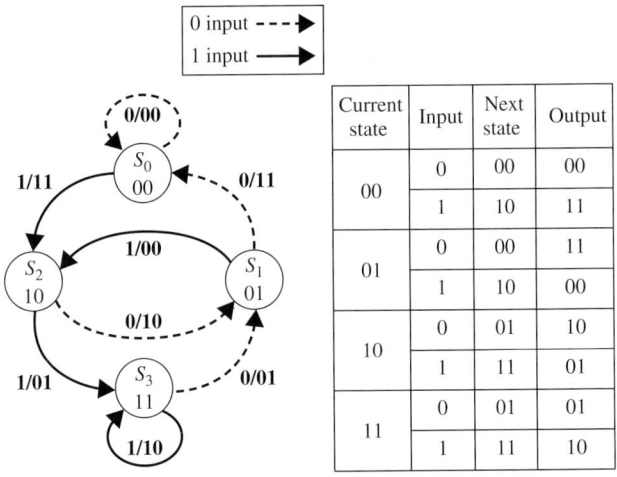

Figure 15.13 State transition diagram for rate 1/2 convolutional encoder.

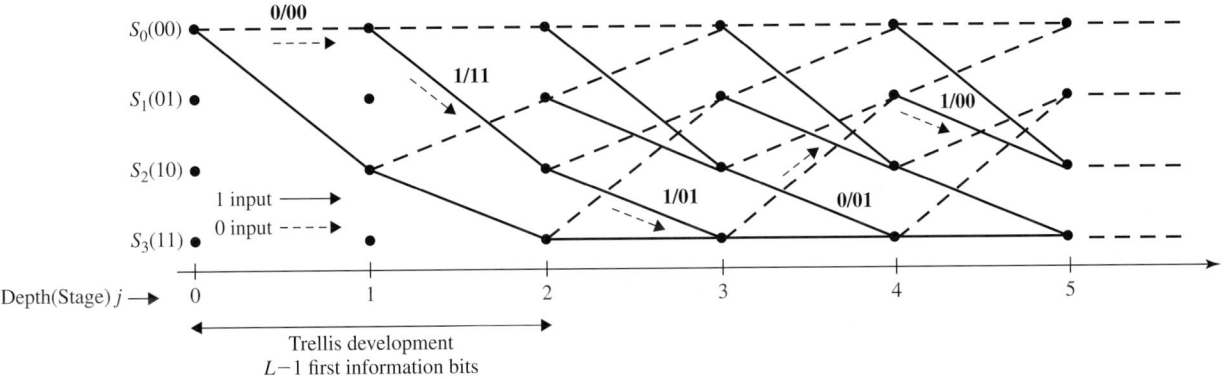

Figure 15.14 Trellis diagram for rate 1/2 convolutional encoder.

a dashed line indicates the state change generated by an input bit 0. The binary pair around each branch indicates input/output bits associated with the corresponding state transition. The trellis contains $L + M$ stages, where M is the length of input information sequence, and L is the constraint length of the code. The **stages** of the trellis are labeled $j = 0, 1, \ldots, L + M - 1$. Stage j is also called the **depth** j. Starting from S_0, it takes $L - 1$ stages for development of the trellis into a fixed structure. The fixed structure prevails after depth L. At this point and thereafter, each of the states can be entered from either of two preceding states. Also from each state, transition can occur to one of two states: one corresponding to an input bit 0 and the other corresponding to an input bit 1. Each input sequence corresponds to a specific path through the trellis. Figure 15.14 also displays the path through the trellis diagram for input bit sequence 01101. The encoding operation starts at state $S_0 = 00$. Because the first information bit is 0, the encoder moves along the dashed line to state $S_0 = 00$. The encoder output bits are 00. Next the bit 1 moves the encoder along the solid line from state $S_0 = 00$ to $S_2 = 10$, generating the output 11. It is easy to see from the figure that the encoder produces the code sequence 00 11 01 01 00 corresponding to the input sequence 01101.

A convolutional code consists of the set of all binary sequences produced by the encoder subject to the constraints imposed by the FSM. In theory, these sequences can be of infinite duration. In practice, it is customary to periodically reset the FSM to a known state (e.g., all-zero state) and encode finite-length frames of input bits. The input sequence is segmented into frames of M bits and appended with $L - 1$ zeros at the end to bring the FSM back to the all-zero state prior to the next frame. The $L - 1$ zeros at the end of the frame are called **tail bits.** There is a **fractional rate loss** due to this overhead. For example, IS-95 uses a $(2, 1, 10)$ convolutional code with $M = 184$ data bits per frame. Therefore, the fractional rate loss due to tails bits overhead in IS-95 is about 5%. Convolutional codes are widely popular in modern digital communication systems. The major applications include:

Satellite and Deep Space Communications

- Odenwalder codes
  - $(2, 1, 8)$ code with generator polynomials $(133, 171)$
  - $(3, 1, 8)$ code with generator polynomials $(133, 145, 171)$

Mobile Communications

- IS-95 CDMA
  - Forward channel (base station to mobile). $(2, 1, 10)$ code with generator polynomials $(753, 561)$
  - Reverse channel (mobile to base station). $(3, 1, 10)$ code with generator polynomials $(557, 663, 771)$
- GSM. $(2, 1, 6)$ with generator polynomials $(31, 33)$
- IS-136 TDMA (USDC). $(2, 1, 7)$ code with generator polynomials $(65, 57)$

15.6.2 Decoding of Convolutional Codes

The ML decoding for convolutional codes entails finding the code sequence $\underline{x}^\ell$ that was most likely to have been transmitted given the received sequence $\underline{y}$. That is, the ML decoder decides that the code sequence $\underline{x}^\ell$ was transmitted if

$$P(\underline{y}|\underline{x}^\ell) \geq P(\underline{y}|\underline{x}^m), \quad m \neq \ell \tag{15.100}$$

Again, we will use log-likelihood function $\log\{P(\underline{y}|\underline{x}^m)\}$ for convenience. Because there is one-to-one correspondence between trellis paths and information sequences, the ML decoding is equivalent to finding a path through the trellis whose code sequence has the largest log-likelihood function. Let $\underline{y} = (\underline{y}_1, \underline{y}_2, \dots, \underline{y}_N)$ be the received sequence consisting of $N = M + L - 1$ subsequences. Due to the independent channel statistics for memoryless channels, the log-likelihood function for a path $\underline{x}^m = (\underline{x}_1^m, \underline{x}_2^m, \dots, \underline{x}_N^m)$ comprised of N branches is given by

$$\log\{P(\underline{y}|\underline{x}^m)\} = \log\left\{\prod_{j=1}^{N} P(\underline{y}_j|\underline{x}_j^m)\right\} = \sum_{j=1}^{N} \log[P(\underline{y}_j|\underline{x}_j^m)] \qquad (15.101)$$

where

$$\underline{y}_j = (\underline{y}_{j1}\ \underline{y}_{j2}, \dots, \underline{y}_{jn}) = \text{received subsequence ("bits") corresponding to the } j\text{th}$$
$$\text{branch in the trellis}$$
$$\underline{x}_j^m = (x_{j1}^m, x_{j2}^m, \dots, x_{jn}^m) = \text{code subsequence ("bits") corresponding to the } j\text{th}$$
$$\text{branch of the } \underline{x}^m \text{ path through the trellis}$$

$\log\{P(\underline{y}|\underline{x}^m)\}$ is called the **path metric** that corresponds to the path $\underline{x}^m$ through the trellis. $P(\underline{y}_j|\underline{x}_j^m)$ is called the **branch metric** for the jth branch of the path $\underline{x}^m$ through the trellis. Equation (15.101) states that the path metric associated with a path $\underline{x}^m$ through the trellis equals the sum of the metrics associated with all branches constituting that path. Again, invoking the DMC assumption, the jth branch metric is given by

$$\log\{P(\underline{y}_j|\underline{x}_j^m)\} = \log\left\{\prod_{i=1}^{n} P(\underline{y}_{ji}|x_{ji}^m)\right\} = \sum_{i=1}^{n} \log P(\underline{y}_{ji}|x_{ji}^m) \qquad (15.102)$$

Substituting (15.102) into (15.101) yields the following expression for the path metric:

$$\log\{P(\underline{y}|\underline{x}^m)\} = \sum_{j=1}^{N}\sum_{i=1}^{n} \log P(\underline{y}_{ji}|x_{ji}^m) \qquad (15.103)$$

Hard-Decision Decoding

In this case, the decision device uses 1-bit quantization to generate the received sequence $\underline{y}$. That is, $\underline{y}_{ji}$ is detected as 0 or 1. If the received sequence $\underline{y}$ and the code sequence $\underline{x}^m$ differ in d_H bit positions, (15.103) can be expressed as

$$\log\{P(\underline{y}|\underline{x}^m)\} = d_H\log_e(p) + (K - d_H)\log_e(1 - p)$$

$$= d_H\log_e\left(\frac{p}{1 - p}\right) + K\log_e(1 - p) \qquad (15.104)$$

where $K = nN = n(M + L - 1)$ is the length of the sequences $\underline{y}$ and $\underline{x}^m$. d_H is the Hamming distance between the received sequence $\underline{y}$ and the code sequence $\underline{x}^m$ being considered. Because $\log_e\left(\dfrac{p}{1 - p}\right) < 0$ for $p < 0.5$, maximizing (15.104) is equivalent to minimizing d_H. Therefore, the ML hard-decision decoding involves finding a path through the trellis whose code sequence is the closest in Hamming distance to the received sequence. As a consequence, the appropriate path metric $c_{HD}(\underline{y}, \underline{x}^m)$ for the

ML hard-decision decoding is the Hamming distance between the received sequence $\underline{y}$ and the code sequence $\underline{x}^m$. That is,

$$c_{HD}(\underline{y}, \underline{x}^m) = d_H(\underline{y}, \underline{x}^m) = w_H(\underline{y} \oplus \underline{x}^m) \tag{15.105}$$

The corresponding branch metric is given by

$$c_{HD}(\underline{y}_j, \underline{x}_j^m) = w_H(\underline{y}_j \oplus \underline{x}_j^m) \tag{15.106}$$

The ML hard-decision decoding computes path metrics $c_{HD}(\underline{y}, \underline{x}^m)$ for all possible sequences through the trellis and selects $\underline{x}^\ell$ for which the path metric is the smallest.

Soft-Decision Decoding

The ML soft-decision sequence decoding entails finding the signal sequence $\underline{s}^\ell$ (corresponding to the code sequence $\underline{x}^\ell$) that is at the minimum Euclidean distance from the unquantized received sequence $\underline{r} = (\underline{r}_1, \underline{r}_2, \ldots, \underline{r}_N)$. Let $\underline{s}_j^m = \sqrt{E_{cb}}(s_{j1}^m, s_{j2}^m, \ldots, s_{jn}^m)$ be the polar signal subsequence transmitted corresponding to the code subsequence $\underline{x}_j^m = (x_{j1}^m, x_{j2}^m, \ldots, x_{jn}^m)$, where $s_{ji}^m = 2x_{ji}^m - 1$. The path metric for the ML soft-decision decoding is the squared Euclidean distance $d_E^2(\underline{r}, \underline{s}^m)$ between the received sequence $\underline{r}$ and the polar signal sequence $\underline{s}^m$ (corresponding to the code sequence $\underline{x}^m$). Due to independent channel statistics for memoryless channels, the path metric for a path $\underline{x}^m$ through the trellis is related to the branch metrics by

$$d_E^2(\underline{r}, \underline{s}^m) = \sum_{j=1}^{N} d_E^2(\underline{r}_j, \underline{s}_j^m) \tag{15.107}$$

where $d_E^2(\underline{r}_j, \underline{s}_j^m)$ is the branch metric for the jth branch corresponding to $\underline{x}^m$ path. As discussed in Section 15.4, the squared Euclidean distance corresponding to the jth branch is given from (15.68) as

$$d_E^2(\underline{r}_j, \underline{s}_j^m) = \sum_{i=1}^{n} \left[r_{ji} - \sqrt{E_{cb}} s_{ji}^m \right]^2 = K - 2\sqrt{E_{cb}} \sum_{i=1}^{n} r_{ji} s_{ji}^m \tag{15.108}$$

where $\underline{r}_j = (r_{j1}, \ldots, r_{jn})$ is the received subsequence corresponding to the jth branch in the trellis. The quantity $K = \sum_{i=1}^{n} (r_{ji}^2 + E_{cb})$ is a positive number that remains constant during the minimization and can therefore be dropped. Thus minimizing the squared Euclidean distance $d_E^2(\underline{r}_j, \underline{s}_j^m)$ in (15.108) is equivalent to maximizing the new branch metric

$$c_{SD}(\underline{r}_j, \underline{s}_j^m) = \sum_{i=1}^{n} r_{ji} \underline{s}_{ji}^m \tag{15.109}$$

Now we can obtain the corresponding path metric $c_{SD}(\underline{r}, \underline{s}^m)$ by using the new branch metric (15.109) as

$$c_{SD}(\underline{r}, \underline{s}^m) = \sum_{j=1}^{N} c_{SD}(\underline{r}_j, \underline{s}_j^m) = \sum_{j=1}^{N} \sum_{i=1}^{n} r_{ji} s_{ji}^m \tag{15.110}$$

Equation (15.97) states that computing the path metric is equivalent to calculating the correlation between the received sequence and the code sequence. The ML decoding computes path metrics $c(\underline{r}, \underline{x}^m)$ for all possible code sequences through the trellis and selects $\underline{x}^\ell$ for which it is the largest.

The problem with ML decoding is that the complexity of computing the path metric grows exponentially with the constraint length of the code, and this computation needs to be done for all possible paths through the trellis. The Viterbi algorithm, discussed in Section 15.6.3, considerably reduces the complexity by applying some optimization concepts from dynamic programming.

15.6.3 The Viterbi Algorithm

The Viterbi algorithm (VA) is an efficient method for performing ML decoding of convolutional codes. It utilizes the trellis diagram to compute the path metrics. For hard-decision decoding, it finds the trellis path having the smallest Hamming distance metric relative to the received sequence. In the case of soft-decision decoding, the minimum Euclidean distance path metric is used to select the optimum path. The Viterbi algorithm is based on the Bellman-Ford Optimality principle from dynamic programming.

Bellman-Ford Optimality Principle

The optimal total path must lie along an optimum subpath from the beginning or end to any intermediate point.

The optimality principle is best explained by an example such as illustrated in Figure 15.15. If the optimal path from node 2 to node 6 includes node 4, then the subpath from node 4 to node 2 must be the minimum-distance path and the subpath from node 4 to node 6 must also be the minimum-distance path.

To understand the application of this principle to ML decoding of convolutional codes, consider a section of the trellis diagram in Figure 15.16. Note that after the trellis has developed into a fixed structure, there are only two branches entering each state. Now if the optimal path at a certain depth in the trellis passes through state S as shown in Figure 15.16, there are two paths that connect previous states, for example, S_1 and S_2 to this state. If we want to see which one of these two branches is a good candidate to minimize (or maximize) the overall path metric, we have to add partial metrics at states S_1 and S_2 to the metrics of the branches connecting these two states to the state S. Then obviously, the subpath that has minimum (or maximum) total metric accumulation up to state S is the **survivor path** at state S (otherwise it could not be the optimum subpath). The other path entering the state ("nonsurvivor path") is discarded. So at every stage in the trellis there are 2^{L-1} survivor paths, one for each encoder state. The Viterbi

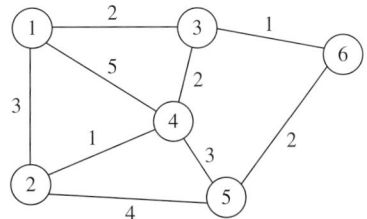

Figure 15.15 Calculation of the optimal (minimum-distance) path.

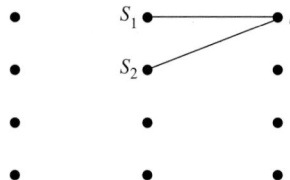

Figure 15.16 Section of code trellis.

algorithm iteratively proceeds in the trellis by eliminating the nonsurvivor paths. At the end, it selects the single survivor path left as the ML path. Trace-back of the ML path on the trellis diagram then provides the ML decoded sequence.

The Viterbi algorithm derives its efficiency from systematically discarding nonsurvivor paths of the trellis from consideration. It must keep track of 2^{L-1} survivor paths and their partial metrics. At each stage, in order to determine the survivor path, 2^L branch metrics must be computed. Thus, the number of computations in decoding and the memory requirements increase exponentially with the constraint length L. This has limited the implementation of convolutional codes to constraint lengths less than 10 in commercial applications. We shall refer to the Figure 15.17 which displays the trellis diagram for the encoder in Figure 15.12. $M = 6$ information bits are assumed. The trellis has been truncated by resetting the encoder with $L - 1 = 2$ tail bits.

Algorithm

Let $C_j(i)$ denote the partial path metric stored for state S_i at depth j. Assume $M = $ total number of information bits processed by the encoder. The received sequence $\underline{y}$ consists of $N = M + L - 1$ n-bit subsequence $\underline{y}_j = (y_{j1}, \dots, y_{jn})$. Place the received sequence $\underline{y}$ at the top of the trellis with the subsequence $\underline{y}_j$ displayed next to the depth j as displayed in Figure 15.17. The values of the received sequence $\underline{y}$ in the figure assume the use of hard-decision decoding.

1. Initialize the trellis. Set $j = 0$ and $C_0(0) = 0$, $C_0(i) = \infty$ for all $i \neq 0$ for hard-decision decoding. For soft-decision decoding, $C_0(i) = -\infty$ for all $i \neq 0$.
2. $j \to j + 1$. Let $\underline{x}_{\ell i} = (x_{\ell i}^1, \dots, x_{\ell i}^n)$ denote the encoder output subsequence accompanied with transition from state S_ℓ to state S_i. Label each branch with the corresponding $\underline{x}_{\ell i}$ subsequence.

   Compute the partial metric for all the paths entering a state by adding the branch metric entering that state to the partial metric of the connecting survivor at the preceding depth. That is,

$$C_j(i) = \begin{cases} \min_\ell \{C_{j-1}(\ell) + d_j(\ell, i)\} & \text{(Hard-decision decoding)} \\ \max_\ell \{C_{j-1}(\ell) + d_j(\ell, i)\} & \text{(Soft-decision decoding)} \end{cases}, i = 0, 1, \dots, 2^{L-1} - 1$$

(15.111)

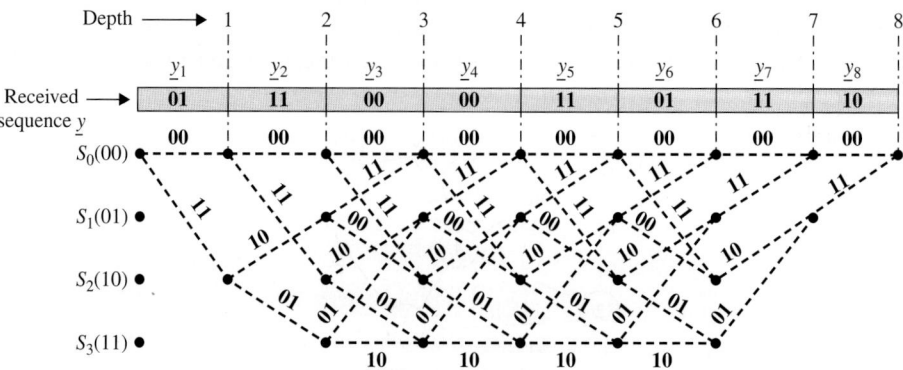

Figure 15.17 Truncated trellis diagram for the encoder in Figure 15.13.

where the metric for a branch originating at state S_ℓ and terminating at state S_i is given by

$$d_j(\ell, i) = \begin{cases} W_H(\underline{X}_{\ell i} \oplus \underline{y}_j) & \text{(Hard-decision decoding)} & (15.112) \\ \\ C_{SD}(\underline{r}_j, \underline{s}_{\ell i}) = \sum_{m=1}^{n} r_{jm} s_{\ell i}^m & \text{(Soft-decision decoding)} & (15.113) \end{cases}$$

$\underline{s}_{\ell i} = (s_{\ell i}^1, s_{\ell i}^2, \ldots, s_{\ell i}^n)$ is polar signal subsequence corresponding to the encoder n-bit output subsequence $\underline{x}_{\ell i} = (x_{\ell i}^1, x_{\ell i}^2 \ldots, x_{\ell i}^n)$. For each state, store the survivor path together with its partial path metric, and eliminate all other paths. Label each node with the corresponding partial path metric.

3. If $j < M + L - 1$, repeat step (2). Otherwise, stop.

The preceding description of the VA presumes that after M information bits, the encoder is reset with a sequence of $(L - 1)$ 0 bits. This allows the decoder to force all paths to state S_0 and complete the decoding.

Example 15.18

For (2, 1, 3) convolution encoder defined in Figure 15.13, apply Viterbi hard-decision decoding to determine the transmitted sequence corresponding to the received sequence 01 11 00 00 11 01 11 10.

Solution

Figure 15.18(a) displays the results of applying the VA at depth 1. We calculate the Hamming distance between the first received subsequence (01) and the encoder output bits on the trellis branches, leaving state S_0 at depth 0 and ending at depth 1 states. These Hamming distances are both 1 and are labeled next to state nodes at depth 1. The decoder stores these Hamming distances and proceeds to depth 2.

Figure 15.18(b) displays the results of applying the VA at depth 2. We see that there are now four paths, one for each state of the encoder. To calculate branch metrics, we calculate the Hamming distance between the second received subsequence (11) and encoder output bits on the trellis branches leading to depth 2 states. The accumulated partial metric for each of the four paths at depth 2 is now determined by adding these branch metrics to metrics noted above the states at depth 1. These partial metrics are now noted above state nodes at depth 2.

Figure 15.18(c) displays the results of applying the VA at depth 3. There are now two paths leading to each state at depth 3. The decoder computes partial metrics for both paths entering each state by adding the corresponding branch metric to the partial metric of the connecting survivor at depth 2. To calculate branch metrics, we calculate the Hamming distance between the third received subsequence (00) and encoder output bits on the trellis branches leading to depth 3 states. The decoder discards the path segment with the larger accumulated partial metric. This leaves one survivor path passing through each of the depth 3 state nodes. The partial metrics for survivor paths are now noted above state nodes at depth 3. In Figure 15.18(d), the surviving paths up to depth 3 are shown by solid lines and the paths not yet decoded by the decoder are shown as dashed lines.

The decoding process moves to depth 4 as illustrated in Figure 15.18(d). The Hamming distances for eight path segments are calculated, and the path segment with the smallest accumulated partial metric is retained as the survivor for each depth 4 state. The survivor paths up to depth 4 are shown by solid lines in Figure 15.18(e).

The decoding process is repeated for depths 5 through 8 as illustrated in Figures 15.18(e) through 15.18(h). Observe that at depth 7 only two paths remain as potential candidates for the ML decoded path. At depth 8 a single path is selected by the algorithm, and decoding is complete.

Figure 15.18 Viterbi algorithm for hard-decision decoding of the received sequence in Example 15.18.

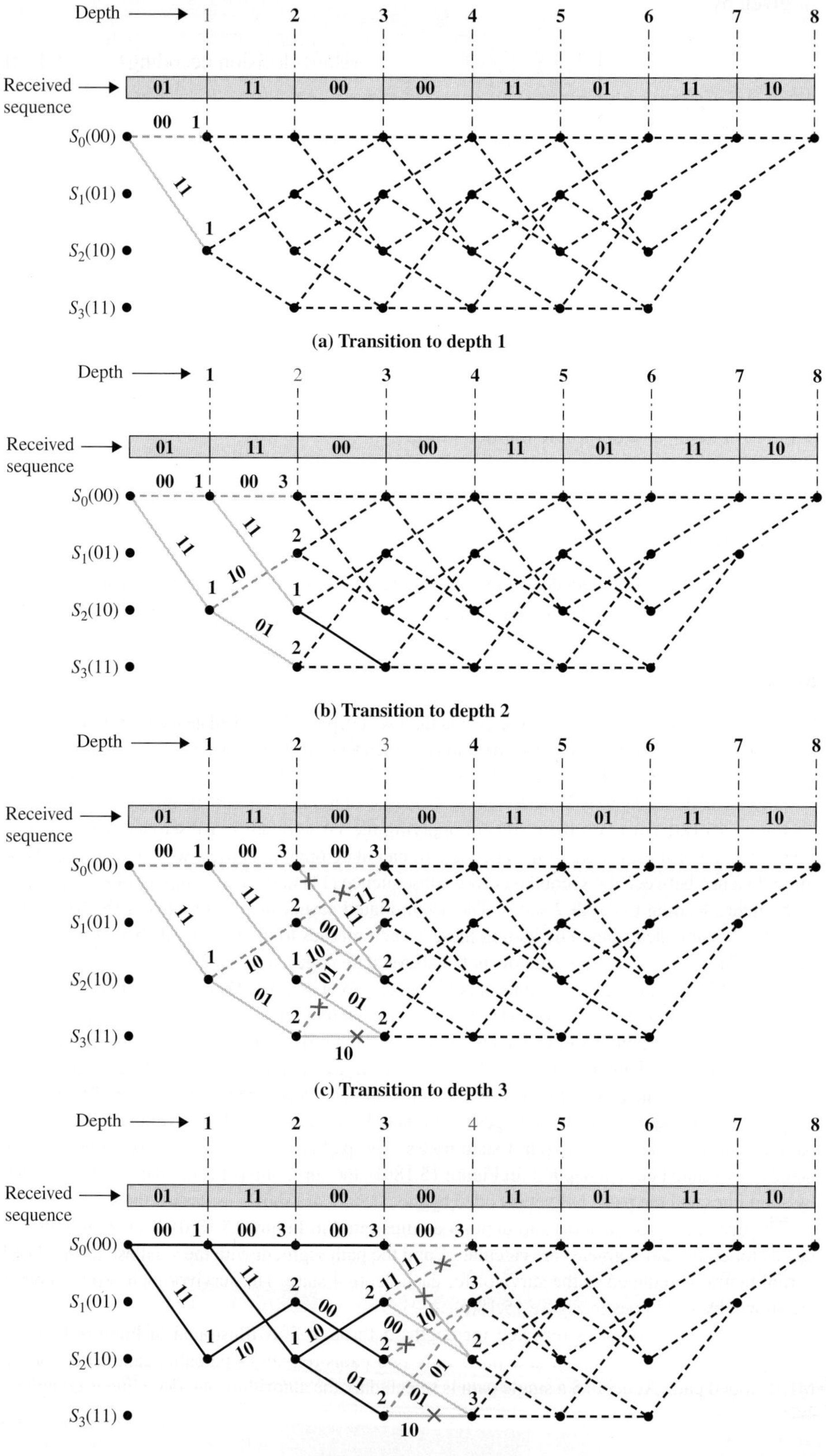

(a) Transition to depth 1

(b) Transition to depth 2

(c) Transition to depth 3

(d) Transition to depth 4

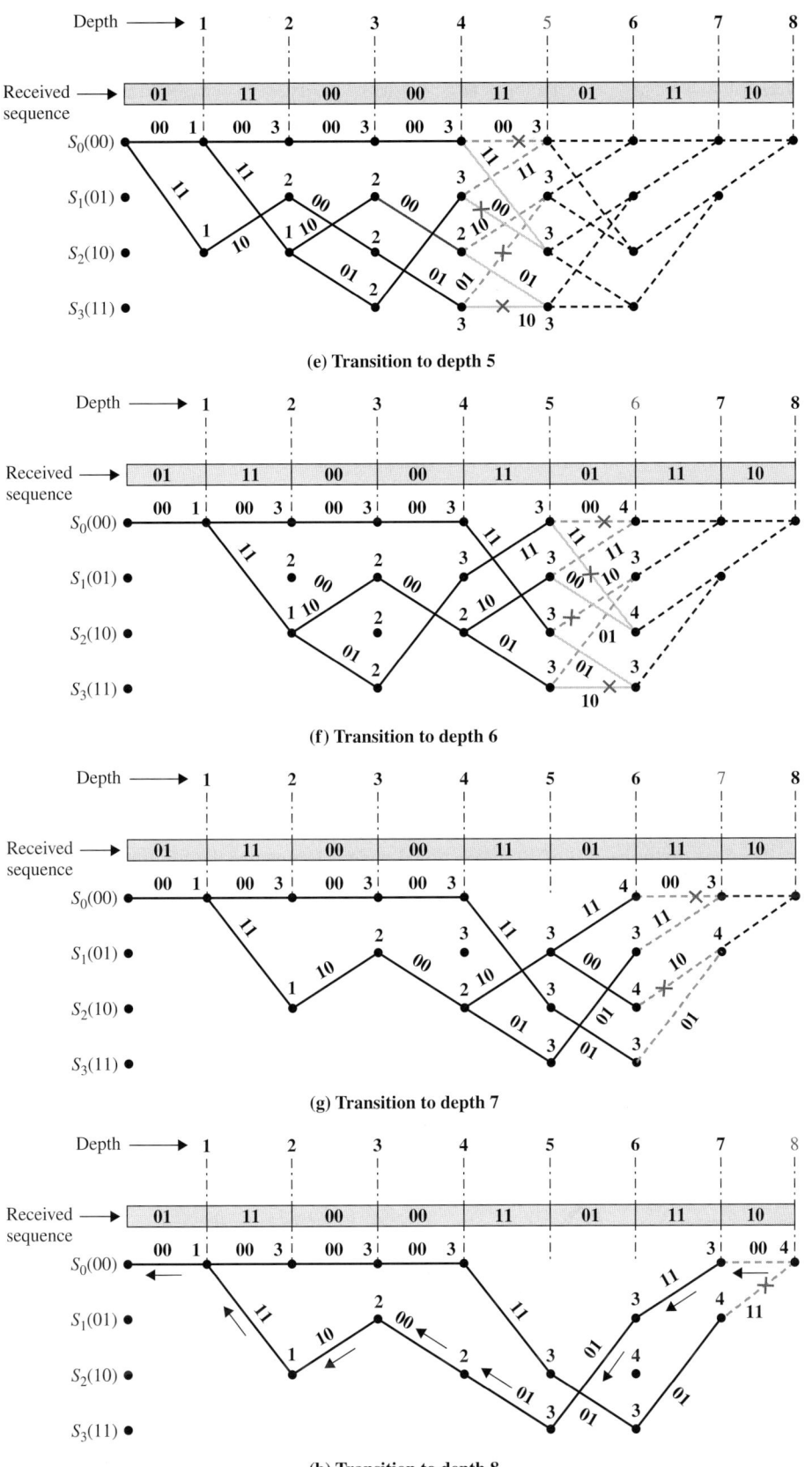

(e) Transition to depth 5

(f) Transition to depth 6

(g) Transition to depth 7

(h) Transition to depth 8

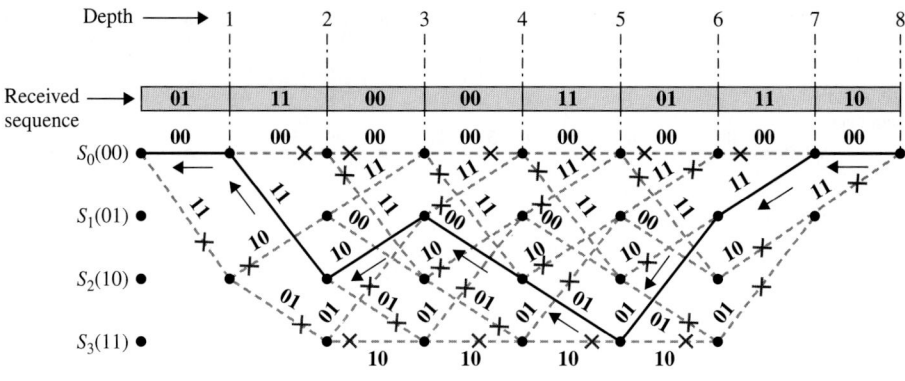

(i) Decoding of the received sequence by traceback

Figure 15.18(i) illustrates the entire VA decoding procedure for the received sequence 01 11 00 00 11 01 11 10. The discarded paths are indicated by the symbol $\times$. The ML decoded sequence is 00 11 10 00 01 01 11 00, whose Hamming distance to the received sequence is 3, and the respective information sequence is 0 1 0 1 1 0 0 0.

15.7　ERROR PERFORMANCE OF CONVOLUTIONAL CODES

Like the block codes, the error correction capability of convolutional codes depends on the distance between codeword sequences. Because convolutional codes are linear, we may assume without loss of generality that the all-zero sequence is transmitted. An error event occurs when a trellis path leaves the all-zero path and remerges with it after visiting one or more non-all-zero states. Figure 15.19 displays several such paths. To determine the minimum distance path, we are interested in enumerating the Hamming (or Euclidean) distance of all paths that diverge from the all-zero path and then merge with it. The **free distance** d_{free} of a convolutional code is defined as the minimum Hamming (or Euclidean) distance of all paths through the trellis to the all-zero path. An (n, k, L) convolutional code can correct t channel errors if d_{free} of the code satisfies

$$d_{\text{free}} > 2t \tag{15.114}$$

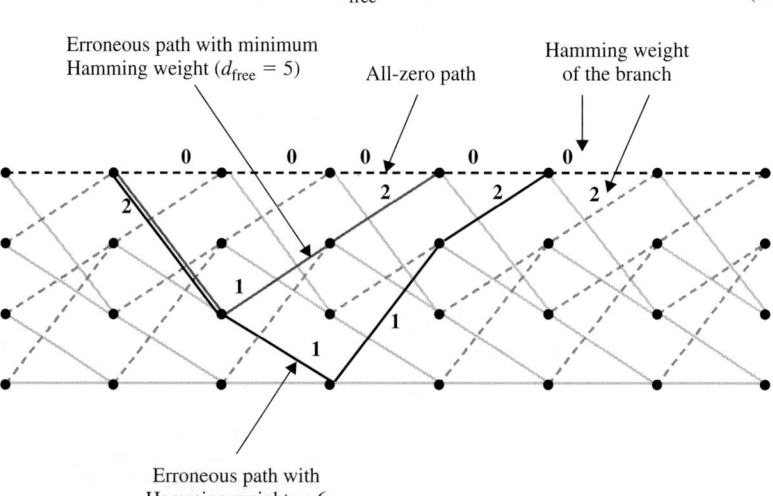

Figure 15.19　Error event paths.

Thus a code with $d_{\text{free}} = 3$ allows all one-bit errors to be corrected. A minimum distance of 5 allows two-bit errors to be corrected as well.

15.7.1 Transfer Function of a Convolutional Code

The computation of d_{free} is facilitated by using the transfer function of a convolutional code. The transfer function of a convolutional code is obtained by modifying its state-transition diagram to represent paths that diverge and remerge with the all-zero path. Figure 15.20 displays the modified state-transition diagram for the encoder in Figure 15.12. Note the following changes in the modified state diagram:

1. The all-zero state is split into two states to distinguish between the start all-zero state (S_0^{start}) and the end all-zero state (S_0^{end}). This makes it possible to represent paths that begin and end in this state.
2. Every branch of the modified state diagram is labeled with the symbol D whose exponent equals the Hamming weight of the encoder output bits generated by the state transition.
3. The exponent of label K represents the number of branches spanned by the path (that is, length of the path) in the process of a state transition.
4. The label J indicates the Hamming weight of the input sequence causing the state transition.

For example, the label of the branch representing transition from S_0^{start} to S_2 is D^2KJ because the Hamming weight of the output code bits is 2 and the transition is caused by an input bit 1. To find the transfer function for this system, the constitutive equations for all states in the system are derived as follows:

$$S_2 = D^2KJS_0^{start} + KJS_1$$

$$S_3 = \frac{DKJS_2}{1 - DKJ}$$

$$S_1 = DKS_3 + DKS_2$$

$$S_0^{end} = D^2KS_1 \tag{15.115}$$

The **transfer function** $T(D, K, J)$, describing the paths from S_0^{start} to S_0^{end}, is defined as

$$T(D, K, J) = \frac{S_0^{end}}{S_0^{start}} \tag{15.116}$$

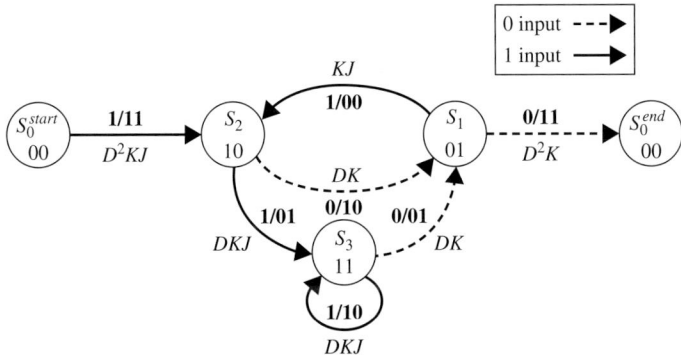

Figure 15.20 Modified state-transition diagram of (2, 1, 3) convolutional code.

Substituting (15.115) into (15.116) and rearranging terms, we obtain

$$T(D, K, J) = \frac{D^5 K^3 J}{1 - DJ(K + K^2)}$$

$$= D^5 K^3 J + D^6(K^4 + K^5)J^2 + D^7(K^5 + K^6 + K^7)J^3 + \ldots \quad (15.117)$$

Each term in the series (15.117) corresponds to a path that diverges from the all-zero path and merges back with it. For example, the first term corresponds to the path with Hamming distance = 5 and path length = 3 and results in a single-bit error (exponent of $J = 1$). The second term corresponds to a path with Hamming distance = 6 and path length = 4 and results in a two-bit error (exponent of $J = 2$). Thus, the transfer function is a convenient method of representing the Hamming distances, path lengths, and associated numbers of bit errors for all paths that diverge and remerge with the all-zero path. Because $d_{\text{free}} = 5$ for the (2, 1, 3) convolutional code, up to two errors in the received sequence are correctable. This is because with two or fewer transmission errors, the received sequence has a Hamming distance of at most 2 to the all-zero sequence versus a Hamming distance of at least 3 to any other code sequence in this code with $d_{\text{free}} = 5$.

15.7.2 Probability of Error for Convolutional Codes

For calculating error probabilities, we again assume that the all-zero sequence is transmitted without any loss of generality.

Viterbi Hard-Decision Decoding

An **error event** occurs if a path that diverges and remerges with the all-zero path accumulates a lower path metric. For an incorrect path to be selected, the received sequence y must be closer to it than the all-zero path. For this to happen, the received sequence y must have at least $\left\lfloor \dfrac{d}{2} + 1 \right\rfloor$ errors in bit positions where the incorrect path with Hamming distance d deviates from the all-zero path. Therefore, the probability of selecting an incorrect path at Hamming distance d from the all-zero path is given from (15.53) as

$$P_2(d) = \sum_{j=\lfloor 0.5d+1 \rfloor}^{d} \binom{d}{j} p^j (1 - p)^{d-j} \quad (15.118)$$

where p is the probability of the bit transmission error. As discussed in Section 15.4, the pairwise probability $P_2(d)$ is upper-bounded by

$$P_2(d) < [4p(1 - p)]^{d/2} \quad (15.119)$$

The **decoding sequence error probability** $P_{se}(e)$ is defined as the probability of selecting an incorrect sequence or path through the trellis. By invoking the union bound as we did in deriving (15.57), we can obtain an upper bound for $P_{se}(e)$ as follows:

$$P_{se}(e) < \sum_{d=d_{\text{free}}}^{\infty} a_d P_2(d) \quad (15.120)$$

where a_d is the number of paths at Hamming distance d that diverge and remerge with the all-zero path. Note that we can use (15.117) to enumerate the number of paths a_d for a given value of Hamming distance d. Substituting (15.119) into (15.120) yields

$$P_{se}(e) < \sum_{d=d_{\text{free}}}^{\infty} a_d [4p(1-p)]^{d/2} \tag{15.121}$$

Equation (15.121) can alternatively be expressed in terms of the transfer function of a convolutional code as

$$P_{se}(e) < T(D, 1, 1)\big|_{D=\sqrt{4p(1-p)}} \tag{15.122}$$

Note that K and J are set to 1 in (15.122) because the length and number of 1 information bits associated with a path do not affect the $P_{se}(e)$ calculation. Equation (15.122) provides an upper bound on the probability of choosing an incorrect path or sequence using Viterbi hard-decision decoding.

To evaluate the probability of decoded bit error P_b, we recall that the exponent of J for a given term in the infinite series representation (15.117) of the transfer function $T(D, K, J)$ indicates the number of 1 bits associated with the corresponding nonzero path. Consequently, the exponent of J equals the number of bit errors associated with the corresponding transfer function term. We can therefore use the transfer function to enumerate not only all the nonzero paths but also associated bit errors. In order to accomplish this, we need to change the exponent of J into a multiplier for each transfer function term in the representation (15.117). Therefore, we differentiate the infinite series (15.117) for the transfer function $T(D, 1, J)$ with respect to J and then set $J = 1$.

$$\frac{dT(D, 1, J)}{dJ}\bigg|_{J=1} = D^5 + (2 \cdot 2)D^6 + (3 \cdot 3)D^7 + \ldots$$

$$= \sum_{d=d_{free}}^{\infty} c_d D^d \tag{15.123}$$

Note that K is set to 1 because path length does affect the probability of decoded bit error calculations. The first term in (15.123) corresponds to the path with Hamming distance $= 5$ and results in a single-bit error. The second term corresponds to a path with Hamming distance $= 6$ and results in a two-bit errors. In general, c_d bit errors are caused by erroneous paths that are at a Hamming distance of d from the all-zero path. Using the coefficients c_d to weight the pairwise probabilities $P_2(d)$, an upper bound on the probability of decoded bit error P_b can be written as

$$P_b \leq \sum_{d=d_{\text{free}}}^{\infty} c_d P_2(d) \tag{15.124}$$

Now substituting (15.119) into (15.124) yields the upper bound

$$P_b < \sum_{d=d_{\text{free}}}^{\infty} c_d [4p(1-p)]^{d/2} \tag{15.125}$$

We can alternatively express the upper bound on P_b in terms of the transfer function of a convolutional code as

$$P_b < \left. \frac{dT(D, 1, J)}{dJ} \right|_{J=1, D=\sqrt{4p(1-p)}} \tag{15.126}$$

Table 15.7 summarizes the characteristics of well-known convolutional codes along with values of c_d for the most likely error events.

Viterbi Soft-Decision Decoding

The pairwise probability $P_2(d)$ of selecting an incorrect path at Hamming distance d from the all-zero path is given from (15.74) as

$$P_2(d) = Q\left(\sqrt{\frac{4E_{cb}d}{2N_o}}\right) \tag{15.74}$$

Substituting (15.74) into (15.120), the upper bound on probability $P_{se}(e)$ can be written as

$$P_{se}(e) < \sum_{d=d_{\text{free}}}^{\infty} a_d Q\left(\sqrt{\frac{2dR_cE_b}{N_o}}\right) \tag{15.127}$$

Applying the Chernoff upper bound for the Q-function, (15.127) can be further simplified for low-error probability channels as

$$P_{se}(e) < \sum_{d=d_{\text{free}}}^{\infty} a_d e^{-dR_cE_b/N_o} \tag{15.128}$$

The upper bound of the probability of decoded bit error P_b is obtained by substituting (15.74) into (15.124) as

$$P_b < \sum_{d=d_{\text{free}}}^{\infty} c_d P_2(d) = \sum_{d=d_{\text{free}}}^{\infty} c_d Q\left(\sqrt{\frac{2dR_cE_b}{N_o}}\right) \approx \sum_{d=d_{\text{free}}}^{\infty} c_d e^{-dR_cE_b/N_o} \tag{15.129}$$

Table 15.7 Characteristics of Popular Convolutional Codes

Code Rate	Constraint Length	Code Generator Polynomials	Free Distance d_{free}	c_d			
				d_{free}	$d_{\text{free}} + 1$	$d_{\text{free}} + 2$	$d_{\text{free}} + 3$
1/2	3	(7, 5)	5	1	4	12	32
1/2	5	(35, 23)	7	4	12	20	72
1/2	7	(171, 133)	10	36	0	211	0
1/2	9	(753, 561)	12	33	0	281	0
1/3	3	(7, 7, 5)	8	3	0	15	0
1/3	5	(37, 33, 25)	12	12	0	12	0
1/3	7	(171, 145, 133)	14	1	0	20	0

The upper bounds in (15.128) and (15.129) can alternatively be expressed in terms of the transfer function of a convolutional code as

$$P_{se}(e) < T(D, 1, 1)|_{D=e^{-R_cE_b/N_o}} \qquad (15.130)$$

$$P_b < \left.\frac{dT(D, 1, J)}{dJ}\right|_{J=1, D=e^{-R_cE_b/N_o}} \qquad (15.131)$$

Figure 15.21 compares the performance of rate 1/2 convolutional code obtained by Simulink simulation for several constraint lengths using the Viterbi hard-decision decoding algorithm. For comparison, the upper bound in (15.129) is plotted as well for each constraint length. The free distance and probability of decoded bit error performance improves with the constraint length. The coding gain at $P_b = 10^{-5}$ is approximately 3.8 dB versus uncoded BPSK for the constraint length of 9. Figure 15.22 illustrates the performance of Viterbi soft-and hard-decision decoding schemes for (8, 2, 7) convolutional code with generator polynomials (171, 133). Soft-decision decoding outperforms hard-decision decoding by better than 2 dB.

15.7.3 Coding Gain

For hard-decision decoding, the probability of decoded bit error P_b for a convolutional code with free distance d_{free} can be approximated from (15.125) for p small as

$$P_b \approx c_{d_{\text{free}}}(4p)^{d_{\text{free}}/2} \qquad (15.132)$$

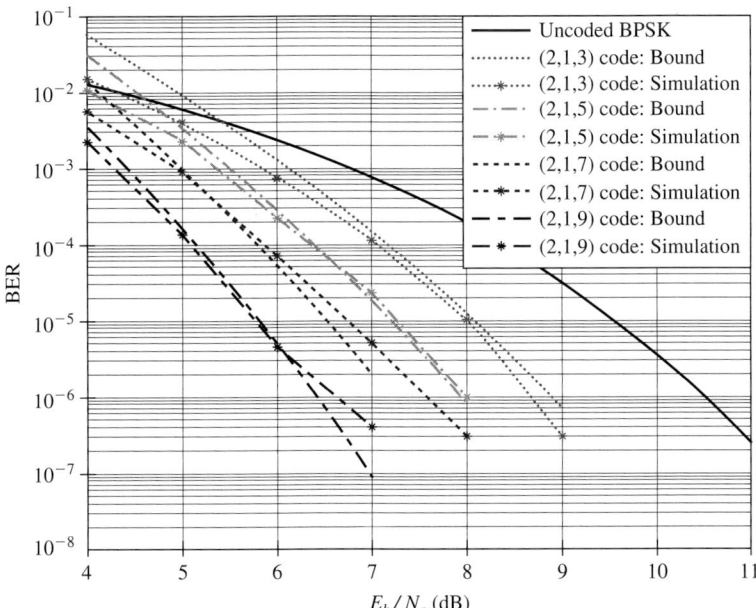

Figure 15.21 Probability of decoded bit error performance of convolutional codes for various constraint lengths.

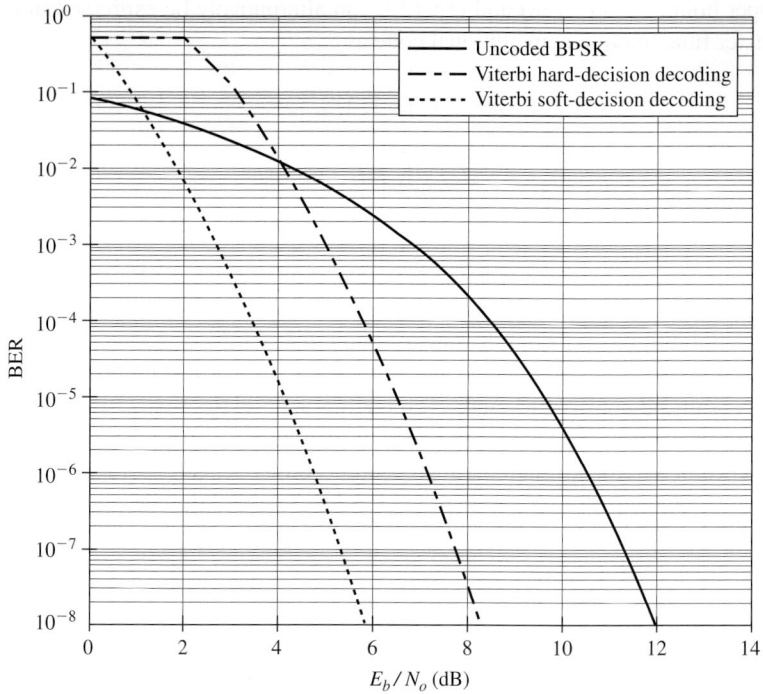

Figure 15.22 Error performance of (8, 2, 7) convolutional code: Viterbi hard- versus soft-decision decoding.

where p = BER of the transmission link. Substituting $p = Q\left(\sqrt{2R_c\left(\dfrac{E_b}{N_o}\right)_{\text{coded}}}\right)$ into (15.132) yields

$$P_b \approx c_{d_{\text{free}}} 2^{d_{\text{free}}} \left(Q\left(\sqrt{2R_c\left(\frac{E_b}{N_o}\right)_{\text{coded}}} \right) \right)^{d_{\text{free}}/2} \approx c_{d_{\text{free}}} 2^{d_{\text{free}}/2} e^{-\frac{R_c d_{\text{free}}}{2}\left(\frac{E_b}{N_o}\right)_{\text{coded}}} \quad (15.133)$$

For an uncoded BPSK system, the BER is approximated by invoking Chernoff bound on the Q-function as

$$P_b = Q\left(\sqrt{\left(\frac{2E_b}{N_o}\right)_{\text{uncoded}}} \right) \approx \frac{1}{2} e^{-\left(\frac{E_b}{N_o}\right)_{\text{uncoded}}} \quad (15.134)$$

To achieve the same probability of decoded bit error P_b, the exponential terms in (15.133) and (15.134) must be equal as discussed in Section 15.4.2. That is,

$$\frac{R_c d_{\text{free}}}{2}\left(\frac{E_b}{N_o}\right)_{\text{coded}} = \left(\frac{E_b}{N_o}\right)_{\text{uncoded}} \quad \text{for large values of } E_b/N_o \quad (15.135)$$

Therefore, the asymptotic coding gain for hard-decision decoding is given by

$$G_{hd} = 10\log_{10}\frac{(E_b/N_o)_{\text{uncoded}}}{(E_b/N_o)_{\text{coded}}} \approx 10\log_{10}\frac{R_c d_{\text{free}}}{2} \quad (15.136)$$

Similarly, it can be shown that for soft-decision decoding, the asymptotic coding gain is given by

$$G_{sd} \approx 10 \log_{10} R_c d_{\text{free}} \qquad (15.137)$$

We conclude by comparing (15.137) with (15.136) that soft-decision decoding offers a 3-dB advantage over hard-decision decoding for convolutional codes as well.

15.8   TURBO CODES

Turbo codes, which achieve performance within a fraction of a dB of the Shannon limit, were first introduced in a landmark paper by Berrou, Glavieux, and Thitimajshima.[5] This remarkable performance is made possible by combining two key techniques: parallel concatenated convolutional coding and **maximum a posteriori probability (MAP)** iterative decoding. The name is derived from the iterative decoding algorithm used to decode these codes where, like a turbo engine, part of the output is reintroduced at the input and processed again.

Turbo codes use two convolutional encoders at the transmitter as illustrated in Figure 15.23. Information bits entering the transmitter are copied to Encoder 1 and Encoder 2. Before entering Encoder 2, the data bits are scrambled by the pseudorandom interleaver. The interleaver (π) is used to permute the input data bits such that the two encoders are operating on the same block of information bits, but in a different order. This encoder structure is called a **parallel concatenation** because the two encoders operate on the same block of input bits as compared to traditional serial concatenation where the second encoder operates on the output bits of the first encoder. Encoder 1 computes parity sequence x_i^1 from the information sequence m_i. Because the interleaver reorders the information sequence, Encoder 2 generates different parity sequence x_i^2 from the scrambled data bits. The encoder output consists of the information sequence and two parity sequences, thus representing a code rate of 1/3. Puncturing (deleting) bits, alternately, from the two parity sequences produces a code rate of 1/2, and other code rates can be achieved by using additional parity generators and/or different puncturing patterns. In essence, the interleaver has the effect of producing some random behavior in the code much as Shannon's random codes would do.

15.8.1   Turbo Decoding

Turbo codes use two decoders that work cooperatively in an iterative fashion to produce more reliable decisions. Figure 15.24 illustrates the basic components of the turbo decoder. Each decoder performs soft input–soft output decoding that assigns a reliability measure for each decoded bit. The reliability measure is in the form of an integer value that indicates how likely the detected bit is to be a 0 or a 1. For example, -7

[5] C. Berrou, M. Glavieux, and P. Thitimajshima, "Near Shannon Limit Error-correcting Coding and Decoding: Turbo Codes," *Proceedings of IEEE International Conference on Communications*, (Geneva, Switzerland, May 1993), 1064–1070; C. Berrou and M. Glavieux, "Near Optimum Error-Correcting Coding and Decoding: Turbo Codes," *IEEE Transactions on Communications* 44 (1996): 1261–1271.

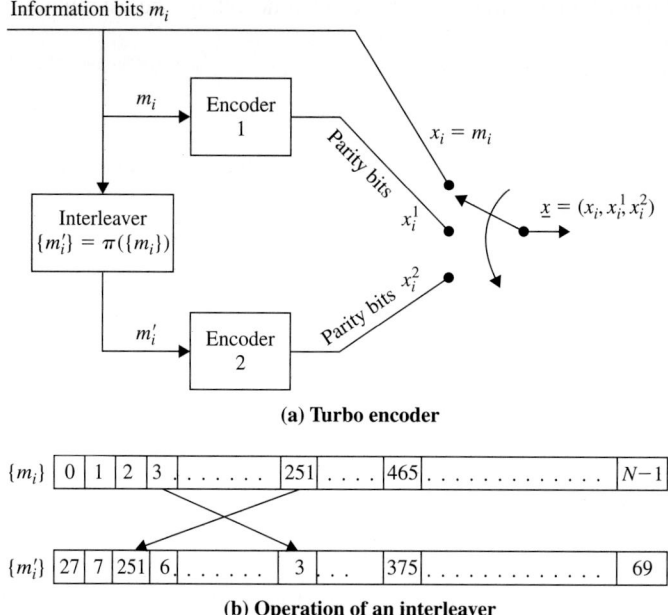

(a) Turbo encoder

(b) Operation of an interleaver

Figure 15.23 Turbo encoder.

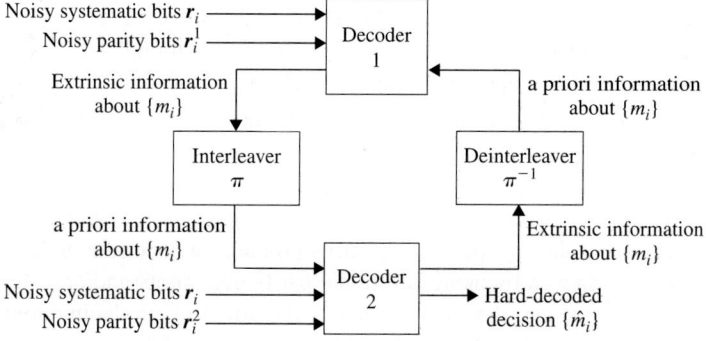

Figure 15.24 Turbo decoder.

means the detected bit is almost certainly a 0; $+7$ means it is almost certainly a 1. The sequence of reliability values generated by one decoder is passed to the other after interleaving or deinterleaving as appropriate. In this way, each decoder takes advantage of the "suggestions" of the other one. After several iterations, the final output is a hard decision on the information bits $\{m_i\}$. Bahl, Cocke, Jelinek, and Raviv[6] developed an algorithm (called the **BCJR algorithm**) that is both soft-input and soft-output. It is also called the MAP or the **a posteriori probability (APP) algorithm.** Another popular soft input–soft output algorithm is a modified version of the Viterbi algorithm discussed

[6] L. Bahl, J. Cocke, F. Jelinek, and J. Raviv, "Optimal Decoding of Linear Codes for Minimizing Symbol Error Rate," *IEEE Transactions on Information Theory* IT-20, (1974): 284–287.

in relation to the decoding of convolutional codes in Section 15.5.3. It is called the **soft-output Viterbi algorithm (SOVA).**[7]

The reliability measure computed by the BCJR decoder is the **log-likelihood ratio (LLR).** It is defined as

$$L(m_i) = \log_e \frac{P(m_i = 1 | \text{inputs})}{P(m_i = 0 | \text{inputs})} \qquad (15.138)$$

where the word *inputs* refers to all the decoder inputs. We observe that the LLR is a function of the a posteriori probabilities of the message bit m_i given our knowledge of all the received signal observations. The LLR provides soft information about m_i as follows:

1. The sign of $L(m_i)$ indicates whether the message bit m_i is likely to take the possible value 1 ($L(m_i) > 0$) or 0($L(m_i) < 0$).
2. The magnitude of $L(m_i)$ is a measure of confidence on how likely the message bit m_i takes the value 1 or 0. A large positive value of $L(m_i)$ increases our confidence that m_i is likely to take the possible value 1 and vice versa.

The output of the BCJR decoder can be expressed as sum of three terms[8]

$$L(m_i) = L_{ch}(m_i) + L_{ex}(m_i) + L_{ap}(m_i) \qquad (15.139)$$

where $L_{ch}(m_i)$ describes the information about the message bit m_i obtained by observing the channel output samples (r_i, r_i^1, r_i^2). $L_{ap}(m_i)$ represents the a priori information about m_i. A positive value of $L_{ap}(m_i)$ would indicate that $m_i = 1$ was likely to have been transmitted, while a negative value of $L_{ap}(m_i)$ would indicate that $m_i = 0$ was likely to have been transmitted. $L_{ex}(m_i)$ is called the **extrinsic information,** and it refers to the new information about the current bit m_i obtained from the a priori and channel information about other bits, invoking the correlation between m_i and these bits. The extrinsic information from one decoder becomes the a priori information for the other decoder.

Figure 15.25 illustrates the detailed implementation of an iterative, rate 1/3 turbo decoder. For polar binary signaling over AWGN, the resulting inputs to Decoder 1, corresponding to the systematic bit x_i and parity bit x_i^1, are given by

$$r_i = \sqrt{E_{cb}}(2x_i - 1) + n_i$$
$$r_i^1 = \sqrt{E_{cb}}(2x_i^1 - 1) + n_i^1 \qquad (15.140)$$

where $E_{cb} = kE_b/n$ is the energy of the coded bit. n_i and n_i^1 are independent and identical Gaussian random variables with mean 0 and variance $N_o/2$. It can be shown that

$$L_{ch}(m_i) = \log_e \frac{f_{r_i}(r_i | x_i = 1)}{f_{r_i}(r_i | x_i = 0)} = \gamma_c r_i \qquad (15.141)$$

---

[7] J. Hagenauer and P. Hoeher, "A Viterbi Algorithm with Soft Decision Outputs and Its Applications, " *Proceedings of IEEE GLOBECOM Conference,* (Dallas, TX, November 1989), 1680–1686.

[8] B. Sklar, "A Primer on Turbo Code Concepts," *IEEE Communications Magazine* 35 (1997): 94–102.

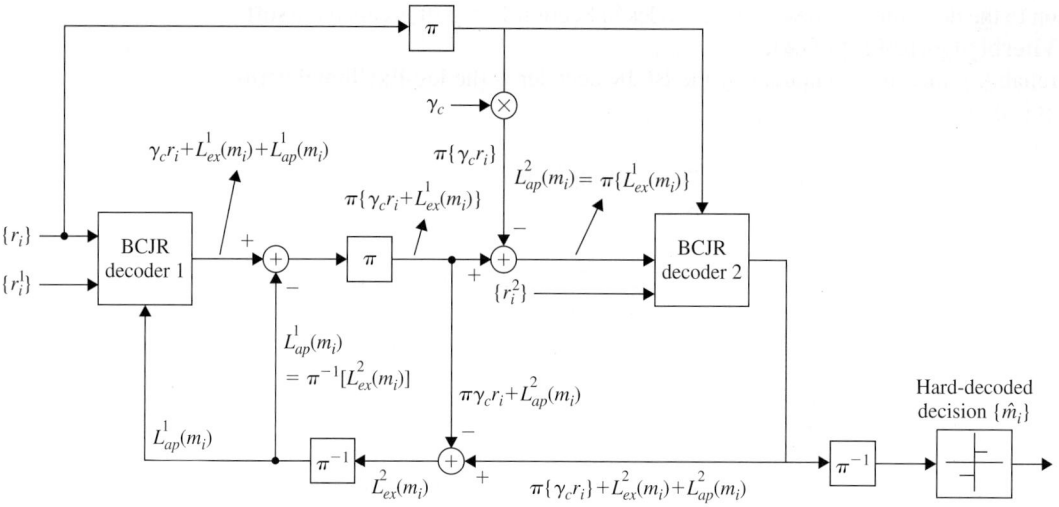

Figure 15.25   Detailed implementation of an iterative, rate 1/3 turbo decoder.

where $\gamma_c = \dfrac{4E_{cb}}{N_o}$ is the channel reliability parameter. For the first iteration, the output of BCJR Decoder 1 is given by

$$L(m_i) = \gamma_c r_i + L_{ex}^1(m_i) + L_{ap}^1(m_i) \tag{15.142}$$

Because we know nothing about the bit m_i at this stage, we set $L_{ap}^1(m_i) = 0$. Note that we subtract $\gamma_c r_i + L_{ap}^1(m_i)$ from $L(m_i)$ to obtain the extrinsic information $L_{ex}^1(m_i)$ from the BCJR Decoder 1. The extrinsic information from Decoder 1 becomes the a priori information for Decoder 2 after the interleaving operation. That is,

$$L_{ap}^2(m_i) = \pi\{L_{ex}^1(m_i)\} \tag{15.143}$$

Note that the interleaver plays an important role in randomizing the burst errors from the decoder. The larger the interleaver, the better the error bursts can be decorrelated. The BCJR Decoder 2 utilizes noisy values r_i and r_i^2, respectively, of the systematic bit x_i and parity bit x_i^2 as well as a priori information sent by Decoder 1. The LLR produced by Decoder 2 is given by

$$L(m_i) = \pi(\gamma_c r_i) + L_{ex}^2(m_i) + L_{ap}^2(m_i) \tag{15.144}$$

The decisions produced by Decoder 2 should have fewer errors because of the information provided by Decoder 1. Turbo decoding proceeds in an iterative fashion as the two decoders alternately update their LLR values. Eventually both decoders should agree on their LLR values to a hard decision on m_i. This corresponds to the event that all the errors are corrected, or there remains an error pattern that cannot be corrected, despite the interleaving and deinterleaving processes. Again, the deinterleaver plays a key role in this effort by randomizing the burst errors from the decoder.

Information bits m_i

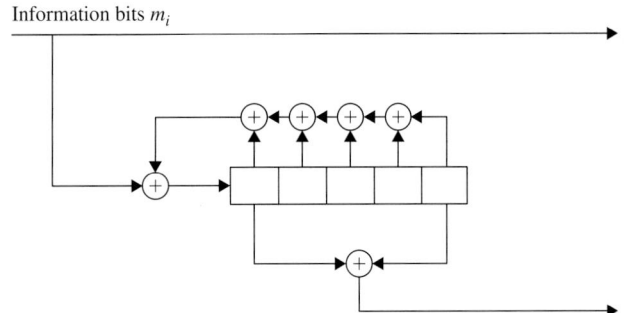

Figure 15.26 A recursive systematic convolutional encoder.

15.8.2   Performance of Turbo Codes

The performance of turbo codes depends on the interleaver size, the interleaver design, the constituent codes, and the number of decoder iterations. To illustrate the impact of various design choices on the performance of turbo codes, we consider the original code by Berrou, Glavieux, and Thitimajshima.[9] The design used the **recursive systematic (RS)** convolutional encoder shown in Figure 15.26. The forward and feedback connections of the RS convolutional encoder are described by the generator polynomial vectors $\underline{g}_1$ = (1 0 0 0 1) and $\underline{g}_2$ = (1 1 1 1 1), respectively. In the octal form, these vectors are represented as 21 and 37, respectively. The encoder incorporated an interleaver of depth $N = 2^{16}$ = 65536. The turbo code is represented using the shorthand notation (37, 21, 65536).

The simulated performance of the code over multiple iterations of the decoder is displayed in Figure 15.27. The decoder converges after approximately 18 iterations. Note that the code achieves a probability of decoded bit error performance of 10^{-6} at an E_b/N_o of 0.9 dB, which is within 0.7 dB of the Shannon limit for binary codes! Figure 15.28 compares the performance of the (37, 21, 65536) turbo code with the NASA standard concatenated code. The latter consists of an inner rate-1/2, constraint length 7 convolutional code with free distance $d_{\text{free}} = 10$ along with an outer (255, 223, 33) RS code. The real coding gain of the NASA code is about 1.6 dB less, even though its rate is lower and its decoding complexity is about the same.

Turbo codes, however, exhibit error floors for moderate to high E_b/N_o values as is evident from Figure 15.27. The probability of decoded bit error performance curve exhibits cliff behavior with increasing E_b/N_o up to a certain point. After this point, the performance curve flattens out. The error floors may be problematic in applications that require very low bit error rates. The error floor can be manipulated by changing the depth of the interleaver. For a given code, increasing the interleaver depth lowers the error floor, and the probability of decoded bit error curve does not flatten until higher SNRs and lower error rates are reached. Conversely, decreasing the interleaver depth results in the error floor being raised, and the probability of decoded bit error curve flattens at slightly lower SNRs and higher error rates. Figure 15.29 illustrates simulations demonstrating the effect of the interleaver depth for (37, 21) turbo code. The disadvantage of increasing the interleaver depth is the corresponding increases in the encoding and decoding delays, which may not be acceptable in some applications.

[9] C. Berrou, M. Glavieux, and P. Thitimajshima, "Near Shannon Limit Error-Correcting Coding and Decoding: Turbo Codes," *Proceedings of IEEE International Conference on Communications,* Geneva, Switzerland (May 1993), 1064–1070; C. Berrou and M. Glavieux, "Near Optimum Error-Correcting Coding and Decoding: Turbo Codes," *IEEE Transactions on Communications* 44 (1996): 1261–1271.

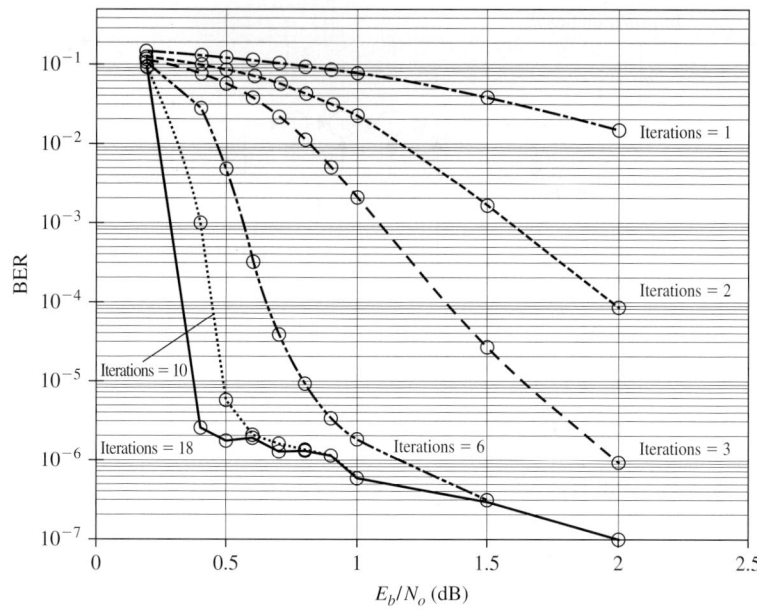

Figure 15.27 Performance of (37, 21, 65536) turbo code for different iterations.

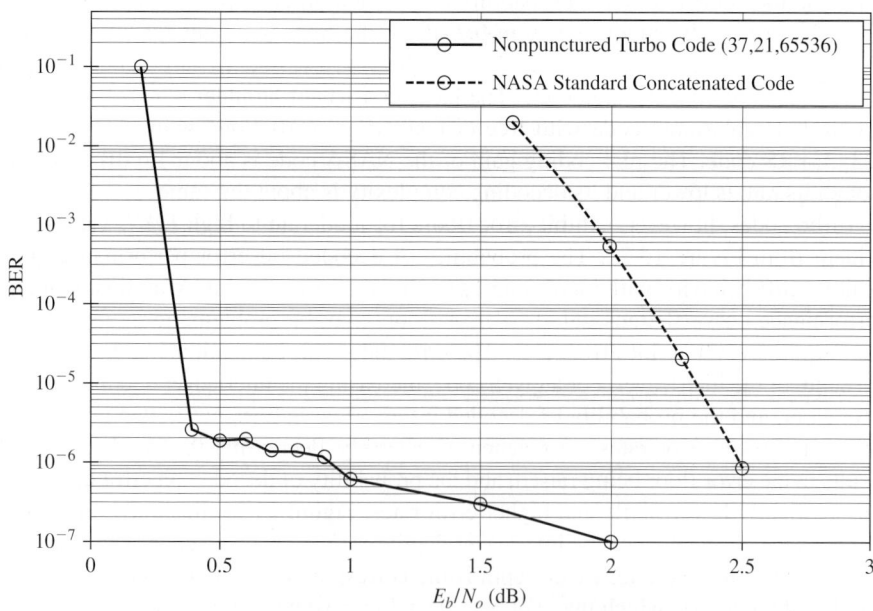

Figure 15.28 Performance comparison of a turbo code and a convolutional code.

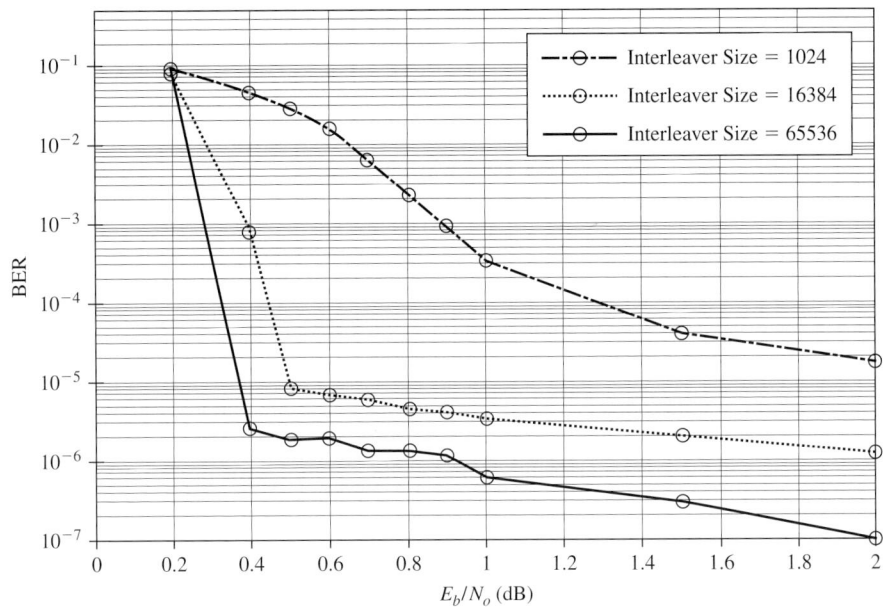

Figure 15.29 Effect of the interleaver depth on the performance of a turbo code.

15.9 TRELLIS-CODED MODULATION

The channel coding techniques considered so far provide coding gain (reduced power) at the expense of increased bandwidth or reduced user data rate. The bandwidth expansion is inversely proportional to the code rate R_c. Shannon's channel coding theorem promised the possibility of simultaneously reducing both power and bandwidth requirements through coding. Trellis-coded modulation (TCM) is a combined coding and modulation scheme that jointly optimizes both power and bandwidth efficiency. As a result, significant coding gains are achieved without bandwidth expansion. TCM, invented by Ungerboeck in the late 1970s, uses M-ary signal sets (e.g., M-PSK or M-QAM) and error correction coding to increase the Euclidean distance between coded sequences.[10]

Figure 15.30 displays unit energy constellations of QPSK and 8-PSK modulation schemes. These signaling systems respectively transmit 2 and 3 information bits/symbol. We observed in Section 11.7 that the minimum squared Euclidean distance, $d_{\min}^2$, decreases as the number signal points in the constellation increases. We know from Section 11.7 that

$$d_{\min}^2 = \begin{cases} 2E_s, & \text{QPSK} \\ 0.586E_s, & \text{8-PSK} \end{cases} \tag{15.145}$$

---

[10] G. Ungerboeck, "Trellis-Coded Modulation with Redundant Signal Sets Part I: Introduction," *IEEE Communications Magazine* 25, (February 1987), 5–11.

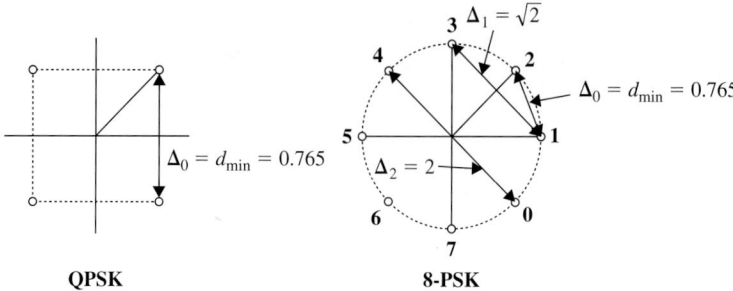

Figure 15.30 Uncoded QPSK and 8-PSK constellations: $E_s = 1$ assumed.

Because there is no correlation between consecutive transmitted symbols, symbol-by-symbol detection is employed at the receiver. As discussed in Chapter 11, reduction in the distance between signal points increases the symbol error probability, as is evident from the nearest-neighbor bound

$$P_e \approx 2Q\left(\sqrt{\frac{d_{min}^2}{2N_o}}\right) \tag{15.146}$$

For $E_s/N_o = 9.6$ dB, QPSK achieves a symbol error rate of 10^{-5}. This degrades to $\sim 10^{-3}$ for 8-PSK. Thus in uncoded systems, it is the Euclidean distance between the signal points in the constellation that determines the probability of error performance.

The key idea in TCM is to transmit sequences of correlated symbols that are separated by large Euclidean distances using a combination of convolutional coding and constellation mapping. At the decoder, sequence detection (as in convolutional codes) rather than symbol-by-symbol detection is used. As discussed in Section 15.6, the probability of detecting an incorrect sequence can be approximated from (15.128) as

$$P_{se}(e) \approx a_{d_{free}} e^{-d_{free}R_c E_b/N_o} \tag{15.147}$$

where $a_{d_{free}}$ denotes the average number of nearest neighbor signal sequences at distance d_{free} that diverge from the transmitted signal sequence and then merge with it. Thus, it is the Euclidean distance between the sequences that determines the coding gain of TCM.

A TCM encoder incorporates the functions of a rate $R_c = k/k + 1$ convolutional encoder followed by a **constellation mapper** that assigns blocks of $(k + 1)$ bits to one of the 2^{k+1}-points in the modulation scheme signal constellation. We will use the example in Figure 15.31 to illustrate the key concepts of TCM. The convolutional encoder is rate 1/2 generating two output bits for each input bit. The state of the convolutional encoder is represented by the contents (m_{i-1}^1, m_{i-2}^1) of the shift register. Therefore, there are four possible states: $S_0 = (0, 0)$, $S_1 = (1, 0)$, $S_2 = (0, 1)$, $S_3 = (1, 1)$. In each symbol interval, a new input bit m_i^1 causes convolutional encoder state transition and generates an output pair (x_i^1, x_i^0). Note that the most significant bit m_i^2 of the input data pair is left uncoded. At each symbol interval, the binary triplet (x_i^2, x_i^1, x_i^0) is assigned one of the eight signal points in the 8-PSK constellation by the mapper. Thus the bandwidth of the modulated signal is not expanded as the symbol rate remains unchanged.

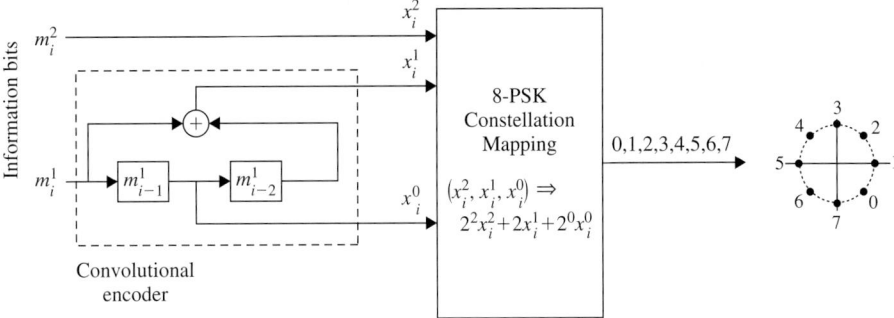

Figure 15.31 TCM encoder.

However, the Euclidean distance between signal points is decreased because an 8-PSK constellation is denser than that of QPSK.

The advantage of the TCM stems from the fact that the convolutional coder allows only certain sequences of successive signal constellation points. As discussed in Section 15.7, the performance of an ML sequence decoder (e.g., Viterbi) is determined by the Euclidean distance between the allowed symbol sequences rather than $d_{\min}$ of the constellation. So if we can exploit the constellation mapping function to map TCM encoder bits (x_i^2, x_i^1, x_i^0) in such a manner that the Euclidean distance between the allowed symbol sequences is increased, coding gain can be obtained compared to the uncoded system, even with a denser signal constellation.

Like convolutional codes, it is useful to consider a trellis diagram representation of a TCM encoder as illustrated in Figure 15.32. The nodes in this transition diagram are the states of the convolutional encoder, and the branches represent the possible transitions between states. The labels along each branch represent the resulting output signal point in the constellation assigned by the mapper. As an example, if the convolution encoder is in state $S_0 = (0, 0)$, the input bit $m_i^1 = 1$ causes a transition to $S_1 = (1, 0)$ while

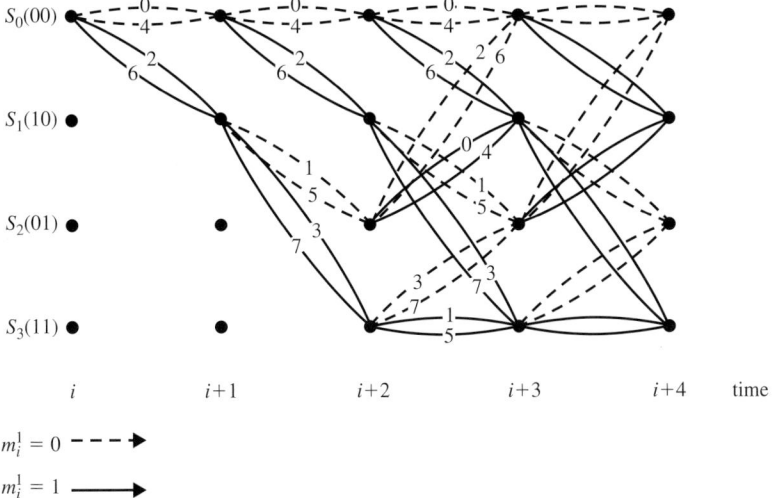

Figure 15.32 Trellis diagram for TCM encoder.

generating the encoder output pair (10). The effect of the uncoded bit m_i^2 is to generate, respectively, the output symbol 2 or 6 depending on its value being 0 or 1. Note that each path through the trellis corresponds to a unique message sequence and is associated with a unique sequence of modulated symbols (i.e., signal points 0, 1, 2, 3, 4, 5, 6, 7). The term *trellis-coded modulation* originates from the fact that the TCM encoded sequences consist of modulated symbols rather than binary digits.

The Mapping Function

The constellation mapper seeks the optimal assignment of constellation signal points so that different symbol sequences are separated by large squared Euclidean distances. Because the free distance, d_{free}, represents the minimum Euclidean distance between two paths through a trellis that diverge from one node and merge later, it has become the major design criterion for trellis codes. Ungerboeck has developed a heuristic design approach to map convolutional encoder transitions to constellation signal points in such a manner that d_{free}^2 is maximized.[11] This mapping is achieved through **set partitioning**. The 2^{k+1}-point constellation with $d_{\min} = \Delta_0$ is successively partitioned into subconstellations such that minimum distances $\Delta_0 < \Delta_1 < \Delta_2 < \ldots$ increase at each stage. Figure 15.33 illustrates the partitioning process for an 8-PSK constellation. The 8-PSK constellation has the minimum Euclidean distance $\Delta_0 = 0.765$. At the next stage, subconstellations B_0 and B_1 have four signal points each, and the minimum Euclidean distance has increased to $\Delta_1 = \sqrt{2}$. Next, subconstellations C_0, C_1, C_2, and C_3 have two signal points each, and the minimum Euclidean distance has increased to $\Delta_2 = 2$. Ungerboeck's design rules can now be stated as follows:

1. Parallel transitions, corresponding to two paths associated with each uncoded bit, are assigned signal points in the subconstellation with the largest Euclidean distance (e.g., C_0, C_1, C_2, and C_3 with $\Delta_2 = 2$ in our 8-PSK example).

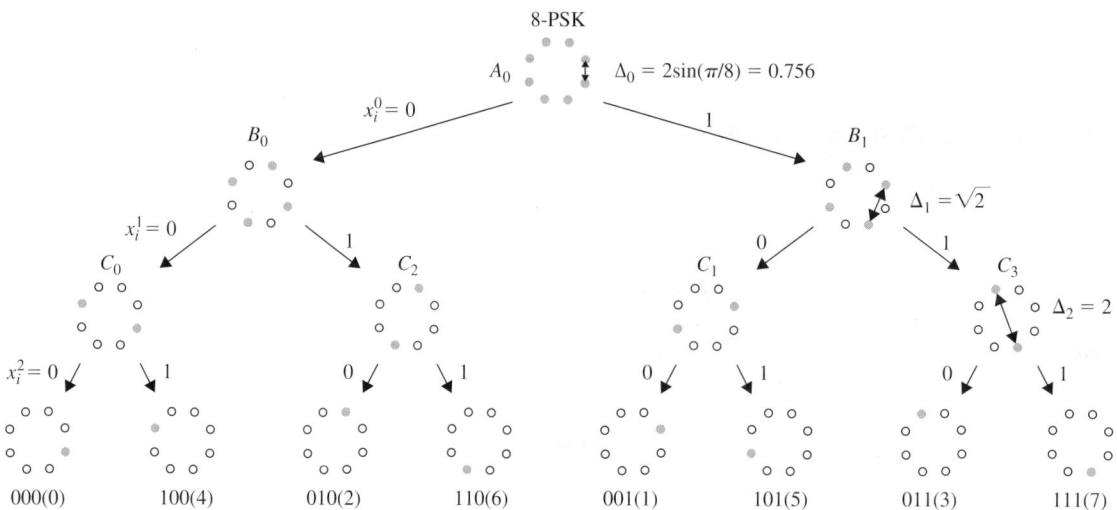

Figure 15.33 Set partitioning of an 8-PSK constellation. (x_i^2, x_i^1, x_i^0)

[11] Ungerboeck, "Trellis-Coded Modulation with Redundant Signal Sets Part I: Introduction," 5–11.

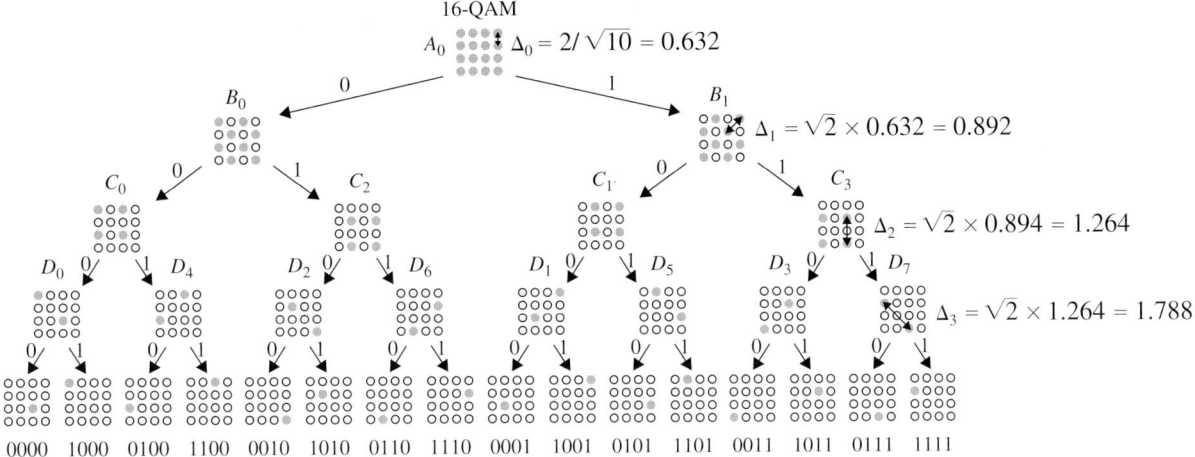

Figure 15.34 Set partitioning of a 16-QAM constellation.

2. Transitions emerging from and converging to the same state are assigned signal points in the subconstellation with the next largest Euclidean distance (e.g., B_0 and B_1 with $\Delta_1 = \sqrt{2}$ in our 8-PSK example).

3. All signal points should occur in the trellis with equal frequency.

Note that the coded bits x_i^0 and x_i^1 are used to decide the subconstellation, and the uncoded bit x_i^2 is used to select the signal point in the subconstellation.

Another example of Ungerboeck's set partitioning rules as applied to a 16-QAM constellation is displayed in Figure 15.34.

15.9.1 Decoding of TCM Codes

To understand the decoding of TCM codes, we have redrawn in Figure 15.35 the trellis diagram for the TCM encoder in Figure 15.31. Note that each transition in the trellis corresponds to a subconstellation (e.g., C_0 or C_1 or C_2 or C_3) rather than a signal point. Because each subconstellation generally contains a number of signal points, the first step in decoding is to find the most likely signal point in each subconstellation. This is accomplished by finding the signal point in each subconstellation that is closest in Euclidean distance to the received signal point. Now we can use the Viterbi algorithm to estimate the most likely path (or corresponding output symbol) sequence which is closest to the received sequence. The Euclidean distance between the received signal point and the most likely signal point in each subconstellation is used as the branch metric.

Performance of TCM Codes

The Viterbi algorithm attempts to find a path through a trellis whose distance is closest to the received symbol sequence. Figure 15.36 displays two candidate paths, one correct one and the other erroneous, that diverge from one node and merge later. If they rejoin in one symbol, they are parallel arms with distance 2 (i.e., $d^2 = 4$). If they go to

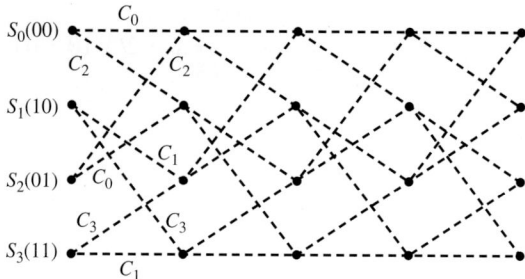

Figure 15.35 Trellis of 8-PSK TCM encoder transitions labeled with subconstellations.

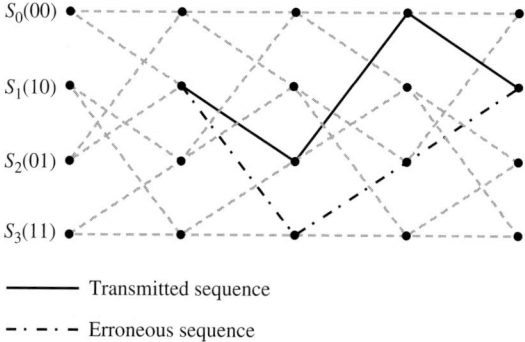

――――― Transmitted sequence

― · ― · ― Erroneous sequence

Figure 15.36 Two possible paths through trellis.

different states in the first transition, they will need at least three symbol intervals to rejoin. The total Euclidean distance between those two paths is

$$d^2 = (d_{\text{leaving same node}})^2 + (d_{\text{entering different nodes}})^2 + (d_{\text{entering same node}})^2$$

$$> \Delta_1^2 + \Delta_0^2 + \Delta_1^2 = 2 + 0.586 + 2 = 4.586 \tag{15.148}$$

All other paths that diverge and remerge are separated by even greater Euclidean distances. Thus the squared free distance, d_{free}^2, is determined by the parallel transitions (i.e., uncoded bit in error) and is equal to 4.

Asymptotic Coding Gain

The asymptotic coding gain of a coded system is defined as

$$\text{Asymptotic coding gain } G = 10 \log_{10} \frac{d_{\text{free}}^2}{d_{\text{min}}^2} \frac{(E_s)_{\text{coded}}}{(E_s)_{\text{uncoded}}} \tag{15.149}$$

If we assume equal powers for coded and uncoded systems, the coding gain of a trellis-coded 8-PSK system is given by

$$G = 10 \log_{10} \frac{d_{\text{free}}^2 \text{ (TCM 8-PSK)}}{d_{\text{min}}^2 \text{ (uncoded 4-PSK)}} = 10 \log_{10} \frac{4}{2} = 3 \text{ dB} \tag{15.150}$$

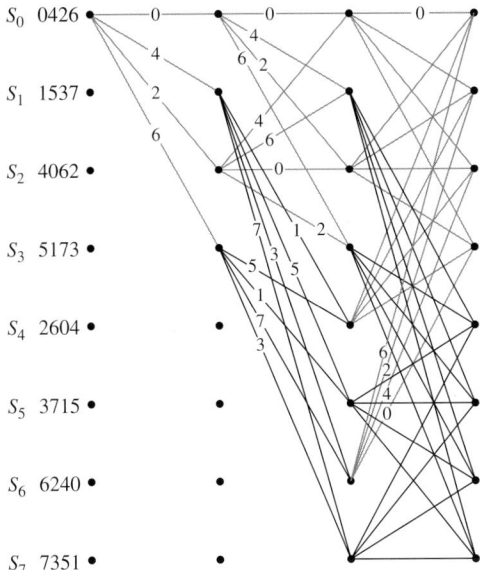

Figure 15.37 Trellis for 8-PSK TCM encoder with 8 states.

Table 15.8 Asymptotic Coding Gains for 8-PSK and 16-QAM TCM

Constraint Length L	Number of States, 2^{L-1}	Coding Gain 8-PSK TCM vs. QPSK	Coding Gain 16-QAM TCM vs. 8-PSK
3	4	3.00	4.36
4	8	3.60	5.33
5	16	4.13	6.12
6	32	4.59	6.12
7	64	5.01	6.79
8	128	5.17	7.37

Hence this simple TCM scheme has 3 dB of asymptotic coding gain when compared to the uncoded QPSK. The coding gain can be improved by eliminating parallel transitions that limited the coding gain to 3 dB. This can be accomplished by increasing the number of states in the convolutional encoder (i.e., constraint length of the rate 1/2 convolutional code). Figure 15.37 shows a trellis for the same code but with the number of states increased to 8 from 4. With more states available, there are no parallel transitions. The list of possible transmission symbols is next to each state label.

Table 15.8 lists the theoretical asymptotic coding gains of four states and up to 128 states of 8-PSK TCM and 16-QAM TCM, which are compared to the uncoded QPSK and 8-PSK, respectively.

Figure 15.38 displays the Simulink simulation results for the probability of decoded bit error performance of 4-, 8-, and 16-state 8-PSK TCM schemes versus uncoded QPSK. The real coding gain at a 10^{-5} bit error rate for 8-PSK TCM with four states is 2.4 dB, versus a 3-dB asymptotic value. The BER performance of 4- and 8-state 16-QAM TCM versus uncoded 8-PSK is shown in Figure 15.39. The real coding gain at a 10^{-5} bit error rate for 4-state 16-QAM is 3.8 dB, versus a 4.36-dB asymptotic value.

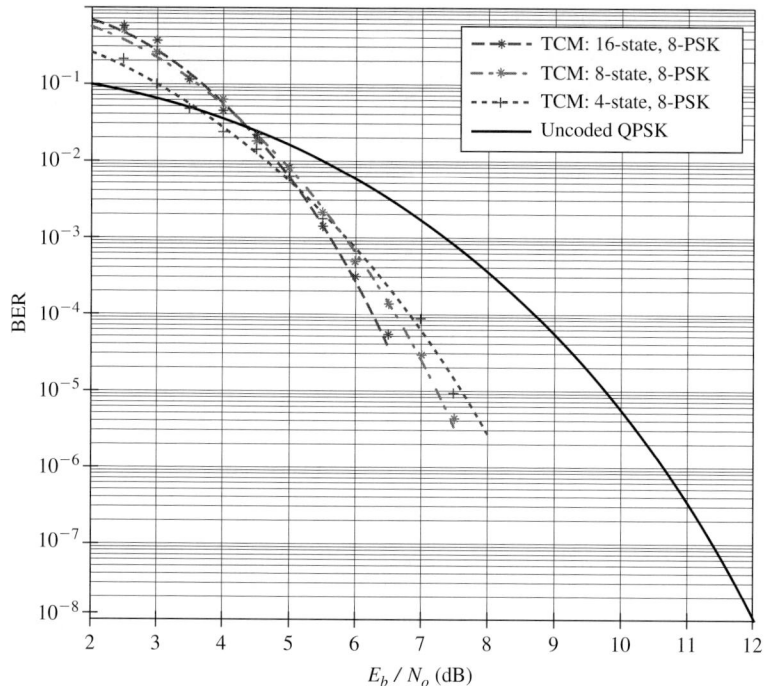

Figure 15.38 8-PSK TCM system performance comparison with uncoded QPSK.

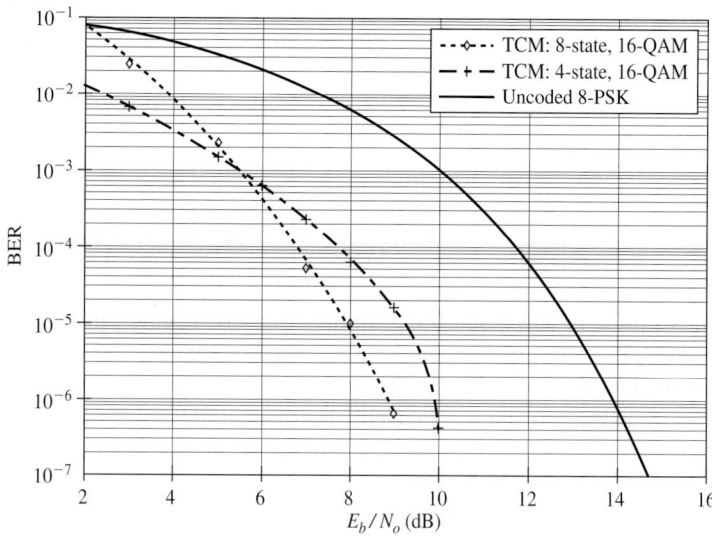

Figure 15.39 16-QAM TCM system performance comparison with uncoded 8-PSK.

FINAL REMARKS

In his landmark 1948 paper, Shannon showed that with the right error-correcting codes, information could be transmitted at speeds up to the channel capacity with arbitrarily low error rates and SNR/bit (E_b/N_o) approaching the Shannon limit. Since then the channel coding has moved from being a mathematical curiosity to being a fundamental element in the design of digital communication and storage systems. Many good codes and efficient decoding schemes have been developed for a variety of applications that achieve performance close to what was promised by Shannon with reasonable implementation complexity. The driving force behind most of the early work in coding was deep space and satellite communications for NASA and military programs. However, it was hard to imagine even two decades ago the pervasive role coding would play in our daily lives through applications such as CD/DVD players, digital TV, cable/ADSL modems, and digital mobile communications. It would be fair to say that without error-correcting codes, the digital media, broadband, and mobile revolution would not have been technically feasible. One should, of course, acknowledge the impact of the semiconductor revolution (i.e., Moore's law) in implementing ever more clever and sophisticated coding algorithms invented by communication engineers.

FURTHER READINGS

Error-control coding is covered in texts [2–5]. Lin [6] is the most comprehensive and up-to-date treatment of the material in the field. Ungerboeck [14] provides an excellent introduction to TCM. Costello [15] is an excellent reference on the applications of coding.

1. Shannon, C. E. "A Mathematical Theory of Communication." *Bell System Technical Journal* 27 (1948): 379–423.

2. Proakis, J., and M. Salehi. *Fundamentals of Communication Systems.* Upper Saddle River, NJ: Prentice Hall, 2005.

3. Haykin, S. *Communication Systems,* 4th ed. Hoboken, NJ: John Wiley, 2000.

4. Ziemer, R., and R. Peterson. *An Introduction to Digital Communication,* 2nd ed., Upper Saddle River, NJ: Prentice Hall, 2001.

5. Proakis, J., and M. Salehi. *Digital Communications,* 5th ed. New York: McGraw-Hill, 2007.

6. Lin, S., and D. Costello. *Error Control Coding,* 2nd ed. Upper Saddle River, NJ: Prentice Hall, 2004.

7. MacWilliams, F., and N. Sloane. *The Theory of Error-Correcting Codes.* Amsterdam: Elsevier, 1977.

8. Viterbi, A. "Convolutional Codes and Their Performance in Communication Systems." *IEEE Transactions on Communications Technology* COM-19 (1971): 751–772.

9. Berrou, C., M. Glavieux, and P. Thitimajshima. "Near Shannon Limit Error-Correcting Coding and Decoding: Turbo Codes." *Proceedings of IEEE International Conference on Communications,* Geneva, Switzerland, May 1993, 1064–1070.

10. Berrou, C., and M. Glavieux. "Near Optimum Error-Correcting Coding and Decoding: Turbo Codes." *IEEE Transactions on Communications* 44 (1996): 1261–1271.

11. Bahl, L., J. Cocke, F. Jelinek, and J. Raviv. "Optimal Decoding of Linear Codes for Minimizing Symbol Error Rate." *IEEE Transactions on Information Theory* IT-20 (1974): 284–287.

12. Hagenauer, J., and P. Hoeher. "A Viterbi Algorithm with Soft Decision Outputs and Its Applications." *Proceedings of IEEE GLOBECOM Conference,* Dallas, TX, November 1989, 1680–1686.

13. Sklar, B. "A Primer on Turbo Code Concepts." *IEEE Communications Magazine* 35, December 1997, 94–102.

14. Ungerboeck, G. "Trellis-Coded Modulation with Redundant Signal Sets Part I: Introduction." *IEEE Communications Magazine* 25, February 1987, 5–11.

15. Costello, D., J. Hagenauer, H. Imai, and S. Wicker. "Applications of Error-Control Coding." *IEEE Transactions on Information Theory* IT-44 (1998): 2531–2560.

PROBLEMS

15.1. Suppose a (3, 1) repetition code is used on a BSC with bit error rate p.

a. Assuming that the receiver makes decision by taking majority vote of the three bits, find the probability of decoding error.

b. How many errors can this code correct and detect?

c. Plot error performance of the (3, 1) code as a function of p.

d. Repeat (a) through (c) for (5, 1) repetition code and compare its performance with the (3, 1) code.

15.2. Consider the (4, 1) repetition code

a. Write generator and parity-check matrices for the code.

b. What is the minimum distance d_{min} of the code? How many errors can this code correct and detect?

15.3. Consider the systematic binary linear (6, 3) code with generator matrix

$$\underline{G} = \begin{pmatrix} 1 & 0 & 0 & \vdots & 1 & 1 & 0 \\ 0 & 1 & 0 & \vdots & 0 & 1 & 1 \\ 0 & 0 & 1 & \vdots & 1 & 0 & 1 \end{pmatrix}$$

a. Determine the parity-check matrix $\underline{H}$ of the code.

b. What is the minimum distance d_{min} of the code? How many errors can this code correct and detect?

c. Using the standard array, show that the code is able to correct one error pattern of Hamming weight 2, in addition to all error patterns of Hamming weight 1.

d. Use the standard array to find the most likely codeword, given that the noisy received codeword is (110101).

e. Now suppose (011101) is transmitted and (101101) is received. What is the decoded word? Comment on your result.

15.4. The parity bits of (7, 3) linear block code are given by

$$b_0 = m_1 + m_2$$
$$b_1 = m_2 + m_3$$
$$b_2 = m_1 + m_2 + m_3$$
$$b_3 = m_1 + m_3$$

    a. Find the generator and parity check matrices $\underline{G}$ and $\underline{H}$ for this code.

    b. What is d_{min} for the code?

    c. List all the codewords for this code.

    d. Construct the standard array and determine the correctable error patterns and their syndromes.

15.5. Consider the systematic binary linear code with the parity-check matrix

$$\underline{H} = \begin{pmatrix} 1\,0 & : & 1\,0\,0 \\ 1\,1 & : & 0\,1\,0 \\ 0\,1 & : & 0\,0\,1 \end{pmatrix}$$

    a. Determine the generator matrix $\underline{G}$ of the code.

    b. Write all the codewords of the code and determine the minimum distance d_{min} of the code. How many errors can this code correct and detect?

    c. Using the standard array, show that the code is able to correct two error patterns of Hamming weight 2, in addition to all error patterns of Hamming weight 1.

    d. What is the asymptotic coding gain with respect to uncoded BPSK modulation?

15.6. Consider the systematic binary linear code with parity-check matrix

$$\underline{H} = \begin{pmatrix} 0\,0\,0\,0\,1\,1\,1\,1\,1\,1 & : & 1\,0\,0\,0 \\ 0\,1\,1\,1\,0\,0\,0\,1\,1\,1 & : & 0\,1\,0\,0 \\ 1\,0\,1\,1\,0\,1\,1\,0\,0\,1\,1 & : & 0\,0\,1\,0 \\ 1\,1\,0\,1\,1\,0\,1\,0\,1\,0\,1 & : & 0\,0\,0\,1 \end{pmatrix}$$

    a. Determine the generator matrix $\underline{G}$ of the code.

    b. Determine the minimum distance d_{min} of the code. How many errors this code can correct and detect?

    c. What is the codeword corresponding to the message vector $\underline{m} = (1\,0\,1\,1\,1\,0\,0\,1\,1\,1)$?

    d. If $\underline{y} = (1\,1\,1\,0\,1\,1\,0\,0\,0\,1\,1\,0\,1\,0)$ is received at the receiver, what is the most likely codeword $\underline{x}$ transmitted?

    e. If $\underline{y} = (0\,1\,1\,0\,1\,0\,1\,0\,1\,1\,1\,0\,1\,1\,0)$ is received at the receiver, what is the most likely message $\underline{m}$ transmitted?

15.7. Prove that an (n, k) block code can correct t errors if its code rate R_c satisfies the following inequality

$$R_c \leq 1 - \frac{1}{n}\log_2\left[\sum_{i=0}^{t}\binom{n}{i}\right]$$

Show that a (63, 39) block code capable of correcting 4 errors can exist. What is the redundancy of the code?

15.8. Consider the generator matrix of the (7, 4, 3) Hamming code given in Example 15.4. The code is extended to an (8, 4) code by adding an overall parity check bit to (7, 4, 3) code.

    a. Find the parity check matrix $\underline{H}$ for this code.

    b. What is d_{min} for the code?

    c. Does the extra check bit increase the error-correcting and error-detecting capabilities of the code?

15.9. Let $g(D) = D^8 + D^7 + D^6 + D^4 + 1$ be the generator polynomial of (15, 7) cyclic block code.

    a. Verify that $g(D)$ can be a generator polynomial of the code.

    b. Determine the code polynomial (codeword) in systematical form for the message $m(D) = D^5 + D^4 + D^2 + 1$.

    c. Is the polynomial $y(D) = D^{14} + D^{11} + D^5 + D^2 + 1$ a codeword?

15.10. Show that for an (n, k) block code, the probability of an undetected error $P_u(e)$ over a BSC with crossover probability p is given by

$$P_u(e) = \sum_{i=1}^{n} A_i p^i (1 - p)^{n-i}$$

where $A_1, A_1, \ldots, A_n$ represents the weight distribution of the code.

Suppose (7, 4) Hamming code is used for error detection over a BSC with crossover probability $p = 10^{-3}$. Compute the probability of an undetected error for this code.

15.11. Consider the $m = 4$ Hamming code.

    a. What is the block length n and d_{min} for the code?

    b. Write the parity check matrix $\underline{H}$ for this code.

    c. Give the set of equations for computing the parity bits in terms of the message bits.

    d. Write an estimate of the probability of decoded bit error if the channel BER $p = 10^{-4}$? Repeat for $p = 10^{-6}$.

15.12. Show that the coding gain for the soft-decision decoded (n, k, d_{min}) block code is given by

$$G_c = 10\log_{10}\left[R_c d_{min} - \frac{k\log_e 2}{E_b/N_o}\right] \text{ dB}$$

where E_b/N_o = uncoded SNR/bit of the link. Calculate the coding gain for (127, 36, 31) BCH code at $E_b/N_o = 8$ dB.

15.13. Consider the extended Golay code (24, 12, 8).

    a. Plot the probability of a codeword error for hard-decision decoding for E_b/N_o in the range 4–14 dB.

    b. Repeat (a) for the soft-decision decoding.

    c. What is the difference in coding gain for the two cases?

15.14. Consider the error-detecting capability of an (n, k) CRC code. Prove the following:

    a. If the generator polynomial $g(D)$ has more than one term, it can detect single errors.

    b. If the generator polynomial $g(D)$ of the code is a primitive polynomial of degree $n - k$, it will detect all double errors as long as the total codeword length doesn't exceed $2^{n-k} - 1$.

    c. If the generator polynomial $g(D)$ of the code has $(1 + D)$ as a factor, it will be able to detect all odd numbers of errors.

15.15. Let $g_1(D) = 1 + D$ and let $g_2(D) = 1 + D + D^3$. Consider the message vector $(1\,0\,0\,1\,0\,1)$.

a. If $g_1(D)$ is used as the generator polynomial, find the codeword.

b. If $g_2(D)$ is used as the generator polynomial, find the codeword.

c. Can $g_2(D)$ detect single errors? Double errors? Triple errors?

d. Find the codeword corresponding the above message vector if $g(D) = g_1(D)g_2(D)$ is the generator polynomial. Comment on the error-detecting capabilities of $g(D)$.

15.16. A rate $R_c = 1/2$ convolution encoder is displayed in Figure P15.1.

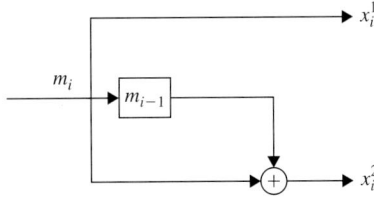

Figure P15.1

a. Find the generators polynomials for this code.

b. Draw the state transition diagram.

c. Is the code systematic? Prove by an example.

d. Draw the decoding trellis to depth 8, and decode the received sequence 1 1 1 0 1 0 0 1 0 0 11 10 11.

e. Draw the modified state transition diagram and determine the corresponding free distance d_{free}.

15.17. A rate $R_c = 1/3$ convolution code is described by the generator polynomials

$$g_1(D) = 1 + D^2$$
$$g_2(D) = 1 + D + D^2$$
$$g_3(D) = 1 + D$$

a. Draw the shift-register convolution encoder for this code.

b. Draw the state transition diagram. What is the constraint length of this code?

c. Draw the trellis diagram and calculate the encoder output sequence corresponding to input sequence 0 1 1 0 1 0.

d. If the input information rate is 1 Mb/s, what is the bit rate of the encoded sequence?

15.18. A rate $R_c = 1/3$ convolutional code is defined by the generator polynomials

$$g_1(D) = 1 + D$$
$$g_2(D) = 1 + D + D^2$$
$$g_3(D) = D^2$$

a. Draw the state transition diagram

b. Determine its transfer function.

c. Calculate d_{free} for the code.

d. Assuming hard-decision decoding and BPSK modulation, plot the probability of decoded bit error for $E_b/N_o = 4 - 11$ dB. Compare it with the performance achieved using soft-decision decoding.

e. What is the coding gain advantage of soft- versus hard-decision decoding at $P_b = 10^{-6}$.

15.19. Consider (2, 1, 3) convolutional code with generator sequences $\underline{g}_1 = (1\ 0\ 1)$ and $\underline{g}_2 = (1\ 1\ 1)$. Use soft-decision Viterbi decoding to find the estimate of the information sequence $\hat{m}$ when the received sequence is

$$\underline{r} = [(-1, -2)\ (2, -1)\ (-1, 3)\ (1, -2)\ (-3, 2)\ (1, 2)]$$

15.20. Consider a TCM scheme shown in Figure P15.2.

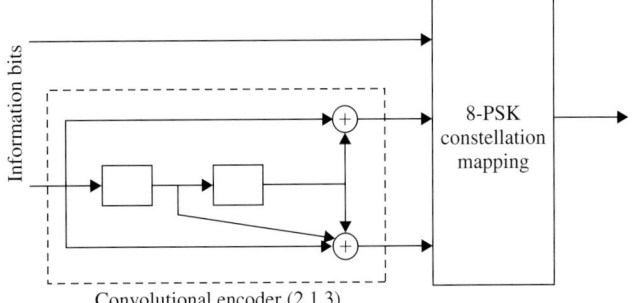

Figure P15.2

a. Assuming that parallel transitions dominate the error probability, what is the coding gain of this trellis code relative to uncoded 8-PSK, given that d_{min} for the 8-PSK is .765?

b. Draw the trellis for this scheme, and assign subsets to the transitions according to the heuristic rules of Ungerboeck.

c. What is the minimum distance error event through the trellis relative to the path generated by the all-zero bit sequence?

d. Assuming that your answer to part (c) is the minimum distance error event for the trellis, what is d_{free} of the code?

MATLAB PROBLEMS

15.21. For (15, 11) Hamming code, write the parity-check matrix $\underline{H}$ and derive the generator matrix $\underline{G}$ from it.

a. List all its codewords.

```
k=11

kk=2^k-1
```

```
m = de2bi(0:kk, k, 'left-msb'); %
2^k message vectors

x=mod(m*G, 2); % 2^k codewords
```

b. Calculate minimum distance d_{min} of the code.

```
d_min=min(sum((x(2:2^k, :))'));
```

c. Construct the syndrome table for the code.

d. Decode the received sequence 1 0 0 0 0 0 0 1 1 1 1 1 1 1 0

15.22. Consider the BER performance of (15, 11) Hamming code using Monte-Carlo simulation.

a. Generate the random bit sequences of length `Nbits`.

```
n = 15; k =11;

Ncodewords = 50,000

Nbits = Ncodewords*k;

bit_sequence= rand(1, Nbits);

bits = round(bit_sequence); % Bit
stream
```

b. Generate (n, k) Hamming codewords.

```
blocks = reshape(bits, k,
Ncodewords)';

cblocks = mod(blocks*G, 2);

cbits = reshape(cblocks', 1,
Ncodewords*n); %Serialize

Ncbits=length(cbits);
```

c. Apply polar mapping to simulate antipodal or BPSK signaling.

```
b_n = 2*cbits-1; % BPSK modulation 0
-> -1; 1 -> 0
```

d. For a given value of E_b/N_o, add AWGN to the transmitted sequence b_n to generate the received sequence r_n.

```
Eb=1;

Ebc=Eb*code_rate;

No = 10^(-EbNo/10); % Noise spectral
density

sigma= sqrt(No/(2*Ebc)); % RMS noise

r_n =b_n + sigma*randn(1, Ncbits);
```

e. The received sequence is hard-decoded and formatted into n-bit received vectors. Calculate syndrome vectors for all received vectors.

```
y = (1+sign(r_n))/2; % hard
decision

yblocks = reshape(y, n,
Ncodewords)';

syndrome = mod(yblocks*H', 2); %
find the syndrome
```

f. Use the syndrome vector calculated in (e) above to locate the error pattern from the syndrome table (Problem 15.21(c)). The corrected received vector is obtained by XORing the error pattern with received code vector. After discarding the parity bits from all corrected received vectors, the decoded bit stream bhat is generated by assembling them in serial format.

```
bhat=[];

for j =1:Ncodewords

index=0;

for i=1:Erows % Erows = number of
error patterns
```

```
if(syndrome_matrix(i, :)==  syndrome
(j, :)), index = i;

end

end

evector= Ematrix(index, :); % Ema-
trix = matrix of error patterns

cblock=xor(yblocks(j, :), evector);

bhat_block(j, :)=cblock(1:k);

bhat=[bhat bhat_block(j, :)];

end
```

g. Perform BER calculations for E_b/N_o values from 0 to 13 dB and plot them. For comparison, also display polar AWGN signaling performance without coding.

15.23. The generator polynomials of a (2, 1, 7) convolutional encoder are (121, 91).

a. Write the generator matrix $\underline{G} = \begin{pmatrix} \underline{g}_1 \\ \underline{g}_2 \end{pmatrix}$ where $\underline{g}_1$ and $\underline{g}_2$ are generator seqeunces.

b. The convolutional encoder may be simulated by the following m-file:

```
[n, L] = size(G);

m = L-1;%length of the shift regis-
terstate = zeros(1, m);% initialize
registers to zero

%

N=length(bits) %N=number of input
bits

%

codedbitstream=[];

for k=1:N

for i=1:n

output(i) = G(i, 1)*bits(k);

for j = 2:L

y=G(i, j)*state(j-1);

output(i) = xor(output(i), y);

end;

end

state = [bits(k), state(1:m-1)];

codedbitstream=[codedbitstream,
output];

end
```

c. Determine the encoder output sequence when the input bit sequence is 0 1 0 1 1 1 0 0 1 0 1 0 0 0 1.

15.24. Consider the BER performance of (2, 1, 3) convolutional code with generator polynomials (7, 5) using Monte-Carlo simulation. Assume that hard Viterbi decoding is used at the receiver.

a. Use frame length `Nbits` = 256 and number of simulations `Nsim` = 1000.

```
k=1;n=2;

code_rate=k/n

L=3; % constraint length

Nsim=1000;

Nbits=256; % frame length

tail_bits =zeros(1:L-1) % tail bits

Nframe = Nbits-L+1

G=[1 1 1;1 0 1];% generator matrix
for (5, 7) polynomials
```

b. Perform BER calculations for SNR/bit values of 0 to 13 dB.

```
Eb=1

Ebc=Eb*code_rate

snr=(0:1:13);

for ii=1:14

error_count=0;

EbNo=snr(ii);

No = 10^(-EbNo/10);% AWGN Noise
spectral density

sigma= sqrt(No/(2*Ebc)); % RMS noise
per sample

for ns=1:Nsim

bit_sequence= rand(1, Nframe);

bits = [round(bit_sequence) tail_
bits]; % Bit

%stream. Append tail bits

cbits=conv_encode(bits, G); % convo-
lutional encoding

Ncbits=length(cbits);
```

```
b_n = 2*cbits-1; % Antipodal mapping
r_n =b_n + sigma*randn(1, Ncbits);
% Add noise

y = (1+sign(r_n))/2; % Hard
decoding

bhat = viterbi_hard_decoder(y);
% Viterbi decoding

% counting the errors

errors = size(find([bits-
bhat(1:Nbits)]), 2);

error_count= error_count + errors;

end; %Nsim

ber(ii) = error_count/(Nbits*Nsim);
% simulated ber

end %snr
```

c. Plot BER versus E_b/N_o. For comparison, display also polar AWGN signaling performance without coding.

15.25. Consider the BER performance of (2, 1, 3) convolutional code in Problem 15.24 with soft Viterbi decoding. Compare the BER performance with hard Viterbi decoding and polar AWGN signaling performance without coding.

15.26. The generator polynomial of (23, 12) Golay code is given by

$$g(D) = 1 + D + D^5 + D^6 + D^7 + D^9 + D^{11}$$

a. Write an m-file for implementing the encoder.

b. What is the output codeword for the message sequence 0 1 1 0 1 0 1 1 1 0 1 0?

c. Compute the error-rate performance of the code for soft- and hard- decision decoding. Use E_b/N_o values 0 to 13 dB. For comparison, display also BPSK AWGN signaling performance without coding.

An Interview with Andrew Viterbi

Courtesy of Andrew Viterbi

Why did you choose a career in the communications field? How did Shannon's work influence your career?

From my middle school years I enjoyed mathematics and made up my mind to enter MIT, which was across the Charles River from my home, and become an engineer. This was the early heyday of electronics and I decided to major in electrical engineering. The department faculty was outstanding even within MIT. Besides Claude Shannon and Norbert Wiener, who seemed unapproachable by undergraduates and beginning graduate students, I was influenced by my professors, circuit and system theory pioneers Ernest A. Guillemin and Samuel J. Mason and communications theorists Robert M. Fano and Y-W Lee. After leaving MIT with my master's degree in 1957, I joined the communication research section at Caltech's Jet Propulsion Lab. There I became gradually more aware of Shannon theory and pursued it further both in my doctoral research and later in my teaching and research at UCLA starting in 1963. By then I had recognized the full impact of Shannon's unparalleled insight.

In your opinion what are the major innovations that have contributed to the phenomenal progress in digital and wireless communications? What has been the impact of the semiconductor revolution?

First and foremost the remarkable semiconductor integration growth predicted by Gordon Moore in 1965 made possible and even inexpensive a generation later what we could only dream of at that time. Then decades of evolution of space and satellite communication led the progress in digital wireless. It is remarkable how the lessons learned with very weak signals received from space were the starting point for creating efficient networks of mobile phones. Furthermore, spread spectrum technology, used since the 1950s by the military to combat hostile interference, found widespread application in cellular voice and data communication in the nineties and beyond.

Your professional career has been unique in the sense that it has spanned working and contributing on both sides of the aisle: academic and industrial. Has this dual relationship been influential toward your successes in solving so many practical problems in the digital wireless, satellite, and space communications?
Early in my career the goal of achieving accurate and efficient communication from space and through satellites drove much of my research. Later I was inspired by achieving the same goal with very large multiuser wireless networks. Having a concrete practical problem to solve always inspired my research efforts. Conversely, believing in the deep concepts developed in our academic research gave us an advantage in selecting and implementing superior innovative communication systems.

Tell us about your invention of the most celebrated Viterbi algorithm? When did you realize its significance and possible impact as we know it today?
It may seem difficult to accept but the so-named algorithm was developed as a critical step in the proof of the ultimate capabilities of convolutional error-correcting codes. It took about 18 months and multiple hours of simulation on a primitive 60s-era mainframe computer by colleagues at Caltech's JPL to establish the potential practical value of the algorithm for space communication. The migration of the algorithm into such diverse fields as magnetic recording, voice and optical character recognition, and genetic sequence analysis followed in subsequent decades.

It seems like we have solved the channel coding problem that emerged from Shannon's seminal work with the invention of low-density parity-check (LDPC) and turbo codes. What are the new frontiers of innovation in the digital communications? Wireless communications?
These powerful codes and their decoding algorithms nearly achieve the Shannon limit for single-channel user-to-user communication. There remain many issues, both theoretical and practical, in perfecting networks of many users both interfering and cooperating with one another. Considerable progress has been made in both spectral and spatial processing, but the field is still open to further innovation.

Who inspired you professionally the most?
Initially my professors mentioned above; then researchers and experienced communication engineers; and finally some of my colleagues and team members who performed the "impossible" in creating a dominant multiple access technology in the face of the skepticism of many.

Do you have any advice for the new generation of students entering the communications field?
Choose a field and a job that you enjoy and you'll never "work" a day in your life.

Dr. Andrew Viterbi is a cofounder and retired Vice Chairman and Chief Technical Officer of QUALCOMM Inc. He spent equal portions of his career in industry, having previously cofounded Linkabit Corp., and worked in academia as professor in the schools of engineering and applied science, first at UCLA and then at UCSD, at which he is now professor emeritus. He is currently president of the Viterbi Group, a technical advisory and investment company. His principal research contribution, the Viterbi algorithm, is used in most digital cellular phones and digital satellite receivers, as well as in such diverse fields as magnetic recording, voice recognition, and DNA sequence analysis. More recently, he concentrated his efforts on establishing CDMA as the multiple access technology of choice for cellular telephony and wireless data communication. Dr. Viterbi has received numerous honors both in the United States and internationally. Among these are seven honorary doctorates from universities in Canada, Israel, Italy, and the United States, the Marconi International Fellowship Award, the IEEE Alexander Graham Bell, the Claude Shannon and the James Clerk Maxwell Awards, the NEC C&C Award, the Eduard Rhein Foundation Award, the Christopher Columbus Medal, the Franklin Medal, the Robert Noyes Semiconductor Industry Award, the Millennium Laureate Award and the IEEE's highest award, the Medal of Honor. He is a member of the National Academy of Engineering and the National Academy of Sciences and is a Fellow of the American Academy of Arts and Sciences. He has received an honorary title from the president of Italy and the National Medal of Science from the president of the United States.

Mathematical Tables

The following tables include a selection of mathematical relationships that are encountered in this text for convenient reference.

TRIGONOMETRIC IDENTITIES

$$\cos u = \frac{e^{ju} + e^{-ju}}{2}$$

$$\sin u = \frac{e^{ju} - e^{-ju}}{2j}$$

$$\cos^2 u + \sin^2 u = 1$$

$$\cos^2 u - \sin^2 u = \cos(2u)$$

$$2 \sin u \cos u = \sin(2u)$$

$$\cos u \cos v = \frac{1}{2} \cos(u - v) + \frac{1}{2} \cos(u + v)$$

$$\sin u \cos v = \frac{1}{2} \sin(u - v) + \frac{1}{2} \sin(u + v)$$

$$\sin u \sin v = \frac{1}{2} \cos(u - v) - \frac{1}{2} \cos(u + v)$$

$$\cos(u \pm v) = \cos u \cos v \mp \sin u \sin v$$

$$\sin(u \pm v) = \sin u \cos v \pm \cos u \sin v$$

$$\cos^2 u = \frac{1}{2} + \frac{1}{2} \cos(2u)$$

$$\cos^{2n} u = \frac{1}{2^{2n}} \left\{ \sum_{k=0}^{n-1} 2 \binom{2n}{k} \cos[2(n-k)u] + \binom{2n}{n} \right\}, \ n \text{ a positive integer}$$

$$\cos^{2n-1} u = \frac{1}{2^{2n-2}} \left\{ \sum_{k=0}^{n-1} \binom{2n-1}{k} \cos(2n - 2k - 1)u \right\}$$

$$\sin^2 u = \frac{1}{2} - \frac{1}{2}\cos(2u)$$

$$\sin^{2n} u = \frac{1}{2^{2n}}\left\{\sum_{k=0}^{n-1}(-1)^{n-k}2\binom{2n}{k}\cos[2(n-k)u] + \binom{2n}{n}\right\}$$

$$\sin^{2n-1} u = \frac{1}{2^{2n-2}}\left[\sum_{k=0}^{n-1}(-1)^{n+k-1}\binom{2n-1}{k}\sin(2n-2k-1)u\right]$$

SERIES EXPANSIONS AND APPROXIMATIONS

$$(x+y)^n = \sum_{k=0}^{n}\binom{n}{k}x^{n-k}y^k, \quad \binom{n}{k} = \frac{n!}{(n-k)!k!}$$

$$(1+x)^n \cong 1 + nx, \; (1-x)^n \cong 1 - nx, \; (1+x)^{1/2} \cong 1 + \frac{1}{2}x, \text{ where } |x| << 1$$

$$e^x = 1 + x + \frac{x^2}{2!} + \frac{x^3}{3!} + \cdots, \quad e^x \cong 1 + x, \; |x| << 1$$

$$\log_2 x = \frac{\log_{10}(x)}{\log_{10} 2}$$

$$\ln(1+x) = x - \frac{x^2}{2!} + \frac{x^3}{3!} - \cdots, \quad \ln(1+x) \cong x, \; |x| << 1$$

$$\sin x = x - \frac{x^3}{3!} + \frac{x^5}{5!} - \cdots, \quad \sin x \cong x - \frac{x^3}{3!}, \; |x| << 1$$

$$\cos x = 1 - \frac{x^2}{2!} + \frac{x^4}{4!} - \cdots, \quad \cos x \cong 1 - \frac{x^2}{2!}, \; |x| << 1$$

$$\tan x = x + \frac{1}{3}x^3 + \frac{2}{15}x^5 + \cdots$$

$$\arcsin x = x + \frac{1}{6}x^3 + \frac{3}{40}x^5 + \cdots$$

$$\arctan x = \begin{cases} x - \frac{1}{3}x^3 + \frac{1}{5}x^5 - \cdots, & |x| < 1 \\ \frac{\pi}{2} - \frac{1}{x} + \frac{1}{3x^3} - \cdots, & x > 1 \end{cases}$$

$$\mathrm{sinc}\, x = 1 - \frac{1}{3!}(\pi x)^2 + \frac{1}{5!}(\pi x)^4 - \cdots$$

$$J_n(x) = \frac{1}{n!}\left(\frac{x}{2}\right)^n - \frac{1}{(n+1)!}\left(\frac{x}{2}\right)^{n+2} + \frac{1}{2!(n+2)!}\left(\frac{x}{2}\right)^{n+4} - \cdots$$

$$J_n(x) \approx \sqrt{\frac{2}{\pi x}} \cos\left(x - \frac{\pi}{4} - \frac{n\pi}{2}\right), \quad x >> 1$$

$$I_0(x) \approx \begin{cases} e^{x^2/4}, & x^2 << 1 \\ e^x/\sqrt{2\pi x}, & x >> 1 \end{cases}$$

Sum of Infinite Series

$$\sum_{n=1}^{\infty} \frac{1}{n}, \quad n \text{ positive integers. Does not converge}$$

$$\sum_{n=1}^{\infty} \frac{1}{n^2} = \frac{\pi^2}{6}, \quad n \text{ positive integers}$$

$$\sum_{n=0}^{\infty} r^n = 1 + r + r^2 + r^3 \ldots = \frac{1}{1-r}, \quad |r| < 1$$

Sum of Finite Series

$$\sum_{m=1}^{M} m = \frac{M(M+1)}{2}$$

$$\sum_{m=1}^{M} m^2 = \frac{M(M+1)(2M+1)}{6}$$

$$\sum_{m=1}^{M} m^3 = \frac{M^2(M+1)^2}{4}$$

$$\sum_{n=0}^{N-1} r^n = \frac{1-r^N}{1-r}, \quad r \neq 1$$

DEFINITE INTEGRALS

$$\int \sin(ax)\, dx = -\frac{1}{a} \cos(ax)$$

$$\int \cos(ax)\, dx = \frac{1}{a} \sin(ax)$$

$$\int \sin^2(ax)\, dx = \frac{x}{2} - \frac{1}{4a} \sin(2ax)$$

$$\int \cos^2(ax)\, dx = \frac{x}{2} + \frac{1}{4a} \sin(2ax)$$

$$\int x \sin(ax)\, dx = a^{-2} \left[\sin(ax) - ax\cos(ax) \right]$$

$$\int x\cos(ax)\,dx = a^{-2}\left[\cos(ax) + ax\sin(ax)\right]$$

$$\int x^m \sin x\,dx = -x^m\cos x + m\int x^{m-1}\cos x\,dx$$

$$\int x^m \cos x\,dx = x^m\sin x - m\int x^{m-1}\sin x\,dx$$

$$\int e^{ax}\,dx = a^{-1}e^{ax}$$

$$\int x^m e^{ax}\,dx = a^{-1}x^m e^{ax} - a^{-1}m\int x^{m-1}e^{ax}\,dx$$

$$\int e^{ax}\sin(bx)\,dx = (a^2 + b^2)^{-1}e^{ax}\left[a\sin(bx) - b\cos(bx)\right]$$

$$\int e^{ax}\cos(bx)\,dx = (a^2 + b^2)^{-1}e^{ax}\left[a\cos(bx) + b\sin(bx)\right]$$

Definite Integrals

$$\int_0^\infty \frac{x^{m-1}}{1 + x^n}\,dx = \frac{\pi/n}{\sin(m\pi/n)},\ n > m > 0$$

$$\int_0^\pi \sin^2(nx)\,dx = \int_0^\pi \cos^2(nx)\,dx = \frac{\pi}{2},\ n\ \text{an integer}$$

$$\int_0^\pi \sin(mx)\sin(nx)\,dx = \int_0^\pi \cos(mx)\cos(nx)\,dx = 0,\ m \neq n, m\ \text{and}\ n\ \text{integer}$$

$$\int_0^\pi \sin(mx)\cos(nx)\,dx = \begin{cases} \dfrac{2m}{m^2 - n^2}, & m + n\ \text{odd} \\ 0, & m + n\ \text{even} \end{cases}$$

$$\int_0^\infty x^{a-1}\cos bx\,dx = \frac{\Gamma(a)}{b^a}\cos\left(\frac{\pi a}{2}\right),\ 0 < |a| < 1,\ b > 0$$

$$\int_0^\infty x^{a-1}\sin bx\,dx = \frac{\Gamma(a)}{b^a}\sin\left(\frac{\pi a}{2}\right),\ 0 < |a| < 1,\ b > 0$$

$$\int_0^\infty x^n e^{-ax}\,dx = \frac{n!}{a^{n+1}}, \quad n \text{ an integer and } a > 0$$

$$\int_0^\infty e^{-a^2 x^2}\,dx = \frac{\sqrt{\pi}}{2|a|}$$

$$\int_0^\infty x^{2n} e^{-a^2 x^2}\,dx = \frac{1 \cdot (3) \cdot (5) \cdots (2n-1)\sqrt{\pi}}{2^{n+1} a^{2n+1}}, \quad a > 0$$

$$\int_0^\infty e^{-ax} \cos(bx)\,dx = \frac{a}{a^2 + b^2}, \quad a > 0$$

$$\int_0^\infty e^{-ax} \sin(bx)\,dx = \frac{b}{a^2 + b^2}, \quad a > 0$$

$$\int_0^\infty e^{-a^2 x^2} \cos(bx)\,dx = \frac{\sqrt{\pi}}{2a} e^{-b^2/4a^2}$$

$$\int_0^\infty x e^{-ax^2} I_0(bx)\,dx = \frac{1}{2a} e^{b^2/4a}, \quad a > 0$$

$$\int_0^\infty \frac{\cos(ax)}{b^2 + x^2}\,dx = \frac{\pi}{2b} e^{-ab}, \quad a > 0,\ b > 0$$

$$\int_0^\infty \frac{x\sin(ax)}{b^2 + x^2}\,dx = \frac{\pi}{2} e^{-ab}, \quad a > 0,\ b > 0$$

$$\int_0^\infty \operatorname{sinc}(x)\,dx = \int_0^\infty \operatorname{sinc}^2(x)\,dx = \frac{1}{2}$$

Abbreviations

AC	Alternating current	FDMA	Frequency-division multiple access
ADC	Analog-to-digital converter	FFT	Fast Fourier transform
ADM	Adaptive delta modulation	FM	Frequency modulation
ANSI	American National Standards Institute	FSK	Frequency shift keying
AM	Amplitude modulation	FT	Fourier transform
ARQ	Automatic-repeat-request	FS	Fourier series
ASCII	American National Standard Code for Information Interchange	HDTV	High definition television
		Hz	Hertz
ASK	Amplitude shift keying	GHz	Giga hertz
ATM	Asynchronous transfer mode	IDTFT	Inverse discrete-time Fourier transform
BER	Bit error rate	IDFT	Inverse discrete Fourier transform
BP	Bandpass	IEEE	Institute of Electrical and Electronics Engineers
BASK	Binary amplitude shift keying	IF	Intermediate frequency
BPSK	Binary phase shift keying	IFT	Inverse Fourier transform
BFSK	Binary frequency shift keying	iid	independent, identically distributed
BSC	Binary symmetric channel		
CATV	Cable television	I/O	Input/output
CDF	Cumulative distribution function	ISI	Inter-symbol interference
CNR	Carrier-to-noise ratio	ITU	International Telecommunications Union
CCITT	Consultative Committee for International Telephone and Telegraph	JPEG	Joint Photographic Experts Group
		kHz	Kilohertz
CT	Continuous-time	km	kilometer
dB	Decibel	LAN	Local area network
DC	Direct current	LED	Light-emitting diode
DFE	Decision feedback equalizer	LMS	Least-mean-square
DTFT	Discrete-time Fourier transform	LNA	Low-noise amplifier
DT	Discrete-time	log	Logarithm
DFT	Discrete Fourier transform	LP	Low-pass
DM	Delta modulation	LTI	Linear time-invariant
DPCM	Differential pulse code modulation	MAP	Maximum *a posteriori* probability
DPSK	Differential phase-shift keying	MMSE	Minimum mean-square error
DSB-SC	Double sideband-suppressed carrier	MPEG	Moving Picture Experts Group
FCC	Federal Communications Commission	ms	Millisecond
FDM	Frequency-division multiplexing	μs	Microsecond

ML	Maximum likelihood	**RF**	Radio frequency
MSK	Minimum shift keying	**RMS**	Root-mean-square
nm	Nanometer	**RZ**	Return-to-zero
ns	Nanosecond	**SDH**	Synchronous digital hierarchy
NRZ	Nonreturn-to-zero	**SER**	Symbol error rate
NTSC	National Television Systems Committee	**SNR**	Signal-to-noise ratio
OQPSK	Offset quadrature phase shift keying	**SONET**	Synchronous optical network
PAM	Pulse amplitude modulation	**TCM**	Trellis-coded modulation
PCM	Pulse code modulation	**TDM**	Time division multiplexing
PDF	Probability density function	**Telco**	Telephone company
PMF	Probability mass function	**TV**	Television
PLL	Phase-lock loop	**UHF**	Ultra-high frequency
PSD	Power spectra density	**VCO**	Voltage-controlled oscillator
PRN	Pseudo-random noise	**VHF**	Very high frequency
PSK	Phase shift keying	**VLSI**	Very large scale integration
QAM	Quadrature amplitude modulation	**VSB**	Vestigial sideband
QoS	Quality of service	**WSS**	Wide-sense stationary
QPSK	Quadrature phase shift keying	**ZFE**	Zero forcing equalizer

List of Symbols

A_c	Amplitude of carrier waveform		$H_R(f)$	Receive filter frequency response
A_m	Amplitude of sinusoidal message waveform		$H_T(f)$	Transmit filter frequency response
B	Bandwidth in Hertz (Hz)		$I(x, y)$	Mutual information between two random variables x and y
B_{abs}	Absolute bandwidth		$I_n(x)$	Modified Bessel function of first kind, order n, argument x
B_T	Transmission bandwidth, or bandwidth of a bandpass signal		$J_n(x)$	Bessel function of first kind, order n, argument x
B_N	Noise-equivalent bandwidth		L	Loss in dB
B_{3dB}	3-dB bandwidth		$\mathscr{L}$	Loss in linear units
BER	Bit error rate		N_o	One-sided power spectral density of white Gaussian noise
C	Channel capacity, bits per second, or capacitance in Farads		NF	Noise figure in dB
D	Deviation ratio, or Symbol rate		P_x	Power in signal $x(t)$
E_x	Energy in signal $x(t)$		P_c	Power in unmodulated carrier
E_b, E_1, E_0, E_s	Energy in bit, energy in bit 1, energy in bit 0, and energy in symbol		P_b	Probability of bit error
f_s	Sampling frequency		P_e	Probability of symbol error
F	Noise figure		P_{cw}	Probability of codeword error
$F_x(x)$	Cumulative distribution function of random variable x		P_{out}, P_{in}	Output and input power (watts)
$F_{xy}(x, y)$	Joint cumulative distribution function of random variables x and y		P_T	Average transmitter power
$\mathscr{G}$	Power gain in linear units		P_R	Average signal power at the predetection filter input
G	Power gain in dB		P_D	Average postdetection signal power
$\mathscr{G}_x(f)$	Power spectral density function of a power signal $x(t)$, Watts/Hz		$P(A)$	Probability of event A
$G_x(f)$	Power spectral density function of random signal $x(t)$, Watts/Hz		$Q(.)$	Gaussian Q-function
$G_{xy}(f)$	Cross-spectral density function of random signal $x(t)$ and $y(t)$		R	Resistance in ohms
			R_b	Bit rate in bits/second
$\underline{G}$	Generator matrix of a block code		R_c	Code rate
$\underline{H}$	Parity-check matrix of a block code		$R_x(t_1, t_2)$	Autocorrelation function of random signal $x(t)$
$H(f)$	Transfer or frequency-response function of an LTI system		$R_{xy}(t_1, t_2)$	Cross-correlation function of random signals $x(t)$ and $y(t)$
$H(x)$	Entropy of random variables x		$\mathscr{R}_x(\tau)$	Time-average autocorrelation function of signal $x(t)$
$H_c(f)$	Channel's frequency response		T	Symbol or pulse period
$H_{eq}(f)$	Equalizer frequency response		T_b	Bit interval or period

T_e	Effective input noise temperature	$\overline{s_n^2}$	Average power in the normalized message signal
T_o	Fundamental period, or standard room temperature (290°K)	$x[n]$	Discrete-time signal or sequence; sampled version of $x(t)$
T_s	Sampling interval or period	$X[k]$	Discrete Fourier transform of sequence $x[n]$
W	Channel bandwidth		
A_n, B_n	Trigonometric Fourier series coefficients	$X(e^{j2\pi fT})$ $X(e^{j\hat{\omega}})$	Discrete-time Fourier transform of sequence $x[k]$
c	Speed of light in kilometer per second	$x^+(t)$	Analytic signal
C_n	nth coefficient for exponential Fourier series	$x^-(t)$	Complex conjugate of $x^+(t)$
c_n	nth equalizer tap gain or coefficient	$y_D(t)$	Demodulator output
$d_{\min}$	Minimum distance, Euclidean or Hamming	α	Attenuation constant, or roll-off factor of raised-cosine or root raised-cosine filter
$d_H(\underline{x}, \underline{y})$	Hamming distance between code words $\underline{x}$ and $\underline{y}$		
f	Frequency	β	Modulation index of FM signal
$f_i(t)$	Instantaneous frequency of an angle-modulated signal	μ	Step size in LMS algorithm
		λ	Wavelength of electromagnetic signal
f_c	Carrier frequency	Δ	Quantization step size
f_{image}	Image frequency	η	Power (or modulation) efficiency of an AM signal, or spectral efficiency of an information-carrying signal in bits per second-Hz
f_{IF}	Intermediate frequency		
f_{LO}l	Local oscillator frequency		
f_m	Sinusoidal message signal frequency		
$f_x(x)$	Probability density function of random variable x	$\delta(t)$	Impulse signal
		m_a	Modulation index of AM signal
$f_{xy}(x, y)$	Joint probability density function of random variables x and y	$\Delta\phi_{\max}$	Maximum phase deviation of an angle-modulated signal
f_s	Sampling rate or frequency	$\Delta f_{\max}$	Maximum frequency deviation of an angle-modulated signal
$h(t)$	Impulse-response of an LTI system		
$h_c(t)$	Impulse-response of a channel	$\Delta\omega_P$	Pull-in (or capture) range of the PLL
$h_{eq}(t)$	Impulse-response of linear equalizer	$\Delta\omega_H$	Hold-in range of the PLL
k_f	Frequency sensitivity of the FM modulator (Hz/volt)	$\Delta\omega_L$	Lock-in range of the PLL
		ζ	Damping factor of the second-order PLL
k_p	Phase sensitivity of the phase modulator (radians/volt)	ω_n	Natural frequency of the second-order PLL
$p_{eq}[k]$	Equalizer output pulse sequence		
p_{ij}	Channel transition probabilities	σ_e^2	Quantizer noise variance
$\text{sinc}(t)$	Sinc signal	$\mathbb{R}$	Field of real numbers
$\text{sgn}(t)$	Signum function	$\mathbb{C}$	Field of complex numbers
t	Time	$\mathbb{C}^n$	Vector space of complex n-tuples
t_d	Delay introduced by the channel	$\mathbb{R}^n$	Vector space of all real n-tuples
$u(t)$	Unit step function	$\mathbb{F}_2$	Field of binary numbers 0 and 1
$s(t)$	Message signal	$\mathbb{F}_2^n$	Vector space of binary n-tuples
$s_n(t)$	Normalized message signal		
$\boldsymbol{s}_n(t)$	Normalized random message signal	$\mathscr{C}$	Error-correcting or Error-detecting code

Index

936